THE WESTERN HERITAGE

Ninth Edition

VOLUME TWO: SINCE 1648

Donald Kagan
YALE UNIVERSITY

Steven Ozment
HARVARD UNIVERSITY

Frank M. Turner
YALE UNIVERSITY

PEARSON

Prentice
Hall

Upper Saddle River, New Jersey 07458

Library of Congress Cataloging-in-Publication Data

Kagan, Donald
    The Western Heritage / Donald Kagan, Steven Ozment, Frank M. Turner.—9th ed.
      p. cm.
    "Combined volume."
    Includes bibliographical references and index.
    ISBN 0-13-195068-1
    1. Civilization, Western—History—Textbooks. I. Ozment, Steven E. II. Turner, Frank M. (Frank Miller), 1944-III. Title.
    CB245.K28 2006
    909'.09821-dc22   2005054962

Vice President/Editorial Director: Charlyce Jones Owen
Executive Editor: Charles Cavaliere
Associate Editor: Emsal Hasan
Editorial Assistant: Maria Guarascio
Editor-in-Chief/Development: Rochelle Diogenes
Development Editor: Gerald Lombardi
Media Editor: Deborah O'Connell
Vice President/Director of Production and Manufacturing:
  Barbara Kittle
Senior Managing Editor: Joanne Riker
Production Liaison: Louise Rothman
Prepress and Manufacturing Manager: Nick Sklitsis
Prepress and Manufacturing Buyer: Benjamin Smith
Director of Marketing: Brandy Dawson
Assistant Marketing Manager: Andrea Messineo
Marketing Assistant: Jennifer Lang
Creative Design Director: Leslie Osher
Senior Art Director: Anne Bonanno Nieglos

Cover and Interior Design: Lisa Delgado
Electronic Artist: Carey Davies
Cartographer: CartoGraphics
Cover Art: An Italian mother in a head scarf with her young
  son and toddler girls with their meager belongings in a bag
  and a suitcase arriving at Ellis Island in New York in 1905.
  Hand colored photo by Lewis Hine. © Bettmann/CORBIS
Director, Image Resource Center: Melinda Reo
Manager, Visual Research: Beth Brenzel
Cover Image Specialist: Karen Sanatar
Photo Researcher: Teri Stratford
Image Coordinator: Robert Farrell
Color Scanning Service: Joe Conti, Greg Harrison, Cory Skidds,
  Rob Uibelhoer, Ron Walko
Composition and Full Service Project Management:
  Caterina Melara/Prepare, Inc.
Printer/Binder: Quebecor World
Cover Printer: Coral Graphics

Credits and acknowledgments borrowed from other sources and reproduced, with permission, in this textbook appear on appropriate page within text.

Pearson Education LTD.
Pearson Education Australia PTY, Limited
Pearson Education Singapore, Pte. Ltd.
Pearson Education North Asia Ltd
Pearson Education, Canada, Ltd
Pearson Educación de Mexico, S.A. de C.V.
Pearson Education–Japan
Pearson Education Malaysia, Pte. Ltd.

PART TIMELINE PHOTO CREDITS:

Part 1 Timeline: page 0, (top) Royal portrait head ("Head of Sargon the Great"). From Nineveh (Kuyunjik). Akkadian, c. 2300–2200 B.C.E. Bronze, h: 12" (30.7 cm). Iraq Museum, Baghdad, Iraq. Scala/Art Resource; (center) © Naturhistorisches Museum Wien; Winfield I. Parks Jr./National Geographic Image Collection; page 1, (top) Peter Harper © The British Museum; (bottom) Anderson/Rudolf Lesch Fine Arts Inc.; page 2, Art Resource, NY; page 3, (top) "Battle of Alexander the Great at Issus." Roman mosaic. Museo Archeologico Nazionale, Naples, Italy. Scala/Art Resources; (bottom) Christopher Rennie/Robert Harding World Imagery.

Part 2 Timeline: page 188, (top) Justinian, detail. c. 547. Mosaic technique. Canali Photobank, Capriolo, Italy; (center) Marvin Trachtenberg; (bottom) Gianni Dagli Orti/Corbis; page 189, (top) Corbis/Bettmann; (center) Torla Evans © The Museum of London; (bottom) Bonaventura Berlinghieri/Art Resource, NY.

Part 3 Timeline: page 288, (top) Thomas Renaut/Getty Images Inc.—Stone Allstock; (center) The Granger Collection, New York; (bottom) Tim Booth © Dorling Kindersley; page 289, (top) Elizabeth I, Armada Portrait, c. 1588 (oil on panel) by George Gower (1540–96) (attr. to). Woburn Abbey, Bedfordshire, UK/Bridgeman Art Library, London/New York; (center) Getty Images Inc.—Hulton Archive Photos;(bottom) Courtesy of the Library of Congress.

Part 4 Timeline: page 548, (top) The Boston Massacre, 5 March 1770: colored engraving, 1770, by Paul Revere after the drawing by Henry Pelham.The Granger Collection, New York; (center) The Bridgeman Art Library International; (bottom) Bildarchiv Preubischer Kulturbesitz; page 549, (top) By Permission of Musee De La Legion D'Honneur, Paris; (center) Ron Case/Getty Images Inc.—Hulton Archive Photos; (bottom) The Granger Collection.

Part 5 Timeline: page 728, (top) NASA/MODIS/NASA/John F. Kennedy Space Center; (center) Getty Images, Inc.—Liaison; (bottom) © Bettmann/Corbis; page 729, (top) Library of Congress; (center) Brown Brothers; (bottom) © Bettmann/CORBIS.

Part 6 Timeline: page 936, (top) Hulton Archives/Getty Images Inc.; (center) Tony Korody/Sygma; (bottom) John Launois/Black Star; page 937, (top) Stevens/SIPA Press; (center) Corbis/Sygma; (bottom) Natalie Behring/Getty Images, Inc.

10 9 8 7 6 5 4 3 2 1
ISBN 0-13-173346-X

BRIEF CONTENTS

CONTENTS

PART 2

THE MIDDLE AGES 476 C.E.–1300 C.E.   188

8   MEDIEVAL SOCIETY: HIERARCHIES, TOWNS, UNIVERSITIES, AND FAMILIES (1000–1300)   256

PART 3

EUROPE IN TRANSITION 1300–1750   288

9   THE LATE MIDDLE AGES: SOCIAL AND POLITICAL BREAKDOWN (1300–1453)   290

PART 4

ENLIGHTENMENT AND REVOLUTION 1700–1850   548

PART 5

TOWARD THE MODERN WORLD 1850–1939   728

24 THE BIRTH OF MODERN EUROPEAN THOUGHT 794

25 IMPERIALISM, ALLIANCES, AND WAR 826

PART 6

GLOBAL CONFLICT, COLD WAR, AND NEW DIRECTIONS 1939–2005   936

Documents

MAPS

ENCOUNTERING THE PAST

A CLOSER LOOK

THE WEST & THE WORLD

PART ICONS
IN THE WESTERN HERITAGE

PART **1**

Written in cuneiform, a writing system developed in ancient Mesopotamia, this is a fragment from a Sumerian tablet listing the disbursement of wages to day laborers. It was composed around 2039 B.C.E., making it one of the oldest examples of writing.   Courtesy of the Library of Congress

PART **2**

Thrown to the lions in 275 C.E. by the Romans for refusing to recant his Christian beliefs, St. Mamai is an important martyr in the iconography of Georgia, a Caucasian kingdom that embraced Christianity early in the fourth century. This gilded silver medallion, made in Georgia in the eleventh century, depicts the saint astride a lion while he bears a cross in one hand, symbolizing his triumphant victory over death and ignorance.   The Tondo of St. Mamai, from the city of Gelati, 11th c. A.D. Courtesy of the Kekelidze, Institute of Manuscripts, Tbilisi, Georgia

PART **3**

Published in 1620, *Novum Organum* ("new organ or instrument") by Francis Bacon is one of the most important works of the scientific revolution. In this and other works Bacon attacked the long-held belief that most truth had already been discovered. This allegorical image, from the frontispiece of *Novum Organum*, shows a ship striking out for unknown territories, seeking, as did Bacon, for a new understanding of the natural world. The ship is flanked by the mythical pillars of Hercules that stand at the point where the Mediterranean meets the Atlantic—the realm of the unknown and unexplored.   Courtesy of the Library of Congress

PART 4

"The Tea-Tax Tempest, or the Anglo-American Revolution." This engraving, made in Germany in 1778, is a satirical, European view of the American Revolution. Father Time on the right uses a magic lantern to project the image of a teapot exploding among British troops as American soldiers advance through the smoke. An Indian on the left (representing America), a black woman (representing Africa), and two seated women (one representing Europe and the other Asia), provide World opinion on the scene.   Courtesy of the Library of Congress

PART 5

This lithograph, created in 1865, served as the frontispiece to a book that surveyed the architecture of New York City immediately following the Civil War. In this cutaway view of the Architectural Iron Works building, the various stages in the manufacture of cast iron are shown while smokestacks above fill the air with black soot, conveying a sense of the hustle and bustle that characterized the industrializing West of the late nineteenth and early twentieth centuries.   Courtesy of the Library of Congress

PART 6

Because they portray all or part of the round Earth on a flat surface, every map projection is distorted to some degree, The interrupted Mollweide projection shown here is often used to show global projections, as the distortion is very severe only at polar latitudes. It thus provides a fairly accurate representation of large parts of the inhabited surface of the Earth. Note how diminutive Europe seems in comparison to other landmasses, a fitting representation of its diminished hegemony in the postcolonial world.

PREFACE

The heritage of Western civilization remains a major point of departure for understanding the twenty-first century. The unprecedented globalization of daily life that is a hallmark of our era has occurred largely through the spread of Western influences. From the sixteenth century onward, the West has exerted vast influences throughout the globe for both good and ill, and today's global citizens continue to live in the wake of that impact. It is the goal of this book to introduce its readers to the Western heritage, so that they may be better informed and more culturally sensitive citizens of the emerging global age.

The attacks upon the mainland of the United States on September 11, 2001, and the subsequent American invasions of Afghanistan and Iraq have concentrated the attention of teachers, students, and informed citizens upon the heritage and future of Western civilization as have no other events since the end of World War II. Whereas previously, commentary about global civilization involved analysis of the spread of Western economic, technological, and political influences, we now must explain how the West has defined itself over many centuries and think about how the West will articulate its core values as it confronts new and daunting challenges. The events of recent years and the hostility that has arisen in many parts of the world to the power and influence of the West require new efforts both to understand how the West sees itself and how other parts of the world see the West.

Twenty years ago, the West still defined itself mainly in terms of the East-West tensions associated with the Cold War. The West is now in the process of defining itself in terms of global rivalries arising from conflict with political groups that are not identical with nation-states, groups that define themselves in terms of opposition to what they understand the West to be. Whether or not we are witnessing a clash of civilizations, as Samuel Huntington, the distinguished Harvard political scientist, contends, we have certainly entered a new era in which citizens of the West need to understand how their culture, values, economy, and political outlooks have emerged. They cannot leave it to those who would attack the West to define Western civilization or to articulate its values.

Since *The Western Heritage* first appeared, we have sought to provide our readers with a work that does justice to the richness and variety of Western civilization and its many complexities. We hope that such an understanding of the West will foster lively debate about its character, values, institutions, and global influence. Indeed, we believe such a critical outlook on their own culture has characterized the peoples of the West since the dawn of history. Through such debates we define ourselves and the values of our culture. Consequently, we welcome the debate and hope that *The Western Heritage*, ninth edition, can help foster an informed discussion through its history of the West's strengths and weaknesses, and the controversies surrounding Western history.

Human beings make, experience, and record their history. In this edition as in past editions, our goal has been to present Western civilization fairly, accurately, and in a way that does justice to that great variety of human enterprise. History has many facets, no one of which alone can account for the others. Any attempt to tell the story of the West from a single overarching perspective, no matter how timely, is bound to neglect or suppress some important parts of that story. Like all authors of introductory texts, we have had to make choices, but we have attempted to provide the broadest possible introduction to Western civilization. To that end, we hope that the many documents included in this book will allow the widest possible spectrum of people to relate their personal experiences over the centuries and will enable our readers to share that experience.

We also believe that any book addressing the experience of the West must also look beyond its historical European borders. Students reading this book come from a wide variety of cultures and experiences. They live in a world of highly interconnected economies and instant communication between cultures. In this emerging multicultural society it seems both appropriate and necessary to recognize how Western civilization has throughout its history interacted with other cultures, both influencing and being influenced by them. Examples of this two-way interaction, such as that with Islam, appear throughout the text. To further highlight the theme of cultural interaction, *The Western Heritage* includes a series of comparative essays, "The West & the World." (For a fuller description, see following.)

GOALS OF THE TEXT

Our primary goal has been to present a strong, clear, narrative account of the central developments in Western history. We have also sought to call attention to certain critical themes:

- The capacity of Western civilization from the time of the Greeks to the present to transform itself through self-criticism.
- The development in the West of political freedom, constitutional government, and concern for the rule of law and individual rights.
- The shifting relations among religion, society, and the state.
- The development of science and technology and their expanding impact on Western thought, social institutions, and everyday life.
- The major religious and intellectual currents that have shaped Western culture.

We believe that these themes have been fundamental in Western civilization, shaping the past and exerting a continuing influence on the present.

Flexible Presentation *The Western Heritage*, ninth edition, is designed to accommodate a variety of approaches to a course in Western civilization, allowing teachers to stress what is most important to them. Some teachers will ask students to read all the chapters. Others will select among them to reinforce assigned readings and lectures.

Integrated Social, Cultural, and Political History *The Western Heritage* provides one of the richest accounts of the social history of the West available today, with strong coverage of family life, the changing roles of women, and the place of the family in relation to broader economic, political, and social developments. This coverage reflects the explosive growth in social historical research in the past three decades, which has enriched virtually all areas of historical study. In this edition we have again expanded both the breadth and depth of our coverage of social history through revisions of existing chapters, the addition of major new material and a new feature, "A Closer Look" (see following), and the inclusion of new documents.

While strongly believing in the study of the social experience of the West, we also share the conviction that internal and external political events have shaped the Western experience in fundamental and powerful ways. The experiences of Europeans in the twentieth century under fascism, national socialism, and communism demonstrate that influence, as has, more recently, the collapse of communism in the former Soviet Union and eastern Europe. We have also been told repeatedly by teachers that no matter what their own historical specialization, they believe that a political narrative gives students an effective tool to begin to understand the past. Consequently, we have sought to integrate the political with the social, cultural, and intellectual.

No other survey text presents so full an account of the religious and intellectual development of the West. People may be political and social beings, but they are also reasoning and spiritual beings. What they think and believe are among the most important things we can know about them. Their ideas about God, society, law, gender, human nature, and the physical world have changed over the centuries and continue to change. We cannot fully grasp our own approach to the world without understanding the intellectual currents of the past and how they influenced our thoughts and conceptual categories.

Clarity and Accessibility Good narrative history requires clear, vigorous prose. As in earlier editions, we have paid careful attention to our writing, subjecting every paragraph to critical scrutiny. Our goal was to make the history of the West accessible to students without compromising vocabulary or conceptual level. We hope this effort will benefit both teachers and students.

THE NINTH EDITION

NEW **A Closer Look** Reflecting the increased use of visual sources to interpret the Western heritage, one illustration per chapter is now examined and analyzed using leader lines to point out important and historically significant details. Examples include a Greek trireme, the cover of the Lindau Gospels, a statue of St. Maurice, and a French imperialist poster from the early twentieth century. This new feature further enhances the already rich visual presentation of *The Western Heritage*.

Encountering the Past Each chapter includes an essay on a significant issue of everyday life or popular culture. These essays explore a variety of subjects including gladiatorial bouts and medieval games, midwivery, smoking in early modern Europe, and the politics of rock music in the late twentieth century. These thirty-one essays, each of which includes an illustration and study questions, expand *The Western Heritage's* rich coverage of social and cultural history. (See p. xxiii for a complete list of the "Encountering the Past" essays.)

The West & The World In this feature, we focus on six subjects that compare Western institutions with those of other parts of the world, or discuss how developments in the West have influenced other cultures. In the ninth edition, the essays are:

Part 1: Ancient Warfare (p. 182)
Part 2: The Invention of Printing in China and Europe (p. 284)
Part 3: The Columbian Exchange (p. 544)
Part 4: The Abolition of Slavery in the Transatlantic Economy (p. 722)
Part 5: Imperialism: Ancient and Modern (p. 870)
Part 6: Energy and the Modern World (p. 1052)

Recent Scholarship As in previous editions, changes in this edition reflect our determination to incorporate the most recent developments in historical scholarship and the concerns of professional historians. Of particular interest are expanded discussions of cultural history, women's history, and the interaction between Islam and the West.

Chapter-By-Chapter Revisions

Chapter 1 Increased coverage of Neolithic Europe, including an entire section on the "Ice man" found in the Alps. A major new section on the Persian Empire has also been added.

Chapter 6 Discussion of Late Antiquity now opens the chapter. Discussion of the Byzantine Empire has been expanded. Coverage of Islam and the early Islamic conquests has been increased.

Chapter 13 An entirely new chapter that examines European political history from the seventeenth to eighteenth centuries.

Chapter 18 Coverage of the French Revolution has been significantly revised and reorganized.

Chapter 25 Discussion of the New Imperialism has been significantly expanded, including a new section on the Scramble for Africa with case-study examinations of colonialism in Egypt, the Belgian Congo, and South Africa.

Chapter 27 New, fuller discussion of Keynesian economics.

Chapter 28 Revised and expanded section on the Holocaust and the destruction of Polish Jewry.

Chapter 29 Updated discussion of post–World War II European political history, especially as regards Russia, the European Union, and the invasions of Afghanistan and Iraq.

Chapter 30 Revised sections on immigration within Europe, Islam in Europe, and terrorism.

Maps and Illustrations The entire map and photo program has been significantly revised. New maps include the Persian Empire, the slave trade, global migration in the nineteenth century, the Holocaust, and the Iraq War. To help students understand the relationship between geography and history, approximately one-half of the maps include relief features. Up to two maps in each chapter feature interactive exercises on the Companion Website that accompanies the text. All maps have been carefully edited for accuracy. The text also contains close to 500 color and black and white illustrations, approximately one-third of which are new to the ninth edition.

Pedagogical Features This edition retains the pedagogical features of the previous edition, including part-opening comparative timelines, a list of key topics at the beginning of each chapter, glossary terms, chapter review questions, and questions accompanying the more than 200 source documents in the text. Each of these features is designed to make the text more accessible to students and to reinforce key concepts.

- **Illustrated timelines** open each of the six parts of the book summarizing, side-by-side, the major events in politics and government, society and economy, and religion and culture.
- **Primary-source documents,** approximately one-third of which are new to this edition, acquaint students with the raw material of history and provide intimate contact with the people of the past and their concerns. Questions accompanying the source documents direct students toward important, thought-provoking issues and help them relate the documents to the material in the text. They can be used to stimulate class discussion or as topics for essays and study groups. In addition, over 200 primary-source documents, with accompanying questions, are found on the Documents in Western Civilization CD-ROM included with all new copies of the text.
- Each chapter includes an **outline**, a list of **key topics**, and an **introduction**. Together these features provide a succinct overview of each chapter.
- **Chronologies** follow each major section in a chapter, listing significant events and their dates.
- **In Perspective** sections summarize the major themes of each chapter and provide a bridge to the next chapter.
- **Chapter Review Questions** help students review the material in a chapter and relate it to broader themes. These too can be used for class discussion and essay topics.

- **Suggested Readings lists** following each chapter have been updated with new titles reflecting recent scholarship.
- **Map Explorations,** prompt students to engage with maps in an interactive fashion. Each Map Exploration is found on the Companion Website for the text.

A Note on Dates and Transliterations This edition of *The Western Heritage* continues the practice of using B.C.E. (before the common era) and C.E. (common era) instead of B.C. (before Christ) and A.D. (anno Domini, the year of the Lord) to designate dates. We also follow the most accurate currently accepted English transliterations of Arabic words. For example, today *Koran* is being replaced by the more accurate *Qur'an;* similarly *Muhammad* is preferable to *Mohammed* and *Muslim* to *Moslem.*

ANCILLARY INSTRUCTIONAL MATERIALS

The ancillary instructional materials that accompany *The Western Heritage* include print and multimedia supplements that are designed to reinforce and enliven the richness of the past and inspire students with the excitement of studying the history of Western civilization.

Print Supplements for the Instructor

Instructor's Manual The Instructor's Manual contains chapter summaries, key points and vital concepts, and information on audio-visual resources that can be used in developing and preparing lecture presentations.

Test-Item File The Test-Item File includes over 1500 multiple-choice, identification, map, and essay test questions.

Prentice Hall Test Manager This commercial-quality computerized test management program, for Windows and Macintosh environments, allows users to create their own tests using items from the printed Test Item File. The program allows users to edit the items in the Test Item File and to add their own questions. Online testing is also available.

Transparency Package This collection of full-color transparency acetates provides the maps, charts, and graphs from the text for use in classroom presentations.

Telecourse Administrative Handbook by Jay Boggis provides instructors with resources for using *The Western Heritage* with the Annenberg/CPB telecourse, The Western Tradition.

Print Supplements for the Student

History Notes, Volumes I and II The Practice Tests include commentaries, definitions, and a variety of exercises designed to reinforce the concepts in the chapter. Practice Tests are free when packed with *The Western Heritage.*

Documents Set, Volumes I and II This carefully selected and edited set of documents provides over 200 additional primary-source readings. Each document includes a brief introduction as well as questions to encourage critical analysis of the reading and to relate it to the content of the text.

Lives and Legacies: Biographies in Western Civilization This two-volume collection provides brief, focused biographies of 60 people, both celebrated and uncelebrated, whose lives provide insight into the heritage of Western civilization. Each biography includes an introduction, pre-reading questions, and suggested readings. Free when bundled with the text.

Penguin Classics Prentice Hall is pleased to provide students significant discounts when copies of *The Western Heritage* are purchased together with titles from the acclaimed Penguin Classics series in Western civilization. Contact your Prentice Hall representative for details.

Prentice Hall Atlas of the Western Civilization This four-color historical atlas produced in collaboration with Dorling Kindersley, provides additional map resources to reinforce concepts in the text.

Understanding and Answering Essay Questions This brief guide suggests helpful study techniques as well as specific analytical tools for understanding different types of essay questions and provides precise guidelines for preparing well-crafted essay answers. This guide is available free to students when shrink-wrapped with the text.

Reading Critically About History: A Guide to Active Reading This guide focuses on the skills needed to learn the essential information presented in college history textbooks. Material covered includes vocabulary skills, recognizing organizational patterns, critical-thinking skills, understanding visual aids, and practice sections. This guide is available free to students when shrink-wrapped with the text.

Telecourse Study Guide, Volumes I and II by Jay Boggis correlates *The Western Heritage* with the Annenberg/CPB telecourse, The Western Tradition.

Media Resources

 Prentice Hall's New Online Resource **OneKey** lets instructors and students in to the best teaching and learning resources—all in one place. This all-inclusive online resource is designed to help you minimize class preparation and maximize teaching time. Conveniently organized by chapter, **OneKey** for *The Western Heritage*, ninth edition, reinforces what students have learned in class and from the text. Among the student resources available for each chapter are: a complete, media-rich e-book version of *The Western Heritage*, ninth edition; quizzes organized by the main subtopics of each chapter; over 200 primary-source documents; and interactive map quizzes.

For instructors, **OneKey** includes images and maps from *The Western Heritage*, ninth edition; instructional material; hundreds of primary-source documents; and PowerPoint presentations.

Prentice Hall One Search with Research Navigator: History 2005 This brief guide focuses on developing critical-thinking skills necessary for evaluating and using online sources. It provides a brief introduction to navigating the Internet with specific references to History Websites. It also provides an access code and instruction on using Research Navigator, a powerful research tool that provides access to three exclusive databases of reliable source material: ContentSelect Academic Journal Database, the New York Times Search by Subject Archive, and Link Library.

Companion Website™ with Grade Tracker (**www.prenhall.com/kagan**) works in tandem with the text and features objectives, study questions, Web links to related Internet resources, document exercises, interactive maps, and map labeling exercises.

World History Document CD-ROM Bound into every new copy of this textbook is a Documents in Western Civilization CD-ROM. This is a powerful resource for research and additional reading that contains more than 200 primary source documents central to Western civilization. Each document provides essay questions that are linked directly to a Website where short-essay answers can be submitted online or printed out. The end of each chapter in *The Western Heritage* includes a list of pertinent documents from the CD-ROM.

ACKNOWLEDGMENTS

We are grateful to the scholars and teachers whose thoughtful and often detailed comments helped shape this revision:

Jennifer Wynot, Metropolitan State College of Denver
William B. Whisenhunt, College of DuPage
Jonathan Perry, University of Central Florida
David Hudson, California State University, Fresno
Wanda L. Scarbro, Pellissippi State Technical Community College
Lynn Lubamersky, Boise State University
Paul J. L. Hughes, Sussex County Community College
Patti Harrold, Edmond Memorial High School
Miriam Pelikan-Pittenger, University of Illinois at Urbana-Champaign

Steven Ozment would like to acknowledge the help of Adam Beaver and Elizabeth Russell. Frank Turner would like to acknowledge the aid of Magnus T. Bernhardsson. Finally, we would like to thank the dedicated people who helped produce this revision. Our acquisitions editor, Charles Cavaliere; our development editor, Gerald Lombardi; our production liaison, Louise Rothman; Lisa Delgado, who created the beautiful new design of this edition; Benjamin D. Smith, our manufacturing buyer; Caterina Melara, production editor; and Teri Stratford, photo researcher.

D.K.
S.O.
F.M.T.

ABOUT THE AUTHORS

DONALD KAGAN is Sterling Professor of History and Classics at Yale University, where he has taught since 1969. He received the A.B. degree in history from Brooklyn College, the M.A. in classics from Brown University, and the Ph.D. in history from Ohio State University. During 1958–1959 he studied at the American School of Classical Studies as a Fulbright Scholar. He has received three awards for undergraduate teaching at Cornell and Yale. He is the author of a history of Greek political thought, *The Great Dialogue* (1965); a four-volume history of the Peloponnesian war, *The Origins of the Peloponnesian War* (1969); *The Archidamian War* (1974); *The Peace of Nicias and the Sicilian Expedition* (1981); *The Fall of the Athenian Empire* (1987); and a biography of Pericles, *Pericles of Athens and the Birth of Democracy* (1991); *On the Origins of War* (1995) and *The Peloponnesian War* (2003). He is coauthor, with Frederick W. Kagan of *While America Sleeps* (2000). With Brian Tierney and L. Pearce Williams, he is the editor of *Great Issues in Western Civilization*, a collection of readings. He was awarded the National Humanities Medal for 2002.

STEVEN OZMENT is McLean Professor of Ancient and Modern History at Harvard University. He has taught Western Civilization at Yale, Stanford, and Harvard. He is the author of eleven books. *The Age of Reform, 1250–1550* (1980) won the Schaff Prize and was nominated for the 1981 National Book Award. Five of his books have been selections of the History Book Club: *Magdalena and Balthasar: An Intimate Portrait of Life in Sixteenth Century Europe* (1986), *Three Behaim Boys: Growing Up in Early Modern Germany* (1990), *Protestants: The Birth of A Revolution* (1992), *The Burgermeister's Daughter: Scandal in a Sixteenth Century German Town* (1996), and *Flesh and Spirit: Private Life in Early Modern Germany* (1999). His most recent publications are *Ancestors: The Loving Family of Old Europe* (2001), *A Mighty Fortress: A New History of the German People* (2004), and "Why We Study Western Civ," *The Public Interest* 158 (2005).

FRANK M. TURNER is John Hay Whitney Professor of History at Yale University and Director of the Beinecke Rare Book and Manuscript Library at Yale University, where he served as University Provost from 1988 to 1992. He received his B.A. degree at the College of William and Mary and his Ph.D. from Yale. He has received the Yale College Award for Distinguished Undergraduate Teaching. He has directed a National Endowment for the Humanities Summer Institute. His scholarly research has received the support of fellowships from the National Endowment for the Humanities and the Guggenheim Foundation and the Woodrow Wilson Center. He is the author of *Between Science and Religion: The Reaction to Scientific Naturalism in Late Victorian England* (1974), *The Greek Heritage in Victorian Britain* (1981), which received the British Council Prize of the Conference on British Studies and the Yale Press Governors Award, *Contesting Cultural Authority: Essays in Victorian Intellectual Life* (1993), and *John Henry Newman: The Challenge to Evangelical Religion* (2002). He has also contributed numerous articles to journals and has served on the editorial advisory boards of *The Journal of Modern History, Isis,* and *Victorian Studies.* He edited *The Idea of a University,* by John Henry Newman (1996) and *Reflections on the Revolution in France* by Edmund Burke (2003). Since 1996 he has served as a Trustee of Connecticut College. In 2003, Professor Turner was appointed Director of the Beinecke Rare Book and Manuscript Library at Yale University.

CHAPTER **13**

EUROPEAN STATE CONSOLIDATION IN THE SEVENTEENTH AND EIGHTEENTH CENTURIES

KEY TOPICS

- The Dutch Golden Age
- The divergent political paths of Britain and France: Parliamentary supremacy and royal absolutism
- Poland's failure to establish a strong central government
- The Habsburg efforts to preserve their holdings
- The emergence of Prussia and Russia as major powers
- Power and decline of the Ottoman Empire

etween the early seventeenth and the mid-twentieth centuries, no region so dominated other parts of the world politically, militarily, and economically as Europe. Such had not been the case before that date and would not be the case after World War II. However, for approximately three and a half centuries, Europe became the chief driving force in one world historical development after another. This era of

Louis XIV of France came to symbolize absolute monarchy though such government was not so absolute as the term implied. This state portrait was intended to convey the grandeur of the king and of his authority. The portrait was brought into royal council meetings when the king himself was absent.   Hyacinthe Rigaud (1659-1743), "Portrait of Louis XIV." Louvre, Paris, France. Photograph © Bridgeman-Giraudon/Art Resource, NY

European dominance, which appears quite temporary in the larger scope of history, also coincided with a shift in power within Europe itself from the Mediterranean, where Spain and Portugal had taken the lead in the conquest and early exploitation of the Americas, to the states of northwest and later north-central Europe.

During the seventeenth and early eighteenth centuries, certain states in northern Europe organized themselves politically so as to be able to dominate Europe and later to influence and even govern other large areas of the world through military might and economic strength. Even within the region of northern Europe, there occurred a sorting out of influence among political states with some successfully establishing long-term positions of dominance and others passing from the scene after relatively brief periods of either military or economic strength.

By the mid-eighteenth century, five major states had come to dominate European politics and would continue to do so until at least World War I. They were Great Britain, France, Austria, Prussia, and Russia. Through their military strength, economic development, and, in some cases, colonial empires, they would affect virtually every other world civilization. Within Europe, these states established their dominance at the expense of Spain, Portugal, the United Provinces of the Netherlands, Poland, Sweden, and the Ottoman Empire. Equally essential to their rise was the weakness of the Holy Roman Empire after the Peace of Westphalia (1648).

In western Europe, Britain and France emerged as the dominant powers. This development represented a shift of influence away from Spain and the United Netherlands. Both of the latter countries had been powerful and important during the sixteenth and seventeenth centuries, but they became politically and militarily marginal during the eighteenth century. Neither, however, disappeared from the map, and both retained considerable economic vitality and influence. Spanish power declined after the War of the Spanish Succession. The case of the Netherlands was more complicated. ■

THE NETHERLANDS: GOLDEN AGE TO DECLINE

The seven provinces that became the United Provinces of the Netherlands emerged as a nation after revolting against Spain in 1572. During the seventeenth century, the Dutch engaged in a series of naval wars with England. Then, in 1672, the armies of Louis XIV invaded the Netherlands. Prince William III of Orange (1650–1702), the grandson of William the Silent (1533–1584) and the hereditary chief executive, or *stadtholder*, of Holland, the most important of the provinces, rallied the Dutch and eventually led the entire European coalition against France. As a part of that strategy, he answered the invitation of Protestant English aristocrats in 1688 to assume, along with his wife Mary, the English throne.

During both the seventeenth and eighteenth centuries, the political and economic life of the Netherlands differed from that of the rest of Europe. The other major nations pursued paths toward strong central government, generally under monarchies, as with France, or in the case of England, under a strong parliamentary system. By contrast, the Netherlands was formally a republic. Each of the provinces retained considerable authority, and the central government, embodied in the States General that met in the Hague, exercised its authority through a kind of ongoing negotiation with the provinces. Prosperous and populous Holland dominated the States General. The Dutch deeply distrusted monarchy and the ambitions of the House of Orange. Nonetheless, when confronted with major military challenges, the Dutch would permit the House of Orange and, most notably, William III to assume dominant leadership. These political arrangements proved highly resilient and allowed the republic to establish itself permanently in the European state system during the seventeenth century. When William died in 1702 and the wars with France ended in 1714, the Dutch reverted to their republican structures.

Although the provinces making up the Netherlands were traditionally identified with the Protestant cause in Europe, toleration marked Dutch religious life. The Calvinist Reformed Church was the official church of the nation, but it was not an established church. There was always a significant number of Roman Catholics and Protestants who did not belong to the Reformed Church. The country also became a haven for Jews. Consequently, while governments in other European states attempted to impose a single religion on their people or tore themselves apart in religious conflict, in the Netherlands peoples of differing religious faiths lived together peacefully.

URBAN PROSPERITY

Beyond the climate of religious toleration, what most amazed seventeenth-century contemporaries about the Dutch Republic was its economic prosperity. Its remarkable economic achievement was built on the foundations of high urban consolidation, transformed agriculture, extensive trade and finance, and an overseas commercial empire.

In the Netherlands, more people lived in cities than in any other area of Europe. Key transformations in Dutch farming that served as the model for the rest of Europe made this urban transformation possible. During the seventeenth century, the Dutch drained and reclaimed land from the sea, which they used for highly profitable farming. Because Dutch shipping provided a steady supply of cheap grain, Dutch farmers themselves could produce more profitable dairy products and beef and cultivate cash products such as tulip bulbs.

Dutch fishermen dominated the market for herring and supplied much of the continent's dried fish. The Dutch also supplied textiles to many parts of Europe. Dutch ships appeared in harbors all over the continent, with their captains purchasing goods that they then transported and resold at a profit to other nations. The overseas trades also supported a vast shipbuilding and ship supply industry. The most advanced financial system of the day supported all of this trade, commerce, and manufacturing.

The final foundation of Dutch prosperity was a seaborne empire. Dutch traders established a major presence in East Asia, particularly in spice-producing areas of Java, the Moluccas, and Sri Lanka. The vehicle for this penetration was the Dutch East Indies Company (chartered in 1602). The company eventually displaced Portuguese dominance in the spice trade of East Asia and for many years prevented English traders from establishing a major presence there. Initially, the Dutch had only wanted commercial dominance of the spice trade, but in time, they moved toward producing the spices themselves, which required them to control many of the islands that now constitute Indonesia. The Netherlands remained the colonial master of this region until after World War II.

ECONOMIC DECLINE

The decline in political influence of the United Provinces of the Netherlands occurred in the eighteenth century. After the death of William III of Britain in 1702, the provinces prevented the emergence of another strong *stadtholder*. Unified political leadership therefore vanished. Naval supremacy slowly but steadily passed to the British. The fishing industry declined, and the Dutch lost their technological superiority in shipbuilding. Countries between which Dutch ships had once carried goods now traded directly with each other.

Similar stagnation overtook the Dutch domestic industries. The disunity of the provinces hastened this economic decline and prevented action that might have halted it.

What saved the United Provinces from becoming completely insignificant in European affairs was their continued financial dominance. Well past the middle of the eighteenth century, Dutch banks continued to finance European trade, and the Amsterdam stock exchange remained an important financial institution.

TWO MODELS OF EUROPEAN POLITICAL DEVELOPMENT

The United Netherlands, like Venice and the Swiss cantons, was a republic governed without a monarch. Elsewhere in Europe monarchy of two fundamentally different patterns predominated in response to the military challenges of international conflict.

The two models became known as *parliamentary monarchy* and *political absolutism*. England embodied the first, and France, the second. Neither model was inevitable for either country, but each resulted from the historical developments and political personalities that molded each nation during the seventeenth century.

The political forces that led to the creation of these two models had arisen from military concerns. During the second half of the sixteenth century, changes in military organization, weapons, and tactics sharply increased the cost of warfare. Because their traditional sources of income could not finance these growing expenses, in addition to the other costs of government, monarchs sought new revenues. Only monarchies that succeeded in

The technologically advanced fleet of the Dutch East India Company, shown here at anchor in Amsterdam, linked the Netherlands' economy with that of southeast Asia.   Andries van Eertvelt (1590–1652), "The Return to Amsterdam of the Fleet of the Dutch East India Company in 1599." Oil on copper. Johnny van Haeften Gallery, London, UK. The Bridgeman Art Library

building a secure financial base that was not deeply dependent on the support of noble estates, diets, or assemblies achieved absolute rule. The French monarchy succeeded in this effort, whereas the English monarchy failed. That success and failure led to the two models of government—*absolutism* in France and *parliamentary monarchy* in England—that shaped subsequent political development in Europe.

The divergent developments of England and France in the seventeenth century would have surprised most people in 1600. It was not inevitable that the English monarchy would have to govern through Parliament or that the French monarchy would avoid dealing with national political institutions that could significantly limit its authority. The Stuart kings of England aspired to the autocracy Louis XIV achieved, and some English political philosophers eloquently defended the divine right of kings and absolute rule. At the beginning of the seventeenth century, the English monarchy was strong. Queen Elizabeth, after a reign of almost forty-five years (1558–1603), was much revered. Parliament met only when the monarch summoned it to provide financial support. France, however, was emerging from the turmoil of its religious wars. The strife of that conflict had torn French society apart. The monarchy was relatively weak. Henry IV, who had become king in 1589, pursued a policy of religious toleration. The French nobles had significant military forces at their disposal and in the middle of the seventeenth century rebelled against the king. These conditions would change dramatically in both nations by the late seventeenth century.

CONSTITUTIONAL CRISIS AND SETTLEMENT IN STUART ENGLAND

JAMES I

In 1603 James VI, the son of Mary Stuart, Queen of Scots, who had been King of Scotland since 1567 succeeded without opposition or incident the childless Elizabeth I as James I of England. He also inherited a large royal debt and a fiercely divided church. A strong believer in the divine right of kings, he expected to rule with a minimum of consultation beyond his own royal court.

Parliament met only when the monarch summoned it, which James hoped to do rarely. In place of parliamentarily approved revenues, James developed other sources of income, largely by levying new custom duties known as *impositions*. Mem-

bers of Parliament regarded this as an affront to their authority over the royal purse, but they did not seek a serious confrontation. Rather, throughout James's reign they wrangled and negotiated.

The religious problem also festered under James. Since the days of Elizabeth, Puritans within the Church of England had sought to eliminate elaborate religious ceremonies and replace the hierarchical episcopal system of church governance under bishops appointed by the king with a more representative Presbyterian form like that of the Calvinist churches in Scotland and on the Continent. At the Hampton Court Conference of January 1604, James rebuffed the Puritans and firmly declared his intention to maintain and even enhance the Anglican episcopacy. Thereafter, both sides had deep suspicions of the other.

Religious dissenters began to leave England. In 1620, Puritan separatists founded Plymouth Colony on Cape Cod Bay in North America, preferring flight from England to Anglican conformity. Later in the 1620s, a larger, better financed group of Puritans left England to found the Massachusetts Bay Colony. In each case, the colonists believed that reformation would or could not go far enough in England and that only in America could they worship freely and organize a truly reformed church.

James's court became a center of scandal and corruption. He governed by favorites, of whom the most influential was the duke of Buckingham, whom rumor made the king's homosexual lover. Buckingham controlled royal patronage and openly sold peerages and titles to the highest bidders—a practice that angered the nobility because it cheapened their rank. There had always been court favorites, but seldom before had a single person so controlled access to the monarch.

James's foreign policy roused further opposition and doubt about his Protestant loyalty. In 1604, he concluded a much-needed peace with Spain, England's longtime adversary. The war had been ruinously expensive, but his subjects considered the peace a sign of pro-Catholic sentiment. James's unsuccessful attempt to relax penal laws against Catholics further increased suspicions, as did his wise hesitancy in 1618 to rush English troops to the aid of German Protestants at the outbreak of the Thirty Years' War. His failed efforts to arrange a marriage between his son Charles and a Spanish princess, and then Charles's marriage in 1625 to Henrietta Marie, the Catholic daughter of Henry IV of France, further increased religious concern. In 1624, shortly before James's death, England again went to war against Spain, largely in response to parliamentary pressures.

KING JAMES I DEFENDS POPULAR RECREATION AGAINST THE PURITANS

The English Puritans believed in strict observance of the Sabbath, disapproving any sports, games, or general social conviviality on Sunday. James I thought these strictures prevented many Roman Catholics from joining the Church of England. In 1618, he ordered the clergy of the Church of England to read the Book of Sports from their pulpits. In this declaration, he permitted people to engage in certain sports and games after church services. His hope was to allow innocent recreations on Sunday while encouraging people to attend the Church of England. Despite the king's good intentions, the order offended the Puritans. The clergy resisted his order and he had to withdraw it.

■ *What motives of state might have led James I to issue this declaration? How does he attempt to make it favorable to the Church of England? Why might so many clergy have refused to read this statement to their congregations?*

With our own ears we heard the general complaint of our people, that they were barred from all lawful recreation and exercise upon the Sunday's afternoon, after the ending of all divine service, which cannot but produce two evils: the one the hindering of the conversion of many [Roman Catholic subjects], whom their priests will take occasion hereby to vex, persuading them that no honest mirth or recreation is lawful or tolerable in our religion, which cannot but breed a great discontentment in our people's hearts, especially as such as are peradventure upon the point of turning [to the Church of England]: the other inconvenience is, that this prohibition barreth the common and meaner sort of people from using such exercises as may make their bodies more able for war, when we or our successors shall have occasion to use them; and in place thereof sets up filthy tipplings and drunkenness, and breeds a number of idle and discontented speeches in their ale-houses. For when shall the common people have leave to exercise, if not upon the Sundays and holy days, seeing they must apply their labor and win their living in all working days? . . .

[A]s for our good people's lawful recreation, our pleasure likewise is, that after the end of divine service our good people be not disturbed, . . . or discouraged from any lawful recreation, such as dancing, either men or women; archery for men, leaping, vaulting, or any other such harmless recreation, or from having of Hay-games, Whitsun-ales, and Morris-dances; and the setting up of May-poles and other sports therewith used; . . . but withal we do here account still as prohibited all unlawful games to be used upon Sundays only, as bear and bull-baitings . . . and at all times in the meaner sort of people by law prohibited, bowling.

And likewise we bar from this benefit and liberty all such known as recusants [Roman Catholics], either men or women, as will abstain from coming to church or divine service, being therefore unworthy of any lawful recreation after the said service, that will not first come to the church and serve God; prohibiting in like sort the said recreations to any that, though [they] conform in religion [i.e., members of the Church of England], are not present in the church at the service of God, before their going to the said recreations.

From Henry Bettenson, ed., *Documents of the Christian Church*, 2nd ed. (London: Oxford University Press, 1963), pp. 400–403. By permission of Oxford University Press.

EARLY CONTROVERSY OVER TOBACCO AND SMOKING

Smoking today is widely condemned throughout the West, but the controversy over tobacco goes back to the earliest European encounter with the plant, which was native to the Americas.

Christopher Columbus on his first voyage in 1492 saw Native Americans smoking tobacco. Later, the first Spanish missionaries associated smoking with pagan religious practices and tried to stop Native Americans from using tobacco. Once tobacco reached Europe in the late sixteenth century, more opposition to smoking arose (although—ironically—some physicians thought it might cure diseases of the lungs and internal organs). As early as 1610, Sir Francis Bacon (1561–1626) noted that smokers found it difficult to stop smoking. The Christian clergy throughout Europe denounced smoking as immoral, and Muslim clerics condemned the practice as contrary to Islam when it spread to the Ottoman Empire. Nonetheless, smoking tobacco in pipes became popular.

The chief British critic of the new practice was none other than King James I (r. 1603–1625). While he defended Sunday sports against Puritan critics who believed any amusements on the Sabbath were sinful, he detested smoking. In 1604, he published his *Counterblaste to Tobacco* in which he declared, "Have you not reason then to be ashamed, and to forbear this filthy novelty. . . ? In your abuse thereof sinning against God, harming yourselves in person . . . and taking thereby the marks . . . of vanity upon you . . . . A custom loathsome to the eye, hateful to the nose, harmful to the brain, dangerous to the lungs, and the black stinking fume thereof, nearest resembling the horrible Stygian smoke of the pit that is bottomless."[1]

To discourage smoking, James's government put a high tax on tobacco. Yet when a brisk trade in smuggled tobacco developed, the government decided to lower the tax to a level where people would not seek to evade it. In 1614, James created a royal monopoly to import tobacco into England, which created a steady government revenue that the increasingly unpopular king badly needed. James, like governments to the present day, may also have regarded this policy as a tax on sin. By 1619, James approved the incorporation of a company of clay pipe makers in London, and 40,000 pounds of tobacco arrived from Virginia the next year. Other European governments would also find tobacco a significant source of tax revenue. Often they would tax tobacco and at the same time attempt to regulate its use, especially among the young.

- *Which groups in Europe in the sixteenth and seventeenth centuries opposed the habit of smoking tobacco? Why did the English government under King James I modify its opposition to tobacco?*

[1]*A Counterblaste to Tobacco* (1604), reprinted by the Rodale Press, London, 1954, p. 36.

Practically from the moment of its introduction into Europe tobacco smoking was controversial. Here a court jester is portrayed as exhaling rabbits from a pipe as three pipe-smoking gentlemen look on.
© Christel Gerstenberg/Corbis

CHARLES I

Parliament had favored the war with Spain but would not adequately finance it because its members distrusted the monarchy. Unable to gain adequate funds from Parliament, Charles I (r. 1625–1649), like his father, resorted to extra-parliamentary measures. These included levying new tariffs and duties, attempting to collect discontinued taxes, and subjecting English property owners to a so-called forced loan (a tax theoretically to be repaid) and then imprisoning those who refused to pay. All these actions, as well as quartering troops in private homes, challenged local political influence of nobles and landowners.

When Parliament met in 1628, its members would grant new funds only if Charles recognized the Petition of Right. This document required that henceforth there should be no forced loans or taxa-

King CHARLES *the* FIRST *in the* HOUSE *of* COMMONS, *demanding the* FIVE *impeached* MEMBERS *to be delivered up to his* AUTHORITY.

One of the key moments in the conflict between Charles I and Parliament occurred in January 1642 when Charles personally arrived at the House of Commons intent on arresting five members who had been responsible for for opposing him. They had already escaped. Thereafter Charles departed London to raise his army. The event was subsequently often portrayed in English art. The present illustration is from an eighteenth-century engraving.
The Granger Collection, New York

tion without the consent of Parliament, that no freeman should be imprisoned without due cause, and that troops should not be billeted in private homes. Charles agreed to the petition, but whether he would keep his word was doubtful. The next year after further disputes, Charles dissolved Parliament and did not recall it until 1640.

Years of Personal Rule   To conserve his limited resources, Charles made peace with France in 1629 and Spain in 1630, again rousing fears that he was too friendly to Roman Catholic powers. To allow Charles to rule without renegotiating financial arrangements with Parliament, his chief advisor Thomas Wentworth (1593–1641; after 1640, earl of Strafford), imposed strict efficiency and administrative centralization in the government and exploited every legal fund-raising device, enforcing previously neglected laws and extending existing taxes into new areas.

Charles might have ruled indefinitely without Parliament had not his religious policies provoked war with Scotland. James I had allowed a wide variety of religious observances in England, Scotland, and Ireland; by contrast, Charles hoped to impose religious conformity at least within England and Scotland. In 1637, Charles and his high-church Archbishop William Laud (1573–1645), against the opposition of both the English Puritans and the Presbyterian Scots, tried to impose on Scotland the English episcopal system and a prayer book almost identical to the Anglican Book of Common Prayer.

The Scots rebelled, and Charles, with insufficient resources for war, was forced in 1640 to call Parliament. It refused even to consider funds for war until the king agreed to redress a long list of political and religious grievances. The king, in response, immediately dissolved that Parliament—hence its name, the Short Parliament (April–May 1640). When the Scots defeated an English army at the Battle of Newburn in the summer of 1640, Charles reconvened Parliament—this time on its terms—for a long and fateful duration.

THE LONG PARLIAMENT AND CIVIL WAR

The landowners and the merchant classes represented in Parliament had long resented the king's financial measures and paternalistic rule. The Puritans in Parliament resented his religious policies and distrusted the influence of his Roman Catholic wife. What became known as the Long Parliament (1640–1660) thus acted with widespread support and general unanimity when it convened in November 1640.

The House of Commons impeached both Strafford and Laud. Both were executed—Strafford in 1641, Laud in 1645. Parliament abolished the courts that had enforced royal policy and prohibited the levying of new taxes without its consent. Finally, Parliament resolved that no more than three years should elapse between its meetings and that the king could not dissolve it without its own consent.

Parliament, however, was sharply divided over religion. Both moderate Puritans (the Presbyterians) and more extreme Puritans (the Independents) wanted to abolish bishops and the Book of Common Prayer. Yet religious conservatives in both houses of Parliament were determined to preserve the Church of England in its current form.

These divisions intensified in October 1641, when Parliament was asked to raise funds for an army to suppress the rebellion in Scotland. Charles's opponents argued that he could not be trusted with an army and that Parliament should become the commander-in-chief of English armed forces. In January 1642, Charles invaded Parliament, intending to arrest certain of his opponents, but they escaped. The king then left London and began to raise an army. Shocked, a majority of the House of Commons passed the Militia Ordinance, which gave Parliament authority to raise an army of its own. The die was now cast. For the next four years (1642–1646), civil war engulfed England with the king's supporters known as Cavaliers and the parliamentary opposition as Roundheads.

OLIVER CROMWELL
AND THE PURITAN REPUBLIC

Two factors led finally to Parliament's victory. The first was an alliance with Scotland in 1643 that committed Parliament to a Presbyterian system of church government. The second was the reorganization of the parliamentary army under Oliver Cromwell (1599–1658), a country squire of iron discipline and strong, independent religious sentiment. Cromwell and his "godly men" were willing to tolerate an established majority church, but only if it permitted Protestant dissenters to worship outside it. (See "John Milton Defends the Freedom to Print Books," page 425.)

Defeated militarily by June 1645, Charles for the next several years tried to take advantage of divisions within Parliament, but Cromwell and his army foiled him. Members who might have been sympathetic to the monarch were expelled from Parliament in December 1648. After a trial by a special court. Charles was executed on January 30, 1649, as a public criminal. Parliament then abolished the monarchy, the House of Lords, and the Anglican Church.

From 1649 to 1660, England became officially a Puritan republic, although Cromwell dominated it.

Oliver Cromwell's New Model Army defeated the royalists in the English Civil War. After the execution of Charles I in 1649, Cromwell dominated the short-lived English republic, conquered Ireland and Scotland, and ruled as Lord Protector from 1653 until his death in 1658. Stock Montage, Inc./Historical Pictures Collection

His army brutally conquered Scotland and Ireland, where his radically Protestant army carried out numerous atrocities against Irish Catholics. As a national leader, however, Cromwell, proved to be no politician. When in 1653, the House of Commons wanted to disband his expensive army of 50,000 men, Cromwell instead disbanded Parliament. He ruled thereafter as Lord Protector.

Cromwell's military dictatorship, however, proved no more effective than Charles's rule and became just as harsh and hated. People deeply resented his Puritan prohibitions of drunkenness, theatergoing, and dancing. Political liberty vanished in the name of religious conformity. When Cromwell died in 1658, the English were ready by 1660 to restore both the Anglican Church and the monarchy.

CHARLES II AND THE RESTORATION OF THE MONARCHY

After negotiations with the army, Charles II (r. 1660–1685) returned to England amid great rejoicing. A man of considerable charm and political skill, Charles set a refreshing new tone after eleven years of somber Puritanism. England returned to the status quo of 1642, with a hereditary monarch, a Parliament of Lords and Commons that met only when the king summoned it, and the Anglican Church, with its bishops and prayer book, supreme in religion.

The king, however, had secret Catholic sympathies and favored religious toleration. He wanted to allow loyal Catholics and Puritans to worship freely. Yet ultra-royalists in Parliament between 1661 and 1665, through a series of laws known as the Clarendon Code, excluded Roman Catholics, Presbyterians, and Independents from the official religious and political life of the nation.

In 1670 by the Treaty of Dover, England and France formally allied against the Dutch, their chief commercial competitor. In a secret portion of this treaty, Charles pledged to announce his conversion to Catholicism as soon as conditions in England permitted this to happen. In return for this announcement (which Charles never made), Louis XIV promised to pay Charles a substantial subsidy. In an attempt to unite the English people behind the war with Holland, and as a sign of good faith to Louis XIV, Charles issued a Declaration

JOHN MILTON DEFENDS FREEDOM TO PRINT BOOKS

Certain Puritans were as concerned about resisting potential tyranny from Parliament as from the monarchy. During the English Civil War, the Parliament passed a very strict censorship measure. In "Areopagitica" (1644), John Milton, later the author of Paradise Lost *(1667), attacked this law and contributed one of the major defenses of the freedom of the press in the history of Western culture. In the passage that follows, he compares the life of a book with the life of a human being.*

■ *Why does Milton think that it may be more dangerous and harmful to attack a book than to attack a person? Was life cheaper and intelligence rarer in his time? Does he have particular kinds of books in mind? What can a book do for society that people cannot?*

I deny not but that it is of greatest concern in the Church and Commonwealth to have a vigilant eye how books demean themselves as well as men; and thereafter to confine, imprison, and do sharpest justice on them as [if they were criminals]; for books are not absolutely dead things, but do contain a progeny of life in them to be as active as that soul was whose progeny they are; nay, they do preserve as in a vial the purest efficacy and extraction of that living intellect that bred them . . . . He who kills a man kills a reasonable creature, God's Image; but he who destroys a good book, kills reason itself, kills the Image of God, as it were . . . . Many a man lives [as] a burden to the Earth; but a good book is the precious life-blood of a master spirit, embalmed and treasured up on purpose to a life beyond life. It is true, no age can restore a life, whereof, perhaps there is no great loss; and revolutions of ages do not oft recover the loss of a rejected truth, for the want of which whole nations fare the worse. We should be wary, therefore, what persecution we raise against the living labours of public men, how we spill that seasoned life of man preserved and stored up in books; since we see a kind of homicide may be thus committed, sometimes a martyrdom, and if it extends to the whole impression, a kind of massacre, whereof the execution ends not in the slaying of an elemental life, but strikes at that ethereal . . . essence, the breath of reason itself; slays an immortality rather than a life.

From J. A. St. John, ed., *The Prose Works of John Milton* (London: H. G. Bohn, 1843–1853), 2:8–9.

ENGLAND IN THE SEVENTEENTH CENTURY

1603   James VI of Scotland becomes James I of England
1604   Hampton Court conference
1611   Publication of the authorized, or King James, version of the English Bible
1625   Charles I becomes English monarch
1628   Petition of Right
1629   Charles I dissolves Parliament and embarks on eleven years of personal rule
1640   April–May, Short Parliament November, Long Parliament convenes
1642   Outbreak of the Civil War
1645   Charles I defeated at Naseby
1648   Pride's Purge
1649   Charles I executed
1649–1660   Various attempts at a Puritan Commonwealth
1660   Charles II restored to the English throne
1670   Secret Treaty of Dover between France and England
1672   Parliament passes the Test Act
1678   Popish Plot
1685   James II becomes king of England
1688   "Glorious Revolution"
1689   William and Mary proclaimed English monarchs
1701   Acts of Settlement provides for Hanoverian succession
1702–1714   Reign of Queen Anne, the last of the Stuarts
1707   Act of Union between England and Scotland
1713   Treaty of Utrecht ends the War of the Spanish Succession
1714   George I becomes king of Great Britain and establishes the Hanoverian dynasty
1721–1742   Robert Walpole dominates British politics
1727   George II becomes king of Great Britain

of Indulgence in 1672, suspending all laws against Roman Catholics and non-Anglican Protestants. Parliament refused to fund the war, however, until Charles rescinded the measure. After he did so, Parliament passed the Test Act requiring all civil and military officials of the crown to swear an oath against the doctrine of transubstantiation—

which no loyal Roman Catholic could honestly do. Parliament had aimed the Test Act largely at the king's brother, James, duke of York, heir to the throne and a recent, devout convert to Catholicism.

In 1678, a notorious liar named Titus Oates swore before a magistrate that Charles's Catholic wife, through her physician, was plotting with Jesuits and Irishmen to kill the king so James could assume the throne. Parliament believed Oates. In the ensuing hysteria, known as the Popish Plot, several innocent people were tried and executed. Riding the crest of anti-Catholic sentiment and led by the earl of Shaftesbury (1621–1683), opposition members of Parliament, called Whigs, made an unsuccessful effort to exclude James from succession to the throne.

More suspicious than ever of Parliament, Charles II turned again to increased customs duties and the assistance of Louis XIV for extra income. By these means, he was able to rule from 1681 to 1685 without recalling Parliament. In those years, Charles drove Shaftesbury into exile, executed several Whig leaders for treason, and bullied local corporations into electing members of Parliament submissive to the royal will. When Charles died in 1685 (after a deathbed conversion to Catholicism), he left James the prospect of a Parliament filled with royal friends.

THE "GLORIOUS REVOLUTION"

When James II (r. 1685–1688) became king, he immediately demanded the repeal of the Test Act. When Parliament balked, he dissolved it and proceeded to appoint Catholics to high positions in both his court and the army. In 1687, he issued another Declaration of Indulgence suspending all religious tests and permitting free worship. In June 1688, James imprisoned seven Anglican bishops who had refused to publicize his suspension of laws against the Catholics. Each of these actions represented a direct royal attack on the local authority of nobles, landowners, the church, and other corporate bodies whose members believed they possessed particular legal privileges.

The English had hoped that James would be succeeded by Mary (r. 1689–1694), his Protestant eldest daughter. She was the wife of William III of Orange, the leader of European opposition to Louis XIV. But on June 20, James II's Catholic second wife gave birth to a son. There was now a Catholic male heir to the throne. The Parliamentary opposition invited William to invade England to preserve its "traditional liberties," that is, the Anglican Church and parliamentary government.

William of Orange arrived with his army in November 1688 and was received without significant opposition by the English people. James fled to France, and Parliament, in 1689, proclaimed William III and Mary II the new monarchs, thus completing the bloodless "Glorious Revolution." William and Mary, in turn, recognized a Bill of Rights that limited the powers of the monarchy and guaranteed the civil liberties of the English privileged classes. Henceforth, England's monarchs would be subject to law and would rule by the consent of Parliament, which was to be called into session every three years. The Bill of Rights also prohibited Roman Catholics from occupying the English throne. The Toleration Act of 1689 permitted worship by all Protestants and outlawed only Roman Catholics and those who denied the Christian doctrine of the Trinity. It did not, however, extend full political rights to persons outside the Church of England.

The measure closing this century of strife was the Act of Settlement (1701), which provided for the English crown to go to the Protestant House of Hanover in Germany if Anne (r. 1702–1714), the second daughter of James II and the heir to the childless William III, died without issue. Thus, at Anne's death in 1714, the Elector of Hanover became King George I of Great Britain (r. 1714–1727) since England and Scotland had been combined in an Act of Union in 1707.

THE AGE OF WALPOLE

George I almost immediately confronted a challenge to his title. James Edward Stuart (1688–1766), the Catholic son of James II, landed in Scotland in December 1715, but met defeat less than two months later.

Despite the victory over the Stuart pretender, the political situation after 1715 remained in flux until Sir Robert Walpole (1676–1745) took over the helm of government. Walpole's ascendancy from 1721 to 1742 was based on royal support, his ability to handle the House of Commons, and his control of government patronage. Walpole maintained peace abroad and promoted the status quo at home. Britain's foreign trade spread from New England to India. Because the central government refrained

Sir Robert Walpole (1676–1745), far left, is shown talking with the Speaker of the House of Commons. Walpole, who dominated British political life from 1721 to 1742, is considered the first prime minister of Britain.   Mansell/TimePix/Getty Images, Inc.

from interfering with the local political influence of nobles and other landowners, they were willing to serve as local government administrators, judges, and military commanders, and to collect and pay the taxes to support a powerful military force, particularly a strong navy. As a result, Great Britain became not only a European power of the first order but eventually a world power.

The power of the British monarchs and their ministers had real limits. Parliament could not wholly ignore popular pressure. Even with the extensive use of patronage, many members of Parliament maintained independent views. Newspapers and public debate flourished. Free speech could be exercised, as could freedom of association. There was no large standing army. There existed significant religious toleration. Walpole's enemies could and did openly oppose his policies, which would not have been possible on the Continent. Consequently, the English state combined considerable military power with both religious and political liberty. British political life became the model for all progressive Europeans who questioned the absolutist political developments of the Continent. Furthermore, many of the political values that had emerged in the British Isles during the seventeenth century also took deep root among their North American colonies.

RISE OF ABSOLUTE MONARCHY IN FRANCE: THE WORLD OF LOUIS XIV

Historians once portrayed Louis XIV's reign (r. 1643–1715) as a time when the French monarchy exerted far-reaching, direct control of the nation at all levels. A somewhat different picture has now emerged.

The French monarchy, which had faced numerous challenges from strong, well-armed nobles and discontented Protestants during the first half of the seventeenth century, only gradually achieved the firm authority for which it became renowned later in the century. The groundwork for Louis XIV's absolutism had been laid by two powerful chief ministers, Cardinal Richelieu (1585–1642) under Louis XIII (r. 1610–1643), and then by Cardinal Mazarin (1602–1661). Both Richelieu and Mazarin attempted to impose direct royal administration on France. Richelieu had also circumscribed many of the political privileges Henry IV had extended to French Protestants in the Edict of Nantes (1598). The centralizing policies of Richelieu and then of Mazarin, however, finally provoked a series of

widespread rebellions among French nobles between 1649 and 1652 known as the *Fronde* (after the slingshots used by street boys).

Though unsuccessful, these rebellions convinced Louis XIV and his advisors that heavy-handed policies could endanger the throne. Thereafter Louis would concentrate unprecedented authority in the monarchy, but he would be more subtle than his predecessors. His genius was to make the monarchy the most important and powerful political institution in France while also assuring the nobles and other wealthy groups of their social standing and influence on the local level. Rather than destroying existing local social and political institutions, Louis largely worked through them. Nevertheless, the king was clearly the senior partner in the relationship.

YEARS OF PERSONAL RULE

On the death of Mazarin in 1661, Louis XIV assumed personal control of the government at the age of twenty-three. He appointed no single chief minister. Rebellious nobles would now be challenging the king directly; they could not claim to be resisting only a bad minister.

Louis devoted enormous personal energy to his political tasks. He ruled through councils that controlled foreign affairs, the army, domestic administration, and economic regulations. Each day he spent hours with the ministers of these councils, whom he chose from families long in royal service or from among people just beginning to rise in the social structure. Unlike the more ancient noble families, the latter had no real or potential power bases in the provinces and depended solely on the king for their standing in both government and society.

Louis made sure, however, that the nobility and other major social groups would benefit from the growth of his own authority. Although he controlled foreign affairs and limited the influence of noble institutions on the monarchy, he never tried to abolish those institutions or limit their local authority. The crown, for example, usually conferred informally with regional judicial bodies, called *parlements*, before making rulings that would affect them. Likewise, the crown would rarely enact economic regulations without consulting local opinion. Louis did, however, clash with the Parlement of Paris, which had the right to register royal laws. In 1673, he curtailed its power by requiring it to register laws before raising any questions about them. Many regional parlements and other authorities, however, had long resented the power of that Parisian body and thus supported the monarch.

VERSAILLES

Louis and his advisors became masters of propaganda and political image creation. Louis never missed an opportunity to impress the grandeur of his crown on the French people but most especially on the French nobility. He did so by the manipulation of symbols. For example, when the *dauphin* (the heir to the French throne) was born in 1662, Louis appeared for the celebration dressed as a Roman emperor. He also dominated the nobility by demonstrating that he could outspend them and create a greater social display than the strongest nobles in the land.

The central element of the image of the monarchy was the palace of Versailles, which, when completed, was the largest secular structure in Europe. More than any other monarch of the day, Louis XIV used the physical setting of his court to exert political control. Versailles, built between 1676 and 1708 on the outskirts of Paris, became Louis's permanent residence after 1682. It was a temple to royalty, designed and decorated to proclaim the glory of the Sun King, as Louis was known. A spectacular estate with magnificent fountains and gardens, it housed thousands of the more important nobles, royal officials, and servants. The stables alone could hold 12,000 horses. Some nobles paid for their own residence at the palace, thus depleting their resources; others required royal patronage to remain in residence. In either case they became dependent on the monarch. Although it consumed over half Louis's annual revenues, Versailles paid significant political dividends.

Because Louis ruled personally, he was himself the chief source of favors and patronage in France. To emphasize his prominence, he organized life at court around every aspect of his own daily routine. Elaborate etiquette governed every detail of life at Versailles. Moments near the king were important to most court nobles because they were effectively excluded from the real business of government. The king's rising and dressing were times of rare intimacy, when nobles could whisper their special requests in his ear. Fortunate nobles held his night candle when he went to his bed.

Some nobles, of course, avoided Versailles. They managed their estates and cultivated their local influence. Many others were simply too poor to cut a figure at court. All the nobility understood, however, that Louis, unlike Richelieu and Mazarin, would not threaten their local social standing. Louis supported France's traditional social structure and the social privileges of the nobility. Yet even the most powerful nobles knew they could strike only a modest figure when compared to the Sun King.

KING BY DIVINE RIGHT

An important source for Louis's concept of royal authority was his devout tutor, the political theorist Bishop Jacques-Bénigne Bossuet (1627–1704). Bossuet defended what he called the "divine right of kings" and cited examples of Old Testament rulers divinely appointed by and answerable only to God. Medieval popes had insisted that only God could judge a pope; so Bossuet argued that only God could judge the king. Although kings might be duty bound to reflect God's will in their rule, yet as God's regents on earth they could not be bound to the dictates of mere nobles and parliaments. Such assumptions lay behind Louis XIV's alleged declaration: *"L'état, c'est moi"* ("I am the state").

Despite these claims, Louis's rule did not exert the oppressive control over the daily lives of his subjects that police states would do in the nineteenth and twentieth centuries. His absolutism functioned primarily in the classic areas of European state action—the making of war and peace, the regulation of religion, and the oversight of economic activity. Even at the height of his power, local institutions, some controlled by townspeople and others by nobles, retained their administrative authority. The king and his ministers supported the social and financial privileges of these local elites. In contrast to the Stuart kings of England, however, Louis firmly prevented them from interfering with his authority on the national level. This system would endure until a financial crisis demoralized the French monarchy in the 1780s.

LOUIS'S EARLY WARS

By the late 1660s, France was superior to any other European nation in population, administrative bureaucracy, army, and national unity. Because of the economic policies of Jean-Baptiste Colbert (1619–1683), his most brilliant minister, Louis could afford to raise and maintain a large and powerful army. His enemies and some later historians claimed that Louis wished to dominate all of Europe, but it would appear that his chief military and foreign policy goal was to achieve secure international boundaries for France. He was particularly concerned to secure its northern borders along the Spanish Netherlands, the Franche-Comté, Alsace, and Lorraine from which foreign armies had invaded France and could easily do so again. Louis was also determined to frustrate Habsburg ambitions that endangered France and, as part of that goal, sought to secure his southern borders toward Spain. Whether reacting to external events or pursuing his own ambitions, Louis's pursuit of French interests threatened and terrified neighboring states and led them to form coalitions against France.

A CLOSER LOOK

Versailles

Louis XIV constructed his great palace at Versailles, as painted here in 1668 by Pierre Patel the Elder (1605–1676), to demonstrate the new centralized power he sought to embody in the French monarchy.

The outer wings, extending from the front of the central structure, housed governmental offices.

The central building is the hunting lodge his father Louis XIII had built earlier in the century. Its interior and that of the wings added to it were decorated with themes from mythology presenting Louis XIV as the "Sun King" around whom all his kingdom revolved.

The gardens and ponds behind the main structure were the sites of elaborate entertainment, concerts, and fireworks.

Pierre Patel, "Perspective View of Versailles." Chateaux de Versailles et de Trianon, Versailles, France. Photo copyright Bridgeman-Giraudon/Art Resource, N.Y.

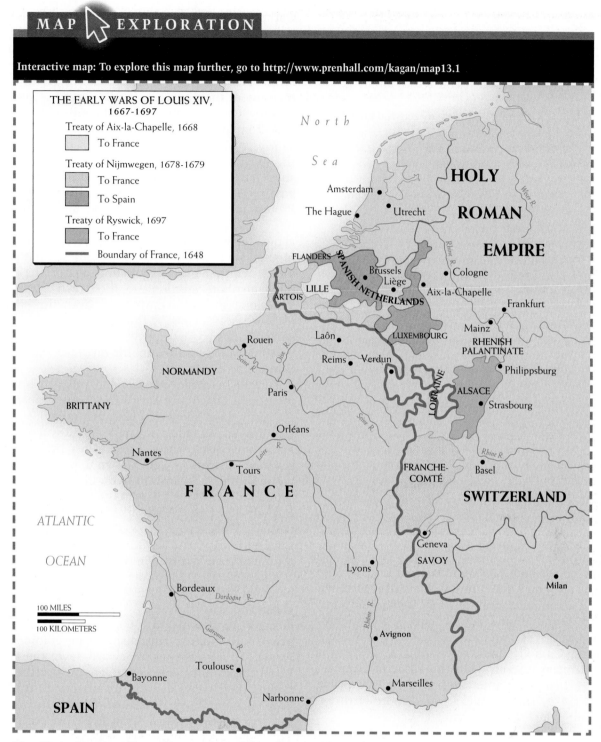

Interactive map: To explore this map further, go to http://www.prenhall.com/kagan/map13.1

Map 13–1 **THE FIRST THREE WARS OF LOUIS XIV**   This map shows the territorial changes resulting from Louis XIV's first three major wars (1667–1697).

The early wars of Louis XIV included conflicts with Spain and the United Netherlands. The first was the War of the Devolution in which Louis supported the alleged right of his first wife, Marie Thérèse, to inherit the Spanish Netherlands. He contended that through complex legal arrangements they should have "devolved" upon her, hence the name of the war. In 1667, Louis's armies invaded Flanders and the Franche-Comté. He was repulsed by the Triple Alliance of England, Sweden, and the United Provinces. By the Treaty of Aix-la-Chapelle (1668), he gained control of certain towns bordering the Spanish Netherlands. (See Map 13–1.)

In 1670, with the secret Treaty of Dover, England and France became allies against the Dutch.

FRANCE FROM LOUIS XIV TO CARDINAL FLEURY

1643	Louis ascends the French throne at the age of five
1643–1661	Cardinal Mazarin directs the French government
1648	Peace of Westphalia
1649–1652	The *Fronde* revolt
1653	The pope declares Jansenism a heresy
1660	Papal ban on Jansenists enforced in France
1661	Louis commences personal rule
1667–1668	War of Devolution
1670	Secret Treaty of Dover between France and Great Britain
1672–1679	French war against the Netherlands
1685	Louis revokes the Edict of Nantes
1688–1697	War of the League of Augsburg
1701	Outbreak of the War of the Spanish Succession
1713	Treaty of Utrecht between France and Great Britain
1714	Treaty of Rastatt between France and the Empire and Holland
1715	Death of Louis XIV
1715–1720	Regency of the duke of Orléans in France
1720	Mississippi Bubble bursts in France
1726–1743	Cardinal Fleury serves as Louis XV's chief minister

Louis invaded the Netherlands again in 1672. The Prince of Orange, the future William III of England, forged an alliance with the Holy Roman Emperor, Spain, Lorraine, and Brandenburg against Louis, now regarded as a menace to the whole of western Europe, Catholic and Protestant alike. The war ended inconclusively with the Peace of Nijmwegen, signed with different parties in successive years (1678, 1679). France gained more territory, including the Franche-Comté.

LOUIS'S REPRESSIVE RELIGIOUS POLICIES

Like Richelieu before him, Louis believed that political unity and stability required religious conformity. To that end he carried out repressive actions against both Roman Catholics and Protestants

Suppression of the Jansenists The French crown and the French Roman Catholic church had long jealously guarded their ecclesiastical independence or "Gallican Liberties" from papal authority in Rome. However, after the conversion to Roman Catholicism of Henry IV in 1593, the Jesuits, fiercely loyal to the authority of the Pope, had monopolized the education of French upper-class men, and their devout students promoted the religious reforms and doctrines of the Council of Trent. As a measure of their success, Jesuits served as confessors to Henry IV, Louis XIII, and Louis XIV.

A Roman Catholic religious movement known as *Jansenism* arose in the 1630s in opposition to the theology and the political influence of the Jesuits. Jansenists adhered to the teachings of St. Augustine (354–430) that had also influenced many Protestant doctrines. Serious and uncompromising, they particularly opposed Jesuit teachings about free will. They believed with Augustine that original sin had so corrupted humankind that individuals could by their own effort do nothing good nor contribute anything to their own salvation. The namesake of the movement, Cornelius Jansen (d. 1638), was a Flemish theologian and the bishop of Ypres. His posthumously published *Augustinus* (1640) assailed Jesuit teaching on grace and salvation as morally lax.

Jansenism made considerable progress among prominent families in Paris. They were opposed to the Jesuits and supported Jansenist religious communities such as the convent at Port-Royal outside Paris. Jansenists, whose Augustinian theology resembled Calvinism, were known to live extremely pious and morally austere lives. In these respects, though firm Roman Catholics, they resembled English Puritans. Also, like the Puritans, the Jansenists became associated with opposition to royal authority, and families of Jansenist sympathies had been involved in the *Fronde*.

On May 31, 1653, Pope Innocent X declared heretical five Jansenist theological propositions on grace and salvation. In 1656, the pope banned Jansen's *Augustinus*. In 1660, Louis permitted the papal bull banning Jansenism to be enforced in France. He also eventually closed down the Port-Royal community. Thereafter, Jansenists either retracted their views or went underground. In 1713, Pope Clement XI issued the bull *Unigenitus* which again extensively condemned Jansenist teaching. The now aged Louis XIV ordered the French church to accept the bull despite internal ecclesiastical opposition.

The theological issues surrounding Jansenism were complex. By persecuting the Jansenists, however, Louis XIV turned his back on the long tradition of protecting the Gallican Liberties of the French Church and fostered within the French Church a core of opposition to royal authority. This had long-term political significance. During the eighteenth century after the death of Louis XIV, the Parlement of Paris and other French judi-

Françoise d'Aubigne, Madame de Maintenon (1635–1719), a mistress to Louis XIV, secretly married him after his first wife's death. The deeply pious Maintenon influenced Louis's policy to make Roman Catholicism France's only religion.   Pierre Mignard (1612–1695), "Portrait of Françoise d'Aubigne, marquise de Maintenon (1635–1719), mistress and second wife of Louis XIV," c. 1694. Oil on canvas, 128 × 97 cm. Inv.: MV 3637. Chateaux de Versailles et de Trianon, Versailles. Bridgeman-Giraudon/Art Resource, NY

cial bodies would reassert their authority in opposition to the monarchy. These courts were sympathetic to the Jansenists because of their common resistance to royal authority. Jansenism, because of its austere morality, then also came to embody a set of religious and moral values that contrasted with what eighteenth-century public opinion saw as the corruption of the mid-eighteenth-century French royal court.

Revocation of the Edict of Nantes   After the Edict of Nantes in 1598, relations between the Catholic majority (nine-tenths of the French population) and the Protestant minority had remained hostile. There were about 1.75 million Huguenots in France in the 1660s (out of an overall population of around 18 million), but their numbers were declining. The French Catholic church had long supported their persecution as both pious and patriotic.

After the Peace of Nijmwegen, Louis launched a methodical campaign against the Huguenots in an effort to unify France religiously. He was also influenced in this policy by his mistress who became his second wife Madame de Maintenon (1635–1719), a deeply pious Catholic who drew Louis toward a much more devout religious observance. Louis hounded Huguenots out of public life, banning them from government office and excluding them from such professions as printing and medicine. He used financial incentives to encourage them to convert to Catholicism. In 1681, he bullied them by quartering troops in their towns. Finally, in October 1685, Louis revoked the Edict of Nantes, and extensive religious repression followed. Protestant churches and schools were closed, Protestant ministers exiled, nonconverting laity were condemned to be galley slaves, and Protestant children were baptized by Catholic priests. (See "Louis XIV Revokes the Edict of Nantes," page 434.)

The revocation was a major blunder. Henceforth, Protestants across Europe considered Louis a fanatic who must be resisted at all costs. More than a quarter million people, many of whom were highly skilled, left France. They formed new communities abroad and joined the resistance to Louis in England, Germany, Holland, and the New World. As a result of the revocation of the Edict of Nantes and the ongoing persecution of Jansenists, France became a symbol of religious repression in contrast to England's reputation for moderate, if not complete, religious toleration.

LOUIS'S LATER WARS

The League of Augsburg and the Nine Years' War After the Treaty of Nijmwegen in 1678–1679, Louis maintained his army at full strength and restlessly probed beyond his borders. In 1681 his forces occupied the free city of Strasbourg on the Rhine River, prompting new defensive coalitions to form against him. One of these, the League of Augsburg, grew to include England, Spain, Sweden, the United Provinces, and the major German states. It also had the support of the Habsburg emperor Leopold I (r. 1658–1705). Between 1689 and 1697, the League and France battled each other in the Nine Years' War, while England and France struggled to control North America.

The Peace of Ryswick, signed in September 1697, which ended the war, secured Holland's borders and thwarted Louis's expansion into Germany.

War of the Spanish Succession   On November 1, 1700, the last Habsburg king of Spain, Charles II (r. 1665–1700), died without direct heirs. Before his death, negotiations had begun among the nations involved to partition his inheritance in a way that would preserve the existing balance of power. Charles II, however, left his entire inheritance to Louis's grandson Philip of Anjou, who became Philip V of Spain (r. 1700–1746).

LOUIS XIV REVOKES
THE EDICT OF NANTES

———※———

Believing a country could not be under one king and one law unless it was also under one religious system, Louis XIV stunned much of Europe in October 1685, by revoking the Edict of Nantes, which had protected the religious freedoms and civil rights of French Protestants since 1598. Compare this document to the one on page 442 in which the elector of Brandenburg welcomes displaced French Protestants into his domains.

■ *What specific actions does this declaration order against Protestants? Does it offer any incentives for Protestants to convert to Catholicism? How does this declaration compare with the English Test Act?*

Art. 1. Know that we . . . with our certain knowledge, full power and royal authority, have by this present, perpetual and irrevocable edict, suppressed and revoked the edict of the aforesaid king our grandfather, given at Nantes in the month of April, 1598, in all its extent . . . together with all the concessions made by [this] and other edicts, declarations, and decrees, to the people of the so-called Reformed religion, of whatever nature they be . . . and in consequence we desire . . . that all the temples of the people of the aforesaid so-called Reformed religion situated in our kingdom . . . should be demolished forthwith.

Art. 2. We forbid our subjects of the so-called Reformed religion to assemble any more for public worship of the above-mentioned religion . . . .

Art. 3. We likewise forbid all lords, of whatever rank they may be, to carry out heretical services in houses and fiefs . . . the penalty for . . . the said worship being confiscation of their body and possessions.

Art. 4. We order all ministers of the aforesaid so-called Reformed religion who do not wish to be converted and to embrace the Catholic, Apostolic, and Roman religion, to depart from our kingdom and the lands subject to us within fifteen days from the publication of our present edict . . . on pain of the galleys.

Art. 5. We desire that those among the said [Reformed] ministers who shall be converted [to the Catholic religion] shall continue to enjoy during their life, and their wives shall enjoy after their death as long as they remain widows, the same exemptions from taxation and billeting of soldiers, which they enjoyed while they fulfilled the function of ministers. . . .

Art. 8. With regard to children who shall be born to those of the aforesaid so-called Reformed religion, we desire that they be baptized by their parish priests. We command the fathers and mothers to send them to the churches for that purpose, on penalty of a fine of 500 livres or more if they fail to do so; and afterwards, the children shall be brought up in the Catholic, Apostolic, and Roman religion. . . .

Art. 10. All our subjects of the so-called Reformed religion, with their wives and children, are to be strongly and repeatedly prohibited from leaving our aforesaid kingdom . . . or of taking out . . . their possessions and effects. . . .

The members of the so-called Reformed religion, while awaiting God's pleasure to enlighten them like the others, can live in the towns and districts of our kingdom . . . and continue their occupation there, and enjoy their possessions . . . on condition . . . that they do not make public profession of [their religion].

S. Z. Ehler and John B. Morrall, eds. and trans., *Church and State Through the Centuries: A Collection of Historic Documents* (New York: Biblo and Tannen, 1967), pp. 209–213. Reprinted by permission of Biblo and Tannen Booksellers and Publishers.

Spain and the vast trade with its American empire appeared to have fallen to France. In September 1701, England, Holland, and the Holy Roman Empire formed the Grand Alliance to preserve the balance of power by once and for all securing Flanders as a neutral barrier between Holland and France and by gaining for the emperor, who was also a Habsburg, his fair share of the Spanish inheritance. Louis soon increased the political stakes by recognizing the Stuart claim to the English throne.

In 1701 the War of the Spanish Succession (1701–1714) began, and it soon enveloped western Europe. France for the first time in Louis's reign went to war with inadequate finances, a poorly equipped army, and mediocre generals. The English, in contrast, had advanced weaponry (flintlock rifles, paper cartridges, and ring bayonets) and superior tactics (thin, maneuverable troop columns rather than the traditional deep ones). John Churchill, the Duke of Marlborough (1650–1722) bested Louis's soldiers in every major engagement, although French arms triumphed in Spain. After 1709 the war became a bloody stalemate.

France finally made peace with England at Utrecht in July 1713, and with Holland and the emperor at Rastatt in March 1714. Philip V remained king of Spain but England got Gibraltar and the island of Minorca, making it a Mediterranean power. (See Map 13–2.) Louis also recognized the right of the House of Hanover the English throne.

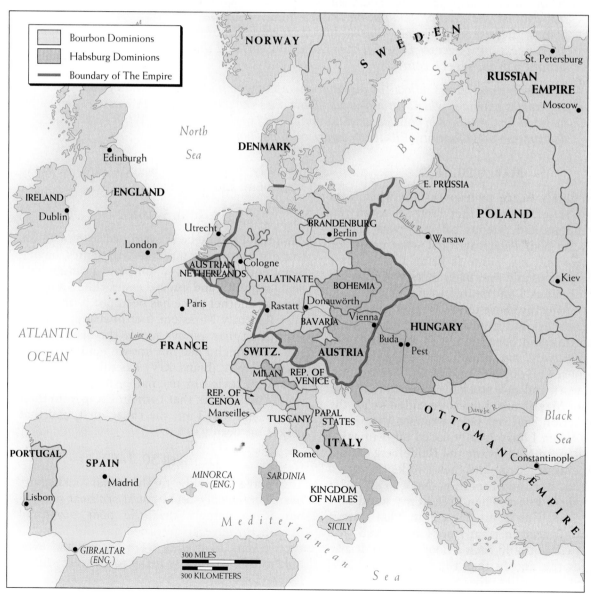

Map 13–2   **EUROPE IN 1714**   The War of the Spanish Succession ended a year before the death of Louis XIV. The Bourbons had secured the Spanish throne, but Spain had forfeited its possessions in Flanders and Italy.

LOUIS XIV'S SISTER-IN-LAW GRIEVES FOR HER HOMELAND

Charlotte Elisabeth, Duchesse d'Orléans (1652–1722), who was married to the brother of Louis XIV of France, had been born the daughter of the Elector of the Palatinate. After her marriage in 1671, she moved to the French court and was never permitted to revisit her homeland. She did, however, carry out an extensive correspondence with friends and family in Germany throughout her life. In August 1688, Louis XIV invaded the Palatinate under the guise of restoring it to his sister-in-law. He had no real purpose except the conquest of the German region. This invasion was important for two reasons. First, it opened a war that continued until 1697. Second, at the onset of the original invasion, the French forces committed enormous atrocities against the civilian population, killing many civilians and destroying their homes. In these letters to her aunt and foster mother, Charlotte Elisabeth recounts her sadness and anger over the plight of these civilians and the difficulty of her own situation in the French court.

■ *How do these letters reflect the plight of a woman who had been required to enter a dynastic marriage when war broke out? How does she report Louis XIV's using her name to further his own political and financial ends in the Palatinate? What kind of destruction was Charlotte Elisabeth aware of in her homeland?*

MARCH 20, 1689

I had barely began to recover somewhat from poor Carllutz's death [her brother] when the horrendous and piteous calamity was visited upon the poor Palatinate, and what pains me most is that my name is being used to cast these poor people into utter misery. And when I cry about it, I am treated to great annoyance and sulking [by those in the French royal court at Versailles]. But to save my life I cannot stop lamenting and bemoaning the thought that I am as it were, my fatherland's ruin, especially when I see all of the Elector's, my late father's, hard work and care suddenly reduced to rubble in poor Mannheim. I am so horrified by all the destruction that has been wrought that every night when I have finally dozed off, I imagine that I am in Mannheim and Heidelberg amidst all the destruction, and then I wake up with a dreadful start and cannot go back to sleep for two whole hours. Then I see in my mind how everything was in my day and in what state it is now, indeed in what state I am myself, and then I cannot hold back a flood of tears. It also grieves me deeply that the King [Louis XIV] waited to inflict the ultimate devastation precisely until I had begged him to spare Mannheim and Heidelberg.

JUNE 5, 1689

Although I should be accustomed by now to the thought of my poor fatherland in flames, having heard nothing else for so long, I still cannot help being regretful and grieved every time I am told that yet another place has been put to the torch . . . . Recently Monsieur [her husband] told me something that annoys me to the depth of my soul and which I had not known before, namely that the King [Louis XIV] has all taxes in the Palatinate levied in my name; now these poor people must think that I am profiting from their misery and that I am the cause of it, and that makes me deeply sad.

OCTOBER 30, 1689

Yesterday I was told something that touched my heart very deeply, and I could not hear it without tears; namely that the poor people of Mannheim have all returned and are living in their cellars as if they were houses and even hold a daily market as if the town were still in its previous state.

FRANCE AFTER LOUIS XIV

Despite its military reverses in the War of the Spanish Succession, France remained a great power. It was less strong in 1715 than in 1680, but it still possessed the largest European population, an advanced, if troubled, economy, and the administrative structure bequeathed it by Louis XIV. Moreover, even if France and its resources had been drained by the last of Louis's wars, the other major states of Europe were similarly debilitated.

Louis XIV was succeeded by his five-year-old great-grandson Louis XV (r. 1715–1774). The young boy's uncle, the duke of Orléans, became regent and remained so until his death in 1720. The regency, marked by financial and moral scandals, further undermined the faltering prestige of the monarchy.

John Law and the Mississippi Bubble   The duke of Orléans was a gambler, and for a time he turned over the financial management of the kingdom to John Law (1671–1729), a Scottish mathematician and fellow gambler. Law believed an increase in the paper-money supply would stimulate France's economic recovery. With the permission of the regent, he established a bank in Paris that issued paper money. Law then organized a monopoly, called the Mississippi Company, on trading privileges with the French colony of Louisiana in North America.

The Mississippi Company also took over the management of the French national debt. The company issued shares of its own stock in exchange for government bonds, which had fallen sharply in value. To redeem large quantities of bonds, Law encouraged speculation in the Mississippi Company stock. In 1719, the price of the stock rose handsomely. Smart investors, however, took their profits by selling their stock in exchange for paper money from Law's bank, which they then sought to exchange for gold. The bank, however, lacked enough gold to redeem all the paper money brought to it.

In February 1720, all gold payments were halted in France. Soon thereafter, Law himself fled the country. The Mississippi Bubble, as the affair was called, had burst. The fiasco brought disgrace on the government that had sponsored Law. The Mississippi Company was later reorganized and functioned profitably, but fear of paper money and speculation marked French economic life for decades.

Renewed Authority of the *Parlements*   The duke of Orléans made a second decision that also lessened the power of the monarchy. He attempted to draw the French nobility once again into the decision-making processes of the government. He set up a system of councils on which nobles were to serve along with bureaucrats. The years of idle noble domestication at Versailles, however, had

Under Louis XV (r. 1715–1774) France suffered major defeats in Europe and around the world and lost most of its North American empire. Louis himself was an ineffective ruler, and during his reign, the monarchy encountered numerous challenges from the French aristocracy.   CORBIS/Bettmann

worked too well, and the nobility seemed to lack both the talent and the desire to govern. The experiment failed. Despite this failure, the great French nobles did not surrender their ancient ambition to assert their rights, privileges, and local influence over those of the monarchy. The chief feature of eighteenth-century French political life was the attempt of the nobility to use its authority to limit the power of the monarchy. The most effective instrument in this process was the previously mentioned *parlements*, or courts dominated by the nobility.

The duke of Orléans reversed the previously noted policy of Louis XIV and formally approved the reinstitution of the full power of the Parlement of Paris to allow or disallow laws. Moreover, throughout the eighteenth century that and other local *parlements* also succeeded in identifying their authority and resistance to the monarchy with wider public opinion. This situation meant that until the revolution in 1789, the *parlements* became natural centers not only for aristocratic but also for popular resistance to royal authority. In a vast transformation from the days of Louis XIV, the *parlements* rather than the monarchy would come to be seen as more nearly representing the nation.

By 1726, the general political direction of the nation had come under the authority of Cardinal Fleury

The impending collapse of John Law's bank triggered a financial panic throughout France. Desperate investors, such as those shown here in the city of Rennes, sought to exchange their paper currency, for gold and silver before the banks' supply of precious metals was exhausted. Collection Musée de Bretagne, Rennes

(1653–1743). He worked to maintain the authority of the monarchy, including ongoing repression of the Jansenists, while continuing to preserve the local interests of the French nobility. Like Walpole in Britain, he pursued economic prosperity at home and peace abroad. Again like Walpole, after 1740, Fleury could not prevent France from entering a worldwide colonial conflict. (See Chapter 17.)

CENTRAL AND EASTERN EUROPE

Central and eastern Europe were economically much less advanced than western Europe. Except for the Baltic ports, the economy was agrarian. There were fewer cities and many more large estates worked by serfs. The states in this region did not possess overseas empires; nor did they engage in extensive overseas trade of any kind, except for supplying grain to western Europe—grain, more often than not, carried on Western European ships.

During the sixteenth and early seventeenth centuries, the political authorities in this region, which lay largely east of the Elbe River, were weak. The almost constant warfare of the seventeenth century had led to a habit of temporary and shifting political loyalties with princes and aristocracies of small states refusing to subordinate them-

selves to central monarchical authorities.

During the last half of the seventeenth century, however, three strong dynasties, whose rulers aspired to the absolutism then being constructed in France, emerged in central and eastern Europe. After the Peace of Westphalia in 1648, the Austrian Habsburgs recognized the basic weakness of the position of the Holy Roman Emperor and started to consolidate their power outside Germany. At the same time, Prussia under the Hohenzollern dynasty emerged as a factor in north German politics and as a major challenger to the Habsburg domination of Germany. Most important, Russia under the Romanov dynasty at the opening of the eighteenth century became a military and naval power of the first order. These three monarchies would dominate central and eastern Europe till the close of World War I in 1918. By contrast, Poland during the eighteenth century became the single most conspicuous example in Europe of a land that failed to establish a viable centralized government.

POLAND: ABSENCE OF STRONG CENTRAL AUTHORITY

In no other part of Europe was the failure to maintain a competitive political position so complete as in Poland. In 1683 King John III Sobieski (r. 1674–1696) had led a Polish army to rescue Vienna from a Turkish siege. Following that spectacular effort, however, Poland became a byword for the dangers of aristocratic independence.

The Polish monarchy was elective, but the deep distrust and divisions among the nobility usually prevented their electing a king from among themselves. Sobieski was a notable exception. Most of the Polish monarchs were foreigners and the tools of foreign powers. The Polish nobles did have a central legislative body called the *Sejm*, or diet. It included only nobles and specifically excluded representatives from corporate bodies, such as the towns. The diet, however, had a practice known as the *liberum veto*, whereby the staunch opposition of any single member, who might have been bribed by a foreign power, could require the body to disband. Such opposition, termed "exploding the diet," was most often the work of a group of dissatisfied nobles rather than of one person. Nonetheless, the requirement of unanimity was a major stumbling block to effective government. The price of this noble liberty would eventually be the disappearance of Poland from the map of Europe in the late eighteenth century.

THE HABSBURG EMPIRE AND THE PRAGMATIC SANCTION

The close of the Thirty Years' War marked a fundamental turning point in the history of the Austrian Habsburgs. Previously, in alliance with their Spanish cousins, they had hoped to bring all of Germany under their control and back to the Catholic fold. In this they had failed, and the decline of Spanish power meant that the Austrian Habsburgs were on their own. (See Map 13–3.)

After 1648, the Habsburg family retained a firm hold on the title of Holy Roman Emperor, but the power of the emperor depended less on the force of arms than on the cooperation he could elicit from the various political bodies in the empire. These included large German units (such as Saxony, Hanover, Bavaria, and Brandenburg) and scores of small German cities, bishoprics, principalities, and territories of independent knights. While establishing their new dominance among the German

states, the Habsburgs also began to consolidate their power and influence within their hereditary possessions outside the Holy Roman Empire, which included the Crown of Saint Wenceslas, encompassing the kingdom of Bohemia (in the modern Czech Republic) and the duchies of Moravia and Silesia; and the Crown of Saint Stephen, which ruled Hungary, Croatia, and Transylvania. Much of Hungary was only liberated from the Turks at the end of the seventeenth century (1699).

Through the Treaty of Rastatt in 1714, the Habsburgs further extended their domains, receiving the former Spanish (thereafter Austrian) Netherlands and Lombardy in northern Italy. Thereafter, the Habsburgs' power and influence would be based primarily on their territories outside of Germany.

In each of their many territories the Habsburgs ruled by virtue of a different title—king, archduke, duke—and they needed the cooperation of the local nobility, which was not always forthcoming. They repeatedly had to bargain with nobles in one part of Europe to maintain their position in another. Their domains were so geographically diverse and the people who lived in them of so many different languages and customs that almost no grounds existed on which to unify them politically. Even Roman Catholicism proved ineffective as a common bond, particularly in Hungary, where

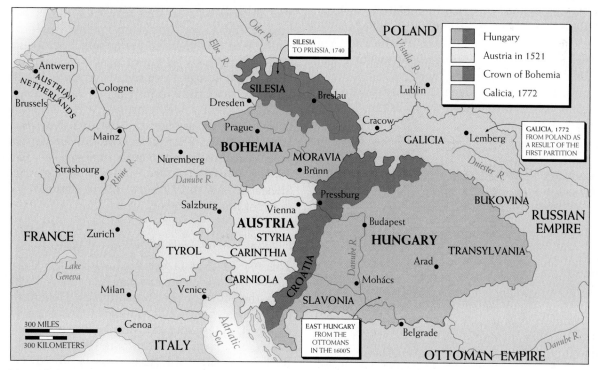

Map 13–3 **THE AUSTRIAN HABSBURG EMPIRE, 1521–1772** The empire had three main units—Austria, Bohemia, and Hungary. Expansion was mainly eastward: eastern Hungary from the Ottomans (17th century) and Galicia from Poland (1772). Meantime, Silesia was lost after 1740, but the Habsburgs remained Holy Roman Emperors.

many Magyar nobles were Calvinist and seemed ever ready to rebel. Over the years the Habsburg rulers established various central councils to chart common policies for their far-flung domains. Virtually all of these bodies, however, dealt with only a portion of the Habsburg holdings.

Despite these internal difficulties, Leopold I (r. 1658–1705) managed to resist the advances of the Ottoman Empire into central Europe, which included a siege of Vienna in 1683, and to thwart the aggression of Louis XIV. He achieved Ottoman recognition of his sovereignty over Hungary in 1699 and extended his territorial holdings over much of the Balkan Peninsula and western Romania. These conquests allowed the Habsburgs to hope to develop Mediterranean trade through the port of Trieste on the northern coast of the Adriatic Sea and helped compensate for their loss of effective power over the Holy Roman Empire. Strength in the East gave them greater political leverage in Germany. Joseph I (r. 1705–1711) continued Leopold's policies.

When Charles VI (r. 1711–1740) succeeded Joseph, a new problem was added to the chronic one of territorial diversity. He had no male heir, and there was only the weakest of precedents for a female ruler of the Habsburg domains. Charles feared that on his death the Austrian Habsburg lands might fall prey to the surrounding powers, as had those of the Spanish Habsburgs in 1700. He was determined to prevent that disaster and to provide his domains with the semblance of legal unity. To those ends, he devoted most of his reign to seeking the approval of his family, the estates of his realms, and the major foreign powers for a document called the *Pragmatic Sanction*.

This instrument provided the legal basis for a single line of inheritance within the Habsburg dynasty

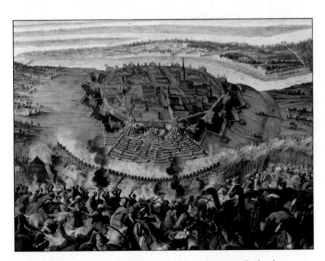

In 1683 the Ottomans laid siege to Vienna. Only the arrival of Polish forces under King John III Sobieski (r. 1674–1696) saved the Habsburg capital.
Dagli Orti/Picture Desk, Inc./Kobal Collection

AUSTRIA AND PRUSSIA IN THE LATE SEVENTEENTH AND EARLY EIGHTEENTH CENTURIES

1640–1688	Reign of Frederick William, the Great Elector
1658–1705	Leopold I rules Austria and resists the Turkish invasions
1683	Turkish siege of Vienna
1688–1713	Reign of Frederick I of Prussia
1699	Peace treaty between Turks and Habsburgs
1711–1740	Charles VI rules Austria and secures agreement to the Pragmatic Sanction
1713–1740	Frederick William I builds up the military power of Prussia
1740	Maria Theresa succeeds to the Habsburg throne
1740	Frederick II violates the Pragmatic Sanction by invading Silesia

through Charles VI's daughter Maria Theresa (r. 1740–1780). Other members of the Habsburg family recognized her as the rightful heir. After extracting various concessions from Charles, the nobles of the various Habsburg domains and the other European rulers also recognized her. Consequently, when Charles VI died in October 1740, he believed that he had secured legal unity for the Habsburg Empire and a safe succession for his daughter. He had indeed established a permanent line of succession and the basis for future legal bonds within the Habsburg holdings. Despite the Pragmatic Sanction, however, his failure to provide his daughter with a strong army or a full treasury left her inheritance open to foreign aggression. Less than two months after his death, the fragility of the foreign agreements became apparent. In December 1740, Frederick II of Prussia invaded the Habsburg province of Silesia in eastern Germany. Maria Theresa had to fight for her inheritance.

PRUSSIA AND THE HOHENZOLLERNS

The rise of Prussia occurred within the German power vacuum created by the Peace of Westphalia. It is the story of the extraordinary Hohenzollern family, which had ruled Brandenburg since 1417. Through inheritance the family had acquired the duchy of Cleves, and the counties of Mark, and Ravensburg in 1614, East Prussia in 1618, and Pomerania in 1648. (See Map 13–4.) Except for Pomerania, none of these lands shared a border with Brandenburg. East Prussia lay inside Poland and outside the authority of the Holy Roman Emperor. All

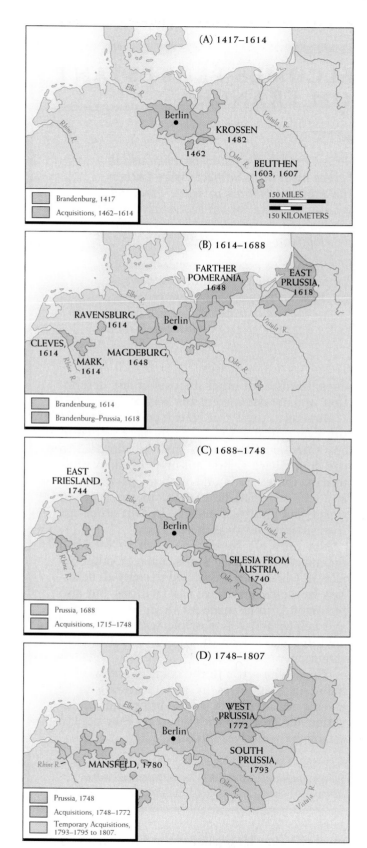

Map 13–4   **EXPANSION OF BRANDEBURG-PRUSSIA**   In the 17th century Brandenburg-Prussia expanded mainly by acquiring dynastic titles in geographically separated lands. In the 18th century it expanded through aggression to the east, seizing Silesia in 1740 and various parts of Poland in 1772, 1793, and 1795.

of the territories lacked good natural resources, and many of them were devastated during the Thirty Years' War. Still, by the late seventeenth century, the scattered Hohenzollern holdings represented a block of territory within the Holy Roman Empire, second in size only to that of the Habsburgs.

The person who began to forge these areas into a modern state was Frederick William (r. 1640–1688), who became known as the Great Elector. He established himself and his successors as the central uniting power by breaking the local noble estates, organizing a royal bureaucracy, and building a strong army. (See "The Great Elector Welcomes Protestant Refugees from France," page 442.)

Between 1655 and 1660, Sweden and Poland fought each other across the Great Elector's holdings in Pomerania and East Prussia. Frederick William had neither an adequate army nor the tax revenues to confront this threat. In 1655, the Brandenburg estates refused to grant him new taxes; however, he proceeded to collect them by military force. In 1659, a different grant of taxes, originally made in 1653, elapsed; Frederick William continued to collect them as well as those he had imposed by his own authority. He used the money to build an army, which allowed him to continue to enforce his will without the approval of the nobility. Similar coercion took place against the nobles in his other territories.

There was, however, a political and social trade-off between the Elector and his various nobles. In exchange for their obedience to the Hohenzollerns, the *Junkers*, or German noble landlords, received the right to demand obedience from their serfs. Frederick William also tended to choose as the local administrators of the tax structure men who would normally have been members of the noble branch of the old parliament. He thus co-opted potential opponents into his service. The taxes fell most heavily on the backs of the peasants and the urban classes. As the years passed, *Junkers* increasingly dominated the army officer corps, and this situation became even more pronounced during the eighteenth century. All officials and army officers took an oath of loyalty directly to the Elector. The army and the Elector thus came to embody the otherwise absent unity of the state. The army made Prussia a valuable potential ally.

Yet even with the considerable accomplishments of the Great Elector, the house of Hohenzollern did not possess a crown. The achievement of a royal title was one of the few state-building accomplishments of Frederick I (r. 1688–1713). This son of the Great Elector was the least "Prussian" of his family during these crucial years. He built palaces, founded Halle University (1694), patronized the arts, and lived luxuriously. In the War of the Spanish Succession, he put his army at the disposal of the Habsburg

THE GREAT ELECTOR WELCOMES PROTESTANT REFUGEES FROM FRANCE

The Hohenzollern dynasty of Brandenburg–Prussia pursued a policy of religious toleration. The family itself was Calvinist, whereas most of its subjects were Lutherans. When Louis XIV of France revoked the Edict of Nantes in 1685, Frederick William, the Great Elector, seized the opportunity to invite French Protestants into his realms. As his proclamation indicates, he wanted to attract persons with productive skills who could aid the economic development of his domains.

■ *In reading this document, do you believe religious or economic concerns more nearly led the elector of Brandenburg to welcome the French Protestants? What specific privileges did the elector extend to them? To what extent were these privileges a welcoming measure, and to what extent were they inducements to emigrate to Brandenburg? In what kind of economic activity does the elector expect the French refugees to engage?*

We, Friedrich Wilhelm, by Grace of God Margrave of Brandenburg . . . Do hereby proclaim and make known to all and sundry that since the cruel persecutions and rigorous ill-treatment in which Our co-religionists of the Evangelical-Reformed faith have for some time past been subjected in the Kingdom of France, have caused many families to remove themselves and to betake themselves out of the said Kingdom into other lands, We now . . . have been moved graciously to offer them through this Edict . . . a secure and free refuge in all Our Lands and Provinces. . . .

Since Our Lands are not only well and amply endowed with all things necessary to support life, but also very well-suited to the reestablishment of all kinds of manufactures and trade and traffic by land and water, We permit, indeed, to those settling therein free choice to establish themselves where it is most convenient for their profession and way of living. . . .

The personal property which they bring with them, including merchandise and other wares, is to be totally exempt from any taxes, customs dues, licenses, or other imposts of any description, and not detained in any way. . . .

As soon as these Our French co-religionists of the Evangelical-Reformed faith have settled in any town or village, they shall be admitted to the domiciliary rights and craft freedoms customary there, gratis and without payments of any fee; and shall be entitled to the benefits, rights, and privileges enjoyed by Our other, native, subjects, residing there. . . .

Not only are those who wish to establish manufacture of cloth, stuffs, hats, or other objects in which they are skilled to enjoy all necessary freedoms, privileges and facilities, but also provision is to be made for them to be assisted and helped as far as possible with money and anything else which they need to realize their intention. . . .

Those who settle in the country and wish to maintain themselves by agriculture are to be given a certain plot of land to bring under cultivation and provided with whatever they need to establish themselves initially. . . .

From C. A. Macartney, ed., *The Habsburg and Hohenzollern Dynasties in the Seventeenth and Eighteenth Centuries* (New York: Walker, 1970), pp. 270–273.

Holy Roman Emperor Leopold I. In exchange, the emperor permitted Frederick to assume the title of "King in Prussia" in 1701.

His successor, Frederick William I (r. 1713–1740), was both the most eccentric monarch to rule the Hohenzollern domains and one of the most effective. He organized the bureaucracy along military lines. The discipline that he applied to the army was fanatical. The Prussian military grew from about 39,000 in 1713 to over 80,000 in 1740, making it the third or fourth largest army in Europe. Prussia's population, in contrast, ranked

CHAPTER 13 ■ EUROPEAN STATE CONSOLIDATION IN THE SEVENTEENTH AND EIGHTEENTH CENTURIES   **443**

thirteenth in size. Separate laws applied to the army and to civilians. Laws, customs, and royal attention made the officer corps the highest social class of the state. Military service thus attracted the sons of *Junkers*. In this fashion the army, the *Junker* nobility, and the monarchy became forged into a single political entity. Military priorities and values dominated Prussian government, society, and daily life as in no other state in Europe. It has often been said that whereas other states possessed armies, the Prussian army possessed its state.

Although Frederick William I built the best army in Europe, he avoided conflict. His army was a symbol of Prussian power and unity, not an instrument for foreign adventures or aggression. At his death in 1740, he passed to his son Frederick II later known as Frederick the Great, (r. 1740–1786) this superb military machine, but not the wisdom to refrain from using it. Almost immediately on coming to the throne, Frederick II upset the Pragmatic Sanction and invaded Silesia. He thus crystallized the Austrian-Prussian rivalry for the control of Germany that would dominate central European affairs for over a century.

RUSSIA ENTERS THE EUROPEAN POLITICAL ARENA

The emergence of Russia in the late seventeenth century as an active European power was a wholly new factor in European politics. Previously, Russia had been considered part of Europe only by courtesy. Before 1673, it did not send permanent ambassadors to western Europe, though it had sent various diplomatic missions since the fifteenth century. Geographically and politically, it lay on the periphery. Hemmed in by Sweden on the Baltic and by the Ottoman Empire on the Black Sea, Russia had no warm-water ports. Its chief outlet for trade to the West was Archangel on the White Sea, which was ice free for only part of the year.

THE ROMANOV DYNASTY

The reign of Ivan IV (r. 1533–1584), later known as Ivan the Terrible, had commenced well but ended badly. About midway in his reign he underwent a personality change that led him to move from a program of sensible reform of law, government, and the army toward violent personal tyranny. A period known as the "Time of Troubles" followed upon his death. In 1613, hoping to end the uncertainty, an assembly of nobles elected as tsar a seventeen-year-old boy named Michael Romanov (r. 1613–1645). Thus began the dynasty that ruled Russia until 1917.

Michael Romanov and his two successors, Aleksei (r. 1654–1676) and Theodore II (r. 1676–1682), brought stability and modest bureaucratic centralization to Russia. The country remained, however, weak and impoverished. After years of turmoil, the *boyars*, the old nobility, still largely controlled the bureaucracy. Furthermore, the government and the tsars faced the danger of mutiny from the *streltsy*, or guards of the Moscow garrison.

PETER THE GREAT

In 1682, another boy—ten years old at the time—ascended the fragile Russian throne as co-ruler with his half brother. His name was Peter (r. 1682–1725), and Russia would never be the same after him. He and the sickly Ivan V had come to power on the shoulders of the *streltsy*, who expected to be rewarded for their support. Violence and bloodshed had surrounded the disputed succession. Matters became even more confused when the boys' sister, Sophia, was named regent. Peter's followers overthrew her in 1689. From that date onward, Peter ruled personally, although in theory he shared the crown until Ivan died in 1696. The dangers and turmoil of his youth convinced Peter of two things: first, the power of the tsar must be made secure from the jealousy of the *boyars* and the greed of the *streltsy*; second, Russian military power must be increased. In both respects, he self-consciously resembled Louis XIV of France, who had experienced the turmoil of the *Fronde* during his youth and resolved to establish a strong monarchy safe from the nobility and defended by a powerful army.

Northwestern Europe, particularly the military resources of the maritime powers, fascinated Peter I, who eventually became known as Peter the Great. In 1697, he made a famous visit in transparent disguise to western Europe. There he dined and talked with the great and the powerful, who considered this almost seven-foot-tall ruler crude. He spent his happiest moments on the trip inspecting shipyards, docks, and the manufacture of military hardware in England and the Netherlands. An imitator of the first order, Peter returned to Moscow determined to copy what he had seen abroad, for he knew warfare would be necessary to make Russia a great power. Yet he understood his goal would require him to confront the long-standing power and traditions of the Russian nobles.

Taming the *Streltsy* and *Boyars* In 1698, while Peter was abroad, the *streltsy* had rebelled. On his return, Peter brutally suppressed the revolt with private tortures and public executions, in which Peter's own ministers took part. Approximately a thousand of the rebels were put to death, and their corpses remained on public display to discourage disloyalty.

Peter the Great (r. 1682–1725), seeking to make Russia a military power, reorganized the country's political and economic structures. His reign saw Russia enter fully into European power politics. The Apotheosis of Tsar Peter the Great 1672–1725 by unknown artist, 1710. Historical Museum, Moscow, Russia/E.T. Archive

Developing a Navy In the mid-1690s, Peter oversaw the construction of ships to protect his interests in the Black Sea against the Ottoman Empire. In 1695, he began a war with the Ottomans and captured Azov on the Black Sea in 1696.[1] Part of the reason for Peter's trip to western Europe in 1697 was to learn how to build still better warships, this time for combat on the Baltic. The construction of a Baltic fleet was essential in Peter's struggles with Sweden that over the years accounted for many of his major steps toward westernizing his realm.

Russian Expansion in the Baltic: The Great Northern War Following the end of the Thirty Years' War in 1648, Sweden had consolidated its control of the Baltic, thus preventing Russian possession of a port on that sea and permitting Polish and German access to the sea only on Swedish terms. The Swedes also had one of the better armies in Europe. Sweden's economy, however, based primarily on the export of iron, was not strong enough to ensure continued political success.

In 1697, Charles XII (r. 1697–1718) came to the Swedish throne. He was headstrong, to say the least, and perhaps insane. In 1700, Peter the Great began a drive to the west against Swedish territory to gain a foothold on the Baltic. In the resulting Great Northern War (1700–1721), Charles XII led a vigorous and often brilliant campaign defeating the Russians at the Battle of Narva (1700). As the conflict dragged on, however, Peter was able to strengthen his forces. By 1709, he decisively defeated the Swedes at the Battle of Poltava in Ukraine. Thereafter, the Swedes could maintain only a holding action against their enemies. Charles himself sought refuge in Turkey and did not return to Sweden until 1714. He was killed under uncertain circumstances four years later while fighting the Danes in Norway. When the Great Northern War came to a close in 1721, the Peace of Nystad confirmed the Russian conquest of Estonia, Livonia, and part of Finland. Henceforth, Russia possessed ice-free ports and a permanent influence on European affairs.

The new military establishment that Peter built would serve the tsar and not itself. He introduced effective and ruthless policies of conscription, drafting an unprecedented 130,000 soldiers during the first decade of the eighteenth century and almost 300,000 troops by the end of his reign. He had adopted policies for the officer corps and general military discipline patterned on those of West European armies.

Peter also made a sustained attack on the *boyars* and their attachment to traditional Russian culture. After his European journey, he personally shaved the long beards of the court *boyars* and sheared off the customary long hand-covering sleeves of their shirts and coats, which had made them the butt of jokes among other European courts. Peter became highly skilled at balancing one group off against another while never completely excluding any as he set about to organize Russian government and military forces along the lines of the more powerful European states.

---

[1] Although Peter had to return Azov to the Ottomans in 1711, its recapture became a goal of Russian foreign policy. See Chapter 18.

Founding St. Petersburg   At one point, the domestic and foreign policies of Peter the Great intersected. This was at the site on the Gulf of Finland where he founded his new capital city of St. Petersburg in 1703. There he built government structures and compelled the *boyars* to construct town houses. He thus imitated those European monarchs who had copied Louis XIV by constructing smaller versions of Versailles. The founding of St. Petersburg went beyond establishing a central imperial court, however; it symbolized a new Western orientation of Russia and Peter's determination to hold his position on the Baltic coast. Moreover, he and his successors employed architects from western Europe for many of the most prominent buildings in and around the city. Consequently, St. Petersburg looked different from the old capital Moscow and other Russian cities.

The Case of Peter's Son Aleksei   Peter's son Aleksei had been born to his first wife whom he had divorced in 1698. Peter was jealous of the young man, who had never demonstrated strong intelligence or ambition. (See "Peter the Great Tells His Son to Acquire Military Skills," page 446.) By 1716, Peter was becoming convinced that his opponents looked to Aleksei as a focus for their possible sedition while Russia remained at war with Sweden. There was some truth to these concerns because the next year Aleksei went to Vienna where he attempted to enter into a vague conspiracy with the Habsburg emperor Charles VI. Compromised

RISE OF RUSSIAN POWER

1533–1584	Reign of Ivan the Terrible
1584–1613	"Time of Troubles"
1613	Michael Romanov becomes tsar
1682	Peter the Great, age ten, becomes tsar
1689	Peter assumes personal rule
1696	Russia captures Azov on the Black Sea from the Turks
1697	European tour of Peter the Great
1698	Peter returns to Russia to put down the revolt of the *streltsy*
1700	The Great Northern War opens between Russia and Sweden; Russia defeated at Narva by Swedish army of Charles XII
1703	St. Petersburg founded
1709	Russia defeats Sweden at the Battle of Poltava
1718	Charles XII of Sweden dies
1718	Aleksei, son of Peter the Great, dies in prison under mysterious circumstances
1721	Peace of Nystad ends the Great Northern War
1721	Peter establishes a synod for the Russian church
1722	Peter issues the Table of Ranks
1725	Peter dies, leaving an uncertain succession

Vue des bords de la Neva en descendant la rivière entre le Palais d'hyver de Sa Majesté Imperiale & les batimens de l'Academie des Sciences

Peter the Great built St. Petersburg on the Gulf of Finland to provide Russia with better contact with western Europe. He moved Russia's capital there from Moscow in 1712. This is an eighteenth-century view of the city.   The Granger Collection

by this trip, Alexsei then returned to Russia surrounded by rumors and suspicions.

Peter, who was investigating official corruption, realized his son might become a rallying point for those he accused. Early in 1718, when Aleksei reappeared in St. Petersburg, the tsar began to look into his son's relationships with Charles VI. Peter discovered that had Aleksei and Charles VI succeeded in organizing a conspiracy, many Russian nobles, officials, and churchmen might have joined them. During this six-month investigation, Peter personally interrogated Aleksei, who was eventually condemned to death and died under mysterious circumstances on June 26, 1718.

PETER THE GREAT TELLS HIS SON TO ACQUIRE MILITARY SKILLS

Enormous hostility existed between Peter the Great and his son Aleksei. Peter believed his son was not prepared to inherit the throne. In October 1715, he composed a long letter to Aleksei in which he berated him for refusing to take military matters seriously. The letter indicates how an early eighteenth-century ruler saw the conduct of warfare as a fundamental part of the role of a monarch. Peter also points to Louis XIV of France as a role model. Peter and Aleksei did not reach an agreement. Aleksei died under mysterious circumstances in 1718, with Peter possibly responsible for his death.

■ *How did Peter use the recent war with Sweden to argue for the necessity of his son acquiring military skills? What concept of leadership does Peter attempt to communicate to his son? Why did Peter see military prowess as the most important ability in a ruler?*

You cannot be ignorant of what is known to all the world, to what degree our people groaned under the oppression of the Swede before the beginning of the present war. . . . You know what it has cost us in the beginning of this war . . . to make ourselves experienced in the art of war, and to put a stop to those advantages which our implacable enemies obtained over us. . . .

But you even will not so much as hear warlike exercises mentioned: though it was by them that we broke through that obscurity in which we were involved, and that we make ourselves known to nations, whose esteem we share at present.

I do not exhort you to make war without lawful reasons: I only desire you to apply yourself to learn the art of it: for it is impossible to govern well without knowing the rules and discipline of it, was it for no other end than for the defense of the country. . . .

You mistake, if you think it is enough for a prince to have good generals to act under his order. Everyone looks upon the head; they study its inclinations and conform themselves to them: all the world own this. . . .

You have no inclination to learn war. You do not apply yourself to it, and consequently you will never learn it: And how then can you command others, and judge of the reward which those deserve who do their duty, or punish others who fail of it? You will do nothing, nor judge of anything but by the assent and help of others, like a young bird that holds up his bill to be fed. . . .

If you think there are some, whose affairs do not fail of success, though they do not go to war themselves; it is true: But they do not go themselves, yet they have an inclination for it, and understand it.

For instance, the late King of France did not always take the field in person; but it is known to what degree he loved war, and what glorious exploits he performed in it, which make his campaigns to be called the theatre and school of the world. His inclinations were not confined solely to military affairs, he also loved mechanics, manufacture and other establishment, which rendered his kingdom more flourishing than any other whatsoever.

From Friedrich C. Weber, *The Present State of Russia* (London, 1722), 2:97–100; *The Global Experience*, 3/3rd ed., Vol. 2 by P. F. Riley, © 1998. Reprinted by permission of Prentice Hall, Inc., Upper Saddle River, NJ.

Reforms of Peter the Great's Final Years The interrogations surrounding Aleksei had revealed greater degrees of court opposition than Peter had suspected. Recognizing he could not eliminate his opponents the way he had attacked the *streltsy* in 1698, Peter undertook radical administrative reforms designed to bring the nobility and the Russian Orthodox Church more closely under the authority of persons loyal to the tsar.

Administrative Colleges In December 1717, while his son was returning to Russia, Peter reorganized his domestic administration to sustain his own personal authority and to fight rampant corruption. To achieve this goal, Peter looked to Swedish institutions called *colleges*—bureaus of several persons operating according to written instructions rather than departments headed by a single minister. He created eight of these colleges to oversee matters such as the collection of taxes, foreign relations, war, and economic affairs. Each college was to receive advice from a foreigner. Peter divided the members of these colleges between nobles and persons he was certain would be personally loyal to himself.

Table of Ranks   Peter made another major administrative reform with important consequences when in 1722 he published a Table of Ranks, which was intended to draw the nobility into state service. That table equated a person's social position and privileges with his rank in the bureaucracy or the military, rather than with his lineage among the traditional landed nobility, many of whom continued to resent the changes Peter had introduced into Russia. Peter thus made the social standing of individual *boyars* a function of their willingness to serve the central state.

Achieving Secular Control of the Church   Peter also moved to suppress the independence of the Russian Orthodox Church where some bishops and clergy had displayed sympathy for the tsar's son. In 1721, Peter simply abolished the position of *patriarch*, the bishop who had been head of the church. In its place he established a government department called the *Holy Synod*, which consisted of several bishops headed by a layman, called the *procurator general*. This body would govern the church in accordance with the tsar's secular requirements. This ecclesiastical reorganization was the most radical transformation of a traditional institution in Peter's reign.

For all the numerous decisive actions Peter had taken since 1718, he still had not settled on a successor. Consequently, when he died in 1725, there was no clear line of succession to the throne. For more than thirty years, soldiers and nobles again determined who ruled Russia. Peter had laid the foundations of a modern Russia, but not the foundations of a stable state.

THE OTTOMAN EMPIRE

On the southeastern borders of Europe and surrounding the southern and eastern shores of the Mediterranean Sea lay the Ottoman Empire. Throughout the sixteenth and seventeenth centuries, Europeans had found themselves in frequent conflict with this empire in the Mediterranean, the Balkans, around the Black Sea, along the borders of Russia, and as far west as Vienna. As Ottoman authority gradually receded during the eighteenth century, the European states on the empire's borders sought to extend their own influence at its expense.

Now that it no longer exists, it is difficult to realize the enormous importance and geographical magnitude of the Ottoman Empire, although its final demise has affected Europe and the United States since the outbreak of the First World War. Governing a remarkably diverse collection of peoples that ranged from Baghdad eastward across the Arabian peninsula, Anatolia, the Balkan peninsula, and across North Africa from Egypt to Algiers, the **Ottoman Empire** was the largest and most stable political entity to arise in or near Europe following the collapse of the Roman Empire. (See Map 13–5, page 448.) It had achieved this power between the eleventh and early sixteenth centuries as Ottoman tribes migrated eastward from the steppes of Asia. In 1453, they conquered Constantinople, thus putting an end to the Byzantine Empire.

RELIGIOUS TOLERATION AND OTTOMAN GOVERNMENT

The Ottoman Empire was the dominant political power in the Muslim world after 1516, when it administered the holy cities of Mecca and Medina as well as Jerusalem, and arranged the safety of Muslim pilgrimages to Mecca. Yet its population was exceedingly diverse ethnically, linguistically, and religiously with significant numbers of Orthodox and Roman Catholic Christians and, after the late fifteenth century, thousands of Jews from Spain.

The Ottomans extended far more religious toleration to their subjects than existed anywhere in Europe. The Ottoman sultans governed their empire through units, called **millets**, of officially recognized religious communities. Various laws and regulations applied to the persons who belonged to a particular millet rather than to a particular administrative territory. Non-Islamic persons in the empire, known as *dhimmis*, or followers of religions tolerated by law, could practice their religion and manage their internal community affairs through their own religious officials, but were second-class citizens generally unable to rise in the service of the empire. *Dhimmis* paid a special poll tax (*jizyah*), could not serve in the military, and were prohibited from wearing certain colors. Their residences and places of worship could not be as large as those of Muslims. Over the years, however, they often attained economic success because they possessed the highest level of commercial skills in the empire. Because the Ottomans discouraged their various peoples from interacting with each other, the Islamic population rarely acquired these and other skills from their non-Islamic neighbors. Thus, for example, when the Ottomans negotiated with European powers, their Greek subjects almost invariably served as the interpreters.

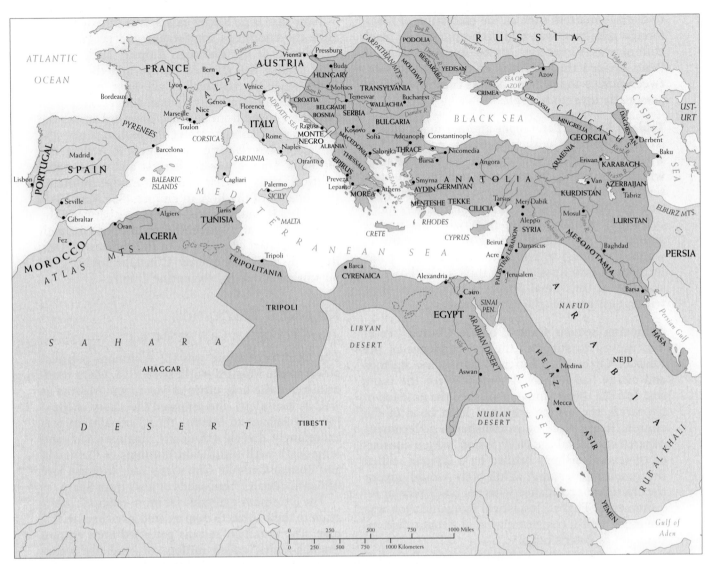

Map 13–5   **THE OTTOMAN EMPIRE IN THE LATE SEVENTEENTH CENTURY.**   By the 1680s the Ottoman Empire had reached its maximum extent, but the Ottoman failure to capture Vienna in 1683 marked the beginning of a long and inexorable decline that ended with the empire's collapse after World War I.

The Ottoman dynasty also kept itself separated from the most powerful families of the empire by recruiting military leaders and administrative officers from groups whom the sultans believed would be personally loyal to them. For example, through a practice known as the *devshirme*, the Ottomans, until the end of the seventeenth century, recruited their most elite troops from Christian communities usually in the Balkans. Christian boys so recruited were raised as Muslims and organized into elite military units, the most famous of which were infantry troops called *Janissaries*. It was thought these troops would be extremely loyal to the sultan and the state because they owed their life and status to the sultan. As a result of this policy, entry into the elite military organizations and advancement in the administrative structures of the empire remained generally closed to the native Islamic population and most especially to members of the most elite Islamic families. Instead, in addition to the army, thousands of persons usually from the outer regions of the empire, who were technically slaves of the sultan, filled government posts and achieved major political influence and status. Thus, in contrast to Europe, few people from the socially leading families gained military, administrative, or political experience in the central institutions of the empire, but remained primarily linked to local government in provincial cities. Paradoxically, many people in the Ottoman Empire believed it was better to be a favored slave of the sultan than a free subject.

The Role of the Ulama   Again in contrast to the long-standing tension between church and state in

Europe, Islamic religious authorities played a significant and enduring role in the political, legal, and administrative life of the Ottoman Empire. The dynasty saw itself as one of the chief protectors of Islamic law (*Shari'a*) and the Sunni traditions of Islam as well as its holy places. Islamic scholars, or *Ulama*, dominated not only Ottoman religious institutions but also schools and courts of law. There essentially existed a trade-off between Ottoman political and religious authorities. The sultan and his administrative officials would consult these Islamic scholars for advice with regard to how their policies and the behavior of their subjects accorded with Islamic law and the Qur'an. In turn, the Ulama would support the Ottoman state while the latter deferred to their judgments. This situation would prove a key factor in the fate of the Ottoman Empire. From the late seventeenth century onward, the Ulama urged the sultans to conform to traditional life even as the empire confronted a rapidly changing and modernizing Europe. The Janissaries also resisted changes that might undermine their own privileged status.

THE END OF OTTOMAN EXPANSION

From the fifteenth century onward, the Ottoman Empire had tried to push further westward into Europe. Even after its naval defeat in 1571 at the Battle of Lepanto, the empire retained control of the eastern Mediterranean and the lands bordering it. Still determined to move toward the west, the Ottomans made their deepest military invasion into Europe in 1683, when they unsuccessfully besieged Vienna. Although that defeat proved to be decisive, many observers at the time thought it the result only of an overreach of power by the Ottomans rather than as a symptom of a deeper decline, which was actually the case.

Gradually, from the seventeenth century onward, the authority of the grand vizier, the major political figure after the sultan, began to grow. This development meant that more and more authority lay with the administrative and military bureaucracy. Rivalries for power among army leaders and nobles, as well as their flagrant efforts to enrich themselves, weakened the effectiveness of the government. About the same time local elites in the various provincial cities of the empire began to assert their own influence. They did not so much reject imperial authority but instead quietly renegotiated its conditions. For example, in the outer European provinces, such as Transylvania, Wallachia, and Moldavia (all parts of modern Romania), the empire depended on the goodwill of local rulers, who paid tribute, but never submitted fully to imperial authority. The same was true in Egypt, Algeria, Tunisia, and elsewhere.

An Ottoman portrayal of the *Devshirme*. This miniature painting from about 1558 depicts the recruiting of young Christian children for the Sultan's elite Janissary corps.
British Library, London, UK/Bridgeman Art Library

External factors also accounted for both the blocking of Ottoman expansion in the late seventeenth century and then its slow decline thereafter. During the European Middle Ages, the Islamic world had far outdistanced Europe in learning, science, and military prowess. From the fifteenth century onward, however, Europeans had begun to make rapid advances in technology, wealth, and scientific knowledge. For example, they designed ships for the difficult waters of the Atlantic and thus eventually opened trade routes to the East around Africa and reached the Americas. As trade expanded, Europeans achieved new commercial skills, founded trading posts in South Asia, established the plantation economies and precious metal mines of the Americas, and became much wealthier. By the seventeenth century, Europeans, particularly the Dutch and Portuguese, imported directly from Asia or America commodities such as spices, sugar, and coffee that they had previously acquired through the Ottoman Empire. By sailing around the Cape of Good Hope in Africa, the Europeans literally circumnavigated the Middle East, which could not match the quantity of raw goods and commodities available in South Asia. During the same decades, Europeans developed greater military and naval power and new weapons.

The Ottoman defeats at Lepanto and Vienna had occurred at the outer limits of their expansion. Then, however, during the 1690s, the Ottomans unsuccessfully fought a league of European states including Austria, Venice, Malta, Poland, and Tuscany, joined by Russia, which, as we have already seen, was emerging as a new aggressive power to the north. In early 1699, the defeated Ottomans negotiated the Treaty of Carlowitz, which required them to surrender significant territory lying not at the edges but at the heart of their empire in Europe, including most of Hungary, to the Habsburgs. This treaty meant not only the loss of territory but also of the revenue the Ottomans had long drawn from those regions. From this time onward, Russia and the Ottomans would duel for control of regions around the Black Sea with Russia achieving ever greater success by the close of the eighteenth century.

Despite these defeats, the Ottomans remained deeply inward looking, continuing to regard themselves as superior to the once underdeveloped European West. Virtually no works of the new European science were translated into Arabic or Ottoman Turkish. Few Ottoman subjects traveled in Europe. The Ottoman leaders, isolated from both their own leading Muslim subjects and from Europe, failed to understand what was occurring far beyond their immediate borders, especially European advances in military technology. When during the eighteenth century the Ottoman Empire began to recognize the new situation, it tended to borrow European technology and import foreign advisers, thus failing to develop its own infrastructure. Moreover, the powerful influence of the Ulama worked against imitation of Christian Europe. Although traditionally opposed to significant interaction with non-Muslims, they did eventually allow non-Muslim teachers into the empire and approved alliances with non-Muslim powers. But the Ulama limited such relationships. For example, in the middle of the eighteenth century, the Ulama persuaded the sultan to close a school of technology and to abandon a printing press he had opened. This influence by Muslim religious teachers occurred just as governments, such as that of Peter the Great, and secular intellectuals across Europe, through the influence of the Enlightenment (see Chapter 17), were increasingly diminishing the influence of the Christian churches in political and economic affairs. Consequently, European intellectuals began to view the once feared Ottoman Empire as a declining power and Islam as a backward-looking religion.

IN PERSPECTIVE

By the second quarter of the eighteenth century, the major European powers were not yet nation-states in which the citizens felt themselves united by a shared sense of community, culture, language, and history. Rather, they were monarchies in which the personality of the ruler and the personal relationships of the great noble families continued to exercise considerable influence over public affairs. The monarchs, except in Great Britain, had generally succeeded in making their power greater than that of the nobility. The power of the aristocracy and its capacity to resist or obstruct the policies of the monarch were not destroyed, however.

In Britain, of course, the nobility had tamed the monarchy, but even there tension between nobles and monarchs would continue throughout the rest of the century.

In foreign affairs, the new arrangement of military and diplomatic power established early in the century prepared the way for two long conflicts. The first was a commercial rivalry for trade and the overseas empire between France and Great Britain. During the reign of Louis XIV, these two nations had collided over the French bid for dominance in Europe. During the eighteenth century, they would duel for control of commerce on other continents. The second arena of warfare would arise in central Europe, where Austria and Prussia fought for the leadership of the German states.

Behind these international conflicts and the domestic rivalry of monarchs and nobles, however, the society of eighteenth-century Europe began to change. The character and the structures of the societies over which the monarchs ruled were beginning to take on some features associated with the modern age. These economic and social developments would eventually transform the life of Europe to a degree beside which the state building of the early eighteenth-century monarchs paled. Parallel to that economic advance, Europeans came to have new knowledge and understanding of nature.

REVIEW QUESTIONS

1. What were the sources of Dutch prosperity and why did the Netherlands decline in the eighteenth century? Why did England and France develop different systems of government and religious policies?

2. Why did the English king and Parliament quarrel in the 1640s? What were the most important issues behind the war between them, and who bears more responsibility for it? What was the Glorious Revolution, and why did it take place?

What role did religion play in seventeenth-century English politics?

3. Why did France become an absolute monarchy? How did Louis XIV consolidate his monarchy? What limits were there on his authority? What was Louis's religious policy? What were the goals of his foreign policy? How did he use ceremony and his royal court to strengthen his authority?

4. How were the Hohenzollerns able to forge their diverse landholdings into the state of Prussia? Who were the major personalities involved in this process and what were their individual contributions? Why was the military so important in Prussia? What major problems did the Habsburgs face and how did they seek to resolve them? Which family, the Hohenzollerns or the Habsburgs, was more successful and why?

5. How and why did Russia emerge as a great power but Poland did not? How were Peter the Great's domestic reforms related to his military ambitions? What were his methods of reform? How did family conflict influence his later policies? Was Peter a successful ruler?

6. What were the strengths and weaknesses of the Ottoman Empire? How did the Ottomans deal with religious minorities? Why did the Empire discourage interaction between its subjects and people from Europe? How did its failure to adapt to modern technology undermine its power?

SUGGESTED READINGS

W. BEIK, *Louis XIV and Absolutism: A Brief Study with Documents* (2000). An excellent volume by a major scholar of absolutism.

J. BREWER, *The Sinews of Power: War, Money and the English State, 1688–1783* (1989). An important study of the financial basis of English power.

P. BURKE, *The Fabrication of Louis XIV* (1992). Examines how Louis XIV used art to forge his public image.

P. COLLINSON, *The Religion of Protestants: The Church in English Society, 1559–1625* (1982). Remains the best introduction to Puritanism.

N. DAVIS, *God's Playground: A History of Poland: The Origins to 1795,* (2005). The recent revision of the classic survey.

J. DE VRIES AND A. VAN DER WOUDE, *The First Modern Economy* (1997). Compares Holland to other European nations.

W. DOYLE, *The Old European Order, 1660–1800* (1992). A broad, thoughtful treatment of the subject.

D. GOFFMAN, *The Ottoman Empire and Early Modern Europe* (2002) An accessible introduction to a complex subject.

L. HUGHES, *Russia in the Age of Peter the Great* (2000). A major overview of the history and society of Peter's time.

C. IMBER, *The Ottoman Empire, 1300–1650: The Structure of Power* (2003). A sweeping analysis based on a broad range of sources.

C. J. INGRAO, *The Habsburg Monarchy, 1618–1815* (2000). The best recent survey.

J. I. ISRAEL, *The Dutch Republic: Its Rise, Greatness, and Fall, 1477–1806* (1995). The major survey of the subject.

M. KISHLANSKY, *A Monarchy Transformed: Britain, 1603–1714* (1996). An important overview.

J. R. MAJOR, *From Renaissance Monarchy to Absolute Monarchy: French Kings, Nobles and Estates* (1994). A major study by a leading scholar exploring the monarchy's relationship to other political and social groups.

D. MCKAY, *The Great Elector: Frederick William of Brandenburg–Prussia* (2001). An account of the origins of Prussian power.

P. K. MONOD, *The Power of Kings: Monarchy and Religion in Europe, 1589–1715* (1999). An important and innovative examination of the roots of royal authority as early modern Europe became modern Europe.

G. PARKER, *The Military Revolution: Military Innovation and the Rise of the West (1500–1800)* (1988). A major work on the impact of military matters on the emergence of centralized monarchies.

H. PHILLIPS, *Church and Culture in Seventeenth-Century France* (1997). A clear examination of the major religious issues confronting France and their relationship to the larger culture.

G. TREASURE, *Louis XIV* (2001). The best, most accessible recent study.

DOCUMENTS CD-ROM

Society and Politics in Early Modern Europe

12.7 Mercantilism

Thought and Culture in Early Modern Europe

13.2 Miguel Cervantes: Chapter 1 from *Don Quixote*
13.3 John Bunyan: from *Pilgrim's Progress*

Absolutism

15.1 Richelieu: Controlling the Nobility
15.2 The Sun King Shines
15.3 Louis XIV: *Mémoires for the Instruction of the Dauphin*
15.4 M. de la Colonie: *The Battle of Schellenberg, 2 July 1704—A French Officer's Account*
15.5 G. M. Trevelyan: Chapter I from *History of England*

14

NEW DIRECTIONS IN THOUGHT AND CULTURE IN THE SIXTEENTH AND SEVENTEENTH CENTURIES

KEY TOPICS

- The astronomical theories of Copernicus, Brahe, Kepler, Galileo, and Newton and the emergence of the scientific worldview
- Impact of the new science on philosophy
- Social setting of early modern science
- Women and the scientific revolution
- Approaches to science and religion
- Witchcraft and witch-hunts

The sixteenth and seventeenth centuries witnessed a sweeping change in the scientific view of the universe. An earth-centered picture gave way to one in which the earth was only another planet orbiting about the sun. The sun itself became one of millions of stars. This transformation of humankind's perception of its place in the larger scheme of things led to a profound rethinking of moral and religious matters,

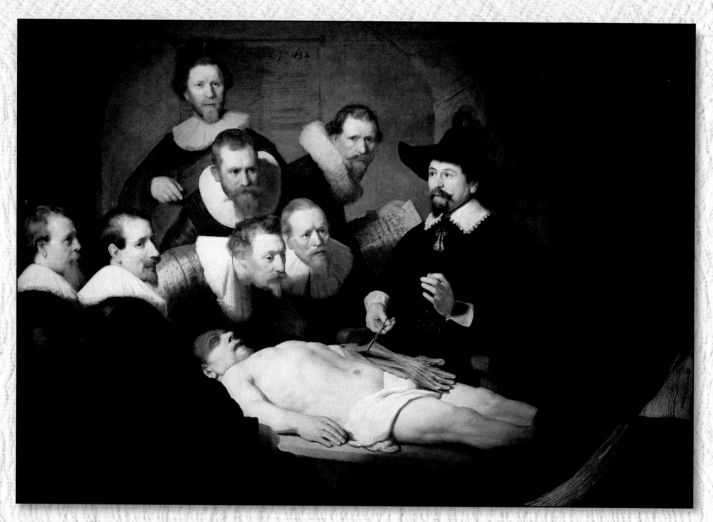

The great Dutch artist Rembrandt van Rijn (1606–1669) recorded the contemporary life of the United Provinces of the Netherlands during its golden age. The new sciences including medicine made much progress in the Netherlands which was a center for publishing and instrument making and known for its religious toleration. *The Anatomy Lesson of Dr. Tulp* (1632) presents the dissection of a cadaver of an executed criminal by the noted Dutch physician Dr. Nicolass Tulp who stands on the right surrounded by other members of the Amsterdam guild of surgeons. Such dissections were a controversial part of new emerging medical education with only one a year permitted in Amsterdam. The dramatic use of light and darkness is characteristic of the painting of the baroque style.   Rembrandt van Rijn (1606–1669). "The Anatomy Lesson of Dr. Tulp." Mauritshuis, The Hague, The Netherlands. SCALA/Art Resource, NY

as well as of scientific theory. Faith and reason needed new modes of reconciliation, as did faith and science. The new ideas and methods of science, usually termed *natural philosophy* at the time, challenged those modes of thought associated with late medieval times: Scholasticism and Aristotelian philosophy.

The impact of the new science that explored the realm of the stars through the newly invented telescope and the world of microorganisms through the newly invented microscope must be viewed in the context of two other factors that simultaneously challenged traditional modes of European thought and culture in the sixteenth and seventeenth centuries. The first of these was the Reformation, which permanently divided the religious unity of central and western Europe and fostered decades of warfare and theological dispute. Although by no means a complete break with medieval thought, the theology of the Reformation did question many ideas associated with medieval Christianity and society. The second factor was the cultural impact of Europe's encounter with the New World of the Americas. The interaction with the Americas meant that Europeans directly or indirectly acquired knowledge of new peoples, plants, and animals wholly different from their own and about which Europeans in neither ancient nor medieval times had any information. Consequently, new uncertainties and unfamiliar vistas confronted many Europeans as they considered their souls, geographical knowledge, and physical nature.

Side by side with this new knowledge and science, however, came a new wave of superstition and persecution. The changing world of religion, politics, and knowledge also created profound fear and anxiety among both the simple and the learned, resulting in the worst witch-hunts in European history. ■

THE SCIENTIFIC REVOLUTION

The process that established the new view of the universe is normally termed the **scientific revolution**. The revolution-in-science metaphor must be used carefully, however. Not everything associated with the "new" science was necessarily new. Sixteenth- and seventeenth-century natural philosophers were often reexamining and rethinking theories and data from the ancient world and the late Middle Ages. Moreover, the word *revolution* normally denotes rapid, collective political change involving many people. The scientific revolution was not rapid. It was a complex movement with many false starts and brilliant people suggesting wrong as well as useful ideas. Nor did it involve more than a few hundred people who labored in widely separated studies and crude laboratories located in Poland, Italy, Denmark, Bohemia, France, and Great Britain. Furthermore, the achievements of the new science were not simply the function of isolated brilliant scientific minds. The leading figures of the scientific revolution often drew on the aid of artisans and craftspeople to help them construct new instruments for experimentation and to carry out those experiments. Thus, the scientific revolution involved older knowledge as well as new discoveries. Additionally, because the practice of science involves social activity as well as knowledge, the revolution also saw the establishment of new social institutions to support the emerging scientific enterprise.

Natural knowledge was only in the process of becoming science as we know it today during the era of the scientific revolution. In fact the word *scientist*, which was only coined in the 1830s, did not yet exist in the seventeenth century, nor did anything resembling the modern scientific career. Individuals devoted to natural philosophy might work in universities or in the court of a prince or even in their own homes and workshops. Only in the second half of the seventeenth century did formal societies and academies devoted to the pursuit of natural philosophy come into existence. Even then the entire process of the pursuit of natural knowledge was a largely informal one.

Yet by the close of the seventeenth century, the new scientific concepts and the methods of their construction were so impressive that they set the standard for assessing the validity of knowledge in the Western world. From the early seventeenth century through the end of the twentieth century, science achieved greater cultural authority in the Western world than any other form of intellectual activity, and the authority and application of scientific knowledge became one of the defining characteristics of modern Western civilization.

Although new knowledge emerged in many areas during the sixteenth and seventeenth centuries, including medicine, chemistry, and natural history, the scientific achievements that most captured the learned imagination and persuaded people of the cultural power of natural knowledge were those that occurred in astronomy.

NICOLAUS COPERNICUS REJECTS AN EARTH-CENTERED UNIVERSE

Nicolaus Copernicus (1473–1543) was a Polish priest and an astronomer who enjoyed a high reputation during his life but who was not known for strikingly original or unorthodox thought. He had been educated first at the University of Kraków in Poland and later in Italy. In 1543, the year of his death, Copernicus published *On the Revolutions of the Heavenly Spheres*, which has been described as "a revolution-making rather than a revolutionary text."[1] What Copernicus did was to provide an

[1] Thomas S. Kuhn, *The Copernican Revolution: Planetary Astronomy in the Development of Western Thought* (New York: Vintage, 1959), p. 135.

intellectual springboard for a complete criticism of the then-dominant view of the position of the earth in the universe. He had undertaken this task to help the papacy reform the calendar, so that it could correctly calculate the date for Easter based on a more accurate understanding of astronomy.

The Ptolemaic System In Copernicus's time, the standard explanation of the place of the earth in the heavens combined the mathematical astronomy of Ptolemy, contained in his work entitled the *Almagest* (150 C.E.), with the physical cosmology of Aristotle. Over the centuries, commentators on Ptolemy's work had developed several alternative **Ptolemaic systems**, on the basis of which they made mathematical calculations relating to astronomy. Most of these writers assumed the earth was the center of the universe, an outlook known as *geocentrism*. Drawing on Aristotle, these commentators assumed that above the earth lay a series of concentric spheres, probably fluid in character, one of which contained the moon, another the sun, and still others the planets and the stars. At the outer regions of these spheres lay the realm of God and the angels. The earth had to be the center because of its heaviness. The stars and the other heavenly bodies had to be enclosed in the spheres so they could move, since nothing could move unless something was actually moving it. The state of rest was presumed to be natural; motion required explanation. This was the astronomy found in such works as Dante's *Divine Comedy*.

The Ptolemaic model gave rise to many problems, which had long been recognized. The most important was the observed motions of the planets. At certain times the planets appeared to be going backwards. The Ptolemaic model accounted for these motions primarily through epicycles. The planet moved uniformly about a small circle (an *epicycle*), and the center of the epicycle moved uniformly about a larger circle (called a *deferent*), with the earth at or near its center. The combination of these two motions, as viewed from the earth, was meant to replicate the changing planetary positions among the fixed stars— and did so to a high degree of accuracy. The circles employed in Ptolemaic systems were not meant to represent the actual paths of anything; that is, they were not orbits. Rather, they were the components of purely mathematical models meant to predict planetary positions. Other intellectual, but nonobservational, difficulties related to the immense speed at which the spheres had to move around the earth. To say the least, the Ptolemaic systems were cluttered. They were

effective, however, as long as one assumed Aristotelian physics to be correct.

Copernicus's Universe Copernicus's *On the Revolutions of the Heavenly Spheres* challenged the Ptolemaic picture in the most conservative manner possible. (See "Copernicus Ascribes Movement to the Earth," page 456.) He adopted many elements of the Ptolemaic model, but transferred them to a *heliocentric* (sun-centered) model, which assumed the earth moved about the sun in a circle. Copernicus's model, which retained epicycles, was actually no more accurate than Ptolemy's. However, Copernicus could claim certain advantages over the ancient model. In particular, the epicycles were smaller. The retrograde motion of the planets was now explained as a result of an optical illusion that arose because people were observing them from earth, which was itself moving. Furthermore, Copernicus argued that the farther planets were from the sun, the longer they took to revolve around it. The length of these individual revolutions made it easier to determine the order of the planets, how they ranked in terms of distance from the sun.

The repositioning of the earth had not been Copernicus's goal. Rather, he appears to have set out to achieve new intelligibility and mathematical elegance in astronomy by rejecting Aristotle's cosmology and by removing the earth from the center of the universe. His system was no more accurate than the existing ones for predicting the location of the planets. He had used no new

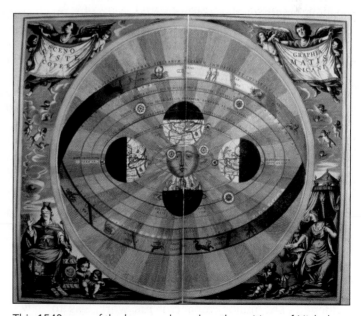

This 1543 map of the heavens based on the writings of Nicholas Copernicus shows the earth and the other planets moving about the sun. Until well into the 1600s, however, astronomers continued to debate whether the sun revolved around the earth.
British Library, London, UK/Bridgeman Art Library

COPERNICUS ASCRIBES MOVEMENT
TO THE EARTH

Copernicus published De Revolutionibus Orbium Caelestium (On the Revolutions of the Heavenly Spheres) *in 1543. In his preface, addressed to Pope Paul III, he explained what had led him to think that the earth moved around the sun and what he thought were some of the scientific consequences of the new theory.*

■ *How does Copernicus justify his argument to the pope? How important was historical precedent and tradition to the pope? Might Copernicus have thought that the pope would be especially susceptible to such an argument, even though what Copernicus proposed (the movement of the earth) contradicted the Bible?*

I may well presume, most Holy Father, that certain people, as soon as they hear that in this book about the Revolutions of the Spheres of the Universe I ascribe movement to the Earthly globe, will cry out that, holding such views, I should at once be hissed off the stage. . . .

So I should like your Holiness to know that I was induced to think of a method of computing the motions of the spheres by nothing else than the knowledge that the Mathematicians [who had previously considered the problem] are inconsistent in these investigations.

For, first, the mathematicians are so unsure of the movements of the Sun and Moon that they cannot even explain or observe the constant length of the seasonal year. Secondly, in determining the motions of these and of the other five planets, they use neither the same principles and hypotheses nor the same demonstrations of the apparent motions and revolutions. . . . Nor have they been able thereby to discern or deduce the principal thing—namely the shape of the Universe and the unchangeable symmetry of its parts. . . .

I pondered long upon this uncertainty of mathematical tradition in establishing the motions of the system of the spheres. At last I began to chafe that philosophers could by no means agree on any one certain theory of the mechanism of the Universe, wrought for us by a supremely good and orderly Creator. . . . I therefore took pains to read again the works of all the philosophers on whom I could lay hand to seek out whether any of them had ever supposed that the motions of the spheres were other than those demanded by the [Ptolemaic] mathematical schools. I found first in Cicero that Hicetas [of Syracuse, fifth century B.C.E.] had realized that the Earth moved. Afterwards I found in Plutarch that certain others had held the like opinion. . . .

Thus assuming motions, which in my work I ascribe to the Earth, by long and frequent observations I have at last discovered that, if the motions of the rest of the planets be brought into relation with the circulation of the Earth and be reckoned in proportion to the circles of each planet, not only do their phenomena presently ensue, but the orders and magnitudes of all stars and spheres, nay the heavens themselves, become so bound together that nothing in any part thereof could be moved from its place without producing confusion of all the other parts of the Universe as a whole.

As quoted in Thomas S. Kuhn, *The Copernican Revolution: Planetary Astronomy in the Development of Western Thought* (New York: Vintage Books, 1959), pp. 137–139, 141–142.

evidence. The major impact of his work was to provide another way of confronting some of the difficulties inherent in Ptolemaic astronomy. The Copernican system did not immediately replace the old astronomy, but it allowed other people who were also discontented with the Ptolemaic view to think in new directions. Indeed, for at least a century, only a minority of natural philosophers and astronomers embraced the Copernican system.

TYCHO BRAHE AND JOHANNES KEPLER MAKE NEW SCIENTIFIC OBSERVATIONS

The Danish astronomer Tycho Brahe (1546–1601) took the next major step toward the conception of a sun-centered system. He did not embrace Copernicus's view of the universe and actually spent most of his life advocating an earth-centered system. He suggested that Mercury and Venus revolved around the sun, but that the moon, the sun, and the other planets revolved around the earth. In pursuit of his own theory, Brahe constructed scientific instruments with which he made more extensive naked-eye observations of the planets than anyone else had ever done. His labors produced a vast body of astronomical data from which his successors could work.

When Brahe died, his assistant, Johannes Kepler (1571–1630), a German astronomer, took possession of these tables. Kepler was a convinced Copernican and a more consistently rigorous advocate of a heliocentric model than Copernicus himself had been. Like Copernicus, Kepler was deeply influenced by Renaissance Neoplatonism, which held the sun in special honor. In keeping with this outlook, Kepler was determined to find in Brahe's numbers mathematical harmonies that would support a sun-centered universe. After much work, Kepler discovered that to keep the sun at the center of things, he must abandon the circular components of Copernicus's model, particularly the epicycles. Based on the mathematical relationships that emerged from his study of Brahe's observations, Kepler set forth the first astronomical model that actually portrayed motion—that is, the path of the planets—and those orbits were elliptical, not circular. Kepler published his findings in his 1609 book entitled *The New Astronomy*. He had used Copernicus's sun-centered universe and Brahe's empirical data to solve the problem of planetary motion.

Kepler had also defined a new problem. None of the available theories could explain why the planetary orbits were elliptical or, for that matter, why planetary motion was orbital at all rather than simply moving off along a tangent. That solution awaited the work of Sir Isaac Newton.

GALILEO GALILEI ARGUES FOR A UNIVERSE OF MATHEMATICAL LAWS

From Copernicus to Brahe to Kepler, there had been little new information about the heavens that might not have been known to Ptolemy. In 1609, however, the same year that Kepler published *The New Astronomy*, an Italian mathematician and natural philosopher named Galileo Galilei (1564–

Galileo Galilei achieved a Europeanwide reputation as a mathematician, instrument maker, and astronomer. His use of the telescope revealed sights of objects in the heavens never previously viewed by human beings. His writings in defense of the Copernican system became increasingly controversial and eventually led to his condemnation by Roman Catholic authorities.
© Bettmann/CORBIS

1642) first turned a telescope on the heavens. Using that recently invented Dutch instrument, he saw stars where none had been known to exist, mountains on the moon, spots moving across the sun, and moons orbiting Jupiter. The heavens were far more complex than anyone had suspected. These discoveries, with some work, could have been accommodated into the Ptolemaic model. Such accommodation would, however, have required a highly technical understanding of Ptolemaic astronomy. Galileo knew that few people who controlled patronage possessed such complex knowledge. Consequently, in the *Starry Messenger* (1610) and *Letters on Sunspots* (1613), he used his considerable rhetorical skills to argue that his newly observed physical evidence, particularly the phases of Venus, required a Copernican interpretation of the heavens.

Galileo's career illustrates that the forging of the new science involved more than just presenting arguments and evidence. In 1610, he had left the University of Padua for Florence, where he became the philosopher and mathematician to the Grand Duke of Tuscany, who was a Medici. Galileo was now pursuing natural philosophy in a princely court and had become dependent on princely patronage. To win such support both for his continued work and for his theories, he named the moons of Jupiter after the Medicis. As a natural philosopher working with the new telescope, he had literally presented recently discovered heavenly bodies to his patron. By his political skills and his excellent prose, he had transformed himself into a high-profile advocate of Copernicanism. Galileo's problems with the Roman Catholic Church (see page 470), arose from both his ideas and his flair for self-advertisement.

Galileo not only popularized the Copernican system, but also articulated the concept of a universe subject to mathematical laws. More than any other writer of the century, he argued that nature displayed mathematical regularity in its most minute details.

Philosophy is written in that great book which ever lies before our eyes—I mean the universe—but we cannot understand it if we do not first learn the language and grasp the symbols in which it is written. This book is written in the mathematical language, and the symbols are triangles, circles, and other geometrical figures, without whose help it is impossible to comprehend a single word of it; without which one wanders through a dark labyrinth.[2]

The universe was rational; however, its rationality was not that of medieval scholastic logic, but of mathematics. Copernicus had thought that the heavens conformed to mathematical regularity; Galileo saw this regularity throughout physical nature.

A world of quantities was replacing one of qualities. All aspects of the world—including color, beauty, and taste—would increasingly be described in terms of the mathematical relationships among quantities. Mathematical models would eventually be applied even to social relations. The new natural philosophy portrayed nature as cold, rational, mathematical, and mechanistic. What was real and lasting was what was mathematically measurable. For many people, the power of the mathematical arguments that appeared irrefutable proved more persuasive than the new information from physical observation that produced so much controversy. Few intellectual shifts have wrought such momentous changes for Western civilization.

[2]Quoted in E. A. Burtt, *The Metaphysical Foundations of Modern Physical Science* (Garden City, NY: Anchor-Doubleday, 1954), p. 75.

ISAAC NEWTON DISCOVERS THE LAWS OF GRAVITATION

The question that continued to perplex seventeenth-century scientists who accepted the theories of Copernicus, Kepler, and Galileo was how the planets and other heavenly bodies moved in an orderly fashion. The Ptolemaic and Aristotelian answer had been the spheres and a universe arranged in the order of the heaviness of its parts. Many unsatisfactory theories had been set forth to deal with the question. It was this issue of planetary motion that the Englishman Isaac Newton (1642–1727) addressed and, in so doing, established a basis for physics that endured for more than two centuries.

In 1687, Newton published *The Mathematical Principles of Natural Philosophy*, better known by its Latin title of *Principia Mathematica*. Much of the research and thinking for this great work had taken place more than fifteen years earlier. Galileo's mathematical bias permeated Newton's thought, as did his view that inertia applied to bodies both at rest and in motion. Newton reasoned that the planets and all other physical objects in the universe moved through mutual attraction, or

Sir Isaac Newton's experiments dealing with light passing through a prism became a model for writers praising the experimental method. CORBIS/Bettmann

gravity. Every object in the universe affected every other object through gravity. The attraction of gravity explained why the planets moved in an orderly, rather than a chaotic, manner. Newton had found that "the force of gravity towards the whole planet did arise from and was compounded of the forces of gravity towards all its parts, and towards every one part was in the inverse proportion of the squares of the distances from the part."[3] Newton demonstrated this relationship mathematically; he made no attempt to explain the nature of gravity itself.

Newton was a mathematical genius, but he also upheld the importance of empirical data and observation. Like Francis Bacon, he believed in empiricism—that one must observe phenomena before attempting to explain them. The final test of any theory or hypothesis for him was whether it described what was actually observed. Newton was a great opponent of the rationalism of the French philosopher René Descartes (see page 461), which he believed included insufficient guards against error. Consequently, as Newton's own theory of universal gravitation became increasingly accepted, so, too, was Baconian empiricism.

PHILOSOPHY RESPONDS TO CHANGING SCIENCE

The revolution in scientific thought contributed directly to a major reexamination of Western philosophy. Several of the most important figures in the scientific revolution, such as Bacon and Descartes, were also philosophers discontented with the scholastic heritage. Bacon stressed the importance of empirical research. Descartes attempted to find certainty through the exploration of his own thinking processes. Newton's interests likewise extended to philosophy; he wrote broadly on many topics, including scientific method and theology.

NATURE AS MECHANISM

If a single idea informed all of these philosophers, though in different ways, it was the idea of *mechanism*. The proponents of the new science sought to explain the world in terms of mechanical metaphors, or the language of machinery. The image to which many of them turned was that of the clock. Johannes Kepler once wrote, "I am

much occupied with the investigation of the physical causes. My aim in this is to show that the machine of the universe is not similar to a divine animated being, but similar to a clock."[4] Nature conceived as machinery removed much of the mystery of the world and the previous assumption of the presence of divine purpose in nature. The qualities that seemed to inhere in matter came to be understood as the result of mechanical arrangement. Some writers came to understand God as a kind of divine watchmaker or mechanic who had arranged the world as a machine that would thereafter function automatically. The drive to a mechanical understanding of nature also meant that the language of science and of natural philosophy would become largely that of mathematics. The emphasis that Galileo had placed on mathematics spread to other areas of thought.

This new mode of thinking transformed physical nature from a realm in which Europeans looked for symbolic or sacramental meaning related to the divine into a realm where they looked for utility or usefulness. Previously, philosophers had often believed a correct understanding of the natural order would reveal divine mysteries or knowledge relating to sacred history. Henceforth, they would tend to see knowledge of nature as revealing nothing beyond itself—nothing about divine purposes for the life of humankind on earth. Natural knowledge became the path toward the physical improvement of human beings through their ability to command and manipulate the processes of nature. Many people associated with the new science also believed such knowledge would strengthen the power of their monarchs.

FRANCIS BACON: THE EMPIRICAL METHOD

Bacon (1561–1626) was an Englishman of almost universal accomplishment. He was a lawyer, a high royal official, and the author of histories, moral essays, and philosophical discourses. Traditionally, he has been regarded as the father of **empiricism** and of experimentation in science. Much of this reputation was actually unearned. Bacon was not a natural philosopher, except in the most amateur fashion. His real accomplishment was setting an intellectual tone and helping create a climate conducive to scientific work.

In books such as *The Advancement of Learning* (1605), the *Novum Organum* (1620), and *The New Atlantis* (1627), Bacon attacked the scholastic

---

[3]Quoted in A. Rupert Hall, *From Galileo to Newton, 1630–1720* (London: Fontana, 1970), p. 300.

[4]Quoted in Steven Shapin, *The Scientific Revolution* (Chicago: University of Chicago Press, 1996), p. 33.

belief that most truth had already been discovered and only required explanation, as well as the scholastic reverence for authority in intellectual life. He believed scholastic thinkers paid too much attention to tradition and to the knowledge of the ancients. He urged contemporaries to strike out on their own in search of a new understanding of nature. He wanted seventeenth-century Europeans to have confidence in themselves and their own abilities rather than in the people and methods of the past. Bacon was one of the first major European writers to champion innovation and change.

Bacon believed that human knowledge should produce useful results—deeds rather than words. In particular, knowledge of nature should be enlisted to improve the human condition. These goals required modifying or abandoning scholastic modes of learning and thinking. Bacon contended, "The [scholastic] logic now in use serves more to fix and give stability to the errors which have their foundation in commonly received notions than to help the search after truth."[5] Scholastic philosophers could not escape from their syllogisms to examine the foundations of their thought and intellectual presuppositions. Bacon urged that philosophers and investigators of nature examine the evidence of their senses before constructing logical speculations. In a famous passage, he divided all philosophers into "men of experiment and men of dogmas" and then observed,

The men of experiment are like the ant, they only collect and use; the reasoners resemble spiders, who make cobwebs out of their own substance. But the bee takes a middle course: it gathers its material from the flowers of the garden and of the field, but transforms and digests it by a power of its own. Not unlike this is the true business of philosophy.[6]

By directing natural philosophy toward an examination of empirical evidence, Bacon hoped it would achieve new knowledge and thus new capabilities for humankind.

Bacon boldly compared himself with Columbus, plotting a new route to intellectual discovery. The comparison is significant, because it displays the consciousness of a changing world that appears so often in writers of the late sixteenth and early seventeenth centuries. They were rejecting the past not from simple contempt or arrogance, but rather from a firm understanding that the world was much more complicated than their medieval forebearers had thought. Neither Europe nor European thought could remain self-contained. Like the new

Sir Francis Bacon (1561–1626), champion of the inductive method of gaining knowledge.   Sir Francis Bacon (1561–1626), champion of the inductive method of gaining knowledge. National Portrait Gallery, London

worlds on the globe, new worlds of the mind were also emerging.

Most of the people in Bacon's day, including the intellectuals influenced by humanism, thought that the best era of human history lay in antiquity. Bacon dissented vigorously from that view. He looked to a future of material improvement achieved through the empirical examination of nature. His own theory of induction from empirical evidence was unsystematic, but his insistence on appealing to experience influenced others whose methods were more productive. He and others of his outlook received almost daily support from the reports not only of European explorers, but also of ordinary seamen who now sailed all over the world and could describe wondrous cultures, as well as plants and animals, unknown to the European ancients.

Bacon believed that expanding natural knowledge had a practical purpose and its goal was human improvement. Some scientific investigation does

[5]Quoted in Franklin Baumer, *Main Currents of Western Thought*, 4th ed. (New Haven, CT: Yale University Press, 1978), p. 281.
[6]Quoted in Baumer, p. 288.

have this character. Much pure research does not. Bacon, however, linked science and material progress in the public mind. This was a powerful idea that still influences Western civilization. It has made science and those who can appeal to the authority of science major forces for change and innovation. Thus, although not making any major scientific contribution himself, Bacon directed investigators of nature to a new method and a new purpose. As a person actively associated with politics, Bacon also believed the pursuit of new knowledge would increase the power of governments and monarchies. Again, his thought in this area opened the way for the eventual strong links between governments and the scientific enterprise.

RENÉ DESCARTES: THE METHOD OF RATIONAL DEDUCTION

Descartes (1596–1650) was a gifted mathematician who invented analytic geometry. His most important contribution, however, was to develop a scientific method that relied more on deduction—reasoning from general principle to arrive at specific facts—than empirical observation and induction.

In 1637, he published his *Discourse on Method*, in which he rejected scholastic philosophy and education and advocated thought founded on a mathematical model. (See "Descartes Explores the Promise of Science," page 462.) The work appeared in French rather than in Latin because Descartes wanted it to have wide circulation and application. In the *Discourse*, he began by saying he would doubt everything except those propositions about which he could have clear and distinct ideas. This approach rejected all forms of intellectual authority, except the conviction of his own reason. Descartes concluded that he could not doubt his own act of thinking and his own existence. From this base, he proceeded to deduce the existence of God. The presence of God was important to Descartes because God guaranteed the correctness of clear and distinct ideas. Since God was not a deceiver, the ideas of God-given reason could not be false.

On the basis of such an analysis, Descartes concluded that human reason could fully comprehend the world. He divided existing things into two basic categories: thinking things and things occupying space—mind and body, respectively. Thinking was the defining quality of the mind, and extension (the property by which things occupy space) was the defining quality of material bodies.

Queen Christina of Sweden (r. 1632–1654), shown here with the French philosopher and scientist René Descartes, was one of many women from the elite classes interested in the New Science. In 1649 she invited Descartes to live at her court in Stockholm, but he died a few months after moving to Sweden.   Pierre-Louis the Younger Dumesnil (1698–1781), "Christina of Sweden (1626-89) and her Court: detail of the Queen and René Descartes (1596-1650) at the Table." Oil on canvas. Chateau de Versailles, France/Bridgeman Art Library

Human reason could grasp and understand the world of extension, which became the realm of the natural philosopher. That world had no place for spirits, divinity, or anything nonmaterial. Descartes separated mind from body to banish nonmaterial matters from the realm of scientific speculation and analysis. Reason was to be applied only to the mechanical realm of matter or to the exploration of itself.

Descartes's emphasis on deduction, rational speculation, and internal reflection by the mind, all of which he explored more fully in his *Meditations* of 1641, have influenced philosophers from his time to the present. His deductive methodology, however, eventually lost favor to **scientific induction**, whereby scientists draw generalizations derived from and test hypotheses against empirical observations.

DESCARTES EXPLORES THE PROMISE OF SCIENCE

In 1637, Descartes published his Discourse on Method. *He wrote against what he believed to be the useless speculations of scholastic philosophy. He championed the careful investigation of physical nature on the grounds that it would expand the scope of human knowledge beyond anything previously achieved and, in doing so, make human beings the masters of nature. This passage contains much of the broad intellectual and cultural argument that led to the ever-growing influence and authority of science from the seventeenth century onward.*

■ How does Descartes compare the usefulness of science with previous speculative philosophy? How does he portray science as an instrument whereby human beings may master nature? What, if any, limits does he place on the extension of scientific knowledge? Why does he place so much emphasis on the promise of science to improve human health?

My speculations were indeed truly pleasing to me; but I recognize that other men have theirs, which perhaps please them even more. As soon, however, as I had acquired some general notions regarding physics, and on beginning to make trial of them in various special difficulties had observed how far they can carry us and how much they differ from the principles hitherto employed, I believed that I could not keep them hidden without grievously sinning against the law which lays us under obligation to promote, as far as in us lies, the general good of all mankind. For they led me to see that it is possible to obtain knowledge highly useful in life, and that in place of the speculative philosophy taught in the Schools we can have a practical philosophy, by means of which, knowing the force and the actions of fire, water, air, and of the stars, of the heavens, and of all the bodies that surround us—knowing them as distinctly as we know the various crafts of the artisans—we may in the same fashion employ them in all the uses for which they are suited, thus rendering ourselves the masters and possessors of na-

ture. This is to be desired, not only with a view to the invention of an infinity of arts by which we would be enabled to enjoy without heavy labor the fruits of the earth and all its conveniences, but above all for the preservation of health, which is, without doubt, of all blessings in this life, the first of all goods and the foundation on which the others rest. For the mind is so dependent on the temper and disposition of the bodily organisms that if any means can ever be found to render men wiser and more capable than they have hitherto been, I believe that it is in the science of medicine that the means must be sought. . . . With no wish to depreciate it, I am yet sure there is no one, even of those engaged in the profession, who does not admit that all we know is almost nothing in comparison with what remains to be discovered; and that we could be freed from innumerable maladies, both of body and of mind, and even perhaps from the infirmities of age, if we had sufficient knowledge of their causes and of the remedies provided by nature.

From René Descartes, *Discourse on Method*, in Norman Kemp Smith, ed., *Descartes's Philosophical Writings* (New York: The Modern Library, 1958), pp. 130–131. Reprinted by permission of Macmillan Press Ltd.

THOMAS HOBBES: APOLOGIST FOR ABSOLUTE GOVERNMENT

Nowhere did the impact of the methods of the new science so deeply affect political thought as in the thought of Thomas Hobbes (1588–1679), the most

original political philosopher of the seventeenth century.

An urbane and much-traveled man, Hobbes enthusiastically supported the new scientific movement. During the 1630s, he visited Paris, where he came to know Descartes, and Italy, where he spent time with Galileo. He took special interest in the works of William Harvey (1578–1657), who was famous for his discovery of the circulation of blood through the body. Hobbes was also a superb classicist. His earliest published work was the first English translation of Thucydides' *History of the Peloponnesian War* and is still being reprinted today. Part of Hobbes's dark view of human nature would appear to derive from Thucydides' historical analysis.

Hobbes had written works of political philosophy before the English Civil War, but the turmoil of that struggle led him in 1651 to publish his influential work *Leviathan*. His aim was to provide a rigorous philosophical justification for a strong central political authority. Hobbes portrayed human beings and society in a thoroughly materialistic and mechanical way. He traced all psychological processes to bare sensation and regarded all human motivations as egoistical, intended to increase pleasure and minimize pain. According to his analysis, human reasoning penetrated to no deeper reality or wisdom than those physical sensations. Consequently, for Hobbes, unlike both previous Christian and ancient philosophers, human beings exist only to meet the needs of daily life, not for higher spiritual ends or for any larger moral purpose. Only a sovereign commonwealth established by a contract between the ruler and the ruled could enable human beings to meet those needs by limiting the free exercise of the natural human pursuit of self-interest with all its potential for conflict.

According to Hobbes human beings in their natural state are inclined to a "perpetual and restless desire" for power. Because all people want and, in their natural state, possess a natural right to everything, their equality breeds enmity, competition, diffidence, and perpetual quarreling—"a war of every man against every man," as Hobbes put it in a famous summary.

In such condition there is no place for industry, because the fruit thereof is uncertain; and consequently no culture of the Earth; no navigation nor use of the commodities that may be imported by sea; no commodious building; no instruments of moving and removing such things as require much force; no knowledge of the face of the Earth; no account of time; no arts; no letters; no society; and, which is worst of all, continual fear and danger of violent death; and the life of man solitary, poor, nasty, brutish, and short.[7]

As seen in this passage, Hobbes, contrary to Aristotle and Christian thinkers like Thomas Aquinas (1225–1274), rejected the view that human beings are naturally sociable. Rather, they are self-centered creatures who lack a master.

Thus, whereas earlier and later philosophers saw the original human state as a paradise from which humankind had fallen, Hobbes saw it as a state of natural, inevitable conflict in which neither safety, security, nor any final authority existed. Human beings in this state of nature were constantly haunted by fear of destruction and death.

Human beings escaped this terrible state of nature, according to Hobbes, only by entering into a particular kind of political contract according to which they agreed to live in a commonwealth tightly ruled by a recognized sovereign. This contract obliged every person, for the sake of peace and self-defense, to agree to set aside personal rights to all things and to be content with as much liberty against others as he or she would allow others against himself or herself. All agreed to live according to a secularized version of the golden rule, "Do not that to another which you would not have done to yourself."[8]

Because, however, words and promises are insufficient to guarantee this agreement, the contract also established the coercive use of force by the sovereign to compel compliance. Believing the dangers of anarchy to be always greater than those of tyranny, Hobbes thought that rulers should be absolute and unlimited in their power, once established as authority. Hobbes's political philosophy has no room for protest in the name of individual conscience or for individual appeal to some other legitimate authority beyond the sovereign. In a reply to critics of his position on sovereign authority, Hobbes pointed out the alternative:

The greatest [unhappiness] that in any form of government can possibly happen to the people in general is scarce sensible in respect of the miseries and horrible calamities that accompany a civil war or that dissolute condition of masterless men, without subjection to laws and a coercive power to tie their hands from rapine and revenge.[9]

The specific structure of this absolute government was not of enormous concern to Hobbes. He believed absolute authority might be lodged in either a monarch or a legislative body, but once that person or body had been granted authority, there existed no argument for appeal. For all practical purposes, obedience to the Hobbesian sovereign was absolute.

Hobbes's argument for an absolute political authority that could assure order aroused sharp opposition. Monarchists objected to his willingness to assign sovereign authority to a legislature. Republicans rejected his willingness to accept a monarchical authority. Many Christian writers,

[7]Thomas Hobbes, *Leviathan*, Parts I and II, ed. by H. W. Schneider (Indianapolis: Bobbs-Merrill, 1958), p. 86, 106–107.

[8]Hobbes, p. 130.
[9]Hobbes, p. 152.

The famous title page illustration for Hobbes's *Leviathan*. The ruler is pictured as absolute lord of his lands, but note that the ruler incorporates the mass of individuals whose self-interests are best served by their willing consent to accept him and cooperate with him.
Rare Books Division, The New York Public Library. Astor, Lenox and Tilden Foundations

including those who supported the divine right of kings, furiously criticized his materialist arguments for an absolute political authority. Other Christian writers attacked his refusal to recognize the authority of either God or the church as standing beside or above his secular sovereign. The religious critique of Hobbes meant that his thought had little immediate practical impact, but his ideas influenced philosophical literature from the late seventeenth century onward.

JOHN LOCKE: DEFENDER OF MODERATE LIBERTY AND TOLERATION

Locke (1632–1704) proved to be the most influential philosophical and political thinker of the seventeenth century. Although he was less original than Hobbes, his political writings became a major source of criticism of absolutism and provided a foundation for later liberal political philosophy in both Europe

and America. His philosophical works dealing with human knowledge became the most important work of psychology for the eighteenth century.

Locke's family had Puritan sympathies, and during the English Civil War his father had fought for the parliamentary forces against the Stuart monarchy. Although a highly intellectual person who was well-read in all the major seventeenth-century natural philosophers, Locke became deeply involved with the tumultuous politics of the English Restoration period. He was a close associate of Anthony Ashley Cooper, the earl of Shaftesbury (1621–1683), considered by his contemporaries to be a radical in both religion and politics. Shaftesbury organized an unsuccessful rebellion against Charles II in 1682, after which both he and Locke, who lived with him, were forced to flee to Holland.

During his years of association with Shaftesbury and the opposition to Charles II, Locke wrote two treatises on government that were eventually pub-

John Locke (1632–1704), defender of the rights of the people against rulers who think their power absolute.
"John Locke (1632-1704)." By courtesy of the National Portrait Gallery, London

lished in 1690. In the first of these, he rejected arguments for absolute government that based political authority on the patriarchal model of fathers ruling over a family. After the publication of this treatise, no major political philosopher again appealed to the patriarchal model. In that regard, though not widely read today, Locke's *First Treatise of Government* proved enormously important by clearing the philosophical decks, so to speak, of a long-standing traditional argument that could not stand up to rigorous analysis.

In his *Second Treatise of Government*, Locke presented an extended argument for a government that must necessarily be both responsible for and responsive to the concerns of the governed. Locke portrayed the natural human state as one of perfect freedom and equality in which everyone enjoyed, in an unregulated fashion, the natural rights of life, liberty, and property. Locke, contrary to Hobbes, regarded human beings in their natural state as creatures of reason and basic goodwill rather than of uncontrolled passion and selfishness. For Locke,

human beings possess a strong capacity for dwelling more or less peacefully in society before they enter a political contract. What they experience in the state of nature is not a state of war, but a condition of competition and modest conflict that requires a political authority to sort out problems rather than to impose sovereign authority. They enter into the contract to form political society to secure and preserve the rights, liberty, and property that they already possess prior to the existence of political authority. In this respect, government exists to protect the best achievements and liberty of the state of nature, not to overcome them. Thus, by its very foundation, Locke's government is one of limited authority.

The conflict that Hobbes believed characterized the state of nature emerged for Locke only when rulers failed to preserve people's natural freedom and attempted to enslave them by absolute rule. The relationship between rulers and the governed is that of trust, and if the rulers betray that trust, the governed have the right to replace them. In this regard, Locke's position resembled that of Thomas Aquinas, who also permitted rebellion when government violated laws of nature.

In his *Letter Concerning Toleration* (1689), Locke used the premises of the as yet unpublished *Second Treatise* to defend extensive religious toleration among Christians, which he saw as an answer to the destructive religious conflict of the past two centuries. To make his case for toleration, Locke claimed that each individual was required to work out his or her own religious salvation and these efforts might lead various people to join different religious groups. For its part, government existed by its very nature to preserve property, not to make religious decisions for its citizens. Governments that attempted to impose religious uniformity thus misunderstood their real purpose. Moreover, government-imposed religious uniformity could not achieve real religious ends, because assent to religious truth must be freely given by the individual's conscience rather than by force. Consequently, Locke urged a wide degree of religious toleration among differing voluntary Christian groups. He did not, however, extend toleration to Roman Catholics, whom he believed to have given allegiance to a foreign prince (i.e., the pope), to non-Christians, or to atheists, whom he believed could not be trusted to keep their word. Despite these limitations, Locke's *Letter Concerning Toleration* established a powerful foundation for the future extension of toleration, religious liberty, and the separation of church and state. His vision of such expansive toleration was partially realized in England after 1688 and most fully in the United States after the American Revolution.

MAJOR WORKS
OF THE SCIENTIFIC REVOLUTION

1543 *On the Revolutions of the Heavenly
      Spheres* (Copernicus)

1605 *The Advancement of Learning* (Bacon)

1609 *The New Astronomy* (Kepler)

1610 *The Starry Messenger* (Galileo)

1620 *Novum Organum* (Bacon)

1632 *Dialogue on the Two Chief World Systems*
      (Galileo)

1637 *Discourse on Method* (Descartes)

1651 *Leviathan* (Hobbes)

1687 *Principia Mathematica* (Newton)

1689 *Letter Concerning Toleration* (Locke)

1690 *An Essay Concerning Human
      Understanding* (Locke)

1690 *Treatises of Government* (Locke)

Finally, just as Newton had set forth laws of astronomy and gravitation, Locke hoped to elucidate the basic structures of human thought. He did so in the most immediately influential of his books, his *Essay Concerning Human Understanding* (1690), which became the major work of European psychology during the eighteenth century. There, Locke portrayed a person's mind at birth as a blank tablet whose content would be determined by sense experience. His vision of the mind has been aptly compared to an early version of behaviorism. It was a reformer's psychology, which contended that the human condition could be improved by changing the environment.

Locke's view of psychology rejected the Christian understanding of original sin, yet he believed his psychology had preserved religious knowledge. He thought such knowledge came through divine revelation in Scripture and also from the conclusions that human reason could draw from observing nature. He hoped this interpretation of religious knowledge would prevent human beings from falling into what he regarded as fanaticism arising from the claims of alleged private revelations and irrationality arising from superstition. For Locke, reason and revelation were compatible and together could sustain a moderate religious faith that would avoid religious conflict.

THE NEW INSTITUTIONS
OF EXPANDING NATURAL
KNOWLEDGE

One of the most fundamental features of the expansion of science was the emerging idea that *genuinely new knowledge* about nature and hu-

mankind could be discovered. In the late Middle Ages, the recovery of Aristotle and the rise of humanistic learning looked back to the ancients to rediscover the kind of knowledge that later Europeans needed. Luther and other Reformers had seen themselves as recovering a better understanding of the original Christian message. By contrast, the proponents of the new natural knowledge and the new philosophy sought to pursue what Bacon called the advancement of learning. New knowledge would be continuously created. This outlook required new institutions.

The expansion of natural knowledge had powerful social implications. Both the new science and the philosophical outlook associated with it opposed Scholasticism and Aristotelianism. These were not simply disembodied philosophical outlooks, but ways of approaching the world of knowledge most scholars in the universities of the day still believed in. Such scholars had a clear, vested interest in preserving those traditional outlooks. As they saw it, they were defending the ancients against the moderns. Not surprisingly, the advanced thinkers of the seventeenth century often criticized the universities. For example, in his *Discourse on Method*, Descartes was highly critical of the education he had received. Hobbes filled the *Leviathan* with caustic remarks about the kind of learning then dominating schools and universities, and Locke advocated educational reform.

Some of the criticism of universities was exaggerated. Medical faculties, on the whole, welcomed the advancement of learning in their fields of study. Most of the natural philosophers had themselves received their education at universities. Moreover, however slowly new ideas might penetrate universities, the expanding world of natural knowledge would be taught to future generations. With that diffusion of science into the universities came new supporters of scientific knowledge beyond the small group of natural philosophers themselves. Universities also provided much of the physical and financial support for teaching and investigating natural philosophy and employed many scientists, the most important of whom was Newton himself. University support of science did, however, vary according to country, with the Italian universities being far more supportive than the French.

Yet because of the reluctance of universities to rapidly assimilate the new science, its pioneers quickly understood that they required a framework for cooperating and sharing of information that went beyond existing intellectual institutions. Consequently, they and their supporters established what have been termed "institutions of sharing" that allowed information and ideas associated with the new science to be gathered, exchanged, and debated.[10] The most famous of these institutions was the Royal Society of London, founded in 1660, whose members consciously saw themselves as following the path Bacon had laid out almost a half century earlier. The Royal Society had been preceded by the Academy of Experiments in Florence in 1657 and was followed by the French Academy of Science in 1666. Germany only slowly overcame the destruction of the Thirty Years' War, and the Berlin Academy of Science was not founded until 1700. In addition to these major institutions, the new science was discussed and experiments were carried out in many local societies and academies.

Colbert was Louis XIV's most influential minister. He sought to expand the economic life of France and to associate the monarchy with the emerging new science from which he hoped might flow new inventions and productive technology. Here he is portrayed presenting members of the French Academy of Science to the monarch. On the founding of the French Academy. Henri Testelin (1616–1695). (after Le Brun). Minister of Finance Colbert presenting the members of the Royal Academy of Science (founded in 1667) to Louis XIV. Study for a tapestry. Photo: Gerard Blot. Chateau de Versailles et de Triaanon, Versailles, France. Reunion des Musees Nationaux/Art Resource, NY

These societies met regularly to hear papers and observe experiments. One of the reasons many early experiments achieved credibility was that they had been observed by persons of social respectability who belonged to one or more of the societies and who, because of their social standing, were presumed to be truthful witnesses of what they had observed. These groups also published information relating to natural philosophy and often organized libraries for their members. Perhaps most important, they attempted to separate the discussion and exploration of natural philosophy from the religious and political conflicts of the day. They intended science to exemplify an arena for the polite exchange of ideas and for civil disagreement and debate. This particular function of science as fostering civility became one of its major attractions.

The activities of the societies also constituted a kind of crossroads between their own members always drawn from the literate classes, and people outside the elite classes, whose skills and practical knowledge might be important for advancing the new science. The latter included craftspeople who could manufacture scientific instruments, sailors whose travels had taken them to foreign parts and who might report on the plants and animals they had seen there, and workers who had practical knowledge of problems in the countryside. In this respect, the expansion of the European economy and the drive toward empires contributed to the growth of the scientific endeavor by bringing back to Europe specimens and experiences that required classification, analysis, and observation.

In good Baconian fashion, the members of the societies presented science as an enterprise that could aid the goals of government and the growth of the economy. For example, mathematicians portrayed themselves as being useful for solving surveying and other engineering problems and for improving armaments. Furthermore, people who had ideas for improving production, navigation, or military artillery might seek the support of the associated societies. In the English context, these people became known as *projectors* and were often regarded as people simply eager to sell their often improbable ideas to the highest bidder. Nonetheless, their activities brought the new science and technology before a wider public.

The work, publications, and interaction of the scientific societies with both the government and private business established a distinct role and presence for scientific knowledge in European social life. By 1700, that presence was relatively modest, but it would grow steadily during the coming decades. The groups associated with the new science saw themselves as championing modern practical achievements of applied knowledge and urging religious toleration, mutual forbearance, and political liberty. Such people would form the social base for the eighteenth-century movement known as the **Enlightenment**.

[10]Lewis Pyenson and Susan Sheets-Pyenson, *Servants of Nature: A History of Scientific Institutions, Enterprises, and Sensibilities* (New York: W. W. Norton, 1999), p. 75.

WOMEN IN THE WORLD OF THE SCIENTIFIC REVOLUTION

The absence of women in the emergence of the new science of the seventeenth century has been a matter of much historical speculation. What characteristics of early modern European intellectual and cultural life worked against extensive contributions by women? Why have we heard so little of the activity by women that did actually occur in regard to the new science?

The same factors that had long excluded women from participating in most intellectual life continued to exclude them from working in the emerging natural philosophy. Traditionally, the institutions of European intellectual life had all but excluded women. Both monasteries and universities had been institutions associated with celibate male clerical culture. Except for a few exceptions in Italy, women had not been admitted to either medieval or early modern European universities; they would continue to be excluded from them until the end of the nineteenth century. Women could and did exercise influence over princely courts where natural philosophers, such as Galileo, sought patronage, but they usually did not determine those patronage decisions or benefit from them. Queen Christina of Sweden (r. 1632–1654), who brought René Descartes to Stockholm to provide the regulations for a new science academy, was an exception. When various scientific societies were founded, women were not admitted to membership. In that regard, there were virtually no social spaces that might have permitted women to pursue science easily.

Yet a few isolated women from two different social settings did manage to engage in the new scientific activity—noblewomen and women from the artisan class. In both cases, they could do so only through their husbands or male relatives.

The social standing of certain noblewomen allowed them to command the attention of ambitious natural philosophers who were part of their husband's social circle. Margaret Cavendish (1623–1673) actually made significant contributions to the scientific literature of the day. As a girl she had been privately tutored and become widely read. Her marriage to the duke of Newcastle introduced her into a circle of natural philosophers. She understood the new science, quarreled with the ideas of Descartes and Hobbes, and criticized the Royal Society for being more interested in novel scientific instruments than in solving practical problems. Her most important works were *Observations Upon Experimental Philosophy* (1666) and *Grounds of Natural Philosophy* (1668). She was the only woman in the seventeenth century to be allowed to visit a meeting of the Royal Society of

Margaret Cavendish, who wrote widely on scientific subjects, was the most accomplished woman associated with the New Science in seventeenth-century England. ImageWorks/Mary Evans Picture Library Ltd.

London. (See "Margaret Cavendish Questions the Fascination with Scientific Instruments".)

Women associated with artisan crafts actually achieved greater freedom to pursue the new sciences than did noblewomen. Traditionally, women had worked in artisan workshops, often with their husbands, and might take over the business when their spouse died. In Germany, much study of astronomy occurred in these settings, with women assisting their fathers or husbands. One German female astronomer, Maria Cunitz, published a book on astronomy that many people thought her husband had written until he added a preface supporting her sole authorship. Elisabetha and Johannes Hevelius constituted a wife-and-husband astronomical team, as did Maria Winkelmann and her husband Gottfried Kirch. In each case, the wife served as the assistant to an artisan astronomer. Although Winkelmann discovered a comet in 1702, it was not until 1930 that the discovery was ascribed to her rather than to her husband. Nonetheless, contemporary philosophers did recognize her abilities and understanding of astronomy. Winkelmann had worked jointly with her husband who was the official astronomer of the Berlin Academy of Sciences and was responsible for an official calendar the academy published. When her husband died in 1710, Winkelmann applied for permission to continue the work, basing her application for the post on the guild's tradition of allowing

MARGARET CAVENDISH QUESTIONS THE FASCINATION WITH SCIENTIFIC INSTRUMENTS

Margaret Cavendish, Duchess of Newcastle, was the most scientifically informed woman of seventeenth-century England. She read widely in natural philosophy and had many acquaintances who were involved in the new science. Although she was enthusiastic about the promise of science, she also frequently criticized some of its leading proponents, including Descartes and Hobbes. She was skeptical of the activities of the newly established Royal Society of London, which she was once permitted to visit. She believed some of its members had become overly enthusiastic about experimentation and new scientific instruments for their own sakes and had begun to ignore the practical questions that she thought science should address. In this respect, her criticism of the Royal Society and its experiments is a Baconian one. She thought the society had replaced scholastic speculation with experimental speculation and that both kinds of speculation ignored important problems of immediate utility.

■ *Why might Margaret Cavendish think that the experiments which were reported about new optical instruments dealt with superficial wonders? Why does she contrast experimental philosophy with the beneficial arts? Do you find a feminist perspective in her comparison of the men of the Royal Society with boys playing with bubbles?*

Art has intoxicated so many men's brains, and wholly imployed their thoughts and bodily actions about phaenomena, or the exterior figure of objects, as all better Arts and Studies are laid aside. . . . But though there be numerous Books written of the wonder of these [experimental optical] Glasses, yet I cannot perceive any such; at best, they are but superficial wonders, as I may call them. But could Experimental Philosophers find out more beneficial Arts then our Fore-fathers have done, either for the better increase of Vegetables and brute Animals to nourish our bodies, or better and commodious contrivances in the Art of Architecture to build us houses, or for the advancing of trade and traffick . . . it would not only be worth their labour, but of as much praise as could be given to them: But, as Boys that play with watry Bubbles . . . are worthy of reproof rather than praise, for wasting their time with useless sports; so those that addict themselves to unprofitable Arts, spend more time than they reap benefit thereby.

From Margaret Cavendish, *Observations Upon Experimental Philosophy;* to which is added, *The Description of a New Blazing World* (London, 1666), pp. 10–11, as quoted in Anna Battigelli, *Margaret Cavendish and the Exiles of the Mind* (Lexington: University of Kentucky Press, 1998), p. 94.

women to continue their husbands' work, in this case the completion of observations required to create an accurate calendar. After much debate, the academy formally rejected her application on the grounds of her gender, although its members knew of her ability and previous accomplishments. Years later, she returned to the Berlin Academy as an assistant to her son, who had been appointed astronomer. Again, the academy insisted that she leave, forcing her to abandon astronomy. She died in 1720.

Such policies of exclusion, however, did not altogether prevent women from acquiring knowledge about scientific endeavors. Margaret Cavendish had composed a *Description of a New World, Called the Blazing World* (1666) to introduce women to the new science. Other examples of scientific writings for a

female audience were Bernard de Fontenelle's *Conversations on the Plurality of Worlds* and Francesco Algarotti's *Newtonianism for Ladies* (1737). During the 1730s, Emilie du Châtelet (1706–1749) aided Voltaire in his composition of an important French popularization of Newton's science. Her knowledge of mathematics was more extensive than his and crucial to his completing his book. She also translated Newton's *Principia* into French, an accomplishment made possible only by her exceptional understanding of advanced mathematics.

Still, with few exceptions, women were barred from science and medicine until the late nineteenth century, and not until the twentieth century did they enter these fields in significant numbers. Not only did the institutions of science exclude them, but also, the ideas associated with medical practice, philosophy, and biology suggested that women and their minds were essentially different from, and inferior to, men. By the early eighteenth century, despite isolated precedents of women pursuing natural knowledge, reading scientific literature, and engaging socially with natural philosophers, it had become a fundamental assumption of European intellectual life that the pursuit of knowledge about nature was a male vocation.

THE NEW SCIENCE AND RELIGIOUS FAITH

For many contemporaries, the new science posed a potential challenge to religion. Three major issues were at stake. First, certain theories and discoveries did not agree with biblical statements about the heavens. Second, who would decide conflicts between religion and science—church authorities or the natural philosophers? Finally, for many religious thinkers, the new science seemed to replace a universe of spiritual meaning and significance with a purely materialistic one. Yet most of the natural philosophers genuinely saw their work as supporting religious belief by contributing to a deeper knowledge of the divine. Their efforts and those of their supporters to reconcile faith and the new science constituted a fundamental factor in the spread of science and its widespread acceptance in educated European circles. The process was not an easy one.

THE CASE OF GALILEO

The condemnation of Galileo by Roman Catholic authorities in 1633 is the single most famous incident of conflict between modern science and religious institutions. For centuries it was interpreted as exemplifying the forces of religion smothering scientific knowledge. More recent research has modified that picture.

The condemnation of Copernicanism and of Galileo occurred at a particularly difficult moment in the history of the Roman Catholic Church. In response to Protestant emphasis on private interpretation of Scripture, the Council of Trent (1545–1563) had stated that only the church itself possessed the authority to interpret the Bible. Furthermore, after the Council, the Roman Catholic Church had adopted a more literalist mode of reading the Bible in response to the Protestant emphasis on the authority of Scripture. Galileo's championing of Copernicanism took place in this particular climate of opinion and practice when the Roman Catholic Church, on the one hand, could not surrender the interpretation of the Bible to a layman and, on the other, had difficulty moving beyond a literal reading of the Bible, lest the Protestants accuse it of abandoning Scripture.

In a *Letter to the Grand Duchess Christina* (1615), Galileo, as a layman, had published his own views about how scripture should be interpreted to accommodate the new science. (See "Galileo Discusses the Relationship of Science to the Bible".) To certain Roman Catholic authorities, his actions resembled that of a Protestant who looked to himself rather than the church to understand the Bible. In 1615 and 1616, he visited Rome and discussed his views openly and aggressively. In early 1616, however, the Roman Catholic Inquisition formally censured Copernicus's views, placing *On the Revolutions of the Heavenly Spheres* in the Index of Prohibited Books. The ground for the condemnation was Copernicus' disagreement with the literal word of the Bible and the biblical interpretations of the Church Fathers. It should be recalled that at the time fully satisfactory empirical evidence to support Copernicus did not yet exist, even in Galileo's mind.

Galileo, who was not on trial in 1616, was formally informed of the condemnation of Copernicanism. Exactly what agreement he and the Roman Catholic authorities reached as to what he would be permitted to write about Copernicanism remains unclear. It appears that he agreed not to advocate that Copernican astronomy was actually physically true, but only to suggest that it could be true in theory.

In 1623, however, a Florentine acquaintance of Galileo's was elected as Pope Urban VIII. He gave Galileo permission to resume discussing the Copernican system, which he did in *Dialogue on the Two Chief World Systems* (1632). The book clearly was designed to defend the physical truthfulness of Copernicanism. Moreover, the voices in the dialogue favoring the older system appeared slow-witted—and those voices presented the views of Pope Urban. Feeling humiliated and betrayed, the pope ordered an investigation of Galileo's book. The actual issue in Galileo's trial of 1633 was whether he had disobeyed the mandate of 1616, and he was held to have done so even though the exact nature of that mandate was less than certain. Galileo was condemned, required to renounce his views, and placed under the equivalent of house arrest in his home near Florence for the last nine years of his life.

Although much more complicated than a simple case of a conflict between science and religion, the condemnation of Galileo cast a long and troubled shadow over the relationship of the emerging new science and the authority of the Roman Catholic Church. The controversy continued into the late twentieth century, when Pope John Paul II formally ordered the reassessment of the Galileo case. In 1992, the Roman Catholic Church admitted that errors had occurred, particularly in the biblical interpretation of Pope Urban VIII's advisers.

GALILEO DISCUSSES THE RELATIONSHIP OF SCIENCE TO THE BIBLE

The religious authorities were often critical of the discoveries and theories of sixteenth- and seventeenth-century science. For years before his condemnation by the Roman Catholic Church in 1633, Galileo had contended that scientific theory and religious piety were compatible. In his Letter to the Grand Duchess Christiana. *(of Tuscany), written in 1615, he argued that God had revealed truth in both the Bible and physical nature and that the truth of physical nature did not contradict the Bible if the latter were properly understood. Galileo encountered difficulties regarding this letter because it represented a layman telling church authorities how to read the Bible.*

■ *Is Galileo's argument based on science or theology? Did the church believe that nature was as much a revelation of God as the Bible was? As Galileo describes them, which is the surer revelation of God, nature or the Bible? Why might the pope reject Galileo's argument?*

The reason produced for condemning the opinion that the Earth moves and the sun stands still is that in many places in the Bible one may read that the sun moves and the Earth stands still. . . .

With regard to this argument, I think in the first place that it is very pious to say and prudent to affirm that the holy Bible can never speak untruth—whenever its true meaning is understood. But I believe nobody will deny that it is often very abstruse, and may say things which are quite different from what its bare words signify. . . .

This being granted, I think that in discussions of physical problems we ought to begin not from the authority of scriptural passages, but from sense experiences and necessary demonstrations; for the holy Bible and the phenomena of nature proceed alike from the divine Word, the former as the dictate of the Holy Ghost and the latter as the observant executrix of God's commands. It is necessary for the Bible, in order to be accommodated to the understanding of every man, to speak many things which appear to differ from the absolute truth so far as the bare meaning of the words is concerned. But Nature, on the other hand, is inexorable and immutable; she never transgresses the laws imposed upon her, or cares a whit whether her abstruse reasons and methods of operation are understandable to men. For that reason it appears that nothing physical which sense-experience sets before our eyes, or which necessary demonstrations prove to us, ought to be called in question (much less condemned) upon the testimony of biblical passages which may have some different meaning beneath their words. For the Bible is not chained in every expression to conditions as strict as those which govern all physical effects; nor is God any less excellently revealed in Nature's actions than in the sacred statements of the Bible. . . .

From this I do not mean to infer that we need not have an extraordinary esteem for the passages of holy Scripture. On the contrary, having arrived at any certainties in physics, we ought to utilize these as the most appropriate aids in the true exposition of the Bible and in the investigation of those meanings which are necessarily contained therein for these must be concordant with demonstrated truths. I should judge the authority of the Bible was designed to persuade men of those articles and propositions which, surpassing all human reasoning, could not be made credible by science, or by any other means than through the very mouth of the Holy Spirit. . . .

But I do not feel obliged to believe that the same God who has endowed us with senses, reason, and intellect has intended to forgo their use and by some other means to give us knowledge which we can attain by them.

From *Discoveries and Opinions of Galileo* by Galileo Galilei, translated by Stillman Drake, copyright © 1957 by Stillman Drake.

A CLOSER LOOK

The Sciences and the Arts

Painters during the seventeenth century were keenly aware that they lived in an age of expanding knowledge of nature and of the world. Adriaen Stalbent (1589–1662) portrayed this close interrelationship of *The Sciences and the Arts*. Across Europe various societies were founded to study the expanding realm of natural knowledge. As in this painting, women only were rarely admitted to the meetings of these societies or to the rooms where the new natural knowledge was pursued or discussed.

On the red, covered table stands an astronomical instrument that natural philosophers used to illustrate the theories of Copernicus, Kepler, and Galileo.

The paintings on the wall illustrate the great masters of the day, some of whom drew on ancient mythological themes, others biblical scenes, and still others contemporary landscapes. Sophisticated viewers would have been able to identify each painting and its artist. The themes from the Bible and ancient mythology here are intended to contrast with the symbols of modern knowledge displayed elsewhere in the room.

On the table on the right stands a globe and volumes of maps that allow observers to trace the explorations of the Americas and other parts of the non-European world.

Adriaen Stalbent (1589–1662) "The Sciences and the Arts." Wood, 93 × 114 cm. Inv. 1405. Museo del Prado, Madrid, Spain. Photograph © Erich Lessing, Art Resource, NY

BLAISE PASCAL: REASON AND FAITH

Blaise Pascal (1623–1662), a French mathematician and a physical scientist who surrendered his wealth to pursue an austere, self-disciplined life, made one of the most influential efforts to reconcile faith and the new science. He aspired to write a work that would refute both dogmatism (which he saw epitomized by the Jesuits) and skepticism. Pascal considered the Jesuits' casuistry (i.e., arguments designed to minimize and excuse sinful acts) a distortion of Christian teach-

ing. He rejected the skeptics of his age because they either denied religion altogether (atheists) or accepted it only as it conformed to reason (deists). He never produced a definitive refutation of the two sides. Rather, he formulated his views on these matters in piecemeal fashion in a provocative collection of reflections on humankind and religion published posthumously under the title *Pensées (Thoughts)*.

Pascal allied himself with the Jansenists, seventeenth-century Catholic opponents of the Jesuits. (See Chapter 13.) His sister was a member of the

Jansenist convent of Port-Royal, near Paris. The Jansenists shared with the Calvinists Saint Augustine's belief in human beings' total sinfulness, their eternal predestination to heaven or hell by God, and their complete dependence on faith and grace for knowledge of God and salvation.

Pascal believed that in religious matters, only the reasons of the heart and a "leap of faith" could prevail. For him, religion was not the domain of reason and science. He saw two essential truths in the Christian religion: A loving God exists, and human beings, because they are corrupt by nature, are utterly unworthy of God. He believed the atheists and the deists of his age had overestimated reason. To Pascal, reason itself was too weak to resolve the problems of human nature and destiny. Ultimately, reason should drive those who truly heeded it to faith in God and reliance on divine grace.

Pascal made a famous wager with the skeptics. It is a better bet, he argued, to believe God exists and to stake everything on his promised mercy than not to do so. This is because, if God does exist, the believer will gain everything, whereas, should God prove not to exist, comparatively little will have been lost by having believed in him.

Convinced that belief in God improved life psychologically and disciplined it morally (regardless of whether God proved in the end to exist), Pascal worked to strengthen traditional religious belief. He urged his contemporaries to seek self-understanding by "learned ignorance" and to discover humankind's greatness by recognizing its misery. He hoped thereby to counter what he believed to be the false optimism of the new rationalism and science.

THE ENGLISH APPROACH TO SCIENCE AND RELIGION

Francis Bacon established a key framework for reconciling science and religion that long influenced the English-speaking world. He argued there were two books of divine revelation: the Bible and nature. In studying nature, the natural philosopher could achieve a deeper knowledge of things divine, just as could the theologian studying the Bible. Because both books of revelation shared the same author, they must be compatible. Whatever discord might first appear between science and religion must eventually be reconciled. Natural theology based on a scientific understanding of the natural order would thus support theology derived from Scripture.

Later in the seventeenth century, with the work of Newton, the natural universe became a realm of law and regularity. Most natural philosophers were devout people who saw in the new picture of physical nature a new picture of God. The Creator of this rational, lawful nature must also be rational.

To study nature was to come to a better understanding of that Creator. Science and religious faith were not only compatible, but mutually supportive. As Newton wrote, "The main Business of Natural Philosophy is to argue from Phaenomena without feigning Hypothesis, and to deduce Causes from Effects, till we come to the very first Cause, which certainly is not mechanical."[11]

The religious thought associated with such deducing of religious conclusions from nature became known as *physico-theology*. This reconciliation of faith and science allowed the new physics and astronomy to spread rapidly. At the very time when Europeans were finally tiring of the wars of religion, the new science provided the basis for a view of God that might lead away from irrational disputes and wars over religious doctrine. Faith in a rational God encouraged faith in the rationality of human beings and in their capacity to improve their lot once liberated from the traditions of the past. The scientific revolution provided the great model for the desirability of change and of criticism of inherited views.

Finally, the new science and the technological and economic innovations associated with its culture came again, especially among English thinkers, to be interpreted as part of a divine plan. By the late seventeenth century, natural philosophy and its practical achievements had become associated in the public mind with consumption and the market economy. Writers such as the Englishman John Ray in *The Wisdom of God Manifested in His Works of Creation* (1690) argued it was evident that God had placed human beings in the world to understand it and then, having understood it, to turn it to productive practical use through rationality. Scientific advance and economic enterprise came to be interpreted in the public mind as the fulfillment of God's plan: Human beings were meant to improve the world. This outlook provided a religious justification for the processes of economic improvement that would characterize much of eighteenth-century Western Europe.

CONTINUING SUPERSTITION

Despite the great optimism among certain European thinkers associated with the new ideas in science and philosophy, traditional beliefs and fears long retained their hold on Western culture. During the sixteenth and seventeenth centuries, many Europeans remained preoccupied with sin, death, and the devil. Religious people, including many among the learned and many who were sympathetic to the emerging scientific ideas, continued to believe in the power of magic and the occult. Until the end of the seventeenth century, almost all Europeans in one way or another believed in the power of demons.

[11]Quoted in Baumer, p. 323.

WITCH-HUNTS AND PANIC

Nowhere is the dark side of early modern thought and culture more strikingly visible than in the witch-hunts and panics that erupted in almost every Western land. Between 1400 and 1700, courts sentenced an estimated 70,000 to 100,000 people to death for harmful magic (*maleficium*) and diabolical witchcraft. In addition to inflicting harm on their neighbors, witches were said to attend mass meetings known as *sabbats*, to which they were believed to fly. They were also accused of indulging in sexual orgies with the devil, who appeared in animal form, most often as a he-goat. Still other charges against them were cannibalism—particularly the devouring of small Christian children—and a variety of ritual acts and practices, often sexual in nature, that denied or perverted Christian beliefs.

Why did witch panics occur in the sixteenth and early seventeenth centuries? The disruptions created by religious division and warfare were major factors. (The peak years of the religious wars were also those of the witch-hunts). Some argue that the Reformation spurred the panics by taking away the traditional defenses against the devil and demons, thus compelling societies to protect themselves preemptively by searching out and executing witches. Political consolidation by secular governments and the papacy played an even greater role, as both aggressively conformed their respective realms in an attempt to eliminate competition for the loyalty of their subjects.

VILLAGE ORIGINS

The roots of belief in witches are found in both popular and elite culture. In village societies, feared and respected "cunning folk" helped people cope with natural disasters and disabilities by magical means. For local people, these were important services that kept village life moving forward in times of calamity. The possession of magical powers, for good or ill, made one an important person within village society. Those who were most in need of security and influence, particularly old, impoverished single or widowed women, often made claims to such authority. In village society witch beliefs may also have been a way to defy urban Christian society's attempts to impose its orthodox beliefs, laws, and institutions on the countryside. Under church persecution local fertility cults, whose semipagan practices were intended to ensure good harvests, acquired the features of diabolical witchcraft.

INFLUENCE OF THE CLERGY

Popular belief in magical power was the essential foundation of the witch-hunts. Had ordinary people not believed that "gifted persons" could help or harm by magical means, and had they not been willing to accuse them, the hunts would never have occurred. However, but the contribution of Christian theologians was equally great. When the church expanded into areas where its power and influence were small, it encountered semipagan cultures rich in folkloric beliefs and practices that predated Christianity. There, it clashed with the cunning men and women, who were respected spiritual authorities in their local communities, the folk equivalents of Christian priests. The Christian clergy also practiced high magic. They could transform bread and wine into the body and blood of Christ (the sacrament of the Eucharist) and eternal penalties for sin into temporal ones (the sacrament of Penance or Confession). They also claimed the power to cast out demons who possessed the faithful.

In the late thirteenth century, the church declared its magic to be the only true magic. Since such powers were not innate to humans, the theologians reasoned, they must come either from God or from the devil. Those from God were properly exercised within and by the church. Any who practiced magic outside and against the church did so on behalf of the devil. From such reasoning grew allegations of "pacts" between nonpriestly magicians and Satan. Attacking accused witches became a way for the church to extend its spiritual hegemony.

In working its will, the church had an important ally in the princes of the age, who were also attempting to extend and consolidate their authority over villages and towns within their lands. As the church sought to supplant folk magic with church magic, the princes sought to supplant customary laws with Roman law. Here the stage was set for a one-sided conflict. Witch trials became one of the ways church and state realized their overlapping goals. To identify, try, and execute witches was a demonstration of absolute spiritual and political authority over a village or a town.

WHO WERE THE WITCHES?

Roughly eighty percent of the victims of witch-hunts were women, most single and aged over forty. This has suggested to some that misogyny fueled the witch-hunts. Inspired by male hatred and sexual fear of strong women, and occurring at a time when women were breaking out from under male control, witch-hunts were a conspiracy of males against females.

A perhaps better argument holds that women were targeted in higher numbers for more common-sensical reasons. (See "Why More Women than Men Are Witches," page 476.) Three groups of women appear especially to have drawn the witch-hunter's attention. The first was widows, who, living alone in the world after the deaths of their husbands, were often dependent on help from others, unhappy, and known to strike out. A second group was midwives, whose work made them unpopular when mothers and newborns died during childbirth. (See "Encountering the Past: Midwives," page 477.) Surviving family members remembered those deaths. Finally, there were women healers and herbalists, who were targeted because their work gave them a moral and spiritual authority over people that the church wished to reserve for its priests. These women found themselves on the front lines in disproportionate numbers when the church declared war on those who practiced magic without its special blessing. Social position, vocation, and influence, not gender per se, put old, single women in harm's way. Nowhere do we find women being randomly rounded up for burning. The witch-hunts targeted specific women.

Three witches charged with practicing harmful magic are burned alive in Baden in southwest Germany. On the left, two of them are feasting with demons at a *sabbat*.   Bildarchiv Preussischer Kulturbesitz

END OF THE WITCH-HUNTS

Several factors helped end the witch-hunts. One was the emergence of a more scientific point of view. In the seventeenth century, mind and matter came to be viewed as two independent realities, making it harder to believe that thoughts in the mind or words on the lips could alter physical things. A witch's curse was mere words. With advances in medicine, the rise of insurance companies, and the availability of lawyers, people gained greater physical security against the physical afflictions and natural calamities that drove the witch panics. Finally, the witch-hunts began to get out of hand. Tortured witches, when asked whom they saw at witches' sabbats sometimes alleged having seen leading townspeople there, and even the judges themselves! At this point the trials ceased to serve the interests of those conducting them, becoming dysfunctional and threatening anarchy as well.

BAROQUE ART

Art historians use the term *baroque* to denote the style associated with seventeenth-century painting, sculpture, and architecture. As with other terms used in art history, the word *baroque* covers a variety of related styles that developed during the century and moved in different directions in different countries. Baroque painters depicted their subjects in a thoroughly naturalistic, rather than an idealized, manner. This faithfulness to nature paralleled the interest in natural knowledge associated with the rise of the new science and the deeper understanding of human anatomy that was achieved during this period. These painters, the

Bernini designed the elaborate Baldacchino that stands under the dome of St. Peter's Basilica. It is one of the major examples of baroque interior decoration.
Scala/Art Resource, NY

WHY MORE WOMEN THAN MEN ARE WITCHES

A classic of misogyny, The Hammer of Witches *(1486), written by two Dominican monks, Heinrich Krämer and Jacob Sprenger, was sanctioned by Pope Innocent VIII as an official guide to the church's detection and punishment of witches. Here, Krämer and Sprenger explain why they believe most witches are women rather than men.*

■ *Why would two Dominican monks say such things about women? What are the biblical passages that they believe justify them? Do their descriptions have any basis in the actual behavior of women in that age? What is the rivalry between married and unmarried people that they refer to?*

Why are there more superstitious women than men? The first [reason] is that they are more credulous; and since the chief aim of the devil is to corrupt faith, therefore he rather attacks them. . . . The second reason is that women are naturally more impressionable and ready to receive the influence of a disembodied spirit. . . . The third reason is that they have slippery tongues and are unable to conceal from their fellow-women those things which by evil arts they know; and since they are weak, they find an easy and secret manner of vindicating themselves by witchcraft. . . . [Therefore] since women are feebler both in mind and body, it is not surprising that they should come more under the spell of witchcraft. For as regards intellect, or the understanding of spiritual things, they seem to be of a different nature from men, a fact which is vouched for by the logic of the authorities, backed by various examples from the Scriptures. . . .

But the natural reason [for woman's proclivity to witchcraft] is that she is more carnal than a man, as is clear from her many carnal abominations. And it should be noted that there was a defect in the formation of the first woman, since she was formed from a bent rib, that is, a rib of the breast, which is bent as it were in a contrary direction to a man. And since through this defect she is an imperfect animal, she always deceives. . . .

As to her other mental quality, her natural will, when she hates someone whom she formerly loved, then she seethes with anger and impatience in her whole soul, just as the tides of the sea are always heaving and boiling. . . .

Truly the most powerful cause which contributes to the increase of witches is the woeful rivalry between married folk and unmarried women and men. This [jealousy or rivalry exists] even among holy women, so what must it be among the others . . . ?

Just as through the first defect in their intelligence women are more prone [than men] to abjure the faith, so through their second defect of inordinate affections and passions they search for, brood over, and inflict various vengeances, either by witchcraft or by some other means. Wherefore it is no wonder that so great a number of witches exist in this sex. . . . [Indeed, witchcraft] is better called the heresy of witches than of wizards, since the name is taken from the more powerful party [that is, the greater number, who are women]. Blessed be the Highest who has so far preserved the male sex from so great a crime.

From *Malleus Maleficarum*, trans. by Montague Summers (Bungay, Suffolk, U.K.: John Rodker, 1928), pp. 41–47. Reprinted by permission.

most famous of whom was Michelangelo Caravaggio (1573–1610), also were devoted to picturing sharp contrasts between light and darkness, which created dramatic scenes in their painting. Consequently both baroque painting and sculpture have been seen as theatrical and intending to draw the observer into an emotional involvement with the subject that is being portrayed.

The work of Baroque artists served both religious and secular ends. Baroque painters, especially in Roman Catholic countries, often portrayed scenes from the Bible and from the lives of saints intended to instruct the observer in religious truths. Artists used the same style of painting, however, to present objects and scenes of everyday life in new realistic detail. Such was the case with

MIDWIVES

Although women in early modern Europe generally found themselves excluded from the world of the new science, midwives across Europe oversaw the delivery of children until well into the eighteenth century. Often known as *wise women* because of their knowledge and medical skills, midwives were among the few women who carried out independent economic and public roles.

Midwifery was a trade, often pursued by elderly or widowed women of the lower social classes, for which women apprenticed for several years. In the 1630s, the Hotel Dieu, a public hospital near Paris, set up a basic course for training midwives. Unlike other skilled workers and tradesmen, however, midwives were not allowed to organize guilds or associations to protect their trade, pass on their skills, and stabilize their incomes. Instead, civil or church authorities, who were invariably men, licensed midwives and often appointed upper-class women, known as honorable women, to supervise them.

Personal respectability and respect for the privacy of the women they attended were essential qualities for successful midwives. They were present at some of the most private moments in the lives of women and their families and were expected not to gossip about family secrets. Furthermore, women from all social classes feared that if their attending midwives were not of good character their own babies might be stillborn or imperfectly formed. Careless or incompetent midwives who injured mother or child could lose their license.

Midwives also performed important religious and civic functions at births. In emergencies they could baptize a frail newborn. They also often registered births and were officially required both to discourage abortion and infanticide and to report those activities when they occurred to the authorities. The respectability of midwives also gave them legal standing to testify to a child's legitimacy or illegitimacy.

Midwifery was one of numerous skills and occupations associated with women in early modern Europe that men took over during the eighteenth century. (See Chapter 16.) Male medical practitioners claimed to possess better training, which was available to them in medical schools, and more professional knowledge about delivering children. Over time, civil and medical authorities began to demand that people who delivered children be trained as doctors in medical schools, which women were not allowed to attend until well into the nineteenth century. In particular, the use of forceps by male surgeons to deliver a child involved a level of training unavailable to women. Yet even as medical professionalization became entrenched, midwives continued to provide their services to the poor and rural populations of Europe.

- *What types of women became midwives in early modern Europe? How did the authorities regulate the practice of midwifery? Why did male professionals gradually replace midwives in delivering babies?*

Linda Schiebinger, *The Mind Has No Sex? Women in the Origins of Modern Science* (Cambridge, MA: Harvard University Press, 1989); Hilary Marland, ed., *The Art of Midwifery: Early Modern Midwives in Europe* (London: Routledge, 1993).

Until well into the eighteenth century, midwives oversaw the delivery of most children in Europe. CORBIS

Dutch painters of still lifes who portrayed all manner of elaborate foodstuffs as well as with artists such Louis LeNain (1593–1648) who painted scenes of French peasant life.

Baroque art became associated, rightly or wrongly, with both Roman Catholicism and absolutist politics. Baroque art first emerged in papal Rome. Gian Lorenzo Bernini's work (1598–1680) in St. Peter's Basilica there was the most famous example of baroque decoration. At the direction of Pope Urban VIII (r. 1623–1644), during whose reign Galileo was condemned, Bernini designed and oversaw the construction of the great tabernacle that stands beneath the church's towering dome and directly over the space where St. Peter is said to be buried. Behind the tabernacle, Bernini also designed a monument to papal authority with the chair of St. Peter resting on the shoulders of four of the church fathers. In front of the cathedral, he designed the two vast colonnades that he said symbolized the arms of the church reaching out to the world. In the church of Santa Maria de la Vittoria in Rome, Bernini created the dramatic sculpture of the Spanish mystic St. Teresa of Avila (1515–1582), depicting her in religious ecstasy.

The association of baroque art with Roman Catholicism had its counterpart in the secular world. Charles I (r. 1625–1649) of England during the 1630s when he ruled as an all-but absolute monarch without calling Parliament employed the Roman Catholic Flemish artist Peter Paul Rubens (1577–1640) to decorate the ceiling of the Banqueting Hall at his palace in London with paintings commemorating his father James I (r. 1603–1625). Rubens was the leading religious painter of the Catholic Reformation. Charles's employment of him fed Puritan suspicions that the king harbored Roman Catholic sympathies. Consequently, it was not by coincidence that Charles I was led to his execution in 1649 through the Rubens-decorated Banqueting Hall to his death on the scaffold erected outside.

The most elaborate baroque monument to political absolutism was Louis XIV's palace at Versailles. (See Chapter 13.) The exterior of the palace was classical in its restrained design. Room after room on the interior, however, was decorated with vast, dramatic paintings and murals presenting Louis as the Sun King. The Hall of Mirrors, which runs across the entire rear of the palace, allowed for a glittering and elaborate play of light whose purpose was to reflect the power of the monarch. In the gardens of Versailles fountains depicted mythical gods as if they had come to pay court or to amuse the Sun King. Monarchs across Europe, Protestant as well as Catholic, who hoped to imitate Louis's absolutism in their own domains, erected similar, if smaller, palaces filled with elaborate decoration. Baroque architecture dominated the capitals of the rulers of the smaller German states as well as the imperial court of the Habsburgs in Vienna.

IN PERSPECTIVE

The scientific revolution and the thought of writers whose work was contemporaneous with it mark a major turning point in the history of Western culture and eventually had a worldwide impact. The scientific and political ideas of the late sixteenth and seventeenth centuries gradually overturned many of the most fundamental premises of the medieval worldview. The sun replaced the earth as the center of the solar system. The solar system itself came to be viewed as one of many possible systems in the universe. The new knowledge of the physical universe gave rise to challenges to the authority of the church and Scripture. Mathematics began to replace theology and metaphysics as the tool for understanding nature.

Parallel to these developments and sometimes related to them, political thought became much less concerned with religious issues. Hobbes's theory of political obligation made virtually no reference to God. Locke's theories about politics recognized God, but paid little attention to Scripture. He also championed greater freedom of religious and political expression. Locke's ideas about psychology emphasized the influence of environment on human character and action. All of these new ideas gradually displaced or reshaped theological and religious modes of thought and placed humankind and life on earth at the center of Western thinking. Intellectuals in the West consequently developed greater self-confidence in their own capacity to shape the world and their own lives.

None of this change came easily, however. The new science and enlightenment were accompanied by new anxieties that were reflected in a growing preoccupation with sin, death, and the devil. The worst expression of this preoccupation was a succession of witch-hunts and trials that took the lives of as many as 100,000 people between 1400 and 1700.

REVIEW QUESTIONS

1. What did Copernicus, Brahe, Kepler, Galileo, and Newton each contribute to the scientific revolution? Which do you think made the most important contributions and why? What did Francis Bacon contribute to the foundation of scientific thought?

2. How would you define the term *scientific revolution*? In what ways was it truly revolutionary? Which is more enduring, a political revolution or an intellectual one?

3. What were the differences between the political philosophies of Thomas Hobbes and John Locke? How did each view human nature? Would you rather live under a government designed by Hobbes or by Locke? Why?

4. Why were women unable to participate fully in the new science? How did family relationships help some women become involved in the advance of natural philosophy?

5. Why did the Catholic Church condemn Galileo? How did Pascal seek to reconcile faith and reason? How did English natural theology support economic expansion?

6. How do you explain the phenomena of witchcraft and witch-hunts in an age of scientific enlightenment? Why did the witch panics occur in the late sixteenth and early seventeenth centuries? How might the Reformation have contributed to them?

SUGGESTED READINGS

R. ASHCRAFT, *Revolutionary Politics and Locke's Two Treatises of Government* (1986). A major study emphasizing the radical side of Locke's thought.

J. BARRY, M. HESTER, AND G. ROBERTS (EDS.), *Witchcraft in Early Modern Europe: Studies in Culture and Belief* (1998). A collection of recent essays.

M. BIAGIOLI, *Galileo Courtier: The Practice of Science in the Culture of Absolutism* (1993). A major revisionist work.

P. DEAR, *Revolutionizing the Sciences: European Knowledge and Its Ambitions, 1500–1700* (2001). A broad-ranging study of both the ideas and institutions of the new science.

M. FEINGOLD, *The Newtonian Moment: Isaac Newton and the Making of Modern Culture* (2004) A superb, well-illustrated volume.

S. GAUKROGER, *Francis Bacon and the Transformation of Early-Modern Philosophy* (2001). An excellent, accessible introduction.

J. GLEIK, *Isaac Newton* (2003) Highly accessible to the general reader.

I. HARRIS, *The Mind of John Locke: A Study of Political Theory in Its Intellectual Setting* (1994). The most comprehensive recent treatment.

J. L. HEILBRON, *The Sun in the Church: Cathedrals as Solar Observatories* (2000). Explores uses made of Roman Catholic cathedrals to make astronomical observations.

K. J. HOWELL, *God's Two Books: Copernican Cosmology and Biblical Interpretation in Early Modern Science* (2002) The clearest discussion of this important subject.

L. JARDINE, *Ingenious Pursuits: Building the Scientific Revolution* (1999). A lively exploration of the interface of personalities, new knowledge, and English society.

KORS AND E. PETERS, EDS., *European Witchcraft, 1100–1700* (1972). Classics of witch belief.

T. S. KUHN, *The Copernican Revolution: Planetary Astronomy in the Development of Western Thought* (1957). Remains the classic work.

B. LEVACK, *The Witch Hunt in Early Modern Europe* (1986). Lucid survey.

P. MACHAMER (ED.), *The Cambridge Companion to Galileo* (1998). Essays that aid the understanding of the entire spectrum of the new science.

J. R. MARTIN, *Baroque* (1977) A classic introduction to Baroque art.

M. OSLER, *Rethinking the Scientific Revolution* (2000). A collection of revisionist essays particularly exploring issues of the interrelationship of the new science and religion.

R. POPKIN, *The History of Scepticism: From Savonarola to Bayle* (2003). A classic study of the fear of loss of intellectual certainty.

L. PYENSON AND S. SHEETS-PYENSON, *Servants of Nature: A History of Scientific Institutions, Enterprises, and Sensibilities* (1999). A history of the settings in which the creation and diffusion of scientific knowledge have occurred.

L. SCHIEBINGER, *The Mind Has No Sex? Women in the Origins of Modern Science* (1989). A major study of the subject.

S. SHAPIN, *The Scientific Revolution* (1996). A readable brief introduction.

T. SORELL, *The Cambridge Companion to Hobbes* (1994). Excellent essays on the major themes of Hobbes's thought.

R. TUCK, *Philosophy and Government 1572–1651* (1993). A continent-wide survey.

R. S. WESTFALL, *The Construction of Modern Science: Mechanisms and Mechanics* (1971). A classic work.

DOCUMENTS CD-ROM

Thought and Culture in Early Modern Europe

13.1 Francis Bacon: from *First Book of Aphorisms*
13.4 Thomas Hobbes: Chapter XIII from *Leviathan*
13.5 Rejecting Aristotle: Galileo Defends the Heliocentric View
13.6 Rethinking the Bible: Galileo Confronts his Critics

CHAPTER 15

SOCIETY AND ECONOMY UNDER THE OLD REGIME IN THE EIGHTEENTH CENTURY

- **MAJOR FEATURES OF LIFE IN THE OLD REGIME**
  Maintenance of Tradition • Hierarchy and Privilege

- **THE ARISTOCRACY**
  Varieties of Aristocratic Privilege • Aristocratic Resurgence

- **THE LAND AND ITS TILLERS**
  Peasants and Serfs • Aristocratic Domination of the Countryside: The English Game Laws

- **FAMILY STRUCTURES AND THE FAMILY ECONOMY**
  Households • The Family Economy • Women and the Family Economy • Children and the World of the Family Economy

- **THE REVOLUTION IN AGRICULTURE**
  New Crops and New Methods • Expansion of the Population

- **THE INDUSTRIAL REVOLUTION OF THE EIGHTEENTH CENTURY**

A Revolution in Consumption • Industrial Leadership of Great Britain • New Methods of Textile Production • The Steam Engine • Iron Production • The Impact of the Agricultural and Industrial Revolutions on Working Women

- **THE GROWTH OF CITIES**
  Patterns of Preindustrial Urbanization • Urban Classes • The Urban Riot

- **THE JEWISH POPULATION: THE AGE OF THE GHETTO**

- **IN PERSPECTIVE**

KEY TOPICS

- The varied privileges and powers of Europe's aristocracies in the Old Regime and their efforts to increase their wealth
- The plight of rural peasants
- Family structure and family economy
- The transformation of Europe's economy by the Agricultural and Industrial Revolutions
- Urban growth and the social tensions that accompanied it
- The strains on the institutions of the Old Regime brought about by social change

During the French Revolution and the turmoil that upheaval spawned, it became customary to refer to the patterns of social, political, and economic relationships that had existed in France before 1789 as the *ancien régime*, or the **Old Regime**. The term has come to be applied generally to the life and institutions of pre-revolutionary Europe. Politically, on the continent, though not in Great Britain, it meant the

During the eighteenth century, most goods were produced in small workshops, such as this iron forge painted by Joseph Wright of Derby (1734–1797), or in the homes of artisans. Not until very late in the century, with the early stages of industrialization, did a few factories appear. In the small early workshops, it would not have been uncommon for the family of the owner to visit, as portrayed in this painting.   "The Iron Forge," 1772 (oil on canvas) by Joseph Wright of Derby (1734–1797). Broadlands Trust, Hampshire, UK/Bridgeman Art Library, London

rule of theoretically absolute monarchies with growing bureaucracies and aristocratically led armies. Economically, a scarcity of food, the predominance of agriculture, slow transport, a low level of iron production, comparatively unsophisticated financial institutions, and, in some cases, competitive commercial overseas empires characterized the Old Regime. Socially, men and women living during the period saw themselves less as individuals than as members of distinct corporate bodies that possessed certain privileges or rights as a group.

Tradition, hierarchy, a corporate feeling, and privilege were the chief social characteristics of the Old Regime. Yet it was by no means a static society. Change and innovation were fermenting in its midst. Farming became more commercialized, and both food production and the size of the population increased. The early stages of the Industrial

Revolution made more consumer goods available, and domestic consumption expanded throughout the century. The colonies in the Americas provided strong demand for European goods and manufactures. Merchants in seaports and other cities were expanding their businesses. By preparing their states for war, European governments put new demands on the resources and the economic organizations of their nations. The spirit of rationality that had been so important to the scientific revolution of the seventeenth century continued to manifest itself in the economic life of the eighteenth century. The Old Regime itself fostered the changes that eventually transformed it into a different kind of society. ■

MAJOR FEATURES OF LIFE IN THE OLD REGIME

Socially, pre-revolutionary Europe was based on (1) aristocratic elites possessing a wide variety of inherited legal privileges; (2) established churches intimately related to the state and the aristocracy; (3) an urban labor force usually organized into guilds; and (4) a rural peasantry subject to high taxes and feudal dues. Of course, the men and women living during this period did not know it was the Old Regime. Most of them earned their livelihoods and passed their lives as their forebearers had done for generations before them and as they expected their children to do after them.

MAINTENANCE OF TRADITION

During the eighteenth century, the past weighed more heavily on people's minds than did the future. Few persons outside the government bureaucracies, the expanding merchant groups, and the movement for reform called the Enlightenment (see Chapter 17) considered change or innovation desirable. This was especially true of social relationships. Both nobles and peasants, for different reasons, repeatedly called for the restoration of traditional, or customary, rights. The nobles asserted what they considered their ancient rights against the intrusion of the expanding monarchical bureaucracies. The peasants, through petitions and revolts, called for the revival or the maintenance of the customary manorial rights that allowed them access to particular lands, courts, or grievance procedures.

Except for the early industrial development in Britain and the accompanying expansion of personal consumption, the eighteenth-century economy was also predominantly traditional. The quality and quantity of the grain harvest remained the most important fact of life for most of the population and the gravest concern for governments.

HIERARCHY AND PRIVILEGE

Closely related to this traditional social and economic outlook was the hierarchical structure of the society. The medieval sense of rank and degree not only persisted, but became more rigid during the century. In several continental cities, sumptuary laws regulating the dress of the different classes remained on the books. These laws forbade persons in one class or occupation from wearing clothes like those worn by their social superiors. The laws, which sought to make the social hierarchy easily visible, were largely ineffective by this time. What really enforced the hierarchy was the corporate nature of social relationships.

Each state or society was considered a community composed of numerous smaller communities. Eighteenth-century Europeans did not enjoy what Americans regard as "individual rights." Instead, a person enjoyed such rights and privileges as were guaranteed to the particular communities or groups of which she or he was a part. The "community" might include the village, the municipality, the nobility, the church, the guild, a university, or the parish. In turn, each of these bodies enjoyed certain privileges, some great and some small. The privileges might involve exemption from taxation or from some especially humiliating punishment, the right to practice a trade or craft, the right of one's children to pursue a particular occupation, or, for the church, the right to collect the tithe.

THE ARISTOCRACY

The eighteenth century was the great age of the aristocracy. The nobility constituted approximately one to five percent of the population of any given country. Yet in every country, it was the single wealthiest sector of the population, had the widest degree of social, political, and economic power, and set the tone of polite society. In most countries, the nobility had their own separate house in the parliament, estates, or diet. Only nobles

A CLOSER LOOK

An Aristocratic Couple

Portraits, such as this one of the English landowner, *Robert Andrews and His Wife*, by Thomas Gainsborough (1728–1788), contain many clues to the aristocratic dominance of landed society.

Andrews's gun and dog indicate his exclusive right to hunt game on his land.

His wife's sitting against the expanse of his landed estate suggests the character of their legal relationship, whereby he could have controlled her property, which would have thus become an extension of his.

© National Gallery, London

The market price of the wheat raised on his estate (known in England as corn) would have been protected by various import laws enacted by the English Parliament whose membership was dominated by landowners such as Andrews himself.

had any kind of representation in Hungary and Poland. Land continued to provide the aristocracy with its largest source of income, but aristocrats did not merely own estates: Their influence was felt throughout social and economic life. In much of Europe, however, manual labor was regarded as beneath a noble. In Spain, it was assumed that even the poorer nobles would lead lives of idleness.

In other nations, however, the nobility often fostered economic innovation and embraced the commercial spirit. Such willingness to change helped protect the nobility's wealth and, in both Great Britain and France, gave them common interest with the commercial classes who were also eager to see the economy grow and protect their property.

VARIETIES OF ARISTOCRATIC PRIVILEGE

To be an aristocrat was a matter of birth and legal privilege. This much the aristocracy had in common across the Continent. In almost every other respect, they differed markedly from country to country.

British Nobility   The smallest, wealthiest, best defined, and most socially responsible aristocracy resided in Great Britain. It consisted of about four hundred families, and the eldest male members of each family sat in the House of Lords. Through the corruptions of the electoral system, these families also controlled many seats in the House of Commons. The estates of the British nobility ranged from a few thousand to fifty thousand acres, from which they received rents. The nobles owned about one-fourth of all the arable land in the country. Increasingly, the British aristocracy invested its wealth in commerce, canals, urban real estate, mines, and even industrial ventures. Because only the eldest son inherited the title (called a "peerage"), the right to sit in the House of Lords, and the land, younger sons moved into commerce, the army, the professions, and the church. British landowners in both houses of Parliament levied taxes and also paid them. They had few significant legal privileges, but their direct or indirect control of local government gave them immense political power and social influence. The aristocracy dominated the society and politics of the English counties. Their country houses, many of which were built in the eighteenth century, were the centers of local society.

French Nobility   The situation of the continental nobilities was less clear cut. In France, the approximately 400,000 nobles were divided between nobles "of the sword," or those whose nobility was derived from military service, and those "of the robe," who had acquired their titles either by serving in the bureaucracy or by having purchased them. The two groups had quarreled in the past, but often cooperated during the eighteenth century to defend their common privileges.

The French nobles were also divided between those who held office or favor with the royal court at Versailles and those who did not. The court nobility reaped the immense wealth that could be gained from holding high office. The nobles' hold on such offices intensified during the century. By the late 1780s, appointments to the church, the army, and the bureaucracy, as well as other profitable positions, tended to go to the nobles already established in court circles. Whereas these well-connected aristocrats were rich, the provincial nobility, called *hobereaux*, were often little better off than wealthy peasants.

Despite differences in rank, origin, and wealth, certain hereditary privileges set all French aristocrats apart from the rest of society. They were exempt from many taxes. For example, most French nobles did not pay the *taille*, or land tax, the basic tax of the Old Regime. The nobles were technically liable for payment of the **vingtième**, or the "twentieth," which resembled an income tax, but they rarely had to pay it in full. The nobles were not liable for the royal *corvées*, or forced labor on public works, which fell on the peasants. In addition to these exemptions, French nobles could collect feudal dues from their tenants and enjoyed exclusive hunting and fishing privileges.

Eastern European Nobilities   East of the Elbe River, the character of the nobility became even more complicated and repressive. Throughout the area, the military traditions of the aristocracy remained important. In Poland, there were thousands of nobles, or *szlachta*, who were entirely exempt from taxes after 1741. Until 1768, these Polish aristocrats possessed the right of life and death over their serfs. Most of the Polish nobility were relatively poor. A few rich nobles who had immense estates exercised political power in the fragile Polish state.

In Austria and Hungary, the nobility continued to possess broad judicial powers over the peasantry through their manorial courts. They also enjoyed various degrees of exemption from taxation. The wealthiest of them, Prince Esterhazy of Hungary, owned ten million acres of land.

In Prussia, after the accession of Frederick the Great in 1740, the position of the Junker nobles became much stronger. Frederick's various wars required their full support. He drew his officers almost wholly from the Junker class. Nobles also increasingly made up the bureaucracy. As in other parts of eastern Europe, the Prussian nobles had extensive judicial authority over the serfs.

In Russia, the eighteenth century saw what amounted to the creation of the nobility. Peter the Great's (r. 1682–1725) linking of state service and noble social status through the Table of Ranks (1722) established among Russian nobles a self-conscious class identity that had not previously existed. Thereafter, they were determined to resist compulsory state service. In 1736, Empress Anna (r. 1730–1740) reduced such service to twenty-five years. In 1762, Peter III (r. 1762) exempted the greatest nobles entirely from compulsory service. In 1785, in the Charter of the Nobility, Catherine the Great (r. 1762–1796) legally defined the rights and privileges of noble men and women in exchange for the assurance that the nobility would serve the state voluntarily. Noble privileges included the right of transmitting noble status to a nobleman's wife and children, the judicial protection of noble rights and property, considerable power over the serfs, and exemption from personal taxes.

ARISTOCRATIC RESURGENCE

The Russian Charter of the Nobility constituted one aspect of the broader European-wide development termed the **aristocratic resurgence**. This was the nobility's reaction to the threat to their social position and privileges that they felt from the expanding power of the monarchies. This resurgence took several forms in the eighteenth century.

First, all nobilities tried to preserve their exclusiveness by making it more difficult to become a noble. Second, they pushed to reserve appointments to the officer corps of the armies, the senior posts in the bureaucracies and government ministries, and the upper ranks of the church exclusively for nobles. By doing this, they hoped to resist the encroaching power of the monarchies.

Third, the nobles attempted to use the authority of existing aristocratically controlled institutions against the power of the monarchies. These institutions included the British Parliament, the French courts, or *parlements*, and the local aristocratic estates and provincial diets in Germany and the Habsburg Empire.

Fourth, the nobility sought to improve its financial position by gaining further exemptions from taxation or by collecting higher rents or long-forgotten feudal dues from the peasantry. The nobility tried to shore up its position by various appeals to traditional and often ancient privileges that had lapsed over time. This aristocratic challenge to the monarchies was a fundamental political fact of the day and a potentially disruptive one.

THE LAND AND ITS TILLERS

Land was the economic basis of eighteenth-century life and the foundation of the status and power of the nobility. Well over three-fourths of all Europeans lived in the country, and few of them ever traveled more than a few miles from their birthplace. Except for the nobility and the wealthier nonaristocratic landowners, most people who dwelled on the land were poor, and in many regions, desperately poor. They lived in various states of economic and social dependency, exploitation, and vulnerability.

PEASANTS AND SERFS

Rural social dependency related directly to the land. The nature of the dependency differed sharply for free peasants, such as English tenants and most French cultivators, and for the serfs of Germany, Austria, and Russia, who were legally bound to a particular plot of land and a particular lord. Yet everywhere, the class that owned most of the land also controlled the local government and the courts. For example, in Great Britain, all farmers and smaller tenants had the legal rights of English citizens. The justices of the peace, however, who presided over the county courts and who could call out the local militia, were always substantial landowners, as were the members of Parliament, who made the laws. In eastern Europe, the landowners presided over the manorial courts. On the Continent, the burden of taxation fell on the tillers of the soil.

Obligations of Peasants The power of the landlord increased as one moved across Europe from west to east. Most French peasants owned some land, but there were a few serfs in eastern France. Nearly all French peasants were subject to certain feudal dues, called *banalités*. These included the required use-for-payment of the lord's, or **seigneur's**, mill to grind grain and his oven to bake bread. The seigneur could also require a certain number of days each year of the peasant's labor. This practice of forced labor was termed the *corvée*. Because French peasants rarely possessed enough land to support their families, they had to rent more land from the seigneur and were also subject to feudal dues attached to those plots. In Prussia and Austria, despite attempts by the monarchies late in the century to improve the lot of the serfs, the landlords continued to exercise almost complete control over them. In many of the Habsburg lands, law and custom required the serfs to provide service, or **robot**, to the lords.

Serfs were worst off in Russia. There, nobles reckoned their wealth by the number of "souls," or male serfs, they owned rather than the size of their acreage. Russian landlords, in effect, regarded serfs merely as economic commodities. They could demand as many as six days a week of labor, known as *barshchina*, from the serfs. Like Prussian and Austrian landlords, they enjoyed the right to punish their serfs. On their own authority, Russian landlords could even exile a serf to Siberia. Serfs had no legal recourse against the orders and whims of their lords. There was little difference between Russian serfdom and slavery.

In southeastern Europe, where the Ottoman Empire held sway, peasants were free, though landlords tried to exert authority in every way. The domain of the landlords was termed a *çift*. The landlord was often an absentee who managed the estate through an overseer. During the seventeenth and eighteenth centuries, these landlords, like those elsewhere in Europe, often became more commercially oriented and turned to the production of crops, such as cotton, vegetables, potatoes, and maize, that they could sell in the market.

A scarcity of labor rather than the recognition of their legal rights supported the independence of the southeastern European peasants. A peasant might migrate from one landlord to another. Because the second landlord needed the peasant's labor, he had no reason to return him to the original landlord. During the seventeenth and eighteenth centuries, however, disorder originating in Constantinople (now Istanbul), the capital, spilled over into the Balkan Peninsula. In this climate, landlords increased their authority by offering their peasants protection from bandits or rebels who might destroy peasant villages. As in medieval times, the manor house or armed enclosure of a local landlord became the peasants' refuge. These landlords also owned all the housing and tools the peasants needed to work the land and also furnished their seed grain. Consequently, despite legal independence, Balkan peasants under

the Ottoman Empire became largely dependent on the landlords, though never to the extent of serfs in eastern Europe or Russia.

Peasant Rebellions   The Russian monarchy itself contributed to the further degradation of the serfs. Peter the Great gave whole villages to favored nobles. Later in the century, Catherine the Great confirmed the authority of the nobles over their serfs in exchange for the landowners' political cooperation. Russia experienced vast peasant unrest, with well over fifty peasant revolts between 1762 and 1769. These culminated in Pugachev's Rebellion between 1773 and 1775, when Emelyan Pugachev (1726–1775) promised the serfs land of their own and freedom from their lords. All of southern Russia was in turmoil until the government brutally suppressed the rebellion. Thereafter, any thought of improving the condition of the serfs was set aside for a generation.

Pugachev's was the largest peasant uprising of the eighteenth century, but smaller peasant revolts or disturbances took place in Bohemia in 1775, in Transylvania in 1784, in Moravia in 1786, and in Austria in 1789. There were almost no revolts in Western Europe, but England experienced many rural riots. Rural rebellions were violent, but the peasants and serfs normally directed their wrath

Eighteenth-century France had some of the best roads in the world, but they were often built with forced labor. French peasants were required to work part of each year on such projects. This system, called the *corvée*, was not abolished until the French Revolution in 1789.   Joseph Vernet, "Construction of a Road." Louvre, Paris, France. Bridgeman-Giraudon/Art Resource, NY

Emelyan Pugachev (1726–1775) led the largest peasant revolt in Russian history. In this contemporary propaganda picture he is shown in chains. An inscription in Russian and German was printed below the picture decrying the evils of revolution and insurrection.
Bildarchiv Preussischer Kulturbesitz

against property rather than persons. The rebels usually sought to reassert traditional or customary rights against practices that they perceived as innovations. Their targets were carefully chosen and included unfair pricing, onerous new or increased feudal dues, changes in methods of payment or land use, unjust officials, or extraordinarily brutal overseers and landlords. Peasant revolts were thus conservative in nature.

ARISTOCRATIC DOMINATION OF THE COUNTRYSIDE: THE ENGLISH GAME LAWS

One of the clearest examples of aristocratic domination of the countryside and of aristocratic manipulation of the law to its own advantage was the English legislation on hunting.

Between 1671 and 1831, English landowners had the exclusive legal right to hunt game animals, including, in particular, hares, partridges, pheasants, and moor fowl. Similar legislation covered other animals such as deer, the killing of which by an unauthorized person became a capital offense in the eighteenth century. By law,

only persons owning a particular amount of landed property could hunt these animals. Excluded from the right to hunt were all persons renting land, wealthy city merchants who did not own land, and poor people in cities, villages, and the countryside. The poor were excluded because the elite believed that allowing them to enjoy the sport of hunting would undermine their work habits. The city merchants were excluded because the landed gentry in Parliament wanted to demonstrate visibly and legally the superiority of landed wealth over commercial wealth. Thus, the various game laws upheld the superior status of the aristocracy and the landed gentry.

The game laws were a prime example of legislation related directly to economic and social status. The gentry who benefited from the laws and whose parliamentary representatives had passed them also served as the local justices of the peace who enforced the laws and punished their violation. The justices of the peace could levy fines and even have poachers impressed into the army. Gentry could also take civil legal action against wealthier poachers, such as rich farmers who rented land, and thus saddle them with immense legal fees. The gentry also employed gamekeepers to protect game from poachers. The gamekeepers were known to kill the dogs belonging to people suspected of poaching. By the middle of the century, gamekeepers had devised guns to shoot poachers who tripped their hidden levers.

A small industry arose to circumvent the game laws, however. Many poor people living either on an estate or in a nearby village would kill game for food. They believed the game actually belonged to the community, and this poaching increased during hard times. Poaching was thus one way for the poor to find food.

Even more important was the black market in game animals that the demand in the cities for this kind of luxury meat sustained. This created the possibility of poaching for profit, and indeed, poaching technically meant stealing or killing game for sale. Local people from both the countryside and the villages would steal the game and then sell it to intermediaries called *higglers*. Later, coachmen took over this function. The higglers and the coachmen would smuggle the game into the cities, where poulterers would sell it at a premium price. Everyone involved made a bit of money along the way. During the second half of the century, English aristocrats began to construct large game preserves. The rural poor, who had lost their rights to communal land as a result of its enclosure by the large landowners, resented these preserves, which soon became hunting grounds to organized gangs of poachers.

Penalties against poaching increased in the 1790s after the outbreak of the French Revolution, but so did the amount of poaching as the economic hardships increased. Britain's participation in the wars of the era put a greater burden on poor people as the demand for food in English cities grew along with their population. By the 1820s, both landowners and reformers called for a change in the law. In 1831, Parliament rewrote the game laws, retaining the landowners' possession of the game, but permitting them to allow other people to hunt it. Poaching continued, but the exclusive right of the landed classes to hunt game had ended.

FAMILY STRUCTURES AND THE FAMILY ECONOMY

In preindustrial Europe, the household was the basic unit of production and consumption. Few productive establishments employed more than a handful of people not belonging to the family of the owner, and those rare exceptions were in cities. Most Europeans, however, lived in rural areas. There, as well as in small towns and cities, the household mode of organization predominated on farms, in artisans' workshops, and in

During the seventeenth century the French Le Nain brothers painted scenes of French peasant life. Although the images softened many of the harsh realities of peasant existence, the clothing and the interiors were based on actual models and convey the character of the life of better off French peasants whose lives would have continued very much the same into the eighteenth century. Erich Lessing/Art Resource, NY

small merchants' shops. With that mode of economic organization, there developed what is known as the **family economy**. Its structure, as described here, had prevailed over most of Europe for centuries.

HOUSEHOLDS

What was a household in the preindustrial Europe of the Old Regime? There were two basic models, one characterizing northwestern Europe and the other eastern Europe.

Northwestern Europe   In northwestern Europe, the household almost invariably consisted of a married couple, their children through their early teenage years, and their servants. Except for the few wealthy people, households usually consisted of not more than five or six members. Furthermore, in these households, more than two generations of a family rarely lived under the same roof. High mortality and late marriage prevented a formation of families of three generations or more. In other words, grandparents rarely lived in the same household as their grandchildren, and families consisted of parents and children. The family structure of northwestern Europe was thus nuclear rather than extended.

Historians used to assume that before industrialization Europeans lived in extended familial settings, with several generations living together in a household. Demographic investigation has now sharply reversed this picture. Children lived with their parents only until their early teens. Then they normally left home, usually to enter the work force of young servants who lived and worked in another household. A child of a skilled artisan might remain with his or her parents to learn a valuable skill; but only rarely would more than one child do so, because children earned more working outside the home.

Those young men and women who had left home would eventually marry and form their own independent households. This practice of moving away from home is known as *neolocalism*. These young people married relatively late. Men were usually over twenty-six, and women over twenty-three. The new couple usually had children as soon after marriage as possible. Frequently, the woman was already pregnant at marriage. Family and community pressure often compelled the man to marry her. In any case, premarital sexual relations were common. The new couple would soon employ a servant, who, together with their growing children, would undertake whatever form of livelihood the household used to support itself.

The word *servant* in this context does not refer to someone looking after the needs of wealthy people. Rather, in preindustrial Europe, a servant was a person—either male or female—who was hired, often under a clear contract, to work for the head of the household in exchange for room, board, and wages. The servant was usually young and by no means always socially inferior to his or her employer. Normally, the servant was an integral part of the household and ate with the family.

Young men and women became servants when their labor was no longer needed in their parents' household or when they could earn more money for their family outside the parental household. Being a servant for several years—often as many as eight or ten years—allowed young people to acquire the productive skills and the monetary savings necessary to begin their own household. These years spent as servants largely account for the late age of marriage in northwestern Europe.

Eastern Europe   As one moved eastward across the Continent, the structure of the household and the pattern of marriage changed. In eastern Europe, both men and women usually married before the age of twenty. Consequently, children were born to much younger parents. Often—especially among Russian serfs—wives were older than their husbands. Eastern European households were generally larger than those in the West. Frequently a rural Russian household consisted of more than nine, and possibly more than twenty, members, with three or perhaps even four generations of the same family living together. Early marriage made this situation more likely. In Russia, marrying involved not starting a new household, but remaining in and expanding one already established.

The landholding structure in eastern Europe accounts, at least in part, for these patterns of marriage and the family. The lords of the manor who owned land wanted to ensure that it would be cultivated, so they could receive their rents. Thus, in Poland, for example, landlords might forbid marriage between their own serfs and those from another estate. They might also require widows and widowers to remarry to assure adequate labor for a particular plot of land. Polish landlords also frowned on the hiring of free laborers—the equivalent of servants in the West—to help cultivate land. The landlords preferred to use other serfs. This practice inhibited the formation of independent households. In Russia, landlords ordered the families of young people in their villages to arrange marriages within a short set time. These lords discouraged single-generation family households because the death or serious illness of one person in such a household might mean the land assigned to it would go out of cultivation.

THE FAMILY ECONOMY

Throughout Europe, most people worked within the family economy. That is to say, the household was the basic unit of production and consumption. Almost everyone lived within a household of some kind because it was virtually impossible for ordinary people to support themselves independently. Indeed, except for members of religious orders, people living outside a household were viewed with great suspicion. They were considered potentially criminal, disruptive, or at least dependent on the charity of others. Everywhere beggars met deep hostility. (See "Rules Are Established for the Berlin Poor House," page 491.)

Depending on their ages and skills, everyone in the household worked. The need to survive poor harvests or economic slumps meant that no one could be idle. Within this family economy, all goods and income produced went to the benefit of the household rather than to the individual family member. On a farm, much of the effort went directly into raising food or producing other agricultural goods that could be exchanged for food. Few Western Europeans, however, had enough land to support their household from farming alone. Thus, one or more family members might work elsewhere and send wages home; for example, the father and older children might work as harvesters, fishermen, or engage in other labor either in the neighborhood or farther from home. If the father was such a migrant worker, his wife and their younger children would have to work the family farm. This was not an uncommon pattern.

The family economy also dominated the life of skilled urban artisans. The father was usually the chief artisan. He normally employed one or more servants, but would expect his children to work in the enterprise also. He usually trained his eldest child in the trade. His wife often sold his wares or opened a small shop of her own. Wives of merchants also frequently ran their husbands' businesses, especially when the husband traveled to purchase new goods. In any case, everyone in the family was involved. If business was poor, family members would look for employment elsewhere—not to support themselves as individuals, but to ensure the survival of the family unit.

In Western Europe, the death of a father often brought disaster to the household. The continuing economic life of the family usually depended on his land or skills. The widow might take on the farm or the business, or his children might do so. The widow usually sought to remarry quickly to restore the labor and skills of a male to the household and to prevent herself from becoming dependent on relatives or charity.

The high mortality rate of the time meant that many households were reconstituted second-family groups that included stepchildren. Because of the advanced age of the widow or economic hard times, however, some households might simply dissolve. The widow became dependent on charity or relatives. The children became similarly dependent or entered the work force as servants earlier than they would have otherwise. In other cases, the situation could be so desperate that they would resort to crime or to begging. The personal, emotional, and economic vulnerability of the family cannot be overemphasized.

In Eastern Europe, the family economy functioned in the context of serfdom and landlord domination. Peasants clearly thought in terms of their families and expanding the land available for cultivation. The village structure may have mitigated the pressures of the family economy, as did the multigenerational family. Dependence on the available land was the chief fact of life. There were many fewer artisan and merchant households, and there was far less geographical mobility than in Western Europe.

WOMEN AND THE FAMILY ECONOMY

The family economy established many of the chief constraints on the lives and personal experiences of women in preindustrial society. Most of the historical research that has been undertaken on this subject relates to Western Europe. There, a woman's life experience was largely the function of her capacity to establish and maintain a household. For women, marriage was an economic necessity, as well as an institution that fulfilled sexual and psychological needs. Outside a household, a woman's life was vulnerable and precarious. Some women became economically independent, but they were the exception. Normally, unless she were an aristocrat or a member of a religious order, a woman probably could not support herself solely by her own efforts. Consequently, a woman devoted much of her life first to maintaining her parents' household and then to devising some means of getting her own household to live in as an adult. Bearing and rearing children were usually subordinate to these goals.

By the age of seven, a girl would have begun to help with the household work. On a farm, this might mean looking after chickens, watering the animals, or carrying food to the adults working the land. In an urban artisan's household, she would do light work, perhaps cleaning or carrying, and later sewing or weaving. The girl would remain in her parents' home as long as she made a

RULES ARE ESTABLISHED
FOR THE BERLIN POOR HOUSE

Poverty was an enormous problem in eighteenth-century Europe, often forcing family members to work away from home and creating thousands of migrant workers and beggars. Governments were hostile to beggars and sometimes to migrant workers, whom they regarded as potential sources of crime and disorder. The regulations for the Berlin Poor House reveal these concerns.

■ *What distinguishes the poor who deserved sympathy from those who did not? How would such a distinction affect social policy? Why might beggars have been regarded as dangers to public order? What attitudes toward work do these regulations display?*

Whereas His Majesty . . . has renewed the prohibition of begging in the streets and in houses and has made all giving of alms punishable; it is decided to inform the public of the present measures for the relief of the poor, and to acquaint it with the main outlines of the above order:

1. In the new workhouse, . . . the genuinely needy and the poor deserving sympathy shall be cared for better than hitherto, but the deliberate beggars shall more resolutely be made to work.

2. The past organization of this house has therefore been totally altered, so that all persons to be received in it shall be divided into two entirely separate main classes, differentiated both in the status of their work and its location, in their dormitory and in their board.

3. The first class is meant for the old and for other persons deserving help and sympathy, who cannot entirely live by their work and do not wish to beg. Those report to the Poor's Chest in the Town Hall of Berlin, with a certificate from the Minister of their Church, showing their hitherto unblemished character, and after their references have been checked, they shall be accepted. They spin in the house as much wool as their age and health permits, and if they spin more than the cost of their keep, the surplus shall be paid out to them. . . .

* * *

5. The second main class is destined for those who do not wish to make use of this benefaction, but would rather live by begging. These deliberate beggars will be arrested by the Poor Law Constables, if necessary with the assistance of the Police, irrespective of age or status, whether they be vagabonds, journeymen, citizens, discharged soldiers, and their wives or children will be sent to the workhouse.

6. Those who are caught begging for the first time shall be put into this class for three months at least, for the second time, for a year, and for the third and later times for several years, according to circumstances, for life.

7. Similarly, this class is destined for those who after due process of law have been sent for punishment as runaway servants and apprentices, for a period of time determined by the Court.

8. All the persons under numbers 5, 6, and 7 shall be forced to spin and prepare wool, and shall be kept on a minimum standard, clearly differentiated from the first class, both in the status and quantity of their work in their board and their lodging.

9. The children shall be cared for separately, . . . and shall receive education for several hours a day. . . .

10. Before a beggar is discharged, he must, in order that he shall not again become a public nuisance, prove an occupation in prospect or the existence of relations or of other persons, who will look after him and will put him up at once. . . .

From *Geschichte der Manufacturen...*, by Kruegeger, as quoted and translated in *Documents of European Economic History*, vol. 1, S. Pollard and C. Holmes, eds., 1968, pp. 166–167, (Edward Arnold).

real contribution to the family enterprise or as long as her labor elsewhere was not more remunerative to the family.

An artisan's daughter might not leave home until marriage, because at home she could learn increasingly valuable skills associated with the trade. The situation was different for the much larger number of girls growing up on farms. Their parents and brothers could often do all the necessary farm work, and a girl's labor at home quickly became of little value to her family. She would then leave home, usually between the age of twelve and fourteen years. She might take up residence on another farm, but more likely she would migrate to a nearby town or city. She would rarely travel more than thirty miles from her parents' household. She would then normally become a servant, once again living in a household, but this time in the household of an employer. Having left home, the young woman's chief goal was to accumulate enough capital for a dowry. Her savings would make her eligible for marriage, because they would allow her to make the necessary contribution to form a household with her husband. Marriage within the family economy was a joint economic undertaking, and the wife was expected to make an immediate contribution of capital to establish the household. A young woman might well work for ten years or more to accumulate a dowry. This practice meant that marriage was usually postponed until her mid- to late twenties.

Within marriage, earning enough money or producing enough farm goods to ensure an adequate food supply dominated women's concerns. Domestic duties, childbearing, and child rearing were subordinate to economic pressures. Consequently, couples tried to limit the number of children they had, usually through the practice of *coitus interruptus*, the withdrawal of the male before ejaculation.

The work of married women differed markedly between city and country and was in many ways a function of their husbands' occupations. If the peasant household had enough land to support itself, the wife spent much of her time literally carrying things for her husband—water, food, seed, harvested grain, and the like. Such landholdings, however, were few. If the husband had to do work besides farming, such as fishing or migrant labor, the wife might actually be in charge of the farm and do the plowing, planting, and harvesting. In the city, the wife of an artisan or a merchant might be in charge of the household finances and help manage the business. When her husband died, she might take over the business and perhaps hire an artisan. Finally, if economic disaster struck the family, it was usually the wife who organized what Olwen Hufton has called the "economy of expedients,"[1] within which family members might be sent off to find work elsewhere or even to beg in the streets.

Despite all this economic activity, women found many occupations and professions closed to them because they were female. They labored with less education than men, because in such a society women at all levels of life consistently found fewer opportunities for education than did men. They often received lower wages than men for the same work. The mechanization of agriculture and the textile industries, which will be discussed later in this chapter, made these disabilities worse.

CHILDREN AND THE WORLD OF THE FAMILY ECONOMY

For women of all social ranks, childbirth meant fear and vulnerability. Contagious diseases endangered both mother and child. Puerperal fever was frequent, as were other infections from unsterilized medical instruments. Not all midwives were skillful practitioners. Furthermore, most mothers gave birth in conditions of immense poverty and wretched housing. Assuming both mother and child survived, the mother might nurse the infant, but often the child would be sent to a wet nurse. The wealthy may have done this for convenience, but economic necessity dictated it for the poor. The structures and customs of the family economy did not permit a woman to devote herself entirely to rearing a child. The wet-nursing industry was well organized, with urban children being frequently transported to wet nurses in the country, where they would remain for months or even years.

The birth of a child was not always welcome. The child might represent another economic burden on an already hard-pressed household, or it might be illegitimate. The number of illegitimate births seems to have increased during the eighteenth century, possibly because increased migration of the population led to fleeting romances.

Through at least the end of the seventeenth century, unwanted or illegitimate births could lead to infanticide, especially among the poor. The parents might smother the infant or expose it to the elements. These practices were one result of both the ignorance and the prejudice surrounding contraception.

---

[1] Olwen Hufton, "Women and the Family Economy in Eighteenth-Century France," *French Historical Studies* 9 (1976): 19.

The late seventeenth and the early eighteenth centuries saw a new interest in preserving the lives of abandoned children. Although foundling hospitals established to care for abandoned children had existed before, their size and number expanded during these years. Two of the most famous were the Paris Foundling Hospital (1670) and the London Foundling Hospital (1739). Such hospitals cared for thousands of children, and the demand for their services increased during the eighteenth century. For example, early in the century, an average of 1,700 children a year were admitted to the Paris Foundling Hospital. In the peak year of 1772, however, that number rose to 7,676 children. Not all of those children came from Paris. Many had been brought to the city from the provinces, where local foundling homes and hospitals were overburdened. The London Foundling Hospital lacked the income to deal with all the children brought to it. In the middle of the eighteenth century, the hospital found itself compelled to choose children for admission by a lottery system.

Sadness and tragedy surrounded abandoned children. Most of them were illegitimate infants from across the social spectrum. Many, however, were left with the foundling hospitals because their parents could not support them. There was a close relationship between rising food prices and increasing numbers of abandoned children in Paris. Parents would sometimes leave personal tokens or saints' medals on the abandoned baby in the vain hope they might one day be able to reclaim the child. Few children were reclaimed. Leaving a child at a foundling hospital did not guarantee its survival. In Paris, only about ten percent of all abandoned children lived to the age of ten.

Despite all of these perils of early childhood, children did grow up and come of age across Europe. The world of the child may not have received the kind of attention it does today, but during the eighteenth century, the seeds of that modern sensibility were sown. Particularly among the upper classes, new interest arose in educating children. In most areas, education remained firmly in the hands of the churches. As economic skills became more demanding, literacy became more valuable, and literacy rates rose during the century. Yet most Europeans remained illiterate. Not until the late nineteenth century was the world of childhood inextricably linked to the process of education. Then children would be reared to become members of a national citizenry. In the Old Regime, they were reared to make their contribution to the economy of their parents' family and then to set up their own households.

THE REVOLUTION IN AGRICULTURE

Thus far, this chapter has examined those groups that sought stability and that, except for certain members of the nobility, resisted change. Other groups, however, wished to pursue significant new directions in social and economic life. The remainder of the chapter considers those forces and developments that would transform European life during the next century. These developments first appeared in agriculture.

The main goal of traditional peasant society was a stability that would ensure the local food supply. Despite differences in rural customs across Europe, the tillers resisted changes that might endanger the sure supply of food, which they generally believed traditional methods of cultivation would provide. The food supply was never certain, and the farther east one traveled, the more uncertain it became. Failure of the harvest meant not only hardship, but death from either outright starvation or malnutrition. People living in the countryside often had more difficulty finding food than did city dwellers, whose local government usually stored reserve supplies of grain.

Poor harvests also played havoc with prices. Smaller supplies or larger demand raised grain prices. Even small increases in the cost of food could exert heavy pressure on peasant or artisan families. If prices increased sharply, many of those families fell back on poor relief from their local government or the church.

Historians now believe that during the eighteenth century bread prices slowly but steadily

The English agricultural improver Jethro Tull devised this seed drill, which increased wheat crops by planting seed deep in the soil rather than just casting it randomly on the surface.   Image Works/Mary Evans Picture Library Ltd.

TURGOT DESCRIBES FRENCH LANDHOLDING

The economy of Europe until the nineteenth century was overwhelmingly rural. That meant that economic growth and political stability depended largely on agricultural production. During the eighteenth century, many observers became keenly aware that different kinds of landholding led to different attitudes toward work and to different levels of production. Robert Jacques Turgot (1727–1781), who later became finance minister of France, analyzed these differences in an effort to reform French agriculture. He was especially concerned with arrangements that encouraged long-term investment. The métayer *system Turgot discusses was an arrangement whereby landowners arranged to have land farmed by peasants who received part of the harvest as payment for working the land. The peasant had no long-term interest in improving the land. Virtually all observers regarded the system as inefficient.*

■ *Why does Turgot favor those farmers who can make investments in the land they rent from a proprietor? What are the structures of the* métayer *system? Why did it lead to poor investments and lower harvests? What is Turgot's attitude toward work and entrepreneurship?*

1. What really distinguishes the area of large-scale farming from the areas of small-scale production is that in the former areas the proprietors find farmers who provide them with a permanent revenue from the land and who buy from them the right to cultivate it for a certain number of years. These farmers undertake all the expenses of cultivation, the ploughing, the sowing and the stocking of the farm with cattle, animals and tools. They are really agricultural entrepreneurs, who possess, like the entrepreneurs in all other branches of commerce, considerable funds, which they employ in the cultivation of land. . . .

They have not only the brawn but also the wealth to devote to agriculture. They have to work, but unlike workers, they do not have to earn their living by the sweat of their brow, but by the lucrative employment of their capital, just as the ship owners of Nantes and Bordeaux employ theirs in maritime commerce.

rose, spurred largely by population growth. Since bread was their main food, this inflation put pressure on the poor. Prices rose faster than urban wages and brought no appreciable advantage to the small peasant producer. However, the rise in grain prices benefited landowners and those wealthier peasants who had surplus grain to sell.

The rising grain prices gave landlords an opportunity to improve their incomes and lifestyle. To achieve those ends, landlords in Western Europe began a series of innovations in farm production that became known as the **Agricultural Revolution**. Landlords commercialized agriculture and thereby challenged the traditional peasant ways of production. Peasant revolts and disturbances often resulted. The governments of Europe, hungry for new taxes and dependent on the goodwill of the nobility, used their armies and militias to smash peasants who defended traditional practices.

NEW CROPS AND NEW METHODS

The drive to improve agricultural production began during the sixteenth and seventeenth centuries in the Low Countries, where the pressures of the growing population and the shortage of land required changes in cultivation. Dutch landlords and farmers devised better ways to build dikes and to drain land, so they could farm more land. They also experimented with new crops, such as clover and turnips, that would increase the supply of animal fodder and restore the soil. These improvements became so famous that early in the seventeenth century English landlords hired Cornelius Vermuyden, a Dutch

CHAPTER 15 ■ SOCIETY AND ECONOMY UNDER THE OLD REGIME IN THE EIGHTEENTH CENTURY

2. *Métayer* System The areas of small-scale farming, that is to say at least four-sevenths of the kingdom, are those where there are no agricultural entrepreneurs, where a proprietor who wishes to develop his land cannot find anyone to cultivate it except wretched peasants who have no resources other than their labor, where he is obliged to make, at his own expense, all the advances necessary for tillage, beasts, tools, sowing, even to the extent of advancing to his *métayer* the wherewithal to feed himself until the first harvest, where consequently a proprietor who did not have any property other than his estate would be obliged to allow it to lie fallow.

After having deducted the costs of sowing and feudal dues with which the property is burdened, the proprietor shares with the *métayer* what remains of the profits, in accordance with the agreement they have concluded. The proprietor runs all the risks of harvest failure and any loss of cattle: he is the real entrepreneur. The *métayer* is nothing more than a mere workman, a farm hand to whom the proprietor surrenders a share of his profits instead of paying wages. But in his work the proprietor enjoys none of the advantages of the farmer who, working on his own behalf, works carefully and diligently; the proprietor is obliged to entrust all his advances to a man who may be negligent or a scoundrel and is answerable for nothing.

This *métayer*, accustomed to the most miserable existence and without the hope and even the desire to obtain a better living for himself, cultivates badly and neglects to employ the land for valuable and profitable production; by preference he occupies himself in cultivating those things whose growth is less troublesome and which provide him with more foodstuffs, such as buckwheat and chestnuts which do not require any attention. He does not worry very much about his livelihood; he knows that if the harvest fails, his master will be obliged to feed him in order not to see his land neglected.

From *Œuvres, et documents les concernant*, by A. M. R. Turgot, ed. by F. Schelle, 5 vols. (Paris, 1914), vol. II, pp. 448–450, *Documents of European Economic History*, as quoted and trans. by S. Pollard and C. Holmes, pp. 38–39, (Edward Arnold, 1968).

engineer, to drain thousands of acres of land around Cambridge.

English landlords provided the most striking examples of eighteenth-century agricultural improvement. They originated almost no genuinely new farming methods, but they popularized ideas developed in the previous century either in the Low Countries or in England. Some of these landlords and agricultural innovators became famous. For example, Jethro Tull (1674–1741) was willing to conduct experiments himself and to finance the experiments of others. Many of his ideas, such as the rejection of manure as fertilizer, were wrong. Others, however, such as using iron plows to turn the earth more deeply and planting wheat by a drill rather than by just casting seeds, were excellent. His methods permitted land to be cultivated for longer periods without having to leave it fallow.

Charles "Turnip" Townsend (1674–1738) encouraged other important innovations. He learned from the Dutch how to cultivate sandy soil with fertilizers. He also instituted crop rotation, using wheat, turnips, barley, and clover. This new system of rotation replaced the fallow field with one sown with a crop that both restored nutrients to the soil and supplied animal fodder. The additional fodder meant that more livestock could be raised. These fodders allowed animals to be fed during the winter and assured a year-round supply of meat. The larger number of animals increased the quantity of manure available as fertilizer for the grain crops. Consequently, in the long run, both animals and human beings had more food.

A third British agricultural improver was Robert Bakewell (1725–1795), who pioneered new methods of animal breeding that produced more and better animals and more milk and meat.

These and other innovations received widespread discussion in the works of Arthur Young (1741–1820), who edited the *Annals of Agriculture*. In 1793, he became secretary of the British Board of Agriculture. Young traveled widely across Europe, and his books are among the most important documents of life during the late eighteenth century.

Enclosure Replaces Open-Field Method Many of the agricultural innovations, which were adopted only slowly, were incompatible with the existing organization of land in England. Small cultivators who lived in village communities still farmed most of the soil. Each farmer tilled an assortment of unconnected strips. The two- or three-field systems of rotation left large portions of land fallow and unproductive each year. Animals grazed on the common land in the summer and on the stubble of the harvest in the winter. Until at least the mid-eighteenth century, the whole community decided what crops to plant. The entire system discouraged improvement and favored the poorer farmers, who needed the common land and stubble fields for their animals. The village method precluded expanding pastureland to raise more animals that would, in turn, produce more manure for fertilizer. Thus, the methods of traditional production aimed at a steady, but not a growing, supply of food.

In 1700, approximately half the arable land in England was farmed by this open-field method. By the second half of the century, the rising price of wheat encouraged landlords to consolidate or enclose their lands to increase production. The **enclosures** were intended to use land more rationally and to achieve greater commercial profits. The process involved the fencing of common lands, the reclamation of previously untilled waste, and the transformation of strips into block fields. These procedures brought turmoil to the economic and social life of the countryside. Riots often ensued.

Because many English farmers either owned their strips or rented them in a manner that amounted to ownership, the larger landlords usually resorted to parliamentary acts to legalize the enclosure of the land, which they owned but rented to the farmers. Because the large landowners controlled Parliament, such measures passed easily. Between 1761 and 1792, almost 500,000 acres were enclosed through acts of Parliament, compared with 75,000 acres between 1727 and 1760. In 1801, a general enclosure act streamlined the process.

The enclosures were controversial at the time and have remained so among historians. They permitted the extension of both farming and innovation, and thus increased food production on larger agricultural units. They also disrupted small traditional communities; they forced off the land independent farmers, who had needed the common pasturage, and poor cottage dwellers, who had lived on the reclaimed wasteland. The enclosures, however, did not depopulate the countryside. In some counties where the enclosures took place, the population increased. New soil had come into production, and services that supported farming also expanded.

The enclosures did not create the labor force for the British Industrial Revolution. What the enclosures most conspicuously displayed was the introduction of the entrepreneurial or capitalistic attitude of the urban merchant into the countryside. This commercialization of agriculture, which spread from Britain slowly across the Continent during the next century, strained the paternal relationship between the governing and governed classes. Previously, landlords had often looked after the welfare of the lower orders through price controls or waivers of rent during hard times. As the landlords became increasingly concerned about profits, they began to leave the peasants to the mercy of the marketplace.

Limited Improvements in Eastern Europe Improving agriculture tended to characterize farm production west of the Elbe River. Dutch farming was efficient. In France, despite the efforts of the government to improve agriculture, enclosures were restricted. Yet many people in France wanted to improve agricultural methods. These new procedures benefited the ruling classes because better agriculture increased their incomes and assured a larger food supply, which discouraged social unrest. (See "Turgot Describes French Landholding," pages 494–495.)

In Prussia, Austria, Poland, and Russia, agricultural improvement was limited. Nothing in the relationship of the serfs to their lords encouraged innovation. In eastern Europe, the chief method of increasing production was to bring previously untilled lands under the plow. The landlords or their agents, and not the villages, normally directed farm management. By extending tillage, the great landlords sought to squeeze more labor from their serfs, rather than greater productivity from the soil. Eastern European landlords, like their western counterparts, sought to increase their profits, but they were less ambitious and successful. The only significant nutritional gain they achieved was the introduction of maize and the potato. Livestock production did not increase significantly.

EXPANSION OF THE POPULATION

The population explosion with which the entire world must contend today had its origins in the eighteenth century. Before that time, Europe's population had experienced dramatic increases, but plagues, wars, or famine had redressed the balance. Beginning in the second quarter of the eighteenth century, the population began to increase steadily. The need to feed this population caused food prices to rise, which spurred agricultural innovation. The need to provide everyday consumer goods for the expanding numbers of people fueled the demand side of the Industrial Revolution.

In 1700, Europe's population, excluding the European provinces of the Ottoman Empire, was probably between 100 million and 120 million people. By 1800, the figures had risen to almost 190 million and by 1850, to 260 million. The population of England and Wales rose from 6 million in 1750 to more than 10 million in 1800. France grew from 18 million in 1715 to about 26 million in 1789. Russia's population increased from 19 million in 1722 to 29 million in 1766. Such extraordinary sustained growth put new demands on all resources and considerable pressure on the existing social organization.

The population expansion occurred across the Continent in both the country and the cities. Only a limited consensus exists among scholars about the causes of this growth. The death rate clearly declined. There were fewer wars and epidemics in the eighteenth century. Hygiene and sanitation also improved. Better medical knowledge and techniques, however, did not contribute much to the decline in deaths. The more important medical advances came after the initial population explosion and would not have affected it directly.

Instead, changes in the food supply itself may have allowed population growth to be sustained. Improved and expanding grain production made one contribution. Another and even more important change was the cultivation of the potato. This tuber was a product of the New World and came into widespread European production during the eighteenth century. (See "The West & The World," page 544.) On a single acre, a peasant family could grow enough potatoes to feed itself for an entire year. This more certain food supply enabled more children to survive to adulthood and rear children of their own.

The impact of the population explosion can hardly be overestimated. It created new demands for food, goods, jobs, and services. It provided a new pool of labor. Traditional modes of production and living had to be revised. More people lived in the countryside than could find employment there. Migration increased. There were also more people who might become socially and politically discontented. Because the population growth fed on itself, these pressures and demands continued to increase. The society and the social practices of the Old Regime literally outgrew their traditional bounds.

THE INDUSTRIAL REVOLUTION OF THE EIGHTEENTH CENTURY

The second half of the eighteenth century witnessed the beginning of the industrialization of the European economy. That achievement of sustained economic growth is termed the ***Industrial Revolution***. Previously, the economy of a province or a country might grow, but growth soon reached a plateau. Since the late eighteenth century, however, the economy of Europe has managed to expand at an almost uninterrupted pace. Depressions and recessions have been temporary, and even during such economic downturns, the Western economy has continued to grow.

At considerable social cost, industrialization made possible the production of more goods and services than ever before in human history. Industrialization in Europe eventually overcame the economy of scarcity. The new means of production demanded new kinds of skills, new discipline in work, and a large labor force. The goods produced met immediate consumer demand and also created new demands. In the long run, industrialization raised the standard of living and overcame the poverty that most Europeans, who lived during the eighteenth century and earlier, had taken for granted. It gave human beings greater control over nature than they had ever known before; yet by the mid-nineteenth century, industrialism would also cause new and unanticipated problems with the environment.

During the eighteenth century, people did not call these economic developments a *revolution.* That term came to be applied to the British economic phenomena only after the French Revolution. Then continental writers observed that what had taken place in Britain was the economic equivalent of the political events in France, hence an Industrial Revolution. It was revolutionary less in its speed, which was on the whole rather slow, than in its implications for the future of European society.

Consumption of all forms of consumer goods increased greatly in the eighteenth century. This engraving illustrates a shop, probably in Paris. Here women, working apparently for a woman manager, are making dresses and hats to meet the demands of the fashion trade. As the document on page 503 demonstrates, some women writers urged more such employment opportunities for women.   Bildarchiv Preussischer Kulturbesitz

A REVOLUTION IN CONSUMPTION

The most familiar side of the Industrial Revolution was the invention of new machinery, the establishment of factories, and the creation of a new kind of work force. Recent studies, however, have emphasized the demand side of the process and the vast increase in both the desire and the possibility of consuming goods and services that arose in the early eighteenth century.

The inventions of the Industrial Revolution increased the supply of consumer goods as never before in history. The supply of goods was only one side of the economic equation, however. An unprecedented demand for the humble goods of everyday life created the supply. Those goods included clothing, buttons, toys, china, furniture, rugs, kitchen utensils, candlesticks, brassware, silverware, pewterware, glassware, watches, jewelry, soap, beer, wines, and foodstuffs. It was the ever-increasing demand for these goods that sparked the ingenuity of designers and inventors. Furthermore, consumer demand seemed unlimited.

Many social factors helped establish the markets for these consumer goods. During the seventeenth century, the Dutch had enjoyed enormous prosperity and had led the way in new forms of consumption. For reasons that are still not clear, during the eighteenth century, first the English and then the people on the Continent came to have more disposable income. This wealth may have resulted from the improvements in agriculture. Those incomes allowed people to buy consumer goods that previous generations had inherited or did not possess. What is key to this change in consumption is that it depended primarily on expanding the various domestic markets in Europe.

This revolution, if that is not too strong a term, in consumption was not automatic. People became persuaded that they needed or wanted new consumer goods. Often, entrepreneurs caused it to happen by developing new methods of marketing. For example, the English porcelain manufacturer Josiah Wedgwood (1730–1795) first attempted to find customers among the royal family and the aristocracy. Once he had gained their business with luxury goods, then he produced a less expensive version of the chinaware for middle-class customers. He also used advertising, opened showrooms in London, and sent salespeople all over Britain with samples and catalogs of his wares. On the Continent, his salespeople used bilingual catalogs. There seemed to be no limit to the markets for consumer goods that social emulation on the one hand and advertising on the other could stimulate.

Furthermore, the process of change in style itself became institutionalized. New fashions and inventions were always better than old ones. If new kinds of goods could be produced, there usually was a market for them. If one product did not find a market, its failure provided a lesson for how to develop a different new product.

This expansion of consumption quietly, but steadily, challenged the social assumptions of the day. Fashion publications made all levels of society aware of new styles. Clothing fashions could be copied. Servants could begin to dress well if not luxuriously. Changes in the consumption of food and drink demanded new kinds of dishware for the home. Tea and coffee became staples. The brewing industry became fully commercialized. Those developments entailed the need for new kinds of cups and mugs and many more of them.

There would always be critics of this consumer economy. The vision of luxury and comfort it offered contrasted with the asceticism of ancient Sparta and contemporary Christian ethics. Yet, the ever-increasing consumption and production of the goods of everyday life became a hallmark of modern Western society from the eighteenth century to our own day. It would be difficult to overestimate the importance of the desire for consumer goods and the higher standard of living that they made possible in Western history after the eighteenth century. The presence and accessibility of such goods became the hallmark of a nation's prosperity. It was the absence of such consumer goods, as well as of civil liberties, that during the 1980s led to such deep discontent with the communist regimes in Eastern Europe and the former Soviet Union.

INDUSTRIAL LEADERSHIP OF GREAT BRITAIN

Great Britain was the home of the Industrial Revolution and, until the middle of the nineteenth century, remained the industrial leader of Europe. Several factors contributed to the early start in Britain.

Great Britain took the lead in the consumer revolution that expanded the demand for goods that could be efficiently supplied. London was the largest city in Europe. It was the center of a world of fashion and taste to which hundreds of thousands, if not millions, of British citizens were exposed each year. In London, these people learned to want the consumer goods they saw on visits for business and pleasure. Newspapers thrived in Britain during the eighteenth century, and the advertising they printed increased consumer wants. The social structure of Britain encouraged people to imitate the lifestyles of their social superiors. It seems to have been in Britain that a world of fashion first developed that led people to want to accumulate goods. In addition to the domestic consumer demand, the British economy benefited from demand from the colonies in North America.

Britain was also the single largest free-trade area in Europe. The British had good roads and waterways without internal tolls or other trade barriers. The country had rich deposits of coal and iron ore. Its political structure was stable, and property was absolutely secure. The sound systems of banking and public credit established a stable climate for investment. Taxation in Britain was heavy, but it was efficiently and fairly collected, largely from indirect taxes. Furthermore, British taxes received legal approval through Parliament, with all social classes and all regions of the nation paying the same taxes. In contrast to the Continent, there was no pattern of privileged tax exemptions.

Finally, British society was mobile by the standards of the time. Persons who had money or could earn it could rise socially. The British aristocracy would receive into its ranks people who had amassed large fortunes. Even persons of wealth who did not join the aristocracy could enjoy their riches, receive social recognition, and exert political influence. No one of these factors preordained the British advance toward industrialism. Together, however, when added to the progressive state of British agriculture, they provided the nation with the marginal advantage to create a new mode of economic production.

NEW METHODS OF TEXTILE PRODUCTION

The industry that pioneered the Industrial Revolution and met the growing consumer demand was the production of textiles for clothing. Textile production is the key example of industrialism emerging to supply the demands of an ever-growing market for everyday goods. Furthermore,

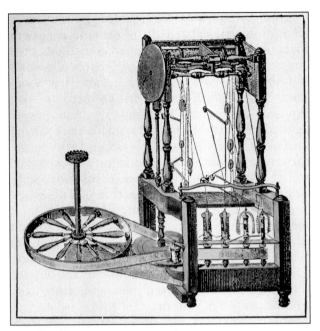

James Hargreave's Spinning Jenny permitted the spinning of numerous spindles of thread on a single machine.
AKG London Ltd.

it illustrates the surprising fact that much of the earliest industrial change took place not in cities, but in the countryside.

Although the eighteenth-century economy was primarily agricultural, manufacturing also permeated rural areas. The peasant family living in a one- or two-room cottage, rather than the factory, was the basic unit of production. The same peasants who tilled the land in spring and summer often spun thread or wove textiles in the winter.

Under what is termed the *domestic*, or putting-out, *system of textile production*, agents of urban textile merchants took wool or other unfinished fibers to the homes of peasants, who spun it into thread. The agent then transported the thread to other peasants, who wove it into the finished product. The merchant sold the wares. In thousands of peasant cottages from Ireland to Austria, there stood a spinning wheel or a hand loom. Sometimes the spinners or weavers owned their own equipment, but more often than not by the middle of the century, the merchant capitalist owned the machinery as well as the raw material.

The domestic system of textile production was a basic feature of this family economy and would continue to be so in Britain and on the Continent well into the nineteenth century. By the mid-eighteenth century, however, production bottlenecks had developed within the domestic system. The demand for cotton textiles was growing more rapidly than production, especially in Britain, which had a large domestic and North American

market for these goods. Inventors devised some of the most famous machines of the early Industrial Revolution to meet consumer demand for cotton textiles.

The Spinning Jenny Cotton textile weavers had the technical capacity to produce the quantity of fabric demanded. The spinners, however, did not have the equipment to produce as much thread as the weavers needed. John Kay's invention of the flying shuttle, which increased the productivity of the weavers, had created this imbalance during the 1730s. Thereafter, manufacturers and merchants offered prizes for the invention of a machine to eliminate this bottleneck.

About 1765, James Hargreaves (d. 1778) invented the **spinning jenny**. Initially, this machine allowed 16 spindles of thread to be spun, but by the close of the century, it could operate 120 spindles.

The Water Frame The spinning jenny broke the bottleneck between the productive capacity of the spinners and the weavers, but it was still a piece of machinery used in the cottage. The invention that took cotton textile manufacture out of the home and put it into the factory was Richard Arkwright's (1732–1792) **water frame**, patented in 1769. This was a water-powered device designed to permit the production of a purely cotton fabric, rather than a cotton fabric containing linen fiber for durability. Eventually Arkwright lost his patent rights, and other manufacturers used his invention freely. As a result, many factories sprang up in the countryside near streams that provided the necessary water power. From the 1780s onward, the cotton industry could meet an ever-expanding demand. Cotton output increased by 800 percent between 1780 and 1800. By 1815, cotton composed 40 percent of the value of British domestic exports and by 1830, just over 50 percent.

The Industrial Revolution had commenced in earnest by the 1780s, but the full economic and social ramifications of this unleashing of human productive capacity were not really felt until the early nineteenth century. The expansion of industry and the incorporation of new inventions often occurred slowly. For example, Edmund Cartwright (1743–1822) invented the power loom for machine weaving in the late 1780s. Yet not until the 1830s were there more power-loom weavers than hand-loom weavers in Britain. Nor did all the social ramifications of industrialism appear immediately. The first cotton mills used water power, were located in the country, and rarely employed more than two dozen workers. Not until the late-century application of the steam engine, perfected by James Watt

(1736–1819) in 1769, to run textile machinery could factories easily be located in or near urban centers. The steam engine not only vastly increased and regularized the available energy, but also made possible the combination of urbanization and industrialization.

THE STEAM ENGINE

More than any other invention, the steam engine permitted industrialization to grow on itself and to expand into one area of production after another. This machine provided for the first time in human history a steady and essentially unlimited source of inanimate power. Unlike engines powered by water or wind, the steam engine, driven by burning coal, provided a portable source of industrial power that did not fail or falter as the seasons of the year changed. Unlike human or animal power, the steam engine depended on mineral energy that never tired. Finally, the steam engine could be applied to many industrial and, eventually, transportation uses.

Thomas Newcomen (1663–1729) in the early eighteenth century had invented the first practical engine to use steam power. When the steam that had been induced into the cylinder condensed, it caused the piston of this device to fall. The Newcomen machine was large and inefficient in its use of energy because both the condenser and the cylinder were heated, and practically untransportable. Despite these problems, English mine operators used the Newcomen machines to pump water out of coal and tin mines. By the third quarter of the eighteenth century, almost a hundred Newcomen machines were operating in the mining districts of England.

During the 1760s, James Watt, a Scottish engineer and machine maker, began to experiment with a model of a Newcomen machine at the University of Glasgow. He gradually understood that separating the condenser from the piston and the cylinder would achieve much greater efficiency. In 1769, he patented his new invention, but transforming his idea into a practical application presented difficulties. His design required precise metalwork. Watt soon found a partner in Matthew Boulton (1728–1809), a successful toy and button manufacturer in Birmingham, the city with the most skilled metalworkers in Britain. Watt and Boulton, in turn, consulted with John Wilkinson (1728–1808), a cannon manufacturer, to drill the precise metal cylinders Watt's design required. In 1776, the Watt steam engine found its first commercial application pumping water from mines in Cornwall.

The use of the steam engine spread slowly because until 1800 Watt retained the exclusive patent rights. He was also reluctant to make further changes to permit the engine to operate more rapidly. Boulton eventually persuaded him to make modifications and improvements that allowed the engines to be used not only for pumping, but also for running cotton mills. By the early nineteenth century, the steam engine had become the prime mover for all industry. With its application to ships and then to wagons on iron rails, the steam engine also revolutionized transportation.

IRON PRODUCTION

The manufacture of high-quality iron has been basic to modern industrial development. Iron is the chief element of all heavy industry and of land or sea transport. Most productive machinery itself is also manufactured from iron. During the early eighteenth century, British ironmakers produced somewhat less than 25,000 tons of iron annually. Three factors held back the production. First, charcoal rather than coke was used to smelt the ore. Charcoal, derived from wood, was becoming scarce as forests in Britain diminished, and it does not burn at as high a temperature as coke, derived from coal. Second, until the perfection of the steam engine, furnaces could not achieve high enough blasts. Finally, the demand for iron was limited. The elimination of the first two problems also eliminated the third.

Eventually, British ironmakers began to use coke, and the steam engine provided new power for the blast furnaces. Coke was an abundant fuel because of Britain's large coal deposits. The steam engine both improved iron production and increased the demand for iron.

In 1784, Henry Cort (1740–1800) introduced a new puddling process, that is, a new method for melting and stirring molten ore. Cort's process allowed the removal of more slag (the impurities that bubbled to the top of the molten metal) and

---

MAJOR INVENTIONS IN THE TEXTILE-MANUFACTURING REVOLUTION

1733 John Kay's flying shuttle
1765 James Hargreaves's spinning jenny (patented 1770)
1769 James Watt's steam engine patent
1769 Richard Arkwright's water frame patent
1787 Edmund Cartwright's power loom

thus the production of purer iron. Cort also developed a rolling mill that continuously shaped the still-molten metal into bars, rails, or other forms. Previously, the metal had to be pounded into these forms.

All these innovations achieved a better, more versatile, cheaper product. The demand for iron consequently grew. By the early nineteenth century, the British produced over a million tons annually. The lower cost of iron, in turn, lowered the cost of steam engines and allowed them to be used more widely.

THE IMPACT OF THE AGRICULTURAL AND INDUSTRIAL REVOLUTIONS ON WORKING WOMEN

The transformation of agriculture and industry led to a series of seemingly modest changes that, taken collectively, diminished the importance and the role of those women already in the work force.

Women had been an important part of traditional European agriculture. They worked in and often were permitted to glean the grain left over after the general harvest. Women also managed industries like milking and cheese production. However, primarily in Western Europe, increasing commercialization and mechanization eroded these traditional roles. Machinery operated by men displaced the work of women in the field and their skills in dairying and home industry, particularly in Britain. Even nonmechanized labor came to favor men. For example, during the late eighteenth century, heavy scythes wielded by men replaced the lighter sickles that women had used to harvest grain. Moreover, the drive to maximize profits led landlords to enclose lands and curtail customary rights like gleaning.

This transformation of farming constricted women's ability to earn their living from the land. Women came to be viewed as opponents of agricultural improvement because these improvements hurt them economically. As a result, proponents of the new agriculture often demeaned the role of women in farming and their related work. Indeed, the vast literature on agricultural improvement specifically advocated removing women from the agricultural work force.

A similar process took place in textile manufacturing, where mechanization deprived many women of one of their most traditional means of earning income. Before mechanization thousands of women worked at spinning wheels to produce thread that hand-loom weavers, who were often their husbands, then wove. The earlier, small spinning jennies did not immediately disrupt this situation because women could use them in the

loft of a home, but the larger ones required a factory setting where men often ran the machinery. As a result, most women spinners were put out of work, and those women who did move into the factory labor force performed less skilled work than men. In the long run, however, the mechanization of spinning left many other women without one of their most traditional means of earning income.

Many working women, displaced from spinning thread or from farming, slowly turned to cottage industries, such as knitting, button making, straw plaiting, bonnet making, or glove stitching, that invariably earned them less than their former occupations had. In later generations, women who earlier would have been spinners or farm workers moved directly into cottage industries. The work and skills these occupations involved were considered inferior; and because it paid so poorly, women who did this work might become prostitutes or engage in other criminal activity. Consequently, the reputations and social standing of many working women suffered.

Among women who did not work in the cottage industries, thousands became domestic servants in the homes of landed or commercial families. During the nineteenth century, such domestic service became the largest area of female employment. It was far more respectable than the cottage industries, but was isolated from the technologically advanced world of factory manufacture or transport.

By the end of the eighteenth century, the work and workplaces of men and women were becoming increasingly separate and distinct. In this respect, many people, such as the English writer Priscilla Wakefield (1750–1832), believed the kinds of employment open to women had narrowed. Wakefield called for new occupations for women. (See "Priscilla Wakefield Demands More Occupations for Women.")

This shift in female employment, or what one historian has termed "this defamation of women workers,"[2] produced several long-term results. First, women's work, whether in cottage industries or domestic service, became associated with the home rather than with places where men worked. Second, the laboring life of most women was removed from the new technologies in farming, transportation, and manufacturing. Woman's work thus appeared traditional, and people assumed women could do only such work. Third, during the nineteenth and early twentieth centuries, Europeans also assumed most women worked only to supplement a husband's income.

[2]Deborah Valenze, *The First Industrial Woman* (New York: Oxford University Press, 1995), p. 183.

PRISCILLA WAKEFIELD DEMANDS MORE OCCUPATIONS FOR WOMEN

At the end of the eighteenth century, Priscilla Wakefield was one of several English women writers who began to demand a wider life for women. She was concerned that women found themselves able to pursue only occupations that paid poorly. They were often excluded from work because of their alleged physical weakness. She also believed women should receive equal wages for equal work. These issues reflected a narrowing of opportunities for women that had occurred in England during the second half of the eighteenth century. As a result of the mechanization of both agriculture and the textile industry, many found traditional occupations were closing to women. Wakefield is thus addressing a general question of opportunities available to women and more recent developments. Many of the issues she raised have yet to be adequately addressed.

■ *What arguments were used at the end of the eighteenth century to limit the kinds of employment that women might enter? Why did women receive less pay than men for similar or the same work? What occupations traditionally filled by men does Wakefield believe women might also pursue?*

Another heavy discouragement to the industry of women, is the inequality of the reward of their labor, compared with that of men; an injustice which pervades every species of employment performed by both sexes.

In employments which depend on bodily strength, the distinction is just; for it cannot be pretended that the generality of women can earn as much as men, when the produce of their labor is the result of corporeal exertion; but it is a subject of great regret, that this inequality should prevail even where an equal share of skill and application is exerted. Male stay-makers, mantua-makers, and hair-dressers, are better paid than female artists of the same professions; but surely it will never be urged as an apology for this disproportion, that women are not as capable of making stays, gowns, dressing hair, and similar arts, as men; if they are not superior to them, it can only be accounted for upon this principle, that the prices they receive for their labor are not sufficient to repay them for the expense of qualifying themselves for their business; and that they sink under the mortification of being regarded as artisans of inferior estimation. . . .

Besides these employments which are commonly performed by women, and those already shown to be suitable for such persons as are above the condition of hard labor, there are some professions and trades customarily in the hands of men, which might be conveniently exercised by either sex. Watchmaking requiring more ingenuity than strength, seems peculiarly adapted to women; as do many parts of the business of stationer, particularly, ruling account books or making pens. The compounding of medicines in an apothecary's shop, requires no other talents than care and exactness; and if opening a vein occasionally be an indispensable requisite, a woman may acquire the capacity of doing it, for those of her own sex at least, without any reasonable objection. . . . Pastry and confectionery appear particularly consonant to the habits of women, though generally performed by men; perhaps the heat of the ovens, and the strength requisite to fill and empty them, may render male assistants necessary; but certain women are most eligible to mix up the ingredients, and prepare the various kinds of cakes for baking. Light turnery and toy-making depend more upon dexterity and invention than force, and are therefore suitable work for women and children. . . .

Farming, as far as respects the theory, is commensurate with the powers of the female mind: nor is the practice of inspecting agricultural processes incompatible with the delicacy of their frames if their constitution be good.

Priscilla Wakefield, *Reflections on the Present Condition of the Female Sex* (1798) (London, 1817), pp. 125–127, as quoted in Bridget Hill, ed., *Eighteenth-Century Women: An Anthology* (London: George Allen & Unwin, 1984), pp. 227–228.

During the eighteenth century farm women normally worked in the home and performed such tasks as churning butter as well as caring for children. As time passed tasks such as making butter were mechanized and women displaced from such work.   Francis Wheatley (RA) (1747-1801) "Morning," signed and dated 1799, oil on canvas, $17^1/_2 \times 21^1/_2$ in. (44.5 × 54.5 cm), Yale Center for British Art, Paul Mellon Collection, USA/Bridgeman Art Library (B1977.14.120)

Finally, because the work women did was considered marginal and only as supplementing a male income, men were paid much more than women. Most people associate the Industrial Revolution with factories, but for many working women, these revolutions led to a life located more in homes than ever before. Indeed, in the nineteenth century, one, though only one, motive behind efforts to restrict the hours and improve the conditions of women in factories was the belief that it was bad for them to be there in the first place. The larger picture of the relationship of the new industrial workplace to family life will be addressed in Chapter 21.

THE GROWTH OF CITIES

Remarkable changes occurred in the pattern of city growth between 1500 and 1800. In 1500, within Europe (excluding Hungary and Russia)

156 cities had a population greater than 10,000. Only four of those cities—Paris, Milan, Venice, and Naples—had populations larger than 100,000. By 1800, 363 cities had 10,000 or more inhabitants, and 17 of them had populations larger than 100,000. The percentage of the European population living in urban areas had risen from just over five percent to just over nine percent. A major shift in urban concentration from southern, Mediterranean Europe to the north had also occurred.

PATTERNS OF PREINDUSTRIAL URBANIZATION

The eighteenth century witnessed a considerable growth of towns, closely related to the tumult of the day and the revolutions with which the century closed. London grew from about 700,000 inhabitants in 1700 to almost one million in 1800. By the time of the French Revolution, Paris had more than 500,000 inhabitants. Berlin's population tripled during the century, reaching 170,000 in 1800. Warsaw had 30,000 inhabitants in 1730, but almost 120,000 in 1794. St. Petersburg, founded in 1703, numbered more than 250,000 inhabitants a century later. The number of smaller cities with 20,000 to 50,000 people also increased considerably. This urban growth must, however, be kept in perspective. Even in France and Great Britain, probably somewhat less than 20 percent of the population lived in cities. And the town of 10,000 inhabitants was much more common than the giant urban center.

These raw figures conceal significant changes that took place in how cities grew and how the population redistributed itself. The major urban development of the sixteenth century had been followed by a leveling off, and even a decline, in the seventeenth. New growth began in the early eighteenth century and accelerated during the late eighteenth and the early nineteenth centuries.

Between 1500 and 1750, major urban expansion took place within already established and generally already large cities. After 1750, the pattern changed with the birth of new cities and the rapid growth of older, smaller cities.

Growth of Capitals and Ports In particular, between 1600 and 1750, the cities that grew most vigorously were capitals and ports. This situation reflects the success of monarchical state building during those years and the consequent burgeoning of bureaucracies, armies, courts, and other groups who lived in the capitals. The growth of port cities, in turn, reflects the expansion of European overseas trade—especially, that of the Atlantic routes. Except for Manchester in England and Lyons in France, the new urban conglomerates were nonindustrial cities.

Furthermore, between 1600 and 1750, cities with populations of fewer than 40,000 inhabitants declined. These included older landlocked trading centers, medieval industrial cities, and ecclesiastical centers. They contributed less to the new political regimes, and the expansion of the putting-out system transferred production from medieval cities to the countryside because rural labor was cheaper than urban labor.

The Emergence of New Cities and the Growth of Small Towns In the mid-eighteenth century, a new pattern emerged. The rate of growth of existing large cities declined, new cities emerged, and existing smaller cities grew. Several factors were at work in the process, which Jan De Vries

has termed "an urban growth from below."[3] First was the general overall population increase. Second, the early stages of the Industrial Revolution, particularly in Britain, occurred in the countryside and fostered the growth of smaller towns and cities located near factories. Factory organization itself led to new concentrations of population.

Cities also grew as a result of the new prosperity of European agriculture, even where there was little industrialization. Improved agricultural production promoted the growth of nearby market towns and other urban centers that served agriculture or allowed more prosperous farmers to have access to consumer goods and recreation. This new pattern of urban growth—new cities and the expansion of smaller existing ones—would continue into the nineteenth century.

URBAN CLASSES

Social divisions were as marked in eighteenth-century cities as they were in nineteenth-century industrial centers. The urban rich were often visibly segregated from the urban poor. Aristocrats and the upper middle class lived in fashionable town houses, often constructed around newly laid-out green squares. The poorest town dwellers usually congregated along the rivers. Small merchants and artisans lived above their shops. Whole families might live in a single room. Modern sanitary facilities were unknown. Pure water was rare. Cattle, pigs, goats, and other animals roamed the streets. All reports on the cities of Europe during this period emphasize both the striking grace and beauty of the dwellings of the wealthy and the dirt, filth, and stench that filled the streets. (See "Encountering the Past: Water, Washing, and Bathing," page 506.)

Poverty was not just an urban problem; it was usually worse in the countryside. In the city, however, poverty was more visible in the form of crime, prostitution, vagrancy, begging, and alcoholism. Many a young man or woman from the countryside migrated to the nearest city to seek a better life, only to discover poor housing, little food, disease, degradation, and finally death. It did not require the Industrial Revolution and the urban factories to make the cities into hellholes for the poor and the dispossessed. The full darkness of London life during the mid-century "gin age," when consumption of that liquor blinded and killed many poor people, is evident in the engravings of William Hogarth (1697–1764).

[3]Jan De Vries, "Patterns of Urbanization in Pre-Industrial Europe, 1500–1800," in H. Schmal, ed., *Patterns of Urbanization since 1500* (London: Croom Helm, 1981), p. 103.

WATER, WASHING, AND BATHING

Before the late nineteenth century, clean water was scarce in Europe. Except for the few households and institutions that had their own wells, water had to be carried from a public fountain or public well. Drought in summer and freezing in winter could lead to shortages.

Governments made little effort to provide water. Everyone assumed that people required little water for their personal use—less than 7.5 liters per day, according to one eighteenth-century commentator. (The average American uses 210 liters per day.) Commerce and agriculture used much more water than individuals: to power mills in the cloth and dye trades, and to quench the thirst of work animals and irrigate fields.

Attitudes toward personal appearance also determined the use of water. In the Middle Ages, public bathhouses were not uncommon. The appearance of the body—cleanliness—was believed to reflect the state of the soul, and townspeople and aristocrats bathed fairly often. However, during the Renaissance and the Reformation, the quality and condition of clothing, not bodily cleanliness, were thought to mirror the soul. Clean clothes also revealed a person's social status—clothes made the man and the woman.

Moreover, from the late Middle Ages through the end of the eighteenth century, etiquette and medical manuals advised people to wash only those parts of their bodies that could be seen in public—the hands, the face, the neck, and the feet. All forms of public bathing were associated with immoral behavior—public bathing meant public nudity, and prostitutes frequented bathhouses.

The switch from woolen to linen clothing accompanied the decline in bathing. By the sixteenth century, easily washable linen clothing had begun to replace woolen garments in much of Western Europe. Clean linen shirts or blouses allowed persons who had not bathed to appear clean. Possession of large quantities of freshly laundered linens was a sign of high social status.

Appearance thus became more important than bodily hygiene. Medical opinion supported these practices. Physicians believed odors or *miasma* (bad air), such as might be found in soiled linens—along with lice, fleas, and other vermin—caused disease. One should therefore change one's shirt every few days but avoid baths, which might let the bad air enter the body through the open pores. Consequently, in an age in which there were practically no personal bathtubs, thousands of shirts were washed each week, almost always by female laundresses, in every city.

Attitudes toward bathing only began to change toward the middle of the eighteenth century when writers argued that frequent bathing might lead to greater health. Large public baths, such as had been known in the ancient world and were a fixture of the Ottoman Empire, revived during the nineteenth century, and the germ theory of disease led health authorities to urge people to bathe often to rid their bodies of germs. The great water projects of the nineteenth century (see Chapter 23) would assure vast quantities of water for personal hygiene.

- *Why did bathing become less frequent after the late Middle Ages? How did the use of linen clothing contribute to this change?*

Daniel Roche, *The Culture of Clothing: Dress and Fashion in the "Ancien Regime"* (Cambridge: Cambridge University Press, 1994); Georges Vigarello, *Concepts of Cleanliness: Changing Attitudes in France since the Middle Ages* (Cambridge: Cambridge University Press, 1988); Alain Corbin, *The Foul and the Fragrant: Odor and the French Social Imagination* (Cambridge, MA: Harvard University Press, 1988).

In the eighteenth century washing linen clothing by hand was a major task of women servants.   J. B. S. Chardin, "The Washerwoman." Nationalmuseum med Prins Eugens Waldemarsudde. Photo: The National Museum of Fine Arts

Also contrasting with the serenity of the aristocratic and upper-commercial-class lifestyle were the public executions that took place all over Europe, the breaking of men and women on instruments of torture in Paris, and the public floggings in Russia. Brutality condoned and carried out by the ruling classes was a fact of everyday life.

The Upper Classes   At the top of the urban social structure stood a generally small group of nobles, large merchants, bankers, financiers, clergy, and government officials. These upper-class men controlled the political and economic affairs of the town. Normally, they constituted a self-appointed and self-electing oligarchy that governed the city through its corporation or city council. Some form of royal charter usually gave the city corporation its authority and the power to select its own members. In a few cities on the Continent, artisan guilds controlled the corporations, but generally, the local nobility and the wealthiest commercial people dominated the councils.

The Middle Class   Another group in the city was the prosperous, but not always immensely wealthy, merchants, trades people, bankers, and professional people. They were the most dynamic element of the urban population and made up the middle class, or bourgeoisie. The concept of the middle class was much less clear cut than that of the nobility. The middle class itself was and would remain diverse and divided, with persons employed in the professions often resentful of those who drew their incomes from commerce. Less wealthy members of the middle class of whatever occupation resented wealthier members who might be connected to the nobility through social or business relationships.

The middle class had less wealth than most nobles, but more than urban artisans. Middle-class people lived in the cities and towns, and their sources of income had little or nothing to do with the land. In one way or another, they all benefited from expanding trade and commerce, whether as merchants, lawyers, or small-factory owners. Theirs was a world in which earning and saving of money enabled rapid social mobility and change in lifestyle. They saw themselves as willing to put their capital and energy to work, whereas they portrayed the nobility as idle. The members of the middle class tended to be economically aggressive and socially ambitious. People often made fun of them for these characteristics and were jealous of their success. The middle class normally supported reform, change, and eco-

nomic growth. They also wanted more rational regulations for trade and commerce, as did some progressive aristocrats.

The middle class was made up of people whose lives fostered the revolution in consumption. On one hand, as owners of factories and of wholesale and retail businesses, they produced and sold goods for the expanding consumer market; on the other hand, members of the middle class were among the chief consumers. It was to their homes that the vast array of new consumer goods made their way. They were also the people whose social values most fully embraced the commercial spirit. They might not enjoy the titles or privileges of the nobility, but they could enjoy material comfort and prosperity. It was this style of life that less well-off people could emulate as they sought to acquire consumer goods for themselves.

During the eighteenth century, the relationship between the middle class and the aristocracy was complicated. On one hand, the nobles, especially in England and France, increasingly embraced the commercial spirit associated with the middle class by improving their estates and investing in cities. On the other hand, wealthy members of the middle class often tried to imitate the lifestyle of the nobility by purchasing landed estates. The aspirations of the middle class for social mobility, however, conflicted with the determination of the nobles to maintain and reassert their own privileges and to protect their own wealth. Middle-class commercial figures—traders, bankers, manufacturers, and lawyers—often found their pursuit of profit and prestige blocked by the privileges of the nobility and its social exclusiveness, by the inefficiency of monarchical bureaucracies dominated by the nobility, or by aristocrats who controlled patronage and government contracts.

The bourgeoisie was not rising to challenge the nobility; rather, both were seeking to increase their existing political power and social prestige. The tensions that arose between the nobles and the middle class during the eighteenth century normally involved issues of power sharing or access to political influence, rather than clashes over values or goals associated with class.

The middle class in the cities also feared the lower urban classes as much as they envied the nobility. The lower orders were a potentially violent element in society, a threat to property, and, in their poverty, a drain on national resources. The lower classes, however, were much more varied than either the city aristocracy or the middle class cared to admit.

This engraving illustrates a metalworking shop such as might have been found in almost any town of significance in Europe. Most of the people employed in the shop probably belonged to the same family. Note that two women are also working. The wife may very well have been the person in charge of keeping the accounts of the business. The two younger boys might be children of the owner or apprentices in the trade, or both.   The Granger Collection, New York

Artisans   Shopkeepers, artisans, and wage earners were the single largest group in any city. They were grocers, butchers, fishmongers, carpenters, cabinetmakers, smiths, printers, hand-loom weavers, and tailors, to give a few examples. They had their own culture, values, and institutions. Like the peasants, they were, in many respects, conservative. Their economic position was vulnerable. If a poor harvest raised the price of food, their own businesses suffered. These urban classes also contributed to the revolution in consumption, however. They could buy more goods than ever before, and, to the extent their incomes permitted, many of them sought to copy the domestic consumption of the middle class.

The lives of these artisans and shopkeepers centered on their work and their neighborhoods. They usually lived near or at their place of employment. Most of them worked in shops with fewer than a half dozen other artisans. Their primary institution had historically been the guild, but by the eighteenth century, the guilds rarely exercised the influence their predecessors had in medieval or early modern Europe.

Nevertheless, the guilds were not to be ignored. They played a conservative role. Rather than seeking economic growth or innovation, they tried to preserve the jobs and skills of their members. In many countries, the guilds still determined who could pursue a craft. To lessen competition, they attempted to prevent too many people from learning a particular skill.

The guilds also provided a framework for social and economic advancement. At an early age, a boy might become an apprentice to learn a craft or trade. After several years, he would be made a journeyman. Still later, if successful and competent, he might become a master. The artisan could also receive social benefits from the guilds, including aid for his family during sickness or the promise of admission for his son. The guilds were the chief protection for artisans against the workings of the commercial market. They were particularly strong in central Europe.

THE URBAN RIOT

The artisan class, with its generally conservative outlook, maintained a rather fine sense of social and economic justice based largely on traditional practices. If they felt that what was economically "just" had been offended, artisans frequently manifested their displeasure by rioting. The most sensitive area was the price of bread, the staple food of the poor. If a baker or a grain merchant announced a price that was considered unjustly high, a riot might well ensue. Artisan leaders would confiscate the bread or grain and sell it for what the urban crowd considered a "just price." They would then give the money paid for the grain or bread to the baker or merchant.

The danger of bread riots restrained the greed of merchants. Such disturbances represented a collective method of imposing the "just price" in place of the price the commercial marketplace set. Thus, bread and food riots, which occurred throughout Europe, were not irrational acts of screaming, hungry people, but highly ritualized social phenomena of the Old Regime and its economy of scarcity.

Other kinds of riots also characterized eighteenth-century society and politics. The riot was a way in which people who were excluded in every other way from the political processes could make their will known. Sometimes religious bigotry led to urban riots. For example, in 1753, London Protestant mobs compelled the government to withdraw an act to legalize Jewish naturalization. In 1780, the same rabidly Protestant spirit manifested itself in the Gordon riots. Lord George Gordon (1751–1793) had raised the specter of an imaginary Catholic plot after the government relieved military recruits from having to take specifically anti-Catholic oaths.

In these riots and in food riots, violence was normally directed against property rather than people. The rioters themselves were not disreputable people but usually small shopkeepers, freeholders, artisans, and wage earners. They usually wanted only to restore a traditional right or practice that seemed endangered. Nevertheless, their actions could cause considerable turmoil and destruction.

During the last half of the century, urban riots increasingly involved political ends. Though often simultaneous with economic disturbances, the political riot always had nonartisan leadership or instigators. In fact, an eighteenth-century "crowd" was often the tool of the upper classes. In Paris, the aristocratic *Parlement* often urged crowd action in its disputes with the monarchy. In Geneva, middle-class citizens supported artisan riots against the local oligarchy. In Great Britain in 1792, the government incited mobs to attack English sympathizers of the French Revolution. Such outbursts indicate that the crowd or mob had entered the European political and social arena well before the revolution in France.

During the Old Regime, European Jews were separated from non-Jews, typically in districts known as ghettos. Relegated to the least desirable section of a city or to rural villages, most lived in poverty. This watercolor painting depicts a street in Kazimlesz, the Jewish quarter of Kraków, Poland. Judaica Collection, Max Berger, Vienna, Austria. Photograph © Erich Lessing/Art Resource, NY

THE JEWISH POPULATION: THE AGE OF THE GHETTO

Although the small Jewish communities of Amsterdam and other Western European cities became famous for their intellectual life and financial institutions, most European Jews lived in Eastern Europe. In the eighteenth century and thereafter, the Jewish population of Europe was concentrated in Poland, Lithuania, and Ukraine, where no fewer than three million Jews dwelled. Perhaps 150,000 Jews lived in the Habsburg lands, primarily Bohemia, around 1760. Fewer than 100,000 Jews lived in Germany. France had approximately 40,000 Jews. England and Holland, each had a Jewish population of fewer than 10,000. There were even smaller groups of Jews elsewhere.

In 1762, Catherine the Great of Russia specifically excluded Jews from a manifesto that welcomed foreigners to settle in Russia. She relaxed the exclusion a few years later, but Jews during her reign often felt they needed assurances of imperial protection for their livelihoods and religious practices against the ordinances of local officials. (See "Belorussian Jews Petition Catherine the Great," page 511.) After the first partition of Poland of 1772, discussed in Chapter 17, the Russian Empire included a large Jewish population, and the number of Jews in Prussia and under Austrian rule also increased.

Jews dwelled in most nations without enjoying the rights and privileges that other subjects had unless monarchs specifically granted them to Jews. Jews were regarded as a kind of resident alien whose residence might well be temporary or changed at the whim of rulers.

No matter where they dwelled, Old Regime Jews lived apart in separate communities from non-Jewish Europeans. These communities might be distinct districts of cities, known as **ghettos**, or in primarily Jewish villages in the countryside. Jews were also treated as a distinct people religiously and legally. In Poland for much of the century, they were virtually self-governing. In other areas, they lived under the burden of discriminatory legislation. Except in England, Jews could not and did not mix in the mainstream of the societies in which they dwelled. This period, which may be said to have begun with the expulsion of the Jews from Spain at the end of the fifteenth century, is known as the age of the ghetto, or separate community.

During the seventeenth century, a few Jews had helped finance the wars of major rulers. These financiers often became close to the rulers and were known as "court Jews." Perhaps the most famous was Samuel Oppenheimer (1630–1703), who helped the Habsburgs finance their struggle against the Turks and the defense of Vienna. However, these loans were often not repaid. The court Jews and their financial abilities became famous. They tended to marry among themselves.

Most European Jews, however, lived in poverty. They occupied the most undesirable sections of cities or poor villages. Some were small-time moneylenders, but most worked at the lowest occupations. Their religious beliefs, rituals, and community set them apart. Virtually all laws and social institutions kept them socially inferior to and apart from their Christian neighbors.

Under the Old Regime, it is important to emphasize that this discrimination was based on religious separateness. Jews who converted to Christianity were welcomed, even if not always warmly, into the major political and social institutions of gentile European society. Until the last two decades of the eighteenth century, in every part of Europe, however, those Jews who remained loyal to their faith were subject to various religious, civil, and social disabilities. They could not pursue the professions freely, they often could not change residence without official permission, and they were excluded from the political structures of the nations in which they lived. Jews could be expelled from their homes, and their property could be confiscated. They could be required to listen to sermons that insulted their religion. Their children could be taken away from them and given Christian instruction. They knew their non-Jewish neighbors might suddenly turn against them and kill them.

In subsequent chapters, it will be shown how the end of the Old Regime brought major changes in the lives of European Jews and in their relationship to the larger culture.

IN PERSPECTIVE

Near the close of the eighteenth century, European society was on the brink of a new era. That society had remained traditional and corporate largely because of an economy of scarcity. Beginning in the eighteenth century, however, the commercial spirit and the values of the marketplace, although not new, were permitted fuller play than ever before in European history.

BELORUSSIAN JEWS PETITION CATHERINE THE GREAT

In the 1780s, through military expansion, Empress Catherine the Great of Russia (see Chapter 17) annexed Belorussia, bringing a new Jewish minority under her imperial government. In response to her decree, governing many aspects of the region's law and economy, Belorussian Jews petitioned the empress to protect certain of their traditional rights regarding the distillation and sale of spirits. They also petitioned for protection in court and for the right to retain their own traditional practices and courts for matters relating to their own community. The petition indicates how in Russia, as elsewhere in Europe, Jews were treated as a people apart. It also illustrates how Jews, like other minorities in Old Regime Europe, sought both to receive the protection of monarchies against arbitrary local officials and to maintain long-standing social practices. The document reveals the Jews' dependence on the goodwill of the non-Jewish community.

■ *How do the petitioners attempt to appeal to long-standing custom to defend their interests? How does the petition suggest that Jewish law and practice, distinct from the rest of the society, governed Jewish social life? In the context of this petition, which non-Jewish authorities may actually or potentially influence Jewish life?*

. . . 2. According to an ancient custom, when the squires built a new village, they summoned the Jews to reside there and gave them certain privileges for several years and then permanent liberty to distill spirits, brew beer and mead, and sell these drinks. On this basis, the Jews built houses and distillation plants at considerable expense. . . . A new decree of Her Imperial Majesty . . . reserved [this right] to the squires. . . . But a decree of the governor-general of Belorussia has now forbidden the squires to farm out distillation in their villages to Jews, even if the squires want to do this. As a result, the poor Jews who built houses in small villages and promoted both this trade and distillation have been deprived of these and left completely impoverished. But until all the Jewish people are totally ruined, the Jewish merchants suffer restraints equally with the poor rural Jews, since their law obliges them to assist all who share their religious faith. They therefore request an imperial decree authorizing the squire, if he wishes, to farm out distillation to Jews in rural areas.

3. Although, with Her Imperial Majesty's permission, Jews may be elected as officials . . . , Jews are allotted fewer votes than other people and hence no Jew can ever attain office. Consequently, Jews have no one to defend them in courts and find themselves in a desperate situation—given their fear and ignorance of Russian—in case of misfortune, even if innocent. To consummate all the good already bestowed, Jews dare to petition that an equal number of electors be required from Jews as from others (or, at least, that in matters involving Jews and non-Jews, a representative from the Jewish community hold equal rights with non-Jews, be present to accompany Jews in court, and attend the interrogation of Jews). But cases involving only Jews (except for promissory notes and debts) should be handled solely in Jewish courts, because Jews assume obligations among themselves, make agreements and conclude all kinds of deals in the Jewish language and in accordance with Jewish rites and laws (which are not known to others). Moreover, those who transgress their laws and order should be judged in Jewish courts. [Similarly, preserve intact all their customs and holidays in the spirit of their faith, as is mercifully assured in the imperial manifesto.]

The newly unleashed commercial spirit led increasingly to a conception of human beings as individuals rather than as members of communities. In particular, that spirit manifested itself in the Agricultural and Industrial Revolutions, as well as in the drive toward greater consumption. Together, those two vast changes in production overcame most of the scarcity that had haunted Europe and the West generally. The accompanying changes in landholding and production would transform the European social structure.

The expansion of population further stimulated change. More people meant more labor, more energy, and more minds contributing to the creation and solution of social difficulties. Cities had to accommodate expanding populations. Corporate groups, such as the guilds, had to confront the existence of a larger labor force. New wealth meant that birth would eventually become less and less a determining factor in social relationships, except for the social roles assigned to the two sexes. Class structure and social hierarchy remained, but the boundaries became more blurred.

Finally, the conflicting ambitions of monarchs, the nobility, and the middle class generated innovation. In the pursuit of new revenues, the monarchs interfered with the privileges of the nobles. In the name of ancient rights, the nobles attempted to secure and expand their existing social privileges. The middle class, in all of its diversity, was growing wealthier from trade, commerce, and the practice of the professions. Its members wanted social prestige and influence equal to their wealth. They resented privileges, frowned on hierarchy, and rejected tradition.

All these factors meant the society of the eighteenth century stood at the close of one era in European history and at the opening of another.

REVIEW QUESTIONS

1. What kinds of privileges separated European aristocrats from other social groups? How did their privileges and influence affect other people living in the countryside? What was the condition of serfs in central and eastern Europe?
2. How would you define the term *family economy*? How did the family economy constrain the lives of women in preindustrial Europe?
3. What caused the Agricultural Revolution? How did the English aristocracy contribute to the Agricultural Revolution? Why did peasants revolt in the eighteenth century?
4. Why did Europe's population increase in the eighteenth century? How did population growth affect consumption?
5. What was the Industrial Revolution and what caused it? Why did Great Britain take the lead in the Industrial Revolution? How did consumers contribute to the Industrial Revolution?
6. How did the distribution of population in cities and towns change? How did the lifestyle of the upper class compare to that of the middle and lower classes? What were some of the causes of urban riots?
7. Where were the largest Jewish populations in eighteenth-century Europe? What was their social and legal position? What were the sources of prejudices against Jews?

SUGGESTED READINGS

J. BLUM, *Lord and Peasant in Russia from the Ninth to the Nineteenth Century* (1961). Remains a classic discussion.
P. DEANE, *The First Industrial Revolution* (1999). A well-balanced and systematic treatment.
P. EARLE, *The Making of the English Middle Class: Business, Community, and Family Life in London, 1660–1730* (1989). The most careful study of the subject.
M. W. FLINN, *The European Demographic System, 1500–1820* (1981). Remains a major summary.
E. HOBSBAWM, *Industry and Empire: The Birth of the Industrial Revolution* (1999). A survey by a major historian of the subject.
K. HONEYMAN, *Women, Gender and Industrialization in England, 1700–1850* (2000). Emphasizes how certain work or economic roles became associated with either men or women.
O. H. HUFTON, *The Poor of Eighteenth-Century France, 1750–1789* (1975). A brilliant study of poverty and the family economy.
A. KAHAN, *The Plow, the Hammer, and the Knout: An Economic History of Eighteenth-Century Russia* (1985). An extensive and detailed treatment.
D. I. KERTZER AND M. BARBAGLI, *The History of the European Family: Family Life in Early Modern Times, 1500–1709* (2001). Broad-ranging essays covering the entire Continent.

S. KING AND G. TIMMONS, *Making Sense of the Industrial Revolution: English Economy and Society, 1700–1850* (2001). Examines the Industrial Revolution through the social institutions that brought it about and were changed by it.

F. E. MANUEL, *The Broken Staff: Judaism Through Christian Eyes* (1992). An important discussion of Christian interpretations of Judaism.

M. OVERTON, *Agricultural Revolution in England: The Transformation of the Agrarian Economy, 1500–1850* (1996). A highly accessible treatment.

P. STEARNS, *The Industrial Revolution in World History* (1998). A broad interpretive account.

D. VALENZE, *The First Industrial Woman* (1995). An elegant, penetrating volume.

E. A. WRIGLEY, *Continuity, Chance and Change: The Character of the Industrial Revolution in England* (1994). A major conceptual reassessment.

DOCUMENTS CD-ROM

Eighteenth-Century Society

16.1 Tortured Execution vs. Prison Rules
16.2 Life in the Eighteenth Century: An Artisan's Journey
16.3 Instructions for a New Law Code
16.4 Jonathan Swift: *A Description of a City Shower*
16.5 The Creation of the Steam Loom
16.6 Protesting the Machines
16.7 G. M. Trevelyan: Chapter XIII from *English Social History*

CHAPTER 16

THE TRANSATLANTIC ECONOMY, TRADE WARS, AND COLONIAL REBELLION

KEY TOPICS

- Europe's mercantilist empires
- Spain's vast colonial empire in the Americas
- Africa, slavery, and the transatlantic plantation economies
- The wars of the mid-eighteenth century in Europe and its colonies
- The struggle for independence in Britain's North American colonies

The mid-eighteenth century witnessed a renewal of European warfare on a worldwide scale. The conflict involved two separate, but interrelated, rivalries. Austria and Prussia fought for dominance in central Europe while Great Britain and France dueled for commercial and colonial supremacy. The wars were long, extensive, and costly in both effort and

General James Wolfe was mortally wounded during his victory over the French at Quebec in 1759. This painting by the American artist Benjamin West (1738–1820) became famous for portraying the dying Wolfe and the officers around him in poses modeled after classical statues.   Getty Images Inc.—Hulton Archive Photos

money. They resulted in a new balance of power on the Continent and on the high seas. Prussia emerged as a great power, and Great Britain gained a world empire.

The expense of these wars led every major European government after the Peace of Paris of 1763 to reconstruct its policies of taxation and finance. Among the results of these policies were the American Revolution, an enlightened absolutism on the Continent, a continuing financial crisis for the French monarchy, and a reform of the Spanish Empire in South America. ■

PERIODS OF EUROPEAN OVERSEAS EMPIRES

Since the Renaissance, European contacts with the rest of the world have gone through four distinct stages. The first was that of the European discovery, exploration, initial conquest, and settlement of the New World. This phase also witnessed the penetration of Southeast Asian markets by Portugal and the Netherlands, which established major imperial outposts and influence in the region. This period closed by the end of the seventeenth century.

During the seventeenth and eighteenth centuries, European maritime nations established overseas empires and set up trading monopolies within them in an effort to magnify their economic strength. As this painting of the Old Custom House Quay in London suggests, trade from these empires and the tariffs imposed on it were expected to generate revenue for the home country. But behind many of the goods carried in the great sailing ships in the harbor and landed on these docks lay the labor of African slaves working on the plantations of North and South America. Samuel Scott "Old Custom House Quay" Collection. V & A Images, The Victoria and Albert Museum, London

The second era—that of the mercantile empires, which are largely the concern of this chapter—was one of colonial trade rivalry among Spain, France, and Great Britain. Although during the sixteenth and seventeenth centuries, differing motives had led to the establishment of overseas European empires, by the eighteenth century they generally existed to foster trade and commerce. These commercial goals, however, often sparked intense rivalry and conflict in key imperial trouble spots. As a result, the various imperial ventures led to the creation of large navies and a series of major naval wars at the mid-century—wars that in turn became linked to warfare on the European continent. The Anglo-French side of the contest has often been compared to a second Hundred Years' War, with theaters of conflict in Europe, the Americas, West Africa, and India.

A fundamental element in these first two periods of European imperial ventures in the Americas was the presence of slavery. By the eighteenth century, the slave population of the New World consisted almost entirely of a black population that had either recently been forcibly imported from Africa or born to slaves whose forebearers had been forcibly imported from Africa. Both the forced migration of so many people from one continent to another and the mid-Atlantic plantation economies that such slave labor supported were unprecedented in history. The creation in the Americas of this slave-based plantation economy led directly to over three centuries of extensive involvement by Europeans and white Americans in the slave trade with Africa—particularly, with the societies of West Africa. In turn, on the American continent the slave trade created extensive communities of Africans from the Chesapeake region of Maryland and Virginia south to Brazil. The Africans brought to the American experience not only their labor, but their languages, customs, and ethnic associations. The Atlantic economy and the societies that arose in the Americas were, consequently, the creation of both Europeans and Africans while, as a result of the Spanish conquest, native Americans were pressed toward the margins of those societies.

Finally, during the second period, both the British colonies of the North American seaboard and the Spanish colonies of Mexico and Central and South America emancipated themselves from European control. This era of independence, part of which is discussed in this chapter and part in Chapter 20, may be said to have closed during the 1820s.

The third stage of European contact with the non-European world occurred in the nineteenth century. During that period, European governments carved out new formal empires involving the direct European administration of indigenous peoples in Africa and Asia. Those nineteenth-century empires also included new areas of European settlement, such as Australia, New Zealand, South Africa, and Algeria. The bases of these empires were trade, national honor, Christian missionary enterprise, and military strategy. Unlike the previous two eras, the nineteenth-century empires were based on formally free labor though they still involved much harsh treatment of non-white indigenous populations.

The last period of the European empire occurred during the mid- and late twentieth century, with the decolonization of peoples who had previously lived under European colonial rule.

During the four-and-one-half centuries before decolonization, Europeans exerted political dominance over much of the rest of the world that was far disproportional to the geographical size or population of Europe. Europeans frequently treated other peoples as social, intellectual, and economic inferiors. They ravaged existing cultures because of greed, religious zeal, or political ambition. These actions are major facts of both European and world history and remain significant factors in the contemporary relationship between Europe and its former colonies, as well as between the United States and those former colonies. What allowed the Europeans initially to exert such influence and domination for so long over so much of the world was not any innate cultural superiority, but a technological supremacy related to naval power and gunpowder. Ships and guns allowed the Europeans to exercise their will almost wherever they chose.

MERCANTILE EMPIRES

Navies and merchant shipping were the keystones of the mercantile empires that were meant to bring profit to a nation rather than to provide areas for settlement. The Treaty of Utrecht (1713) estab-

lished the boundaries of empire during the first half of the eighteenth century.

Except for Brazil, which Portugal governed, and Dutch Guiana, Spain controlled all of mainland South America. In North America, it ruled Florida, Mexico, California, and the Southwest. The Spanish also governed Central America and the islands of Cuba, Puerto Rico, Trinidad, and the eastern part of Hispaniola that is today the Dominican Republic.

The British Empire consisted of the colonies along the North Atlantic seaboard, Nova Scotia, Newfoundland, Bermuda, Jamaica, and Barbados. Britain also possessed a few trading stations on the Indian subcontinent.

The French domains covered the Saint Lawrence River valley and the Ohio and Mississippi River valleys. They included the West Indian islands of Saint Domingue (modern Haiti on the western part of Hispaniola), Guadeloupe, and Martinique, and also stations in India and on the West Coast of Africa. To the French and British merchant communities, India appeared as a vast potential market for European goods, as well as the source of calico cloth and spices that were in much demand in Europe.

The Dutch controlled Surinam, or Dutch Guiana, in South America, Cape Colony in what is today South Africa, and trading stations in West Africa, Sri Lanka, and Bengal in India. Most importantly, they also controlled the trade with Java in what is now Indonesia. The Dutch had opened these markets largely in the seventeenth century and had created a vast trading empire far larger in extent, wealth, and importance than the geographical size of the United Netherlands would have led one to expect. The Dutch had been daring sailors and they made important technological innovations in sailing.

All of these powers and the Danes also possessed numerous smaller islands in the Caribbean. In the eighteenth century, the major rivalries existed among the Spanish, the French, and the British.

MERCANTILIST GOALS

If any formal economic theory lay behind the conduct of eighteenth-century empires, it was mercantilism, that practical creed of hard-headed businesspeople. The terms *mercantilism* and *mercantile system* were invented by later opponents and critics of the system whereby governments heavily regulated trade and commerce in hope of increasing national wealth. Economic writers believed this system necessary for a nation to gain a favorable trade balance of gold and silver bullion. They regarded bullion as the measure of a country's wealth, and a nation was truly wealthy only if it amassed more bullion than its rivals.

The mercantilist statesmen and traders regarded the world as an arena of scarce resources and economic limitations. Mercantilist thinking assumed that only modest levels of economic growth were possible. Such thinking predated the expansion of agricultural and later industrial productivity discussed in the previous chapter. Before such sustained economic growth began, the wealth of one nation was assumed to grow or increase largely at the direct expense of another nation. That is to say, the wealth of one state might expand only if its armies or navies conquered the domestic or colonial territory of another state and thus gained the productive capacity of that area, or if a state expanded its trading monopoly over new territory, or if, by smuggling, it could intrude on the trading monopoly of another state.

From beginning to end, the economic well-being of the home country was the primary concern of mercantilist writers. Colonies existed to provide markets and natural resources for the industries of the home country. In turn, the home country was to protect and administer the colonies. Both sides assumed the colonies were the inferior partner in the relationship. The home country and its colonies were to trade exclusively with each other. To that end, governments tried to forge trade-tight systems of national commerce through navigation laws, tariffs, bounties to encourage production, and prohibitions against trading with the subjects of other monarchs. National monopoly was the ruling principle.

Mercantilist ideas had always been neater on paper than in practice. By the early eighteenth century, mercantilist assumptions were far removed from the economic realities of the colonies. The colonial and home markets simply did not mesh. Spain could not produce enough goods for South America. Economic production in the British North American colonies challenged English manufacturing and led to British attempts to limit certain colonial industries, such as iron and hat making.

Colonists of different countries wished to trade with each other. English colonists could buy sugar more cheaply from the French West Indies than from English suppliers. The traders and merchants of one nation always hoped to break the monopoly of another. For all these reasons, the eighteenth century became what one historian many years ago termed the "golden age of smugglers."[1] Gov-

ernments could not control their subjects' activities. Clashes among colonists could and did bring about conflict between European governments.

FRENCH–BRITISH RIVALRY

Major flash points existed between France and Britain in North America. Their colonists quarreled endlessly with each other. Both groups of settlers coveted the lower Saint Lawrence River valley, upper New England, and, later, the Ohio River valley. There were other rivalries over fishing rights, the fur trade, and alliances with Native Americans.

The heart of the eighteenth-century colonial rivalry in the Americas, however, lay in the West Indies. These islands, close to the American continents, were the jewels of the empire. The West Indies raised tobacco, cotton, indigo, coffee, and, above all, sugar, for which there existed huge markets in Europe. These commodities were becoming part of daily life, especially in Western Europe. They represented one aspect of those major changes in consumption that marked eighteenth-century European culture. Sugar in particular had become a staple rather than a luxury. It was used in coffee, tea, and cocoa, for making candy and preserving fruits, and in the brewing industry. There seemed no limit to its uses, no limit to consumer demand for it, and, for a time, almost no limit to the riches it might bring to plantation owners. Only slave labor allowed the profitable cultivation of these products during the seventeenth and eighteenth centuries. (See "Encountering the Past: Sugar Enters the Western Diet," page 526.)

India was another area of French–British rivalry. In India, both France and Britain traded through privileged chartered companies that enjoyed a legal monopoly. The East India Company was the English institution; the French equivalent was the *Compagnie des Indes*. The trade of India and Asia figured only marginally in the economics of the empire. Nevertheless, enterprising Europeans always hoped to develop profitable commerce with India. Others regarded India as a springboard into the even larger potential market of China. The original European footholds in India were trading posts called *factories*. They existed through privileges granted by various Indian governments.

Two circumstances in the mid-eighteenth century changed this situation in India. First, the administration and government of several Indian states had decayed. Second, Joseph Dupleix (1697–1763) for the French and Robert Clive (1725–1774) for the British saw the developing power vacuum as providing opportunities for ex-

[1]Walter Dorn, *Competition for Empire, 1740–1763* (New York: Harper, 1940), p. 266.

panding the control of their respective companies. To maintain their own security and to expand their privileges, each of the two companies began in effect to take over the government of some of the regions. Each group of Europeans hoped to checkmate the other.

The Dutch maintained their extensive commercial empire further to the east in what today is Indonesia. By the eighteenth century, the other European powers more or less acknowledged Dutch predominance in that region.

THE SPANISH COLONIAL SYSTEM

Spanish control of its American Empire involved a system of government and a system of monopolistic trade regulation. Both were more rigid in appearance than in practice. Actual government was often informal, and the trade monopoly was frequently breached. Until the mid-eighteenth century, the primary purpose of the Spanish Empire was to supply Spain with the precious metals mined in the New World.

COLONIAL GOVERNMENT

Because Queen Isabella of Castile (r. 1474–1504) had commissioned Columbus, the technical legal link between the New World and Spain was the crown of Castile. Its powers both at home and in America were subject to few limitations. The Castilian monarch assigned the government of America to the Council of the Indies, which, with the monarch, nominated the viceroys of New Spain (Mexico) and Peru. These viceroys served as the chief executives in the New World and carried out the laws issued by the Council of the Indies.

Each of the viceroyalties was divided into several subordinate judicial councils, known as *audiencias.* There was also a variety of local officers, the most important of which were the *corregidores,* who presided over municipal councils. All of these officers represented a vast array of patronage, which the monarchy usually bestowed on persons born in Spain. Virtually all power flowed from the top of this political structure downward; in effect, local initiative or self-government scarcely existed.

TRADE REGULATION

The colonial political structures functioned largely to support Spanish commercial self-interests. The *Casa de Contratación* (House of Trade) in Seville regulated all trade with the New World. Cádiz was the only port authorized for use in the American trade. The *Casa* was the most influential institution of the Spanish Empire. Its members worked closely with the *Consulado* (Merchant Guild) of Seville and other groups involved with American commerce in Cádiz.

A complicated system of trade and bullion fleets administered from Seville maintained Spain's trade monopoly. Each year, a fleet of commercial vessels (the *flota*), controlled by Seville merchants and escorted by warships, carried merchandise from Spain to a few specified ports in America, including Portobello, Veracruz, and Cartagena on the Atlantic coast. (See "Visitors Describe the Portobello Fair," page 520.) There were no authorized ports on the Pacific Coast. Areas far to the south, such as Buenos Aires on the Río de la Plata, received goods only after the shipments had been unloaded at one of the authorized ports. After selling their wares, the ships were loaded with silver and gold bullion; they usually spent the winter in heavily fortified Caribbean ports, and then sailed back to Spain. The *flota* system always worked imperfectly, but trade outside it was illegal. Regulations prohibited the Spanish colonists within the American Empire from establishing direct trade with each other and from building their own shipping and commercial industry. Foreign merchants were also forbidden to breach the Spanish monopoly.

COLONIAL REFORM UNDER THE SPANISH BOURBON MONARCHS

A crucial change occurred in the Spanish colonial system in the early eighteenth century. The War of the Spanish Succession (1701–1714) and the Treaty of Utrecht (1713) replaced the Spanish Habsburgs with the Bourbons of France on the Spanish throne. Philip V (r. 1700–1746) and his successors tried to use French administrative skills to reassert the imperial trade monopoly, which had decayed under the last Spanish Habsburgs, and thus to improve the domestic economy and revive Spanish power in Europe.

Under Philip V, Spanish coastal patrol vessels tried to suppress smuggling in American waters. (See "Buccaneers Prowl the High Seas," page 521.) An incident arising from this policy led to war with England in 1739, the year in which Philip established the viceroyalty of New Granada in the area that today includes Venezuela, Colombia, and Ecuador. The goal was to strengthen the royal government there.

VISITORS DESCRIBE THE PORTOBELLO FAIR

The Spanish tried to restrict all trade within their Latin American Empire to a few designated ports. Each year, a fair was held in some of these ports. The most famous such port was Portobello on the Isthmus of Panama. In the 1730s, two visitors described the event. This fair was the chief means of facilitating trade between the western coast of South America and Spain.

■ *What products were sold at the fair? How does this passage illustrate the inefficiency of monopoly trade in the Spanish Empire and the many chances for smuggling?*

The town of Portobello, so thinly inhabited, by reason of its noxious air, the scarcity of provisions, and the soil, becomes, at the time of the [Spanish] galleons one of the most populous places in all South America. . . .

The ships are no sooner moored in the harbour, than the first work is, to erect, in the square, a tent made of the ship's sails, for receiving its cargo; at which the proprietors of the goods are present, in order to find their bales, by the marks which distinguish them. These bales are drawn on sledges, to their respective places by the crew of every ship, and the money given them is proportionally divided.

Whilst the seamen and European traders are thus employed, the land is covered with droves of mules from Panama, each drove consisting of above a hundred, loaded with chests of gold and silver, on account of the merchants of Peru. Some unload them at the exchange, others in the middle of the square; yet, amidst the hurry and confusion of such crowds, no theft, loss, or disturbance is ever known. He who has seen this place during the *tiempo muerto,* or dead time, solitary, poor, and a perpetual silence reigning everywhere; the harbour quite empty, and every place wearing a melancholy aspect; must be filled with astonishment at the sudden change, to see the bustling multitudes, every

house crowded, the square and streets encumbered with bales and chests of gold and silver of all kinds; the harbour full of ships and vessels, some bringing by the way of Rio de Chape the goods of Peru, such as *cacao, quinquina,* or Jesuit's bark, Vicuña wool, and bezoar stones; others coming from Carthagena, loaded with provisions; and thus a spot, at all times detested for its deleterious qualities, becomes the staple of the riches of the old and new world, and the scene of one of the most considerable branches of commerce in the whole earth.

The ships being unloaded, and the merchants of Peru, together with the president of Panama, arrived, the fair comes under deliberation. And for this purpose the deputies of the several parties repair on board the commodore of the galleons, where, in the presence of the commodore, and the president of Panama, . . . the prices of the several kinds of merchandizes are settled. . . . The purchases and sales, as likewise the exchanges of money, are transacted by brokers, both from Spain and Peru. After this, every one begins to dispose of his goods; the Spanish brokers embarking their chests of money, and those of Peru sending away the goods they have purchased, in vessels called *chatas* and *bongos,* up the river Chagres. And thus the fair of Portobello ends.

From George Juan and Antonio de Ulloa, *A Voyage to South America,* Vol. 1 (London, 1772), pp. 103–110, as quoted in Benjamin Keen, ed., *Readings in Latin-American Civilization, 1492 to the Present* (New York: Houghton Mifflin, 1955), pp. 107–108.

The great mid-century wars exposed the vulnerability of the Spanish empire to naval attack and economic penetration. As an ally of France, Spain emerged as one of the defeated powers in 1763. Government circles became convinced that the colonial system had to be reformed.

Charles III (r. 1759–1788), the most important of the imperial reformers, attempted to reassert Spain's control of the empire. Like his Bourbon predecessors, Charles emphasized royal ministers rather than councils. Thus, the role of both the Council of the Indies and the *Casa de*

BUCCANEERS PROWL THE HIGH SEAS

By no means did all of the trade in the Caribbean Sea occur at the Portobello fair described on page 520. Piracy was a major problem for transatlantic trade. There was often a fine line between freewheeling buccaneering pirates operating for their own gain and privateers who in effect worked for various European governments that wanted to penetrate the commercial monopoly of the Spanish Empire. Alexander Exquemelin was a ship's surgeon who for a time plied his trade on board a pirate ship and then later settled in Holland. His account of those days emphasizes the careful code of conduct among the pirates themselves and the harshness of their behavior toward both those on ships they captured and poor farmers and fishermen whom they robbed and virtually enslaved.

■ *How did the restrictive commercial policy of the Spanish Empire encourage piracy and privateering? Was there a code of honor among the pirates? What kinds of people may have suffered most from piracy? To what extent did pirates have any respect for individual freedom? How romantic was the real world of pirates?*

When a buccaneer is going to sea he sends word to all who wish to sail with him. When all are ready, they go on board, each bringing what he needs in the way of weapons, powder, and shot.

On the ship, they first discuss where to go and get food supplies. . . . The meat is either [salted] pork or turtle. . . . Sometimes they go and plunder the Spaniards' *corrales*, which are pens where they keep perhaps a thousand head of tame hogs. The rovers . . . find the house of the farmer . . . [whom] unless he gives them as many hogs as they demand, they hang . . . without mercy. . . .

When a ship has been captured, the men decide whether the captain should keep it or not: if the prize is better than their own vessel, they take it and set fire to the other. When a ship is robbed, nobody must plunder and keep the loot to himself. Everything taken . . . must be shared . . . , without any man enjoying a penny more than his fair share. To prevent deceit, before the booty is distributed everyone has to swear an oath on the Bible that he has not kept for himself so much as the value of a sixpence. . . . And

should any man be found to have made a false oath, he would be banished from the rovers, and never be allowed in their company. . . .

When they have captured a ship, the buccaneers set the prisoners on shore as soon as possible, apart from two or three whom they keep to do the cooking and other work they themselves do not care for, releasing these men after two or three years.

The rovers frequently put in for fresh supplies at some island or other, often . . . lying off the south coast of Cuba. . . . Everyone goes ashore and sets up his tent, and they take turns to go on marauding expeditions in their canoes. They take prisoner . . . poor men who catch and set turtles for a living, to provide for their wives and children. Once captured, these men have to catch turtle for the rovers as long as they remain on the island. Should the rovers intend to cruise along a coast where turtle abound, they take the fishermen along with them. The poor fellows may be compelled to stay away from their wives and families four or five years, with no news whether they are alive or dead.

Alexander O. Exquemelin, *The Buccaneers of America*, trans. by Alexis Brown, (Baltimore: Penguin Books, 1969), pp. 70–72.

Contratación diminished. After 1765, Charles abolished the monopolies of Seville and Cádiz and permitted other Spanish cities to trade with America. He also opened more South American and Caribbean ports to trade and authorized commerce between Spanish ports in America. In 1776, he organized a fourth viceroyalty in the region of Río de la Plata, which included much of present-day Argentina, Uruguay, Paraguay, and Bolivia. (See Map 16–1, page 522.)

MAP ▷ EXPLORATION

Interactive map: To explore this map further, go to http://www.prenhall.com/kagan/map16.1

DISPUTED BY
ENGLAND,
RUSSIA,
AND SPAIN

VICEROYALTY
OF
NEW SPAIN

Rio Grande

A T L A N T I C

O C E A N

EFFECTIVE FRONTIER OF
SPANISH SETTLEMENT

Gulf of Mexico

Mexico
City
Veracruz

Santo Domingo
Caribbean Sea

Portobelo   Cartagena   Caracas

VICEROYALTY OF
NEW GRANADA
Separated From
Viceroyalty of
Peru,
1717, 1739

GUIANA

Bogotá

Quito

Amazon R.

VICEROYALTY
OF
PERU

VICEROYALTY
OF
BRAZIL

Pernambuco

Lima

Bahia

P A C I F I C

O C E A N

Portosi

São Paulo

Rio de Janeiro

VICEROYALTY
OF
LA PLATA
Separated From the
Viceroyalty of Peru,
1776

Santiago

Buenos
Aires

AUDIENCIA
OF CHILE

Claimed but not
settled by Spain

Map 16–1   VICEROYALTIES IN LATIN AMERICA IN 1780   The late eighteenth-century viceroyalties in Latin America display the effort of the Spanish Bourbon monarchy to establish more direct control of the colonies. They sought this control through the introduction of more royal officials and by establishing more governmental districts.

The Silver Mines of Potosí. Worked by conscripted Indian laborers under extremely harsh conditions, these mines provided Spain with a vast treasure in silver.   Hulton/Corbis-Bettmann

To increase the efficiency of tax collection and end bureaucratic corruption, Charles III introduced the institution of the *intendant* into the Spanish Empire. These loyal, royal bureaucrats were patterned on the French *intendants* made so famous and effective as agents of French royal administration under the absolutism of Louis XIV.

The late-eighteenth-century Bourbon reforms did stimulate the imperial economy. Trade expanded and became more varied. These reforms, however, also brought the empire more fully under direct Spanish control. Many **peninsulares** (persons born in Spain) entered the New World to fill new posts, which were often the most profitable jobs in the region. Expanding trade brought more Spanish merchants to Latin America. The economy remained export oriented, and their economic life was still organized to benefit Spain. As a result of these policies, the **creoles** (persons of European descent born in the Spanish colonies) came to feel they were second-class subjects. In time, their resentment would provide a major source of the discontent leading to the wars of independence in the early nineteenth century. The imperial reforms of Charles III were the Spanish equivalent of the new colonial measures the British government undertook after 1763, which, as will be seen later in this chapter, led to the American Revolution.

BLACK AFRICAN SLAVERY, THE PLANTATION SYSTEM, AND THE ATLANTIC ECONOMY

Within various parts of Europe itself, slavery had existed since ancient times. Before the eighteenth century, little or no moral or religious stigma was attached to slave owning or slave trading. It had a continuous existence in the Mediterranean world, where only the sources of slaves changed over the centuries. After the conquest of Constantinople in 1453, the Ottoman Empire forbade the exportation of white slaves from regions under its control. The Portuguese then began to import African slaves into the Iberian Peninsula from the Canary Islands and West Africa. Black slaves from Africa were also not uncommon in other parts of the Mediterranean, and a few found their way into northern Europe. There they might be used as personal servants or displayed because of the novelty of their color in royal courts or in wealthy homes.

Yet, from the sixteenth century onward, first within the West Indies and the Spanish and Portuguese settlements in South America and then in the British colonies on the South Atlantic seaboard of North America, slave labor became a fundamental social and economic factor. The development of those plantation economies based on slave labor led to an unprecedented interaction between the peoples of Europe and Africa and between the European settlers in the Americas and Africa. From that point onward, Africa and Africans were drawn into the Western experience as never before in history.

THE AFRICAN PRESENCE IN THE AMERICAS

Once they had encountered and begun to settle the New World, the Spanish and Portuguese faced a severe shortage of labor. They and most of the French and English settlers who came later had no intention of undertaking manual work themselves. At first, they used Native Americans as laborers, but during the sixteenth century as well as afterward, disease killed hundreds of thousands of the native population. As a result, labor soon became scarce. The Spanish and Portuguese then turned to the labor of imported African slaves. Settlers in the English colonies of North America during the seventeenth century turned more slowly to slavery, with the largest number coming to the Chesapeake Bay region of Virginia and Maryland and then later into the low country of the Carolinas. Which African peoples became sold into slavery during any given decade largely depended on internal African warfare and state-building. This remained the case until the end of the transatlantic slave trade in the nineteenth century.

The major sources for slaves were slave markets on the West African Coast from Senegambia to Angola. Slavery and an extensive slave trade had ex-

isted in West Africa for centuries. Just as particular social and economic conditions in Europe had led to the voyages of exploration and settlement, political and military conditions in Africa and warfare among various African nations similarly created a supply of slaves that certain African societies were willing to sell to Europeans. European slave traders did not confront a passive situation in West Africa over which they exercised their will by force and commerce. Rather, they encountered dynamic African societies working out their own internal historic power relationships and rivalries in which Africans sold and acquired other Africans from different regions and nations as slaves.

The West Indies, Brazil, and Sugar   To grasp the full impact of the forced immigration of Africans to the Americas, we must take into account both regions and the entire picture of the transatlantic economy. Far more slaves were imported into the West Indies and Brazil than into North America. Although citizens of the United States mark the beginning of slavery in 1619 with the arrival of African slaves on a Dutch ship in Jamestown, Virginia, over a century of slave trading in the West Indies and South America had preceded that event. Indeed, by the late sixteenth century, Africans had become a major social presence in the West Indies and in the major cities of both Spanish and Portuguese South America. Their presence and influence in these regions would grow over the centuries. African labor and African immigrant slave communities were the most prominent social features of these regions, making the development of their economies and cultures what one

This eighteenth-century print shows bound African captives being forced to a slaving port. It was largely African middlemen who captured slaves in the interior and marched them to the coast.   North Wind Picture Archives

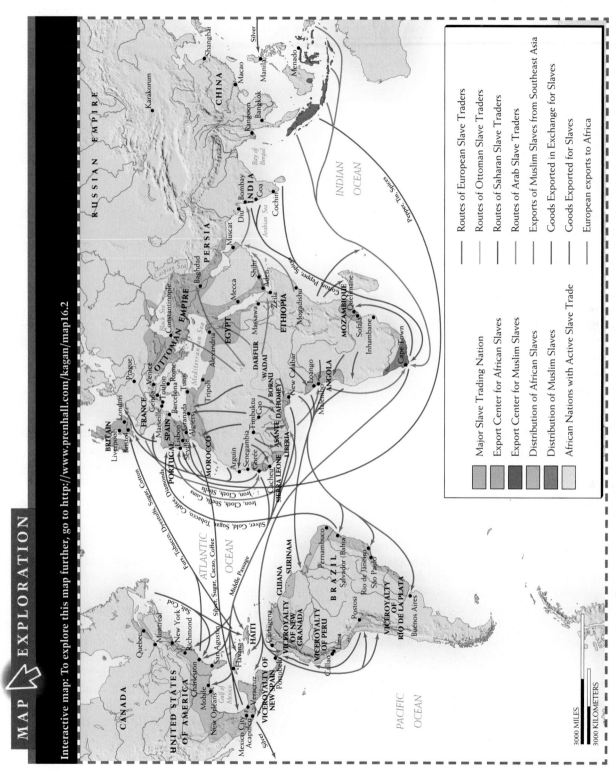

Legend:

- Routes of European Slave Traders
- Routes of Ottoman Slave Traders
- Routes of Saharan Slave Traders
- Routes of Arab Slave Traders
- Exports of Muslim Slaves from Southeast Asia
- Goods Exported in Exchange for Slaves
- Goods Exported for Slaves
- European exports to Africa

- Major Slave Trading Nation
- Export Center for African Slaves
- Export Center for Muslim Slaves
- Distribution of African Slaves
- Distribution of Muslim Slaves
- African Nations with Active Slave Trade

Map 16–2   THE SLAVE TRADE, 1400–1860   Slavery is an ancient institution and complex slave-trading routes were in existence in Africa, the Middle East, and Asia for centuries, but it was the need to supply labor for the plantations of the Americas that led to the greatest movement of peoples across the face of the earth.

SUGAR ENTERS THE WESTERN DIET

Before the European discovery of the Americas, sugar was a luxury product that only the wealthy could afford. Because it requires subtropical temperatures and heavy rainfall, sugarcane could not be grown in Europe. Sugar had to be imported, at great expense, from the Arab world or from the Spanish and Portuguese islands off the coast of Africa, which were too arid for the plant to flourish.

The Caribbean, however, is ideal for sugarcane. Columbus carried it to the New World in 1493, and within about a decade sugar was being cultivated—by slaves—on Santo Domingo.

Yet, sugar production did not begin to soar until Britain and France established themselves in the Caribbean in the seventeenth century and the demand for sugar began to grow in Europe, first slowly and then insatiably. By the eighteenth century, the small British and French islands in the Caribbean where sugar was produced by African slave labor had become some of the most valuable real estate on earth.

Whereas the North American colonies imported Caribbean molasses to make rum, Europeans desired sugar to sweeten other foods. Sugar, the largest colonial import into Britain, embodied the mercantile policy of a closed economic system. It was raised in British colonies, paid for by British exports, shipped on British ships, insured by British firms, refined in British cities, and consumed on British tables.

The voracious demand for sugar as a sweetener was tied up with three other tropical products—coffee, tea, and chocolate—that European consumers began to drink in enormous quantities in the seventeenth and eighteenth centuries. Each of these beverages is a stimulant, which helps explain their popularity, but by themselves they taste bitter. Sugar made them palatable to European consumers. The demand for sugar and these drinks became mutually reinforcing. As the markets for coffee, chocolate, and especially tea grew in England and the English colonies, so did the demand for sugar.

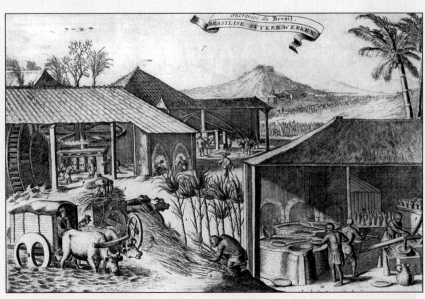

Sugar was both raised and processed on plantations such as this one in Brazil.
© Hulton-Deutsch Collection/CORBIS

As the production of sugar rose, its price fell. The cheaper sugar became, the more of it Europeans consumed. By the end of the eighteenth century, tea with sugar was cheaper than beer or milk, and it had become the most popular drink among the British poor (while remaining an elegant drink for the wealthy). Moreover, because sugar had originally been a luxury item, people felt they were improving their standard of living if they consumed more of it.

During the nineteenth century, sugar consumption continued to expand, and sugar became even cheaper when free-trade policies reduced protective import duties and when the French began to manufacture it from sugar beets, which could easily be grown in Europe. Nineteenth-century Westerners developed the custom of ending a meal with dessert, food usually sweetened with sugar.

- *How did the colonization of the Americas affect the European demand for sugar? Why did sugar consumption increase so rapidly in Europe during the eighteenth and nineteenth centuries?*

Sidney Mintz, *Sweetness and Power: The Place of Sugar in Modern History* (New York: Penguin Books, 1985).

historian has described as "a Euro-African phenomenon."[2] In these places, African slaves equaled or more generally surpassed the numbers of white European settlers in what soon constituted multiracial societies. Someone passing through the marketplace of these towns and cities would have heard a vast number of African, as well as European, languages. Although Native American labor continued to be exploited on the South American continent, it was increasingly a marginal presence in the ever-expanding African slave-based plantation economy of the Atlantic seaboard, the Caribbean, and offshore islands.

Within much of Spanish South America, the numbers of slaves declined during the late seventeenth century, and slavery became somewhat less fundamental there than elsewhere. Slavery continued to expand its influence, however, in Brazil and in the Caribbean through the spreading cultivation of sugar to meet the demand of the European market. By the close of the seventeenth century, the Caribbean islands were the world center for the production of sugar and the chief supplier for the ever-growing demand for it. The opening of new areas of cultivation and other economic enterprises required additional slaves during the eighteenth century, a period of major slave importation. The growing prosperity of sugar islands that had begun to be exploited in the late seventeenth century, as well as the new sugar, coffee, and tobacco regions of Brazil, where gold mining also required additional slaves, accounts for this increase in slave commerce and allowed higher prices to be paid for slaves. In Brazil, the West Indies, and the southern British colonies, prosperity and slavery went hand in hand.

A vast increase in the number of Africans brought as slaves to the Americas occurred during the eighteenth century, with most arriving in the Caribbean or Brazil. Early in the century, as many as 20,000 new Africans a year arrived in the West Indies as slaves. By 1725, it has been estimated that almost 90 percent of the population of Jamaica consisted of black slaves. After the mid-century, the numbers were even larger. The influx of new Africans in most areas—even in the British colonies—meant the numbers of new forced immigrants outnumbered the slaves of African descent already present.

Newly imported African slaves were needed because the fertility rate of the earlier slave population was low and the death rate high from disease, overwork, and malnutrition. The West Indies

proved to be a particularly difficult region in which to secure a stable, self-reproducing slave population. The conditions for slaves there led to high rates of mortality with new slaves coming primarily from the ongoing slave trade. A similar situation prevailed in Brazil. Restocking through the slave trade meant the slave population of those areas consisted of African-born persons rather than of persons of African descent. Consequently, one of the key factors in the social life of many of the areas of American slavery during the eighteenth century was the presence of persons newly arrived from Africa, carrying with them African languages, religion, culture, and local African ethnic identities that they would infuse into the already existing slave communities. Thus, the eighteenth century witnessed an enormous new African presence throughout the Americas.

SLAVERY AND THE TRANSATLANTIC ECONOMY

Different nations dominated the slave trade in different periods. During the sixteenth century, the Portuguese and the Spanish were most involved. The Dutch supplanted them during most of the seventeenth century. Thereafter, during the late seventeenth and eighteenth centuries, the English were the chief slave traders. French traders also participated in the trade.

Slavery touched most of the economy of the transatlantic world. (See Map 16–2, page 525). Colonial trade followed roughly a geographic triangle. European goods—often guns—were carried to Africa to be exchanged for slaves, who were then taken to the West Indies, where they were traded for sugar and other tropical products, which were then shipped to Europe. Not all ships covered all three legs of the triangle. Another major trade pattern existed between New England and the West Indies with New England fish, rum, or lumber being traded for sugar. At various times, the prosperity of such cities as Amsterdam, Liverpool, England, and Nantes, France, rested largely on the slave trade. Cities in the British North American colonies, such as Newport, Rhode Island, profited from slavery sometimes by trading in slaves, but more often by supplying other goods to the West Indian market. All the shippers who handled cotton, tobacco, and sugar depended on slavery, though they might not have had direct contact with the institution, as did all the manufacturers and merchants who produced finished products for the consumer market.

As had been the case during previous centuries, eighteenth-century political turmoil in Africa, such as the civil wars in the Kingdom of Kongo, increased the supply of slaves during that period.

[2]John Thornton, *Africa and the Africans in the Making of the Atlantic World, 1400–1800*, 2nd ed. (Cambridge, UK: Cambridge University Press, 1998), p. 140.

These Kongo wars had originated in a dispute over succession to the throne in the late seventeenth century and continued into the eighteenth. Some captives were simply sold to European slave traders calling at ports along the West African coast. Other African leaders conducted slave raids, so their captives could be sold to finance the purchase of more weapons. Similar political unrest and turmoil in the Gold Coast area (modern Ghana) during the eighteenth century increased the supply of African captives to be sold into American slavery. Consequently, warfare in West Africa, often far into the interior, and the economic development of the American Atlantic seaboard were closely related.

THE EXPERIENCE OF SLAVERY

The Portuguese, Spanish, Dutch, French, and English slave traders forcibly transported several million (perhaps more than nine million; the exact numbers are disputed) Africans to the New World—the largest forced intercontinental migration in human history. During the first four centuries of settlement, far more black slaves came involuntarily to the New World than did free European settlers or European indentured servants. The conditions of slaves' passage across the Atlantic were wretched. Quarters were unspeakably cramped, food was bad, disease was rampant. Many Africans died during the crossing. (See "A Slave Trader Describes the Atlantic Passage," page 530.) There were always more African men than women transported, so it was difficult to preserve traditional African extended family structures. During the passage and later, many Africans attempted to recreate such structures among themselves, even if they were not actually related by direct family ties.

In the Americas, the slave population was divided among new Africans recently arrived, old Africans who had lived there for some years, and creoles who were the descendants of earlier generations of African slaves. Plantation owners preferred the two latter groups, who were already accustomed to the life of slavery. They sold for higher prices. The newly arrived Africans were subjected to a process known as *seasoning*, during which they were prepared for the laborious discipline of slavery and made to understand that they were no longer free. The process might involve receiving new names, acquiring new work skills, and learning, to some extent, the local European language. Some newly arrived Africans worked in a kind of apprentice relationship to an older African slave of similar ethnic background. Other slaves were broken into slave labor through work on field gangs. Occasionally, plantation owners preferred to buy younger Africans, whom they thought might be more easily acculturated to the labor conditions of the Americas. Generally, North American plantation owners were only willing to purchase such recently arrived Africans seasoned in the West Indies.

Language and Culture　The plantation to which the slaves eventually arrived always lay in a more or less isolated rural setting, but its inhabitants could usually visit their counterparts on other plantations or in nearby towns on market days. Within the sharply restricted confines of slavery, the recently arrived Africans were able, at least for a time, to sustain elements of their own culture and social structures. From the West Indies southward throughout the eighteenth century, there were more people whose first language was African rather than European. For example, Coromantee was the predominant language on Jamaica. In South Carolina and on St. Domingue, most African slaves spoke Kikongo to each other. It would take more than two generations for the colonial language to dominate, and even then the result was often a dialect combining an African and a European language.

Through these languages, Africans on plantation estates could organize themselves into nations with similar, though not necessarily identical, ethnic ties to regions of West Africa. The loyalty achieved through a shared African language in the American setting created a solidarity among African slaves that was wider than what in Africa had probably been a primary loyalty to a village. These nations that the plantation experience organized and sustained also became the basis for a wide variety of religious communities among African slaves that had roots in their African experience. In this manner, some Africans maintained a loyalty to the Islamic faith of their homeland.

Many of the African nations on plantations, such as those of Brazil, organized lay religious brotherhoods that carried out various kinds of charitable work within the slave communities. In the Americas, the various African nations would elect their own kings and queens, who might preside over gatherings of the members of the nation drawn from various plantations.

The shared language of a particular African nation in the Americas enabled the slaves to communicate among themselves during revolts such as that in South Carolina in 1739, in Jamaica in the early 1760s, and, most successfully, during the Haitian Revolution of the 1790s. In the South Carolina revolt, the slave owners believed their slaves had communicated among themselves by playing

African drums. In the aftermath of the revolt, the owners attempted to suppress such drum playing in the slave community.

Daily Life The life conditions of plantation slaves differed from colony to colony. Black slaves living in Portuguese areas had the fewest legal protections. In the Spanish colonies, the church attempted to provide some protection for black slaves, but devoted more effort toward the welfare of Native Americans. Slave codes were developed in the British and the French colonies during the seventeenth century, but they provided only the most limited protection to slaves while assuring dominance to their owners. Slave owners always feared a revolt, and legislation and other regulations were intended to prevent one. All slave laws favored the master rather than the slave. Slave masters were permitted to whip slaves and inflict other harsh corporal punishment. Furthermore, slaves were often forbidden to gather in large groups lest they plan a revolt. In most of these slave societies, the law did not recognize slave marriages. Legally, the children of slaves were slaves, and the owner of their parents owned them too.

The daily life of most slaves during these centuries involved hard agricultural labor, poor diet, and inadequate housing. Owners could separate slave families, or their members could be sold separately after owners died. The slaves' welfare and their lives were sacrificed to the continuing expansion of the sugar, rice, and tobacco plantations that made their owners wealthy and that produced goods for European consumers. Scholars have sometimes concluded that slaves in one area lived better than in another. Today, it is generally accepted that all the slaves in plantation societies led exposed and difficult lives with little variation among them.

Conversion to Christianity Most African slaves transported to the Americas were, like the Native Americans, eventually converted to Christianity. In the Spanish, French, and Portuguese domains, they became Roman Catholics. In the English colonies, most became Protestants of one denomination or another. Both forms of Christianity preached to slaves to accept both their slavery and a natural social hierarchy with their masters at the top.

Slaves on the plantations of the American South were the chattel property of their masters, and their lives were grim. Some artists sought to disguise this harsh reality by depicting the lighter moments of slave society as in this scene of slaves dancing.   Getty Images Inc.—Hulton Archive Photos

Although organized African religion eventually disappeared in the Americas, especially in the British colonies, some African religious practices survived in muted forms, gradually separated from African religious belief. These included an African understanding of nature and the cosmos, and the belief in witches and other people with special spiritual powers, such as conjurers, healers, and voodoo practitioners. Although slaves did manage to mix Christianity with their previous African religions, their conversion to Christianity was nonetheless another example, like that of the Native Americans, of the crushing of a set of non-European cultural values in the context of the New World economies and social structures.

European Racial Attitudes The European settlers in the Americas and the slave traders also carried with them prejudices against black Africans. Many Europeans considered Africans to be savages or less than civilized. Still others looked down on them simply because they were slaves. Both Christians and Muslims had shared these attitudes in the Mediterranean world, where slavery had existed for so long. Furthermore, many European languages and cultures attached negative connotations to the idea and image of blackness. In virtually all these plantation societies, race was an important element in keeping black slaves in subservience. Although racial thinking about slavery became important primarily in the nineteenth century, that slaves were black and masters were white was as fundamental to the system as that slaves were chattel property.

A SLAVE TRADER DESCRIBES
THE ATLANTIC PASSAGE

During 1693 and 1694, Captain Thomas Phillips carried slaves from Africa to Barbados on the ship Hannibal. *The financial backer of the voyage was the Royal African Company of London, which held an English crown monopoly on slave trading. Phillips sailed to the west coast of Africa, where he purchased the Africans who were sold into slavery by an African king. Then he set sail westward.*

■ *Who are the various people described in this document who in one way or another were involved in or profited from the slave trade? What dangers did the Africans face on the voyage? What contemporary attitudes could have led this captain to treat and think of his human cargo simply as goods to be transported? What are the grounds of his self-pity for the difficulties he met?*

Having bought my complement of 700 slaves, 480 men and 220 women, and finish'd all my business at Whidaw [on the Gold Coast of Africa], I took my leave of the old king and his *cappasheirs* [attendants], and parted, with many affectionate expressions on both sides, being forced to promise him that I would return again the next year, with several things he desired me to bring from England. . . . I set sail the 27th of July in the morning, accompany'd with the East-India Merchant, who had bought 650 slaves, for the Island of St. Thomas . . . from which we took our departure on August 25th and set sail for Barbadoes.

We spent in our passage from St. Thomas to Barbadoes two months eleven days, from the 25th of August to the 4th of November following: in which time there happened such sickness and mortality among my poor men and Negroes. Of the first we buried 14, and of the last 320, which was a great detriment to our voyage, the Royal African Company losing ten pounds by every slave that died, and the owners of the ship ten pounds ten shillings, being the freight agreed on to be paid by the charter-party for every Negro delivered alive ashore to the African Company's agents at Barbadoes. . . . The loss in all amounted to near 6500 pounds sterling.

The distemper which my men as well as the blacks mostly died of was the white flux, which was so violent and inveterate that no medicine would in the least check it, so that when any of our men were seized with it, we esteemed him a dead man, as he generally proved. . . .

The Negroes are so incident to [subject to] the small-pox that few ships that carry them escape without it, and sometimes it makes vast havoc and destruction among them. But tho' we had 100 at a time sick of it, and that it went thro' the ship, yet we lost not above a dozen by it. All the assistance we gave the diseased was only as much water as they desir'd to drink, and some palm-oil to annoint their sores, and they would generally recover without any other helps but what kind nature gave them. . . .

But what the smallpox spar'd, the flux swept off, to our great regret, after all our pains and care to give them their messes in due order and season, keeping their lodgings as clean and sweet as possible, and enduring so much misery and stench so long among a parcel of creatures nastier than swine, and after all our expectations to be defeated by their mortality. . . .

No gold-finders can endure so much noisome slavery as they do who carry Negroes; for those have some respite and satisfaction, but we endure twice the misery; and yet by their mortality our voyages are ruin'd, and we pine and fret ourselves to death, and take so much pains to so little purpose.

From Thomas Phillips, "Journal," *A Collection of Voyages and Travels*, Vol. 6, ed. by Awnsham and John Churchill (London, 1746), as quoted in Thomas Howard, ed., *Black Voyage: Eyewitness Accounts of the Atlantic Slave Trade* (Boston: Little, Brown, and Company, 1971), pp. 85–87.

A CLOSER LOOK

The Slave Ship *Brookes*
This print records the main decks of the 320-ton slave ship *Brookes*.

The average space for each African destined for slavery in the Americas was 78 inches by 16 inches. The Africans were normally shackled to assure discipline and to prevent their injuring the crew. Iron shackles also prevented Africans from committing suicide on the voyage.

The ship measured 25 feet wide and 100 feet long.

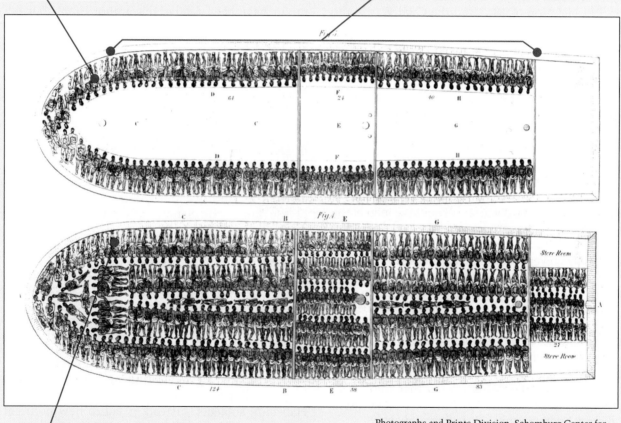

Photographs and Prints Division, Schomburg Center for Research in Black Culture, The New York Public Library, Astor, Lenox and Tilden Foundations

Through the most inhumane use of space efficiency, 609 slaves could be crammed onboard for the nightmarish passage to America. A Parliamentary inquiry in 1788 found that the ship had been designed to carry no more than approximately 450 persons.

(See "A Slave Trader Describes the Atlantic Passage".)

The plantations that stretched from the middle Atlantic colonies of North America through the West Indies and into Brazil constituted a vast corridor of slave societies in which social and economic subordination was based on both involuntary servitude and race. These societies had not existed before the European discovery and exploitation of the Americas. In its complete dependence on slave labor and racial differences, this kind of society was unique in both European and world history. As already noted, its social and economic influence touched not only the plantation societies themselves, but West Africa, Western Europe, and New England. It existed from the sixteenth century through the late nineteenth century, when the emancipation of slaves had been completed through the slave revolt of Saint Domingue (1794), the British outlawing of the slave trade (1807), the Latin American wars of independence, the Emancipation Proclamation of 1863 and the Civil War in the United States, and the Brazilian emancipation of 1888. To the present day, every society in which plantation slavery once existed still contends with the long-term effects of that institution.

MID-EIGHTEENTH-CENTURY WARS

From the standpoint of international relations, the state system of the mid-eighteenth century was quite unstable and tended to lead the major states of Europe into prolonged warfare. The statesmen of the period generally assumed that warfare could further national interests. No forces or powers saw it in their interest to prevent war or maintain peace. Because professional armies and navies fought eighteenth-century wars before the French Revolution, the conflicts rarely affected civilian populations deeply. Wars did not lead to domestic political or social upheaval, and peace did not bring international stability. Consequently, nations often viewed periods of peace at the conclusion of a war simply as opportunities to recoup their strength, so that they could start fighting again to seize another nation's territory or disrupt another empire's trading monopoly.

The two fundamental areas of great power rivalry were the overseas empires and central and eastern Europe. Conflict in one of these regions repeatedly overlapped with conflict in the other, and this interaction influenced strategy and the pattern of alliances among the great powers.

THE WAR OF JENKINS'S EAR

By the mid-eighteenth century, the West Indies had become a hotbed of trade rivalry and illegal smuggling. Much to British chagrin, the Spanish government took its own alleged trading monopoly seriously and maintained coastal patrols, which boarded and searched English vessels to look for contraband.

In 1731, during one such boarding operation, there was a fight, and the Spaniards cut off the ear of an English captain named Robert Jenkins. Thereafter he carried about his severed ear preserved in a jar of brandy. This incident was of little importance until 1738, when Jenkins appeared before the British Parliament, reportedly brandishing his ear as an example of Spanish atrocities to British merchants in the West Indies. The British merchant and West Indian planters lobbied Parliament to relieve Spanish intervention in their trade. Sir Robert Walpole (1676–1745), the British prime minister, could not resist these pressures. In late 1739, Britain went to war with Spain. This war might have been a relatively minor event, but because of developments in continental European politics, it became the opening encounter to a series of European wars fought across the world until 1815.

THE WAR OF THE AUSTRIAN SUCCESSION (1740–1748)

In December 1740, after being king of Prussia for less than seven months, Frederick II (r. 1740–1786) seized the Austrian province of Silesia in eastern Germany. The invasion shattered the provisions of the Pragmatic Sanction (see Chapter 13) and upset the continental balance of power. The young king of Prussia had treated the House of Habsburg simply as another German state rather than as the leading power in the region. Silesia itself rounded out Prussia's possessions, and Frederick was determined to keep his ill-gotten prize.

Maria Theresa Preserves the Habsburg Empire The Prussian seizure of Silesia could have marked the opening of a general hunting season on Habsburg holdings and the beginning of revolts by Habsburg subjects. Instead, it led to new political allegiances. Maria Theresa's (r. 1740–1780) great achievement was not the reconquest of Silesia, which eluded her, but the preservation of the Habsburg Empire as a major political power.

She was then just twenty-three and had succeeded to the Habsburg realms only two months before the invasion. She won loyalty and support from her various subjects not merely through her heroism, but by granting new privileges to the nobility. Most significantly, the empress recognized Hungary as the most important of her crowns and promised the Magyar nobility local

Maria Theresa of Austria provided the leadership that saved the Habsburg Empire from possible disintegration after the Prussian invasion of Silesia in 1740.
Martin van Meytens: "Kaiserin Maria Theresia mit ihrer Familie auf der SchloBterasse von Schobrunn." Kunsthistorisches Museum, Vienna, Austria

autonomy. She thus preserved the Habsburg state, but at considerable cost to the power of the central monarchy.

Hungary would continue to be, as it had been in the past, a particularly troublesome area in the Habsburg Empire. When the monarchy was strong and secure, it could ignore guarantees made to Hungary. When the monarchy was threatened, or when the Magyars could stir up enough opposition, the Habsburgs promised new concessions.

France Draws Great Britain into the War The war over the Austrian succession and the British–Spanish commercial conflict could have remained separate disputes. What united them was the role of France. Just as British merchant interests had pushed Sir Robert Walpole into war, aggressive court aristocrats compelled the elderly Cardinal Fleury (1653–1743), first minister of Louis XV (r. 1715–1774), to abandon his planned naval attack on British trade and instead to support the Prussian aggression against Austria, the traditional enemy of France. This was among the more fateful decisions in French history.

In the first place, aid to Prussia consolidated a new and powerful state in Germany. That new power could, and indeed later did, endanger France. Second, the French move against Austria brought Great Britain into the continental war, as Britain sought to make sure the Low Countries remained in the friendly hands of Austria, not France. In 1744, the British–French conflict expanded beyond the Continent when France supported Spain against Britain in the New World. As a result, French military and economic resources were badly divided. France could not bring sufficient strength to the colonial struggle. Having chosen to continue the old struggle with Austria, France lost the struggle for the future against Great Britain. The war ended in a stalemate in 1748 with the Treaty of Aix-la-Chapelle. Prussia retained Silesia, and Spain renewed Britain's privilege from the Treaty of Utrecht (1713) to import slaves into the Spanish colonies.

THE "DIPLOMATIC REVOLUTION" OF 1756

Although the Treaty of Aix-la-Chapelle had brought peace in Europe, France and Great Britain continued to struggle unofficially in the Ohio River valley and in upper New England. These clashes were the prelude to what is known in American history as the French and Indian War, which formally erupted in the summer of 1755.

Before war commenced again in Europe, however, a dramatic shift of alliances took place, in part, as a result of the events in North America. The British king, George II (r. 1727–1760), who was also the Elector of Hanover in Germany, thought the French might attack Hanover in response to the conflict in America. In January 1756, Britain and

Prussia signed the Convention of Westminster, a defensive alliance aimed at preventing the entry of foreign troops into the German states. Whereas George II feared a French attack on Hanover, Frederick II feared an alliance of Russia and Austria. The convention meant that Great Britain, the ally of Austria since the wars of Louis XIV, had now joined forces with Austria's major eighteenth-century enemy.

Maria Theresa was despondent over this development. It delighted her foreign minister, Prince Wenzel Anton Kaunitz (1711–1794), however. He had long hoped for an alliance with France to help dismember Prussia. The Convention of Westminster made possible this alliance, which would have been unthinkable a few years earlier. France was agreeable because Frederick had not consulted with its ministers before coming to his understanding with Britain. So, in May 1756, France and Austria signed a defensive alliance. Kaunitz had succeeded in completely reversing the direction that French foreign policy had followed since the sixteenth century. France would now fight to restore Austrian supremacy in central Europe.

THE SEVEN YEARS' WAR (1756–1763)

Once again, however, Frederick II precipitated a European war that extended into a colonial theater.

Frederick the Great Opens Hostilities   In August 1756, Frederick II opened what would become the Seven Years' War by invading Saxony. Frederick considered this to be a preemptive strike against a conspiracy by Saxony, Austria, and France to destroy Prussian power. He regarded the invasion as a continuation of the defensive strategy of the Convention of Westminster. The invasion itself, however, created the very destructive alliance that Frederick feared. In the spring of 1757, France and Austria made a new alliance dedicated to the destruction of Prussia. Sweden, Russia, and many of the smaller German states joined them.

Two factors in addition to Frederick's stubborn leadership (it was after this war that he came to be called Frederick the Great) saved Prussia. First, Britain furnished considerable financial aid. Second, in 1762, Empress Elizabeth of Russia (r. 1741–1762) died. Her successor was Tsar Peter III (he was murdered the same year), whose admiration for Frederick was boundless. He immediately made peace with Prussia, thus relieving Frederick of one enemy and allowing him to hold off Austria and France. The Treaty of Hubertusburg of 1763 ended the continental conflict with no significant changes in prewar borders. Silesia remained Pruss-

ian, and Prussia clearly stood among the ranks of the great powers.

William Pitt's Strategy for Winning North America
The survival of Prussia was less impressive to the rest of Europe than were the victories of Great Britain in every theater of conflict. The architect of these victories was William Pitt the Elder (1708–1778), a person of colossal ego and administrative genius. Although he had previously criticized British involvement with the Continent, once he became secretary of state in charge of the war in 1757, he pumped huge sums into the coffers of Frederick the Great. He regarded the German conflict as a way to divert French resources and attention from the colonial struggle. He later boasted of having won America on the plains of Germany.

North America was the center of Pitt's real concern. Put simply, he wanted all of North America east of the Mississippi for Great Britain, and that was what he won. He sent more than 40,000 regular English and colonial troops against the French in Canada. Never had so many soldiers been devoted to colonial warfare. He achieved unprecedented cooperation with the American colonies, whose leaders realized they might finally defeat their French neighbors.

The French government was unwilling and unable to direct similar resources against the English in America. Their military administration was corrupt, the military and political commands in Canada were divided, and France could not adequately supply its North American forces. In September 1759, on the Plains of Abraham, overlooking the valley of the Saint Lawrence River at Quebec City, the British army under James Wolfe defeated the French under Louis

---

CONFLICTS OF THE MID–EIGHTEENTH CENTURY

1713	Treaty of Utrecht
1739	Outbreak of War of Jenkins's Ear between England and Spain
1740	War of the Austrian Succession commences
1748	Treaty of Aix-la-Chapelle
1756	Convention of Westminster between England and Prussia
1756	Seven Years' War opens
1757	Battle of Plassey
1759	British forces capture Quebec
1763	Treaty of Hubertusburg
1763	Treaty of Paris

The English artist Francis Hayman in 1760 portrayed the victory in 1757 of Robert Clive over the Siraj-ud-daulah, the Mughal Nawab of Bengal, at Plassey. The victory brought English domination of the Indian subcontinent for almost two centuries. Note the manner in which this English artist clearly makes the victory one of the West over the East by contrasting the English horse and the Indian elephant and the contrasting dress of the protagonists. Clive had won the battle largely through bribing many of the Nawab's troops and potential allies.
The Granger Collection, New York

Joseph de Montcalm. The French Empire in Canada was ending.

Pitt's colonial vision, however, extended beyond the Saint Lawrence valley and the Great Lakes basin. The major islands of the French West Indies fell to British fleets. Income from the sale of captured sugar helped finance the British war effort. British slave interests captured the bulk of the French slave trade. Between 1755 and 1760, the value of the French colonial trade fell by more than 80 percent. In India, the British forces under the command of Robert Clive defeated France's Indian allies in 1757 at the Battle of Plassey. This victory opened the way for the eventual conquest of Bengal in northeast India and later of all of India by the British East India Company. Never had Great Britain or any other European power experienced such a complete worldwide military victory.

The Treaty of Paris of 1763   The Treaty of Paris of 1763 reflected somewhat less of a victory than Britain had won on the battlefield. Pitt was no longer in office. George III (r. 1760–1820) and Pitt had quarreled over policy, and the minister had departed. His replacement was the earl of Bute (1713–1792), a favorite of the new monarch. Bute was responsible for the peace settlement. Britain received all of Canada, the Ohio River valley, and the eastern half of the Mississippi River valley. Britain returned Pondicherry and Chandernagore in India and the West Indian sugar islands of Guadeloupe and Martinique to the French.

The Seven Years' War had been a vast conflict. Tens of thousands of soldiers and sailors had been killed or wounded. Major battles had been fought around the globe. At great internal sacrifice, Prussia had permanently wrested Silesia from Austria and had turned the Holy Roman Empire into an empty shell. Habsburg power now depended largely on the Hungarian domains. France, though still having sources of colonial income, was no longer a great colonial power. The Spanish Empire remained largely intact, but the British were still determined to penetrate its markets.

In India, the British East India Company continued to impose its own authority on the decaying indigenous governments. The ramifications of that situation would extend until the mid-twentieth century. In North America, the British government faced the task of organizing its new territories. From this time until World War II, Great Britain was a world power, not just a European one.

The quarter century of warfare also caused a long series of domestic crises among the European powers. Defeat convinced many in France of the necessity for political and administrative reform. The financial burdens of the wars had astounded all contemporaries. Every power had to increase its revenues to pay its war debt and finance its preparation for the next combat. Nowhere did this search for revenue lead to more far-ranging consequences than in the British colonies in North America.

THE AMERICAN REVOLUTION AND EUROPE

The revolt of the British colonies in North America was an event in both transatlantic and European history. It erupted from problems of revenue collection common to all the major powers after the Seven Years' War. The War of the American Revolution also continued the conflict between France and Great Britain. The French support of the Americans deepened the existing financial and administrative difficulties of the French monarchy.

RESISTANCE TO THE IMPERIAL SEARCH FOR REVENUE

After the Treaty of Paris of 1763, the British government faced two imperial problems. The first was the sheer cost of maintaining their empire, which the British felt they could no longer carry alone. The national debt had risen considerably, as had domestic taxation. Since the American colonies had been the chief beneficiaries of the conflict, the British felt it was rational for the colonies henceforth to bear part of the cost of their protection and administration. The second problem was the vast expanse of new territory in North America that the British had to organize. This included all the land from the mouth of the Saint Lawrence River to the Mississippi River, with its French settlers and, more importantly, its Native Americans. (See Map 16–3.)

The British drive for revenue began in 1764 with the passage of the Sugar Act under the ministry of George Grenville (1712–1770). The measure attempted to produce more revenue from imports into the colonies by the rigorous collection of what was actually a lower tax. Smugglers who violated the law were to be tried in admiralty courts without juries. The next year, Parliament passed the Stamp Act, which put a tax on legal documents and other items such as newspapers. The British considered these taxes legal, because Parliament had approved the decision to collect them, and fair, because the money was to be spent in the colonies.

The Americans responded that they alone, through their colonial assemblies, had the right to tax themselves and that they were not represented in Parliament. Furthermore, the expenditure in the colonies of the revenue Parliament levied did not reassure the colonists. They feared that if their colonial government was financed from outside, they would lose control over it. In October 1765, the Stamp Act Congress met in America and drew up a protest to the crown. There was much disorder in the colonies, particularly in Massachusetts, roused by groups known as the Sons of Liberty. The colonists agreed to refuse to import British goods. In 1766, Parliament

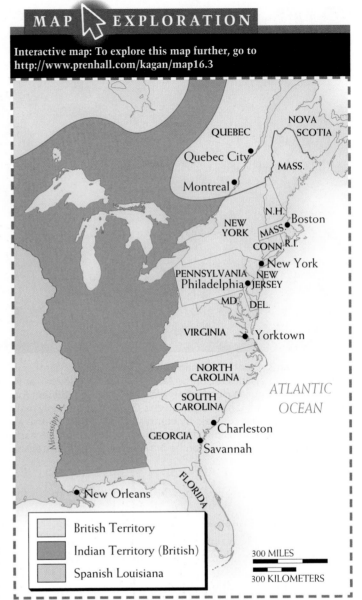

MAP ◤ EXPLORATION

Interactive map: To explore this map further, go to
http://www.prenhall.com/kagan/map16.3

Map 16–3   **NORTH AMERICA IN 1763**   In the year of the victory over France, the English colonies lay along the Atlantic seaboard. The difficulties of organizing authority over the previous French territory in Canada and west of the Appalachian Mountains would contribute to the coming of the American Revolution.

repealed the Stamp Act, but through the Declaratory Act said it had the power to legislate for the colonies.

The Stamp Act crisis set the pattern for the next ten years. Parliament, under the leadership of a royal minister, would approve revenue or administrative legislation. The Americans would then resist by reasoned argument, economic pressure, and violence. Then the British would repeal the legislation, and the process would begin again. Each time, tempers on both sides became more frayed and positions more irreconcilable. With each clash, the Americans more fully developed their own thinking about political liberty.

THE CRISIS AND INDEPENDENCE

In 1767, Charles Townshend (1725–1767), as Chancellor of the Exchequer, the British finance minister, led Parliament to pass a series of revenue acts relating to colonial imports. The colonists again resisted. The ministry sent over its own customs agents to administer the laws. To protect these new officers, the British sent troops to Boston in 1768. The obvious tensions resulted. In March 1770, the Boston Massacre, in which British troops killed five citizens, took place. That same year, Parliament repealed all of the Townshend duties except the one on tea.

In May 1773, Parliament passed a new law relating to the sale of tea by the East India Company. The measure permitted the direct importation of tea into the American colonies. It actually lowered the price of tea while retaining the tax imposed without the colonists' consent. In some cities, the colonists refused to permit the unloading of the tea; in Boston, a shipload of tea was thrown into the harbor.

The British ministry of Lord North (1732–1792) was determined to assert the authority of Parliament over the colonies. During 1774, Parliament passed a series of laws known in American history as the **Intolerable Acts**. These measures closed the port of Boston, reorganized the government of Massachusetts, allowed troops to be quartered in private homes, and removed the trials of royal customs officials to England. The same year, the Quebec Act extended the boundaries of Quebec to include the Ohio River valley. The Americans regarded the Quebec Act as an attempt to prevent their mode of self-government from spreading beyond the Appalachian Mountains.

During these years, citizens critical of British policy had established committees of correspondence throughout the colonies. They made the various sections of the eastern seaboard aware of common problems and encouraged united action. In September 1774, these committees organized the First Continental Congress in Philadelphia. This body hoped to persuade Parliament to restore self-government in the colonies and abandon its direct supervision of colonial affairs. Conciliation, however, was not forthcoming. By April 1775, the Battles of Lexington and Concord had been fought. In June, the colonists suffered defeat at the Battle of Bunker Hill. Despite that defeat, the colonial assemblies began to meet under their own authority rather than under that of the king.

The Second Continental Congress gathered in May 1775. It still sought conciliation with Britain, but the pressure of events led it to begin to conduct the government of the colonies. By August 1775,

George III had declared the colonies in rebellion. During the winter, Thomas Paine's (1737–1809) pamphlet *Common Sense* galvanized public opinion in favor of separation from Great Britain. A colonial army and navy were organized. In April 1776, the Continental Congress opened American ports to the trade of all nations. On July 4, 1776, the Continental Congress adopted the Declaration of Independence. Thereafter, the War of the American Revolution continued until 1781, when the forces of George Washington defeated those of Lord Cornwallis at Yorktown. Early in 1778, however, the war had widened into a European conflict when Benjamin Franklin (1706–1790) persuaded the French government to support the rebellion. In 1779, the Spanish also joined the war against Britain. The 1783 Treaty of Paris concluded the conflict, and the thirteen American colonies finally established their independence.

AMERICAN POLITICAL IDEAS

The political ideas of the American colonists had largely arisen out of the struggle of the seventeenth-century English aristocrats and gentry against the absolutism of the Stuart monarchs. The American colonists looked to the English Revolution of 1688 as having established many of their own fundamental political liberties, as well as those of the English. The colonists claimed that, through the measures imposed from 1763 to 1776, George III and the British Parliament were attacking those liberties and dissolving the bonds of moral and political allegiance that had formerly united the two peoples. Consequently, the colonists employed a theory that had developed to justify an aristocratic rebellion to support their own popular revolution.

These Whig political ideas, largely derived from the writings of John Locke, were, however, only a part of the English ideological heritage that affected the Americans. Throughout the eighteenth century, they had become familiar with a series of British political writers called the Commonwealthmen, who held republican political ideas that had their intellectual roots in the most radical thought of the Puritan revolution. During the early eighteenth century, these writers, the most influential of whom were John Trenchard (1662–1723) and Thomas Gordon (d. 1750) in *Cato's Letters* (1720–1723), had relentlessly criticized the government patronage and parliamentary management of Sir Robert Walpole and his successors. They argued that such government was corrupt and it undermined liberty. They regarded much parliamentary taxation as simply a means of financing political corruption. They also considered standing armies instruments of tyranny. In Great Britain,

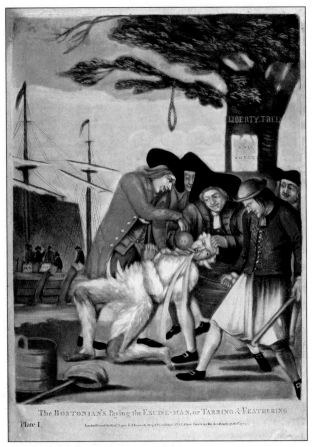

Many Americans fiercely objected to the British Parliament's attempts to tax the colonies. This print of a British tax collector being tarred and feathered warned officials of what could happen to them if they tried to collect these taxes. Philip Dawe (c. 1750-C.1785), "The Bostonians paying the Excise-Man or Tarring & Feathering." London, 1774. Colored Engraving. The Gilder Lehman Collection on deposit at the Pierpont Morgan Library. GL 4961.01. Photography: Joseph Zehavi. The Pierpont Morgan Library/Art Resource, NY

this republican political tradition had only a marginal impact. The writers were largely ignored because most British subjects regarded themselves as the freest people in the world. Three thousand miles away, however, colonists read the radical books and pamphlets and often accepted them at face value. The policy of Great Britain toward America following the Treaty of Paris of 1763 and certain political events in Britain had made many colonists believe the worst fears of the Commonwealthmen were coming true. All of these events coincided with the accession of George III to the throne.

EVENTS IN GREAT BRITAIN

George III believed that a few powerful Whig families and the ministries they controlled had bullied and dominated his two immediate royal predecessors. George III also believed he should have ministers of his own choice and Parliament should function under royal, rather than aristocratic, management. When George appointed the Earl of Bute as his first minister after William Pitt resigned in 1761, he ignored the great Whig families that had run the country since 1715. The king sought the aid of politicians whom the Whigs hated. Moreover, he tried to use the same kind of patronage techniques Walpole developed to control of the House of Commons.

Between 1761 and 1770, George tried one minister after another, but each, in turn, failed to gain enough support from the various factions in the House of Commons. Finally, in 1770, he turned to Lord North, who remained the king's first minister until 1782. The Whig families and other political spokespersons claimed that George III was attempting to impose a tyranny. What they meant was that the king was attempting to curb the power of a particular group of the aristocracy. George III certainly was seeking to restore more royal influence to the government of Great Britain, but he was not trying to make himself a tyrant.

The Challenge of John Wilkes Then, in 1763 began the affair of John Wilkes (1725–1797). This London political radical and member of Parliament published a newspaper called *The North Briton*. In issue number 45, Wilkes strongly criticized Lord Bute's handling of the peace negotiations with France. Wilkes was arrested under the authority of a general warrant issued by the secretary of state. He pleaded the privileges of a member of Parliament and was released. The courts also later ruled that the vague kind of general warrant by which he had been arrested was illegal. The House of Commons, however, ruled that issue number 45 of *The North Briton* constituted libel, and it expelled Wilkes. He soon fled the country and was outlawed. Throughout these procedures Wilkes enjoyed widespread support.

In 1768, Wilkes returned to England and was reelected to Parliament, but the House of Commons, under the influence of George III's friends, refused to seat him. He was elected three more times. After the fourth election, the House of Commons simply ignored the results and seated the government-supported candidate. As had happened earlier, large, unruly demonstrations of shopkeepers, artisans, and small-property owners supported Wilkes as did aristocratic politicians who wished to humiliate George III. "Wilkes and Liberty" became the slogan of political radicals and many noble opponents of the monarch. Wilkes was finally seated in 1774, after having become the lord mayor of London.

The American colonists followed these developments closely. Events in Britain confirmed their fears about a monarchical and parliamentary conspiracy against liberty. The king, as their Whig friends told them, was behaving like a tyrant. The Wilkes affair displayed the arbitrary power of the monarch, the corruption of the House of Commons, and the contempt of both for popular electors. That same monarch and Parliament were attempting to overturn the traditional relationship of Great Britain to its colonies by imposing parliamentary taxes. The same government had then landed troops in Boston, changed the government of Massachusetts, and undermined the traditional right of jury trial. All of these events fulfilled too exactly the portrait of political tyranny that had developed over the years in the minds of articulate colonists.

Movement for Parliamentary Reform   The political influences between America and Britain operated both ways. The colonial demand for no taxation without representation and the criticism of the adequacy of the British system of representation struck at the core of the eighteenth-century British political structure. British subjects at home who were no more directly represented in the House of Commons than were the Americans could adopt the colonial arguments. The colonial questioning of the tax-levying authority of the House of Commons was related to the protest of John Wilkes. Both the Americans and Wilkes were challenging the power of the monarch and the authority of Parliament. Moreover, both the colonial leaders and Wilkes appealed over the head of legally constituted political authorities to popular opinion and popular demonstrations. Both were protesting the power of a largely self-selected aristocratic political body. The British ministry was fully aware of these broader political implications of the American troubles.

The American colonists also demonstrated to Europe how a politically restive people in the Old Regime could fight tyranny and protect political liberty. They established revolutionary, but orderly, political bodies that could function outside the existing political framework: the congress and the convention. These began with the Stamp Act Congress of 1765 and culminated in the Constitutional Convention of 1787. The legitimacy of these congresses and conventions lay not in existing law, but in the alleged consent of the governed. This approach represented a new way to found a government.

Toward the end of the War of the American Revolution, calls for parliamentary reform arose in Britain itself. The method proposed for changing the system was the extra-legal Association Movement.

The Yorkshire Association Movement   By the close of the 1770s, many in Britain resented the mismanagement of the American war, the high taxes, and Lord North's ministry. In northern England in 1778, Christopher Wyvil (1740–1822), a landowner and retired clergyman, organized the Yorkshire Association Movement. Property owners, or freeholders, of Yorkshire met in a mass meeting to demand moderate changes in the corrupt system of parliamentary elections. They organized corresponding societies elsewhere. They intended that the association examine, and suggest reforms for, the entire government. The Association Movement was thus a popular attempt to establish an extra-legal institution to reform the government. (See "Major Cartwright Calls for the Reform of Parliament," page 540.)

The movement collapsed during the early 1780s because its supporters, unlike Wilkes and the American rebels, were not willing to appeal for broad popular support. Nonetheless, the agitation of the Association Movement provided many people with experience in political protest. Several of its younger figures lived to raise the issue of parliamentary reform after 1815.

Parliament was not insensitive to the demands of the Association Movement. In April

The surrender of Lord Cornwallis' British army at Yorktown, Virginia, in 1781 to American and French forces under George Washington ended Britain's hopes of suppressing the American Revolution.   John Trumbull (American 1756–1843), "The Surrender of Lord Cornwallis at Yorktown, 19 October 1781," 1787–c. 1828. Oil on canvas, 53.3 × 77.8 × 1.9 cm (21 × 30 ⅝ × ¾ in.) Yale University Art Gallery, Trumbull Collection

MAJOR CARTWRIGHT CALLS FOR THE REFORM OF PARLIAMENT

During the American Revolution there were many demands in England to reform Parliament. In this pamphlet of 1777, Major John Cartwright demands that many more English citizens be allowed to vote for members of the House of Commons. He also heaps contempt on the opponents of reform. Note how he declares that no political authority in Britain has the power to establish the unjust situation he describes.

■ *What does Cartwright mean by "corruption"? How does he believe Britain has been deprived of its liberties? Why does he prefer an annual election of Parliament to elections every seven years? How does he illustrate the wrongful state of representation under the present system?*

Suffering as we do, from a deep parliamentary corruption, it is no time to tamper with silly correctives, and trifle away the life of public freedom: but we must go to the bottom of the stinking sore and cleanse it thoroughly: we must once more infuse into the constitution the vivifying sprit of liberty and expel the very last dregs of this poison. *Annual parliaments* with an *equal representation of the commons* are the only specifics in this case: and they would effect a radial cure. That a house of commons, formed as ours is, should maintain septennial elections [i.e., elections every seven years], and laugh at every other idea is no wonder. The wonder is, that the British nation which, but the other day, was the greatest nation on earth, should be so easily laughed out of its liberties. . . .

Those who now claim the *exclusive* right of sending to parliament the 513 representatives for about six million souls (amongst whom are one million five hundred thousand males, *competent as electors*) consist of about two hundred and fourteen thousand persons; and 254 of these representatives are elected by 5,723. . . . Their pretended rights are many of them, derived from *royal favour;* some from antient usage and prescription; and some indeed from act of parliament; but neither the most authentic acts of royalty, nor precedent, nor prescription, nor even parliament can establish any flagrant injustice; much less can they strip one million two hundred and eighty-six thousand of an inalienable right, to vest it in a number amounting to only one-seventh of that multitude. . . .

From *Legislative Rights of the Commonality Vindicated,* by John Carwright (1740–1824), in "The English Radical Tradition", 1763–1914, (London: Adam and Charles Black, 1966), pp. 32–33.

1780, the Commons passed a resolution that called for lessening the power of the crown. In 1782, Parliament adopted a measure for "economical" reform, which abolished some patronage at the disposal of the monarch. These actions, however, did not prevent George III from appointing a minister of his own choice. In 1783, shifts in Parliament obliged Lord North to form a ministry with Charles James Fox (1749–1806), a longtime critic of George III. The monarch was most unhappy with the arrangement.

In 1783, the king approached William Pitt the Younger (1759–1806), son of the victorious war minister, to manage the House of Commons. During the election of 1784, Pitt received immense patronage support from the crown and constructed a House of Commons favorable to the monarch. Thereafter, Pitt sought to formulate trade policies that would give his ministry broad popularity. In 1785, he attempted one measure of modest parliamentary reform. When it failed, the young prime minister, who had been only twenty-four at the time of his appointment, abandoned the cause of reform.

By the mid-1780s, George III had achieved part of what he had sought since 1761. He had reasserted the influence of the monarchy in political affairs. It proved a temporary victory, because his own mental illness, which would eventually require a regency, weakened the royal power. The cost of his years of dominance had been high, however. On both sides of the Atlantic, the issue of popular sovereignty had been widely discussed. The American colonies had been lost. Economically, this loss did not prove disastrous. British trade with America after independence actually increased.

BROADER IMPACT OF THE AMERICAN REVOLUTION

The Americans—through their state constitutions, the Articles of Confederation, and the federal Constitution adopted in 1788—had demonstrated to Europe the possibility of government without kings and hereditary nobilities. They had established the example of a nation in which written documents based on popular consent and popular sovereignty—rather than on divine law, natural law, tradition, or the will of kings—were the highest political and legal authority. The political novelty of these assertions should not be ignored.

As the crisis with Britain unfolded during the 1760s and 1770s, the American colonists had come to see themselves first as preserving traditional English liberties against the tyrannical crown and corrupt Parliament and then as developing a whole new sense of liberty. By the mid-1770s, the colonists had rejected monarchical government and embraced republican political ideals. They would govern themselves through elected assemblies without any monarchical authority. Once a constitution was adopted, they would insist on a Bill of Rights specifically protecting a whole series of civil liberties. The Americans would reject the aristocratic social hierarchy that had existed in the colonies. They would embrace democratic ideals—even if the franchise remained limited. They would assert the equality of white male citizens not only before the law, but in ordinary social relations. They would reject social status based on birth and inheritance and assert the necessity of the liberty for all citizens to improve their social standing and economic lot by engaging in free commercial activity. They did not free their slaves, nor did they address issues of the rights of women or of Native Americans. Yet in making their revolution, the American colonists of the eighteenth century produced a society more free than any the world had ever seen and one that would eventually expand the circle of political and social liberty. In all these respects, the American Revolution was a genuinely radical movement, whose influence would widen as Americans

EVENTS IN BRITAIN AND AMERICA RELATING TO THE AMERICAN REVOLUTION

1760	George III becomes king
1763	Treaty of Paris concludes the Seven Years' War
1763	John Wilkes publishes issue number 45 of *The North Briton*
1764	Sugar Act
1765	Stamp Act
1766	Stamp Act repealed and Declaratory Act passed
1767	Townshend Acts
1768	Parliament refuses to seat John Wilkes after his election
1770	Lord North becomes George III's chief minister
1770	Boston Massacre
1773	Boston Tea Party
1774	Intolerable Acts
1774	First Continental Congress
1775	Second Continental Congress
1776	Declaration of Independence
1778	France enters the war on the side of America
1778	Yorkshire Association Movement founded
1781	British forces surrender at Yorktown
1783	Treaty of Paris concludes War of the American Revolution

moved across the continent and as other peoples began to question traditional modes of European government.

IN PERSPECTIVE

During the sixteenth and seventeenth centuries, the West European maritime powers established extensive commercial, mercantile empires in North and South America. The point of these empires was to extract wealth and to establish commercial advantage for the colonial power. Spain had the largest of these empires, but by the end of the seventeenth century, Britain and France had also each established a major American presence. As a vast plantation economy emerged, significant portions of these American empires became economically dependent on slave labor, drawn from the forced importation of Africans. Through this large slave labor force, African linguistic, social, and religious influences became major cultural factors in these regions.

During the eighteenth century, the great European powers engaged in warfare over their American empires and over their power in India. These colonial wars became entangled in dynastic wars in central and eastern Europe and resulted in worldwide mid-century European conflict.

In the New World, Britain, France, and Spain battled for commercial dominance. France and Britain also clashed in India. By the third quarter of the century, Britain had ousted France from its major holdings in North America and from any significant presence in India. Spain, though no longer a military power of the first order, had managed to maintain its vast colonial empire in Latin America and much of its monopoly over the region's trade.

On the Continent, France, Austria, and Prussia collided over conflicting territorial and dynastic ambitions. Britain used the continental wars to divert France from the colonial arena. With British aid, Prussia had emerged in 1763 as a major continental power. Austria had lost territory to Prussia, while France had accumulated a vast debt.

The mid-century conflicts, in turn, led to major changes in all the European states. Each of the monarchies needed more money and tried to govern itself more efficiently. This problem led Britain to attempt to tax the North American colonies, which led to a revolution and the colonies' independence. Already deeply in debt, the French monarchy aided the Americans, fell into a deeper financial crisis, and soon clashed sharply with the nobility as royal ministers tried to find new revenues. That clash eventually unleashed the French Revolution. Spain moved to administer its Latin American empire more efficiently, which increased revolutionary discontent in the early nineteenth century. In preparation for future wars, the rulers of Prussia, Austria, and Russia pursued a mode of activist government known as Enlightened Absolutism (see Chapter 17). In that regard, the mid-eighteenth-century wars set in motion most of the major political developments of the next half century.

REVIEW QUESTIONS

1. What were the fundamental ideas associated with mercantile theory? Did they work? Which European country was most successful in establishing a mercantile empire? Least successful? Why?
2. What were the main points of conflict between Britain and France in North America, the West Indies, and India? How did the triangles of trade function among the Americas, Europe, and Africa?
3. How was the Spanish colonial empire in the Americas organized and managed? What changes did the Bourbon monarchs institute in the Spanish Empire?
4. What was the nature of slavery in the Americas? How was it linked to the economies of the Americas, Europe, and Africa? Why was the plantation system unprecedented? How did the plantation system contribute to the inhumane treatment of slaves?
5. What were the results of the Seven Years' War? Which countries emerged in a stronger position and why?
6. How did European ideas and political developments influence the American colonists? How did their actions, in turn, influence Europe? What was the relationship between American colonial radicals and contemporary political radicals in Great Britain?

SUGGESTED READINGS

B. BAILYN, *The Ideological Origins of the American Revolution* (1992). An important work illustrating the role of English radical thought in the perceptions of the colonists.

C. A. BAYLY, *Imperial Meridian: The British Empire and the World, 1780–1830* (1989). A major study of the empire after the loss of America.

I. BERLIN, *Many Thousands Gone: The First Two Centuries of Slavery in North America* (1998). The most extensive recent treatment emphasizing the differences in the slave economy during different decades.

R. BLACKBURN, *The Making of New World Slavery from the Baroque to the Modern, 1492–1800* (1997). An extraordinary work.

M. A. BURKHOLDER and L. L. JOHNSON, *Colonial Latin America* (2004). A standard synthesis.

L. COLLEY, *Britons: Forging the Nation, 1707–1837* (1992). Important discussions of the recovery from the loss of America.

D. B. DAVIS, *The Problem of Slavery in the Age of Revolution, 1770–1823* (1975). A major work on both European and American history.

J. J. ELLIS, *His Excellency: George Washington* (2004) A biography that explores the entire era of the American Revolution.

R. HARMS, *The Diligent: A Voyage through the Worlds of the Slave Trade* (2002). A powerful narrative of the voyage of a French slave trader.

H. S. KLEIN, *The Atlantic Slave Trade* (1999). A succinct synthesis based on recent literature.

P. LANGFORD, *A Polite and Commercial People: England, 1717–1783* (1989). An excellent survey covering social history, politics, the overseas wars, and the American Revolution.

P. MAIER, *American Scripture: Making the Declaration of Independence* (1997). Replaces previous works on the subject.

A. PAGDEN, *Lords of All the World: Ideologies of Empire in Spain, Britain, and France, 1492–1830* (1995). One of the few comparative studies of the empires during this period.

J. THORNTON, *Africa and the Africans in the Making of the Atlantic World, 1400–1800*, 2nd ed. (1998). A discussion of the role of Africans in the emergence of the transatlantic economy.

G. S. WOOD, *The American Revolution: A History* (2002). A major interpretation.

DOCUMENTS CD-ROM

Europe and the Americas in the Eighteenth Century

17.1 Slaves in the City
17.2 Demands from a Slave Rebellion
17.3 The Stamp Act: "Unconstitutional and Unjust"
17.4 "Declaration of Sentiments": American Women Want Independence Too
17.6 Thomas Paine: from "Common Sense"
17.7 John Adams: *Thoughts on Government*

The Enlightenment

18.6 Medicine from Turkey: The Small Pox Vaccination

THE COLUMBIAN EXCHANGE: DISEASE, ANIMALS, AND AGRICULTURE

The European encounter with the Americas produced remarkable ecological transformations that have shaped the world to the present moment. The same ships that carried Europeans and Africans to the New World also transported animals, plants, and germs that had never before appeared in the Americas. There was a similar transport back to Europe and Africa. Alfred Crosby, the leading historian of the process, has named this cross-continental flow "the Columbian exchange."

DISEASES ENTER THE AMERICAS

With the exception of a few ships that had gone astray or, in the case of the Vikings, that had gone in search of new lands, the American continents had been biologically separated from Europe, Africa, and Asia for tens of thousands of years. In the Americas no native animals could serve as major beasts of burden except for the llama, which could not transport more than about a hundred pounds. Nor did animals constitute a major source of protein for Native Americans, whose diets consisted largely of maize, beans, peppers, yams, and potatoes. At the same time, the American continents included areas of vast grassland without grazing animals that would have transformed those plants into animal protein. Moreover, it also appears that native peoples had lived on the long-isolated American continents without experiencing major epidemics.

By the second voyage of Columbus (1493), that picture began to change in remarkable ways. On his return voyage to Hispaniola and other islands of the Caribbean, Columbus brought a number of animals and plants that were previously unknown to the New World. The men on all his voyages and those on subsequent European voyages also carried diseases novel to the Americas.

The diseases thus transported by Europeans ultimately accounted for the conquest of the people of the Americas as much as the advanced European weaponry. Much controversy surrounds the question of the actual size of the populations of Native Americans in the Caribbean islands, Mexico, Peru, and the North Atlantic coast. All accounts present those populations as quite significant, with those of Mexico in particular numbering many millions. Yet in the first two centuries after the encounter, wherever Europeans went either as settlers or as conquerors, extremely large numbers of Native Americans died from diseases they had never before encountered. The most deadly such disease was smallpox, which destroyed millions of people. Beyond the devastation wrought by that disease, bubonic plague, typhoid, typhus, influenza, measles, chicken pox, whooping cough, malaria, and diphtheria produced deadly results in more localized epidemics. For example, an unknown disease, but quite possibly typhus, caused major losses among the Native Americans of New England between approximately 1616 and 1619.

Native Americans appear to have been highly susceptible to these diseases because, with no earlier exposure, they lacked immunity. Wherever such outbreaks are recorded, Europeans either contracted or died from them at a much lower rate than the Native Americans. These diseases would continue to victimize Native Americans at a higher rate than Americans of European descent through the end of the nineteenth century when smallpox and measles still killed large numbers of the Plains Indian peoples of North America.

Although many historical and medical questions still surround the subject, it appears almost certain that syphilis, which became a rampant venereal disease in Europe at the close of the fifteenth century and eventually spread around the globe, originated in the New World. It seems to have been an entirely new disease, spawned through a mutation when the causal agent for yaws migrated from the Americas to new climatic settings in Europe. Until the discovery of penicillin in the 1940s, syphilis remained a major concern of public health throughout the world.

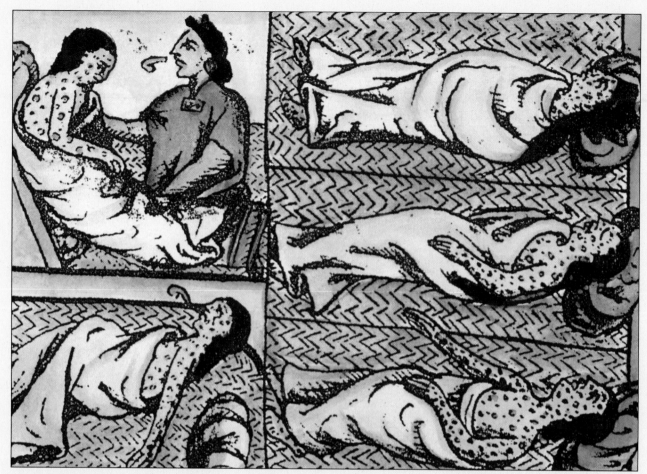

Nothing so destroyed the life of the Native Americans whom the Spanish encountered as the introduction of smallpox. With no immune defenses to this new disease, millions of Native Americans died of smallpox during the sixteenth and seventeenth centuries.   The Granger Collection.

ANIMALS AND AGRICULTURE

The introduction of European livestock to the Americas quite simply revolutionized the agriculture of two continents. The most important new animals were pigs, cattle, horses, goats, and sheep. Once transported to the New World, these animals multiplied at unprecedented rates. The place where this first occurred was in the islands of the Caribbean, during the first forty years of Spanish settlement and exploitation. This situation established the foundation for the later Spanish conquest of both Mexico and Peru by providing the Spanish with strong breeds of animals, especially horses, acclimated to the Americas when they set out to conquer the mainland of South America.

The horse became first the animal of the conquest and then the animal of colonial Latin American culture. Native Americans had no experience with such large animals who would obey the will of a human rider. The mounted Spanish horseman

struck fear into these people, and for good reason. After the conquest, however, the Americas from Mexico southward became the largest horse-breeding region of the world, with ranches raising thousands of animals. Horses became relatively cheap, and even Native Americans could acquire them. By the nineteenth century, the possession of horses would allow the Plains Indians of North America to resist the advance of their white conquerors.

The flourishing of pigs, cattle, and sheep allowed a vast economic exploitation of the Americas. These animals produced enormous quantities of hides and wool. Their presence in such large numbers also meant the Americas from the sixteenth century through the present would support a diet more plentiful in animal protein than anywhere else in the world.

Europeans also brought their own plants to the New World, including peaches, oranges, grapes, melons, bananas, rice, onions, radishes, and various

Within one year of Columbus's encounter with the Americas, the event had been captured in a woodcut published in Giuliano Dati's *Narrative of Columbus* (1493). Columbus's several voyages, and those of later Europeans as well, introduced not only European warfare but began a vast ecological exchange of plants, animals, and diseases between the Old and New Worlds.   The Granger Collection.

green vegetables. Socially, for three centuries the most significant of these was sugarcane, whose cultivation created the major demand for slavery throughout the transatlantic plantation economy. Nutritionally, European wheat would, over the course of time, allow the Americas not only to feed themselves, but also to export large amounts of grain throughout the world. This American production of wheat on the vast plains of the two continents contrasted sharply with the difficulty Europeans faced raising grain in the northern and northeastern parts of the Continent, particularly in Russia.

No significant animals from the Americas, except the turkey, actually came to be raised in Europe. The Americas did send to Europe, however, a series of plants that eventually changed the European diet: maize, potatoes, sweet potatoes, peppers, beans, manioc (tapioca), peanuts, squash, pumpkin, pineapple, cocoa, and tomatoes. All of these, to a greater or lesser degree, eventually entered the diet of Europeans and of European settlers and their descendants in the Americas. Maize and the potato, however, had the most transform-

ing impact. Each of these two crops became a major staple in European farming, as well as in the European diet. Both crops grow rapidly, supplying food quickly and steadily if not attacked by disease. Tobacco, we should note, originated in the Americas, too.

Maize was established as a crop in Spain within thirty years of the country's encounter with the New World. A century and a half later it was commonplace in the Spanish diet, and its cultivation had spread to Italy and France. Maize produced more grain for the seed and farming effort than wheat did. Throughout Europe, maize was associated primarily with fodder for animals. As early as the eighteenth century, travelers noted the presence of polenta in the peasant diet, and other forms of maize dishes, such as fried mush, spread.

The potato established its European presence more slowly than maize. The Spanish encountered the potato only when Pizarro conquered Peru, where it was a major part of the Native American food supply. It was adopted slowly by Europeans because it needed to be raised in climates more temperate than that of Spain and the Mediterranean. It appears to have become a major peasant food in Scotland, Ireland, and parts of Germany during the eighteenth century. It became more widely cultivated elsewhere in Europe only after new strains of the plant were imported from Chile in the late nineteenth century. In the middle of the seventeenth century, Irish peasants were urged to cultivate the potato as a major source of cheap nutrition that could grow in quantity on a small plot. The food shortages arising from the wars of Louis XIV and then during the eighteenth century led farmers in northern European to adopt the potato for similar reasons. It was nutrient insurance against failure of the grain harvest. There is good reason to believe the cultivation of the potato was one of the major causes of the population increase in eighteenth- and nineteenth-century Europe. It was the quintessential food of the poor.

Many tragedies arose from the encounter between the people of the Americas and those of Europe, as well as from the forging of new nations and civilizations in the Americas. Yet, one of the last chapters of those tragedies to arise as a direct fall-out of the Columbian exchange three centuries earlier was the Irish famine of the 1840s. Irish peasants had become almost wholly dependent on the potato as a source of food. In the middle of the 1840s, an American parasite infected the Irish potato crop. The result of the failure of the crop was the death of hundreds of thousands of Irish peasants and the migration of still more hundreds of thousands to the Americas and elsewhere in the world.

- *Define the Columbian exchange. What was the impact of European diseases on the Americas? Why was the impact so profound? Why could so many European crops grow well in the Americas? What was the cultural impact of animals taken from Europe to the Americas? How did food from the Americas change the diet of Europe and then later, as Europeans immigrated, the diet of the entire world?*

PART 4: ENLIGHTENMENT AND REVOLUTION
1700–1850

1713–1824

Politics and Government

1713	Treaty of Utrecht
1713–1740	Frederick William I builds Prussian military
1720–1740	Walpole in England, Fleury in France
1740–1748	War of the Austrian Succession
1756–1763	Seven Years' War
1772	First Partition of Poland
1775–1783	American Revolution
1789	Gathering of the Estates General at Versailles; fall of the Bastille, Declaration of the Rights of Man and Citizen
1793	Louis XVI executed, Second Partition of Poland
1793–1794	Reign of Terror
1795	Third Partition of Poland
1799	Napoleon named First Consul in France

The Boston Massacre

Society and Economy

1733	John Kay's flying shuttle
1750s	Agricultural Revolution in Britain
1763	British establish dominance in India
1763–1789	Enlightened absolutist rulers seek to spur economic growth
1765	James Hargreaves's spinning jenny
1769	Richard Arkwright's waterframe
1773–1775	Pugachev's Rebellion
1787	Edmund Cartwright's power loom
1789–1802	Revolutionary legislation restructures French political and economic life
1794–1824	Wars of independence in Latin America break the colonial system

Hargreave's Spinning Jenny

Religion and Culture

1721	Montesquieu, *Persian Letters*
1733	Voltaire, *Letters on the English*
1738	Voltaire, *Elements of the Philosophy of Newton*
1739	Wesley begins field preaching
1748	Hume, *Inquiry into Human Nature*
1748	Montesquieu, *Spirit of the Laws*
1751	First volume of Diderot's *Encyclopedia*
1762	Rousseau, *The Social Contract* and *Émile*
1763	Voltaire, *Treatise on Tolerance*
1774	Goethe, *The Sorrows of Young Werther*
1776	Smith, *Wealth of Nations*
1779	Lessing, *Nathan the Wise*
1781	Joseph II adopts toleration in Austria
1781	Kant, *The Critique of Pure Reason*

Voltaire

1804–1848

1804	Napoleonic Code; Napoleon crowned emperor
1805	Third Coalition formed against France, battles of Trafalgar and Austerlitz
1806	Napoleon establishes the Continental System
1808	Spanish resistance to Napoleon stiffens
1812	Napoleon invades Russia; meets defeat
1814	Congress of Vienna opens
1815	Napoleon defeated at Waterloo
1821	Greek Revolution begins
1825	Decembrist Revolt in Russia
1829	Catholic Emancipation Act in Great Britain
1830	Revolution in France, Belgium, and Poland Serbia gains independence
1832	Great Reform Bill in Britain
1848	Revolutions sweep across Europe

Napoleon Bonaparte

1810	Abolition of serfdom in Prussia
1825	Stockton and Darlington Railway opens
1828–1850	First European police departments
1833	English Factory Act to protect children
1834	German Zollverein established
1846	Corn Laws repealed in Britain
1848	Serfdom abolished in Austria and Hungary

Queen Victoria's railway
carriage

1790	Civil Constitution of the Clergy; Burke, *Reflections on the Revolution in France*
1792	Wollstonecraft, *Vindication of the Rights of Woman*
1802	Napoleon, *Concordat with the Papacy*
1806	Hegel, *Phenomenology of Mind*
1807	Fichte, *Addresses to the German Nation*
1808	Goethe, *Faust, Part I*
1817	Ricardo, *Principles of Political Economy*
1819	Byron, *Don Juan*
1829	Catholic Emancipation Act in Great Britain
1830–1842	Comte, *The Positive Philosophy*
1830	Lyell, *Principles of Geology*
1843	Kierkegaard, *Fear and Trembling*
1848	Marx and Engels, *Communist Manifesto*

Karl Marx

CHAPTER **17**

THE AGE OF ENLIGHTENMENT:

Eighteenth-Century Thought

KEY TOPICS

- The intellectual and social background of the Enlightenment
- The philosophes of the Enlightenment and their agenda of intellectual and political reform
- Enlightenment writers' attitude toward religion
- The Philosophes' political thought
- Efforts of "enlightened" monarchs in central and eastern Europe to increase the economic and military strength of their domains
- The partition of Poland by Prussia, Russia, and Austria

During the eighteenth century, the conviction began to spread throughout the expanding literate sectors of European society that economic improvement and political reform were both possible and desirable. This attitude is now commonplace, but it came into its own only after 1700. It represents one of the primary continuing intellectual inheritances from that age.

The salon of Madame Marie Thérèse Geoffrin (1699–1777) was one of the most important Parisian gathering spots for Enlightenment writers during the middle of the eighteenth century. Well-connected women such as Madame Geoffrin were instrumental in helping the philosophes they patronized to bring their ideas to the attention of influential people in French society and politics.   Chateaux de Malmaison et Bois-Preau, Rueil-Malmaison. Bridgeman-Giraudon/Art Resource, NY

The movement of people and ideas that fostered such thinking is called the Enlightenment.

Inspired by the scientific revolution and prepared to challenge traditional intellectual and theological authority, Enlightenment writers believed that human beings can comprehend the operation of physical nature and mold it to achieve material and moral improvement, economic growth, and adminis-trative reform. They advocated agricultural improvement, commercial society, expanding consumption, and the application of innovative rational methods to traditional social and economic practices. The rationality of the physical universe became a standard against which they measured and criticized the customs and traditions of society. In religious matters they generally advocated a policy of toleration that opposed the claims to exclusive religious privilege of state-supported established churches whether Roman Catholic or Protestant. As the criticisms of Enlightenment writers penetrated every corner of contemporary society, politics, and religious opinion, the spirit of innovation and improvement came to characterize modern Europe and Western society.

Some of the ideas and outlooks of the Enlightenment had a direct impact on rulers in central and eastern Europe. These rulers, whose policies became known by the term *enlightened absolutism*, sought to centralize their authority so as to reform their countries. They often attempted to restructure religious institutions and to sponsor economic growth. Although they frequently associated themselves with the Enlightenment, many of their military and foreign policies were in direct opposition to enlightened ideals. Nonetheless, both the Enlightenment writers and these monarchs were forces for modernization in European life. ■

FORMATIVE INFLUENCES ON THE ENLIGHTENMENT

The Newtonian worldview, the political stability and commercial prosperity of Great Britain after 1688, the need for administrative and economic reform in France after the wars of Louis XIV, and the consolidation of what is known as a *print culture* were the chief factors that fostered the ideas of the Enlightenment and the call for reform throughout Europe.

IDEAS OF NEWTON AND LOCKE

Isaac Newton (1642–1727) and John Locke (1632–1704) were the major intellectual forerunners of the Enlightenment. The achievements of the Scientific Revolution from Copernicus to Newton had persuaded natural philosophers and then many other writers that traditions of thought inherited from both the ancient and medieval Christian worlds were incorrect or confused and needed to be challenged. Newton's formulation of the law of universal gravitation exemplified the newly perceived power of the human mind. Newtonian physics had portrayed a pattern of mechanical and mathematical rationality in the physical world. During the eighteenth century, thinkers from a variety of backgrounds began to apply this insight to society. If nature was rational, they reasoned, society, too, should be organized rationally. Furthermore, Newton had encouraged natural philosophers to approach the study of nature directly and to avoid metaphysics and supernaturalism. He had insisted on the use of empirical experience to check rational speculation. This emphasis on concrete experience became a key feature of Enlightenment thought.

As explained in Chapter 14, Newton's success in physics had inspired his fellow countryman John Locke to explain human psychology in terms of experience. In *An Essay Concerning Human Understanding* (1690), Locke argued that all humans enter the world a **tabula rasa**, or blank page. Personality is the product of the sensations that impinge on an individual from the external world throughout his or her life. Thus, experience, and only experience, shapes character. This essentially behaviorist theory implied that human nature is changeable and can be molded by modifying the surrounding physical and social environment. Locke's was thus a reformer's psychology that suggested the possibility of improving the human condition. Locke's psychology also, in effect, rejected the Christian doctrine that sin permanently flawed human beings. By contrast, Locke's thought implied that human beings need not wait for the grace of God or other divine aid to better their lives. They can take charge of their own destiny.

THE EXAMPLE OF BRITISH TOLERATION AND POLITICAL STABILITY

Newton's physics and Locke's psychology provided the theoretical basis for a reformist approach to society. The domestic stability of Great Britain after the Revolution of 1688 furnished a living example of a society in which, to many contemporaries, enlightened reforms appeared to benefit everyone. England permitted religious toleration to all except Unitarians and Roman Catholics, and even they were not actively persecuted. Relative freedom of the press and free speech prevailed. The authority of the monarchy was limited, and political sovereignty resided in Parliament. The courts protected citizens from arbitrary government action. The army was small. Furthermore, the domestic economic life of Great Britain displayed far less regulation than that of France or other continental nations. As reformist observers on the Continent noted, these liberal policies had produced neither disorder nor instability, but rather economic prosperity, political stability, and a loyal citizenry.

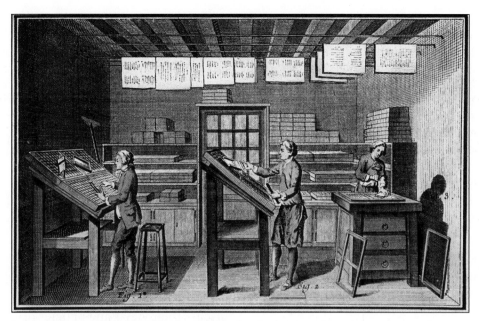

Printing shops were the productive centers for the book trade and newspaper publishing that spread the ideas of the Enlightenment.   The Granger Collection

This view may have been idealized, but England was nonetheless significantly freer than any other European nation at the time. Many writers of the continental Enlightenment contrasted what they regarded as the wise, progressive features of English life with the absence of religious toleration, the extensive literary censorship, the possibility of arbitrary arrest, the overregulation of the economy, and the influence of aristocratic military values in their own nations and most particularly in France.

THE EMERGENCE OF A PRINT CULTURE

The Enlightenment flourished in a *print culture,* that is, a culture in which books, journals, newspapers, and pamphlets had achieved a status of their own. In the past, print culture had deeply influenced the intellectual and religious movements associated with Renaissance humanism, the Reformation, and the Counter-Reformation. During the seventeenth century, a lively world of publication had arisen, which many governments sought to censor. During the eighteenth century, the volume of printed material—books, journals, magazines, and daily newspapers—increased sharply throughout Europe, notably in Britain. Prose came to be valued as highly as poetry, and the novel emerged as a distinct literary genre.

One of the driving forces behind this expansion of printed materials was the increase in literacy that occurred across Europe. Significantly more people especially in the urban centers of Western and central Europe could read. As a result, the printed word became the chief vehicle for communicating information and ideas and would remain so until the electronic revolution of our own day.

A growing concern with everyday life and material concerns—with secular as opposed to religious issues—accompanied this expansion of printed forms. Toward the end of the seventeenth century, half the books published in Paris were religious; by the 1780s, only about ten percent were. Novels often came to provide the moral and social instruction that books of piety once furnished. An English journal observed unhappily in 1790: "Novels spring into existence like insects on the banks of the Nile; and, if we may be indulged in another comparison, cover the shelves of circulating libraries, as locusts crowd the fields of Asia. Their great and growing number is a serious evil; for, in general, they exhibit delusive views of human life; and while they amuse, frequently they poison the mind."[1] People may have thus criticized the moral influence of the novel but did not deny its influence.

Books were not inexpensive in the eighteenth century, but they, and the ideas they conveyed, circulated in a variety of ways to reach a broad public. Private and public libraries, as the previous quotation noted, grew in number, allowing single copies to reach many readers. Authors might also publish the same material in different formats.

[1]Quoted T. C. W. Blanning, *The Culture of Power and the Power of Culture: Old Regime Europe 1660–1789* (Oxford: Oxford University Press, 2002) in p. 151.

The English essayist, critic, and dictionary author Samuel Johnson (1709–1784), for example, published as books a collection of essays that had first appeared in newspapers or journals. The number of the latter publications also expanded throughout the century.

Within both aristocratic and middle-class society, people were increasingly expected to be familiar with books and secular ideas. Popular publications, such as *The Spectator*, begun in 1711 by Joseph Addison (1672–1719) and Richard Steele (1672–1729), fostered the value of polite conversation and the reading of books. Coffeehouses became centers for discussing writing and ideas. (See "Encountering the Past: Coffeehouses and Enlightenment".) The lodges of Freemasons, the meeting places for members of a movement that began in Britain and spread to the Continent, provided another site for discussing secular ideas in secular books.

The expanding market for printed matter allowed writers to earn a living from their work for the first time, making authorship an occupation. Parisian ladies who hosted fashionable salons sought out popular writers. Some writers, notably Alexander Pope (1688–1744) in England and Voltaire in France, grew wealthy, providing an example for their young colleagues. In a challenge to older aristocratic values, status for authors in this new print culture was based on merit and commercial competition, not heredity and patronage.

A division, however, soon emerged between high and low literary culture. Successful authors of the Enlightenment addressed themselves to monarchs, nobles, the upper middle classes, and professional groups, and they were read and accepted in these upper levels of society. Other aspiring authors found social and economic disappointment. They lived marginally, writing professionally for whatever newspaper or journal that would pay for their work. Many of these lesser writers grew resentful, blaming a corrupt society for their lack of success. From their anger, they often espoused radical ideas or took moderate Enlightenment ideas to radical extremes, transmitting them in this embittered form to their often lower-class audience.

An expanding, literate public and the growing influence of secular printed materials created a new and increasingly influential social force called *public opinion*. This force—the collective effect on political and social life of views circulated in print and discussed in the home, the workplace, and centers of leisure—seems not to have existed before the middle of the eighteenth century. Books and newspapers could have thousands of readers, who in effect supported the writers whose works they bought, as they discussed their ideas and circulated them widely. The writers, in turn, had to answer only to their readers. The result changed the cultural and political climate in Europe. In 1775, a new member of the French Academy declared:

A tribunal has arisen independent of all powers and that all powers respect, that appreciates all talents, that pronounces on all people of merit. And in an enlightened century, in a century in which each citizen can speak to the entire nation by way of print, those who have a talent for instructing men and a gift for moving them—in a word, men of letters—are, amid the public dispersed, what the orators of Rome and Athens were in the middle of the public assembled.[2]

Governments could no longer operate wholly in secret or with disregard to the larger public sphere. They, as well as their critics, had to explain and discuss their views and policies openly.

Continental European governments sensed the political power of the new print culture. They regulated the book trade, censored books and newspapers, confiscated offending titles, and imprisoned offending authors. The eventual expansion of freedom of the press represented also an expansion of the print culture—with its independent readers, authors, and publishers—and the challenge it posed to traditional intellectual, social, and political authorities.

THE PHILOSOPHES

The writers and critics who flourished in the expanding print culture and who took the lead in forging the new attitudes favorable to change, championed reform, and advocated toleration were known as the **philosophes**. Not usually philosophers in a formal sense, these figures sought rather to apply the rules of reason, criticism, and common sense to nearly all the major institutions, economic practices, and exclusivist religious policies of the day. The most famous of their number included Voltaire, Montesquieu, Diderot, D'Alembert, Rousseau, Hume, Gibbon, Smith, Lessing, and Kant. (See "Immanuel Kant Defines Enlightenment," page 556.)

A few of these philosophes, particularly those in Germany, were university professors. Most, however, were free agents who might be found in London coffeehouses, Edinburgh drinking spots, the salons of fashionable Parisian ladies, the country houses of reform-minded nobles, or the courts

[2]Chrétien-Guillaume Malesherbes, as quoted in Roger Chartier, *The Cultural Origins of the French Revolution*, trans. by Lydia G. Cochran (Durham, NC: Duke University Press, 1991), pp. 30–31.

COFFEEHOUSES AND ENLIGHTENMENT

The ideas of the Enlightenment not only spread through books and journals. They took on a life of their own in public discussions in what was a new popular institution of European social life—the coffeehouse.

Coffee, originally imported into Europe from the Ottoman Empire, is the chief Turkish contribution to the Western diet. Coffeehouses had long existed in the Muslim world, encouraged by the Islamic prohibition on alcoholic drink. The first European coffeehouse appeared in Venice in the 1640s, and the first coffeehouse in Vienna opened its doors in 1683 with coffee left behind when the Turks abandoned their siege of the city.

By the middle of the eighteenth century, thousands of coffeehouses dotted European cities and towns. Customers were attracted to them in part because the coffeehouses did not serve alcoholic beverages, which made unruly behavior less likely than in taverns. (The practice of tipping began in the coffeehouses of London. The word *tips* originated as an acronym for "to insure prompt service.")

Throughout Europe, the coffeehouse provided a social for the open, spontaneous discussion of events, politics, literature, and ideas—but only for men (respectable women did not enter coffeehouses). By furnishing copies of newspapers and others journals, the proprietors of coffeehouses linked their customers to the growing print culture just as today's Internet cafés link customers to the World Wide Web. In London coffeehouses, members of the Royal Society and other men associated with the new science mixed with merchants and bankers. Some London coffeehouse proprietors invited learned persons to lecture, usually for a fee, on Newtonian physics, the mechanical philosophy, ethics, and the relationship of science and religion. One historian has described these lecturers as "the philosophical brotherhood of the coffeehouses."[1]

[1]Larry Stewart, *The Rise of Public Science. Rhetoric Technology, and Natural Philosophy in Newtonian Britain, 1660–1750* (Cambridge: Cambridge University Press, 1992), p. 145.

In France the philosophes, such as Voltaire, Rousseau, and Diderot, looked to the café as a place to meet other writers. By 1743, a German commented, "A coffeehouse is like a political stock exchange, where the most gallant and wittiest heads of every estate come together. They engage in wide-ranging and edifying talk, issue well-founded judgments on matters concerning the political and the scholarly world, converse sagaciously about the most secret news from all courts and states, and unveil the most hidden truths."[2]

One irony, however, should be noted about the eighteenth-century European coffeehouses. Although they provided one of the chief locations for the public discussion of the ideas of the Enlightenment, which fostered greater liberty of thought in Europe, the coffee and sugar consumed in these establishments were cultivated by slave labor on plantations in the Caribbean and Brazil. The coffeehouse was one of many institutions of European life that was connected to the transatlantic plantation slave economy.

- *How did coffeehouses help spread the ideas of the Enlightenment? How was the consumption of coffee related to the transatlantic slave trade?*

[2]Quoted in James Van Horn Melton, *The Rise of the Public in Enlightenment Europe* (Cambridge: Cambridge University Press, 2001), p. 243.

Business, science, religion, and politics were discussed in London coffeehouses such as this. Permission of the Trustees of the British Museum

555

IMMANUEL KANT DEFINES ENLIGHTENMENT

Kant was one of the most important German philosophers associated with the Enlightenment. His work is more fully discussed in Chapter 19. The passage here is from one of his articles, written in 1784, for a broad audience. He equates Enlightenment with the courage of the individual to use his or her reason. He indicates that this is difficult because so many people have come by habit to depend on others for guidance. He discusses the freedom that the use of reason requires.

■ *What authorities should the liberated intellect have the courage to question? Why does Kant believe intellectual liberation requires effort and the rejection of laziness and cowardice? Why does Kant link enlightenment with freedom?*

Enlightenment is man's emergence from his self-imposed nonage. Nonage is the inability to use one's own understanding without another's guidance. This nonage is self-imposed if its causes lie not in lack of understanding but in indecision and lack of courage to use one's own mind without another's guidance. Dare to know! (*Sapere aude*) "Have the courage to use your own understanding," is therefore the motto of the Enlightenment.

Laziness and cowardice are the reasons why such a large part of mankind gladly remain minors all their lives, long after nature has freed them from external guidance. They are the reasons why it is so easy for others to set themselves up as guardians. It is so comfortable to be a minor. If I have a book that thinks for me, a pastor who acts as my conscience, a physician who prescribes my diet, and so on—then I have no need to exert myself. I have no need to think, if only I can pay; others will take care of that disagreeable business for me. . . .

Thus it is very difficult for the individual to work himself out of the nonage which has become almost second nature to him. He has even grown to like it and is at first really incapable of using his own understanding, because he has never been permitted to try it. Dogmas and formulas, these mechanical tools designed for reasonable use—or rather abuse—of his natural gifts, are the fetters of an everlasting nonage. The man who casts them off would make an uncertain leap over the narrowest ditch, because he is not used to such movement. That is why there are only a few men who walk firmly, and who have emerged from nonage by cultivating their own minds.

It is more nearly possible, however, for the public to enlighten itself; indeed, if it is only given freedom, enlightenment is almost inevitable. There will always be a few independent thinkers, even among the self-appointed guardians of the multitude. Once such men have thrown off the yoke of nonage, they will spread about them the spirit of a reasonable appreciation of man's value and of his duty to think for himself. . . .

This enlightenment requires nothing but freedom—and the most innocent of all that may be called "freedom": freedom to make public use of one's reason in all matters.

Immanuel Kant, "What Is Enlightenment?" trans. by Peter Gray, in *Introduction to Contemporary Civilization in the West*, 2nd ed., Vol. 2 (New York: Columbia University Press, 1954), pp. 1071–1072.

of the most powerful monarchs on the Continent. In eastern Europe, they were often royal bureaucrats. They were not an organized group; they disagreed on many issues and did not necessarily like or respect each other. Their relationship to one another and to lesser figures of the same turn of mind has been compared with that of a family, which, despite quarrels and tensions, preserves a basic unity.[3]

The philosophes drew the bulk of their readership from the prosperous commercial and profes-

[3] Peter Gay, *The Enlightenment: An Interpretation*, Vol. 1 (New York: Knopf, 1967), p. 4.

sional urban classes. These people as well as forward-looking aristocrats discussed the reformers' writings and ideas in local philosophical societies, Freemason lodges, and clubs. These readers had enough income to buy and the leisure to read the philosophes' works. Although the writers of the Enlightenment did not consciously champion the goals or causes of the middle class, they did provide an intellectual ferment and a major source of ideas that could be used to undermine existing social practices and political structures based on aristocratic privilege. They taught their contemporaries, including reform-minded aristocrats, how to pose pointed, critical questions. Moreover, the philosophes generally supported the expansion of trade, the improvement of agriculture and transport, and the invention of new manufacturing machinery that were transforming the society and the economy of the eighteenth century and enlarging the business and commercial classes.

The chief bond among the philosophes was their common desire to reform religion, political thought, society, government, and the economy for the sake of human liberty. As the historian Peter Gay once suggested, this goal included "freedom from arbitrary power, freedom of speech, freedom of trade, freedom to realize one's talents, freedom of aesthetic response, freedom, in a word, of moral man to make his way in the world."[4] Though challenged over the last three centuries, no other single set of ideas has done so much to shape and define the modern Western world.

Statue of Voltaire by Jean-Antoine Houdon (Theatre Francais, Paris).
Musee Lambinet, Versailles/Giraudon/Art Resource, NY

VOLTAIRE—FIRST AMONG THE PHILOSOPHES

By far the most influential of the philosophes was François-Marie Arouet, known to posterity by his pen name Voltaire (1694–1778). During the 1720s, Voltaire had offended first the French monarch and then certain nobles by his politically and socially irreverent poetry and plays. He was arrested and twice briefly imprisoned, in comfortable conditions, in the Bastille, the royal prison-fortress in Paris. In 1726, to escape the wrath of a powerful aristocrat whom he had offended, Voltaire went into exile in England. There he visited its best literary circles, observed its tolerant intellectual and religious climate, relished the freedom he felt in its moderate political atmosphere, and admired its science and economic prosperity. In 1727, he also witnessed the elaborate funeral of Sir Isaac Newton. The next year Voltaire returned to France and, in 1733, published *Letters on the English*, which appeared in French the next year. The book praised the virtues of the English, especially their religious liberty, and implicitly criticized the abuses of French society. The Parlement of Paris condemned

[4]Gay, p. 3.

the book, and the authorities harassed Voltaire. He moved to Cirey from which, if necessary, he could easily escape France into what was then the nearby independent duchy of Lorraine. There he lived with Countess Emilie de Chatelet (1706–1749), the brilliant mathematician, discussed in Chapter 14, who became his mistress. In 1738, with her considerable help, he published *Elements of the Philosophy of Newton*, which more than any other single book popularized the thought of Isaac Newton across the continent. In 1749, Madame de Chatelet died.

Shortly thereafter, Voltaire took up residence for three years in Berlin at the court of Frederick the Great of Prussia with whom he had corresponded for several years. The residency ended unhappily with Voltaire fleeing to France. For a time he settled in Switzerland near Geneva, but clashed with local conservative Calvinist clergy over his sponsoring plays in the theater in his home. Thereafter he acquired the estate of Ferney, just across the French border, but close enough to flee to Geneva should the French authorities bother him. His extremely popular plays, essays, histories, and stories along with his far-flung correspondence made him the literary dictator of Europe. For the rest of his long life, he turned the venom of his satire and sarcasm against one evil after another in French and European life.

In 1755 a huge earthquake struck Lisbon, Portugal killing at least 60,000 people. Voltaire wrote a deeply pessimistic poem commemorating the event. Other contemporary writers questioned his pessimism arguing for a more optimistic view of life and nature. In 1759, Voltaire replied in the novel *Candide*, his still widely read satire attacking war, religious persecution, and what he considered unwarranted optimism about the human condition. Like most of the philosophes, Voltaire believed human society could and should be improved, but he was never certain that reform, if achieved, would be permanent. In that respect his thought reflected the broader pessimistic undercurrent of the Enlightenment. As his fellow philosophe Jean d'Alembert wrote, "Barbarism lasts for centuries; it seems that it is our natural element; reason and good taste are only passing."[5]

In his later years, as will be seen in the next section, Voltaire also became a major voice attacking religious persecution and advocating toleration. He died in 1778 in Paris after a triumphal return to that city, which he had not seen for decades.

[5] Jean Le Rond d'Alembert, *Preliminary Discourse to the Encyclopedia of Diderot*, trans. by Richard N. Schwab (Indianapolis: ITT Bobbs-Merrill Educational Publishing, 1985), p. 103.

THE ENLIGHTENMENT AND RELIGION

For many, but not all, philosophes of the eighteenth century, ecclesiastical institutions, especially in their frequently privileged position as official parts of the state, were the chief impediment to human improvement and happiness. Voltaire's cry, "Crush the Infamous Thing," summed up the attitude of a number of philosophes toward the churches and Christianity. Almost all varieties of Christianity, but especially Roman Catholicism, felt their criticism as also did both Judaism and Islam.

The critical philosophes complained that both established and non-established Christian churches hindered the pursuit of a rational life and the scientific study of humanity and nature. Both Roman Catholic and Protestant clergy taught that humans were basically depraved, becoming worthy only through divine grace. According to the doctrine of original sin—either Protestant or Catholic—meaningful improvement in human nature on earth was impossible. Religion thus turned attention away from this world to the world to come. For example, the philosophes argued that the Calvinist doctrine of predestination denied that virtuous behavior in this life could affect the fate of a person's soul after death. Mired in conflicts over obscure doctrines, the churches promoted intolerance and bigotry, inciting torture, war, and other forms of human suffering.

With this attack, the philosophes were challenging not only a set of ideas, but also some of Europe's most powerful institutions. The churches were deeply enmeshed in the power structure of the Old Regime. They owned large amounts of land and collected tithes from peasants before any secular authority collected its taxes. Most clergy were legally exempt from taxes and made only annual voluntary grants to the government. The upper clergy in most countries were relatives or clients of aristocrats. High clerics were actively involved in politics. Bishops served in the British House of Lords and on the Continent, cardinals and bishops advised rulers or were sovereign princes themselves. In Protestant countries, the leading local landowner usually appointed the parish clergyman. In Britain and on the Continent, membership in the state church conferred political and social advantages. Those who did not belong to it were often excluded from political life, the universities, and the professions. Clergy frequently provided intellectual justification for the social and political status quo, and they were active agents of religious and literary censorship.

DEISM

The philosophes, although critical of many religious institutions and frequently anticlerical, did not oppose all religion. In Scotland, for example, the enlightened historian William Robertson (1721–1793) was the head of the Scottish Presbyterian Kirk. In England, Anglican clergymen did much to popularize the thought of Newton. In France, several of the leading philosophes were Catholic priests. What the philosophes sought, however, was religion without fanaticism and intolerance, a religious life that would largely substitute human reason for the authority of churches. The Newtonian worldview had convinced many writers that nature was rational. Therefore, the God who had created nature must also be rational, and the religion through which that God was worshiped should be rational. Most of them believed the life of religion and of reason could be combined, giving rise to a set of ideas known as **deism**.

The title of one of the earliest deist works, *Christianity Not Mysterious* (1696) by John Toland (1670–1722), indicates the general tenor of this religious outlook. Toland and later deist writers promoted religion as a natural and rational, rather than a supernatural and mystical, phenomenon. In this respect they differed from Newton and Locke, both of whom regarded themselves as Christians (though not necessarily theologically orthodox ones). Newton believed God could interfere with the natural order, whereas the deists regarded God as a kind of divine watchmaker who had created the mechanism of nature, set it in motion, and then departed. Most of the deist writers were also strongly anticlerical and were for that reason regarded as politically radical.

The deists' creed had two major points. The first was a belief in the existence of God, which they thought the contemplation of nature could empirically justify. Joseph Addison's poem on the spacious firmament (1712) illustrates this idea:

The spacious firmament on high,
With all the blue ethereal sky,
And spangled heav'n, a shining frame,
Their great Original proclaim:
Th' unwearied Sun, from day to day,
Does his Creator's power display,
And publishes to every land
The work of an Almighty hand.

Because nature provided evidence of a rational God, that deity must also favor rational morality. So the second point in the deists' creed was a belief in life after death, when rewards and punishments would be meted out according to the virtue of the lives people led on this earth.

Deism was empirical, tolerant, reasonable, and capable of encouraging virtuous living. Voltaire wrote,

The great name of Deist, which is not sufficiently revered, is the only name one ought to take. The only gospel one ought to read is the great book of Nature, written by the hand of God and sealed with his seal. The only religion that ought to be professed is the religion of worshiping God and being a good man.[6]

Deists hoped that wide acceptance of their faith would end rivalry among the various Christian sects and with it religious fanaticism, conflict, and persecution. They also felt deism would remove the need for priests and ministers, who, in their view, were often responsible for fomenting religious differences and denominational hatred. Deistic thought led some contemporaries to believe God had revealed himself in different ways and that many religions might embody divine truth.

TOLERATION

As discussed in Chapter 14, John Locke had set forth a strong argument for toleration in his *Letter Concerning Toleration* of 1689. Except in England, however, toleration remained the exception during the eighteenth century. Continuing in Locke's spirit, the philosophes presented religious toleration as a primary social condition for the virtuous life. Again Voltaire took the polemical lead in championing this cause. In 1762, the Roman Catholic political authorities in the city of Toulouse ordered the execution of a Huguenot named Jean Calas, who had been accused of murdering his son to prevent him from converting to Roman Catholicism. Calas was viciously tortured and publicly strangled without ever confessing his guilt. The confession would not have saved his life, but it would have given the Catholics good propaganda to use against Protestants.

Voltaire learned of the case only after Calas's death. He made the dead man's cause his own. In 1763, he published his *Treatise on Tolerance* and hounded the authorities for a new investigation. Finally, in 1765, the judicial decision against the unfortunate man was reversed. For Voltaire, the case illustrated the fruits of religious fanaticism and the need for rational reform of judicial processes.

---

[6]Quoted in J. H. Randall, *The Making of the Modern Mind*, rev. ed. (New York: Houghton Mifflin, 1940), p. 292.

In 1779, the German playwright and critic Gotthold Lessing (1729–1781) wrote *Nathan the Wise*, a plea for toleration not only of different Christian sects, but also of religious faiths other than Christianity. The premise behind all of these calls for toleration was, in effect, that life on earth and human relationships should not be subordinated to religious zeal that permitted one group of people to persecute, harm, or repress other groups.

RADICAL ENLIGHTENMENT CRITICISM OF CHRISTIANITY

Some philosophes went beyond the formulation of a rational religious alternative to Christianity and the advocacy of toleration to attack the churches and the clergy with vehemence. The Scottish philosopher David Hume (1711–1776), argued in "Of Miracles," a chapter in his *Inquiry into Human Nature* (1748), that no empirical evidence supported the belief in divine miracles central to much of Christianity. For Hume, the greatest miracle was that people believed in miracles. Voltaire repeatedly questioned the truthfulness of priests and the morality of the Bible. In his *Philosophical Dictionary* (1764), he humorously pointed out inconsistencies in biblical narratives and immoral acts of the biblical heroes. In *The Decline and Fall of the Roman Empire* (1776), Edward Gibbon (1737–1794), the English historian, explained the rise of Christianity in terms of natural causes rather than the influence of miracles and piety.

A few philosophes went further. Baron d'Holbach (1723–1789) and Julien Offray de La Mettrie (1709–1751) embraced positions close to atheism and materialism. Theirs was distinctly a minority position, however. Most of the philosophes sought not the abolition of religion, but its transformation into a humane force that would encourage virtuous living. In the words of the title of a work by the German philosopher Immanuel Kant (1724–1804), they sought to pursue *Religion within the Limits of Reason Alone* (1793).

JEWISH THINKERS IN THE AGE OF ENLIGHTENMENT

Despite their emphasis on toleration, the philosophes' criticisms of traditional religion often reflected an implicit contempt not only for Christianity but also, and sometimes more vehemently, for Judaism and, as we see later, for Islam as well. Their attack on the veracity of biblical miracles and biblical history undermined the au-

The Dutch Jewish philosopher Baruch Spinoza was deeply influenced by the new science of the mid-seventeenth century. In his writings, Spinoza argued for rationality over traditional spiritual beliefs. Library of Congress

thority of the Hebrew scriptures as well as the Christian. They often aimed their satirical barbs at personalities from the Hebrew scriptures. Some philosophes characterized Judaism as a more primitive faith than Christianity and one from which philosophical rationalism provided a path of escape. The Enlightenment view of religion thus served in some ways to further stigmatize Jews and Judaism in the eyes of non-Jewish Europeans.

Enlightenment values also, however, allowed certain Jewish intellectuals to rethink the relationship of their communities to the wider European culture from which they had largely lived apart. Two major Jewish writers—one a few decades before the opening of the Enlightenment and one toward the close—entered the larger debate over religion and the place of Jews in European life. These were Baruch Spinoza (1632–1677), who lived in the Netherlands, and Moses Mendelsohn (1729–1786), who lived in Germany. Spinoza set the example for a secularized version of Judaism, and Mendelsohn established the main outlines of an assimilationist position. Although their approaches displayed certain similarities, there were also important differences.

The new science of the mid-seventeenth century deeply influenced Spinoza, the son of a Jewish merchant of Amsterdam. Like his contemporaries, Hobbes and Descartes, he looked to the power of human reason to reconceptualize traditional thought. In that regard his thinking reflected the age of scientific revolution and looked toward the later Enlightenment.

In his *Ethics*, the most famous of his works, Spinoza so closely identified God and nature, or the spiritual and material worlds, that contemporaries condemned him. Many thought he drew God and nature too intimately into a single divine substance, leaving little room for the possibility of a distinctly divine revelation to humankind in scripture. Both Christians and Jews also believed Spinoza's near pantheistic position (the idea that God is not a distinct personality but that everything in the universe is) meant that human beings might not be personally responsible for their actions and that there could be no personal, individual immortality of the human soul after death. During his lifetime the controversial character of his writings led both Jews and Protestants to criticize him as an atheist. When he was twenty-four, his own synagogue excommunicated him, and thereafter he lived apart from the Amsterdam Jewish community.

In his *Theologico-Political Treatise* (1670), Spinoza directly anticipated much of the religious criticism of the Enlightenment and its attacks on the power of superstition in human life. Spinoza described the origins of religion in thoroughly naturalistic terms. He believed the Hebrew Bible provided Jews with divine legislation but not with specially revealed theological knowledge. In this respect, he was calling on both Jews and Christians to use their own reason in religious matters and to read the Bible like other ancient books. Spinoza's extensive rational and historical criticism of the biblical narratives disturbed Christian and Jewish contemporaries who saw him as a writer seeking to lead people away from all religion. He actually argued, however, that the formally organized religious institutions of both Christianity and Judaism led people away from the original teaching of scripture and encouraged them to persecute those who disagreed with the leaders of their respective churches and synagogues.

Because of Spinoza's excommunication from his synagogue, the philosophes considered him a martyr for rationality against superstition. He also symbolized Jews who, through the use of their critical reason, separated themselves from traditional Judaism and attempted to enter mainstream society to pursue a secular existence

with little or no regard for their original faith. Consequently, his life and his writings, as one commentator has stated, "made it possible for defenders of the Enlightenment to advocate toleration of Jews while simultaneously holding Judaism in contempt."[7] This stance of championing toleration while condemning Judaism itself would later characterize the outlook of many non-Jewish Europeans regarding the assimilation of Jews into European civic life. It was, however, an outlook that Jewish communities themselves could not welcome without considerable modification.

Moses Mendelsohn, the leading Jewish philosopher of the eighteenth century, was known as the "Jewish Socrates." Writing almost a century after Spinoza, he also advocated the entry of Jews into modern European life. In contrast to Spinoza, however, Mendelsohn argued that a Jew could combine loyalty to Judaism with adherence to rational, Enlightenment values. Mendelsohn could hold this position in part because of the influence of Lessing's arguments for toleration. Indeed, Mendelsohn had been the chief model for Lessing's character *Nathan the Wise*.

Mendelsohn's most influential work was *Jerusalem; or, On Ecclesiastical Power and Judaism* (1783) in which he argued both for extensive religious toleration and for maintaining the religious distinction of Jewish communities. Mendelsohn urged that religious diversity within a nation did not harm loyalty to the government; therefore, governments should be religiously neutral and Jews should enjoy the same civil rights as other subjects. Then, in the spirit of the deists, he presented Judaism as one of many religious paths revealed by God. Jewish law and practice were intended for the moral benefit of Jewish communities; other religions similarly served other people. Consequently, various communities should be permitted to practice their religious faith alongside other religious groups.

Unlike Spinoza, Mendelsohn wished to advocate religious toleration while genuinely sustaining the traditional religious practices and faith of Judaism. Nevertheless, Mendelsohn believed Jewish communities should not have the right to excommunicate their members over differences in theological opinions or even if their members embraced modern secular ideas. He thus sought both toleration of Jews within European society

---

[7] Steven B. Smith, *Spinoza, Liberalism, and the Question of Jewish Identity* (New Haven, CT: Yale University Press, 1997), p. 166.

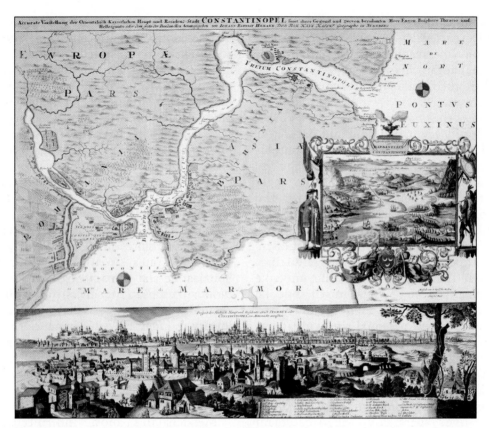

Few Europeans visited the Ottoman Empire. What little they knew about it came from reports of travelers and from illustrations such as this view of Constantinople, the empire's capital.   © Historical Picture Archive/CORBIS

and toleration by Jews of a wider spectrum of opinion within their own communities. His hope was that the rationalism of the Enlightenment would provide the foundation for both types of toleration. Mendelsohn thus set forth a far more extensive vision of religious toleration than had John Locke almost a century earlier. Locke had contended that while the state should tolerate many different religious communities, each should retain the right of excommunication over its members (see Chapter 14).

ISLAM IN ENLIGHTENMENT THOUGHT

Unlike Judaism, Islam, except in the Balkan Peninsula, had few adherents in eighteenth-century Europe. Although European merchants traded with the Ottoman Empire or with those parts of South Asia where Islam prevailed, most Europeans came to know what little they did know about the Islamic world and Islam as a religion through books—the religious commentaries of Christian missionaries, histories, and the reports of travelers—that, with rare exceptions, were hostile to Islam and deeply misleading.

Islam continued to be seen as a rival to Christianity. European writers, such as Pascal in his *Pensées* (see Chapter 14), repeated what other Christian critics had said for centuries. They portrayed Islam as a false religion and Muhammed as an impostor and a false prophet because he had not performed miracles. Furthermore, they also attacked Islam as an exceptionally carnal or sexually promiscuous religion because of its teaching that heaven was a place of sensuous delights, its permission for a man to have more than one wife, Muhammed's own polygamy, and the presence of harems in the Islamic world.

Christian authors also ignored the Islamic understanding of the life and mission of Muhammed. They referred to Islam as Muhammedanism, thus implying that Muhammed was divine rather than a human being with whom God had chosen to communicate. Muslims consider the suggestion that Muhammed was divine to be blasphemous.

European universities did endow professorships to study Arabic during the seventeenth century, but these university scholars generally agreed with theological critics that Islam too often embodied religious fanaticism. Even relatively well-informed works based on knowledge of Arabic and Islamic sources, such as Barthélemy d'Herbelot's *Bibliothèque orientale* (*Oriental Library*), a reference book published in 1697, Simon Ockley's *History of the Saracens* (1718), and George Sale's introduction to the first full English translation of the Qur'an (1734) were largely hostile to their subject. All of these books continued to be reprinted and remained influential well into the nineteenth century, demonstrating how little disinterested information Europeans had about Islam.

Enlightenment philosophes spoke with two voices regarding Islam. Voltaire indicated his opinion along with that of many of his contemporaries in the title of his 1742 tragedy, *Fanaticism, or Mohammed the Prophet*. Although he sometimes spoke well of the Qur'an, Voltaire declared in a later historical work, "We must suppose that Muhammed, like all enthusiasts, violently impressed by his own ideas, retailed them in good faith, fortified them with fancies, deceived himself in deceiving others, and finally sustained with deceit a doctrine he believed to be good."[8] Thus, for Voltaire, Muhammed and Islam in general represented simply one more example of the religious fanaticism he had so often criticized among Christians.

Some Enlightenment writers, however, spoke well of the Islamic faith. The deist John Toland, who opposed prejudice against both Jews and Muslims, contended that Islam derived from early Christian writings and was thus a form of Christianity. These views so offended most of his contemporaries that Toland became known as a "Mohametan" Christian. Edward Gibbon, who blamed Christianity for contributing to the fall of the Roman Empire, wrote with respect of Muhammed's leadership and Islam's success in conquering so vast a territory in the first century of its existence. Other commentators approved of Islam's tolerance and the charitable work of Muslims.

Some philosophes criticized Islam on cultural and political grounds. In *The Persian Letters* (1721), supposedly written by two Muslim Persians visiting Europe, the young philosophe Charles de Montesquieu used Islamic culture as a foil to criticize his own European society. Yet, by the time he wrote his more influential *Spirit of the Laws* (1748), discussed more fully later in this chapter, Montesquieu associated Islamic society with the passivity that he ascribed to people subject to political despotism. Like other Europeans, Montesquieu believed the excessive influence of Islamic religious leaders prevented the Ottoman Empire from adapting itself to new advances in technology.

One of the most positive commentators on eighteenth-century Islam was a woman. Between 1716 and 1718, Lady Mary Wortley Montagu (1689–1762) lived in Istanbul with her husband, the British ambassador to Turkey. She wrote a series of letters about her experiences there that were published the year after her death. In these *Turkish Embassy Letters*, she praised much about Ottoman society and urged the English to copy the Turkish practice of vaccination against smallpox. Unlike European males, Montagu had access to the private quarters of women in Istanbul. In contrast to the constraints under which English women found themselves, she thought upperclass Turkish women were remarkably free and well treated by their husbands despite having to wear clothing that completely covered them in public. In fact, Montagu thought the anonymity these coverings bestowed allowed Turkish women to move freely about Istanbul. She also considered the magnificent Ottoman architecture better than anything in Western Europe. Montagu repeatedly criticized the misinformation that prevailed in Europe about the Ottoman Empire and declared that many of the hostile comments about Islam and Islamic morality were simply wrong.

Nevertheless, the European voices demanding fairness and expressing empathy for Islam were rare throughout the eighteenth century. As one historian has commented, "The basic Christian attitude was still what it had been for a millennium: a rejection of the claim of Muslims that Muhammad was a prophet and the Qur'an the word of God, mingled with a memory of periods of fear and conflict, and also, a few thinkers and scholars apart, with legends, usually hostile and often contemptuous."[9]

Muslims were not curious about the Christian West themselves. Only a handful of Muslims from the Ottoman Empire visited Western Europe in the eighteenth century, and no Islamic writers showed much interest in contemporary European authors. The Ulama, the Islamic religious establishment, reinforced these attitudes. They taught that God's revelations to Muhammad meant Islam had replaced Christianity as a religion and therefore there was little for Muslims to learn from Christian culture.

---

[8]Quoted in Theodore Besterman, *Voltaire* (New York: Harcourt, Brace, & World, 1969), p. 409.

[9]A. Hourani, *Islam in European Thought* (Cambridge: Cambridge University Press, 1991), p. 136.

THE ENLIGHTENMENT AND SOCIETY

THE *ENCYCLOPEDIA*: FREEDOM AND ECONOMIC IMPROVEMENT

The mid-century witnessed the publication of the *Encyclopedia*, one of the greatest monuments of the Enlightenment and its most monumental undertaking in the realm of print culture. Under the heroic leadership of Denis Diderot (1713–1784) and Jean Le Rond d'Alembert (1717–1783), the first volume appeared in 1751. Eventually, numbering seventeen volumes of text and eleven of plates (illustrations), the project was completed in 1772. No other work of the Enlightenment so illustrated the movement's determination to probe life on earth rather than in the religious realm. As one writer in the *Encyclopedia* observed, "Man is the unique point to which we must refer everything, if we wish to interest and please amongst considerations the most arid and details the most dry."[10] The use of the word *man* in this passage was not simply an accident of language. Most philosophes, as we shall see later in the chapter, were thinking primarily of men, not women, when they framed their reformist ideas.

The *Encyclopedia*, in part a collective plea for freedom of expression, reached fruition only after many attempts to censor it and halt its publication. It was the product of the collective effort of more than a hundred authors, and its editors had at one time or another solicited articles from all the major French philosophes. It included the most advanced critical ideas of the time on religion, government, and philosophy. To avoid official censure, these ideas often had to be hidden in obscure articles or under the cover of irony. The *Encyclopedia* also included numerous important articles and illustrations on manufacturing, canal building, ship construction, and improved agriculture, making it an important source of knowledge about eighteenth-century social and economic life.

[10]Quoted in F. L. Baumer, *Main Currents of Western Thought*, 4th ed. (New Haven, CT: Yale University Press, 1978), p. 374.

Between 14,000 and 16,000 copies of various editions of the *Encyclopedia* were sold before 1789. The project had been designed to secularize learning and to undermine intellectual assumptions that lingered from the Middle Ages and the Reformation. The articles on politics, ethics, and society ignored divine law and concentrated on humanity and its immediate well-being. The Encyclopedists looked to antiquity rather than to the Christian centuries for their intellectual and ethical models. For them, the future welfare of humankind lay not in pleasing God or following divine commandments, but rather in harnessing the power and resources of the earth and in living at peace with one's fellow human beings. The good life lay here and now and was to be achieved through the application of reason to human relationships. The publication of the *Encyclopedia* spread Enlightenment thought more fully over the Continent, penetrating German and Russian intellectual and political circles.

BECCARIA AND REFORM OF CRIMINAL LAW

Although the term did not appear until later, the idea of *social science* originated with the Enlightenment. Philosophes hoped to end human cruelty by discovering social laws and making people aware of them. These concerns are most evident in the philosophes' work on law and prisons.

In 1764, Marquis Cesare Beccaria (1738–1794), an Italian aristocrat and philosophe, published *On Crimes*

Denis Diderot was the heroic editor of the *Encylopedia* published in seventeen volumes of text and eleven of prints between 1751 and 1772. Through its pages many of the chief ideas of the Enlightenment reached a broad audience of readers. Réunion des Musées Nationaux/Art Resource, NY

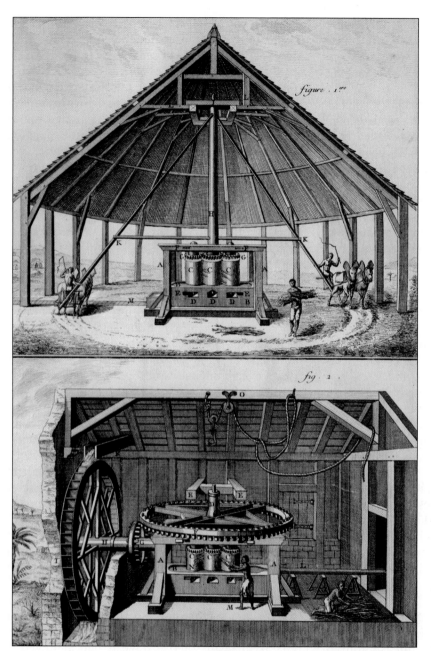

Denis Diderot in the *Encyclopedia* included illustrations of machinery and working people from across the globe. Diderot was also deeply hostile to slavery. This engraving illustrated a sugar mill and sugar boiling house run with slave labor in the New World. The sugar produced in such mills was used in the European coffee houses where the ideas of the philosophes were often discussed.   University of Virginia Library

and Punishments, in which he applied critical analysis to the problem of making punishments both effective and just. He wanted the laws of monarchs and legislatures—that is, positive law—to conform with the rational laws of nature. He rigorously and eloquently attacked both torture and capital punishment. He thought the criminal justice system should ensure a speedy trial and certain punishment and the intent of punishment should be to deter further crime. The purpose of laws was not to impose the will of God or some other ideal of perfection, but to secure the greatest good or happiness for the greatest number of human beings. This utilitarian philosophy based on happiness in this life permeated most Enlightenment writing on practical reforms.

THE PHYSIOCRATS AND ECONOMIC FREEDOM

Economic policy was another area in which the philosophes saw existing legislation and administration preventing the operation of natural social laws. They believed mercantilist legislation (designed to protect a country's trade from external competition) and the regulation of labor by governments and guilds actually hampered the expansion of trade, manufacture, and agriculture. In France, these economic reformers were called the **phys-iocrats**. Their leading spokespeople were François Quesnay (1694–1774) and Pierre Dupont de Nemours (1739–1817).

The physiocrats believed the primary role of government was to protect property and to permit its owners to use it freely. They argued that agriculture was the basis on which all economic production depended. They favored the consolidation of small peasant holdings into larger, more efficient farms. Here, as elsewhere, the rationalism of the Enlightenment was closely connected to the spirit of improvement that influenced so much of eighteenth-century European economic life.

ADAM SMITH ON ECONOMIC GROWTH AND SOCIAL PROGRESS

The most important economic work of the Enlightenment was Adam Smith's (1723–1790) *Inquiry into the Nature and Causes of the Wealth of Nations* (1776). Smith, who was for a time a professor at Glasgow University in Scotland, believed economic liberty was the foundation of a natural economic system. As a result, he urged that the mercantile system of England—including the navigation acts governing colonial trade, the bounties the government gave to favored merchants and industries, most tariffs, trading monopolies, and the domestic regulation of labor and manufacture—be abolished. These regulations were intended to preserve the wealth of the nation, to capture wealth from other nations, and to maximize the work available for the nation's laborers. Smith argued, however, that they hindered the expansion of wealth and production. The best way to encourage economic growth, he maintained, was to unleash individuals to pursue their own selfish economic interests. As self-interested individuals sought to enrich themselves by meeting the needs of others in the marketplace, the economy would expand. Consumers would find their wants met as manufacturers and merchants competed for their business.

Mercantilism assumed that the earth's resources were limited and scarce, so one nation could acquire wealth only at the expense of others. Smith's book challenged this assumption. He saw the resources of nature—water, air, soil, and minerals—as boundless. To him, they demanded exploitation for the enrichment and comfort of humankind. In effect, Smith was saying the nations and peoples of Europe need not be poor.

Smith is usually regarded as the founder of **laissez-faire** economic thought and policy, which favors a limited role for the government in economic life. *The Wealth of Nations* was, however, a complex book. Smith was no simple dogmatist. For example, he did not oppose all government activity in the economy. The state, he argued, should provide schools, armies, navies, and roads. It should also undertake certain commercial ventures, such as opening dangerous new trade routes that were economically desirable, but too expensive or risky for private enterprise.

Within *The Wealth of Nations*, Smith, like other Scottish thinkers of the day, embraced an important theory of human social and economic development, known as the *four-stage theory*. According to this theory, human societies can be classified as hunting and gathering, pastoral or herding, agricultural, or commercial. The hunters and gatherers have little or no settled life. Pastoral societies are groups of nomads who tend their herds and develop some private property. Agricultural or farming societies are settled and have clear-cut property arrangements. Finally, the commercial state includes advanced cities, the manufacture of numerous items for wide consumption, extensive trade between cities and the countryside, as well as elaborate forms of property and financial arrangements. Smith and other Scottish writers described the passage of human society through these stages as a movement from barbarism to civilization.

The four-stage theory implicitly evaluated the later stages of economic development and the people dwelling in them as higher, more progressive, and more civilized than the earlier ones. A social theorist using this theory could thus quickly look at a society and, on the basis of the state of its economic development and organizations, rank it in terms of the stage it had achieved. In fact, the commercial stage, the highest rank in the theory, described society as it appeared in northwestern Europe. Thus, Smith's theory allowed Europeans to look about the world and always find themselves dwelling at the highest level of human achievement. To Europeans, this outlook helped justify their economic and imperial domination of the world during the following century. They repeatedly portrayed themselves as bringing a higher level of civilization to people elsewhere who, according to the four-stage theory, lived in lower stages of human social and economic development. Europeans thus imbued with the spirit of the Enlightenment presented themselves as carrying out a civilizing mission to the rest of the world.

POLITICAL THOUGHT OF THE PHILOSOPHES

Nowhere was the philosophes' reformist agenda, as well as tensions among themselves, so apparent as in their political thought. Most philosophes were discontented with certain political features of their countries, but French philosophes were especially discontented. There, the corruption around the royal court, the blundering of the bureaucracy, the less-than-glorious mid-century wars, and the power of the church seemed to make all problems worse. Consequently, the most important political thought of the Enlightenment occurred in France. The French philosophes, however, were divided over how to solve their country's problems. Their proposed solutions spanned a wide political spectrum, from aristocratic reform to democracy to absolute monarchy.

MONTESQUIEU AND *SPIRIT OF THE LAWS*

Charles Louis de Secondat, baron de Montesquieu (1689–1755), was a lawyer, a noble of the robe, and a member of a provincial *parlement*. He also belonged to the Bordeaux Academy of Science, before which he presented papers on scientific topics.

Although living comfortably within the bosom of French society, he saw the need for reform. In 1721, as already noted, he published *The Persian Letters* to satirize contemporary institutions. Behind the humor lay the cutting edge of criticism and an exposition of the cruelty and irrationality of European life. About a decade after this volume appeared, Montesquieu, like Voltaire, visited England and deeply admired English institutions.

In his most enduring work, *Spirit of the Laws* (1748), Montesquieu held up the example of the British constitution as the wisest model for regulating the power of government. Montesquieu's *Spirit of the Laws*, perhaps the single most influential book of the century, exhibits the internal tensions of the Enlightenment. In it, Montesquieu pursued an empirical method, taking illustrative examples from the political experience of both ancient and modern nations. From these, he concluded that no single set of political laws could apply to all peoples at all times and in all places. The good political life depended rather on the relationship among many political variables. Whether the best form of government for a country was a monarchy or a republic, for example, depended on that country's size, population, social and religious customs, economic structure, traditions, and climate. Only a careful examination and evaluation of these elements could reveal what mode of government would most benefit a particular people.

For France, Montesquieu favored a monarchical government tempered and limited by various intermediary institutions, including the aristocracy, the towns, and the other corporate bodies that enjoyed liberties the monarch had to respect. These corporate bodies might be said to represent segments of the general population and thus of public opinion. In France, he regarded the aristocratic courts, or *parlements*, as a major example of an intermediary association. Their role was to limit the power of the monarchy and thus to preserve the liberty of its subjects.

In championing these aristocratic bodies and the general oppositional role of the aristocracy, Montesquieu was a political conservative. He adopted this conservatism in the hope of achieving reform, however, for he believed the oppressive and inefficient absolutism of the monarchy accounted for the degradation of French life.

One of Montesquieu's most influential ideas was that of the division of power in government. For his model of a government with authority wisely separated among different branches, he took contemporary Great Britain. There, he believed, executive power resided in the king, legislative power in the Parliament, and judicial power in the courts. He thought any two branches could check and balance the power of the other. His perception of the eighteenth-century British constitution was incorrect because he failed to see how patronage and electoral corruption allowed a handful of powerful aristocrats to dominate the government. Moreover, he was also unaware of the emerging cabinet system, which was slowly making the executive power a creature of the Parliament.

Nevertheless, Montesquieu's analysis illustrated his strong belief that monarchs should be subject to constitutional limits on their power and that a separate legislature, not the monarch, should formulate laws. For this reason, although he set out to defend the political privileges of the French aristocracy, Montesquieu's ideas have had a profound effect on the constitutional form of liberal democracies for more than two centuries.

ROUSSEAU: A RADICAL CRITIQUE OF MODERN SOCIETY

Jean-Jacques Rousseau (1712–1778) held a different view of the exercise and reform of political power from Montesquieu's. Rousseau was a strange, isolated genius who never felt particularly comfortable with the other philosophes. His own life was troubled. He could form few close friendships. He sired numerous children, whom he abandoned to foundling hospitals. Yet perhaps more than any other writer of the mid-eighteenth century, he transcended the political thought and values of his own time. Rousseau hated the world and the society in which he lived. It seemed to him impossible for human beings living according to the commercial values of his time to achieve moral, virtuous, or sincere lives. In 1750, in his *Discourse on the Moral Effects of the Arts and Sciences*, he contended that the process of civilization and the Enlightenment had corrupted human nature. In 1755, in his *Discourse on the Origin of Inequality*, Rousseau blamed much of the evil in the world on the uneven distribution of property.

Among the philosophes of the Enlightenment Jean Jacques Rousseau set forth the most democratic and egalitarian political ideas. This bust was created by the French sculptor Jean-Antoine Houdon after Rousseau's death mask.   Réunion des Musées Nationaux/Art Resource, NY

In both works, Rousseau brilliantly and directly challenged the social fabric of the day. He questioned the concepts of material and intellectual progress and the morality of a society in which commerce and industry were regarded as the most important human activities. The other philosophes generally believed life would improve if people could enjoy more of the fruits of the earth or could produce more goods. Rousseau raised the more fundamental question of what constitutes the good life. This question has haunted European social thought ever since the eighteenth century.

Rousseau carried these same concerns into his political thought. His most extensive discussion of politics appeared in *The Social Contract* (1762). Although the book attracted little immediate attention, by the end of the century it was widely read in France. Compared with Montesquieu's *Spirit of the Laws, The Social Contract* is an abstract book. It does not propose specific reforms, but outlines the kind of political structure that Rousseau believed would overcome the evils of contemporary politics and society.

In the tradition of John Locke, most eighteenth-century political thinkers regarded human beings as individuals and society as a collection of individuals pursuing personal, selfish goals. These writers wished to liberate individuals from the undue bonds of government. Rousseau picked up the stick from the other end. His book opens with the declaration, "All men are born free, but everywhere they are in chains."[11] The rest of the volume is a defense of the chains of a properly organized society over its members.

Rousseau suggested that society is more important than its individual members, because they are what they are only by virtue of their relationship to the larger community. Independent human beings living alone can achieve little. Through their relationship to the larger community, they become moral creatures capable of significant action. The question then becomes: What kind of community allows people to behave morally? In his two previous discourses, Rousseau had explained that the contemporaneous European society was not such a community; it was merely an aggregate of competing individuals whose chief social goal was to preserve selfish independence despite all potential social bonds and obligations.

Rousseau envisioned a society in which each person could maintain personal freedom while behaving as a loyal member of the larger community.

[11]Jean-Jacques Rousseau, *The Social Contract and Discourses*, trans. by G. D. H. Cole (New York: Dutton, 1950), p. 3.

Drawing on the traditions of Plato and Calvin, he defined freedom as obedience to law. In his case, the law to be obeyed was that created by the general will. In a society with virtuous customs and morals in which citizens have adequate information on important issues, the concept of the general will is normally equivalent to the will of a majority of voting citizens. Democratic participation in decision making would bind the individual citizen to the community. Rousseau believed the general will, thus understood, must always be right and that to obey the general will is to be free. This argument led him to the notorious conclusion that under certain circumstances some people must be forced to be free. Rousseau's politics thus constituted a justification for radical direct democracy and for collective action against individual citizens.

Rousseau had, in effect, attacked the eighteenth-century cult of the individual and the fruits of selfishness. He stood at odds with the commercial spirit that was transforming the society in which he lived. Rousseau would have disapproved of the main thrust of Adam Smith's *Wealth of Nations*, which he may or may not have read, and would no doubt have preferred a study on the virtue of nations. Smith wanted people to be prosperous; Rousseau wanted them to be good even if being good meant they might remain poor. He saw human beings not as independent individuals, but as creatures enmeshed in necessary social relationships. He believed loyalty to the community should be encouraged. As one device to that end, he suggested a properly governed society should decree a civic religion based on the creed of deism. Such a shared religion could, he argued, help unify a society even if it had to be enforced by repressive legislation.

Rousseau had only a marginal impact on his own time. The other philosophes questioned his critique of material improvement. Aristocrats and royal ministers could hardly be expected to welcome his proposal for radical democracy. Too many people were either making or hoping to make money to appreciate his criticism of commercial values. He proved, however, to be a figure to whom later generations returned. Leading figures in the French Revolution were familiar with his writing, and he influenced writers in the nineteenth and twentieth centuries who were critical of the general tenor and direction of Western culture. Rousseau hated much about the emerging modern society in Europe, but he contributed much to modernity by exemplifying for later generations the critic who dared to question the very foundations of social thought and action.

ENLIGHTENED CRITICS OF EUROPEAN EMPIRES

Most European thinkers associated with the Enlightenment favored the extension of European empires across the world. Like the Scottish writers who embraced the four-stage theory, they believed that the extension of the political structures and economies of northwestern Europe amounted to the spread of progress and civilization. The Scottish commentators and their followers were not without their criticisms of European civilization and of excessive economic regulation in contemporary empires, but on the whole, they believed European civilization superior to that of other cultures.

A few Enlightenment voices, however, did criticize the European empires on moral grounds, especially the European conquest of the Americas, the treatment of Native Americans, and the enslavement of Africans on the two American continents. The most important of these critics were Denis Diderot and two German philosophers, Immanuel Kant and Johann Gottlieb Herder (1744–1803). (See "Denis Diderot Condemns European Empires," page 570.)

What ideas allowed these figures from the Enlightenment to criticize their empires? As Sankar Muthu has recently written, "The first and most basic idea is that human beings deserve some modicum of moral and political respect simply because of the fact that they are human."[12] In other words, the Enlightenment critics of their empires argued for a form of shared humanity that the sixteenth-century European conquerors and their successors in the Americas and in other areas of imperial conquest had ignored. Immanuel Kant wrote, "When America, the Negro countries, the Spice Islands, the Cape, and so forth were discovered, they were to them [the Europeans], countries belonging to no one, since they counted the inhabitants as *nothing*."[13] Kant, Diderot, and Herder rejected this dismissive outlook and the harsh policies that had flowed from it. They believed no single definition of human nature could be made the standard throughout the world and then used to dehumanize people whose appearance or culture differed from it.

A second of these critical ideas was the conviction that the people whom Europeans had encountered

---

[12]Sankar Muthu, *Enlightenment Against Empire* (Princeton: Princeton University Press, 2003), p. 268. This section draws primarily from this excellent recent book.

[13]Quoted in Muthu, *Enlightenment Against Empire*, p. 267.

DENIS DIDEROT CONDEMNS EUROPEAN EMPIRES

Denis Diderot was one of the most prolific writers of the Enlightenment. He is most famous as the editor of the Encyclopedia. *Some of his writings were published without being directly attributed to him. Among these were his contributions to Abbé G. T. Raynal's* History of the Two Indies, *published in various editions after 1772. Diderot's contributions appear to have been made in 1780. Raynal's entire* History *was critical of the European colonial empires that had arisen since the Spanish encounter with the New World. Diderot particularly condemned the inhumane treatment of the native populations of the Americas, the greed all Europeans displayed, and the various forms of forced labor.*

■ *What is the basis for Diderot's view that Europeans have behaved tyrannically? How does he portray the behavior of Europeans in foreign areas? What specific social results does he associate with European greed?*

Let the European nations make their own judgment and give themselves the name they deserve. . . . Their explorers arrive in a region of the New World unoccupied by anyone from the Old World, and immediately bury a small strip of metal on which they have engraved these words: *This country belongs to us.* Any why does it belong to you?

. . . You have no right to the natural products of the country where you land, and you claim a right over your fellow-men. Instead of recognizing this man as a brother you only see him as a slave, a beast of burden. Oh my fellow citizens! You think like that and you behave like that; and you have ideas of justice, a morality, a holy religion . . . in common with whose whom you treat so tryannically. This reproach should especially be addressed to the Spaniards.

* * *

Beyond the Equator a man is neither English, Dutch, French, Spanish, nor Portuguese. He retains only those principles and prejudices of his native country which justify or excuse his conduct. He crawls when he is weak; he is violent when strong; he is in a hurry to acquire, in a hurry to enjoy, and capable of every crime which will lead him most quickly to his goals. He is a domestic tiger returning to the forest; the thirst for blood takes hold of him once more. This is how all the Europeans, every one of them, indistinctly, have appeared in the countries of the New World. There they have assumed a common frenzy—the thirst for gold.

* * *

The Spaniard, the first to be thrown up by the waves onto the shores of the New World, thought he had no duty to people who did not share his color, customs, or religion. He saw in them only tools for his greed, and he clapped them in irons. These weak men, not used to work, soon died in the foul air of the mines, or in other occupations which were virtually as lethal. Then people called for slaves from Africa. Their number has gone up as more land has been cultivated. The Portuguese, Dutch, English, French, Danes, all the nations, free or subjected, have without remorse sought to increase their fortune in the sweat, blood and despair of these unfortunates. What a horrible system!

From "Extracts from the Histoire des Deux Indes", "6 Principles of Colonisation", (Book Eight, Ch. I; IV, 105–8), pgs. 176–177, "7 National Character at Home and Overseas", (Book Nine, Ch. I; IV, 233–5), pg. 178, "14 Slavery and Liberty", (Book Eleven, Ch. 24, V, 275–8), pg. 178 in *Political Writings* by Denis Diderot, trans. by John Hope Mason and Robert Wokler. © Cambridge University Press 1992. Reprinted with the permission of Cambridge University Press.

in the Americas had possessed cultures that should have been respected and understood rather than destroyed. Some Europeans in the early years of the encounter with America had argued that while the native peoples were human, their way of life was too degraded to treat them as the human equals of Europeans. In the late eighteenth century, Herder rejected such a view, "'European culture' is a mere abstraction, an empty concept. Where does or did it actually exist in its entirety? In which nation? In which period? . . . Only a misanthrope could regard European culture as the universal condition of our species. The culture of *man* is not the culture of the *European*; it manifests itself according to time and place in every people."[14] For Herder, human beings living in different societies possessed the capacity as human beings to develop in culturally different fashions. He thus embraced an outlook later known as cultural relativism.

A third idea, closely related to the second, was that human beings may develop distinct cultures possessing intrinsic values that cannot be compared, one to the detriment of another, because each culture possesses deep inner social and linguistic complexities that make any simple comparison impossible. Indeed, Diderot, Kant, and Herder argued that being a human includes the ability to develop a variety of distinctly different cultures.

These arguments critical of empire often involved criticism of New World slavery and were part of the anti-slavery movement to be discussed in Chapter 20. Whereas the antislavery arguments took strong hold in both Europe and America from the late eighteenth century onward, the arguments critical of empires did not. They remained isolated from the rest of Enlightenment political thought and would not be strongly revived until new anticolonial voices were raised in Europe and the non-European world at the close of the nineteenth century.

WOMEN IN THE THOUGHT AND PRACTICE OF THE ENLIGHTENMENT

Women, especially in France, helped significantly to promote the careers of the philosophes. In Paris, the salons of women such as Marie-Thérèse Geoffrin (1699–1777), Julie de Lespinasse (1733–1776),

14Quoted in F. M. Barnard, *Self-Direction and Political Legitimacy: Rousseau and Herder* (Oxford: Clarendon Press, 1988), p. 227.

MAJOR WORKS OF THE ENLIGHTENMENT AND THEIR PUBLICATION DATES

1670 Spinoza's *Theologico-Political Treatise*

1677 Spinoza's *Ethics* (published posthumously)

1687 Newton's *Principia Mathematica*

1690 Locke's *Essay Concerning Human Understanding*

1696 Toland's *Christianity Not Mysterious*

1721 Montesquieu's *Persian Letters*

1733 Voltaire's *Letters on the English*

1738 Voltaire's *Elements of the Philosophy of Newton*

1748 Montesquieu's *Spirit of the Laws*

1748 Hume's *Inquiry into Human Nature,* with the chapter "Of Miracles"

1750 Rousseau's *Discourse on the Moral Effects of the Arts and Sciences*

1751 First volume of the *Encyclopedia,* edited by Diderot

1755 Rousseau's *Discourse on the Origin of Inequality*

1759 Voltaire's *Candide*

1762 Rousseau's *Social Contract* and *Émile*

1763 Voltaire's *Treatise on Tolerance*

1764 Voltaire's *Philosophical Dictionary*

1764 Beccaria's *On Crimes and Punishments*

1776 Gibbon's *Decline and Fall of the Roman Empire*

1776 Smith's *Wealth of Nations*

1779 Lessing's *Nathan the Wise*

1783 Mendelsohn's *Jerusalem; or, On Ecclesiastical Power and Judaism*

1792 Wollstonecraft's *Vindication of the Rights of Woman*

1793 Kant's *Religion within the Limits of Reason Alone*

---

and Claudine de Tencin (1689–1749) gave the philosophes access to useful social and political contacts and a receptive environment in which to circulate their ideas. Association with a fashionable salon brought philosophes increased social status and added luster and respectability to their ideas. Philosophes clearly enjoyed the opportunity to be the center of attention that a salon provided, and their presence at them could boost the sales of their works. The women who organized the salons were well connected to political figures who could help protect the philosophes and secure royal pensions for them. The marquise de Pompadour (1721–1764), the mistress of King

ROUSSEAU ARGUES FOR SEPARATE SPHERES FOR MEN AND WOMEN

Rousseau published Émile, *a novel about education, in 1762. In it, he made one of the strongest and most influential arguments of the eighteenth century for distinct social roles for men and women. Furthermore, he portrayed women as fundamentally subordinate to men. In the next document, Mary Wollstonecraft, a contemporary, presents a rebuttal.*

■ *How does Rousseau move from the physical differences between men and women to an argument for distinct social roles and social spheres? What would be the proper kinds of social activities for women in Rousseau's vision? What kind of education would he think appropriate for women?*

There is no parity between the two sexes in regard to the consequences of sex. The male is male only at certain moments. The female is female her whole life or at least during her whole youth. Everything constantly recalls her sex to her; and, to fulfill its functions well, she needs a constitution which corresponds to it. She needs care during her pregnancy; she needs rest at the time of childbirth; she needs a soft and sedentary life to suckle her children; she needs patience and gentleness, a zeal and an affection that nothing can rebuff in order to raise her children. She serves as the link between them and their father; she alone makes him love them and gives him the confidence to call them his own. How much tenderness and care is required to maintain the union of the whole family! And, finally, all this must come not from virtues but from tastes, or else the human species would soon be extinguished.

The strictness of the relative duties of the two sexes is not and cannot be the same. When woman complains on this score about unjust man-made inequality, she is wrong. This inequality is not a human institution—or, at least, it is the work not of prejudice but of reason. It is up to the sex that nature has charged with the bearing of children to be responsible for them to the other sex. Doubtless it is not permitted to anyone to violate his faith, and every unfaithful husband who deprives his wife of the only reward of the austere duties of her sex is an unjust and barbarous man. But the unfaithful woman does more; she dissolves the family and breaks all the bonds of nature. . . .

Once it is demonstrated that man and woman are not and ought not be constituted in the same way in either character or temperament, it follows that they ought not to have the same education. In following nature's directions, man and woman ought to act in concert, but they ought not to do the same things. The goal of their labors is common, but their labors themselves are different, and consequently so are the tastes directing them. . . .

The good constitution of children initially depends on that of their mothers. The first education of men depends on the care of women. Men's morals, their passions, their tastes, their pleasures, their very happiness also depend on women. Thus the whole education of women ought to relate to men. To please men, to be useful to them, to make herself loved and honored by them, to raise them when young, to care for them when grown, to counsel them, to console them, to make their lives agreeable and sweet—these are the duties of women at all times, and they ought to be taught from childhood. So long as one does not return to this principle, one will deviate from the goal, and all the precepts taught to women will be of no use for their happiness or for ours.

Louis XV, played a key role in overcoming efforts to censor the *Encyclopedia*. She also hindered the publication of works attacking the philosophes. Other salon hostesses distributed the writings of the philosophes among their friends. Madame de Tencin promoted Montesquieu's *Spirit of the Laws* in this way.

Despite this help and support from the learned women of Paris, the philosophes were on the whole not strong feminists. Many urged better and broader education for women. They criticized the education women did receive as overly religious, and they tended to reject ascetic views of sexual relations. In general, however, they displayed traditional views toward women and advocated no radical changes in their social condition.

Montesquieu, for example, maintained, in general, that the status of women in a society was the result of climate, the political regime, culture, and women's physiology. He believed women were not naturally inferior to men and should have a wider role in society. He showed himself well aware of the kinds of personal, emotional, and sexual repression European women endured in his day. He sympathetically observed the value placed on women's appearance and the prejudice women met as they aged. In *The Persian Letters*, he included a long exchange about the repression of women in a Persian harem, condemning by implication the restrictions on women in European society. Yet Montesquieu's willingness to consider social change for women in European life had limits. Although in the *Spirit of the Laws* he indicated a belief in the equality of the sexes, he still retained a traditional view of marriage and family and expected men to dominate those institutions. Furthermore, although he supported the right of women to divorce and opposed laws that oppressed them, he upheld the ideal of female chastity.

The views about women expressed in the *Encyclopedia* were less generous than those of Montesquieu. The *Encyclopedia* suggested ways to improve women's lives, but in general, it did not emphasize that the condition of women needed reform. Almost all the contributors were men, and the editors, Diderot and d'Alembert, evidently saw no need to include many articles by women. Most of the articles that dealt with women specifically or discussed women in connection with other subjects often emphasized their physical weakness and inferiority, usually attributed to menstruation or childbearing. Some contributors favored the social equality of women, others opposed it, and still others were indifferent. The articles conveyed a general sense that women were reared to be frivolous and unconcerned with important issues. The Encyclopedists discussed women primarily within a family context—as daughters, wives, and mothers—and presented motherhood as a woman's most important occupation. On sexual behavior, the Encyclopedists upheld an unquestioned double standard.

In contrast to the articles, however, illustrations in the *Encyclopedia* showed women deeply involved in the economic activities of the day. The illustrations also portrayed the activities of lower-class and working-class women, about whom the articles had little to say.

One of the most surprising and influential analyses of the position of women came from Jean-Jacques Rousseau. This most radical of all Enlightenment political theorists urged a traditional and conservative role for women. In his novel *Émile* (1762) (discussed again in Chapter 19), he set forth a radical version of the view that men and women occupy separate spheres. He declared that women should be educated for a position subordinate to men, emphasizing especially women's function in bearing and rearing children. In his vision, there was little else for women to do but make themselves pleasing to men. He portrayed them as weaker and inferior to men in virtually all respects, except perhaps for their capacity for feeling and giving love. He excluded them from political life. Only men were to populate the world of citizenship, political action, and civic virtue. Women were relegated to the domestic sphere. (See "Rousseau Argues for Separate Spheres for Men and Women".) Many of these attitudes were not new—some have roots as ancient as Roman law—but Rousseau's powerful presentation and the influence of his other writings gave them new life in the late eighteenth century. Rousseau deeply influenced many leaders of the French Revolution, who, as shall be seen in the next chapter, often incorporated his view on gender roles in their policies.

Paradoxically, despite these views and despite his own ill treatment of the women who bore his many children, Rousseau achieved a vast following among women in the eighteenth century. He is credited with persuading thousands of upper-class women to breast-feed their own children rather than putting them out to wet nurses. One explanation for this influence is that his writings, although they did not advocate liberating women or expanding their social or economic roles, did stress the importance of their emotions. He portrayed the domestic life and the role of wife and mother as a noble and fulfilling vocation, giving middle- and upper-class women a sense that their

MARY WOLLSTONECRAFT CRITICIZES ROUSSEAU'S VIEW OF WOMEN

Mary Wollstonecraft published A Vindication of the Rights of Woman in 1792, thirty years after Rousseau's Émile had appeared. In this pioneering feminist work, she criticizes and rejects Rousseau's argument for distinct and separate spheres for men and women. She portrays that argument as defending the continued bondage of women to men and as hindering the wider education of the entire human race.

■ *What criticisms does Wollstonecraft direct against Rousseau's views? Why does Wollstonecraft emphasize a new kind of education for women?*

The most perfect education . . . is such an exercise of the understanding as is best calculated to strengthen the body and form the heart. Or, in other words, to enable the individual to attain such habits of virtue as will render it independent. In fact, it is a farce to call any being virtuous whose virtues do not result from the exercise of its own reason. This was Rousseau's opinion respecting men: I extend it to women. . . .

I may be accused or arrogance; still I must declare what I firmly believe, that all the writers who have written on the subject of female education and manners from Rousseau to Dr. Gregory [a Scottish physician], have contributed to render women more artificial, weak characters, than they would otherwise have been; and, consequently, more useless members of society. . . .

Strengthen the female mind by enlarging it, and there will be an end to blind obedience; but, as blind obedience is ever sought for by power, tyrants and sensualists are in the right when they endeavour to keep women in the dark, because the former only wants slaves, and the latter a play-thing. The sensualist, indeed, has been the most dangerous of tyrants, and women have been duped by their lovers, as princes by their ministers, whilst dreaming that they reigned over them. . . .

Rousseau declares that a woman should never, for a moment, feel herself independent, that she should be governed by fear to exercise her natural cunning, and made a coquettish slave in order to render her a more alluring object of desire, a sweeter companion to man,

daily occupations had a purpose. He assigned them a degree of influence in the domestic sphere that they could not have competing with men outside it.

In 1792, in A *Vindication of the Rights of Woman,* Mary Wollstonecraft (1759–1797) brought Rousseau before the judgment of the rational Enlightenment ideal of progressive knowledge. The immediate incentive for this essay was

Mary Wollstonecraft in her Vindication of the Rights of Woman defended equality of women with men on the grounds of men and women sharing the capacity of human reason. CORBIS/Bettmann

whenever he chooses to relax himself. He carries the arguments, which he pretends to draw from the indications of nature, still further, and insinuates that truth and fortitude, the cornerstones of all human virtue, should be cultivated with certain restrictions, because, with respect to the female character, obedience is the grand lesson which ought to be impressed with unrelenting rigour.

What nonsense! When will a great man arise with sufficient strength of mind to put away the fumes which pride and sensuality have thus spread over the subject! If women are by nature inferior to men, their virtues must be the same in quality, if not in degree, or virtue is a relative idea; consequently, their conduct should be founded on the same principles, and have the same aim.

Connected with man as daughters, wives, and mothers, their moral character may be estimated by their manner of fulfilling those simple duties; but the end, the grand end of their exertions should be to unfold their own faculties and acquire the dignity of conscious virtue. . . .

But avoiding . . . any direct comparison of the two sexes collectively, or frankly acknowledging the inferiority of women according to the present appearance of things, I shall only insist that men have increased that inferiority till women are almost sunk below the standard of rational creatures. Let their faculties have room to unfold, and their virtues to gain strength, and then determine where the whole sex must stand in the intellectual scale. . . .

I . . . will venture to assert, that till women are more rationally educated, the progress of human virtue and improvement in knowledge must receive continual checks. . . .

The mother, who wishes to give true dignity of character to her daughter, must, regardless of the sneers of ignorance, proceed on a plan diametrically opposite to that which Rousseau has recommended with all the deluding charms of eloquence and philosophical sophistry: for his eloquence renders absurdities plausible, and his dogmatic conclusions puzzle, without convincing, those who have not ability to refute them.

From Mary Wollstonecraft, *A Vindication of the Rights of Woman*, ed. by Carol H. Poston (New York: W.W. Norton, 1975), pp. 21, 22, 24–26, 35, 40, 41.

her opposition to certain policies of the French Revolution, unfavorable to women, that Rousseau had inspired. Wollstonecraft (who, like so many women of her day, died of puerperal fever, a form of blood poisoning caused by unsanitary conditions during childbirth) accused Rousseau and others after him who upheld traditional roles for women of attempting to narrow women's vision and limit their experience. She argued that to confine women to the separate domestic sphere because of supposed limitations of their physiology was to make them the sensual slaves of men. Confined in this separate sphere, they were the victims of male tyranny, their obedience was blind, and they could never achieve their own moral or intellectual identity. Denying good education to women would impede the progress of all humanity. With these arguments, Wollstonecraft was demanding for women the kind of liberty that male writers of the Enlightenment had been championing for men for more than a century. In doing so, she placed herself among the philosophes and broadened the agenda of the Enlightenment to include the rights of women as well as those of men. (See "Mary Wollstonecraft Criticizes Rousseau's View of Women".)

ROCOCO AND NEOCLASSICAL STYLES IN EIGHTEENTH-CENTURY ART

Two contrasting styles dominated eighteenth-century European art and architecture. The Rococo style embraced lavish, often lighthearted decoration with an emphasis on pastel colors and the play of light. Neoclassicism embodied a return to figurative and architectural models drawn from the Renaissance and the ancient world. The Rococo became associated with the aristocracies of the

Old Regime while Neoclassicism recalled ancient republican values that implicitly criticized the Old Regime and, toward the end of the century, was embraced by the French Revolution and Napoleon.

Rococo architecture and decoration originated in early eighteenth-century France. After Louis XIV's death in 1715, the Regent Philippe d'Orleans (1674–1723) and the French aristocracy spent less time at Versailles and began to enjoy the diversions of Paris. There, wealthy French aristocrats built houses known as *hôtels*. Their designers compensated for the relatively small scale and nondescript exteriors of these mansions with interiors that were elaborately decorated and painted in light colors to make the rooms seem brighter and more spacious. It was in such aristocratic urban settings that fashionable Parisian hostesses held the salons the philosophes attended. Louis XV also liked Rococo art, and he had both Madame de Pompadour and other mistresses painted, sometimes in compromising poses, by Rococo artists, especially Francois Boucher (1700–1770). Consequently Rococo also became known as the Style of Louis XV, suggesting a social and political world more accommodating to the French aristocracy and less religiously austere than that of Louis XIV.

Beyond such domestic and personally intimate settings in France, the Rococo style spread across Europe and was adapted to many public buildings and churches. One of the most spectacular Rococo spaces was the Imperial Hall (*Kaisarsaal*) built in Würzburg, Bavaria to the design of Balthasar Neumann (1687–1753) with ceilings painted with scenes from Greek mythology by the Venetian Gian Battista Tiepolo (1696–1770).

The paintings associated with Rococo art often portrayed the aristocracy, and particularly the French aristocracy, at play. Artists depicted what were known as *fêtes galantes* or scenes of elegant parties in lush gardens. The paintings showed not reality, but an idealized landscape with carefree men and women pursuing a life of leisure, romance, and seduction. Among the most prominent of such artists was Jean-Antoine Watteau (1684–1721) in whose *Pilgrimage to Isle of Cithera* young lovers embark to pay homage to the goddess Venus. Other artists such as Boucher and Jean-Honoré Fragonard (1732–1806) produced works filled with female nudes and with men and women in sexually suggestive poses.

As the eighteenth century wore on, the way of life illustrated in Rococo paintings and of more popular prints produced from them convinced many people in France that the monarchy, the court, and the aristocracy were frivolous and decadent. In reality, as seen in Chapter 15, many

Antoine Watteau, "Embarkation for Cythera," (1717).　Oil on canvas. 129 × 194 cm. Louvre, Paris, France/Giraudon-Bridgeman Art Library

The color, the light, and the elaborate decorative details associated with rococo style is splendidly exemplified in the Imperial Hall (Kaisarsaal) built in Würzburg, Bavaria according to the design of Balthasar Neumann (1687–1753).   Dorothea Zwicker-Berberich

French and European aristocrats were hardworking and disciplined, and Louis XVI, who succeeded Louis XV in 1774, was a well-intentioned, pious, and highly moral monarch. Nonetheless, the light-hearted carelessness of Rococo art increased hostility toward the political and social elites of the Old Regime.

Contemporaries, moreover, did not have to wait for the tumult of the French Revolution to view art that directly criticized the society Rococo art portrayed. The mid-eighteenth century witnessed a new admiration for the art of the ancient world. In 1755, Johann Joachim Winckelmann (1717–1768), a German archaeologist, published *Thoughts on the Imitation of Greek Works in Painting and Sculpture*, followed in 1764 by *The History of Ancient Art*. In both works he either directly or indirectly contrasted the superficiality of the Rococo with the seriousness of ancient art and architecture. His books and the simultaneous rediscovery and partial excavation of the ancient Roman cities of Pompeii and Herculaneum in southern Italy fostered the rise of *Neoclassicism* in art and architecture. This movement constituted a return to themes, topics, and styles drawn from antiquity itself and from the Renaissance appeal to antiquity.

The popularity of the city of Rome as a destination for artists and aristocratic tourists contributed to the rise of Neoclassicism. European aristocrats who came to Italy in the mid-eighteenth century on what was called "the Grand Tour" increasingly admired both the ancient and Renaissance art that was on view there and the Neoclassical works that contemporary artists were producing there. Not only did these wealthy and influential travelers purchase paintings and statues to bring home with them, but they also commissioned architects to rebuild their own houses and public buildings in Neoclassical style.

Figures in Neoclassical paintings rarely suggest movement and often seem to stand still in a kind of tableau illustrating a moral theme. These paintings were didactic rather than emotional or playful. Their subject matter was usually concerned with public life or public morals, rather than depicting intimate family life, daily routine, or the leisure activity favored by Rococo painters.

Many Neoclassical painters used scenes of heroism and self-sacrifice from ancient history to draw

A CLOSER LOOK

An Eighteenth-Century Artist Appeals to the Ancient World

Jacques Louis David completed *The Oath of the Horatii* in 1784. Like many of his other works, it used themes from the supposedly morally austere ancient Roman Republic to criticize the political life of his own day. David intended the painting to contrast ancient civic virtue with the luxurious aristocratic culture of contemporary France.

The Horatii take an oath their father administers to protect the Roman Republic against enemies even if it means sacrificing their own lives. One of these enemies is romantically involved with one of their sisters in the right of the painting. Patriotism must be upheld over other relationships.

Jacques-Louis David, "Oath of the Horatii." 1784–85. © Reunion des Musees Nationaux, Paris, France/Art Resource, NY

The sisters and mother of the Horatii weep in a separate part of the scene. The emotion of the women and their uncertain policital loyalty suggests that civic virtue pertains only to men.

The sharp division of the painting with a male world on the left and a female world on the right illustrates how eighteenth-century republican thinkers, such as Rousseau, excluded women from civic life and political participation.

The Pantheon in Paris (construction commencing l758) embodied the
neoclassical style used for a Jesuit Church. After the French Revolution it
became a national monument where famous figures of the Enlightenment
and Revolution were buried. The bodies of both Voltaire and Rousseau
were transferred there during the l790s.   Jacques Germain Soufflot (1713-1780),
Facade of the Pantheon (formerly Church of Ste. Genevieve), 1757. Pantheon, Paris, France.
© Bridgeman-Giraudon/Art Resource, NY

contemporary moral and political lessons. Such
scenes provided a sharp moral contrast to the
works of Watteau or Boucher in which lovers seek
only pleasure and escape from care.

Other Neoclassical artists intended their paintings to be a form of direct political criticism.
Jacques-Louis David (1748–1825), the foremost
French Neoclassical painter, used ancient republican themes in the 1780s to emphasize the corruption of French monarchical government. His
Oath of the Horatii in 1784 illustrates a scene,
derived from the ancient Roman historian Livy,
of soldiers taking an oath to die for the Roman
Republic. The painting, also portrays the concept
of separate spheres for men and women. The
brothers are taking the oath to defend the republic with their lives. The women in the scene appear emotional and incapable of entering the

masculine civic life of the republic. David painted
many similar scenes from the ancient Roman Republic and later became an artistic champion of
the French Revolution and Napoleon (who, ironically, made him a baron).

The philosophes themselves became the subjects of Neoclassical artists. The French sculptor
Jean Antoine Houdon (1741–1828) produced numerous portraits in stone of leading philosophes
including Voltaire and Rousseau as well as American admirers of the Enlightenment such as Benjamin Franklin (1706–1790) and Thomas Jefferson
(1743–1826). Such statues furnished a gallery of
writers who had criticized the Old Regime or embodied modern republican values.

Even religious structures built in the Neoclassical style were, by the end of the century, transformed to monuments to the Enlightenment and

Revolution. Modeled on its ancient pagan namesake in Rome, the Pantheon in Paris was begun in 1758 as a Jesuit church. During the French Revolution, the new government transformed it into a national monument where the remains of French heroes could be interred. Voltaire's remains were placed there in 1791 and Rousseau's in 1794.

ENLIGHTENED ABSOLUTISM

Most of the philosophes favored neither Montesquieu's reformed and revived aristocracy nor Rousseau's democracy as a solution to contemporary political problems. Like other thoughtful people of the day in other stations and occupations, they looked to the existing monarchies. Because of his personal clash with aristocrats as a young writer and his general distrust of democratic ideas, Voltaire was a strong monarchist. In 1759, he published a *History of the Russian Empire under Peter the Great*, which declared, "Peter was born, and Russia was formed."[15] Voltaire and other philosophes, such as Diderot, who visited Catherine II of Russia, and the physiocrats, some of whom were ministers to Louis XV and Louis XVI, did not wish to limit the power of monarchs. Rather, they sought to use that power to rationalize economic and political structures and liberate intellectual life. Most philosophes were not opposed to power if they could find a way to use it for their own purposes or if they could profit in one way or another from their personal relationships to strong monarchs.

During the last third of the century, some observers believed that several European rulers had embraced many of the reforms the philosophes advocated. Historians use the term *enlightened absolutism* for this form of monarchical government in which the central absolutist administration was strengthened and rationalized at the cost of other, lesser centers of political power, such as the aristocracy, the church, and the parliaments or diets that had survived from the Middle Ages. The monarchs most closely associated with it are Frederick II (r. 1740–1786) of Prussia, Joseph II of Austria (r. 1765–1790), and Catherine II (r. 1762–1796) of Russia. Each had complicated relationships to the community of enlightened writers.

Frederick II corresponded with the philosophes, gave Voltaire and other philosophes places at his court, and even wrote history, political tracts, literary criticism, and music. Catherine II, adept at what would later be called public relations, consciously sought to create the image of being an enlightened ruler. She read and cited the works of the philosophes, subsidized Diderot, and corresponded with Voltaire, lavishing compliments on him, all in the hope that she would receive favorable comments from them, as she indeed did. Joseph II continued numerous initiatives begun by his mother, Maria Theresa (r. 1740–1780). He imposed a series of religious, legal, and social reforms that contemporaries believed he had derived from the philosophes' suggestions.

The relationship between these rulers and the writers of the Enlightenment was, however, more complicated than these appearances suggest. The humanitarian and liberating zeal of the Enlightenment writers was only part of what motivated the policies of the rulers. Frederick II, Joseph II, and Catherine II were also determined to play major diplomatic and military roles in Europe. In no small measure, they adopted Enlightenment policies favoring the rational economic and social integration of their realms because these policies also increased their military strength and political power. As explained in Chapter 13, all the major European states had emerged from the Seven Years' War knowing they would need stronger armies for future wars and increased revenues to finance these armies. The search for new revenues and internal political support was one of the incentives prompting the "enlightened" reforms of the monarchs of Russia, Prussia, and Austria. Consequently, they and their advisers used rationality to pursue goals most philosophes admired, but also to further what some philosophes considered irrational militarism. The flattery of monarchs could bend the opinions of a philosophe. For example, Voltaire, who had written against war, could praise the military expansion of Catherine's Russia because it appeared in his mind to bring civilization to peoples he regarded as uncivilized and because he enjoyed being known as a literary confidant of the empress.

FREDERICK THE GREAT OF PRUSSIA

More than any other ruler of the age, Frederick the Great of Prussia embodied enlightened absolutism. Drawing upon the accomplishments of his Hohenzollern forebearers, he forged a state that commanded the loyalty of the military, the junker nobility, the Lutheran clergy, a growing bureaucracy recruited from an educated middle class, and

---

[15] Quoted in Larry Wolff, *Inventing Eastern Europe: The Map of Civilization on the Mind of the Enlightenment* (Palo Alto, CA: Stanford University Press, 1994), p. 200.

Frederick II of Prussia became known as Frederick the Great after his victories in the Seven Years Wars. This portrait of 1763 shows him at the time of those triumphs when he had permanently secured the position of Prussia as a major Europe power. He was equally interested in the economic development of Prussia.   Erich Lessing/Art Resource, NY

university professors. Because the authority of the Prussian monarchy and the military were so strong and because the nobles, bureaucracy, clergy, and professors were so loyal, Frederick had the confidence to permit a more open discussion of Enlightenment ideas and to put into effect more Enlightenment values, such as extensive religious toleration, than any other continental ruler. Consequently, in marked contrast to France, Prussians sympathetic to the Enlightenment tended to support the state rather than criticize it.

Promotion Through Merit   Reflecting an important change in the European view of the ruler, Frederick frequently described himself as "the first servant of the State" contending that his own personal and dynastic interests should always be subordinate to the good of his subjects. Like earlier Hohenzollern rulers, he protected the local social and political interests of the Prussian nobility as well as their role in the army, but he also required nobles who sought positions in his well-paid bureaucracy to qualify for those jobs by merit. By 1770, a Prussian Civil Service Commission oversaw the education and examinations required for all major government appointments. Frederick thus made it clear that merit rather than privilege of birth would determine who served the Prussian state.

During his reign Frederick created few new nobles, and those persons whom he did ennoble earned their titles by merit, for having served the king and the state well. This policy of ennobling

MARIA THERESA AND JOSEPH II OF AUSTRIA DEBATE TOLERATION

In 1765, Joseph, the eldest son of the Empress Maria Theresa, became co-regent with his mother. He believed some religious toleration should be introduced into the Habsburg realms. Maria Theresa, whose opinions on many political issues were advanced, refused to consider toleration. This exchange of letters sets forth their sharply differing positions. The toleration of Protestants that is in dispute related only to Lutherans and Calvinists. Maria Theresa died in 1780; the next year Joseph issued on edict of toleration.

■ *How does Joseph define toleration, and why does Maria Theresa believe it is the same as religious indifference? Why does Maria Theresa fear that toleration will bring about political as well as religious turmoil? Why does Maria Theresa think that Joseph's belief in toleration has come from Joseph's acquaintance with wicked books?*

JOSEPH TO MARIA THERESA, JULY 20, 1777

It is only the word "toleration" which has caused the misunderstanding. You have taken it in quite a different meaning [from mine expressed in an earlier letter]. God preserve me from thinking it a matter of indifference whether the citizens turn Protestant or remain Catholic, still less, whether they cleave to, or at least observe, the cult which they have inherited from their fathers! I would give all I possess if all the Protestants of your states would go over to Catholicism.

The word "toleration," as I understand it, means only that I would employ any person, without distinction of religion, in purely temporal matters, allow them to own property, practice trades, be citizens, if they were qualified and if this would be of advantage to the State and its industry. Those who, unfortunately, adhere to a false faith, are far further from being converted if they remain in their own country than if they migrate into another, in which they can hear and see the convincing truths of the Catholic faith. Similarly, the undisturbed practice of their religion makes them far better subjects and causes them to avoid irreligion, which

only for merit and Frederick's protecting the nobility's local social interests and leadership of the army meant that Prussia did not experience the conflicts between the aristocracy and the monarchy that troubled other eighteenth-century European states.

Frederick felt comfortable in the intellectual life of his day and personally participated in the culture of the Enlightenment. He favored the Prussian universities and allowed professors wide latitude to discuss new ideas. In turn, Prussian professors were virtually unanimous in their praise and support of Frederick.

Because the Prussian state required academic training for appointment to positions of authority, nobles attended the universities. There they studied with middle-class Prussians who were training to serve the state either as Protestant clergy or bureaucrats. Consequently, nobles, clergy, and bureaucrats in Prussia shared a similar educational background that combined a moderate exposure to Enlightenment ideas with broadly shared religious values and loyalty to the state.

Religious Toleration No single policy so associated Frederick with the Enlightenment as that of full religious toleration. Continuing the Hohenzollern policy of toleration for foreign workers who brought important skills into Prussia, Frederick allowed Catholics and Jews to settle in his predominantly Lutheran country, and he protected the Catholics living in Silesia after he conquered that province from the Habsburgs in the 1740s. (See Chapter 13.) He even stated that he

is a far greater danger to our Catholics than if one lets them see others practice their religion unimpeded.

MARIA THERESA TO JOSEPH, LATE JULY 1777

Without a dominant religion? Toleration, indifference are precisely the true means of undermining everything, taking away every foundation; we others will then be the greatest losers.... He is no friend of humanity, as the popular phrase is, who allows everyone his own thoughts. I am speaking only in the political sense, not as a Christian, nothing is so necessary and salutary as religion. Will you allow everyone to fashion his own religion as he pleases? No fixed cult, no subordination to the Church—what will then become of us? The result will not be quiet and contentment; its outcome will be the rule of the stronger and more unhappy times like those which we have already seen. A manifesto by you to this effect can produce the utmost distress and make you responsible for many thousands of souls. And what are my own sufferings, when I see you entangled in opinions so erroneous? What is at stake is not only the welfare of the State but your own salvation....

Turning your eyes and ears everywhere, mingling your spirit of contradiction with the simultaneous desire to create something, you are ruining yourself and dragging the Monarchy down with you into the abyss.... I only wish to live so long as I can hope to descend to my ancestors with the consolation that my son will be as great, as religious as his forebearer, that he will return from his erroneous views, from those wicked books whose authors parade their cleverness at the expense of all that is most holy and most worthy of respect in the world, who want to introduce an imaginary freedom which can never exist and which degenerates into license and into complete revolution.

As quoted in C. A. Macartney, ed., *The Habsburg and Hohenzollern Dynasties in the Seventeenth and Eighteenth Centuries* (New York: Walker, 1970), pp. 151–153. Reprinted by permission of Walker and Co.

would be willing to build mosques for Turks should they move into his country. His religious toleration won the strong support of philosophers, such as Immanuel Kant and Moses Mendelsohn. Frederick nonetheless tended to appoint Protestants to most key positions in the bureaucracy and army.

Administrative and Economic Reforms Frederick also ordered a new codification of Prussian law, which was completed after his death. His objective was to rationalize the existing legal system and make it more efficient, eliminating regional peculiarities, reducing aristocratic influence, abolishing torture, and limiting the number of capital crimes. The other enlightened monarchs shared this concern for legal reform, which they saw as a way to extend and strengthen royal power.

The mid-century wars had inflicted considerable economic damage on Prussia. Thereafter, Frederick used the power of the state to foster economic growth. He continued the longstanding Hohenzollern policy of importing workers from outside Prussia. He sought to develop Prussian agriculture. Under state supervision, swamps were drained, new crops introduced, and peasants encouraged and sometimes compelled to migrate where they were needed. For the first time in Prussia, potatoes and turnips became important crops. Frederick also established a land-mortgage credit association to help landowners raise money for agricultural improvements. Despite these efforts, however, most Prussians did not prosper under Frederick's reign, and the burden of taxation, reflecting his protection of the interests of the nobles, fell disproportionately on peasants and townspeople.

JOSEPH II OF AUSTRIA

No eighteenth-century ruler so embodied rational, impersonal force as did the emperor Joseph II of Austria. He was the son of Maria Theresa and co-ruler with her from 1765 to 1780. Thereafter, he ruled alone until his death in 1790. Joseph was an austere and humorless person. During much of his life, he slept on straw and ate little but boiled beef. He prided himself on a narrow, passionless rationality, which he sought to impose by his own will on the various Habsburg domains. Despite his personal eccentricities and cold personality, Joseph II sincerely wished to improve the lot of his people. He was much less a political opportunist and cynic than either Frederick the Great of Prussia or Catherine the Great of Russia. Nonetheless, the ultimate result of his well-intentioned efforts was a series of aristocratic and peasant rebellions extending from Hungary to the Austrian Netherlands.

Centralization of Authority   As explained in Chapter 13, of all the rising states of the eighteenth century, Austria was the most diverse in its people and problems. The historian Robert Palmer likened the Habsburg domains to "a vast holding company."[16] The Habsburgs never succeeded in creating either a unified administrative structure or a strong aristocratic loyalty to the dynasty. To preserve the monarchy during the War of the Austrian Succession (1740–1748), Maria Theresa had guaranteed the aristocracy considerable independence, especially in Hungary.

During and after the conflict, however, she took steps to strengthen the power of the crown outside of Hungary, building more of a bureaucracy than had previous Habsburg rulers. In Austria and Bohemia, the empress imposed a much more efficient system of tax collection that extracted funds even from the clergy and the nobles. She also established central councils to deal with governmental problems. To assure her government a supply of educated officials, she sought to bring all educational institutions into the service of the crown and expanded primary education on the local level.

Maria Theresa was concerned about the welfare of the peasants and serfs. She brought them some

relief by expanding the authority of the royal bureaucracy over the local power of the nobility and limiting the amount of labor, or *robot*, landowners could demand from peasants. Her motives were less humanitarian than to assure a good pool from which to draw military recruits. In these policies and in her desire to stimulate prosperity and military strength by royal initiative, Maria Theresa anticipated the policies of her son.

Joseph II was more determined than his mother, and his projected reforms were more wide ranging. He aimed to extend his territories at the expense of Poland, Bavaria, and the Ottoman Empire. His greatest ambition, however, was to increase the authority of the Habsburg emperor over his various realms. He sought to overcome the pluralism of the Habsburg holdings by imposing central authority on areas of political and social life in which Maria Theresa had wisely chosen not to interfere.

In particular, Joseph sought to reduce Hungarian autonomy. To avoid having to guarantee Hungary's existing privileges or extend new ones at the time of his coronation, he refused to have himself crowned king of Hungary and even had the Crown of Saint Stephen, symbol of the Hungarian state, sent to the Imperial Treasury in Vienna. He reorganized local government in Hungary to increase the authority of his own officials. He also required the use of German in all governmental matters.

Ecclesiastical Policies   Another target of Joseph's royal absolutism was the church. Since the reign of Charles V (r. 1510–1558), the Habsburgs had been the most important dynastic champions of Roman Catholicism. Maria Theresa was devout, but she had not allowed the church to limit her authority. Although she had attempted to discourage certain of the more extreme modes of Roman Catholic popular religious piety, such as public flagellation, she was adamantly opposed to religious toleration. (See "Maria Theresa and Joseph II of Austria Debate Toleration", page 582.)

Joseph II was also a practicing Catholic, but based on both Enlightenment values and pragmatic politics, he favored a policy of toleration. In October 1781, Joseph extended freedom of worship to Lutherans, Calvinists, and the Greek Orthodox. They were permitted to have their own places of worship, to sponsor schools, to enter skilled trades, and to hold academic appointments and positions in the public service. Joseph also granted the right of private worship to Jews and relaxed the financial and social burdens imposed on them, though he did not give Jews full equality with other Habsburg subjects.

---

[16]Robert R. Palmer, *The Age of Democratic Revolution*, Vol. 1 (Princeton, NJ: Princeton University Press, 1959), p. 103.

Above all, Joseph sought to bring the Roman Catholic Church directly under royal control. He forbade the bishops of his realms to communicate directly with the pope. Since he considered religious orders that did not run schools or hospitals to be unproductive, he dissolved more than six hundred monasteries, confiscated their lands, and used some of their revenue to found new parishes in areas where there was a shortage of priests. He also reorganized the training of priests. The emperor believed that the traditional Roman Catholic seminaries, which were run by the various dioceses, instilled in priests too great a loyalty to the papacy and too little concern for their future parishioners. They were, therefore, replaced by eight general seminaries under government supervision whose training emphasized parish duties. In effect, Joseph's policies made Roman Catholic priests the employees of the state, ending the influence of the Roman Catholic Church as an independent institution in Habsburg lands. In many respects, his ecclesiastical policies, known as *Josephinism*, prefigured those of the French Revolution.

Economic and Agrarian Reform Like Frederick of Prussia, Joseph sought to improve the economic life of his domains. He abolished many internal tariffs, encouraged road building, and improved river transport. He personally inspected farms and manufacturing districts. Joseph also reconstructed the judicial system to make laws more uniform and rational and to lessen the influence of local landlords. All of these improvements were expected to bring new unity to the state and more taxes into the imperial coffers in Vienna.

Joseph's policies toward serfdom and the land were a far-reaching extension of those Maria Theresa had initiated. During his reign, he introduced reforms that touched the very heart of the rural social structure. He did not abolish the authority of landlords over their peasants, but he did seek to make that authority more moderate and subject to the oversight of royal officials. He abolished serfdom as a legally sanctioned state of servitude. He granted peasants a wide array of personal freedoms, including the right to marry, to engage in skilled work, and to have their children learn a skill without having to secure the landlord's permission.

Joseph reformed the procedures of the manorial courts and opened avenues of appeal to royal officials. He also encouraged landlords to change land leases, so that peasants could more easily inherit land or transfer it to other peasants. His goal in all

of these efforts to reduce traditional burdens on peasants was to make them more productive and industrious farmers.

Near the end of his reign, Joseph proposed a new and daring system of land taxation. He decreed in 1789 that all proprietors of the land were to be taxed regardless of social status. No longer were the peasants alone to bear the burden of taxation. He commuted *robot* into a monetary tax, only part of which was to go to the landlord, the rest reverting to the state. Angry nobles blocked the implementation of this decree, and it died with Joseph in 1790. This and other of Joseph's earlier measures, however, brought turmoil throughout the Habsburg realms. Peasants revolted over disagreements with landlords about their newly granted rights. The nobles of the various Habsburg realms protested the taxation scheme. The Magyars resisted Joseph's centralization measures in Hungary and forced him to rescind them.

Joseph was succeeded by his brother Leopold II (r. 1790–1792). Although sympathetic to Joseph's goals, Leopold was forced to repeal many of the most controversial decrees, such as that on taxation. In other areas, Leopold considered his brother's policies simply wrong. For example, he

---

RUSSIA FROM PETER THE GREAT THROUGH CATHERINE THE GREAT

1725	Death of Peter the Great
1725–1727	Catherine I
1727–1730	Peter II
1730–1741	Anna
1740–1741	Ivan VI
1741–1762	Elizabeth
1762	Peter III
1762	Catherine II (the Great) becomes empress
1767	Legislative commission summoned
1769	War with Turkey begins
1773–1775	Pugachev's Rebellion
1772	First Partition of Poland
1774	Treaty of Kuchuk-Kainardji ends war with Turkey
1775	Reorganization of local government
1783	Russia annexes Crimea
1785	Catherine issues the Charter of the Nobility
1793	Second Partition of Poland
1795	Third Partition of Poland
1796	Death of Catherine the Great

returned political and administrative power to local nobles because he thought it expedient for them to have a voice in government. Still, he did not repudiate his brother's program wholesale. He retained, in particular, Joseph's religious policies and maintained as much political centralization as he thought possible.

CATHERINE THE GREAT OF RUSSIA

Joseph II never grasped the practical necessity of forging political constituencies to support his policies. Catherine II, who had been born a German princess, but who became empress of Russia, understood only too well the fragility of the Romanov dynasty's base of power.

After the death of Peter the Great in 1725, the court nobles and the army repeatedly determined the Russian succession. As a result, the crown fell primarily into the hands of people with little talent. Peter's wife, Catherine I, ruled for two years (1725–1727) and was succeeded for three years by Peter's grandson, Peter II. In 1730, the crown devolved on Anna, a niece of Peter the Great. During 1740 and 1741, a child named Ivan VI, who was less than a year old, was the nominal ruler. Finally, in 1741, Peter the Great's daughter Elizabeth came to the throne. She held the title of empress until 1762, but her reign was not notable for new political departures or sound administration. Her court was a shambles of political and romantic intrigue. Much of the power the tsar possessed at the opening of the century had vanished.

At her death in 1762, Elizabeth was succeeded by her nephew Peter III. He was a weak ruler whom many contemporaries considered mad. He

Catherine the Great ascended to the Russian throne after the murder of her husband. She tried initially to enact major reforms, but she never intended to abandon absolutism. She assured nobles of their rights and by the end of her reign had imposed press censorship.
The Granger Collection

immediately exempted the nobles from compulsory military service and then rapidly made peace with Frederick the Great, for whom he held unbounded admiration. That decision probably saved Prussia from military defeat in the Seven Years' War. The one positive feature of this unbalanced creature's life was his marriage in 1745 to a young German princess born in the small duchy of Anhalt Zerbst. This was the future Catherine the Great.

For almost twenty years, Catherine lived in misery and frequent danger at the court of Elizabeth. During that time, she befriended important nobles and read widely the books of the philosophes. She was a shrewd person whose experience in a court crawling with rumors, intrigue, and conspiracy had taught her how to survive. She exhibited neither love nor fidelity toward her demented husband. A few months after his accession as tsar, Peter was deposed and murdered with Catherine's approval, if not her aid, and she was immediately proclaimed empress.

Catherine's familiarity with the Enlightenment and the general culture of Western Europe convinced her Russia was backward and that it needed major reforms to remain a great power. She understood that any significant reform must have a wide base of political and social support, especially since she had assumed the throne through a palace coup. In 1767, she summoned a legislative commission to advise her on revising the law and government of Russia. There were more than five hundred delegates, drawn from all sectors of Russian life. Before the commission convened, Catherine issued a set of instructions, partly written by herself. They contained many ideas drawn from the political writings of the philosophes. The commission considered the instructions as well as other ideas and complaints its members raised.

Russian law, however, was not revised for more than half a century. In 1768, Catherine dismissed the commission before several of its key committees had reported. Yet the meeting had not been useless, for it had gathered a vast amount of information about the conditions of local administration and economic life throughout Russia. The inconclusive debates and the absence of programs from the delegates themselves suggested that most Russians saw no alternative to an autocratic monarchy, and Catherine had no intention of departing from absolutism.

Limited Administrative Reform Catherine carried out limited reforms on her own authority. She gave strong support to the rights and local power of the nobility. In 1775, she reorganized local government to solve problems the legislative commission had brought to light. She put most local offices in the hands of nobles rather than creating a royal bureaucracy. In 1785, Catherine issued the Charter of the Nobility, which guaranteed nobles many rights and privileges. In part, the empress had to favor the nobles because they could topple her from the throne. Moreover, Russia's educated class was too small to provide an independent bureaucracy, and the treasury could not afford an army strictly loyal to the crown. So Catherine wisely made a virtue of necessity. She strengthened the stability of her crown by making convenient friends with her nobles.

Economic Growth Part of Catherine's program was to continue the economic development begun under Peter the Great. She attempted to suppress internal barriers to trade. Exports of grain, flax, furs, and naval stores grew dramatically. She also favored the expansion of the small Russian urban middle class that was so vital to trade. Through all of these departures, Catherine tried to maintain ties of friendship and correspondence with the philosophes. She knew that if she treated them kindly, they would be sufficiently flattered to give her a progressive reputation throughout Europe.

Territorial Expansion Catherine's limited administrative reforms and her policy of economic growth had a counterpart in the diplomatic sphere. The Russian drive for warm-water ports continued. (See Map 17–1, page 588.) This goal required warfare with the Turks. In 1769, as a result of a minor Russian incursion, the Ottoman Empire declared war on Russia. The Russians responded with a series of strikingly successful military moves.

During 1769 and 1770, the Russian fleet sailed all the way from the Baltic Sea into the eastern Mediterranean. The Russian army won several major victories that by 1771 gave Russia control of Ottoman provinces on the Danube River and the Crimean coast of the Black Sea. The conflict dragged on until 1774, when the Treaty of Kuchuk-Kainardji gave Russia a direct outlet on the Black Sea, free navigation rights in its waters, and free access through the Bosporus. Crimea became an independent state, which Catherine painlessly annexed in 1783. Finally, under this treaty Catherine, as empress of Russia, was made the protector of the Orthodox Christians living in the Ottoman Empire. In the future this would cause conflict

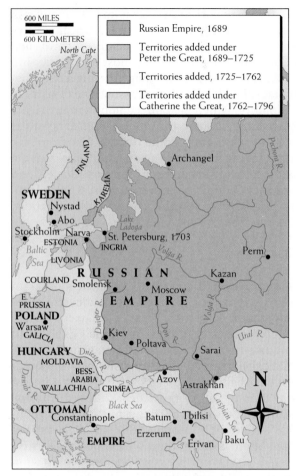

Map 17–1 **EXPANSION OF RUSSIA, 1689–1796** The overriding territorial aim of the two most powerful Russian monarchs of the 18th century, Peter the Great (in the first quarter of the century) and Catherine the Great (in the last half of the century) was to secure navigable outlets to the sea in both the north and the south for Russia's vast empire; hence Peter's push to the Baltic Sea and Catherine's to the Black Sea. Russia also expanded into Central Asia and Siberia during this time period.

with France whose monarch had previously been recognized as the protector of Roman Catholic Christians in the empire.

THE PARTITION OF POLAND

The Russian military successes increased Catherine's domestic political support, but they made the other states of eastern Europe uneasy. These anxieties were overcome by an extraordinary division of Polish territory known as the First Partition of Poland.

The Russian victories along the Danube River were most unwelcome to Austria, which also harbored ambitions of territorial expansion in that direction. At the same time, the Ottoman Empire

was pressing Prussia for aid against Russia. Frederick the Great made a proposal to Russia and Austria that would give each something it wanted, prevent conflict among the powers, and save appearances. After long, complicated secret negotiations, Russia agreed to abandon the conquered Danubian provinces. In compensation, it received a large portion of Polish territory with almost 2 million inhabitants. As a reward for remaining neutral, Prussia annexed most of the territory between East Prussia and Prussia proper. This land allowed Frederick to unite two previously separate sections of his realm. Finally, Austria took Galicia in southern Poland, with its important salt mines, and other Polish territory with more than 2.5 million inhabitants. (See Map 17–2.)

In September 1772, the helpless Polish aristocracy, paying the price for maintaining internal liberties at the expense of developing a strong central government, ratified this seizure of nearly one-third of Polish territory. The loss was not necessarily fatal to Poland's continued existence, and it inspired a revival of national feeling. Attempts were made to strengthen the Polish state and reform its feeble central government, but they proved to be too little and too late. Poland was no match for its stronger, more ambitious neighbors. The partition of Poland clearly demonstrated that any nation without a strong monarchy, bureaucracy, and army could no longer compete within the European state system. It also demonstrated that the major powers in eastern Europe were prepared to settle their own rivalries at the expense of such a weak state. If Polish territory had not been available to ease tensions, international rivalries might have led to warfare among Russia, Austria, and Prussia.

As shall be seen in Chapter 18, the wars and social upheaval that followed the outbreak of the French Revolution gave Russia and Prussia an excuse to partition Poland again in 1793, and Russia, Prussia, and Austria partitioned it a third time in 1795, removing it from the map of Europe for more than a century. Each time, the great powers contended they were saving themselves, and by implication the rest of Europe, from Polish anarchy. The fact was that Poland's political weakness left it vulnerable to plunderous aggression by its more powerful neighbors.

THE END OF THE EIGHTEENTH CENTURY IN CENTRAL AND EASTERN EUROPE

During the last two decades of the eighteenth century, all three regimes based on enlightened absolutism became more conservative and politically

Map 17–2 **PARTITIONS OF POLAND, 1772, 1793, AND 1795.**   The callous eradication of Poland from the map displayed 18th-century power politics at its most extreme. Poland, without a strong central government, fell victim to the strong absolute monarchies of central and eastern Europe.

repressive. In Prussia and Austria, the innovations of the rulers stirred resistance among the nobility. In Russia, fear of peasant unrest was the chief factor.

Frederick the Great of Prussia grew remote during his old age, leaving the aristocracy to fill important military and administrative posts. A reaction to Enlightenment ideas also set in among Prussian Lutheran writers.

In Austria, Joseph II's plans to restructure society and administration in his realms provoked growing frustration and political unrest, with the nobility calling for an end to innovation. In response, Joseph turned increasingly to censorship and his secret police.

Russia faced a peasant uprising, the Pugachev Rebellion, between 1773 and 1775, and Catherine the Great never fully recovered from the fears of social and political upheaval that it raised. Once

the French Revolution broke out in 1789, the Russian empress censored books based on Enlightenment thought and sent offensive authors into Siberian exile.

By the close of the century, fear of, and hostility to, change permeated the ruling classes of central and eastern Europe. This reaction had begun before 1789, but the events in France bolstered and sustained it for almost half a century. Paradoxically, nowhere did the humanity and liberalism of the Enlightenment encounter greater rejection than in those states that had been governed by "enlightened" rulers.

IN PERSPECTIVE

The writers of the Enlightenment, known as *philosophes*, charted a major new path in modern European and Western thought. They operated within a print culture that made public opinion into a distinct, cultural force. Admiring Newton and the achievements of physical science, they tried to apply reason and the principles of science to the cause of social reform. They also believed that passions and feelings are essential parts of human nature. Throughout their writings they championed reasonable moderation in social life. More than any other previous group of Western thinkers, they opposed the authority of the established churches and especially of Roman Catholicism. Most of them championed some form of religious toleration. They also sought to achieve a science of society that could discover how to maximize human productivity and material happiness. The great dissenter among them was Rousseau, who also wished to reform society, but in the name of virtue rather than material happiness.

The political influence of these writers was diverse and far-reaching. The founding fathers of the American republic looked to them for political guidance, as did moderate liberal reformers throughout Europe, especially within royal bureaucracies. The autocratic rulers of eastern Europe consulted the philosophes in the hope that Enlightenment ideas might allow them to rule more efficiently. The revolutionaries in France would honor them. This diverse assortment of followers illustrates the diverse character of the philosophes themselves. It also shows that Enlightenment thought cannot be reduced to a single formula. Rather, it should be seen as an outlook that championed change and reform, giving central place to humans and their welfare on earth rather than to God and the hereafter.

REVIEW QUESTIONS

1. How did the Enlightenment change basic Western attitudes toward reform, faith, and reason? What were the major formative influences on the philosophes? How important were Voltaire and the *Encyclopedia* in the success of the Enlightenment?

2. Why did the philosophes consider organized religion to be their greatest enemy? What were the basic tenets of deism? How did Jewish writers contribute to Enlightenment thinking about religion? What are the similarities and differences between the Enlightenment evaluation of Islam and its evaluations of Christianity and Judaism?

3. What were the attitudes of the philosophes toward women? What was Rousseau's view of women? What were the separate spheres he imagined men and women occupying? What were Mary Wollstonecraft's criticisms of Rousseau's view?

4. How did the views of the mercantilists about the earth's resources differ from those of Adam Smith in his book *The Wealth of Nations*? Why might Smith be regarded as an advocate of the consumer? How did his theory of history work to the detriment of less economically advanced non-European peoples? How did some Enlightenment writers criticize European empires?

5. How did the political views of Montesquieu differ from those of Rousseau? Was Montesquieu's view of England accurate? Was Rousseau a child of the Enlightenment or its enemy? Which did Rousseau value more, the individual or society?

6. Were the enlightened monarchs true believers in the ideals of the philosophes, or was their enlightenment a mere veneer? Was their power really absolute? What motivated their reforms? What does the partition of Poland indicate about the spirit of enlightened absolutism?

SUGGESTED READINGS

D. D. BIEN, *The Calas Affair: Persecution, Toleration, and Heresy in Eighteenth-Century Toulouse* (1960). The standard treatment of the famous case.

T. C. W. BLANNING, *The Culture of Power and the Power of Culture: Old Regime Europe 1660–1789* (2002). A remarkable synthesis of the interaction of political power and culture in France, Prussia, and Austria.

J. BUCHAN, *Crowded with Genius: The Scottish Enlightenment* (2003). A lively, accessible introduction.

S. FEINER, *The Jewish Enlightenment* (2002). An extensive, challenging pan-European treatment of the subject.

P. GAY, *The Enlightenment: An Interpretation*, 2 vols. (1966, 1969). A classic.

D. GOODMAN, *The Republic of Letters: A Cultural History of the French Enlightenment* (1994). Concentrates on the role of salons.

J. I. ISRAEL, *Radical Enlightenment: Philosophy and the Making of Modernity* (2001). A controversial account of the most radical strains of thought in Enlightenment culture.

C. A. KORS, *Encyclopedia of the Enlightenment* (2002). A major reference work on all of the chief intellectual themes of the era.

J. P. LEDONNE, *The Russian Empire and the World, 1700–1917* (1996). Explores the major reasons for Russian expansion from the eighteenth to the early twentieth centuries.

G. MACDONAGH, *Frederick the Great* (2001). A thoughtful and accessible biography.

D. MACMAHON, *Enemies of the Enlightenment: The French Counter-Enlightenment and the Making of Modernity* (2001). A fine exploration of French writers critical of the philosophes.

I. DE MADARIAGA, *Russia in the Age of Catherine the Great* (1981). The best discussion in English.

J. V. H. MELTON, *The Rise of the Public in Enlightenment Europe* (2001). Explores the social basis of print culture with an excellent bibliography.

S. MUTHU, *Enlightenment Against Empire* (2003) A challenging volume covering the critique of the empire.

R. PORTER, *The Creation of the Modern World: The Untold Story of the British Enlightenment* (2000). Seeks to shift the center of the Enlightenment from France to England.

P. RILEY, *The Cambridge Companion to Rousseau* (2001). Excellent accessible essays by major scholars.

E. ROTHCHILD, *Economic Sentiments: Adam Smith, Condorcet, and the Enlightenment* (2001). A sensitive account of Smith's thought and its relationship to the social questions of the day.

A. M. WILSON, *Diderot* (1972). A splendid biography of the person behind the *Encyclopedia* and other major Enlightenment publications.

L. WOLFF, *Inventing Eastern Europe: The Map of Civilization on the Mind of the Enlightenment* (1994). A remarkable study of how Enlightenment writers recast the understanding of this part of the Continent.

P. ZAGORIN, *How the Idea of Religious Toleration Came to the West* (2003) A major discussion of the subject from early modern Europe to the Enlightenment.

DOCUMENTS CD-ROM

The Enlightenment

18.1 John Locke: Chapter I from *Essay Concerning Human Understanding*

18.2 David Hume: *Of the Dignity or Meanness of Human Nature*

18.3 Charles Montesquieu: Book 4 from *The Spirit of the Laws*

18.4 The *Encyclopédie*

18.5 A Doctor Criticizes Midwives

18.7 Adam Smith: Division of Labor

CHAPTER 18

THE FRENCH REVOLUTION

KEY TOPICS

■ The financial crisis that impelled the French monarchy to call the Estates General
■ The transformation of the Estates General into the National Assembly, the Declaration of the Rights of Man and Citizen, and the reconstruction of the political and ecclesiastical institutions of France
■ The second revolution, the end of the monarchy, and the turn to more radical reforms
■ The war between France and the rest of Europe
■ The Reign of Terror, the Thermidorian Reaction, and the establishment of the Directory

In the spring of 1789 political turmoil soon resulting in revolution erupted in France. The events of that year marked the beginning of a new political order in France and eventually throughout the West. The French Revolution brought to the foreground the principles of civic equality and popular sovereignty that challenged the major political and social institutions of Europe and that in evolving forms have continued to

On July 14, 1789, crowds stormed the Bastille, a prison in Paris. This event, whose only practical effect was to free a few prisoners, marked the first time the populace of Paris redirected the course of the revolution.

Anonymous, France, 18th century, "Siege of the Bastille, 14 July, 1789." Musée de la Ville de Paris, Musée Carnavalet, Paris, France. Bridgeman–Giraudon/Art Resource, NY

shape and reshape Western political and social life to the present day. During the 1790s the forces the revolution unleashed would cause small-town provincial lawyers and Parisian street orators to exercise more influence over the fate of the Continent than aristocrats, royal ministers, or monarchs. Citizen armies commanded by people of low birth and filled by conscripted village youths would defeat armies composed of professional soldiers led by officers of noble birth. The king and queen of France, as well as thousands of French peasants and shopkeepers, would be executed. The existence of the Roman Catholic faith in France and indeed of Christianity itself would be challenged.

Finally Europe would embark on almost a quarter-century of war that would eventually extend across the continent and result in millions of casualties. ■

THE CRISIS OF THE FRENCH MONARCHY

Although the French Revolution would shatter many of the political, social, and ecclesiastical structures of Europe, its origins lay in a much more mundane problem. By the late 1780s, the French royal government could not command sufficient taxes to finance itself. The monarchy's unsuccessful search for adequate revenues led it into ongoing conflicts with aristocratic and ecclesiastical institutions. Eventually, the resulting deadlock was so complete that Louis XVI and his ministers were required to summon the French Estates General, which had not met since 1614. Once the deputies to that body gathered, a new set of issues and problems quickly emerged that led to the revolution itself. Yet, none of this would have occurred if the monarchy had not reached a state of financial crisis that meant it could no longer function within the limits and practices of existing political institutions.

THE MONARCHY SEEKS NEW TAXES

The French monarchy emerged from the Seven Years' War (1756–1763) defeated, deeply in debt, and unable thereafter to put its finances on a sound basis. French support of the American revolt against Great Britain further deepened the financial difficulties of the government. On the eve of the revolution, the interest and payments on the royal debt amounted to just over one-half of the entire budget. Given the economic vitality of France, the debt was neither overly large nor disproportionate to the debts of other European powers. The problem lay with the inability of the royal government to tap the nation's wealth through taxes to service and repay the debt. Paradoxically, France was a rich nation with an impoverished government.

The debt was symptomatic of the failure of the late-eighteenth-century French monarchy to come to terms with the political power of aristocratic institutions and, in particular, the *parlements*. As explained in Chapter 13, French absolutism had always involved a process of ongoing negotiation between the monarchy and local aristocratic interests. This process had become more difficult after the death of Louis XIV (r. 1643–1715) when the aristocracy had sought to reclaim parts of the influence it had lost. Nonetheless, for the first half of the century, the monarchy had retained most of its authority.

For twenty-five years after the Seven Years' War, however, a standoff occurred between the monarchy and the aristocracy, as one royal minister after another attempted to devise new tax schemes that would tap the wealth of the nobility, only to be confronted by opposition from both the *Parlement* of Paris and provincial *parlements*. Both Louis XV (r. 1715–1774) and Louis XVI (r. 1774–1792) lacked the character, resolution, and political skills to resolve the dispute. In place of a consistent policy for dealing with the growing debt and aristocratic resistance to change, the monarchy hesitated, retreated, and even lied.

In 1770, Louis XV appointed René Maupeou (1714–1792) as chancellor. The new minister was determined to break the *parlements* and increase taxes on the nobility. He abolished the *parlements* and exiled their members to different parts of the country. He then began an ambitious program to make the administration more efficient. What ultimately doomed Maupeou's policy was less the resistance of the nobility than the unexpected death from smallpox of Louis XV in 1774. His successor, Louis XVI, in an attempt to regain what he conceived to be popular support, dismissed Maupeou, restored all the *parlements*, and confirmed their old powers.

Although the *parlements* spoke for aristocratic interests, they appear to have enjoyed public support. By the second half of the eighteenth century, many French nobles shared with the wealthy professional and commercial classes similar economic interests and similar goals for administrative reforms that would support economic growth. Both groups regarded the lumbering institutions of monarchical absolutism as a burden. Moreover, throughout these initial and later disputes with the monarchy, the *parlements*, though completely dominated by the aristocracy, used the language of liberty and reform to defend their cause. They portrayed the monarchy as despotic—that is, as acting arbitrarily in defiance of the law. Here they drew on the ideas and arguments of many Enlightenment writers, such as Montesquieu and the physiocrats, discussed in Chapter 16.

The monarchy was unable to rally public opinion to its side because it had lost much of its moral authority. The sexually scandalous life of Louis XV was known throughout France, and the memory of his behavior lingered long after his death. Marie Antoinette (1755–1793), the wife of Louis XVI, also rightly or wrongly, gained a reputation for sexual misconduct and personal extravagance. She became the subject of numerous prurient prints and pamphlets that circulated throughout Paris and beyond. Louis XVI's own faithfulness to his queen and upright morals could not outweigh the monarchy's reputation for scandal. Furthermore, Louis XVI and his family continued to live at Versailles, rarely leaving its grounds to mix with his subjects and with the aristocracy, who now, unlike in the days of Louis XIV, often dwelled in Paris or on their estates. Hence, the French monarch stood at a distinct popular disadvantage in his clashes first with the *parlements* and later with other groupings of the aristocracy.

In all these respects, the public image and daily reality of the French monarchy were much more problematical than that of other contemporary monarchs. Frederick II of Prussia and Joseph II of Austria genuinely saw themselves, and were seen by their subjects, as patriotic servants of the state. George III of Great Britain, despite all his political difficulties, was regarded by most Britons as having a model character and as seeking the economic improvement of his nation. All three had reputations for personal frugality, and they moved frequently among the people they governed.

NECKER'S REPORT

France's successful intervention on behalf of the American colonists against the British only worsened the financial problems of Louis XVI's government. By 1781, as a result of the aid to America, its debt was larger, and its sources of revenues were unchanged. The new royal director-general of finances, Jacques Necker (1732–1804), a Swiss banker, then produced a public report in 1781 that suggested the situation was not so bad as had been feared. He argued that if the expenditures for the American war were removed, the budget was in surplus. Necker's report also revealed that a large portion of royal expenditures went to pensions for aristocrats and other royal court favorites. This revelation angered

Well-meaning but weak and vacillating, Louis XVI (r. 1774–1792) stumbled from concession to concession until he finally lost all power to save his throne.   Joseph Siffred Duplessis (1725–1802), "Louis XVI". Versailles, France. Photograph copyright Bridgeman–Giraudon/Art Resource, NY

court aristocratic circles, and Necker soon left office. His financial sleight of hand, nonetheless, made it more difficult for government officials to claim a real need to raise new taxes.

CALONNE'S REFORM PLAN
AND THE ASSEMBLY OF NOTABLES

The monarchy hobbled along until 1786. By this time, Charles Alexandre de Calonne (1734–1802) was the minister of finance. Calonne proposed to encourage internal trade, to lower some taxes, such as the *gabelle* on salt, and to transform the *corvée*, peasants' labor services on public works, into money payments. He also sought to remove internal barriers to trade and reduce government regulation of the grain trade. More importantly, Calonne wanted to introduce a new land tax that all landowners would have to pay regardless of their social status. If this tax had been imposed, the monarchy could have abandoned other indirect taxes. The government would also have had less need to seek additional taxes that required approval from the aristocratically dominated *parlements*. Calonne also intended to establish new local assemblies made up of landowners to approve land taxes; in these assemblies the voting power would have depended on the amount of land a person owned rather than on his social status. All these proposals would have undermined both the political and the social power of the French aristocracy. Other of his proposals touched the economic privileges of the French Church. These policies reflected much advanced economic and administrative thinking of the day.

The monarchy, however, had little room to maneuver. The creditors were at the door, and the treasury was nearly empty. Calonne needed public support for such bold new undertakings. In February 1787, he met with an Assembly of Notables, nominated by the royal ministry from the upper ranks of the aristocracy and the church, to seek support for his plan. The Assembly adamantly refused to give it. There was some agreement that reform and greater fairness in taxation was necessary, but the Assembly did not trust the information they had received from Calonne. In his place they called for the reappointment of Necker, who they believed had left the country in sound fiscal condition. Finally, they claimed that only the Estates General of France, a medieval institution that had not met since 1614, could consent to new taxes. The notables believed that calling the Estates General, which had been traditionally organized to allow aristocratic and church dominance, would actually allow the nobility to have a direct role in governing the country alongside the monarchy. The issue was less the nobility not wishing to reform tax structure than its determination to acquire power at the expense of the monarchy and to direct reforms itself.

DEADLOCK AND THE CALLING OF THE ESTATES GENERAL

Again, Louis XVI backed off. He replaced Calonne with Étienne Charles Loménie de Brienne (1727–1794), archbishop of Toulouse and the chief opponent of Calonne at the Assembly of Notables. Once in office, Brienne found, to his astonishment, that the financial situation was as bad as his predecessor had asserted. Brienne himself now sought to reform the land tax. The *Parlement* of Paris, however, in its self-appointed role as the embodiment of public opinion, took the new position that it lacked authority to authorize the tax and that only the Estates General could do so. Shortly thereafter, Brienne appealed to the Assembly of the Clergy to approve a large subsidy to fund that part of the debt then coming due for payment. The clergy, like the *Parlement* dominated by aristocrats, not only refused the subsidy, but also reduced the voluntary contribution, or *don gratuit*, that it paid to the government in lieu of taxes.

As these unfruitful negotiations were taking place at the center of political life, local aristocratic *parlements* and estates in the provinces were making their own demands. They wanted to restore the privileges they had enjoyed during the early seventeenth century, before Richelieu and Louis XIV had crushed their independence. Furthermore, bringing the financial crisis to a new point of urgency, bankers refused in the summer of 1788 to extend necessary short-term credit to the government. Consequently, in July 1788, the king, through Brienne, agreed to convoke the Estates General the next year. Brienne resigned, and Necker replaced him. Some kind of political reform was coming, but what form it would take and how it would happen would be largely determined by the conflicts that emerged from summoning the Estates General.

THE REVOLUTION OF 1789

THE ESTATES GENERAL BECOMES THE NATIONAL ASSEMBLY

The Estates General had been called because of the political deadlock between the French monarchy and the vested interests of aristocratic institutions and the church. Almost immediately after it was summoned, however, the three groups, or estates, represented within it clashed with each other. The First Estate was the clergy, the Second Estate the nobility, and the **Third Estate** was, theoretically, everyone else in the kingdom, although its representatives were drawn primarily from wealthy members of the commercial and professional middle classes. All the representatives in the Estates General were men. During the widespread public discussions preceding the meeting of the Estates General, representatives of the Third Estate made it clear they would not permit the monarchy and the aristocracy to decide the future of the nation.

A comment by a priest, the Abbé Siéyès (1748–1836), in a pamphlet published in 1789, captures the spirit of the Third Estate's representatives: "What is the Third Estate? Everything. What has it been in the political order up to the present? Nothing. What does it ask? To become something."[1] The spokesmen for the Third Estate became more determined to assert their role less from any preexisting conflicts with the nobility than from the conflicts that emerged during the debates and electioneering for the Estates General in late 1788 and early 1789.

Debate over Organization and Voting Before the Estates General gathered, a public debate over its proper organization drew the lines of basic disagreement. The aristocracy made two important attempts to limit the influence of the Third Estate. First, a reconvened Assembly of Notables demanded that each estate have an equal number of representatives. Second, in September 1788, the *Parlement* of Paris ruled that voting in the Estates General should be conducted by order rather than by head— that is, each estate, or order, in the Estates General, rather than each individual member, should have one vote. This procedure would in all likelihood have ensured the aristocratically dominated First and Second Estates could always outvote the Third by a vote of two estates to one estate. Both moves raised doubt about the aristocracy's previously declared concern for French liberty and revealed it as a group hoping to maintain its privileged influence no matter what government reforms might be enacted. Spokesmen for the Third Estate immediately denounced the arrogant claims of the aristocracy.

In many respects the interests of the aristocracy and the most prosperous and well-educated members of the Third Estates had converged during the eighteenth century, and many nobles had married husbands and wives from the elite of the Third Estate. Yet a fundamental social distance separated the members of the two orders. Many aristocrats were much richer than members of the Third Estate, and noblemen had all but monopolized the high command in the army and navy. The Third

[1] Quoted in Leo Gershoy, *The French Revolution and Napoleon* (New York: Appleton-Century-Crofts, 1964), p. 102.

Estate had also experienced various forms of political and social discrimination from the nobility. The resistance of the nobility to voting by head confirmed the suspicions and resentments of the members of the Third Estate, who tended to be well-off, but not enormously rich, lawyers. The stance of both the reconvened Assembly of Notables and the *Parlement* of Paris regarding the composition and functioning of the forthcoming Estates General meant that the elected members of the Third Estate would approach the gathering with a newly awakened profound distrust of the nobility and of the aristocratically dominated church.

Doubling the Third   In the face of widespread public uproar over the aristocratic effort to dominate composition and procedures of the Estates General, the royal council eventually decided that strengthening the Third Estate would best serve the interests of the monarchy and the cause of fiscal reform. In December 1788, the council announced the Third Estate would elect twice as many representatives as either the nobles or the clergy. This so-called doubling of the Third Estate meant it could easily dominate the Estates General if voting proceeded by head rather than by order. The council correctly assumed that liberal nobles and clergy would support the Third Estate, confirming that, despite social differences, these groups shared important interests and reform goals. The method of voting had not yet been decided when the Estates General gathered at Versailles in May 1789.

The *Cahiers de Doléances*   When the representatives came to the royal palace, they brought with them **cahiers de doléances**, or lists of grievances, registered by the local electors, to be presented to the king. Many of these lists have survived and provide considerable information about the state of France on the eve of the revolution. The documents criticized government waste, indirect taxes, church taxes and corruption, and the hunting rights of the aristocracy. They included calls for periodic meetings of the Estates General, more equitable taxes, more local control of administration, unified weights and measures to facilitate trade and commerce, and a free press. The overwhelming demand of the *cahiers* was for equality of rights among the king's subjects. Yet it is also clear that the *cahiers* that originated among the nobility were not radically different from those of the Third Estate. There was broad agreement that the French government needed major reform, that greater equality in taxation and other matters was desirable, and that many aristocratic privileges must be abandoned. (See "The Third Estate of a French City Petitions the King," page 600.) The *cahiers* drawn up before May 1789 indicate that the three estates

could have cooperated to reach these goals. But that conflict among the estates, rather than cooperation, was to be the case became clear almost from the moment the Estates General opened.

The Third Estate Creates the National Assembly
The complaints, demands, and hopes for reform expressed in the *cahiers* could not, however, be discussed until the questions of the organization and voting in the Estates General had been decided. From the beginning, the Third Estate, whose members consisted largely of local officials, professionals, and other persons of property, refused to sit as a separate order as the king desired. For several weeks there was a standoff. Then, on June 1, the Third Estate invited the clergy and the nobles to join them in organizing a new legislative body. A few priests did so. On June 17, that body declared itself the National Assembly, and on June 19 by a narrow margin, the Second Estate voted to join the Assembly.

The Tennis Court Oath   At this point, Louis XVI hoped to reassert a role in the proceedings. He intended to call a "Royal Session" of the Estates General for June 23, and closed the room where the National Assembly had been gathering. On June 20, finding themselves thus unexpectedly locked out of their usual meeting place, the National Assembly moved to a nearby indoor tennis court. There, its members took an oath to continue to sit until they had given France a constitution. This was the famous Tennis Court Oath. Louis XVI ordered the National Assembly to desist, but many clergy and nobles joined the Assembly in defiance of the royal command.

On June 27, the king, now having completely lost control of the events around him, capitulated and formally requested the First and Second Estates to meet with the National Assembly, where voting would occur by head rather than by order. The Third Estate because of the doubling of its membership had twice as many members as either of the other estates that joined them. Had nothing further occurred, the government of France would have already been transformed. Henceforth, the monarchy could govern only in cooperation with the National Assembly, and the National Assembly would not be a legislative body organized according to privileged orders. The National Assembly, which renamed itself the National Constituent Assembly because of its intention to write a new constitution, was composed of a majority of members drawn from all three orders, who shared liberal goals for the administrative, constitutional, and economic reform of the country. The revolution in France against government by privileged hereditary orders, however, rapidly extended beyond events occurring at Versailles.

A CLOSER LOOK

Challenging the French Political Order

This late eighteenth-century cartoon satirizes the French social and political structure as the events and tensions leading up to the outbreak of the French Revolution unfolded. This image embodies the highly radical critique of the French political structure that erupted from about 1787 when the nobility and church refused to aid the financial crisis of the monarchy.

Louis XVI is portrayed as the chief rider of the poor citizen holding a whip and declaring that feudal dues and the rights of the landowners should prevail. This positioning of the king suggests that the cartoon was drawn after the calling of the Estates General when, until the representation of the Third Estate was doubled, Louis was seen as siding with the church and nobility against the people. Prior to then, he had been seen as a paternal protector of the French people.

Behind the king ride a Roman Catholic bishop and a noble magistrate. The former holds a document associating the clergy with religious persecution and protection of church property. The noble holds a statement championing the powers of the aristocratic *parlements*.

At the bottom of the heap is a poor, blinded ordinary French citizen in the chains of taxation and feudal obligations. The image suggests that the chains of obligation and the orders of privilege maintaining the chains need to be removed.

CORBIS/Bettmann

This painting of the Tennis Court Oath, June 20, is by Jacques-Louis David (1748–1825). In the center foreground are members of different estates joining hands in cooperation as equals. The presiding officer is Jean-Sylvain Bailly, soon to become mayor of Paris.   Jacques-Louis David, "Oath of the Tennis Court, the 20th of June 1789." Chateaux de Versailles et de Trianon, Versailles, France. Bridgeman–Giraudon/Art Resource, NY

FALL OF THE BASTILLE

Two new forces soon intruded on the scene. First, Louis XVI again attempted to regain the political initiative by mustering royal troops near Versailles and Paris. On the advice of Queen Marie Antoinette, his brothers, and the most conservative aristocrats at court, he seemed to be contemplating the use of force against the National Constituent Assembly. On July 11, without consulting Assembly leaders, Louis abruptly dismissed Necker, his minister of finance. Louis's gathering troops and dismissal of Necker marked the beginning of a steady, but consistently poorly executed, royal attempt to undermine the Assembly and halt the revolution. Most of the National Constituent Assembly wished to establish some form of constitutional monarchy, but from the start, Louis's refusal to cooperate thwarted that effort. The king fatally decided to throw in his lot with the conservative aristocracy against the emerging forces of reform drawn from across the social and political spectrum.

The second new factor to impose itself on the events at Versailles was the populace of Paris, which numbered more than 600,000 people. The mustering of royal troops created anxiety in the city, where throughout the winter and spring of 1789 high prices for bread, which was the staple food of the poor, had produced riots. Those Parisians who had elected representatives to the Third Estate had continued to meet after the elections. By June they were organizing a citizen militia and collecting arms. They regarded the dismissal of Necker as the opening of a royal offensive against the National Constituent Assembly and the city. They intended to protect the Assembly and the revolution it had begun.

On July 14, large crowds of Parisians, most of them small shopkeepers, tradespeople, artisans, and wage earners, marched to the Bastille to get weapons for the militia. This great fortress, with ten-foot-thick walls, had once held political prisoners. Through miscalculations and ineptitude by the governor of the fortress, the troops in the Bastille fired into the crowd, killing ninety-eight people and

THE THIRD ESTATE OF A FRENCH CITY PETITIONS THE KING

The cahiers de doléances *were the lists of grievances brought to Versailles in 1789 by members of the Estates General. This particular cahier originated in Dourdan, a city in central France, and reflects the complaints of the Third Estate. The first two articles refer to the organization of the Estates General. The other articles ask the king to grant various forms of equality before the law and in taxation. Most of the* cahiers *of the Third Estate included these demands for equality.*

■ *Which of the following petitions relate to political rights and which to economic equality? The slogan most associated with the French Revolution was "Liberty, Equality, Fraternity." Which of these petitions represents each of these values?*

The order of the third estate of the City . . . of Dourdan . . . supplicates [the king] to accept the grievances, complaints, and remonstrances which it is permitted to bring to the foot of the throne, and to see therein only the expression of its zeal and the homage of its obedience.

It wishes:

1. That his subjects of the third estate, equal by such status to all other citizens, present themselves before the common father without other distinction which might degrade them.

2. That all the orders, already united by duty and common desire contribute equally to the needs of the State, also deliberate in common concerning its needs.

3. That no citizen lose his liberty except according to law: that, consequently, no one be arrested by virtue of special orders, or, if imperative circumstances necessitate such orders that the prisoner be handed over to regular courts of justice within forty-eight hours at the latest.

12. That every tax, direct or indirect, be granted only for a limited time, and that every collection beyond such term be regarded as peculation, and punished as such.

15. That every personal tax be abolished; that thus the capitation [a poll tax] and the taille [tax from which nobility and clergy were exempt] and its accessories be merged with the vingtièmes [an income tax] in a tax on land and real or nominal property.

16. That such tax be borne equally, without distinction, by all classes of citizens and by all kinds of property, even feudal . . . rights.

17. That the tax substituted for the corvée be borne by all classes of citizens equally and without distinction. That said tax, at present beyond the capacity of those who pay it and the needs to which it is destined, be reduced by at least one-half.

From John Hall Stewart, *Documentary Survey of the French Revolution*, 1st Edition, © 1951. Reprinted by permission of Pearson Education, Inc., Upper Saddle River, NJ.

wounding many others. Thereafter, the crowd stormed the fortress. They released the seven prisoners inside, none of whom was a political prisoner, and killed several troops and the governor.

On July 15, the militia of Paris, by then called the National Guard, offered its command to a young liberal aristocrat, the Marquis de Lafayette (1757–1834). This hero of the American Revolution gave the guard a new insignia: the red and blue stripes from the colors of the coat of arms of Paris, separated by the white stripe of the royal flag. The emblem be-

came the revolutionary *cockade* (badge) and eventually the tricolor flag of revolutionary France.

The attack on the Bastille marked the first of many crucial *journées*, days on which the populace of Paris redirected the course of the revolution. The fall of the fortress signaled that the National Constituent Assembly alone would not decide the political future of the nation. As the news of the taking of the Bastille spread, similar disturbances took place in provincial cities. A few days later, Louis XVI again bowed to the force of events and personally visited Paris, where he wore the revolutionary *cockade* and recognized the organized electors as the legitimate government of the city. The king also recognized the National Guard and thus implicitly admitted that he lacked the military support to turn back the revolution. The citizens of Paris were, for the time being, satisfied. They also had established themselves as an independent political force with which other political groups might ally for their own purposes.

THE "GREAT FEAR" AND THE NIGHT OF AUGUST 4

Simultaneous with the popular urban disturbances, a movement known as the "Great Fear" swept across much of the French countryside. Rumors that royal troops would be sent into the rural districts intensified the peasant disturbances that had begun during the spring. The Great Fear saw the burning of *châteaux*, the destruction of legal records and documents, and the refusal to pay feudal dues. The peasants were determined to take possession of food supplies and land that they considered to be rightfully theirs. They were reclaiming rights and property they had lost through administrative tightening of the collection of feudal dues during the past century as well as venting their anger against the injustices of rural life. Their targets were both aristocratic and ecclesiastical landlords.

On the night of August 4, 1789, aristocrats in the National Constituent Assembly attempted to halt the spreading disorder in the countryside. By prearrangement, several liberal nobles and clerics rose in the Assembly and renounced their feudal rights, dues, and tithes. In a scene of great emotion, they surrendered hunting and fishing rights, judicial authority, and legal exemptions. These nobles and clerics gave up what they had already lost and what they could not have regained without civil war in the rural areas. Many of them later received financial compensation for their losses. Nonetheless, after the night of August 4, all French citizens were subject to the same and equal laws. Furthermore, since the sale of government offices was also abolished, the events of that night opened political and military positions, careers, and advancement to talent rather than basing them exclusively on birth or wealth. This dramatic session of the Assembly effectively abolished the major social institutions of the Old Regime and created an unforeseen situation that required a vast legal and social reconstruction of the nation. Without those renunciations, the constructive work of the National Constituent Assembly would have been much more difficult and certainly much more limited. (See "The National Assembly Decrees Civic Equality in France," page 602.)

Both the attack on the Bastille and the Great Fear displayed characteristics of the urban and rural riots that had occurred often in eighteenth-century France. Louis XVI first thought the turmoil over the Bastille was simply another bread riot. Indeed, the popular disturbances were only partly related to the events at Versailles. A deep economic downturn had struck France in 1787 and continued into 1788. The harvests for both years had been poor, and the food prices in 1789 were higher than at any time since 1703. Wages had not kept up with the rise in prices. Throughout the winter of 1788–1789, an unusually cold one, many people suffered from hunger. Wage and food riots had erupted in several cities. These economic problems fanned the fires of revolution.

The political, social, and economic grievances of many sections of the country became combined. The National Constituent Assembly could look to the popular forces as a source of strength against the king and the conservative aristocrats. When the various elements of the Assembly later quarreled among themselves, however, the resulting factions would appeal for support to the politically sophisticated and well-organized shopkeeping and artisan classes. They, in turn, would demand a price for their cooperation.

THE DECLARATION OF THE RIGHTS OF MAN AND CITIZEN

In late August 1789, the National Constituent Assembly decided that before writing a new constitution, it should publish a statement of broad political principles. On August 27, the Assembly issued the Declaration of the Rights of Man and Citizen. This declaration drew on the political language of the Enlightenment and the Declaration of Rights that the state of Virginia had adopted in June 1776.

The French declaration proclaimed that all men were "born and remain free and equal in rights." The natural rights so proclaimed were "liberty, property, security, and resistance to oppression." Governments existed to protect those rights. All political sovereignty resided in the nation and its representatives. All citizens were to be equal before the law and were to be "equally admissible to all public dignities, offices, and employments, according to their capacity, and with no other distinction than that of their virtues and talents." There were to be due process of law and presumption of innocence until proof of guilt. Freedom of religion was affirmed. Taxation was to be apportioned equally according to the capacity to pay. Property constituted "an inviolable and sacred right."[2]

---

[2]Quoted in Georges Lefebvre, *The Coming of the French Revolution*, trans. by R. R. Palmer (Princeton, NJ: Princeton University Press, 1967), pp. 221–223.

THE NATIONAL ASSEMBLY DECREES CIVIC EQUALITY IN FRANCE

These famous decrees of August 4, 1789, in effect created civic equality in France. The special privileges previously possessed or controlled by the nobility were removed.

■ *What institutions and privileges are included in "the feudal regime"? How do these decrees recognize that the abolition of some privileges and former tax arrangements will require new kinds of taxes and government financing to support religious, educational, and other institutions?*

1. The National Assembly completely abolishes the feudal regime. It decrees that, among the rights and dues . . . all those originating in real or personal serfdom, personal servitude, and those which represent them, are abolished without indemnification; all other are declared redeemable, and that the price and mode of redemption shall be fixed by the National Assembly. . . .
2. The exclusive right to maintain pigeon-houses and dove-cotes is abolished. . . .
3. The exclusive right to hunt and to maintain unenclosed warrens is likewise abolished. . . .
4. All manorial courts are suppressed without indemnification.
5. Tithes of every description and the dues which have been substituted for [them] . . .

are abolished on condition, however, that some other method be devised to provide for the expenses of divine worship, the support of the officiating clergy, the relief of the poor, repairs and rebuilding of churches and parsonages, and for all establishments, seminaries, schools, academies, asylums, communities, and other institutions, for the maintenance of which they are actually devoted. . . .

6. The sale of judicial and municipal offices shall be suppressed forthwith. . . .
7. Pecuniary privileges, personal or real, in the payment of taxes are abolished forever. . . .
8. All citizens, without distinction of birth, are eligible to any office or dignity, whether ecclesiastical, civil or military. . . .

From Frank Maloy Anderson, ed. and trans., *The Constitutions and Other Select Documents Illustrative of the History of France, 1789–1907,* 2nd. ed., rev. and enl. (Minneapolis: H. W. Wilson, 1908), pp. 11–13.

The Declaration of the Rights of Man and Citizen was directed in large measure against specific abuses of the old French monarchical and aristocratic regime, but it was framed in abstract universalistic language applicable to other European nations. In this respect, the ideas set forth in the declaration like those of the Protestant reformers three centuries earlier could jump across national borders and find adherents outside France. The two most powerful, universal political ideas of the declaration were civic equality and popular sovereignty. The first would challenge the legal and social inequities of European life, and the second would assert that governments must be responsible to the governed. These two principles, in turn, could find themselves in tension with the declaration's principle of the protection of property.

It was not accidental that the Declaration of the Rights of Man and Citizen specifically applied to men and not to women. As discussed in Chapter 16, much of the political language of the Enlightenment, and especially that associated with Rousseau, separated men and women into distinct gender spheres. According to this view, which influenced legislation during the revolution, men were suited for citizenship, women for motherhood and the domestic life. Nonetheless, in the charged atmosphere of the summer of 1789, many politically active and informed Frenchwomen hoped the guarantees of the declaration would be extended to them. They were particularly concerned with property, inheritance, family, and divorce. Some people saw in the declaration a framework within which women might eventually enjoy the rights and protection of citizenship. Those hopes would be disappointed.

The Women of Paris marched to Versailles on October 5, 1789. The following day the royal family was forced to return to Paris with them. Henceforth, the French government would function under the constant threat of mob violence.   Anonymous, 18th CE, "To Versailles, to Versailles". The women of Paris going to Versailles, 7 October, 1789. French. Musée de la Ville de Paris, Musée Carnavalet, Paris, France. Photograph copyright Bridgeman–Giraudon/Art Resource, NY

THE PARISIAN WOMEN'S MARCH ON VERSAILLES

Louis XVI stalled before ratifying both the Declaration of the Rights of Man and Citizen and the aristocratic renunciation of feudalism. His hesitations fueled suspicions that he might again try to resort to force. Moreover, bread remained scarce and expensive. On October 5, some 7,000 Parisian women armed with pikes, guns, swords, and knives marched to Versailles demanding more bread. They milled about the palace, and many stayed the night. Intimidated, the king agreed to sanction the decrees of the Assembly. The next day he and his family appeared on a balcony before the crowd. Deeply suspicious of the monarch and believing that he must be kept under the watchful eye of the people, the Parisians demanded that Louis and his family return to Paris with them. The monarch had no real choice. On October 6, 1789, his carriage followed the crowd into the city, where he and his family settled in the old palace of the Tuileries in the heart of Paris.

The National Constituent Assembly also soon moved to Paris. Thereafter, both Paris and France remained relatively stable and peaceful until the summer of 1792. A decline in the price of bread in late 1789 helped to calm the atmosphere.

THE RECONSTRUCTION OF FRANCE

In Paris, the National Constituent Assembly set about reorganizing France. In government, it pursued a policy of constitutional monarchy; in administration, rationalism; in economics, unregulated freedom; and in religion, anticlericalism. Throughout its proceedings and following the principles of the Declaration of the Rights of Man and Citizen, the Assembly was determined to protect property in all its forms. The Assembly sought to limit the impact on the national life of those French people who had no property or only small amounts of it. Although championing civic equality before the law, the Assembly, with the aristocrats and middle-class elite united, spurned social equality and extensive democracy. It thus charted a general course that, to a greater or lesser degree, nineteenth-century liberals across Europe would follow.

POLITICAL REORGANIZATION

In the Constitution of 1791, the National Constituent Assembly established a constitutional monarchy. The major political authority of the nation would be a unicameral Legislative Assembly, in which all laws would originate. The monarch was allowed a suspensive veto that could delay, but not halt, legislation. The Assembly also had the power to make war and peace.

Active and Passive Citizens The constitution provided for an elaborate system of indirect elections to thwart direct popular pressure on the government. The citizens of France were divided into active and passive categories. Only active citizens—that is, men paying annual taxes equal to three days of local labor wages—could vote. They chose electors, who then, in turn, voted for the members of the legislature. Further property qualifications were required to serve as an elector or member of the legislature. Only about 50,000 citizens of a population of about 25 million could qualify as electors or members of the Legislative Assembly. Women could neither vote nor hold office.

These constitutional arrangements effectively transferred political power from aristocratic wealth to all forms of propertied wealth in the nation. The accumulation of wealth from land and commercial property, not hereditary privilege or the purchase of titles or offices, would open the path to political authority. These new political arrangements based on property rather than birth reflected the changes in French society over the past century and allowed more social and economic interests to have a voice in governing the nation.

Olympe de Gouges's Declaration of the Rights of Woman The laws that excluded women from voting and holding office did not pass unnoticed. In 1791, Olympe de Gouges (d. 1793), a butcher's daughter from Montauban in northwest France who became a major revolutionary radical in Paris, composed a Declaration of the Rights of Woman, which she ironically addressed to Queen Marie Antoinette. Much of the document reprinted the Declaration of the Rights of Man and Citizen, adding the word *woman* to the various original clauses. That strategy demanded that women be regarded as citizens and not merely as daughters, sisters, wives, and mothers of citizens. Olympe de Gouges further outlined rights that would permit women to own property and require men to recognize the paternity of their children. She called for equality of the sexes in marriage and improved education for women. She declared, "Women, wake up; the *tocsin* of reason is being heard throughout the whole universe; discover your rights."[3] Her declaration illustrated how the simple listing of rights in the Declaration of the Rights of Man and Citizen created a structure of universal civic expectations even for those it did not cover. The Na-

tional Assembly had established a set of values against which it could itself be measured. It provided criteria for liberty, and those to whom it had not extended full liberties could demand to know why and could claim the revolution was incomplete until they too enjoyed those freedoms.

Departments Replace Provinces In reconstructing the local and judicial administration, the National Constituent Assembly applied the rational spirit of the Enlightenment. It abolished the ancient French provinces, such as Burgundy and Brittany, and established in their place eighty-three administrative units called departments, or *départements*, of generally equal size named after rivers, mountains, and other geographical features. The departments in turn were subdivided into districts, cantons, and communes. Elections for departmental and local assemblies were also indirect. This administrative reconstruction proved to be permanent. The departments still exist in twenty-first-century France. (See Map 18–1, page 606.)

All the ancient judicial courts, including the seigneurial courts and the *parlements*, were also abolished and replaced by uniform courts with elected judges and prosecutors. Procedures were simplified, and the most degrading punishments, such as branding, torture, and public flogging, were removed from the books.

ECONOMIC POLICY

In economic matters, the National Constituent Assembly continued the policies Louis XVI's reformist ministers had formerly advocated. It suppressed the guilds and liberated the grain trade. The Assembly established the metric system to provide the nation with uniform weights and measures. (See "Encountering the Past: The Metric System," page 605.)

Workers' Organizations Forbidden The new policies of economic freedom and uniformity disappointed both peasants and urban workers. In 1789, the Assembly placed the burden of proof on the peasants to rid themselves of the residual feudal dues for which compensation was to be paid. On June 14, 1791, the Assembly crushed the attempts of urban workers to protect their wages by enacting the Chapelier Law, which forbade workers' associations. The Assembly saw the efforts of workers to organize in such a way as to resemble the abolished guilds of the Old Regime and thus to oppose the new values of political and social individualism, which the revolution championed. Peasants and workers were henceforth to be left to the freedom and mercy of the marketplace.

Confiscation of Church Lands While these various reforms were being put into effect, the financial

---

[3] Quoted in Sara E. Melzer and Leslie W. Rabine, eds., *Rebel Daughters: Women and the French Revolution* (New York: Oxford University Press, 1992), p. 88.

THE METRIC SYSTEM

Much about the era of the French Revolution seems alien to us today. One French regime followed another amidst confusion, violence, and bloodshed. Yet one thing that the revolutionaries did still touches the lives of virtually all Europeans and, if the U.S. Congress has its way, will touch everyone in the United States as well. In 1795, the French revolutionary government decreed a new standard for weights and measures—the metric system.

Inspired by the rationalism of the eighteenth-century Enlightenment, the metric system was intended to bring the order and simplicity of a system based on ten to the chaos of different weights and measures used in the various regions of prerevolutionary France. For its adherents, the republic marked the dawn of a new era in human history in which the triumph of science would replace the reign of superstition and obscurity. A new system of uniform weights and measures would also further one of the revolutionaries' political goals: centralization. With one set of weights and measures in use throughout the country, France would be closer to becoming a single "indivisible" republic.

Astronomy, which relied on the rational application of mathematics to measure the heavens, provided the basis for the new system of distance or length. Astronomers had devised methods to measure the arch of meridians—the highest point reached by the sun—around the earth. So the revolutionary authorities took the meridian in the latitude of Paris, which is 45°, as their standard for measuring the meter. The meter was to be one ten-millionth of one quarter of that meridian. All other measurements of length were then defined as decimal fractions or multiples of the meter.

1 centimeter (cm) = 10 millimeters (mm)
1 decimeter (dm) = 10 centimeters
1 meter = 100 centimeters
1 kilometer (km) = 1,000 meters

The standard for measuring weights was the gram, which constituted the weight of a cube of pure water measuring 0.01 meter on each side. Each measure of weight was defined as a decimal fraction or multiple of a gram. So a kilogram is 1,000 grams.

The metric system was soon adopted by scientists, but in their everyday lives, the population of France clung to their old, familiar weights and measures. Change, however "rational," did not come easily and was resisted. In 1812, Napoleon, bowing to popular sentiment, brought back the old units, but in 1840, the French government reimposed the metric system. Thereafter, rationality—and convenience—triumphed, and by the close of the nineteenth century, the metric system was used throughout continental Europe and had been introduced into Latin America. In the twentieth century it was adopted throughout Asia and Africa.

Today, the United States remains the great exception. Despite efforts by scientists, engineers, and doctors, who all use the metric system in their work, people in the United States still prefer to measure in inches, feet, yards, and miles and to weigh in ounces and pounds. Perhaps without even being aware of it, they are rejecting a system introduced during the French Revolution.

Jean-Baptiste Delambre (1749–1822) was one of the French astronomers whose measurements of the arch of meridians formed the basis for establishing the length of the meter. Image Works/Mary Evans Picture Library Ltd.

- *Why did the French revolutionary government introduce the metric system? How did the metric system reflect the ideas of the Enlightenment? Why has most of the world accepted this system?*

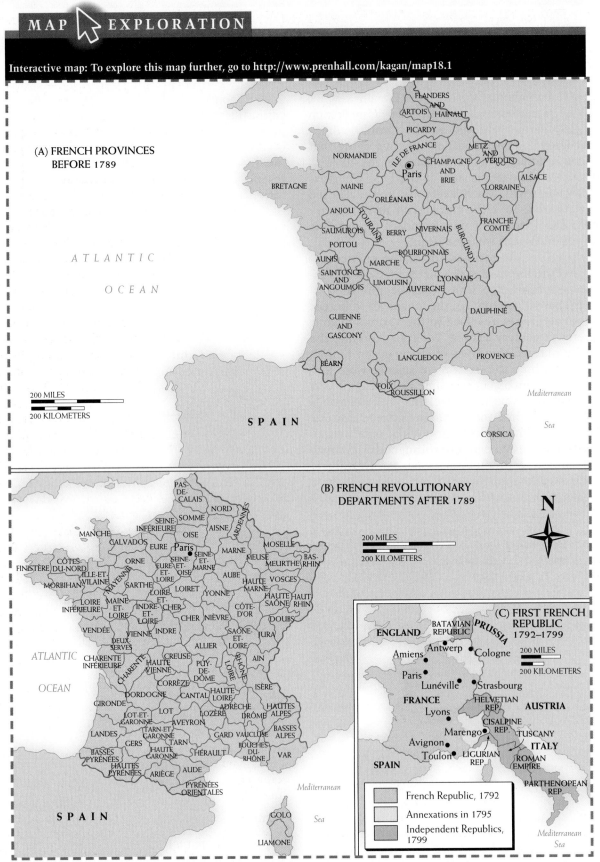

MAP ↖ EXPLORATION

Interactive map: To explore this map further, go to http://www.prenhall.com/kagan/map18.1

(A) FRENCH PROVINCES
BEFORE 1789

(B) FRENCH REVOLUTIONARY DEPARTMENTS AFTER 1789

(C) FIRST FRENCH REPUBLIC 1792–1799

French Republic, 1792
Annexations in 1795
Independent Republics, 1799

Map 18–1 **FRENCH PROVINCES AND THE REPUBLIC** In 1789, the National Constituent Assembly redrew the map of France. The ancient provinces (A) were replaced with a larger number of new, smaller departments (B). This redrawing of the map was part of the assembly's effort to impose greater administrative rationality in France. The borders of the republic (C) changed as the French army conquered new territory.

The *assignats* were government bonds that were backed by confiscated church lands. They circulated as money. When the government printed too many of them, inflation resulted and their value fell.   Bildarchiv Preussischer Kulturbesitz

crisis that had occasioned the calling of the Estates General persisted. The Assembly did not repudiate the royal debt, because it was owed to the bankers, the merchants, and the commercial traders of the Third Estate. The National Constituent Assembly had suppressed many of the old, hated indirect taxes and had substituted new land taxes, but these proved insufficient. Moreover, there were not enough officials to collect those taxes, and many people simply evaded them in the general confusion of the day. The continuing financial problem led the Assembly to take what may well have been, for the future of French life and society, its most decisive action. The Assembly decided to finance the debt by confiscating and then selling the land and property of the Roman Catholic Church in France. The results were further inflation, religious schism, and civil war. In effect, the National Constituent Assembly had opened a new chapter in the relations of church and state in Europe.

The *Assignats* Having chosen to plunder the church, the Assembly authorized the issuance of ***assignats***, or government bonds, in December 1789. Their value was guaranteed by the revenue to be generated from the sale of church property. Initially, a limit was set on the quantity of *assignats* to be issued. The bonds, however, proved so acceptable to the public that they began to circulate as currency. The Assembly decided to issue an ever-larger number of them to liquidate the national debt and to create a large body of new property owners with a direct stake in the revolution. Within a few months, however, the value of the *assignats* began to fall and inflation increased, putting new stress on the urban poor. Fluctu-

ation in the worth of this currency would plague the revolutionary government throughout the 1790s.

THE CIVIL CONSTITUTION OF THE CLERGY

The confiscation of church lands required an ecclesiastical reconstruction. In July 1790, the National Constituent Assembly issued the Civil Constitution of the Clergy, which transformed the Roman Catholic Church in France into a branch of the secular state. This legislation reduced the number of bishoprics from 135 to 83, making one diocese for each of the new departments. It also provided for the election of pastors and bishops, who henceforth became salaried employees of the state. The Assembly, which also dissolved all religious orders in France except those that cared for the sick or ran schools, consulted neither Pope Pius VI (r. 1775–1799) nor the French clergy about these sweeping changes. The king approved the measure only with the greatest reluctance.

The Civil Constitution of the Clergy was the major blunder of the National Constituent Assembly. It embittered relations between the French church and the state, a problem that has persisted to the present day. The measure immediately created immense opposition within the French church, even from bishops who had long championed Gallican liberties over papal domination. In the face of this resistance, the Assembly unwisely ruled that all clergy must take an oath to support the Civil Constitution. Only seven bishops and a little less than half the lower clergy did so. In reprisal, the Assembly designated those clergy who had not taken the oath as "refractory" and removed them from their clerical functions.

Angry reactions were swift. Refractory priests celebrated Mass in defiance of the Assembly. In February 1791, Pope Pius condemned not only the Civil Constitution of the Clergy, but also the Declaration of the Rights of Man and Citizen. That condemnation marked the opening of a Roman Catholic offensive against the revolution and liberalism that continued throughout the nineteenth century. Within France itself, the pope's action created a crisis of conscience and political loyalty for all sincere Catholics. Religious devotion and revolutionary loyalty became incompatible for many people. French citizens were divided between those who supported the constitutional priests and those who, like the royal family, followed the refractory clergy.

THE REVOLUTIONARY GOVERNMENT FORBIDS WORKERS' ORGANIZATIONS

The Chapelier Law of June 14, 1791, was one of the most important pieces of revolutionary legislation. It was directed against the guilds, those organizations that had protected skilled workers under the Old Regime. The law rejected collective action by labor, emphasizing instead the worker as an individual. The principles of this legislation prevented effective labor organization in France for well over half a century.

■ *Why are workers' organizations declared to be contrary to the principles of liberty? Why were guilds seen as one of the undesirable elements of the Old Regime? What coercive powers are to be brought to bear against workers' organizations? After this legislation, how could workers confront the operation of the market economy?*

1. Since the abolition of all kinds of corporations of citizens of the same occupation and profession is one of the fundamental bases of the French Constitution, reestablishment thereof under any pretext or form whatsoever is forbidden.

2. Citizens of the same occupation or profession, entrepreneurs, those who maintain open shop, workers, and journeymen of any craft whatsoever may not, when they are together, name either president, secretaries, or trustees, keep accounts, pass decrees or resolutions, or draft regulations concerning their alleged common interests. . . .

4. If, contrary to the principles of liberty and the Constitution, some citizens associated in the same professions, arts, and crafts hold deliberations or make agreements among themselves tending to refuse by mutual consent or to grant only at a determined price the assistance of their industry or their labor, such deliberations and agreements, whether accompanied by oath or not, are declared unconstitutional, in contempt of liberty and the Declaration of the Rights of Man, and noneffective; administrative and municipal bodies shall be required so to declare them. . . .

8. All assemblies composed of artisans, workers, journeymen, day laborers, or those incited by them against the free exercise of industry and labor appertaining to every kind of person and under all circumstances arranged by private contract, or against the action of police and the execution of judgments rendered in such connection, as well as against public bids and auctions of divers enterprises, shall be considered as seditious assemblies, and as such shall be dispersed by the depositories of the public force, upon legal requisitions made thereupon, and shall be punished according to all the rigor of the laws concerning authors, instigators, and leaders of the said assemblies, and all those who have committed assaults and acts of violence.

From John Hall Stewart *Documentary Survey of the French Revolution*, 1st Edition, © 1951. Reprinted by permission of Pearson Education, Inc., Upper Saddle River, NJ.

COUNTERREVOLUTIONARY ACTIVITY

The revolution had other enemies besides the pope and devout Catholics. As it became clear that the old political and social order was undergoing fundamental and probably permanent change, many aristocrats, eventually over 16,000, left France. Known as the **émigrés**, they settled in countries near the French border, where they sought to foment counterrevolution. Among the most important of their number was the king's younger brother, the count of Artois (1757–1836). In the summer of 1791, his agents and the queen persuaded Louis XVI to attempt to flee the country.

Flight to Varennes   On the night of June 20, 1791, Louis and his immediate family, disguised as servants, left Paris. They traveled as far as Varennes on their way to Metz in eastern France where a royalist military force was waiting for them. At Varennes the king was recognized, and his flight was halted. On June 24, a company of soldiers es-

In June 1791, Louis XVI and his family attempted to flee France. They were recognized in the town of Varennes, where their flight was halted and they were returned to Paris. This ended any realistic hope for a constitutional monarchy. © Bettmann/CORBIS

corted the royal family back to Paris. Eventually the leaders of the National Constituent Assembly, determined to save the constitutional monarchy, announced the king had been abducted from the capital. This convenient public fiction could not cloak the reality that the king was now the chief counterrevolutionary in France and that the constitutional monarchy might not last long. Profound distrust now dominated the political scene.

Declaration of Pillnitz Two months later, on August 27, 1791, under pressure from the *émigrés*, Emperor Leopold II (r. 1790–1792) of Austria, who was the brother of Marie Antoinette, and King Frederick William II (r. 1786–1797) of Prussia issued the Declaration of Pillnitz. The two monarchs promised to intervene in France to protect the royal family and to preserve the monarchy if the other major European powers agreed. This provision rendered the declaration meaningless because, at the time, Great Britain would not have given its consent. The declaration was, however, taken seriously in France, where the revolutionaries saw the nation surrounded by aristocratic and monarchical foes seeking to undo all that had been accomplished since 1789.

THE END OF THE MONARCHY: A SECOND REVOLUTION

The National Constituent Assembly drew to a close in September 1791, having completed its task of reconstructing the government and the administration of France. The Assembly had passed a measure that forbade any of its own members to sit in the Legisla-

tive Assembly the new constitution established. That new Assembly filled with entirely new members met on October 1 and immediately had to confront the challenges flowing from the resistance to the Civil Constitution of the Clergy, the king's flight, and the Declaration of Pillnitz.

EMERGENCE OF THE JACOBINS

Ever since the original gathering of the Estates General, deputies from the Third Estate had organized themselves into clubs composed of politically like-minded persons. The most famous and best organized of these clubs were the **Jacobins** because the group met in a former Dominican priory dedicated to St. Jacques (James) in Paris. The Jacobins had also established a network of local clubs throughout the provinces. They had been the most advanced political group in the National Constituent Assembly and had pressed for a republic rather than a constitutional monarchy. They drew their political language from the most radical thought of the Enlightenment, most particularly Rousseau's emphasis on equality, popular sovereignty, and civic virtue. Such thought and language became all the more effective because the events of 1789 to 1791 had destroyed the old political framework, and the old monarchical political vocabulary was less and less relevant. The rhetoric of republicanism filled that vacuum and for a time supplied the political values of the day. The flight of Louis XVI in the summer of 1791 and the Declaration of Pillnitz led renewed demands for a republic.

Factionalism plagued the Legislative Assembly throughout its short life (1791–1792). A group of Jacobins known as the *Girondists* (because many of them came from the department of the Gironde in southwest France) assumed leadership of the Assembly.[4] They were determined to oppose the forces of counterrevolution. They passed one measure ordering the *émigrés* to return or suffer the loss of their property and another requiring the refractory clergy to support the Civil Constitution or lose their state pensions. The king vetoed both acts.

Furthermore, on April 20, 1792, the Girondists led the Legislative Assembly to declare war on Austria, by this time governed by Francis II (r. 1792–1835) and allied to Prussia. This decision launched a period of

---

[4]The Girondists are also frequently called the Brissotins after Jacques-Pierre Brissot (1754–1793), their chief spokesperson in early 1792.

armed conflict across Western Europe that with only brief intervals of peace lasted until the final defeat of France at Waterloo in June 1815.

The Girondists believed the war would preserve the revolution from domestic enemies and bring the most advanced revolutionaries to power. Paradoxically, Louis XVI and other monarchists also favored the war. They thought the conflict would strengthen the executive power (the monarchy). The king also hoped that foreign armies might defeat French forces and restore the Old Regime. Both sides were playing a dangerously, deluded political game. The war radicalized French politics and within months led to what is usually called the second revolution, which overthrew the constitutional monarchy and established a republic.

With the outbreak of war, the country and the revolution seemed in danger. As early as March 1791, a group of women led by Pauline Léon had petitioned the Legislative Assembly for the right to bear arms and to fight to protect the revolution. Léon also wanted women to serve in the National Guard. These demands to serve, voiced in the universal language of citizenship, illustrated how the rhetoric of the revolution could be used to challenge traditional social roles and the concept of separate social spheres for men and women. Furthermore, the pressure of war raised the possibility that the nation could not meet its military needs if it honored the idea of separate spheres. Once the war began, some Frenchwomen did enlist in the army and served with distinction. (See "French Women Petition to Bear Arms," page 611.)

Initially, the war effort went poorly. In July 1792, the duke of Brunswick, commander of the Prussian forces, issued a manifesto threatening to destroy Paris if the French royal family were harmed. This statement stiffened support for the war and increased distrust of the king.

Late in July, under radical working-class pressure, the government of Paris passed from the elected council to a committee, or *commune*, of representatives from the sections (municipal wards) of the city. Thereafter the Paris commune became an independent political force casting itself in the role of the protector of the gains of the revolution against both internal and external enemies. Its activities and forceful modes of intimidation largely accounted for the dominance of the city of Paris over many of the future directions of the revolutionary government for the next three years.

On August 10, 1792, a large crowd invaded the Tuileries palace and forced Louis XVI and Marie Antoinette to take refuge in the Legislative Assembly. The crowd fought with the royal Swiss guards. When Louis was finally able to call off the troops, several hundred of them and many Parisian citizens lay dead in the most extensive violence since the fall of the Bastille. Thereafter the royal family was imprisoned in comfortable quarters, but the king was allowed to perform none of his political functions. The recently established constitutional monarchy no longer had a monarch.

THE CONVENTION AND THE ROLE OF THE *SANS-CULOTTES*

The September Massacres Early in September, the Parisian crowd again made its will felt. During the first week of the month, in what are known as the September Massacres, the Paris Commune summarily executed or murdered about 1,200 people who were in the city jails. Some of these people were aristocrats or priests, but most were simply common criminals. The crowd had assumed the prisoners were all counterrevolutionaries. News of this event along with the massacre of the Swiss guards as well as the imprisonment of the royal family spread rapidly across Europe, rousing new hostility toward the revolutionary government.

The Paris Commune then compelled the Legislative Assembly to call for the election by universal male suffrage of still another new assembly to write a democratic constitution. That body, called the **Convention** after the American Constitutional Convention of 1787, met on September 21, 1792. The previous day, the French army filled with patriotic recruits willing to die for the revolution had halted the Prussian advance at the Battle of Valmy in eastern France. Victory on the battlefield had confirmed the victory of democratic forces at home. As its first act, the Convention declared France a republic—that is, a nation governed by an elected assembly without a monarch.

Goals of the *Sans-culottes* The second revolution had been the work of Jacobins more radical than the Girondists and of the people of Paris known as the ***sans-culottes***. The name of this group means "without breeches" and derived from the long trousers that, as working people, they wore instead of aristocratic knee breeches. The *sans-culottes* were shopkeepers, artisans, wage earners, and, in a few cases, factory workers. The persistent food shortages and the revolutionary inflation reflected in the ongoing fall of the value of the *assignats* had made their difficult lives even more burdensome. The politics of the Old Regime had ignored them, and the policies of the National Constituent Assembly had left them victims of unregulated economic liberty. The government, however, required their labor and their lives if the war was to succeed. From the summer of 1792 until the summer of 1794, their attitudes, desires, and ideals were the primary factors in the internal development of the revolution.

FRENCH WOMEN PETITION TO BEAR ARMS

—m—

The issue of women serving in the revolutionary French military appeared early in the revolution. In March 1792, Pauline Léon petitioned the National Assembly on behalf of more than three hundred Parisian women for the right to bear arms and train for military service for the revolution. Similar requests were made during the next two years. Some womed did serve in the military, but in 1793, legislation forbade women to participate in military service. Legislators argued that women belonged in the domestic sphere and military service would lead them to abandon family duties.

■ *How does this petition challenge the concept of citizenship in the Declaration of the Rights of Man and Citizen? How do these petitioners relate their demand to bear arms to their role as women in French society? How do the petitioners relate their demands to the use of all national resources against the enemies of the revolution?*

Patriotic women come before you to claim the right which any individual has to defend his life and liberty. . . .

We are *citoyennes* [female citizens], and we cannot be indifferent to the fate of the fatherland. . . .

Yes, Gentlemen, we need arms, and we come to ask your permission to procure them. May our weakness be no obstacle; courage and intrepidity will supplant it, and the love of the fatherland and hatred of tyrants will allow us to brave all dangers with ease. . . .

No, Gentlemen, We will [use arms] only to defend ourselves the same as you; you cannot refuse us, and society cannot deny the right nature gives us, unless you pretend the Declaration of Rights does not apply to women and that they should let their throats be cut like lambs, without the right to defend themselves. For can you believe the tyrants would spare us? . . . Why then not terrorize aristocracy and tyranny with all the resources of civic effort and the pure zeal, zeal which cold men can well call fanaticism and exaggeration, but which is only the natural result of a heart burning with love for the public weal? . . .

If, for reasons we cannot guess, you refuse our just demands, these women you have raised to the ranks of *citoyennes* by granting that to their husbands, these women who have sampled the promises of liberty, who have conceived the hope of placing free men in the world, and who have sworn to live free or die—such women, I say, will never consent to concede the day to

slaves; they will die first. They will uphold their oath, and a dagger aimed at their breasts will deliver them from the misfortunes of slavery! They will die, regretting not life, but the uselessness of their death; regretting, moreover, not having been able to drench their hands in the impure blood of the enemies of the fatherland and to avenge some of their own!

But, Gentlemen, let us cast our eyes away from these cruel extremes. Whatever the rages and plots of aristocrats, they will not succeed in vanquishing a whole people of united brothers armed to defend their rights. We also demand only the honor of sharing their exhaustion and glorious labors and of making tyrants see that women also have blood to shed for the service of the fatherland in danger.

Gentlemen, here is what we hope to obtain from your justice and equity:

1. Permission to procure pikes, pistols, and sabres (even muskets for those who are strong enough to use them), within police regulations.
2. Permission to assemble on festival days and Sundays on the Champ de la Fédération, or in other suitable places, to practice maneuvers with these arms.
3. Permission to name the former French Guards to command us, always in conformity with the rules which the mayor's wisdom prescribes for good order and public calm.

From *Women in Revolutionary Paris, 1789–1795: Selected Documents Translated With Notes And Commentary.* Translated with notes and commentary by Darline Gay Levy, Harriet Branson Applewhite, and Mary Durham Johnson. Copyright 1979 by the Board of Trustees of the University of Illinois. Used with permission of the editors and the University of Illinois Press.

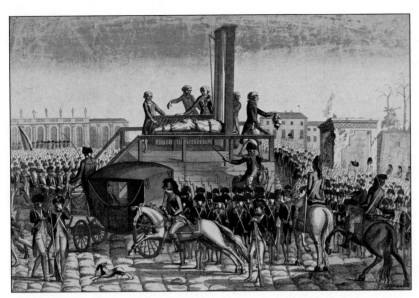

On January 21, 1793, the Convention executed Louis XVI by guillotine.
Cliché Bibliothèque Nationale de France, Paris

The *sans-culottes* generally knew what they wanted. The Parisian tradespeople and artisans sought immediate relief from food shortages and rising prices through price controls. The economic hardship of their lives made them impatient to see their demands met. They believed all people have a right to subsistence, and they resented most forms of social inequality. This attitude made them intensely hostile to the aristocracy and the original leaders of the revolution of 1789 from the Third Estate, who, they believed, simply wanted to share political power, social prestige, and economic security with the aristocracy. The *sans-culottes'* hatred of inequality did not take them so far as to demand the abolition of property. Rather, they advocated a community of small property owners who would also participate in the political nation.

In politics they were anti-monarchical, strongly republican, and suspicious even of representative government. They believed the people should make the decisions of government to an extent as great as possible. In Paris, where their influence was most important, the *sans-culottes* had gained their political experience in meetings of the Paris sections. The Paris Commune organized the previous summer was their chief political vehicle and crowd action their chief instrument of action.

The Policies of the Jacobins The goals of the *sans-culottes* were not wholly compatible with those of the Jacobins, republicans who sought representative government. Jacobin hatred of the aristocracy and hereditary privilege did not extend to a general suspicion of wealth. Basically, the Jacobins favored an unregulated economy. From the time of Louis XVI's flight to Varennes onward, however, the more extreme Jacobins began to cooperate with leaders of the Parisian *sans-culottes* and the Paris Commune to overthrow the monarchy. Once the Convention began to deliberate, these Jacobins, known as the *Mountain* because their seats were high up in the assembly hall, worked with the *sans-culottes* to carry the revolution forward and to win the war. This willingness to cooperate with the forces of the popular revolution separated the Mountain from the Girondists, who were also members of the Jacobin Club.

Execution of Louis XVI By the spring of 1793, several issues had brought the Mountain and its *sans-culottes* allies to dominate the Convention and the revolution. In December 1792, Louis XVI was put on trial as mere "Citizen Capet," the original medieval name of the royal family. The Girondists looked for a way to spare his life, but the Mountain defeated the effort. An overwhelming majority convicted Louis of conspiring against the liberty of the people and the security of the state. Condemned to death by a smaller majority, he was beheaded on January 21, 1793.

The next month, the Convention declared war on Great Britain and Holland, and a month later on Spain. Soon thereafter, the Prussians renewed their offensive and drove the French out of Belgium. To make matters worse, General Dumouriez (1739–1823), the Girondist victor of Valmy, deserted to the enemy. Finally, in March 1793, a royalist revolt led by aristocratic officers and priests erupted in the Vendée in western France and roused much popular support. Thus, the revolution found itself at war with most of Europe and much of the French nation. The Girondists had led the country into the war, but had been unable either to win it or to suppress the enemies of the revolution at home. The Mountain stood ready to take up the task.

EUROPE AT WAR WITH THE REVOLUTION

Initially, the rest of Europe had been ambivalent toward the revolutionary events in France. Those people who favored political reform regarded the revolution as wisely and rationally reorganizing a corrupt and inefficient government. The major foreign governments thought that the revolution meant France would cease to be an important factor in European affairs for years.

EDMUND BURKE ATTACKS THE REVOLUTION

In 1790, however, the Irish-born writer and British statesman Edmund Burke (1729–1799) argued a different position in *Reflections on the Revolution in France*. Burke condemned the reconstruction of the French administration as the application of a blind rationalism that ignored the historical realities of political development and the concrete complexities of social relations. He also forecast further turmoil as people without political experience tried to govern France, predicted the possible deaths of Louis XVI and Marie Antoinette at the hands of the revolutionaries, and forecast that the revolution would end in military despotism. As the revolutionaries proceeded to attack the church, the monarchy, and finally the rest of Europe, Burke's ideas came to have many admirers.

Thomas Paine, the hero of the American Revolution, composed *The Rights of Man* (1791–1792) in direct response to Burke and in defense of the revolutionary principles. Paine declared, "From what we now see, nothing of reform on the political world ought to be held improbable. It is an age of revolutions, in which everything may be looked for."[5] Paine's volume sold more copies at the time in England, but Burke's exercised more influence in the long run and was immediately published widely on the continent where it became a handbook of European conservatives.

By the outbreak of the war with Austria in April 1792, the other European monarchies recognized, along with Burke, the danger of both the ideas and the aggression of revolutionary France. In response, one government after another turned to repressive domestic policies. (See "Burke Denounces the Extreme Measures of the French Revolution".)

SUPPRESSION OF REFORM IN BRITAIN

In Great Britain, William Pitt the Younger (1759–1806), the prime minister, who had unsuccessfully supported moderate reform of Parliament during the 1780s, turned against both reform and popular movements. The government suppressed the London Corresponding Society, founded in 1792 as a working-class reform group. In Birmingham, the government sponsored mob action to drive Joseph Priestley (1733–1804), a famous chemist and a radical political thinker, out of the country. In early 1793, Pitt secured parliamentary approval for acts suspending *habeas corpus* and making the writing of certain ideas treasonable. With less success, Pitt also attempted to curb freedom of the press. All political groups who dared oppose the government faced being associated with sedition.

[5] Thomas Paine, *Political Writings*, Revised Student Edition, Bruce Kuklick, ed. (Cambridge: Cambridge University Press, 1997), p. 153

THE SECOND AND THIRD PARTITIONS OF POLAND, 1793, 1795

The final two partitions of Poland, already noted in Chapter 16, occurred as a direct result of fears by the eastern powers that the principles of the French Revolution were establishing themselves in Poland. After the first partition in 1772, Polish leaders had commenced reforms to provide for a stronger state. In 1791, a group of nobles known as the Polish Patriots actually issued a new constitution that substituted an hereditary for an elective monarchy, provided for real executive authority in the monarch and his council, established a new bicameral diet, and eliminated the *liberum veto*. The Polish government also adopted equality before the law and religious toleration. Frederick William II of Prussia (r. 1786–1797) promised to defend the new Polish constitutional order because he believed that a stronger Poland was in Prussia's interest against the growing Russian power. Catherine the Great of Russia also understood that a reformed Polish state would diminish Russian influence in Poland and eastern Europe.

In April 1792, conservative Polish nobles who opposed the reforms invited Russia to restore the old order. The Russian army quickly defeated the reformist Polish forces led by Tadeusz Kosciuszko (1746–1817), a veteran of the American Revolution. In response to the Russian invasion, Frederick William II moved his troops from the west where they were confronting the French revolutionary army to his eastern frontier with Poland. That transfer of Prussian troops proved crucial to the important later French victories in the autumn of 1792. However, rather than protecting Poland as he had promised, Frederick William reached an agreement with Catherine early in 1793 to carry out a second partition of Poland. The reformed constitution was abolished, and the new Polish government remained under the influence of Russia.

In the spring of 1794, Polish officers mutinied against efforts to unite their forces with the Russian army. Kosciuszko, who had been in France and Germany since his defeat in 1792, returned to Poland to lead these troops. Initially he was successful. As the rebellion expanded, the language and symbols of the French Revolution appeared in Polish cities. Before long, Prussia, Austria, and Russia sent troops into Poland. On November 4 in the single bloodiest day of combat in the decade, Russian troops killed well over 10,000 Poles outside Warsaw. Kosciuszko ended up in a Russian prison, and the next year the three eastern powers portioned what remained of Poland among them. Polish officers and troops who escaped Poland after the last partition later fought with the armies of the French Revolution and Napoleon against the forces of the partitioning powers.

BURKE DENOUNCES THE EXTREME MEASURES OF THE FRENCH REVOLUTION

Edmund Burke was the most important foreign critic of the French Revolution. His first critique, Reflections on the Revolution in France, *appeared in 1790. In 1796, he composed* Letters on a Regicide Peace, *which opposed a proposed peace treaty between Great Britain and revolutionary France. In that work, he summarized what he regarded as the worst evils of the revolutionary government: the execution of the king, the confiscation of property of the church and nobles, and de-Christianization (see page 618).*

■ *To which of the major events in the French Revolution does Burke refer? Why, by 1796, would Burke and others have emphasized the religious policies of the revolution? Did Burke exaggerate the evils of the revolution? Who was Burke trying to persuade?*

A government of the nature of that set up at our very door has never been hitherto seen, or ever imagined in Europe. . . . France, since her revolution, is under the sway of a sect, whose leaders have deliberately, at one stroke, demolished the whole body of that jurisprudence which France had pretty nearly in common with other civilized countries. . . .

Its foundation is laid in regicide, in Jacobinism, and in atheism, and it has joined to those principles a body of systematic manners, which secures their operation. . . .

I call a commonwealth regicide, which lays it down as a fixed law of nature, and a fundamental right of man, that all government, not being a democracy, is an usurpation. That all kings, as such, are usurpers; and for being kings may and ought to be put to death, with their wives, families, and adherents. That commonwealth which acts uniformly upon those principles . . . —this I call regicide by establishment.

Jacobinism is the revolt of the enterprising talents of a country against its property. When private men form themselves into associations for the purpose of destroying the pre-existing laws and institutions of their country; when they secure to themselves an army, by dividing amongst the people of no property the estates of the ancient and lawful proprietors, when a state recognizes those acts; when it does not make confiscations for crimes, but makes crimes for confiscations; when it has its principal strength, and all its resources, in such a violation of property . . . —I call this Jacobinism by establishment.

I call it atheism by establishment, when any state, as such, shall not acknowledge the existence of God as a moral governor of the world; . . . —when it shall abolish the Christian religion by a regular decree;—when it shall persecute with a cold, unrelenting, steady cruelty, by every mode of confiscation, imprisonment, exile, and death, all its ministers;—when it shall generally shut up or pull down churches; when the few buildings which remain of this kind shall be opened only for the purpose of making a profane apotheosis of monsters, whose vices and crimes have no parallel amongst men. . . When, in the place of that religion of social benevolence, and of individual self-denial, in mockery of all religion, they institute impious, blasphemous, indecent theatric rites, in honour of their vitiated, perverted reason, and erect altars to the personification of their own corrupted and bloody republic; . . . when wearied out with incessant martyrdom, and the cries of a people hungering and thristing for religion, they permit it, only as a tolerated evil—I call this atheism by establishment.

When to these establishments of regicide, of Jacobinism, and of atheism, you add the correspondent system of manners, no doubt can be left on the mind of a thinking man concerning their determined hostility to the human race.

From *The Works of the Right Honourable Edmund Burke* (London: Henry G. Bohn, 1856), 5: 206–208.

THE REIGN OF TERROR

WAR WITH EUROPE

The French invasion of the Austrian Netherlands (Belgium) and the revolutionary reorganization of that territory in 1792 roused the rest of Europe to active hostility. In November 1792, the Convention declared it would aid all peoples who wished to cast off aristocratic and monarchical oppression. The Convention had also proclaimed the Scheldt River in the Netherlands open to the commerce of all nations and thus had violated a treaty that Great Britain had made with Austria and Holland. The British were on the point of declaring war on France over this issue when the Convention issued its own declaration of hostilities against Britain in February 1793.

By April 1793, when the Jacobins began to direct the French government, the nation was at war with Austria, Prussia, Great Britain, Spain, Sardinia, and Holland. The governments of these nations, allied in what is known as the First Coalition, were attempting to protect their social structures, political systems, and economic interests against the aggression of the revolution.

This widening of the war in the winter and spring of 1792–1793 brought new, radical political actions within France as the revolutionary government mobilized itself and the nation for the conflict. Throughout France, there was the sense that a new kind of war had erupted. In this war the major issue was not protection of national borders as such, but rather the defense of the bold new republican political and social order that had emerged since 1789. The French people understood that the achievements of the revolution were in danger. To protect those achievements, the government took extraordinary actions that touched almost every aspect of national life. Thousands of people from all walks of life including peasants, nobles, clergy, business and professional people, one-time revolutionary leaders as well as the king and queen were arbitrarily arrested and, in many cases, executed. The immediate need to protect the revolution from enemies, real or imagined, from across the spectrum of French political and social life was considered more important than the security of property or even of life. These actions to protect the revolution and silence dissent came to be known as the **Reign of Terror**. (See "The Paris Jacobin Club Alerts the Nation to Internal Enemies of the Revolution," page 616.)

THE REPUBLIC DEFENDED

To mobilize for war, the revolutionary government organized a collective executive in the form of powerful committees. These, in turn, sought to organize all French national life on a wartime footing. The result was an immense military effort dedicated both to protecting and promoting revolutionary ideals.

The Committee of Public Safety   In April 1793, the Convention established a Committee of General Security and a Committee of Public Safety to carry out the executive duties of the government. The latter committee eventually enjoyed almost dictatorial power. All of the revolutionary leaders who served on the Committee of Public Safety were convinced republicans who had long opposed the more vacillating policies of the Girondists. They saw their task as saving the revolution from mortal enemies at home and abroad. They enjoyed a working political relationship with the *sans-culottes* of Paris, but this was an alliance of expediency for the committee.

The *Levée en Masse*   The major problem for the Convention was to wage the war and at the same time to secure domestic support for the war effort. In early June 1793, the Parisian *sans-culottes* invaded the Convention and successfully demanded the expulsion of the Girondist members. That action further radicalized the Convention and gave the Mountain complete control. On June 22, the Convention approved a fully democratic constitution, but delayed its implementation until the conclusion of the war. In fact, it was never implemented. On August 23, Lazare Carnot (1753–1823), the member of the Committee of Public Safety in charge of the military, began a mobilization for victory by issuing a ***levée en masse***, a military requisition on the entire population, conscripting males into the army and directing economic production to military purposes. The Convention decreed:

> From this moment until that in which the enemy shall have been driven from the soil of the Republic, all Frenchmen are in permanent requisition for the service of the armies.
> The young men shall go to battle; the married men shall forge arms and transport provisions; the women shall make tents and clothing and shall serve in the hospitals; the children shall turn old linen into lint; the aged shall betake themselves to the public places in order to arouse the courage of the warriors and preach the hatred of kings and the unity of the Republic.[6]

Following the *levée en masse*, the Convention on September 29, 1793, established a ceiling on prices in accord with *sans-culotte* demands. During these same months, the armies of the revolution also successfully crushed many of the counterrevolutionary disturbances in the provinces. Never before had Europe seen a nation organized in this way,

[6]Frank Maloy Anderson, ed. and trans., *The Constitutions and Other Select Documents Illustrative of the History of France, 1789–1907*, 2nd ed., rev. and enl. (Minneapolis: H. W. Wilson, 1908), pp. 184–185.

THE PARIS JACOBIN CLUB ALERTS THE NATIONS TO INTERNAL ENEMIES OF THE REVOLUTION

By early 1793, the revolutionary groups in Paris stood sharply divided amongst themselves. The Girondists (also known as Brissotins), who had led the nation into war, faced military reversals. General Dumouriez, a former revolutionary commander, had changed sides and was leading an army against France. At this point, on April 5, the radical Jacobin Club of Paris sent a circular to its provincial clubs, painting a dire picture of the fate of the revolution. While Dumouriez was marching against Paris, they accused members of the government and its administrators of conspring to betray the revolution. The circular suggested that some people were cooperating with England in the war against France. The Jacobins also portrayed as counterrevolutionaries all those political figures who had opposed the execution of Louis XVI. The Paris Jacobins then called on their allies in the provinces to defend the revolution and to take vengeance against its internal enemies. The distortion of the motives of political enemies, the appeal to a possible reversal of the revolution, and the accusations of internal conspiracy served to justify the demand for justice against enemies of the revolution. The accusations embodied in this circular and the fears it sought to arouse represented the kind of thinking that informed the suspension of legal rights and due process associated with the Reign of Terror.

■ *How did the Jacobins use the war to call for actions against their own domestic political enemies? What real and imagined forces did they see threatening the revolution? How did this circular constitute a smear campaign by one group of revolutionaries against other groups? What actions did the Jacobins seek?*

Friends, we are betrayed! To arms! To arms! The terrible hour is at hand when the defenders of the *Patrie* must vanquish or bury themselves under the bloody ruins of the Republic. Frenchmen, never was your liberty in such great peril! At last our enemies have put

nor one defended by a citizen army, which, by late 1794, with over a million men, had become larger than any ever organized in European history.

Other events within France astounded Europeans even more. The Reign of Terror had begun. Those months of quasi-judicial executions and murders stretching from the autumn of 1793 to the midsummer of 1794 are probably the most famous or infamous period of the revolution. They can be understood only in the context of the war on one hand and the revolutionary expectations of the Convention and the *sans-culottes* on the other.

THE "REPUBLIC OF VIRTUE" AND ROBESPIERRE'S JUSTIFICATION OF TERROR

The presence of armies closing in on the nation made it easy to dispense with legal due process. The people who sat in the Convention and those sitting on the Committee of Public Safety, however, did not see their actions simply in terms of expediency made necessary by war. They also believed they had created something new in world history, a "republic of virtue." In this republic, civic virtue largely understood in terms of Rousseau's *Social Contract*, the sacrifice of one's self and one's interest for the good of the republic, would replace selfish aristocratic and monarchical corruption. The republic of virtue manifested itself in many ways: in the renaming of streets from the egalitarian vocabulary of the revolution; in republican dress copied from that of the *sans-culottes* or the Roman Republic; in the absence of powdered wigs; in the suppression of plays and other literature that were insufficiently republican; and in a general attack against crimes, such as prostitution, that were supposedly characteristic of aristocratic society. Yet the core value of the republic of virtue in line with Rousseau's thought was the upholding of the public over the private good or the championing of the general will over individual

the finishing touch to their foul perfidy, and to complete it their accomplice Dumouriez is marching on Paris. . . .

But Brothers, not all your dangers are to be found there! . . . You must be convinved of a grievous truth! Your greatest enemies are in your midst, they direct your operations. O Vengeance !!! . . .

Yes, brothers and friends, yes, it is in the Senate that parricidal hands tear at your vitals! Yes, the counterrevolution is in the Government. . . . , in the National Conventional. It is there, at the center of your security and your hope, that criminal delegates hold the threads of the web that they have woven with the horde of despots who come to butcher us! . . . It is there that a sacrilegious cabal is directed by the English court . . . and others. . . .

Let us rise! Yes, let us rise! Let us arrest all the enemies of our revolution, and all suspected persons. Let us exterminate, without pity, all conspirators, unless we wish to be exterminated ourselves. . . .

Let the departments, the districts, the municipalities, and all the popular societies unite and concur in protesting to the Convention, by dispatching thereto a veritable rain of petitions manifesting the formal wish for the immediate

recall of all unfaithful members who have betrayed their duty by not wishing the death of the tyrant, and, above all, against those who have led astray so many of their colleagues. Such delegates are traitors, royalists, or fatuous men. The Republic condemns the friends of kings! . . .

Let us all unite equally to demand that the thunder or indictments be loosed against generals who are traitors to the Republic, against prevaricating ministers, against postal administrators, and against all unfaithful agents of the government. Therein lies our most salutary means of defence; but let us repel the traitors and tyrants.

The center of their conspiracy is here: it is in Paris that our perfidious enemies wish to consummate their crime. Paris, the cradle, the bulwark of liberty, is, without doubt, the place where they have sworn to annihilate the holy cause of humanity under the corpses of patriots.

From John Hall Stewart, *Documentary Survey of the French Revolution*, 1st Edition, © 1951. Reprinted by permission of Pearson Education, Inc., Upper Saddle River, NJ.

interests. It was in the name of the public good that the Committee of Public Safety carried out the policies of the terror.

The person who embodied this republic of virtue defended by terror was Maximilien de Robespierre (1758–1794), who, by late 1793, had emerged as the dominant figure on the Committee of Public Safety. This utterly selfless revolutionary figure has remained controversial from his day to the present. From the beginning of the revolution, he had favored a republic. The Jacobin Club provided his primary forum and base of power. A shrewd and sensitive politician, Robespierre had opposed the war in 1792 because he feared it might aid the monarchy. He depended largely on the support of the *sans-culottes* of Paris, but he continued to dress as he had before the revolution in powdered wig and knee breeches. For him, the republic of virtue meant whole-hearted support of the republican government, the renunciation of selfish gains

from political life, and the assault on foreign and domestic enemies of the revolution. Portraying revolutionary France as endangered on all sides, he told the Convention early in 1794,

Without, all the tyrants encircle you; within, all the friends of tyranny conspire—they will conspire until crime has been robbed of hope. We must smother the internal and external enemies of the Republic or perish with them. Now, in this situation, the first maxim of your policy ought to be to lead the people by reason and the people's enemies by terror. If the mainspring of popular government in peacetime is virtue, amid revolution it is at the same time [both] virtue and *terror*: virtue, without which terror is fatal; terror, without which virtue is impotent. Terror is nothing but prompt, severe, inflexible justice; it is therefore an emanation of virtue. It is less a special principle than a consequence of the general principle of democracy applied to our country's most pressing needs.[7]

[7]Quoted in Richard T. Bienvenu, *The Ninth of Thermidor: The Fall of Robespierre* (New York: Oxford University Press, 1968), p. 38.

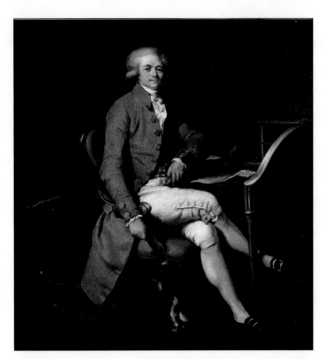

Maximilien Robespierre (1758–1794) emerged as the most powerful revolutionary figure in 1793 and 1794, dominating the Committee of Public Safety. He considered the Terror essential for the success of the revolution.
Musée des Beaux-Arts, Lille. Bridgeman–Giraudon/Art Resource, NY

Robespierre and those who supported his policies were among the first of a succession of secular ideologues of the left and the right who, in the name of humanity, would bring so much suffering to Europe in the following two centuries. The policies associated with terror in the name of republican virtue included the exclusion of women from active political life, the de-Christianization of France, and the use of revolutionary tribunals to dispense justice to alleged enemies of the republic.

REPRESSION OF THE SOCIETY OF REVOLUTIONARY REPUBLICAN WOMEN

Revolutionary women established their own distinct institutions during these months. In May 1793, Pauline Léon and Claire Lacombe founded the Society of Revolutionary Republican Women. Its purpose was to fight the internal enemies of the revolution. Its members saw themselves as militant citizens. Initially, the Jacobin leaders welcomed the organization. Members of the society and other women filled the galleries of the Convention to hear the debates and cheer their favorite speakers. The society became increasingly radical, however. Its members sought stricter controls on the price of food and other commodities, worked to ferret out food hoarders, and brawled with working market women whom they thought to be insufficiently revolutionary. The women of the society also demand-

ed the right to wear the revolutionary *cockade* that male citizens usually wore in their hats. By October 1793, the Jacobins in the Convention had begun to fear the turmoil the society was causing and banned all women's clubs and societies. The debates over these decrees show that the Jacobins believed the society opposed many of their economic policies, but the deputies used Rousseau's language of separate spheres for men and women to justify their exclusion of women from active political life.

There were other examples of repression of women in 1793. Olympe de Gouges, author of the Declaration of the Rights of Woman, opposed the Terror and accused Jacobins of corruption. She was guillotined in November 1793. The same year, women were formally excluded from serving in the French army and from the galleries of the Convention. The exclusion of women from public political life was part of the establishment of the Jacobin republic of virtue, because in such a republic men would be active citizens in the military and political sphere and women would be active only in the domestic sphere.

DE-CHRISTIANIZATION

The most dramatic step taken by the republic of virtue, and one that illustrates its imposition of political values to justify the Terror, was an the Convention's attempt to de-Christianize France. In November 1793, the Convention proclaimed a new calendar dating from the first day of the French Republic. There were twelve months of thirty days each, with names associated with the seasons and climate. Every tenth day, rather than every seventh, was a holiday. Many of the most important events of the next few years became known by their dates on the revolutionary calendar.[8] In November 1793, the Convention decreed the Cathedral of Notre Dame in Paris to be a "Temple of Reason."

The legislature then sent trusted members, known as deputies on mission, into the provinces to enforce de-Christianization by closing churches, persecuting clergy and believers (both Roman Catholic and Protestant), occasionally forcing priests to marry, and sometime simply by killing priests and nuns. Churches were desecrated, torn down, or used as barns or warehouses. This radical religious policy attacking both clergy and religious property roused enormous popular opposition and alienated parts of the French provinces from the revolutionary government in Paris. Robespierre

---

[8] From summer to spring, the months of the revolutionary calendar were Messidor, Thermidor, Fructidor, Vendémiaire, Brumaire, Frimaire, Nivose, Pluviose, Ventose, Germinal, Floreal, and Prairial.

personally opposed de-Christianization because he was convinced it would prove a political blunder that would erode loyalty to the republic.

REVOLUTIONARY TRIBUNALS

The Reign of Terror manifested itself in revolutionary tribunals that the Convention established during the summer of 1793. The mandate of these tribunals, the most prominent of which was in Paris, was to try the enemies of the republic, but the definition of who was an "enemy" shifted as the months passed. It included those who might aid other European powers, those who endangered republican virtue, and, finally, good republicans who opposed the policies of the dominant faction of the government. The Terror of the revolutionary tribunals systematized and channeled the popular resentment that had manifested itself in the September Massacres of 1792. Those whom the tribunal condemned in Paris were beheaded on the guillotine, a recently invented instrument of efficient and supposedly humane execution. (The drop of the blade of the guillotine was certain to sever the head of the condemned at once, whereas beheading by axe or sword could, and often did, require multiple blows and cause unnecessary pain.)

On the way to her execution in 1793, Marie Antoinette was sketched from life by Jacques-Louis David as she passed his window. Jacques Louis David (1748–1825), "Marie-Antoinette brought to the guillotine (after a drawing by David who witnessed the execution)." Pen drawing. 1793. Bibliotheque Nationale, Paris, France. Bridgeman-Giraudon/Art Resource, NY

Other modes of execution, such as mass shootings and drowning, were used in the provinces.

The first victims of the Terror were Marie Antoinette, other members of the royal family, and aristocrats, who were executed in October 1793. Girondist politicians who had been prominent in the Legislative Assembly followed them. These executions took place in the same weeks that the Convention had moved against the Society of Revolutionary Republican Women, whom it had also seen as endangering Jacobin control.

In early 1794, the Terror moved to the provinces, where the deputies on mission presided over the summary execution of thousands of people, most of whom were peasants, who had allegedly supported internal opposition to the revolution. One of the most infamous incidents occurred in Nantes on the west coast of France, where several hundred people, including many priests, were simply tied to rafts and drowned in the river Loire. The victims of the Terror were now coming from every social class, including the *sans-culottes.*

THE END OF THE TERROR

Revolutionaries Turn Against Themselves In Paris during the late winter of 1794, Robespierre began to orchestrate the Terror against republican political figures of the left and right. On March 24, he secured the execution of certain extreme *sans-culottes* leaders known as the *enragés.* They had wanted further measures to regulate prices, secure social equality, and press de-Christianization. Robespierre then turned against other republicans in the Convention. Most prominent among them was Jacques Danton (1759–1794), who had provided heroic national leadership in the dark days of September 1792 and who had later served briefly on the Committee of Public Safety before Robespierre joined the group. Danton and others were accused of being insufficiently militant on the war, profiting monetarily from the revolution, and rejecting the link between politics and moral virtue. Danton was executed in April 1794. Robespierre thus exterminated the leadership of both groups that might have threatened his position. Finally, on June 10, he secured passage of the Law of 22 Prairial, which permitted the revolutionary tribunal to convict suspects without hearing substantial evidence against them. The number of executions was growing steadily.

Fall of Robespierre In May 1794, at the height of his power, Robespierre, considering the worship of "Reason" too abstract for most citizens, replaced it with the "Cult of the Supreme Being." This deistic cult reflected Rousseau's vision of a civic religion that would induce morality among citizens. Robespierre, however, did not long preside over his new religion.

The Festival of the Supreme Being, which took place in June 1794, inaugurated Robespierre's new civic religion. Its climax occurred when a statue of Atheism was burned and another statue of Wisdom rose from the ashes.   Pierre-Antoine Demachy, "Festival of the Supreme Being at the Champ de Mars on June 8, 1794". Musée de la Ville de Paris, Musée Carnavalet, Paris, France. Bridgeman–Giraudon/Art Resource, NY

On July 26, Robespierre made an ill-tempered speech in the Convention, declaring that other leaders of the government were conspiring against him and the revolution. Similar accusations against unnamed persons had preceded his earlier attacks. No member of the Convention could now feel safe. On July 27—the Ninth of Thermidor on the revolutionary calendar—members of the Convention, by prearrangement, shouted him down when he rose to make another speech. That night Robespierre was arrested, and the next day he and approximately 80 of his supporters were executed. The revolutionary *sans-culottes* of Paris did not try to save him because he had deprived them of their chief leaders. He had also recently supported a measure to cap workers' wages. Other Jacobins turned against him because, after Danton's death, they feared they would be his next victims. Robespierre had destroyed rivals for leadership without creating supporters for himself. He had also for months tried to persuade the Paris populace that the Convention itself was harboring enemies of the revolution. Assured by the Convention that Robespierre had sought dictatorial powers, Parisians saw him as one more of those internal enemies. Robespierre was the unwitting creator of his own destruction.

THE THERMIDORIAN REACTION

The fall of Robespierre might simply have been one more shift in the turbulent politics of the revolution, but instead it proved to be a major turning point. The members of the Convention used the event to reassert their authority over the executive power of Committee of Public Safety. Within a short time, the Reign of Terror, which had claimed more than 25,000 victims, came to a close. It no longer seemed necessary since the war abroad was going well and the republican forces had crushed the provincial uprisings.

This tempering of the revolution, called the **Thermidorian Reaction**, because of its association with the events of 9 Thermidore, consisted of the destruction of the machinery of terror and the establishment of a new constitutional regime. It resulted from a widespread feeling that the revolution had become too radical. In particular, it displayed a weariness of the Terror and a fear that the *sans-culottes* had become too powerful. The influence of generally wealthy middle-class and professional people soon replaced that of the *sans-culottes*.

In the weeks and months after Robespierre's execution, the Convention allowed the Girondists who

THE CONVENTION ESTABLISHES THE WORSHIP OF THE SUPREME BEING

—⁓⁓—

On May 7, 1794, the Convention passed an extraordinary piece of revolutionary legislation. It established the worship of the Supreme Being as a state cult. Although the law drew on the religious ideas of deism, the point of the legislation was to provide a religious basis for the new secular French state. Pay particular attention to Article 6 which outlines the political and civic values that the Cult of the Supreme Being was supposed to nurture.

■ *How does this declaration reflect the ideas of the Enlightenment? Why has it been seen as establishing a civil religion? What personal and social values was this religion supposed to nurture?*

1. The French people recognize the existence of the Supreme Being and the immortality of the soul.
2. The recognize that the worship worthy of the Supreme Being is the observance of the duties of man.
3. The place in the forefront of such duties detestation of bad faith and tyranny, punishment of tyrants and traiters, succoring of unfortunates, respect of weak persons defence of the oppressed, doing to others all the good that one can, and being just towards everyone.
4. Festivals shall be instituted to remind man of the concept of the Divinity and of the dignity of his being.
5. They shall take their names from the glorious events of our Revolution, or from the virtues most dear and most useful to man, or from the greatest benefits of nature. . . .

6. On the days of *décade* the name given to a particular day in each month of the revolutionary calendar] it shall celebrate the following festivals:

   To the Supreme Being and to nature; to the human race; to the French people; to the benefactors of humanity; to the martyrs of liberty; to liberty and equality; to the Republic; to the liberty of the world; to the love of the *Patrie* [Fatherland]; to the hatred of tyrants and traitors; to truth; to justice; to modesty; to glory and immortality; to friendship; to frugality; to courage; to good faith; to heroism; to disinterestedness; to stoicism; to love; to conjugal love; to paternal love; to maternal tenderness; to filial piety; to infancy; to youth; to manhood; to old age; to misfortune; to agriculture; to industry: to our forefathers; to posterity; to happiness.

From John Hall Stewart, *Documentary Survey of the French Revolution*, 1st Edition, © 1951. Reprinted by permission of Pearson Education, Inc., Upper Saddle River, NJ.

had been in prison or hiding to return to their seats. A general amnesty freed political prisoners. The Convention restructured the Committee of Public Safety and diminished its power while repealing the notorious Law of 22 Prairial. Some, though by no means all, of the people responsible for the Terror were removed from public life. The Paris Commune was outlawed, and its leaders and deputies on mission were executed. The Paris Jacobin Club was closed, and Jacobin clubs in the provinces were forbidden to correspond with each other.

The executions of former terrorists marked the beginning of "the white terror." Throughout the country, people who had been involved in the Reign of Terror were attacked and often murdered. Jacobins were executed with little more due process than they had extended to their victims a few months earlier. The Convention itself approved some of these trials. In other cases, gangs of youths who had aristocratic connections or who had avoided serving in the army roamed the streets, beating known Jacobins. In Lyons, Toulon, and Marseilles, these so-called "bands of Jesus" dragged suspected terrorists from prisons and murdered them much as alleged royalists had been murdered during the September Massacres of 1792.

The republic of virtue gave way, if not to one of vice, at least to one of frivolous pleasures. The dress of the *sans-culottes* and the Roman Republic disappeared among the middle class and the aristocracy. New plays appeared in the theaters, and prostitutes again roamed the streets of Paris. Families of victims of the Reign of Terror gave parties in which they appeared with shaved necks, like the victims of the guillotine, and with red ribbons tied about them. Although the Convention continued to favor the Cult of the Supreme Being, it allowed Catholic services to be held. Many refractory priests returned to the country. One of the unanticipated results of the Thermidorian Reaction was a genuine revival of Catholic worship.

The Thermidorian Reaction also saw the repeal of legislation that had been passed in 1792 making divorce more equitable for women. As the passage of that measure suggests, the reaction did not extend women's rights or improve their education. The Thermidorians and their successors had seen enough attempts at political and social change. They sought to return family life to its status before the outbreak of the revolution. Political authorities and the church were determined to reestablish separate spheres for men and women and to reinforce traditional gender roles. As a result, Frenchwomen may have had less freedom after 1795 than before 1789.

ESTABLISHMENT OF THE DIRECTORY

The Thermidorian Reaction led to still another new constitution. The democratic constitution of 1793, which had never gone into effect, was abandoned. In its place, the Convention issued the Constitution of the Year III, which reflected the Thermidorian determination to reject *both* constitutional monarchy and democracy. In recognition of the danger of a legislature with only one chamber and unlimited authority, this new document provided for a legislature of two houses. Members of the upper body, or Council of Elders, were to be men over forty years of age who were either husbands or widowers. The lower Council of Five Hundred was to consist of men of at least thirty who could be either married or single. The executive body was to be a five-person Directory whom the Elders would choose from a list the Council of Five Hundred submitted. Property qualifications limited the franchise, except for soldiers, who were permitted to vote whether they had property or not.

Historically, the term *Thermidor* has come to be associated with political reaction. That association requires considerable qualification. By 1795, the political structure and society of the Old Regime in France based on rank and birth had given way permanently to a political system based on civic equality and social status based on property ownership. People who had never been allowed direct, formal access to political power had, to different degrees, been granted it. Their entrance into political life had given rise to questions of property distribution and economic regulations that could not again be ignored. Representation was an established principle of politics. Henceforth, the question before France and eventually before all of Europe would be which new groups would be permitted representation. In the *levée en masse*, the French had demonstrated to Europe the power of the secular ideal of nationhood and of the willingness of citizen soldiers to embrace self-sacrifice.

The post-Thermidorian course of the French Revolution did not undo these stunning changes in the political and social contours of Europe. What triumphed in the Constitution of the Year III was the revolution of the holders of property. For this reason the French Revolution has often been considered a victory of the bourgeoisie, or middle class. The property that won the day, however, was not industrial wealth, but the wealth stemming from commerce, the professions, and land. The largest new propertied class to emerge from the revolutionary turmoil was the peasantry, who, as a result of the destruction of aristocratic privileges, now owned their own land. Unlike peasants liberated from traditional landholding in other parts of Europe during the next century, French peasants had to pay no monetary compensation either to their former landlords or to the state.

REMOVAL OF THE *SANS-CULOTTES* FROM POLITICAL LIFE

The most decisively reactionary element in the Thermidorian Reaction and the new constitution was the removal of the *sans-culottes* from political life. With the war effort succeeding, the Convention severed its ties with the *sans-culottes*. True to their belief in an unregulated economy, the Thermidorians repealed the ceiling on prices. As a result, the winter of 1794–1795 brought the worst food shortages of the period. There were many food riots, which the Convention suppressed to prove that the era of the *sans-culottes journées* had come to a close. Royalist agents, who aimed to restore the monarchy, tried to take advantage of their discontent. On October 5, 1795—13 Vendémiaire—the sections of Paris led by the royalists rose up against the Convention. The government turned the artillery against the royalist rebels. A general named Napoleon Bonaparte (1769–1821) commanded the cannon, and with a "whiff of grapeshot," he dispersed the crowd.

By the Treaties of Basel in March and June 1795, the Convention concluded peace with Prussia and Spain. The legislators, however, feared a resurgence of both radical democrats and royalists in the

THE FRENCH REVOLUTION

1787
February–May Unsuccessful negotiations with the Assembly of Notables
1788
August 8 Louis XVI summons the Estates General
December 27 Approval of doubling of the Third Estate membership
1789
May 5 The Estates General opens at Versailles
June 17 The Third Estate declares itself the National Assembly
June 20 The National Assembly takes the Tennis Court Oath
July 14 Fall of the Bastille in the city of Paris
Late July The Great Fear spreads in the countryside
August 4 The nobles surrender their feudal rights at a meeting of the National Constituent Assembly
August 27 Declaration of the Rights of Man and Citizen
October 5–6 Parisian women march to Versailles and force Louis XVI and his family to return to Paris
1790
July 12 Civil Constitution of the Clergy adopted
July 14 A new political constitution is accepted by the king
1791
June 14 Chapelier Law
June 20–24 Louis XIV and his family attempt to flee France and are stopped at Varennes
August 27 The Declaration of Pillnitz
October 1 The Legislative Assembly meets
1792
April 20 France declares war on Austria
August 10 The Tuileries palace is stormed, and Louis XVI takes refuge with the Legislative Assembly
September 2–7 The September Massacres
September 20 France wins the Battle of Valmy
September 21 The Convention meets, and the monarchy is abolished
1793
January 21 King Louis XVI is executed

February 1 France declares war on Great Britain
March Counterrevolution breaks out in the Vendée
April The Committee of Public Safety is formed
June 22 The Constitution of 1793 is adopted, but not implemented
July Robespierre enters the Committee of Public Safety
August 23 *Levée en masse* proclaimed
September 29 Maximum prices set on food and other commodities
October 16 Queen Marie Antoinette is executed
October 30 Women's societies and clubs banned
November 10 The Cult of Reason is proclaimed; the revolutionary calendar, beginning on September 22, 1792, is adopted
1794
March 24 Execution of the leaders of the *sans-culottes* known as the *enragés*
April 6 Execution of Danton
May 7 Cult of the Supreme Being proclaimed
June 8 Robespierre leads the celebration of the Festival of the Supreme Being
June 10 The Law of 22 Prairial is adopted
July 27 The Ninth of Thermidor and the fall of Robespierre
July 28 Robespierre is executed
August 1 Repeal of the Law of 22 Prairial
August 10 Reorganization of the Revolutionary Tribunal
November 12 Closing of Jacobin Club in Paris
1795
May 31 Abolition of Revolutionary Tribunal
August 22 The Constitution of the Year III establishes the Directory
September 23 Two-Thirds Law Adopted
1796
May 10 Babeuf's Conspiracy of Equals
1799
November 9 Napoleon's (8 Brumaire) coup d'état overthrows the Directory

Gracchus Babeuf was executed in 1797 for leading the "Conspiracy of Equals," a radical plot to overthrow the Directory and redistribute property among all French citizens. © Michael Nicholson/CORBIS

upcoming elections for the Council of Five Hundred. Consequently, the Convention ruled that at least two-thirds of the new legislature must have served in the Convention itself, thus rejecting the decision the National Constituent Assembly had made in 1791 when it forbade its members to be elected to the new Legislative Assembly. The Two-Thirds Law, which sought to foster continuity but also clearly favored politicians already in office, quickly undermined public faith in the new constitutional order.

The Directory faced almost immediate social unrest. During the spring of 1796 in Paris, Gracchus Babeuf (1760–1797) led the Conspiracy of Equals. He and his followers called for more radical democracy and for more equality of property. They declared at one point, "The aim of the French Revolution is to destroy inequality and to re-establish the general welfare . . . . The Revolution is not complete, because the rich monopolize all the property and govern exclusively, while the poor toil like slaves, languish in misery, and count for nothing in the state."[9] In a sense, they were correct. The Directory intended to resist any further social changes in France that might endanger property or political stability. Babeuf was arrested, tried, and executed. This

minor plot became famous decades later, when European socialists attempted to find their historical roots in the French Revolution.

The suppression of the *sans-culottes*, the narrow franchise of the constitution, the Two-Thirds Law, and the Catholic royalist revival presented the Directory with challenges that it was never able to overcome. Because France remained at war with Austria and Great Britain, it needed a broader-based active loyalty than it was able to command. Instead, the Directory came to depend on the power of the army to govern France. All soldiers could vote. Moreover, within the army that the revolution had created and sustained were ambitious officers who were eager for power. As will be seen in the next chapter, the instability of the Directory, the growing role of the army, and the ambitions of its leaders held profound consequences not only for France but for the entire Western world.

━━━∞∞∞━━━

IN PERSPECTIVE

The French Revolution is the central political event of modern European history. It unleashed political and social forces that shaped Europe and much of the rest of the world for the next two centuries. The revolution began with a clash between the monarchy and the nobility. Once the Estates General gathered, however, the traditional boundaries of eighteenth-century political life could not contain the discontent. The Third Estate, in all of its diversity, demanded real influence in government. Initially, that meant the participation of middle-class members of the Estates General, but soon the people of Paris and the peasants made their own demands known. Thereafter, popular nationalism exerted itself on French political life and the destiny of Europe.

Revolutionary legislation and popular uprisings in Paris, the countryside, and other cities transformed the social as well as the political life of the nation. Nobles surrendered traditional social privileges. The church saw its property confiscated and its operations brought under state control. For a time, there was an attempt to de-Christianize France. Vast amounts of landed property changed hands, and France became a nation of peasant landowners. Urban workers lost the protection they had enjoyed under the guilds and became more subject to the forces of the marketplace.

Violence accompanied many of the revolutionary changes. Thousands died during the Reign of Terror. France also found itself at war with virtually the rest of Europe. Resentment, fear, and a new desire for stability eventually brought the Terror to

[9]Quoted in John Hall Stewart, *A Documentary Survey of the French Revolution* (New York: Macmillan, 1966), pp. 656–657.

an end. That desire for stability, combined with a determination to defeat the foreign enemies of the revolution and to carry it abroad, would, in turn, work to the advantage of the army. Eventually, Napoleon Bonaparte would claim leadership in the name of stability and national glory.

REVIEW QUESTIONS

1. Why has France been called a rich nation with an impoverished government? How did the financial weaknesses of the French monarchy lay the foundations of the revolution of 1789?
2. What were Louis XVI's most serious mistakes during the French Revolution? Had he been a more able ruler, could the French Revolution have been avoided or a constitutional monarchy succeeded? Did the revolution ultimately have little to do with the competence of the monarch?
3. How was the Estates General transformed into the National Assembly? How does the Declaration of the Rights of Man and Citizen reflect the social and political values of the eighteenth-century Enlightenment? How were France and its government reorganized in the early years of the revolution? Why has the Civil Constitution of the Clergy been called the greatest blunder of the National Assembly?
4. Why were some political factions dissatisfied with the constitutional settlement of 1791? What was the revolution of 1792 and why did it occur? Who were the *sans-culottes*, and how did they become a factor in the politics of the period? How influential were they during the Terror in particular? Why did the *sans-culottes* and the Jacobins cooperate at first? Why did that cooperation end?
5. Why did France go to war with Austria in 1792? What were the benefits and drawbacks for France of fighting an external war in the midst of a domestic political revolution?
6. What were the causes of the Terror? How did the rest of Europe react to the French Revolution and the Terror? How did events in France influence the last two partitions of Poland?
7. A motto of the French Revolution was "equality, liberty, and fraternity." How did the revolution both support and violate this motto? Did French women benefit from the revolution? Did French peasants benefit from it?

SUGGESTED READINGS

D. ANDRESS, *The French Revolution and the People* (2004). Explores the direct impact of the policies and experience of the revolution on ordinary people especially in the countryside.
N. ASTON, *Christianity and Revolutionary Europe c. 1750–1830* (2002). Continent-wide survey of the impact of revolution on religion.

K. M. BAKER AND C. LUCAS (EDS.), *The French Revolution and the Creation of Modern Political Culture*, 3 vols. (1987). A splendid collection of original articles on politics during the revolution.
T. C. BLANNING, *The Revolutionary Wars, 1787–1802* (1996). Essential for understanding the role of the army and the revolution.
W. DOYLE, *The Oxford History of the French Revolution* (2003). A broad, complex narrative with an excellent bibliography.
A. FORREST, *Revolutionary Paris, the Provinces and the French Revolution* (2004). A clear presentation of the tensions between the center of the revolution and the provinces.
C. HAYDEN AND W. DOYLE, EDS., *Robespierre* (1999). Essays evaluating Robespierre's ideas, career, and reputation.
P. HIGONNET, *Goodness beyond Virtue: Jacobins During the French Revolution* (1998). An outstanding work that clearly relates political values to political actions.
D. JORDON, *The King's Trial: Louis XVI vs. the French Revolution* (1979) A gripping account of the event.
E. KENNEDY, *A Cultural History of the French Revolution* (1989). An important examination of the role of the arts, schools, clubs, and intellectual institutions.
S. E. MELZER AND L. W. RABINE (EDS.), *Rebel Daughters: Women and the French Revolution* (1997). Essays exploring the role and image of women in the revolution.
C. C. O'BRIEN, *The Great Melody: A Thematic Biography of Edmund Burke* (1992). The best recent biography.
R. R. PALMER, *The Age of Democratic Revolution: A Political History of Europe and America, 1760–1800*, 2 vols. (1959, 1964). Still an impressive survey of the political turmoil in the transatlantic world.
T. TACKETT, *Becoming a Revolutionary: The Deputies of the French National Assembly and the Emergence of a Revolutionary Culture (1789–1790)* (1996). The best study of the early months of the revolution.

DOCUMENTS CD-ROM

The French Revolution

19.1 The Declaration of the Rights of Man and Citizen
19.2 "Declaration of the Rights of Women and the Female Citizen"
19.3 Petition of Women of the Third Estate
19.4 Robespierre: Justification of Terror
19.5 Louis XVI: *A Royal Reform Proposal, 1787*
19.6 Edmund Burke: *The Moral Imagination*

CHAPTER 19

THE AGE OF NAPOLEON AND THE TRIUMPH OF ROMANTICISM

KEY TOPICS

- Napoleon's rise, his coronation as emperor, and his administrative reforms
- Napoleon's conquests, the creation of a French Empire, and Britain's enduring resistance
- The invasion of Russia and Napoleon's decline
- The reestablishment of a European order at the Congress of Vienna
- Romanticism and the reaction to the Enlightenment
- Islam and Romanticism

B y the late 1790s, the French people, especially property owners, who now included the peasants, longed for stability. The Directory was not providing it. Only the army was able to take charge of the nation as a symbol of both order and the popular values of the revolution. The most politically astute general was Napoleon Bonaparte, who had been a radical during the early revolution, a victorious commander in

This portrait of Napoleon on his throne by Jean Ingres (1780–1867) shows him in the splendor of an imperial monarch who embodies the total power of the state.

Jean Auguste Dominique Ingres (1780-1867), "Napoleon on His Imperial Throne," 1806. Oil on canvas, 259 × 162 cm. Musee des Beaux-Arts, Rennes. Photograph © Erich Lessing/Art Resource, NY

Italy, and a supporter of the repression of revolutionary disturbances after Thermidor.

Once in power, Napoleon consolidated many of the achievements of the revolution. He also repudiated much of it by establishing an empire. Thereafter, his ambitions drew France into wars of conquest and liberation across the Continent. For over a decade, Europe was at war, with only brief periods of armed truce. Through his conquests

Napoleon spread many of the ideas and institutions of the revolution and overturned much of the old political and social order. He also provoked popular nationalism in opposition to French domination. This new force and the great alliances that opposed France eventually defeated Napoleon.

Throughout these Napoleonic years, new ideas and sensibilities, known by the term *Romanticism*, grew across Europe. Many of the ideas had originated in the eighteenth century, but they flourished in the turmoil of the French Revolution and the Napoleonic Wars. The revolution spurred the imagination of poets, painters, and philosophers.

Some Romantic ideas, such as nationalism, supported the revolution; others, such as the emphasis on history and religion, opposed its values. ■

THE RISE OF NAPOLEON BONAPARTE

The chief threat to the Directory came from royalists, who hoped to restore the Bourbon monarchy by legal means. Many of the *émigrés* had returned to France. Their plans for a restoration drew support from devout Catholics and from those citizens disgusted by the excesses of the revolution. Monarchy promised stability. The spring elections of 1797 replaced most incumbents with constitutional monarchists and their sympathizers, thus giving them a majority in the national legislature.

To preserve the republic and prevent a peaceful restoration of the Bourbons, the antimonarchist Directory staged a *coup d'état* on 18 Fructidor (September 4, 1797). They put their own supporters into the legislative seats their opponents had won. They then imposed censorship and exiled some of their enemies. At the request of the Directors, Napoleon Bonaparte, the general in charge of the French invasion of Italy, had sent a subordinate to Paris to guarantee the success of the coup. In 1797, as in 1795, the army and Bonaparte had saved the day for the government installed in the wake of the Thermidorian Reaction.

Napoleon Bonaparte was born in 1769 to a poor family of lesser nobles at Ajaccio, on the Mediterranean island of Corsica. Because France had annexed Corsica in 1768, he went to French schools and, in 1785, obtained a commission as a French artillery officer. He favored the revolution and was a fiery Jacobin. In 1793, he played a leading role in recovering the port of Toulon from the British. As a reward for his service, he was appointed a brigadier general. During the Thermidorian Reaction, his defense of the new regime on 13 Vendémiaire won him a command in Italy.

EARLY MILITARY VICTORIES

By 1795, French arms and diplomacy had shattered the enemy coalition, but France's annexation of Belgium guaranteed continued fighting with Britain and Austria. The invasion of Italy aimed to deprive Austria of its rich northern Italian province of Lombardy. In a series of lightning victories, Bonaparte crushed the Austrian and Sardinian armies. On his own initiative, and against the

wishes of the government in Paris, he concluded the Treaty of Campo Formio in October 1797. The treaty took Austria out of the war and crowned Napoleon's campaign with success. Before long, France dominated all of Italy and Switzerland.

In November 1797, the triumphant Bonaparte returned to Paris as a hero and to confront France's only remaining enemy, Britain. He judged it impossible to cross the Channel and invade England at that time. Instead, he chose to attack British interests through the eastern Mediterranean by capturing Egypt from the Ottoman Empire. By this strategy, he hoped to drive the British fleet from the Mediterranean, cut off British communications with India, damage British trade, and threaten the British Empire.

Napoleon easily overran Egypt, but the invasion was a failure. Admiral Horatio Nelson (1758–1805) destroyed the French fleet at Abukir on August 1, 1798. The French army was cut off from France. To make matters worse, the situation in Europe was deteriorating. The invasion of Egypt had alarmed Russia, which had its own ambitions in the Near East. The Russians, the Austrians, and the Ottomans joined Britain to form the Second Coalition against France. In 1799, the Russian and Austrian armies defeated the French in Italy and Switzerland and threatened to invade France.

Napoleon's venture into Egypt in 1798 and 1799 marked the first major West European assault on the Ottoman Empire. It occurred less than a quarter century after Russia, under Catherine the Great, had taken control of the Crimea in the Treaty of Kuchuk-Kainardji. (See Chapter 17.) Significantly, British, not Ottoman forces, drove the French out of Egypt. As shall be seen in Chapter 22, after Napoleon's invasion, the Ottoman Empire realized that it had to reform itself if it was to resist other European encroachments.

THE CONSTITUTION OF THE YEAR VIII

Economic troubles and the dangerous international situation eroded the Directory's fragile support. One of the Directors, the Abbé Siéyès (1748–1836), proposed a new constitution. The author of the pamphlet *What Is the Third Estate?* (1789) now wanted an executive body independent of the whims of electoral politics, a government based on the principle of "confidence from below, power from above." The change would require another *coup d'état* with military support. News of France's misfortunes had reached Napoleon in Egypt. Without orders and leaving his army behind, he returned to France in October 1799 to popular acclaim. Soon he joined Siéyès. On 19 Brumaire (November 10, 1799), his troops ensured the success of the coup.

Siéyès appears to have thought that Napoleon could be used and then dismissed, but he misjudged his man. The proposed constitution divided executive authority among three consuls. Bonaparte quickly pushed Siéyès aside, and in December 1799, he issued the Constitution of the Year VIII. Behind a screen of universal male suffrage that suggested democratic principles, a complicated system of checks and balances that appealed to republican theory, and a Council of State that evoked memories of Louis XIV, the new constitution established the rule of one man—the First Consul, Bonaparte. To find an appropriate historical analogy, we must go back to Caesar and Augustus in ancient Rome, and to the Greek tyrants of the sixth century B.C.E. The career of Bonaparte, however, pointed forward to the dictators of the twentieth century. He was the first modern political figure to use the rhetoric of revolution and nationalism, to back it with military force, and to combine these elements into a mighty weapon of imperial expansion in the service of his own power.

THE CONSULATE IN FRANCE (1799–1804)

The **Consulate** in effect ended the revolution in France. The leading elements of the Third Estate—that is, officials, landowners, doctors, lawyers, and financiers—had achieved most of their goals by 1799. They had abolished hereditary privilege, and the careers thus opened to talent allowed them to achieve wealth, status, and security for their property. The peasants were also satisfied. They had gained the land they had always wanted and had destroyed oppressive feudal privileges. The newly established dominant classes had little or no desire to share their new privileges with the lower social orders. Bonaparte seemed just the person to give them security. When he submitted his constitution to the voters in a plebiscite, they overwhelmingly approved it.

SUPPRESSING FOREIGN ENEMIES AND DOMESTIC OPPOSITION

Throughout much of the 1790s, the pressures of warfare, particularly conscription, had accounted for much French internal instability. Bonaparte justified the public's confidence in himself by making peace with France's enemies. Russia had already left the Second Coalition. A campaign in Italy brought another victory over Austria at Marengo in 1800. The Treaty of Luneville early in 1801 took Austria out of the war. Britain was now alone and, in 1802, concluded the Treaty of Amiens, which brought peace to Europe.

Bonaparte also restored peace and order at home. He used generosity, flattery, and bribery to win over enemies. He issued a general amnesty and employed men from all political factions. He required only that they be loyal to him. Men who had been radicals during the Reign of Terror, or who had fled the Terror and favored constitutional monarchy, or who had been high officials under Louis XVI occupied some of the highest offices.

Bonaparte, however, ruthlessly suppressed opposition. He established a highly centralized administration in which prefects responsible to the government in Paris managed all departments. He employed secret police. He stamped out the royalist rebellion in the west and made the rule of Paris effective in Brittany and the Vendée for the first time in years.

Napoleon also used and invented opportunities to destroy his enemies. A plot on his life in 1804 provided an excuse to attack the Jacobins, though it was the work of the royalists. Also in 1804, he violated the sovereignty of the German state of Baden to seize and execute the Bourbon duke of Enghien (1772–1804). The duke was accused of participation in a royalist plot, though Bonaparte knew him to be innocent. The action was a flagrant violation of international law and of due process. Charles Maurice de Talleyrand-Périgord (1754–1838), Bonaparte's foreign minister, later termed the act "worse than a crime—a blunder" because it provoked foreign opposition. It was popular with the former Jacobins, however, for it seemed to preclude the possibility of a Bourbon restoration. The executioner of a Bourbon was not likely to restore the royal family. The execution also seems to have put an end to royalist plots.

CONCORDAT WITH THE ROMAN CATHOLIC CHURCH

No single set of revolutionary policies had aroused so much domestic opposition as those regarding the French Catholic Church; nor were there any other policies to which fierce supporters of the revolution seemed so attached. When the French armies had invaded Italy, they had driven Pope Pius VI (r. 1775–1799) from Rome, and he eventually died in exile in France. In 1801, to the shock and dismay of his anticlerical supporters, Napoleon concluded a concordat with Pope Pius VII (r. 1800–1823).

The agreement was possible because Pius VII, before becoming pope, had written that Christianity was compatible with the ideals of equality and democracy. The concordat gave Napoleon what he most wanted. The agreement required both the refractory clergy and those who had accepted the revolution to resign. Their replacements received their spiritual investiture from the pope, but the state named the bishops and paid their salaries and the salary of one priest in each parish. In return, the church gave up its claims to its confiscated property.

The concordat declared, "Catholicism is the religion of the great majority of French citizens." This was merely a statement of fact and fell far short of what the pope had wanted: religious dominance for the Roman Catholic Church. The clergy had to swear an oath of loyalty to the state. The Organic Articles of 1802, which the government issued on its own authority without consulting the pope, established the supremacy of state over church. Similar laws were applied to the Protestant and Jewish communities, reducing still further the privileged position of the Catholic Church. (See "Napoleon Makes Peace with the Papacy".)

THE NAPOLEONIC CODE

In 1802, a plebiscite ratified Napoleon as consul for life, and he soon produced another constitution that granted him what amounted to full power. He thereafter set about reforming and codifying French law. The result was the Civil Code of 1804, usually known as the Napoleonic Code.

The Napoleonic Code safeguarded all forms of property and tried to secure French society against internal challenges. All the privileges based on birth that the revolution had overthrown remained abolished.

The conservative attitudes toward labor and women that had emerged during the revolution also received full support. Workers' organizations remained forbidden, and workers had fewer rights than their employers. Fathers were granted extensive control over their children and husbands over their wives. However, primogeniture—the right of an eldest son to inherit most or all of his parents' property—remained abolished, and property was distributed among all children, males and females, but married women needed their husbands' consent to dispose of their own property. Divorce remained more difficult for women than for men. Before this code, French law had differed from region to region. That confused set of laws had given women opportunities to protect their interests. The universality of the Napoleonic Code ended that.

ESTABLISHING A DYNASTY

In 1804, Bonaparte seized on a bomb attack on his life to make himself emperor. He argued that establishing a dynasty would make the new regime secure and make further attempts on his life useless. Another new constitution declared Napoleon Bonaparte Emperor of the French, instead of First Consul of the Republic. A plebiscite also overwhelmingly ratified this constitution.

To conclude the drama, Napoleon invited Pope Pius VII to Notre Dame to take part in the coronation. At the last minute, however, the pope agreed that Napoleon should crown himself. The emperor would not allow anyone to think his power and authority depended on the church. Henceforth, he was called Napoleon I.

NAPOLEON'S EMPIRE (1804–1814)

Between his coronation as emperor and his final defeat at Waterloo (1815), Napoleon conquered most of Europe. France's victories changed the map of the Continent. The wars put an end to the Old Regime and its feudal trappings throughout Western Europe and forced the eastern European states to reorganize themselves to resist Napoleon's armies.

Everywhere, Napoleon's advance unleashed the powerful force of nationalism, discussed more fully in Chapter 20. His weapon was the militarily mobilized French nation, one of the achievements of the revolution. Napoleon could put 700,000 men under arms at one time, risk 100,000 troops in a single battle, endure heavy losses, and fight again. He could conscript citizen soldiers in unprecedented numbers, thanks to their loyalty to the nation and to him. No single enemy could match such resources. Even coalitions were unsuccessful, until Napoleon's mistakes led to his own defeat.

CONQUERING AN EMPIRE

The Peace of Amiens (1802) between France and Great Britain was merely a truce. Napoleon's unlimited ambitions shattered any hope that it might last. He sent an army to restore the rebellious colony of Haiti to French rule. This move aroused British fears that he was planning a new French empire in America, because Spain had restored Louisiana to France in 1801. More serious were his interventions in the Dutch Republic, Italy, and Switzerland and his reorganization of Germany. The Treaty of Campo Formio had required a redistribution of territories along the Rhine River, and the petty princes of the region engaged in a scramble to enlarge their holdings. Among the results

NAPOLEON MAKES PEACE WITH THE PAPACY

In the 1790s, after the passage of the Civil Constitution of the Clergy (1790), anticlerical violence, popular resistance, and papal condemnation had created turmoil and instability in France. Departing from the religious policies of the previous revolutionary governments, Napoleon concluded a concordat with Pope Pius VII in 1801. This document was the cornerstone of Napoleonic religious policy. The concordat allowed the Roman Catholic Church to function freely in France only within the limits of church support for the government as indicated in the oath included in Article 6.

■ *Why was it to Napoleon's political advantage to make this agreement with the papacy? What privileges or advantages does the church achieve in the document? Would the highest loyalty of a bishop who took the oath in Article 6 reside with the church or the French state?*

The Government of the French Republic recognizes that the Roman, catholic and apostolic religion is the religion of the great majority of French citizens.

His Holiness likewise recognizes that this same religion has derived and in this moment again expects the greatest benefit and grandeur from the establishment of the catholic worship in France and from the personal profession of it which the consuls of the Republic make.

In consequence, after this mutual recognition, as well for the benefit of religion as for the maintenance of internal tranquility, they have agreed as follows:

1. The catholic, apostolic and Roman religion shall be freely exercised in France: its worship shall be public, and in conformity with the police regulations which the government shall deem necessary for the public tranquility. . . .

4. The First Consul of the Republic shall make appointments, within the three months which shall follow the publication of the bull of His Holiness, to the archbishoprics and bishoprics of the new circumscription. His Holiness shall confer the canonical institution, following the forms established in relation to France before the change of government. . . .

6. Before entering upon their functions, the bishops shall take directly, at the hands of the First Consul, the oath of fidelity which was in use before the change of government, expressed in the following terms:

> "I swear and promise to God, upon the holy scriptures, to remain in obedience and fidelity to the government established by the constitution of the French Republic. I also promise not to have any intercourse, nor to assist by any counsel, nor to support any league, either within or without, which is inimical to the public tranquility; and if, within my diocese or elsewhere, I learn that anything to the prejudice of the state is being contrived, I will make it known to the government."

From Maloy Anderson, ed. and trans., *The Constitutions and Other Select Documents Illustrative of the History of France, 1789–1907*, 2nd ed., rev. and enl. (Minneapolis: H. W. Wilson, 1908), pp. 296–297.

---

were the reduction of Austrian influence and the emergence of fewer, but larger, German states in the West, all dependent on Napoleon.

British Naval Supremacy   Alarmed by these developments, the British issued an ultimatum. When Napoleon ignored it, Britain declared war in May 1803. William Pitt the Younger returned to office as prime minister in 1804 and began to construct the Third Coalition. By August 1805, he had persuaded Russia and Austria to move once more against France. A great naval victory soon raised the fortunes of the allies. On October 21, 1805, the British admiral Lord Nelson destroyed the combined French and Spanish fleets at the Battle of Trafalgar off the Spanish coast. Nelson died in the battle, but the British lost no ships. Trafalgar ended all French hope of invading Britain and guaranteed British control of the sea for the rest of the war. (See "Encountering the Past: Sailors and Canned Food," page 634.)

Napoleonic Victories in Central Europe   On land the story was different. Even before Trafalgar, Napoleon had marched to the Danube River to

A CLOSER LOOK

The Coronation of Napoleon

Jacques-Louis David recorded the elaborate coronation of Napoleon in a monumental painting that revealed the enormous political and religious tensions of that event, which involved the kind of ritual and ceremony associated with the monarchy of the ancient regime.

Napoleon's mother sits in a balcony-like setting and presides over her son's establishment of a new reigning dynasty in France and across Europe, through the placement of relatives on various thrones.

Napoleon is about to place a crown on the head of his wife Josephine whom he will later divorce because she and he were unable to conceive an heir for his new dynasty. He would then marry the daughter of the Habsburg emperor.

Jacques Louis David (1748–1825), "Consecration of the Emperor Napoleon I and Coronation of Empress Josephine," 1806–07. Louvre, Paris. Bridgeman–Giraudon/Art Resource, NY

To the right sits Pope Pius VII who observes the event, but is not a real participant. Napoleon and the Pope had signed a Concordat that restored much of the standing but by no means all of the prerevolutionary authority of the Roman Catholic Church in France. The pope understood that at that moment in France as well as throughout Europe his authority was largely subject to the wishes of the French emperor.

In this early-nineteenth-century cartoon, England, personified by a caricature of William Pitt, and France, personified by a caricature of Napoleon, are carving out their areas of interest around the globe.   Bildarchiv Preussischer Kulturbesitz

attack his continental enemies. In mid-October he forced an Austrian army to surrender at Ulm and occupied Vienna. On December 2, 1805, in perhaps his greatest victory, Napoleon defeated the combined Austrian and Russian forces at Austerlitz. The Treaty of Pressburg that followed won major concessions from Austria. The Austrians withdrew from Italy and left Napoleon in control of everything north of Rome. He was recognized as king of Italy.

Napoleon also made extensive political changes in Germany. In July 1806, he organized the Confederation of the Rhine, which included most of the western German princes. Their withdrawal from the Holy Roman Empire led Francis II to dissolve that ancient political body and henceforth to call himself Emperor Francis I of Austria.

Prussia, which had remained neutral up to this point, now foolishly went to war against France. Napoleon's forces quickly crushed the famous Prussian army at Jena and Auerstädt on October 14, 1806. Two weeks later, Napoleon was in Berlin. There, on November 21, he issued the Berlin Decrees, forbidding his allies from importing British goods. On June 13, 1807, Napoleon defeated the Russians at Friedland and occupied East Prussia. The French emperor was master of all Germany.

Treaty of Tilsit   Unable to fight another battle and unwilling to retreat into Russia, Tsar Alexander I (r. 1801–1825) was ready to make peace. He and Napoleon met on a raft in the Niemen River while the two armies and the nervous king of Prussia watched from the bank. On July 7, 1807, they signed the Treaty of Tilsit, which confirmed France's gains. Prussia lost half its territory. Only the support of Alexander saved it from extinction. Prussia openly and Russia secretly became allies of Napoleon.

Napoleon organized conquered Europe much like the estate of a Corsican family. The great French Empire was ruled directly by the head of the clan, Napoleon. On its borders lay satellite states ruled by members of his family. His stepson ruled Italy for him, and three of his brothers and his brother-in-law were made kings of other conquered states. Napoleon denied a kingdom only to his brother Lucien, of whose wife he disapproved. The French emperor expected his relatives to take orders without question. When they failed to do so, he rebuked and even punished them. This establishment of the Napoleonic family as the collective sovereigns of Europe provoked political opposition that needed only encouragement and assistance to flare up into serious resistance.

THE CONTINENTAL SYSTEM

After the Treaty of Tilsit, such assistance could come only from Britain, and Napoleon knew he must defeat the British before he could feel safe. Unable to compete with the British navy, he continued the economic warfare the Berlin Decrees had begun. He planned to cut off all British trade with the European continent and thus to cripple British commercial and financial power. He hoped to cause domestic unrest and drive Britain from the war. The Milan Decree of 1807 went further and attempted to stop neutral nations from trading with Britain. (See Map 19–1, page 635.)

Despite initial drops in exports and domestic unrest, the British economy survived. British control of the seas assured access to the growing markets of North and South America and of the eastern Mediterranean. At the same time, the Continental System badly hurt the European economies. Napoleon rejected advice to turn his empire into a free-trade area. Such a policy would have been both popular and helpful. Instead, his tariff policies favored France, increased the resentment of foreign merchants, and made them less willing to enforce the system and more ready to engage in smuggling. It was, in part, to prevent smuggling that Napoleon invaded Spain in 1808. The resulting peninsular campaign in Spain and Portugal helped bring on his ruin.

EUROPEAN RESPONSE TO THE EMPIRE

Wherever Napoleon ruled, he imposed the Napoleonic Code and abolished hereditary social distinctions. Feudal privileges disappeared, and the peasants were freed from serfdom and manorial dues. In the towns, the guilds and the local

SAILORS AND CANNED FOOD

In 1803, during the Napoleonic wars, the French navy undertook a secret experiment—provisioning a few of its naval vessels involved in long overseas voyages or blockades with food preserved by the then novel process of canning. The results were excellent; the crews thrived; and the French government ordered more canned goods.

Until the discovery of canning, the chief methods for preserving food were drying, salting, pickling, smoking, fermenting, and condensing. Most of these techniques are still used, but they strongly alter the taste of food and destroy some of its nutritive value. Although vitamins were unknown in the eighteenth century, military authorities did know that something in fresh fruit and vegetables kept their men healthy. In the 1790s, the French government offered a reward to anyone who could invent a method of preserving food that would make it both nearer in taste and texture to fresh products and more nourishing for sailors and soldiers who often suffered from scurvy and malnutrition from their rations of dried bread and salted meat. The desired food would allow naval vessels to stay at sea longer without having to put into port for fresh food and armies to campaign without having to live off the land.

Nicholas Appert, a French chef, was determined to produce preserved food that would be both tasty and healthful. In 1795, he established what amounted to a small food preservation laboratory on the outskirts of Paris. He eventually discovered that if he filled glass jars with fresh vegetables, fruit, soups, or meat, added water or a sauce, sealed the jars with tight stoppers, and then cooked them in a hot water bath, the result was a tasty preserved food that lasted indefinitely as long as the jars remained sealed. Although Appert did not know it, one reason the food remained unspoiled was that his process killed any microbes in it.

Although many fine French foods are still canned in jars, the process quickly took a new turn in Great Britain where the navy as well as food producers were interested in it. Appert published a book on his method in 1810, and by 1813 an Eng-

Nicholas Appert (1749–1841) invented canning as a way of preserving food nutritiously. Canned food could be transported over long distances without spoiling.
Private Collection/Bridgeman Art Library

lish company began canning in tins, which were less expensive and more durable than glass jars. Soon other canning companies appeared in Europe, including those that produced canned sardines. By mid-century, millions of people, particularly in Western Europe and North America, were eating canned food. By 1900, canned goods had become what they remain today—part of everyday life around the world. The basic process used in canning is still the one Appert devised in the 1790s.

- *What advantages did canning have over other methods of preserving food? Why was the military interested in it? How did canning become a part of everyday life?*

Source: Sue Shephard, *Pickled, Potted, and Canned: How the Art and Science of Food Processing Changed the World* (New York: Simon & Schuster, 2000).

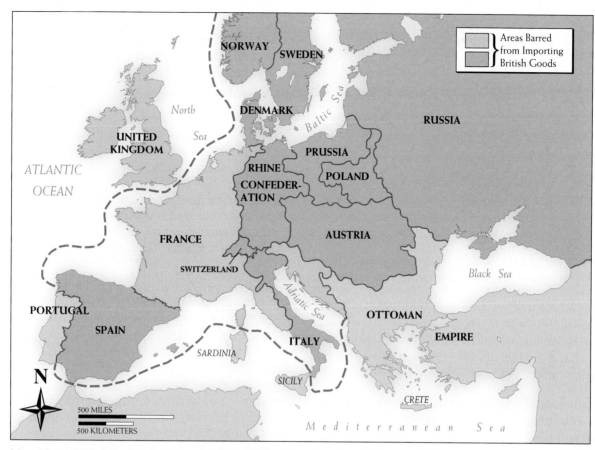

Map 19–1 **THE CONTINENTAL SYSTEM, 1806–1810** Napoleon hoped to cut off all British trade with the European continent and thereby drive the British from the war.

oligarchies that had been dominant for centuries were dissolved or deprived of their power. The established churches lost their traditional independence and were made subordinate to the state. Toleration replaced monopoly of religion by an established church. Despite these reforms, however, it was always clear that Napoleon's policies were intended first for his own glory and that of France. The Continental System demonstrated that Napoleon's rule was intended to enrich France, rather than Europe generally. Consequently, before long, the conquered states and peoples grew restive. (See "Napoleon Advises His Brother to Rule Constitutionally," page 636.)

GERMAN NATIONALISM AND PRUSSIAN REFORM

The German response to Napoleon's success was particularly interesting and important. There had never been a unified German state. The great German writers of the Enlightenment, such as Immanuel Kant and Gotthold Lessing, were neither deeply politically engaged nor nationalistic.

At the beginning of the nineteenth century, the Romantic Movement had begun to take hold. One of its basic features in Germany was the emergence of nationalism, which went through two distinct stages there. Initially, nationalistic writers emphasized the unique and admirable qualities of German culture, which, they argued, arose from the history of the German people. Such cultural nationalism prevailed until Napoleon's humiliation of Prussia at Jena in 1806.

At that point many German intellectuals began to urge resistance to Napoleon on the basis of German nationalism. The French conquest endangered the independence and achievements of all German-speaking people. Many nationalists also criticized the German princes, who ruled selfishly and inefficiently and who seemed ever ready to lick Napoleon's boots. Only a people united through its language and culture could resist the French onslaught. No less important in forging a German national sentiment was the example of France itself, which had attained greatness by enlisting the active support of the entire people in the patriotic cause. Henceforth, many Germans sought to solve their internal political problems by attempting to establish a unified German state, reformed to harness the energies of the entire people.

NAPOLEON ADVISES HIS BROTHER TO RULE CONSTITUTIONALLY

As Napoleon swept through Europe, he set his relatives on the thrones of various conquered kingdoms and then imposed written constitutions on them. In this letter of November 1807, Napoleon sent his brother Jerome (1784–1860) a constitution for the Kingdom of Westphalia in Germany. The letter shows how Napoleon spread the political ideas and institutions of the French Revolution across Europe. Napoleon ignored, however, the nationalistic resentment that French conquest aroused, even when that conquest brought more liberal political institutions. Such nationalism would contribute to his downfall.

■ *What benefits does Napoleon believe his conquest and subsequent rule by his brother will bring to their new subjects? Why does he believe that these, rather than military victory, will achieve new loyalty? How does Napoleon suggest playing off the resentment of the upper classes to consolidate power? What is the relationship between having a written constitution such as Napoleon is sending his brother and the power of public opinion that he mentions toward the close of the letter?*

I enclose the constitution for your Kingdom. You must faithfully observe it. I am concerned for the happiness of your subjects, not only as it affects your reputation, and my own, but also for its influence on the whole European situation.

Don't listen to those who say that your subjects are so accustomed to slavery that they will feel no gratitude for the benefits you give them. There is more intelligence in the Kingdom of Westphalia than they would have you believe; and your throne will never be firmly established except upon the trust and affection of the common people. What German opinion impatiently demands is that men of no rank, but of marked ability, shall have an equal claim upon your favour and your employment, and that every trace of serfdom, or of a feudal hierarchy between the sovereign and the lowest class of his subjects shall be done away with. The benefits of the Code Napoleon, public trial, and the introduction of juries, will be the leading features of your Government. And to tell you the truth, I count more upon their effects, for the extension and consolidation of your rule, than upon the most resounding victories. I want your subjects to enjoy a degree of liberty, equality, and prosperity hitherto unknown to the German people. . . . Such a method of government will be a stronger barrier between you and Prussia than the Elbe, the fortresses, and the protection of France. What people will want to return under the arbitrary Prussian rule, once it has tasted the benefits of a wise and liberal administration? In Germany, as in France, Italy, and Spain, people long for equality and liberalism. I have been managing the affairs of Europe long enough now to know that the burden of the privileged classes was resented everywhere. Rule constitutionally. Even if reason, and the enlightenment of the age, were not sufficient cause, it would be good policy for one in your position; and you will find that the backing of public opinion gives you a great natural advantage over the absolute kings who are your neighbors.

From J. M. Thompson, ed., *Napoleon's Letters* (London: Dent, 1954), pp. 190–191, as quoted in Maurice Hutt, ed., *Napoleon* (Englewood Cliffs, NJ: Prentice-Hall, 1972), p. 34.

After Tilsit, only Prussia could arouse such patriotic feelings. Elsewhere German rulers were either under Napoleon's thumb or collaborating with him. Defeated, humiliated, and diminished, Prussia continued to resist, however feebly. To Prussia fled German nationalists from other states, calling for reforms and unification that King Frederick William III (r. 1797–1840) and the Junker nobility in fact feared and hated. Reforms came about despite such opposition because the defeat at Jena had shown that the Prussian state had to change to survive.

The Prussian administrative and social reforms were the work of Baron vom Stein (1757–1831) and Prince von Hardenberg (1750–1822). Neither of these reformers intended to reduce the autocratic power of the Prussian monarch or to end the dominance of the Junkers, who formed the bulwark of the state and of the officer corps. Rather, they wanted to fight French power with their own version of the French weapons. As Hardenberg declared,

Our objective, our guiding principle, must be a revolution in the better sense, a revolution leading directly to the great goal, the elevation of humanity through the wisdom of those in authority . . . . Democratic rules of conduct in a monarchical administration, such is the formula . . . which will conform most comfortably with the spirit of the age.[1]

Although the reforms came from the top, they wrought important changes in Prussian society.

Stein's reforms broke the Junker monopoly of landholding. Serfdom was abolished. However, unlike in the western German states where all remnants of serfdom simply disappeared, in Prussia the Junkers ensured that vestiges of the system survived. Former Prussian serfs were free to leave the land if they chose, but those who stayed had to continue to perform manorial labor. They could obtain the ownership of the land they worked only if they forfeited a third of it to the lord. The result was that Junker holdings grew larger. Some peasants went to the cities to find work, others became agricultural laborers, and some did actually become small freeholding farmers. In Prussia and elsewhere, serfdom had ended, but the rise in the numbers of landless laborers created new social problems.

Military reforms sought to increase the supply of soldiers and to improve their quality. Jena had shown that an army of free patriots commanded by officers chosen on merit rather than by birth could defeat an army of serfs and mercenaries commanded by incompetent nobles. To remedy the situation, the Prussian reformers abolished inhumane military punishments, sought to inspire patriotic feelings in the soldiers, opened the officer corps to

commoners, gave promotions on the basis of merit, and organized war colleges that developed new theories of strategy and tactics.

These reforms soon enabled Prussia to regain its former power. Because Napoleon strictly limited the size of its army to 42,000 men, however, Prussia could not introduce universal conscription until it broke with Napoleon in 1813. Before that date, the Prussians evaded the limit by training one group each year, putting them into the reserves, and then training a new group the same size. Prussia could thus boast an army of 270,000 by 1814.

THE WARS OF LIBERATION

Spain In Spain more than elsewhere in Europe, national resistance to France had deep social roots. Spain had achieved political unity as early as the sixteenth century. The Spanish peasants were devoted to the ruling dynasty and especially to the Roman Catholic Church. France and Spain had been allies since 1796. In 1807, however, a French army came into the Iberian Peninsula to force Portugal to abandon its traditional alliance with Britain. The army stayed in Spain to protect lines of supply and communication. Napoleon used a revolt that broke out in Madrid in 1808 as a pretext to depose the Spanish Bourbons and to place his brother Joseph (1768–1844) on the Spanish throne. Attacks on the privileges of the church increased public outrage. Many members of the upper classes were prepared to collaborate with Napoleon, but the peasants, urged on by the lower clergy and the monks, rebelled.

In Spain, Napoleon faced a new kind of warfare. Guerrilla bands cut lines of communication, killed stragglers, destroyed isolated units, and then disappeared into the mountains. The British landed an army under Sir Arthur Wellesley (1769–1852), later the duke of Wellington, to support the Spanish insurgents. Thus began the long peninsular campaign that would drain French strength from elsewhere in Europe and hasten Napoleon's eventual defeat.

Austria The French troubles in Spain encouraged the Austrians to renew the war in 1809. Since their defeat at Austerlitz, they had sought a war of revenge. The Austrians counted on Napoleon's distraction in Spain, French war weariness, and aid from other German princes. Napoleon was fully in command in France, however, and the German princes did not move. The French army marched swiftly into Austria and won the Battle of Wagram. The resulting Peace of Schönbrunn deprived Austria of much territory and 3.5 million subjects.

Another spoil of victory was the Austrian archduchess Marie Louise (1791–1847), daughter of

[1]Quoted in Geoffrey Brunn, *Europe and the French Imperium* (New York: Harper & Row, 1938), p. 174.

Goya y Lucientes, Francisco de Goya, recorded Napoleon's troops executing Spanish guerilla fighters who had rebelled against the French occupation in *The Third of May, 1808.* Francisco de Goya, "Los fusilamientos del 3 de Mayo, 1808." 1814. Oil on canvas, 8'6" × 11'4".
© Museo Nacional del Prado, Madrid

Emperor Francis I. Napoleon's wife, Josephine de Beauharnais (1763–1814), was forty-six and had borne him no children. His dynastic ambitions, as well as the desire for a royal marriage, led him to divorce Josephine and marry the eighteen-year-old Marie Louise. Napoleon had also considered marrying the sister of Tsar Alexander, but had received a polite rebuff.

THE INVASION OF RUSSIA

The failure of Napoleon's marriage negotiations with Russia emphasized the shakiness of the Franco-Russian alliance concluded at Tilsit. Russian nobles disliked the alliance because of the liberal politics of France and because the Continental System prohibited timber sales to Britain. Only French aid in gaining Constantinople could justify the alliance in their eyes, but Napoleon gave them no help against the Ottoman Empire. The organization of the Polish Duchy of Warsaw as a Napoleonic satellite on the Russian doorstep and its enlargement with Austrian territory in 1809 after the Battle of Wagram angered Alexander. Napoleon's annexation of Holland in violation of the Treaty of Tilsit, his recognition of the French marshal Bernadotte (1763–1844) as the future King Charles XIV of Sweden, and his marriage to Marie Louise further disturbed the tsar. At the end of 1810, Russia withdrew from the Continental System and began to prepare for war. (See Map 19–2.)

Napoleon was determined to end the Russian military threat. He amassed an army of more than 600,000 men, including a core of Frenchmen and more than 400,000 other soldiers drawn from the rest of his empire. He intended the usual short campaign crowned by a decisive battle, but the Russians retreated before his advance. His vast superiority in numbers—the Russians had only about 160,000 troops—made it foolish for them to risk a battle. Instead they followed a "scorched-earth" policy, destroying all food and supplies as they retreated. The so-called Grand Army of Napoleon could not live off the country, and the expanse of Russia made supply lines too long to maintain. Terrible rains, fierce heat, shortages of food and water, and the courage of the Russian rear guard eroded the morale of Napoleon's army. Napoleon's advisers urged him to abandon the venture, but he feared an unsuccessful campaign would undermine his position in the empire and in France. He pinned his faith on the Russians' unwillingness to abandon Moscow without a fight.

In September 1812, Russian public opinion forced the army to give Napoleon the battle he wanted despite the canny Russian general Mikhail Kutuzov's (1745–1813) wish to let the Russian winter defeat the invader. At Borodino, not far west of Moscow, the bloodiest battle of the Napoleonic era cost the French 30,000 casualties and the Russians almost twice as many. Yet the Russian army was not destroyed. Napoleon won nothing substantial, and the battle was regarded as a defeat for him.

Fires set by the Russians soon engulfed Moscow and left Napoleon far from home with a badly diminished army lacking adequate supplies as winter came to a vast and unfriendly country. After capturing the burned city, Napoleon addressed several peace offers to Alexander, but the tsar ignored them. By October, what was left of the Grand Army was forced to retreat. By December, Napoleon realized the Russian fiasco would encourage plots against him at home. He returned to Paris, leaving the remnants of his army to struggle westward. Perhaps only 100,000 of the original 600,000 survived their ordeal.

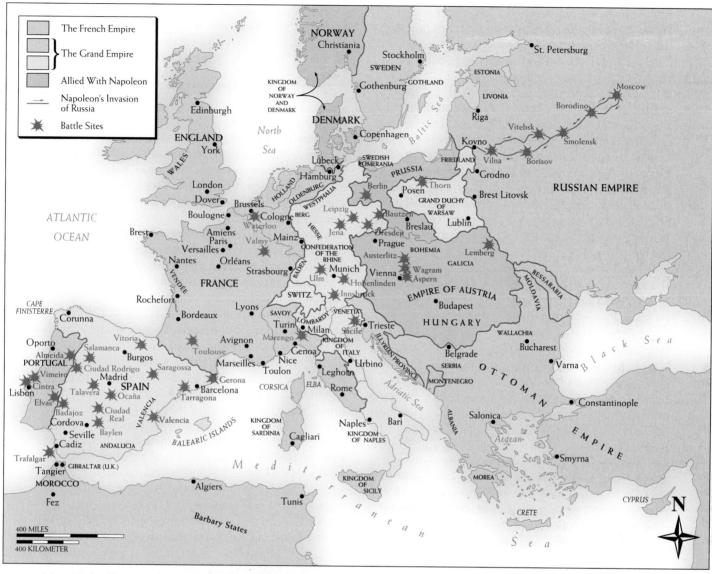

Map 19–2 **NAPOLEONIC EUROPE IN LATE 1812** By mid-1812 the areas shown in peach were incorporated into France, and most of the rest of Europe was directly controlled by or allied with Napoleon. But Russia had withdrawn from the failing Continental System, and the decline of Napoleon was about to begin.

EUROPEAN COALITION

Even as the news of the disaster reached the West, the final defeat of Napoleon was far from certain. He was able to put down his opponents in Paris and raise another 350,000 men. Neither the Prussians nor the Austrians were eager to risk another contest with Napoleon, and even the Russians hesitated. The Austrian foreign minister, Prince Klemens von Metternich (1773–1859), would have been glad to make a negotiated peace that would leave Napoleon on the throne of a shrunken and chastened France rather than see Russia dominate Europe. Napoleon might have negotiated a reasonable settlement had he been willing to make concessions that

would have split his jealous opponents. He would not consider that solution, however. As he explained to Metternich,

Your sovereigns born on the throne can let themselves be beaten twenty times and return to their capitals. I cannot do this because I am an upstart soldier. My domination will not survive the day when I cease to be strong, and therefore feared.[2]

In 1813, patriotic pressure and national ambition brought together the last and most powerful coalition against Napoleon. The Russians drove westward, and Prussia and then Austria joined

[2] Quoted in Felix Markham, *Napoleon and the Awakening of Europe* (New York: Macmillan, 1965), pp. 115–116.

them. Vast amounts of British money assisted them. From Spain, Wellington marched his army into France. Napoleon's new army was inexperienced and poorly equipped. His generals had lost confidence in him and were tired. The emperor himself was worn out and sick. Still, he waged a skillful campaign in central Europe and defeated the allies at Dresden. In October, however, the combined armies of the enemy decisively defeated him at Leipzig in what the Germans called the Battle of the Nations. In March 1814, the allied armies marched into Paris. A few days later, Napoleon abdicated and went into exile on the island of Elba, off the coast of central Italy. (See "A German Writer Describes the War of Liberation".)

THE CONGRESS OF VIENNA AND THE EUROPEAN SETTLEMENT

Fear of Napoleon and hostility to his ambitions had held the victorious coalition together. As soon as he was removed, the allies pursued their separate ambitions. The key person in achieving eventual agreement among them was Robert Stewart, Viscount Castlereagh (1769–1822), the British foreign secretary. Even before the victorious armies had entered Paris, he brought about the signing of the Treaty of Chaumont on March 9, 1814. It provided for the restoration of the Bourbons to the French throne and the contraction of France to its frontiers of 1792. Even more importantly, Britain, Austria, Russia, and Prussia agreed to form a Quadruple Alliance for twenty years to preserve whatever settlement they agreed on. Remaining problems—and there were many—and final details were left for a conference to be held at Vienna.

TERRITORIAL ADJUSTMENTS

The Congress of Vienna assembled in September 1814, but did not conclude its work until November 1815. Although a glittering array of heads of state attended the gathering, the four great powers conducted the important work of the conference. The only full session of the congress met to ratify the arrangements the big four made. The easiest problem the great powers faced was France. All the victors agreed that no single state should be allowed to dominate Europe, and all were determined to prevent France from doing so again. The restoration of the French Bourbon monarchy, which was temporarily popular, and a nonvindictive boundary settlement were designed to keep France calm and satisfied.

The powers also strengthened the states around France's borders to serve as barriers to renewed French expansion. They established the kingdom of the Netherlands, which included Belgium and Luxembourg, in the north and added the important port of Genoa to strengthen Piedmont in the south. Prussia was given important new territories along the Rhine River to deter French aggression in the West. Austria gained full control of northern Italy to prevent a repetition of Napoleon's conquests there. As for the rest of Germany, most of Napoleon's territorial arrangements were left untouched. The venerable Holy Roman Empire, which had been dissolved in 1806, was not revived. (See Map 19–3.) In all these areas, the congress established the rule of legitimate monarchs and rejected any hint of the republican and democratic policies that had flowed from the French Revolution.

On these matters agreement was not difficult, but the settlement of eastern Europe sharply divided the victors. Alexander I of Russia wanted all of Poland under his rule. Prussia was willing to give it to him in return for all of Saxony, which had been allied with Napoleon. Austria, however, was unwilling to surrender its share of Poland or to see Prussian power grow or Russia penetrate deeper into central Europe. The Polish-Saxon question almost caused a new war among the victors, but

Map 19–3 **THE GERMAN STATES AFTER 1815** As noted, the German states were also recognized.

A GERMAN WRITER DESCRIBES THE WAR OF LIBERATION

The German resistance to Napoleon as his army retreated from Moscow was the first time in modern German history that people from virtually all German-speaking lands cooperated together. The memory of that action became one of the defining moments in the emergence of a sense of German nationhood. Ernest Moritz Arndt (1769–1860) described the excitement and enthusiasm of that moment. This passage was frequently reprinted in German history textbooks for more than a century.

■ *Why does Arndt claim each of these various groups wanted war? How does Arndt suggest the possibility of a united nation that did not yet actually exist?*

Fired with enthusiasm, the people rose, "with God for King and Fatherland." Among the Prussians there was only one voice, one feeling, one anger and one love, to save the Fatherland and to free Germany. The Prussians wanted war; war and death they wanted; peace they feared because they could hope for no honorable peace from Napoleon. War, war, sounded the cry from the Carpathians to the Baltic, from the Niemen to the Elbe. War! cried the nobleman and landed proprietor who had become impoverished. War! that peasant who was driving his last horse to death . . . . War! the citizen who was growing exhausted from quartering soldiers and paying taxes. War! the widow who was sending her only son to the front. War! the young girl who, with tears of pride and pain, was leaving her betrothed. Youths who were hardly able to bear arms, men with gray hair, officers who on account of wounds and mutilations had long ago been honorably discharged, rich landed proprietors and officials, fathers of large families and managers of extensive businesses—all were unwilling to remain behind. Even young women, under all sorts of disguises, rushed to arms; all wanted to drill, arm themselves and fight and die for the Fatherland. . . .

The most beautiful thing about all this holy zeal and happy confusion was that all differences of position, class, and age were forgotten . . . that the one great feeling for the Fatherland, its freedom and honor, swallowed all other feelings, caused all other considerations and relationships to be forgotten.

Snyder, Louis L., translator. *Documents of German History.* Copyright © 1958 by Rutgers, the State University. Reprinted by permission of Rutgers University Press.

defeated France provided a way out. The wily Talleyrand, now representing France at Vienna, suggested the weight of France added to that of Britain and Austria might bring Alexander to his senses. When news of a secret treaty among the three leaked out, the tsar agreed to become ruler of a smaller Poland, and Prussia settled for only part of Saxony. Thereafter, France was included as a fifth great power in all deliberations.

THE HUNDRED DAYS
AND THE QUADRUPLE ALLIANCE

Napoleon's return from Elba on March 1, 1815, further united the victors. The French army was still loyal to the former emperor, and many of the French people preferred his rule to that of the restored Bourbons. The coalition seemed to be dissolving in Vienna. Napoleon seized the opportunity, escaped to France, and soon regained power. He promised a liberal constitution and a peaceful foreign policy. The allies were not convinced. They declared Napoleon an outlaw (a new device under international law) and sent their armies to crush him. Wellington, with the crucial help of the Prussians under Field Marshal von Blücher (1742–1819), defeated Napoleon at Waterloo in Belgium on June 18, 1815. Napoleon again abdicated and was exiled on Saint Helena, a tiny Atlantic island off the coast of Africa, where he died in 1821.

LE CONGRÈS.

In this political cartoon of the Congress of Vienna, Tallyrand simply watches which way the wind is blowing, Castlereagh hesitates, while the monarchs of Russia, Prussia, and Austria form the dance of the Holy Alliance. The king of Saxony holds on to his crown and the republic of Geneva pays homage to the kingdom of Sardinia. Bildarchiv Preussischer Kulturbesitz

The Hundred Days, as the period of Napoleon's return is called, frightened the great powers and made the peace settlement harsher for France. In addition to some minor territorial adjustments, the victors imposed a war indemnity and an army of occupation on France. Alexander proposed a Holy Alliance, whereby the monarchs promised to act together in accordance with Christian principles. Austria and Prussia signed; but Castlereagh thought it absurd, and England abstained. The tsar, who was then embracing mysticism, believed his proposal a valuable tool for international relations. The Holy Alliance soon became a symbol of extreme political reaction.

England, Austria, Prussia, and Russia renewed the Quadruple Alliance on November 20, 1815. Henceforth, it was as much a coalition for maintaining peace as for pursuing victory over France. A coalition for such a purpose had never existed in European diplomacy before. It represented an important new departure in European affairs. Unlike eighteenth-century diplomacy, certain powers were determined to prevent war. The statesmen at Vienna had seen the armies of the French Revolution and Napoleon overturning the political and social order of much of the Continent. Their nations had experienced unprecedented destruction and had had to raise enormous military forces. They knew war affected not just professional armies and navies, but entire civilian populations. They were determined to prevent any more such upheaval and destruction.

Consequently, the chief aims of the Congress of Vienna were to prevent a recurrence of the Napoleonic nightmare and to arrange a lasting peace. The leaders of Europe had learned that a treaty should secure not victory, but peace. The diplomats aimed to establish a framework for stability, rather than to punish France. The great powers sought to ensure that each of them would respect the Vienna settlement and not use force to change it.

The Congress of Vienna achieved its goals. France accepted the new situation without undue resentment, in part because the new international order recognized it as a great power. The victorious powers settled difficult problems reasonably. They established a new legal framework whereby treaties were made between states rather than between monarchs. The treaties remained in place when a monarch died. Furthermore, during the quarter century of warfare, European leaders had come to calculate the nature of political and economic power in new ways that went beyond the simple vision of gaining a favorable balance of trade that had caused so many eighteenth-century wars. They took into account their natural resources and economies, their systems of education, and the possibility that general growth in agriculture, commerce, and industry would benefit all states and not one at the expense of others.

The congress has been criticized for failing to recognize and provide for the great forces that would stir the nineteenth century—nationalism and democracy. Such criticism is inappropriate. At the time nationalist pressures were relatively rare; the general desire was for peace. The settlement, like all such agreements, aimed to solve past ills, and in that it succeeded. The statesmen at Vienna would have had to have a super-human ability to have anticipated future problems or to have yielded to forces of which they disapproved and that they believed threatened international peace and stability. The measure of the success of the Vienna settlement is that it remained essentially intact for almost half a century and prevented general war for a hundred years. (See Map 19–4, page 644.)

NAPOLEONIC EUROPE

1797	Napoleon concludes the Treaty of Campo Formio
1798	Nelson defeats the French navy in the harbor of Abukir in Egypt
1799	Consulate established in France
1801	Concordat between France and the papacy
1802	Treaty of Amiens
1803	War renewed between France and Britain
1804	Execution of Duke d'Enghien
1804	Napoleonic Civil Code issued
1804	Napoleon crowned as emperor
1805 (October 21)	Nelson defeats French and Spanish fleet at Trafalgar
1805 (December 2)	Austerlitz
1806	Jena
1806	Continental System established by Berlin Decrees
1807	Friedland
1807	Treaty of Tilsit; Russia becomes an ally of Napoleon
1808	Beginning of Spanish resistance to Napoleonic domination
1809	Wagram
1809	Napoleon marries Archduchess Marie Louise of Austria
1812	Invasion of Russia and French defeat at Borodino
1813	Leipzig (Battle of the Nations)
1814	Treaty of Chaumont (March) establishes Quadruple Alliance
1814 (September)	Congress of Vienna convenes
1815 (March 1)	Napoleon returns from Elba
1815 (June 18)	Waterloo
1815 (September 26)	Holy Alliance formed at Congress of Vienna
1815 (November 20)	Quadruple Alliance renewed at Congress of Vienna
1821	Napoleon dies on Saint Helena

THE ROMANTIC MOVEMENT

The years of the French Revolution and the conquests of Napoleon saw the emergence of a new and important intellectual movement throughout Europe. **Romanticism**, in its various manifestations, was a reaction against much of the thought of the Enlightenment. Romantic writers and artists saw the imagination or some such intuitive intellectual faculty supplementing reason as a means to perceive and understand the world. Many of them urged a revival of Christianity, so that it would once again permeate Europe as it had during the Middle Ages. Unlike the philosophes, the Romantics liked the art, literature, and architecture of medieval times. They were also deeply interested in folklore, folk songs, and fairy tales. Dreams, hallucinations, sleepwalking, and other phenomena that suggested the existence of a world beyond that of empirical observation, sensory data, and discursive reasoning fascinated the Romantics.

ROMANTIC QUESTIONING OF THE SUPREMACY OF REASON

The Romantic Movement had roots in the individualism of the Renaissance, Protestant devotion and personal piety, sentimental novels of the eighteenth century, and dramatic German poetry of the **Sturm and Drang** (literally, "storm and stress") movement, which rejected the influence of French rationalism on German literature. However, two writers who were also closely related to the Enlightenment provided the immediate intellectual foundations for Romanticism: Jean-Jacques Rousseau and Immanuel Kant raised questions about whether the rationalism so dear to the philosophes was sufficient to explain human nature and be the bedrock principle for organizing human society.

ROUSSEAU AND EDUCATION

We already pointed out in Chapter 17, that Jean-Jacques Rousseau, though sharing in the reformist spirit of the Enlightenment, opposed many of its other facets. Rousseau's conviction that society and material prosperity had corrupted human nature profoundly influenced Romantic writers.

Rousseau set forth his view on how the individual could develop to lead a good and happy life uncorrupted by society in his novel *Émile* (1762), a work that was for a long time far more influential than *The Social Contract*. (See Chapter 17.) In *Émile*, Rousseau stressed the difference between children and adults. He distinguished the stages of human maturation and urged that children be raised with maximum individual freedom. Each child should be allowed to grow freely, like a plant, and to learn by trial and error what reality is and how best to deal with it. The parent or teacher would help most by providing the basic necessities of life and warding off what was manifestly harmful. Beyond that, the adult should stay completely out of the way, like a gardener who waters and weeds a garden but otherwise lets nature take its course. As noted in Chapter 17, Rousseau thought that, because of their physical differences, men and women would naturally grow into social roles with different spheres of activity.

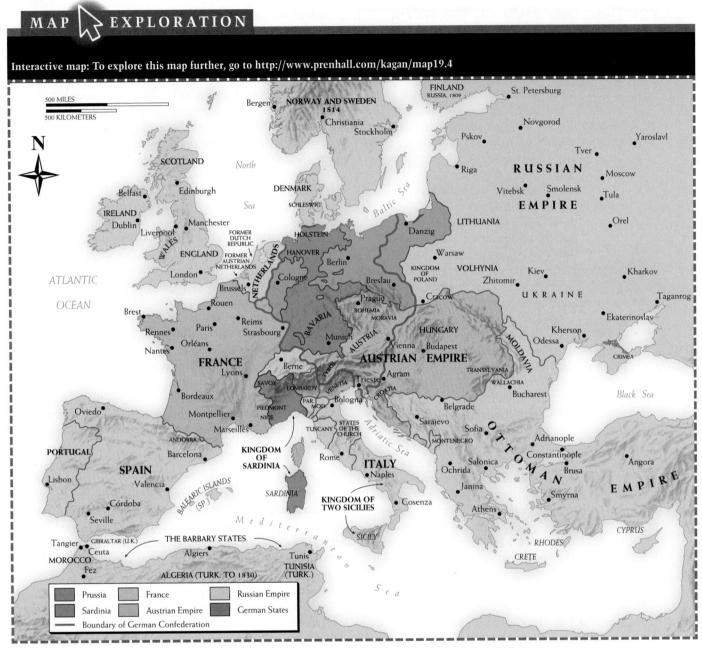

Interactive map: To explore this map further, go to http://www.prenhall.com/kagan/map19.4

Map 19–4 **EUROPE 1815, AFTER THE CONGRESS OF VIENNA** The Congress of Vienna achieved the post-Napoleonic territorial adjustments shown on the map. The most notable arrangements dealt with areas along France's borders (the Netherlands, Prussia, Switzerland, and Piedmont) and in Poland and northern Italy.

Rousseau also thought that adults should allow the child's sentiments, as well as its reason, to flourish. To Romantic writers, this concept of human development vindicated the rights of nature over those of artificial society. They thought such a form of open education would eventually lead to a natural society. In its fully developed form, this view of life led the Romantics to value the uniqueness of each individual and to explore childhood in great detail. Like Rousseau, the Romantics saw humankind, nature, and society as organically interrelated.

KANT AND REASON

Immanuel Kant (1724–1804) wrote the two greatest philosophical works of the late eighteenth century: *The Critique of Pure Reason* (1781) and *The Critique of Practical Reason* (1788). He sought to accept the rationalism of the Enlightenment and to still preserve a belief in human freedom, immortality, and the existence of God. Against Locke and other philosophers who saw knowledge rooted in sensory experience alone, Kant argued for the subjective character of human knowledge. For Kant, the human mind does not simply reflect the world around it like a passive mirror; rather, the mind actively imposes on the world of sensory experience "forms of sensibility" and "categories of understanding." The mind itself generates these categories. In other words, the human mind perceives the world as it does because of its own internal mental categories. This meant that human perceptions are as much the product of the mind's own activity as of sensory experience.

Kant found the sphere of reality that was accessible to pure reason to be limited. He believed, however, that beyond the phenomenal world of sensory experience, over which "pure reason" was master, there existed what he called the "noumenal" world. This world is a sphere of moral and aesthetic reality known by "practical reason" and conscience. Kant thought all human beings possess an innate sense of moral duty or an awareness of what he called a **categorical imperative**. This term refers to an inner command to act in every situation as one would have all other people always act in the same situation. Kant regarded the existence of this imperative of conscience as incontrovertible proof of humankind's natural freedom. On the basis of humankind's moral sense, Kant postulated the existence of God, eternal life, and future rewards and punishments. He believed that reason alone could not prove these transcendental truths. Still, he was convinced they were realities to which every reasonable person could attest.

To many Romantic writers, Kantian philosophy refuted the narrow rationality of the Enlightenment. Whether they called it "practical reason," "fancy," "imagination," "intuition," or simply "feeling," the Romantics believed that the human mind had the power to penetrate beyond the limits of largely passive human understanding as set forth by Hobbes, Locke, and Hume. Most Romantics also believed poets and artists possess these powers in abundance. Other Romantic writers appealed to the limits of human reason to set forth new religious ideas or political thought that was often at odds with Enlightenment writers.

ROMANTIC LITERATURE

The term *Romantic* appeared in English and French literature as early as the seventeenth century. Neoclassical writers then used the word to describe literature they considered unreal, sentimental, or excessively fanciful. In the eighteenth century, the English writer Thomas Warton (1728–1790) associated Romantic literature with medieval romances. In Germany, a major center of the Romantic literary movement, Johann Gottfried Herder (1744–1803) used the terms *Romantic* and *Gothic* interchangeably. In both England and Germany, the term came to be applied to all literature that did not observe classical forms and rules and gave free play to the imagination.

As an alternative to such dependence on the classical forms, August Wilhelm von Schlegel (1767–1845) praised the "Romantic" literature of Dante, Petrarch, Boccaccio, Shakespeare, the Arthurian legends, Cervantes, and Calderón. According to Schlegel, Romantic literature was to classical literature what the organic and living were to the merely mechanical. He set forth his views in *Lectures on Dramatic Art and Literature* (1809–1811).

The Romantic Movement had peaked in Germany and England before it became a major force in France under the leadership of Madame de Staël (1766–1817) and Victor Hugo (1802–1885). (See "Madame de Staël Describes the New Romantic Literature of Germany," page 646.) So influential was the classical tradition in France that not until 1816 did a French writer openly declare himself a Romantic. That was Henri Beyle (1783–1842), who wrote under the pseudonym Stendhal. He praised Shakespeare and criticized his own countryman, the seventeenth-century classical dramatist Jean Racine (1639–1699).

THE ENGLISH ROMANTIC WRITERS

The English Romantics believed poetry was enhanced by freely following the creative impulses of the mind. In this belief, they directly opposed Lockean psychology, which regarded the mind as a passive receptor and poetry as a mechanical exercise of "wit" following prescribed rules. For Samuel Taylor Coleridge (1772–1834), the artist's imagination was God at work in the mind. As Coleridge expressed his views, the imagination was "a repetition in the finite mind of the eternal act of creation in the infinite I AM." Poetry thus could not be considered idle play. Rather, it was the highest of human acts, humankind's self-fulfillment in a transcendental world.

Coleridge was the master of Gothic poems of the supernatural, such as "The Rime of the Ancient Mariner," which relates the story of a sailor cursed for killing an albatross. The poem treats the subject as a crime against nature and God and raises the issues of guilt, punishment, and the redemptive possibilities of humility and penance. At the end of the poem, the mariner discovers the unity and beauty of all things. Having repented, he is delivered from his awful curse, which has been symbolized by the dead albatross hung around his neck:

O happy living things! no tongue
Their beauty might declare:
A spring of love gushed from my heart,
And I blessed them unaware . . .
The self-same moment I could pray;
And from my neck so free
The Albatross fell off, and sank
Like lead into the sea.

MADAME DE STAËL DESCRIBES THE NEW ROMANTIC LITERATURE OF GERMANY

Anne-Louise-Germaine de Staël, known generally as Madame de Staël, was the daughter of Jacques Necker, the finance minister of Louis XVI. She was also the friend of major French political liberals and a critic of Napoleonic absolutism. More importantly for European literary life, Madame de Staël visited Germany, read the emerging German Romantic literature, and introduced it to both French- and English-speaking Europe in her book Concerning Germany *(1813). In the passage that follows, she endorses the new literature then emerging in Germany. She points to the novelty of this Romantic poetry and then relates it to a new appreciation of Christianity and the middle ages. The Christian features she associates with the poetry represent one strain among many of the religious revival that followed the de-Christianizing religious policies of the French Revolution.*

■ *How does de Staël characterize the new Romantic school of poetry? Why does she contrast it with the literature that had its roots in ancient Greece and Rome? Why does she believe the new literature will continue to grow? What is the relationship of the middle ages to the new poetry and other examples of the fine arts touched by Romantic sensibilities?*

The word *romantic* has been lately introduced in Germany, to designate that kind of poetry which is derived from the songs of the Troubadours; that which owes its birth to the union of chivalry and Christianity. If we do not admit that the empire of literature has been divided between paganism and Christianity, the north and the south, antiquity and the middle ages, chivalry and the institutions of Greece and Rome, we shall never succeed in forming a philosophical judgment of ancient and of modern taste.

Some French critics have asserted that German literature is still in its infancy; this opinion is entirely false: men who are best skilled in the knowledge of languages, and the works of the ancients, are certainly not ignorant of the defects and advantages attached to the species of literature which they either adopt or reject; but their character, their habits, and their modes of reasoning, have led them to prefer that which is founded on the recollection of chivalry, on the wonders of the middle ages, to that which has for its basis the mythology of the Greeks. The literature of romance is alone capable of further improvement, because, being rooted in our own soil, that alone can continue to grow and acquire fresh life: it expresses our religion; it recalls our history; its origin is ancient, although not of classical antiquity. Classic poetry, before it comes home to us, must pass through our recollections of paganism; that of the Germans is the Christian era of the fine arts; it employs our personal impressions to excite strong and vivid emotions; the genius by which it is inspired addresses itself immediately to our hearts; of all phantoms at once the most powerful and the most terrible. . . .

The new school maintains the same system in the fine arts as in literature, and affirms that Christianity is the source of all modern genius; the writers of this school also characterize, in a new manner, all that in Gothic architecture agrees with the religious sentiments of Christians. It does not follow however from this, that the moderns can and ought to construct Gothic churches; . . . it is only of consequence to us, in the present silence of genius, to lay aside the contempt which has been thrown on all the conceptions of the middle ages.

From Madame De Staël, *Concerning Germany* (London, John Murray, 1814) as quoted in Howard E. Hugo, ed., *The Romantic Reader* (Viking, 1957), pp. 64–66.

Wordsworth William Wordsworth (1770–1850) was Coleridge's closest friend. Together they published *Lyrical Ballads* in 1798 as a manifesto of a new poetry that rejected the rules of eighteenth-century criticism. Among Wordsworth's most important later poems is his "Ode on Intimations of Immortality" (1803), written in part to console Coleridge, who was suffering a deep personal crisis. Its subject is the loss of poetic vision, something Wordsworth also felt then in himself. Nature, which he had worshipped, no longer spoke freely to him, and he feared it might never speak to him again:

There was a time when meadow, grove, and stream,
The earth, and every common sight,
To me did seem
Appareled in celestial light,
The glory and the freshness of a dream.
It is not now as it hath been of yore—
Turn whereso'er I may,
By night or day,
The things which I have seen I now can
see no more.

He had lost what he believed all human beings lose in the necessary process of maturation: their childlike vision and closeness to spiritual reality. For both Wordsworth and Coleridge, childhood was the bright period of creative imagination. Wordsworth held a theory of the soul's preexistence in a celestial state before its creation. The child, being closer in time to its eternal origin and undistracted by worldly experience, recollects the supernatural world much more easily. Aging and urban living corrupt and deaden the imagination, making one's inner feelings and the beauty of nature less important. In his book-length poem *The Prelude* (1850), Wordsworth presented a long autobiographical account of the growth of the poet's mind.

Lord Byron A true rebel among the Romantic poets was Lord Byron (1788–1824). In Britain, even most of the other Romantic writers distrusted and disliked him. He had little sympathy for their views of the imagination. Outside England, however, Byron was regarded as the embodiment of the new person the French Revolution had created. He rejected the old traditions (he was divorced and famous for his many love affairs) and championed the cause of personal liberty. Byron was outrageously skeptical and mocking, even of his own beliefs. In *Childe Harold's Pilgrimage* (1812), he created a brooding, melancholy Romantic hero. In *Don Juan* (1819), he wrote with ribald humor, acknowledged nature's cruelty as well as its beauty, and even expressed admiration for urban life.

THE GERMAN ROMANTIC WRITERS

Much Romantic poetry was also written on the Continent, but almost all major German Romantics wrote at least one novel. Romantic novels often were highly sentimental and borrowed material from medieval romances. The characters of Romantic novels were treated as symbols of the larger truth of life. Purely realistic description was avoided. The first German Romantic novel was Ludwig Tieck's (1773–1853) *William Lovell* (1793–1795). It contrasts the young Lovell, whose life is built on love and imagination, with those who live by cold reason alone and who thus become easy prey to unbelief, misanthropy, and egoism. As the novel rambles to its conclusion, a mixture of philosophy, materialism, and skepticism, administered to him by two women he naively loves, destroys Lovell.

Schlegel Friedrich Schlegel (1767–1845) wrote a progressive early Romantic novel, *Lucinde* (1799) that attacked prejudices against women as capable of being little more than lovers and domestics. Schlegel's novel reveals the ability of the Romantics to become involved in the social issues of their day. He depicted Lucinde as the perfect friend and companion, as well as the unsurpassed lover, of the hero. Like other early Romantic novels, the work shocked contemporary morals by frankly discussing sexual activity and by describing Lucinde as equal to the male hero.

Goethe Towering above all of these German writers stood Johann Wolfgang von Goethe (1749–1832). Perhaps the greatest German writer of modern times, Goethe defies easy classification. Part of his literary production fits into the Romantic mold,

---

PUBLICATION DATES OF MAJOR ROMANTIC WORKS

1762 Rousseau's *Emile*
1774 Goethe's *Sorrows of Young Werther*
1781 Kant's *Critique of Pure Reason**
1788 Kant's *Critique of Practical Reason**
1798 Wordsworth and Coleridge's *Lyrical Ballads*
1799 Schlegel's *Lucinde*
1799 Schleiermacher's *Speeches on Religion to Its Cultured Despisers*
1802 Chateaubriand's *Genius of Christianity*
1806 Hegel's *Phenomenology of Mind*
1808 Goethe's *Faust*, Part I
1812 Byron's *Childe Harold's Pilgrimage*
1819 Byron's *Don Juan*
1825 Scott's *Tales of the Crusaders*
1841 Carlyle's *On Heroes and Hero-Worship*

* Kant's books were not themselves part of the Romantic Movement, but they were fundamental to later Romantic writers.

and part of it was a condemnation of Romantic excesses. The book that made his early reputation was *The Sorrows of Young Werther*, published in 1774. This novel, like many in the eighteenth century, is a series of letters. The hero falls in love with Lotte, who is married to another man. The letters explore their relationship with the sentimentalism that was characteristic of the age. Eventually Werther and Lotte part, but in his grief, Werther takes his own life. This novel became popular throughout Europe. Romantic authors admired its emphasis on feeling and on living outside the bounds of polite society.

Goethe's masterpiece was *Faust*, a long dramatic poem. Part I, published in 1808, tells the story of Faust, who makes a pact with the devil—he will exchange his soul for greater knowledge than other human beings possess. As the story progresses, Faust seduces a young woman named Gretchen. She dies, but is received into heaven as the grief-stricken Faust realizes he must continue to live.

In Part II, completed in 1832, Faust is taken through a series of adventures involving witches and mythological characters. At the conclusion, however, he dedicates his life, or what remains of it, to the improvement of humankind. He feels this goal will allow him to overcome the restless striving that induced him to make the pact with the devil. That new knowledge breaks the pact. Faust dies and is received by angels.

ROMANTIC ART

The art of the Romantic Era, like its poetry and philosophy, stood largely in reaction to that of the eighteenth century. Whereas the Rococo artists had looked to Renaissance models and Neo-Classical painters to the art of the ancient world, Romantic painters often portrayed scenes from medieval life. For them, the Middle Ages represented the social stability and religious reverence that was disappearing from their own era.

THE CULT OF THE MIDDLE AGES AND NEO-GOTHICISM

Like many early Romantic artists, the English landscape painter John Constable (1776–1837) was politically conservative. In *Salisbury Cathedral, from the Meadows*, he portrayed a stable world in which neither political turmoil nor industrial development challenged the traditional dominance of the church and the landed classes. Although the clouds and sky in the painting depict a severe storm, the works of both nature and humankind present a powerful sense of enduring order. The trees clearly have withstood this storm as they have withstood others for many years. The cathedral, built in the Middle Ages, has also stood majestically intact for centuries. Like many English conservatives of his day, Constable saw the church and the British constitution as intimately related. Religious institutions were barriers to political radicalism. In his private letters, Constable associated liberal reformers with the devil, leading some scholars to suggest that the lightning striking the back roof of the cathedral symbolizes those evil forces and that the rainbow, arching over the entire scene and giving it a sacramental nature, indicates God's blessing for the traditional order of nature and society.

Constable and other Romantics tended to idealize rural life because they believed it was connected to the medieval past and was opposed to the increasingly urban, industrializing, commercial society that was developing around them. In fact, the rural landscape and rustic society that Constable

John Constable's *Salisbury Cathedral from the Meadows* displays the appeal of Romantic art to both medieval monuments and the sublime power of nature. John Constable (1776–1837), "Salisbury Cathedral from the Meadows," 1831. Oil on canvas, 151.8 × 189.9. © The National Gallery, London

At the castle of Neuschwanstein King Ludwig II of Bavaria erected the most extensive neo-gothic monument of central Europe.   Josaf Beck/Getty Images, Inc.–Taxi

depicted in his paintings had already largely disappeared from England.

Medieval structures not only appeared in Romantic painting. The Neo-Gothic revival in architecture dotted the European landscape with modern imitations of them. Many medieval cathedrals were restored during this era, and new churches were designed to resemble their medieval forerunners. The British Houses of Parliament built in 1836–1837 were the most famous public buildings in the Neo-Gothic style, but town halls, schools, and even railroad stations were designed to look like medieval buildings, while aristocratic country houses were rebuilt to resemble medieval castles.

The single most remarkable nineteenth-century Neo-Gothic structure was the castle of Neuschwanstein constructed between 1869 and 1886 on a mountain in southern Germany by King Ludwig II of Bavaria (r. 1864–1886). The cost of this castle, the interior of which was never completed, almost bankrupted the Bavarian monarchy.

NATURE AND THE SUBLIME

Beyond their attraction to history, Romantic artists also sought to portray nature in all of its majestic power as no previous generation of European artists had ever done. Moreover, like Romantic poets, the artists of the era were drawn toward the mysterious and unruly side of nature rather than toward the rational Newtonian order that had prevailed during the Enlightenment. Their works often sought to portray what they and others termed *the sublime*—that

is, subjects from nature that aroused strong emotions, such as fear, dread, and awe, and raise questions about whether and how much we control our lives. Painters often traveled to remote areas such as the Scottish Highlands, the mountains of Wales, or the Swiss Alps to portray unruly and dangerous scenes from nature that would immediately grip and engage the viewer's emotions.

Romantics saw nature as a set of infinite forces that overwhelmed the smallness of humankind. For example, in 1824, the German artist Caspar David Friedrich (1774–1840) in *The Polar Sea* painted the plight of a ship trapped and crushed by the force of a vast polar ice field. In direct contrast to eighteenth-century artists' portrayal of sunny Enlightenment, Friedrich also painted numerous scenes in which human beings stand shrouded in the mysterious darkness of night where moonlight and torches cast only fitful illumination.

An artist who similarly understood the power of nature but also depicted the forces of the new industrialism that was challenging them was Joseph Mallord William Turner (1775–1851) whose painting *Rain, Steam and Speed—The Great Western Railway* of 1844 illustrated the recently invented railway engine barreling through an enveloping storm. In this scene the new technology is both part of the natural world and strong enough to dominate it.

Friedrich's and Turner's paintings taken together symbolize the contradictory forces affecting Romantic artists—the sense of the power, awe, and mastery of nature coupled with the sense that the advance of industry represented a new kind of awesome human power that could challenge or even surpass the forces of nature itself.

RELIGION IN THE ROMANTIC PERIOD

During the Middle Ages, the foundation of religion had been the authority of the church. The Reformation leaders had appealed to the authority of the Bible. Then, many Enlightenment writers attempted to derive religion from the rational nature revealed by Newtonian physics. Other Enlightenment figures attacked religion in general and Christianity in particular. Romantic religious thinkers, in contrast, sought the foundations of religion in the inner emotions of humankind. Reacting to the anticlericalism of both the Enlightenment and the French Revolution, these thinkers also saw religious faith, experience, and institutions as central to human life. Their forerunners were the mystics of Western Christianity. One of the first great examples of a religion characterized by Romantic impulses—Methodism—arose in mid-eighteenth century England during the Enlightenment and became one of the most powerful forces in transatlantic religion during the nineteenth century.

METHODISM

Methodism originated in the middle of the eighteenth century as a revolt against deism and rationalism in the Church of England. The Methodist revival formed an important part of the background of English Romanticism. The leader of the Methodist movement was John Wesley (1703–1791). His mother, Susannah Wesley, who bore eighteen children, had carefully supervised his education and religious development.

While at Oxford University studying to be an Anglican priest, Wesley organized a religious group known as the Holy Club. He soon left England for missionary work in the new colony of Georgia in America, where he arrived in 1735. While he was crossing the Atlantic, a group of German Mora-

Caspar David Friedrich's *The Polar Sea* illustrated the power of nature to diminish the creations of humankind as seen in the wrecked ship on the right of the painting.
Kunsthalle, Hamburg, Germany/A.K.G., Berlin/SuperStock

vians on the ship deeply impressed him with their unshakable faith and confidence during a storm. Wesley, who had despaired of his life, concluded they knew far better than he the meaning of justification by faith. When he returned to England in 1738, Wesley began to worship with Moravians in London. There, in 1739, he underwent a conversion experience that he described in the words, "My heart felt strangely warmed." From that point on, he felt assured of his own salvation.

Wesley discovered he could not preach his version of Christian conversion and practical piety in Anglican church pulpits. Therefore, late in 1739, he began to preach in the open fields near the cities and towns of western England. Thousands of humble people responded to his message of repentance and good works. Soon he and his brother Charles (1707–1788), who became famous for his hymns, began to organize Methodist societies. By the late eighteenth century, the Methodists had become a separate church. They ordained their own clergy and sent missionaries to America, where they eventually achieved their greatest success and influence.

Methodism stressed inward, heartfelt religion and the possibility of Christian perfection in this life. John Wesley described Christianity as "an inward principle . . . the image of God impressed on a created spirit, a fountain of peace and love springing up into everlasting life."[3] True Christians were those who were "saved in this world from all sin, from all unrighteousness . . . and now in such a sense perfect as not to commit sin and . . . freed from evil thoughts and evil tempers."[4]

John Wesley (1703–1791) was the founder of Methodism. He emphasized the role of emotional experience in Christian conversion. CORBIS/Bettmann

[3] Quoted in Albert C. Outler, ed., *John Wesley: A Representative Collection of His Writings* (New York: Oxford University Press, 1964), p. 220.
[4] Ibid.

Joseph Mallord William Turner's *Rain, Steam, and Speed—The Great Western Railway* captured the tensions many Europeans felt between their natural environment and the new technology of the industrial age.   Joseph Mallord William Turner, 1775–1851, "Rain, Steam, and Speed—The Great Western Railway 1844". Oil on canvas, 90.8 × 121.9. © The National Gallery, London

Many people, weary of the dry rationalism that derived from deism, found Wesley's ideal relevant to their own lives. The Methodist preachers emphasized the role of enthusiastic, emotional experience as part of Christian conversion. After Wesley, religious revivals became highly emotional in style and content.

NEW DIRECTIONS IN CONTINENTAL RELIGION

Similar religious developments based on feeling appeared on the Continent. After the Thermidorian Reaction, a strong Roman Catholic revival took place in France. Its followers disapproved of both the religious policy of the revolution and the anticlericalism of the Enlightenment. The most important book to express these sentiments was *The Genius of Christianity* (1802) by Viscount François René de Chateaubriand (1768–1848). In this work, which became known as the "bible of Romanticism," Chateaubriand argued that the essence of religion is "passion." The foundation of faith in the church was the emotion that its teachings and sacraments inspired in the heart of the Christian.

Against the Newtonian view of the world and of a rational God, the Romantics found God immanent in nature. No one stated the Romantic religious ideal more eloquently or with greater impact on the modern world than Friedrich Schleiermacher

(1768–1834). In 1799, he published *Speeches on Religion to Its Cultured Despisers*. It was a response to Lutheran orthodoxy, on the one hand, and to Enlightenment rationalism, on the other. The advocates of both were the "cultured despisers" of real, or heartfelt, religion. According to Schleiermacher, religion was neither dogma nor a system of ethics. It was an intuition or feeling of absolute dependence on an infinite reality. Religious institutions, doctrines, and moral activity expressed that primal religious feeling only in a secondary, or indirect, way.

Although Schleiermacher considered Christianity the "religion of religions," he also believed every world religion was unique in its expression of the primal intuition of the infinite in the finite. He thus turned against the universal natural religion of the Enlightenment, which he termed "a name applied to loose, unconnected impulses," and defended the meaningfulness of the numerous world religions. Every such religion was seen to be a unique version of the emotional experience of dependence on an infinite being. In so arguing, Schleiermacher interpreted the religions of the world in the same way that other Romantic writers interpreted the variety of unique peoples and cultures.

ROMANTIC VIEWS OF NATIONALISM AND HISTORY

A distinctive feature of Romanticism, especially in Germany, was its glorification of both the individual person and individual cultures. Behind these views lay the philosophy of German idealism, which understood the world as the creation of subjective egos. J. G. Fichte (1762–1814), an important German philosopher and nationalist, identified the individual ego with the Absolute that underlies all existing things. According to him and similar philosophers, the world is truly the creation of humankind. The world is as it is because especially strong persons conceive of it in a particular way and impose their wills on the world and other people. Napoleon served as the contemporary example of such a great person. This philosophy has ever since served to justify the glorification of great persons and their actions in overriding all opposition to their will and desires.

HERDER AND CULTURE

In addition to this philosophy, the influence of new historical studies lay behind the German glorification of individual cultures. German Romantic writers went in search of their own past in reaction to the copying of French manners in eighteenth-century Germany, the impact of the French Revolution, and the imperialism of Napoleon. An early leader in this effort was Johann Gottfried Herder (1744–1803), already discussed in Chapter 17, as a critic of European colonialism. Herder resented French cultural dominance in Germany. In 1778, he published an influential essay entitled "On the Knowing and Feelings of the Human Soul." In it, he vigorously rejected the mechanical explanation of nature so popular with Enlightenment writers. He saw human beings and societies as developing organically, like plants, over time. Human beings were different at different times and places.

Herder revived German folk culture by urging the collection and preservation of distinctive German songs and sayings. His most important followers in this work were the Grimm brothers, Jakob (1785–1863) and Wilhelm (1786–1859), famous for their collection of fairy tales. Believing each language and culture were the unique expression of a people, Herder opposed both the concept and the use of a "common" language, such as French, and "universal" institutions, such as those Napoleon had imposed on Europe. These, he believed, were forms of tyranny over the individuality of a people. Herder's writings led to a broad revival of interest in history and philosophy. Although initially directed toward identifying German origins, such work soon expanded to embrace other world cultures. Eventually the ability of the Romantic imagination to be at home in any age or culture spurred the study of non-Western religion, comparative literature, and philology.

HEGEL AND HISTORY

The most important philosopher of history in the Romantic period was the German, Georg Wilhelm Friedrich Hegel (1770–1831). He is one of the most complicated and significant philosophers in the history of Western civilization.

Hegel believed ideas develop in an evolutionary fashion that involves conflict. At any given time, a predominant set of ideas, which he termed the **thesis**, holds sway. Conflicting ideas, which Hegel termed the **antithesis**, challenge the thesis. As these patterns of thought clash, a **synthesis** emerges that eventually becomes the new thesis. Then the process begins all over again. Periods of world history receive their character from the patterns of thought that predominate during them. (See "Hegel Explains the Role of Great Men in History," page 653.)

Several important philosophical conclusions followed from this analysis. One of the most significant was the belief that all periods of history have been of almost equal value because each was, by definition, necessary to the achievements of those that came later. Also, all cultures are valuable because each contributes to the necessary clash of values and ideas that allows humankind to develop. Hegel discussed these concepts in *The Phenomenology of Mind* (1806), *Lectures on the Philosophy of History* (1822–1831), and other works, many of which were published only after his death. During his lifetime, his ideas became widely known through his university lectures at Berlin.

ISLAM, THE MIDDLE EAST, AND ROMANTICISM

The new religious, literary, and historical sensibilities of the Romantic period modified the European understanding of both Islam and the Arab world while at the same time preserving long-standing attitudes.

The energized Christianity associated with Methodist-like forms of Protestantism, on the one hand, and Chateaubriand's emotional Roman Catholicism, on the other, renewed the traditional sense of necessary conflict between Christianity and Islam. Chateaubriand wrote a travelogue of his journey from Paris to Jerusalem in 1811. A decade later, when he was a member of the French parliament, he invoked the concept of a crusade against the Muslim world in a speech on the danger posed by the Barbary pirates of North Africa.

Indeed, the medieval Crusades against Islam fired the Romantic imagination. Nostalgic European artists painted from a Western standpoint the great moments of the Crusades including the bloody capture of Jerusalem. Stories from those conflicts filled historical novels such as *Tales of the Crusaders* (1825) by Sir Walter Scott (1771–1832). Although they presented heroic images of Muslim warriors, these paintings and novels ignored the havoc that the crusaders had visited on the peoples of the Middle East.

The general nineteenth-century association of nationalistic aspirations with Romanticism also cast the Ottoman Empire and with it Islam in an unfavorable political light. Romantic poets and intellectuals championed the cause of the Greek Revolution (see Chapter 20) and revived older charges of Ottoman despotism.

By contrast, other Romantic sensibilities induced Europeans to see the Muslim world in a more positive fashion. The Romantic emphasis on the value of literature drawn from different cultures and ages allowed many nineteenth-century European readers to enjoy the stories from *The Thousand and One*

HEGEL EXPLAINS THE ROLE OF GREAT MEN IN HISTORY

Hegel believed that behind the development of human history from one period to the next lay the mind and purpose of what he termed the World-Spirit, *a concept somewhat like the Christian God. Hegel thought particular heroes from the past (such as Caesar) and in the present (such as Napoleon) were the unconscious instruments of that spirit. In this passage from his lectures on the philosophy of history, Hegel explained how these heroes could change history. All these concepts are characteristic of the Romantic belief that human beings and human history are always intimately connected with larger, spiritual forces at work in the world. The passage also reflects the widespread belief of the time that the world of civic or political action pertained to men and that of the domestic sphere belonged to women.*

■ *How might the career of Napoleon have inspired this passage? What are the antidemocratic implications of this passage? In this passage, do great men make history or do historical developments make great men? Why do you think Hegel does not associate this power of shaping history with women as well as men? In that regard, note how he relates history with political developments rather than with those of the private social sphere.*

Such are all great historical men—whose own particular aims involve those large issues which are the will of the World-Spirit. They may be called Heroes, inasmuch as they have derived their purposes and their vocation, not from the calm, regular course of things, sanctioned by the existing order, but from a concealed fount—one which has not attained to phenomenal, present existence—from that inner Spirit, still hidden beneath the surface, which, impinging on the outer world as on a shell, bursts it in pieces, because it is another kernel than that which belonged to the shell in question. They are men, therefore, who appear to draw the impulse of their life from themselves; and whose deeds have produced a condition of things and a complex of historical relations which appear to be only their interest, and their work.

Such individuals had no consciousness of the general Idea they were unfolding, while prosecuting those aims of theirs; on the contrary, they were practical, political men. But at the same time they were thinking men, who had an insight into the requirements of the time—what was ripe for development. This was the very Truth for their age, for their world; the species next in order, so to speak, and which was already formed in the womb of time. It was theirs to know this nascent principle; the necessary, directly sequent step in progress, which their world was to take; to make this their aim, and to expend their energy in promoting it. World historical men—the Heroes of an epoch—must, therefore, be recognized as its clear-sighted ones; their deeds, their words are the best of that time.

From G. W. F. Hegel, *The Philosophy of History*, trans. by J. Sibree (New York: Dover, 1956), pp. 30–31. Reprinted by permission.

Nights, which first appeared in English in 1778 from a French translation. As poets across Europe rejected classicism in literature in favor of folk stories and fairy tales, they saw the *Arabian Nights* as mysterious and exotic. In 1859, Edward FitzGerald (1809–1883) published his highly popular translation of the *Rubáiyát of Omar Khayyám* of Nishapur, a Persian poet of the twelfth century.

Herder's and Hegel's concepts of history gave both the Arab peoples and Islam distinct roles in history. For Herder, Arab culture was one of the numerous communities that composed the human race and manifested the human spirit. The Prophet Muhammad, while giving voice to the ancient spirit of the Arab people, had drawn them from a polytheistic faith to a great monotheistic vision. For Hegel, Islam represented an important stage of the development of the world spirit. However, Hegel believed Islam had fulfilled its role in history and no longer had any significant part to play.

When Napoleon invaded Egypt in 1799, he met stiff resistance. On July 25, however, the French won a decisive victory. This painting of that battle by Baron Antoine Gros (1771–1835) emphasizes French heroism and Muslim defeat. Such an outlook was typical of European views of Arabs and the Islamic world. Antoine Jean Gros (1771–1835). Detail, "Battle of Aboukir, July 25, 1799," c. 1806. Oil on canvas. Chateau de Versailles et de Trianon, Versailles, France. Bridgeman–Giraudon/Art Resource, NY

These outlooks, which penetrated much nineteenth-century intellectual life, made it easy for Europeans to believe that Islam could, for all practical purposes, be ignored or reduced to a spent historical force.

The British historian and social commentator Thomas Carlyle (1795–1881) attributed new, positive qualities to Muhammad himself. Carlyle disliked the Enlightenment's disparagement of religion and spiritual values. He was also drawn to German theories of history. In his book *On Heroes and Hero-Worship* (1841), Carlyle presented Muhammad as the embodiment of the hero as prophet. He repudiated the traditional Christian and general Enlightenment view of Muhammad as an impostor. (See Chapter 17.) To Carlyle, Muhammad was straightforward and sincere. Carlyle's understanding of religion was similar to Schleiermacher's, and thus in his pages, Muhammad appeared as a person who had experienced God subjectively and had communicated a sense of the divine to others. Although friendly to Muhammad from a historical standpoint, Carlyle nonetheless saw him as one of many great religious figures and not, as Muslims believed, as the last of the prophets through whom God had spoken.

The person whose actions in the long run did perhaps the most to reshape the idea of both Islam and the Middle East in the European imagination was Napoleon himself. With his Egyptian expedition of 1798, the first European military invasion of the Near East since the Crusades, the study of the Arab world became an important activity within French intellectual life. For his invasion of Egypt to succeed, Napoleon believed he must make it clear he had no intention of destroying Islam, but rather sought to liberate Egypt from the military clique that governed the country in the name of the Ottoman Empire. To that end, he took with him scholars of Arabic and Islamic culture whom he urged to converse with the most educated people they could meet. Napoleon personally met with the local Islamic leaders and had all of his speeches and proclamations translated into classical Arabic. Such cultural sensitivity and the serious efforts of the French scholars to learn Arabic and study the Qur'an impressed Egyptian scholars. (When the French sought to levy new taxes, however, the Egyptians' enthusiasm waned.)

It was on this expedition that the famous Rosetta Stone was discovered. Now housed in the British Museum, it eventually led to the decipherment of ancient Egypt's hieroglyphic writing. Napoleon's scholars also published a twenty-three volume *Description of Egypt* (1809–1828), which concentrated largely on ancient Egypt. Their approach suggested the history of the Ottoman Empire needed to be related first to the larger context of Egyptian history and that Islam, although enormously important, was only part of a larger cultural story. The implication was that if Egypt and Islam were to be understood, it would be through European—if not necessarily Christian—categories of thought.

Two cultural effects in the West of Napoleon's invasion were an increase in the number of European visitors to the Middle East and a demand for architecture based on ancient Egyptian models. Perhaps the most famous example of this fad is the Washington Monument in Washington, D.C., which is modeled after ancient Egyptian obelisks.

IN PERSPECTIVE

Romantic ideas made a major contribution to the emergence of nationalism, which proved to be one of the strongest motivating forces of the nineteenth and twentieth centuries. The writers of the Enlightenment had generally championed a cosmopolitan outlook on the world. By contrast, the Romantic thinkers emphasized the individuality and worth of each separate people and culture. A people or a nation was defined by a common language, history, and customs and by the possession of a historical homeland. This cultural nationalism gradually became transformed into a political creed. It came to be widely believed that every people, ethnic group, or nation should constitute a separate political entity and that only when it so existed could the nation be secure in its own character.

France under the revolutionary government and Napoleon had demonstrated the power of nationhood. Other peoples came to desire similar strength and confidence. Napoleon's toppling of ancient political structures, such as the Holy Roman Empire, proved the need for new political organization in Europe. By 1815, only a few Europeans aspired to this, but as time passed, peoples from Ireland to Ukraine came to share these yearnings. The Congress of Vienna could ignore such feelings, but for the rest of the nineteenth century, as shall be seen in subsequent chapters, statesmen had to confront the growing power these feelings had unleashed.

REVIEW QUESTIONS

1. How did Napoleon rise to power? What groups supported him? What were his major domestic achievements? Did his rule fulfill or betray the French Revolution?
2. What regions made up Napoleon's realm, and what was the status of each region within it? Did his administration show foresight, or was the empire a burden he could not afford?
3. Why did Napoleon decide to invade Russia? Why did the operation fail?
4. What were the results of the Congress of Vienna? Was the Vienna settlement a success?
5. Why did Romantic writers champion feelings over reason? What questions did Rousseau and Kant raise about reason?
6. Why was poetry important to Romantic writers? How did the Romantic concept of religion differ from Reformation Protestantism and Enlightenment deism? How did Romantic ideas and sensibilities modify European ideas of Islam and the Middle East? What were the cultural results of Napoleon's invasion of Egypt?

SUGGESTED READINGS

M. H. ABRAMS, *The Mirror and the Lamp: Romantic Theory and the Critical Tradition* (1958). A classic on Romantic literary theory.

E. BEHLER, *German Romantic Literary Theory* (1993). A clear introduction to a difficult subject.

F. C. BEISER, *Enlightenment, Revolution, and Romanticism: The Genesis of Modern German Political Thought, 1790–1800* (1992). The best recent study of the subject.

G. E. BENTLEY, *The Stranger from Paradise: A Biography of William Blake* (2001). Now the standard work.

N. BOYLE, *Goethe* (2001). A challenging two-volume biography.

M. BROERS, *Europe under Napoleon 1799–1815* (2002). Examines the subject from the standpoint of those Napoleon conquered.

T. CHAPMAN, *Congress of Vienna: Origins, Processes, and Results* (1998). A clear introduction to the major issues.

P. DWYER, *Talleyrand* (2002). A useful account of his diplomatic influence.

S. ENGLUND, *Napoleon: A Political Life* (2004). A thoughtful recent biography.

C. ESDAILE *The Peninsular War: A New History* (2003). A narrative of the Napoleonic wars in Spain.

A. FORREST, *Napoleon's Men: The Soldiers of the Revolution and Empire* (2002). An examination of the troops rather than their commander.

H. HONOUR, *Romanticism* (1979). Still the best introduction to Romantic art, well illustrated.

S. KÖRNER, *Kant* (1955). A classic brief, clear introduction.

J. LUSVASS, *Napoleon on the Art of War* (2001). A collection of Napoleon's own writings.

J. J. MCGANN AND J. SODERHOLM (EDS.), *Byron and Romanticism* (2002). Essays on the poet who most embodied Romantic qualities to the people of his time.

R. MUIR, *Tactics and the Experience of Battle in the Age of Napoleon* (1998). A splendid account of troops in battle.

T. PINKARD, *Hegel: A Biography* (2000). A long but accessible study.

P. W. SCHROEDER, *The Transformation of European Politics, 1763–1848* (1994). A major synthesis of the diplomatic history of the period, emphasizing the new departures of the Congress of Vienna.

I. WOLOCH, *Napoleon and His Collaborators: The Making of a Dictatorship* (2001). A key study by one of the major scholars of the subject.

DOCUMENTS CD-ROM

Napoleon and the Birth of Romanticism

20.1 A View from the Field: A Napoleonic Soldier
20.2 A View from the Field: A British Soldier
20.3 The French View
20.4 The Arab View
20.5 Jean-Jacques Rousseau: from *Emile*
20.6 Samuel Taylor Coleridge: from *Aids to Reflection*

CHAPTER 20

THE CONSERVATIVE ORDER AND THE CHALLENGES OF REFORM (1815–1832)

KEY TOPICS

- The challenges of nationalism and liberalism to the conservative order in the early nineteenth century
- The domestic and international politics of the conservative order from the Congress of Vienna through the 1820s
- The Wars of Independence in Latin America
- The revolutions of 1830 on the Continent and the passage of the Great Reform Bill in Britain

The Congress of Vienna was followed by a decade in which conservative political forces controlled virtually all of Europe. In the international arena, these forces sought to maintain peace and to prevent the outbreak of war that would unleash destruction and disorder. They did so through unprecedented forms of cooperation and mutual consultation. Domestically, they sought to maintain the authority of monarchies

In 1830, revolution again erupted in France as well as elsewhere on the Continent. Engène Delacroix's *Liberty Leading the People* was the most famous image recalling that event. Note how he portrays persons from different social classes and occupations joining the revolution led by the figure of Liberty. Eugène Delacroix (1798–1863), "Liberty Leading the People," 1830. Oil on canvas, 260 × 325 cm—RF 129. Louvre—Department des Peintures, Paris, France. Photograph © Erich Lessing/Art Resource, NY

and aristocracies after the turmoil the French Revolution and Napoleon had wrought. Two sets of critics challenged this conservative order. Nationalists wished to redraw the map of Europe according to the boundaries of nationalities or ethnic groups. Liberals sought moderate political reform and freer economic markets. The goals of nationalists and liberals threatened the dominance of landed aristocracies and the rule of monarchs who governed by

virtue of dynastic inheritance rather than nationality. The efforts of Europe's Latin American colonies to gain independence also challenged the status quo.

For the first fifteen years after the Congress of Vienna, the forces of conservatism were successful, except for the failure of Spain and Portugal to retain control of Latin America. In the late 1820s, however, the conservatives faced stronger challenges. Thereafter, certain major liberal goals were achieved when a revolution occurred in France in 1830 and a sweeping reform bill passed through the British Parliament in 1832. During the same period, however, Russia and other countries in eastern and central Europe continued to resist political and social change. ■

THE CHALLENGES OF NATIONALISM AND LIBERALISM

Observers have frequently regarded the nineteenth century as the great age of "isms." Throughout the Western world, secular ideologies began to take hold of the learned and popular imaginations in opposition to the political and social status quo. These included nationalism, liberalism, republicanism, socialism, and communism. A noted historian once called all such words "trouble-breeding and usually thought-obscuring terms."[1] They are just that if we use them as an excuse to avoid thinking or if we fail to see the variety of opinions each of them conceals.

THE EMERGENCE OF NATIONALISM

Nationalism proved to be the single most powerful European political ideology of the nineteenth and early twentieth centuries. It has reasserted itself in present-day Europe following the collapse of communist governments in eastern Europe and in the former Soviet Union. As a political outlook, nationalism was and is based on the relatively modern concept that a nation is composed of people who are joined together by the bonds of a common language, as well as common customs, culture, and history, and who, because of these bonds, should be administered by the same government. That is to say, nationalists in the past and the present contend that political and ethnic boundaries should coincide. Political units had not been so defined or governed earlier in European history. The idea came into its own during the late eighteenth and the early nineteenth centuries.

Opposition to the Vienna Settlement   Early nineteenth-century nationalism directly opposed the principle upheld at the Congress of Vienna that legitimate monarchies or dynasties, rather than ethnicity, provide the basis for political unity. Nationalists naturally protested multinational states such as the Austrian and Russian empires. They also objected to peoples of the same ethnic group, such as Germans and Italians, dwelling in political units smaller than that of the ethnic nation. Consequently, nationalists challenged both the domestic and the international order of the Vienna settlement.

Behind the concept of nationalism usually, though not always, lay the idea of popular sovereignty, since the qualities of peoples, rather than their rulers, determine a national character. This aspect of nationalism, however, frequently led to confusion or conflict because of the presence of minorities. Within many territories in which one national group has predominated, there have also existed significant minority ethnic enclaves that the majority has had every intention of governing with or without their consent. In some cases, a nationalistically conscious group would dominate in one section of a country, but people of the same ethnicity in another region would not have nationalistic aspirations. The former might then attempt to impose their aspirations on the latter.

Creating Nations   In fact, it was nationalists who actually created nations in the nineteenth century. During the first half of the century, a particular, usually small, group of nationalistically minded writers or other intellectual elites, using the printed word, spread a nationalistic concept of the nation. These groups were frequently historians who chronicled a people's past, or writers and literary scholars who established a national literature by collecting and publishing earlier writings in the people's language. In effect, they gave a people a sense of their past and a literature of their own. As time passed, schoolteachers spread nationalistic ideas by imparting a nation's official language and history. These small groups of early nationalists established the cultural beliefs and political expectations on which the later mass-supported nationalism of the second half of the century would grow.

Which language to use in the schools and in government offices was always a point of contention for nationalists. In France and Italy, official versions of the national language were imposed in the schools and they replaced local dialects. In parts of Scandinavia and eastern Europe, nationalists attempted to resurrect from earlier times what they regarded as purer versions of the national language.

[1] Arthur O. Lovejoy, *The Great Chain of Being: A Study in the History of an Idea* (New York: Harper Torchbooks, 1963), p. 6.

Often, modern scholars or linguists virtually invented these resurrected languages. This process of establishing national languages led to far more linguistic uniformity in European nations than had existed before the nineteenth century. Yet even in 1850, perhaps less than half of the inhabitants of France spoke the official French language.

Language could become such an effective cornerstone in the foundation of nationalism thanks largely to the emergence of the print culture discussed in Chapter 17. The presence of a great many printed books, journals, magazines, and newspapers "fixed" language in a more permanent fashion than did the spoken word. This uniform language found in printed works could overcome regional spoken dialects and establish itself as dominant. In most countries, spoken and written proficiency in the official, printed language became a path to social and political advancement. The growth of a uniform language helped persuade people who had not thought of themselves as constituting a nation that in fact they were one.

Meaning of Nationhood   Nationalists used a variety of arguments and metaphors to express what they meant by *nationhood*. Some argued that gathering, for example, Italians into a unified Italy or Germans into a unified Germany, thus eliminating or at least federating the petty dynastic states that governed those regions, would promote economic and administrative efficiency. Adopting a tenet from political liberalism, certain nationalist writers suggested that nations determining their own destinies resembled individuals exploiting personal talents to determine their own careers. Some nationalists claimed that nations, like biological species in the natural world, were distinct creations of God. Other nationalists claimed a place for their nations in the divine order of things. (see "Mazzini Defines Nationality," page 660.) Throughout the nineteenth century, for example, Polish nationalists portrayed Poland as the suffering Christ among nations, thus implicitly suggesting that Poland, like Christ, would experience resurrection and a new life.

A significant difficulty for nationalism was, and is, determining which ethnic groups could be considered nations, with claims to territory and political autonomy. In theory, any of them could, but in reality, nationhood came to be associated with groups that were large enough to support a viable economy, that had a significant cultural history, that possessed a cultural elite that could nourish and spread the national language, and that had the military capacity to conquer other peoples or to establish and protect their own independence. Throughout the century many smaller ethnic groups claimed to fulfill these criteria, but could not effectively achieve either independence or recognition. They could and did, however, create domestic unrest within the political units they inhabited.

Regions of Nationalistic Pressure   During the nineteenth century, nationalists challenged the political status quo in six major areas of Europe. England had brought Ireland under direct rule in 1800, abolishing the separate Irish Parliament and allowing the Irish to elect members to the British Parliament in Westminster. Irish nationalists, however, wanted independence or at least larger measures of self-government. The "Irish problem," as it was called, would haunt British politics for the next two centuries. German nationalists sought political unity for all German-speaking peoples, challenging the multinational structure of the Austrian Empire and pitting Prussia and Austria against each other. Italian nationalists sought to unify Italian-speaking peoples on the Italian peninsula and to drive out the Austrians. Polish nationalists, targeting primarily their Russian rulers, struggled to restore Poland as an independent nation. In eastern Europe, a host of national groups, including Hungarians, Czechs, Slovenes, and others, sought either independence or formal recognition within the Austrian Empire. Finally, in southeastern Europe on the Balkan peninsula and eastward, national groups, including Serbs, Greeks, Albanians, Romanians, and Bulgarians, sought independence from Ottoman and Russian control.

Although there were never disturbances in all six areas at the same time, any one of them had the potential to erupt into turmoil for much of the nineteenth century and beyond. In each area, nationalist activity ebbed and flowed. The dominant governments often thought they needed only to repress the activity or ride it out until stability returned. Over the course of the century, however, nationalists changed the political map and political culture of Europe.

EARLY-NINETEENTH-CENTURY POLITICAL LIBERALISM

The word *liberal*, as applied to political activity, entered the European and American vocabulary during the nineteenth century. Its meaning has varied over time. Nineteenth-century European conservatives often regarded as *liberal* almost anyone or anything that challenged their own political, social, or religious values. For twenty-first-century Americans, the word *liberal* carries with it meanings and connotations that have little or nothing to do with its significance to nineteenth-century Europeans. European conservatives of the

MAZZINI DEFINES NATIONALITY

No political force in the nineteenth and twentieth centuries was stronger than nationalism. It eventually replaced loyalty to a dynasty with loyalty based on ethnic considerations. It received new standing after World War I when the self-determination of nations became one of the cornerstones of the Paris Peace Treaties. Still later, former European colonies embraced this powerful idea. In the passage that follows, written in 1835, the Italian nationalist and patriot Giuseppe Mazzini (1805–1872) explains his understanding of nationalism. Note how he combines a generally democratic view of politics with a religious concept of the divine destiny of nations. Once in power, however, nationalist states in Europe and the rest of the world were often not democratic.

■ *What qualities of a people does Mazzini associate with nationalism? How and why does Mazzini relate nationalism to divine purposes? How does this view of nationality relate to the goals of liberal freedoms? How might these ideals of nationalism lead to international or domestic conflict?*

The essential characteristics of a nationality are common ideas, common principles and a common purpose. A nation is an association of those who are brought together by language, by given geographical conditions or by the role assigned them by history, who acknowledge the same principles and who march together to the conquest of a single definite goal under the rule of a uniform body of law.

The life of a nation consists in harmonious activity (that is, the employment of all individual abilities and energies comprised within the association) towards this single goal. . . .

But nationality means even more than this. Nationality also consists in the share of mankind's labors which God assigns to a people. This mission is the task which a people must perform to the end that the Divine Idea shall be realized in this world; it is the work which gives a people its rights as a member of Mankind; it is the baptismal rite which endows a people with its own character and its rank in the brotherhood of nations. . . .

Nationality depends for its very existence upon its sacredness within and beyond its borders.

If nationality is to be inviolable for all, friends and foes alike, it must be regarded inside a country as holy, like a religion, and outside a country as a grave mission. It is necessary too that the ideas arising within a country grow steadily, as part of the general law of Humanity which is the source of all nationality. It is necessary that these ideas be shown to other lands in their beauty and purity, free from any alien mixture, from any slavish fears, from any skeptical hesitancy, strong and active, embracing in their evolution every aspect and manifestation of the life of the nation. These ideas, a necessary component in the order of universal destiny, must retain their originality even as they enter harmoniously into mankind's general progress.

The people must be the basis of nationality; its logically derived and vigorously applied principles its means; the strength of all its strength; the improvement of the life of all and the happiness of the greatest possible number its results; and the accomplishment of the task assigned to it by God its goal. This is what we mean by nationality.

From Herbert H. Rowen, ed., *From Absolutism to Revolution, 1648–1848*, 2nd ed. © 1969. Reprinted by permission of Prentice-Hall, Inc., Upper Saddle River, NJ, pp. 277–280.

last century saw liberals as more radical than they actually were; present-day Americans often think of nineteenth-century liberals as more conservative than they were.

Political Goals   Nineteenth-century liberals derived their political ideas from the writers of the Enlightenment, the example of English liberties, and the so-called principles of 1789 embodied in the French Declaration of the Rights of Man and Citizen. They sought to establish a political framework of legal equality, religious toleration, and freedom of the press. Their general goal was a political structure that would limit the arbitrary power of government against the persons and property of individual citizens. They generally believed the legitimacy of government emanated from the freely given consent of the governed. The popular basis of such government was to be expressed through elected representative, or parliamentary, bodies. Most importantly, free government required government ministers to be responsible to the representatives rather than to the monarch. Liberals sought to achieve these political arrangements through written constitutions. They wanted to see constitutionalism and constitutional governments installed across the Continent.

These goals may seem limited, and they were. Responsible constitutional government, however, existed nowhere in Europe in 1815. Even in Great Britain, the cabinet ministers were at least as responsible to the monarch as to the House of Commons. Conservatives were suspicious of written constitutions, associating them with the French Revolution and Napoleon's regimes. They were also certain that no written constitution could embody all the political wisdom needed to govern a state.

Those who espoused liberal political structures often were educated, relatively wealthy people, usually associated with the professions or commercial life, but who were excluded in one manner or another from the existing political processes. Because of their wealth and education, they felt their exclusion was unjustified. Liberals were often academics, members of the learned professions, and people involved in the rapidly expanding commercial and manufacturing segments of the economy. They believed in, and were products of, a career open to talent. The monarchical and aristocratic regimes, as restored after the Congress of Vienna, often failed both to recognize their new status sufficiently and to provide for their economic and professional interests.

Although liberals wanted broader political participation, they did not advocate democracy. What they wanted was to extend representation to the propertied classes. Second only to their hostility to the privileged aristocracies was their contempt for the lower, unpropertied classes. Liberals transformed the eighteenth-century concept of aristocratic liberty into a new concept of privilege based on wealth and property rather than birth. As the French liberal theorist Benjamin Constant (1767–1830) wrote in 1814,

Those whom poverty keeps in eternal dependence are no more enlightened on public affairs than children, nor are they more interested than foreigners in national prosperity, of which they do not understand the basis and of which they enjoy the advantages only indirectly. Property alone, by giving sufficient leisure, renders a man capable of exercising his political rights.[2]

By the middle of the century, this widely shared attitude meant that throughout Europe liberals had separated themselves from both the rural peasant and the urban working class, a division that was to have important consequences.

Economic Goals   The economic goals of nineteenth-century liberals also divided them from working people. The manufacturers of Great Britain, the landed and manufacturing middle class of France, and the commercial interests of Germany and Italy, following the Enlightenment ideas of Adam Smith, sought to abolish the economic restraints associated with mercantilism or the regulated economies of enlightened absolutists. They wanted to manufacture and sell goods freely. To that end, they favored the removal of international tariffs and internal barriers to trade. Economic liberals opposed the old paternalistic legislation that established wages and labor practices by government regulation or by guild privileges. They saw labor as simply one more commodity to be bought and sold freely.

Liberals wanted an economic structure in which people were at liberty to use whatever talents and property they possessed to enrich themselves. Such a structure, they contended, would produce more goods and services for everyone at lower prices and provide the basis for material progress.

Because the social and political circumstances of various countries differed, the specific programs of liberals also differed from one country to another. In Great Britain, the monarchy was already limited, and most individual liberties had been secured. With reform, Parliament could provide more nearly representative government. Links between land, commerce, and industry were in place.

---

[2]Quoted in Frederick B. Artz, *Reaction and Revolution, 1814–1832* (New York: Harper, 1934), p. 94.

France also already had many structures liberals favored. The Napoleonic Code gave France a modern legal system. French liberals could justify calls for greater rights by appealing to the widely accepted "principles of 1789." As in England, representatives of the different economic interests in France had worked together. The problem for liberals in both countries was to protect civil liberties, define the respective powers of the monarch and the elected legislature, and expand the electorate moderately while avoiding democracy. (See "Benjamin Constant Discusses Modern Liberty.")

The complex political situation in German-speaking Europe was different from that in France or Britain, and German liberalism differed accordingly from its French and British counterparts. In the German states and Austria, monarchs and aristocrats offered stiffer resistance to liberal ideas, leaving German liberals with less access to direct political influence. A sharp social divide separated the aristocratic landowning classes, which filled the bureaucracies and officer corps, from the small middle-class commercial and industrial interests. Little or no precedent existed for middle-class participation in the government or the military, and there was no strong tradition of civil or individual liberty. From the time of Martin Luther in the 1500s through Kant and Hegel in the late eighteenth century, freedom in Germany had meant conformity to a higher moral law rather than participation in politics.

Most German liberals favored a united Germany and looked either to Austria or to Prussia as the instrument of unification. As a result, they were more tolerant of a strong state and monarchical power than other liberals were. They believed that unification would lead to a freer social and political order. The monarchies in Austria and Prussia refused to cooperate with these dreams of unification, frustrating German liberals and forcing them to settle for more modest achievements, such as lowering internal trade barriers.

Relationship of Nationalism to Liberalism Nationalism was not necessarily or even logically linked to liberalism. Indeed, nationalism could be, and often was, directly opposed to liberal political values. Some nationalists wanted their own particular ethnic group to dominate minority national or ethnic groups within a particular region. This was true of the Magyars, who sought political control over non-Magyar peoples living within the historical boundaries of Hungary. Nationalists also often defined their own national group in opposition to other national groups whom they might regard as cultural inferiors or

historical enemies. This darker side of nationalism would emerge starkly in the second half of the nineteenth century and would poison European political life for much of the twentieth century. Furthermore, conservative nationalists might seek political autonomy for their own ethnic group, but have no intention of establishing liberal political institutions thereafter.

Nonetheless, although liberalism and nationalism were not identical, they were often compatible. By espousing representative government, civil liberties, and economic freedom, nationalist groups in one country could gain the support of liberals elsewhere in Europe who might not otherwise share their nationalist interests. Many nationalists in Germany, Italy, and much of the Austrian Empire adopted this tactic. Some nationalists took other symbolic steps to arouse sympathy. Nationalists in Greece, for example, made Athens their capital because they believed it would associate their struggle for independence with ancient Athenian democracy, which English and French liberals revered.

CONSERVATIVE GOVERNMENTS: THE DOMESTIC POLITICAL ORDER

Despite the challenges of liberalism and nationalism, the domestic political order that the restored conservative institutions of Europe established, particularly in Great Britain and eastern Europe, showed remarkable staying power. Not until World War I did their power and pervasive influence come to an end.

CONSERVATIVE OUTLOOKS

The major pillars of nineteenth-century **conservatism** were legitimate monarchies, landed aristocracies, and established churches. The institutions themselves were ancient, but the self-conscious alliance of throne, land, and altar was new. In the eighteenth century, these groups had often quarreled. Only the upheavals of the French Revolution and the Napoleonic era transformed them into natural, if sometimes reluctant, allies. In that sense, conservatism as an articulated outlook and set of cooperating institutions was as new a feature on the political landscape as nationalism and liberalism.

The more theoretical political and religious ideas of the conservative classes were associated with thinkers such as Edmund Burke (see Chapter 18) and Friedrich Hegel (see Chapter 19).

BENJAMIN CONSTANT DISCUSSES MODERN LIBERTY

In 1819, the French liberal theorist Benjamin Constant (1767–1830) delivered lectures on the character of ancient and modern liberty. In this passage, he emphasizes the close relationship of modern liberty to economic freedom and a free private life. He then ties the desire for a free private life to the need for a representative government. Modern life did not leave people enough time to make the political commitment that the ancient Greek polis had required. Consequently, modern citizens turned over much of their political concern and activity to representatives. In this discussion Constant set forth the desire of nineteenth-century liberals to maximize private freedom and to minimize areas of life in which the government might interfere. His argument also provides a foundation for rejecting direct democracy, which he and other liberals associated with the reign of terror and with Napoleon's plebiscites.

■ *According to Constant, what are the ways in which a modern citizen is free of government control and interference? How does he defend a representative government? On the basis of this passage, do you believe that Constant was opposed to a democratic government?*

[Modern liberty] is, for each individual, the right not to be subjected to anything but the law, not to be arrested, or detained, or put to death, or mistreated in any manner, as a result of the arbitrary will of one or several individuals. It is each man's right to express his opinions, to choose and exercise his profession, to dispose of his property and even abuse it, to come and go without obtaining permission and without having to give an account of either his motives or his itinerary. It is the right to associate with other individuals, either to confer about mutual interests or profess the cult that he and his associates prefer or simply to fill his days and hours in the manner most conforming to his inclinations and fantasies. Finally, it is each man's right to exert influence on the administration of government, either through the election of some or all of its public functionaries, or through remonstrances, petitions, and demands which authorities are more or less obliged to take into account. . . .

Just as the liberty we now require is distinct from that of the ancients, so this new liberty itself requires an organization different from that suitable for ancient liberty. For the latter, the more time and energy a man consecrated to the exercise of his political rights, the more free he believed himself to be. Given the type of liberty to which we are now susceptible, the more the exercise of our political rights leaves us time for our private interests, the more precious we find liberty to be. From this . . . stems the necessity of the representative system. The representative system is nothing else than an organization through which a nation unloads on several individuals what it cannot and will not do for itself. Poor men handle their own affairs; rich men hire managers. This is the story of ancient and modern nations. The representative system is the power of attorney given to certain men by the mass of the people who want their interests defended but who nevertheless do not always have the time to defend these interests themselves.

Benjamin Constant, *Making of Modern Liberalism*. New Haven, CT: Yale University Press, 1984, pp. 66, 74.

Conservatives shared other, less formal attitudes forged by the revolutionary experience. The execution of Louis XVI at the hands of radical democrats convinced most monarchs they could trust only aristocratic governments or governments of aristocrats in alliance with the wealthiest middle-class and professional people. The European aristocracies believed that no form of genuinely representative government would protect their property and influence. All conservatives spurned the idea of a written constitution unless they were permitted to write the document themselves. Even then, some rejected the concept.

The churches equally distrusted popular movements, except their own revivals. Ecclesiastical leaders throughout the Continent regarded themselves as entrusted with the educational task of supporting the social and political status quo. They also feared and hated most of the ideas associated with the Enlightenment, because those rational concepts and reformist writings enshrined the critical spirit and undermined revealed religion.

Conservative aristocrats retained their former arrogance, but not their former privileges or their old confidence. They saw themselves as surrounded by enemies and as standing permanently on the defensive against the forces of liberalism, nationalism, and popular sovereignty. They knew that political groups that hated them could topple them. They also understood that revolution in one country could spill over into another.

All of the nations of Europe in the years immediately after 1815 confronted problems arising directly from their entering an era of peace after a quarter century of armed conflict. The war effort, with its loss of life and property and its need to organize people and resources, had distracted attention from other problems. The wartime footing had allowed all the belligerent governments to exercise firm control over their populations. War had fueled economies and had furnished vast areas of employment in armies, navies, military industries, and agriculture. The onset of peace meant citizens could raise new political issues and that economies were no longer geared to supplying military needs. Soldiers and sailors came home and looked for jobs as civilians. The vast demands of the military effort on industries subsided and caused unemployment. The young were no longer growing up in a climate of war and could think about other issues. For all of these reasons, the conservative statesmen who led every major government in 1815 confronted new pressures that would cause various degrees of domestic unrest and would lead them to resort to differing degrees of repression.

LIBERALISM AND NATIONALISM RESISTED IN AUSTRIA AND THE GERMANIES

The early-nineteenth-century statesman who, more than any other epitomized conservatism, was the Austrian prince Metternich (1773–1859). This devoted servant of the Habsburg emperor had been, along with Britain's Viscount Castlereagh (1769–1822), the chief architect of the Vienna settlement. It was Metternich who seemed to exercise chief control over the forces of European reaction.

Dynastic Integrity of the Habsburg Empire   The Austrian government could make no serious compromises with the new political forces in Europe. To no other country were the programs of liberalism and nationalism potentially more dangerous. Germans and Hungarians, as well as Poles, Czechs, Slovaks, Slovenes, Italians, Croats, and other ethnic groups, peopled the Habsburg domains. Through client governments, Austria also dominated those parts of the Italian peninsula that it did not rule directly.

For Metternich and other Austrian officials, the recognition of the political rights and aspirations of any of the various national groups would mean

Prince Klemens von Metternich (1773–1859) epitomized nineteenth-century conservatism.   Sir Thomas Lawrence (1769–1830), "Clemens Lothar Wenzel, Prince Metternich" (1773–1859), RCIN 404948, OM 905 WC 206. The Royal Collection © 2003, Her Majesty Queen Elizabeth II

the probable dissolution of the empire. If Austria permitted representative government, Metternich feared the national groups would fight their battles internally at the cost of Austria's international influence.

To safeguard dynastic integrity, Austria had to dominate the newly formed German Confederation to prevent the formation of a German national state that might absorb the German-speaking heart of the empire and exclude the other realms the Habsburgs governed. The Congress of Vienna had created the German Confederation to replace the defunct Holy Roman Empire. It consisted of thirty-nine states under Austrian leadership. Each state remained more or less autonomous, but Austria was determined to prevent any movement toward constitutionalism in as many of them as possible.

Defeat of Prussian Reform   An important victory for this holding policy came in Prussia in the years immediately after the Congress of Vienna. In 1815, Frederick William III (r. 1797–1840), caught up in the exhilaration that followed the War of Liberation, as Germans called the last part of their conflict with Napoleon, had promised some form of constitutional government. After stalling, he formally reneged on his pledge in 1817. Instead, he created a new Council of State, which, although it improved administrative efficiency, was responsible to him alone.

In 1819, the king moved further from reform. After a major disagreement over the organization of the army, he replaced his reform-minded ministers with hardened conservatives. On their advice, in 1823, Frederick William III established eight provincial estates, or diets. These bodies were dominated by the Junkers and exercised only an advisory function. The old bonds linking monarchy, army, and landholders in Prussia had been reestablished. The members of this alliance would oppose the threats the German nationalists posed to the conservative social and political order.

Student Nationalism and the Carlsbad Decrees
To widen their bases of political support, the monarchs of three southern German states—Baden, Bavaria, and Württemberg—had granted constitutions after 1815. None of these constitutions, however, recognized popular sovereignty, and all defined political rights as the gift of the monarch. Yet in the aftermath of the defeat of Napoleon, many young Germans continued to cherish nationalist and liberal expectations.

University students who had grown up during the days of the reforms of Stein and Hardenberg and had read the writings of early German nationalists made up the most important of these groups. Many of them or their friends had fought Napoleon. When they went to the universities, they continued to dream of a united Germany. They formed *Burschenschaften*, or student associations. Like student groups today, these clubs served numerous social functions, one of which was to replace old provincial attachments with

In May 1820, Karl Sand, a German student and a member of a *Burschenschaft*, was executed for his murder of the conservative playwright August von Kotzebue the previous year. In the eyes of many young German nationalists, Sand was a political martyr.   Bildarchiv Preussischer Kulturbesitz

loyalty to the concept of a united German state. It should also be noted that these clubs were often anti-Semitic. (See Encountering the Past: Gymnastics and German Nationalism.)

In 1817, in Jena, one such student club organized a large celebration for the fourth anniversary of the Battle of Leipzig and the tercentenary of Luther's Ninety-five Theses. There were bonfires, songs, and processions as more than five hundred people gathered for the festivities. The event made German rulers uneasy, for the student clubs included a few republicans.

Two years later, in March 1819, a student named Karl Sand, a *Burschenschaft* member, assassinated the conservative dramatist August von Kotzebue, who had ridiculed the *Burschenschaft* movement. Sand, who was tried and publicly executed, became a nationalist martyr. Although Sand had acted alone, Metternich used the incident to suppress institutions associated with liberalism.

In July 1819, Metternich persuaded the major German states to issue the Carlsbad Decrees, which dissolved the *Burschenschaften*. The decrees also provided for university inspectors and press censors. (See "Metternich Discusses Sources of Political Unrest.") The next year the German Confederation issued the Final Act, which limited the subjects that the constitutional chambers of

METTERNICH DISCUSSES SOURCES OF POLITICAL UNREST

Prince Klemens von Metternich (1773–1859) was the chief minister of the Austrian empire and the statesman who most opposed change in Europe after the Congress of Vienna. In 1819, he was attempting to suppress political activity in the universities. As he explained in this letter, he did not fear students as such but rather the future adults who, as students, had been taught liberal political ideas. He also considered lawyers more politically dangerous than professors.

■ *According to Metternich, what is the difference between people who conspire against things and those who conspire against theories? Why does he fear the role of universities as a source of revolutionary disturbance? Why does he consider the press the greatest danger?*

That the students' folly declines or tunes to some other side than that of politics does not surprise me. This is in the nature of things. The student, taken in himself, is a child, and the *Burschenshaft* [student fraternity] is an unpractical puppet show. Then, I have never ... spoken of students, but all my aim has been directed at the professors. Now, the professors, singly or united, are most unsuited to be conspirators. People only conspire profitably against things, not against theories. ... Where they are political, they must be supported by deed, and the deed is the overthrow of existing institutions. ...

This is what learned men and professors cannot manage, and the class of lawyers is better suited to carry it on. I know hardly one learned man who knows the value of property; while, on the contrary, the lawyer class is always rummaging about in the property of others. Besides, the professors are, nearly without exception, given up to theory; while no people are more practical than lawyers.

Consequently, I have never feared that the revolution would be engendered by the universities; but that at them a whole generation of revolutionaries must be formed, unless the evil is restrained, seems to me certain. I hope that the most mischievous symptoms of the evil at the universities may be met, and that perhaps from its own peculiar sources, for the measures of the Government will contribute to this less than the weariness of the students, the weakness of the professors, and the different direction which the studies may take. ...

The greatest and consequently the most urgent evil now is the press.

From *Memoirs of Prince Metternich*, vol. 3, trans. by Mrs. Napier (New York: Scribner: 1880–1881), pp. 286–288.

GYMNASTICS AND GERMAN NATIONALISM

Today citizens take great pride in the performance of their nations' athletes in the Olympics. This modern link between athletics and nationalism originated in early nineteenth-century Germany with the *Turnverein*, or gymnastic movement.

Its founder was Friedrich Ludwig Jahn (1778–1852), later known as Turnvater Jahn on the grounds that he was the father of the movement, which he described as "Love of the Fatherland through Gymnastics." He was also an innovator in gymnastic equipment, credited with inventing the parallel bars and improving the pommel vault.

Jahn became a fervent patriot when he saw the German states and particularly Prussia humiliated by Napoleon. He attacked what he regarded as foreign influences on German life, including that of German Jews. Jahn was convinced that Germans must cultivate their bodily strength to overcome external enemies. In 1811, he established an open-air gymnasium in a meadow near Berlin. The young men who attended this gymnasium and others that he soon founded throughout the German states saw themselves as an advanced nationalistic guard.

After the defeat of Napoleon in 1815, gymnastic clubs spread across Germany, fostered nationalist sentiment, and challenged the social and political status quo. The clubs embodied social equality. All members wore plain gray exercise uniforms that

Jahn had designed and addressed each other with the familiar "Du." Conservatives were suspicious. They saw these early gymnastic clubs as a state within the various disunited German states. For a time Prussia banned gymnastics and sent Jahn to prison.

During the 1840s, however, the gymnastic movement revived. Germany soon had tens of thousands of adult gymnasts, and the clubs became increasingly nationalistic, often excluding Jews. After German unification in 1870, national festivals often featured gymnastic performances, and national monuments had areas for gymnastic display. Political figures from Bismarck to Hitler cultivated their links to the gymnastic societies. The connection between gymnastics and German nationalism was so strong that even liberal Germans who immigrated to the United States founded *Turnvereins* in their new homes.

- *What factors turned Jahn to nationalism? Why did he associate nationalism with physical strength? How could the* Turnverein *movement spread easily in the Germanies?*

Liah Greenfeld, *Nationalism: Five Roads to Modernity* (Cambridge, MA: Harvard University Press, 1992), 367–70; Matthew Levinger, *Enlightened Nationalism: The Transformation of Prussian Political Culture, 1806–1848* (New York: Oxford University Press, 2000), George L. Mosse, *The Nationalization of the Masses: Political Symbolism and Mass Movements in Germany from the Napoleonic Wars through the Third Reich*, p. 128 (New York: New American Library, 1975).

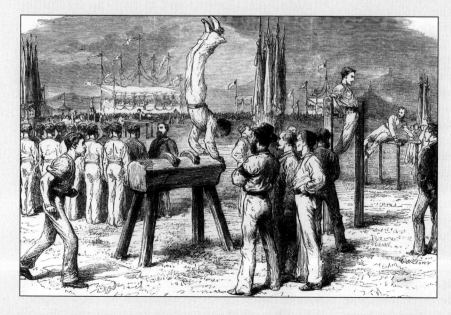

Turnvater Jahn encouraged German gymnasts to use athletic equipment in their exercises. Here at a Bonn gymnastic festival of 1872 an athlete works out on a Pommel Horse, a piece of athletic equipment that pre-dated Jahn but the design of which he improved. Also note the athletic clothing which emphasizes egalitarian social relations among the athletes. CORBIS/Bettmann

Bavaria, Württemberg, and Baden could discuss. The measure also asserted the right of the monarchs to resist demands of constitutionalists. For many years thereafter, the secret police of the various German states harassed potential dissidents. In the opinion of the princes, these included almost anyone who sought even moderate social or political change.

POSTWAR REPRESSION IN GREAT BRITAIN

The years 1819 and 1820 marked a high tide for conservative influence and repression in western as well as eastern Europe. After 1815, Great Britain experienced two years of poor harvests. At the same time, discharged sailors and soldiers and out-of-work industrial workers swelled the ranks of the unemployed.

Lord Liverpool's Ministry and Popular Unrest The Tory ministry of Lord Liverpool (1770–1828) was unprepared to deal with these problems of postwar dislocation. Instead, it sought to protect the interests of the landed and wealthy classes. In 1815, Parliament passed a Corn Law to maintain high prices for domestically produced grain (called "corn" in Britain) by levying import duties on foreign grain. The next year, Parliament replaced the income tax that only the wealthy paid with excise or sales taxes on consumer goods that both the wealthy and the poor paid. These laws continued a legislative trend that marked the abandonment by the British ruling class of its traditional role of paternalistic protector of the poor. In 1799, the Combination Acts had outlawed workers' organizations or unions. During the war, wage protection had been removed. Many in the taxpaying classes wanted to abolish the Poor Law that provided public relief for the destitute and unemployed.

In light of these policies and the postwar economic downturn, it is hardly surprising that the lower social orders began to doubt the wisdom of their rulers and to demand political changes. Mass meetings called for the reform of Parliament. Reform clubs were organized. Radical newspapers, such as William Cobbett's *Political Registrar*, demanded change. In the hungry, restive agricultural and industrial workers, the government could see only images of continental *sans-culottes* ready to hang aristocrats from the nearest lamppost. Government ministers regarded radical leaders, such as Cobbett (1763–1835), Major John Cartwright (1740–1824), and Henry "Orator" Hunt (1773–1835), as demagogues who were seducing the people away from allegiance to their natural leaders.

The government's answer to the discontent was repression. In December 1816, an unruly mass meeting took place at Spa Fields near London. This disturbance gave Parliament an excuse to pass the Coercion Acts of March 1817, which temporarily suspended *habeas corpus* and extended existing laws against seditious gatherings.

"Peterloo" and the Six Acts This initial repression, in combination with improved harvests, calmed the political landscape for a time. By 1819, however, the people were restive again. In the industrial north, well-organized mass meetings demanded the reform of Parliament. The radical reform campaign culminated on August 16, 1819, with a meeting in the industrial city of Manchester at Saint Peter's Fields. Royal troops and the local militia were on hand to ensure order. As the speeches were about to begin, a local magistrate ordered the militia to move into the audience. The result was panic and death. At least eleven people in the crowd were killed; scores were injured. The event became known as the Peterloo Massacre, a phrase that drew a contemptuous comparison with Wellington's victory at Waterloo.

Peterloo had been the act of local officials, whom the Liverpool ministry felt it must support. The cabinet also decided to act once and for all to end these troubles. Most of the radical leaders were arrested and imprisoned. In December 1819, a few months after the German Carlsbad Decrees, Parliament passed a series of laws called the Six Acts, which (1) forbade large unauthorized, public meetings, (2) raised the fines for seditious libel, (3) speeded up the trials of political agitators, (4) increased newspaper taxes, (5) prohibited the training of armed groups, and (6) allowed local officials to search homes in certain disturbed counties. In effect, the Six Acts attempted to prevent radical leaders from agitating and to give the authorities new powers.

Two months after the passage of the Six Acts, the Cato Street Conspiracy was unearthed. Under the guidance of a possibly demented man named Arthur Thistlewood (1770–1820), a group of extreme radicals had plotted to blow up the entire British cabinet. The plot was foiled. The leaders were arrested and tried, and five of them were hanged. Although little more than a half-baked plot, the conspiracy helped discredit the movement for parliamentary reform.

BOURBON RESTORATION IN FRANCE

The abdication of Napoleon in 1814 opened the way for a restoration of Bourbon rule in the homeland of the great revolution. The new king was the former count of Provence and a brother of Louis XVI. The son of the executed monarch had died in

The French Bourbons were restored to the throne in 1815 but would rule only until 1830. This picture shows Louis XVIII, seated, second from left, and his brother, the count of Artois, who would become Charles X, standing on the left. Notice the bust of Henry IV in the background, placed there to associate the restored rulers with their popular late-sixteenth–early-seventeenth-century forebearer. Bildarchiv Preussischer Kulturbesitz

prison. Royalists had regarded the dead boy as Louis XVII, and so his uncle became Louis XVIII (r. 1814–1824). This fat, awkward man had become a political realist during his more than twenty years of exile. He understood he could not turn back the clock to 1789. France had undergone too many irreversible changes. Consequently, Louis XVIII agreed to become a constitutional monarch, but under a constitution of his own making called the Charter.

The Charter The Charter provided for a hereditary monarchy and a bicameral legislature. The monarch appointed the upper house, the Chamber of Peers, modeled on the British House of Lords; a narrow franchise with a high property qualification elected the lower house, the Chamber of Deputies. The Charter guaranteed most of the rights the Declaration of the Rights of Man and Citizen had enumerated. There was to be religious toleration, but Roman Catholicism was designated the official religion of the nation. Most importantly for thousands of French people at all social levels who had profited from the revolution, the Charter promised not to challenge the property rights of the current owners of land that had been confiscated from aristocrats and the church. With this provision, Louis XVIII hoped to reconcile to his regime those who had benefited from the revolution.

Ultraroyalism This moderate spirit did not penetrate deeply into the ranks of royalist supporters whose families had suffered during the revolution.

Rallying around Louis' brother and heir, the count of Artois (1757–1836), those people who were more royalist than the monarch now demanded their revenge. In the months after Napoleon's final defeat at Waterloo, royalists in the south and west carried out a White Terror against former revolutionaries and supporters of the deposed emperor. The king could do little or nothing to halt this bloodbath. Similar extreme royalist sentiment could be found in the Chamber of Deputies. The ultraroyalist majority elected in 1816 proved so dangerously reactionary that the king soon dissolved the chamber. The second election returned a more moderate majority. Several years of political give-and-take followed, with the king making mild accommodations to liberals.

In February 1820, however, the duke of Berri, son of Artois and heir to the throne after his father, was murdered by a lone assassin. The ultraroyalists persuaded Louis XVIII that the murder was the result of his ministers' cooperation with liberal politicians, and the king responded with repressive measures. New electoral laws gave wealthy electors two votes. Press censorship was imposed, and people suspected of dangerous political activity were made subject to easy arrest. By 1821, the government placed secondary education under the control of the Roman Catholic bishops.

All these actions revealed the basic contradiction of the French restoration. By the early 1820s, the veneer of constitutionalism had worn away. Liberals were being driven out of politics and into a near illegal status.

THE CONSERVATIVE INTERNATIONAL ORDER

At the Congress of Vienna, the major powers—Russia, Austria, Prussia, and Great Britain—had agreed to consult with each other from time to time on matters affecting Europe as a whole. Such consultation was one of the new departures in international relations the Congress achieved. The vehicle for this consultation was a series of postwar congresses, or conferences. Later, as differences arose among the powers, the consultations became more informal. This new arrangement for resolving mutual foreign policy issues was known as the *Concert of Europe*. It prevented one nation from taking a major action in international affairs without working in concert with and obtaining the assent of the others. The initial goal of the Concert of Europe was to maintain the balance of power against new French aggression and against the military might of Russia. The Concert continued to function, however, on large and small issues until the third quarter of the century. Its goal—a novel one in European affairs—was to maintain the peace. In that respect, although the great powers sought to maintain conservative domestic governments, they were taking genuinely new steps to regulate their international relations.

THE CONGRESS SYSTEM

In the years immediately after the Congress of Vienna, the new congress system of mutual cooperation and consultation functioned well. The first congress took place in 1818 at Aix-la-Chapelle in Germany near the border of Belgium. As a result of this gathering, the four major powers removed their troops from France, which had paid its war reparations, and readmitted France to good standing among the European nations. Despite unanimity on these decisions, the conference was not without friction. Tsar Alexander I (r. 1801–1825) suggested that the Quadruple Alliance (see Chapter 19) agree to uphold the borders and the existing governments of all European countries. Castlereagh, representing Britain, flatly rejected the proposal. He contended the Quadruple Alliance was intended only to prevent future French aggression. These disagreements appeared somewhat academic until revolutions broke out in southern Europe.

THE SPANISH REVOLUTION OF 1820

When the Bourbon Ferdinand VII of Spain (r. 1814–1833) was placed on his throne after Napoleon's downfall, he had promised to govern according to a

THE PERIOD OF POLITICAL REACTION

1814	French monarchy restored
1815	Russia, Austria, Prussia form Holy Alliance
1815	Russia, Austria, Prussia, and Britain renew Quadruple Alliance
1818	Congress of Aix-la-Chapelle
1819 (July)	Carlsbad Decrees
1819 (August 16)	Peterloo Massacre
1819 (December)	Great Britain passes Six Acts
1820 (January)	Spanish revolution
1820 (October)	Congress of Troppau
1821 (January)	Congress of Laibach
1821 (February)	Greek revolution
1822	Congress of Verona
1823	France helps crush Spanish revolution

written constitution. Once in power, however, he ignored his pledge, dissolved the *Cortés* (the parliament), and ruled alone. In 1820, army officers who were about to be sent to suppress revolution in Spain's Latin American colonies rebelled. In March, Ferdinand once again announced he would abide by the provisions of the constitution. For the time being, the revolution had succeeded.

Almost at the same time, in July 1820, revolution erupted in Naples, where the king of the Two Sicilies quickly accepted a constitution. There were other, lesser revolts in Italy, but none of them succeeded.

These events frightened the ever-nervous Metternich. Italian disturbances were especially troubling to him. Austria hoped to dominate the peninsula to provide a buffer against the spread of revolution on its own southern flank. The other powers were divided on the best course of action. Britain opposed joint intervention in either Italy or Spain. Metternich turned to Prussia and Russia, the other members of the Holy Alliance formed in 1815, for support. The three eastern powers, along with unofficial delegations from Britain and France, met at the Congress of Troppau in late October 1820. Led by Tsar Alexander, the members of the Holy Alliance issued the Protocol of Troppau. This declaration asserted that stable governments might intervene to restore order in countries experiencing revolution. Yet even Russia hesitated to authorize Austrian intervention in Italian affairs. That decision was finally reached in January 1821 at the Congress of Laibach. Shortly thereafter,

Austrian troops marched into Naples and restored the absolutist rule of the king of the Two Sicilies. From then on, Metternich attempted to foster policies that would improve the efficient administration of the various Italian governments so as to increase their support among their subjects.

The final postwar congress took place in October 1822 at Verona. Its primary purpose was to resolve the situation in Spain. Once again, Britain balked at joint action. Shortly before the meeting, Castlereagh had committed suicide. George Canning (1770–1827), the new foreign minister, was much less sympathetic to Metternich's goals. At Verona, Britain, in effect, withdrew from continental affairs. Austria, Prussia, and Russia agreed to support French intervention in Spain. In April 1823, a French army crossed the Pyrenees and within a few months suppressed the Spanish revolution. French troops remained in Spain to prop up King Ferdinand until 1827.

What did not happen in Spain, however, was as important for the new international order as what did happen. France did not use its intervention as an excuse to aggrandize its power or increase its territory. The same had been true of all the other interventions under the congress system. The great powers authorized these interventions to preserve or restore conservative regimes, not to conquer territory for themselves. Their goal was to maintain the international order established at Vienna. Such a situation stood in sharp contrast to the alliances to invade or confiscate territory that the European powers had made during the eighteenth century and the wars of the French Revolution and Napoleon. This new mode of international restraint through formal and informal consultation prevented war among the great powers until the middle of the century and averted a general European conflict until 1914. As one historian has commented, "The statesmen of the Vienna generation . . . did not so much fear war because they thought it would bring revolution as because they had learned from bitter experience that war was revolution."[3]

The Congress of Verona and the Spanish intervention had a second diplomatic result. The new British foreign minister, George Canning, was much more interested in British commerce and trade than Castlereagh had been. Thus Canning sought to prevent the extension of European reaction to Spain's colonies in Latin America, which were then in revolt (see page 673). He intended to exploit these South American revolutions to break

Spain's old trading monopoly with its colonies and gain access for Britain to Latin American trade. To that end, he supported the American Monroe Doctrine in 1823, prohibiting further colonization and intervention by European powers in the Americas. Britain soon recognized the Spanish colonies as independent states. Through the rest of the century, British commercial interests dominated Latin America. Canning may thus be said to have brought the War of Jenkins's Ear (1739) to a successful conclusion.

REVOLT AGAINST OTTOMAN RULE IN THE BALKANS

The Greek Revolution of 1821   While the powers were plotting conservative interventions in Italy and Spain, a third Mediterranean revolt erupted—in Greece. The Greek revolution became one of the most famous of the century because it attracted the support and participation of many illustrious writers. Liberals throughout Europe, who were seeing their own hopes crushed at home, imagined that the ancient Greek democracy was being reborn. Lord Byron went to fight in Greece and died there in 1824 (of cholera). Philhellenic ("pro-Greek") societies were founded in nearly every major country. The struggle was posed in the eighteenth-century Enlightenment terms of Western liberal Greek freedom against the Asian oriental despotism of the Ottoman Empire.

As discussed in Chapter 13, the Ottoman Empire had not changed its fundamental political or economic structures during the eighteenth century even as the major European states grew richer and more powerful. Ottoman weakness and instability troubled European diplomacy throughout the nineteenth century, raising what was known as "the Eastern Question": What should the European powers do about the Ottoman inability to assure political and administrative stability in its possessions in and around the eastern Mediterranean? Most of the major powers had a keen interest in those territories. Russia and Austria coveted land in the Balkans. France and Britain were concerned with the empire's commerce and with control of key naval positions in the eastern Mediterranean. Also at issue was the treatment of the Christian inhabitants of the empire and access to the Christian shrines in the Holy Land. The goals of the great powers often conflicted with the desire for independence of the many national groups in the Ottoman Empire. Yet, because the powers had little desire to strengthen the empire, they were often more sympathetic to nationalistic aspirations there than elsewhere in Europe.

[3]Paul W. Schroeder, *The Transformation of European Politics, 1763–1848* (Oxford: Clarendon Press, 1994), p. 802.

A CLOSER LOOK

An English Poet Appears as an Albanian

The famous English poet, George Gordon, Lord Byron (1788–1824) was one of many European liberals who went to Greece to aid the cause of its independence. He died there of fever in 1824.

His portrait here in Albanian dress was intended to demonstrate his willingness to exchange Western European clothes for what many of his contemporaries would have regarded as the exotic garb of the Balkan peoples. The costume also suggested that Byron, whose personal life was regarded as scandalous, did not intend to see his cultural identity shaped solely by England.

The portrait also demonstrated that Byron, the Romantic poet, saw himself capable of embodying many different personalities.

Byron's association with liberal causes indicated that Romantic writers, who were often seen as supporting conservatism, could also embrace liberal movements.

The Granger Collection, NY

These conflicting interests, as well as mutual distrust, prevented any direct intervention in Greek affairs for several years. Eventually, however, Britain, France, and Russia concluded that an independent Greece would benefit their strategic interests and would not threaten their domestic security. In 1827, they signed the Treaty of London, demanding Turkish recognition of Greek independence, and sent a joint fleet to support the Greek revolt. In 1828, Russia sent troops into the Ottoman holdings in what is today Romania, ultimately gaining control of that territory in 1829 with the Treaty of Adrianople. The treaty also stipulated the Turks would allow Britain, France, and Russia to decide the future of Greece. In 1830, a second Treaty of London declared Greece an independent kingdom. Two years later, Otto I (r. 1832–1862), the son of the king of Bavaria, was chosen to be the first king of the new Greek kingdom.

Serbian Independence   The year 1830 also saw the establishment of a second independent state on the Balkan peninsula. Since the late eighteenth century, Serbia had sought independence from the Ottoman Empire. During the Napoleonic wars, its fate had been linked to Russian policy and Russian relations with the Ottoman Empire. Between 1804 and 1813, a remarkable Serbian leader, Kara George (1762–1817), had led a guerrilla war against the Ottomans. This ultimately unsuccessful revolution helped build national self-identity and attracted the interest of the great powers.

In 1815 and 1816, a new leader, Milos Obrenovitch (1780–1860), succeeded in negotiating greater administrative autonomy for some Serbian territory, but most Serbs lived outside the borders of this new entity. In 1830, the Ottoman sultan formally granted independence to Serbia, and by the late 1830s, the major powers granted it diplomatic recognition. Serbia's political structure, however, remained in doubt for many years.

In 1833, Milos, now a hereditary prince, pressured the Ottoman authorities to extend the borders of Serbia, which they did. These new boundaries persisted until 1878. Serbian leaders continued to seek additional territory, however, creating tensions with Austria. The status of minorities, particularly Muslims, within Serbian territory, was also a problem.

In the mid-1820s, Russia, which like Serbia was a Slav state and Eastern Orthodox in religion, became Serbia's formal protector. In 1856, Serbia came under the collective protection of the great powers, but the special relationship between Russia and Serbia would continue until the First World War and would play a decisive role in the outbreak of that conflict.

THE WARS OF INDEPENDENCE IN LATIN AMERICA

The wars of the French Revolution and, more particularly, those of Napoleon sparked movements for independence from European domination throughout Latin America. In less than two decades, between 1804 and 1824, France was driven from Haiti, Portugal lost control of Brazil, and Spain was forced to withdraw from all of its American empire except Cuba and Puerto Rico. Three centuries of Iberian colonial government over the South American continent ended. These wars brought to a conclusion the era of European political domination and direct economic exploitation of the American continents that had begun with the encounter between the peoples of the New World and Spain at the end of the fifteenth century. The period of transatlantic history beginning with the American Revolution and ending with the Latin American Wars of Independence thus constituted the first era of decolonization from European rule. (See Map 20-1, on page 674.)

REVOLUTION IN HAITI

Between 1791 and 1804, the French colony of Haiti achieved independence. This event was of key importance for two reasons. First, it was sparked by policies of the French Revolution overflowing into its New World Empire. Second, the Haitian Revolution demonstrated that slaves of African origins could lead a revolt against white masters and mulatto freemen. The example of the Haitian Revolution for years thereafter terrified slaveholders throughout the Americas.

The relationship between slaves and masters on Haiti had been filled with violence throughout the eighteenth century. The French colonial masters had frequently used racial divisions between black slaves and mulatto freemen to their own political advantage. Once the French Revolution had broken out in France, the French National Assembly in 1791 decreed that free property-owning mulattos on Haiti should enjoy the same rights as white plantation owners. The Colonial Assembly in Haiti resisted the orders from France.

In 1791, a full-fledged slave rebellion shook Haiti. It arose as a result of a secret conspiracy among the slaves. François-Dominique Toussaint L'Ouverture (1743?–1803), himself a former slave, quickly emerged as its leader. The rebellion involved enormous violence and loss of life on both sides. Although the slave rebellion collapsed, mulattos and free black people on Haiti, who hoped to gain the rights the French National Assembly had promised, then took up arms against the white

Interactive map: To explore this map further, go to http://www.prenhall.com/kagan/map20.1

Map 20–1 **LATIN AMERICA IN 1830**   By 1830 most of Latin America had been liberated from Europe. This map shows the initial borders of the states of the region with the dates of their independence. The United Provinces of La Plata formed the nucleus of what later became Argentina.

Toussaint L'Ouverture (1746–1803) began the revolt that led to Haitian independence in 1804.   Stock Montage

colonial masters. French officials sent by the revolutionary government in Paris soon backed them. Slaves now came to the aid of an invading French force, and in early 1793, the French abolished slavery in Haiti.

By this time both Spain and Great Britain were attempting to intervene in Haitian events to expand their own influence in the Caribbean. Both were opposed to the end of slavery and both coveted Haiti's rich sugar-producing lands. Toussaint L'Ouverture and his force of ex-slaves again supported the French against the Spanish and the British. By 1800, his army had achieved dominance throughout the island of Hispanola. He imposed an authoritarian constitution on Haiti and made himself Governor-General for life, but he preserved formal ties with France.

The French government under Napoleon distrusted L'Ouverture and feared that his example would undermine French authority elsewhere in the Caribbean and North America. In 1802, Napoleon sent an army to Haiti and eventually captured L'Overture, who was sent back to France where he died in prison in 1803. Other Haitian

military leaders of slave origin, the most important of whom was Jean-Jacques Dessalines (1758–1806), continued to resist. When Napoleon found himself again at war with Britain in 1803, he decided to abandon his American empire, selling Louisiana to the United States and withdrawing his forces from Haiti. Thus, the Haitian slave-led rebellion became the first successful assault on colonial government in Latin America. France formally recognized Haitian independence in 1804.

WARS OF INDEPENDENCE ON THE SOUTH AMERICAN CONTINENT

Haiti's revolution, which involved the popular uprising of a repressed social group, proved to be the great exception in the Latin American drive for liberty from European masters. Generally speaking, on the South American continent, the Creole elite—merchants, landowners, and professional people of Spanish descent—led the movements against Spain and Portugal. Few Native Americans, black people, mestizos, mulattos, or slaves became involved in or benefited from the end of Iberian rule. Indeed, the example of the Haitian slave revolt haunted the Creoles, as did the revolts of Indians in the Andes in 1780 and 1781. The Creoles were determined that any drive for political independence from Spain and Portugal should not cause social disruption or the loss of their own privileges. In this respect, the Creole revolutionaries were not unlike American revolutionaries in the southern colonies, who wanted to reject British rule but keep their slaves, or French revolutionaries, who wanted to depose the king but not to extend liberty to the French working class.

Creole Discontent   Creole discontent with Spanish colonial government had many sources. (The Brazilian situation will be discussed separately. See page 678.) Latin American merchants wanted to trade more freely within the region and with North American and European markets. They wanted commercial regulations that would benefit them rather than Spain. They had also resented increases in taxation by the Spanish crown.

Creoles resented Spanish policies that favored *peninsulares*—white people born in Spain—for political patronage, including appointments in the colonial government, church, and army. The Creoles believed the *peninsulares* secured all the best positions. Seen in this light, the royal patronage system represented another device with which Spain extracted wealth and income from America to benefit its own people in Europe rather than its colonial subjects.

Creole leaders had read the Enlightenment philosophes and regarded their reforms as potentially beneficial to the region. They were also well aware of the events and the political philosophy of the American Revolution. To transform Creole discontent into revolt against the Spanish government required more, however, than reform programs and revolutionary examples. That transforming event occurred in Europe when Napoleon invaded Portugal in 1807 and made his own brother king of Spain in 1808. The Portuguese royal family fled to Brazil and established its government there, but the Bourbon monarchy of Spain had, for the time being, been overthrown. That situation created an imperial political vacuum throughout Spanish Latin America and gave Creole leaders both the opportunity and the necessity to act.

The Creole elite feared a liberal Napoleonic monarchy in Spain would attempt to impose reforms in Latin America that would harm their economic and social interests. They also feared a French-controlled Spain would try to drain the region of the wealth and resources Napoleon needed for his wars. To protect their interests and to seize the opportunity to direct their own political destiny, between 1808 and 1810 Creole *juntas*, or political committees, claimed the right to govern different regions of Latin America. Many of them insincerely declared they were ruling in the name of the deposed Spanish Bourbon monarch Ferdinand VII. After the establishment of these local *juntas*, Spain never effectively reestablished its authority in South America, although it would take ten years or more of politically and economically exhausting warfare before Latin American independence became permanent. The establishment of the *juntas* also ended the privileges of the *peninsulares*, whose welfare had always depended on the favors of the Spanish crown. Creoles now took over positions in the government and army.

San Martín in Río de la Plata   The vast size of Latin America, its geographical barriers, its distinct regional differences, and the absence of an even marginally integrated economy meant there would be several different paths to independence. The first region to assert itself was the Río de la Plata, or modern Argentina. The center of revolt was the city of Buenos Aires, whose citizens, as early as 1806, had fought off a British invasion and thus had learned they could protect themselves rather than have to rely on Spain. In 1810, the *junta* in Buenos Aires not only thrust off Spanish authority, but also sent forces into Paraguay and Uruguay to liberate them from Spain. These armies were defeated, but Spain nevertheless lost control of both areas. Paraguay asserted its own independence. Brazil took over Uruguay.

These early defeats did not discourage the Buenos Aires government, which determined to liberate Peru, the stronghold of royalist power and loyalty on the continent. By 1817, José de San Martín (1778–1850), the leading general of the Río de la Plata forces, led an army in a daring march over the Andes Mountains and occupied Santiago in Chile, where the Chilean independence leader Bernardo O'Higgins (1778–1842) was established as the supreme dictator. From Santiago, San Martín organized a fleet that, in 1820, carried his army by sea to Peru. The next year, San Martín drove royalist forces from Lima and became Protector of Peru.

Simon Bolívar's Liberation of Venezuela   While the army of San Martín had been liberating the southern portion of the continent, Simón Bolívar (1783–1830) had been pursuing a similar task in the north. Bolívar had been involved in the organization of a liberating *junta* in Caracas, Venezuela, in 1810. He was a firm advocate of both independence and a republic. Between 1811 and 1814, civil war broke out throughout Venezuela as both royalists, on one hand, and slaves and *llaneros* (Venezuelan cowboys), on the other, challenged the authority of the republican government. Bolívar had to go into exile first in Colombia and then in Jamaica. In 1816, with help from Haiti, he returned to the continent. He first captured Bogotá, capital of New Granada (including modern Colombia, Bolivia, and Ecuador), to secure a base for an attack on Venezuela. The tactic worked. By the summer of 1821, Bolívar's forces captured Caracas, and he was named president.

A year later, in July 1822, the armies of Bolívar and San Martín joined as they moved to liberate Quito, the capital of what is today Ecuador. At a famous meeting in Guayaquil, the two liberators sharply disagreed about the future political structure of Latin America. San Martín believed the peoples of the region required monarchies; Bolívar maintained his republicanism. Not long after the meeting, San Martín quietly retired from public life and went into exile in Europe. Meanwhile, Bolívar deliberately allowed the political situation in Peru to fall into confusion, and in 1823, he sent in troops to establish his control. On December 9, 1824, at the Battle of Ayacucho, the liberating army crushed the main Spanish royalist forces. This battle marked the end of Spain's effort to retain its South American empire.

Simón Bolívar. Bolívar was the liberator of much of Latin America. He inclined toward a policy of political liberalism.   © Christie's Images/CORBIS

INDEPENDENCE IN NEW SPAIN

The drive for independence in New Spain, which included present-day Mexico as well as Texas, California, and the rest of the southwest United States, illustrates better than in any other region the socially conservative outcome of the Latin American colonial revolutions. As elsewhere, a local governing *junta* was organized in 1808. Before it had undertaken any significant measures, however, a Creole priest, Miguel Hidalgo y Costilla (1753–1811) in 1810, issued a call for rebellion to the Indians in his parish. They and other repressed groups of black and mestizo urban and rural workers responded. Father Hidalgo set forth a program of social reform, including hints of changes in landholding. Soon he stood at the head of a loosely organized group of 80,000 followers, who captured several major cities and then marched on Mexico City. Hidalgo's forces and the royalist army that opposed them committed many atrocities. In July 1811, the revolutionary priest was captured and executed. Leadership of his movement then fell to José María Morelos y Pavón (1765–1815), a mestizo priest. Far more radical than Hidalgo, he called for an end to forced labor and for substantial land reforms. He was executed in 1815, ending five years of popular uprising.

The uprising and its demand for fundamental social reforms united all conservative political groups in Mexico, both Creole and Spanish. These groups opposed any kind of reform that might diminish their privileges. In 1820, however, an unexpected challenge arose to their recently achieved security. As already discussed, the revolution in Spain had forced Ferdinand VII to accept a liberal constitution. Conservative Mexicans feared the new liberal monarchy would attempt to impose liberal reforms on Mexico. Therefore, for the most conservative of reasons, they rallied behind a former royalist general, Augustín de Iturbide (1783–1824), who declared Mexico independent of Spain in 1821. Shortly thereafter, Iturbide was declared emperor. His own regime did not last long, but he had created an independent Mexico, governed by groups determined to resist significant social reform.

BRAZILIAN INDEPENDENCE

Brazilian independence, in contrast to that of Spanish Latin America, came relatively simply and peacefully. As already noted, the Portuguese royal family, along with several thousand government officials and members of the court, fled to Brazil in 1807. Their arrival immediately transformed Rio de Janeiro into a royal city. The prince regent João addressed many of the local complaints, equivalent to those of the Spanish Creoles, by, for example, taking measures that expanded trade. In 1815, he made Brazil a kingdom, which meant it was no longer to be regarded merely as a colony of Portugal. This change was in many respects long overdue, since Brazil was far larger and more prosperous than Portugal itself. Then, in 1820, a revolution occurred in Portugal, and its leaders demanded João's return to Lisbon. They also demanded the return of Brazil to colonial status. João, who had become King João VI in 1816 (r. 1816–1826), returned to Portugal, but left his son Dom Pedro as regent in Brazil and encouraged him to be sympathetic to the political aspirations of the Brazilians. In September 1822, Dom Pedro embraced the cause of Brazilian independence against the recolonizing efforts of Portugal. By the end of the year, he had become emperor of an independent Brazil, which remained a monarchy under his son and successor Dom Pedro II (r. 1831–1889) until 1889. Thus, in contrast to virtually all other nations of Latin America, Brazil achieved independence in a way that left no real dispute as to where the center of political authority lay.

Two other factors aided the peaceful transition to independence in Brazil. First, the political and social elite of Brazil wanted to avoid the destruction that the wars of independence had unleashed in the Spanish American Empire. Second, these leaders had every intention of preserving slavery. The wars of independence elsewhere had generally led to the abolition of slavery or moved the new states closer to abolishing it. Warfare in Brazil might have caused social turmoil with similar consequences.

THE CONSERVATIVE ORDER SHAKEN IN EUROPE

During the first half of the 1820s, the restored conservative order had, in general, successfully resisted the forces of liberalism. The two exceptions to this success, the Greek Revolution and the Latin American wars of independence, both occurred on the periphery of the European world. Beginning in the mid-1820s, however, the conservative govern-

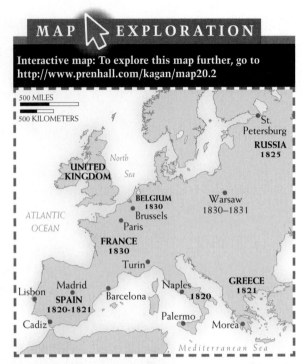

MAP EXPLORATION

Interactive map: To explore this map further, go to http://www.prenhall.com/kagan/map20.2

Map 20–2 **CENTERS OF REVOLUTION, 1820–1831**   The conservative order imposed by the great powers in post-Napoleonic Europe was challenged by various uprisings and revolutions, beginning in 1820–1821 in Spain, Naples, and Greece and spreading to Russia, Poland, France, and Belgium later in the decade.

ments of Russia, France, and Great Britain faced new political discontent. (See Map 20–2.) In Russia the result was suppression, in France revolution, and in Britain, accommodation. Belgium emerged as a newly indepent state.

RUSSIA: THE DECEMBRIST REVOLT OF 1825

Tsar Alexander I had come to the throne in 1801 after a palace coup against his father, Tsar Paul (r. 1796–1801). After flirting with Enlightenment ideas, Alexander turned permanently away from reform. Both at home and abroad, he took the lead in suppressing liberalism and nationalism. There would be no significant challenge to tsarist autocracy until his death.

Unrest in the Army   As Russian forces drove Napoleon's army across Europe and then occupied defeated France, many Russian officers were exposed to the ideas of the French Revolution and the Enlightenment. Some of them, realizing how economically backward and politically stifled their own nation remained, developed reformist sympathies. Unable to express themselves openly because of Alexander's repressive policies, they

When the Moscow regiment refused to swear allegiance to Nicholas, he ordered the cavalry and artillery to attack them. Although a total failure, the Decembrist Revolt came to symbolize the yearnings of all Russian liberals in the nineteenth century for a constitutional government.   "The Insurrection of the Decembrists at Senate Square, St. Petersburg on 14th December, 1825" (w/c on paper) by Russian School (19th century). Private Collection/Archives Charmet/Bridgeman Art Library

formed secret societies. One of these, the Southern Society, led by an officer named Pestel, advocated representative government and the abolition of serfdom. Pestel himself even favored limited independence for Poland and democracy. Another secret society, the Northern Society, was more moderate. It favored constitutional monarchy and the abolition of serfdom, but wanted to protect the interests of the aristocracy. Both societies were small and often in conflict with each other. They agreed only that Russia's government must change. Sometime during 1825, they apparently decided to carry out a *coup d'état* in 1826.

Dynastic Crisis In late November 1825, Tsar Alexander I died unexpectedly. His death created two crises. The first was dynastic. Alexander had no direct heir. His brother Constantine (1779–1831), the next in line to the throne and at the time the commander of Russian forces in occupied Poland, had married a woman who was not of royal blood. He had thus excluded himself from the throne and was more than willing to renounce any

claim to it. Through a series of secret instructions made public only after his death, Alexander had named his younger brother, Nicholas (r. 1825–1855), as the new tsar.

Once Alexander was dead, the legality of these instructions became uncertain. Constantine acknowledged Nicholas as tsar, and Nicholas acknowledged Constantine. This family muddle continued for about three weeks, during which, to the astonishment of all Europe, Russia actually had no ruler. Then, in early December, the army command told Nicholas about a conspiracy among certain officers. Able to wait no longer, Nicholas had himself declared tsar, much to the delight of the by-now-exasperated Constantine.

The second crisis then unfolded. Junior officers had indeed plotted to rally the troops under their command to the cause of reform. On December 26, 1825, the army was to take the oath of allegiance to Nicholas, who was less popular than Constantine and regarded as more conservative. Most regiments took the oath, but the Moscow regiment, whose chief officers, surprisingly, were not secret society members, marched into the Senate Square in Saint Petersburg and refused to swear allegiance. Instead, they called for a constitution and Constantine as tsar. Attempts to settle the situation peacefully failed. Late in the afternoon, Nicholas ordered the cavalry and the artillery to attack the insurgents. More than sixty people were killed. Early in 1826, Nicholas himself presided over the commission that investigated the Decembrist Revolt and the secret army societies. Five of the plotters were executed, and more than a hundred others were exiled to Siberia.

Although the Decembrist Revolt failed completely, it was the first rebellion in modern Russian history whose instigators had had specific political goals. They wanted a constitutional government and the abolition of serfdom. As the century passed, the political martyrdom of the Decembrists came to symbolize the yearnings of the never numerous Russian liberals.

The Autocracy of Nicholas I Although Nicholas was neither an ignorant nor a bigoted reactionary, he came to symbolize the most extreme form of nineteenth-century autocracy. He knew economic growth and social improvement in Russia required reform, but he was afraid of change. In 1842, he told his State Council, "There is no doubt that serfdom, in its present form, is a flagrant evil which everyone realizes, yet to attempt to remedy it now would be, of course, an evil more disastrous."[4] To remove serfdom would necessarily, in his view, have undermined the nobles' support of the tsar. So Nicholas turned his back on this and practically all other reforms. Literary and political censorship and a widespread system of surveillance by secret police flourished throughout his reign. There was little attempt to forge even an efficient and honest administration. Nicholas' only significant reform was a codification of Russian law, published in 1833.

Official Nationality In place of reform, Nicholas and his closest advisers embraced a program called Official Nationality. Presiding over this program was Count S. S. Uvarov, minister of education from 1833 to 1849. Its slogan, published repeatedly in government documents, newspapers, journals, and schoolbooks, was "Orthodoxy, Autocracy, and Nationalism." The Russian Orthodox church was to provide the basis for morality, education, and intellectual life. The church, which, since the days of Peter the Great, had been an arm of the secular government, controlled the schools and universi-

ties. Young Russians were taught to accept their place in life and to spurn social mobility.

Autocracy meant the unrestrained power of the tsar as the only authority that could hold the vast expanse of Russia and its peoples together. Political writers stressed that only under the autocracy of Peter the Great, Catherine the Great, and Alexander I had Russia prospered and exerted a major influence on world affairs.

Through the glorification of Russian nationality, Russians were urged to see their religion, language, and customs as a source of perennial wisdom that separated them from the moral corruption and political turmoil of the West. This program alienated serious Russian intellectuals from the tsarist government.

Revolt and Repression in Poland Nicholas I was also extremely conservative in foreign affairs, as became apparent in Poland in the 1830s. Most of Poland, which had been partitioned in the late eighteenth century and ceased to exist as an independent state, remained under Russian domination after the Congress of Vienna, but was granted a constitutional government with a parliament, called the diet, that had limited powers. Under this arrangement, the tsar also reigned as king of Poland. Both Alexander and Nicholas delegated their brother, the Grand Duke Constantine, to run Poland's government. Although both tsars frequently infringed on the constitution and quarreled with the Polish diet, this arrangement held through the 1820s. Nevertheless, Polish nationalists continued to agitate for change.

In late November 1830, after news of the French and Belgian revolutions of that summer had reached Poland, a small insurrection of soldiers and students broke out in Warsaw. Disturbances soon spread throughout the country. On December 18, the Polish diet declared the revolution a nationalist movement. Early the next month, the diet deposed Nicholas as king of Poland. The tsar sent troops into the country and suppressed the revolt. In February 1832, Nicholas issued the Organic Statute, declaring Poland to be an integral part of the Russian Empire. Although this statute guaranteed certain Polish liberties, in practice, the Russian government systematically ignored them. The Polish uprising had confirmed the tsar's worst fears. Henceforth Russia and Nicholas became the gendarme of Europe, ever ready to provide troops to suppress liberal and nationalist movements.

REVOLUTION IN FRANCE (1830)

The Polish revolt was the most distant of several disturbances that flowed from the overthrow of the Bourbon dynasty in France during July

---

[4]Quoted in Michael T. Florinsky, *Russia: A History and an Interpretation*, Vol. 2 (New York: Macmillan, 1953), p. 755.

1830. When Louis XVIII had died in 1824, his brother, the count of Artois, the leader of the ultraroyalist faction, succeeded him as Charles X (r. 1824–1830). The new king was a firm believer in rule by divine right.

The Reactionary Policies of Charles X   Charles X's first action was to have the Chamber of Deputies in 1824 and 1825 indemnify aristocrats who had lost their lands in the revolution. He did this by lowering the interest rates on government bonds to create a fund to pay an annual sum to the survivors of the *émigrés* who had forfeited land. Middle-class bondholders, who lost income, resented this measure. Charles also restored the rule of primogeniture, whereby only the eldest son of an aristocrat inherited the family domains. To support the Roman Catholic Church, he enacted a law that punished sacrilege with imprisonment or death. Liberals disapproved of all of these measures.

In the elections of 1827, the liberals gained enough seats in the Chamber of Deputies to compel the king to compromise. He appointed a less conservative ministry. Laws against the press were eased as was government dominance of education. Liberals, however, wanted a genuinely constitutional regime and remained unsatisfied. In 1829, the king replaced his moderate ministry with an ultraroyalist cabinet headed by the Prince de Polignac (1780–1847). The opposition, in desperation, opened negotiations with the liberal Orléans branch of the royal family.

The July Revolution   In 1830, Charles X called for new elections, in which the liberals scored a stunning victory. Instead of accepting the new Chamber of Deputies, the king and his ministers decided to attempt a royalist seizure of power. In June and July 1830, Polignac sent a naval expedition against Algiers, which was nominally under Ottoman rule but had in fact become a pirate state whose ships preyed on the merchant vessels of all nations. News of the capture of Algiers and the founding of a French Empire in North Africa reached Paris on July 9. Taking advantage of the euphoria this victory created, Charles issued the Four Ordinances on July 25, 1830, staging what amounted to a royal *coup d'état*. These ordinances restricted freedom of the press, dissolved the recently elected Chamber of Deputies, limited the franchise to the wealthiest people in the country, and called for new elections.

The Four Ordinances provoked swift and decisive popular reaction. Liberal newspapers called on the nation to reject the monarch's actions. The workers of Paris, burdened since 1827 by an economic downturn, erected barricades in the streets. The king called out troops, and although more than 1,800 people died during the ensuing battles, the army was not able to gain control of Paris.

On July 5, 1830 French forces captured Algiers, which France would continue to rule until 1962. Note how this drawing contrasts the power and modernity of the French conquerors with the almost medieval appearance of the Algerian defenses.   Roger Viollet/Getty Images, Inc.–Liaison

On August 2, Charles X abdicated and went into exile in England. The Chamber of Deputies named a new ministry composed of constitutional monarchists. In an act that finally ended the rule of the Bourbon dynasty, it also proclaimed Louis Philippe (r. 1830–1848), the duke d'Orléans, the new king instead of the Count de Chambord, the infant grandson of Charles X in whose favor Charles had abdicated.

In the Revolution of 1830, the liberals of the Chamber of Deputies had filled a power vacuum the Paris uprising and the failure of effective royal action had created. Had Charles X provided himself with sufficient troops in Paris, the outcome could have been different. Moreover, had the liberals, who favored a constitutional monarchy, not acted quickly, the workers and shopkeepers of Paris might have attempted to form a republic. By seizing the moment, the middle class, the bureaucrats, and the moderate aristocratic liberals overthrew the restoration monarchy and still avoided a republic. These liberals feared a new popular revolution such as the one that had swept France in 1792. They had no desire for another *sans-culotte* republic. A fundamental political and social tension thus underlay the new monarchy. The revolution had succeeded thanks to a temporary alliance between hard-pressed laborers and the prosperous middle class, but these two groups soon realized that their basic goals were different.

Monarchy under Louis Philippe Politically, the July Monarchy, as the new regime was called, was more liberal than the restoration government. Louis Philippe was called the "king of the French" rather than "king of France." The tricolor flag of the revolution replaced the white flag of the Bourbons. The new constitution was regarded as a right of the people rather than as a concession of the monarch. Catholicism became the religion of a majority of the people rather than "the official religion." The new government was strongly anticlerical. Censorship was abolished. The franchise became wider, but remained restricted. The king had to cooperate with the Chamber of Deputies; he could not dispense with laws on his own authority.

Socially, however, the Revolution of 1830 proved conservative. The hereditary peerage was abolished in 1831, but the everyday economic, political, and social influence of the landed oligarchy continued. Money was the path to power and influence in the government. There was much corruption.

Most importantly, the liberal monarchy displayed little or no sympathy for the lower and working classes. In 1830, the workers of Paris had called for the protection of jobs, better wages, and the preservation of the traditional crafts, rather than for the usual goals of political liberalism. The government of Louis Philippe ignored their demands and their plight. The laboring classes of Paris and the provincial cities seemed just one more possible source of disorder. In late 1831, troops suppressed a workers' revolt in Lyons. In July 1832, an uprising occurred in Paris during the funeral of a popular Napoleonic general. Again the government called out troops, and more than eight hundred people were killed or wounded. In 1834, a large strike by silk workers in Lyons was crushed. Such discontent might be smothered for a time, but unless the government addressed the social and economic conditions that created it, new turmoil would eventually erupt.

The new French government of 1830 was only too happy to retain the control of the city of Algiers that Charles X had achieved less than a month before his overthrow. The occupation of Algeria gave French merchants in Marseilles new economic ties to North Africa. Moreover, the French quickly dismantled the structures of the Ottoman government that had survived in Algeria and set out to conquer and administer the interior of the country, which was larger than France itself and where Ottoman rule had never penetrated. By the 1850s, the French had extended their rule, after constant warfare against Muslim tribesmen, as far as the northern Sahara desert. France now had a vast new empire, and French citizens and other Europeans also began to settle in Algeria in large numbers, especially in the cities. In the second half of the nineteenth century, the French government came to regard Algeria, despite its overwhelmingly Muslim population, as not a colony but an integral part of France itself. This was to have serious repercussions after World War II when a pro-independence movement developed among Muslim Algerians.

BELGIUM BECOMES INDEPENDENT (1830)

The July Revolution in Paris sent sparks to other political tinder on the Continent. The revolutionary fires first flared in neighboring Belgium. The former Austrian Netherlands, Belgium had been merged with the kingdom of Holland in 1815. The two countries differed in language, religion, and economy, however, and the Belgian upper classes never reconciled themselves to Dutch rule.

On August 25, 1830, disturbances broke out in Brussels after the performance of an opera about a rebellion in Naples against Spanish rule. To end the rioting, the municipal authorities and people from the propertied classes formed a provisional national government. When compromise between the Belgians and the Dutch failed, King William I of Holland (r. 1815–1840) sent troops and ships against Belgium. By November 10, 1830, the Dutch had been defeated. A national congress then wrote a liberal Belgian constitution, which was issued in 1831.

Although the major powers saw the revolution in Belgium as upsetting the boundaries the Congress of Vienna had established, they were not inclined to intervene to reverse it. Russia was preoccupied with the Polish revolt. Prussia and the other German states were suppressing small uprisings in their own domains. The Austrians were busy putting down disturbances in Italy. France under Louis Philippe hoped to dominate an independent Belgium. Britain could tolerate a liberal Belgium, as long as it was free of foreign domination.

In December 1830, Lord Palmerston (1784–1865), the British foreign minister, persuaded representatives of the powers in London to recognize Belgium as an independent and neutral state. In July 1831, Prince Leopold of Saxe-Coburg (r. 1831–1865), who had connections to the British royal family and married the daughter of Louis Philippe, became king of the Belgians. The Convention of 1839 guaranteed Belgian neutrality, which remained an article of faith in European international relations for almost a century.

Both Belgium and Serbia gained independence in 1830, and ironically, diplomatic crises involving both nations led to World War I. The assassination of an Austrian archduke by a Serbian nationalist in Sarajevo in 1914 triggered the war, and Germany's violation of Belgian neutrality brought Britain into it.

THE GREAT REFORM BILL IN BRITAIN (1832)

In Great Britain, the revolutionary year of 1830 saw the election of a House of Commons that debated the first major bill to reform Parliament. The death of George IV (r. 1820–1830) and the accession of William IV (r. 1830–1837) required the calling of a parliamentary election, held in the summer of 1830. Historians once believed the July revolution in France influenced voting in Britain, but close analysis of the time and character of individual county and borough elections has shown otherwise. The passage of the Great Reform Bill, which became law in 1832, was the result of a series of events different from those that occurred on the Continent. In Britain, the forces of conservatism and reform accommodated each other.

Political and Economic Reform   Several factors contributed to this spirit of compromise. First, the commercial and industrial class was larger in Britain than in other countries. No government, could ignore their economic interests without damaging British prosperity. Second, Britain's liberal Whig aristocrats, who regarded themselves as the protectors of constitutional liberty, had a long tradition of favoring moderate reforms that would make revolutionary changes unnecessary. Early Whig sympathy for the French Revolution reduced their influence. After 1815, however, they reentered the political arena. Finally, British law, tradition, and public opinion all showed a strong respect for civil liberties.

In 1820, the year after the passage of the notorious Six Acts, Lord Liverpool shrewdly reshaped his cabinet. Although they were conservatives, the new members of the government also believed it had to accommodate itself to the changing social and economic life of the nation. They favored greater economic freedom and repealed the Combination Acts that had prohibited labor organizations.

Catholic Emancipation Act   English determination to maintain the union with Ireland brought about another key reform. England's relationship to Ireland was similar to that of Russia to Poland or Austria to its several national groups. In 1800, fearful that Irish nationalists might again rebel as they had in 1798 and perhaps turn Ireland into a base for a French invasion, William Pitt the Younger had persuaded Parliament to pass the Act of Union between Ireland and England. Ireland now sent a hundred members to the House of Commons. Only Protestant Irishmen, however, could be elected to represent their overwhelmingly Roman Catholic nation.

During the 1820s, under the leadership of Daniel O'Connell (1775–1847), Irish nationalists organized the Catholic Association to agitate for Catholic emancipation. In 1828, O'Connell secured his own election to Parliament, where he could not legally take his seat. The duke of Wellington, who was now prime minister, realized that henceforth Ireland might elect an overwhelmingly Catholic delegation. If they were not seated, civil war might erupt across the Irish Sea. Consequently, in 1829, Wellington and Robert Peel steered the Catholic Emancipation Act through Parliament. Roman Catholics could now become members of Parliament. This measure, together with the repeal in 1828 of restrictions against Protestant nonconformists, ended the Anglican monopoly on British political life.

Catholic emancipation was a liberal measure passed for the conservative purpose of preserving order in Ireland. It included a provision raising the property qualification to vote in Ireland, so that only the wealthier Irish could vote. Nonetheless, this measure alienated many of Wellington's Anglican Tory supporters in the House of Commons. The election of 1830 returned many supporters of parliamentary reform to Parliament. Even some Tories supported reform, because they thought only a corrupt House of Commons could have passed Catholic emancipation. The Tories, consequently, were badly divided, and the Wellington ministry soon fell. King William IV then turned to the leader of the Whigs, Earl Grey (1764–1845), to form a government.

Legislating Change   The Whig ministry presented the House of Commons with a major reform bill that had two broad goals. The first was to replace "rotten boroughs," or boroughs that had few voters, with representatives for the previously unrepresented manufacturing districts and cities. Second, the number of voters in England and Wales was to be increased by about 50 percent

EVENTS ASSOCIATED WITH LIBERAL REFORM AND REVOLUTION

1824	Charles X becomes king of France
1825	Decembrist Revolt in Russia
1828	Repeal of restrictions against British Protestant nonconformists
1829	Catholic Emancipation Act passed in Great Britain; Ottoman Sultan grants independence to Serbia
1830 (July 9)	News of French colonial conquest in Algeria reaches Paris
1830 (July 25)	Charles X issues the Four Ordinances
1830 (August 2)	Charles X abdicates; Louis Philippe proclaimed king
1830 (August 25)	Belgian revolution
1830 (November 29)	Polish revolution
1832	Organic Statute makes Poland an integral part of Russian Empire
1832	Great Reform Bill passed in Great Britain

Beginning in the 1820s Daniel O'Connell revolutionized the organization of Irish politics. He created grass roots organization and collected funds to finance Irish nationalist activities. He was also known as one of the great public speakers of his generation. Here he is portrayed addressing a political gathering in County Meath, Ireland.   Getty Images Inc.—Hulton Archive Photos

through a series of new franchises. In 1831, the House of Commons narrowly defeated the bill. Grey called for a new election and won a majority in favor of the bill. The House of Commons passed the reform bill, but the House of Lords rejected it. Mass meetings were held throughout the country. Riots broke out in several cities. Finally, William IV agreed to create enough new peers to give a third reform bill a majority in the House of Lords. Under this pressure, the measure became law in 1832.

The **Great Reform Bill** expanded the size of the English electorate, but it was not a democratic measure. It increased the number of voters by more than 200,000, or almost 50 percent, but it kept a property qualification for the franchise. (Gender was also a qualification. No thought was given to enfranchising women.) Some members of the working class actually lost the right to vote because certain old franchise rights were abolished. New urban boroughs were created to allow the growing cities to have a voice in the House of Commons. Yet the passage of the reform act did not, as was once thought, constitute the triumph of middle-class interests in England: For every new

THOMAS BABINGTON MACAULAY DEFENDS THE GREAT REFORM BILL

Macaulay (1800–1859) was a member of the House of Commons, which passed the Great Reform Bill in 1831, only to have the House of Lords reject it before another measure was enacted in 1832. His speeches in support of the bill reflect his views on the need for Parliament to give balanced representation to major elements in the population without embracing democracy. His arguments had wide appeal.

■ *Who does Macaulay think should be represented in Parliament? Why does he oppose universal suffrage? Why does he regard the Reform Bill as "a measure of conservation"? Why would Metternich have seen little or nothing conservative about the measure?*

[T]he principle of the ministers] is plain, rational, and consistent. It is this—to admit the middle class to a large and direct share in the Representation, without any violent shock to the institutions of our country. . . . I hold it to be clearly expedient, that in a country like this, the right of suffrage should depend on a pecuniary qualification. Every argument . . . which would induce me to oppose Universal Suffrage, induces me to support the measure which is now before us. I oppose Universal Suffrage, because I think that it would produce a destructive revolution. I support this measure, because I am sure that it is our best security against a revolution. . . . I . . . do entertain great apprehension for the fate of my country. I do in my conscience believe, that unless this measure, or some similar measure, be speedily adopted, great and terrible calamities will befall us. Entertaining this opinion, I think myself bound to state it, not as a threat, but as a reason. I support this measure as a means of Reform: But I support it still more as a measure of conservation. That we may exclude those whom it is necessary to exclude, we must admit those whom it may be safe to admit. . . . All history is full of revolutions, produced by causes similar to those which are now operating in England. A portion of the community which had been of no account, expands and becomes strong. It demands a place in the system, suited, not to its former weakness, but to its present power. If this is granted, all is well. If this is refused, then comes the struggle between the young energy of one class, and the ancient privileges of another . . . . Such . . . is the struggle which the middle classes in England are maintaining against an aristocracy of mere locality.

From *Hansard's Parliamentary Debates*, 3rd series, Vol. 2, pp. 1191–1197.

urban electoral district, a new rural district was also drawn, and the aristocracy was expected to dominate rural elections. What the bill permitted was a wider variety of property to be represented in the House of Commons. (See "Thomas Babington Macaulay Defends the Great Reform Bill".)

The success of the reform bill reconciled previously unrepresented property owners and economic interests to the political institutions of the country. The act laid the groundwork for further orderly reforms of the church, municipal government, and commercial policy. By admitting into the political forum people who sought change and giving them access to the legislative process, it made revolution in Britain unnecessary. Great Britain thus maintained its traditional institutions of government while allowing an increasingly diverse group of people to influence them.

IN PERSPECTIVE

Through the Congress System, the major powers had responded to pressures on the Vienna Settlement without going to war against each other or allowing any state or group of states to annex territory. In the fifteen years between the conclusion of the Congress of Vienna and the Revolution of 1830 in France, no revolutionary disturbance had succeeded in Europe except for the Greek revolt that broke out in 1821. In Russia, the Decembrist Revolt of 1825 failed almost before it had begun. The only truly successful revolutionary activity during these years occurred in Latin America, where wars of independence ended Spain's and Portugal's centuries-old colonial domination.

Nonetheless, during the 1820s, liberal political ideas and some liberal political figures began to make inroads into the otherwise conservative domestic order. In 1830, revolution and reform again began to move across Europe. The French replaced the Bourbons with a more liberal monarchy. Belgium also achieved independence under a liberal government. Perhaps most importantly, Britain moved slowly toward a more liberal position. During the 1820s, Britain had become unenthusiastic about a political role that placed it in opposition to all change. For its own commercial reasons, it favored independence for Latin America. Popular pressures at home led the British aristocratic leadership to enact a moderate reform bill in 1832. Thereafter, Britain would be viewed as the leading liberal state in Europe and one that would support nationalistic causes.

REVIEW QUESTIONS

1. What is nationalism? What were the goals of nationalists? What difficulties did nationalists confront in realizing those goals? Why was nationalism a special threat to the Austrian Empire? What areas saw significant nationalist movements between 1815 and 1830? Which were successful and which unsuccessful?

2. What were the tenets of liberalism? Who were the liberals, and how did liberalism affect the political developments of the early nineteenth century? What is the relationship of liberalism to nationalism?

3. What difficulties did the conservatives in Austria, Prussia, and Russia face after the Napoleonic wars? How did they attempt to solve those difficulties at home and in international affairs? What were the aims of the Concert of Europe? How did the Congress of Vienna change international relations?

4. What were the main reasons for Creole discontent with Spanish rule, and to what extent did Enlightenment political philosophy influence the Creole leaders? Who were some of the primary leaders of Latin American independence?

Why was Brazil's path to independence different from that of Spanish America?

5. What were the main provisions of the constitution of the restored monarchy in France? What did Charles X hope to accomplish? Why did revolution break out in France in 1830? What did this revolution achieve and what problems did it fail to resolve?

6. Why did Britain avoid a revolution in the early 1830s? What was the purpose of the Great Reform Bill? What did it achieve? Would you call it a "revolutionary" document?

7. By approximately 1830, how had European political ambitions and the ideas of liberalism and nationalism begun to undermine the Ottoman Empire? Which Ottoman territories were lost by that date?

SUGGESTED READINGS

B. ANDERSON, *Imagined Communities*, rev. ed. (1991). An influential and controversial discussion of nationalism.

M. BERDAHL, *The Politics of the Prussian Nobility: The Development of a Conservative Ideology, 1770–1848* (1988). A major examination of German conservative outlooks.

A. BRIGGS, *The Making of Modern England* (1959). Classic survey of English history during the first half of the nineteenth century.

A. CRAITU, *Liberalism under Siege: The Political Thought of the French Doctrinaires* (2003). An outstanding study of early nineteenth-century French liberalism.

M. F. CROSS AND D. WILLIAMS, (EDS.), *French Experience from Republic to Monarchy, 1792–1824: New Dawns in Politics, Knowledge and Culture* (2000). Essays on French culture from the revolution through the restoration.

D. DAKIN, *The Struggle for Greek Independence* (1973). An excellent explanation of the Greek independence question.

L. DUBOIS, *Avengers of the New World: The Story of the Haitian Revolution* (2004). An analytic narrative likely to replace others.

E. J. EVANS, *Britain Before the Reform Act: Politics and Society, 1815–1832* (1995). Explores the forces that resisted and pressed for reform.

W. FORTESCUE, *Revolution and Counter-Revolution in France, 1815–1852* (2002). A helpful brief survey.

E. GELLNER, *Nations and Nationalism* (1983). A major theoretical work.

L. GREENFELD, *Nationalism: Five Roads to Modernity* (1992). A major comparative study.

R. HARVEY, *Liberators: Latin America's Struggle for Independence* (2002). An excellent, lively treatment.

E. J. HOBSBAWM, *Nations and Nationalism since 1780: Programme, Myth, Reality*, rev. ed. (1992). Emphasizes intellectual factors.

C. JELAVICH AND B. JELAVICH, *The Establishment of the Balkan National States, 1804–1920* (1977). A standard, clear introduction.

M. B. LEVINGER, *Enlightened Nationalism: The Transformation of Prussian Political Culture, 1806–1848* (2002). A major work based on the most recent scholarship.

C. A. MACARTNEY, *The Habsburg Empire, 1790–1918* (1971). Remains an important survey.

P. MANENT, *An Intellectual History of Liberalism* (1994). A penetrating, succinct study.

P. PILBEAM, *The 1830 Revolution in France* (1991). Emphasizes the Restoration's accommodation to various interest groups.

N. V. RIASANOVSKY, *Nicholas I and Official Nationality in Russia, 1825–1855* (1959). Remains a lucid discussion of the conservative ideology that made Russia the major opponent of liberalism.

J. SHEEHAN, *German History, 1770–1866* (1989). A long work that is now the best available survey of the subject.

A. B. ULAM, *Russia's Failed Revolutionaries* (1981). Contains a useful discussion of the Decembrists as a background for other nineteenth-century Russian revolutionary activity.

DOCUMENTS CD-ROM

Reaction, Reform, and Revolt

21.1 "Sentiments of a Nation": A Mexican Call for Independence
21.2 Thomas MacAulay: *A Radical War-Song*
21.3 Alexis de Tocqueville: *The New Social Morality*
21.4 Simon Bolívar's Political Ideas

21

ECONOMIC ADVANCE AND SOCIAL UNREST (1830–1850)

- **TOWARD AN INDUSTRIAL SOCIETY**
  Population and Migration
  Railways

- **THE LABOR FORCE**
  The Emergence of a Wage-Labor Force • Working-Class Political Action: The Example of British Chartism

- **FAMILY STRUCTURES AND THE INDUSTRIAL REVOLUTION**
  The Family in the Early Factory System

- **WOMEN IN THE EARLY INDUSTRIAL REVOLUTION**
  Opportunities and Exploitation in Employment • Changing Expectations in the Working-Class Marriage

- **PROBLEMS OF CRIME AND ORDER**
  New Police Forces • Prison Reform

- **CLASSICAL ECONOMICS**
  Malthus on Population • Ricardo on Wages • Government Policies Based on Classical Economics

- **EARLY SOCIALISM**
  Utopian Socialism • Anarchism • Marxism

- **1848: YEAR OF REVOLUTIONS**
  France: the Second Republic and Louis Napoleon • The Habsburg Empire: Nationalism Resisted • Italy: Republicanism Defeated • Germany: Liberalism Frustrated

- **IN PERSPECTIVE**

KEY TOPICS

- The development of industrialism and its effects on the organization of labor and the family
- The changing role of women in industrial society
- The establishment of police forces and reform of prisons
- Early developments in European socialism
- The revolutions of 1848

By 1830, Europe was headed toward an industrial society. Only Great Britain had already attained that status, but the pounding of new machinery and the grinding of railway engines soon began to echo across much of the Continent. Yet what characterized the second quarter of the century was not the triumph of industrialism but the final protests of those

In 1848 Ana Ipatescu helped to lead Transylvanian revolutionaries against Russian rule. Transylvania is part of present day Romania. The revolutions of 1848 in Eastern Europe were primarily uprisings of nationalist groups. Although generally repressed in the revolutions of that year, subject nationalities would prove a source of political upheaval and unrest in the region throughout the rest of the century, ultimately providing the spark for the outbreak of World War I.   The Art Archive/Picture Desk, Inc./Kobal Collection

economic groups who opposed it. Intellectually, the period saw the formulation of the major creeds supporting and criticizing the newly emerging society.

These were years of uncertainty for almost everyone. Even the most confident entrepreneurs knew the trade cycle could bankrupt them within weeks. For the industrial workers and the artisans, unemployment became a haunting and recurring problem. For the peasants, the question was sufficiency of food. It was a period of self-conscious transition that culminated in 1848 with a continent-wide outbreak of revolution. People knew one mode of life was passing, but no one knew what would replace it. ■

TOWARD AN INDUSTRIAL SOCIETY

The Industrial Revolution had begun in eighteenth-century Great Britain with the advances in textile production described in Chapter 15. Natural resources, adequate capital, native technological skills, a growing food supply, a social structure that allowed considerable mobility, and strong foreign and domestic demand for goods had given Britain an edge in achieving a vast new capacity for production in manufacturing. British factories and recently invented machines allowed producers to furnish customers with a greater number of consumer products of a higher quality and for lower prices than those of any competitors. Also, the French Revolution and the wars of Napoleon had finally destroyed the French Atlantic trade and thus disrupted continental economic life for two decades. The Latin American wars of independence opened the markets of South America to British goods. In North America, both the United States and Canada demanded British products. Through its control of India, Britain commanded the markets of southern Asia. British banks similarly dominated the international financial markets.

The British textile industry was a vast worldwide economic network. For much of its supply of raw cotton, this industry depended on the labor of American slaves, although Britain itself had been trying to end the slave trade since 1807. In turn, the finished textiles were shipped all over the world along sea-lanes the British navy protected. The wealth that Britain gained through textile production and its other industries of iron making, shipbuilding, china production, and the manufacture of other finished goods was invested all over the world, but especially in the United States and Latin America. This enormous activity provided the economic foundation for British dominance of the world scene throughout the nineteenth century.

Despite their economic lag, the continental nations were beginning to make material progress. By the 1830s, in Belgium, France, and Germany, the number of steam engines in use was growing steadily. Exploitation of the coalfields of the Ruhr and the Saar basins had begun. Coke was replacing charcoal in iron and steel production.

Industrial areas on the Continent were generally less concentrated than in Britain; nor did the Continent have large manufacturing districts, such as the British Midlands. Major pockets of production, such as Lyons, Rouen, and Lille in France and Liege in Belgium, did exist in Western Europe, but most continental manufacturing still took place in the countryside. New machines were integrated into the existing domestic system. The slow pace of continental imitation of the British example meant that, at midcentury, peasants and urban artisans remained more important politically than industrial factory workers.

POPULATION AND MIGRATION

While the process of industrialization spread, the population of Europe continued to grow on the base of the eighteenth-century population explosion. The number of people in France rose from 32.5 million in 1831 to 35.8 million in 1851. During approximately the same period, the population of Germany rose from 26.5 million to 33.5 million and that of Britain from 16.3 million to 20.8 million. More and more of the people of Europe lived in cities. By midcentury, one-half of the population of England and Wales and one-quarter of the population of France and Germany had become town dwellers. Eastern Europe, by contrast, remained overwhelmingly rural, with little industrial manufacturing.

The sheer numbers of human beings put considerable pressure on the physical resources of the cities. Migration from the countryside meant that existing housing, water, sewers, food supplies, and lighting were completely inadequate. Slums with indescribable filth grew, and disease, especially cholera, ravaged the population. Crime increased and became a way of life for those who could make a living in no other manner. Human misery and degradation in many early-nineteenth-century cities seemed to have no bounds.

The situation in the countryside was scarcely better. During the first half of the century, the productive use of the land remained the basic fact of life for most Europeans. The enclosures of the late eighteenth century, the land redistribution of the French Revolution, and the emancipation of serfs in Prussia and later in Austria (1848) and Russia (1861) commercialized landholding. Liberal reformers had hoped the legal revolution in ownership would transform peasants into progressive, industrious farmers. Instead, most peasants became conservative landholders without enough land to make agricultural innovations or, oftentimes, even to support themselves.

It is important to note the differing dates of rural emancipation across Europe. In England, France, and the Low Countries, persons living in the countryside could move freely between country and town. In Germany, eastern Europe, and Russia, such migration was difficult until the serfs were emancipated. Even when emancipation did occur, as throughout Germany early in the century, it did not make migration simple. So from Germany eastward, the pace of industrialization was much slower, in part because of the absence of a fluid market for free labor moving to the cities.

The specter of poor harvests still haunted Europe. The worst such experience of the century

MAP **EXPLORATION**

Interactive map: To explore this map further, go to http://www.prenhall.com/kagan/map21.1

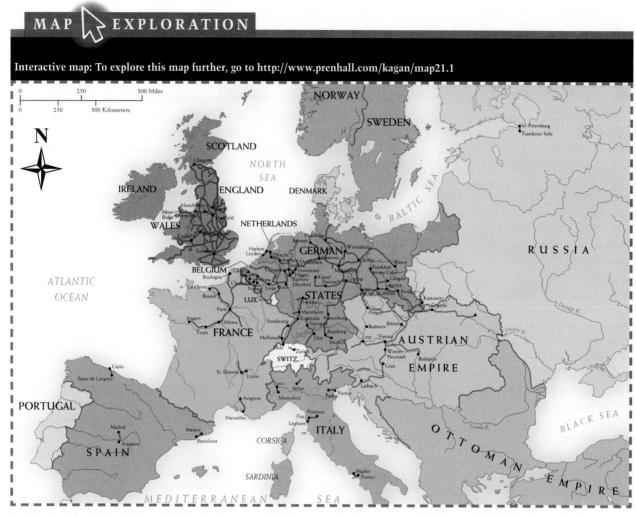

Map 21–1 **EUROPEAN RAILROADS IN 1850** A midcentury Britain had the most extensive rail network, and the most industrialized economy, in Europe, but rail lines were expanding rapidly in France, the German states, and Austria. Southern and eastern Europe had few railways, and the Ottoman Empire had none.

was the Irish famine of 1845 to 1847. Perhaps as many as half a million Irish peasants with no land or small plots simply starved when disease blighted the potato crop. Hundreds of thousands emigrated. (See "Encountering the Past: The Potato and the Great Hunger in Ireland, page 693.) By midcentury, the revolution in landholding led to greater agricultural production. It also resulted in a vast uprooting of people from the countryside into cities and from Europe into the rest of the world. The countryside thus provided many of the workers for the new factories, as well as people with few economic skills who slowly emigrated to cities in hope of finding work.

RAILWAYS

Industrial advance itself had also contributed to this migration. The 1830s and 1840s opened the first great age of railway building. The Stockton and Darlington Line opened in England in 1825. By 1830, another major line had been built between Manchester and Liverpool and had several hundred passengers a day. Belgium had undertaken railway construction by 1835. The first French line opened in 1832, but serious construction came only in the 1840s. Germany entered the railway age in 1835. At midcentury, Britain had 9,797 kilometers of railway, France 2,915, and Germany 5,856. (See Map 21–1.)

The railroads, plus canals and improved regular roads, meant people could leave the place of their birth more easily than ever before. The improvement in transportation also allowed cheaper and more rapid passage of raw materials and finished products.

Railways epitomized the character of the industrial economy during the second quarter of the century. They represented investment in capital goods rather than in consumer goods. Consequently,

George Stephenson (1781–1848) invented the locomotive in 1814, but the "Rocket," his improved design shown here, did not win out over other competitors until 1829. In the following two decades the spread of railways transformed the economy of Western Europe.   Image Works/Mary Evans Picture Library Ltd.

there was a shortage of consumer goods at cheap prices. This favoring of capital over consumer production was one reason the working class was often unable to purchase much for its wages. The railways in and of themselves also brought about still more industrialization. Embodying the most dramatic application of the steam engine, they sharply increased demand for iron and steel and then for a more skilled labor force. The new iron and steel capacity soon permitted the construction of ironclad ships and iron machinery rather than ships and machinery made of wood. These new capital industries led to the formation of vast industrial fortunes that would be invested in still newer enterprises. Industrialism had begun to grow on itself.

THE LABOR FORCE

The composition and experience of the early nineteenth-century labor force was varied. No single description could include all the factory workers, urban artisans, domestic craftspeople, household servants, miners, countryside peddlers, farm workers, or railroad workers. Some of the work force was reasonably well off and enjoyed steady employment and decent wages. Other workers were the "laboring poor," who held jobs, but earned little more than subsistence wages. Then there were those, such as the women and children who worked nearly naked in the mines of Wales, whose conditions of life shocked Europe when a parliamentary report in the 1840s publicized them. Fur-

thermore, the conditions of workers varied from decade to decade and from industry to industry within any particular decade.

Although historians have traditionally emphasized the role and experience of industrial factory workers, only the textile-manufacturing industry became thoroughly mechanized and moved into the factory setting during the first half of the century. Far more of the nonrural, nonagricultural work force consisted of skilled artisans living in cities or small towns. They were attempting to maintain the value of their skills and control over their trades in the face of changing features of production. All these working people faced possible unemployment, with little or no provision for their security. During their lives, they confronted the dissolution of many of the traditional social ties of custom and community.

THE EMERGENCE OF A WAGE-LABOR FORCE

During the nineteenth century, artisans as well as factory workers eventually came to participate in a wage-labor force in which their labor became a commodity of the labor marketplace. This process has often been termed *proletarianization.* In the process of becoming wage laborers, artisans gradually lost both significant ownership of the means of production, such as tools and equipment, and of control over the conduct of their own trades. The process occurred most rapidly wherever the factory system arose displacing previous skilled labor. The factory owner provided the financial capital to construct the factory, to purchase the machinery, and to secure the raw materials. The factory workers contributed their labor for a wage. The process could also occur outside the factory setting if a new invention, such as a mechanical printing press, could do the work of several artisans within an urban or rural workshop setting.

Factory workers also had to submit to various kinds of factory discipline that was virtually always unpopular and difficult to impose. This discipline meant the demands for a smooth operation of the machinery largely determined working conditions. Closing of factory gates to late workers, fines for such lateness, dismissal for drunkenness, and

THE POTATO AND THE GREAT HUNGER IN IRELAND

Any agricultural economy that depends on a single product is in a precarious position. If the people that economy supports also depend on a single source of food, they also stand on the edge of catastrophe—they have nothing to fall back on if their only source of food fails. That kind of catastrophe occurred in Ireland, which was under British rule in the 1840s when the potato crop failed.

So many people starved in the Irish Famine that the workhouses could not shelter them all.   Private Collection/Bridgeman Art Library

During the eighteenth century, almost half of the Irish population came to depend on the potato, which had been brought to Europe from South America in the seventeenth century, as virtually their only food. On less than one acre, an Irish peasant could raise enough potatoes to feed ten other people for a year and pay his rent (few Irish peasants owned their own land).

Before the 1840s, there had been isolated potato failures in parts of Ireland, but never a general failure. Then in l845, a mysterious blight, caused by a fungus, struck potato crops across Ireland. The potato vines withered in the fields, and potatoes in storage became moldy and inedible. Half the crop was lost. The Irish, with modest aid from the British government, survived, but in 1846 the blight reappeared and destroyed the entire crop. The crop of 1847 was better, but the blight came again in 1848.

This series of Irish potato crop failures was the worst natural disaster to strike nineteenth-century Europe. Without potatoes, Irish tenants could not pay their rent. Landlords drove starving tenants off their farms. Disease spread, and tens of thousands died.

In 1846, in response to the Irish famine, the British government repealed the tariffs on imported grain known as the Corn Laws and enacted a program of public works to employ the dispossessed, but the help was inadequate. Most economists and politicians believed government aid caused more harm than good, and the government was reluctant to provide charity. The 1847 Irish Poor Relief Act required anyone who occupied more than one-quarter acre of land to enter a government-run workhouse before receiving poor relief, but the scale of the disaster overwhelmed the workhouses.

To escape the famine, soon known as The Great Hunger, many of the Irish poor emigrated, primarily to the United States and Britain itself. Much of Ireland became depopulated. The census of 1841 counted 8,197,000 people in Ireland; ten years later, death and emigration had cut the population by more than 1.5 million. By 1901, more waves of emigration had reduced it to 4,459,000. The population had still not recovered to prefamine levels at the dawn of the twenty-first century: In 2000, the combined population of the Irish Republic and British-ruled Northern Ireland was only 5,460,000. Alone among the nations of Europe, Ireland has fewer inhabitants today than it did in the nineteenth century.

- *Why was the failure of the potato crop such a disaster for Ireland? How did the famine affect the Irish population?*

R. N. Salaman, *The History and Social Influence of the Potato* (Cambridge: Cambridge University Press, 1985); Cecil Woodham-Smith, *The Great Hunger: Ireland 1845–1849* (New York: Harper & Row, 1962).

public scolding of faulty laborers were attempts to create human discipline that would match the mechanical regularity of the cables, wheels, and pistons. The factory worker had no direct say about the quality of the product or its price.

For all the difficulties of workers in factory conditions, however, their economic situation was often better than that of textile workers who resisted the factory mode of production. In particular, English hand-loom weavers, who continued to work in their homes, experienced decades of declining trade and growing poverty in their failing attempt to compete with power looms.

Urban artisans in the nineteenth century entered the wage-labor force more slowly than factory workers, and machinery had little to do with the process. The emergence of factories in and of itself did not harm urban artisans. Many even prospered from the development. For example, the construction and maintenance of the new machines generated major demand for metalworkers, who consequently did well. The actual erection of factories and the expansion of cities benefited all craftspeople in the building trades, such as carpenters, roofers, joiners, and masons. The lower prices for machine-made textiles aided artisans involved in making clothing, such as tailors and hatters, by reducing the costs of their raw materials. Where the urban artisans encountered difficulty and where they found their skills and livelihood threatened was in the organization of production.

In the eighteenth century, a European town or city workplace had usually consisted of a few artisans laboring for a master. They labored first as apprentices and then as journeymen, according to established guild regulations and practices. The master owned the workshop and the larger equipment, and the apprentices and journeymen owned their tools. The journeyman could expect eventually to become a master. This guild system had allowed workers to exercise a considerable degree of control over labor recruitment and training, the pace of production, the quality of the product, and its price. The guild functioned to protect the integrity of the craft and the prosperity of the craftsmen.

In the nineteenth century, it became increasingly difficult for artisans to exercise corporate or guild direction and control over their trades. The legislation of the French Revolution had outlawed such organizations in France. Across Europe, political and economic liberals disapproved of labor and guild organizations and attempted to ban them. These thinkers believed guilds raised the price of both labor and products to the disadvantage of owners of capital and consumers.

Other destructive forces were also at work. The masters often found themselves under increased competitive pressure from larger, more heavily capitalized establishments or from the introduction of machine production into a previously craft-dominated industry. In many workshops masters began to follow a practice, known in France as *confection*, whereby goods, such as shoes, clothing, and furniture, were produced in standard sizes and styles rather than by special orders for individual customers.

This practice increased the division of labor in the workshop. Each artisan produced a smaller part of the more-or-less uniform final product. Thus, less skill was required of each artisan, and the particular skills a worker possessed became less valuable. To increase production and reduce costs, masters also tried to lower the wages they paid for piecework. Those attempts often led to work stoppages or strikes. Migrants from the countryside or small towns into the cities created, in some cases, a surplus of relatively unskilled workers. They were willing to work for lower wages or under less favorable and protected conditions than traditional artisans. This situation made it much more difficult for urban journeymen ever to hope to become masters in charge of their own workshops. Increasingly, these artisans became lifetime wage laborers whose skills were simply bought and sold in the marketplace.

WORKING-CLASS POLITICAL ACTION: THE EXAMPLE OF BRITISH CHARTISM

By midcentury, such artisans, proud of their skills and frustrated in their social and economic expectations, became the most radical political element in the European working class. From at least the 1830s onward, these artisans took the lead in one country after another in attempting to formulate new ways to protect their social and economic interests.

By the late 1830s, many British workers linked the solution of their economic plight to a program of political reform known as **Chartism**. In 1836, William Lovett (1800–1877) and other London radical artisans formed the London Working Men's Association. In 1838, the group issued the Charter, demanding six specific reforms. The Six Points of the Charter included universal male suffrage, annual election of the House of Commons, the secret ballot, equal electoral districts, and the abolition of property qualifications for and the payment of salaries to members of the House of Commons.

For more than ten years, the Chartists, who were never tightly organized, agitated for their reforms. On three occasions the Charter was presented to Parliament, which refused to pass it. Petitions with millions of signatures were presented to the House of Commons. Strikes were called. The Chartists

In the 1830s and 1840s, the Chartists circulated petitions throughout Britain demanding political reform. Here the petitions are being taken to Parliament in a vast ceremonious procession. Museum of London

published a newspaper, the *Northern Star*. Feargus O'Connor (1794–1855), the most important Chartist leader, made speeches across Britain. Despite this vast activity, Chartism as a national movement failed. Its ranks were split between those who advocated violence and those who wanted to use peaceful tactics. On the local level, however, the Chartists scored several successes and controlled the city councils in Leeds and Sheffield.

As prosperity returned after the depression of the late 1830s and early 1840s, many working people abandoned the movement. Chartists' demonstrations in 1848 fizzled. Nevertheless, Chartism was the first large-scale European working-class political movement. It had specific goals and largely working-class leadership. Eventually, several of the Six Points became law (for example, the secret ballot was enacted in 1872). Continental working-class observers saw in Chartism the kind of mass movement that workers must eventually adopt if they were to improve their situation.

FAMILY STRUCTURES AND THE INDUSTRIAL REVOLUTION

It is more difficult to generalize about the European working-class family structure in the age of early industrialism than under the Old Regime. Industrialism developed at different rates across the Continent, and the impact of industrialism cannot be separated from that of migration and urbanization. Furthermore, industrialism did not touch all families directly; the structures and customs of many peasant families changed little for much of the nineteenth century.

Much more is known about the relationships of the new industry to the family in Great Britain than elsewhere. Many of the British developments foreshadowed those in other countries as the factory system spread.

THE FAMILY IN THE EARLY FACTORY SYSTEM

Contrary to what historians and other observers once believed, the adoption of new machinery and factory production did not destroy the working-class family. Before the late-eighteenth-century revolution in textile production in England, the individual family involved in textiles was the chief unit of production. The earliest textile-related inventions, such as the spinning jenny, did not change that situation. As noted in Chapter 15, the new machine was initially simply brought into the home to spin the thread. It was the mechanization of weaving that led to the major change. The father who became a machine weaver was then employed in a factory. His work was thus separated from his home. Although one should not underestimate the changes and pressures in family life that occurred when the father left for the factory, the structure of early English factories allowed the father to preserve certain of his traditional family roles as they had existed before the factory system.

In the domestic system of the family economy, the father and mother had worked with their children in textile production as a family unit. They had trained and disciplined the children within the home setting. Their home life and their economic life were largely the same. Moreover, in the home setting, the wife who worked as a spinner might have earned as much or even more than her

A CLOSER LOOK

The Great Exhibition in London

The Great Exhibition of 1851 was held in London to celebrate progress in industry and commerce achieved through the new industrial order. Its organizers invited governments and businesses from around the globe to display the products they manufactured. The organizers generally supported free trade and believed the displays would demonstrate the value of peaceful commerce.

Note the construction of the building known as the Crystal Palace. The structural iron symbolized the possibility of using new kinds of building materials. The vast quantities of glass demonstrated that a once scarce luxury good could now be produced in large quantities for everyday consumption. In the past such structures of iron and glass had been used only for small greenhouses to raise plants on aristocratic estates.

The crowds in the picture and the even larger crowds who actually attended the Great Exhibition demonstrated that, after a quarter century of social turmoil and political discontent in Europe, large numbers of people could gather peacefully in public.

London's Crystal Palace during the International Exhibition of 1851. Victoria & Albert Museum, London, Great Britain/Art Resource, NY

The classical statues to the left were present to show that the new consumer goods industrialism made possible were compatible with an ongoing culture of elite art.

husband. Early factory owners and supervisors permitted the father to employ his wife and children as his assistants. Thus, parental training and discipline could be transferred from the home into the early factory. In some cases, in both Britain and France, whole families would move near a new factory so that the family as a unit could work there. Despite those accommodations to family life, family members still had to face the new work discipline of the factory setting. Moreover, women assisting their husbands in the factory often did less skilled work than they had in their homes. (See page 699.)

A major shift in this family and factory structure began in the mid-1820s in England and had been more or less completed by the mid-1830s. As spinning and weaving were put under one roof, the size of factories and of the machinery grew. These newer machines required fewer skilled operators, but many relatively unskilled attendants. This became the work of unmarried women and children. Factory owners found these workers would accept lower wages and were less likely than adult men to try to form worker organizations or unions.

Factory wages for the more skilled adult males, however, became sufficiently high to allow some fathers to remove their children from the factory and send them to school. The children who were left working in the factories as assistants were often the children of the economically depressed hand-loom weavers. The wives of the skilled operatives also usually no longer worked in the factories. So the original links of the family in the British textile factory that had existed for well over a quarter century largely disappeared. Men were supervising women and children who did not belong to their families.

Concern for Child Labor   At this point in the 1830s, workers became concerned about the plight of child laborers because parents were no longer exercising discipline over their own children in the factories. The English Factory Act of 1833 forbade the employment of children under age nine, limited the workday of children aged nine to thirteen to nine hours a day, and required the factory owner to pay for two hours of education a day for these children. The effect was further to divide work and home life. The workday for adults and older teenagers remained twelve hours. Younger children often worked in relays of four or six hours. Consequently, the parental link was thoroughly broken. The education requirement began the process of removing nurturing and training from the home and family to a school, where a teacher rather than the parents was in charge of education.

After passage of the English Factory Act, many British workers demanded shorter workdays for adults. They desired to reunite, in some manner, the workday of adults with that of their children or at least to allow adults to spend more time with their children. In 1847, Parliament mandated a ten-hour workday. By present standards, this was long. At that time, however, it allowed parents and children more hours together as a domestic unit, since their relationship as a work or production unit had ceased wherever the factory system prevailed. By the mid-1840s, in the lives of industrial workers, the roles of men as breadwinners and as fathers and husbands had become distinct in the British textile industry. Furthermore, reformers' concerns about the working conditions of women in factories and in mines arose in part from the relatively new view that the place of women was in the home rather than in an industrial or even agrarian workplace.

Changing Economic Role for the Family   What occurred in Britain presents a general pattern for what would happen elsewhere with the spread of industrial capitalism and public education. The European family was passing from being the chief unit of both production and consumption to becoming the chief unit of consumption alone. This development did not mean the end of the family as an economic unit. Parents and children, however, now came to depend on sharing wages often derived from several sources, rather than on sharing work in the home or factory.

Ultimately, the wage economy meant that families were less closely bound together than in the past. Because wages could be sent over long distances to parents, children might now move farther away from home. Once they moved far away, the economic link was, in time, often broken. In contrast, when a family settled in an industrial city, the wage economy might, in that or the next generation, actually discourage children from leaving home as early as they had in the past. Children could find wage employment in the same city and then live at home until they had accumulated enough savings to marry and begin their own household. That situation meant children often remained with their parents longer than in the past.

WOMEN IN THE EARLY INDUSTRIAL REVOLUTION

As noted in Chapter 15, the industrial economy ultimately produced an immense impact on the home and family life of women. First, it eventually took most productive work out of the home and allowed many families to live on the wages of the male spouse. That transformation prepared the

WOMEN INDUSTRIAL WORKERS EXPLAIN THEIR ECONOMIC SITUATION

In 1832, there was much discussion in the British press about factory legislation. Most of that discussion concerned the employment of children, but the Examiner *newspaper suggested that factory laws should also, in time, eliminate women's employment in factories. That article provoked the following letter to the editor, composed by or on behalf of women factory workers, which stated why women needed such employment and the unattractive alternatives.*

■ *What reasons do these women give to prove why they need to hold manufacturing jobs? What changes in production methods have led women from the home to the factory? How does the situation of these women relate to the possibility of their marrying?*

Sir,

Living as we do, in the densely populated manufacturing districts of Lancashire, and most of us belonging to that class of females who earn their bread either directly or indirectly by manufactories, we have looked with no little anxiety for your opinion on the Factory Bill. . . . You are for doing away with our services in manufactories altogether. So much the better, if you had pointed out any other more eligible and practical employment for the surplus female labour, that will want other channels for a subsistence. If our competition were withdrawn, and short hours substituted, we have no doubt but the effects would be as you have stated, "not to lower wages, as the male branch of the family would be enabled to earn as much as the whole had done," but for the thousands of females who are employed in manufactories, who have no legitimate claim on any male relative for employment or support, and who have, through a variety of circumstance, been early thrown on their own resources for a livelihood, what is to become of them?

In this neighbourhood, hand-loom has been almost totally superseded by power-loom weaving, and no inconsiderable number of females, who must depend on their own exertions, or their parishes for support, have been forced, of necessity into the manufactories, from their total inability to earn a livelihood at home.

It is a lamentable fact, that, in these parts of the country, there is scarcely any other mode of employment for female industry, if we except servitude and dressmaking. Of the former of these, there is no chance of employment for one-twentieth of the candidates that would rush into the field, to say nothing of lowering the wages of our sisters of the same craft; and of the latter, galling as some of the hardships of manufactories are (of which the indelicacy of mixing with the men is not the least), yet there are few women who have been so employed, that would change conditions with the ill-used genteel little slaves, who have to lose sleep and health, in catering to the whims and frivolities of the butterflies of fashion.

We see no way of escape from starvation, but to accept the very tempting offers of the newspapers, held out as baits to us, fairly to ship ourselves off to Van Dieman's Land [Tasmania] on the very delicate errand of husband hunting, and having safely arrived at the "Land of Goshen," jump ashore, with a "Who wants me?" . . .

The Female Operatives of Todmorden

From *The Examiner*, February 26, 1832, as quoted in Ivy Pinchbeck, *Women Workers and the Industrial Revolution, 1750–1850* (New York: Augustus M. Kelley, 1969), pp. 199–200.

As textile production became increasingly automated in the nineteenth century, textile factories required fewer skilled workers and more unskilled attendants. To fill these unskilled positions, factory owners turned increasingly to unmarried women and widows, who worked for lower wages than men and were less likely to form labor organizations.   Bildarchiv Preussischer Kulturbesitz

way for a new concept of gender-determined roles in the home and in domestic life generally. Women came to be associated with domestic duties, such as housekeeping, food preparation, child rearing and nurturing, and household management, or with poorly paid, largely unskilled cottage industries. Men came to be associated almost exclusively with supporting the family. Children were raised to conform to these expected gender patterns. Previously, this domestic division of labor into separate male and female spheres had prevailed only among the relatively small middle class and the gentry. During the nineteenth century, that division came to characterize the working class as well.

OPPORTUNITIES AND EXPLOITATION IN EMPLOYMENT

Because the early Industrial Revolution had begun in textile production, women and their labor were deeply involved from the start. Although both spinning and weaving were still domestic industries, women usually worked in all stages of pro-

duction. Hand spinning was virtually always a woman's task. At first, when spinning was moved into factories and involved large machines, men often displaced women. Furthermore, the higher wages male cotton-factory workers commanded allowed many married women not to work or to work only to supplement their husbands' wages.

Women in Factories   With the next generation of machines in the 1820s, however, unmarried women rapidly became employed in the factories, where they often constituted the majority of workers. Their new jobs, however, often demanded fewer skills than those they had previously exercised in the home production of textiles. Women's factory work also required fewer skills than most work men did. Tending a machine required less skill than spinning or weaving or acting as forewoman. There was thus a certain paradox in the impact of the factory on women: It opened many new jobs to them, but lowered the level of skills they needed to have. The supervisors of women were almost invariably men.

Moreover, almost always, the women in the factories were young, single women or widows. Upon marriage or perhaps after the birth of the first child, young women usually found their husbands earned enough money for them to leave the factory. Sometimes the factory owners, who disliked employing married women because of the likelihood of pregnancy, the influence of their husbands, and the duties of child rearing, no longer wanted them. Widows might return to factory work because they lacked their husbands' former income.

Work on the Land and in the Home   In Britain and elsewhere by midcentury, industrial factory work still accounted for less than half of all employment for women. The largest group of employed women in France continued to work on the land. In England, they were domestic servants. Throughout Western Europe, domestic cottage industries, such as lace making, glove making, garment making, and other kinds of needlework, employed many women. In almost all such cases, their conditions of labor were harsh, whether they worked in their homes or in sweatshops. It cannot be overemphasized that all work by women commanded low wages and involved low skills. They had virtually no effective modes to protect themselves from exploitation. The charwoman, hired by the day to do rough house cleaning or washing, was a common sight across the Continent and symbolized the plight of working women.

The low wages of female workers in all areas of employment sometimes led them to become prostitutes to supplement their wage income. This situation prevailed across Europe throughout the century. In 1844, Louise Aston (1814–1871), a German political radical, portrayed this situation in a poem looking at the experience of a Silesian weaver as she confronts a factory owner on whom her family depends to purchase the cloth they have woven:

The factory owner has come,
And he says to me: "My darling child,
I know your people
Are living in misery and sorrow;
So if you want to lie with me
For three or four nights,
See this shiny gold coin!
It's yours immediately."[1]

Such sexual exploitation of women was hardly new to European society, but the particular pressures of the transformation of the economy from one of skilled artisans to that of unskilled factory workers made many women especially vulnerable. (See "Women Industrial Workers Explain Their Economic Situation," page 698.)

CHANGING EXPECTATIONS IN THE WORKING-CLASS MARRIAGE

Moving to cities and entering the wage economy gave women wider opportunities for marriage. Cohabitation before marriage was not uncommon. Parents had less to do with arranging marriages than in the past. (See "A Frenchwoman Writes to Her Father about Marriage.") Marriage now usually meant a woman would leave the work force to live on her husband's earnings. If all went well, that arrangement might improve her situation. If the husband became ill or died, however, or if he deserted his wife, she would have to reenter the market for unskilled labor at an advanced age.

Despite these changes, many of the traditional practices associated with the family economy survived into the industrial era. As a young woman came of age, both family needs and her desire to marry still directed what she would do with her life. The most likely early occupation for a young woman was domestic service. A girl born in the country normally migrated to a nearby town or city for such employment, often living initially with a relative. As in the past, she would try to earn enough in wages to give herself a dowry, so she might marry and set up her own household. If she became a factory worker, she would probably live in a supervised dormitory. These dormitories

helped attract young women to work in a factory by convincing parents their daughters would be safe.

The life of young women in the cities was more precarious than earlier. There were fewer family and community ties. There were also perhaps more available young men. These men, who worked for wages rather than in the older apprenticeship structures, were more mobile, so relationships between men and women often were more fleeting. In any case, illegitimate births increased; fewer women who became pregnant before marriage found the father willing to marry them.

Marriage in the wage industrial economy was also different in certain respects from marriage in earlier times. It still involved starting a separate household, but the structure of gender relationships within the household was different. Marriage was less an economic partnership. The husband's wages might well be able to support the entire family. The wage economy and the industrialization separating workplace from home made it difficult for women to combine domestic duties with work. When married women worked, it was usually in the nonindustrial sector of the economy. More often than not, the children rather than the wife were sent to work. This may help explain the increase in the number of births within marriages, as children in the wage economy usually were an economic asset. Married women worked outside the home only when family needs, illness, or widowhood forced them to.

In the home, working-class women were by no means idle. Their domestic duties were an essential factor in the family wage economy. If work took place elsewhere, someone had to be directly in charge of maintaining the home. Homemaking came to the fore when a life at home had to be organized separately from the place of work. Wives were concerned primarily with food and cooking, but they were also often in charge of the family's finances. The role of the mother expanded when the children still living at home became wage earners. She was now providing home support for her entire wage-earning family. She created the environment to which the family members returned after work. The longer period of home life of working children may also have increased and strengthened familial bonds of affection between those children and their hardworking homebound mothers. In all these respects, the culture of the working-class marriage and family tended to imitate the family patterns of the middle and upper classes, whose members had often accepted the view of separate gender spheres set forth by Rousseau and popularized in hundreds of novels, journals, and newspapers.

[1] As quoted in Lia Secci, "German Women Writers and the Revolution of 1848," in John C. Fout, ed., *German Women in the Nineteenth Century: A Social History* (New York: Holmes & Meier, 1984), p. 162.

A FRENCHWOMAN WRITES TO HER FATHER ABOUT MARRIAGE

Stéphanie Jullien was a young middle-class woman whose father wished her to marry a man who was courting her. She had already rejected one suitor, and her father was concerned about her future. In this letter to her father, she explains why she wants to delay her decision. Ultimately, she did marry the man in question, and the marriage appears to have been happy.

■ *How does Stéphanie Jullien distinguish between these vocational and social opportunities available to a woman from those available to a man? What are her expectations of marriage? What does the letter also tell you about her relationship to her father? Compare this letter with the preceding letter by English working-class women. What problems do the women share? How are their lives different? What does a comparison of the two letters tell you about the difference in class experience in the early nineteenth century?*

You men have a thousand occupations to distract you: society, business, politics, and work absorb you, exhaust you, upset you . . . . As for us women who, as you have said to me from time to time, have only the roses in life, we feel more profoundly in our solitude and in our idleness the sufferings that you can slough off. I don't want to make a comparison here between the destiny of man and the destiny of woman: each sex has its own lot, its own troubles, its own pleasures. I only want to explain to you that excess of moroseness of which you complain and of which I am the first to suffer. . . . I am not able to do anything for myself and for those around me. I am depriving my brothers in order to have a dowry. I am not even able to live alone, being obliged to take from others, not only in order to live but also in order to be protected, since social convention does not allow me to have independence. And yet the world finds me guilty of being the only person that I am at liberty to be; not having useful or productive work to do, not having any calling except marriage, and not being able to look by myself for someone who will suit me, I am full of cares and anxieties. . . .

I am asking for more time [before responding to a marriage proposal]. It is not too much to want to see and know a man for ten months, even a year when it is a matter of passing one's life with him. There is no objection to make, you say. But the most serious and the most important presents itself: I do not love him. Don't think I am talking about a romantic and impossible passion or an ideal love, neither of which I ever hope to know. I am talking of a feeling that makes one want to see someone, that makes his absence painful and his return desirable, that makes one interested in what another is doing, that makes one want another's happiness almost in spite of oneself, that makes, finally, the duties of a woman toward her husband pleasures and not efforts. It is a feeling without which marriage would be hell, a feeling that cannot be born out of esteem, and which to me, however, seems to be the very basis of conjugal happiness. I can't feel these emotions immediately. . . . Let me have some time. I want to love, not out of any sense of duty, but for myself and for the happiness of the one to whom I attach my life, who will suffer if he only encounters coldness in me, when he brings me love and devotion.

From the Jullien Family Papers, 39 AP 4, Archives Nationales, Paris, trans. by Barbara Corrado Pope, as quoted in Erna Olafson Hellerstein, Leslie Parker Hume, and Karen M. Offen, eds., *Victorian Women: A Documentary Account of Women's Lives in Nineteenth-Century England, France, and the United States* (Stanford, Calif.: Stanford University Press, 1981), pp. 247–248. Reprinted by permission of Barbara Corrado Pope.

PROBLEMS OF CRIME AND ORDER

Throughout the nineteenth century, the political and economic elite in Europe were profoundly concerned about social order. The revolutions of the late eighteenth and early nineteenth centuries made them fearful of future disorder and threats to life and property. Industrialization and urbanization also contributed to this problem of order. Thousands of Europeans migrated from the countryside to the towns and cities. There, they often encountered poverty or unemployment and general social frustration and disappointment. Cities became associated with criminal activity, especially crimes against property, such as theft and arson. Throughout the first sixty years of the nineteenth century, crime appears to have increased slowly but steadily before more or less reaching a plateau.

Historians and social scientists are divided about the reasons for this rise in the crime rate. So little is known about crime in rural settings that comparisons with the cities are difficult. Moreover, crime statistics in the nineteenth century are problematic. No two nations kept them in the same manner. Different legal codes and systems of

London policeman. Professional police forces did not exist before the early nineteenth century. The London police force was created in 1828.   Peter Newark's Pictures

judicial administration were in effect in different areas of the Continent, thus giving somewhat different legal definitions of what constituted criminal activity. The result has been confusion, difficult research, and tentative conclusions.

NEW POLICE FORCES

From the propertied, elite classes, two major views about containing crime and criminals emerged during the nineteenth century: Better systems of police and prison reform. The result of these efforts was the triumph in Europe of the idea of a policed society in which a paid, professionally trained group of law-enforcement officers keeps order, protects property and lives, investigates crime, and apprehends offenders. These officers are distinct from the army and are charged specifically with domestic security. It is to them that the civilian population normally turns for law enforcement. A key feature of the theory of a policed society is that the visible presence of law-enforcement officers may prevent crime. These police forces, again at least in theory, did not perform a political role, although many countries often ignored that distinction. Police forces also became one of the largest groups of municipal government employees.

Professional police forces did not really exist until the early nineteenth century. They differed from one country to another in both authority and organization, but their creation proved crucial to the emergence of an orderly European society. The prefect of Paris, who was the chief administrative official of that city, set forth the principles that lay behind the founding of all of these new police units when he announced that "Safety by day and night, free traffic movement, clean streets, the supervision of and precaution against accidents, the maintenance of order in public places, the seeking out of offences and their perpetrators. . . . The municipal police is a parental police."[2]

Professional police forces appeared in Paris in 1828. The next year, the British Parliament passed legislation sponsored by Sir Robert Peel (1788–1850) that placed police on London streets. They were soon known as *bobbies* or, more disparagingly, as Peelers, after the sponsor of the legislation. Berlin deployed similar police departments after the Revolution of 1848. All of these forces were distinguished by an easily recognizable uniform. Police on the Continent carried guns; those in Britain did not.

Although citizens sometimes viewed police with suspicion, especially in Britain where many

[2] Quoted in Clive Emsley, *Policing and Its Context, 1750–1870* (London: Macmillan, 1983), p. 58.

people opposed the creation of a professional police force as a threat to traditional British liberties, by the end of the century, most Europeans regarded the police as their protectors. Persons from the upper and middle classes felt police made their property more secure. Persons from the working class also frequently turned to the police to protect their lives and property and to aid them in emergencies. Of course, most people hated and feared political or secret police wherever governments, especially in Russia, created them.

PRISON REFORM

Before the nineteenth century, European prisons were local jails or state prisons, such as the Bastille. Governments also sent criminals to prison ships, called *hulks*. Some Mediterranean nations sentenced prisoners to naval galleys, where, chained to their benches, they rowed until they died or were eventually released. In prisons, inmates lived under wretched conditions. Men, women, and children were housed together. Persons guilty of minor offenses were left in the same room with those guilty of the most serious offenses.

Beginning in the late eighteenth century, the British government sentenced persons convicted of the most serious offenses to **transportation**. Transportation to the colony of New South Wales in Australia was regarded as an alternative to capital punishment, and the British used it until the mid-nineteenth century, when the colonies began to object. Thereafter, the British government housed long-term prisoners in public works prisons in Britain.

By the close of the eighteenth century and in the early nineteenth century, reformers, such as John Howard (1726–1790) and Elizabeth Fry (1780–1845) in England and Charles Lucas (1803–1889) in France, exposed the horrendous conditions in prisons and demanded change. Reform came slowly because of the expense of constructing new prisons and a lack of sympathy for criminals.

In the 1840s, however, both the French and the English undertook several bold efforts at prison reform. These efforts would appear to indicate a shift in opinion whereby crime was seen not as an assault on order or on authority but as a mark of a character fault in the criminal. Thereafter, part of the goal of imprisonment was to rehabilitate or transform the prisoner. The result of this change was the creation of exceedingly repressive prison systems designed according to the most advanced scientific modes of understanding criminals and criminal reform.

Europeans used various prison models originally established in the United States. All these experiments depended on separating prisoners from each other. One was known as the *Auburn system* after Auburn Prison in New York State. According to it, prisoners were separated from each other during the night but could associate while working during the day. The other was the *Philadelphia system*, in which prisoners were kept rigorously separated from each other at all times.

The chief characteristics of these systems were an individual cell for each prisoner and long periods of separation and silence among prisoners. The most famous example of this kind of prison in Europe was Pentonville Prison near London. There, each prisoner occupied a separate cell and was never allowed to speak to or see another prisoner. Each prisoner wore a mask when in the prison yard; in the chapel, each had a separate stall. The point of the system was to induce self-reflection in which the prisoners would think about their crimes and eventually decide to repudiate their criminal tendencies. As time passed, the system

In many prisons, treadmills like these were the only source of exercise available to English prisoners.   Bildarchiv Preussischer Kulturbesitz

became more relaxed because the intense isolation often led to mental collapse.

In France, imprisonment became more repressive as the century passed. The French constructed prisons similar to Pentonville in the 1840s. In 1875, the French also adopted a firm, general policy of isolating inmates. France constructed sixty prisons based on this principle by 1908. Prisoners were supposed to be trained in a trade or skill while in prison so they could reemerge as reformed citizens.

The vast increase in repeat offenses led the French government in 1885, long after the British had abandoned the practice, to sentence serious repeat offenders to transportation to places such as the infamous Devil's Island off the coast of South America. Transportation was intended literally to purge the nation of its worst criminals and to ensure they would never return.

These attempts to create a police force and to reform prisons illustrate the concern about order and stability by European political and social elites that developed after the French Revolution. On the whole, their efforts succeeded. By the end of the century, an orderly society had been established, and the new police and prisons had no small role in that development.

CLASSICAL ECONOMICS

Economists whose thought derived largely from Adam Smith's *Wealth of Nations* (1776) dominated private and public discussions of industrial and commercial policy. Their ideas are often associated with the phrase *laissez-faire* (a French phrase that means roughly "let people do as they please"). Although they thought the government should perform many important functions, the classical economists favored economic growth through competitive free enterprise. They conceived of society as consisting of atomistic individuals whose competitive efforts met consumers' demands in the marketplace. They believed the mechanism of the marketplace should govern most economic decisions. They believed most government action to be mischievous and corrupt. The government should maintain a sound currency, enforce contracts, protect property, impose low tariffs and taxes, and leave the remainder of economic life to private initiative. The economists naturally assumed the state would maintain enough armed forces and naval power to protect the nation's economic structure and foreign trade. With emphasis on thrift, competition, and personal industriousness, the political economists voice appealed to the middle classes.

MALTHUS ON POPULATION

The classical economists had complicated and pessimistic ideas about the working class. Thomas Malthus (1766–1834) and David Ricardo (1772–1823), probably the most influential of all these writers, suggested, in effect, that nothing could improve the condition of the working class. In 1798, Malthus published the first edition of his *Essay on the Principle of Population*. His ideas have haunted the world ever since. He contended that population must eventually outstrip the food supply. Although the human population grows geometrically, the food supply can expand only arithmetically. There was little hope of averting the disaster, in Malthus's opinion, except through late marriage, chastity, and contraception, the last of which he considered a vice. It took three-quarters of a century for contraception to become a socially acceptable method of containing the population explosion.

Malthus contended that the immediate plight of the working class could only become worse. If wages were raised, the workers would simply produce more children, who would, in turn, consume both the extra wages and more food. Later in his life, Malthus suggested, in a more optimistic vein, that if the working class could be persuaded to adopt a higher standard of living, their increased wages might be spent on consumer goods rather than on begetting more children.

RICARDO ON WAGES

In his *Principles of Political Economy* (1817), David Ricardo transformed the concepts of Malthus into the "iron law of wages." If wages were raised, parents would have more children. They, in turn, would enter the labor market, thus expanding the number of workers and lowering wages. As wages fell, working people would produce fewer children. Wages would then rise, and the process would start all over again. Consequently, in the long run, wages would always tend toward a minimum level. These arguments simply supported employers in their natural reluctance to raise wages and also provided strong theoretical support for opposing labor unions. Journals, newspapers, and even short stories, such as Harriet Martineau's (1802–1876) series entitled *Illustrations of Political Economy*, spread the ideas of the economists to the public in the 1830s.

GOVERNMENT POLICIES BASED ON CLASSICAL ECONOMICS

The working classes of France and Great Britain, needless to say, resented the attitudes of the economists, but the governments embraced them.

Louis Philippe (1773–1850) and his minister François Guizot (1787–1874) told the French to go forth and enrich themselves. People who simply displayed sufficient energy need not be poor. A number of the French middle class did just that. The July Monarchy (1830–1848) saw the construction of major capital-intensive projects, such as roads, canals, and railways. Little, however, was done about the poverty in the cities and the countryside.

In Germany, the middle classes made less headway. After the Napoleonic wars, however, the Prussian reformers had seen the desirability of abolishing internal tariffs that impeded economic growth. In 1834, all the major German states, except Austria, formed the **Zollverein**, or free trading union. Classical economics had less influence in Germany because of the tradition dating from the enlightened absolutism of state direction of economic development. The German economist Friedrich List (1789–1846) argued for this approach to economic growth during the second quarter of the century.

Britain was the home of the major classical economists, and their policies were widely accepted. The utilitarian thought of Jeremy Bentham (1748–1832) increased their influence. Although **utilitarianism** did not originate with him, Bentham sought to create codes of scientific law that were founded on the principle of utility, that is, the greatest happiness for the greatest number. In his *Fragment on Government* (1776) and *The Principles of Morals and Legislation* (1789), Bentham explained the application of the principle of utility would overcome the special interests of privileged groups who prevented rational government. He regarded the existing legal and judicial systems as burdened by traditional practices that harmed the very people the law should serve. The application of reason and utility would remove the legal clutter that prevented justice from being realized. He believed the principle of utility could be applied to other areas of government administration.

Bentham gathered round him political disciples who combined his ideas with those of classical economics. In 1834, the reformed House of Commons passed a new Poor Law that followers of Bentham had prepared. This measure established a Poor Law Commission that set out to make poverty the most undesirable of all social situations. Government poor relief was to be disbursed only in workhouses. Life in the workhouse was consciously designed to be more unpleasant than life outside. Husbands and wives were separated, the food was bad, and the enforced work was distasteful. The social stigma of the workhouse was even worse. The law and its administration presupposed

---

MAJOR WORKS OF ECONOMIC AND POLITICAL COMMENTARY

1776 Adam Smith, *The Wealth of Nations*

1798 Thomas Malthus, *Essay on the Principle of Population*

1817 David Ricardo, *Principles of Political Economy*

1830s Harriet Martineau, *Illustrations of Political Economy*

1839 Louis Blanc, *The Organization of Labor*

1845 Friedrich Engels, *The Condition of the Working Class in England*

1848 Karl Marx and Friedrich Engels, *The Communist Manifesto*

---

that people would not work because they were lazy. The laboring class, not unjustly, regarded the workhouses as new "bastilles."

The second British monument to applied classical economics was the repeal of the Corn Laws in 1846. The Anti-Corn Law League, organized by manufacturers, had sought this goal for more than six years. The League wanted to abolish the tariffs protecting the domestic price of grain. That change would lead to lower food prices, which would then allow lower wages at no real cost to the workers. In turn, the prices on British manufactured goods could also be lowered to strengthen their competitive position in the world market.

The actual reason for Sir Robert Peel's repeal of the Corn Laws in 1846 was the Irish famine. Peel had to open British ports to foreign grain to feed the starving Irish. He realized the Corn Laws could not be reimposed. Peel accompanied the abolition measure with a program for government aid to modernize British agriculture and to make it more efficient. The repeal of the Corn Laws was the culmination of the lowering of British tariffs that had begun during the 1820s. It marked the opening of an era of free trade that continued until the twentieth century.

EARLY SOCIALISM

During the twentieth century, the socialist movement, in the form of either communist or social democratic political parties, constituted one of the major political forces in Europe. Less than 150 years ago, the advocates of socialism lacked any meaningful political following, and their doctrines appeared blurred and confused to most of their contemporaries. It is important to understand their early ideas and then to see (as shall be seen in later chapters) how those ideas, which for many years appeared on the margins of European political life, came to assume great importance in the late nineteenth century and beyond.

The early socialists generally applauded the new productive capacity of industrialism. They denied, however, that the free market could adequately produce and distribute goods the way the classical economists claimed. In the capitalist order, the socialists saw primarily mismanagement, low wages, misdistribution of goods, and suffering arising from the unregulated industrial system. Moreover, the socialists thought human society should be organized as a community, rather than merely as a conglomerate of atomistic, selfish individuals.

UTOPIAN SOCIALISM

Among the earliest people to define the social question were a group of writers whom their critics called the **utopian socialists**. They were considered utopian because their ideas were often visionary and because they frequently advocated the creation of ideal communities. They were called socialists because they questioned the structures and values of the existing capitalistic framework. In some cases, they actually deserved neither description. A significant factor in the experience of almost all of these groups was the discussion, and sometimes the practice, of radical ideas about sexuality and the family. People who might have been sympathetic to their economic concerns were profoundly unsympathetic to their views on free love and open family relationships.

Saint-Simonianism   Count Claude Henri de Saint-Simon (1760–1825) was the earliest of the socialist pioneers. As a young, liberal French aristocrat, he had fought in the American Revolution. Later he welcomed the French Revolution, during which he made and lost a fortune. By the time of Napoleon's ascendancy, he had turned to a career of writing and social criticism and a concern for order.

Above all else, Saint-Simon believed modern society would require rational management. Private wealth, property, and enterprise should be subject to an administration other than that of its owners. His ideal government would have consisted of a large board of directors organizing and coordinating the activity of individuals and groups to achieve social harmony. In a sense, he was the ideological father of technocracy. Not the *redistribution* of wealth, but its *management* by experts, would alleviate the poverty and social dislocation of the age.

When Saint-Simon died in 1825, he had persuaded only a handful of people his ideas were correct.

Nonetheless, Saint-Simonian societies were always centers for lively discussion of advanced social ideals. Some of the earliest debates in France over feminism took place within these societies. During the late 1820s and 1830s, the Saint-Simonians became well known for advocating sexuality outside marriage. Several of Saint-Simon's disciples also became leaders in the French railway industry during the 1850s.

Owenism   The major British contributor to the early socialist tradition was Robert Owen (1771–1858), a self-made cotton manufacturer. In his early twenties, Owen became a partner in one of the largest cotton factories in Britain at New Lanark, Scotland. Owen was a firm believer in the environmentalist psychology of the Enlightenment that had flowed from the thought of John Locke. If human beings were placed in the correct surroundings, they and their character could be improved. Moreover, Owen saw no incompatibility between creating a humane industrial environment and making a good profit.

At New Lanark, he put his ideas into practice. Workers were provided with good quarters. Recreational possibilities abounded, and the children received an education. There were several churches, although Owen himself was a notorious freethinker on matters of religion and sex. In the factory itself, rewards were given for good work. His plant made a fine profit. Visitors flocked from all over Europe to see what Owen had done through enlightened management.

In numerous articles and pamphlets, as well as in letters to influential people, Owen pleaded for a reorganization of industry based on his own successful model. He envisioned a series of communities shaped like parallelograms in which factory workers and farm workers might live together and produce their goods in cooperation. During the 1820s, Owen sold his New Lanark factory and then went to the United States, where he established the community of New Harmony, Indiana. When quarrels among the members led to the community's failure, he refused to give up his reformist causes. He returned to Britain, where he became the moving force behind the organization of the Grand National Union, an attempt to draw all British trade unions into a single body. It collapsed along with other labor organizations during the early 1830s.

Fourierism   Charles Fourier (1772–1837) was Owen's French intellectual counterpart. He was a commercial salesperson who never succeeded in attracting the same kind of public attention as Owen. He wrote his books and articles and waited at home each day at noon, hoping to meet a patron

MR OWEN'S INSTITUTION, NEW LANARK.
(Quadrille Dancing.)

Robert Owen, the Scottish industrialist and early socialist, created an ideal industrial community at New Lanark, Scotland. He believed deeply in the power of education and saw that the children of workmen received sound educations.   Picture Desk, Inc./Kobal Collection

who would undertake his program. No one ever arrived to meet him. Fourier believed the industrial order ignored the passionate side of human nature. Social discipline ignored all the pleasures that human beings naturally seek.

Fourier advocated the construction of communities, called *phalanxes*, in which liberated living would replace the boredom and dullness of industrial existence. Agrarian rather than industrial production would predominate in these communities. Sexual activity would be relatively free, and marriage was to be reserved only for later life. Fourier also urged that no person be required to perform the same kind of work for the entire day. People would be both happier and more productive if they moved from one task to another. Through his emphasis on the problem of boredom, Fourier isolated one of the key difficulties of modern economic life.

Saint-Simon, Owen, and Fourier expected some existing government to carry out their ideas. They failed to confront the political difficulties their envisioned social transformations would arouse. Other figures paid more attention to the politics of

the situation. In 1839, Louis Blanc (1811–1882) published *The Organization of Labor*. Like other socialist writers, this Frenchman demanded an end to competition, but he did not seek a wholly new society. He called for political reform that would give the vote to the working class. Once so empowered, workers could use the vote to turn the political processes to their own economic advantage. A state controlled by a working-class electorate would finance workshops to employ the poor. In time, such workshops might replace private enterprise, and industry would be organized to ensure jobs. Blanc recognized the power of the state to improve life and the conditions of labor. The state itself could become the great employer of labor.

ANARCHISM

Other writers and activists of the 1840s, however, rejected both industry and the dominance of government. These were the **anarchists**. They are usually included in the socialist tradition, although they do not exactly fit there. Some favored programs of violence and terrorism; others were peaceful. Auguste Blanqui (1805–1881) was a major spokesperson for terror. He spent most of his adult life in jail. Seeking to abolish both capitalism and the state, Blanqui urged the development of a professional revolutionary vanguard to attack capitalist society. His ideas for the new society were vague, but in his call for professional revolutionaries, he foreshadowed Lenin.

Pierre-Joseph Proudhon (1809–1865) represented the other strain of anarchism. In his most famous work, *What Is Property?* (1840), Proudhon attacked the banking system, which rarely extended credit to small-property owners or the poor. He wanted credit expanded to allow such people to engage in economic enterprise that would not involve unfair or unearned profits. Society should be organized on the basis of mutualism, which amounted to a system of small businesses and other cooperative enterprises among which there would be peaceful cooperation and exchanges of goods based on mutual recognition of the labor each area of production required. With such a social system, the state as the protector of property would be unnecessary. Later in the century, anarchists would favor a wide variety of cooperative businesses whose point was to favor the community good over that of the individual as well as to afford an essential fairness in exchange. Proudhon's ideas later influenced the French labor movement, which was generally less directly political in its activities than the labor movements in Britain and Germany.

MARXISM

The mode of socialist thought that eventually exerted more influence over modern European history than any other was **Marxism**. During the late nineteenth century, its ideas permeated the major continental socialist parties. With the Bolshevik Revolution of November 1917, the communist strain of Marxist thought came to dominate the Soviet Union and, after World War II, Eastern Europe and revolutionary movements in the colonial and post-colonial world. With the collapse of the Soviet Union and of the communist governments in Eastern Europe in the last twenty years of the twentieth century, it is difficult for many people to recapture the power that Marx's political and social vision exerted over Europe and other parts of the world for more than a hundred years.

Too often, the history of European socialism has been regarded as a linear development leading naturally or necessarily to the late-nineteenth-century triumph of Marxism within the major socialist po-

Karl Marx's socialist philosophy eventually triumphed over most alternative versions of socialism in Europe, but his monumental work became subject to varying interpretations, criticisms, and revisions that continue to this day.   Bildarchiv Preussischer Kulturbesitz

litical parties. Nothing could be further from the truth. Marxist socialist ideas did eventually triumph over much, though not all, of Europe, but only through competition with other socialist formulas and largely as a result of the political situation in Germany during the last quarter of the nineteenth century. At midcentury, the ideas of Karl Marx were simply one more contribution to a heady mixture of concepts and programs criticizing the emerging industrial capitalist society. Marxism differed from its competitors in its claims to scientific accuracy, its rejection of reform, and its call for revolution, though the character of that revolution was not well defined. Furthermore, Marx set the emergence of the industrial work force in the context of a world historical development from which he drew sweeping political conclusions.

Karl Marx (1818–1883) was born in Germany in the Prussian Rhineland. His family was Jewish, but his father had converted to Lutheranism, and Judaism played no role in his education. Marx's middle-class parents sent him to the University of

Berlin, where he became deeply involved in Hegelian philosophy and radical politics. In 1842 and 1843, he edited the radical *Rhineland Gazette* (*Rheinische Zeitung*). Soon the Prussian authorities drove him from his native land. He lived as an exile, first in Paris, then in Brussels, and finally, after 1849, in London.

Partnership with Engels In 1844, Marx met Friedrich Engels (1820–1895), another young middle-class German, whose father owned a textile factory in Manchester, England. The next year Engels published *The Condition of the Working Class in England*, which presented a devastating picture of industrial life. The two men became fast friends. Late in 1847, they were asked to write a pamphlet for a newly organized and ultimately short-lived secret Communist League. *The Communist Manifesto*, published in German, appeared early in 1848. Marx, Engels, and the League had adopted the name *communist* because it was much more self-consciously radical than socialist. Communism implied the outright abolition of private property, rather than a less extensive rearrangement of society. Despite its later vast influence throughout the world, the *Manifesto*, a work of fewer than fifty pages, was at the time of its publication and for many years thereafter just one more political tract. Moreover, neither Marx nor his thought had any effect on the revolutionary events of 1848, which will be discussed more fully later in this chapter.

Sources of Marx's Ideas Marx derived the major ideas of the *Manifesto* and of his later work, including *Capital* (vol. 1, 1867), from German Hegelianism, French utopian socialism, and British classical economics. Marx applied to concrete historical, social, and economic developments Hegel's abstract philosophical concept that thought develops from the clash of thesis and antithesis into a new intellectual synthesis. For Marx, the conflict between dominant and subordinate social groups led to the emergence of a new dominant social group. These new social relationships, in turn, generated new discontent, conflict, and development. The French utopian socialists had depicted the problems of capitalist society and had raised the issue of property redistribution. Both Hegel and Saint-Simon led Marx to see society and economic conditions as developing through historical stages. The classical economists had produced the analytical tools for an empirical, scientific examination of the industrial capitalist society.

Using the intellectual tools of Hegel, the French utopian socialists, and the British classical econo-

mists provided, Marx fashioned a philosophy that gave a special role or function to the new industrial work force as the single most important driving force of contemporary history. Marx later explained to a friend:

What I did that was new was to prove: (1) that the existence of classes is bound up with particular historical phases in the development of production; (2) that the class struggle necessarily leads to the dictatorship of the proletariat; (3) that this dictatorship itself only constitutes the transition to the abolition of all classes and to a classless society.[3]

In the *Communist Manifesto* and his numerous other writings, Marx equated the fate of the proletariat—that is, the new industrial labor force—with the fate of humanity itself. According to Marx, as the proletariat came to liberate itself from its bondage to the capitalist mode of industrial production, such liberation would eventually amount to the liberation of all humanity. It was this utopian vision of human emancipation, no matter how much the actual later development of the European and world economy failed to conform to Marx's predictions, that drew many people from Europe and elsewhere to embrace much of his thought and to base their political actions on their understanding of his philosophy. Besides this wider vision, however, the details of Marx's argument were also important for later nineteenth-century and twentieth-century European political life.

Revolution Through Class Conflict In the *Communist Manifesto*, Marx and Engels contended that human history must be understood rationally and as a whole. History is the record of humankind's coming to grips with physical nature to produce the goods necessary for survival. That basic productive process determines the structures, values, and ideas of a society. Historically, the organization of the means of production has always involved conflict between the classes that owned and controlled the means of production and the classes that worked for them. That necessary conflict has provided the engine for historical development; it is not an accidental by-product of mismanagement or bad intentions. Thus, piecemeal reforms cannot eliminate the social and economic evils inherent in the very structures of production. To achieve that, a radical social transformation is required. The development of capitalism will make such a revolution inevitable.

In Marx's and Engels's eyes, the class conflict that had characterized previous Western history

[3] Albert Fried and Ronald Sanders, eds., *Socialist Thought: A Documentary History* (Garden City, NY: Anchor Doubleday, 1964), p. 295.

had become simplified during the early nineteenth century into a struggle between the bourgeoisie and the proletariat, or between the middle class associated with industry and commerce, on the one hand, and the workers, on the other. The character of capitalism itself ensured the sharpening of the struggle. Capitalist production and competition would steadily increase the size of the unpropertied proletariat. Large-scale mechanical production crushed both traditional and smaller industrial producers into the ranks of the proletariat. As the business structures grew larger and larger, the competitive pressures would squeeze out smaller middle-class units. Competition among the few remaining giant concerns would lead to more intense suffering for the proletariat. The process also meant the proletariat itself would continue to expand to include more and more people. As this ever-expanding body of workers suffered increasingly from the competition among the ever-enlarging firms, Marx contended, they would eventually begin to foment revolution. Finally, they would overthrow the few remaining owners of the means of production. For a time, the workers would organize the means of production through a dictatorship of the proletariat. This would eventually give way to a propertyless and classless communist society.

This proletarian revolution was inevitable, according to Marx and Engels. The structure of capitalism required competition and consolidation of enterprise. Although the class conflict involved in the contemporary process resembled that of the past, it differed in one major respect: The struggle between the capitalistic bourgeoisie and the industrial proletariat would culminate in a wholly new society that would be free of class conflict. The victorious proletariat, by its very nature, could not be a new oppressor class: "The proletarian movement is the self-conscious, independent movement of the immense majority, in the interest of the immense majority."[4] The result of the proletarian victory would be "an association in which the free development of each is the condition for the free development of all."[5] The victory of the proletariat over the bourgeoisie would represent the culmination of human history. For the first time in human history, one group of people would not be oppressing another. (See "Karl Marx and Friedrich Engels Describe the Class Struggle.)

The economic environment of the 1840s had conditioned Marx's analysis. The decade had seen much unemployment and deprivation. During the later part of the century, however, European and American capitalism did not collapse as he had predicted, nor did the middle class become proletarianized. Rather, the industrial system benefited more and more people. Nonetheless, within a generation of the publication of the *Communist Manifesto*, Marxism had captured the imagination of many socialists, especially in Germany, and large segments of the working class. Marxist doctrines appeared to be based on the empirical evidence of hard economic fact. Marxism's scientific claim helped spread the ideology as science became more influential during the second half of the century. At its core, however, the attraction of the ideology was its utopian vision of ultimate human liberation, no matter how illiberal or authoritarian the governments that embraced the Marxist vision in the twentieth century were.

1848: YEAR OF REVOLUTIONS

In 1848, a series of liberal and nationalistic revolutions erupted across the Continent. (See Map 21–2, page 712.) No single factor caused this general revolutionary groundswell; rather, similar conditions existed in several countries. Severe food shortages had prevailed since 1846. Grain and potato harvests had been poor. The famine in Ireland was simply the worst example of a more widespread situation. The commercial and industrial economy was also depressed. Unemployment was widespread. Systems of poor relief were overburdened. These difficulties, added to the wretched living conditions in the cities, heightened the frustration and discontent of the urban artisan and laboring classes.

The dynamic force for change in 1848 originated, however, not with the working classes, but with the political liberals, who were generally drawn from the middle classes. Throughout the Continent, liberals were pushing for their program of a more representative government, civil liberty, and unregulated economic life. The repeal of the English Corn Laws and the example of peaceful agitation by the Anti-Corn Law League encouraged them. The liberals on the Continent wanted to pursue similar peaceful tactics. To put additional pressure on their governments, however, they began to appeal for the support of the urban working classes. The latter, however, wanted improved working and economic conditions, rather than a more liberal government. Moreover, their tactics were frequently violent rather than peaceful. The temporary alliance of liberals and workers in several states overthrew or severely shook the old order; then the allies began to fight each other.

[4]Robert C. Tucker, ed., *The Marx-Engels Reader* (New York: W. W. Norton, 1972), p. 353.

[5]Ibid.

KARL MARX AND FRIEDRICH ENGELS DESCRIBE THE CLASS STRUGGLE

The Communist Manifesto (1848) is arguably the most influential political pamphlet of modern European history. In that relatively brief document, Karl Marx and Friedrich Engels portrayed human history as developing from ancient times to the present through a series of economic class struggles. In the contemporary world, they saw the complex struggles of the past reduced to a head-on economic, political, and social clash between the bourgeoisie, or capital-owning class, and the proletariat, or workers. Both groups had emerged in the course of history. The bourgeoisie had arisen from medieval townsmen asserting their liberty against feudal landowners and then against other groups of aristocrats. In turn, as the bourgeoisie came to dominate the economy and invest their capital in modern industry, they produced the contemporary wage-labor force. Over time this labor force came to see that its interests opposed that of its economic masters. The result was to be the final class conflict of history because, as Marx and Engels argued, the proletariat, unlike any previous group seeking to establish its liberty, was so large that its victory was also the victory of humanity itself.

■ *Whom do Marx and Engels portray as the previous enemies of the bourgeoisie? How did bourgeois economic development and dominance lead to a society based on the "cash nexus"? Why is the bourgeoisie responsible for the emergence of the proletariat? Why is the victory of the proletariat inevitable?*

The history of all hitherto existing society is the history of class struggles. . . .

Our epoch, the epoch of the bourgeoisie, possesses, however, this distinctive feature: it has simplified the class antagonisms. Society as a whole is more and more splitting up into two great hostile camps, into two great classes directly facing each other: Bourgeoisie and Proletariat. . . .

Each step in the development of the bourgeoisie was accompanied by a corresponding political advance of that class. . . .

The bourgeoisie, wherever it has gotten the upper hand, has put an end to all feudal, patriarchal, idyllic relations. It has pitilessly torn asunder the motley feudal ties that bound man to his "natural superiors," and has left remaining no other nexus between man and man than naked self-interest, than callous "cash payment." . . .

The proletariat goes through various stages of development. With its birth begins its struggle with the bourgeoisie. . . .

But with the development of industry the proletariat not only increases in number; it becomes concentrated in greater masses, its strength grows, and it feels that strength more. The various interests and conditions of life within the ranks of the proletariat are more and more equalized, in proportion as machinery obliterates all distinctions of labour, and nearly everywhere reduces wages to the same low level. . . .

The bourgeoisie finds itself involved in a constant battle. . .

Of all the classes that stand face to face with the bourgeoisie today, the proletariat alone is a really revolutionary class. . . .

All previous historical movements were movements of minorities, or in the interest of minorities. The proletarian movement is the self-conscious, independent movement of the immense majority, in the interest of the immense majority. . . .

The advance of industry, whose involuntary promoter is the bourgeoisie, replaces the isolation of the labourers, due to competition, by their revolutionary combination, due to association. The development of Modern Industry, therefore, cuts from under its feet the very foundation on which the bourgeoisie produces and appropriates products. What the bourgeoisie, therefore, produces, above all, is its own grave-diggers. Its fall and the victory of the proletariat are equally inevitable. . . .

The proletarians have nothing to lose but their chains. They have a world to win.

Karl Marx and Friedrich Engels, *The Communist Manifesto*, in Lawrence H. Simon, ed., Karl Marx, *Selected Writings* (Indianapolis: Hackett Publishing Company, Inc, l994), pp. 158, 159, 160, 161, 165, 166–167, 168, 169, 186. © 1994 International Publishers Co. Reprinted by permission of International Publishers Co., Inc./New York.

Map 21–2 **CENTERS OF REVOLUTION IN 1848–1849** The revolution that toppled the July monarchy in Paris in 1848 soon spread to Austria and many of the German and Italian states. Yet by the end of 1849, most of these uprisings had been suppressed.

gressive Europeans. Without exception, the revolutions failed to establish genuinely liberal or national states. The conservative order proved stronger and more resilient than anyone had expected. Moreover, the liberal middle-class political activists in each country discovered they could no longer push for political reform without also raising the social question. The liberals refused to follow political revolution with social reform and thus isolated themselves from the working classes. Once separated from potential mass support, the liberal revolutions became an easy prey for the armies of the reactionary classes.

FRANCE: THE SECOND REPUBLIC AND LOUIS NAPOLEON

As had happened twice before, the revolutionary tinder first blazed in Paris. The liberal political opponents of the corrupt regime of Louis Philippe and his minister Guizot organized a series of political banquets. They used these occasions to criticize the government and demand further admission for them and their middle-class supporters to the political process. The poor harvests of 1846 and 1847 and the resulting high food prices and unemployment brought working-class support to the liberal campaign. On February 21, 1848, the government forbade further banquets. A large one had been scheduled for the next day. On February 22, disgruntled Parisian workers paraded through the streets demanding reform and Guizot's ouster. The next morning the crowds grew, and by afternoon, Guizot had resigned. The crowds erected barricades, and numerous clashes occurred between the citizenry and the municipal guard. On February 24, 1848, Louis Philippe abdicated and fled to England.

The National Assembly and Paris Workers The liberal opposition, led by the poet Alphonse de Lamartine (1790–1869), organized a provisional

Finally, outside France, nationalism was an important common factor in the uprisings. Germans, Hungarians, Italians, Czechs, and smaller national groups in eastern Europe sought to create national states that would reorganize or replace existing political entities. The Austrian Empire, as usual, was the state nationalism most profoundly endangered. At the same time, various national groups clashed with each other during these revolutions.

The immediate results of the 1848 revolutions were stunning. Never in a single year had Europe known so many major uprisings. The French monarchy fell, and other thrones were shaken. Yet the revolutions proved to be a false spring for pro-

During the February days of the French Revolution of 1848, crowds in Paris burned the throne of Louis Philippe.   Bildarchiv Preussischer Kulturbesitz

government. The liberals intended to call an election for an assembly that would write a republican constitution. The various working-class groups in Paris, however, had other ideas: They wanted a social as well as a political revolution. Led by Louis Blanc, they demanded representation in the cabinet. Blanc and two other radical leaders became ministers. Under their pressure, the provisional government organized national workshops to provide work and relief for thousands of unemployed workers.

On Sunday, April 23, an election based on universal male suffrage chose the new National Assembly. The result was a legislature dominated by moderates and conservatives. In the French provinces, many people resented the Paris radicals and were frightened by their ideas. The church and the local notables still exercised considerable influence. Peasants feared that Parisian socialists would confiscate their small farms. The new conservative National Assembly had little sympathy for the expensive national workshops, which they incorrectly perceived to be socialistic.

Throughout May, government troops and the unemployed workers and artisans of Paris clashed. As a result, the assembly closed the workshops to new entrants and planned to eject many enrolled workers. By late June, barricades again appeared in Paris. On June 24, under orders from the government, General Louis Cavaignac (1802–1857), with troops drawn largely from the conservative countryside, moved to destroy the barricades and quell disturbances. During the next two days, more than four hundred people were killed. Thereafter, troops hunted down another 3,000 persons in street fighting. The drive for social revolution had ended.

Emergence of Louis Napoleon   The so-called June Days confirmed the political predominance of conservative property holders in French life. They wanted a state that was safe for small property. Late in 1848, the election for president confirmed this search for social order. The new president was Louis Napoleon Bonaparte (1808–1873), a nephew of the great emperor. For most of his life, he had been an adventurer living outside of France. Twice he had attempted to lead a coup against the July Monarchy. The disorder of 1848 gave him a new opportunity to enter French political life. After the corruption of Louis Philippe and the turmoil of the early months of the Second Republic, the voters turned to the name of Bonaparte as a source of stability and greatness.

The election of the "Little Napoleon" doomed the Second Republic. Louis Napoleon was dedicated to his own fame rather than to republican institutions. He was the first of the modern dictators who, by playing on unstable politics and social insecurity, changed European life. He quarreled with the National Assembly and claimed that he, rather than they, represented the will of the nation. In 1851, the assembly refused to amend the constitution to allow the president to run for reelection. Consequently, on December 2, 1851, the anniversary of the great Napoleon's victory at Austerlitz, Louis Napoleon seized power. Troops dispersed the assembly, and the president called for new elections. More than 200 people died resisting the coup, and more than 26,000 persons were arrested throughout the country. Almost 10,000 persons who opposed the coup were transported to Algeria.

Yet, in the plebiscite of December 21, 1851, more than 7.5 million voters supported the actions of Louis Napoleon and approved a new constitution that consolidated his power. Only about 600,000 citizens dared to vote against him. A year later, in December 1852, an empire was proclaimed, and Louis Napoleon became Emperor Napoleon III. Again a plebiscite approved the action. For the second time in just over fifty years, France had turned from republicanism to Caesarism.

Frenchwomen in 1848   The years between the February Revolution of 1848 and the Napoleonic coup of 1851 saw major feminist activity by Frenchwomen. Especially in Paris, women seized the opportunity of the collapse of the July Monarchy to voice demands for reform of their social conditions. They joined the wide variety of political clubs that emerged in the wake of the revolution. Some of these clubs emphasized women's rights. Some women even tried unsuccessfully to vote in the elections of 1848. Both middle-class and working-class women were involved in these activities. The most radical group of women called themselves the Vesuvians, after the volcano in Italy. They claimed it was time for the demands of women to erupt like pent-up lava. They demanded full domestic household equality between men and women, the right of women to serve in the military, and similarity in dress for both sexes. They also conducted street demonstrations. The radical character of their demands and actions lost them the support of more moderate women.

Certain Parisian women quickly attempted to use for their own cause the liberal freedoms that suddenly had become available. They organized the *Voix des femmes (The Women's Voice)*, a daily newspaper that addressed issues of concern to women. The newspaper insisted that improving the lot of men would not necessarily improve the condition of women. They soon organized a society with the same name as the newspaper. Many of the women involved in the newspaper and society had earlier been involved in Saint-Simonian or Fourierist groups. Members of the *Voix des femmes* group were relatively conservative feminists. They cooperated with male political groups, and they urged the integrity of the family and fidelity in marriage. They furthermore warmly embraced the maternal role for women, but tried to use it to raise the importance of women in society. Because motherhood and child rearing are so important to a society, they argued, women must receive better education, economic security, equal civil rights, property rights, and the rights to work and vote. The provisional government made no move to enact these rights, although some members of the assembly supported the women's groups. The emphasis on family and motherhood represented, in part, a defensive strategy to prevent conservative women and men from accusing the advocates of women's rights of seeking to destroy the family and traditional marriage.

The fate of French feminists in 1848 was similar to that of the radical workers. They were thoroughly defeated and their efforts wholly frustrated. Once the elections were held that spring, the new government expressed no sympathy for their causes. The closing of the national workshops adversely affected women workers as well as men and blocked one outlet that women had used to make their needs known. The conservative crackdown on political clubs closed another arena in which women had participated. Women were soon specifically forbidden to participate in political clubs either by themselves or with men. These repressive actions repeated what had happened to politically active Frenchwomen and their organizations in 1793.

At this point, women associated with the *Voix des femmes* attempted to organize workers' groups to improve the economic situation for working-class women. Two leaders of this effort, Jeanne Deroin (d. 1894) and Pauline Roland (1805–1852), were arrested, tried, and imprisoned for these activities. The former eventually left France; the lat-

THE REVOLUTIONARY CRISIS OF 1848 TO 1851

1848

February 22–24	Revolution in Paris forces the abdication of Louis Philippe
February 26	National workshops established in Paris
March 3	Kossuth attacks the Habsburg domination of Hungary
March 13	Revolution in Vienna
March 15	The Habsburg emperor accepts the Hungarian March Revolution Laws in Berlin
March 18	Frederick William IV of Prussia promises a constitution; revolt against Austria in Milan
March 19	Frederick William IV is forced to salute the corpses of slain revolutionaries in Berlin
March 22	Piedmont declares war on Austria
April 23	Election of the French National Assembly
May 15	Worker protests in Paris lead the National Assembly to close the national workshops
May 17	Habsburg emperor Ferdinand flees from Vienna to Innsbruck
May 18	The Frankfurt Assembly gathers to prepare a German constitution
June 2	Pan-Slavic Congress gathers in Prague
June 17	Austrian troops suppress a Czech revolution in Prague
June 23–26	Troops of the National Assembly suppress a workers' insurrection in Paris
July 24	Austria defeats Piedmont
September 17	General Jellachich invades Hungary
October 31	Vienna falls to General Windischgraetz
November 15	Papal minister Rossi is assassinated in Rome
November 16	Revolution in Rome
November 25	Pope Pius IX flees Rome
December 2	Habsburg Emperor Ferdinand abdicates and Francis Joseph becomes emperor
December 10	Louis Napoleon is elected president of the Second French Republic

1849

January 5	General Windischgraetz occupies Budapest
February 2	The Roman Republic is proclaimed
March 12	War is resumed between Piedmont and Austria
March 23	Piedmont is defeated, and Charles Albert abdicates the crown of Piedmont in favor of Victor Emmanuel II
March 27	The Frankfurt Parliament completes a constitution for Germany
March 28	The Frankfurt Parliament elects Frederick William IV of Prussia to be emperor of Germany
April 21	Frederick William IV of Prussia rejects the crown offered by the Frankfurt Parliament
June 18	Troops disperse the remaining members of the Frankfurt Parliament
July 3	French troops overthrow the Roman Republic
August 9–13	Austria, aided by Russian troops, defeats the Hungarians

1851

December 2	*Coup d'état* of Louis Napoleon

ter was sent off to Algeria during the repression after the coup of Louis Napoleon. By 1852, the entire feminist movement that had sprung up in 1848 had been eradicated.

THE HABSBURG EMPIRE: NATIONALISM RESISTED

The events of February 1848 in Paris immediately reverberated throughout the Habsburg domains. The empire was susceptible to revolutionary challenge on every score. Its government rejected liberal institutions. Its borders cut across national lines. Its society perpetuated serfdom. During the 1840s, even Metternich had urged reform, but none was forthcoming. In 1848, the regime confronted rebellions in Vienna, Prague, Hungary, and Italy. The disturbances that broke out in Germany also threatened Habsburg predominance.

The Vienna Uprising The Habsburg troubles began on March 3, 1848, when Louis Kossuth (1802–1894), a Magyar nationalist and member of the Hungarian diet, attacked Austrian domination, called for the independence of Hungary, and demanded a responsible ministry under the Habsburg dynasty. Ten days later, inspired by Kossuth's speeches, students led a

Louis Kossuth, a Magyar nationalist, seeking to raise troops to fight for Hungarian independence during the revolutionary disturbances of 1848.
Bildarchiv Preussischer Kulturbesitz

series of disturbances in Vienna. The army failed to restore order. Metternich resigned and fled the country. The feeble-minded Emperor Ferdinand (r. 1835–1848) promised a moderately liberal constitution. Unsatisfied, the radical students then formed democratic clubs to press the revolution further. On May 17, the emperor and the imperial court fled to Innsbruck. The government of Vienna at this point lay in the hands of a committee of more than two hundred persons concerned primarily with alleviating the economic plight of the city's workers.

What the Habsburg government most feared was not the urban rebellions but an uprising of the serfs in the countryside. Already a few serfs had invaded manor houses and burned property records. Consequently, almost immediately after the Vienna uprising, the imperial government emancipated the serfs in much of Austria. The Hungarian diet also abolished serfdom in March 1848. These actions smothered the most serious potential threat to order in the empire. The emancipated serfs now had little reason to support the revolutionary movement in the cities. These emancipations were one of the most important permanent results of the Revolutions of 1848.

The Magyar Revolt The Vienna revolt had emboldened the Hungarians. The Magyar leaders of the Hungarian March Revolution were primarily liberals supported by nobles who wanted their aristocratic liberties guaranteed against the central government in Vienna. The Hungarian diet passed the March Laws, which mandated equality of religion, jury trials, the election of the lower chamber of the diet, a relatively free press, and payment of taxes by the nobility. Emperor Ferdinand approved these measures because in the spring of 1848 he could do little else.

The Magyars also hoped to establish a separate Hungarian state within the Habsburg domains. They would exercise local autonomy while Ferdinand remained their emperor. As part of this scheme for a partially independent state, the Hungarians attempted to annex Transylvania, Croatia, and other eastern territories of the Habsburg Empire. That annexation would have brought Romanians, Croatians, and Serbs under Magyar government. These national groups resisted the drive toward Magyarization, especially the imposition on them, for the purposes of the government and administration, of the Hungarian language. The national groups whom the Hungarians were now repressing believed the Habsburgs offered them a better chance to preserve their national or ethnic identity, their languages, and their economic self-interest. In late March, the Vienna government sent Count Joseph Jellachich (1801–1859) to aid the national groups who were rebelling against the rebellious Hungarians. By early September 1848, he was invading Hungary with the support of the national groups who were resisting Magyarization. These events in Hungary represented a prime example of the clash between liberalism and nationalism. The Hungarian March Laws would have created a state that was liberal in political structure but would not have allowed autonomy to the non-Magyar peoples within its borders.

Czech Nationalism In the mid-March 1848, with Vienna and Budapest in revolt, Czech nationalists demanded that the Czech provinces of Bohemia and Moravia be permitted to constitute an autonomous Slavic state within the empire similar to that just enacted in Hungary. Conflict immediately developed, however, between the Czechs and the Germans living in these regions. The Czechs summoned a congress of Slavs, including Poles, Ruthenians, Czechs, Slovaks, Croats, Slovenes, and Serbs, which met in Prague in early June. Under the leadership of Francis Palacky (1798–

1876), this first Pan-Slavic Congress called for the national equality of Slavs within the Habsburg Empire. The manifesto also protested the repression of all Slavic peoples under Habsburg, Hungarian, German, and Ottoman domination. The document raised the vision of a vast east European Slavic nation or federation of Slavic states that would extend from Poland south and eastward through Ukraine and within which Russian interests would surely dominate. Although such a state never came into being, the prospect of a unified Slavic people freed from Ottoman, Habsburg, and German control was an important political factor in later European history. Russia would use Pan-Slavism as a tool to attempt to gain the support of nationalist minorities in eastern Europe and the Balkans and to bring pressure against both the Habsburg Empire and Germany. (See "The Pan-Slavic Congress Calls for the Liberation of Slavs," page 718.)

On June 12, the day the Pan-Slavic Congress closed, a radical insurrection broke out in Prague. General Prince Alfred Windischgraetz (1787–1862), whose wife had been killed by a stray bullet, moved his troops against the uprising. The Prague middle class was happy to see the radicals suppressed, which was finalized by June 17. The Germans in the area approved the smothering of Czech nationalism. The policy of "divide and conquer" had succeeded.

Rebellion in Northern Italy While repelling the Hungarian and Czech bids for autonomy, the Habsburg government also faced war in northern Italy. A revolt against Habsburg domination began in Milan on March 18. Five days later, the Austrian commander General Count Joseph Wenzel Radetzky (1766–1858) retreated from the city. King Charles Albert of Piedmont (r. 1831–1849), who wanted to annex Lombardy (the province of which Milan is the capital), aided the rebels. The Austrian forces fared badly until July, when Radetzky, reinforced by new troops, defeated Piedmont and suppressed the revolt. For the time being, Austria held its position in northern Italy.

Vienna and Hungary remained to be recaptured. In midsummer, the emperor returned to the capital. A newly elected assembly was trying to write a constitution, and within the city, the radicals continued to press for concessions. The imperial government decided to reassert its control. When a new insurrection occurred in October, the imperial army bombarded Vienna and crushed the revolt. On December 2, Emperor Ferdinand, clearly too feeble to govern, abdicated in favor of his young nephew Francis Joseph (r. 1848–1916). Real power now lay with Prince Felix Schwarzenberg

(1800–1852), who intended to use the army with full force.

On January 5, 1849, troops occupied Budapest. By March the triumphant Austrian forces had imposed military rule over Hungary, and the new emperor repudiated the recent constitution. The Magyar nobles attempted one last revolt. In August, Austrian troops, reinforced by 200,000 soldiers that Tsar Nicholas I of Russia (r. 1825–1855) happily furnished, finally crushed the Hungarians. Croatians and other nationalities that had resisted Magyarization welcomed the collapse of the revolt. The imperial Habsburg government survived its gravest internal challenge because of the divisions among its enemies and its own willingness to use military force with a vengeance.

ITALY: REPUBLICANISM DEFEATED

The brief war between Piedmont and Austria in 1848 marked only the first stage of the Italian revolution. Many Italians hoped King Charles Albert of Piedmont would drive Austria from the peninsula and thus prepare the way for Italian unification. The defeat of Piedmont was a sharp disappointment to them. Liberal and nationalist hopes then shifted to the pope. Pius IX (r. 1846–1878) had a liberal reputation. He had reformed the administration of the Papal States. Nationalists believed a united Italian state might emerge under his leadership.

In Rome, however, as in other cities, political radicalism was on the rise. On November 15, 1848, a democratic radical assassinated Count Pelligrino Rossi (r. 1787–1848), the liberal minister of the Papal States. The next day, popular demonstrations forced the pope to appoint a radical ministry. Shortly thereafter, Pius IX fled to Naples for refuge. In February 1849, the radicals proclaimed the Roman Republic. Republican nationalists from all over Italy, including Giuseppe Mazzini (1805–1872) and Giuseppe Garibaldi (1807–1882), two of the most prominent, flocked to Rome. They hoped to use the new republic as a base of operations to unite the rest of Italy under a republican government.

In March 1849, radicals in Piedmont forced Charles Albert to renew the patriotic war against Austria. After the almost immediate defeat of Piedmont at the Battle of Novara, the king abdicated in favor of his son, Victor Emmanuel II (r. 1849–1878). The defeat meant the Roman Republic must defend itself alone. The troops that attacked Rome and restored the pope came from France. The French wanted to prevent the rise of a strong, unified state on their southern border. Moreover, protection of the pope was good

THE PAN-SLAVIC CONGRESS CALLS FOR THE LIBERATION OF SLAVS

The first Pan-Slavic Congress met in Prague in June 1848. It called for the political reorganization of the Austrian Empire and most of eastern Europe. Its calls for changes in the national standing of the various Slavic peoples would have affected the Russian, Austrian, and Ottoman empires, as well as some of the then disunited states of Germany. The national aspirations the congress voiced would affect Europe from that time to the present. Note that the authors of the manifesto recognize that the principle of nationality, as adapted to the political life of Slavic peoples, is relatively new in 1848.

■ *How did the authors apply the individual freedoms associated with the French Revolution to the fate of individual nations? What areas of Europe would these demands have changed? What potential differences among the Slavic peoples does the manifesto ignore or gloss over?*

The Slavic Congress in Prague is something unheard-of, in Europe as well as among the Slavs themselves. For the first time since our appearance in history, we, the scattered members of a great race, have gathered in great numbers from distant lands in order to become reacquainted as brothers and to deliberate our affairs peacefully. We have understood one another not only through our beautiful language, spoken by eighty million, but also through the consonance of our hearts and the similarity of our spiritual qualities. . . .

It is not only in behalf of the individual within the state that we raise our voices and make known our demands. The nation, with all its intellectual merit, is as sacred to us as are the rights of an individual under natural law. . . .

In the belief that the powerful spiritual stream of today demands new political forms and that the state must be re-established upon altered principles, if not within new boundaries, we have suggested to the Austrian Emperor, under whose constitutional government we, the majority [of Slavic peoples] live, that he transform his imperial state into a union of equal nations. . . .

We raise our voices vigorously in behalf of our unfortunate brothers, the Poles, who were robbed of their national identity by insidious force. We call upon the governments to rectify this curse and these old onerous and hereditary sins in their administrative policy, and we trust in the compassion of all Europe. . . . We demand that the Hungarian Ministry abolish without delay the use of inhuman and coercive means toward the Slavic races in Hungary, namely the Serbs, Croats, Slovaks, and Ruthenians, and that they promptly be completely assured of their national rights. Finally, we hope that the inconsiderate policies of the Porte will no longer hinder our Slavic brothers in Turkey from strongly claiming their nationality and developing it in a natural way. If, therefore, we formally express our opposition to such despicable deeds, we do so in the confidence that we are working for the good of freedom. Freedom makes the peoples who hitherto have ruled more just and makes them understand that injustice and arrogance bring disgrace not to those who must endure it but to those who act in such a manner.

From the "Manifesto of the First Pan-Slavic Congress," trans. by Max Riedlsperger from I. I. Udalzow, *Aufzeichnungen über die Geschichte des nationalen und politischen Kampfes in Böhme im Jahre 1848* (Berlin: Rutten & Loening, 1953), pp. 223–226, as quoted in Stephen Fischer-Galati, ed., *Man, State, and Society in East European History.* Copyright © 1970 by Praeger Publishers. Reproduced by permission of Greenwood Publishing Group, Inc., Westport, CT.

domestic politics for the French Republic and its president, Louis Napoleon. In early June 1849, 10,000 French soldiers laid siege to Rome. By the end of the month, the Roman Republic had dissolved. Garibaldi attempted to lead an army north against Austria, but he was defeated. On July 3, Rome fell to the French forces, which stayed there to protect the pope until 1870.

Pius IX renounced his liberalism. He became one of the arch conservatives of the next quarter century. Leadership for Italian unification would have to come from another direction.

GERMANY: LIBERALISM FRUSTRATED

The revolutionary contagion had also spread rapidly through the German states. Insurrections calling for liberal government and greater German unity erupted in Wurtemburg, Saxony, Hanover, and Bavaria where King Ludwig I (r. 1825–1848) was forced to abdicate in favor of his son. The major revolution, however, occurred in Prussia.

Revolution in Prussia By March 15, 1848, large popular disturbances had erupted in Berlin. Frederick William IV (r. 1840–1861), believing the trouble stemmed from foreign conspirators, refused to turn his troops on the Berliners. He even announced limited reforms. Nevertheless, on March 18, several citizens were killed when troops cleared a square near the palace.

The monarch was still hesitant to use his troops forcefully, and the government was divided and confused. The king called for a Prussian constituent assembly to write a constitution. The next day, as angry Berliners crowded around the palace, Frederick William IV appeared on the balcony to salute the corpses of his slain subjects. He made further concessions and implied that henceforth Prussia would helped unify Germany. For all practical purposes, the Prussian monarchy had capitulated.

Frederick William IV appointed a cabinet headed by David Hansemann (1790–1864), a widely respected moderate liberal. The Prussian constituent assembly, however, proved to be radical and democratic. As time passed, the king and his conservative supporters decided to ignore the assembly. The liberal ministry resigned and a conservative one replaced it. In April 1849, the assembly was dissolved, and the monarch proclaimed his own constitution. One of its key elements was a system of three-class voting. All adult males were allowed to vote. They voted, however, according to three classes arranged by ability to pay taxes. Thus the largest taxpayers, who constituted only about 5 percent of the population, elected one-third of the Prussian Parliament. This system prevailed in Prussia until 1918. In the revised Prussian constitution of 1850, the ministry was responsible to the king alone. Moreover, the Prussian army and officer corps swore loyalty directly to the monarch.

The Frankfurt Parliament While Prussia was moving from revolution to reaction, other events were unfolding in Germany as a whole. On May 18, 1848, representatives from all the German states gathered in Saint Paul's Church in Frankfurt to revise the organization of the German Confederation. The Frankfurt Parliament intended to write a moderately liberal constitution for a united Germany. The liberal character of the Frankfurt Parliament alienated both German conservatives and the German working class. The very existence of the parliament, representing as it did a challenge to the existing political order, offended the conservatives. The Frankfurt Parliament's refusal to restore the protection the guilds had once afforded cost it the support of the industrial workers and artisans. The liberals were too attached to the concept of a free labor market to offer meaningful legislation to workers. This failure marked the beginning of a profound split between German liberals and the German working class. For the rest of the century, German conservatives would be able to play on that division.

As if to demonstrate its disaffection from workers, in September 1848, the Frankfurt Parliament called in troops of the German Confederation to suppress a radical insurrection in the city. The liberals in the parliament wanted nothing to do with workers who erected barricades and threatened the safety of property.

The Frankfurt Parliament also floundered on the issue of unification. Members differed over whether to include Austria in a united Germany. The "large German [*grossdeutsch*] solution" favored Austria's inclusion, whereas the "small German [*kleindeutsch*] solution" advocated its exclusion. The latter formula prevailed because Austria rejected the whole notion of German unification, which raised too many other nationality problems within the Habsburg domains. Consequently, the Frankfurt Parliament looked to Prussian, rather than Austrian, leadership.

On March 27, 1849, the parliament produced its constitution. Shortly thereafter, its delegates offered the crown of a united Germany to Frederick William IV of Prussia. He rejected the offer, asserting that kings ruled by the grace of God rather than by the permission of man-made constitutions. On his refusal, the Frankfurt Parliament began to dissolve. Not long afterward, troops drove off the remaining members.

German liberals never fully recovered from this defeat. The Frankfurt Parliament had alienated the artisans and the working class without gaining any compensating support from the conservatives. The liberals had proved themselves to be awkward, hesitant, unrealistic, and ultimately dependent on the armies of the monarchies. They had failed to unite Germany or to confront effectively the realities of political power in the German states.

The various revolutions did manage to extend the franchise in some of the German states and to establish conservative constitutions. The gains were not negligible, but they were a far cry from the hopes of March 1848.

IN PERSPECTIVE

The first half of the nineteenth century witnessed unprecedented social change in Europe. The foundations of the industrial economy were laid. That emerging economy changed virtually every existing institution. Railways crossed the Continent. New consumer goods became available. Family patterns changed, as did the social and economic expectations of women. The crowding of cities presented new social and political problems. The new concern about crime and the establishment of police forces brought issues of social order to the foreground. An urban working class became one of the chief facts of both political and social life. The ebb and flow of the business cycle increased economic anxiety for workers and property owners alike.

While all these fundamental social changes took place, Europe was also experiencing continuing political strife. The turmoil of 1848 through 1850 ended the era of liberal revolution that had begun in 1789. Liberals and nationalists discovered that rational argument and small, local insurrections would not achieve their goals. The political initiative passed for a time to the conservative political groups. Henceforth, nationalists were less romantic and more hardheaded. Railways, commerce, guns, soldiers, and devious diplomacy, rather than language and cultural heritage, became the future weapons of national unification. The working class also adopted new tactics and a new organization. The era of the riot and urban insurrection was ending; in the future, workers would turn to trade unions and political parties to achieve their political and social goals.

Perhaps most importantly after 1848, the European middle class ceased to be revolutionary. It became increasingly concerned about protecting its property against radical political and social movements associated with socialism and, as the century passed, with Marxism. The middle class remained politically liberal only so long as liberalism seemed to promise economic stability and social security for its own style of life.

Finally, as will be seen more fully in the next chapter, the revolutions of 1848 also changed European conservatism. Metternich's conservative policies had not prevented the upheavals of 1848. In the following decades, European conservatives would find new ways to adapt some of the new forces of European politics to their ends. They would embrace their own forms of nationalism and even democratic structures to ensure that they remained dominant over much of Europe.

REVIEW QUESTIONS

1. What inventions were particularly important in the development of industrialism? How did industrialism change society? Why were the years covered in this chapter so difficult for artisans? How was the European labor force transformed into a wage-labor workforce?

2. How did the industrial economy change the working-class family? What roles and duties did various family members assume? How did the role of women change in the new industrial era?

3. What were the goals of the working class in the new industrial society, and how did they differ from middle-class goals? Why did the working class and the middle class pursue different goals?

4. Why did European states create police forces in the nineteenth century? How and why did prisons change during this era?

5. How would you define socialism? What were the chief ideas of the early socialists? How did the ideas of Karl Marx differ from those of the socialists? What historical role did Marx assign to the proletariat?

6. What factors, old and new, led to the widespread outbreak of the revolutions in 1848? Were the causes in the various countries essentially the same, or did each have its own particular set of circumstances? Why did these revolutions fail throughout Europe? What roles did liberals and nationalists play in the revolutions? Why did they sometimes clash?

SUGGESTED READINGS

B. S. ANDERSON AND J. P. ZINSSER, *A History of Their Own: Women in Europe from Prehistory to the Present*, vol. 2 (1988). A wide-ranging survey.

I. BERLIN, *Karl Marx: His Life and Environment*, 4th ed. (1996). A classic introduction.

E. D. BROSE, *The Politics of Technological Change in Prussia: Out of the Shadow of Antiquity, 1809–1848* (1993). Examines how various social groups understood the economic growth and industrialization of Prussia.

R. B. CARLISLE, *The Proffered Crown: Saint-Simonianism and the Doctrine of Hope* (1987). The best treatment of the broad social doctrines of Saint-Simonianism.

J. COFFIN, *The Politics of Women's Work* (1996). Examines the subject in France.

I. DEAK, *The Lawful Revolution: Louis Kossuth and the Hungarians, 1848–1849* (1979). The most significant study of the topic in English.

J. F. C. HARRISON, *Quest for the New Moral World: Robert Owen and the Owenites in Britain and America* (1969). The standard work.

D. I. KERTZER AND M. BARBAGLI (EDS.), *Family Life in the Long Nineteenth Century, 1789–1913: The History of the European Family* (2002). Wide-ranging collection of essays.

K. KOLAKOWSKI, *Main Currents of Marxism: Its Rise, Growth, and Dissolution*, 3 vols. (1978). An important and comprehensive survey.

D. LANDES, *The Unbound Prometheus: Technological Change and Industrial Development in Western Europe from 1750 to the Present* (1969). Classic one-volume treatment of technological development in a broad social and economic context.

H. PERKIN, *The Origins of Modern English Society, 1780–1880* (1969). A provocative attempt to look at the society as a whole.

J. D. RANDERS-PEHRSON, *Germans and the Revolution of 1848–1849* (2001). An exhaustive treatment of the subject.

W. H. SEWELL, JR., *Work and Revolution in France: The Language of Labor from the Old Regime to 1848* (1980). A fine analysis of French artisans.

J. SPERBER, *The European Revolution, 1841–1851* (1993). An excellent synthesis.

E. P. THOMPSON, *The Making of the English Working Class* (1964). A classic work.

D. WINCH, *Riches and Poverty: An Intellectual History of Political Economy in Britain, 1750–1834* (1996). A superb survey from Adam Smith through Thomas Malthus.

DOCUMENTS CD-ROM

Reaction, Reform and Revolt

21.5 Karl Marx and Friedrich Engels: *The Communist Manifesto*

21.6 Michael Harrington, from *Socialism: Past and Future*

21.7 Anarchism: Michael Bakunin

Industrialization

22.1 Extolling the Virtues of the Manufacturer

22.2 Child Labor Inquiry

22.6 Improving the Poor?

THE ABOLITION OF SLAVERY IN THE TRANSATLANTIC ECONOMY

One of the most important developments during the age of Enlightenment and revolution was the opening of a crusade to abolish chattel slavery in the transatlantic economy. The antislavery movement constituted the greatest and most extensive achievement of liberal reformers during the eighteenth and nineteenth centuries. Indeed, it marked the first time in the history of the world that a society actually tried to abolish slavery. This achievement came as the result of the impact of Christian ethics, Enlightenment ideals, slave revolts, revolutionary wars in America and Europe, civil war in the United States, and economic dislocation in the slave economies themselves. In 1750, almost no one seriously questioned the existence of slavery, but, by 1888, the institution no longer existed in the transatlantic economy.

Chattel slavery—the ownership of one human being by another—had existed in the West as well as elsewhere in the world since ancient times and had received intellectual and religious justification throughout the history of the West. Both Plato and Aristotle provided arguments for slavery based on the assertion that persons in bondage were intended by nature to be slaves. Christian writers similarly accommodated themselves to the institution. They contended that the most harmful form of slavery was the enslavement of the soul to sin rather than the enslavement of the physical body. They also argued that genuine freedom was realized through one's relationship to God and that problems relating to the injustices of inequality would be solved in the hereafter. Christian scholastic thinkers in the Middle Ages portrayed slavery as part of the natural and necessary hierarchy of the universe.

SLAVERY SPREADS TO THE AMERICAS

Although a vast slave trade existed throughout the Mediterranean world through the end of the Middle Ages, slavery was no longer a dominant institution on the European continent or within the European economy. The European encounter with America at the end of the fifteenth century radically transformed this situation. The American continent and the West Indies presented opportunities for achieving great wealth, but a major labor shortage existed in these regions. Eventually slavery provided the means to resolve this labor shortage.

The establishment and maintenance of slavery in the transatlantic economy drew Europeans and Americans into various relationships with Africa. About the same time as the encounter with America, Europeans made contact with areas of West Africa where slavery already existed. This region became the chief source of slaves imported into the Americas. Four centuries later, during the antislavery movement, Europeans would seek to change the African economy by ending its dependence on the slave trade. Those efforts led to the penetration of Africa by European traders, missionaries, and finally colonial forces and administrators.

Although at one time or another slaves labored throughout the Americas, the system of slavery became primarily identified with the plantation economy stretching from Maryland south to Brazil, where tropical products, initially primarily sugar, were produced by slave labor. This plantation economy existed from approximately the late sixteenth through the late nineteenth centuries. The slaves on whose labor this economy was based included Native Americans enslaved within both the Spanish Empire and North America, and Africans forcibly imported into the Americas. Consequently, the slaves were virtually always of a different race from their masters. Race itself soon became part of the justification for the social hierarchy of the plantation world. In and of itself, the fact of slavery in the Americas was not unusual to the Western experience or to that of other societies in Africa or Asia. Slavery had existed at most times and places in human history. Far more unusual in the history of the West, and for that matter in the experience of all other societies that had held and continued to hold slaves, was the emergence after 1760 of an international movement to abolish chattel slavery in the transatlantic economy.

THE CRUSADE AGAINST SLAVERY

The eighteenth-century crusade against slavery originated in a profound change in the religious and intellectual outlooks on slavery among small but influential groups in both America and Europe. The entire thrust of Enlightenment reasoning to the extent that it challenged or questioned the wisdom of existing institutions gnawed away at the older defenses of slavery, most particularly the concept of an unchanging social hierarchy. Although some writers associated with the Enlightenment, including John Locke, were reluctant to question slavery and even defended it, the general Enlightenment rhetoric of equality stood in sharp contrast to the radical inequality of slavery. Montesquieu sharply satirized slavery in *The Spirit of the Laws* (1748). Similarly, the emphasis of Adam Smith in *The Wealth of Nations* (1776) on free labor and efficiency of free markets undermined defenses of slavery.

Within much eighteenth-century literature, there emerged a tendency to idealize primitive peoples living in cultures very different from those of Europe. Previously such peoples had been regarded as backward and rebellious. Now numerous writers portrayed them as embodying a lost human virtue. This expanding body of literature transformed the way many people thought about slavery and allowed some Europeans to look on African slaves in the Americas as having been betrayed and robbed of an original innocence. Additionally, much eighteenth-century European ethical thinking, as well as later romantic poetry, emphasized empathy and feeling. In such a climate, attitudes toward slavery were transformed. Once considered to be the natural and deserved result of some deficiency in slaves themselves, slavery now grew to be regarded as undeserved and unacceptable. The same kind of ethical thinking led reformers to believe that by working against slavery, for virtually the first time defined as an unmitigated evil, they would realize their own highest ethical character.

Religious movements became the single most important cultural force to foster the antislavery crusade. The evangelical religious revival associated with Methodism and with other forms of Protestant preaching emphasized the conversion experience and the change of heart as a sign of hav-

After 1807, the British Royal Navy patrolled the West African coast attempting to intercept slave-trading ships. In 1846, the British ship HMS *Albatross* captured a Spanish slave ship, the *Albañoz*, and freed the slaves. A British officer depicted the appalling conditions in the slave hold in this watercolor.   The Granger Collection, New York

ing received salvation. In 1774, John Wesley, the founder of Methodism, attacked slaveholding in *Thoughts on Slavery*. Turning against slaveholding and slave trading by plantation owners and slave traders served to illustrate one clear example of such a change of heart. Some slaveholders and slave traders feared they might be endangering their own salvation by their association with the institution. John Newton, a former slave trader who underwent an evangelical conversion, wrote the hymn "Amazing Grace."

The initial religious protest against slavery originated among English Quakers, a radical Protestant religious group founded by George Fox in the seventeenth century. By the early eighteenth century, it had solidified itself into a small but relatively wealthy sect in England. Members of Quaker congregations at that time actually owned slaves in the West Indies and participated in the transatlantic slave trade. During the Seven Years' War (1756–1763), however, many Quakers experienced economic hardship. Furthermore, the war created other difficulties for the English population as a whole. Certain Quakers decided the presence of the evil of slavery in the world explained these troubles. They then sought to remove this evil from their own lives and that of their congregations and began to take action against the whole system of slavery that characterized the transatlantic economy.

Just as the slave system was a transatlantic affair, so was the crusade against it. Quakers in both Philadelphia and England soon moved against the institution. The most influential of the early antislavery writers was Anthony Benezet, a Philadelphia Quaker, whose most important publications were *Some Considerations on the Keeping of Negroes* (1754) and *A Short Account of That Part of Africa Inhabited by the Negroes* (1762). The latter work emphasized the manner in which the slave trade degraded African society itself. Benezet also drew heavily on Montesquieu. This may not be surprising because Enlightenment writers often admired the English Quakers as exemplifying a religion of tolerance and reason.

By the earliest stages of the American Revolution a small group of reformers, normally spearheaded by Quakers, had established an antislavery network. They published pamphlets, sermons, and books on the subject. The Society for the Relief of Free Negroes Illegally Held in Bondage, the first antislavery society in the world, was founded in Philadelphia in 1775 and, when reorganized in 1784 as the Pennsylvania Abolition Society, Benjamin Franklin became its president. In 1787, the Committee for the Abolition of the Slave Trade was organized in England. In France, the Société des Amis des Noirs was founded in 1778.

The turmoil of the American Revolution and the founding of the American republic gave these groups the occasion for some of their earliest successes. Emancipation gradually, but nonetheless steadily, spread among the northern states. In 1787, the Continental Congress forbade the presence of slavery in the newly organized Northwest Territory north of the Ohio River. What is important so far as the crusade against slavery is concerned is the disappearance of slavery in approximately half of the new nation and the commitment not to extend it to an important new territory. Despite these American developments, Great Britain became and remained the center for the antislavery movement. In 1772, a decision by the chief justice affirmed that slaves brought into Great Britain could not forcibly be removed. The decision, though of less immediate importance than some thought at the time, gave further impetus to the small but growing group of antislavery reformers.

During the early 1780s, the antislavery reformers in Great Britain decided to work toward ending the slave trade rather than the institution of slavery. The horrors of the slave trade caught the public's attention in 1783 when the captain of the slave ship *Zong* threw more than 130 slaves overboard in order to collect insurance. For the reformers, attacking the trade rather than the institution appeared a less radical and a more achievable reform. To many, the slave trade appeared to be a more obvious crime than the holding of slaves, which seemed a more nearly passive act. Furthermore, attacking slavery itself involved serious issues of property rights that might alienate potential supporters of the abolition of the slave

The slave revolt on the French Island of St. Domingue achieved the largest emancipation of slaves in the eighteenth century. In this print, Toussaint-L'Ouverture leads the revolt. CORBIS

trade. The antislavery groups also believed that if the trade was ended, planters would have to treat their remaining slaves more humanely.

By the end of the 1780s, the English Quakers were joined by evangelical Christians from the Church of England to form the Society for the Abolition of the Slave Trade. The most famous of the new leaders was William Wilberforce who, for the rest of his life, fought the slave trade. Year after year, he introduced a bill to abolish the slave trade. Finally, in 1807, he saw it passed.

SLAVE REVOLTS

While the British reformers worked for the abolition of the slave trade, slaves themselves in certain areas took matters into their own hands. The largest emancipation of slaves to occur in the eighteenth century came on the island of Saint Domingue (Haiti), France's wealthiest colony, as a result of the slave revolt of 1794 led by Toussaint L'Ouverture and Jean-Jacques Dessalines. The revolt in Haiti and Haiti's eventual independence in 1804 stood as a warning to slave owners throughout the West Indies. (See Chapter 20.) There would be other slave revolts such as those in Virginia led by Gabriel Prosser in 1800 and by Nat Turner in 1831, in South Carolina led by Denmark Vesey in 1822, in British-controlled Demarra in 1823 and 1824, and in Jamaica in 1831. Each of these was brutally suppressed.

ECONOMIC PRESSURES

Through the conclusion of the Seven Years' War, the West Indies interest group had been one of the most powerful in the British Parliament. During the second half of the eighteenth century and beyond, new and different economic interest groups began to displace the influence of that group. Within the West Indies themselves the planters were experiencing soil exhaustion and new competition from newly tilled islands controlled by France and other new islands opened for sugar cultivation. Some older plantations were being abandoned while others operated with low profitability. Now with the new islands under cultivation there was a glut of sugar on the market, and as a consequence the price was falling.

Under these conditions some British West Indies planters, for reasons that had nothing to do with religion or humanitarianism, began to favor curtailing the slave trade. Without new slaves, French planters would lack the labor they needed to exploit their islands. During the Napoleonic Wars, the British captured a number of the valuable French islands. In order to protect the planters on the older British West Indies islands, in 1805, the British cabinet issued Orders in Council, which forbade the importation of slaves into the newly acquired French islands. By 1807, the abolition sentiment was strong enough for Parliament to pass Wilberforce's measure prohibiting slave trading from any British port.

The suppression of this trade through the navy became one of the fundamental pillars of nineteenth-century British foreign policy. Throughout the rest of the Napoleonic era the British attempted to draw allies into a policy of forbidding the slave trade. They also attempted unsuccessfully to incorporate the abolition of the slave trade into the settlement of the Congress of Vienna. In addition, the British navy maintained squadrons of ships around the coast of West Africa to halt slave traders. Although the French and Americans also patrolled the West African coast, neither was deeply committed to ending the slave trade. Nonetheless, in 1824, the American Congress made slave trading a capital offense.

The French invasion of Spain in 1808, as discussed in Chapter 21, provided the spark for the Latin American wars of independence. The leaders of these movements had been influenced by the liberal ideas of the Enlightenment and were, thus, generally predisposed to disapprove of slavery. The political groups seeking independence from Spain also sought the support of slaves by promises of emancipation. Furthermore, the newly independent nations needed good relations with Britain to support their economies, and, consequently, most of them very quickly freed their slaves to gain such support. The actual freeing of slaves was gradual and often came some years after the emancipation legislation. Despite the gradual nature of this abolition, slavery would disappear by approximately the middle of the nineteenth century from all of the newly independent nations of Latin America. The great exception was Brazil.

ABOLISHING SLAVERY IN THE NEW WORLD

British reformers gradually recognized that the abolition of the slave trade had not actually improved the lot of slaves. In 1823, they adopted as a new goal the gradual emancipation of slaves. The chief voices calling for this change were those of William Wilberforce and Thomas Clarkson, who were active in founding the Abolition Society.

The savagery with which West Indian planters put down slave revolts in 1823 and 1824 and again in 1831 strengthened the resolve of the antislavery reformers. By 1830, the reformers had abandoned the goal of gradual abolition and demanded the complete abolition of slavery. In 1833, after the passage of the Reform Bill in Great Britain, they achieved that goal when Parliament abolished the right of British subjects to hold slaves. In the British West Indies, 750,000 slaves were freed within a few years.

The other old colonial powers in the New World tended to be much slower in their own abolition of slavery. Portugal did little or nothing about slavery in Brazil, and when that nation became independent of Portugal, its new government continued slavery. Portugal ended slavery elsewhere in its American possessions in 1836; the Swedes, in 1847; the Danes, in 1848; but the Dutch not until 1863. France had witnessed a significant antislavery movement throughout the first half of the century, but slavery was not abolished in its West Indian possessions until the revolution of 1848.

During the first thirty years of the nineteenth century, the institution of slavery revived and achieved strong new footholds in the transatlantic world. These areas were the lower south of the United States for the cultivation of cotton, Brazil for the cultivation of coffee, and Cuba for the cultivation of sugar. World demand for these products made the slave system economically viable in these regions. Consequently, despite the drive to emancipation, which had succeeded in the northern states of the United States, slavery persisted in much of the Caribbean and in most of Latin America.

An antislavery movement had existed in the United States since the end of the eighteenth century, but it took on a new life in the early 1830s. The British abolition of slavery in the West Indies served as an inspiration to a new generation of American antislavery leaders, the most famous of whom was William Lloyd Garrison. He and other American abolitionists raised the question of slavery throughout the 1830s and 1840s. It was, however, the disposition of lands the United States had acquired in the Mexican War of 1847 that placed slavery at the heart of the American political debate. For over a decade the question of slavery sharply divided Americans. The election of Lincoln in 1860 brought those sectional tensions to a head, and the American Civil War erupted in the spring of 1861. In 1863, Lincoln issued the Emancipation Proclamation, which ended slavery in the combatant states. The passage of the Thirteenth Amendment to the American Constitution in 1865 abolished slavery in the United States.

The end of slavery in the United Sates left both Cuba, the most important remaining possession of the Spanish Empire in the Americas, and Brazil with slave economies. In 1868, an insurgency against Spanish colonial policy broke out in Cuba and lasted for ten years. This war disrupted much of the Cuban economy and saw some planters move toward using free labor. The Spanish forces attacked other planters by freeing their slaves. In 1870, the Spanish government passed a measure for gradual emancipation of slaves in both Cuba and Puerto Rico. In subsequent years, the sugar economy collapsed, making slavery unprofitable. Abolitionist agitation grew in Spain, and slavery was abolished in its New World colonies in 1886.

Brazil, under British pressure, had effectively ended the slave trade in 1850, but the question of the abolition of slavery was postponed for many years. In 1871, as a result of abolitionist agitation and because the Emperor Pedro II opposed slavery, a law providing for an extremely gradual abolition of slavery was passed. During the next two decades, abolitionist sentiment grew, and public figures from across the political spectrum voiced opposition to slavery. In 1888, Isabel Christiana, then regent while her father Pedro II was in Europe for medical treatment, signed a law abolishing slavery in Brazil without any form of compensation to the slave owners.

The abolition of slavery in Brazil ended a system of forced labor that had characterized the transatlantic economy for almost four hundred years. Wherever slavery had existed, however, its presence left and would continue to leave long-term consequences for the realization of equality and social justice. The end of slavery, consequently, did not end the problems that slavery created in the transatlantic world.

AFRICA AND THE END OF SLAVERY

The transatlantic slave trade itself had adversely affected the life of Africa both through the vast loss of population over the centuries as well as through the undermining of African society through the internal slave trade. Similarly, the crusade against transatlantic slavery had drawn Europeans much more deeply into the affairs of the African continent. The various efforts by antislavery groups began to impact Africa in the first half of the nineteenth century. Their goal was to transform the

African economy by substituting new peaceful trade in tropical goods for the slave trade. The reformers hoped to spread both free trade and Christianity into Africa. "Christianity and civilization" and "Christianity and commerce" were popular slogans of the day. Missionaries and traders saw themselves as natural allies in the cause.

The first effort in this direction was the resettlement of black slaves or children of black slaves into Africa. In 1787, the British established a colony of poor free blacks from Britain in Sierra Leone. The effort went badly, but a few years later former slaves once owned by British loyalists in America were settled there. Then former slaves from the Caribbean were brought to Sierra Leone. The colony became relatively successful only after 1807, when the British navy landed slaves rescued from captured slave trading ships. Sierra Leone, though quite small, became a place on the coast of West Africa where Christianity and commerce rather than the slave trade flourished. The French established a smaller experiment at Libreville in Gabon. The most famous and lasting attempt to resettle former black slaves in Africa was the establishment of Liberia by the efforts of the American Colonization Society after 1817. Liberia became an independent republic in 1847. All of these efforts to move former slaves back to Africa had only modest success, but they did affect the life of West Africa.

Other antislavery reformers were less interested in establishing outposts for the settlement of former slaves than in transforming the African economy itself. In 1841, the African Civilization Society under the leadership of Thomas Fowell Buxton sent a group of paddle-steamer ships up the Niger River in the hope of creating the basis for new trade with Africa. The goal was to establish free trade between Britain and Africa in which the manufactured goods of the former, most particularly textiles, would be exchanged for tropical agricultural goods produced by Africans. The expedition failed because most of its members died of disease. Yet the impulse to penetrate Africa for purposes of spreading trade and Christianity would continue for the rest of the century.

The antislavery movement marked the first of the intrusions of the European powers well beyond the coast of West Africa into the heart of the continent. After the American Civil War finally halted any large-scale demand for slaves from Africa, the antislavery reformers began to focus on ending the slave trade in East Africa and the Indian Ocean. This drive against slavery and the slave trade in Africa itself became one of the rationales for European interference in Africa during the second half of the nineteenth century and served as one of the foundations for the establishment of the late-century colonial empires.

The crusade against slavery in the transatlantic economy eventually touched most of the world. It radically transformed the economies and societies of both North and South America. It led to a transformation of the African economy and eventually to a significant European presence in the life of African societies. Efforts to eradicate slavery, particularly the efforts by British reformers, caused the spread of the reform movement into Asia. Slavery has not been abolished throughout the world, and antislavery societies still exist, though they receive little publicity. Yet the abolition of slavery in the transatlantic world stands as one of the most permanent achievements of the forces of eighteenth-century Enlightenment and revolution.

■ *What were the justifications of slavery prior to the eighteenth century? What religious and intellectual developments led some Europeans and some Americans to question and criticize the institution of slavery? Why did antislavery reformers first concentrate on the abolition of the slave trade? How did both slavery and antislavery lead Americans and Europeans to become involved with Africa? How did that involvement change between approximately 1600 and 1870?*

1850–1900

Politics and Government

1854–1856	Crimean War
1861	Proclamation of the Kingdom of Italy
1867	Austro-Hungarian Dual Monarchy founded
1869	Suez Canal completed
1870	Franco-Prussian War; French Republic proclaimed
1871	German Empire proclaimed; Paris Commune
1880s	Britain establishes Protectorate in Egypt
1882	Italy, Germany, Austria form Triple Alliance
1894	Dreyfus convicted in France; Nicholas II becomes tsar of Russia
1898	Germany begins to build a battleship navy
1904	Britain and France in Entente Cordiale
1908–1909	Bosnian crisis

NASA photo of Suez Canal

Society and Economy

1850–1910	Height of European outward migration
1853–1870	Haussmann redesigns Paris
1857	Bessemer steelmaking process
1861	Serfdom abolished in Russia
1870	Education Act and first Irish Land Act, Britain
1875	Public Health and Artisan Dwelling Acts, Britain
1881	Second Irish Land Act
1886	Daimler invents internal combustion engine
1894	Union of German Women's Organizations founded
1901	National Council of French Women founded
1903	Third Irish Land Act; British Women's Social and Political Union founded; Wright brothers fly the first airplane

The construction of the Eiffel Tower

Religion and Culture

1850–1880	Jewish emancipation in much of Europe
1853–1854	Gobineau, *Essay on the Inequality of the Human Races*
1857	Flaubert, *Madame Bovary*
1859	Darwin, *On the Origin of Species*
1864	Pius IX, *Syllabus of Errors*
1867	Mill, *The Subjection of Women*
1871	Darwin, *The Descent of Man*; Religious tests abolished at Oxford and Cambridge
1872	Nietzsche, *The Birth of Tragedy*
1873–1876	Bismarck's *Kulturkampf*
1879	Ibsen, *A Doll's House*
1880s	Growing anti-Semitism in Europe
1880	Zola, *Nana*
1883	Nietzsche, *Thus Spake Zarathustra*
1892	Ibsen, *The Master Builder*
1896	Herzl, *The Jewish State*
1899	Bernstein, *Evolutionary Socialism*

Charles Darwin

1900–1939

1911	Second Moroccan crisis
1912	Third Irish Home Rule Bill passed
1912–1913	First and Second Balkan Wars
1914–1918	World War I
1917	Russian Revolution; Bolsheviks seize power
1919	Paris Peace Conference; Weimar constitution proclaimed in Germany
1922	Mussolini takes power in Italy
1923	France invades the Ruhr; Hitler's Beer Hall *Putsch*; first Labour government in Britain
1931	National Government formed in Great Britain
1933	Hitler appointed chancellor of Germany
1935	Nuremburg Laws; Italy invades Ethiopia
1936	Popular Front in France; purge trials in the Soviet Union; Spanish Civil War begins
1938	Munich Conference; *Kristallnacht* in Germany
1939	Germany invades Poland, starts World War II

Bolshevik uprising

1906	Land redemption payments canceled for Russian peasants
1907	Women vote on national issues in Norway
1918	Vote granted to some British women
1921	Soviet Union begins New Economic Policy
1923	Rampant inflation in Germany
1926	General strike in Great Britain
1928	Britain extends full franchise to women
1928–1933	First Five-Year Plan and agricultural collectivization in the Soviet Union
1929	Wall Street crash
1932	Lausanne Conference ends German reparations
mid-1930s	Nazis stimulate German economy through public works and defense spending

Stock market crash, Wall Street, N.Y.

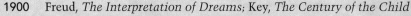

1900	Freud, *The Interpretation of Dreams*; Key, *The Century of the Child*
1902	Lenin, *What Is to Be Done?*
1905	Weber, *The Protestant Ethic and the Spirit of Capitalism*; Termination of the Napoleonic Concordat in France
1910	Pope Pius X requires anti-Modernist oath
1920	Keynes, *Economic Consequences of the Peace*
1922	Joyce, *Ulysses*
1924	Hitler, *Mein Kampf*
1929	Woolf, *A Room of One's Own*
1936	Keynes, *General Theory of Employment, Interest, and Money*
1937	Orwell, *Road to Wigan Pier*
1938	Sartre, *Nausea*

Virginia Woolf

CHAPTER 22

THE AGE OF NATION-STATES

- ■ **THE CRIMEAN WAR (1853–1856)**
  Peace Settlement and Long-Term Results

- ■ **REFORMS IN THE OTTOMAN EMPIRE**

- ■ **ITALIAN UNIFICATION**
  Romantic Republicans • Cavour's Policy • The New Italian State

- ■ **GERMAN UNIFICATION**
  Bismarck • The Franco-Prussian War and the German Empire (1870–1871)

- ■ **FRANCE: FROM LIBERAL EMPIRE TO THE THIRD REPUBLIC**
  The Paris Commune • The Third Republic • The Dreyfus Affair

- ■ **THE HABSBURG EMPIRE**
  Formation of the Dual Monarchy • Unrest of Nationalities

- ■ **RUSSIA: EMANCIPATION AND REVOLUTIONARY STIRRINGS**
  Reforms of Alexander II • Revolutionaries

- ■ **GREAT BRITAIN: TOWARD DEMOCRACY**
  The Second Reform Act (1867) • Gladstone's Great Ministry (1868–1874) • Disraeli in Office (1874–1880) • The Irish Question

- ■ **IN PERSPECTIVE**

KEY TOPICS

- ■ Reforms in the Ottoman Empire
- ■ The unification of Italy and Germany
- ■ The shift from empire to republic in France
- ■ The emergence of a dual monarchy in Austria-Hungary
- ■ Reforms in Russia, including the emancipation of the serfs
- ■ The emergence of Great Britain as the exemplary liberal state and its confrontation with Irish nationalists

T he revolutions of 1848 collapsed in defeat for both liberalism and nationalism. In the 1850s, conservative regimes were entrenched across the Continent. Yet only a quarter century later, many of the major goals of early-nineteenth-century liberals and nationalists had been reached. Italy and Germany were each united under conservative constitutional monarchies.

The proclamation of the German Empire in the Hall of Mirrors at Versailles, January 18, 1871, after the defeat of France in the Franco-Prussian War. Kaiser Wilhelm I is standing at the top of the steps under the flags. Bismarck is in the center in a white uniform.   Bildarchiv Preussischer Kulturbesitz

The Habsburg emperor accepted constitutional government and recognized the liberties of the Magyars of Hungary. In Russia, the tsar emancipated the serfs. France had become a republic. Liberalism and even democracy flourished in Great Britain. The Ottoman Empire also undertook major reforms.

Paradoxically, most of these developments occurred under conservative political leadership.

War and competition with other states compelled some governments to pursue new policies at home as well as abroad. They had to find novel methods to maintain the loyalty of their subjects. Some conservative leaders preferred to carry out a popular policy on their own terms, so that they, rather than the liberals, would receive credit. Other leaders acted as they did because they had no choice. ■

THE CRIMEAN WAR (1853–1856)

As has so often been true in modern European history, the impetus for change originated in war. The Crimean War (1853–1856) was rooted in the long-standing desire of Russia to extend its influence over the Ottoman Empire. Two disputes led to the conflict. First, as noted in Chapter 17, the Russians had, since the time of Catherine the Great (r. 1762–1796), been given protective oversight of Orthodox Christians in the Empire, and France had similar oversight of Roman Catholics. In 1851, yielding to French pressure, the Ottoman sultan had assigned care of certain holy places in Palestine to Roman Catholics. This decision angered the Russians and damaged Russian prestige. Second, Russia wanted to extend its control over the Ottoman provinces of Moldavia and Walachia (now in Romania). In the summer of 1853, the Russians used their right to protect Orthodox Christians in the Ottoman Empire as the pretext to occupy the two provinces. Shortly thereafter, the Ottoman Empire declared war on Russia.

Of far more significance to the great powers than the protection of Christian sites in Palestine was the fate of the weak Ottoman Empire. The Russian government envisioned the eventual breakup of the empire and hoped to extend its influence at Ottoman expense. Both France and Britain, though recognizing the difficulties of the Ottoman government and using it to their own advantage when the opportunity presented itself, opposed Russian expansion in the eastern Mediterranean, where they had extensive naval and commercial interests. The French emperor Napoleon III (r. 1852–1870) also thought an activist foreign policy would shore up domestic support for his regime.

On March 28, 1854, France and Britain declared war on Russia in alliance with the Ottomans. Much to the disappointment of Tsar Nicholas I, Austria and Prussia remained neutral. The Austrians had their own ambitions in the Balkans, and, for the moment, Prussia followed Austrian leadership.

Both sides conducted the conflict ineptly, a fact that became widely known in Western Europe because the Crimean War was the first to be covered by war correspondents and photographers. The ill-equipped and poorly commanded armies became bogged down along the Crimean coast of the Black Sea. In September 1855, after a long siege, the Russian fortress of Sevastopol finally fell to the French and British. Thereafter, both sides moved to end the war.

PEACE SETTLEMENT AND LONG-TERM RESULTS

In March 1856, a conference in Paris concluded the Treaty of Paris. This treaty required Russia to surrender territory near the mouth of the Danube River, to recognize the neutrality of the Black Sea, and to renounce its claims to protect Orthodox Christians in the Ottoman Empire. Even before the conference, Austria had forced Russia to withdraw from Moldavia and Walachia. The image of an invincible Russia that had prevailed across Europe since the close of the Napoleonic Wars was shattered.

Also shattered was the Concert of Europe (see Chapter 20), as a means of dealing with international relations on the Continent. Following the successful repression of the 1848 uprisings, the great powers feared revolution less than they had earlier in the century, and, consequently, they displayed much less reverence for the Vienna settlement. As historian Gordon Craig put it, "After 1856, there were more powers willing to fight to overthrow the existing order than there were to take up arms to defend it."[1] As a result, for about twenty-five years after the Crimean War, European affairs were unstable, producing a period of adventurism in foreign policy. While these events reshaped Western Europe, however, the Ottoman Empire over whose fate the Crimean War had been fought undertook reforms. These need to be considered before we return to the events in Europe.

REFORMS IN THE OTTOMAN EMPIRE

The short-lived Napoleonic invasion of the Ottoman province of Egypt in 1798–1799 (see Chapter 19), sparked a drive for change in the Ottoman Empire. In 1839, under pressure from imperial bureaucrats who had studied in Europe, the sultan issued a decree, called the *Hatt-i Sharif of Gülhane*, that attempted to reorganize the empire's administration and military along European lines. This decree opened what became known as the *Tanzimat* (meaning reorganization) era of the Ottoman Empire, lasting from 1839 to 1876. The reforms, which were drawn up by administrative councils and not issued arbitrarily by the sultan, liberalized the economy, ended the practice of tax farming, and sought to eliminate corruption. The *Hatt-i Sharif* was particularly remarkable for extending civic equality to Ottoman subjects regard-

[1] *The New Cambridge Modern History*, Vol. 10 (Cambridge, UK: Cambridge University Press, 1967), p. 273.

less of their religion. Muslims, Christians, and Jews were now equal before the law. The empire also made it much easier for Muslims to enter into commercial agreements with non-Muslims, both within the empire and from abroad.

Another reform decree, called the *Hatti-i Hümayun*, was promulgated in 1856 at the close of the Crimean War. Under the influence of Britain and France, it spelled out the rights of non-Muslims more explicitly, giving them equal obligations with Muslims for military service and equal opportunity for state employment and admission

to state schools. The decree also abolished torture and allowed foreigners to acquire some forms of property. In time, printing presses and Western-oriented schools appeared in the empire mainly via Christian missionaries, many of whom were Americans. For the first time in its long history, the Ottoman Empire actually sought to copy European legal and military institutions and the secular values flowing from liberalism.

The imperial government took these steps to gain the loyalty of its Christian subjects at a time when nationalism was making increasing inroads

A CLOSER LOOK

The Crimean War Recalled

The wars of the third quarter of the nineteenth century brought European armies once again to the foreground in European culture and art. Beginning with the Crimean War (1853–1856) and ending with those of German unification (1870), the armed forces of the various nations states reforged European political life. Artists might record even the most difficult moments of warfare. Here, Elizabeth Thompson, Lady Butler, portrayed *Roll Call after an Engagement, Crimea.* She completed the work in 1874 two decades after the war, and Queen Victoria purchased it.

A certain nostalgia for the comradeship of soldiers even under the most difficult circumstances penetrates this scene at a time when Britain had not engaged in a major war for many years.

The abilities of the aristocratic officers leading the British army had been discredited, so Butler here portrays ordinary troops.

The ill-equipment of the troops during the war had been a public scandal, and the evident suffering of these troops recalls that.

Lady Elizabeth Thompson Butler (1846–1933), "The Roll Call: Calling the Roll after an Engagement, Crimea (unframed)." The Royal Collection © 2003, Her Majesty Queen Elizabeth II. Photo by SC

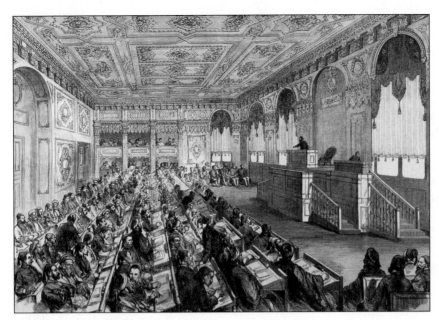

Ottoman reformers established a parliament in 1877, but the sultan retained most political authority. *Illustrated London News* of April 14, 1877. Mary Evans Picture Library Ltd.

among them. In effect, during this reform era the Ottoman government broke down the millet system (see Chapter 13) and sought to define all its citizens as Ottoman subjects rather than as members of particular religious communities.

However, putting these reforms into practice proved difficult. In some regions of the empire, especially in Egypt and Tunis, local rulers were virtually independent of Istanbul. They carried out their own modernizing reforms, often working closely with European powers. In the capital itself, power struggles developed among courtiers, European-oriented administrators and army officers, merchants who prospered from the changes, and the *ulema*, which sought to maintain the rule of Islamic law. Because of these tensions, as well as growing nationalism in various regions, the Ottoman Empire failed to achieve genuine political strength and stability. Many Ottomans questioned the wisdom of Tanzimat and warned that replacing long-standing Islamic institutions with European ones would lead to disaster.

The Balkan wars of the late 1870s, which resulted in either the independence of, or Russian or Austrian dominance over, most of the empire's European holdings, demonstrated the inability of the Ottoman Empire to master its own destiny. (See Chapter 26.) The response to these foreign defeats resulted in greater efforts to modernize the army and the economy and to build railways and telegraphs. In 1876, reformers persuaded the sultan to proclaim an Ottoman constitution on the grounds that European political arrangements

as well as technology accounted for European strength. The constitution called for a parliament consisting of an elected chamber of deputies and an appointed senate (these met for the first time in 1877) but left the sultan's power mostly intact. Nonetheless, a new sultan soon rejected even these limited steps toward constitutionalism and dismissed the parliament. In 1908, military officers carried out a revolution against the authority, though not the person of the sultan. Another group of reformist officers, known as the *Young Turks*, came to the fore with another program to modernize the empire. They were still in charge when World War I broke out, and their decision to enter the war on the side of the Central Powers in November 1914 led to the empire's defeat and collapse. (See Chapter 26.)

One of the underlying themes of all of these attempts at reform and modernization from 1839 to 1914 was the increasing secularization of the government, which sought less to question the Islamic foundations of society than to reduce the influence of the Muslim religious authorities on the state.

ITALIAN UNIFICATION

Nationalists had long wanted to unite the small, mostly absolutist principalities of the Italian peninsula into a single state. During the first half of the century, however, opinion differed about how to achieve Italian unification.

ROMANTIC REPUBLICANS

One approach to the issue was *romantic republicanism*. After the Congress of Vienna, secret republican societies were founded throughout Italy, the most famous of which was the **Carbonari** ("charcoal burners"). They were ineffective.

After the failure of nationalist uprisings in Italy in 1831, the leadership of romantic republican nationalism passed to Giuseppe Mazzini (1805–1872). He became the most important nationalist leader in Europe and brought new fervor to the cause. He once declared, "Nationality is the role assigned by God to a people in the work of humanity. It is its mission, its task on earth, to the end that God's thought may be realized in the world."[2] In 1831, he founded the Young Italy Society to drive Austria from the peninsula and establish an Italian republic.

During the 1830s and 1840s, Mazzini and his fellow republican Giuseppe Garibaldi (1807–1882) led insurrections. Both were involved in the ill-fated Roman Republic of 1849. Throughout the 1850s, they continued to conduct what amounted to guerrilla warfare. Because both men spent much time in exile, they became well known across the Continent and in the United States.

Republican nationalism frightened moderate Italians, who wanted to rid themselves of Austrian domination but not to establish a republic. For a time, these people had hoped the papacy would sponsor unification. That solution became impossible after the experience of Pius IX with the Roman Republic in 1849. Consequently, at mid-century, "Italy" remained a geographical expression rather than a political entity.

Yet by 1860, the Italian peninsula was transformed into a nation-state under a constitutional monarchy. Count Camillo Cavour (1810–1861), the prime minister of Piedmont—not of romantic republicans—made this possible. His method was a force of arms tied to secret diplomacy. The spirit of Machiavelli must have smiled over the enterprise.

CAVOUR'S POLICY

Piedmont (officially styled the Kingdom of Sardinia), in northwestern Italy, was the most independent state on the peninsula. The Congress of Vienna had restored the kingdom as a buffer between French and Austrian ambitions. As has been seen, during 1848 and 1849, King Charles Albert of Piedmont, after having promulgated a conservative constitution, twice unsuccessfully fought Austria. After the second defeat, he abdicated in favor of his son, Victor Emmanuel I (r. 1849–1878). In 1852, the new monarch chose Cavour as his prime minister.

A cunning statesman, Cavour had begun political life as a conservative, but had gradually moved toward a moderately liberal position. He had made a fortune by investing in railroads, reforming agriculture on his estates, and editing a newspaper. He was deeply imbued with the ideas of the Enlightenment, classical economics, and utilitarianism. Cavour was a nationalist of a new breed who had no respect for Mazzini's ideals. A strong monarchist, Cavour rejected republicanism. Economic and material progress, not romantic ideals, required a large, unified state on the Italian peninsula.

[2]Quoted in William L. Langer, *Political and Social Upheaval, 1832–1852* (New York: Harper Torchbooks, 1969), p. 115.

Cavour believed that if Italians proved themselves to be efficient and economically progressive, the great powers might decide that Italy could govern itself. As premier, he promoted free trade, railway construction, expansion of credit, and agricultural improvement. He believed that such material and economic bonds, rather than fuzzy romantic yearnings, must unite the Italians. Cavour also recognized the need to capture the loyalties of those Italians who believed in other varieties of nationalism. He thus fostered the Nationalist Society, which established chapters in other Italian states to press for unification under the leadership of Piedmont. Finally, the prime minister believed only French intervention could defeat Austria and unite Italy. The accession of Napoleon III in France seemed to open the way for such aid.

French Sympathies   Cavour used the Crimean War to bring Italy into European politics. In 1855, Piedmont sent 10,000 troops to help France and Britain capture Sebastopol. This small but significant participation in the war allowed Cavour to raise the Italian question at the Paris conference. He left Paris with no diplomatic reward, but his intelligence and political capacity had impressed everyone, especially Napoleon III. During the rest

Count Camillo Cavour (1810–1861) used an opportunistic alliance with France against Austria and military interventions in the Papal States and southern Italy to secure Italian unification under King Victor Emmanuel II of Piedmont, rather than as the republic that Mazzini and Garibaldi had advocated.   © Archivo Iconografico, S.A./CORBIS

of the decade, he achieved further international respectability for Piedmont by opposing Mazzini, who was still attempting to lead nationalist uprisings. By 1858, Cavour represented a moderate liberal, monarchist alternative to both republicanism and reactionary absolutism in Italy.

Cavour bided his time. Then, in January 1858, an Italian named Felice Orsini attempted to assassinate Napoleon III. The incident heightened the emperor's interest in the Italian issue. He saw himself continuing his more famous uncle's liberation of the peninsula. He also saw Piedmont as a potential ally against Austria. In July 1858, Cavour and Napoleon III met at Plombières in southern France. Riding alone in a carriage, with the emperor at the reins, the two men plotted to provoke a war in Italy that would permit them to defeat Austria. A formal treaty in December 1858 confirmed the agreement.

War with Austria   In early 1859, tension grew between Austria and Piedmont as Piedmont mobilized its army. On April 22, Austria demanded that Piedmont demobilize. That allowed Piedmont to claim that Austria was provoking a war. France intervened to aid its ally. On June 4, the Austrians were defeated at Magenta, and on June 24 at Solferino. Meanwhile, revolutions had broken out in Tuscany, Modena, Parma, and the Romagna provinces of the Papal States.

With the Austrians in retreat and the new revolutionary regimes calling for union with Piedmont, Napoleon III feared too extensive a Piedmontese victory. On July 11, he concluded peace with Austria at Villafranca. Piedmont received Lombardy, but Venetia remained under Austrian control. Cavour felt betrayed by France, but the war had driven Austria from most of northern Italy. Later that summer, Parma, Modena, Tuscany, and the Romagna voted to unite with Piedmont. (See Map 22–1.)

Garibaldi's Campaign   At this point, the forces of romantic republican nationalism compelled Cavour to pursue the complete unification of northern and southern Italy. In May 1860, Garibaldi landed in Sicily with more than 1,000 troops, who had been outfitted in the north. He captured Palermo and prepared to attack the mainland. By September he controlled the city and kingdom of Naples, probably the most corrupt example of Italian absolutism. For more than two decades Garibaldi had hoped to form a republican Italy, but Cavour forestalled him. He rushed Piedmontese troops south to confront Garibaldi. On the way, they conquered the rest of the Papal States except the area around Rome, which French troops saved for the pope. Garibaldi's nationalism won out over his republicanism, and he accepted Piedmontese domination. In late 1860, Naples and Sicily voted to join the Italian kingdom. In response to the help received from France and Napoleon III's concern over the new large nation-state on his borders, Piedmont ceded Savoy and Nice, where much of the population spoke French, to France.

Giuseppe Garibaldi. The charismatic leader can be seen on the right urging on his troops in the rout of Neapolitan forces at Calatafimi, Sicily in 1860.   Bildarchiv Preussischer Kulturbesitz

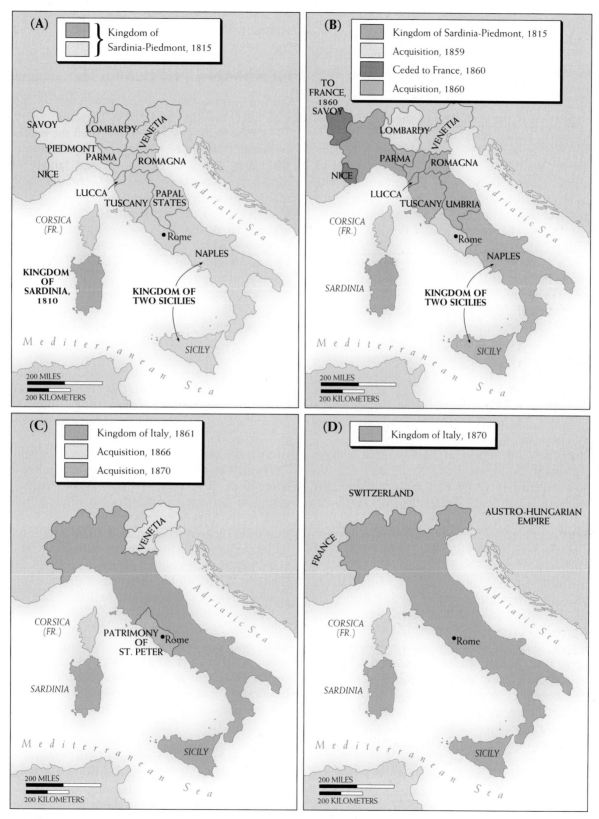

Map 22–1   **THE UNIFICATION OF ITALY**   Beginning with the association of Sardinia and Piedmont by the Congress of Vienna in 1815, unification was achieved through the expansion of Piedmont between 1859 and 1870. Both Cavour's statesmanship and the campaigns of ardent nationalists played large roles.

THE NEW ITALIAN STATE

In March 1861, Victor Emmanuel II was proclaimed king of Italy. Three months later Cavour died. The new state more than ever needed his skills, because Piedmont had, in effect, not so much united Italy as conquered it. The republicans resented the treatment of Garibaldi. The clericals were appalled at the conquest of the Papal States. In the south, armed resistance against the imposition of Piedmontese-style administration continued until 1866. The economies and societies of north and south Italy were incompatible. The south was rural, poor, and backward. The north was industrializing, and its economy was increasingly linked to that of the rest of Europe. The social structures of the two regions reflected these differences, with large landholders and peasants dominant in the south and an urban working class emerging in the north.

The political framework of the united Italy could not overcome these problems. The constitution, which was that promulgated for Piedmont in 1848, provided for a conservative constitutional monarchy. Parliament consisted of two houses: a senate appointed by the king and a chamber of deputies elected on a narrow franchise. Ministers were responsible to the monarch, not to Parliament. These arrangements did not foster vigorous parliamentary life. Political leaders often simply avoided major problems. In place of efficient, progressive government, such as Cavour had brought to Piedmont, a system called *transformismo* developed. Bribery, favors, or a seat in the cabinet "transformed" political opponents into government supporters. Italian politics became a byword for corruption.

The unification was not complete. Many Italians believed other territories should be added to their nation. The most important of these were Venetia and Rome. The former was gained in 1866 in return for Italy's alliance with Prussia in the Austro-Prussian War. French troops continued to guard Rome and the papacy until the troops were withdrawn during the Franco-Prussian War of 1870. The Italian state then annexed Rome and made it the capital. The papacy confined itself to the Vatican and remained hostile to the Italian state until the Lateran Accord of 1929. (See Chapter 27.)

By 1870, only the small province of Trent and the city of Trieste, both ruled by Austria, remained outside Italy. In and of themselves, these areas were not important, and their inhabitants were a mix of Italians, Germans, and Slavs, but they fueled the continued hostility of Italian nationalists toward Austria. The desire to liberate *Italia irre-denta*, or "unredeemed Italy," was one reason for the Italian support of the Allies against Austria and Germany during World War I.

GERMAN UNIFICATION

German unification was the most important political development in Europe between 1848 and 1914. (See Map 22–2.) It transformed the balance of economic, military, and international power. Moreover, the way it was created largely determined the character of the new German state. Germany was united by the conservative army, the monarchy, and the prime minister of Prussia, who wanted to outflank Prussian liberals. A unified Germany, which two generations of German liberals had sought, was actually achieved for the most illiberal of reasons.

During the 1850s, German unification seemed remote. The political structure of the German-speaking lands was the German Confederation, which had been established at the Congress of Vienna. It was a loose federation of 39 states of differing size and strength whose appointed representatives met in a central diet in Frankfurt. The two by far strongest states were Austria and Prussia. During the 1850s, Austria presided over the diet of the German Confederation. The major states continued to trade with each other through the *Zollverein* (tariff union), and railways linked their economies. Frederick William IV of Prussia had given up thoughts of unification under Prussian leadership. Austria continued to oppose any union that might lessen its influence. Liberal nationalists had not recovered from the humiliations of 1848 and 1849, so they could do little or nothing for unification. What quickly overturned this static situation was a series of domestic political changes and problems within Prussia.

In 1858, Frederick William IV was adjudged insane, and his brother William assumed the regency. William I (r. 1861–1888), who became king in his own right in 1861, was less idealistic than his brother and more of a Prussian patriot. In the usual Hohenzollern tradition, his first concern was to strengthen the Prussian army. In 1860, his war minister and chief of staff proposed to enlarge the army, to increase the number of officers, and to extend the period of conscription from two to three years. The Prussian Parliament, created by the Constitution of 1850, refused to approve the necessary taxes. The liberals, who dominated the body, sought to avoid placing additional power in the hands of the monarchy. For two years, monarch and Parliament were deadlocked.

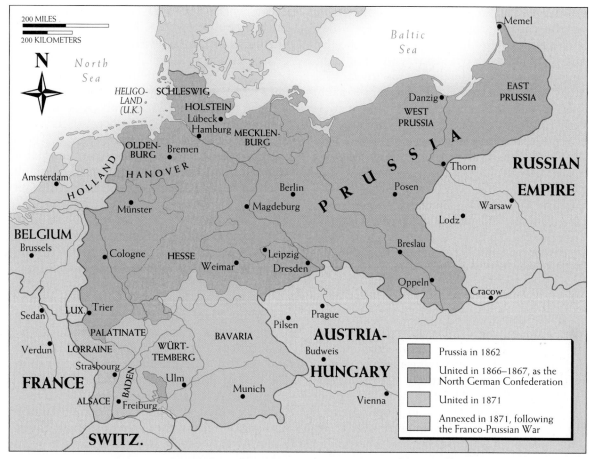

Map 22–2 **THE UNIFICATION OF GERMANY**   Under Bismarck's leadership, and with the strong support of its royal house, Prussia used diplomatic and military means, on both the German and international stages, to forcibly unify the German states into a strong national entity.

BISMARCK

In September 1862, William I turned for help to the person who, more than any other single individual, shaped the next thirty years of European history: Otto von Bismarck (1815–1898). Bismarck came from Junker (noble landlord) stock. He attended a university and displayed an interest in German unification. During the 1840s, he was elected to the provincial diet, where he was so reactionary he disturbed even the king. Yet he had made his mark. From 1851 to 1859, Bismarck served as the Prussian representative to the German Confederation. Later he became Prussian ambassador to Russia and was ambassador to France when William I appointed him prime minister.

Although Bismarck entered public life as a reactionary, he had mellowed into a conservative. He opposed parliamentary government, but not a constitutionalism that preserved a strong monarchy. He understood that Prussia—and later, Germany—must have a strong industrial base. His years in Frankfurt arguing with his Austrian counterpart

had hardened his Prussian patriotism. In politics, he was a pragmatist who put more trust in power and action than in ideas. As he declared in his first speech as prime minister, "Germany is not looking to Prussia's liberalism but to her power. . . . The great questions of the day will not be decided by speeches and majority decisions—that was the mistake of 1848–1849—but by iron and blood."[3] Yet this same minister, after having led Prussia into three wars, spent the next nineteen years seeking to preserve peace.

Upon becoming prime minister in 1862, Bismarck immediately moved against the liberal Parliament. He contended that even without new financial levies, the Prussian constitution permitted the government to carry out its functions on the basis of previously granted taxes. Therefore, taxes could be collected and spent despite the parliamentary refusal to vote them. The army and

[3]Quoted in Otto Pflanze, *Bismarck and the Development of Germany: The Period of Unification: 1815–1871* (Princeton, NJ: Princeton University Press, 1963), p. 177.

most of the bureaucracy supported this interpretation of the constitution. In 1863, however, new elections sustained the liberal majority in the Parliament. Bismarck had to find a way to attract popular support away from the liberals and toward the monarchy and the army. He, therefore, set about uniting Germany through the conservative institutions of Prussia. In effect, Bismarck embraced the cause of German nationalism as a strategy to enable Prussian conservatives to outflank Prussian liberals.

The Danish War (1864) Bismarck's vision of a united Germany did not include all German-speaking lands. That is to say, he pursued a *kleindeutsch*, or small German, solution to unification. He intended to exclude Austria from any future united German state. This goal required complex diplomacy.

The Schleswig-Holstein problem gave Bismarck the handle for his policy. The kings of Denmark had longed ruled these two northern duchies, which had never actually having become part of Denmark itself. Their populations were a mixture of Germans and Danes. Holstein, where Germans predominated, belonged to the German Confederation. In 1863, the Danish Parliament moved to incorporate both duchies into Denmark. The smaller states of the German Confederation proposed an all-German war to halt this move. Bismarck, however, wanted Prussia to act alone or only in cooperation with Austria. Together, the two large states easily defeated Denmark in 1864.

The Danish defeat increased Bismarck's personal prestige and strengthened his political hand. Over the next two years, he managed to maneuver Austria into war with Prussia. In August 1865, the two powers negotiated the Convention of Gastein, which put Austria in charge of Holstein and Prussia in charge of Schleswig. Bismarck then mended other diplomatic fences. He had gained Russian sympathy in 1863 by supporting Russia's suppression of a Polish revolt, and he persuaded Napoleon III to promise neutrality in an Austro-Prussian conflict. In April 1866, Bismarck promised Italy Venetia if it attacked Austria in support of Prussia when war broke out. Now Bismarck had to provoke his war.

The Austro-Prussian War (1866) Constant Austro-Prussian tensions had arisen over the administration of Schleswig and Holstein. Bismarck ordered the Prussian forces to be as obnoxious as possible to the Austrians. On June 1, 1866, Austria appealed to the German Confederation to intervene in the dispute. Bismarck claimed that this request violated the 1864 alliance and the Convention of Gastein. The Seven Weeks' War, which resulted in the summer of 1866, led to the decisive defeat of Austria at Königgrätz in Bohemia.

The Treaty of Prague, which ended the conflict on August 23, was lenient toward Austria, which only lost Venetia, ceded as promised to Napoleon III, who in turn ceded it to Italy. Austria refused to give Venetia directly to Italy because the Austrians had crushed the Italians during the war. The treaty permanently excluded the Austrian Habsburgs from German affairs. Prussia had thus established itself as the only major power among the German states.

The North German Confederation In 1867, Prussia annexed Hanover, Hesse Kassel, Nassau, and the city of Frankfurt, all of which had all supported Austria during the war, and deposed their rulers. Under Prussian leadership, all Germany north of the Main River now formed the North German Confederation. Each state retained its own local government, but all military forces were under federal control. The president of the federation was the king of Prussia, represented by his chancellor, Bismarck. A legislature consisted of two houses: a federal council, or **Bundesrat**, composed of members appointed by the governments of the states, and a lower house, or **Reichstag**, chosen by universal male suffrage.

Bismarck, the great conservative chancellor, unlike German liberals, actually embraced a democratic franchise because he sensed that the peasants would vote for conservatives Moreover, the *Reichstag* had little real power, because the ministers were responsible only to the monarch. The *Reichstag* could not even originate legislation. The chancellor had to propose all laws. The legislature did have the right to approve military budgets, but these were usually submitted to cover several years at a time. The constitution of the North German Confederation, which, after 1871, became the constitution of the German Empire, possessed some of the appearances, but none of the substance, of liberalism. Germany was, in effect, a military monarchy.

Bismarck's spectacular successes overwhelmed the liberal opposition in the Prussian Parliament. The liberals were split between those who prized liberalism and those who supported unification. In the end, nationalism proved more attractive. In 1866, the Prussian Parliament retroactively approved the military budget that it had rejected earlier. Bismarck had crushed the Prussian liberals by making the monarchy and the army the most popular institutions in the country. The drive toward German national unification had achieved his domestic Prussian political goal.

THE FRANCO-PRUSSIAN WAR AND THE GERMAN EMPIRE (1870–1871)

Bismarck now wanted to complete unification by bringing the states of southern Germany—Bavaria, Wurtemberg, Baden, and Hesse Darmstadt—into the newly established confederation. Spain gave him the excuse. In 1868, a military coup deposed the corrupt Bourbon queen of Spain, Isabella II (r. 1833–1868). To replace her, the Spaniards chose Prince Leopold of Hohenzollern-Sigmaringen, a Catholic cousin of William I of Prussia. On June 19, 1870, Leopold accepted the Spanish crown with Prussian blessings. Bismarck knew that France would object strongly to a Hohenzollern Spain.

On July 2, the Spanish government announced Leopold's acceptance, and the French reacted as expected. France sent its ambassador to Prussia Count Vincent Benedetti (1817–1900) to consult with William I, who was vacationing at Bad Ems. They discussed the matter at several meetings. On July 12, Leopold's father renounced his son's candidacy for the Spanish throne, fearing the issue would cause war between Prussia and France. William was relieved that conflict had been avoided, and he had not had to order Leopold to renounce the Spanish throne.

There the matter might have rested had it not been for the impetuosity of the French and the guile of Bismarck. On July 13, the French government instructed Benedetti to ask William for assurances he would tolerate no future Spanish candidacy for Leopold. The king refused, but said he might take the question under further consideration. Later that day he sent Bismarck, who was in Berlin, a telegram reporting the substance of the meeting. The peaceful resolution of the controversy had disappointed the chancellor, who desperately wanted a war with France to complete unification. The king's telegram gave him a new opportunity to provoke war. Bismarck released an edited version of the dispatch. The revised Ems telegram made it appear that William had insulted the French ambassador. The idea was to goad France into declaring war.

The French government fell for Bismarck's bait and declared war on July 19. Napoleon III was sick and not eager for war, but his government believed victory over the North German Confederation would renew popular

GERMAN AND ITALIAN UNIFICATION

1854	Crimean War opens
1855	Cavour leads Piedmont into the war on the side of France and England
1856	Treaty of Paris concludes the Crimean War
1858	(January 14) Attempt to assassinate Napoleon III
1858	(July 20) Secret conference between Napoleon III and Cavour at Plombières
1859	War of Piedmont and France against Austria
1860	Garibaldi lands his forces in Sicily and invades southern Italy
1861	(March 17) Proclamation of the Kingdom of Italy
1861	(June 6) Death of Cavour
1862	Bismarck becomes prime minister of Prussia
1864	Danish War
1865	Convention of Gastein
1866	Austro-Prussian War
1866	Austria cedes Venetia to Italy
1867	North German Confederation formed
1870	(June 19–July 12) Crisis over Hohenzollern candidacy for the Spanish throne
1870	(July 13) Bismarck publishes the edited Ems dispatch
1870	(July 19) France declares war on Prussia
1870	(September 1) France defeated at Sedan and Napoleon III captured
1870	(September 4) French Republic proclaimed
1870	(October 2) Italian state annexes Rome
1871	(January 18) Proclamation of the German Empire at Versailles
1871	(March 28–May 28) Paris Commune
1871	(May 23) Treaty of Frankfurt ratified between France and Germany

The Prussian victory at the battle of Sedan in September 1870 brought about the collapse of the regime of Louis Napoleon in France and sealed the Prussian accomplishment of the unification of Germany. In this contemporary photograph the Prussian infantry is making an advance.   Getty Images Inc.—Hulton Archive Photos

HEINRICH VON TREITSCHKE DEMANDS THE ANNEXATION OF ALSACE AND LORRAINE

The Franco-Prussian War witnessed outbursts of extreme nationalistic rhetoric on both sides. One such voice was that of the German historian Heinrich von Treitschke (1834–1896). In a newspaper article, he demanded the annexation of Alsace and Lorraine from France. He did so even though the population of Alsace wished to remain part of France and German was not the dominant language in the region. He appealed to an earlier time when the region had been German in language and culture, and he asserted that "might makes right" to assure German domination. Read this passage in conjunction with Lord Acton's condemnation of nationalism. (See "Lord Acton Condemns Nationalism," p. 749.)

■ *On what grounds does Treitschke base the German claim to Alsace and Lorraine? Why does he contend it is proper to ignore the wishes of the people involved? What, if any, political morality informs his views?*

The sense of justice to Germany demands the lessening of France. . . .

What is demanded by justice is, at the same time, absolutely necessary for our security. . . .

Every State must seek the guarantees of its own security in itself alone. . . .

In view of our obligation to secure the peace of the world, who will venture to object that the people of Alsace and Lorraine do not want to belong to us? The doctrine of the right of all the branches of the German race to decide on their own destinies, the plausible solution of demagogues without a fatherland, shiver to pieces in presence of the sacred necessity of these great days. These territories are ours by the right of the sword, and we shall dispose of them in virtue of a higher right—the right of the German nation, which will not permit its lost children to remain strangers to the German Empire. We Germans, who know Germany and France, know better than these unfortunates themselves what is good for the people of Alsace. . . . Against their will we shall restore them to their true selves. We have seen with joyful wonder the undying power of the moral forces of history, manifested far too frequently in the immense

support for the empire. Once the conflict erupted, the southern German states, honoring treaties of 1866, joined Prussia against France, whose defeat was not long in coming. On September 1, at the Battle of Sedan, the Germans not only beat the French army but also captured Napoleon III. By late September, Paris was besieged; it finally capitulated on January 28, 1871.

Ten days earlier, in the Hall of Mirrors at the Palace of Versailles, the German Empire had been proclaimed. The German princes requested William to accept the title of German emperor. The princes remained heads of their respective states within the new empire. Through the peace settlement with France, Germany annexed Alsace and part of Lorraine and forced the French to pay a large indemnity. (See "Heinrich von Treitschke Demands the Annexation of Alsace and Lorraine.")

Both the fact and the manner of German unification produced long-range effects in Europe. A powerful new state had been created in north central Europe. It was rich in natural resources and talented citizens. Militarily and economically, the German Empire would be far stronger than Prussia had been alone. The unification of Germany was also a blow to European liberalism, because the new state was a conservative creation. Conservative politics were now backed not by a weak Austria or an economically retrograde Russia, but by the strongest state on the Continent.

The two nations most immediately affected by German and Italian unification were France and Austria. The emergence of the two new unified states revealed French and Habsburg weakness. Each had to change. France returned to republican government, and the Habsburgs came to terms with their Magyar subjects.

changes of these days, to place much confidence in the value of a mere popular disinclination. The spirit of a nation lays hold, not only of the generation which lives beside it, but of those who are before and behind it. We appeal from the mistaken wishes of the men who are there today to the wishes of those who were there before them. We appeal to all those strong German men who once stamped the seal of our German nature on the language and manners, the art and the social life of the Upper Rhine. Before the nineteenth century closes, the world will recognize that . . . we were only obeying the dictates of national honor when we made little account of the preferences of the people who live in Alsace today. . . .

At all times the subjection of a German race to France has been an unhealthy thing; today it is an offence against the reason of History—a vassalship of free men to half-educated barbarians. . . .

There is no perfect identity between the political and national frontier of any European country. Not one of the great Powers, and Germany no more than the rest of them, can ever subscribe to the principle that "language alone decides the formation of States." It would be impossible to carry that principle into effect. . . .

The German territory which we demand is ours by nature and by history. . . . In the tempests of the great Revolution the people of Alsace, like all the citizens of France, learned to forget their past. . . .

Most assuredly, the task of reuniting there the broken links between the ages is one of the heaviest that has ever been imposed upon the political forces of our nation. . . .

The people of Alsace are already beginning to doubt the invincibility of their nation, and at all events to divine the mighty growth of the German Empire. Perverse obstinacy, and a thousand French intrigues creeping in the dark, will make every step on the newly conquered soil difficult for us: but our ultimate success is certain, for on our side fights what is stronger than the lying artifices of the stranger—nature herself and the voice of common blood.

From Heinrich von Treitschke, "What We Demand from France" (1870), in Heinrich von Treitschke, *Germany, France, Russia and Islam* (New York: G. P. Putnam's Sons, 1915), pp. 100, 102, 106, 109, 120, 122, 134–135, 153, 158.

FRANCE: FROM LIBERAL EMPIRE TO THE THIRD REPUBLIC

Historians divide the reign of Napoleon III (r. 1852–1870) into the years of the authoritarian empire and those of the liberal empire. The year of division is 1860. After the coup in December 1851, Napoleon III had controlled the legislature, censored the press, and harassed political dissidents. His support came from the army, property owners, the French Catholic Church, peasants, and businesspeople. They approved the security he ensured for property, his protection of the pope, and his economic program. French victory in the Crimean War had confirmed the emperor's popularity.

From the late 1850s onward, Napoleon III began to modify his policy. In 1860, he concluded a free-trade treaty with Britain and permitted freer debate in the legislature. By the late 1860s, he had relaxed the press laws and permitted labor unions. In 1870, he allowed the leaders of the moderates in the legislature to form a ministry, and he also agreed to a liberal constitution that made the ministers responsible to the legislature.

Napoleon III's liberal concessions sought to shore up domestic support to compensate for his failures in foreign policy. By 1860, he had lost control of the diplomacy of Italian unification. Between 1861 and 1867, he had supported a disastrous military expedition against Mexico led by Archduke Maximilian of Austria that ended in defeat and Maximilian's execution. In 1866, France had watched passively while Bismarck and Prussia reorganized German affairs. The war of 1870 against Germany had been the French government's last and most disastrous attempt to shore up its foreign policy and secure domestic popularity.

The Second Empire, but not the war, came to an inglorious end with the Battle of Sedan in September 1870. The emperor was captured and then allowed to go to England, where he died in 1873. Shortly after news of Sedan reached Paris, a republic was proclaimed and a government of national defense established. Paris itself was soon under Prussian siege, and the government moved to Bordeaux. Paris finally surrendered in January 1871, but France had been ready to sue for peace long before.

THE PARIS COMMUNE

The division between the provinces and Paris became sharper after the fighting with Germany stopped. Monarchists dominated the new National Assembly elected in February. For the time being, the assembly gave executive power to Adolphe Thiers (1797–1877), who had been active in French politics since 1830. He negotiated a settlement with Prussia (the Treaty of Frankfurt), which was officially ratified on May 23.

Many Parisians, having suffered during the siege, resented what they regarded as a betrayal by the monarchist National Assembly sitting at Versailles. The Parisians elected a new municipal government, called the *Paris Commune*, which was formally proclaimed on March 28, 1871. The Commune intended to administer Paris separately from the rest of France. Radicals and socialists of all stripes participated in the Commune. In April, the National Assembly surrounded Paris with an army. On May 8, this army bombarded the city. On May 21, it broke through the city's defenses. During the next seven days, the troops killed about 20,000 inhabitants while the communards shot scores of hostages.

The Paris Commune became a legend throughout Europe. Marxists regarded it as a genuine proletarian government that the French bourgeoisie had suppressed. This interpretation is mistaken. The Commune, though of shifting composition, was dominated by petty bourgeois members. The socialism of the Commune had its roots in Blanqui's and Proudhon's anarchism rather than in Marx's concept of class conflict. The Commune wanted not a worker's state, but a nation of relatively independent, radically democratic enclaves. Its suppression thus represented not only the protection of property, but also the triumph of the centralized nation-state. Just as the armies of Piedmont and Prussia had united the small states of Italy and Germany, the army of the French National Assembly destroyed the particularistic political tendencies of Paris and, by implication, those of any other French community.

THE THIRD REPUBLIC

The National Assembly backed into a republican form of government against its will. Its monarchist majority was divided in loyalty between the House of Bourbon and the House of Orléans. They could have surmounted this problem, because the Bourbon claimant, the count of Chambord, had no children and agreed to accept the Orléanist heir as his successor. Chambord refused to become king, however, if France retained the revolutionary tricolor flag. Even the conservative monarchists would not return to the white flag of the Bourbons, which symbolized extreme political reaction.

While the monarchists quarreled among themselves, events marched on. By September 1873, the indemnity had been paid, and the Prussian occupation troops had withdrawn. Thiers was ousted from office because he had displayed clear republican sentiments. The monarchists wanted a more sympathetic executive. They elected as president a conservative army officer, Marshal Patrice MacMahon (1808–1893), who was expected to prepare for a monarchist restoration. In 1875, the National Assembly, still monarchist in sentiment, but unable to find a king, decided to regularize the political system. It adopted a law that provided for a Chamber of Deputies elected by universal male suffrage, a Senate chosen indirectly, and a president elected by the two legislative houses. This rather simple republican system had resulted from the bickering and frustration of the monarchists.

After numerous quarrels with the Chamber of Deputies, MacMahon resigned in 1879. His departure meant that dedicated republicans controlled

---

MAJOR DATES IN THE HISTORY OF THE THIRD FRENCH REPUBLIC

1870	Defeat by Prussia and proclamation of republic
1871	Paris Commune
1873	Prussian occupation troops depart
1873	Marshal MacMahon elected president
1875	Major political institutions of Third Republic organized
1879	MacMahon resigns as president
1894	Captain Dreyfus convicted
1906	Dreyfus's conviction set aside

the national government despite lingering opposition from the church, wealthy families, and a part of the army.

The political structure of the Third Republic proved much stronger than many citizens suspected at the time. It survived challenges from persons such as General Georges Boulanger (1837–1891), who would have imposed stronger executive authority. It also survived several scandals, such as those involving sales of awards of the Legion of Honor and widespread corruption of politicians and journalists by a company that tried to construct a canal in Panama, that made its politics appear increasingly sleazy. The institutions of the republic, however, allowed new ministers to replace those whose corruption was exposed.

THE DREYFUS AFFAIR

The greatest trauma of the Third Republic occurred over what became known as the *Dreyfus affair*. On December 22, 1894, a French military court found Captain Alfred Dreyfus (1859–1935) guilty of passing secret information to the German army. The evidence against him was flimsy and was later revealed to have been forged. Someone in the officer corps had been passing documents to the Germans, and it suited the army investigators

to accuse Dreyfus, who was Jewish. After Dreyfus had been sent to Devil's Island, a notorious prison in French Guiana, however, secrets continued to flow to the German army. In 1896, a new head of French counterintelligence reexamined the Dreyfus file and found evidence of forgery. A different officer was implicated, but a military court acquitted him of all charges.

By then the affair had provoked near-hysterical public debate. The army, the French Catholic Church, political conservatives, and vehemently anti-Semitic newspapers contended that Dreyfus was guilty. Such anti-Dreyfus opinion was dominant at the beginning of the affair. In 1898, however, the novelist Emile Zola (1840–1902) published a newspaper article entitled *"J'accuse"* ("I accuse"), in which he contended that the army had denied due process to Dreyfus and had suppressed or forged evidence. Zola was convicted of libel and fled to England to avoid serving a one-year prison sentence.

Zola was only one of numerous liberals, radicals, and socialists who had begun to demand a new trial for Dreyfus. Although these forces of the political left had come to Dreyfus's support rather slowly, they soon realized his cause could aid their own public image. They portrayed the conservative institutions of the nation as having denied

The prosecution of Captain Alfred Dreyfus, who is shown here standing on the right at his military trial, provoked the most serious crisis of the Third Republic.   © Bettman/CORBIS

Dreyfus the rights belonging to any citizen of the republic. They also claimed, and properly so, that Dreyfus had been framed to protect the guilty persons, who were still in the army. In August 1898, further evidence of forged material came to light. The officer responsible for those forgeries committed suicide in jail, but a new military trial again convicted Dreyfus. The president of France immediately pardoned him, however, and eventually, in 1906, a civilian court set aside the results of both military trials.

The Dreyfus case divided France as no issue had done since the Paris Commune. By its conclusion, the conservatives were on the defensive. They had allowed themselves to persecute an innocent person and to manufacture false evidence against him to protect themselves from disclosure. They had also embraced violent anti-Semitism. On the political left, radicals, republicans, and socialists developed an informal alliance, which outlived the Dreyfus case itself. These groups realized that the political left had to support republican institutions to achieve its goals. Nonetheless, the political, religious, and racial divisions and suspicions growing out of the Dreyfus affair continued to divide the Third Republic until France's defeat by Germany in 1940.

THE HABSBURG EMPIRE

After 1848, the Habsburg Empire was a problem both to itself and for the rest of Europe. An ungenerous critic remarked that a standing army of soldiers, a kneeling army of priests, and a crawling army of informers supported the empire. In the age of national states, liberal institutions, and industrialism, the Habsburg domains remained primarily dynastic, absolutist, and agrarian. The Habsburg response to the revolts of 1848–1849 had been to reassert absolutism. Emperor Francis Joseph (r. 1848–1916) was honest, conscientious, and hardworking, but unimaginative. He reacted to events but rarely commanded them.

During the 1850s, his ministers attempted to impose a centralized administration on the empire. The system amounted to a military and bureaucratic regime dominated by German-speaking Austrians. The Vienna government abolished internal tariffs in the empire. It divided Hungary, which had been so revolutionary in 1848, into military districts. The Roman Catholic Church acquired control of education. National groups, such as the Croats and Slovaks, who had supported the empire against the Hungarians, received no rewards for their loyalty. Although this system provoked resentment, it eventually floundered because of setbacks in foreign affairs.

Austrian refusal to support Russia during the Crimean War meant the new tsar Alexander II (r. 1855–1881) would no longer help preserve Habsburg rule in Hungary, as Nicholas I had done in 1849. An important external prop of Habsburg power for the past half century thus disappeared. The Austrian defeat in 1859 at the hands of France and Piedmont and the subsequent loss of territory in Italy confirmed the necessity for a new domestic policy. For seven years the emperor, the civil servants, the aristocrats, and the politicians tried to construct a viable system of government.

The coronation of Francis Joseph of Hungary in 1867 is depicted in this painting. The so-called Ausgleich, or Compromise, of 1867 transformed the Habsburg Empire into a dual monarchy in which Austria and Hungary became almost separate states except for defense and foreign affairs. Bildarchiv der Oesterreichischen Nationalbibliothek, Wien

FORMATION OF THE DUAL MONARCHY

In 1860, Francis Joseph issued the October Diploma, which created a federation among the states and provinces of the empire. There were to be local diets dominated by the landed classes and a single imperial parliament. The Magyar nobility of Hungary, however, rejected the plan.

Consequently, in 1861, the emperor issued the February Patent, which set up an entirely different form of government. It established a bicameral imperial parliament, or *Reichsrat*, with an upper chamber appointed by the emperor and an indirectly elected lower chamber. Again, the Magyars refused to cooperate in a system designed to give political dominance in the empire to German-speaking Austrians. The Magyars sent no delegates to

MAJOR DATES IN THE LATE-NINETEENTH-CENTURY HABSBURG EMPIRE

1848 Francis Joseph becomes emperor
1859 defeat by France and Piedmont
1860 October Diploma
1861 February Patent
1866 Defeat by Prussia
1867 Compromise between emperor and Hungary, establishing the Dual Monarchy
1897 Ordinances giving equality of language between Germans and Czechs in Austria
1907 Universal male suffrage introduced for Austria

the legislature. Nevertheless, for six years, the February Patent governed the empire, and it prevailed in Austria proper until 1918. Ministers were responsible to the emperor, not the *Reichsrat*, and civil liberties were not guaranteed. Armies could be levied and taxes raised without parliamentary consent. When the *Reichsrat* was not in session, the emperor could simply rule by decree.

Meanwhile, secret negotiations between the emperor and the Magyars produced no concrete result until the Prussian defeat of Austria in the summer of 1866 and the consequent exclusion of Austria from German affairs. Francis Joseph now had to come to terms with the Magyars. The subsequent **Ausgleich**, or Compromise, of 1867 transformed the Habsburg Empire into a dual monarchy known as Austria-Hungary.

Francis Joseph was crowned king of Hungary in Budapest in 1867. Except for the common monarch, army, and foreign relations, Austria and Hungary became almost wholly separate states. They shared ministers of foreign affairs, defense, and finance, but the other ministers were different for each state. There were also separate parliaments. Each year, sixty parliamentary delegates from each state met to discuss mutual interests. Every ten years, Austria and Hungary renegotiated their trade relationship. This cumbersome machinery, unique in European history, reconciled the Magyars to Habsburg rule. They had achieved the free hand they had long wanted in Hungary.

UNREST OF NATIONALITIES

The Compromise of 1867 introduced two different principles of political legitimacy into the two sections of the Habsburg Empire. In Hungary, political loyalty was based on nationality because Hungary had been recognized as a distinct part of the monarchy on the basis of nationalism. In effect, Hungary was a Magyar nation under the Habsburg emperor. In the rest of the Habsburg domains, the principle of legitimacy meant dynastic loyalty to the emperor. Many of the other nationalities wished to achieve the same type of settlement that the Hungarians had won, or to govern themselves, or as time went on, to unite with fellow nationals who lived outside the empire. (See Map 22–3, page 748.)

Many of these other national groups—including the Czechs, the Ruthenians, the Romanians, and the Croatians—opposed the Compromise of 1867 that, in effect, had permitted the German-speaking Austrians and the Hungarian Magyars to dominate all other nationalities within the empire. The most vocal critics were the Czechs of Bohemia. They favored a policy of "trialism," or triple monarchy, in which the Czechs would have a position similar to that of the Hungarians. In 1871, Francis Joseph was willing to accept this concept. The Magyars, however, vetoed it lest they be forced to make similar concessions to their own subject nationalities. Furthermore, the Germans of Bohemia were afraid the Czech language would be imposed on them.

For more than twenty years, generous patronage and posts in the bureaucracy placated the Czechs. By the 1890s, however, Czech nationalism again became more strident. In 1897, Francis Joseph gave the Czechs and the Germans equality of language in various localities. Thereafter, the Germans in the Austrian *Reichsrat* opposed these measures by disrupting Parliament. The Czechs replied in kind. By the turn of the century, this obstructionism, which included the playing of musical instruments in the *Reichsrat*, had paralyzed parliamentary life. The emperor ruled by imperial decree through the bureaucracy. In 1907, Francis Joseph introduced universal male suffrage in Austria (but not in Hungary), but this action did not eliminate the chaos in the *Reichsrat*. In effect, by 1914, constitutionalism was a dead letter in Austria. It flourished in Hungary, but only because the Magyars relentlessly exercised political supremacy over all other competing national groups except Croatia, which was permitted considerable autonomy.

There is reason to believe nationalism became stronger during the last quarter of the nineteenth century. Language became the single most important factor in defining a nation. The expansion of education made this possible. In all countries where nationalistic groups prospered, their membership was dominated by intellectuals, students, and educated members of the middle class, all of whom were literate in the literary version of particular national languages. Furthermore, during

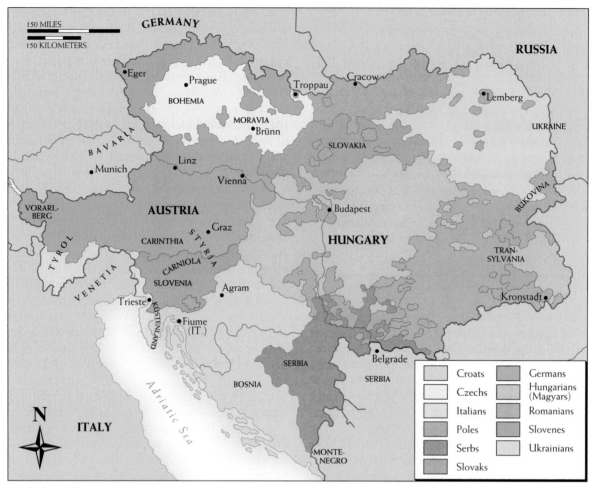

Map 22–3 NATIONALITIES WITHIN THE HABSBURG EMPIRE The patchwork appearance reflects the unusual problem of the numerous ethnic groups that the Habsburgs could not meld into a modern national state. Only the Magyars were recognized in 1867, leaving nationalist Czechs, Slovaks, and the others chronically dissatisfied.

these same years, as will be seen in Chapter 24, racial thinking became important in Europe. Racial thought maintained there was a genetic basis for ethnic and cultural groups that had hitherto been generally defined by a common history and culture. Once language and race became the ways to define an ethnic or national group, the lines between such groups became much more sharply drawn. (See "Lord Acton Condemns Nationalism.")

The unrest of the various nationalities within the Habsburg Empire not only caused internal political difficulties; it also became a major source of political instability for all of central and eastern Europe. Each of the nationality problems normally had ramifications for both foreign and domestic policy. Both the Croats and the Poles wanted an independent state in union with their fellow nationals who lived outside the empire—and in the case of the Poles, with fellow nationals in the Russian Empire and Germany. Other national groups, such

as Ukrainians, Romanians, Italians, and Bosnians, saw themselves as potentially linked to Russia, Romania, Serbia, Italy, or a yet-to-be established south Slavic, or Yugoslav, state. Many of these nationalities looked to Russia to protect their interests or influence the government in Vienna. The Romanians were also concerned about the Romanian minority in Hungary. Serbia sought to expand its borders to include Serbs who lived within Habsburg or Ottoman territory. Out of these Balkan tensions emerged much of the turmoil that would spark the First World War. Many of the same ethnic tensions account for warfare in the former Yugoslavia.

The dominant German population of Austria proper was generally loyal to the emperor. A part of it, however, yearned to join the new German Empire. These Austro-Germans often hated the non-German national groups of the empire, and many of them were anti-Semites. Such attitudes would influence the young Adolf Hitler.

LORD ACTON CONDEMNS NATIONALISM

Lord Acton (1834–1902) was an important nineteenth-century English historian and commentator on contemporary religious and political events. He was deeply concerned with the character and preservation of liberty. His was one of the earliest voices to warn against the dangers of nationalism.

■ *Why does Acton see the principle of nationality as dangerous to liberty? Why does he see nationalism as a threat to minority groups and to democracy?*

The greatest adversary of the rights of nationality is the modern theory of nationality. By making the State and the nation commensurate with each other in theory, it reduces practically to a subject condition all other nationalities that may be within the boundary. It cannot admit them to an equality with the ruling nation which constitutes the State, because the State would then cease to be national, which would be a contradiction of the principle of its existence. According, therefore, to the degree of humanity and civilization in that dominant body which claims all the rights of the community, the inferior races are exterminated, or reduced to servitude, or outlawed, or put in a condition of dependence.

If we take the establishment of liberty for the realization of moral duties to be the end of civil society, we must conclude that those states are substantially the most perfect which, like the British and Austrian Empires, include various distinct nationalities without oppressing them. Those in which no mixture of races has occurred are imperfect; and those in which its effects have disappeared are decrepit. A State which is incompetent to satisfy different races condemns itself; a State which labors to neutralize, to absorb, or to expel them, destroys its own vitality; a State which does not include them is destitute of the chief basis of self-government. The theory of nationality, therefore, is a retrograde step in history. . . .

[N]ationality does not aim either at liberty or prosperity, both of which it sacrifices to the imperative necessity of making the nation the mold and measure of the State. Its course will be marked with material as well as moral ruin, in order that a new invention may prevail over the works of God and the interests of mankind. There is no principle of change, no phrase of political speculation conceivable, more comprehensive, more subversive, or more arbitrary than this. It is a confutation of democracy, because it sets limits to the exercise of the popular will, and substitutes for it a higher principle.

From John Emerich Edward Dalbert-Acton, First Baron Acton, *Essays in the History of Liberty*, ed. by J. Rufus Fears (Indianapolis: Liberty Classics, 1985), pp. 431–433.

For the next century of European and even world history, the significance of this nationalist unrest within the late-nineteenth-century Habsburg Empire and its neighbors can hardly be overestimated. Nationality problems touched all four of the great central and eastern European empires—the German, the Russian, the Austrian, and the Ottoman. The first three had large Polish populations, and Russia, Austria, and the Ottomans had many minority groups. Each nationality regarded its own aspirations and discontents as more important than the larger good or even survival of the empires that they inhabited. The weakness of the Ottoman Empire allowed both Austria and Russia to compete in the Balkans for influence and thus further inflame nationalistic resentments. Such nationalistic stirrings affected the fate of all four empires from the 1860s through the outbreak of World War I. The government of each of these empires would be overturned during the war, and the Habsburg monarchy and the Ottoman Empire would disappear. These same unresolved problems of central and eastern European nationalism would then lead directly to World War II. They continue to fester today.

RUSSIA: EMANCIPATION AND REVOLUTIONARY STIRRINGS

Russia changed remarkably during the last half of the nineteenth century. The government finally addressed the long-standing problem of serfdom and undertook a broad range of administrative reforms. During the same period, however, radical revolutionary groups began to organize. These groups tried to draw the peasants into revolutionary activity and assassinated government officials, including the tsar. The government's response was renewed repression.

REFORMS OF ALEXANDER II

Russia's defeat in the Crimean War and its humiliation in the Treaty of Paris compelled the government to reconsider its domestic policies. Nicholas I died in 1855 during the conflict. His son Alexander II (r. 1855–1881), who had traveled extensively in Russia and been well prepared to rule, was familiar with the difficulties the nation faced. The debacle of the war had made reform both necessary and possible. Alexander II took advantage of this turn of events to institute the most extensive restructuring of Russian society and administration since Peter the Great. Like Peter, Alexander imposed his reforms from the top.

Abolition of Serfdom   In every area of economic and public life, a profound cultural gap separated Russia from the rest of Europe. Nowhere was this more apparent than in the survival of serfdom. In Russia, the institution had changed little since the eighteenth century, although every other nation on the Continent had abandoned it. Russian landowners still had a free hand with their serfs, and the serfs had little recourse against the landlords. In March 1856, at the conclusion of the Crimean War, Alexander II announced his intention to abolish serfdom. He had decided that its abolition was necessary if Russia was to remain a great power.

Serfdom was economically inefficient. There was always the threat of revolt, and the serfs forced into the army had performed poorly in the Crimean War. Moreover, nineteenth-century moral opinion condemned serfdom. Only Russia, Brazil, and certain portions of the United States among the Western nations retained such forms of involuntary servitude. For five years, government commissions wrestled over how to implement the tsar's desire. Finally, in February 1861, despite opposition from the nobility and the landlords, Alexander II ended serfdom.

The actual emancipation law was a disappointment, however, because land did not accompany freedom. Serfs immediately received the personal right to marry without their landlord's permission, as well as the rights to buy and sell property, to sue in court, and to pursue trades. What they did not receive was free title to their land. They had to pay the landlords over a period of forty-nine years for allotments of land that were frequently too small to support them. They were also charged interest during this period. The former serfs, who were now free peasant farmers, made the payments to the government, which had already reimbursed the landlords for their losses. The peasants would not receive title to the land until the debt was paid.

The procedures were so complicated and the results so limited that many serfs believed real emancipation was still to come. The redemption payments led to almost unending difficulty. Poor harvests made it impossible for many peasants to keep up with the payments, and they fell increasingly behind in their debt. The situation was not remedied until 1906, when, during the widespread revolutionary unrest following the Japanese defeat of Russia in 1905, the government grudgingly completed the process of emancipation by canceling the remaining debts.

Reform of Local Government and the Judicial System   The abolition of serfdom required the reorganization of local government and the judicial system. The authority of village communes replaced that of the landlord over the peasant. The village elders settled family quarrels, imposed fines, issued internal passports that were legally required for peasants to move from one locale to another, and collected taxes. Often, also, the village commune, not individual peasants, owned the land. The nobility were given a larger role in

---

**MAJOR DATES
IN LATE-NINETEENTH-CENTURY
RUSSIA**

1855	Alexander II becomes tsar
1856	Defeat in Crimean War
1861	Serfdom abolished
1863	Suppression of Polish rebellion
1864	Reorganization of local government
1864	Reform of judicial system
1874	Military enlistment period reduced
1878	Attempted assassination of military governor of Saint Petersburg
1879	Land and Freedom splits
1881	The People's Will assassinates Alexander II
1881	Alexander III becomes tsar
1894	Nicholas II becomes tsar

local administration through a system of provincial and county *zemstvos*, or councils, organized in 1864. These councils were to oversee local matters, such as bridge and road repair, education, and agricultural improvement. The *zemstvos*, however, were underfunded, and many of them remained ineffective.

The flagrant inequities and abuses of the pre-emancipation judicial system could not continue. In 1864, Alexander II issued a new statute on the judiciary that for the first time introduced Western European legal principles into Russia. These included equality before the law, impartial hearings, uniform procedures, judicial independence, and trial by jury. The new system was far from perfect. The judges were not genuinely independent, and the tsar could increase as well as reduce sentences. Certain offenses, such as those involving the press, were not tried before a jury. Nonetheless, the new courts were both more efficient and less corrupt than the old system.

Military Reform   The government also reformed the army. Russia possessed the largest army on the Continent, but it had floundered badly in the Crimean War. The usual period of service for a soldier was twenty-five years. Villages had to provide quotas of serfs to serve in the army. Often, recruiters simply seized serfs from their families. Once in the army, recruits rarely saw their homes again. Life in the army was harsh, even by the brutal standards of most mid-century armies. In the 1860s, the army lowered the period of service to fifteen years and relaxed discipline slightly. In 1874, the enlistment period was lowered to six years of active duty and nine years in the reserves. All males were subject to military service after the age of twenty.

Repression in Poland   Alexander's reforms became more measured shortly after the Polish Rebellion of 1863. As in 1830, Polish nationalists attempted to overthrow Russian dominance. Once again the Russian army suppressed the rebellion. Alexander II then moved to Russify Poland. In 1864, he emancipated the Polish serfs to punish the politically restive Polish nobility. Russian law, language, and administration were imposed on all areas of Polish life. Henceforth, until the close of World War I, Poland was treated as merely another Russian province.

As the Polish suppression demonstrated, Alexander II was a reformer only within the limits of his own autocracy. His changes in Russian life failed to create new loyalty to, or gratitude for, the government among his subjects. The serfs felt their emancipation had been inadequate. The nobles and the wealthier educated segments of Russian society resented the tsar's persistent refusal to allow them a meaningful role in government and policy-making. Consequently, although Alexander II became known as the Tsar Liberator, he was never popular. He could be indecisive and closed minded. These characteristics became more pronounced after 1866, when an attempt was made on his life. Thereafter, Russia increasingly became a police state. This new repression fueled the activity of radical groups within Russia. Their actions, in turn, made the autocracy more reactionary.

REVOLUTIONARIES

The tsarist regime had long had its critics. One of the most prominent was Alexander Herzen (1812–1870), who lived in exile. From London, he published a newspaper called *The Bell*, in which he set forth reformist positions. The initial reforms of Alexander II had raised great hopes among Russian students and intellectuals, but they soon became discontented with the limited character of the reforms. Drawing on the ideas of Herzen and other radicals, these students formed a revolutionary movement known as *populism*. They sought a social revolution based on the communal life of the Russian peasants. The chief radical society was called *Land and Freedom*.

In the early 1870s, hundreds of young Russian men and women took their revolutionary message into the countryside. They intended to live with the peasants, to gain their trust, and to teach them about the peasant's role in the coming revolution. The bewildered and distrustful peasants turned most of the youths over to the police. In the winter of 1877–1878, almost two hundred students were tried. Most were acquitted or given light sentences, because they had been held for months in preventive detention and because the court believed a display of mercy might lessen public sympathy for the young revolutionaries. The court even suggested the tsar might wish to pardon those students given heavier sentences. The tsar refused and let it be known he favored heavy penalties for all persons involved in revolutionary activity.

Thereafter, the revolutionaries decided the tsarist regime must be attacked directly. They adopted a policy of terrorism. In January 1878, Vera Zasulich (1849–1919) attempted to assassinate the military governor of Saint Petersburg. A jury acquitted her because the governor she had shot had a reputation for brutality. Some people also believed Zasulich had a personal rather than a political grievance against her victim. Nonetheless, the verdict further encouraged the terrorists.

Tsar Alexander II (r. 1855–1881) was assassinated on March 1, 1881. The assassins first threw a bomb that wounded several Imperial guards. When the tsar stopped his carriage to see the wounded, the assassins threw a second bomb, killing him.   Bildarchiv Preussischer Kulturbesitz

In 1879, Land and Freedom split into two groups. One advocated educating the peasants, and it soon dissolved. The other, known as *The People's Will*, was dedicated to the overthrow of the autocracy. Its members decided to assassinate the tsar himself. (See "The People's Will Issues a Revolutionary Manifesto.") Several attempts failed, but on March 1, 1881, a bomb hurled by a member of The People's Will killed Alexander II. Four men and two women were sentenced to death for the deed. All of them had been willing to die for their cause. The emergence of such dedicated revolutionary opposition was as much a part of the reign of Alexander II as were his reforms. The limited character of those reforms convinced many Russians that the autocracy could never truly redirect Russian society.

The reign of Alexander III (r. 1881–1894) strengthened that pessimism. He possessed all the autocratic and repressive characteristics of his grandfather, Nicholas I, and none of the better qualities of his father, Alexander II. Some slight improvements were made to conditions in Russian factories, but Alexander III sought primarily to roll back his father's reforms. He favored the centralized bureaucracy over the *zemstvos*. He strengthened the secret police and increased censorship of the press. In effect, he confirmed all the evils that the revolutionaries saw as inherent in autocratic government. His son, Nicholas II (r. 1894–1917), would discover that autocracy could not survive the pressures of the twentieth century.

GREAT BRITAIN: TOWARD DEMOCRACY

While the continental nations became unified and struggled toward internal political restructuring, Great Britain symbolized the confident liberal state. Britain was not without its difficulties and domestic conflicts, but it seemed able to deal with them through its existing political institutions. The general prosperity of the third quarter of the century mitigated the social hostility of the 1840s. All classes shared a belief in competition and individualism. Even the leaders of trade unions during these years asked mainly to receive more of the fruits of prosperity and to have their social respectability acknowledged. Parliament itself remained an institution through which new groups and interests were absorbed into the existing political processes. In short, the British did not have to create new liberal institutions and then learn how to live within them. (See "Encountering the Past: The Arrival of Penny Postage," page 754.)

THE PEOPLE'S WILL ISSUES A REVOLUTIONARY MANIFESTO

In the late 1870s, an extreme revolutionary movement appeared in Russia calling itself The People's Will. *It advocated the overthrow of the tsarist government and the election of an Organizing Assembly to form a government based on popular representation. It directly embraced terrorism as a path toward its goal of the Russian people governing themselves. Members of this group assassinated Alexander II in 1881.*

■ *Which of the group's seven demands might be associated with liberalism, and which go beyond liberalism in their radical intent? Why does the group believe it must engage in terrorism as well as propaganda? Would any reforms by the Russian government have satisfied this group or dissuaded them from terrorist action?*

Although we are ready to submit wholly to the popular will, we regard it as none the less our duty, as a party, to appear before the people with our program. . . . It is as follows:

1. Perpetual popular representation . . . having full power to act in all national questions.
2. General local self-government, secured by the election of all officers, and the economic independence of the people.
3. The self-controlled village commune as the economic and administrative unit.
4. Ownership of the land by the people.
5. A system of measures having for their object the turning over to the laborers of all mining works and factories.
6. Complete freedom of conscience, speech, association, public meeting, and electioneering activity.
7. The substitution of a territorial militia for the army. . . .

In view of the stated aim of the party its operations may be classified as follows:

1. Propaganda and agitation. Our propaganda has for its object the popularization, in all social classes, of the idea of a political and popular revolution as a means of social reform, as well as popularization of the party's own program. Its essential features are criticism of the existing order of things, and a statement and explanation of revolutionary methods. The aim of agitation should be to incite the people to protest as generally as possible against the present state of affairs, to demand such reforms as are in harmony with the party's purposes, and, especially, to demand the summoning of an Organizing Assembly. . . .

2. Destructive and terroristic activity. Terroristic activity consists in the destruction of the most harmful persons in the Government, the protection of the party from spies, and the punishment of official lawlessness and violence in all the more prominent and important cases in which such lawlessness and violence are manifested. The aim of such activity is to break down the prestige of Governmental power, to furnish continuous proof of the possibility of carrying on a contest with the Government, to raise in that way the revolutionary spirit of the people and inspire belief in the practicability of revolution, and, finally, to form a body suited and accustomed to warfare.

Quoted in George Kennan, *Siberia and the Exile System*, Vol. 2 (New York: The Century Co., 1891), pp. 495–499.

THE SECOND REFORM ACT (1867)

By the early 1860s, most observers realized the franchise would again have to be expanded. The prosperity and social respectability of the working class convinced many politicians that the workers deserved the vote. Organizations such as the Reform League, led by John Bright (1811–1889), agitated for parliamentary action. In 1866, Lord Russell's Liberal ministry introduced a reform bill

THE ARRIVAL OF PENNY POSTAGE

While the armies of the great powers were redrawing the map of Europe during the middle of the nineteenth century, new forms of administration were drawing people closer together. One of the most important of these innovations was the development of postal systems for delivering mail inexpensively. The British government took the lead.

Sending letters and newspapers through the mail had become increasingly expensive, and the British postal service ran large deficits. Other countries had similar problems. At that time the weight of the item to be mailed and the distance over which it had to be carried determined how much it cost to mail it. Furthermore, the person receiving the letter or packet, not the sender, had to pay the postage. Many officials had the privilege of franking their letters and thus paying nothing. The system encouraged resentment and schemes to avoid paying postage. Some people could not afford the postage on letters sent to them. Others put symbols on the outside of a letter, so the recipient could refuse to accept the letter but still "get the message."

Rowland Hill (1795–1879), an English reformer, proposed a simple new procedure in 1837. The price of postage would be lowered, would be uniform for most letters and newspapers regardless of distance, and would be prepaid by the sender. Franking by government officials would also end.

In 1840, the system, known as the Uniform Penny Post, began. Within two years the volume of British mail grew from approximately 75 million items to 196.5 million and, by 1849, to 329 million. The reduced cost of postage meant almost everyone could afford to send letters and postcards. It also led to a huge increase in the size of the government work force. In Britain and most countries, the number of postal workers was soon rivaled only by the number of soldiers and sailors.

Hill had also suggested a small, self-adhesive stamp be attached to a letter to indicate the postage had been paid. The first such stamp bore only the words POSTAGE ONE PENNY. It paid for letters up to one-half ounce. A two-penny stamp was used for letters that weighed an ounce.

With the new British postal system, the volume of mail vastly increased as did the number of postal workers involved in sorting and delivering it. Image Works/Mary Evans Picture Library Ltd.

Other nations soon issued their own stamps. It soon became as important for governments to prevent the forging of postage stamps as currency. Consequently, stamps were printed from engraved steel plates to which small changes were made from time to time. Those changes, introduced to prevent fraud or to commemorate famous people and events, together with the sheer number of national postal systems with their own stamps, gave rise to the hobby of stamp collecting.

The rise of the modern postal system also fostered international cooperation. A treaty signed in Berne, Switzerland, in 1874, established what became the Universal Postal Union, which is still functioning. It mandates that the postage paid in the sender's nation assures delivery of a letter or package anywhere in the world.

- *What changes did Rowland Hill introduce into the British postal service? How did those changes affect the quantity of mail and the size of the government work force?*

M.J. Daunton, "Rowland Hill and the Penny Post," *History Today*, August 1985; "Post, and Postal Service," *Encyclopedia Britannica*, 11th ed.

that a coalition of traditional Conservatives and antidemocratic Liberals defeated. Russell resigned, and the Conservative Lord Derby (1799–1869) replaced him. A surprise then occurred.

The Conservative ministry, led in the House of Commons by Benjamin Disraeli (1804–1881), introduced its own reform bill in 1867. As the debate proceeded, Disraeli accepted one amendment after another and expanded the electorate well beyond the limits the Liberals had earlier proposed. The final measure increased the number of voters from approximately 1,430,000 to 2,470,000. Britain had taken a major step toward democracy. Large numbers of male working-class voters had been admitted to the electorate.

Disraeli hoped the Conservatives would receive the gratitude of the new voters. Because reform was inevitable, it was best for the Conservatives to enjoy the credit for it. Like his contemporary Bismarck, Disraeli was prepared to embrace democracy. He thought that eventually significant portions of the working class would support Conservative candidates who were responsive to social issues. He also thought the growing suburban middle class would become more conservative. In the long run, his intuition proved correct. The Conservative Party dominated British politics in the twentieth century.

The immediate election of 1868, however, dashed Disraeli's hopes. William Gladstone (1809–1898) became the new prime minister. Gladstone had begun political life in 1833 as a strong Tory, but over the next thirty-five years, he became steadily more liberal. He had supported Robert Peel, free trade, repeal of the Corn Laws, and efficient administration. As chancellor of the exchequer (finance minister) during the 1850s and early 1860s, he had lowered taxes and government expenditures. He had also championed Italian nationalism. Yet he had opposed a new reform bill until the early 1860s. In 1866, he had been Russell's spokesperson in the House of Commons for the unsuccessful Liberal reform bill.

GLADSTONE'S GREAT MINISTRY (1868–1874)

Gladstone's ministry of 1868 to 1874 witnessed the culmination of classical British liberalism. Those institutions that remained the preserve of the aristocracy and the Anglican church were opened to people from other classes and religious denominations. In 1870, competitive examinations for the civil service replaced patronage. In 1871, the purchase of officers' commissions in the

army was abolished. The same year, Anglican religious requirements for the faculties of Oxford and Cambridge universities were removed. The Ballot Act of 1872 introduced voting by secret ballot.

The most momentous measure of Gladstone's first ministry was the Education Act of 1870. For the first time in British history, the government assumed the responsibility for establishing and running elementary schools. Previously, British education had been a task relegated to the religious denominations, which received small amounts of state support for the purpose. Henceforth, the government would establish schools where religious denominations had not done so.

These reforms were typically liberal. They sought to remove abuses without destroying institutions and to permit all able citizens to compete on the grounds of ability and merit. They tried to avoid the potential danger to a democratic state of an illiterate citizenry. These reforms were also a mode of state building, because they reinforced loyalty to the nation by abolishing sources of discontent.

DISRAELI IN OFFICE (1874–1880)

The liberal policy of creating popular support for the nation by extending political liberties and reforming abuses had its conservative counterpart in concern for social reform. Disraeli succeeded Gladstone as prime minister in 1874, when the election produced sharp divisions among Liberal Party voters over religion, education, and the sale of alcohol.

The two men differed on most issues. Whereas Gladstone looked to individualism, free trade, and competition to solve social problems, Disraeli believed in paternalistic legislation to protect the weak and ease class antagonisms.

Disraeli talked a better line than he produced. He had few specific programs or ideas. The significant social legislation of his ministry stemmed primarily from the efforts of his home secretary, Richard Cross (1823–1914). The Public Health Act of 1875 consolidated previous legislation on sanitation and reaffirmed the duty of the state to interfere with private property to protect health and physical well-being. Through the Artisan Dwelling Act of 1875, the government became actively involved in providing housing for the working class. That same year, in an important symbolic gesture, the Conservative majority in Parliament gave new protection to British trade unions and allowed them to raise picket lines. The Gladstone ministry, although recognizing the legality of unions, had refused such protection.

A House of Commons debate. William Ewart Gladstone, standing on the right, is attacking Benjamin Disraeli, who sits with legs crossed and arms folded. Gladstone served in the British Parliament from the 1830s through the 1890s. Four times the Liberal Party prime minister, he was responsible for guiding major reforms through Parliament. Disraeli, regarded as the founder of modern British conservatism, served as prime minister from 1874 to 1880. Image Works/Mary Evans Picture Library Ltd.

THE IRISH QUESTION

In 1880, a second Gladstone ministry took office after an agricultural depression and an unpopular foreign policy undermined the Conservative government. In 1884, with Conservative cooperation, a third reform act gave the vote to most male farm workers. The major issue of the decade, however, was Ireland. From the late 1860s onward, Irish nationalists had sought to achieve **home rule** for Ireland, by which they meant Irish control of local government.

During his first ministry, Gladstone addressed the Irish question through two major pieces of legislation. In 1869, he disestablished the Church of Ireland, the Irish branch of the Anglican church. Henceforth, Irish Roman Catholics would not pay taxes to support the hated Protestant church, to which few of the Irish belonged. Second, in 1870, the Liberal ministry sponsored a land act that provided compensation to those Irish tenant farmers who were evicted and loans for those who wished to purchase their land. Throughout the 1870s, the Irish question continued to fester. Land remained the center of the agitation. Today, Irish economic development seems more complicated, and who owns the land seems less important than the methods of management and cultivation. Never-

theless, the organization of the Irish Land League in the late 1870s led to intense agitation and intimidation of landlords, who were often Protestants of English descent. The leader of the Irish movement for a just land settlement and for home rule was Charles Stewart Parnell (1846–1891). In 1881, the second Gladstone ministry passed another Irish land act that strengthened tenant rights. It was accompanied, however, by a Coercion Act to restore law and order to Ireland.

By 1885, Parnell had organized eighty-five Irish members of the House of Commons into a tightly disciplined party that often voted as a bloc. They frequently disrupted Parliament to gain attention for the cause of home rule. They bargained with the two English political parties. In the election of 1885, the Irish Party emerged holding the balance of power between the English Liberals and Conservatives. Irish support could decide which party took office. (See "Parnell Calls for Home Rule for Ireland.") In December 1885, Gladstone announced his support of home rule for Ireland. Parnell gave his votes to a Liberal ministry. The home rule issue then split the Liberal Party. In 1886, a group known as the Liberal Unionists joined with the Conservatives to defeat home rule. Gladstone called for a new election, but the

PARNELL CALLS FOR HOME RULE FOR IRELAND

Since 1800, Ireland had been governed as part of Great Britain, sending representatives to the British Parliament in Westminster. Throughout the century, there had been tension and violent conflict between the Irish and their English governors. Agitation for home rule, whereby the Irish would directly control many of their own affairs, reached a peak in the 1880s. Charles Stewart Parnell was the chief leader for the cause of Irish nationalism during that decade. His program at the time was home rule for Ireland, by which he meant Irish administration of Irish domestic affairs while preserving an ill-defined union with England. In 1885, he made a speech outlining the resentments the Irish had felt toward the English since the Act of Union of 1800. He also drew direct parallels between the relationship of Ireland to England and that of Hungary to Austria. The efforts to achieve home rule failed during the nineteenth century.

■ *How does Parnell say the Act of Union affected Irish sentiment toward England? What parallel does he draw with Hungary and Austria? Why might Parnell be regarded as a moderate nationalist?*

It is not possible for human intelligence to forecast the future in the matter; but we can point to this—we can point to the fact that under 85 years of parliamentary connection with England, Ireland has become intensely disloyal and intensely disaffected; that notwithstanding the Whig policy of so-called conciliation, alternative conciliation and coercion . . . that disaffection has broadened, deepened, and intensified from day to day. Am I not, then, entitled to assume that one of the roots of this disaffection and feeling of disloyalty is the assumption by England of the management of our affairs. It is admitted that the present system can't go on, and what are you going to put in its place? My advice to English statesmen considering this question would be this—trust the Irish people altogether or trust them not at all. . . . Whatever chance the English rulers may have of drawing to themselves the affection of the Irish people lies in destroying the abominable system of legislative union between the two countries by conceding fully and freely to Ireland their right to manage her own affairs. It is impossible for us to give guarantees, but we can point to the past; we can show that the record of English rule is a constant series of steps from bad to worse, that the condition of English power is more insecure and more unstable at the present moment than it has ever been. We can point to the example of other countries; of Austria and of Hungary—to the fact that Hungary having been conceded self-government became one of the strongest factors in the Austrian empire. We can show the powers that have been freely conceded in the colonies [such as Canada and Australia have led to loyalty] . . . I am confident that the English statesman who is great enough . . . to carry out these teachings . . . to give Ireland full legislative liberty, full power to manage her own domestic concerns will be regarded in the future by his countrymen as one who has removed the greatest peril to the English empire—a peril, I firmly believe, which if not removed will find some day . . . an opportunity of revenging itself to the destruction of the British empire for the misfortunes, the oppressions, and the misgovernment of our country.

From Charles Stewart Parnell, "Speech at Wicklow," October 5, 1885, as quoted in Raymond Phineas Stearns, *Pageant of Europe: Sources and Selections from the Renaissance to the Present Day* (New York: Harcourt, Brace and Company, 1948), pp. 634–635.

MAJOR DATES
IN LATE-NINETEENTH-CENTURY BRITAIN

1867   Second Reform Act
1868   Gladstone becomes prime minister
1869   Disestablishment of Church of Ireland
1870   Education Act and first Irish Land Act
1871   Purchase of army officers' commissions abolished
1871   Religious tests abolished at Oxford and Cambridge
1872   Secret Ballot Act
1874   Disraeli becomes prime minister
1875   Public Health Act and Artisan Dwelling Act
1880   Beginning of Gladstone's second ministry
1881   Second Irish Land Act and Irish Coercion Act
1884   Third Reform Act
1885   Gladstone announces support of Irish home rule
1886   Home Rule Bill defeated and Lord Salisbury becomes the Conservative prime minister
1892   Gladstone begins his third ministry; second Irish Home Rule Bill defeated
1903   Third Irish Land Act
1912   Third Irish Home Rule Bill passed
1914   Provisions of Irish Home Rule Bill suspended because of the outbreak of World War I

Liberals were defeated. They remained divided, and Ireland remained firmly under English administration.

The new Conservative ministry of Lord Salisbury (1830–1903) attempted to reconcile the Irish to British rule through public works and administrative reform. The policy, which was tied to further coercion, had only marginal success. In 1892, Gladstone returned to power. A second Home Rule Bill passed the House of Commons but was defeated in the House of Lords. There the Irish question stood until after the turn of the century. The Conservatives sponsored a land act in 1903 that carried out the final transfer of land to tenant ownership. Ireland became a country of small farms. In 1912, a Liberal ministry passed the third Home Rule Bill. Under the provisions of the House of Lords Act of 1911, which curbed the power of the Lords, the bill had to pass the Commons three times over the Lords' veto to become law. The third passage occurred in the summer of 1914, but the implementation of home rule was suspended for the duration of World War I.

The Irish question affected British politics in a manner not unlike that of the Austrian nationalities problem. Normal British domestic issues could not be resolved because of the political divisions Ireland created. The split of the Liberal Party proved especially harmful to the cause of further social and political reform. People who could agree about reform could not agree about Ireland, and the Irish problem seemed more important. Because the two traditional parties failed to deal with the social questions by the turn of the century, a newly organized Labour Party began to fill the vacuum.

IN PERSPECTIVE

Between 1850 and 1875, the major contours of the political systems that would dominate Europe until World War I had been drawn. These systems and political arrangements solved, so far as such matters can be solved, many of the political problems that had troubled Europeans during the first half of the nineteenth century. On the whole, the concept of the nation-state had triumphed. Support for governments no longer stemmed from loyalty to dynasties, but from citizen participation. Moreover, the unity of nations was now based on ethnic, cultural, linguistic, and historical bonds. The parliamentary governments of Western Europe were different from the autocracies of eastern Europe, but both political systems had been compelled to recognize the force of nationalism and the larger role of citizens in political affairs. Only Russia failed to make such concessions. In Russia the only concession to popular opinion had been the emancipation of the serfs.

Future discontent would arise primarily from the demands of labor to enter the political processes and the unsatisfied aspirations of subject nationalities. These two sources of unrest would trouble Europe for the next forty years and would eventually undermine the political structures created during the late nineteenth century.

REVIEW QUESTIONS

1. Why did the Ottoman Empire attempt to reform itself between 1839 and 1914? What was the result of these efforts?
2. Why was it so difficult to unify Italy? What groups wanted unification? Why did Cavour succeed? What did Garibaldi contribute to Italian unification?

3. How and why did Bismarck unify Germany? Why had earlier attempts failed? How did German unification affect the rest of Europe?

4. What events led to the establishment of the Third Republic in France? What were the objectives of the Paris Commune? How did the Dreyfus affair affect the Third Republic?

5. What problems did Austria share with other eastern European empires? Were they solved? Why did the Habsburgs agree to the Compromise of 1867? Was it a success?

6. What reforms did Alexander II institute in Russia? Did they solve Russia's domestic problems? Why did the abolition of serfdom not satisfy the peasants? What were the goals of *The Peoples' Will?*

7. How did the policies of the British Liberal and Conservative parties differ between 1860 and 1890? Why was Irish home rule such a divisive issue in British politics?

SUGGESTED READINGS

I. T. BEREND, *History Derailed: Central and Eastern Europe in the Long Nineteenth Century* (2003). The best one-volume treatment of the complexities of this region.

D. BLACKBOURN, *The Long Nineteenth Century: A History of Germany, 1780–1918* (1998). An outstanding survey based on up-to-date scholarship.

R. BLAKE, *Disraeli* (1967). Remains the best biography of the man.

J. BLUM, *Lord and Peasant in Russia from the Ninth to the Nineteenth Century* (1961). A clear discussion of emancipation in the later chapters.

M. CLARK, *The Italian Risorgimento* (1998). A brief overview based on recent scholarship.

R. B. EDGERTON, *Death or Glory: The Legacy of the Crimean War* (2000). Multifaceted study of a mismanaged war that transformed European politics.

R. KEE, *The Green Flag: A History of Irish Nationalism* (2001). A vast survey.

D. LANGEWIESCHE, *Liberalism in Germany* (1999). A broad survey that is particularly good on the problems unification caused for German Liberals.

D. C. LIEVAN, *The Russian Empire and Its Rivals* (2001). Explores the imperial side of Russian government.

H. C. G. MATTHEW, *Gladstone, 1809–1898* (1998). A superb biography.

N. M. NAIMARK, *Terrorists and Social Democrats: The Russian Revolutionary Movement under Alexander III* (1983). Useful discussion of a complicated subject.

P. G. NORD, *The Republican Moment: Struggles for Democracy in Nineteenth-Century France* (1996). A major examination of nineteenth-century French political culture.

J. P. PARRY, *The Rise and Fall of Liberal Government in Victorian Britain* (1994). An outstanding study.

O. PFLANZE, *Bismarck and the Development of Germany*, 3 vols. (1990). A major biography and history of Germany for the period.

R. PRICE, *The French Second Empire: An Anatomy of Political Power* (2001). This volume along with the following title are the most comprehensive recent study.

R. PRICE, *People and Politics in France, 1848–1870* (2004).

J. RIDLEY, *Garibaldi* (2001). An extensive biography of a remarkable personality.

A. SKED, *Decline and Fall of the Habsburg Empire 1815–1918* (2001). A major, accessible survey of a difficult subject.

D. M. SMITH, *Cavour* (1984). An excellent biography.

DOCUMENTS CD-ROM

Industrialization

22.3 Women Miners
22.4 A Factory Girl: Countering the Stereotypes
22.5 A View from Downstairs: A Servant's Life

CHAPTER 23

THE BUILDING OF EUROPEAN SUPREMACY:

Society and Politics to World War I

- **POPULATION TRENDS AND MIGRATION**

- **THE SECOND INDUSTRIAL REVOLUTION**
  New Industries • Economic Difficulties

- **THE MIDDLE CLASSES IN ASCENDANCY**
  Social Distinctions Within the Middle Class

- **LATE-NINETEENTH-CENTURY URBAN LIFE**
  The Redesign of Cities • Urban Sanitation • Housing Reform and Middle-Class Values

- **VARIETIES OF LATE-NINETEENTH-CENTURY WOMEN'S EXPERIENCES**
  Women's Social Disabilities • New Employment Patterns for Women • Working-Class Women • Poverty and Prostitution • Women of the Middle Class • The Rise of Political Feminism

- **JEWISH EMANCIPATION**
  Differing Degrees of Citizenship • Broadened Opportunities

- **LABOR, SOCIALISM, AND POLITICS TO WORLD WAR I**
  Trade Unionism • Democracy and Political Parties • Karl Marx and the First International • Great Britain: Fabianism and Early Welfare Programs • France: "Opportunism" Rejected • Germany: Social Democrats and Revisionism • Russia: Industrial Development and the Birth of Bolshevism

- **IN PERSPECTIVE**

KEY TOPICS

- The transformation of European life by the Second Industrial Revolution
- Urban sanitation, housing reform, and the redesign of cities
- The condition of women in late-nineteenth-century Europe and the rise of political feminism
- The emancipation of the Jews
- The development of labor politics and socialism in Europe to the outbreak of World War I
- Industrialization and political unrest in Russia

The growth of industrialism between 1860 and 1914 increased Europe's productive capacity to unprecedented and unparalleled levels. New steel mills, railways, shipyards, and chemical plants reflected an expanding supply of capital goods in the second half of the nineteenth century. By the first decade of the twentieth century, the age of the automobile, the airplane, the bicycle, the refrigerated ship, the telephone,

Women only gradually gained access to secondary and university education during the second half of the nineteenth century and the early twentieth century. Young women on their way to school, the subject of this 1880 English painting, would thus have been a new sight when it was painted.   Sir George Clausen (RA) (1852–1944), "Schoolgirls, Haverstock Hill," signed and dated 1880, oil on canvas, 20$\frac{1}{2}$ × 30$\frac{3}{8}$ in. (52 × 77.2 cm), Yale Center for British Art/Paul Mellon Collection, USA/Bridgeman Art Library (B1985.10.1). Courtesy of the Estate of Sir George Clausen

the radio, the typewriter, and the electric light bulb had dawned. The world's economies, based on the gold standard, became increasingly interdependent. European manufactured goods and financial capital flowed into markets all over the globe. In turn, Europeans imported foreign raw materials and foodstuffs. Within Europe itself, the eastern and southern European countries tended to import finished goods from the west and the north and to export agricultural products.

During this half century, European political, economic, and social life assumed many of its current characteristics. Nation-states with large electorates, political parties, and centralized bureaucracies emerged. Business adopted large-scale corporate structures, and the labor force organized itself into trade unions. The number of white-collar workers increased. Western Europe became predominately urban. Socialism strongly affected the political life of all nations. The foundations of the welfare state and of vast military establishments were laid. Taxation increased accordingly.

Europe had also quietly become dependent on the resources and markets of the rest of the world. Changes in the weather in Kansas, Argentina, or New Zealand might now affect the European economy. Before World War I, however, Europe's industrial, military, and financial supremacy concealed that dependency. Many Europeans assumed their supremacy to be natural and permanent, but the twentieth century would reveal it to have been temporary. ■

POPULATION TRENDS AND MIGRATION

The proportion of Europeans in the world's total population was apparently greater around 1900—estimated at about 20 percent—than ever before or since. The number of Europeans had risen from approximately 266 million in 1850 to 401 million in 1900 and to 447 million in 1910. Thereafter, birth and death rates declined or stabilized in Europe and other developed regions, and population growth began to slow in those areas but not elsewhere. The result has been a persistent demographic differential between the developed and undeveloped world—stable or slowly growing populations in developed countries and large, rapidly growing populations in undeveloped regions—that contributes to the world's present food and resource crisis.

Europe's peoples were on the move in the latter half of the century as never before (See Map 23–1). The mid-century emancipation of peasants lessened the authority of landlords and made legal movement and migration easier. Railways, steamships, and better roads increased mobility. Cheap land and better wages accompanied economic development in Europe, North America, Latin America, and Australia, enticing people to move from regions where they had little prospect of improving their lives to regions that held or seemed to hold opportunity. In Europe itself the main migration continued to be from the countryside into urban areas. During this era, Europeans also left their own continent in record numbers. Between 1846 and 1932, more than 50 million Europeans left their homelands. The major areas to benefit from this movement were the United States, Canada, Australia, South Africa, Brazil, Algeria, and Argentina. At midcentury, most of the emigrants were from Great Britain (especially Ireland), Germany, and Scandinavia. After 1885, migration from southern and eastern Europe rose. This exodus helped relieve the social and population pressures on the Continent. The outward movement of peoples, in conjunction with Europe's economic and technological superiority, contributed heavily to the Europeanization of the world. Not since the sixteenth century had European civilization had such an impact on other cultures.

THE SECOND INDUSTRIAL REVOLUTION

During the third quarter of the nineteenth century, the gap that had long existed between British and continental economic development closed. (See Map 23–2, page 764.) The basic heavy industries of Belgium, France, and Germany expanded rapidly. In particular, the growth of the German industry was stunning. German steel production surpassed Britain's in 1893 and was nearly twice that of Britain by the outbreak of World War I. This emergence of an industrial Germany was the major fact of European economic and political life at the turn of the century.

MAJOR DATES OF THE SECOND INDUSTRIAL REVOLUTION

1856–1870	Passage of laws permitting joint stock companies: 1856, Britain; 1863, France; 1870, Prussia
1857	Bessemer process for making steel
1873	Beginning of major economic downturn
1876	Alexander Graham Bell invents the telephone
1879	Edison perfects the electric light bulb
1881	First electric power plant in Britain
1885	Gottlieb Daimler invents the internal combustion engine
1889	Daimler's first automobile
1895	Diesel engine invented
1895	Wireless telegraphy invented
1890s	First major impact of petroleum
1903	Wright brothers make first successful airplane flight
1909	Henry Ford manufactures the Model T

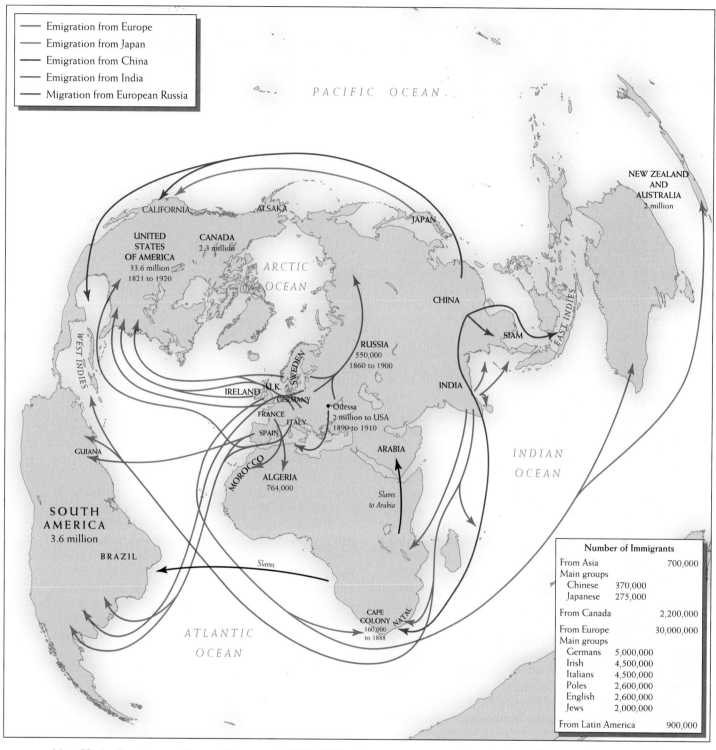

Legend:
- Emigration from Europe
- Emigration from Japan
- Emigration from China
- Emigration from India
- Migration from European Russia

PACIFIC OCEAN

CALIFORNIA   ALSAKA   JAPAN

UNITED STATES OF AMERICA
33.6 million
1821 to 1920

CANADA
2.3 million

ARCTIC OCEAN

CHINA

NEW ZEALAND AND AUSTRALIA
2 million

WEST INDIES

RUSSIA
550,000
1860 to 1900

SIAM

EAST INDIES

SWEDEN

IRELAND   U.K.

GERMANY

FRANCE

ITALY

SPAIN

Odessa
2 million to USA
1890 to 1910

INDIA

INDIAN OCEAN

GUIANA

MOROCCO

ALGERIA
764,000

ARABIA

Slaves to Arabia

SOUTH AMERICA
3.6 million

BRAZIL

Slaves

CAPE COLONY
160,000
to 1888

NATAL

ATLANTIC OCEAN

Number of Immigrants		
From Asia		700,000
Main groups		
Chinese	370,000	
Japanese	275,000	
From Canada		2,200,000
From Europe		30,000,000
Main groups		
Germans	5,000,000	
Irish	4,500,000	
Italians	4,500,000	
Poles	2,600,000	
English	2,600,000	
Jews	2,000,000	
From Latin America		900,000

Map 23–1   **PATTERNS OF GLOBAL MIGRATION, 1840–1900**   Emigration was a global process by the late 19th century. But more immigrants went to the United States than to every other nation combined.

NEW INDUSTRIES

Initially, the economic expansion of the third quarter of the century involved the spread of industries similar to those pioneered earlier in Great Britain. In particular, the expansion of railway systems on the Continent spurred economic growth. Thereafter, however, wholly new industries emerged. This latter development is usually termed the ***Second Industrial Revolution***. The first Industrial Revolution was associated with textiles, steam, and iron; by contrast, the second was associated with steel, chemicals, electricity, and oil.

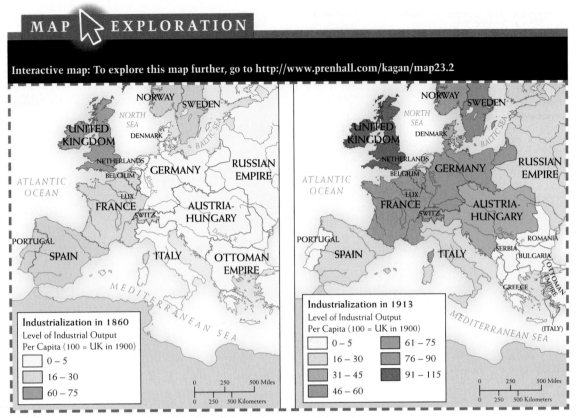

MAP 🔺 EXPLORATION

Interactive map: To explore this map further, go to http://www.prenhall.com/kagan/map23.2

Industrialization in 1860
Level of Industrial Output
Per Capita (100 = UK in 1900)

0 – 5	
16 – 30	
60 – 75	

Industrialization in 1913
Level of Industrial Output
Per Capita (100 = UK in 1900)

0 – 5	61 – 75
16 – 30	76 – 90
31 – 45	91 – 115
46 – 60	

Map 23–2 **EUROPEAN INDUSTRIALIZATION, 1860–1913**   In 1860 Britain was far more industrialized than other European countries. But in the following half century, industrial output rose significantly, if unevenly, across much of Western Europe, especially in the new German Empire. The Balkan states and the Ottoman Empire, however, remained economically backward.

In the 1850s, Henry Bessemer (1830–1898), an English engineer, discovered a new process, named after him, for manufacturing steel cheaply in large quantities. In 1860, Great Britain, Belgium, France, and Germany combined produced 125,000 tons of steel. By 1913, the figure had risen to over 32 million tons.

The chemical industry also came of age during this period. The Solway process of alkali production replaced the older Leblanc process, allowing the recovery of more chemical by-products. The new process permitted increased production of sulfuric acid and laundry soap. New dyestuffs and plastics were also developed. Formal scientific research played an important role in this growth of the chemical industry, marking the beginning of a direct link between science and industrial development. As in so many other aspects of the Second Industrial Revolution, Germany was a leader in forging this link, fostering scientific research and education.

The most significant change for industry and, eventually, for everyday life involved the application of electrical energy to production. Electricity was the most versatile and transportable source of power ever discovered. It could be delivered almost anywhere to run either large or small machinery, making the locations of factories more flexible and factory construction more efficient. The first major public power plant was constructed in 1881 in Great Britain. Soon electric poles, lines, and generating stations dotted the European landscape. Homes began to use electric lights. Streetcar and subway systems were electrified.

In 1885, the German engineer Gottlieb Daimler (1834–1900), improving a previous prototype, invented the modern internal combustion engine. By 1889, he had mounted it on a carriage body specifically designed to incorporate a still more improved internal combustion engine, and the automobile was born. France initially took the lead in auto manufacturing, but for many years, the car remained a novelty item that only the wealthy could afford. It was the American, Henry Ford (1863–1947), who later made the automobile accessible to the masses. No single invention so transformed the mobility of large numbers of people first through the automobile itself and then through trolleys and buses. The automobile industry, furthermore, created a vast new demand for steel and the materials that went into other auto parts and established an ever growing demand for petroleum products that continues to this day. Then as now, Europe depended on imported supplies of oil. The major oil companies were Standard Oil of the United States, British Shell Oil, and Royal Dutch Petroleum.

458 M. FOURNIER'S "MORS."
The Winner of the Race from Paris
to Berlin. 1901

The invention and commercialization of automobiles soon led to auto races in Europe and North America. Here Henri Fournier, the winner of the 1901 Paris to Berlin Motor Car Race, sits in his winning racing car manufactured by the Paris-based auto firm of Emile and Louis Mors.   Getty Images Inc.– Hulton Archive Photos

ECONOMIC DIFFICULTIES

Despite the multiplication of new industries, the second half of the nineteenth century was not a period of uninterrupted or smooth economic growth. Both industry and agriculture generally prospered from 1850 to 1873, but in the last quarter of the century, economic advance slowed. Bad weather and foreign competition put grave pressures on European agriculture and caused many European peasants to emigrate to other parts of the world.

As new farming regions developed in the United States, Canada, Argentina, Australia, and New Zealand, products from those areas challenged the market for home-produced European agricultural goods. Refrigerated ships could bring meat and dairy products to Europe from all over the world. Grain could be grown more economically on the plains of North America, Argentina, and Ukraine than it could in Western Europe, and railways and steamships made it easy and cheap to ship it across continents and oceans. These developments lowered the prices of consumer goods, but put great pressure on European agriculture.

Several large banks failed in 1873, and the rate of capital investment slowed. Some industries then entered a two-decade-long period of stagnation that many contemporaries regarded as a depression. Overall, however, the general standard of living in the industrialized nations improved in the second half of the nineteenth century. Both prices and wages, as well as profits, fell, so real wages generally held firm and even rose in some countries. Yet many workers still lived and labored in abysmal conditions. There were pockets of *unemployment* (a word that was coined during this period), and

strikes and other forms of labor unrest were common. These economic difficulties fed the growth of trade unions and socialist political parties.

The new industries produced consumer goods, and expansion in consumer demand brought the economy out of stagnation by the end of the century. (See "Encountering the Past: Bicycles: Transportation, Freedom, and Sport," page 767.) Lower food prices eventually allowed all classes to spend more on consumer goods. Urbanization naturally created larger markets. People living in cities simply saw more things they wanted to buy than they would have encountered in the countryside. New forms of retailing and marketing appeared—department stores, chain stores, mail-order catalogs, and advertising—simultaneously stimulating and feeding consumer demand. (See "Paris Department Stores Expand Their Business," page 766.) Imperialism also opened new markets overseas for European consumer goods.

THE MIDDLE CLASSES IN ASCENDANCY

The sixty years before World War I were the age of the middle classes. The London Great Exhibition of 1851 held in the Crystal Palace displayed the products and the new material life they had forged. Thereafter, the middle classes became the arbiter of consumer taste. After the revolutions of 1848, the middle classes ceased to be a revolutionary group. Once the question of social equality and equality of property had been raised, large and small property owners across the Continent moved to protect what they possessed against demands from socialists and other working-class groups.

SOCIAL DISTINCTIONS WITHIN THE MIDDLE CLASSES

The middle classes, never perfectly homogeneous, grew increasingly diverse. Their most prosperous members—the owners and managers of great businesses and banks—lived in splendor that rivaled, and sometimes exceeded, that of the aristocracy. In Britain some of them, such as W. H. Smith (1825–1891), the owner of railway newsstands, were made members of the House of Lords. The Krupp family of Germany who owned huge steel works in the Rhineland were pillars of the state and were ennobled by the German emperor and received visits from the imperial court.

Only a few hundred families gained such wealth. Beneath them were the comfortable small entrepreneurs and professional people, whose incomes permitted private homes, large quantities of furniture, pianos, pictures, books, journals, education

PARIS DEPARTMENT STORES EXPAND THEIR BUSINESS

—m—

The department store in Europe and the United States became a major retailing institution in the last half of the nineteenth century. It was one of the reasons for the expansion in late-century consumer demand. This description, written by E. Levasseur in 1907, follows the growth of such stores in Paris and explains why they exerted such economic power. Note how many of their sales techniques stores still use today.

■ Why should French governments have favored the growth of department stores? Where did these stores stand in the process of economic production and sales? Why was the volume of sales so important? What kinds of people might have benefited from the jobs available in these stores? Why might these stores have hurt small retailers?

It was in the reign of Louis Philippe [1830–1848] that department stores for fashion goods and dresses . . . began to be distinguished. The type was already one of other notable developments of the Second Empire; it became one of the most important ones of the Third Republic. These stores have increased in number and several of them have become extremely large. Combining in their different departments all articles of clothing, toilet articles, furniture and many other ranges of goods, it is their special object so to combine all commodities as to attract and satisfy customers who will find conveniently together an assortment of a mass of articles corresponding to all their various needs. They attract customers by permanent display, by free entry into the shops, by periodic exhibitions, by special sales, by fixed prices, and by their ability to deliver the goods purchased to customers' homes, in Paris and to the provinces. Turning themselves into direct intermediaries between the producer and the consumer, even producing sometimes some of their articles in their own workshops, buying at lowest prices because of their large orders and because they are in a position to profit from bargains, working with large sums, and selling to most of their customers for cash only, they can transmit these benefits in lowered selling prices. They can even decide to sell at a loss, as an advertisement or to get rid of out-of-date fashions.

The success of these department stores is only possible thanks to the volume of their business, and this volume needs considerable capital and a very large turnover. Now capital, having become abundant, is freely combined nowadays in large enterprises. . . . [T]he large urban agglomerations, the ease with which goods can be transported by the railways, the diffusion of some comforts to strata below the middle classes, have all favoured these developments. . . .

According to the tax records of 1891, these stores in Paris, numbering 12, employed 1,708 persons and rated their site values at 2,159,000 francs; the largest had then 542 employees. These same stores had, in 1901, 9,784 employees; one of them over 2,000 and another over 1,600; their site value was doubled.

From *Documents of European Economic History*, Vol. 3 by Sidney Pollard and Colin Holmes, pp. 95–96. (London: Edward Arnold, 1972.)

for their children, and vacations. Also in this group were the shopkeepers, schoolteachers, librarians, and others who had either a bit of property or a skill derived from education that provided respectable nonmanual employment.

Finally, there was a wholly new element—"white-collar workers"—who formed the lower middle class, or **petite bourgeoisie**. They included secretaries, retail clerks, and lower-level bureaucrats in business and government. They often had working-class origins and might even belong to unions, but they had middle-class aspirations and consciously sought to distance themselves from a lower class lifestyle. They pursued educational opportunities and chances for even the slightest career advancement for themselves and, especially, for their children. Many of them spent much of their disposable income on consumer goods, such

BICYCLES: TRANSPORTATION, FREEDOM, AND SPORT

Before the car, came the bicycle. Bicycles were the first mass-produced, affordable machines for individual travel. Between 1880 and 1900, they took Europe and North America by storm. For the first time in history, individual men and, significantly, women had a machine that enabled them to travel on their own for work or pleasure. Bicycles had an immense impact on Western society.

The first functioning bicycles had been invented in Germany about 1817, but they were clumsy and dangerous. Made of wood, these machines lacked pedals and tires. They had to be pushed along the ground, and their riders could not control their speed. It took another eighty years for the modern bicycle to take shape. Pedals were introduced in the 1860s. Metal frames, solid rubber tires, and chain drives, which increased speed, appeared in the 1870s. In the 1880s, the ride became much smoother when John Boyd Dunlop, an Irish physician, invented the pneumatic tire, and in France, the Michelin brothers introduced the inner tube. (Before then, the ride was so rough that bicycles were sometimes called "boneshakers.") By the 1890s, the "safety bicycle" with its now familiar triangular frame and chain drive attached to the pedal and back wheel was being mass produced across Europe and North America, and men and women of the working class could afford them. By 1900, male workers of modest means across Europe were riding bicycles to work.

By increasing individual mobility, the bicycle made it easier to get to work, to hold a job farther from home, and to move about one's city or town or reach the countryside. New clothing designs, especially "bloomers," trousers worn under skirts, (designed before the bicycle) permitted women to bicycle while maintaining modesty. In the 1890s, feminists like Marie Pognon in France and Susan B. Anthony in the United States hailed the "egalitarian and leveling bicycle" for the freedom it gave women.

By 1914, there were millions of cyclists across the transatlantic world. Europeans and Americans organized cycling clubs with distinctive uniforms. Some of these clubs, such as the English Clarion Cycling Clubs, the French Union Sportive du Parti Socialiste, and the German *Solidaritet*, used cy-

The bicycle helped liberate women's lives, but as this poster suggests, it also was associated with glamour and fashion. © Archivo Iconografico, S.A./CORBIS

cling trips to spread literature for left-wing causes. Other groups cycled for pleasure. The kinds of touring clubs that now exist for automobiles were first organized for cyclists, as were many of the early European travel guides such as the French *Guides Michelin*, which first appeared in 1900. Then as now, Michelin made tires and stood to sell more of them the more people toured the countryside.

Bicycle racing quickly became a competitive sport. The most famous professional racer in the world was Marshall Walter "Major" Taylor, an African American who raced in both the United States and Europe. Paris and other French cities built velodromes for indoor cycle racing, which was one of the official sports of the first modern Olympics in 1896. In 1903, *L'Auto*, a French sports paper, organized the first Tour de France race to increase its circulation. Six riders raced a 2,500 km-course over 19 days.

- *Why did bicycles become so popular in Europe in the late nineteenth century? What advantages did bicycles bring to women?*

Eugen Weber, *France: Fin de Siècle* (Cambridge, MA: Harvard University Press, 1986), pp. 103–104, 195–206; Will and Terra Hanger, "Bicycles," *History Magazine*, October/November 2001.

as stylish clothing and furniture, that were distinctively middle class in appearance.

Significant tensions and social anxieties marked relations among the various middle-class groups. Small shopkeepers resented the power of the great capitalists, with their department stores and mail-order catalogs. There is some evidence that the professions were becoming overcrowded. People who had only recently attained a middle-class lifestyle feared losing it in bad economic times. Nonetheless, in the decades immediately before World War I, the middle classes set the values and goals for most of society.

LATE-NINETEENTH-CENTURY URBAN LIFE

Europe became more urbanized than ever in the latter half of the nineteenth century as migration to the cities continued. Between 1850 and 1911, urban dwellers rose from 25 to 44 percent of the population in France and from 30 to 60 percent of the population in Germany. Similar increases occurred in other Western European countries.

The rural migrants to the cities were largely uprooted from traditional social ties. They often faced poor housing, social anonymity, and, because they rarely possessed the right kinds of skills, unemployment. People from different ethnic backgrounds found themselves in proximity to one another and had difficulty mixing socially. Competition for jobs generated new varieties of political and social discontent, such as the anti-Semitism directed at the thousands of Russian Jews who had migrated to Western Europe. Indeed, much of the political anti-Semitism of the latter part of the century had its roots in the problems urban migration generated.

THE REDESIGN OF CITIES

The inward urban migration placed new social and economic demands on already strained city resources and gradually transformed the patterns of urban living. National and municipal governments redesigned the central portions of many large European cities during the second half of the century. Previously, the central urban areas had been places where people from all social classes both lived and worked. From the middle of the century onward, planners transformed these districts into areas where businesses, government offices, large stores, and theaters were located, but where fewer people resided. Commerce, trade, government, and leisure activities now dominated central cities.

The New Paris The most famous and extensive transformation of a major city occurred in Paris. Like so many other European cities, Paris had expanded from the Middle Ages onward with little or no design or planning. Great public buildings and squalid hovels stood near each other. The Seine River was an open sewer. The streets were narrow, crooked, and crowded. It was impossible to cross easily from one part of the city to another either on foot or by carriage. In 1850, an accurate map of the city did not even exist. Of more concern to the government of Napoleon III (r. 1852–1870), the city's streets had for sixty years provided battlegrounds for urban insurrections that had threatened or toppled French governments on numerous occasions, most recently in 1848.

Napoleon III personally determined to redesign Paris. He appointed Baron Georges Haussmann (1809–1891), who, as prefect of the Seine from 1853 to 1870, oversaw a vast urban reconstruction program. Whole districts were destroyed to open the way for the broad boulevards and streets that became the hallmark of modern Paris. Much, though by no means all, of the purpose of this street planning was political. The wide vistas not only were beautiful, but they also allowed for the quick deployment of troops to put down riots. The eradication of the many small streets and alleys removed areas where barricades could be, and had been, erected.

The project was also political in another sense. In addition to the new boulevards, parks such as the Bois de Boulogne and major public buildings such as the Paris Opera were also constructed or completed. These projects, along with the demolition and street building, created thousands of government jobs. Many other laborers found employment in the private construction that accompanied the public works.

Further rebuilding and redesign occurred under the Third Republic after the destruction that accompanied the suppression of the Commune in 1871. Many department stores, office complexes, and largely middle-class apartment buildings were constructed. By the late 1870s, mechanical trams were operating in Paris. After much debate, construction of a subway system (the *métro*) began in 1895, long after that of London (1863). Near the close of the century, new railway stations were also erected to link the refurbished central city to the suburbs.

In 1889, the Eiffel Tower was built, originally as a temporary structure for the international trade exposition of that year. Not all the new structures of Paris bespoke the impact of middle-class commerce and the reign of iron and steel, however. Between 1873 and 1914, the Roman Catholic Church oversaw the construction of the Basilica of the Sacred Heart (*Sacré Cœur*) high atop Montmartre as an act of national penance for the sins that had supposedly led to French defeat in the Franco-Prussian War (1870–1871). Those two landmarks—the Eiffel Tower

The Eiffel Tower, shown under construction in this painting, was to become a symbol of the newly redesigned Paris and its steel structure a symbol of French industrial strength.   Getty Images, Inc.—Liaison

and the Basilica of the Sacred Heart—symbolized the social and political divisions between liberals and conservatives in the Third Republic.

Development of Suburbs   Commercial development, railway construction, and slum clearance displaced many city dwellers and raised urban land values and rents. Consequently, both the middle classes and the working class began to seek housing elsewhere. The middle classes looked for neighborhoods removed from urban congestion. The working class looked for affordable housing. The result, in virtually all countries, was the development of suburbs surrounding the city proper. These suburbs housed families whose breadwinners worked in the central city or in a factory located within the city limits. European suburbs, unlike those that developed in the United States, often consisted of apartment buildings or private houses built closely together with small gardens.

The expansion of railways with cheap workday fares and the introduction of mechanical and, later, electric tramways, as well as subways, allowed tens of thousands of workers from all classes to move daily between the city and the outlying suburbs. For hundreds of thousands of Europeans, home and work became more physically separated than ever before.

URBAN SANITATION

The efforts of governments and of the increasingly conservative middle classes to maintain public order after 1848 led to a growing concern with the problems of public health and housing for the poor.

A widespread feeling arose that only when the health and housing of the working class were improved would middle-class health also be secure and the political order stable.

Impact of Cholera   Concerns with health and housing first manifested themselves as a result of the great cholera epidemics of the 1830s and 1840s. Unlike many other common deadly diseases of the day that touched only the poor, cholera struck all classes, and the middle class demanded a solution. Before the development of the bacterial theory of disease late in the century, physicians and sanitary reformers believed that miasmas in the air spread the infections that led to cholera and other diseases. These miasmas, which could be detected by their foul odors, were believed to arise from filth. The way to get rid of the dangerous, foul-smelling air was to clean up the cities.

During the 1840s, many physicians and some government officials began to publicize the dangerous unsanitary conditions associated with overcrowding in cities and with businesses, such as basement slaughterhouses. In 1840, Louis René Villermé (1782–1863) published his *Tableau de l'état physique et moral des ouvriers* (*Catalog of the Physical and Moral State of Workers*) about urban working-class conditions in France. (See "A French Physician Describes a Slum in Lille," page 771.) In 1842, Edwin Chadwick's (1800–1890) *Report on*

GROWTH OF MAJOR EUROPEAN CITIES (FIGURES IN THOUSANDS)

	1850	1880	1910
Berlin	419	1,122	2,071
Birmingham	233	437	840
Frankfurt	65	137	415
London	2,685	4,470	7,256
Madrid	281	398	600
Moscow	365	748	1,533
Paris	1,053	2,269	2,888
Rome	175	300	542
Saint Petersburg	485	877	1,962
Vienna	444	1,104	2,031
Warsaw	160	339	872

the Sanitary Condition of the Labouring Population shocked the English public. In Germany, Rudolf Virchow (1821–1902) published similar findings. These and various other private reports and those by public commissions closely linked the issues of wretched living conditions and public health. They also argued that sanitary reform would remove the dangers. The reports, incidentally, now provide some of the best information available about working-class living conditions in the mid-nineteenth century.

New Water and Sewer Systems   The proposed solution to the health hazard was cleanliness, to be achieved through new water and sewer systems. These facilities were constructed slowly, usually first in capital cities and then much later in provincial centers. Some major urban areas did not have good water systems until after 1900. Nonetheless, the building of such systems was one of the major health and engineering achievements of the second half of the nineteenth century. The sewer system of Paris was a famous part of Haussmann's rebuilding program. In London, the construction of the Albert Embankment along the Thames involved not only large sewers discharging into the river, but gas mains and water pipes as well; all were encased in thick walls of granite and concrete, one of the new

A major feature of the reconstruction of mid-nineteenth-century Paris under the Emperor Napoleon II was a vast new sewer system to provide for drainage in the city. Sewer workmen could travel the length of the structure on small rail cars. Even today tourists still may visit parts of the mid-city Paris sewer system.   Nadar/Getty Images

building materials of the day. Wherever these sanitary facilities were installed, the mortality rate dropped considerably—not because they prevented miasmas, but because they disposed of human waste and provided clean water free of harmful bacteria for people to drink, cook with, and bathe in.

Expanded Government Involvement in Public Health   The concern with public health led to an expansion of governmental power on various levels. In Britain the Public Health Act of 1848, in France the Melun Act of 1851, and various laws in the still-disunited German states, as well as later legislation, introduced new restraints on private life and enterprise. This legislation allowed medical officers and building inspectors to enter homes and businesses in the name of public health. The state could condemn private property for posing health hazards. Private land could be excavated to construct the sewers and water mains required to protect the public. New building regulations restrained the activities of private contractors.

Full acceptance at the close of the century of the bacterial theory of disease associated with the discoveries of Louis Pasteur (1822–1895) in France, Robert Koch (1843–1910) in Germany, and Joseph Lister (1827–1912) in Britain increased public concern about cleanliness. Throughout Europe, issues related to the maintenance of public health and the physical well-being of the population repeatedly opened the way for new modes of government intervention in the lives of citizens.

HOUSING REFORM AND MIDDLE-CLASS VALUES

The information about working-class living conditions the sanitary reformers revealed also led to heated debates over the housing problem. The wretched dwellings of the poor were themselves a cause of poor sanitation and thus became a newly perceived health hazard. Furthermore, the domestic arrangements of the poor, whose large families might live in a single room without any personal privacy, shocked middle-class reformers and bureaucrats. A single toilet might serve a whole block of tenements. After the revolutions of 1848, the overcrowding in housing and the social discontent that it generated were also seen to pose a political danger.

Middle-class reformers thus turned to housing reform to solve the medical, moral, and political dangers slums posed. Decent housing would foster a good home life, in turn leading to a healthy, moral, and politically stable population. As A. V. Huber, one of the early German housing reformers, declared,

A FRENCH PHYSICIAN DESCRIBES A SLUM IN LILLE

—⚬—

It is difficult to conceive of the world before the sanitation movement. The work of medical doctors frequently carried them into working-class areas in industrial cities that other members of the middle class rarely visited. Louis Villermé, a French physician, described the slums and the general living conditions of industrial workers. This passage, published in 1840, describes a particularly notorious section of Lille, a cotton-manufacturing town in northern France.

■ *What does Villermé find most disturbing about the scene he describes? How is his description possibly designed to call forth sympathy and concern from a middle-class reader? How might the conditions described have led the poor of France toward socialism or radical politics? How would addressing the problems described have increased the role of government?*

The poorest live in the cellars and attics. These cellars . . . open onto the streets or courtyards, and one enters them by a stairway which is very often at once the door and the window. . . . Commonly the height of the ceiling is six or six and a half feet at the highest point, and they are only ten to fourteen or fifteen feet wide.

It is in these somber and sad dwellings that a large number of workers eat, sleep, and even work. The light of day comes an hour later for them than for others, and the night an hour earlier.

Their furnishings normally consist, along with the tools of their profession, of a sort of cupboard or a plank on which to deposit food, a stove . . . a few pots, a little table, two or three poor chairs, and a dirty pallet of which the only pieces are a straw mattress and scraps of a blanket. . . .

In their obscure cellars, in their rooms, which one would take for cellars, the air is never renewed, it is infected; the walls are plastered with garbage. . . . If a bed exists, it is a few dirty, greasy planks; it is damp and putrescent straw; it is a coarse cloth whose color and fabric are hidden by a layer of grime; it is a blanket that resembles a sieve. . . . The furniture is dislocated, worm-eaten, covered with filth. Utensils are thrown in disorder all over the dwelling. The windows, always closed, are covered by paper and glass, but so black, so smoke-encrusted, that the light is unable to penetrate . . . everywhere are piles of garbage, of ashes, of debris from vegetables picked up from the streets, of rotten straw; of animal nests of all sorts; thus, the air is unbreathable. One is exhausted, in these hovels, by a stale, nauseating, somewhat piquant odor, odor of filth, odor of garbage. . . .

And the poor themselves, what are they like in the middle of such a slum? Their clothing is in shreds, without substance, consumed, covered, no less than their hair, which knows no comb, with dust from the workshops. And their skin? . . . It is painted, it is hidden, if you wish, by indistinguishable deposits of diverse exudations.

From Louis René Villermé, *Tableau de l'état physique et moral des ouvriers employés dans les manufactures de coton, de laine et de soie* (Paris, 1840), as quoted and trans. in William H. Sewell, Jr., *Work and Revolution in France: The Language of Labor from the Old Regime to 1848* (Cambridge, UK.: Cambridge University Press, 1980), p. 224.

Certainly it would not be too much to say that the home is the communal embodiment of family life. Thus the purity of the dwelling is almost as important for the family as is the cleanliness of the body for the individual. Good or bad housing is a question of life and death if ever there was one.[1]

[1]Quoted in Nicholas Bullock and James Read, *The Movement for Housing Reform in Germany and France, 1840–1914* (Cambridge, UK: Cambridge University Press, 1985), p. 42.

Later advocates of housing reform, such as Jules Simon (1814–1896) in France, saw good housing as leading to good family life and, ultimately, to strong patriotic feeling. It was widely believed that providing the poor and the working class with adequate, respectable, cheap housing would alleviate social and political discontent. It was also believed that the personal saving and investment that was required to

MAJOR DATES RELATING TO SANITATION REFORM

1830s and 1840s	Cholera epidemics
1840	Villermé's *Catalog of the Physical and Moral State of Workers*
1842	Chadwick's *Report on the Sanitary Condition of the Labouring Population*
1848	British Public Health Act
1851	French Melun Act

own a home would lead the working class to adopt the thrifty habits of the middle classes.

Private philanthropy made the first attack on the housing problem. Companies operating on low profit margins or making low-interest loans encouraged housing for the poor. Firms such as the German Krupp Armaments concern that sought to ensure a contented, healthy, and stable work force, constructed model housing projects and industrial communities.

By the mid-1880s, the migration into cities had made housing a political issue. Legislation in England in 1885 lowered the interest rates to construct cheap housing, and soon thereafter local governments began public housing projects. In Germany, action on housing came later in the century through the initiative of local municipalities. In 1894, France made inexpensive credit available to construct housing for the poor. None of these governments, however, adopted wide-scale housing experiments.

Nonetheless, by 1914, the housing problem had been fully recognized if not adequately addressed. The goal of housing reform across Western Europe came to be to provide homes for the members of the working class that would allow them to enjoy a family life more or less like that of the middle class. Such a home would be in the form of a detached house or an affordable city apartment with several rooms, a private entrance, and separate toilet facilities.

VARIETIES OF LATE-NINETEENTH-CENTURY WOMEN'S EXPERIENCES

Late-nineteenth-century women and men led lives that reflected their social rank. Yet, within each rank, the experience of women was distinct from that of men. Women remained, generally speaking, economically dependent and legally inferior, whatever their social class.

WOMEN'S SOCIAL DISABILITIES

In the mid-nineteenth century, virtually all European women faced social and legal disabilities in three areas: property rights, family law, and education. By the close of the century, there had been some improvement in each area.

Women and Property Until the last quarter of the century in most European countries, married women could not own property in their own names, no matter what their social class. For all practical purposes, upon marriage, women lost to their husbands' control any property they owned or that they might inherit or earn by their own labor. Their legal identities were subsumed in their husbands' identities, and they had no independent standing before the law. The courts saw the theft of a woman's purse as a theft of her husband's property. Because private property and wage earning were the bases of European society, these disabilities put married women at a great disadvantage, limiting their freedom to work, to save, and to move from one location to another.

Reform of women's property rights came slowly. By 1882, Great Britain had passed the Married Woman's Property Act, which allowed married women to own property in their own right. In France, however, a married woman could not even open a savings account in her own name until 1895, and married French women did not gain possession of the wages they earned until 1907. In 1900, Germany allowed women to take jobs without their husbands' permission, but except for her wages, a German husband retained control of most of his wife's property. Similar laws prevailed elsewhere in Europe.

Family Law European family law also disadvantaged women. Legal codes required wives to "give obedience" to their husbands. The Napoleonic Code and the remnants of Roman law still in effect made women legal minors throughout Europe. Divorce was difficult everywhere for most of the century. In England before 1857, each divorce required a separate act of Parliament. Thereafter, couples could divorce, with difficulty, through the Court of Matrimonial Causes. Most nations did not permit divorce by mutual consent. French law forbade divorce between 1816 and 1884. Thereafter, the majority of nations recognized a legal cause for divorce—cruelty or injury—which had to be proven in court. In Great Britain, adultery was the usual cause for divorce, but to obtain a divorce, a woman had to prove her husband's adultery plus other offenses, whereas a man only had to prove his wife's adultery. In Germany, only adultery or serious maltreatment was recognized as reasons for divorce. Across Europe, some version of the double standard prevailed whereby husbands' extramarital sexual relations were tolerated to a much greater degree than those of wives. Everywhere, divorce required hearings in court and the presentation of legal proof, making the process expensive and more difficult for women, who did not control their own property.

The authority of husbands also extended to children. A husband could take children away from their mother and give them to someone else to rear. Only a father, in most countries, could permit his daughter to marry. In some countries, he could virtually force his daughter to marry the man of his choice. In cases of divorce and separation, courts normally awarded the husband authority over and custody of children, no matter how he had treated them previously.

The issues surrounding the sexual and reproductive rights of women that have been so widely debated recently could hardly be discussed in the nineteenth century. Until well into the twentieth century, both contraception and abortion were illegal. The law surrounding rape normally worked to the disadvantage of women. Wherever they turned with their problems—whether to physicians or lawyers—women confronted an official or legal world that men almost wholly populated and controlled.

Educational Barriers Throughout the nineteenth century, women had less access to education than men had and what was available to them was inferior to that available to men. Not surprisingly, there were many more illiterate women than men. Most women were educated only enough for the domestic lives they were expected to lead.

University and professional education remained reserved for men until at least the third quarter of the century. In Switzerland, the University of Zurich first opened its doors to women in the 1860s. The University of London admitted women for degrees in 1878. Women's colleges were founded at Cambridge during the last quarter of the century. Women could take Oxford and Cambridge university examinations, but were not awarded degrees at Oxford until 1920 and at Cambridge until 1921. In France, women could not attend lectures at the Sorbonne until 1880. Just before the turn of the century, universities and medical schools in the Austrian Empire allowed women to matriculate, but Prussian universities did not admit women until after 1900. Russian women did not attend universities before 1914, but other institutions that awarded degrees were open to them. Italian universities proved themselves more open to both women students and women instructors than similar institutions elsewhere in Europe. In many countries, more foreign than native women attended university classes. This was especially the case in Zurich, where many Russian women studied for medical

degrees. Many of the American women who founded or taught in the first women's colleges in the United States studied at European universities.

The absence of a system of private or public secondary education for women prevented most of them from gaining the qualifications they needed to enter a university whether or not the university prohibited them. Evidence suggests that educated, professional men feared that admitting women would overcrowd their professions. Women who attended universities and medical schools, like the young Russian women who studied medicine at Zurich, were sometimes labeled political radicals.

By the turn of the century, some men in the educated elites feared the challenge educated women posed to traditional gender roles in the home and workplace. Restricting women's access to secondary and university education helped bar them from social and economic advancement. Women would benefit only marginally from the expansion of professional employment that occurred during the late nineteenth and early twentieth centuries. Some women did enter the professions, particularly medicine, but their number remained few. Most nations refused to allow women to become lawyers until after World War I.

School teaching at the elementary level, which had come to be seen as a "female job" because of its association with the nurturing of children, became a professional haven for women. Trained at institutions designed particularly for elementary schoolteachers, usually known as normal schools, women schoolteachers at the elementary level were regarded as educated, but not as university educated. Higher education remained largely the province of men.

The few women who pioneered in the professions and on government commissions and school boards or who dispersed birth control information faced social obstacles, humiliation, and often outright bigotry. These women and their male supporters were challenging that clear separation into male and female spheres that had emerged in middle-class European social life during the nineteenth century. Women themselves were often hesitant to support feminist causes or expanded opportunities for females because they had been so thoroughly acculturated into the recently stereotyped roles. Many women, as well as men, saw a real conflict between family responsibilities and feminism.

NEW EMPLOYMENT PATTERNS FOR WOMEN

During the Second Industrial Revolution, two major developments affected the economic lives of women. The first was the large-scale expansion in the variety of jobs available to women outside the better paying learned professions. The second was the withdrawal of many married women from the

Women working in the London Central Telephone Exchange. The invention of the telephone opened new employment opportunities for women. Image Works/Mary Evans Picture Library Ltd.

work force. These two seemingly contradictory developments require explanation.

Availability of New Jobs The expansion of governmental bureaucracies, the emergence of corporations and other large businesses, and the vast growth of retail stores opened many new employment opportunities for women. The need for elementary school teachers, usually women, grew as governments adopted compulsory education laws. Technological inventions and innovations, such as the typewriter and, eventually, the telephone exchange, also fostered female employment. Women by the thousands became secretaries and clerks for governments and private businesses. Thousands more became shop assistants.

Although these jobs did open new and often better employment opportunities for women, they nonetheless required low-level skills and involved minimal training. They were occupied primarily by unmarried women or widows. Women rarely occupied more prominent positions.

Employers continued to pay women low wages, because they assumed, although they often knew better, that a woman did not need to live on what she herself earned, but could expect additional financial support from her father or her husband. Consequently, a woman who did need to support herself independently could seldom find a job that paid an adequate income—or a position that paid as well as one a man who was supporting himself held.

Withdrawal from the Labor Force Most of the women filling the new service positions were young and unmarried. Upon marriage, or certainly after the birth of her first child, a woman normally withdrew from the labor force. Either she did not work or she worked at some occupation that she could pursue at home. This pattern was not new, but it had become significantly more common by the end of the nineteenth century. The kinds of industrial occupations that women had filled in the mid-nineteenth century, especially textile and garment making, were shrinking. Married or unmarried women thus had fewer opportunities for employment in those industries. Employers in offices and retail stores preferred young, unmarried women whose family responsibilities would not interfere with their work. The decline in the number of children being born also meant that fewer married women were needed to look after other women's children.

The real wages paid to male workers increased during this period, so families had a somewhat reduced need for a second income. Also, thanks to improving health conditions, men lived longer than before, so the death of their husbands was less likely to thrust wives into the work force. The smaller size of families also lowered the need for supplementary wages. Working children stayed at home longer and continued to contribute to the family's wage pool.

Finally, the cultural dominance of the middle class established a pattern of social expectations, especially for wives. The more prosperous a working-class family became, the less involved in employment its women were supposed to be. Indeed, the less income-producing work a wife did, the more prosperous and stable the family was considered.

Yet behind these generalities stands the enormous variety of social and economic experiences late-nineteenth-century women actually encountered. As might be expected, the chief determinant of these individual experiences was social class.

WORKING-CLASS WOMEN

Although the textile industry and garment making were much less dominant than earlier in the century, they continued to employ many women. The German clothing-making trade illustrates the kind of vulnerable economic situation that women could encounter as a result of their limited skills and the way the trade was organized. The system of manufacturing mass-made clothes of uniform sizes in Germany was designed to require minimal capital investment by manufacturers and to protect them from risk. A major manufacturer would produce clothing through what was called a *putting-out system.* The manufacturer would purchase the material and then put it out for tailoring. Usually, numerous independently owned, small sweatshops or workers in their homes made the clothing. It was seldom made in a factory.

In Berlin in 1896, this system employed more than 80,000 garment workers. When business was good and demand strong, employment for these women was high. As the seasons shifted or business slackened, however, less and less work was put out, idling many of them. In effect, the workers who actually sewed the clothing carried much of the risk of the enterprise. Some women did work in clothing factories, but they, too, were subject to layoffs. Furthermore, women in the clothing trade were nearly always in positions less skilled than those of the male tailors or the middlemen who owned the workshops.

The expectation of separate social and economic spheres for men and women and the definition of women's chief work as pertaining to the home contributed mightily to the exploitation of women workers outside the home. Because their wages were regarded merely as supplementing their husbands' wages, they became particularly vulnerable to the kind of economic exploitation that characterized the German putting-out system for clothing production and similar systems elsewhere. Women were nearly always treated as casual workers everywhere in Europe.

POVERTY AND PROSTITUTION

A major, but little recognized, social fact of most nineteenth-century cities was the presence of a surplus of working women who did not fit the stereotype of wife or daughter supplementing a family's income. Almost always many more women were seeking employment than there were jobs. The economic vulnerability of women and the consequent poverty many of them faced were among the chief causes of prostitution. Every major late-nineteenth-century European city had thousands of prostitutes.

Prostitution was, of course, not new. It had always been one way for poor women to find income. In the late nineteenth century, however, it was closely related to the difficulty encountered by indigent women who were trying to make their way in an overcrowded female labor force. On the Continent, prostitution was generally legalized and subject to governmental and municipal regulations that male legislatures and councils passed and male police and physicians enforced. In Britain, prostitution received only minimal regulation.

Many myths and misunderstandings have surrounded the subject of prostitution. The most recent studies of prostitution in England emphasize that most prostitutes were active on the streets for only a few years, from their late teens to about age twenty-five. Many were poor women who had recently migrated from nearby rural areas. Others were born in the towns where they became prostitutes. Certain cities—those with large army garrisons or naval bases or those, like London, with large transient populations—attracted prostitutes. Far fewer prostitutes worked in manufacturing towns, where there were more opportunities for steady employment and community life was more stable.

Women who became prostitutes usually came from families of unskilled workers and had minimal skills and education themselves. Many had been servants. They also often were orphans or came from broken homes. Contrary to many sensational late-century newspaper accounts, there were few child prostitutes. Furthermore, middle-class employers or clients rarely seduced women into prostitution, although working-class women were always potentially subject to sexual exploitation. The customers of poor working-class prostitutes were primarily working-class men.

WOMEN OF THE MIDDLE CLASS

A vast social gap separated poor working-class women from their middle-class counterparts. As their fathers' and husbands' incomes permitted, middle-class women participated in the vast expansion of consumerism and domestic comfort that marked the late nineteenth and the early twentieth centuries.

They filled their homes with manufactured items, including clothing, china, furniture, carpets, drapery, wallpaper, and prints. They enjoyed all the improvements of sanitation and electricity. They could command the services of numerous domestic servants. They moved into the fashionable new houses being constructed in the rapidly expanding suburbs.

The Cult of Domesticity For the middle classes, the distinction between work and family, defined by gender, had become complete and constituted the model for all other social groups. Middle-class women, if at all possible, did not work. More than any other women, they became limited to the roles of wife and mother. As a result, they might enjoy great domestic luxury and comfort, but their lives, talents, ambitions, and opportunities for applying their intelligence were sharply circumscribed.

Middle-class women became, in large measure, the product of a particular understanding of social life. Home life was to be different from the life of business and the marketplace. The home was to be a private place of refuge, a view scores of women's journals across Europe set forth.

As studies of the lives of middle-class women in northern France have suggested, this image of the middle-class home and of the role of women in the home is different from the one that had existed earlier in the nineteenth century. During the first half of the century, many middle-class wives contributed directly to their husbands' business, handling accounts or correspondence. These women also frequently left the task of rearing their children to nurses and governesses. The reasons for the change during the century are not certain, but it appears that men began to insist on doing business exclusively with other men. Magazines and books for women began to praise motherhood, domesticity, religion, and charity as the proper work of women in accordance with the concept of separate spheres.

For middle-class Frenchwomen, as well as for middle-class women elsewhere, the home came to be seen as the center of virtue, children, and the respectable life. Marriages were usually arranged to benefit the family economically. Romantic marriage was viewed as a danger to social stability. Most middle-class women in northern France married by the age of twenty-one and were expected to have children soon after marriage. The first child was often born within the first year. Rearing and nurturing her children was a woman's chief task. Her only experience or training was for the role of dutiful daughter, wife, and mother.

Within the home, a middle-class woman largely directed the household. She oversaw virtually all domestic management and child care. She was in charge of the home as a unit of consumption, which

Department stores, such as Bon Marche in Paris, sold wide selections of consumer goods under one roof. These modern stores increased the economic pressure on small traditional merchants who specialized in selling only one kind of good. (See "Paris Department Stores Expand their Business," page 766.) Image Works/Mary Evans Picture Library Ltd.

is why so much advertising was directed toward women. All this domestic activity, however, occurred within the bounds of the approved middle-class lifestyle that set strict limits on a woman's initiative. In her conspicuous position within the home and family, a woman symbolized first her father's and then her husband's worldly success.

Religious and Charitable Activities The cult of domesticity in France and elsewhere assigned firm religious duties to women, which the Roman Catholic Church strongly supported. Women were expected to attend Mass frequently and assure the religious instruction of their children. They were charged with observing meatless Fridays and participation in religious observances. Prayer was a major part of their daily lives. They internalized those portions of the Christian religion that stressed meekness and passivity. In other countries, religion and religious activities also became part of the expected work of women. This close association between religion and a strict domestic life for women was one reason for later tension between feminism and religious authorities.

Another important role for middle-class women was the administration of charity. Women were considered especially qualified for this work because of their presumed innate spirituality and their capacity to instill domestic and personal discipline. Middle-class women were often in charge of clubs for poor youth, societies to protect poor young women, schools for infants, and societies for visiting the poor. Women were supposed to be particularly interested in the problems of poor women, their families, and their children. Often, to receive charity from middle-class women, a recipient who was poor had to demonstrate good character. By the end of the century, middle-class women seeking to expand their spheres of activity became social workers for the church, for private charities, or for the government. These vocations were a natural extension of the roles society assigned to them.

The following obituary of a French lady who died in the late nineteenth century illustrates how these vocations and virtues received public praise for women who fulfilled them:

The poor were the object of her affectionate interest, especially the shameful poor, the fallen people. She sought them out and helped them with perfect discretion which doubled the value of her benevolent interest. To those whom she could approach without fear of bruising their dignity, she brought, along with alms to assure their existence, consolation of the most serious sort—she raised their courage and their hopes. To others, each Sunday, she opened all the doors of her home, above all when her children were still young. In making them distribute these alms with her, she hoped to initiate them early into practices of charity. In the last years of her life, the St. Gabriel Orphanage gained her interest. Not only did she accomplish a great deal with her generosity, but she also took on the task of maintaining the clothes of her dear orphans in good order and in good repair. When she appeared in the courtyard of the establishment at recreation time, all her protégés surrounded her and lavished her with manifestations of their profound respect and affectionate gratitude.[2]

As will be seen in the immediately following sections, many ideas and social forces would challenge the values this obituary celebrates, but the role for upper-middle-class women that it illustrates would dominate European life for decades to come.

Sexuality and Family Size Historians have come to realize that the world of the middle-class wife and her family was much more complicated than they once thought. Neither all wives nor their families conformed to the stereotypes. Recent studies suggest that the middle classes of the nineteenth century enjoyed sexual relations within marriage far more than was once thought. Diaries, letters, and even early medical and sociological sex surveys indicate that sexual enjoyment rather than sexual repression was fundamental to middle-class marriages. Much of the inhibition about sexuality

stemmed from the dangers of childbirth, which, in an age of limited sanitation and anesthesia, were widely and rightly feared, rather than from any dislike or disapproval of sex itself.

One of the major changes in this regard during the second half of the century was the acceptance of a small family size among the middle classes. The birthrate in France dropped throughout the nineteenth century. It began to fall in England steadily from the 1870s onward. During the last decades of the century, new contraceptive devices became available, which middle-class couples used. One of the chief reasons for the apparently conscious decision of couples to limit their family size was to maintain a relatively high level of material consumption. Children had become much more expensive to rear, and at the same time, more material comforts had become available. Fewer children probably meant more attention for each of them, possibly increasing the emotional bonds between mothers and their children.

THE RISE OF POLITICAL FEMINISM

Plainly, liberal society and its values had neither automatically nor inevitably improved the lot of women. In particular, they did not give women the vote or access to political activity. In Catholic countries, male liberals feared that granting the vote to women would benefit political conservatives, because men thought that priests exercised undue control over women. A similar apprehension existed about the alleged influence of the Anglican clergy over women in England and Protestant pastors in parts of Germany. Consequently, anticlerical liberals often had difficulty working with feminists.

Obstacles to Achieving Equality Women also were often reluctant to support feminist causes. Political issues relating to gender were only one of several priorities for many women. Some were sensitive to their class and economic interests. Others subordinated feminist political issues to national unity and patriotism. Still others would not support particular feminist organizations because they objected to their tactics. The various social and tactical differences among women often led to sharp divisions within the feminists' own ranks. Except in England, it was often difficult for working-class and middle-class women to cooperate. Roman Catholic feminists were uncomfortable with radical secularist feminists. There were other disagreements about which goals were most important for improving women's legal and social conditions.

Although liberal society and law presented women with many obstacles, they also provided feminists with many of their intellectual and political tools. As early as 1792 in Britain, Mary

[2]Quoted in Bonnie G. Smith, *Ladies of the Leisure Class: The Bourgeoises of Northern France in the Nineteenth Century* (Princeton, NJ: Princeton University Press, 1981), pp. 147–148. Copyright © 1981 by Princeton University Press. Reprinted by permission of Princeton University Press.

MAJOR DATES IN LATE-NINETEENTH-CENTURY AND EARLY-TWENTIETH-CENTURY WOMEN'S HISTORY

1857	Revised English divorce law
1865	University of Zurich admits women for degrees
1869	John Stuart Mill's *The Subjection of Women*
1878	University of London admits women as candidates for degrees
1882	English Married Woman's Property Act
1894	Union of German Women's Organizations founded
1901	National Council of French Women founded
1903	British Women's Social and Political Union founded
1907	Norway permits women to vote on national issues
1910	British suffragettes adopt radical tactics
1918	Vote extended to some British women
1919	Weimar constitution allows German women to vote
1920–1921	Oxford and Cambridge Universities award degrees to women
1922	French Senate defeats bill extending vote to women
1928	Britain extends vote to women on same basis as men

Wollstonecraft (1759–1797), in *The Vindication of the Rights of Woman*, had applied the revolutionary doctrines of the rights of man to the predicament of the members of her own sex. (See Chapter 17.) John Stuart Mill (1806–1873), together with his wife, Harriet Taylor (1804–1858), extended the logic of liberal freedom to the position of women in *The Subjection of Women* (1869). The arguments for utility and efficiency so dear to middle-class liberals could be used to expose the human and social waste implicit in the inferior role assigned to women.

Furthermore, the socialist criticism of capitalist society often, though by no means always, included a harsh indictment of the social and economic position to which women had been relegated. The earliest statements in support of feminism arose from critics of the existing order who were often people who had unorthodox opinions about sexuality, family life, and property. This hardened resistance to the feminist message, especially on the Continent.

These difficulties prevented continental feminists from raising the massive public support or mounting the large demonstrations that feminists in Britain and the United States could. Everywhere in Europe, however, including Britain, the feminist cause was badly divided over both goals and tactics. (See "An English Feminist Defends the Female Franchise.")

Votes for Women in Britain   Europe's most advanced women's movement was in Britain. There, Millicent Fawcett (1847–1929) led the moderate National Union of Women's Suffrage Societies. She believed Parliament would grant women the vote only if it were convinced they would be respectable and responsible in their political activity. In 1908, the National Union could rally almost half a million women in London. Fawcett's husband Henry Fawcett (1833–1884) was a Liberal Party cabinet minister and economist who also supported women's suffrage. Her tactics were those of English liberals.

Emmeline Pankhurst (1858–1928) led a much more radical branch of British feminists. Pankhurst's husband, who died near the close of the century, had been active in both labor and Irish nationalist politics. Irish nationalists had developed numerous disruptive political tactics. Early labor politicians had also sometimes confronted the police over the right to hold meetings. In 1903, Pankhurst and her daughters, Christabel and Sylvia, founded the Women's Social and Political Union. For years they and their followers, known derisively as **suffragettes**, lobbied publicly and privately for extending the vote to women. By 1910, having failed to move the government, they turned to the violent tactics of arson, breaking windows, and sabotage of postal boxes. They marched en masse on Parliament. The Liberal government of Prime Minister Herbert Asquith (1852–1928) imprisoned demonstrators and force-

Emmeline Pankhurst (1857–1928) was frequently arrested for forcibly advocating votes for British women.   Hulton Archive Photos/Getty Images Inc.

AN ENGLISH FEMINIST DEFENDS THE FEMALE FRANCHISE

—⚭—

Frances Power Cobbe (1822–1904) wrote widely about religious and social issues. She had been a feminist since early adulthood. In this letter to a British feminist magazine in 1884, she explains why women should seek the vote.

■ What motives does Cobbe assign to the pursuit of the right to vote? Why does she emphasize "womanliness" as an issue that must not be allowed to undermine the cause of women? What does Cobbe think about violence? Why would later British advocates of votes for women turn to violent tactics?

If I may presume to offer an old woman's counsel to the younger workers in our cause, it would be that they should adopt the point of view—that it is before all things our duty to obtain the franchise. If we undertake the work in this spirit, and with the object of using the power it confers, whenever we gain it, for the promotion of justice and mercy and the kingdom of God upon earth, we shall carry on all our agitation in a corresponding manner, firmly and bravely, and also calmly and with generous good temper. And when our opponents come to understand that this is the motive underlying our efforts, they, on their part, will cease to feel bitterly and scornfully toward us, even when they think we are altogether mistaken. . . .

The idea that the possession of political rights will destroy "womanliness," absurd as it may seem to us, is very deeply rooted in the minds of men; and when they oppose our demands, it is only just to give them credit for doing so on grounds which we should recognize as valid, if their premises were true. It is not so much that our opponents (at least the better part of them) despise women, as that they really prize, what women now are in the home and in society, so highly that they cannot bear to risk losing it by any serious change in their condition. These fears are futile and faithless, but there is nothing in them to affront us. To remove them, we must not use violent words, for every such violent word confirms their fears; but, on the contrary, show the world that while the revolutions wrought by men have been full of bitterness and rancor and stormy passions, if not of bloodshed, we women will at least strive to accomplish our great emancipation calmly and by persuasion and reason.

From letter to the *Woman's Tribune*, May 1, 1884, quoted in Frances Power Cobbe, *Life of Frances Power Cobbe by Herself*, Vol. 2 (Boston: Houghton Mifflin, 1894), pp. 532–533.

fed those who went on hunger strikes in jail. The government refused to extend the franchise. Only in 1918, and then as a result of their contribution to the war effort in World War I, did British women over age thirty receive the vote. (Men could vote at age twenty-one.)

Political Feminism on the Continent   The contrast between the women's movement in Britain and those in France and Germany shows how advanced the British women's movement was. In France, when Hubertine Auclert (1848–1914) began campaigning for the vote in the 1880s, she stood virtually alone. During the 1890s, several women's organizations emerged. In 1901, the National Council of French Women (CNFF) was organized among upper-middle-class women, but it did not support the vote for women for several years. French Roman Catholic feminists such as Marie Mauguet (1844–1928) supported the franchise. Almost all French feminists, however, rejected violence. Nor were they ever able to organize mass rallies. The leaders of French feminism believed women could achieve the vote through careful legalism. In 1919, the French Chamber of Deputies passed a bill granting the vote to women, but in 1922, the French Senate defeated the bill. French women did not receive the right to vote until after World War II.

In Germany, feminist awareness and action were even more underdeveloped. German law actually forbade German women from engaging in political activity. Because no group in the German Empire enjoyed extensive political rights, women were not certain they would benefit from demanding them. Any such demand would be regarded as subversive not only of the state, but also of society.

In 1894, the Union of German Women's Organizations (BDFK) was founded. By 1902, it was supporting the right to vote. But its main concern was improving women's social conditions, increasing their access to education, and extending their right to other protections. The BDKF also tried to gain women's admittance to political or civic activity on the municipal level. Its work usually included education, child welfare, charity, and public health. The German Social Democratic Party supported women's suffrage, but the German authorities and German Roman Catholics so disdained the socialists, that its support only made suffrage more suspect in their eyes. Women received the vote in Germany only in 1919, under the constitution of the Weimar Republic after the German defeat in war and revolution at home.

Throughout Europe before World War I, women demanded rights widely and vocally. Their tactics and the success they achieved, however, varied from country to country depending on political and class structures. Before World War I, only Norway (1907) allowed women to vote on national issues.

JEWISH EMANCIPATION

The emancipation of European Jews from the narrow life of the ghetto into a world of equal or nearly equal citizenship and social status was a major accomplishment of political liberalism and had an enduring impact on European life. Emancipation, slow and never fully completed, began in the late eighteenth century and continued throughout the nineteenth. It moved at different paces in different countries.

DIFFERING DEGREES OF CITIZENSHIP

In 1782, Joseph II, the Habsburg emperor, issued a decree that placed the Jews of his empire under more or less the same laws as Christians. In France, the National Assembly recognized Jews as French citizens in 1789. During the turmoil of the Napoleonic Wars, Jewish communities in Italy and Germany were allowed to mix on a generally equal footing with the Christian population. These steps toward political emancipation were always uncertain and were frequently limited or abrogated when rulers or governments changed. Certain freedoms were granted, only to be partially withdrawn later. Even countries that had given Jews political rights did not permit them to own land and often subjected them to discrimina-

tory taxes. Nonetheless, during the first half of the century, Jews in Western Europe, and to a much lesser extent in central and eastern Europe, began to gain equal or more nearly equal citizenship.

In Russia, and in Poland under Russian rule, the traditional modes of prejudice and discrimination continued unabated until World War I. Russian rule treated Jews as aliens. The government undermined Jewish community life, limited the publication of Jewish books, restricted areas where Jews could live, required Jews to have internal passports to move about the country, banned Jews from many forms of state service, and excluded Jews from many institutions of higher education. The state allowed the police and right-wing nationalist groups to conduct *pogroms*—organized riots—against Jewish neighborhoods and villages.

BROADENED OPPORTUNITIES

After the revolutions of 1848, European Jews saw a general improvement in their situation that lasted for several decades. In Germany, Italy, the Low Countries, and Scandinavia, Jews attained full citizenship. After 1858, Jews in Great Britain could sit in Parliament. Austria-Hungary extended full legal rights to Jews in 1867. Indeed, from about 1850 to 1880, relatively little organized or overt prejudice was expressed against Jews in Western Europe. They entered the professions and other occupations once closed to them. They participated fully in literary and cultural life. They were active in the arts and music. They became leaders in science and

Because many major financial institutions of nineteenth-century Europe were owned by wealthy Jewish families, antisemitic political figures often blamed them for economic hard times. The most famous such family was the Rothschilds who controlled banks in several countries. The head of the London branch was Lionel Rothschild (1808–1879). He was elected to Parliament several times, but was not seated because he would not take the required Christian oath. After the requirement of that oath was abolished in 1858, he sat in Parliament from 1858 to 1874.
Getty Images Inc.– Hulton Archive Photos

education. Jews intermarried freely with non-Jews as legal, secular prohibitions against such marriages were repealed during the last quarter of the century.

Outside of Russia, Jewish politicians entered cabinets and served in the highest offices of the state. Politically, Jews often were aligned with liberal parties because these groups had championed equal rights. Later in the century, especially in eastern Europe, many Jews became associated with socialist parties.

The prejudice that had been associated with Christian religious attitudes toward Jews seemed to have dissipated, although it still appeared in Russia and other parts of eastern Europe. Hundreds of thousands of European Jews migrated from these regions to Western Europe and the United States. Almost anywhere in Europe, Jews might encounter prejudice on a personal level. Yet in Western Europe, including England, France, Italy, Germany, and the Low Countries, the legalized persecution and discrimination that had so haunted Jews in the past seemed to have ended.

That newfound security began to erode during the last two decades of the nineteenth century. Anti-Semitic voices began to be heard in the 1870s, attributing the economic stagnation of the decade to Jewish bankers and financial interests. In the 1880s, organized **anti-Semitism** erupted in Germany, as it did in France at the time of the Dreyfus affair. As will be seen in the next chapter, these developments gave rise to the birth of Zionism, initially a minority movement within the Jewish community. Most Jewish leaders believed the attacks on Jewish life were merely temporary recurrences of older forms of prejudice; they felt their communities would remain safe under the liberal legal protections that had been extended during the century. That analysis would be proved disastrously wrong in the 1930s and 1940s.

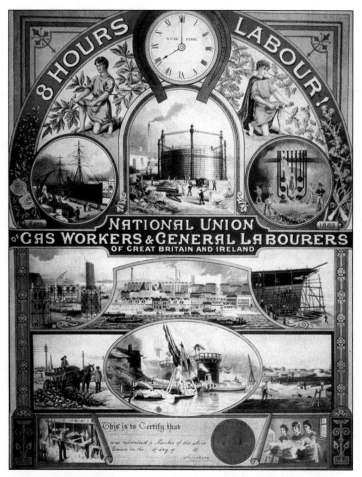

Trade unions continued to grow in late-nineteenth-century Great Britain. The effort to curb the unions eventually led to the formation of the Labour Party. The British unions often had quite elaborate membership certificates, such as this one for the National Union of Gas Workers and General Labourers of Great Britain and Ireland.   The Granger Collection

LABOR, SOCIALISM, AND POLITICS TO WORLD WAR I

The late-century industrial expansion further changed the life of the labor force. In all industrializing continental countries, the numbers of the urban proletariat rose. The proportion of artisans and highly skilled workers declined, and for the first time, factory wage earners predominated. The number of unskilled workers in shipping, transportation, and building also grew.

Workers still had to look to themselves to improve their lot. After 1848, however, European workers stopped rioting in the streets to voice their grievances. They also stopped trying to revive the old paternal guilds and similar institutions. After midcentury, workers turned to new institutions and ideologies. Chief among these were trade unions, democratic political parties, and socialism.

TRADE UNIONISM

Trade unionism came of age when governments extended legal protections to unions during the second half of the century. Unions became fully legal in Great Britain in 1871 and were allowed to picket in 1875. In France, Napoleon III at first used troops against strikes, but as his political power waned, he allowed weak labor associations in 1868. The Third French Republic fully legalized unions in 1884. In Germany, unions were permitted to function with little disturbance after 1890. Union participation in the political process was at first marginal. As long as the representatives of the traditional governing classes looked after labor interests, members of the working class rarely sought office themselves.

Unions directed their mid-century organizational efforts toward skilled workers and the immediate improvement of wages and working conditions. By the close of the century, industrial unions for unskilled workers were being organized. Employers intensely opposed these large unions of thousands of workers. Unions frequently had to engage in long strikes to convince employers to accept their demands. Europe suffered a rash of strikes in the decade before World War I as unions sought to keep wages in line with inflation. Despite union advances, however, and the growth of union membership (in 1910 to approximately three million in Britain, two million in Germany, and 977,000 in France), most of Europe's labor force was never unionized in this period. What the unions did represent for workers was a new collective form of association to confront economic difficulties and improve security.

DEMOCRACY AND POLITICAL PARTIES

Except for Russia, all the major European states adopted broad-based, if not perfectly democratic, electoral systems in the late nineteenth century. Great Britain passed its second voting reform act in 1867 and its third in 1884. Bismarck brought universal male suffrage to the German Empire in 1871. The French Chamber of Deputies was democratically elected. Universal male suffrage was adopted in Switzerland in 1879, in Spain in 1890, in Belgium in 1893, in the Netherlands in 1896, and in Norway in 1898. Italy finally fell into line in 1912. The broadened franchise meant politicians could no longer ignore workers, and discontented groups could now voice their grievances and advocate their programs within the institutions of government rather than from the outside.

The advent of democracy brought organized mass political parties like those already in existence in the United States to Europe for the first time. In the liberal European states with narrow electoral bases, most voters had been people of property who knew what they had at stake in politics. Organization had been minimal. The expansion of the electorate brought into the political process many people whose level of political consciousness, awareness, and interest was low. This electorate had to be organized and taught about power and influence in the liberal democratic state.

The organized political party—with its workers, newspapers, offices, social life, and discipline—was the vehicle that mobilized the new voters. The largest single group in these mass electorates was the working class. The democratization of politics presented the socialists with opportunities and required the traditional ruling classes to vie with the socialists for the support of the new voters.

During these years, socialism as a political ideology and plan of action opposed nationalism. The problems of class were supposed to be transnational, and socialism was supposed to unite the working classes across national borders. European socialists, however, badly underestimated the emotional drawing power of nationalism. Many workers had both socialist and nationalist sympathies, which were rarely in conflict with each other. When the outbreak of war in 1914 did bring them into conflict, however, nationalist feelings prevailed.

The major question for late-century socialist parties throughout Europe was whether revolution or democratic reform would improve the life of the working class. This question sharply divided all socialist parties and especially those whose leadership adhered to the intellectual legacy of Karl Marx. The Bolshevik Revolution of November 1917 would transform socialist debates and actions and render many of the disputes of the late nineteenth century and early twentieth centuries moot. During those decades, however, the dispute over whether to achieve socialism through revolution or reform sharply shaped socialist thought, party programs, and political behavior and influenced not only socialism but the larger European political arena.

KARL MARX
AND THE FIRST INTERNATIONAL

Karl Marx himself took into account the new realities that developed during the third quarter of the century. Although he continued to predict the disintegration of capitalism, his practical, public political activity reflected a different approach.

In 1864, a group of British and French trade unionists founded the International Working Men's Association. Known as the First International, its membership encompassed a vast array of radical political types, including socialists, anarchists, and Polish nationalists. In the inaugural address for the First International, Marx approved workers and trade unions' efforts to reform the conditions of labor within the existing political and economic processes. In his private writings he often criticized such reformist activity, but these writings were not made public until near the end of the century, years after his death.

The violence involved in the rise and suppression of the Paris Commune (see Chapter 22), which Marx had declared a genuine proletarian uprising, cast a pall over socialism throughout Europe. British trade unionists, who received legal protections in

1871, wanted no connection with the events in Paris. The French authorities used the uprising to suppress socialist activity. Under these pressures, the First International held its last European congress in 1873. It soon transferred its offices to the United States, where it was dissolved in 1876.

The short-lived First International had a disproportionately great impact on the future of European socialism. Throughout the late 1860s, the organization gathered statistics, kept labor groups informed of mutual problems, provided a forum to debate socialist doctrine, and extravagantly proclaimed (and overstated) its own influence over contemporary events. From these debates and activities, Marxism emerged as the single most important strand of socialism. Marx and his supporters defeated or drove out anarchists and advocates of other forms of socialism. The apparently scientific character of Marxism made it attractive at a time when science was more influential than at any previous period in European history. Marx's thought deeply impressed German socialists, who were to establish the most powerful socialist party in Europe, and became the chief vehicle for preserving and developing it. The full development of German socialism, however, also involved the influence of non-Marxist socialists in Great Britain.

GREAT BRITAIN: FABIANISM AND EARLY WELFARE PROGRAMS

Neither Marxism nor any other form of socialism made significant progress in Great Britain, the most advanced industrial society of the day. There trade unions grew steadily, and their members normally supported Liberal Party candidates. The "new unionism" of the late 1880s and the 1890s organized the dockworkers, the gas workers, and similar unskilled groups. In 1892, Keir Hardie (1856–1915) became the first independent working man to be elected to Parliament, but the small socialist Independent Labour Party founded a year later remained ineffective. Until 1901, labor's general political activity remained limited. In that year, however, the House of Lords, which also acts as Britain's highest court, through the Taff Vale decision, removed the legal protection previously accorded union funds. The Trades Union Congress responded by launching the Labour Party. In the election of 1906, the fledgling party sent twenty-nine members to Parliament. Their goals as trade unionists, however, did not yet include socialism. In this same period, the British labor movement became more militant. In scores of strikes before the war, workers fought for wages to meet the rising cost of living. The government took a larger role than ever before in mediating these strikes,

Beatrice and Sidney Webb. These most influential British Fabian Socialists, shown in a photograph from the late 1920s, wrote many books on governmental and economic matters, served on special parliamentary commissions, and agitated for the enactment of socialist policies. CORBIS/Bettmann

which in 1911 and 1912 involved the railways, the docks, and the coal mines.

British socialism itself remained primarily the preserve of non-Marxist intellectuals. The **Fabian** Society, founded in 1884, was Britain's most influential socialist group. The society took its name from Q. Fabius Maximus (d. 203 B.C.E.), the Roman general whose tactics against Hannibal involved avoiding direct conflict that might lead to defeat. The name reflected the society's gradualist approach to major social reform. Its leading members were Sidney Webb (1859–1947) and Beatrice Webb (1858–1943), H. G. Wells (1866–1946), Graham Wallas (1858–1932), and George Bernard Shaw (1856–1950). Many Fabians were civil servants who believed the problems of industry, the expansion of ownership, and the state direction of production could be solved and achieved gradually, peacefully, and democratically. They sought to educate the country about the rational wisdom of socialism. They were particularly interested in modes of collective ownership on the municipal level, the so-called gas-and-water socialism.

The British government and the Liberal and Conservative parties responded slowly to these pressures. In 1903, Joseph Chamberlain (1836–1914) launched his unsuccessful campaign to match foreign tariffs and to finance social reform through higher import duties. The campaign split the Conservative Party. After 1906, the Liberal Party, led by Sir Henry Campbell-Bannerman (1836–1908) and, after 1908, by Herbert Asquith, pursued a two-pronged policy. Fearful of losing seats in Parliament to the new Labour Party, they restored the former protection of the unions. Then, after 1909, with Chancellor of the Exchequer David Lloyd George (1863–1945) as its guiding light, the Liberal ministry undertook a broad program of social legislation that included establishing labor exchanges, regulating certain trades, such as tailoring and lace making, and passing the National Insurance Act of 1911, which provided unemployment benefits and health care.

The financing of these programs brought the Liberal majority in the House of Commons into conflict with the Conservative-dominated House of Lords. The result was the Parliament Act of 1911, which allowed the Commons to override the legislative veto of the upper chamber. The new taxes and social programs meant that in Britain, the home of nineteenth-century liberalism, the state was taking on an expanded role in the life of its citizens. The early welfare legislation was only marginally satisfactory to labor, many of whose members still thought they could gain more from the direct action of strikes.

FRANCE: "OPPORTUNISM" REJECTED

French socialism was a less united and more politically factionalized movement than socialism in other countries. At the turn of the century, Jean Jaurès (1859–1914) and Jules Guesde (1845–1922) led the two major factions of French socialists. Jaurès believed socialists should cooperate with middle-class Radical ministries to ensure the enactment of needed social legislation. Guesde opposed this policy, arguing that socialists could not, with integrity, support a bourgeois cabinet they were theoretically dedicated to overthrowing. The government's response to the Dreyfus affair brought the quarrel to a head. In 1899, seeking to unite all supporters of Dreyfus, Prime Minister René Waldeck-Rousseau (1846–1904) appointed the socialist Alexander Millerand (1859–1943) to the cabinet.

The Second International had been founded in 1889 in a new effort to unify the various national socialist parties and trade unions. By 1904, the Amsterdam Congress of the Second International debated the issue of *opportunism*, as such participation by socialists in cabinets was termed. The Congress condemned opportunism in France and

ordered French socialists to form a single party. Jaurès accepted the decision. Thereafter French socialists began to work together, and by 1914, the recently united Socialist Party had become the second largest group in the Chamber of Deputies. Jaurès was assassinated in 1914 in a Paris cafe at the outbreak of World War I. Thereafter in the patriotism of the war effort, French socialist leaders participated in the wartime cabinet. After the war the French socialist movement split with socialists not again serving in a French cabinet until the Popular Front Government of 1936. (See Chapter 28.)

The French labor movement, with deep roots in anarchism, was uninterested in either politics or socialism. French workers usually voted socialist, but the unions themselves, unlike those in Britain, avoided active political participation. The main labor union, Confédération Générale du Travail, founded in 1895, regarded itself as a rival to the socialist parties. Its leaders sought to improve the workers' conditions through direct action. They embraced the doctrines of syndicalism, which had been most persuasively expounded by Georges Sorel (1847–1922) in *Reflections on Violence* (1908). This book enshrined the general strike as a device to unite workers and gain them power. The strike tactic often conflicted with the socialist belief in aiding labor through state action. Strikes were common in France between 1905 and 1914, and the middle-class Radical ministry used troops to suppress them on more than one occasion.

GERMANY: SOCIAL DEMOCRATS AND REVISIONISM

The negative judgment the Second International rendered against French socialist participation in bourgeois ministries reflected a policy of permanent hostility to nonsocialist governments that the German Social Democratic Party, or SPD, had already adopted. The organizational success of this party, more than any other single factor, kept Marxist socialism alive during the late nineteenth and early twentieth centuries.

The SDP had been founded in 1875. Its origins lay in the labor agitation of Ferdinand Lasalle (1825–1864), who wanted workers to participate in German politics. Wilhelm Liebknecht (1826–1900) and August Bebel (1840–1913), who were Marxists that opposed reformist politics, soon joined the party. Thus, from its founding, the SPD was divided between those who advocated reform and those who advocated revolution.

Bismarck's Repression of the SPD Twelve years of persecution under Bismarck forged the character of the SPD. The so-called Iron Chancellor believed socialism would undermine German politics and society. He used an assassination attempt on Emperor William I (r. 1861–1888) in 1878, in which the socialists were not involved, to steer antisocialist laws through the *Reichstag.* The measures suppressed the organization, meetings, newspapers, and other public activities of the SPD. Thereafter, to remain a socialist meant to remove oneself from the mainstream of respectable German life and possibly to lose one's job. The antisocialist legislation proved politically counterproductive. From the early 1880s onward, the SPD steadily polled more and more votes in elections to the *Reichstag.*

As simple repression failed to wean German workers from socialist loyalties, Bismarck undertook a program of social welfare legislation. In 1883, the German Empire adopted a health insurance measure. The next year the Reichstag enacted accident insurance legislation. Finally, in 1889, Bismarck sponsored a plan for old age and disability pensions. These programs, to which both workers and employers contributed, represented a paternalistic, conservative alternative to socialism. The state itself would organize a system of social security that did not require any change in the system of property holding or politics. Germany became the first major industrial nation to enjoy this kind of welfare program.

The Erfurt Program   After forcing Bismarck's resignation mainly because of differences over foreign policy, Emperor William II (r. 1888–1918) allowed the antisocialist legislation to expire, hoping to build new political support among the working class. Even under the repressive laws, members of the SPD could sit in the *Reichstag.* With the repressive measures lifted, the party needed to decide what attitude to assume toward the German Empire.

The answer came in the Erfurt Program of 1891, formulated under the political guidance of Bebel and the ideological tutelage of Karl Kautsky (1854–1938). In good Marxist fashion, the program declared the imminent doom of capitalism and the necessity of socialist ownership of the means of production. The party intended to pursue these goals through legal political participation rather than by revolutionary activity. Kautsky argued that because capitalism by its very nature must collapse, the immediate task for socialists was to improve workers' lives rather than work for revolution, which was inevitable. So, although in theory the SPD was vehemently hostile to the German Empire, in practice the party functioned within its institutions. The SPD members of the *Reichstag* maintained clear political consciences by refusing to enter the cabinet (to which they were not invited anyway) and by refraining for many years from voting in favor of the military budget.

The Debate over Revisionism   The dilemma of the SPD, however, generated the most important challenge within the socialist movement to the orthodox Marxist analysis of capitalism and the socialist revolution. The author of this socialist heresy, Eduard Bernstein (1850–1932), had lived in Britain and was familiar with the Fabians. Bernstein questioned whether Marx and his later orthodox followers, such as Kautsky, had been correct in their pessimistic appraisal of capitalism and the necessity of revolution. In *Evolutionary Socialism* (1899), Bernstein pointed to conditions that did not meet orthodox Marxists' expectations. The standard of living was rising in Europe. Stockholding was making the ownership of capitalist industry more widespread. The middle class was not falling into the ranks of the proletariat and was not identifying its problems with those of the workers. The inner contradictions of capitalism had simply not developed the way Marx had predicted. Moreover, the extension of the franchise to the working class meant that parliamentary methods might achieve revolutionary social change. For Bernstein, social reform through democratic institutions replaced revolution as the path to a humane socialist society. (See "Eduard Bernstein Criticizes Orthodox Marxism," page, 786.)

Bernstein's doctrines, known as **Revisionism**, generated heated debate among German socialists, who finally condemned them. His critics argued that evolution toward social democracy might be possible in liberal, parliamentary Britain, but not in authoritarian, militaristic Germany, with its feeble *Reichstag.* Nonetheless, while still calling for revolution, the SPD pursued a course of action similar to what Bernstein advocated. Its trade union members, prospering within the German economy, did not want revolution. Its grassroots members wanted to be patriotic Germans as well as good socialists. Its leaders feared anything that might renew the persecution they had experienced under Bismarck.

Consequently, the SPD worked for electoral gains, expansion of its membership, and short-term political and social reform. It prospered and became one of the most important institutions of imperial Germany. Even middle-class Germans voted for it to oppose the illiberal institutions of the empire. In August 1914, after long debate among themselves, the SPD members of the *Reichstag* unanimously voted for the war credits that would finance Germany's participation in World War I.

RUSSIA: INDUSTRIAL DEVELOPMENT AND THE BIRTH OF BOLSHEVISM

In the 1890s, Russia entered the industrial age and confronted many of the problems that the more advanced nations of the Continent had experienced

EDUARD BERNSTEIN CRITICIZES ORTHODOX MARXISM

Eduard Bernstein was responsible for the emergence of Revisionism within the German Social Democratic Party. He was a dedicated socialist who recognized that Marx's Communist Manifesto *(1848) had not predicted the actual future of the European working classes. Bernstein believed the capitalist system would not suddenly collapse and that socialists should change their tactics to achieve political rights and pursue reform instead of revolution. [Compare this document with the passages from* The Communist Manifesto *in Chapter 21.]*

■ *According to Bernstein, what specific predictions in the* Communist Manifesto *failed to materialize? Why is the advance of democracy important to his argument? Why does he see the extension of political rights to German workers as so important?*

I set myself against the notion that we have to expect shortly a collapse of the bourgeois economy, and that social democracy should be induced by the prospect of such an imminent, great, social catastrophe to adapt its tactics to that assumption. . . .

The adherents of this theory of a catastrophe, base it especially on the conclusion of the *Communist Manifesto.* This is a mistake in every respect. . . .

Social conditions have not developed to such an acute opposition of things and classes as is depicted in the *Manifesto.* . . . The number of members of the possessing classes is today not smaller but larger. The enormous increase of social wealth is not accompanied by a decreasing number of large capitalists but by an increasing number of capitalists of all degrees. . . .

In all advanced countries we see the privileges of the capitalist bourgeoisie yielding step by step to democratic organizations. . . . Factory legislation, the democratizing of local government and the extension of its area of work, the freeing of trade unions and systems of co-operative trading from legal restrictions, the consideration of standard conditions of labour in the work undertaken by public authorities—all these characterize this phase of the evolution. . . .

The conquest of political power by the working classes, the expropriation of capitalists, are not ends in themselves but only means for the accomplishment of certain aims and endeavours. As such they are demands in the program of social democracy. . . . Nothing can be said beforehand as to the circumstances of their accomplishment; we can only fight for their realization. But the conquest of political power necessitates the possession of political rights; and the most important problem of tactics which German social democracy has at the present time to solve, appears to me to be to devise the best ways for the extension of the political and economic rights of the German working classes.

From Eduard Bernstein, *Evolutionary Socialism: A Criticism and Affirmation, 1899* (New York: Schocken Books, 1961), pp. xxiv–xxvi, xxix–xxx.

fifty or seventy-five years earlier. Unlike those other countries, Russia had to deal with political discontent and economic development simultaneously. Russian socialism reflected that peculiar situation.

Witte's Program for Industrial Growth Tsar Alexander III (r. 1881–1894) and, after him, Nicholas II (r. 1894–1917) were determined that Russia should become an industrial power. Only by doing so, they believed, could the country maintain its position as a great power. Count Sergei Witte (1849–1915) led Russia into the industrial age. After a career in railways and other private business, he was appointed first minister of communications and then finance minister in 1892. Witte, who pursued a policy of planned economic development, protective tariffs, high taxes, putting Russia's currency on the gold standard, and efficiency in government and business, epitomized the nineteenth-century modernizer. He established a strong financial relationship with the French money market, which enabled Russia to finance its modernization program with French loans and which later led to diplomatic cooperation and an alliance between Russia and France.

Witte favored heavy industries. Between 1890 and 1904, the Russian railway system grew from 30,596 to 59,616 kilometers. The 5,000-mile-long Trans-Siberian Railroad was completed in 1903. Coal output more than tripled during the same period. Pig-iron production increased from 928,000 tons in 1890 to 4,641,000 tons in 1913. During the same period, steel production rose from 378,000 to 4,918,000 tons. Textile manufacturing continued to expand and was still the single largest industry. The factory system spread extensively.

Industrialism, however, also brought social discontent to Russia, as it had elsewhere. Landowners felt that foreign capitalists were earning too much of the profit. The peasants saw their grain exports and tax payments finance development that did not measurably improve their lives. A small, but significant, industrial proletariat emerged. In 1900, Russia had approximately three million factory workers. Their working and living conditions were poor. They enjoyed little state protection, and trade unions were illegal. In 1897, Witte did enact an 11.5-hour workday, but needless to say, discontent and strikes continued.

Similar social and economic problems arose in the countryside. Russian agriculture had not prospered after the emancipation of the serfs in 1861. The peasants remained burdened with redemption payments for the land they farmed, local taxes, excessive national taxes, and falling grain prices. Peasants did not own their land as individuals, but communally through the *mir*, or village. They farmed the land inefficiently through strip farming or by tilling small plots. Many free peasants with too little land to support their families had to work on large estates owned by nobles or for more prosperous peasant farmers, known as **kulaks**. Between 1860 and 1914, the population of European Russia rose from about 50 million to around 103 million people. Land hunger and discontent spread among the peasants and sparked frequent uprisings in the countryside.

New political developments accompanied economic changes. The membership and intellectual roots of the Social Revolutionary Party, founded in 1901, reached back to the Populists of the 1870s. The new party opposed industrialism and looked to the communal life of rural Russia as a model for the future. In 1903, the Constitutional Democratic Party, or Cadets, was formed. This liberal party drew its members from those who participated in local councils called **zemstvos**. Modeling themselves on the liberal parties of Western Europe, the Cadets wanted a constitutional monarchy under a parliamentary regime with civil liberties and economic progress.

Lenin's Early Thought and Career   The situation of Russian socialists differed radically from that of socialists in other major European countries. Russia had no representative institutions and only a

In this photograph taken in 1895, Lenin sits at the table among a group of other young Russian radicals from Saint Petersburg.   CORBIS/Bettmann

small working class. The compromises and accommodations achieved elsewhere were meaningless in Russia, where socialists believed that in both theory and practice they must be revolutionary. The repressive policies of the tsarist regime required the Russian Social Democratic Party, founded in 1898, to function in exile. The party members greatly admired the German Social Democratic Party and adopted its Marxist ideology.

The leading late-nineteenth-century Russian Marxist was Gregory Plekhanov (1857–1918), who wrote from exile in Switzerland. At the turn of the century, his chief disciple was Vladimir Ilyich Ulyanov (1870–1924), who later took the name of Lenin. The future leader of the communist revolution was the son of a high bureaucrat. His older brother, while a student in Saint Petersburg, had become involved in radical politics; arrested for participating in a plot against Alexander III, he was executed in 1887. In 1893, Lenin moved to Saint Petersburg, where he studied law. Soon he, too, was drawn to the revolutionary groups among the factory workers. He was arrested in 1895 and exiled to Siberia. In 1900, after his release, Lenin left Russia for the West. He spent most of the next seventeen years in Switzerland.

There, Lenin became deeply involved in the disputes of the exiled Russian Social Democrats. They all considered themselves Marxists, but they differed on what a Marxist revolution would mean for primarily rural Russia and on how to structure their own party. Unlike the backward-looking Social Revolutionaries, the Social Democrats were modernizers who favored industrial development. Looking to Karl Marx's writings, most Russian Social Democrats believed Russia must develop a large proletariat before the Marxist revolution could come. They also hoped to build a mass political party like the German SPD.

Lenin dissented from both these ideas. In *What Is to Be Done?* (1902), he condemned any accommodations, such as those the German SPD practiced. He also criticized trade unionism that settled for short-term reformist gains rather than work for true revolutionary change for the working class. Lenin further rejected the concept of a mass democratic party composed of workers. Instead, he declared that revolutionary consciousness would not arise spontaneously from the working class. Rather, "people who make revolutionary activity their profession" must carry that consciousness to the workers.[3] Only a small, tightly organized, elite party could possess the proper dedication to revolution and resist penetration by police spies. The guiding principle of that party should be "the strictest secrecy, the strictest selection of members, and the training of professional revolutionaries."[4] Lenin thus rejected both Kautsky's view that revolution was inevitable and Bernstein's view that democratic means could achieve revolutionary goals. Lenin substituted the small, professional, nondemocratic revolutionary party for Marx's proletariat as the instrument of revolutionary change. (See "Lenin Argues for the Necessity of a Secret and Elite Party of Professional Revolutionaries.")

In 1903, at the London Congress of the Russian Social Democratic Party, Lenin forced a split in the party ranks. He and his followers lost many votes on questions put before the congress, but near its close they mustered a slim majority. Thereafter Lenin's faction assumed the name **Bolsheviks**, meaning "majority," and the other, more moderate, democratic revolutionary faction came to be known as the **Mensheviks**, or "minority." There was, of course, a considerable public relations advantage to the name *Bolshevik*. (In 1912, the Bolsheviks organized themselves as a separate party.)

A fundamental organizational difference had existed between what in 1903 were the two chief factions of the Russian Social Democratic Party. The Mensheviks wanted a party with a mass membership, similar to the German SDP and other West European socialist parties, which would function democratically. The Bolsheviks intended the party to consist of elite professional revolutionaries who would provide centralized leadership for the working class. Lenin believed a mass party functioning in a democratic fashion would seek only to reform workers' wages, hours, and living conditions, whereas he wanted a revolution that would transform Russia.

In 1905, Lenin complemented his organizational theory with a program for revolution in Russia. In *Two Tactics of Social Democracy in the Bourgeois-Democratic Revolution,* he urged the socialist revolution to unite the proletariat and the peasantry. Lenin grasped better than any other revolutionary the profound discontent in the Russian countryside. He believed the tsarist government probably could not suppress an alliance of workers and peasants in rebellion.

Lenin's two principles—an elite party and a dual social revolution—guided later Bolshevik activity. The Bolsheviks ultimately seized power in November 1917, transforming the political landscape of the twentieth century, but they did so only after the turmoil of World War I had undermined support

---

[3]Quoted in Albert Fried and Ronald Sanders, eds., *Socialist Thought: A Documentary History* (Garden City, NY: Anchor Doubleday, 1964), p. 459.

[4]Fried and Sanders, p. 468.

LENIN ARGUES FOR THE NECESSITY OF A SECRET AND ELITE PARTY OF PROFESSIONAL REVOLUTIONARIES

Social democratic parties in Western Europe had mass memberships and were generally democratic organizations. In this passage from What Is to Be Done? (1902), Lenin explains why the autocratic political conditions of Russia demanded a different kind of organization for the Russian Social Democratic Party. Lenin's ideas became the guiding principles of Bolshevik organization. Note Lenin's difference with both Marx's Communist Manifesto and Bernstein's revisitionist views.

■ *What does Lenin mean by "professional revolutionaries"? Why does Russia need such revolutionaries? How does Lenin reconcile his antidemocratic views to the goal of aiding the working class?*

I assert that it is far more difficult [for government police] to unearth a dozen wise men than a hundred fools. This position I will defend, no matter how much you instigate the masses against me for my "anti-democratic" views, etc. As I have stated repeatedly, by "wise men," in connection with organization, I mean professional revolutionaries, irrespective of whether they have developed from among students or working men. I assert: (1) that no revolutionary movement can endure without a stable organization of leaders maintaining continuity; (2) that the broader the popular mass drawn spontaneously into the struggle, which forms the basis of the movement and participates in it, the more urgent the need for such an organization, and the more solid this organization must be . . . ; (3) that such an organization must consist chiefly of people professionally engaged in revolutionary activity; (4) that in an autocratic state [such as Russia], the more we confine the membership of such an organization to people who are professionally engaged in revolutionary activity and who have been professionally trained in the art of combating the political police, the more difficult will it be to unearth the organization; and (5) the greater will be the number of people from the working class and from other social classes who will be able to join the movement and perform active work in it. . . .

The only serious organization principle for the active workers of our movement should be the strictest secrecy, the strictest selection of members, and the training of professional revolutionaries.

From Albert Fried and Ronald Sanders, eds., *Socialist Thought: A Documentary History* (Garden City, NY: Anchor Doubleday, 1964), pp. 460, 468.

for the tsar and only after other political forces had already toppled the tsarist government in February 1917. Before World War I, the Bolsheviks constituted the odd man out in European socialist politics; they exerted no significant prewar influence on members of other socialist groups, who, in general, ignored them. For their part, the Bolsheviks responded by scorning the West European socialist parties that worked within their nations' political systems. Between 1900 and the outbreak of World War I, the government of Nicholas II managed to confront political upheaval more or less successfully.

The Revolution of 1905 and its Aftermath   The quarrels among the exiled Russian socialists and Lenin's doctrines had no immediate influence on events in Russia. Industrialization continued to stir resentment. In 1903, Nicholas II dismissed Witte, hoping to quell the criticism. The next year, in response to conflicts over Manchuria and Korea, Russia went to war against Japan, partly in hopes the conflict would rally public opinion to the tsar. Instead, the Russians lost the war, and the government faced an internal political crisis. The Japanese captured Port Arthur, Russia's naval base on the coast of China, early in 1905. A few

A CLOSER LOOK

Bloody Sunday, St. Petersburg 1905

On Bloody Sunday, January 22, 1905, troops of Tsar Nicholas II fired on a peaceful procession of workers at the Winter Palace who sought to present a petition for better working and living conditions. The scene portrayed here depicts one of the enduring images of events leading to the subsequent Russian Revolutions of 1905 and 1917. It figured in at least two movies: the 1925 anti-tsarist Soviet silent film called "The Ninth of January," and "Nicholas and Alexandra," the lavish 1971 movie that was sympathetic to the tsar and blamed Bloody Sunday on frightened and incompetent officials. While Nicholas had not ordered the troops to fire and was not even in St. Petersburg on Bloody Sunday, the event all but destroyed any chance of reconciliation between the tsarist government and the Russian working class.

The workers are visibly defenseless in the face of the rifles being fired at them.

Bildarchiv Preussischer Kulturbesitz

Although the square before the Winter Palace toward the right of the troops is large and might have allowed an escape route of sorts for the workers' procession, the troops forced the crowd into an area of narrow escape.

The view is the one that officials in the Winter Palace, which lay behind the row of troops with rifles, would have seen.

days later, on January 22, a Russian Orthodox priest named Father George Gapon led several hundred workers to present a petition to the tsar to improve industrial conditions. The petioners did not know that the tsar was not even in Saint Petersburg, but as they approached the Winter Palace, troops opened fire, killing approximately forty people and wounding hundreds of others. As word of this massacre spread, and large, angry crowds gathered elsewhere in the city, the military shot more people. The final death toll was approximately 200 killed and 800 wounded, though at the time rumors made the numbers much larger. The day, soon known as Bloody Sunday, marked a turning point. Vast numbers of ordinary Russians came to believe they could no longer trust the tsar or his government.

During the next ten months, revolutionary disturbances spread throughout Russia. Sailors mutinied, workers went on strike, peasants revolted, and property was attacked. The uncle of Nicholas II was assassinated in Moscow. Liberal leaders of the Constitutional Democratic Party from the *zemstvos* demanded political reform. University students went on strike. Social Revolutionaries and Social Democrats agitated among urban working groups. In early October 1905, strikes broke out in Saint Petersburg, and for all practical purposes, worker groups, called **soviets**, controlled the city. Nicholas II, who had recalled Witte, issued the October

MAJOR DATES IN THE DEVELOPMENT OF SOCIALISM

1864 International Working Men's Association (the First International) founded
1875 German Social Democratic Party founded
1876 First International dissolved
1878 German antisocialist laws passed
1884 British Fabian Society founded
1889 Second International founded
1891 German antisocialist laws permitted to expire
1891 German Social Democratic Party's Erfurt Program
1895 French Confédération Générale du Travail founded
1899 Eduard Bernstein's *Evolutionary Socialism*
1902 The British Labour Party founded
1902 Lenin's *What Is to Be Done?*
1903 Bolshevik-Menshevik split
1904 "Opportunism" rejected at the Amsterdam Congress of the Second International

Manifesto, which promised Russia a constitutional government.

Early in 1906, Nicholas II announced the creation of a representative body, the **Duma**, with two chambers. He reserved to himself, however, ministerial appointments, financial policy, and military and foreign affairs. The April elections returned a highly radical group of representatives. The tsar then replaced Witte with P. A. Stolypin (1862–1911), who had little sympathy for parliamentary government. Stolypin persuaded Nicholas to dissolve the Duma. A second assembly was elected in February 1907. Again, cooperation proved impossible, and the tsar dissolved that Duma in June. A third Duma, elected in late 1907 on the basis of a more conservative franchise, proved sufficiently pliable for the tsar and his minister. Thus, within two years of the 1905 Revolution, Nicholas II had recaptured much of the ground he had conceded.

Stolypin set about repressing rebellion, removing some causes of the revolt, and rallying property owners behind the tsarist regime. Early in 1907, special field courts-martial condemned almost 700 rebellious peasants to death. Before undertaking this repression, Stolypin, in November 1906, had canceled any redemptive payments that the peasants still owed the government from the emancipation of the serfs in 1861. He took this step to encourage peasants to assume individual proprietorship of the land they farmed and to abandon the communal system of the *mirs.* Stolypin believed farmers would be more productive working for themselves. Combined with a program to instruct peasants on how to farm more efficiently, this policy improved agricultural production. However, many peasant smallholders sold their land and joined the industrial labor force.

The moderate liberals who sat in the Duma approved of the new land measures. They liked the idea of competition and individual property ownership. The Constitutional Democrats wanted a more genuinely parliamentary mode of government, but they compromised out of fear of new revolutionary disturbances. Hatred of Stolypin was still widespread, however, among the country's older conservative groups, and industrial workers remained antagonistic to the tsar. In 1911, Stolypin was assassinated by a Social Revolutionary, who may have been a police agent in the pay of conservatives. Nicholas II found no worthy successor. His government simply muddled along.

Meanwhile, at court, the monk Grigory Efimovich Rasputin (1871?–1916) gained ascendancy with the tsar and his wife because of his alleged

MAJOR DATES IN TURN-OF-THE-CENTURY RUSSIAN HISTORY

1892	Witte appointed finance minister
1895	Lenin arrested and sent to Siberia
1897	11.5-hour workday established
1898	Russian Social Democratic Party founded
1900	Lenin leaves Russia for western Europe
1901	Social Revolutionary Party founded
1903	Constitutional Democratic Party (Cadets) founded
1903	Bolshevik-Menshevik split
1903	Witte dismissed
1904	Russo-Japanese War begins
1905 (January)	Japan defeats Russia
1905 (January 22)	Revolution breaks out in Saint Petersburg after Bloody Sunday
1905 (October 20)	General strike
1905 (October 26)	October Manifesto establishes constitutional government
1906 (May 10)	First Duma meets
1906 (June)	Stolypin appointed prime minister
1906 (July 21)	Dissolution of first Duma
1906 (November)	Land redemption payments canceled for peasants
1907 (March 5–16)	Second Duma seated and dismissed in June
1907	Franchise changed and a third Duma elected, which sits until 1912
1911	Stolypin assassinated by a Social Revolutionary
1912	Fourth Duma elected
1914	World War I breaks out

power to heal the tsar's hemophilic son Alexis, the heir to the throne, when medicine proved unable to help the boy. The undue influence of this strange, uncouth man, as well as continued social discontent and conservative resistance to any further liberal reforms, undermined the position of the tsar and his government after 1911. Once again, as in 1904, he and his ministers thought that some bold move in foreign policy might bring the regime the popular support it desperately needed.

IN PERSPECTIVE

From 1860 through 1914, two apparently contradictory developments emerged in European social life. On one hand, the lifestyle of the urban middle classes became the model to which much of society aspired. The characteristics of this lifestyle included a relatively small family living in its own house or large apartment, servants, and a wife who did not earn an income. The middle classes, in general, benefited from the many material comforts that the Second Industrial Revolution had generated.

During the same period, the forces of socialism and labor unions assumed a new and major role in European political life. Their leaders demanded greater social justice and a fairer distribution of the vast quantities of consumer goods Europe was producing. Some socialists sought in one way or another to work within existing political systems. Others—particularly, those in Russia—advocated revolution. The growth in wealth and the availability of new goods and services magnified the injustices the poor suffered, and the contrast between them and the middle classes, and made the demands of labor and the socialists more strident. In Russia, the strains of the early stages of industrialization intensified social unrest. These strains, compounded by the humiliating defeat in a war against Japan, triggered the unsuccessful revolution of 1905.

The working class, however, was not alone in seeking change. Women, for the first time in European history, began in significant ways to demand a political role and to protest the gender inequalities embedded in law and family life. They were beginning to enter the professions and were taking a significant role in the service economy, such as the new telephone companies. These changes, as much as the demands of socialists, would, in time, raise questions about the adequacy of the much admired late-nineteenth-century middle-class lifestyle.

REVIEW QUESTIONS

1. How did the Second Industrial Revolution transform European society? What new industries developed, and which do you think had the greatest impact in the twentieth century? Why did European economic growth slacken in the second half of the nineteenth century?

2. Why were European cities redesigned during the late nineteenth century? Why were housing and health key issues for urban reform?

3. What was the status of European women in the second half of the nineteenth century? Why did they grow discontented with their lot? What factors led to change? To what extent had they improved their position by 1914? What tactics did they use to effect change? Was the emancipation of women inevitable? How did women approach their situation differently from country to country?

4. What were the major characteristics of Jewish emancipation in the nineteenth century?

5. What was the status of the European working classes in 1860? Had it improved by 1914? Why did trade unions and organized mass political parties grow? Why were the debates over "opportunism" and "revisionism" important to the Western European socialist parties?

6. What were the benefits and drawbacks of industrialization for Russia? Were the tsars wise to attempt to modernize their country, or should they have left it as it was? How did Lenin's view of socialism differ from that of the socialists in Western Europe?

SUGGESTED READINGS

A. ASCHER AND P. A. STOLYPIN, *The Search for Stability in Late Imperial Russia* (2000). A broad-ranging biography based on extensive research.

P. BIRNBAUM, *Jewish Destinies: Citizenship, State, and Community in Modern France* (2000). Explores the subject from the French Revolution to the present.

T. W. CLYMAN AND J. VOWLES, *Russia through Women's Eyes: Autobiographies from Tsarist Russia* (1996). A splendid collection of relatively brief memoirs.

G. CROSSICK AND S. JAUMAIN (EDS.), *Cathedrals of Consumption: The European Department Store, 1850–1939* (1999). Essays on the development of a new mode of distribution of consumer goods.

A. GEIFMAN, *Thou Shalt Kill: Revolutionary Terrorism in Russia, 1894–1917* (1993). An examination of political violence in late imperial Russia.

R. F. HAMILTON, *Marxism, Revisionism, and Leninism: Explication, Assessment, and Commentary* (2000). A contribution by a historically-minded sociologist.

J. HARSIN, *Policing Prostitution in Nineteenth-Century Paris* (1985). A major study of this significant subject in French social history.

G. HIMMELFARB, *Poverty and Compassion: The Moral Imagination of the Late Victorians* (1991). The best examination of late Victorian social thought.

E. HOBSBAWM, *The Age of Empire, 1875–1914* (1987). A stimulating survey that covers cultural as well as political developments.

S. S. HOLTON, *Feminism and Democracy: Women's Suffrage and Reform Politics in Britain, 1900–1918* (1986). An excellent treatment of the subject.

T. HOPPEN, *The Mid-Victorian Generation, 1846–1886* (1998). The most extensive treatment of the subject.

M. MALIA, *Russia under Western Eyes: From the Bronze Horseman to the Lenin Mausoleum* (2000). A brilliant work on how Western intellectuals understood Russia.

E. D. RAPPAPORT, *Shopping for Pleasure: Women in the Making of London's West End* (2001). A study of the rise of department stores in London.

H. ROGGER, *Jewish Policies and Right-Wing Politics in Imperial Russia* (1986). A learned examination of Russian anti-Semitism.

M. L. ROZENBLIT, *The Jews of Vienna, 1867–1914: Assimilation and Identity* (1983). Covers the cultural, economic, and political life of Viennese Jews.

R. SERVICE, *Lenin: A Biography* (2002). Based on new sources and will no doubt become the standard biography.

D. SORKIN, *The Transformation of German Jewry, 1780–1840* (1987). An examination of Jewish emancipation in Germany.

G. P. STEENSON, *Not One Man! Not One Penny!: German Social Democracy, 1863–1914* (1999). An extensive survey.

N. STONE, *Europe Transformed* (1984). A sweeping survey that emphasizes the difficulties of late-nineteenth-century liberalism.

A. THORPE, *A History of the British Labour Party* (2001). From its inception to the twenty-first century.

J. R. WALKOWITZ, *Prostitution and Victorian Society: Women, Class, and the State* (1980). A work of great insight and sensitivity.

DOCUMENTS CD-ROM

Nineteenth-Century Society

23.1 The Church Weighs In: *Rerum Novarum*
23.2 Women Without Power Change the System
23.3 Sex in Society
23.4 John Stuart Mill: from *The Subjection of Women*
23.5 Bernard Shaw: Act III from *Mrs. Warren's Profession*
23.6 Gertrude Himmelfarb: from *Poverty and Compassion*

CHAPTER 24

THE BIRTH OF MODERN EUROPEAN THOUGHT

KEY TOPICS

During the same period that the modern nation-state developed and the Second Industrial Revolution laid the foundations for modern life, the ideas that marked European thought for much of the twentieth century and beyond took shape. Like previous intellectual changes, these arose from earlier patterns of thought. The Enlightenment provided late-nineteenth-century Europeans with a heritage of

Darwin's theories about the evolution of humankind from the higher primates aroused enormous controversy. This caricature shows him with a monkey's body holding a mirror to an apelike creature.
National History Museum, London, UK/Bridgeman Art Library

rationalism, toleration, cosmopolitanism, and an appreciation of science. Romanticism led them to value feelings, imagination, national identity, and the autonomy of the artistic experience.

By 1900, these strands of thought had become woven into a new fabric. Many of the traditional intellectual signposts were disappearing. Christianity had experienced the most severe intellectual attack in its history. The picture of the physical world prevailing since Newton had undergone major modification. Darwin and Freud had challenged the special place that Western thinkers had assigned to humankind. Writers began to question rationality. The humanitarian ideals of liberalism and socialism gave way to aggressive nationalism. European intellectuals were more daring than ever before, but they were also probably less certain and optimistic. ■

THE NEW READING PUBLIC

The social context of intellectual life changed in the latter part of the nineteenth century. For the first time in Europe, a mass reading public came into existence as more people than ever before became drawn into the world of print culture. In 1850, about half the population of Western Europe and a much higher proportion of Russians were illiterate. That situation changed during the next half century.

ADVANCES IN PRIMARY EDUCATION

Literacy on the Continent improved steadily from the 1860s onward as governments financed education. Hungary provided elementary education in 1868, Britain in 1870, Switzerland in 1874, Italy in 1877, and France between 1878 and 1881. The already advanced education system of Prussia was extended throughout the German Empire after 1871. By 1900, in Britain, France, Belgium, the Netherlands, Germany, and Scandinavia, approximately 85 percent or more of the people could read, but Italy, Spain, Russia, Austria-Hungary, and the Balkans still had illiteracy rates of between 30 and 60 percent.

The new primary education in the basic skills of reading, writing, and elementary arithmetic reflected and generated social change. Both liberals and conservatives regarded such minimal training as necessary for orderly political behavior by the newly enfranchised voters. They also hoped that literacy would create a more productive labor force. This side of the educational crusade embodied the Enlightenment faith that right knowledge would lead to right action.

Literacy and its extension, however, soon became a force in its own right. The school-teaching profession grew rapidly in numbers and prestige and, as noted in Chapter 23, became a major area for the employment of women. Those people who learned to read soon discovered that much of the education that led to better jobs and political influence was still open only to those who could afford it. Having created systems of primary education, the major nations had to give further attention to secondary education by the time of World War I. In another generation, the question would become one of democratic university instruction.

Public education became widespread in Europe during the second half of the nineteenth century and women came to dominate the profession of school teaching, especially at the elementary level. This 1905 photograph shows English schoolchildren going through morning drills. © Hulton-Deutsch Collection/CORBIS

READING MATERIAL FOR THE MASS AUDIENCE

The expanding literate population created a vast market for new reading material. The number of newspapers, books, magazines, mail-order catalogs, and libraries grew rapidly. Cheap mass-circulation newspapers, such as *Le Petit Journal* of Paris and the *Daily Mail* and *Daily Express* of London, enjoyed their first heyday. Such newspapers carried advertising that alerted readers to the new consumer products available through the Second Industrial Revolution. Other publishers produced newspapers with specialized political or religious viewpoints. The number of monthly and quarterly journals for families, women, and freethinking intellectuals increased. Probably more people with different ideas could get into print in the late nineteenth century than ever before in European history. In addition, more people could read their ideas than ever before.

Because many of the new readers were only marginally literate and still ignorant about many subjects, the books and journals catering to them were often mediocre. The cheap newspapers prospered on stories of sensational crimes and political scandal and on pages of advertising. Religious journals depended on denominational rivalry. A brisk market existed for pornography. Newspapers with editorials on the front page became major factors in the emerging mass politics. The news could be managed, but in Central Europe more often by the government censor than by the publisher.

Critics pointed to the low level of public taste, but the new education, the new readers, and the myriad of new books and journals permitted a popularization of knowledge that has become a hallmark of our world. The new literacy was the intellectual parallel of the railroad and the steamship. People could leave their original intellectual surroundings because literacy is not an end in itself, but leads to other skills and other knowledge.

SCIENCE AT MIDCENTURY

In about 1850, Voltaire (1694–1778) would have felt at home in a general discussion of scientific concepts. The basic Newtonian picture of physical nature that he had popularized still prevailed. Scientists continued to believe that nature operates as a vast machine according to mechanical principles. At mid century, learned persons regarded the physical world as rational, mechanical, and dependable. Experiment and observation could reveal its laws objectively. Scientific theory purportedly described physical nature as it really existed. Moreover, by 1850, science had a strong institutional life in French and German universities and in new professional societies. William Whewell of Cambridge University had invented the word "scientist" in the early 1830s, and it was in common use by the end of the century. (See Encountering the Past: The Birth of Science Fiction, page 798.)

COMTE, POSITIVISM, AND THE PRESTIGE OF SCIENCE

During the early nineteenth century, science had continued to establish itself as the model for all human knowledge. The French philosopher Auguste Comte (1798–1857), a late child of the Enlightenment and a onetime follower of Saint-Simon, developed **positivism**, a philosophy of human intellectual development that culminated in science. In *The Positive Philosophy* (1830–1842), Comte argued that human thought had developed in three stages. In the first, or theological, stage, physical nature was explained in terms of the action of divinities or spirits. In the second, or metaphysical, stage, abstract principles were regarded as the operative agencies of nature. In the final, or positive stage, explanations of nature became matters of exact description of phenomena, without recourse to an unobservable operative principle.

Physical science had, in Comte's view, entered the positive stage, and similar thinking should penetrate other areas of analysis. In particular, Comte believed that positive laws of social behavior could be discovered in the same fashion as laws of physical nature. He is, thus, generally regarded as the father of sociology. Works like Comte's helped convince learned Europeans that all knowledge must resemble scientific knowledge.

From the mid-nineteenth century onward, the links of science to the technology of the Second Industrial Revolution made the general European public aware of science and technology as never before. The British Fabian socialist Beatrice Webb (1858–1943) recalled this situation from her youth:

Who will deny that the men of science were the leading British intellectuals of that period; that it was they who stood out as men of genius with international reputations; that it was they who were the self-confident militants of the period; that it was they who were routing the theologians, confounding the mystics, imposing their theories on philosophers, their inventions on capitalists, and their discoveries on medical men; whilst they were at the same time snubbing the artists, ignoring the poets, and even casting doubts on the capacity of the politicians?[1]

Her remarks would have applied in every industrialized nation in Europe. Writers spoke of a religion of science that would explain all nature without resorting to supernaturalism. Popularizers, such as Thomas Henry Huxley (1825–1895) in Britain and Ernst Haeckel (1834–1919) in Germany, worked to gain government support of scientific research and to include science in the schools and universities.

[1] Beatrice Webb, *My Apprenticeship* (London: Longmans, Green, 1926), pp. 130–131.

THE BIRTH OF SCIENCE FICTION

During the Renaissance many European writers composed works about fantasy voyages to distant lands. In the seventeenth century, authors published some two hundred accounts of trips to the moon. Throughout the nineteenth century, other authors told tales of fantastic voyages into space or beneath the earth.

However, the real father of today's works of popular science fiction was Jules Verne (1828–1905). His *Five Weeks in a Balloon* (1863), a tale of a balloon trip across Africa, sold so well that a French publisher immediately gave Verne a contract to write two such stories each year for a magazine. So influential was Verne's image of the future that the United States named its first atomic submarine the *Nautilus* after the vessel the mysterious Captain Nemo commanded in Verne's *Twenty Thousand Leagues under the Sea* (1870).

Verne prided himself on his scientific veracity. He also located his stories in his own age. Readers felt they were experiencing a contemporary adventure.

Toward the turn of the century, science fiction found another master in the English novelist H. G. Wells (1866–1946), who in 1895 published *The Time Machine* in which the characters travel through time. Wells's first success was rapidly followed by *The Island of Dr. Moreau* (1896) about a mad surgeon's inhuman experiments on animals, and *The War of the Worlds* (1898) about a Martian invasion of the earth. Wells invented many of the devices, such as new stars appearing near the solar system, Martians and other planetary creatures unfriendly to humans, machinery that goes astray, and strange diseases, that would become the stock in trade for later science fiction writers.

Verne, Wells, and their many imitators, published their stories in cheap illustrated magazines with mass circulations. Consequently, science fiction immediately entered popular culture. Throughout the twentieth century popular movies and television series were made based on the stories of both Verne and Wells. In 1938, when Orson Welles (1915–1985) broadcast Wells's *War of the Worlds* over the radio, many Americans actually believed Martians had landed in New Jersey. The

Captain Nemo's submarine confronts a giant octopus in Verne's *Twenty Thousand Leagues under the Sea.*
© Bettman/CORBIS

works of Verne and Wells continue to influence the writing of science fiction.

- *Why is Jules Verne considered the father of modern science fiction? What enduring plot devices did H. G. Wells introduce? Why did science fiction become so popular?*

P. Nichols and J. Clute, *The Encyclopedia of Science Fiction* (New York: St. Martin's Press, 1995); Dieter Wuckel and Bruce Cassidy, *The Illustrated History of Science Fiction* (New York: Ungar, 1986); David Kyle, *A Pictorial History of Science Fiction* (London: Hamlyn, 1976).

DARWIN'S THEORY OF NATURAL SELECTION

In 1859, Charles Darwin (1809–1882) published *On the Origin of Species*, which carried the mechanical interpretation of physical nature into the world of living things. The book was one of the seminal works of Western thought and earned Darwin the honor of being regarded as the "Newton of biology." Both Darwin and his book have been much misunderstood. He did not originate the concept of evolution, which had been discussed widely before he wrote. What he and Alfred Russel Wallace (1823–1913) did, working independently, was to formulate the principle of natural selection, which explained how species had changed or evolved over time. Earlier writers had believed evolution might occur; Darwin and Wallace explained how it could occur.

Drawing on Malthus, the two scientists contended that more living organisms come into existence than can survive in their environment. Those organisms with a marginal advantage in the struggle for existence live long enough to propagate. This principle of survival of the fittest Darwin called **natural selection**. It was naturalistic and mechanistic, requiring no guiding mind behind the development in organic nature. What neither Darwin nor anyone else in his day could explain was the origin of those chance variations that provided some living things with the marginal chance for survival. Only after 1900, when the work on heredity of the Austrian monk, Gregor Mendel (1822–1884), received public attention, did the mystery of those variations begin to be unraveled.

Darwin and Wallace's theory represented the triumph of naturalistic explanation, which removed the idea of purpose from organic nature. Eyes were not made for seeing according to the rational wisdom and purpose of God, but had developed mechanistically over time. Thus, the theory of evolution through natural selection not only contradicted the biblical narrative of the Creation, but also undermined both the deistic argument for the existence of God from the design of the universe and the whole concept of fixity in nature or the universe at large. The world was a realm of flux. The idea that physical and organic nature might be constantly changing allowed people to believe that society, values, customs, and beliefs should also change.

In 1871, in *The Descent of Man*, Darwin applied the principle of evolution by natural selection to human beings. Darwin was hardly the first person to treat human beings as animals, but he contended that humankind's moral nature and religious sentiments, as well as its physical frame, had developed naturalistically largely in response to the requirements of survival. Neither the origin nor the character of humankind, in Darwin's view, required the existence of a god for their explanation. Not since Copernicus had removed the earth from the center of the universe had the pride of Western human beings received so sharp a blow.

Darwin's theory of evolution by natural selection was controversial from the moment *On the Origin of Species* appeared. It encountered criticism from both the religious and the scientific communities. By the end of the century, scientists widely accepted the concept of evolution but not yet Darwin's mechanism of natural selection. The acceptance of the latter really dates from the 1920s and 1930s, when Darwin's theory was combined with modern genetics.

SCIENCE AND ETHICS

One area in which science came to have a new significance was social thought and ethics. Philosophers applied the concept of the struggle for survival to human social relationships. The phrase "survival of the fittest" predated Darwin and reflected the competitive outlook of classical economics. Darwin's use of the phrase gave it the prestige associated with advanced science.

The most famous advocate of evolutionary ethics was Herbert Spencer (1820–1903), a British philosopher. Spencer, a strong individualist, believed human society progresses through competition. If the weak receive too much protection, the rest of humankind is the loser. In Spencer's work, struggle against one's fellow human beings became a kind of ethical imperative. The concept could be applied to justify not aiding the poor and the working class or to justify the domination of colonial peoples or to advocate aggressive competition among nations. Evolutionary ethics and similar concepts, all of which are usually termed *social Darwinism*, often came close to saying that "might makes right."

One of the chief opponents of such thinking was Thomas Henry Huxley, the great defender of Darwin. In 1893, Huxley declared that the physical process of evolution was at odds with human ethical development. The struggle in nature only showed how human beings should not behave. (See "T. H. Huxley Criticizes Evolutionary Ethics," page 800.)

T. H. HUXLEY CRITICIZES
EVOLUTIONARY ETHICS

T. H. Huxley (1825–1895) was a British scientist who had been among Darwin's strongest defenders. He was also an outspoken advocate for the advancement of science in the late nineteenth century. Huxley, however, became a major critic of social Darwinism, which attempted to deduce ethical principles from evolutionary processes involving struggle in nature. Drawing a strong distinction between the cosmic process of evolution and the social process of ethical development, he argued in Evolution and Ethics *(1893) that human ethical progress occurs through combating the cosmic process.*

■ What does Huxley mean by the "cosmic process"? Why does he equate "social progress" with the "ethical process"? In this passage, does Huxley present human society as part of nature or as something that may be separate from nature?

Men in society are undoubtedly subject to the cosmic process. As among other animals, multiplication goes on without cessation, and involves severe competition for the means of support. The struggle for existence tends to eliminate those less fitted to adapt themselves to the circumstances of their existence. The strongest, the most self-assertive, tend to tread down the weaker. But the influence of the cosmic process on the evolution of society is the greater the more rudimentary its civilization. Social progress means a checking of the cosmic process at every step and the substitution for it of another, which may be called the ethical process; the end of which is not the survival of those who may happen to be the fittest, in respect of the whole of the conditions which obtain, but of those who are ethically the best.

As I have already urged, the practice of that which is ethically best—what we call goodness or virtue—involves a course of conduct which, in all respects, is opposed to that which leads to success in the cosmic struggle for existence. In place of ruthless self-assertion it demands self-restraint; in place of thrusting aside, or treading down, all competitors, it requires that the individual shall not merely respect, but shall help his fellows; its influence is directed, not so much to the survival of the fittest, as to the fitting of as many as possible to survive. It repudiates the gladiatorial theory of existence.

It is from neglect of these plain considerations that the fanatical individualism of our time attempts to apply the analogy of cosmic nature to society. . . .

Let us understand, once for all, that the ethical progress of society depends, not on imitating the cosmic process, still less in running away from it, but in combating it.

From T. H. Huxley, *Evolution and Ethics* (London: Macmillan & Co., 1893), as quoted in Franklin L. Baumer, *Main Currents of Western Thought: Readings in Western European Intellectual History from the Middle Ages to the Present*, 3rd ed., rev. (New York: Alfred A. Knopf, 1970), pp. 561–562.

CHRISTIANITY AND THE CHURCH UNDER SIEGE

The nineteenth century was one of the most difficult periods in the history of the organized Christian churches. Many European intellectuals left the faith. The secular, liberal nation-states attacked the influence of the church. The expansion of population and the growth of cities challenged its organizational capacity. Yet during all of this turmoil, the Protestant and Catholic churches remained popular.

INTELLECTUAL SKEPTICISM

The intellectual attack on Christianity challenged its historical credibility, its scientific accuracy, and its morality. The philosophes of the Enlightenment had delighted in pointing out contradictions in the Bible. The historical scholarship of the nineteenth century brought new issues to the foreground.

History   In 1835, David Friedrich Strauss (1808–1874) published *The Life of Jesus*, in which he questioned whether the Bible provides any genuine historical evidence about Jesus. Strauss contended the story of Jesus is a myth that arose from the particular social and intellectual conditions of first-century Palestine. Jesus' character and life represent the aspirations of the people of that time and place, rather than events that actually occurred. Other authors also published skeptical examinations of the life of Jesus.

During the second half of the century, scholars such as Julius Wellhausen (1844–1918) in Germany, Ernst Renan (1823–1892) in France, and William Robertson Smith (1847–1894) in Great Britain contended that human authors had written and revised the books of the Bible with the problems of Jewish society and politics in mind. The Bible was not an inspired book, but had, like the Homeric epics, been written by normal human beings in a primitive society. This questioning of the historical validity of the Bible caused more literate men and women to lose faith in Christianity than any other single cause.

Science   Science also undermined Christianity. This blow was particularly cruel because many eighteenth-century writers had led Christians to believe the scientific examination of nature buttressed their faith. William Paley's (1743–1805) *Natural Theology* (1802) and books by numerous scientists had enshrined that belief. The geology of Charles Lyell (1797–1875) suggested the earth is much older than the biblical records contend. By looking to natural causes to explain floods, mountains, and valleys, Lyell removed the miraculous hand of God from the physical development of the earth. Darwin's theory cast doubt on the Creation. His ideas and those of other writers suggested that the moral nature of humankind can be explained without appeal to God. Finally, anthropologists, psychologists, and sociologists proposed that religious sentiments are just one more set of natural phenomena.

Morality   Other intellectuals questioned the morality of Christianity. The issue of immoral biblical stories was again raised. The morality of the Old Testament God, his cruelty and unpredictability, did not fit well with the tolerant, rational values of liberals. They also wondered about the morality of the New Testament God, who would sacrifice for his own satisfaction the only perfect being ever to walk the earth. Many of the clergy began to wonder if they could preach doctrines they felt to be immoral.

From another direction, writers like Friedrich Nietzsche (1844–1900) in Germany portrayed Christianity as a religion that glorified weakness rather than the strength life required. Christianity demanded a useless and debilitating sacrifice of the flesh and spirit, rather than heroic living and daring. Nietzsche once observed, "War and courage have accomplished more great things than love of neighbor."[2]

These skeptical currents created a climate in which Christianity lost much of its intellectual respectability. Fewer educated people joined the clergy. Many found they could live with little or no reference to Christianity. The secularism of everyday life proved as harmful to the faith as the direct attacks. This situation was especially prevalent in the cities, which were growing faster than the capacity of the churches to meet the challenge. Whole generations of the urban poor grew up with little or no experience of the church as an institution or of Christianity as a religious faith.

CONFLICT BETWEEN CHURCH AND STATE

The secular state of the nineteenth century clashed with both the Protestant and the Roman Catholic churches. Liberals disliked the dogma and the political privileges of the established churches. National states were often suspicious of the supranational character of the Roman Catholic Church. The primary area of conflict between the state and the churches, however, was education. Previously, most education in Europe had taken place in church schools. The churches feared that future generations would emerge from the new state-financed schools without any religious teaching. From 1870 through the turn of the century, all the major countries debated religious education.

Great Britain   In Great Britain, the Education Act of 1870 provided for state-supported schools run by elected school boards, whereas earlier the government had given small grants to religious schools. The new schools were to be built in areas where the religious denominations did not provide satisfactory education. There was rivalry both between the Anglican church and the state and between the Anglican church and the Nonconformist denominations—that is, those Protestant denominations that were not part of the Church of England. All the churches opposed improvements in education because these increased the costs of church schools. In the Education Act of 1902, the government provided state support for both religious and

[2]Walter Kaufmann, ed. and trans., *The Portable Nietzsche* (New York: Viking, 1967), p. 159.

nonreligious schools, but imposed the same educational standards on each.

France The British conflict was calm compared with that in France, which had a dual system of Catholic and public schools. Under the Falloux Law of 1850, the local priest provided religious education in the public schools. The conservative French Catholic Church and the Third French Republic loathed each other. Between 1878 and 1886, a series of educational laws sponsored by Jules Ferry (1832–1893) replaced religious instruction in the public schools with civic training. The number of public schools was expanded, and members of religious orders could no longer teach in them. After the Dreyfus affair, the French Catholic Church again paid a price for its reactionary politics. The Radical government of Pierre Waldeck-Rousseau (1846–1904), drawn from pro-Dreyfus groups, suppressed the religious orders. In 1905, the Napoleonic Concordat was terminated, and church and state were separated.

Germany and the *Kulturkampf* The most extreme church-state conflict occurred in Germany during the 1870s. At unification, the German Catholic hierarchy wanted freedom for the churches guaranteed in the constitution. Bismarck left the matter to the federal states, but he soon felt the Roman Catholic Church and the Catholic Center Party threatened the unity of the German Empire. In 1870 and 1871, he removed the clergy from overseeing local education in Prussia and set education under state direction. This secularization of education represented the beginning of a concerted attack on the Catholic Church in Germany.

The "May Laws" of 1873, which applied to Prussia, but not to the entire German Empire, required priests to be educated in German schools and universities and to pass state examinations. The state could veto the appointments of priests. The legislation abolished the disciplinary power of the pope and the church over the clergy and transferred it to the state. Many of the clergy refused to obey these laws, and by 1876, Bismarck had either arrested or expelled all Catholic bishops from Prussia.

In the end, Bismarck's *Kulturkampf* ("cultural struggle") against the Catholic Church failed. By the end of the 1870s, he abandoned his attack. He had gained state control of education and civil laws governing marriage only at the price of provoking Catholic resentment against the German state. The *Kulturkampf* was probably his greatest blunder.

AREAS OF RELIGIOUS REVIVAL

The German Catholic resistance to the intrusions of the secular state illustrates the continuing vitality of Christianity during this period of intellectual and political hardship for the church. In Great Britain, both the Anglican church and the Nonconformist denominations expanded and raised vast sums for new churches and schools. In Ireland, the 1870s saw a Catholic devotional revival. In France, after the defeat by Prussia, priests organized special pilgrimages to shrines for thousands of penitents who believed France had been defeated because of their sins. The cult of the miracle of Lourdes grew during these years. Churches of all denominations gave more attention to the urban poor.

In effect, the last half of the nineteenth century witnessed the final great effort to Christianize Europe. It was well organized, well led, and well financed. It failed only because the population of Europe had outstripped the resources of the churches. The vitality of the churches accounts, in part, for the intense hostility of their enemies.

THE ROMAN CATHOLIC CHURCH AND THE MODERN WORLD

The most striking feature of Christian religious revival was the resilience of the papacy. The brief hope for a liberal pontificate from Pope Pius IX (r. 1846–1878) vanished when he fled the turmoil in Rome in November 1848. In the 1860s, embittered by the process of Italian unification, he launched a counteroffensive against liberalism. In 1864, he issued the *Syllabus of Errors*, which set the Catholic Church squarely against contemporary science, philosophy, and politics.

In 1869, the pope summoned the First Vatican Council. The next year, through the political manipulations of the pontiff and against opposition from many bishops, the council promulgated the dogma of **papal infallibility** when speaking officially on matters of faith and morals. No earlier pope had asserted such centralized authority within the church. The First Vatican Council ended in 1870, when Italian troops occupied Rome at the outbreak of the Franco-Prussian War. Thereafter the territory of the papacy was limited to the Vatican City, and the papacy made no formal accommodation to the Italian state until 1929. Pius IX and many other Roman Catholics believed the Catholic Church could only sustain itself in the modern world of nation-states with large electorates by centering the authority of the church in the papacy itself. The spiritual authority of the papacy became a substitute for its lost political and temporal authority.

Pius IX was succeeded by Leo XIII (r. 1878–1903). Leo, who was sixty-eight years old at the time of his election, sought to make accommodations to the modern age and to address its great social questions. He looked to the philosophy of Thomas Aquinas (1225–1274) to reconcile the claims of faith and reason.

Leo's most important pronouncement on public issues was the encyclical *Rerum Novarum* (1891). In that document, he defended private property, religious education, and religious control of the marriage laws, and he condemned socialism and Marxism, but he also declared that employers should treat their employees justly, pay them proper wages, and permit them to organize labor unions. The pope supported laws to protect work-ers and urged that modern society be organized in corporate groups that would include people from various classes who would cooperate according to Christian principles. The corporate society, based on medieval social organization, was to be an alternative to both socialism and competitive capitalism. On the basis of Leo XIII's pronouncements, democratic Catholic political parties and Catholic trade unions were founded throughout Europe. (See "Leo XII Considers the Social Question in European Politics," page 804.)

His successor Pius X (r. 1903–1914) hoped to resist modern thought and restore traditional devotional life. Between 1903 and 1907, he condemned Catholic modernism, a movement of modern biblical criticism within the church, and in 1910 he required all priests to take an anti-Modernist oath. The struggle between Catholicism and modern thought was resumed.

A CLOSER LOOK

Conflict Between Church and State in Germany
The conflict between the German imperial government and the German Roman Catholic Church was among the most intense church-state encounters of the late nineteenth century. Here the tumultuous event is somewhat trivialized as Bismarck and the Pope are portrayed attempting to checkmate each other.

The chess game is intended to illustrate how Bismarck sought to remove major German church leaders from public life.

The Pope has fewer and fewer pieces on the board. Those Bismarck has captured have been placed in the box on the left denoted by an indistinct German word suggesting imprisonment. The German government had sent some Catholic clergy to prison.

The chess piece in the Pope's hand is called *Encyclical*, indicating the official statement that the Pope could issue against the German government.

Bildarchiv Preussischer Kulturbesitz

LEO XIII CONSIDERS THE SOCIAL QUESTION IN EUROPEAN POLITICS

In his 1891 encyclical Rerum Novarum, *Pope Leo XIII provided the Catholic Church's answer to secular calls for social reforms. The pope denied the socialist claim that class conflict is the natural state of affairs. He urged employers to seek just and peaceful relations with workers.*

■ *How does Leo XIII reject the concept of class conflict? What responsibilities does he assign to the rich and to the poor? Are the responsibilities of the two classes equal? What kinds of social reform might emerge from these ideas?*

The great mistake that is made in the matter now under consideration is to possess oneself of the idea that class is naturally hostile to class; that rich and poor are intended by Nature to live at war with one another. So irrational and so false is this view that the exact contrary is the truth. . . . Each requires the other; capital cannot do without labour, nor labour without capital. Mutual agreement results in pleasantness and good order; perpetual conflict necessarily produces confusion and outrage. Now, in preventing such strife as this, and in making it impossible, the efficacy of Christianity is marvelous and manifold . . . . Religion teaches the labouring man and the workman to carry out honestly and well all equitable agreements freely made; never to injure capital, or to outrage the person of an employer; never to employ violence in representing his own cause, or to engage in riot or disorder; and to have nothing to do with men of evil principles, who work upon the people with artful promises and raise hopes which usually end in disaster and in repentance when too late. Religion teaches the rich man and the employer that their work people are not their slaves; that they must respect in every man his dignity as a man and as a Christian; that labour is nothing to be ashamed of, if we listen to right reason and to Christian philosophy, but is an honourable employment, enabling a man to sustain his life in an upright and creditable way; and that it is shameful and inhuman to treat men like chattels to make money by, or to look upon them merely as so much muscle or physical power. Thus, again, Religion teaches that, as among the workman's concerns are Religion herself and things spiritual and mental, the employer is bound to see that he has time for the duties of piety; that he be not exposed to corrupting influences and dangerous occasions; and that he be not led away to neglect his home and family or to squander his wages. Then, again, the employer must never tax his work people beyond their strength, nor employ them in work unsuited to their sex or age. His great and principal obligation is to give every one that which is just.

As quoted in F. S. Nitti, *Catholic Socialism*, trans. by Mary Mackintosh (London: S. Sonnenschein, 1895), p. 409.

ISLAM AND LATE-NINETEENTH-CENTURY EUROPEAN THOUGHT

The few European thinkers who wrote about Islam in the late nineteenth century discussed it using the same scientific and naturalistic scholarly methods they applied to Christianity and Judaism. They interpreted Islam as a historical phenomenon without any reference to the supernatural, and the Qur'an received the same kind of critical historical analysis that was being directed toward the Bible.

Islam, like the other great world religions, was seen as a product of a particular culture. In the works of scholars such as the influential French writer Ernest Renan, Islam was, like Judaism, a manifestation of the ancient Semitic mentality, which had given rise to a powerful monotheistic vision. Renan, and sociologists such as Max Weber, also dismissed Islam as a religion and culture incapable of developing science and closed to new ideas.

However, Renan's views were opposed in a French journal by Jamal al-din Al-Afghani

(1839–1897), an Egyptian intellectual, who argued that over time Islam, which had arisen 600 years after Christianity, would eventually produce cultures as modern as those in Europe. Al-Afghani was one of the rare Islamic writers who directly contested a European thinker.

The European racial and cultural outlooks that denigrated nonwhite peoples and their civilizations were also directed toward the Arab world. European authors who championed white racial superiority looked to India and the Aryan civilization that was supposed to have risen there and later influenced northern European life as the source of Europe's cultural superiority.

Christian missionaries reinforced these anti-Islamic attitudes. They blamed Islam for Arab economic backwardness, for mistreating women, and for condoning slavery. They also often came into conflict with Islamic religious authorities. Because the penalty for abjuring Islam is death, the missionaries made few converts among Muslims. So they turned their efforts to founding schools and hospitals, hoping these Christian foundations would eventually lead some Muslims to Christianity. Few Muslims converted, but these institutions did educate young Arabs in Western science and medicine, and many of their students became leaders in the Middle East. Eventually, as missionary families came to live for long periods of time among Arabs, they became more sympathetic to Arab political aspirations.

Within the Islamic world, and especially in the decaying Ottoman Empire, as political leaders continued to champion Western scientific education and technology, they confronted a variety of responses from religious thinkers. Some of these thinkers sought to combine modern thought with Islam. For example, the Salafi, or the salafiyya movement, believed there was no inherent contradiction between science and Islam. They believed Muhammad had wisely and properly addressed the issues of his day, and a reformed Islamic faith could do so again. The Arab world should cease imitating the West and modernize itself on the basis of a pure, restored Islamic faith. The Salafi emphasized a rational reading of the Qur'an and saw Ottoman decline as the result of Muslim religious error. This outlook, which had originally sought to reconcile Islam with the modern world, eventually led many Muslims in the twentieth century to oppose Western influence.

Other Islamic religious leaders simply rejected the West and modern thought. They included the Mahdist movement in Sudan, the Sanussiya in Libya, and the Wahhabi movement in the Arabian peninsula. Such religious-based opposition was strongest in those portions of the Middle East

where the European presence was least direct, which is to say outside of Morocco, Algeria, Egypt, and Tunisia, which for all intents and purposes were under the control of Western powers by 1900, and Turkey, where Ottoman leaders had long been deeply involved with the West.

TOWARD A TWENTIETH-CENTURY FRAME OF MIND

The last quarter of the nineteenth century and the first decade of the twentieth century were the crucible of modern Western thought. Philosophers, scientists, psychologists, and artists began to portray physical reality, human nature, and society in ways different from those of the past. Their new concepts challenged the major presuppositions of mid-nineteenth-century science, rationalism, liberalism, and bourgeois morality.

SCIENCE: THE REVOLUTION IN PHYSICS

The changes in the scientific worldview originated within the scientific community itself. By the late 1870s, discontent existed over the excessive realism of mid-century science. It was thought that many scientists believed their mechanistic models, solid atoms, and absolute time and space actually described the real universe.

In 1883, Ernst Mach (1838–1916) published *The Science of Mechanics*, in which he urged that scientists consider their concepts descriptive not of the physical world, but of the sensations the scientific observer experiences. Scientists could describe only the sensations, not the physical world that underlay those sensations. In line with Mach, the French scientist Henri Poincaré (1854–1912) urged that the theories of scientists be regarded as hypothetical constructs of the human mind rather than as true descriptions of nature. In 1911, Hans Vaihinger (1852–1933) suggested the concepts of science be considered "as if" descriptions of the physical world. By World War I, few scientists believed they could portray the "truth" about physical reality. Rather, they saw themselves as recording the observations of instruments and as offering useful hypothetical or symbolic models of nature.

X Rays and Radiation Discoveries in the laboratory paralleled the philosophical challenge to nineteenth-century science. With those discoveries, the comfortable world of supposedly "complete" nineteenth-century physics vanished forever. In December 1895, Wilhelm Roentgen (1845–1923) published a paper on his discovery of X rays, a form of energy that penetrated various opaque materials. Major steps in the exploration of radioactivity followed within months of the publication of his paper.

In 1896, Henri Becquerel (1852–1908) discovered that uranium emitted a similar form of energy. The next year, J. J. Thomson (1856–1940), at Cambridge University, formulated the theory of the electron. The interior world of the atom had become a new area for human exploration. In 1902, Ernest Rutherford (1871–1937) explained the cause of radiation through the disintegration of the atoms of radioactive materials. Shortly thereafter, he speculated on the immense store of energy present in the atom.

Theories of Quantum Energy, Relativity, and Uncertainty   The discovery of radioactivity and discontent with the existing mechanical models led to revolutionary theories in physics. In 1900, Max Planck (1858–1947) pioneered the articulation of the quantum theory of energy, according to which energy is a series of discrete quantities, or packets, rather than a continuous stream. In 1905, Albert Einstein (1879–1955) published his first epoch-making papers on **relativity** in which he contended that time and space exist not separately, but rather as a combined continuum. Moreover, the measurement of time and space depends on the observer as well as on the entities being measured.

In 1927, Werner Heisenberg (1901–1976) set forth his uncertainty principle, according to which the behavior of subatomic particles is a matter of statistical probability rather than of exactly determinable cause and effect. Much that had seemed unquestionable about the physical universe had now become ambiguous.

The mathematical complexity of twentieth-century physics meant science would rarely again be successfully popularized. At the same time, through applied technology and further research in chemistry, physics, and medicine, science affected daily living more than ever before. Scientists from the late nineteenth century onward became the most successful group of Western intellectuals in gaining the financial support of governments and private institutions for the pursuit of their research. They did so by relating the success of science to the economic progress, military security, and the health of their nations. Science, through research, medicine, and technological change, has thus affected modern life more significantly than any other intellectual activity.

LITERATURE: REALISM AND NATURALISM

Between 1850 and 1914, the moral certainties of middle-class Europeans changed no less radically than their concepts of the physical universe. The

Marie Curie (1869–1934) and Pierre Curie (1859–1906) were two of the most important figures in the advance of physics and chemistry. Marie was born in Poland but worked in France for most of her life. She is credited with the discovery of radium, for which she was awarded the Nobel Prize in Chemistry in 1911.   Ullstein Bilderdienst

realist movement in literature portrayed the hypocrisy, brutality, and the dullness that underlay bourgeois life. The **realist** and **naturalist** writers brought scientific objectivity and observation to their work. By using the mid-century cult of science so vital to the middle class, they confronted readers with the harsh realities of life. Realism rejected the romantic idealization of nature, the poor, love, and polite society. Realist novelists portrayed the dark side of life, almost, some people thought, for its own sake.

Earlier writers, including Charles Dickens (1812–1870) and Honoré de Balzac (1799–1850), had portrayed the cruelty of industrial life and of a society based on money. Other authors, such as George Eliot (born Mary Ann Evans, 1819–1880), paid close attention to the details of her characters. These authors' work had, however, included imagination and artistry. A better morality was possible through Christian or humane values or, for Eliot, through an appreciation of humanity arising from Auguste Comte's thought.

The major figures of late-century realism examined the dreary and unseemly side of life without being certain whether a better life was possible. In good Darwinian fashion, they portrayed human beings as subject to the passions, the materialistic determinism, and the pressures of the environment like any other animals. Most of them, however, also saw society itself as perpetuating evil.

Flaubert and Zola   Critics have often considered Gustave Flaubert's (1821–1880) *Madame Bovary* (1857), with its story of colorless provincial life and a woman's hapless search for love in and outside of marriage, as the first genuinely realistic novel. The work portrayed life without heroism, purpose, or even civility.

The author who turned realism into a movement, however, was Emile Zola (1840–1902). He found artistic inspiration in Claude Bernard's (1813–1878) *Introduction to the Study of Experimental Medicine* (1865). Zola argued that he could write an experimental novel in which he would observe and report the characters and their actions as the scientist might relate a laboratory experiment. He once declared, "I have simply done on living bodies the work of analysis which surgeons perform on corpses."[3] He believed absolute physical and psychological determinism ruled human events in the way it did the physical world.

Between 1871 and 1893, Zola published twenty novels exploring subjects normally untouched by writers: alcoholism, prostitution, adultery, labor strife. He refused to turn his readers' thoughts away from the ugly aspects of life. Nothing in his purview received the light of hope or the aura of romance. Although critics faulted his taste and moralists condemned his subject matter, Zola enjoyed a worldwide following. As noted in Chapter 22, he took a leading role in the defense of Captain Dreyfus.

Ibsen and Shaw   The Norwegian playwright Henrik Ibsen (1828–1906) carried realism into the dramatic presentation of domestic life. He sought to strip away the illusory mask of middle-class morality. His most famous play is *A Doll's House* (1879). Its chief character, Nora, has a narrow-minded husband who cannot tolerate independence of character or thought on her part. She finally leaves him, slamming the door behind her. In *Ghosts* (1881), a respectable woman must deal with a son suffering from syphilis inherited from

Emile Zola of France was the master of the realistic novel.
Emile Zola, 1840–1902. Franzosischer Schriftsteller. Gemalde von Edouard Manet, 1868. Original: Paris, Louvre. Photograph: Lauros–Giraudon. © Bildarchiv Preussischer Kulturbesitz, Berlin

her husband. In *The Master Builder* (1892), an aging architect kills himself while trying to impress a young woman. Ibsen's works were controversial. He dared to attack sentimentality, the ideal of the female "angel of the house," and the cloak of respectability that hung so insecurely over the middle-class family.

One of Ibsen's greatest champions was the Irish writer George Bernard Shaw (1856–1950), who spent most of his life in England. Shaw defended Ibsen's work and made his own realistic onslaught against romanticism and false respectability. In *Mrs. Warren's Profession* (1893), he dealt with prostitution. In *Arms and the Man* (1894) and *Man and Superman* (1903), he heaped scorn on the romantic ideals of love and war, and in *Androcles and the Lion* (1913), he pilloried Christianity.

Realist writers believed it their duty to portray reality and the commonplace. In dissecting what they considered the "real" world, they helped change the moral perception of the good life. They refused to let public opinion dictate what they wrote about or how they treated their subjects. By presenting their audiences with unmentionable subjects, they sought to remove the veneer of hypocrisy that had forbidden such discussion. They hoped to destroy illusions and compel the

[3]Quoted in George J. Becker, *Documents of Modern Literary Realism* (Princeton, NJ: Princeton University Press, 1963), p. 159.

public to face reality. That change in itself seemed good. Few of the realist writers who raised these problems posed solutions to them. They often left their readers unable to sustain old values and uncertain about where to find new ones.

MODERNISM IN LITERATURE

From the 1870s onward throughout Europe, a new multifaceted movement, usually called **modernism**, touched all the arts. Like realism, modernism was critical of middle-class society and morality. Modernism, however, was not deeply concerned with social issues. What drove the modernists was a concern for the aesthetic or the beautiful. Across the spectrum of the arts, modernists tried to break the received forms and to create new forms. To many contemporaries, the new forms seemed formless. The English essayist Walter Pater (1839–1903) set the tone of the movement when he declared in 1877 that all art "constantly aspires to the condition of music."

Among the chief proponents of modernism in England were the members of the Bloomsbury Group, including authors Virginia Woolf (1882–1941) and Leonard Woolf (1880–1969), artists Vanessa Bell (1879–1961) and Duncan Grant (1885–1978), the historian and literary critic Lytton Strachey (1880–1932), and the economist John Maynard Keynes (1883–1946). These authors challenged the values of their Victorian forebearers. In *Eminent Victorians* (1918), Strachey used a series of biographical sketches to heap contempt on his subjects. Grant and Bell looked to the modern artists on the Continent for their models. **Keynesian economics** eventually challenged much of the structure of nineteenth-century economic theory. In both personal practice and theory, the Bloomsbury Group rejected what they regarded as the repressive sexual morality of their parents' generation.

No one charted these changing sensibilities with more eloquence than Virginia Woolf. Her novels, such as *Mrs. Dalloway* (1925) and *To the Lighthouse* (1927), portrayed individuals seeking to make their way in a world with most of the nineteenth-century social and moral certainties removed.

On the Continent, one of the major practitioners of modernism in literature was Marcel Proust (1871–1922). In his seven-volume novel *In Search of Time Past* (*A la Recherche du Temps Perdu*), published between 1913 and 1927, he adopted a stream-of-consciousness format that allowed him to explore his memories. He would concentrate on a single experience or object and then allow his mind to wander through all the thoughts and memories it

Virginia Woolf charted the changing sentiments of a world with most of the nineteenth-century social and moral certainties removed. In *A Room of One's Own*, quoted in the document selection on p. 823, she also challenged some of the accepted notions of feminist thought, asking whether women writers should bring to their work any separate qualities they possessed as women, and concluding that men and women writers should strive to share each other's sensibilities.   Hulton Archive Photos/Getty Images, Inc.

evoked. In Germany, Thomas Mann (1875–1955), through a long series of novels, the most famous of which were *Buddenbrooks* (1901) and *The Magic Mountain* (1924), explored both the social experience of middle-class Germans and how they dealt with the intellectual heritage of the nineteenth century. In *Ulysses* (1922), James Joyce (1882–1941), who was born in Ireland, but spent much of his life on the Continent, transformed not only the novel, but also the structure of the paragraph.

Modernism in literature arose before World War I and flourished after the war, nourished by the turmoil and social dislocation it created. The war removed many of the old political structures and social expectations. After its appalling violence, readers found themselves much less shocked by

Marcel Proust's multivolume *In Search of Time Past*, (*A la Recherche du Temps Perdu*) which was published between 1913 and 1927, was one of the most significant modernist novels. © Bettmann/CORBIS

upheavals in literary forms and the moral content of novels and poetry.

THE COMING OF MODERN ART

The last quarter of the nineteenth century witnessed a series of new departures in Western art that transformed painting and later sculpture in a revolutionary manner that has continued to the present day.

Impressionism This fundamental change in European painting arose primarily in Paris. Two major characteristics marked this new style of painting. First, instead of portraying religious, mythological, and historical themes, painters began to depict modern life itself, focusing on the social life and leisured activities of the urban middle and lower middle classes. Second, many of these artists were fascinated with light, color, and the representation through painting itself of momentary, largely unfocused, visual experience whether of social life or of landscape. Contemporaries called these paintings *impressionistic* and considered them curious and artistically shocking when they were first displayed in Paris. During the twentieth century these paintings would become the most popular works visited in both European and American art museums.

The new paintings of modern life by the impressionists, including Edward Manet (1837–1883), Claude Monet (1840–1926), Camille Pissaro (1830–1903), Pierre-Auguste Renoir (1841–1919), and Edgar Degas (1834–1917), recorded Parisians attending cafés, dance halls, concerts, picnics, horse races, boating excursions, and beach parties. The backdrop for these works was Paris as it had been reconstructed under Napoleon III (r. 1852–1870) into a city of wide boulevards, parks, and places for middle-class leisure.

The sites included in these paintings allowed people from different classes to mix socially while pursuing a leisure activity. One such meeting place was the Folies-Bergère, a café/concert hall where patrons could enjoy a variety of popular entertainment, including singers, musicians, dancers, gymnasts, and animal shows. Paris had many such establishments, but the Folies-Bergère was one of the largest and most expensive.

In *A Bar at the Folies-Bergère*, first displayed in 1882, Edouard Manet painted a young barmaid standing behind a table holding liquor and wine bottles and in front of a large mirror that reflects the activity occurring in front of her. (Manet actually painted this picture in his studio with a woman who worked as a barmaid posing as his model.) The table, together with its bottles, fruit, vase, and flowers, constitutes a formal still-life composition, but unlike traditional still lifes, this one shows objects of commercial consumption in a setting where leisure itself is commercially consumed. The mirror reflects the table and its contents, the music hall itself with the legs of a trapeze artist appearing in the top left corner, the audience for the performance, the back of the barmaid, and a man she is serving. Manet took great pains to paint the interior light of the hall, which appears to be coming from the newly invented electric light bulbs.

One of the great questions of the painting is the meaning and expression of the barmaid. The hubbub and restlessness of the reflected audience and the noise and excitement of the performance do not register on her face. The barmaid's expression may suggest the anonymity of so many social encounters in modern urban life. Because it was commonly assumed in Paris that many barmaids and shop girls needed to supplement their meager wages through prostitution, scholars have suggested that the woman in this painting, like the liquor and the fruit, is simply another object of commerce.

Post-impressionism By the 1880s, the impressionists had had an enormous impact on contemporary art. Their work was followed by that of

Édouard Manet (1832–1883), *A Bar at the Folies-Bergère*, 1882.   Oil on canvas, 96 × 130 cm.
Signed dated. Courtauld gift 1932. Courtauld Institute Gallery, London

younger artists who drew upon their techniques but also attempted often to relate the achievement of impressionism to earlier artistic traditions. Form and structure rather than the effort to record the impression of the moment played a major role in their work. This later group of artists has been described as ***post-impressionists***, though they should best be understood as a continuation of the previous movement rather than a reaction against it. The chief figures associated with postimpressionism are Georges Seurat, Paul Cezanne, Vincent Van Gogh, and Paul Gauguin.

Georges Seurat (1859–1891) was a young French painter who read extensively in contemporary scientific works about light, color, and vision. These studies led him to a technique of painting known as pointillism whereby the artist applied small dots or points of paint to the canvas. Through this laborious process he hoped to decompose colors into their basic units leaving it to the eye of the viewer to mix those dots into the desired color or shade of color. Seurat is counted among the first postimpressionists because he saw himself bring-

ing the new painting of modern life back into touch with earlier artistic traditions. He once described his painting *A Sunday Afternoon on the Island of the Grande Jatte (1884–1886)* as "a new version of Phidias's Panathenaic procession [on the Parthenon frieze in Athens], with 'the moderns moving about . . . friezelike, stripped down to their essentials.'"[4]

Seurat also introduced implicit social commentary into the previous impressionist portrayal of leisured activity. The Grande Jatte was an island in the Seine beyond Paris where on Sundays Parisians would gather. In Seurat's painting, shadows in the foreground suggest that all is not entirely sunny for the largely middle-class afternoon crowd. The boatman smoking the pipe indicates a brooding working-class presence in the foreground of their lives. All of the figures resemble the mannequins that appeared in the fashionable new Paris department

[4]Quoted in T. J. Clark, *The Painting of Modern Life: Paris in the Art of Manet and His Followers* (Princeton: Princeton University Press, 1984), p. 266.

stores. Except for the one child who is running, the figures appear almost mechanical, like the manufacturing processes that produced their clothing and their other domestic consumer goods. These figures, compared by one contemporary critic to lead soldiers, stand bored and perhaps puzzled by their situation of comfort, leisure, and ease.

In reaction to the impressionists' fascination with light, Paul Cezanne (1839–1906), working largely in isolation, attempted to bring form and solidity back into his paintings of still life and of the landscape of Provence. Displaying a new sensitivity to non-Western peoples and their art, Paul Gauguin (1848–1903) produced works portraying peoples living in the South Pacific.

Georges Seurat, "A Sunday Afternoon on the Island of La Grande Jatte," 1884–86. Oil on Canvas. 6'9½ × 10'1¼ (2.07 × 3.08 m). Helen Birch Bartlett Memorial Collection. Photograph © 2005, The Art Institute of Chicago. All Rights Reserved

Other artists collected African masks or studied such objects in the anthropological museum in Paris. Whereas Cezanne had given artists a new way of looking at and then shaping reality, the art of Africa and of the Pacific gave artists examples of remarkable works that had no relationship to the long-standing Western artistic tradition.

Cubism   The single most important new departure in early-twentieth-century Western art was *cubism*, a term first coined to describe the paintings of Pablo Picasso (1881–1973) and Georges Braque (1882–1963).

For over 500 years, painting in the West had sought to reproduce the appearance of reality. From the time of the Renaissance, paintings functioned as a kind of window on an artistic depiction of the real world. Even the Impressionists and Post-Impressionists essentially stood in this tradition.

Beginning in 1907, Picasso and Braque rejected the idea of a painting as constituting a window onto the real world. Rather, they saw painting as an autonomous realm of art itself with no purpose beyond itself. Braque once commented, "The painter thinks in forms and colors. The aim is not to reconstitute an anecdotal fact but to constitute a pictorial fact. . . . One does not imitate the appearance; the appearance is the result."[5] Echoing the art of ancient Egypt, medieval primitives, and Africa, Picasso and Braque represented only two dimensions in their painting. They made little or no effort to go beyond the flatness of the surface itself. They at-

tempted to include at one time on a single surface as many different perspectives, angles, or views of the object painted as possible. "Reality" was the construction of their experience of multiple perceptions. The space in the paintings was literally the space of two dimensions filled with geometric shapes as well as geometric voids. The shapes stand dismantled, set in new and usually unexpected positions, communicating a sense of dislocation.

Braque's still life *Violin and Palette* (1909 and 1910) represents the cubist determination to present "a new, completely non-illusionistic and non-imitative method of depicting the visual world."[6] Various shapes seem to flow into other shapes. Portions of the violin and of the palette are recognizable, but as shapes, not as objects in and of themselves. The violin appears at one moment from a host of perspectives, but the violin has interest only in its relationship to the other shapes of color in the painting. As we move to the right of the painting, no elements reproduce a recognizable object. The painting exists as its own world and as the construction of the artist. Throughout the painting Braque is literally taking apart the violin and other objects, so that he and the viewer can analyze them. As one commentator explained in 1919 in regard to cubism, "[T]he true picture will constitute an individual object, which will possess an existence of its own apart from the subject that has inspired it."[7] The elements of the palette, the

[5]Quoted in Max Kozloff, *Cubism/Futurism* (New York: Charterhouse, 1973), p. 11.

[6]Edward F. Fry, *Cubism* (New York: McGraw-Hill, 1966), p. 38.
[7]Maurice Raynal, "Some Intentions of Cubism," 1919, as quoted in Fry, *Cubism*, p. 153.

Georges Braque, *Violin and Palette (Violon et Palette)*, 1909–1910.   Autumn 1909. Oil on canvas. 91.7 × 42.8 cm (36¹/₈ × 16⁷/₈ inches). Solomon R. Guggenheim Museum, New York, 54.1412. Photograph by Lee B. Ewing © The Solomon R. Guggenheim Foundation, New York. © 2004 Artists Rights Society (ARS), New York/ADAGP, Paris

modernists in literature had reshaped the portrayal of social and moral experience and the new physics had reconceptualized nature itself.

FRIEDRICH NIETZSCHE AND THE REVOLT AGAINST REASON

During the second half of the century, philosophers began to question the adequacy of rational thinking to address the human situation. No writer better exemplified this new attitude than the German philosopher Friedrich Nietzsche (1844–1900). His books remained unpopular until late in his life, when his brilliance had deteriorated into insanity. He was wholly at odds with the values of the age and attacked Christianity, democracy, nationalism, rationality, science, and progress. He sought less to change values than to probe their sources in the human character. He wanted not only to tear away the masks of respectable life, but to explore how human beings made such masks.

His first important work was *The Birth of Tragedy* (1872) in which he urged that the nonrational aspects of human nature are as important and noble as the rational characteristics. He insisted on the positive function of instinct and ecstasy in human life. To limit human activity to strictly rational behavior was to impoverish human life. In this work, Nietzsche regarded Socrates as one of the major contributors to Western decadence because of the Greek philosopher's appeal for rationality. In Nietzsche's view, the strength for the heroic life and the highest artistic achievement arises from sources beyond rationality.

In later works, such as the prose poem *Thus Spake Zarathustra* (1883), Nietzsche criticized democracy and Christianity. Both would lead only to the mediocrity of sheepish masses. He announced the death of God and proclaimed the coming of the *Overman* (Übermensch), who would embody heroism and greatness. The term was frequently interpreted as some mode of superman or super race, but such was not Nietzsche's intention. He was critical of contemporary racism and anti-Semitism. He sought a return to the heroism that he associated with Greek life in the Homeric age. He thought the values of Christianity and of bourgeois morality prevented humankind from achieving life on a heroic level.

Two of Nietzsche's most profound works are *Beyond Good and Evil* (1886) and *The Genealogy of Morals* (1887). Both are difficult books. Nietzsche sought to discover not what is good and what is evil, but the social and psychological sources of the judgment of good and evil. He de-

violin, and the notes of a musical score floating on folded paper tents hold interest and meaning in this painting only because they are in the painting, not because they are imitations of a violin, a palette, or a musical score.

The cubist painters sought to redirect the artistic portrayal of reality in the same manner that

DATES OF MAJOR WORKS OF FICTION

1857 Flaubert, *Madame Bovary*
1877 Zola, *L'Assommoir*
1879 Ibsen, *A Doll's House*
1880 Zola, *Nana*
1881 Ibsen, *Ghosts*
1892 Ibsen, *The Master Builder*
1893 Shaw, *Mrs. Warren's Profession*
1894 Shaw, *Arms and the Man*
1901 Mann, *Buddenbrooks*
1903 Shaw, *Man and Superman*
1913 Shaw, *Androcles and the Lion*
1913 Proust, first volume of *In Search of Time Past*
1922 Joyce, *Ulysses*
1924 Mann, *The Magic Mountain*
1925 Woolf, *Mrs. Dalloway*
1927 Woolf, *To the Lighthouse*

clared, "There are no moral phenomena at all, but only a moral interpretation of phenomena."[8] He dared to raise the question of whether morality itself was valuable: "We need a critique of moral values; the value of these values themselves must first be called in question."[9] In Nietzsche's view, morality was a human convention that had no independent existence. For Nietzsche, this discovery liberated human beings to create life-affirming values instead. Christianity, utilitarianism, and middle-class respectability could, in good conscience, be abandoned. Human beings could create a new moral order that would glorify pride, assertiveness, and strength rather than meekness, humility, and weakness.

In his appeal to feelings and emotions and in his questioning of the adequacy of rationalism, Nietzsche drew on the Romantic tradition. The kind of creative impulse that earlier Romantics had considered the gift of artists Nietzsche saw as the burden of all human beings. The character of the human situation that this philosophy urged on its contemporaries was that of an ever-changing flux in which nothing but change itself was permanent. Human beings had to forge from their own will and determination the values that were to exist in the world.

[8] *The Basic Writings of Nietzsche*, ed. and trans. by Walter Kaufman (New York: The Modern Library, 1968), p. 275.
[9] Kaufman, p. 456.

THE BIRTH OF PSYCHOANALYSIS

A determination to probe beneath the surface or public appearance united the major figures of late-nineteenth-century science, art, and philosophy. They sought to discern the undercurrents, tensions, and complexities that lay beneath the calm surfaces of hard atoms, respectable families, rationality, and social relationships. As a result of their theories and discoveries, educated Europeans could never again view the surface of life with complacency or even with much confidence. No intellectual development more exemplified this trend than psychoanalysis through the work of Sigmund Freud (1856–1939).

Development of Freud's Early Theories Freud was born into an Austrian Jewish family that settled in Vienna. He planned to become a lawyer, but soon moved to study physiology and medicine. In 1886, he opened his medical practice in Vienna, where he lived until the Nazis drove him out in 1938. Freud conducted all his research and writing from the base of his medical practice. His earliest medical interests had been psychic disorders, to which he sought to apply the critical method of science. In late 1885, he studied in Paris with Jean-Martin Charcot (1825–1893), who used hypnosis to treat hysteria. In Vienna, he collaborated with another physician, Josef Breuer (1842–1925), and in 1895, they published *Studies in Hysteria*.

In the mid-1890s, Freud abandoned hypnosis and allowed his patients to talk freely and spontaneously about themselves. He found that they associated their particular neurotic symptoms with experiences related to earlier experiences, going back to childhood. He also noted that sexual matters were significant in his patients' problems. For a time, he thought that perhaps sexual incidents during childhood accounted for their illnesses.

By 1897, however, Freud had rejected this view. In its place he formulated a theory of infantile sexuality, according to which sexual drives and energy already exist in infants and do not simply emerge at puberty. For Freud, human beings are sexual creatures from birth through adulthood. He thus questioned in the most radical manner the concept of childhood innocence. He also portrayed the little acknowledged matter of sexuality as one of the bases of mental order and disorder.

Freud's Concern with Dreams During the same decade, Freud also examined the psychic phenomena of dreams. Romantic writers had taken dreams seriously, but few psychologists had examined them scientifically. Freud believed the seemingly irrational content of dreams must have a reasonable, scientific explanation. His research led him to reconsider the general nature of the human mind. He concluded that dreams allow unconscious wishes, desires, and drives that had been excluded from everyday conscious life to enjoy freer play in the mind. "The dream," he wrote, "is the [disguised] fulfillment of a [suppressed, repressed] wish."[10] During the waking hours, the mind represses or censors certain wishes, which are as important to the individual's psychological makeup as conscious thought is. In fact, Freud argued, unconscious drives and desires contribute to conscious behavior. Freud developed these concepts and related them to his idea of infantile sexuality in his most important book, *The Interpretation of Dreams*, published in 1900.

Freud's Later Thought   In later books and essays, Freud developed a new model of the internal organization of the mind as an arena of struggle and conflict among three entities: the id, the superego, and the ego. The **id** consists of amoral, irrational, driving instincts for sexual gratification, aggression, and general physical and sensual pleasure. The **superego** embodies the external moral imperatives and expectations imposed on the personality by society and culture. The **ego** mediates between the impulses of the id and the asceticism of the superego and allows the personality to cope with the inner and outer demands of its existence. Consequently, everyday behavior displays the activity of the personality as its inner drives are partially repressed through the ego's coping with external moral expectations, as interpreted by the superego.

In his acknowledgment of the roles of instinct, will, dreams, and sexuality, Freud reflected the Romantic tradition of the nineteenth century. In other respects, however, he was a son of the Enlightenment. Like the philosophes, he was a realist who wanted human beings to live free of fear and illusions by rationally understanding themselves and their world. He saw the personalities of human beings as being determined by finite physical and mental forces in a finite world. He was hostile to religion and spoke of it as an illusion. Freud, like the writers of the eighteenth century, wished to see civilization and humane behavior prevail. More fully than those predecessors, however, he understood the immense sacrifice of instinctual drives required for rational civilized behavior. It has been a grave misreading of Freud to see him as urging humankind to thrust off all repression. He

In 1909 Freud and his then-devoted disciple Carl Jung visited Clark University in Worchester, Massachusetts, during Freud's only trip to the United States. Here Freud sits on the right holding a cane. Jung is sitting on the far left.   Archives of the History of American Psychology—The University of Akron. Courtesy Clark University, Special Collections

did indeed believe that excessive repression could lead to a mental disorder, but he also believed civilization and the survival of humankind required some repression of sexuality and aggression. Freud thought the sacrifice and struggle were worthwhile, but he was pessimistic about the future of civilization in the West.

Divisions in the Psychoanalytic Movement   By 1910, Freud had gathered around him a small, but able, group of disciples. Several of his early followers soon moved toward theories of which the master disapproved. The most important of these dissenters was Carl Jung (1875–1961), a Swiss whom for many years Freud regarded as his most promising student. Before World War I, the two men, however, had come to a parting of the ways. Jung questioned the primacy of sexual drives in forming personality and in contributing to mental disorder. He also put less faith in reason.

Jung believed the human subconscious contains inherited memories from previous generations. These collective memories, as well as the personal experience of an individual, constitute his or her soul. Jung regarded human beings in the twentieth century as alienated from these useful collective memories. In *Modern Man in Search of a Soul* (1933) and other works, Jung tended toward mysticism and saw positive values in religion. Freud was highly critical of most of Jung's work. If Freud's thought derived primarily from the Enlightenment, Jung's was more dependent on Romanticism.

By the 1920s, the psychoanalytic movement had become even more fragmented. Nonetheless, it in-

---

[10]*The Basic Writings of Sigmund Freud*, trans. by A. A. Brill (New York: The Modern Library, 1938), p. 235.

fluenced not only psychology, but also sociology, anthropology, religious studies, and literary theory. In recent years, psychoanalysis has confronted very considerable criticism. Whether or not it survives as a model for understanding human behavior, however, it profoundly influenced the intellectual life of the twentieth century.

RETREAT FROM RATIONALISM IN POLITICS

Nineteenth-century liberals and socialists agreed that rational analysis could discern the problems of society and prepare solutions. These thinkers felt that, once given the vote, individuals would behave according to their rational political self-interest. Education would improve the human condition. By 1900, these views had come under attack. Political scientists and sociologists painted politics as frequently irrational. Racial theorists questioned whether rationality and education could affect human society at all.

Weber   During this period, however, one major social theorist was impressed by the role of reason in human society. The German sociologist Max Weber (1864–1920) regarded the emergence of rationalism throughout society as the major development of human history. Such rationalization displayed itself in the rise of both scientific knowledge and bureaucratic organization.

Weber saw bureaucratization as the basic feature of modern social life. He used this view to oppose Marx's concept of the development of capitalism as the driving force in modern society. Bureaucratization involved the division of labor as each individual fit into a particular role in much larger organizations. Furthermore, Weber believed that in modern society people derive their own self-images and sense of personal worth from their positions in these organizations.

Weber also contended—again, in contrast to Marx—that noneconomic factors might account for major developments in human history. For example, in his best known essay, *The Protestant Ethic and the Spirit of Capitalism* (1905), Weber traced much of the rational character of capitalist enterprise to the ascetic religious doctrines of Puritanism. The Puritans, in his opinion, worked for worldly success less for its own sake than to assure themselves that they stood among the elect of God. The theory has generated historical research and debate from its publication to the present.

Theorists of Collective Behavior   In his emphasis on the individual and on the dominant role of rationality, Weber differed from many contemporary

social scientists, such as Gustave LeBon (1841–1931), Emile Durkheim (1858–1917), and Georges Sorel (1847–1922) in France, Vilfredo Pareto (1848–1923) in Italy, and Graham Wallas (1858–1932) in England. LeBon was a psychologist who explored the activity of crowds and mobs. He believed that crowds behave irrationally. In *Reflections on Violence* (1908), Sorel argued that people do not pursue rationally perceived goals but are led to action by collectively shared ideals. Durkheim and Wallas became deeply interested in the necessity of shared values and activities in a society. These elements, rather than a logical analysis of the social situation, bind human beings together. Instinct, habit, and affections, instead of reason, direct human social behavior. Besides playing down the function of reason in society, all of these theorists emphasized the role of collective groups in politics rather than that of the individual, formerly championed by liberals.

RACISM

The same tendencies to question or even to deny the constructive activity of reason in human affairs and to sacrifice the individual to the group manifested themselves in theories of race. **Racism** had long existed in Europe. Renaissance explorers had displayed prejudice against nonwhite peoples. Since at least the eighteenth century, biologists and anthropologists had classified human beings according to the color of their skin, their language, and their stage of civilization. After late-eighteenth-century linguistic scholars observed similarities between many of the European languages and Sanskrit, they postulated the existence of an ancient race called the Aryans, who had spoken the original language from which the rest derived. During the Romantic period, writers had called the different cultures of Europe races.

The debates over slavery in the European colonies and the United States had given further opportunity for the development of racial theory. In the late nineteenth century, however, race emerged as a single dominant explanation of the history and the character of large groups of people. What transformed racial thinking at the end of the century was its association with the biological sciences. The prestige associated with biology and science in general became transferred to racial thinking, whose advocates now claimed to possess a materialistic, scientific basis for their thought. They came to claim that racial science could support a hierarchy of superior and inferior races within Europe and among the various peoples outside Europe.

Gobineau Count Arthur de Gobineau (1816–1882), a reactionary French diplomat, enunciated the first important theory of race as the major determinant of human history. In his four-volume *Essay on the Inequality of the Human Races* (1853–1854), Gobineau portrayed the troubles of Western civilization as the result of the long degeneration of the original white Aryan race. He claimed it had unwisely intermarried with the inferior yellow and black races, thus diluting the greatness and ability that originally existed in its blood. Gobineau saw no way to reverse this degeneration. (See " Alexis de Tocqueville Forecasts the Danger of Gobineau's Racial Thought".)

Gobineau's essay remained little known for years. However, a growing literature by anthropologists and explorers spread racial thinking. In the wake of Darwin's theory, thinkers applied the concept of survival of the fittest to races and nations. The recognition of the animal nature of humankind made the racial idea all the more persuasive.

ALEXIS DE TOCQUEVILLE FORECASTS THE DANGER OF GOBINEAU'S RACIAL THOUGHT

Alexis de Tocqueville is best known for having written Democracy in America *(4 vols., 1835, 1840). He was also a major historian of the French Revolution, a politician, and an important commentator on the events and ideas of his time. He knew Arthur de Gobineau and read the first volume of the latter's* Essay on the Inequality of the Human Races *shortly after it was published in 1853. Tocqueville then wrote Gobineau a letter in which he sharply criticized the idea of the racial determination of human actions. Tocqueville also pointed to how dangerous it would be if the idea ever influenced the political life of nations with mass electorates.*

■ *Why does Tocqueville see Gobineau's idea as a kind of materialistic determinism? Why does he think Gobineau's views are wrong? Why does he see political danger in racial thinking?*

Your doctrine is rather a sort of fatalism, of predestination, if you wish, but at any rate, very different from that of St. Augustine, from the Jansenists, and from the Calvinists. . . . You continually speak about races regenerating or degenerating, losing, or acquiring through an infusion of new blood social capacities which they have not previously had. . . . I must frankly say that, to me, this sort of predestination is a close relative of the purest materialism. And be assured that should the masses, whose reasoning always follows the most beaten tracks, accept your doctrines, it would lead them straight from races to individuals and from social capacities to all sorts of potentialities. Whether the element of fatality should be introduced into the material order of things, or whether God willed to make different kinds of men so that He imposed special burdens of race on some, withholding from them a capacity for certain feelings, for certain thoughts, for certain habits, for certain qualities—all this has nothing to do with my own concern with the practical consequences of these philosophical doctrines. The consequence of both theories is that of a vast limitation, if not a complete abolition, of human liberty. Thus I confess that after having read your book I remain, as before, opposed in the extreme to your doctrines. I believe that they are probably quite false; I know that they are certainly very pernicious. Surely among the different families which compose the human race there exist certain tendencies, certain proper aptitudes resulting from thousands of different causes. But that these tendencies, that these capacities should be insuperable has not only never been proved, but no one will ever be able to prove it, since to do so one would need to know not only the past but also the future.

From Alexis de Tocqueville to Arthur de Gobineau, 17 November 1853, in Alexis de Tocqueville, *The European Revolution and Correspondence with Gobineau*, edited by J. Lukacs (Gloucester, MA: Peter Smith, 1968), pp. 227–228.

Chamberlain   At the close of the century, Houston Stewart Chamberlain (1855–1927), an Englishman who settled in Germany, drew together these strands of racial thought into the two volumes of his *Foundations of the Nineteenth Century* (1899). He championed the concept of biological determinism through race, but believed that through genetics the human race could be improved and even that a superior race could be developed. (See "H. S. Chamberlain Exalts the Role of Race".)

Chamberlain was anti-Semitic. He pointed to the Jews as the major enemy of European racial regeneration. Chamberlain's book and the works on which it drew aided the spread of anti-Semitism in European political life. Also in Germany, the writings of Paul de Lagarde (1827–1891) and Julius Langbehn (1851–1907) emphasized the supposed racial and cultural dangers posed by the Jews to German national life.

Late-Century Nationalism   Racial thinking was one part of a wider late-century movement toward more aggressive nationalism. Previously, nationalism had in general been a movement among European literary figures and liberals. The former had sought to develop what they regarded as the historically distinct qualities of particular national or ethnic literatures. The liberal nationalists had hoped to redraw the map of Europe to reflect ethnic boundaries. The drive for the unification of

H. S. CHAMBERLAIN EXALTS THE ROLE OF RACE

Houston Stewart Chamberlain's Foundations of the Nineteenth Century *(1899) was one of the most influential late-century works of racial thought. Chamberlain believed that most people in the world are racially mixed and this mixture weakens those human characteristics most needed for physical and moral strength. He also believed people who were assured of their racial purity could act with the most extreme self-confidence and arrogance. Chamberlain's views had a major influence on the Nazi Party in Germany and on others who wished to establish their alleged racial superiority for political purposes.*

■ *What does Chamberlain mean by "Race" in this passage? How, in his view, does race, as opposed to character or environment, determine human nature? How might a nationalist use these ideas?*

Nothing is so convincing as the consciousness of the possession of Race. The man who belongs to a distinct, pure race, never loses the sense of it. The guardian angel of his lineage is ever at his side, supporting him where he loses his foothold, warning him like the Socratic Daemon where he is in danger of going astray, compelling obedience, and forcing him to undertakings which, deeming them impossible, he would never have dared to attempt. Weak and erring like all that is human, a man of this stamp recognises himself, as others recognise him, by the sureness of his character, and by the fact that his actions are marked by a certain simple and peculiar greatness, which finds its explanation in his distinctly typical and superpersonal qualities. Race lifts a man above himself; it endows him with extraordinary—I might almost say supernatural—powers, so entirely does it distinguish him from the individual who springs from the chaotic jumble of peoples drawn from all parts of the world: and should this man of pure origin be perchance gifted above his fellows, then the fact of Race strengthens and elevates him on every hand, and he becomes a genius towering over the rest of mankind, not because he has been thrown upon the earth like a flaming meteor by a freak of nature, but because he soars heavenward like some strong and stately tree, nourished by thousands and thousands of roots—no solitary individual, but the living sum of untold souls striving for the same goal.

From Houston Stewart Chamberlain, *Foundations of the Nineteenth Century*, Vol. 1, trans. by John Lees (London: John Lane, 1912), p. 269.

Italy and Germany had been major causes, as had been the liberation of Poland from foreign domination. The various national groups of the Habsburg Empire had also sought emancipation from Austrian domination.

From the 1870s onward, however, nationalism became a movement with mass support, well-financed organizations, and political parties. Nationalists often redefined nationality in terms of race and blood. The new nationalism opposed the internationalism of both liberalism and socialism. The ideal of nationality was used to overcome the pluralism of class, religion, and geography. The nation replaced religion for many secularized people. It sometimes became a secular religion in the hands of state schoolteachers, who were replacing the clergy as the instructors of youth. Nationalism of this aggressive, racist variety became the most powerful ideology of the early twentieth century and would reemerge after the collapse of communism in the 1990s.

Some Europeans also used racial theory to support harsh, condescending treatment of colonial peoples in the late nineteenth and early twentieth centuries. They were convinced that white Europeans were racially superior to the peoples of color whom they governed and that these peoples would always be inferior to them. Similar racial theory also informed attitudes toward peoples of color in the West itself as was the case with the inferiority ascribed to African Americans and Native Americans in the United States.

ANTI-SEMITISM AND THE BIRTH OF ZIONISM

Political and racial anti-Semitism, which cast such dark shadows across the twentieth century, developed, in part, from the prevailing atmosphere of racial thought and the retreat from rationality in politics. Religious anti-Semitism dated from at least the Middle Ages. Since the French Revolution, West European Jews had gradually gained entry into civil life. Popular anti-Semitism, however, survived, with the Jewish community being identified with money and banking interests. During the last third of the century, as finance capitalism changed the economic structure of Europe, many non-Jewish Europeans threatened by the changes became hostile toward the Jewish community.

Anti-Semitic Politics   In Vienna, Mayor Karl Lueger (1844–1910) used anti-Semitism as a major attraction for his Christian Socialist Party. In Germany, the ultraconservative Lutheran chaplain

Adolf Stoecker (1835–1909) revived anti-Semitism. The Dreyfus affair in France focused a new hatred toward the Jews.

To this ugly atmosphere, racial thought contributed the belief that no matter to what extent Jews assimilated themselves into the culture of their country, their Jewishness—and thus their alleged danger to society—would remain. For racial thinkers, the problem of race was not in the character, but in the blood of the Jew. An important Jewish response to this new, rabid outbreak of anti-Semitism was the launching in 1896 of the **Zionist** movement to found a separate Jewish state. Its founder was the Austro-Hungarian Theodor Herzl (1860–1904).

Herzl's Response   The conviction in 1894 of Captain Dreyfus in France and the election of Karl Lueger in 1895 as mayor of Vienna, as well as personal experiences of discrimination, convinced Herzl that liberal politics and the institutions of the liberal state could not protect the Jews in Europe or ensure that they would be treated justly. In 1896, Herzl published *The Jewish State*, in which he called for a separate state in which all Jews might be assured of those rights and liberties that they

Theodor Herzl's visions of a Jewish state would eventually lead to the creation of the state of Israel in 1948.
CORBIS/Bettmann

should be enjoying in the liberal states of Europe. Furthermore, Herzl followed the tactics of late-century mass democratic politics by directing his appeal particularly to the poor Jews who lived in the ghettos of Eastern Europe and the slums of Western Europe. The original call to Zionism thus combined a rejection of the anti-Semitism of Europe and a desire to realize some of the ideals of both liberalism and socialism in a state outside Europe. (See "Herzl Calls for a Jewish State".)

HERZL CALLS FOR A JEWISH STATE

In 1896, Theodor Herzl published his pamphlet The Jewish State. *Herzl lived in France during the turmoil and anti-Semitism associated with the Dreyfus affair. He became convinced that only the establishment of a separate state for Jews would halt the outbreaks of anti-Semitism that characterized late-nineteenth-century European political and cultural life. Following the publication of this pamphlet, Herzl began to organize the Zionist movement among Jews in both Eastern and Western Europe.*

■ *Why does Herzl define what he calls the Jewish Question as a national question? What objections does he anticipate to the founding of a Jewish state? Why does he believe the founding of a Jewish state will be an effective move against anti-Semitism?*

The idea which I develop in this pamphlet is an age-old one: the establishment of a Jewish State.

The world resounds with outcries against the Jews, and this is what awakens the dormant idea. . . .

I believe I understand anti-Semitism, a highly complex movement. I view it from the standpoint of a Jew, but without hatred or fear. I think I can discern in it the elements of vulgar sport, of common economic rivalry, of inherited prejudice, of religious intolerance—but also of a supposed need for self-defense. To my mind, the Jewish Question is neither a social nor a religious one, even though it may assume these and other guises. It is a national question, and to solve it we must first of all establish it as an international political problem which will have to be settled by the civilized nations of the world in council.

We are a people, one people.

Everywhere we have sincerely endeavored to merge with the national communities surrounding us and to preserve only the faith of our fathers. We are not permitted to do so. . . .

And will some people say that the venture is hopeless, because even if we obtain the land and the sovereignty only the poor people will go along? They are the very ones we need first! Only desperate men make good conquerors.

Will anybody say, Oh yes, if it were possible it would have been done by now?

It was not possible before. It is possible now. As recently as a hundred, even fifty years ago it would have been a dream. Today it is all real. The rich, who have an epicurean acquaintance with all technical advance, know very well what can be done with money. And this is how it will be: Precisely the poor and plain people, who have no idea of the power that man already exercises over the forces of Nature, will have the greatest faith in the new message. For they have never lost their hope of the Promised Land. . . .

Now, all this may seem to be a long-drawn-out affair. Even in the most favorable circumstances it might be many years before the founding of the State is under way. In the meantime, Jews will be ridiculed, offended, abused, whipped, plundered, and slain in a thousand different localities. But no; just as soon as we begin to implement the plan, anti-Semitism will immediately grind to a halt everywhere.

From Theodor Herzl, *The Jewish State* (New York: The Herzl Press, 1970), pp. 27, 33, 109, as quoted in William W. Hallo, David B. Ruderman, and Michael Stanislawski, eds., *Heritage: Civilization and the Jews: Source Guide* (New York: Praeger, 1984), pp. 234–235.

WOMEN AND MODERN THOUGHT

The ideas that so shook Europe from the publication of *The Origin of Species* through the opening of World War I produced, at best, mixed results for women. Within the often radically new ways of thinking about the world, views of women and their roles in society often remained remarkably unchanged.

ANTIFEMINISM IN LATE-CENTURY THOUGHT

The influence of biology on the thinking of intellectuals during the late nineteenth century and their own interest in the nonrational side of human behavior led many of them to sustain what had become stereotyped views of women. The emphasis on biology, evolution, and reproduction led intellectuals to concentrate on women's mothering role. Their interest in the nonrational led them to reassert the traditional view that feeling and the nurturing instinct are basic to women's nature. Many late-century thinkers and writers of fiction also often displayed fear and hostility toward women, portraying them as creatures susceptible to overwhelming and often destructive feelings and instincts. A genuinely misogynist strain emerged in late-century fiction and painting.

Much of the biological thought that challenged religious ideas and the accepted wisdom in science actually reinforced the traditional view of women as creatures weaker and less able than men. Darwin himself held such views of women, and he expressed them directly in his scientific writings. Medical thought of the late century similarly sustained these views. Whatever social changes were to be wrought through science, significant changes in the organization of the home and the relationship between men and women were not among them.

This conservative and hostile perception of women manifested itself in several ways within the scientific community. In London in 1860, the Ethnological Society excluded women from its discussions on the grounds that the subject matter of the customs of primitive peoples was unfit for women and that women were amateurs whose presence would lower the level of the discussion. T. H. Huxley took the lead in this exclusion, as he had in a previous exclusion of women from meetings of the Geological Society. Male scientists also believed women should not discuss reproduction or other sexual matters. Huxley, in public lectures, claimed to have found scientific evidence of the inferiority of women to men. Karl Vogt (1817–1895), a leading German anthropologist, held similar views about the character of women. Darwin would repeat the ideas of both Huxley and Vogt in his *Descent of Man.* Late-Victorian anthropologists tended likewise to assign women, as well as nonwhite races, an inferior place in the human family. Still, despite their otherwise conservative views on gender, both Darwin and Huxley supported the expansion of education for women.

The position of women in Freud's thought is controversial. Many of his earliest patients, on whose histories he developed his theories, were women. Critics have claimed, nonetheless, that Freud portrayed women as incomplete human beings who might be inevitably destined to unhappy mental lives. He saw the natural destiny of women as motherhood and the rearing of sons as their greatest fulfillment.

The first psychoanalysts were trained as medical doctors, and their views of women reflected contemporary medical education, which, like much of the scientific establishment, tended to portray women as inferior. Distinguished women psychoanalysts, such as Karen Horney (1885–1952) and Melanie Klein (1882–1960), would later challenge Freud's views on women, and other writers would try to establish a psychoanalytic basis for feminism. Nonetheless, the psychoanalytic profession would remain dominated by men, as would academic psychology. Because psychology increasingly influenced child rearing and domestic relations law in the twentieth century, it, ironically, gave men a large impact in the one area of social activity that women had dominated.

The social sciences of the late nineteenth and early twentieth centuries similarly reinforced traditional gender roles. Most major theorists believed that women's role in reproduction and child rearing demanded a social position inferior to men. Auguste Comte, whose thought in this area owed much to Rousseau, portrayed women as biologically and intellectually inferior to men. Herbert Spencer, although an advocate for improving women's lot, thought they could never achieve equality with men. Emile Durkheim portrayed women as creatures of feeling and family rather than of intellect. Max Weber favored improvements in the condition of women, but did not really support significant changes in their social roles or in their relationship to men. Virtually all of the early sociologists took a conservative view of marriage, the family, child rearing, and divorce.

NEW DIRECTIONS IN FEMINISM

The close of the century witnessed a revival of feminist thought in Europe that would grow in the twentieth century. The role of feminist writers during these years was difficult. Many women's organizations, as seen in Chapter 23, concentrated on achieving the vote for women, but feminist writers and activists raised other questions as well. Women confronted their problems as women in a variety of ways, not just by seeking the vote. Some organizations redefined ways of thinking about women and their relationships to men and society. Few of these groups were large, and their victories were rare. Nonetheless, by the early 1900s, they had defined the issues that would become more fully and successfully explored after World War II.

Sexual Morality and the Family   In various nations, middle-class women began to challenge the double standard of sexual morality and the traditional male-dominated family. This often meant challenging laws about prostitution.

Between 1864 and 1886, English prostitutes were subject to the Contagious Diseases Acts. The police in certain cities with naval or military bases could require any woman identified as, or suspected of being, a prostitute to undergo an immediate internal medical examination for venereal disease. Those found to have a disease could be confined for months to locked hospitals (women's hospitals for the treatment of venereal diseases) without legal recourse. The law took no action against their male customers. Indeed, the purpose of the laws was to protect men, presumably sailors and soldiers, and not the women themselves, from infection.

These laws angered English middle-class women who believed the harsh working conditions and the poverty imposed on so many working-class women were the true causes of prostitution. They framed the issue in the context of their own efforts to prove that women are as human and rational as men and thus properly subject to equal treatment. They saw poor women being made victims of the same kind of discrimination that prevented women of their class from entering the universities and professions. The Contagious Diseases Acts assumed that women were inferior to men and treated them as less than rational human beings. The laws literally put women's bodies under the control of male customers, male physicians, and male law-enforcement personnel. They denied to poor women the freedoms that all men enjoyed in English society.

By 1869, the Ladies' National Association for the Repeal of the Contagious Diseases Acts, a distinctly middle-class organization led by Josephine Butler (1828–1906), began actively to oppose those laws. The group achieved the suspension of the acts in 1883 and their repeal in 1886. Government and police regulation of prostitution roused similar movements in other nations, which adopted the English movement as a model. In Vienna during the 1890s, the General Austrian Women's Association, led by Auguste Ficke (1833–1916), combated the legal regulation of prostitution, which would have put women under the control of police authorities. In Germany, women's groups divided between those who would have penalized prostitutes and those who saw them as victims of male society. By the turn of the century, the latter had come to dominate, although tensions between the groups would remain for some time.

The feminist groups that demanded the abolition of laws that punished prostitutes without questioning the behavior of their customers were challenging the double standard and, by extension, the traditional relationship of men and women in marriage. In their view, marriage should be a free

Josephine Butler (1828–1906) was an English reformer who campaigned relentlessly to repeal the Contagious Diseases Acts.   Getty Images Inc.—Hulton Archive Photos

PUBLICATION DATES OF MAJOR NONFICTION WORKS

1830 Lyell, *Principles of Geology*

1830–1842 Comte, *The Positive Philosophy*

1835 Strauss, *The Life of Jesus*

1853–1854 Gobineau, *Essay on the Inequality of the Human Races*

1859 Darwin, *The Origin of Species*

1864 Pius IX, *Syllabus of Errors*

1865 Bernard, *An Introduction to the Study of Experimental Medicine*

1871 Darwin, *The Descent of Man*

1872 Nietzsche, *The Birth of Tragedy*

1883 Mach, *The Science of Mechanics*

1883 Nietzsche, *Thus Spake Zarathustra*

1891 Leo XIII, *Rerum Novarum*

1893 Huxley, *Evolution and Ethics*

1896 Herzl, *The Jewish State*

1899 Chamberlain, *The Foundations of the Nineteenth Century*

1900 Freud, *The Interpretation of Dreams*

1900 Key, *The Century of the Child*

1905 Weber, *The Protestant Ethic and the Spirit of Capitalism*

1908 Sorel, *Reflections on Violence*

1929 Woolf, *A Room of One's Own*

1933 Jung, *Modern Man in Search of a Soul*

union of equals with men and women sharing responsibility for their children. In Germany, the Mothers' Protection League (*Bund für Mutterschutz*) contended that both married and unmarried mothers required the help of the state, including leaves for pregnancy and child care. This radical group emphasized the need to rethink all sexual morality. In Sweden, Ellen Key (1849–1926), in *The Century of the Child* (1900) and *The Renaissance of Motherhood* (1914), maintained that motherhood is so crucial to society that the government, rather than husbands, should support mothers and their children.

Virtually all turn-of-the-century feminists in one way or another supported wider sexual freedom for women, often claiming it would benefit society as well as improve women's lives. Many of the early advocates of contraception had also been influenced by social Darwinism. They hoped that limiting the number of children would allow more healthy and intelligent children to survive. Such was the outlook of Marie Stopes (1880–1958), an Englishwoman who pioneered contraception clinics in the poor districts of London.

Women Defining Their Own Lives For Josephine Butler and Auguste Ficke, as well as other continental feminists, achieving legal and social equality for women would be one step toward transforming Europe from a male-dominated society to one in which both men and women could control their own destinies. Ficke wrote, "Our final goal is therefore not the acknowledgment of rights, but the elevation of our intellectual and moral level, the development of our personality."[11] Increasingly, feminists would concentrate on freeing and developing women's personalities through better education and government financial support for women engaged in traditional social roles, whether or not they had gained the vote.

Some women also became active within socialist circles. There they argued that the socialist transformation of society should include major reforms for women. Socialist parties usually had all-male leadership. By the close of the century, most male socialist leaders, including Lenin and later Stalin, were intolerant of demands for changes in the family or greater sexual freedom for either men or women. Nonetheless, socialist writings began to include calls for improvements in the economic situation of women that were compatible with more advanced feminist ideals.

It was within literary circles, however, that feminist writers often most clearly articulated the problems that they now understood themselves to face. Distinguished women authors were actually doing, on a more or less equal footing, something that men had always done, leading some to wonder whether simple equality was the main issue. Virginia Woolf's *A Room of One's Own* (1929) became one of the fundamental texts of twentieth-century feminist literature. In it, she meditated first on the difficulties that women of both brilliance and social standing encountered in being taken seriously as writers and intellectuals. She concluded that a woman who wishes to write requires both a room of her own, meaning a space not dominated by male institutions, and an adequate independent income. Woolf was concerned with more than asserting the right of women to participate in intellectual life, however. Establishing a new stance for feminist writers, she asked whether women, as writers, must imitate men or whether they should bring to their endeavors the separate intellectual and psychological qualities they possessed as women. As she had challenged some of the literary conventions of the traditional novel in her fiction,

---

[11]Quoted in Harriet Anderson, *Utopian Feminism: Women's Movements in Fin-de-Siècle Vienna* (New Haven, CT: Yale University Press, 1992), p. 13.

she challenged some of the accepted notions of feminist thought in *A Room of One's Own* and concluded that male and female writers must actually be able to think as both men and women and share the sensibilities of each. In this sense, she sought to open the whole question of gender definition. (See "Virginia Woolf Urges Women to Write".)

VIRGINIA WOOLF URGES WOMEN TO WRITE

In 1928, Virginia Woolf, the English novelist, delivered two papers at women's colleges at Cambridge University that became the basis for A Room of One's Own, *published a year later. There, discussing the difficulty a woman writer confronted in finding women role models, she outlined obstacles that women faced in achieving the education, the time, and the income that would allow them to write. In the passage that follows, which closes her essay, she urges women to begin to write so future women authors would have models. She then presents an image of Shakespeare's sister, who, lacking such models, had not written anything, but who, through the collective efforts of women, might in the future emerge as a great writer because she would have the literary models of the women Woolf addressed to follow and to imitate.*

■ *How does Woolf's fiction of Shakespeare's sister establish a benchmark for women writers? What does Woolf mean by the common life through which women will need to work to become independent writers? Why does she emphasize the need for women to have both income and space if they are to become independent writers?*

A thousand pens are ready to suggest what you should do and what effect you will have. My own suggestion is a little fantastic, I admit; I prefer, therefore, to put it in the form of fiction.

I told you in the course of this paper that Shakespeare had a sister; but do not look for her in Sir Sidney Lee's life of the poet. She died young—alas, she never wrote a word. She lies buried where the omnibuses now stop, opposite the Elephant and Castle [a London intersection]. Now my belief is that this poet who never wrote a word and was buried at the cross-roads still lives. She lives in you and in me, and in many other women who are not here to-night, for they are washing up the dishes and putting the children to bed. But she lives; for great poets do not die; they are continuing presences; they need only the opportunity to walk among us in the flesh. This opportunity, as I think, it is now coming within your power to give her. For my belief is that if we live another century or so—I am talking of the common life which is the real life and not of the little separate lives which we live as individuals—and have five hundred [pounds income] a year each of us and rooms of our own; if we have the habit of freedom and the courage to write exactly what we think; if we escape a little from the common sitting-room and see human beings not always in their relation to each other but in relation to reality; and the sky, too, and the trees or whatever it may be in themselves; . . . if we face the fact, for it is a fact, that there is no arm to cling to, but that we go alone and that our relation is to the world of reality and not only to the world of men and women, then the opportunity will come and the dead poet who was Shakespeare's sister will put on the body which she has so often laid down. Drawing her life from the lives of the unknown who were her forerunners, as her brother did before her, she will be born. As for her coming without that preparation, without that effort on our part, without that determination that when she is born again she shall find it possible to live and write her poetry, that we cannot expect, for that would be impossible. But I maintain that she would come if we worked for her, and that so to work, even in poverty and obscurity, is worthwhile.

From Virginia Woolf, *A Room of One's Own* (London: The Hogarth Press, 1974), pp. 170–172.

By World War I, feminism in Europe, fairly or not, had become associated in the popular imagination with challenges to traditional gender roles and sexual morality and with either socialism or political radicalism. So when extremely conservative political movements arose between the world wars, their leaders often emphasized traditional roles for women and traditional ideas about sexual morality. Lenin and Stalin would follow a similar path in the Soviet political experiment. (See Chapters 26 and 27.)

IN PERSPECTIVE

By the opening of the twentieth century, European thought had achieved contours that seem familiar to us today. Science had revolutionized thinking about nature. Physicists had transformed the traditional views of matter and energy as they probed the mysteries of the atom. Evolutionary biology had revealed that human beings are not distinct from the natural order. Many believed science would provide a new basis for ethics and morality. Christianity had experienced its most severe challenge in modern times from science, history, philosophy, and the secular national states.

Nonreligious thinkers and writers also assailed the primacy of reason. Nietzsche and Freud, in their different ways, questioned whether human beings are rational creatures at all. Weber and other social and political theorists doubted that politics could ever be entirely rational. All these developments challenged the rational values of the Enlightenment.

The racial theorists questioned whether mind and character were as important as racial characteristics allegedly carried in the blood. Racial thinking also allowed some Europeans to believe they were inherently superior to non-Europeans, Jews, and ethnic minorities in Europe itself.

Turn-of-the-century feminists demanded equal treatment for women under the law and contended that the relationship between men and women within marriage required rethinking. They set forth much of the feminist agenda for the twentieth century.

REVIEW QUESTIONS

1. Why was science dominant in the second half of the nineteenth century? How did the scientific outlook change between 1850 and 1914? What was positivism? How did Darwin and Wallace's theory of natural selection affect ethics, Christianity, and European views of human nature?

2. Why was Christianity attacked in the late nineteenth century? Why was Leo XIII regarded as a liberal pope? Why was the papacy itself so resilient?

3. Why did Europeans feel superior toward Islam? How did Islamic thinkers respond to the European challenge?

4. How did social conditions of literature change in the late nineteenth century? What was the significance of the explosion of literary matter? How did the realists undermine middle-class morality? How did literary modernism differ from realism?

5. What were the major movements associated with the rise of modern art?

6. How did Nietzsche and Freud challenge traditional morality?

7. Why were many late-nineteenth-century intellectuals afraid of and hostile to women? How did Freud view the position of women? What social and political issues affected women in the late nineteenth and early twentieth centuries? What new directions did feminism take?

8. What was the character of late-nineteenth-century racism? How did it become associated with anti-Semitism?

9. How did many ideas associated with modernism conflict with feminist goals? What were new departures in turn of the century feminism?

SUGGESTED READINGS

M. ADAS, *Machines as the Measure of Men: Science, Technology, and Ideologies of Western Dominance* (1989). The best single volume on racial thinking and technological advances as forming ideologies of European colonial dominance.

C. ALLEN, *The Human Christ: The Search for the Historical Jesus* (1998). A broad survey of the issue for the past two centuries.

M. D. BIDDIS, *Father of Racist Ideology: The Social and Political Thought of Count Gobineau* (1970). Sets the subject in the more general context of nineteenth-century thought.

P. BOWLER, *Evolution: The History of an Idea* (2003). An outstanding survey.

J. BURROW, *The Crisis of Reason: European Thought, 1848–1914* (2000). The best overview available.

T. J. CLARK, *The Painting of Modern Life: Paris in the Art of Manet and His Followers* (1984). A classic.

F. J. COPPA, *The Modern Papacy since 1789* (1999). A straightforward survey.

B. DENVIR, *Post-Impressionism* (1992). A brief introduction.

R. HARRIS, *Lourdes: Body and Soul in a Secular Age* (1999). A sensitive discussion of Lourdes in its religious and cultural contexts.

R. HELMSTADTER (ED.), *Freedom and Religion in the Nineteenth Century* (1997). Major essays on the relationship of church and state.

R. L. HERBERT, *Impressionism: Art, Leisure, and Parisian Society* (1988). Emphasizes the social setting of impressionist art.

J. HODGE AND G. RADICK, *The Cambridge Companion to Darwin* (2003). A far-ranging collection of essays with a good bibliography.

A. HOURANI, *Arab Thought in the Liberal Age 1789–1939* (1967). A classic account, clearly written and accessible to the nonspecialist.

J. KÖHLER, *Zarathustra's Secret: The Interior Life of Friedrich Nietzsche* (2002). A controversial new biography.

W. LACQUEUR, *A History of Zionism* (1989). The most extensive one-volume treatment.

M. LEVENSON, *The Cambridge Companion to Modernism* (1999). Excellent essays on a wide range of subjects.

M. R. O'CONNELL, *Critics on Trial: An Introduction to the Catholic Modernist Crisis* (1994). An extensive, accessible account.

A. PAIS, *Subtle Is the Lord: The Science and Life of Albert Einstein* (1983). The most accessible biography.

P. G. J. PULZER, *The Rise of Political Anti-Semitism in Germany and Austria* (1989). A sound discussion of anti-Semitism and Central European politics.

R. ROSENBLUM, *Cubism and 20th Century Art* (2001) A well-informed introduction

C. E. SCHORSKE, *Fin de Siècle Vienna: Politics and Culture* (1980). Classic essays on the creative intellectual climate of Vienna.

W. SMITH, *Politics and the Sciences of Culture in Germany, 1840–1920* (1991). A major survey of the interaction between science and the social sciences.

D. VITAL, *A People Apart: The Jews in Europe 1789–1939* (1999). A broad and deeply researched volume.

A. N. WILSON, *God's Funeral* (1999). Explores the thinkers who contributed to religious doubt during the nineteenth and twentieth centuries.

DOCUMENTS CD-ROM

Nineteenth-Century Thought

24.1 George Elliot: Essay on Margaret Fuller and Mary Wollstonecraft
24.2 An Advocate for Science Education
24.3 Sex in Society
24.4 Auguste Comte: from *The Age of Ideology*
24.5 Friedrich Nietzsche: from *The Age of Ideology*
24.6 Sir Edmund Gosse: from *Father and Son*

CHAPTER 25

IMPERIALISM, ALLIANCES, AND WAR

- **EXPANSION OF EUROPEAN POWER AND THE NEW IMPERIALISM**
  The New Imperialism • Motives for the New Imperialism • The "Scramble for Africa" • Asia

- **EMERGENCE OF THE GERMAN EMPIRE AND THE ALLIANCE SYSTEMS (1873–1890)**
  Bismarck's Leadership • Forging the Triple Entente (1890–1907)

- **WORLD WAR I**
  The Road to War (1908–1914) • Sarajevo and the Outbreak of War (June–August 1914) • Strategies and Stalemate: 1914–1917

- **THE RUSSIAN REVOLUTION**
  The Provisional Government • Lenin and the Bolsheviks • The Communist Dictatorship

- **THE END OF WORLD WAR I**
  Germany's Last Offensive • The Armistice • The End of the Ottoman Empire

- **THE SETTLEMENT AT PARIS**
  Obstacles the Peacemakers Faced • The Peace • Evaluating the Peace

- **IN PERSPECTIVE**

KEY TOPICS

- The economic, cultural, and strategic factors behind Europe's New Imperialism in the late nineteenth and early twentieth centuries
- The formation of alliances and the search for strategic advantage among Europe's major powers
- The origins and course of World War I
- The Russian Revolution
- The peace treaties ending World War I

D uring the second half of the nineteenth century, and especially after 1870, Europe exercised unprecedented influence and control over the rest of the world. North and South America, as well as Australia and New Zealand, almost became part of the European world as great streams of European immigrants populated them. Until the nineteenth century, Asia (with the significant exception of India) and most of

The use of poison gas (by both sides) during the First World War and its dreadful effects—blinding, asphyxiation, burned lungs—came to symbolize the horrors of modern war. This painting shows a group of British soldiers being guided to the rear after they were blinded by mustard gas on the Western Front.

John Singer Sargent, *Gassed*, 1918–1919. Imperial War Museum, London

Africa had gone their own ways, having little contact with Europe. In the latter part of that century, however, European nations divided almost all of Africa among them. Europe also imposed its economic and political power across Asia. By the next century, European dominance had brought every part of the globe into a single world economy. Events in any corner of the world had significant effects thousands of miles away.

These developments might have been expected to lead to greater prosperity and good fortune. Instead, they helped foster competition and hostility among the great powers of Europe and bring on a terrible war that undermined Europe's strength and its influence in the world. The peace settlement, proclaimed as "a peace without victors," disillusioned idealists in the West. It treated Germany almost as harshly as Germany would have treated its foes if it had been victorious. Also, the new system failed to provide realistic and effective safeguards against a return to power of a vengeful Germany. The withdrawal of the United States into a disdainful isolation from world affairs destroyed the basis for keeping the peace on which the hopes of Britain and France relied. The frenzy for imperial expansion that seized Europeans in the late nineteenth century had done much to destroy Europe's peace and prosperity and its dominant place in the world. ■

EXPANSION OF EUROPEAN POWER AND THE NEW IMPERIALISM

The explosive developments in nineteenth-century science, technology, industry, agriculture, transportation, communication, and military weapons provided the chief sources of European power. They made it possible for a few Europeans (or Americans) to impose their will, by force or the threat of force, on other peoples many times their number. Institutional as well as material advantages allowed Westerners to have their way. The growth of national states that commanded the loyalty, service, and resources of their inhabitants to a degree previously unknown was a Western phenomenon. It permitted the European nations to deploy their resources more effectively than ever before.

The Europeans also possessed another, less tangible, weapon: They considered their civilization and way of life to be superior to all others. This gave them a self-confidence that was often unpleasantly arrogant and fostered their expansionist mood.

The expansion of European influence was not new. Spain, Portugal, France, Holland, and Britain had controlled territories overseas for centuries, but by the mid-nineteenth century, only Great Britain still had extensive holdings. The first half of the century was generally hostile to colonial expansion. The loss of the American colonies had sobered even the British. The French acquired Algeria and part of Indochina, and the British added territory to their holdings in Canada, India, Australia, and New Zealand. The dominant doctrine of free trade, however, opposed political interference in other lands as economically unprofitable.

Britain ruled the waves and had great commercial advantages as a result of being the first country to experience the Industrial Revolution. Therefore, the British were usually content to trade and invest overseas without annexations. Yet they were prepared to interfere forcefully if a less industrialized country interfered with their trade. Still, at midcentury, in Britain as elsewhere, most people opposed further political or military involvement overseas.

In the last third of the century, however, the European states swiftly spread their control over perhaps ten million square miles and 150 million people—about one-fifth of the world's land area and one-tenth of its population. During this period, European expansion went forward with great speed, and participation in it came to be regarded as necessary for a great power. The movement has been called the **New Imperialism**.

An American cartoonist in 1888 depicted John Bull (England) as the octopus of imperialism, grabbing land on every continent. *The Granger Collection*

THE NEW IMPERIALISM

The word *imperialism* is now used so loosely that it has almost lost real meaning. It may be useful to offer a definition that might be widely accepted: "the policy of extending a nation's authority by territorial acquisition or by establishing economic and political hegemony over other nations."[1] That definition seems to apply equally well to ancient Egypt and Mesopotamia and to the European performance in the late nineteenth century, but the latter case had new elements. Previous imperialisms had taken the form either of seizing land and settling it with the conqueror's people or of establishing trading centers to exploit the resources of the dominated area. The New Imperialism did not completely abandon these devices, but it also introduced new ones.

The usual pattern of the New Imperialism was for a European nation to invest capital in a "less industrialized" country, to develop its mines and agriculture, to build railroads, bridges, harbors, and telegraph systems, and to employ many natives in the process. This transformed the local economy and culture. To safeguard its investments, the dominant European state would make favorable arrangements with the local government, either by loaning it money or by intimidating it.

If these arrangements proved inadequate, the dominant power would establish more direct political control. Sometimes this meant full annexation and direct rule as a colony, or it could be a protectorate status, whereby the local ruler became a figurehead controlled by the dominant European state and maintained by its military power. In other instances, the European state established "spheres of influence" in which it received special commercial and legal privileges without direct political involvement.

MOTIVES FOR THE NEW IMPERIALISM

The predominant interpretation of the motives for the New Imperialism has been economic, in the form given by the English radical economist J. A. Hobson (1858–1928) and later adapted by Lenin. As Lenin put it, "Imperialism is the monopoly stage of capitalism,"[2] the last stage of a dying system. Competition inevitably eliminates inefficient capitalists and therefore leads to monopoly. Powerful industrial and financial capitalists soon run out of profitable areas of investment in their own countries and persuade their governments to gain colonies in "less developed" countries. Here they can find higher profits from their investments, new markets for their products, and safe sources of raw materials.

Facts do not support this viewpoint, however. The European powers did invest considerable capital abroad, but not in a way that fit the model of Hobson and Lenin. Britain, for example, made heavier investments abroad before 1875 than during the next two decades. Only a small percentage of British and European investments overseas, moreover, went to their new colonies. Most capital went into other European countries or to older, well-established areas like the United States, Canada, Australia, and New Zealand. Even when countries did invest in new areas, they often did not invest in their own colonies.

The facts are equally discouraging for those who emphasize the need for markets and raw materials. Colonies were not usually important markets for the great imperial nations, and all these states were forced to rely on areas that they did not control as sources of vital raw materials. It is not even clear that control of the new colonies was particularly profitable, though Britain, to be sure, benefited greatly from its rule of India. It is also true that some European businesspeople and politicians hoped colonial expansion would cure the great depression of 1873 to 1896.

Nevertheless, as one of the leading students of the subject has said, "No one can determine whether the accounts of empire ultimately closed with a favorable cash balance."[3] That is true of the European imperial nations collectively, but it is certain that for some of them, like Italy and Germany, empire was a losing proposition. Some individuals (like King Leopold II of the Belgians, in the Congo) and companies, of course, made great profits from particular colonial ventures, but such people were able to influence national policy only occasionally. Economic motives certainly played a part, but a full understanding of the New Imperialism requires a search for other motives.

At the time, advocates of imperialism gave various justifications for it. Some argued that the advanced European nations had a duty to bring the benefits of their higher culture and superior civilization to more so-called backward peoples. (See "Social Darwinism and Imperialism," page 832.) Religious groups demanded that Western governments support Christian missionaries politically and even militarily. Some politicians and diplomats supported imperialism as a tool of social policy. In Germany, for instance, some people suggested that imperial expansion would deflect public interest away from domestic politics and social reform. Yet Germany acquired few colonies, and such considerations played little, if any, role in its colonial policy. In Britain, Joseph Chamberlain (1836–1914), the colonial secretary from 1895 to 1903, argued for the empire as a source of profit

---

[1]*American Heritage Dictionary of the English Language*, 3rd ed. (New York: Houghton Mifflin, 1993), p. 681.

[2]V. I. Lenin, *Imperialism, the Highest Stage of Capitalism* (New York: International Publishers, 1939), p. 88.

[3]D. K. Fieldhouse, *The Colonial Empires* (New York: Delacorte, 1966), p. 393.

and economic security that would finance a great program of domestic reform and welfare, but these arguments were made well after Britain had acquired most of its empire. Another apparently plausible justification for imperialism was that colonies would attract a European country's surplus population. In fact, most European emigrants went to areas their countries did not control, chiefly the Americas and Australia.

THE "SCRAMBLE FOR AFRICA"

All of these motives were on display in the late nineteenth century, when European imperial powers expanded their economic and political control

of Africa. During this so-called "Scramble for Africa," which occurred between the late 1870s and about 1900, the European powers sought to maximize their control of African territory and raw materials. Motivated by intense economic and political competition, they rationalized their expansionary policies on both religious and cultural grounds. The imperial powers eventually divided almost all the continent among themselves. The short- and long-term consequences were complex and in most cases devastating for the Africans. Among the long-term effects was that European control forcibly integrated African societies into the modern world economy. In the process, new forms of social organizations emerged and

A CLOSER LOOK

The French in Morocco

Many imperialists—European, American, and Asian—claimed altruistic motives for their acquisition of colonies. The French, especially, have always taken pride in bringing "French civilization" to the lands France ruled. This cover of a magazine appeared in November 1911, the year when the French decision to extend and tighten their control of Morocco sparked a serious international crisis. It is a good example of how France justified its colonial empire as a *mission civilitrice,* a vocation to bring civilization to "backward" peoples.

The illustration reveals the arrogance of such imperial pretensions. In the top right-hand corner, a French officer in a pith helmet gives orders to a saluting African soldier.

The message at the bottom of the page says, "France will be able to freely bring civilization, prosperity, and peace" to Morocco.

The central figure on the cover is a shining Marianne, the symbol of the French Republic, carrying a horn of plenty from which gold coins spill out. Marianne is far larger than the Moroccans, who look at her in wonder and admiration at the benefits that French rule will bring.

The Granger Collection

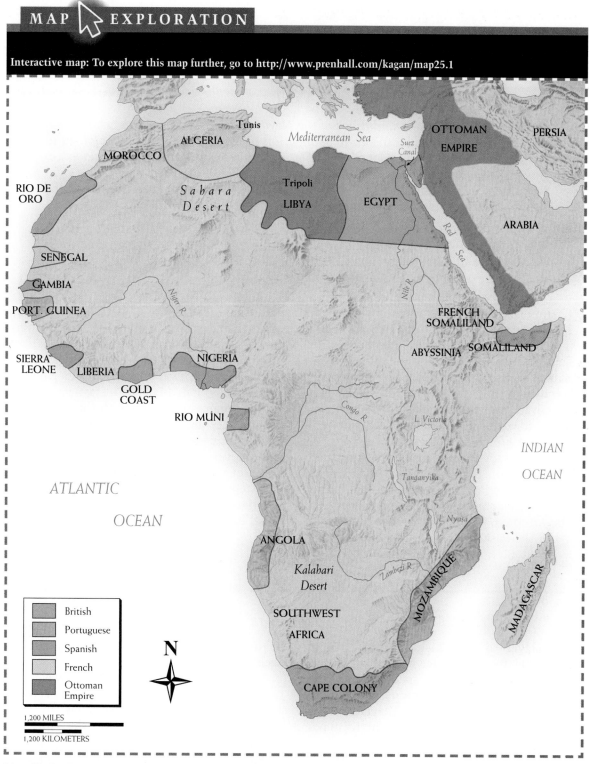

Interactive map: To explore this map further, go to http://www.prenhall.com/kagan/map25.1

Map 25–1 **IMPERIAL EXPANSION IN AFRICA TO 1880**   Until the 1880s, few European countries held colonies in Africa, mostly on its fringes.

new market economies and political structures developed that would later form the basis for the modern, postcolonial African nations.

For centuries, European slave-trading bases had dotted the African coastline, but few Europeans had penetrated the interior. This changed in the late 1870s. (See Map 25-1.) The Congress of Vienna had prohibited the Atlantic slave trade in 1815, a ban that Western, primarily British, naval patrols enforced along the African coast. Those patrols and the abolition of slavery in the Americas during the nineteenth century meant that Africa was no longer a source for slave labor except in Central and East Africa where Arab slave traders continued

SOCIAL DARWINISM AND IMPERIALISM

—〰—

One of the intellectual foundations of the New Imperialism was the doctrine of social Darwinism, a pseudoscientific application of Darwin's ideas about biology to nations and races. The impact of social Darwinism was substantial. In the selection that follows, an Englishman, Karl Pearson (1857–1936), attempts to connect concepts from evolutionary theory—the struggle for survival and the survival of the fittest—to the development of human societies.

■ *How does the author connect Darwin's ideas to the concept of human progress? Is it reasonable to equate biological species with human societies, races, or nations? How do the author's ideas justify imperial expansion? What arguments can you make against the author's assertions?*

History shows me one way, and one way only, in which a state of civilisation has been produced, namely, the struggle of race with race, and the survival of the physically and mentally fitter race. This dependence of progress on the survival of the fitter race, terribly black as it may seem to some of you, gives the struggle for existence its redeeming features; it is the fiery crucible out of which comes the finer metal. You may hope for a time when the sword shall be turned into the ploughshare, when American and German and English traders shall no longer compete in the markets of the world for raw materials, for their food supply, when the white man and the dark shall share the soil between them, and each till it as he lists. But, believe me, when that day comes mankind will no longer progress; there will be nothing to check the fertility of inferior stock; the relentless law of heredity will not be controlled and guided by natural selection. Man will stagnate. . . . The path of progress is strewn with the wreck of nations; traces are everywhere to be seen of the hecatombs of inferior races, and of victims who found not the narrow way to the greater perfection. Yet these dead peoples are, in very truth, the stepping stones on which mankind has arisen to the higher intellectual and deeper emotional life of today.

From Karl Pearson, *National Life from the Standpoint of Science*, 2nd ed. (Cambridge, UK: Cambridge University Press, 1907), pp. 21, 26–27, 64.

to export slaves to the Muslim world until at least the 1890s. Instead, Africa became an important supplier of raw materials, such as ivory, rubber, minerals, and, notably, diamonds and gold to the West. The British, French, Belgians, Germans, Italians, and Portuguese sought to maximize their access to these resources. The competition was so fierce and the scramble for African territories so frantic and volatile that the imperial powers were constantly negotiating with each other about how to parcel Africa among them without the contest leading to war. To set the rules, the German chancellor Otto von Bismarck, called a conference in Berlin in 1884–1885 that mapped out a European-controlled Africa. African colonies had become both trophies for European powers and possible bargaining chips in their economic and political competition with each other. (See Map 25–2.)

The imperial scramble for Africa was not based on a universal policy, and each power acquired and administered its new possessions in different ways. Their goal, however, was the same: to gain control, or at least dominance, through diplomacy or superior force and then either to place Europeans directly in charge of administering the territories or, in some cases, to compel local rulers to accept European "advisors" who would exercise the real authority. The Europeans justified their activities by claiming that this was a civilizing mission—that they were bringing civilization to "savage" and "backward" natives. In fact, the European powers ran Africa primarily for their own benefit.

Interactive map: To explore this map further, go to http://www.prenhall.com/kagan/map25.2

MAP EXPLORATION

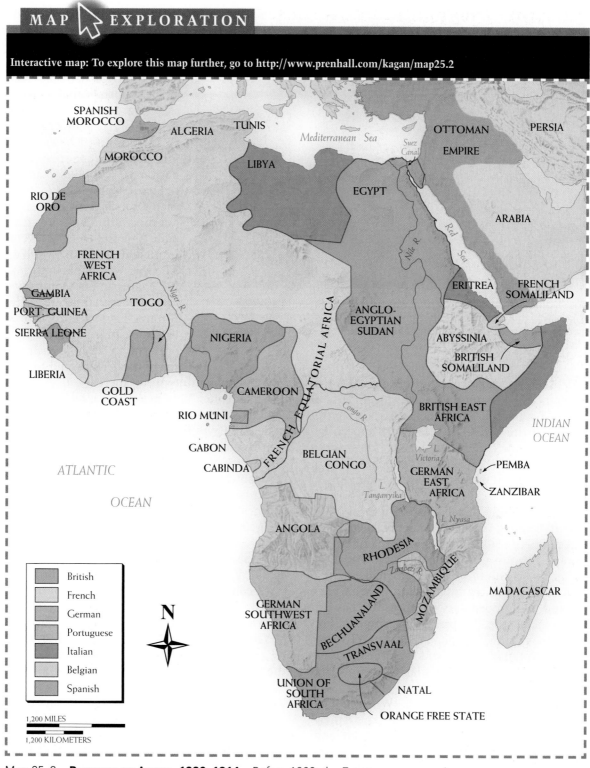

Map 25–2 **PARTITION OF AFRICA, 1880–1914** Before 1880, the European presence in Africa was largely the remains of early exploration by old imperialists and did not penetrate the heart of the continent. By 1914, the occupying powers included most large European states; only Liberia and Abyssinia (Ethiopia) remained independent.

North Africa In North Africa, the experience of European imperialism was slightly different from that in sub-Saharan Africa. Because much of North Africa was still technically part of the Ottoman Empire, the European powers secured their interests primarily in two ways: through economic penetration (investments and loans) and diplomatic pressure. Force, however, was always an option.

The opening of the Suez Canal in 1869 was a major engineering achievement that linked Asia to Europe. It also became a major international waterway benefiting all maritime states reducing the distance from London to Bombay in half.   Key Color/Index Stock Imagery, Inc.

By 1914, European powers controlled all of North Africa. France had begun the conquest of Algeria in 1830 (see Chapter 20). The French also took control of Tunisia in the early 1880s and of Morocco between 1901 and 1912. Italy seized Libya from Turkey in 1911–1912. Egypt, the richest North African country, fell under the control of Britain.

Egypt   Egypt was an unusual case. For most of the nineteenth century, it had been a semi-independent province of the Ottoman Empire under the hereditary rule of a Muslim dynasty. The Khedives, as these rulers were titled, had tried to modernize the country by building new harbors, roads, and a European-style army. To pay for these projects, the Egyptian government borrowed money from European creditors. To earn the money to repay these loans, it forced farmers to plant cash crops, particularly cotton that could be sold on the international market. This proved to be a mixed blessing. When cotton prices were high, for example, during the American Civil War (1861–1865), which cut off supplies of cotton from the Southern states, the Egyptian economy boomed, and government revenues soared. When cotton prices fell, as they did after the Civil War, so did Egyptian revenue. Ultimately, the Egyptian government became utterly dependent on European creditors. The construction of the Suez Canal was the final blow to Egypt's finances.

The Suez Canal was opened in 1869. Built by French engineers with European capital, it was one of the most remarkable engineering feats of the day. The canal connected the Mediterranean to the Red Sea, which meant that ships from Europe no longer had to sail around Africa to reach Asia. In particular, the canal reduced the shipping distance from India to Britain from about 12,000 miles to 7,000 miles. The canal therefore increased the speed of international contacts and, by reducing shipping costs, made many goods on the world market more affordable. Yet the tangible benefits to Egypt were not immediately clear. By 1876, the Khedive was bankrupt; most of his shares in the company that ran the canal were sold to Britain. Egypt's European creditors took more than 50 per cent of Egyptian revenue each year to repay their loans and forced the Egyptian government to increase taxes to raise more revenue. This provoked a rebellion, and in 1881, the Egyptian army took over the government to defend Egypt from foreign exploitation.

An uncooperative Egyptian government was, however, not in the best interests of the European superpowers. Britain sent a fleet and army to Egypt that easily defeated the Egyptians and established seventy years of British supremacy in the country.

Egypt never became an official part of the British Empire. The Khedives, who became kings after Egypt severed its ties with Turkey during the First World War, continued to reign, but the British exercised control through a relatively small number of British administrators and soldiers. The British used their experience from India to run Egypt.

Their primary goal was stability: Egypt had to repay its debts, and Britain was to retain control of the Suez Canal, which the British regarded as their "lifeline" to their empire in India and the Far East. They built a naval base at Alexandria and installed a large garrison in Cairo. They established municipal governments that were responsible for taxation and public services and further expanded cotton cultivation. They also prevented the Egyptians from establishing a textile industry that would compete with Britain's own textile mills.

Economically, this meant that while the Egyptian economy grew and tax revenues increased, per capita income actually declined among Egyptians, most of whom were peasant farmers who owned little or no land. Politically, it led to the growth of Egyptian nationalism and to increasing demands that the British leave Egypt.

The Belgian Congo   Perhaps the most remarkable story in the European scramble for Africa was the acquisition of the Belgian Congo. In the 1880s, the lands drained by the vast Congo River and its tributaries became the personal property of King Leopold II of Belgium (r. 1865–1909). As a young monarch, he had become determined that Belgium, despite its small territory, must acquire colonies. No doubt he was inspired by the great commercial wealth that the neighboring Netherlands had accumulated from its long history of colonial trade.

The Belgian government, however, had no interest at that time in acquiring colonies. So despite being a constitutional monarch, Leopold used his own wealth and political guile to realize his colonial ambitions. He did so under the guise of humanitarian concern for Africans. In 1876, he gathered explorers, geographers, and antislavery reformers in Brussels and formed the International African Association. He then recruited the English-born journalist and explorer Henry Morton Stanley (1841–1904) to undertake a major expedition into the Congo. Stanley had previously made a great reputation by crossing Africa from east to west. Between 1879 and 1884, Stanley explored the Congo and on Leopold's behalf made "treaties" with local rulers who had no idea what they were signing. Leopold then won diplomatic recognition for those treaties and for his own allegedly humanitarian efforts in the region first from the United States and then in 1885 from a conference of European powers held in Berlin. The larger, stronger European states were willing to let Leopold govern the Congo to keep one another out. Leopold, thus, personally became the ruler of an African domain that was over seventy times the size of Belgium itself. Only after the Belgian government gave him an interest-free loan that he needed to pay for his activities in the Congo did he agree to bequeath the Congo to Belgium upon his death.

Although Leopold continued to cultivate the image of a humanitarian ruler by holding antislavery conferences in Belgium and manipulating public relations, his goal in the Congo was economic exploitation of the most brutal kind. Leopold's administration used slave labor, intimidation, torture, mutilation, and mass murder to extract rubber and ivory from what became known as the Congo Free State. Eventually, beginning with the African-American reporter George Washington Williams (1849–1891) and culminating with an international outcry led by the English journalist E. D. Morel (1873–1924) and the diplomat Roger Casement (1864–1916), Leopold's crimes were exposed, and he formally turned the Congo over to Belgium in 1908.

The cruelties in the Congo, which became the basis for Joseph Conrad's classic novel *Heart of Darkness* (1902), were recorded for posterity in photographs, eyewitness accounts, and newspaper articles, and by an official Belgian commission.

Elephant tusks in Central Africa. Ivory was a prized possession used for decorative purposes and jewelry.
Caravan with Ivory, French Congo, (now the Republic of the Congo). Robert Visser (1882–1894). c. 1890–1900, postcard, collotype. Publisher unknown, ©1900. Postcard 1912. Image No. EEPA 1985-140792. Eliot Elisofon Photographic Archives. National Museum of African Art/Smithsonian Institution

The most responsible historical estimates suggest that the exploitation Leopold's administration carried out halved the population of the Congo in about thirty years. Millions of Africans died of murder, exploitation, starvation, and disease.

Southern Africa   South Africa's fertile pastures and farm land and its vast deposits of coal, iron ore, gold, diamonds, and copper made it appealing to a host of people. The Afrikaners or Boers, descendants of seventeenth- and eighteenth-century Dutch settlers, had long inhabited the area around the Cape of Good Hope, and the British started to settle there after Britain took over from the Dutch during the Napoleonic Wars.

Though the British met with considerable native resistance, as they expanded in southern Africa, from the Zulu, Shona, and Ndebele peoples, they eventually established colonies in what is now South Africa, Botswana, Zambia, and Zimbabwe. In 1910, after a series of bloody wars with the white Afrikaners, who consistently resented and opposed British rule, the British formed a pact with them that guaranteed the rule of the European minority over the majority black and nonwhite population. Africans and people of mixed race whom the British referred to as "colored" were forbidden to own land, denied the right to vote, and excluded from positions of power. To preserve their political power and economic privileges, the white elite of South Africa eventually enforced a policy of racial apartheid—"separateness"—that turned the country into a totally segregated land. The result was decades of oppression, racial tensions, and economic exploitation.

ASIA

In Asia, the emergence of Japan as a great power frightened the other powers that were interested in China. (See Map 25–3.), The Russians were building a railroad across Siberia to Vladivostok and were afraid of any threat to Manchuria. Together with France and Germany, they applied diplomatic pressure that forced Japan out of the Liaotung Peninsula in northern China and its harbor, Port Arthur. All pressed feverishly for concessions in China. Fearing that China, its markets, and its investment opportunities would soon be closed to U.S. citizens, the United States proposed the Open Door Policy in 1899. This policy opposed foreign annexations in China and allowed entrepreneurs of all nations to trade there on equal terms. British support helped win acceptance of the policy by all the powers except Russia.

The United States had only recently emerged as a force in international affairs. After freeing itself of British rule and consolidating its independence during the Napoleonic Wars, the Americans had busied themselves with westward expansion on the North American continent until the end of the nineteenth century. The Monroe Doctrine of 1823 had, in effect, made the entire Western Hemisphere an American protectorate. Cuba's attempt to gain independence from Spain was the spark for the new U.S. involvement in international affairs. Sympathy for the Cuban cause, U.S. investments on the island, the desire for Cuban sugar, and concern over the island's strategic importance in the Caribbean all helped persuade the United States to fight Spain.

Victory in the Spanish-American War of 1898 brought the United States an informal protectorate over Cuba and the annexation of Puerto Rico and drove Spain completely out of the Western Hemisphere. The United States forced Spain to sell the Philippine Islands and Guam, and Germany bought the other Spanish islands in the Pacific. The United States and Germany also divided Samoa between them. France and Britain took the remaining Pacific islands. The United States had dominated Hawaii for some time and annexed it in 1898, five years after an American-backed coup had overthrown the native Hawaiian monarchy. This burst of activity after the Spanish-American War made the United States an imperial and Pacific power.

EXPANSION OF EUROPEAN POWER AND THE NEW IMPERIALISM

1869	Suez Canal completed
1875	Britain gains control of the Suez Canal
1879–1884	Leopold II establishes his personal rule in the Congo
1882	France controls Algeria and Tunisia
1880s	Britain establishes protectorate over Egypt
1884–1885	Germany establishes protectorate over Southwest Africa (Namibia), Togoland, the Cameroons, and East Africa (Tanzania)
1898	Spanish-American War: United States acquires Puerto Rico, Philippines, and Guam, annexes Hawaiian Islands, and establishes protectorate over Cuba
1899	United States proposes Open Door Policy in Far East
1899–1902	Boer War in South Africa
1908	Belgium takes over the Congo from Leopold II

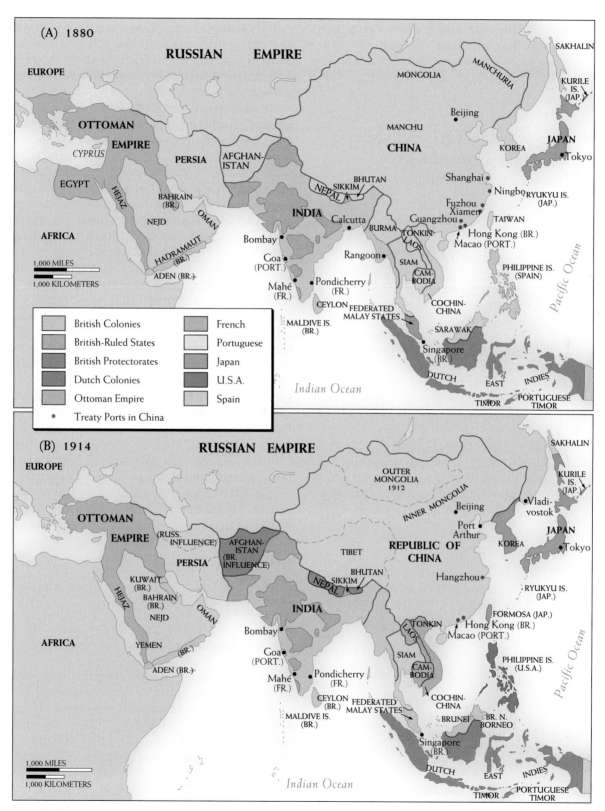

Map 25–3 **ASIA, 1880–1914** As in Africa, the decades before World War I saw imperialism spread widely and rapidly in Asia. Two new powers, Japan and the United States, joined the British, French, and Dutch in extending control both to islands and to the mainland and in exploiting an enfeebled China.

Thus, by the turn of the century, most of the world had come under the control of the industrialized West. The one remaining area of great vulnerability was the Ottoman Empire. Its fate, however, was closely tied up with European developments and must be treated in that context.

EMERGENCE OF THE GERMAN EMPIRE AND THE ALLIANCE SYSTEMS (1873–1890)

Prussia's victories over Austria and France and its creation of a large, powerful German Empire in 1871 revolutionized European diplomacy. A vast new political unit had united the majority of Germans to form a nation of great and growing population, wealth, industrial capacity, and military power. Its sudden appearance created new problems and upset the balance of power that the Congress of Vienna had forged. Britain and Russia retained their positions, although the Crimean War had weakened the latter.

Austria, however, had been severely weakened, and the forces of nationalism threatened it with disintegration. The Franco-Prussian War and the German annexation of Alsace-Lorraine badly damaged French power and prestige. The French were afraid of their powerful new neighbor as well as resentful of their defeat, their loss of territory, and the loss of France's traditional position as the dominant Western European power.

BISMARCK'S LEADERSHIP

Until 1890, Bismarck continued to guide German policy. After 1871, he insisted Germany was a satisfied power and wanted no further territorial gains, and he meant it. He wanted to avoid a new war that might undo his achievement. He tried to assuage French resentment by pursuing friendly relations and by supporting French colonial aspirations. He also prepared for the worst. If France could not be conciliated, it must be isolated. Bismarck sought to prevent an alliance between France and any other European power—especially Austria or Russia—that would threaten Germany with a war on two fronts.

War in the Balkans Bismarck's first move was to establish the Three Emperors' League in 1873. The League brought together the three great conservative empires of Germany, Austria, and Russia. The league soon collapsed over Austro-Russian rivalry in the Balkans that arose from the Russo-Turkish War that broke out in 1877. The tottering Ottoman Empire was held together chiefly because the European powers could not agree about how to partition it. Ottoman weakness encouraged Serbia and Montenegro to come to the aid of their fellow Slavs in Bosnia and Herzegovina when they revolted against Turkish rule. Soon the rebellion spread to Bulgaria.

Then Russia entered the fray and turned it into a major international crisis. The Russians hoped to pursue their traditional policy of expansion at Ottoman expense and especially to achieve their most cherished goal: control of Constantinople and the Dardanelles. Russian intervention also reflected the influence of the Pan-Slavic movement, which sought to unite all the Slavic peoples, even those under Austrian or Ottoman rule, under the protection of Holy Mother Russia.

The Ottoman Empire was soon forced to sue for peace. The Treaty of San Stefano of March 1878 was a Russian triumph. The Slavic states in the Balkans were freed of Ottoman rule, and Russia itself obtained territory and a large monetary indemnity. The settlement, however, alarmed the other great powers. Austria feared that the Slavic victory and the increase in Russian influence in the Balkans would threaten its own Balkan provinces. The British were alarmed both by the effect of the Russian victory on the European balance of power and by the possibility of Russian control of the Dardanelles, which would make Russia a Mediterranean power and threaten Britain's control of the Suez Canal. Disraeli was determined to resist, and British public opinion supported him. A music-hall song that became popular gave the language a new word for super patriotism: *jingoism*.

We don't want to fight,
But by jingo if we do,
We've got the men,
We've got the ships,
We've got the money too!
The Russians will not have Constantinople!

The Congress of Berlin Britain and Austria forced Russia to agree to an international conference at which the other great powers would review the provisions of San Stefano. The resulting Congress of Berlin met in June and July 1878 under the presidency of Bismarck. The choice of site and presiding officer were a clear recognition of Germany's new importance and of Bismarck's claim that Germany wanted no new territory and sought to preserve the peace.

Bismarck referred to himself as an "honest broker," and the title was justified. He wanted to avoid a war between Russia and Austria into which he feared Germany would be drawn with nothing to gain and much to lose. From the collapsing Ottoman Empire, he wanted nothing. "The Eastern Question," he said, "is not worth the healthy bones of a single Pomeranian musketeer."[4]

The decisions of the congress were a blow to Russian ambitions. Bulgaria, a Russian client, was reduced in size by two-thirds and deprived of access to the Aegean Sea. Austria-Hungary was given Bosnia and Herzegovina to "occupy and administer," although those provinces remained formally under Ottoman rule. Britain received Cyprus, and France was encouraged to occupy Tunisia. These territories were compensation for the gains that Russia was permitted to keep. Germany asked for nothing, but still earned Russian resentment. The Russians believed they had saved Prussia in 1807 from complete destruction by Napoleon and had expected German gratitude. They were bitterly disappointed, and the Three Emperors' League was dead.

The Berlin settlement also annoyed the Balkan states. Romania wanted Bessarabia, which Russia kept; Bulgaria wanted the borders of the Treaty of San Stefano; and Greece wanted more Ottoman territory. The major trouble spot, however, was in the south Slavic states of Serbia and Montenegro. They resented the Austrian occupation of Bosnia and Herzegovina, as did many of the natives of those provinces. The south Slavic question, no less than the estrangement between Russia and Germany, was a threat to the peace of Europe.

German Alliances with Russia and Austria For the moment, Bismarck could ignore the Balkans, but he could not ignore the breach in his eastern alliance system. With Russia alienated, he concluded a secret treaty with Austria in 1879. This Dual Alliance provided that Germany and Austria would come to each other's aid if Russia attacked either of them. If another country attacked one of them, each promised at least to maintain neutrality.

The treaty was for five years and was renewed regularly until 1918. As the anchor of German policy, it was criticized at the time, and in retrospect, some have considered it an error. It appeared to tie German fortunes to those of the troubled Austro-Hungarian Empire and thus to borrow trouble for Germany. In addition, by isolating the Russians, it pushed them to seek alliances in the West.

Bismarck was fully aware of these dangers, but discounted them with good reason. He never allowed the alliance to drag Germany into Austria's Balkan quarrels. As he put it, in any alliance there is a horse and a rider, and he meant Germany to be

the rider. He made it clear to the Austrians that the alliance was purely defensive and Germany would never be a party to an attack on Russia. "For us," he said, "Balkan questions can never be a motive for war."

Bismarck believed that monarchical, reactionary Russia would not seek an alliance either with republican, revolutionary France or with increasingly democratic Britain. In fact, he expected the Austro-German negotiations to frighten Russia into seeking closer relations with Germany, and he was right. By 1881, he had renewed the Three Emperors' League on a firmer basis. The three powers promised to maintain friendly neutrality in case a fourth power attacked any of them. Other clauses included the right of Austria to annex Bosnia-Herzegovina whenever it wished and the support of all three powers for closing the Dardanelles to all nations in case of war.

The agreement allayed German fears of a Russian-French alliance and Russian fears of a combination of Austria and Britain against it, of Britain's fleet sailing into the Black Sea, and of a hostile combination of Germany and Austria. Most importantly, the agreement reduced the tension in the Balkans between Austria and Russia.

The Triple Alliance In 1882, Italy, ambitious for colonial expansion and angered by the French occupation of Tunisia, asked to join the Dual Alliance. The provisions of its entry were defensive and directed against France. Bismarck's policy was now a complete success. He was allied with three of the great powers and friendly with the other, Great Britain, which held aloof from all alliances. France was isolated and no threat. Bismarck's diplomacy was a great achievement, but an even greater challenge was to maintain this complicated system of secret alliances in the face of the continuing rivalries among Germany's allies. Despite a war in 1885 between Serbia and Bulgaria that again estranged Austria and Russia, he succeeded.

Although the Three Emperors' League lapsed, the Triple Alliance (Germany, Austria, and Italy) was renewed for another five years. To restore German relations with Russia, Bismarck negotiated the Reinsurance Treaty of 1887, in which both powers promised to remain neutral if either was attacked. All seemed smooth, but a change in the German monarchy upset Bismarck's arrangements. (See "Bismarck Explains His Foreign Policy," page 840.)

In 1888, William II (r. 1888–1918) came to the German throne. He was twenty-nine years old, ambitious, and impetuous. He was imperious by temperament and believed he ruled by divine right. An injury at birth had left him with a withered left

---

[4]Quoted in Hajo Holborn, *A History of Modern Germany, 1840–1945* (New York: Knopf, 1969), p. 239.

BISMARCK EXPLAINS HIS FOREIGN POLICY

Otto von Bismarck, chancellor of the new German Empire, guided German foreign policy in the years from its establishment of the empire in 1871 until his dismissal from office in 1890. In that period and for another quarter-century, Europe was free of war among the great powers. The system of alliances Bismarck took the lead in creating is often given credit for preserving that peace. The following passage from his memoirs, written in his retirement, sets forth in retrospect his intentions in creating this system.

■ *What alliances made up Bismarck's system? How were they meant to preserve the peace? What is Bismarck's stated purpose for avoiding a war in Europe? Were there other reasons too?*

The Triple Alliance which I originally sought to conclude after the peace of Frankfurt, and about which I had already sounded Vienna and St. Petersburg, from Meaux, in September 1870, was an alliance of the three emperors with the further idea of bringing into it monarchical Italy. It was designed for the struggle which, as I feared, was before us; between the two European tendencies which Napoleon called Republican and Cossack, and which I, according to our present ideas, should designate on the one side as the system of order on a monarchical basis, and on the other as the social republic to the level of which the antimonarchical development is wont to sink, either slowly or by leaps and bounds, until the conditions thus created become intolerable, and the disappointed populace are ready for a violent return to monarchical institutions in a Cæsarean form. I consider that the task of escaping from this *circulus vitiosus*, or, if possi-

ble, of sparing the present generation and their children an entrance into it, ought to be more closely incumbent on the strong existing monarchies, those monarchies which still have a vigorous life, than any rivalry over the fragments of nations which people the Balkan peninsula. If the monarchical governments have no understanding of the necessity for holding together in the interests of political and social order, but make themselves subservient to the chauvinistic impulses of their subjects, I fear that the international revolutionary and social struggles which will have to be fought out will be all the more dangerous, and take such a form that the victory on the part of monarchical order will be more difficult. Since 1871 I have sought for the most certain assurance against those struggles in the alliance of the three emperors, and also in the effort to impart to the monarchical principle in Italy a firm support in that alliance.

Otto von Bismarck, *Reflections and Reminiscences*, ed. by Theodore S. Hamerow (New York: Harper Torchbooks, 1968), pp. 236–237.

arm. He compensated for this disability with vigorous exercise, a military bearing, and an often embarrassingly bombastic rhetoric.

Like many Germans of his generation, William II was filled with a sense of Germany's destiny as the leading power of Europe. He wanted recognition of at least equality with Britain, the land of his mother and of his grandmother, Queen Victoria. To achieve a "place in the sun," he and his contemporaries wanted a navy and colonies like Britain's. These aims, of course, ran counter to

Bismarck's limited continental policy. When William argued for a navy as a defense against a British landing in North Germany, Bismarck replied, "If the British should land on our soil, I should have them arrested." This was only one example of the great distance between the young emperor, or kaiser, and his chancellor. In 1890, William used a disagreement over domestic policy to dismiss Bismarck.

As long as Bismarck held power, Germany was secure, and the great European powers remained at

Bismarck and the young Kaiser William II meet in 1888. The two disagreed over many issues, and in 1890 William dismissed the aged chancellor.   German Information Center

peace. Although he made mistakes, there was much to admire in his understanding and management of international relations in the hard world of reality. He had a clear and limited idea of his nation's goals. He resisted pressures for further expansion with few and insignificant exceptions. He understood and used the full range of diplomatic weapons: appeasement and deterrence, threats and promises, secrecy and openness. He understood the needs and hopes of other countries and, where possible, tried to help them satisfy their needs or used those countries to his own advantage. His system of alliances created a stalemate in the Balkans and ensured German security.

During Bismarck's time, Germany was a force for European peace and was increasingly understood to be so. This position would not, of course, have been possible without its great military power. It also required, however, the leadership of a statesman who was willing and able to exercise restraint and who understood what his country needed and what was possible.

FORGING THE TRIPLE ENTENTE (1890–1907)

Franco-Russian Alliance Almost immediately after Bismarck's retirement, his system of alliances collapsed. His successor was General Leo von Caprivi (1831–1899), who had once asked, "What kind of jackass will dare to be Bismarck's successor?" Caprivi refused the Russian request to renew the Reinsurance Treaty, in part because he felt incompetent to continue Bismarck's complicated policy and in part because he wished to draw Germany closer to Britain, but Britain remained aloof, and Russia was alienated.

Even Bismarck had assumed that ideological differences would prevent a Franco-Russian alliance. Political isolation and the need for foreign capital, however, drove the Russians toward France. The French, who were even more isolated, encouraged their investors to pour capital into Russia if it would help produce security against Germany. In 1894, France and Russia signed a defensive alliance against Germany.

Britain and Germany Britain now became the key to the international situation. Colonial rivalries pitted the British against the Russians in Central Asia and against the French in Africa. Traditionally, Britain had also opposed Russian control of Constantinople and the Dardanelles and French control of the Low Countries. There was no reason to think Britain would soon become friendly to its traditional rivals or abandon its accustomed friendliness toward the Germans.

Yet within a decade of William II's accession, Germany had become the enemy in British minds. Before the turn of the century, popular British thrillers about imaginary wars portrayed the French as the invader; after the turn of the century, the enemy was usually Germany. This remarkable transformation has often been attributed to economic rivalry between Germany and Britain, in which Germany challenged and even overtook British production in various materials and markets. Certainly, Germany made such gains, and many Britons resented them. Yet the problem was not a serious cause of hostility, and it waned during the first decade of the century. The real problem lay in the foreign and naval policies of the German emperor and his ministers.

William II admired Britain's colonial empire and mighty fleet. At first, Germany tried to win the British over to the Triple Alliance, but when Britain clung to its "splendid isolation," German policy changed. The idea was to demonstrate Germany's worth as an ally by withdrawing support and even making trouble for Britain. This odd manner of gaining an ally reflected the kaiser's confused feelings toward Britain, which mixed dislike and jealousy with admiration. Many Germans, especially in the intellectual community, shared these feelings. Like William, they were eager for Germany to pursue a "world policy" rather than Bismarck's limited one that confined German interests to Europe. They, too, saw England as the barrier to German ambitions. Their influence in the schools, the universities, and the press guaranteed popular approval of hostility to Britain.

In Africa, the Germans blocked British attempts to build a railroad from Capetown to Cairo. They also openly sympathized with the Boers of South Africa in their resistance to British expansion. In 1896, William congratulated Paul Kruger (1825–1904), president of the Boer Transvaal Republic, for repulsing a British raid "without having to appeal to friendly powers [i.e., Germany] for assistance."

In 1898, William began to realize his dream of a German navy with the passage of a naval law providing for nineteen battleships. In 1900, a second law doubled that figure. The architect of the new navy was Admiral Alfred von Tirpitz (1849–1930), who openly proclaimed that Germany's naval policy was aimed at Britain. His "risk" theory argued that Germany could build a fleet strong enough, not to defeat the British, but to do enough damage to make the British navy inferior to that of other powers like France or the United States. The theory was, in fact, absurd, because as Germany's fleet became menacing, the British would certainly build enough ships to maintain their advantage, and Britain had greater financial resources than Germany.

The naval policy, therefore, was doomed to failure. Its main results were to waste German resources and to begin a great naval race with Britain. Eventually, the threat the German navy posed so antagonized and alarmed British opinion that the British abandoned their traditional policies.

At first, however, Britain was not unduly concerned. The general hostility of world opinion during the Boer War (1899–1902), in which their great empire crushed a rebellion by South African farmers, embarrassed the British, and their isolation no longer seemed so splendid. The Germans had acted with restraint during the war. Between 1898 and 1901, Joseph Chamberlain, the colonial secretary, made several attempts to conclude an alliance with Germany. The Germans, confident that a British alliance with France or Russia was impossible, refused and held out for greater concessions.

The Entente Cordiale The first breach in Britain's isolation came in 1902, when it concluded an alliance with Japan to defend British interests in the Far East against Russia. Next, Britain abandoned its traditional antagonism toward France and in 1904 concluded a series of agreements with the French, collectively called the Entente Cordiale. It was not a formal treaty and had no military provisions, but it settled all outstanding colonial differences between the two nations. In particular, Britain gave France a free hand in Morocco in return for French recognition of British control over Egypt. The Entente Cordiale was a long step toward aligning the British with Germany's great potential enemy.

Britain's new relationship with France was surprising, but in 1904, hardly anyone believed the British whale and the Russian bear would ever come together. The Russo-Japanese War of 1904–1905 made such a development seem even less likely, because Britain was allied with Russia's enemy, but Britain had behaved with restraint, and their unexpected defeat, which also led to the Russian Revolution of 1905, humiliated the Russians. Although the revolution was put down, it weakened Russia and reduced British apprehensions about Russian power. The British were also concerned that Russia might again drift into the German orbit.

The First Moroccan Crisis At this point, Germany decided to test the new understanding between Britain and France. In March 1905, Emperor William II landed at Tangier, made a speech in favor of Moroccan independence, and by implication asserted Germany's right to participate in Morocco's destiny. This was a challenge to France. Germany's chancellor, Prince Bernhard von Bülow (1849–1929), intended to show France how weak it was. He also hoped to gain colonial concessions.

The Germans demanded an international conference to show their power more dramatically. The conference met in 1906 at Algeciras in Spain. Austria sided with its German ally, but Spain, which also had claims in Morocco, Italy, Russia and the United States, voted with Britain and France. The Germans had overplayed their hand, receiving trivial concessions, and the French position in Morocco was confirmed. German bullying had, moreover, driven Britain and France closer together. In the face of the threat of a German attack on France, Sir Edward Grey (1862–1933), the British foreign secretary, without making a firm commitment, authorized conversations between the British and French general staffs. Their agreements became morally binding as the years passed. By 1914, French and British military and naval plans were so mutually dependent that the two countries were effectively, if not formally, allies.

British Agreement with Russia Britain's fear of Germany's growing naval power, its concern over German ambitions in the Near East (as represented by the German-sponsored plan to build a railroad from Berlin to Baghdad), and its closer relations with France made it desirable for Britain to become more friendly with France's ally, Russia. With French support, in 1907 the British concluded an agreement with Russia much like the Entente Cordiale with France. It settled Russo-British quarrels in Central Asia and opened the door for wider cooperation. The Triple Entente, an informal, but powerful, association of Britain, France, and Russia, was now ranged against the Triple Alliance. Italy was an unreliable ally, however, which meant two great land powers and Great Britain encircled Germany and Austria-Hungary.

William II and his ministers had turned Bismarck's nightmare of the prospect of a two-front war with France and Russia into a reality. They had made it more horrible by adding Britain to their foes. The equilibrium that Bismarck had worked so hard to achieve was destroyed. Britain would no longer support Austria in restraining Russian ambitions in the Balkans. Germany, increasingly alarmed by a sense of being encircled, was less willing to restrain the Austrians for fear of alienating them, too. In the Dual Alliance of Germany and Austria, the rider was now less clear.

Bismarck had built his alliance system to maintain peace, but the new alliance increased the risk of war and made the Balkans a likely spot for it to break out. Bismarck's diplomacy had left France isolated and impotent. The new arrangement associated France with the two greatest powers in Europe besides Germany. The Germans could rely only on Austria, and Austria's troubles made it less likely to provide aid than to need it.

WORLD WAR I

THE ROAD TO WAR (1908–1914)

The weak Ottoman Empire still controlled the central strip of the Balkan Peninsula running west from Constantinople to the Adriatic. North and south of it were the independent states of Romania, Serbia, Montenegro, and Greece, as well as Bulgaria, technically still part of the empire, but legally autonomous and practically independent. The Austro-Hungarian Empire included Croatia and Slovenia and, since 1878, had "occupied and administered" Bosnia and Herzegovina.

Except for the Greeks and the Romanians, most of the inhabitants of the Balkans spoke variants of the same Slavic language and felt a cultural and historical kinship with one another. For centuries Austrians, Hungarians, or Turks had ruled them, and the nationalism that characterized late-nineteenth-century Europe made many of them eager for independence. The more radical among them longed for a union of the south Slavic, or Yugoslav, peoples in a single nation. They looked to independent Serbia as the center of the new nation and hoped to detach all the Slavic provinces (especially Bosnia, which bordered on Serbia) from Austria. Serbia believed its destiny was to unite the Slavs at the expense of Austria, as Piedmont had united the Italians and Prussia the Germans.

In 1908, a group of modernizing reformers called the Young Turks seized power in the Ottoman Empire. Their actions threatened to breath new life into the empire and to interfere with the plans of the European jackals to pounce on the Ottoman corpse. These events brought on the first of a series of Balkan crises that would eventually lead to war.

The Bosnian Crisis In 1908, the Austrian and Russian governments decided to act quickly before Turkey became strong enough to resist. They struck a bargain in which Russia agreed to support the Austrian annexation of Bosnia and Herzegovina in return for Austrian backing for opening the Dardanelles to Russian warships.

Austria, however, declared the annexation before the Russians could act. The British and French, eager for the favor of the Young Turks, refused to agree to the Russian demand to open the Dardanelles. The Russians were humiliated and furious, but too weak to do anything but protest. The Austrian annexation of Bosnia enraged Russia's "little brothers," the Serbs.

Germany had not been warned in advance of Austria's plans and was unhappy because the action threatened their relations with Russia and Turkey. Germany felt so dependent on the Dual Alliance, however, that it nevertheless assured Austria of its support. Austria had been given a free hand, and to some extent, Vienna was now making German policy. It was a dangerous precedent. Also, the failure of Britain and France to support Russia strained the Triple Entente. This made it harder for them to oppose Russian interests in the future if they were to keep Russian friendship.

The Second Moroccan Crisis The second Moroccan crisis, in 1911, emphasized the French and British need for mutual support. When France sent an army to Morocco, Germany took the opportunity to "protect German interests" there as a means to extort colonial concessions in the French Congo. To add force to their demands, the Germans sent the gunboat *Panther* to the Moroccan port of Agadir, purportedly to protect German citizens there. Once again, as in 1905, the Germans went too far. The *Panther*'s visit to Agadir provoked a strong reaction in Britain. For some time Anglo-German relations had been growing worse, chiefly because the naval race had intensified. In 1907, Germany had built its first dreadnought, a new type of battleship that Britain had launched in 1906. In 1908, Germany had passed still another naval law that accelerated the challenge to British naval supremacy.

These actions threatened Britain's security. Britain had to increase taxes to pay for new armaments just when its liberal government was launching its expensive program of social legislation. Negotiations failed to persuade William II and Tirpitz to slow down naval construction.

In this atmosphere, the British heard of the *Panther*'s arrival in Morocco. They wrongly believed the Germans meant to turn Agadir into a naval base on the Atlantic. The crisis passed when France yielded some insignificant bits of the Congo and Germany recognized the French protectorate over Morocco. Britain drew closer to France. The British made plans to send an expeditionary force to defend France in case Germany attacked, and the British and French navies agreed to cooperate. Without any formal treaty, the German naval construction and the Agadir crisis had turned the Entente Cordiale into a de facto alliance. If Germany attacked France, Britain must defend the French, for its own security was inextricably tied up with that of France.

War in the Balkans   The second Moroccan crisis also provoked another crisis in the Balkans. Italy sought to gain colonies and to take its place among the great powers. It wanted Libya, which, though worth little before the discovery of oil in the 1950s, was at least available. Italy feared that the recognition of the French protectorate in Morocco would encourage France to move into Libya also. So, in 1911, Italy attacked the Ottoman Empire to preempt the French, and forced Turkey to cede Libya and the Dodecanese Islands in the Aegean. The Italian victory encouraged the Balkan states to try their luck. In 1912, Bulgaria, Greece, Montenegro, and Serbia jointly attacked the Ottoman Empire and won easily. (See Map 25–4.) After this First Balkan War, the victors fell out among themselves over the division of Macedonia, and in 1913 a Second Balkan War erupted. This time, Turkey and Romania joined Serbia and Greece against Bulgaria and stripped away much of what the Bulgarians had gained in 1878 and 1912.

After the First Balkan War, the alarmed Austrians were determined to limit Serbian gains and especially to prevent the Serbs from gaining a port on

---

THE COMING OF WORLD WAR I

1871	The end of the Franco-Prussian War; creation of the German Empire; German annexation of Alsace-Lorraine
1873	The Three Emperors' League (Germany, Russia, and Austria-Hungary)
1875	The Russo-Turkish War
1878	The Congress of Berlin
1879	The Dual Alliance between Germany and Austria
1881	The Three Emperors' League is renewed
1882	Italy joins Germany and Austria in the Triple Alliance
1888	William II becomes the German emperor
1890	Bismarck is dismissed
1894	The Franco-Russian alliance
1898	Germany begins to build a battleship navy
1899–1902	Boer War
1902	The British alliance with Japan
1904	The Entente Cordiale between Britain and France
1904–1905	The Russo-Japanese War
1905–1906	The first Moroccan crisis
1907	The British agreement with Russia
1908–1909	The Bosnian crisis
1911	The second Moroccan crisis
1911	Italy attacks Turkey
1912–1913	The First and Second Balkan wars
1914	Outbreak of World War I

---

the Adriatic. This policy meant keeping Serbia out of Albania, but the Russians backed the Serbs, and tensions mounted. An international conference sponsored by Britain in early 1913 resolved the dispute in Austria's favor and called for an independent principality of Albania. Austria, however, felt humiliated by the public airing of Serbian demands, and the Serbs defied the powers and continued to occupy parts of Albania. Finally, in October 1913, Austria issued an ultimatum, and Serbia withdrew its forces from Albania.

During this crisis, many officials in Austria had wanted an all-out attack on Serbia to remove its threat to the empire once and for all. Emperor Francis Joseph and the heir to the throne, Archduke Francis Ferdinand had resisted those demands. At the same time, Pan-Slavic sentiment in Russia pressed Tsar Nicholas II to take a firm

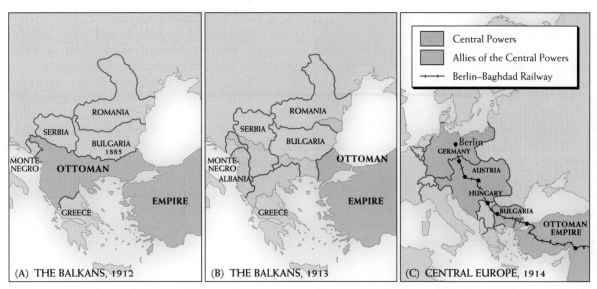

Map 25–4 **THE BALKANS, 1912–1913**   Two maps show the Balkans (a) before and (b) after the two Balkan wars; note the Ottoman retreat. In (c), we see the geographical relationship of the Central Powers and their Bulgarian and Turkish allies.

stand, but Russia once again let Austria have its way with Serbia. Throughout the crisis, Britain, France, Italy, and Germany restrained their allies, although each worried about appearing to be too reluctant to help its friends.

The lessons learned from this crisis of 1913 influenced behavior in the final crisis in 1914. As in 1908, the Russians had been embarrassed by their passivity; and their allies were more reluctant to restrain them again. The Austrians were embarrassed by the results of accepting an international conference and were determined not to do it again. They had gotten better results from threatening to use force; they and their German allies did not miss the lesson.

SARAJEVO AND THE OUTBREAK OF WAR (JUNE–AUGUST 1914)

The Assassination   On June 28, 1914, a young Serbian nationalist shot and killed Archduke Francis Ferdinand, heir to the Austrian throne, and his wife as they drove in an open car through the Bosnian capital of Sarajevo. The assassin was a member of a conspiracy hatched by a political terrorist society called Union or Death, better known as the Black Hand. The chief of intelligence of the Serbian army's general staff had helped plan and prepare the crime. Though his role was not known at the time, it was generally believed throughout Europe that Serbian officials were involved. The glee of the Serbian press after the assassination lent support to that belief.

The archduke was not popular in Austria, and his funeral evoked little grief. He had been known

to favor a form of federal government for Austria that would have raised the status of the Slavs in the empire. This position alienated the conservatives among the Habsburg officials and the Hungarians. It also threatened the radical nationalists' dream of an independent south Slav state.

Germany and Austria's Response   News of the assassination produced outrage everywhere in Europe except in Serbia. To those Austrians who had long favored an attack on Serbia, the opportunity seemed irresistible, but it was never easy for the Dual Monarchy to make a decision. Conrad von Hotzendorf (1852–1925), chief of the Austrian general staff, urged an attack, as he had often done before. Count Stefan Tisza (1861–1918), speaking for Hungary, resisted. Count Leopold von Berchtold (1863–1942), the Austro-Hungarian foreign minister, felt the need for strong action, but he knew German support would be required in the likely event that Russia should intervene to protect Serbia. Moreover, nothing could be done without Tisza's approval, and only German support could persuade the Hungarians to accept a war. The question of peace or war against Serbia, therefore, had to be answered in Berlin.

William II and Chancellor Theobald von Bethmann-Hollweg (1856–1921) readily promised German support for an attack on Serbia. It has often been said that they gave the Austrians a "blank check," but their message was more specific than that. They urged the Austrians to move swiftly while the other powers were still angry at Serbia. They also made the Austrians feel they would view a failure to act as evidence of Austria-Hungary's weakness and uselessness as an ally. Therefore, the

Above: The Austrian archduke Francis Ferdinand and his wife in Sarajevo on June 28, 1914. Later in the day the royal couple were assassinated by young revolutionaries trained and supplied in Serbia, igniting the crisis that led to World War I. Below: Moments after the assassination the Austrian police captured one of the assassins.
Brown Brothers

Austrians never wavered in their determination to make war on Serbia. They hoped, with the protection of Germany, to fight Serbia alone, but they were prepared to risk a general European conflict. The Germans also knew they risked a general war, but they too hoped to "localize" the fight between Austria and Serbia.

Some scholars believe Germany had long been plotting war, and some even think a specific plan for war in 1914 was set in motion as early as 1912. The vast body of evidence on the crisis of 1914, however, gives little support to such notions. The German leaders plainly reacted to a crisis they had not foreseen and just as plainly made decisions in response to events. The decision to support Aus-

tria, however, made war difficult, if not impossible, to avoid. The emperor and chancellor made that decision without significant consulting of either their military or diplomatic advisers.

William II reacted violently to the assassination. He was moved by his friendship for the archduke and by outrage at an attack on royalty. A different provocation would probably not have moved him so much. Bethmann-Hollweg was less emotional, but under severe pressure. To resist the decision would have meant flatly opposing the emperor. The German army suspected the chancellor of being soft. It would have been difficult for him to take a conciliatory position. Important military leaders, especially General Helmut von Moltke (1848–1916), Chief of the General Staff since 1906, had come to believe that the growing power of Russia threatened Germany. Moltke repeatedly spoke of the need for a decisive war against Russia, and its allies if necessary, "the sooner the better." His influence would be important at key moments in the crisis.

Bethmann-Hollweg, like many other Germans, also feared for the future. Russia was recovering its strength and would reach a military peak in 1917. The Triple Entente was growing closer and more powerful, and Germany's only reliable ally was Austria. The chancellor recognized the danger of supporting Austria, but he believed it to be even more dangerous to withhold that support. If Austria did not crush Serbia, it might collapse before the onslaught of Slavic nationalism backed by Russia. If Germany did not defend its ally, the Austrians might look elsewhere for help. His policy was one of calculated risk.

Unfortunately, the calculations proved to be incorrect. Bethmann-Hollweg hoped the Austrians would strike swiftly and present the powers with a fait accompli while the outrage of the assassination was still fresh, and he hoped German support would deter Russia. Failing that, he was prepared for a continental war against France and Russia. This policy, though, depended on British neutrality, and the German chancellor convinced himself the British would stand aloof.

The Austrians, however, were slow to act. They did not even deliver their deliberately unacceptable ultimatum to Serbia until July 23, when the general hostility toward Serbia had begun to subside. Serbia further embarrassed the Austrians by returning so soft and conciliatory an answer that even the mercurial German emperor thought it removed all reason for war, but the Austrians were determined not to turn back. On July 28, they declared war on Serbia, even though the army would not be ready to attack until mid-August.

The Triple Entente's Response The Russians, previously so often forced to back off, responded angrily to the Austrian demands on Serbia. The most conservative elements of the Russian government feared that war would lead to revolution, as it had in 1905, but nationalists, Pan-Slavs, and most of the politically conscious classes in general demanded action. The government responded by ordering partial mobilization, against Austria only. This policy was militarily impossible, but its intention was to put diplomatic pressure on Austria to refrain from attacking Serbia.

Mobilization of any kind, however, was a dangerous weapon because it was generally understood to be equivalent to an act of war. In fact, only Germany's war plan made mobilization the first and irrevocable start of a war. It required a quick victory in the west before the Russians were ready to act. Even partial Russian mobilization seemed to jeopardize this plan and put Germany in great danger. From this point on, the general staff pressed for German mobilization and war. Their claim of military necessity soon became irresistible.

France and Britain were not eager for war. France's president and prime minister were on their way back from a long-planned state visit to Russia when the crisis flared on July 23. The Austrians had, in fact, delivered their ultimatum to the Serbs precisely when these two men would be at sea. Had they been in Paris, they might have tried to restrain the Russians. In their absence and without consulting his government, the French ambassador to Russia gave the Russians the same assurances of support that Germany had given Austria. The British worked hard to resolve the crisis by traditional means: a conference of the powers. Austria, still smarting from its humiliation after the London Conference of 1913, would not hear of it. The Germans privately supported the Austrians, but publicly took on a conciliatory tone to placate the British.

Soon, however, Bethmann-Hollweg realized what he should have known from the first: If Germany attacked France, Britain must fight. Until July 30, his public appeals to Austria for restraint were a sham. Thereafter, he sincerely tried to persuade the Austrians to negotiate and avoid a general war, but it was too late. The Austrians could not turn back without losing their own self-respect and the respect of the Germans.

On July 30, Austria ordered mobilization against Russia. Bethmann-Hollweg resisted the enormous pressure to mobilize, not because he hoped to avoid war, but because he wanted Russia to mobilize against Germany first and appear to be the aggressor. Only in that way could he win the support of the German nation for war, especially the backing of pacifist Social Democrats. His luck was good for a change. The news of Russian general mobilization came only minutes before Germany would have mobilized in any case. Germany then declared war on Russia on August 1. The Schlieffen Plan went into effect. The Germans occupied Luxembourg on August 2 and invaded Belgium, which resisted, on August 3—the same day Germany declared war on France. (See "The Kaiser's Comments on the Outbreak of the World War," pages 848–849.) The invasion of Belgium violated the treaty of 1839 in which the British had joined the other powers in guaranteeing Belgian neutrality. This factor undermined sentiment in Britain for neutrality and united the nation against Germany, which then invaded France. On August 4, Britain declared war on Germany.

The Great War had begun. As Sir Edward Grey, the British foreign secretary, put it, the lights were going out all over Europe. They would come on again, but Europe would never be the same.

Although debate on the causes of the war continues, the most common opinion today is that German ambitions for a higher place in the international order under the new kaiser William II led to a new challenge to the status quo. German bullying resulted in a series of crises that led to the final crisis in July 1914, when Germany supported—indeed, pushed—its only reliable ally Austria into a war against Serbia that touched off the world war.

The deeper causes of that war are seen to be Germany's new ambitions to become a world power like Great Britain and to become the dominant power on the European continent. Germany's decision to build a battleship navy threatened Britain's interests and security. In response, the British launched an expensive and unwelcome naval race to maintain their superiority at sea and abandoned their cherished "splendid isolation" and long-standing competitions with France and Russia. In an unprecedented reversal of policy, they made an alliance with Japan and agreements with France and Russia to form the "Triple Entente," which grew from a set of colonial accords to an informal, but visible, check on German ambitions. This new international configuration alarmed Germany, which complained that jealous and hostile forces were "encircling" it. The Germans feared the growing power of the country's enemies, but Germany did not seriously attempt to ease the tension. Instead, a new arms race ensued, and Germany assumed a rigid stance in the final crisis that ended in war.

THE KAISER'S COMMENTS ON THE OUTBREAK OF THE WORLD WAR

—◆m◆—

On July 30, 1914, the German Foreign Office received the news that Russian mobilization had been started and would not be stopped. German strategy, based on the Schlieffen Plan, required an immediate mobilization and a swift attack on France before the weight of the Russian armies in the east could take full effect. The telegram from the German ambassador in Saint Petersburg, therefore, meant that war had come. The Kaiser, as usual, filled the margins of the document with his comments. On this occasion, he concluded with a long note that reveals his own understanding of the situation.

■ *What was the significance of mobilization on which the Kaiser places so much emphasis? Why does the Kaiser focus so much anger on England? In 1914, why was Great Britain aligned with its traditional rivals, France and Russia, against Germany?*

If mobilization can no longer be retracted— WHICH IS NOT TRUE—why, then, did the Czar appeal for my mediation three days afterward without mention of the issuance of the mobilization order? That shows plainly that the mobilization appeared to him to have been precipitate, and that after it he made this move *pro forma* in our direction for the sake of quieting his uneasy conscience, although he knew that it would no longer be of any use, as he did not feel himself to be strong enough to STOP the mobilization. Frivolity and weakness are to plunge the world into the most frightful war, which eventually aims at the destruction of Germany. For I have no doubt left about it: England, Russia and France have AGREED among themselves—after laying the foundation of the *casus foederis* for us through Austria—to take the Austro-Serbian conflict for an EXCUSE for waging a WAR OF EXTERMINATION against us. Hence Grey's [Sir Edward Grey, The British Foreign Secretary] cynical observation to Lichnowsky [The German Ambassador to Britain] "as long as the war is CONFINED to Russia and Austria, England would sit quiet, only when we and France MIXED INTO IT would he be compelled to make an active move against us ("); i.e., either we are shamefully to betray our allies, SACRIFICE them to Russia—thereby breaking up the Triple Alliance, or we are to be attacked in common by the Triple Entente for our FIDELITY TO OUR ALLIES and punished, whereby they will satisfy their jealousy by joining in totally RUINING us. That is the real naked situation *in nuce* which, slowly

STRATEGIES AND STALEMATE: 1914–1917

Throughout Europe, jubilation greeted the outbreak of war. No general war had been fought since Napoleon, and few understood the horrors of modern warfare. The dominant memory was of Bismarck's swift and decisive campaigns, in which the costs and casualties were light and the rewards great. After years of crises and resentments, war came as a release of tension. The popular press had increased public awareness of, and interest in, foreign affairs and had fanned the flames of patriotism. The prospect of war moved even a rational man of science like Sigmund Freud to say, "My whole libido goes out to Austria-Hungary."

Both sides expected to take the offensive, force a battle on favorable ground, and win a quick victory. The Triple Entente powers—or the Allies, as they called themselves—held superiority in numbers and financial resources, as well as command of the sea. (See Figure 25–1, page 850.) Germany and Austria, the Central Powers, had the advantages of possessing internal lines of communication and having launched their attack first.

Germany's war plan, was based on ideas developed by Count Alfred von Schlieffen (1833–1913), chief of the German general staff from 1891 to 1906. (See Map 25–5, page 851.) It aimed to outflank the French frontier defenses by sweeping through Belgium to the Channel and then wheeling to the south

and cleverly set going, certainly by Edward VII, has been carried on, and systematically built up by disowned conferences between England and Paris and Petersburg; finally brought to a conclusion by George V and set to work. And thereby the stupidity and ineptitude of our ally is turned into a snare for us. So the famous "CIRCUMSCRIPTION" of Germany has finally become a complete fact, despite every effort of our politicians and diplomats to prevent it. The net has been suddenly thrown over our head, and England sneeringly reaps the most brilliant success of her persistently prosecuted purely ANTI-GERMAN WORLD-POLICY, against which we have proved ourselves helpless, while she twists the noose of our political and economic destruction out of our fidelity to Austria, as we squirm ISOLATED in the net. A great achievement, which arouses the admiration even of him who is to be destroyed as its result! Edward VII is stronger after his death than am I who am still alive! And there have been people who believed that England could be won over or pacified, by this or that puny measure!!! Unremittingly, relentlessly she has pursued her object, with notes, holiday proposals, scares, Haldane, etc., until this point was reached. And we walked into the net and even went into the one-ship-program in construction with the ardent hope of thus pacifying England!!! All my warnings, all my pleas were voiced for nothing. Now comes England

so-called gratitude for it! From the dilemma raised by our fidelity to the venerable old Emperor of Austria we are brought into a situation which offers England the desired pretext for annihilating us under the hypocritical cloak of justice, namely, of helping France on account of the reputed "balance of power" in Europe, i.e., playing the card of all the European nations in England's favor against us! This whole business must now be ruthlessly uncovered and the mask of Christian peaceableness publicly and brusquely torn from its face in public, and the pharisaical hypocrisy exposed on the pillory!! And our consuls in Turkey and India, agents, etc., must fire the whole Mohammedan world to fierce rebellion against this hated, lying, conscienceless nation of shop-keepers; for if we are to be bled to death. England shall at least lose India.

From *Outbreak of the World War: German Documents Collected by Karl Kautsky*, by Max Montgelas and Walther Schücking, No. 401 (1924), pp. 348–350, trans. by Carnegie Endowment for International Peace. Reprinted by permission of Carnegie Endowment for International Peace.

and east to envelop the French and crush them against the German fortresses in Lorraine. The secret of success lay in making the right wing of the advancing German army immensely strong and deliberately weakening the left opposite the French frontier. The weakness of the left was meant to draw the French into attacking the wrong place while the war was decided on the German right. In the east, the Germans planned to stand on the defensive against Russia until France had been crushed, a task they thought would take only six weeks.

The apparent risk, besides the violation of Belgian neutrality and the consequent alienation of Britain, lay in weakening the German defenses against a direct attack across the frontier. The

strength of German fortresses and the superior firepower of German howitzers made that risk more theoretical than real. The true danger was that the German striking force on the right through Belgium would not be powerful enough to make the swift progress vital to success. The execution of the plan fell to Count Helmuth von Moltke, the nephew of Bismarck's most effective general. Moltke added divisions to the left wing and even weakened the Russian front for the same purpose. For reasons still debated, the plan failed by a narrow margin.

The War in the West The French had also put their faith in the offensive, but with less reason

	POPULATION (TOTAL)	SOLDIERS POTENTIALLY AVAILABLE	MILITARY EXPENDITURES (1913–1914)	BATTLESHIPS IN SERVICE OR BEING BUILT	CRUISERS	SUBMARINES	MERCHANT SHIPS (TONS)
GREAT BRITAIN	Overseas Emp. 390 Million 45,000,000	711,000	250,000,000	64	121	64	20,000,000
FRANCE	Overseas Emp. 58 Million 40,000,000	1,250,000	185,000,000	28	34	73	2,000,000
ITALY	Overseas Emp. 2 Million 35,000,000	750,000	50,000,000	14	22	12	1,750,000
RUSSIA	164,000,000	1,200,000	335,000,000	16	14	29	750,000
BELGIUM	7,500,000	180,000	13,750,000				
ROMANIA	7,500,000	420,000	15,000,000				
GREECE	5,000,000	120,000	3,750,000				
SERBIA	5,000,000	195,000	5,250,000				
MONTE-NEGRO	500,000						
UNITED STATES	92,000,000	150,000	150,000,000	37	35	25	4,500,000
GERMANY	65,000,000	2,200,000	300,000,000	40	57	23	5,000,000
AUSTRIA-HUNGARY	50,000,000	810,000	110,000,000	16	12	6	1,000,000
OTTOMAN EMPIRE	20,000,000	360,000	40,000,000				
BULGARIA	4,500,000	340,000	5,500,000				

FIGURE 25–1   Relative strengths of the combatants in World War I.

French troops advancing on the Western Front. This scene of trench warfare characterizes the 20th century's first great international conflict. The trenches were protected by barbed wire and machine guns, which gave defenders the advantage.
Hulton/CORBIS-Bettmann

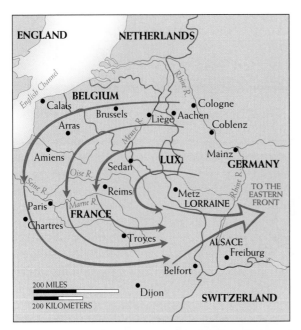

Map 25–5 **THE SCHLIEFFEN PLAN OF 1905** Germany's grand strategy for quickly winning the war against France in 1914 is shown by the wheeling arrows on the map. In the original plan, the crushing blows at France were to be followed by the release of troops for use against Russia on Germany's eastern front. The plan, however, was not adequately implemented, and the war on the western front became a long contest in place.

than the Germans. They underestimated the numbers and effectiveness of the German reserves and overestimated what the courage and spirit of their own troops could achieve. Courage and spirit could not defeat machine guns and heavy artillery. The French offensive on Germany's western frontier failed totally. This defeat probably was preferable to a partial success, because it released troops for use against the main German army. As a result, the French and the British were able to stop the German advance on Paris at the Battle of the Marne in September 1914. (See Map 25–6, page 852, and Map 25–7, page 853.)

Thereafter, the nature of the war in the west became one of position instead of movement. Both sides dug in behind a wall of trenches protected by barbed wire that stretched from the North Sea to Switzerland. Strategically placed machine-gun nests made assaults difficult and dangerous. Both sides, nonetheless, attempted massive attacks preceded by artillery bombardments of unprecedented and horrible force and duration. Still, the defense was always able to recover and to bring up reserves fast enough to prevent a breakthrough.

Assaults that cost hundreds of thousands of lives produced advances of only hundreds of yards. Even poison gas proved ineffective. In 1916, the

British tanks moving toward the Battle of Cambrai in Flanders late in 1917. Tanks were impervious to machine-gun fire. Had they been used in great numbers, they might have broken the stalemate in the west.   Bildarchiv Preussischer Kulturbesitz

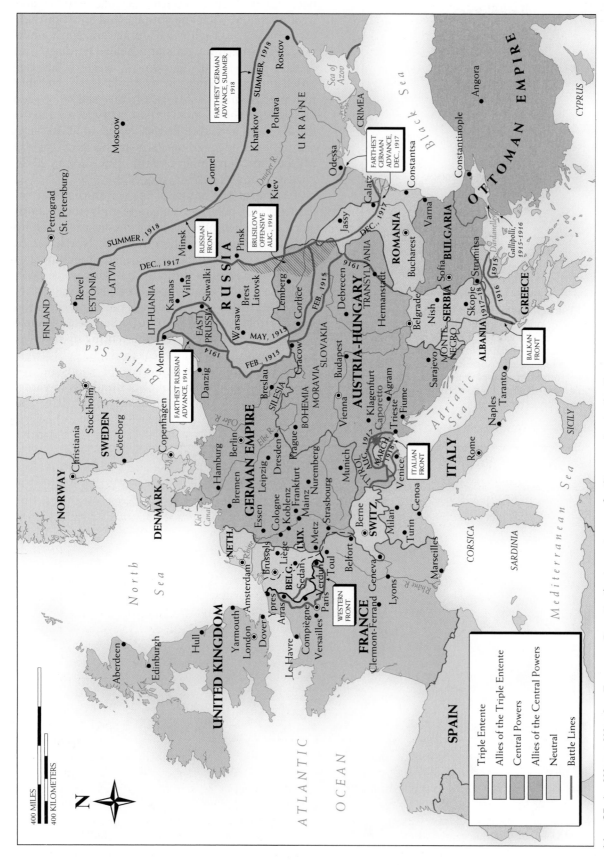

Map 25–6 **WORLD WAR I IN EUROPE** Despite the importance of military action in the Far East, in the Arab world, and at sea, the main theaters of activity in World War I were in the European areas.

SPAIN

ATLANTIC
OCEAN

North
Sea

UNITED KINGDOM

Aberdeen
Edinburgh
Hull
Yarmouth
London
Dover
Le Havre
Ypres
Arras
Compiègne
Versailles
Paris
FRANCE
Clermont-Ferrand
Lyons
Geneva

WESTERN
FRONT

NETH.
Amsterdam
Brussels
BELG.
Liège
Sedan
Verdun
Toul
Belfort
LUX.
Metz

NORWAY
Christiania

SWEDEN
Göteborg
Stockholm

DENMARK
Copenhagen

Baltic Sea

Kiel
Canal

GERMAN EMPIRE
Hamburg
Bremen
Berlin
Essen
Cologne
Koblenz
Frankfurt
Mainz
Nuremberg
Strasbourg
Leipzig
Dresden
Prague
Munich
SWITZ.
Berne
Milan
Turin
Genoa

ITALY
Rome
Naples
Taranto

CORSICA
SARDINIA
SICILY

Mediterranean Sea

Rhône R.
Marseilles

FINLAND

Moscow

Petrograd
(St. Petersburg)

Revel
ESTONIA
LATVIA
LITHUANIA
Kaunas
Vilna
Memel
Danzig
EAST PRUSSIA
Suwalki
Minsk
Pinsk

RUSSIA

Gomel

Kharkov
Poltava
Rostov

Kiev
Odessa
UKRAINE
CRIMEA

Sea of Azov

Black Sea

FARTHEST GERMAN ADVANCE, SUMMER, 1918
SUMMER, 1918
SUMMER, 1918

RUSSIAN FRONT
DEC., 1917

BRUSILOV'S OFFENSIVE AUG., 1916

FARTHEST GERMAN ADVANCE, DEC., 1917

FARTHEST RUSSIAN ADVANCE, 1914

Warsaw
Brest Litovsk
Lemberg
Gorlice
Cracow
Breslau
SILESIA
Oder R.
Elbe R.
BOHEMIA
MORAVIA
SLOVAKIA
Vienna
Budapest

AUSTRIA-HUNGARY

TRANSYLVANIA
Debrecen
Hermanstadt

ROMANIA
Bucharest
Galatz
Jassy
Constantsa
Varna

BULGARIA
Sofia
SERBIA
Belgrade
Nish
Skopje
Strumitsa
MONTE NEGRO
ALBANIA
Sarajevo

GREECE

Gallipoli, 1915–1916
Dardanelles

Constantinople

OTTOMAN EMPIRE
Angora

CYPRUS

Klagenfurt
Caporetto
Trieste
Agram
Fiume
Venice
TYROL
AUG., 1917
MARCH, 1918
ITALIAN FRONT

Adriatic Sea

BALKAN FRONT

Dnieper R.

FEB., 1915
MAY, 1915
FEB., 1915
1914
1916
1915
1916
1917–18
DEC., 1917

9161
9161
9161

N

400 MILES
400 KILOMETERS

Triple Entente
Allies of the Triple Entente
Central Powers
Allies of the Central Powers
Neutral
Battle Lines

852

MAP EXPLORATION

Interactive map: To explore this map further, go to
http://www.prenhall.com/kagan/map25.7

Map 25–7 **THE WESTERN FRONT, 1914–1918**   This
map shows the crucial western front in detail.

British introduced the tank, which eventually proved to be the answer to the machine gun. The Allied command was slow to understand this, however, and until the end of the war, defense was supreme. For three years after its establishment, the western front moved only a few miles in either direction.

The War in the East   In the east, the war began auspiciously for the Allies. The Russians advanced into Austrian territory and inflicted heavy casualties, but Russian incompetence and German energy soon reversed the situation. A junior German officer, Erich Ludendorff (1865–1937), under the command of the elderly general Paul von Hindenburg (1847–1934), destroyed or captured an entire Russian army at the Battle of Tannenberg and defeated another one at the Masurian Lakes. In 1915, the Central Powers pressed their advantage in the east and drove into the Baltic states and Russian Poland, inflicting more than two million casualties in a single year.

As the battle lines hardened, both sides sought new allies. Turkey (because of its hostility to Russia) and Bulgaria (the enemy of Serbia) joined the Central Powers. Both sides bid for Italian support with promises of the spoils of victory. Because the Austrians held what the Italians wanted most, the Allies could promise more. In a secret treaty of 1915, they agreed to deliver to Italy after victory most of *Italia irredenta* (i.e., the South Tyrol, Trieste, and some of the Dalmatian Islands), plus colonies in Africa and a share of the Turkish Empire. By the spring of 1915, Italy was engaging Austrian armies. The Italian campaign weakened Austria and diverted some German troops, but the Italian alliance never produced significant results. Romania joined the Allies in 1916 but was quickly defeated and driven from the war.

In the Far East, Japan honored its alliance with Britain and entered the war. The Japanese quickly overran the German colonies in China and the Pacific and used the opportunity to put pressure on China. Both sides also appealed to nationalistic sentiment in areas the enemy held. The Germans supported nationalist movements among the Irish, the Flemings in Belgium, and the Poles and Ukrainians under Russian rule. They even tried to persuade the Turks to lead a Muslim uprising against the British in Egypt and India, and against the French and Italians in North Africa. The Allies made the same appeals with greater success. They sponsored movements of national autonomy for the Czechs, the Slovaks, the south Slavs, and against the Poles that were under Austrian rule. They also favored a movement of Arab independence from Turkey. Guided by Colonel T. E. Lawrence (1888–1935), this last scheme proved especially successful later in the war.

In 1915, the Allies tried to break the deadlock on the western front by going around it. The idea came chiefly from Winston Churchill (1874–1965), first lord of the British admiralty. He proposed to attack the Dardanelles and capture Constantinople. This policy supposedly would knock Turkey from the war, bring help to the Balkan front, and ease communications with Russia. The plan was daring, but promising, and in its original form, it presented little risk. British naval superiority and the element of surprise might force the straits and capture Constantinople by purely naval action. Even if the scheme failed, the fleet could just sail away.

The success of Churchill's plan depended on timing, speed, and daring leadership, but all of these were lacking. Worse, the execution of the attack was inept and overly cautious. Troops were landed, and as Turkish resistance continued, the Allied commitment increased. Before the campaign was abandoned, the Allies lost almost

150,000 men and diverted three times that number from more useful occupations.

Return to the West Both sides turned back to the west in 1916. General Erich von Falkenhayn (1861–1922), who had succeeded Moltke in September 1914, attacked the French stronghold of Verdun. His plan was not to break through the French line, but to inflict enormous casualties on the French, who would have to defend Verdun against superior firepower from several directions. He, too, underestimated the superiority of the defense. The French held Verdun with comparatively few men and inflicted almost as many casualties as they suffered. The commander of Verdun, Henri Pétain (1856–1951), became a national hero, and "They shall not pass" became a slogan of national defiance.

The Allies tried to end the impasse by launching a major offensive along the River Somme in July. Aided by a Russian attack in the east that drew off some German strength and by an enormous artillery bombardment, they hoped at last to break through. Once again, the defense was superior. Enormous casualties on both sides brought no result. The war on land dragged on with no end in sight.

The War at Sea As the war continued, control of the sea became more important. The British ignored the distinction between war supplies (which were contraband according to international law) and food or other peaceful cargo (which was not subject to seizure). They imposed a strict blockade meant to starve out the enemy, regardless of international law. The Germans responded with submarine warfare meant to destroy British shipping and starve the British. They declared the waters around the British Isles a war zone, where even neutral ships would not be safe. Both policies were unwelcome to neutrals, and especially to the United States, which conducted extensive trade in the Atlantic. Yet the sinking of neutral ships by German submarines was both more dramatic and more offensive than the British blockade.

In May 1915, a German submarine torpedoed the British liner *Lusitania*. Among the 1,200 who drowned were 118 Americans. President Woodrow Wilson (1856–1924) warned Germany that a repetition would have grave consequences; the Germans desisted for the time being, rather than further anger the United States. This development gave the Allies a considerable advantage. The German fleet that had cost so much money and had caused so much trouble played no significant part in the war. The only major battle it fought was at Jutland in 1916. The battle resulted in a standoff and confirmed British domination of the surface of the sea.

America Enters the War In December 1916, President Woodrow Wilson intervened to try to bring about a negotiated peace. Neither side, however, was willing to renounce war aims that its opponent found acceptable. The war seemed likely to continue until one or both sides reached exhaustion.

Two events early in 1917 changed the situation radically. On February 1, the Germans announced the resumption of unrestricted submarine warfare, which led the United States to break off diplomatic relations. On April 6, the United States declared war on Germany. One of the deterrents to an earlier American intervention had been the presence of the autocratic tsarist Russia among the Allies. Wilson could conceive of the war only as an idealistic crusade "to make the world safe for democracy." That problem was resolved in March 1917 by a revolution in Russia that overthrew the tsarist government.

THE RUSSIAN REVOLUTION

No political faction planned or led the March Revolution in Russia. It was the result of the collapse of the monarchy's ability to govern. Although public opinion in Russia had strongly supported the country's entry into the war, the conflict overtaxed Russia's resources and the efficiency of the tsarist government.

Nicholas II was weak and incompetent and suspected of being under the domination of his German wife and the insidious peasant faith healer Rasputin, whom a group of Russian noblemen assassinated in 1916. Military and domestic failures produced massive casualties, widespread hunger, strikes by workers, and disorganization in the army. The peasant discontent that had plagued the countryside before 1914 did not subside during the conflict. In 1915, the tsar took personal command of the armies on the German front, which kept him away from the capital. In his absence, corrupt and incompetent ministers increasingly discredited the government even in the eyes of conservative monarchists. All political factions in the Duma, Russia's parliament, were discontented.

THE PROVISIONAL GOVERNMENT

In early March 1917, strikes and worker demonstrations erupted in Petrograd, as Saint Petersburg had been renamed. The ill-disciplined troops in the city refused to fire on the demonstrators. (See "The Outbreak of the Russian Revolution," pages 856–857.) The tsar abdicated on March 15. The government of Russia fell into the hands of members of the Duma, who soon formed a provisional government composed chiefly of Constitutional Democrats (Cadets) with Western sympathies.

At the same time, the various socialist groups, including both Social Revolutionaries and Social Democrats of the Menshevik wing, began to organize soviets, councils of workers and soldiers. Initially, they allowed the provisional government to function without actually supporting it. As relatively orthodox Marxists, the Mensheviks believed that Russia had to have a bourgeois stage of development before it could have a revolution of the proletariat. They were willing to work temporarily with the Constitutional Democrats in a liberal regime, but they became estranged when the Cadets failed to control the army or to purge "reactionaries" from the government.

In this climate, the provisional government decided to remain loyal to Russia's alliances and continue the war. The provisional government thus accepted tsarist foreign policy and associated itself with the main source of domestic suffering and discontent. The collapse of the last Russian offensive in the summer of 1917 sealed its fate. Disillusionment with the war, shortages of food and other ne-

cessities at home, and the peasants' demands for land reform undermined the government. This occurred even after the moderate socialist Alexander Kerensky (1881–1970) became prime minister. Moreover, discipline in the army had disintegrated.

LENIN AND THE BOLSHEVIKS

Ever since April, the Bolshevik wing of the Social Democratic Party had been working against the provisional government. The Germans, in their most successful attempt at subversion, had rushed the brilliant Bolshevik leader V. I. Lenin (1870–1924) in a sealed train from his exile in Switzerland across Germany to Petrograd. They hoped he would cause trouble for the revolutionary government.

Lenin saw the opportunity to achieve the political alliance of workers and peasants he had discussed before the war. In speech after speech, he hammered away on the theme of peace, bread, and land. The Bolsheviks demanded that all political power go to the soviets, which they controlled. The failure of the summer offensive encouraged them to attempt a coup, but the effort was a

Petrograd munitions workers demonstrating in 1917.   Ria-Novosti/Sovfoto/Eastfoto

THE OUTBREAK OF THE RUSSIAN REVOLUTION

The Russian Revolution of March 1917 started with a series of ill-organized demonstrations in Petrograd. These actions and the ineffectuality of the government's response are described in the memoirs of Maurice Paléologue (1859–1944), the French ambassador.

■ *What elements contributing to the success of the March Revolution emerge from this selection? Why might the army have been unreliable? Why did the two ambassadors think a new ministry should be appointed? What were the grievances of the revolutionaries? Why is there no discussion of the leaders of the revolution? What role did the emperor (tsar) play in these events?*

MONDAY, MARCH 12, 1917

At half-past eight this morning, just as I finished dressing, I heard a strange and prolonged din which seemed to come from the Alexander Bridge. I looked out: there was no one on the bridge, which usually presents such a busy scene. But, almost immediately, a disorderly mob carrying red flags appeared at the end which is on the right bank of the Neva, and a regiment came towards it from the opposite side. It looked as if there would be a violent collision, but on the contrary the two bodies coalesced. The army was fraternizing with revolt.

Shortly afterwards, someone came to tell me that the Volhynian regiment of the Guard had mutinied during the night, killed its officers and was parading the city, calling on the people to take part in the revolution and trying to win over the troops who still remain loyal.

At ten o'clock there was a sharp burst of firing, and flames could be seen rising somewhere on the Liteïny Prospekt which is quite close to the embassy. Then silence. Accompanied by my military attaché, Lieutenant-Colonel Lavergne, I went out to see what was happening. Frightened inhabitants were scattering through the streets. There was indescribable confusion at the corner of the Liteïny. Soldiers were helping civilians to erect a barricade. Flames mounted from the Law Courts. The gates of the arsenal burst open with a crash. Suddenly the crack of machine-gun fire split the air: it was the regulars who had just taken up position near the Nevsky Prospekt. The revolutionaries replied. I had seen enough to have no doubt as to what was coming. Under a hail of bullets I returned to the embassy with Lavergne who had walked calmly and slowly to the hottest corner out of sheer bravado.

failure. Lenin fled to Finland, and his chief collaborator, Leon Trotsky (1879–1940), was imprisoned.

The failure of a right-wing countercoup gave the Bolsheviks another chance. Trotsky, released from prison, led the powerful Petrograd soviet. Lenin returned in October, insisted to his doubting colleagues that the time was ripe to take power, and by the extraordinary force of his personality persuaded them to act. Trotsky organized the coup that took place on November 6 and concluded with an armed assault on the provisional government. The Bolsheviks, almost as much to their own astonishment as to that of the rest of the

world, had come to rule Russia. (See "An Eyewitness Account of the Bolsheviks' Seizure of Power," pages 858–859.)

THE COMMUNIST DICTATORSHIP

The victors moved to fulfill their promises and to assure their own security. The provisional government had decreed an election for late November to select a Constituent Assembly. The Social Revolutionaries won a large majority over the Bolsheviks. When the assembly gathered in January, it met for only a day before the Red Army, controlled by the

About half-past eleven I went to the Ministry for Foreign Affairs, picking up Buchanan [the British ambassador to Russia] on the way.

I told Pokrovski [the Russian foreign minister] everything I had just witnessed.

"So it's even more serious than I thought," he said.

But he preserved unruffled composure, flavoured with a touch of skepticism, when he told me of the steps on which the ministers had decided during the night:

"The sitting of the Duma has been prorogued to April and we have sent a telegram to the Emperor, begging him to return at once. With the exception of M. Protopopov [the Minister of the Interior, in charge of the police], my colleagues and I all thought that a dictatorship should be established without delay; it would be conferred upon some general whose prestige with the army is pretty high, General Russky for example."

I argued that, judging by what I saw this morning, the loyalty of the army was already too heavily shaken for our hopes of salvation to be based on the use of the "strong hand," and that the immediate appointment of a ministry inspiring confidence in the Duma seemed to me more essential than ever, as there is not a moment to lose. I reminded Pokrovski that in 1789, 1830, and 1848, three French dynasties were overthrown because they were too late in realiz-

ing the significance and strength of the movement against them. I added that in such a grave crisis the representative of allied France had a right to give the Imperial Government advice on a matter of internal politics.

Buchanan endorsed my opinion.

Pokrovski replied that he personally shared our views, but that the presence of Protopopov in the Council of Ministers paralyzed action of any kind.

I asked him:

"Is there no one who can open the Emperor's eyes to the real situation?"

He heaved a despairing sigh.

"The Emperor is blind!"

Deep grief was writ large on the face of the honest man and good citizen whose uprightness, patriotism and disinterestedness I can never sufficiently extol.

From Maurice Paléologue, *An Ambassador's Memoirs* (London: Doubleday & Company, Inc., and Hutchinson Publishing Group, Ltd., 1924), pp. 221–225.

Bolsheviks, dispersed it. All other political parties also ceased to function in any meaningful fashion. In November and January, the Bolshevik government nationalized the land and turned it over to its peasant proprietors. Factory workers were put in charge of their plants. The state seized banks and repudiated the debt of the tsarist government. Property of the church reverted to the state.

The Bolshevik government also took Russia out of the war, which they believed benefited only capitalism. They signed an armistice with Germany in December 1917 and in March 1918 accepted the Treaty of Brest-Litovsk, by which Russia yielded

Poland, Finland, the Baltic states, and Ukraine. Some territory in the Transcaucasus region went to Turkey. The Bolsheviks also agreed to pay a heavy war indemnity.

These terms were a high price to pay for peace, but Lenin had no choice. Russia was incapable of renewing the war effort, and the Bolsheviks needed time to impose their rule. Moreover, Lenin believed that the war and the Russian example would soon lead to communist revolutions across Europe.

The new Bolshevik government met major domestic resistance. Civil war erupted between Red Russians, who supported the revolution, and

AN EYEWITNESS ACCOUNT OF THE BOLSHEVIKS' SEIZURE OF POWER

John Reed was an American newspaperman who was in Russia during the Revolution of 1917, an enthusiastic convert to Communism, a supporter of the Bolsheviks, and an ardent admirer of Lenin. In the following selections from his account of the Bolshevik revolution he described Lenin's qualities and the part Lenin played in overthrowing the Provisional Government.

■ *What was the Provisional government? How did it come into being? Why was it under pressure in November 1917? Which groups were vying for power? What program gave gave victory to the Bolsheviks?*

THURSDAY, OCT. 26/NOV. 8

The Congress was to meet at one o'clock, and long since the great meeting-hall had filled, but by seven there was yet no sign of the presidium.... The Bolshevik and Left Social Revolutionary factions were in session in their own rooms. All the livelong afternoon Lenin and Trotzky had fought against compromise. A considerable part of the Bolsheviki were in favour of giving way so far as to create a joint all-Socialist government. "We can't hold on!" they cried. "Too much is against us. We haven't got the men. We will be isolated, and the whole thing will fall." So Kameniev, Riazanov and others.

But Lenin, with Trotzky beside him, stood firm as a rock. "Let the compromisers accept our programme and they can come in! We won't give way an inch. If there are comrades here who haven't the courage and the will to dare what we dare, let him leave with the rest of the cowards and conciliators! Backed by the workers and soldiers we shall go on."

At five minutes past seven came word from the left Socialist Revolutionaries to say that they would remain in the Military Revolutionary Committee. "See!" said Lenin, "They are following."...

It was just 8:40 when a thundering wave of cheers announced the entrance of the presidium with Lenin—great Lenin—among them. A short, stocky figure, with a big head set down in his shoulders, bald and bulging. Little eyes, a snubbish nose, wide, generous mouth, and heavy chin; clean-shaven now, but already beginning to bristle with the well-known beard of his past and future. Dressed in shabby clothes, his trousers much too long for him. Unimpressive, to be the idol of a mob, loved and revered as perhaps few leaders in history have been.

White Russians, who opposed it. In the summer of 1918, the Bolsheviks murdered the tsar and his family. Loyal army officers continued to fight the revolution and received aid from Allied armies. Under the leadership of Trotsky, however, the Red Army eventually overcame the domestic opposition. By 1921, Lenin and his supporters were in firm control.

THE END OF WORLD WAR I

The collapse of Russia and the Treaty of Brest-Litovsk were the zenith of German success. The Germans controlled eastern Europe and its resources, especially food, and by 1918 they were free to concentrate their forces on the western front. These developments would probably have been decisive without American intervention. Still, American troops would not arrive in significant numbers for about a year, and both sides tried to win the war in 1917.

An Allied attempt to break through in the west failed disastrously. Losses were heavy and the French army mutinied. The Austrians, supported by the Germans, defeated the Italians at Caporetto and threatened to overrun northern Italy, until they were checked with the aid of Allied troops. The deadlock continued, but time was running out for the Central Powers.

A strange popular leader—a leader purely by virtue of intellect; colourless, humourless, uncompromising and detached, without picturesque idiosyncrasies—but with the power of explaining profound ideas in simple terms, of analysing a concrete situation. And combined with shrewdness, the greatest intellectual audacity.

. . .

Other speakers followed, apparently without any order. A delegate of the coal-miners of the Don Basin called upon the Congress to take measures against Kaledin, who might cut off coal and food from the capital. Several soldiers just arrived from the Front brought the enthusiastic greetings of their regiments.

. . . Now Lenin, gripping the edge of the reading stand, letting his little winking eyes travel over the crowd as he stood there waiting, apparently oblivious to the long-rolling ovation, which lasted several minutes. When it finished, he said simply, "We shall now proceed to construct the Socialist order!" Again that overwhelming human roar.

"The first thing is the adoption of practical measures to realise peace.... We shall offer peace to the peoples of all the belligerent countries upon the basis of the Soviet terms—no annexations, no indemnities, and the right of self-determination of peoples. At the same time, according to our promise, we shall publish and repudiate the secret treaties.... The question of War and Peace is so clear that I think that I may, without preamble, read the project of a Proclamation to the Peoples of All the Belligerent Countries...."

His great mouth, seeming to smile, opened wide as he spoke; his voice was hoarse—not unpleasantly so, but as if it had hardened that way after years and years of speaking—and went on monotonously, with the effect of being able to go on forever.... For emphasis he bent forward slightly. No gestures. And before him, a thousand simple faces looking up in intent adoration....

It was exactly 10:35 when Kameniev asked all in favour of the proclamation to hold up their cards. One delegate dared to raise his hand against, but the sudden sharp outburst around him brought it swiftly down.... Unanimous.

At two o'clock the Land Decree was put to vote, with only one against and the peasant delegates were wild with joy.... So plunged the Bolsheviki ahead, irresistible, over-riding hesitation and opposition—the only people in Russia who had a definite programme of action while the others talked for eight long months....

From John Reed, *Ten Days That Shook the World* (New York: Boni and Liveright, 1919), pp. 123–129.

GERMANY'S LAST OFFENSIVE

In March 1918, the Germans decided to gamble everything on one last offensive. (This decision was taken chiefly by Ludendorff, second in command to Hindenburg, but the real leader of the army.) The German army reached the Marne again, but got no farther. They had no more reserves, and the entire nation was exhausted. In contrast, the arrival of American troops in ever-increasing numbers bolstered the Allies. An Allied counteroffensive proved irresistible. As the exhausted Austrians collapsed in Italy, and Bulgaria and Turkey dropped out of the war, the German high command knew the end was imminent.

Ludendorff was determined to make peace before the German army was thoroughly defeated in the field and to make civilians responsible for ending the war. For some time, he had been the effective ruler of Germany under the aegis of the emperor. He now allowed a new government to be established on democratic principles and to seek peace immediately. The new government, under Prince Max of Baden, asked for peace on the basis of the **Fourteen Points** that President Wilson had declared as the American war aims. These were idealistic principles, including self-determination for nationalities, open diplomacy, freedom of the seas, disarmament, and the establishment of the League of Nations to keep the

MAJOR CAMPAIGNS AND EVENTS OF WORLD WAR I

August 1914	Germans attack in West
August–September 1914	First Battle of the Marne
1914	Battles of Tannenberg and the Masurian Lakes
April 1915	British land at Gallipoli, start of Dardanelles campaign
May 1915	Germans sink British ship *Lusitania*
February 1916	Germans attack Verdun
May–June 1916	Battle of Jutland
February 1917	Germans declare unrestricted submarine warfare
March 1917	Russian Revolution
April 1917	United States enters war
November 1917	Bolsheviks seize power
March 1918	Treaty of Brest-Litovsk
March 1918	German offensive in the West
November 1918	Armistice

peace. Wilson insisted he would deal only with a democratic German government because he wanted to be sure he was dealing with the German people and not merely their rulers.

THE ARMISTICE

The disintegration of the German army forced William II to abdicate on November 9, 1918. The majority branch of the Social Democratic Party proclaimed a republic to prevent their radical Leninist wing from setting up a soviet government. Two days later, this republican, socialist-led government signed the armistice that ended the war by accepting German defeat. The German people were, in general, unaware their army had been defeated and was crumbling. No foreign soldier stood on German soil. Many Germans expected a negotiated and mild settlement. The real peace was different and embittered the Germans. Many of them came to believe Germany had not been defeated but had been tricked by the enemy and

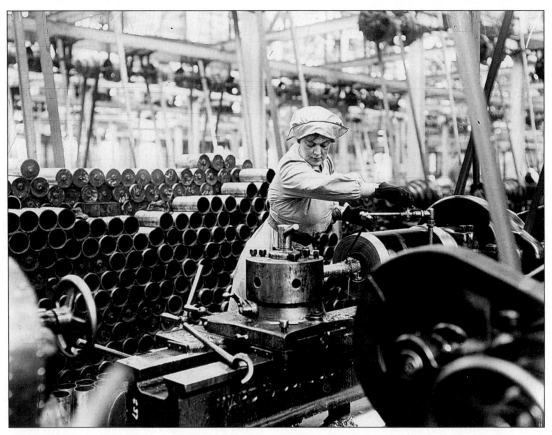

Women munitions workers in England. World War I demanded more from the civilian populations than had previous wars, resulting in important social changes. The demands of the munitions industries and a shortage of men (so many of whom were in uniform) brought many women out of traditional roles at home and into factories and other war-related work.
Getty Images Inc.–Hulton Archive Photos

betrayed—even stabbed in the back—by republicans and socialists at home.

The victors rejoiced, but they also had much to mourn. The casualties on all sides came to about ten million dead and twice as many wounded. The economic and financial resources of the European states were badly strained. The victorious Allies, formerly creditors to the world, became debtors to the new American colossus, which the calamities of war had barely touched.

The Great War, as contemporaries called it, the First World War to those who lived through its horrible offspring, lasted more than four years, doing terrible damage. Battle casualties alone counted more than 4 million dead and 8.3 million wounded among the Central Powers and 5.4 million dead and 7 million wounded from their opponents, and millions of civilians died from the war and causes arising from it. Among the casualties also were the German, Austro-Hungarian, Russian, and Turkish empires. The American intervention in 1917 thrust the United States into European affairs with a vengeance, and the collapse of the Russian autocracy brought the Bolshevik revolution and the reality of a great communist state. Disappointment, resentment, and economic dislocations caused by the war brought various forms of fascism to Italy, Germany, and other countries. The comfortable nineteenth-century assumptions of inevitable progress based on reason, science and technology, individual freedom, democracy, and free enterprise gave way in many places to cynicism, nihilism, dictatorship, statism, official racism, and class warfare. It is widely agreed that the First World War was the mother of the Second and to most of the horrors of the rest of the century.

These kinds of changes affected the colonial peoples the European powers ruled, and overseas empires would never again be as secure as they had seemed before the war. Europe was no longer the center of the world, free to interfere when it wished or to ignore the rest of the world if it chose. The memory of that war lived on to shake the nerve of the victorious Western powers as they faced the new conditions of the postwar world.

THE END OF THE OTTOMAN EMPIRE

At the outbreak of World War I in August 1914, the Ottoman Empire was neutral, but many military officers, the so-called Young Turks who had taken control of the Ottoman government in 1909, were pro-German. After hesitating for three months, the Turks decided to enter the war on the German side in November 1914. This decision ultimately brought about the end of the Ottoman Empire. Early victories gave way to defeat after defeat at the hands of the Russians and the British, the latter assisted by Arabs from the Arabian peninsula and neighboring lands, most notably Hussein (1856–1931), *sherif* (ruler or emir) of Mecca, the city of Muhammad. The British drove the Ottomans out of Palestine and advanced deep into Mesopotamia, as far north as the oil fields of Mosul in modern Iraq. By October 30, 1918, Turkey was out of the war. In November, an Allied fleet sailed into the harbor of Constantinople and landed troops who occupied the city. The Ottoman government was helpless.

The peace treaty signed in Paris in 1920 between Turkey and the Allies dismembered the Ottoman Empire, placing large parts of it, particularly the areas Arabs inhabited, under the control of

The Allies promoted Arab efforts to secure independence from Turkey in an effort to remove Turkey from the war. Delegates to the peace conference of 1919 in Paris included British colonel T. E. Lawrence, who helped lead the rebellion, and representatives from the Middle Eastern region. Prince Feisal, the third son of King Hussein, stands in the foreground of this picture; Colonel T. E. Lawrence is in the middle row, second from the right; and Brigadier General Nuri Pasha Said of Baghdad is second from the left. CORBIS/Bettmann

Britain and France. In Mesopotamia the British created the state of Iraq, which, along with Palestine, became British mandates. Syria and Lebanon became French mandates. (**Mandates** were territories that were legally administered under the auspices of the League of Nations, but were in effect ruled as colonies.) A Greek invasion of the Turkish homeland in Anatolia in 1919 provoked a nationalist reaction, bringing the young general Mustafa Kemal (1881–1938), who later took the name Ataturk, meaning "Father of the Turks," to power. He drove the Greeks out of Anatolia and compelled the victorious powers to make a new arrangement sealed by the treaty of Lausanne in 1923. Ataturk abolished the Ottoman sultanate and deposed the last caliph. The new Republic of Turkey abandoned most of the old Ottoman Empire but became fully independent of control by the European powers and sovereign in its Anatolian homeland. Under Ataturk and his successors, Turkey, although its population was overwhelmingly Muslim, became a secular state and a force for stability in the region.

Ataturk (1881–1938), the father of the Turkish Republic, sought to modernize his country by forcing Turks to adopt western ways, including the Latin alphabet. Here he is shown teaching the alphabet as president in 1928.
Turkish Cultural Office

The Arab portions of the old empire, however, were a different story. Divided into a collection of artificial states that had no historical reality, governed or dominated as client regimes by the British and French, they were relatively quiet during the 1920s and 1930s. The weakening of Britain and France during and after the Second World War, however, and their subsequent abandonment of control in the Middle East would create problems in the latter part of the century.

THE SETTLEMENT AT PARIS

The representatives of the victorious states gathered at Versailles and other Parisian suburbs in the first half of 1919. Wilson speaking for the United States, David Lloyd George (1863–1945) for Britain, Georges Clemenceau (1841–1929) for France, and Vittorio Emanuele Orlando (1860–1952) for Italy made up the Big Four. Japan also had an important part in the discussions. The diplomats who met in Paris had a far more difficult task than those who had sat at Vienna a century earlier. Both groups attempted to restore order to the world after long and costly wars. At the earlier conference, however, Metternich and his associates could confine their thoughts to Europe. France had acknowledged defeat and was willing to take part in and uphold the Vienna settlement. The diplomats at Vienna were not much affected by public opinion; and they could draw the new map of Europe along practical lines determined by the realities of power and softened by compromise.

OBSTACLES THE PEACEMAKERS FACED

The negotiators at Paris in 1919 were less fortunate. They represented constitutional, generally democratic governments, and public opinion had become a mighty force. Though there were secret sessions, the conference often worked in the full glare of publicity. Nationalism had become almost a secular religion, and Europe's many ethnic groups could not be relied on to remain quiet while the great powers distributed them on the map. Moreover, propaganda and especially the intervention of Woodrow Wilson had transformed World War I into a moral crusade to achieve a peace that would be just as well as secure. (See "Encountering the Past: War Propaganda and the Movies.") The Fourteen Points set forth the right of nationalities to self-determination as an absolute value; but in fact no one could draw the map of Europe to match ethnic groups perfectly with their homelands. All these elements made compromise difficult.

Wilson's idealism, moreover, came into conflict with the more practical war aims of the victorious

War Propaganda and the Movies: Charlie Chaplin

The vast scope of the First World War required support. As the war stretched on and its costs increased, all the competing nations intensified propaganda campaigns to justify the huge expenditure of lives and resources. Sometimes this took the form of painting the enemy in brutal and lurid colors to provoke hatred, and sometimes it took the form of sympathetic images of patriotism and sacrifice for a noble cause. These efforts, sponsored both by government and private agencies, saturated the lives of everyone—men, women, and even children—while the war lasted.

At first, most of the propaganda came in the form of writing—newspaper articles and pamphlets, justifying the war and demonizing the enemy. Soon, however, verbal efforts gave way to more emotionally powerful visual devices such as posters,

Charlie Chaplin in *Shoulder Arms.* © Sunset Boulevard/ Corbis Sygma

cartoons, and caricatures. By the middle of the war, however, the relatively new medium of film became the most powerful weapon of propaganda. Graphically and dramatically, movies showed the enemy as either horrible or ridiculous and one's own soldiers and people as brave and noble. Such images could reach rich and poor, literate and illiterate, young and old, with great emotional effect.

Both sides produced films that became enormously popular, but none more so than those Charlie Chaplin (1889–1977) did for the Allies. Born in England, he came to America as a vaudeville star in 1914 and was already famous when the war broke out. His tragicomic character, the tramp, in many variations, had universal appeal. His wartime films had amazing effects: They helped sell great quantities of Liberty Bonds (which the American government used to help pay for its involvement in the war), raised the morale of civilians, and even eased the miseries of shell-shocked soldiers.

Chaplin's 1918 movie *Shoulder Arms* was his greatest wartime success. It gave a comic picture of the difficulties of basic training for American recruits and portrays the Germans as bumbling fools. In the film, Chaplin's character, exhausted by the rigors of drilling, falls asleep. He wakes up at the front, where he deceives the enemy by pretending to be a tree, captures first a German unit and finally the kaiser, all by himself.

The Germans, too, soon learned the propaganda value of films, which were more completely in the hands of the government than those made in the Allied states. The German army made comedies, melodramas, and newsreels and showed them both to the troops and the civilian public. The German government thought movies so important that even during the freezing, brutal winter of 1917–1918 when fuel supplies were at a premium, it gave movie theaters special priority to use coal and electricity, but there was no German Charlie Chaplin.

- *What were the purposes of propaganda in the war? What were the advantages of using movies in the war effort?*

powers and with many of the secret treaties that had been made before and during the war. The British and French people had been told that Germany would be made to pay for the war. Russia had been promised control of Constantinople in return for recognizing the French claim to Alsace-Lorraine and British control of Egypt. Romania had been promised Transylvania at the expense of Hungary.

Some of the agreements contradicted others. Italy and Serbia had competing claims in the Adriatic. During the war, the British had encouraged Arab hopes of an independent Arab state carved out of the Ottoman Empire. Those plans, however, contradicted the Balfour Declaration (1917), in which the British seemed to accept Zionist ideology and to promise the Jews a national home in Palestine. Both of these plans conflicted with an Anglo-French agreement to divide the Near East between themselves.

The continuing national goals of the victors presented further obstacles to an idealistic "peace without victors." France was painfully conscious of its numerical inferiority to Germany and of the low birthrate that would keep it inferior. So France was naturally eager to weaken Germany permanently and preserve French superiority. Italy continued to seek *Italia irredenta*, Britain looked to its imperial interests, and Japan pursued its own advantage in Asia. The United States insisted on freedom of the seas, which favored American commerce, and on its right to maintain the Monroe Doctrine.

Finally, the peacemakers of 1919 faced a world still in turmoil. The greatest immediate threat appeared to be the spread of Bolshevism. While civil war distracted Lenin and his colleagues, the Allies landed small armies in Russia to help overthrow the Bolshevik regime. The revolution seemed likely to spread as communist governments were established in Bavaria and Hungary. A communist uprising led by the "Spartacus group" had to be suppressed in Berlin. The worried Allies even allowed an army of German volunteers to fight the Bolsheviks in the Baltic states.

Fear of the spread of communism affected the diplomats at Versailles, but it was far from dominant. The Germans played on such fears to get better terms, but the Allies, especially the French, would not hear of it. Fear of Germany remained the chief concern for France. More traditional and more immediate interests governed the policies of the other Allies.

THE PEACE

The Paris settlement consisted of five separate treaties between the victors and the defeated powers. Formal sessions began on January 18,

Britain's David Lloyd George, France's Georges Clemenceau, and America's Woodrow Wilson (l. to r.) were the dominant figures at the Paris peace conference in 1919. © Bettmann/CORBIS

1919, and the last treaty was signed on August 10, 1920. (See Map 25–8.) Wilson arrived in Europe to unprecedented popular acclaim. Liberals and idealists expected a new kind of international order achieved in a new and better way, but they were soon disillusioned. "Open covenants openly arrived at" soon gave way to closed sessions in which Wilson, Clemenceau, and Lloyd George made arrangements that seemed cynical to outsiders.

The notion of "a peace without victors" became a mockery when the Soviet Union (as Russia was now called) and Germany were excluded from the peace conference. The Germans were simply presented with a treaty and compelled to accept it, fully justified in their complaint that the treaty had been dictated, not negotiated. The principle of national self-determination was violated many times and was unavoidable. Still, their exclusion from decisions angered the diplomats from the small nations. The undeserved adulation accorded Wilson on his arrival gradually turned into equally undeserved scorn. He had not abandoned his ideals lightly, but had merely given way to the irresistible force of reality.

Map 25–8 **WORLD WAR I PEACE SETTLEMENT IN EUROPE AND THE MIDDLE EAST** The map of central and eastern Europe, as well as that of the Middle East, underwent drastic revision after World War I. The enormous territorial losses suffered by Germany, Austria-Hungary, the Ottoman Empire, Bulgaria, and Russia were the other side of the coin represented by gains for France, Italy, Greece, and Romania and by the appearance or reappearance of at least eight new independent states from Finland in the north to Yugoslavia in the south. The mandate system for former Ottoman territories outside Turkey proper laid foundations for several new, mostly Arab, states in the Middle East. In Africa, the mandate system placed the former German colonies under British, French, and South African rule. (See Map 25–2, page 833.)

The League of Nations   Wilson could make unpalatable concessions without abandoning his ideals because he put great faith in a new instrument for peace and justice: the **League of Nations**. Its covenant was an essential part of the peace treaty. The league was to be not an international government, but a body of sovereign states that agreed to pursue common policies and to consult in the common interest, especially when war threatened. The members promised to submit differences among themselves to arbitration, an international court, or the League Council. Refusal to abide by the results would justify economic sanctions and even military intervention by the league. The league was unlikely to be effective, however, because it had no armed forces at its disposal. Furthermore, any action required the unanimous consent of its council, consisting permanently of Britain, France, Italy, the United States, and Japan, as well as four other states that had temporary seats. The Covenant of the League bound its members to "respect and preserve" the territorial integrity of all its members; this was generally seen as a device to ensure the security of the victorious powers. The exclusion of Germany and the Soviet Union from the League Assembly further undermined its claim to evenhandedness.

Colonies   Another provision of the covenant dealt with colonial areas. These were called mandates and were placed under the "tutelage" of one of the great powers under league supervision and encouraged to advance toward independence. This provision had no teeth, and little advance was made. Provisions for disarmament were equally ineffective. Members of the league remained fully sovereign and continued to pursue their national interests. Only Wilson put much faith in the league's future ability to produce peace and justice. To get the other states to agree to the league, he approved territorial settlements that violated his own principles.

Germany   In the West, the main territorial issue was the fate of Germany. Although a united Germany was less than fifty years old, no one seems to have thought of undoing Bismarck's work and dividing the country into its component parts. The French wanted to set the Rhineland up as a separate buffer state, but Lloyd George and Wilson would not permit it. Still, they could not ignore France's need for protection against a resurgent Germany. France received Alsace-Lorraine and the right to work the coal mines of the Saar for fifteen years. Germany west of the Rhine and fifty kilometers east of it was to be a demilitarized zone. Allied troops could stay on the west bank for fifteen years.

The treaty also provided that Britain and the United States would help France if Germany attacked it. Such an attack was made more unlikely by the permanent disarmament of Germany. Its army was limited to 100,000 men on long-term service, its fleet was reduced to a coastal defense force, and it was forbidden to have warplanes, submarines, tanks, heavy artillery, or poison gas. As long as these provisions were observed, France would be safe.

The East   The settlement in the East reflected the collapse of the great defeated empires that had ruled it for centuries. Germany lost part of Silesia, and East Prussia was cut off from the rest of Germany by a corridor carved out to give the revived state of Poland access to the sea. The Austro-Hungarian Empire disappeared entirely, giving way to five small successor states. Most of its German-speaking people were gathered in the Republic of Austria, cut off from the Germans of Bohemia and forbidden to unite with Germany.

The Magyars were left with the much-reduced kingdom of Hungary. The Czechs of Bohemia and Moravia joined with the Slovaks and Ruthenians to the east to form Czechoslovakia, and this new state included several million unhappy Germans plus Poles, Magyars, and Ukrainians. The southern Slavs were united in the Kingdom of Serbs, Croats, and Slovenes, or Yugoslavia. Italy gained Trentino, which included tens of thousands of German speakers, and the port of Trieste. Romania was enlarged by receiving Transylvania from Hungary and Bessarabia from Russia. Bulgaria lost territory to Greece and Yugoslavia. Russia lost vast territories in the west. Finland, Estonia, Latvia, and Lithuania became independent states, and most of Poland was carved out of formerly Russian soil.

Reparations   Perhaps the most debated part of the peace settlement dealt with **reparations** for the damage Germany did during the war. Before the armistice, the Germans promised to pay compensation "for all damages done to the civilian population of the Allies and their property." The Americans judged the amount would be between $15 billion and $25 billion and that Germany would be able to pay that amount. France and Britain, however, who worried about repaying their war debts to the United States, were eager to have Germany pay the full cost of the war, including pensions to survivors and dependents.

There was a general agreement that Germany could not afford to pay such a huge sum, whatever it might be, and the conference did not specify an amount. In the meantime, Germany was to pay $5 billion annually until 1921. At that time, a final figure would be set, which Germany would have to pay in thirty years. The French did not regret the outcome. Either Germany would pay and be bled into impotence, or Germany would refuse to pay and French intervention would be warranted.

To justify these huge reparation payments, the Allies inserted the notorious **war guilt clause** (Clause 231) into the treaty:

The Allied and Associated Governments affirm, and Germany accepts, the responsibility of Germany and her allies for causing all the loss and damage to which the Allied and Associated Governments and their nationals have been subjected as a consequence of the war imposed upon them by aggression of Germany and her allies.

The Germans, of course, did not believe they were solely responsible for the war and bitterly resented the charge. They had lost territories containing badly needed natural resources. Yet they were presented with an astronomical and apparently unlimited reparations bill. To add insult to injury, they were required to admit to a war guilt they did not feel.

Finally, to heap insult upon insult, they were required to accept the entire treaty as the victors wrote it, without negotiation. Germany's prime minister Philipp Scheidmann (1865–1939) spoke of the treaty as the imprisonment of the German people and asked, "What hand would not wither that binds itself and us in these fetters?" There was no choice, however. The Social Democrats and the Catholic Center Party formed a new government, and their representatives signed the treaty. These parties formed the backbone of the Weimar government that ruled Germany until 1933. They never overcame the stigma of having accepted the Treaty of Versailles.

EVALUATING THE PEACE

Few peace settlements have undergone more severe attacks than the one negotiated in Paris in 1919. It was natural that the defeated powers should object to it, but the peace soon came under bitter criticism in the victorious countries as well. Many of the French objected that the treaty tied French security to promises of aid from the unreliable Anglo-Saxon countries. In England and the United States, a wave of bitter criticism arose in liberal quarters because the treaty seemed to violate the idealistic and liberal aims that the Western leaders had professed.

It was not a peace without victors. It did not put an end to imperialism, but attempted to promote the national interests of the winning nations. It violated the principles of national self-determination by leaving significant pockets of minorities outside the borders of their national homelands.

The Economic Consequences of the Peace The most influential economic critic of the treaty was John Maynard Keynes (1883–1946), a brilliant British economist who took part in the peace conference. He resigned in disgust when he saw the direction it was taking. His book, *The Economic Consequences of the Peace* (1920), was a scathing attack, especially on reparations and the other economic aspects of the peace. It was also a skillful assault on the negotiators and particularly on Wilson, whom Keynes depicted as a fool and a hypocrite. Keynes argued that the Treaty of Versailles was both immoral and unworkable. He called it a Carthaginian peace, referring to Rome's destruction of Carthage after the Third Punic War. He argued that such a peace would bring economic ruin and war to Europe unless it was repudiated.

Keynes's argument had a great effect on the British, who were already suspicious of France and glad of an excuse to withdraw from continental affairs. The decent and respectable position came to be one that supported revision of the treaty in favor of Germany. In the United States, the book fed the traditional tendency toward isolationism and gave powerful weapons to Wilson's enemies. Wilson's own political mistakes helped prevent American ratification of the treaty. Thus, America was out of the League of Nations and not bound to defend France. Britain, therefore, was also free from its obligation to France. France was left to protect itself without adequate means to do so for long.

Many of the attacks on the Treaty of Versailles are unjustified. It was not a Carthaginian peace. Germany was neither dismembered nor ruined. Reparations could be and were scaled down. Until the great world depression of the 1930s, the Germans recovered prosperity. Complaints against the peace should also be measured against the peace that the victorious Germans had imposed on Russia at Brest-Litovsk and their plans for a European settlement if they had won. Both were far more severe than anything enacted at Versailles. The attempt to achieve self-determination for nationalities was less than perfect, but it was the best effort Europe had ever made to do so.

Divisive New Boundaries and Tariff Walls The peace, nevertheless, was unsatisfactory in important ways. The elimination of the Austro-Hungarian Empire, however inevitable, created serious problems. Economically, it was disastrous. New borders and tariff walls separated raw materials from manufacturing areas and producers from their markets. In hard times, this separation created friction and hostility that aggravated other quarrels the peace treaties also created. Poland contained unhappy

German, Lithuanian, and Ukrainian minorities, and Czechoslovakia and Yugoslavia were collections of nationalities that did not find it easy to live together. Territorial disputes in Eastern Europe promoted further tension.

Moreover, the peace rested on a victory that Germany did not admit. The Germans felt cheated rather than defeated. The high moral principles the Allies proclaimed undercut the validity of the peace, for it plainly fell far short of those principles.

Failure to Accept Reality   Finally, the great weakness of the peace was its failure to accept reality. Germany and Russia must inevitably play an important part in European affairs, yet the settlement and the League of Nations excluded them. Given the many discontented parties, the peace was not self-enforcing; yet no satisfactory machinery to enforce it was established. The League of Nations was never a serious force for this purpose. It was left to France, with no guarantee of support from Britain and no hope of help from the United States, to defend the new arrangements. Finland, the Baltic states, Poland, Romania, Czechoslovakia, and Yugoslavia were expected to be a barrier to the westward expansion of Russian communism and to help deter a revival of German power. Most of these states, however, would have to rely on France in case of danger, and France was simply not strong enough to protect them if Germany revived.

The tragedy of the Treaty of Versailles was that it was neither conciliatory enough to remove the desire for revision, even at the cost of war, nor harsh enough to make another war impossible. The only hope for a lasting peace was that Germany would remain disarmed while the more obnoxious clauses of the peace treaty were revised. Such a policy required continued attention to the problem, unity among the victors, and farsighted leadership; but none of these was consistently present during the next two decades.

IN PERSPECTIVE

The outburst of European imperialism in the late the nineteenth century brought the Western countries into contact with almost all the inhabited areas of the world. The growth of industry, increased ease of transportation and communication, and the burgeoning of a world economic system all brought previously remote and isolated places into the orbit of the West.

By the time of the outbreak of the war, European nations had divided Africa among themselves for exploitation. India had long been a British colony.

The desirable parts of China were under European commercial control. Indochina was under French rule, and the powers had divided the islands of the Pacific. Much of the Near East was under the nominal control of the dying Ottoman Empire but under European influence. The Monroe Doctrine made Latin America a protectorate of the United States. Japan, pushed out of its isolation, had itself become an imperial power at the expense of China and Korea.

Yet the world the New Imperialism created did not last long. What began as yet another Balkan War involving the European powers became a general war that profoundly affected much of the rest of the world. As the terrible war of 1914–1918 dragged on, the real motives that had driven the European powers to fight gave way to public affirmations of the principles of nationalism and self-determination. The peoples under colonial rule took the public statements—and promises sometimes made to them in private—seriously and sought to win their independence and nationhood.

Mostly, the peace settlement disappointed them. The establishment of the League of Nations and the system of mandates changed little. The British Empire grew even larger as it inherited vast territories from the defeated German and the defunct Ottoman empires. The French retained and expanded their holdings in Africa and the Near East. Japanese imperial ambitions were rewarded at the expense of China and Germany.

A glance at the new map of the world could give the impression that the old imperial nations, especially Britain and France, were more powerful than ever, but that impression would be superficial and misleading. The great Western European powers had paid an enormous price in lives, money, and will for their victory in the war. Colonial peoples pressed for the rights that the West proclaimed as universal, but denied to their colonies; and some influential minorities in the countries that ruled those colonies sympathized with colonial aspirations for independence. Tension between colonies and their ruling nations was a cause of serious instability in the world the Paris treaties of 1919 created.

REVIEW QUESTIONS

1. To what areas of the world did Europe extend its power after 1870? How and why did European attitudes toward imperialism change after 1870? What features differentiate the New Imperialism from previous imperialistic movements? What features did they have in common?

2. What role in the world did Bismarck envisage for the new Germany after 1871? How suc-

cessful was he in carrying out his vision? Was he wise to tie Germany to Austria-Hungary?

3. Why and in what stages did Britain abandon its policy of "splendid isolation" at the turn of the century? Were the policies it pursued instead wise ones, or should Britain have followed a different course altogether?

4. How did developments in the Balkans lead to the outbreak of World War I? What was the role of Serbia? Of Austria? Of Russia? What was the aim of German policy in July 1914? Did Germany want a general war?

5. Why did Germany lose World War I? Could Germany have won, or was victory never a possibility? What were the benefits of Versailles to Europe, and what were its drawbacks? Was the settlement too harsh or too conciliatory? Could it have secured lasting peace in Europe? How might it have been improved?

6. Why did Lenin succeed in establishing Bolshevik rule in Russia? What role did Trotsky play? Was it wise policy for Lenin to take Russia out of the war?

SUGGESTED READINGS

L. ALBERTINI, *The Origins of the War of 1914*, 3 vols. (1952, 1957). Discursive, but invaluable.

V. R. BERGHAHN, *Germany and the Approach of War in 1914* (1973). Stresses the importance of Germany's naval program.

S. B. FAY, *The Origins of the World War*, 2 vols. (1928). The best and most influential of the revisionist accounts.

N. FERGUSON, *The Pity of War* (1999). An analytic study of the First World War with controversial interpretations, especially of why it began and why it ended.

F. FISCHER, *Germany's Aims in the First World War* (1967). An influential interpretation that stirred an enormous controversy by emphasizing Germany's role in bringing on the war.

D. FROMKIN, *Europe's Last Summer: Who Started the Great War in 1914?* (2004). A lively and readable account of the outbreak of the war based on the latest scholarship.

H. HERWIG, *The First World War: Germany and Austria, 1914–18* (1997). A fine study of the war from the losers' perspective.

A. HOCHSCHILD, *King Leopold's Ghost: A Study of Greed, Terror, and Heroism in Colonial Africa* (1999). A well-informed account of a tragedy.

J. N. HORNE, *Labour at War: France and Britain, 1914–1918* (1991). Examines a major issue on the home fronts.

J. KEEGAN, *The First World War* (1999). A vivid and readable narrative.

P. KENNEDY, *The Rise of the Anglo-German Antagonism, 1860–1914* (1980). An unusual and thorough analysis of the political, economic, and cultural roots of important diplomatic developments.

D. C. B. LIEVEN, *Russia and the Origins of the First World War* (1983). A good account of the forces that shaped Russian policy.

A. MOMBAUER, *The Origins of the First World War: Controversies and Consensus* (2002). A discussion and evaluation of historians' shifting views regarding the responsibility for the outbreak of the war.

W. J. MOMMSEN, *Theories of Imperialism* (1980). A study of the debate on the meaning of imperialism.

Z. STEINER, *Britain and the Origins of the First World War* (1977). A perceptive and informed account of British foreign policy before the war.

D. STEVENSON, *Cataclysm: The First World War as Political Tragedy* (2004). Analyzes the bankruptcy of reason that precipitated the war and kept it going.

H. STRACHAN, *The First World War* (2004). A one-volume version of the massive three-volume magisterial account now underway.

S. R. WILLIAMSON, Jr., *Austria-Hungary and the Origins of the First World War* (1991). A valuable study of a complex subject.

DOCUMENTS CD-ROM

Nationalism and Imperialism

World War I

IMPERIALISM:
ANCIENT AND MODERN

The concept of "empire" does not win favor today, and the word *imperialism*, derived from it, has carried an increasingly pejorative meaning since it was coined in the nineteenth century. Both words imply forcible domination by a nation or a state that exploits an alien people for its own benefit. Although, in our time, the charge of imperialism arises whenever a large and powerful nation influences weaker ones, exertion of influence alone is not imperialism. To be true to historical experience, one nation's actions toward another are imperialistic only if the dominant nation exerts both political and military control over the weaker one. In that sense, the last great empire in the modern world was the conglomeration of republics and ostensibly independent satellite states dominated by Russia prior to the USSR's collapse, but the Russians and the other imperial powers after World War II took no public pride in their domination. In our day, ruling an "empire" or engaging in "imperialism" is generally considered among the worst acts a nation can commit.

Such views are rare, perhaps unique, in the history of civilization. A major source for this opinion is the Christian religious tradition, especially parts of the New Testament that deprecate power and worldly glory and praise humility. In fact, Christianity was not hostile to power and empire, for it took control of the Roman Empire in the fourth century C.E. and has lived comfortably with "empire" until our own century. The rise of democracy and nationalism in the last two centuries may have been more influential in changing attitudes toward imperialism, because these movements exalt the freedom and autonomy of a people. Perhaps the modern disdain for empire building has its principal origins in the extraordinary horror of modern warfare and the historical knowledge that competition for empire has often led to war.

If, however, we are to understand the widespread experience of empire throughout history, we must be alert to the great gap that separates the views of most people throughout history from our current opinions. The earliest empires go back more than 4,000 years to the valleys of the Nile and the Tigris-Euphrates, and empires arose later in China, Japan, India, Iran, and Central and South America, among other areas. Typically, they were led by rulers who were believed to be gods or the representatives of gods, or at least were godlike in their ability to rule over many people. To their own people they brought wealth and prosperity, power, and reflected glory, all considered highly desirable. No one appears to have questioned the propriety of conquering another people and taking their lands, property, and persons to benefit the conquerors. Empire seemed to be part of the order of things—good for the rulers, usually bad for the ruled.

THE GREEKS: AMBIGUITIES OF POWER

In most respects, the Greeks resembled other ancient peoples in their attitudes toward power, conquest, empire, and the benefits that came with them. Their Olympian gods held sway over earth, heaven, and the underworld because of victorious wars over other deities, and they gloried in their rule. The heroes in the epic poems that formed the Greek system of values won glory and honor through battle, conquest, and rule over other people. They viewed the world as a place of intense competition in which victory and domination, which brought fame and glory, were the highest goals, whereas defeat and subordination brought ignominy and shame.

When the legendary world of aristocratic heroes gave way to the world of city-states (*poleis*), competition was elevated from contests among individuals, households, and clans to contests and wars among *poleis*. In 416 B.C.E., more than a decade after the death of Pericles (c. 490–429 B.C.E.), Athenian spokesmen explained to some Melian officials their view of international relations: "Of the gods we believe, and of men we know, that by a necessity of their nature they always rule wherever they have the power"[1].

[1] Thucydides 5.105

Although their language was shockingly blunt, it reflected the views of most Greeks.

Yet this was also a dramatic presentation of the morally problematic status of the Athenian Empire. The Athenians' harsh statement would have struck a sympathetic chord among the Greeks. They appreciated power and the security and glory it can bring, but their own historical experience was different from that of other ancient nations. Their culture had been shaped by small autonomous, independent city-states, and they considered freedom natural for people raised in such an environment. Citizens, they believed, should be free in their persons, free to maintain their own constitutions, laws, and customs, and their city-states should be free to conduct their own foreign relations and to compete for power and glory. The free, autonomous *polis*, they though, was greater than the mightiest powers in the world, and the sixth-century B.C.E. poet Phocylides was prepared to compare it to the great Assyrian Empire: "A little *polis* living orderly in a high place is greater than block-headed Nineveh" (Fragment 5).

When *poleis* fought one another, the victor typically took control of a piece of border land that was usually the source of the dispute. They did not normally enslave the defeated enemy or annex and occupy its land. In these matters, as in many others, the Greeks distinguished themselves from alien peoples who did not speak Greek and were not shaped by the Greek cultural tradition. These people were called barbarians, *barbaroi*, because their speech sounded to the Greeks like "bar bar." Because they had not been raised as people in free communities, but lived as subjects to a ruler, they were, it seemed, slaves by nature. To the Greeks, then, dominating and enslaving such people was perfectly acceptable. Greeks, however, viewed themselves as naturally free, as they demonstrated by creating and living in the free institutions of the *polis*. To rule over such people, to deny them their freedom and autonomy, would be wrong—so the Greeks thought, but they did not always act accordingly. The early Spartans, for instance, had changed the status of the conquered Greeks of Laconia and Messenia to *Helots*, or slaves of the state.

The Greeks shared still another belief that interfered with the comfortable acceptance of great power and empire: They thought any good thing amassed by humans to excess, beyond moderation, eventually led to *hubris*, a condition of wanton violence arising from arrogant pride in one's greatness. Those overcome by hubris were thought to have overstepped the limits established for human

The philosopher–emperor Marcus Aurelius was compelled to spend much of his time fighting against tribal invaders on Rome's northern frontiers. This relief from the triumphal arch dedicated to him in Rome (176–180) shows him mounted, on campaign. Nimatallah/Art Resource

beings, to have shown contempt for the gods and, thereby, to have incurred *nemesis*, or divine anger and retribution. The great example to the Greeks of the fifth century of the workings of hubris and nemesis was the fate of Xerxes (r. 486–465 B.C.E.), Great King of the Persian Empire. His power became so great, it filled him with a blind arrogance that led him to try to extend his rule over the Greek mainland and thus brought disaster to himself and his people. When, therefore, the Athenians undertook the leadership of a Greek alliance after the Persian War, and that leadership brought them wealth and power and, in fact, turned into what was frankly acknowledged to be an empire, their response was ambiguous and contradictory. These developments were a source of pride and gratification, but also of embarrassment and, to some Athenians, shame.

The Ottoman Turks began to overrun the Balkans in the mid-1300s. In 1526, Sultan Suleyman the Magnificent destroyed a Hungarian army at the Battle of Mohacs. The Ottoman Empire ruled most of the Balkans until the late nineteenth century. Sultan Suleyman battles the Mohacs. Lokman, The Military Campaigns of Suleyman the Magnificent. Ms. Hunemame. Ottoman dynasty. Topkapi Palace Museum, Istanbul, Turkey. Giraudon/Art Resource, NY

The Macedonian conquest of the Greek city-states in 338 B.C.E. marked a return to an older attitude toward empire. Alexander the Great (r. 340–323 B.C.E.) conquered the vast Persian Empire, itself the successor of empires that had stretched from the Nile to the Indus valley. The death of Alexander led to its division and eventual absorption by the emergent Roman Empire by the second century B.C.E.

THE ROMANS: A THEORY OF EMPIRE

The Romans had fewer hesitations about the desirability of imperial power than the Greeks. Their culture, which arose from a world of farmers ac-customed to hard work, deprivation, and subordination to authority, venerated the military virtues. Roman society valued power, glory, and the responsibilities of leadership, even domination, without embarrassment. In time, the Romans formulated a theory of empire that claimed Roman rule brought great advantages to its subjects: prosperity, justice, the rule of law, and, most valuable of all, peace. In the words of their great epic poet Virgil (70–19 B.C.E.), it was the Roman practice "To humble the arrogant and be sparing to their subjects."[2] These claims had considerable foundation, and the Romans could not have ruled so vast an

[2] Virgil, Aeneid 6.850

empire with a relatively small army for more than half a millennium if their subjects had not enjoyed these benefits. Some of the conquered had a different viewpoint, however. As one British chieftain put it in the first century C.E.: "They make a wilderness and call it peace."[3]

MUSLIMS, MONGOLS, AND OTTOMANS

The rise of Islam in the seventh century C.E. produced a new kind of empire that derived its energy from religious zeal. Bursting out of Arabia, the Muslim armies swiftly gained control of most of the territory held by the old Persian Empire, North Africa, and Spain.

In the twelfth and thirteenth centuries, the great Mongol Empire, at its height, dominated Eurasia from the Pacific to central Europe, ruling Russia for more than two centuries. As in most ancient empires, the Mongols demanded taxes and military service from the conquered. They also imposed their rule over the mighty and long-standing Chinese Empire, parts of India, and much of the Islamic world before their power declined.

Still another great empire that spanned Europe and Asia was that of the Ottomans, a Turkish people, originally from central Asia. In the fourteenth century, they established a kingdom in Anatolia (Asia Minor) and soon conquered the ancient Byzantine Empire, seizing Constantinople in 1453. In the next century, the Ottoman Empire dominated southeastern Europe, the Black Sea, North Africa from Morocco to Egypt, Palestine, Syria and Arabia, Mesopotamia and Iraq, and Kurdistan and Georgia in the Caucasus. As late as 1683, Ottoman armies threatened to take Vienna and push into western Europe. Over the next two centuries, however, Ottoman power declined as the European national states grew stronger. Russia, in particular, inflicted defeats that left Turkey in the late nineteenth century, "the sick man of Europe."

EUROPEAN EXPANSION

Europe, divided first by feudalism, then by the emergence of multiple nascent national states, had been the victim of Islamic imperial expansion during the Middle Ages, first at the hands of the Arabs, then the Turks. The crusades had produced small and transitory conquests. It was only in the late 1400s that Europeans began the economic and political expansion that culminated in their command of much of the planet by 1900. The first phase of European expansion involved the "discovery," exploration, conquest, exploitation, and settlement of the Americas. It was made possible by important developments in naval and military technology, the dynamism inherent in early commercial and financial capitalism, and the freedom to compete for wealth and power unleashed by the division into separate states.

Spain and Portugal took the lead, founding empires in Central and South America, sometimes conquering existing empires ruled by native peoples. In Central America, the Aztecs exacted labor and taxes from their subject peoples, using some of them as human sacrifices. In the Andes, the Incas ruled a great empire that also required military service and forced labor from its subjects. Both Native American empires were overthrown by Spain, which then established a vast American empire whose resources, especially gold and silver, formed the basis of the great Spanish Empire in Europe. Portugal exploited the agricultural and mineral riches of Brazil using slaves imported from Africa.

The seventeenth century saw the establishment of European trading posts and then colonies on the Indian subcontinent and in the East Indies, chiefly by the Dutch, British, and French. In North America, Spain held Mexico, Florida, and California. Of more lasting significance were French and British settlements in Canada and what was to become the United States. The British colonies, especially, represented a special kind of European overseas settlement in which concern for commerce was less important than the acquisition of land for farming.

The wars of the eighteenth century ultimately cleared North America and India of French competition, leaving both as British monopolies and important bases of what would become a worldwide British Empire. The largest and most populous empire in the history of the world, it included colonies of one sort or another on all the inhabited continents; "the sun," as the saying went, "never set on the British Empire." Whether European colonialism was profitable for the imperial powers is still controversial, but Great Britain certainly benefited more than the others. Unlike most colonial powers, the British imported great quantities of natural resources from their colonies and carried on a high percentage of their trade with them. Even more singular, the British Empire included such self-governing areas as Canada, Australia, New Zealand, and South Africa, ruled by emigrants from Britain who remained loyal to the mother country and were willing to assist it in wartime. "The jewel in Britain's imperial crown," as another saying went, "was India." With a population of some 300 million,

---

[3] Tacitus, Agricola 30

European imperialism ultimately rested on the willingness to use force. When anti-British agitation mounted in India after World War I, General Reginald Dyer's troops fired on unarmed Indian demonstrators at Amritsar. More than 300 Indians were killed. UPI/CORBIS

it contained perhaps 80 percent of the empire's subjects and provided much of the imperial profit.

At the height of its power in the mid-ninteenth century, it is remarkable how little money and effort Britain needed to spend to maintain these desired conditions. The cost of its armed services, including its great navy, during these years was only about two to three percent of its gross national product—a low figure compared with other nations, and incredibly low considering Britain's status as the world's greatest empire. The British army was the smallest among the European powers: By 1880 it numbered fewer than a quarter of a million men—less than half the size of France's and barely a quarter of Russia's.

France returned to its imperial pursuits after its defeat in the Napoleonic Wars, especially in North Africa and Southeast Asia, and in the last quarter of the century, Germany and Italy joined the competition for colonies. The latter part of the century brought the European partition of Africa and the establishment of European economic and political power throughout Asia. Modernized Japan, too, became a colonial power, modeling itself on the imperialist policies of the European powers. (See Chapter 26.)

By the next century, European dominance had created a single global economy and had made events in any corner of the world significant thousands of miles away. The possession of colonies became part of the definition of a great power, and the competition for colonies helped bring on World War I.

TOWARD DECOLONIZATION

The weakening of the European colonial powers in World War II began the process of decolonization. The economic value of most colonies had proved to be much smaller than anticipated, and the colonial powers lacked both the capacity and the incentive to restore their former rule. Nationalist movements in the old colonies, moreover, would make such attempts costly and unpleasant. These movements flourished under the banner of national self-determination, self-government, and independence, ideas that came from and were cherished by the European colonial powers themselves. The example of Nazi Germany, moreover, had discredited theories of racial superiority that had justified much of European imperial rule. For European imperialism the handwriting was on the wall, although some colonial powers held on more fiercely than others. The French, for instance, fought at great cost—but in vain—to retain Algeria and Indochina. By the 1970s, a postcolonial world had emerged, and the concept of empire had become unclean. (See Chapter 29.)

- *What were the major ancient attitudes toward imperialism? What are the major modern attitudes? How do you account for the differences? What justifications and explanations have modern people used in connection with imperialism? Which do you think are the most important? Do you think ancient and modern reasons for imperialism are fundamentally different?*

CHAPTER 26

POLITICAL EXPERIMENTS OF THE 1920S

KEY TOPICS

- Economic and political disorder in the aftermath of World War I
- The Soviet Union's far-reaching political and social experiment
- Mussolini and the Fascist seizure of power in Italy
- French determination to enforce the Versailles treaty
- First Labour government and general strike in Britain
- The development of authoritarian governments in most of the successor states of the Habsburg Empire
- Reparations, inflation, political turmoil, and the rise of Nazism in the German Weimar Republic

E xperimentation in politics and the pursuit of normality in economic life marked the decade following the conclusion of the Paris treaties, or Versailles settlement, as they were also known. These treaties, as examined in Chapter 26, established a bold new experiment in European diplomatic relations. The Paris settlement instituted the League of Nations and imposed economic and military terms that fostered

Anxiety over the spread of the Bolshevik revolution was a fundamental factor of European politics during the 1920s and 1930s. Images like this Soviet portrait of Lenin as a heroic revolutionary conjured fears among people in the rest of Europe of a political force determined to overturn their social, political, and economic institutions.   Bildarchiv Preussischer Kulturbesitz

friction among all the powers—and in Germany deep resentment. Germany, after suffering a humiliating military defeat, jettisoned the imperial monarchy and set out on the experiment of the Weimar Republic, which had many determined and violent opponents. Through war and revolution the Habsburg Empire collapsed and was replaced by small successor states, only one of which, Czechoslovakia, became a generally successful democracy. In Russia, the Bolsheviks, after seizing control of the government in 1917 and then winning a civil war, reorganized every aspect of life, transforming the state into the Soviet Union. In Italy, the political turmoil and social strains of the postwar era resulted in the emergence of the authoritarian movement known as Fascism. In Great Britain, most of Ireland established itself as an independent nation. All of these transformations involved domestic violence for at least five years after the close of the Great War itself.

Many of these political experiments failed, and the economic and social normality so many Europeans sought proved elusive. By the close of the 1920s, the political path had been paved for the nightmares of brutally authoritarian governments and international aggression that were to mark the 1930s and 1940s. Yet many of the people who had survived the Great War had hoped and worked for a better outcome. Authoritarianism and aggression were not the inescapable destiny of Europe. They emerged from the failure to secure alternative modes of democratic political life and stable international relations and from the inability to achieve long-term economic prosperity. ■

POLITICAL AND ECONOMIC FACTORS AFTER THE PARIS SETTLEMENT

In 1919, experimental political regimes studded the map of Europe. From Ireland to Russia, new governments were seeking to gain the active support of their citizens and to solve the grievous economic problems the war had caused. In the Soviet Union, the Bolsheviks regarded themselves as forging a new kind of civilization, one built on achieving communism. To that end, they constructed a vast authoritarian state apparatus.

The situation was different elsewhere on the Continent. In many, though not all, countries, the turn to liberal democracy resulted in women and previously disenfranchised males being given the right to vote. For the first time in European history, governments had become responsible to mass electorates. Even where the authoritarian, military empires of Germany and Austria-Hungary had previously held sway, democratically elected parliamentary governments took form. Their goals were more modest and less utopian than those of the Bolsheviks. Yet to pursue parliamentary politics where it had never been meaningfully practiced proved no simple task. The Wilsonian vision of democratic, self-determined nations foundered on the harsh realities of economics, aggressive nationalism, and political conservatism. Too often, nations that had been given democratic parliamentary government lacked both the will and the political skill to make the new system work. Many of the constitutional arrangements, themselves structurally flawed, contained the seeds of their own destruction. Moreover, in many of the new democracies, important sectors of the citizenry believed parliamentary politics was inherently corrupt or feeble. Economics and politics were more intimately connected than ever before. The economic and social anxieties of the electorate, as well as nationalistic ambitions, could, and eventually did, overcome political scruples.

DEMANDS FOR REVISION OF THE PARIS SETTLEMENT

The Paris peace treaties themselves became hotly contested domestic political issues. Usually, the objections arose from nationalistic concerns and resentments. Germany had been humiliated. The arrangements for reparations led to endless international haggling over payments. Various minority national groups in the successor states of eastern Europe also felt they had been treated unjustly or been denied self-determination. There were important demands for further border adjustments because significant national minorities, particularly German, still resided outside national boundaries as drawn in Paris. On the other side, the victorious powers, and especially France, often believed the provisions of the treaty were not being adequately enforced. Thus, throughout the 1920s, calls either to revise or to enforce the Paris treaties contributed to domestic political turmoil across the Continent. Many political figures were willing to fish in these troubled international waters for a large catch of domestic votes.

POSTWAR ECONOMIC PROBLEMS

Along with the move toward political experimentation and the demands for revision of the new international order, there existed a widespread desire to return to the economic prosperity of the prewar years. After 1918, however, it was impossible to restore in the economic realm what American president Warren Harding (1865–1923) would term *normalcy*. During the Great War, Europeans had turned the military and industrial power that they had created during the previous century against themselves. What had been "normal" in economic and social life before 1914 could not be reestablished.

The casualties from the war numbered in the millions. (See Table 26–1.) This represented not only a waste of human life and talent, but also the loss of producers and consumers.

TABLE 26–1 Total Casualties in the First World War			
Country	Dead	Wounded	Total Killed as a Percentage of Population
France	1,398,000	2,000,000	3.4
Belgium	38,000	44,700	0.5
Italy	578,000	947,000	1.6
British Empire	921,000	2,090,000	1.7
Romania	250,000	120,000	3.3
Serbia	278,000	133,000	5.7
Greece	26,000	21,000	0.5
Russia	1,811,000	1,450,000	1.1
Bulgaria	88,000	152,000	1.9
Germany	2,037,000	4,207,000	3.0
Austria-Hungary	1,100,000	3,620,000	1.9
Turkey	804,000	400,000	3.7
United States	114,000	206,000	0.1

Source: Niall Ferguson, The Pity of War (New York: Basic Books, 1998).

Another casualty of the conflict was the financial dominance and independence of Europe. In 1914, Europe had been the financial and credit center of the world. By 1918, European states were deep in debt to each other and to the United States. The Bolsheviks had repudiated the debt of the tsarist government, much of which was owed to French creditors. Other nations could not pursue this revolutionary course. The Paris settlement had imposed heavy financial obligations on Germany and its allies. The United States refused to ask reparations from Germany, but did demand repayment of war debts from its own allies.

On one hand, the reparation and debt structure meant no nation was fully in control of its own economic life. On the other hand, the absence of international economic cooperation meant that, more than ever, individual nations felt compelled to pursue or to try to pursue selfish, nationalistic economic aims. It was perhaps the worst of all possible international economic worlds.

The market and trade conditions that had prevailed before 1914 had also changed radically. Much of Europe's transport facilities, mines, and industry had been damaged or destroyed. Russia all but withdrew from the European economic order. The division of eastern and central Europe into a multitude of small states broke up the trade region formerly encompassed by Germany and Austria-Hungary. Most of these new states had weak economies hardly capable of competing in modern economic life. The new political boundaries separated raw materials from the factories that used them. Railway systems on which finished and unfinished products traveled might now lie under the control of two or more nations. Political and economic nationalism went together. Nations raised new customs barriers where before there had been none.

International trade also followed novel patterns. The United States became less dependent on European production and was now a major competitor. During the war, the belligerents had been forced to sell many of their investments on other continents to finance the conflict. As a consequence, European dominance over the world economy weakened. Slow postwar economic growth or even the decline of economic activity within colonies or former colonies lowered the international demand for European goods. The United States and Japan began to penetrate markets in Latin America and Asia that European producers and traders had dominated.

NEW ROLES FOR GOVERNMENT AND LABOR

The war had given labor new prominence. In every country, the unions had supported the war effort and ensured labor peace for wartime production. In turn, their members had received better wages, and their leaders had been admitted to high political councils. This wartime cooperation of unions and labor leaders with national governments destroyed the internationalism of the prewar labor movement. It also, however, meant that henceforth governments could not ignore the demands of labor. After the war, many wages fell, but rarely to prewar levels. European workers intended to receive their just share of the fruits of their labor. Collective bargaining and union recognition brought on by the war were also there to stay. This improvement in both the status and the influence of labor was one of the most significant changes to flow from World War I. In reaction to it, middle-class European voters became increasingly conservative. Those same middle-class voters were often deeply apprehensive about the Communist government in the newly established Soviet Union.

During the civil war in the Soviet Union, hunger and starvation haunted the countryside. Here a group of malnourished children posed for a photograph.
Bildarchiv Preussischer Kulturbesitz

THE SOVIET EXPERIMENT BEGINS

The consolidation of the Bolshevik revolution in Russia and its formation of the Soviet Union of Socialist Republics was the single most transforming new element on the post–World War I European international scene. The Soviet Union eventually constituted the most extensive and durable of all the twentieth-century authoritarian governments that came to power in the political turmoil of the World War and its aftermath. The Communist Party of the Soviet Union retained power from 1917 until the end of 1991. It was neither a mass party nor a nationalistic one. Its early membership rarely exceeded one percent of the Russian population. For several years after 1917, the party faced widespread domestic opposition, and the communist leaders long felt their hold on the country was insecure. Yet the communists also regarded their government and their revolution not as local events in a national history, but as epoch-making events in the history of the world and the development of humanity. Communism was an exportable commodity that could disrupt the political life of other nations, and throughout the history of the Soviet Union, its leaders sought to export its ideology and doctrines. Fear of communism and a determination to stop its spread became one of the leading political forces in Western Europe and the United States for most of the rest of the century.

WAR COMMUNISM

Within the Soviet Union, the Red Army, under the organizational direction of Leon Trotsky (1879–1940), eventually suppressed internal and foreign military opposition to the new government. The White Russian armies, which fought the Red Army for several years, could not adequately organize themselves, and Allied help was insufficient to defeat the Bolsheviks. Yet the military threat allowed the Bolsheviks to pursue authoritarian policies more rapidly than they might otherwise have been able to do. Within months of the revolution, a new secret police, known as the *Cheka*, appeared. Throughout the civil war, Lenin had declared that the Bolshevik Party, as the vanguard of the revolution, was imposing the dictatorship of the proletariat. Political and economic administration became highly centralized. All major decisions flowed from the top in a nondemocratic manner. Under the economic policy of war communism, the revolutionary government confiscated and then ran the banks, the transport system, and heavy industry. The state also seized grain from the peasants to feed the army and the workers in the cities. The fact of the civil war permitted the Bolsheviks to suppress resistance to this economic policy. Throughout the period of the civil war, the government headed by Lenin repressed all actual or potential sources of opposition. (See "Trotsky Urges the Use of Terrorism.")

War communism aided the victory of the Red Army. The revolution had survived and triumphed. The policy, however, generated domestic opposition to the Bolsheviks, who in 1920 numbered only about 600,000 members. The alliance of workers and peasants under the slogan "Peace, Bread, and Land" had begun to come apart at the seams. Many Russians were no longer willing to make the sacrifices the central party bureaucrats demanded. In 1920 and 1921, strikes occurred in many factories. Discontented peasants resisted the requisition of grain as they had since 1918. In March 1921, the Baltic fleet mutinied. The Red Army crushed the rebellion with grave loss of life.

THE NEW ECONOMIC POLICY

Under these difficult conditions, Lenin made a strategic retreat. In March 1921, following the naval mutiny and in the face of continuing peasant resistance to the requisition of grain needed to feed the urban population, he outlined the **New Economic Policy (NEP)**. Apart from what he termed "the commanding heights" of banking, heavy

TROTSKY URGES THE USE OF TERROR

Leon Trotsky led the Red Army to victory in the brutal civil war that followed the Bolshevik revolution. He became a major opponent, and later a victim, of Stalin. In 1920, he explained how terror and intimidation must be used to achieve communist revolution. He contends that capitalist society itself came to power through the use of force and that only force will allow the working class to establish its dominance. He argues that there is no real moral argument against the use of terror and violence. In particular, he directs his remarks toward liberals, who thought parliamentary means could achieve social change, and against the German Marxist socialists, the Kautskians, who had argued that historical forces would bring about the revolution of the working class without the use of violence. Trotsky's words help explain the fear of Bolshevism that swept across Europe immediately after World War I, a fear right-wing politicians manipulated during the 1920s and 1930s.

■ *How does Trotsky's justification of terror compare with that associated with the Reign of Terror during the French Revolution? How might the circumstances of the Russian civil war have led Trotsky to these views? Did the communist terror Trotsky advocated differ from the repressive police policies of the tsars?*

The problem of revolution, as of war, consists in breaking the will of the foe, forcing him to capitulate and to accept the conditions of the conqueror. The will, of course, is a fact of the physical world, but in contradistinction to a meeting, a dispute, or a congress, the revolution carries out its object by means of the employment of material resources—though to a lesser degree than war. The bourgeoisie itself conquered power by means of revolts, and consolidated it by the civil war. In the peace period, it retains power by means of a system of repression. As long as class society, founded on the most deep-rooted antagonisms, continues to exist, repression remains a necessary means of breaking the will of the opposing side.

Even if, in one country or another, the dictatorship of the proletariat grew up within the external framework of democracy, this would by no means avert the civil war. The question as to who is to rule the country, i.e., of the life or death of the bourgeoisie, will be decided on either side, not by references to the paragraphs of the constitution, but by the employment of all forms of violence. . . .

The question of the form of repression, or of its degree, of course, is not one of "principle." It is a question of expediency. . . .

Terror can be very efficient against a reactionary class which does not want to leave the scene of operations. Intimidation is a powerful weapon of policy, both internationally and internally. A victorious war, generally speaking, destroys only an insignificant part of the conquered army, intimidating the remainder and breaking their will. The revolution works in the same way: it kills individuals, and intimidates thousands. In this sense, the Red Terror is not distinguishable from the armed insurrection, the direct continuation of which it represents. The State terror of a revolutionary class can be condemned "morally" only by a man who, as a principle, rejects (in words) every form of violence whatsoever—consequently, every war and every uprising. For this one has to be merely and simply a hypocritical Quaker.

"But, in that case, in what do your tactics differ from the tactics of Tsarism?" we are asked by the high priests of Liberalism and Kautskianism.

You do not understand this, holy men? We shall explain to you. The terror of Tsarism was directed against the proletariat. The gendarmerie of Tsarism throttled the workers who were fighting for the Socialist order. Our Extraordinary Commissions shoot landlords, capitalists, and generals who are striving to restore the capitalist order. Do you grasp this—distinction? Yes? For us Communists it is quite sufficient.

From Leon Trotsky, *Terrorism and Communism*, 1920; English trans., *Dictatorship vs. Democracy: A Reply to Karl Kautsky* (New York: Workers' Party of America, 1922), pp. 54, 57–59, as quoted in Robert V. Daniels, *A Documentary History of Communism*, rev. ed., Vol. 1 (Hanover, NH, and London: University Press of New England, 1984), pp. 121–122.

industry, transportation, and international commerce, the government would tolerate private enterprise. In particular, peasants could farm for profit. They would pay taxes like other citizens, but they could sell their grain on the open market. The NEP was in line with Lenin's conviction that the Russian peasantry held the key to the success of the revolution.

After 1921, the countryside did become more stable, and a more secure food supply seemed assured for the cities. Similar free enterprise flourished within light industry and domestic retail trade. The NEP, however, was not fully successful, because there were virtually no consumer goods for the peasants to purchase with the money they received for their grain. Yet by 1927, industrial production had reached its 1913 level. The revolution seemed to have transformed Russia into a land of small, if frequently discontented, family farmers and owners of small private shops and businesses.

STALIN VERSUS TROTSKY

The NEP had caused disputes within the Politburo, the governing committee of the Communist Party. Some members considered the partial return to capitalism a betrayal of Marxist principles. These frictions increased when Lenin's firm hand disappeared. In 1922, he suffered a stroke and never again dominated party affairs. In 1924, he died.

The resulting power vacuum led to an intense struggle for the leadership of the party. Two factions emerged. One was led by Leon Trotsky, the other by Joseph Stalin (1879–1953), who had become general secretary of the party in 1922. Shortly before his death, Lenin had criticized both men, but was especially harsh toward Stalin. Stalin's

Leon Trotsky led the Bolshevik Army to victory over the opponents of the Russian Revolution. He and Stalin later quarreled over the direction of the revolution. Trotsky lost the struggle with Stalin, who later ordered his execution.
Underwood & Underwood/CORBIS

power base, however, lay with the party membership and in the day-to-day management of party affairs. Consequently, he was able to withstand the posthumous strictures of Lenin.

Trotsky's Position The issue between the two factions was power within the party, but the struggle was fought out over the question of Russia's path toward industrialization and the future of the communist revolutionary movement. Trotsky, speaking for what became known as the left wing, urged rapid industrialization financed through the expropriation of farm production. Agriculture should be collectivized, and the peasants should be made to pay for industrialization. Trotsky further argued that the revolution in Russia could succeed only if new revolutions took place elsewhere. Russia needed the skills and wealth of other nations to build its own economy. As Trotsky's influence within the party waned, he also demanded that party members be permitted to criticize the government and the party. Trotsky was, however, a latecomer to the advocacy of open discussion. When he had controlled the Red Army, he had been an unflinching disciplinarian.

Stalin's Rise Stalin had been born into a poor family. Unlike the other early Bolshevik leaders, he had not spent a long period of exile in Western Europe and was much less intellectual and internationalist in his outlook. He was also more brutal. During his tenure as commissar of nationalities, Stalin's handling of various recalcitrant national groups within Russia after the revolution had shocked even Lenin, though not enough for Lenin to dismiss him. As the party general secretary, a post that party intellectuals disdained as merely clerical, Stalin amassed power through his command of bureaucratic and administrative methods. He was neither a brilliant writer nor an effective public speaker. He did, however, master the crucial, if dull, details of party structure, including admission to the party and promotion within it. That mastery gained him the support of the lower levels of the party apparatus when he clashed with other leaders.

During the mid-1920s, a Communist Party faction known as the right wing opposed Trotsky's drive for rapid industrialization. Its chief ideological voice was that of Nikolai Bukharin (1888–1938), the editor of *Pravda* (*Truth*), the official party newspaper. In the face of the uncertain economic recovery, the right wing pressed for the continuation of Lenin's NEP and for relatively slow industrialization. At the time, this position represented a policy based largely on decentralized economic planning and tolerating modest free enterprise and small landholdings. Stalin manipulated these intraparty rivalries.

In the mid-1920s, Stalin expediently supported Bukharin's position on economic development. In 1924, he also enunciated, in opposition to Trotsky, the doctrine of "socialism in one country," which contended that socialism (meaning communism) could be achieved in Russia alone. Russian success did not depend on the fate of revolutions elsewhere. Stalin thus nationalized the previously international scope of the Marxist revolution. He cunningly used his control over the Central Committee of the Communist Party to edge out Trotsky and his supporters.

By 1927, Trotsky had been removed from all his offices, expelled from the party, and exiled to Siberia. In 1929, he was forced out of Russia, and eventually he moved to Mexico, where he was murdered in 1940 by one of Stalin's agents. With Trotsky defeated, Stalin was firmly in control of the Soviet state. It remained to be seen where he would take it and what "socialism in one country" would mean in practice.

THE THIRD INTERNATIONAL

The Bolshevik revolution in Russia was a transforming event for the internal history of socialism as well as for Russia and international affairs. The event stunned West European socialists. In the West, prior to the war, as discussed in Chapter 23, social democratic parties had debated among

A CLOSER LOOK

Bolshevik Visions of World Revolution

The Bolshevik revolution spread fear of ongoing revolution across Western Europe and beyond. Much of this fear was a response to aggressive Soviet propaganda that the Comintern, established in 1919 to sponsor and organize communist parties outside the Soviet Union, carried out. This poster celebrates the international aims of the Bolshevik revolution and the Soviet Union.

The blazing red banner proclaims to a group of workers "You have nothing to lose but your chains, but the world will soon be yours."

The banner is stretched around the world from Moscow over the North Pole, across the Americas, to Australia. It casts a red shadow over Africa and Asia.

A group of workers of many different races and nationalities listens to a Soviet orator.

Russian propaganda poster celebrating 1st May: "You have nothing to lose but your chains, but the world will soon be yours." Museum of the Revolution, Moscow, Russia/Bridgeman Art Library, London

themselves whether to participate in parliamentary structures. They had regarded the Russian Bolsheviks as eccentric, politically marginal Marxist extremists. The Bolshevik victory consequently required West European social democrats to rethink their position within the world of international socialism. For their part, the Bolsheviks regarded such reformist social democrats as enemies. The Bolsheviks intended to establish themselves as the international leaders of Marxism.

To that end, in 1919, the Soviet communists founded the Third International of the European socialist movement, better known as the *Comintern*. The Comintern worked to make the Bolshevik model of socialism, as Lenin had developed it, the rule for all socialist parties outside the Soviet Union. In 1920, the Comintern imposed its Twenty-one Conditions on any socialist party that wished to join it. These conditions included acknowledging Moscow's leadership, rejecting reformist or revisionist socialism, repudiating previous socialist leaders, and adopting the Communist Party name. In effect, the Comintern sought to destroy democratic socialism, which it accused of having betrayed the working class through reform policies and parliamentary accommodation.

The decision whether to accept these conditions split every major European socialist party. As a result, separate communist and social democratic parties emerged in many countries. The communist parties modeled themselves after the Soviet party, and Moscow dictated their policies. The social democratic parties attempted to pursue both

ALEXANDRA KOLLONTAI DEMANDS A NEW FAMILY LIFE IN THE SOVIET UNION

While Lenin sought to consolidate the Bolshevik revolution against internal and external enemies, there existed within the young Soviet Union a vast utopian impulse to change and reform virtually every social institution that had existed before the revolution or that the communists associated with capitalist society. Alexandra Kollontai (1872–1952) was a spokesperson of the extreme political left within the early Soviet Union. In communist circles, there had been much speculation on how the end of bourgeois society might change the structure of the family and the position of women. In the passage that follows, written in 1920, Kollontai states one of the most radical visions of this change. During the years immediately after the revolution, rumors circulated in the West about sexual and family experimentation in the Soviet Union. Statements such as this one fostered such rumors. Kollontai herself later became a supporter of Stalin and a Soviet diplomat.

■ *Why did Kollontai see the restructuring of the family as essential to establishing a new kind of communist society? Would these changes make people loyal to that society? What changes in society does the kind of economic independence she seeks for women presuppose? What might childhood be like if the state, rather than their parents, assumed responsibility for children?*

There is no escaping the fact: the old type of family has seen its day. It is not the fault of the Communist State, it is the result of the changed conditions of life. The family is ceasing to be a necessity of the State, as it was in the past; on the contrary, it is worse than useless, since it needlessly holds back the female workers from more productive and far more serious work. . . . But on the ruins of the former family we shall soon see a new form rising which will involve altogether different relations between men and women, and which will be a union of affection and comradeship, a union of two equal members of the Communist society, both of them free, both of them independent, both of them workers. No more domestic "servitude"

social reform and liberal parliamentary politics. Throughout the 1920s and early 1930s, the communists and social democrats fought each other more intensely than they fought either capitalism or conservative political parties. Their fierce conflict was one of the fundamental features of the interwar European political landscape.

These policies of the Comintern and the resulting divisions of the West European socialist parties directly affected the rise of the fascists and the Nazis in Western Europe. It is difficult to overestimate the fears that Soviet political rhetoric and Communist Party activity aroused in Europe during the 1920s and 1930s. Conservative and right-wing political groups manipulated and exaggerated these fears. The presence of separate communist parties in Western Europe meant that right-wing politicians always had a convenient target they could justly accuse of seeking to overthrow the government and to impose Soviet-style political and economic systems in their nations. Furthermore, right-wing politicians also accused the democratic socialist parties of supporting policies that might facilitate a communist takeover. The division of the European political left also meant that right-wing political movements rarely had to confront a united left.

WOMEN AND THE FAMILY IN THE EARLY SOVIET UNION

Communist views toward women and the family assumed that the traditional family embodied middle-class capitalist values, which were at odds of women. No more inequality within the family. No more fear on the part of the woman lest she remain without support or aid with little ones in her arms if her husband should desert her. The woman in the Communist city no longer depends on her husband but on her work. It is not her husband but her robust arms which will support her. There will be no more anxiety as to the fate of her children. The State of the Workers will assume responsibility for these. Marriage will be purified of all its material elements, of all money calculations, which constitute a hideous blemish on family life in our days. . . .

The woman who is called upon to struggle in the great cause of the liberation of the workers—such a woman should know that in the new State there will be no more room for such petty divisions as were formerly understood: "These are my own children, to them I owe all my maternal solicitude, all my affection; those are your children, my neighbour's children; I am not concerned with them. I have enough to do with my own." Henceforth the worker-mother, who is conscious of her social function, will rise to a point where she no longer differentiates between yours and mine; she must remember that there are henceforth only our children, those of the Communist State, the common possession of all the workers.

The Worker's State has need of a new form of relation between the sexes. The narrow and exclusive affection of the mother for her own children must expand until it embraces all the children of the great proletarian family. In place of the indissoluble marriage based on the servitude of woman, we shall see rise the free union, fortified by the love and mutual respect of the two members of the Workers' State, equal in their rights and in their obligations. In place of the individual and egotistic family there will arise a great universal family of workers, in which all the workers, men and women, will be, above all, workers, comrades.

From Alexandra Kollontai, *Communism and the Family*, as reprinted in Rudolf Schlesinger, ed. and trans., *Changing Attitudes in Soviet Russia; Documents and Readings.* Reprinted by permission of Taylor & Francis Book, Ltd.

with what was socially good and with the liberty of the proletariat. In the early years of the Russian Revolution, this outlook led to utopian projections of what the life of women and the family would resemble under socialism. The most famous such utopian writer was Alexandra Kollontai (1872–1952). In *Communism and the Family* (1918) and other works, she envisioned a new kind of family that she thought would liberate both women and men. Her views included both the expansion of sexual freedom and the radical sharing of tasks about the home between wives and husbands. She wanted to replace what she regarded as egoistic, exploitative family relationships with families based on love and comradeship. (See "Alexandra Kollantai Demands a New Family Life," pages 884–885.) Few people in the Soviet Union, even among the communists, agreed with Kollontai, but her views became well known and were often assumed to reflect those of a wide spectrum of the Soviet leadership and citizenry. At a time when the Soviet Union was isolated from the rest of the world, people on the outside could imagine that Kollontai's radical social vision constituted the reality of the bold new life being forged there. As will be seen later in this chapter and in the next, both Italian fascists and German Nazis contrasted their own traditionalist views of women with these radical views.

Family Legislation from Reform to Repression
Soon after achieving power in late 1917, the Bolsheviks began to issue laws that affected women. Divorce became far easier, marriage was no longer a religious ceremony, and legitimate and illegitimate children were given the same rights. Women were given more protection in the workplace and within marriage. Abortion was legalized in 1920. All of these measures were enacted to create a socialist society. Women obtained high positions in the Communist Party, and more women voted, but in fact, women had no significant impact on Soviet government.

The dislocations flowing from the civil war, the confiscation of property, shifting economic policies, and the general reordering of Soviet society during the 1920s seriously disrupted Soviet family life. Domestic violence appears to have been common. The birthrate fell. There were more abortions and more abandoned children. The new divorce law made it easy for husbands to leave their wives, but a housing shortage forced divorced couples often to continue to live together.

From the 1920s on, women could become leaders in the party and the economy, though they seldom achieved the top ranks. Educational opportunities for women were readily available, yet women who worked, even those who had professional careers, were still expected to do the housework, and there was no significant structure of state-run child care. Typically, women were paid less than men. Throughout the history of the Soviet Union, the chronic shortage of consumer goods affected women more than any other group. It was they who most often had to stand in the long lines, cope with an absence of food, clothing, and other goods, and somehow make their own lives and those of their families hang together.

THE FASCIST EXPERIMENT IN ITALY

Italy witnessed the first authoritarian political experiment in Western Europe that arose in part from fears of the spread of Bolshevism. From the Italian fascist movement of Benito Mussolini (1883–1945) came the general terms *fascist*, and **fascism**, frequently used to describe a number of right-wing dictatorships that arose across Europe between the wars.

Historians and political scientists disagree about the exact meaning of *fascism* as a political term. Most scholars do agree, however, that the governments regarded as fascist were antidemocratic, anti-Marxist, antiparliamentary, and frequently anti-Semitic. These governments claimed to hold back the spread of Bolshevism, which, because of Soviet rhetoric and the agitation of domestic communist parties, seemed at the time a real threat. The fascist regimes sought to make the world safe for the middle class, small businesses, owners of moderate amounts of property, and small farmers. The fascist regimes rejected the political inheritance of the French Revolution and of nineteenth-century liberalism. Fascists believed that normal parliamentary politics and parties sacrificed national honor and greatness to petty disputes. They wanted to overcome the class conflict of Marxism and the party conflict of liberalism by uniting the various groups and classes within the nation to achieve great national purposes. As Mussolini declared in 1931, "The fascist conception of the state is all-embracing, and outside of the state no human or spiritual values can exist, let alone be desirable."[1] The fascist governments were usually

---

[1] Quoted in Denis Mack Smith, *Italy: A Modern History* (Ann Arbor: University of Michigan Press, 1959), p. 412.

single-party dictatorships characterized by terrorism and police surveillance. In contrast to the Communist Party of the Soviet Union, their base was mass political parties. Fascist movements were invariably nationalistic in response to the feared international expansion of communism.

Fascist political movements drew upon the scorn for reason in political life that many late-nineteenth-century thinkers had voiced. These movements, wherever they arose, also championed the cult of the great leaders following again the ideas of heroic leadership that nineteenth-century writers such as Hegel had portrayed as being necessary to effect real changes in history. Those intellectuals had often condoned or even advocated violence to bring about historical change. (See Chapters 19 and 24.) In Italy the memories of Garibaldi and his red shirts and in Germany a cult that had developed around Bismarck's unification of Germany through warfare helped pave the way for mass movements devoted to a single leader who appeared larger than life, claimed to embody the will and destiny of the nation, and used force to gain political ends. The first of these leaders was Mussolini who to a greater or lesser extent became a model for others across the Continent. Because he has later often been made the object of ridicule and because Hitler overshadowed him in the 1930s, it is easy to forget the enormous impact Mussolini and Italian fascism made on the politics of the 1920s.

THE RISE OF MUSSOLINI

The Italian *Fasci di Combattimento*, or "Bands of Combat," was founded in 1919 in Milan. Its members came largely from Italian war veterans who felt the Paris conference had cheated Italy of the hard-won fruits of victory. They especially resented Italy's failure to gain Fiume (now Rijeka in Slovenia) on the northeast coast of the Adriatic Sea. They also feared the spread of socialism and the effects of inflation within Italy itself.

Their leader, Benito Mussolini, had been born the son of a blacksmith. He had worked as a schoolteacher and a day laborer before becoming active in Italian socialist politics. By 1912, he had become editor of the socialist newspaper *Avanti* (meaning "forward"). In 1914, Mussolini broke with the socialists and supported Italian entry into the war on the side of the Allies. His interventionist position lost him the editorship of *Avanti*. He had in effect moved from championing the proletariat to championing the nation.

Nationalism replaced socialism as his ideology for a national revolution that would transform what he and many others regarded as a weak liberal state into a strong united Italy. He soon established his own paper, *Il Popolo d'Italia* (*The People of Italy*). Later he served in the army and was wounded fighting the Austrians in the Alps during World War I. In 1919, Mussolini was simply one of many more or less prominent Italian politicians, and his Fasci organization was just one more small political group in a country full of them. As a politician, Mussolini was an opportunist par excellence. He could change his ideas and principles to suit every new occasion. Action for him was always more important than thought or rational justification. His one real goal was political survival. (See "Mussolini Heaps Contempt on Political Liberalism," page 888.)

Postwar Italian Political Turmoil Postwar Italian politics was a muddle. During the war, the Italian Parliament had virtually ceased to function, and ministers ruled by decree. Many Italians, however, were already dissatisfied with the parliamentary system. Italian nationalists—not just Mussolini's followers—felt Italy had not been treated as a great power at the peace conference and had not received the territories it deserved.

The main spokesperson for this discontent was the extreme nationalist writer Gabriele D'Annunzio (1863–1938). In 1919, he seized Fiume with a force of patriotic Italians. The Italian army eventually drove him out, but D'Annunzio had shown how a nongovernmental military force could be put to political use. Moreover, the use of force against D'Annunzio embarrassed the Italian government and made it appear less patriotic than the ultranationalists.

Between 1919 and 1921, Italy also experienced considerable internal social turmoil. Industrial strikes were common, and workers occupied factories. Peasants seized uncultivated land from large estates. Parliamentary and constitutional government seemed incapable of dealing with this unrest. The Socialist Party had captured a plurality of seats in the lower house of the Italian parliament, the Chamber of Deputies, in the 1919 election. The sharp division between socialists and communists had not yet emerged, and the Socialist Party included many people who were soon to become communists. A new Catholic Popular Party had also done well in the election. Both appealed to the working and agrarian classes. Neither party, however, would cooperate with the other; parliamentary deadlock resulted. Under these conditions, many

MUSSOLINI HEAPS CONTEMPT ON POLITICAL LIBERALISM

The political tactics of the Italian fascists wholly disregarded the liberal belief in the rule of law and the consent of the governed. In 1923, Mussolini explained why the fascists hated and repudiated these liberal principles. Note his emphasis on the idea of the twentieth century as a new historical epoch requiring a new kind of politics and his undisguised praise of force in politics.

■ *Which nineteenth-century liberal political leaders might Mussolini have been attacking? Why might Mussolini's audience have been receptive to these views? What events or developments within liberal states allowed Mussolini to portray liberalism as corrupt and powerless?*

Liberalism is not the last word, nor does it represent the definitive formula on the subject of the art of government. . . . Liberalism is the product and the technique of the 19th century. . . . It does not follow that the Liberal scheme of government, good for the 19th century, for a century, that is, dominated by two such phenomena as the growth of capitalism and the strengthening of the sentiment of nationalism, should be adapted to the 20th century, which announces itself already with characteristics sufficiently different from those that marked the preceding century. . . .

I challenge Liberal gentlemen to tell if ever in history there has been a government that was based solely on popular consent and that renounced all use of force whatsoever. A government so constructed there has never been and never will be. Consent is an ever-changing thing like the shifting sand on the sea coast. It can never be permanent: It can never be complete. . . . If it be accepted as an axiom that any system of government whatever creates malcontents, how are you going to prevent this discontent from overflowing and constituting a menace to the stability of the State? You will

prevent it by force. By the assembling of the greatest force possible. By the inexorable use of this force whenever it is necessary. Take away from any government whatsoever force—and by force is meant physical, armed force—and leave it only its immortal principles, and that government will be at the mercy of the first organized group that decides to overthrow it. Fascism now throws these lifeless theories out to rot. . . . The truth evident now to all who are not warped by [liberal] dogmatism is that men have tired of liberty. They have made an orgy of it. Liberty is today no longer the chaste and austere virgin for whom the generations of the first half of the last century fought and died. For the gallant, restless and bitter youth who face the dawn of a new history there are other words that exercise a far greater fascination, and those words are: order, hierarchy, discipline. . . .

Know then, once and for all, that Fascism knows no idols and worships no fetishes. It has already stepped over, and, if it be necessary, it will turn tranquilly and step again over, the more or less putrescent corpse of the Goddess of Liberty.

From Benito Mussolini, "Force and Consent" (1923), as trans. in Jonathan F. Scott and Alexander Baltzly, eds., *Readings in European History since 1814* (New York: F. S. Crofts, 1931), pp. 680–682.

Italians honestly, and still others conveniently, believed or feared that the social upheaval and political paralysis would lead to a communist revolution.

Early Fascist Organization Initially, Mussolini was uncertain of the direction of the political winds. He first supported the factory occupations and land seizures. Never one to be concerned with consistency, however, he soon reversed himself. He had discovered that many upper-class and middle-class Italians, pressured by inflation and fearing the loss of their property, had no sympathy for the workers or the peasants. They wanted order, rather than some vague form of social justice that might harm their own interests. Moreover, Mussolini was coming to see any social group that pursued its own goals as undermining great national purposes and national unity. The socialists became easy and obvious targets because they had always supported internationalism as well as working-class interests.

Consequently, Mussolini and his fascists took direct action in the face of government inaction. They formed local squads of terrorists who disrupted Socialist Party meetings, beat up socialist leaders, and intimidated socialist supporters. They attacked strikers and farm workers and protected strikebreakers. Conservative landowners and businessmen were grateful. The officers and institutions of the law simply ignored the crimes of the fascist squads. By early 1922, the fascists were intimidating local officials through arson, beatings, and murder in cities such as Ferrara, Ravenna, and Milan. They controlled the local government in much of northern Italy.

March on Rome In the election of 1921, Italian voters sent Mussolini and thirty-four of his followers to the Chamber of Deputies. Their importance grew as the local fascists gained more direct power. The movement now had hundreds of thousands of supporters. In October 1922, the fascists, dressed in their characteristic black shirts, began a rather haphazard march on Rome, which became known as the Black Shirt March. King Victor Emmanuel III (r. 1900–1946), because of both personal and political concerns, refused to sign a decree that would have authorized the army to stop the marchers. Probably no other single decision so ensured a fascist seizure of power. The cabinet resigned in protest. On October 29, the monarch telegraphed Mussolini, who had stayed in Milan rather than join the black shirts, and asked him to become prime minister. The next day, Mussolini arrived in Rome by sleeping car and greeted his followers as the head of the government when they entered the city. Although the march on Rome became a famous moment in fascist history, Mussolini would not have achieved authority if he had not made allies within the political system during the months preceding the march.

Technically, Mussolini had come into office by legal means. The monarch had the constitutional authority to appoint the prime minister. Mussolini, however, had no majority or even near majority in the Chamber of Deputies. Behind the legal facade of his coming to power lay months of terrorist disruption and intimidation and the threat of the fascist march itself. The nonfascist politicians, whose ineptitude had prepared the way for Mussolini, believed his ministry, like others since 1919, would be brief. They did not understand that he was not a traditional Italian politician.

THE FASCISTS IN POWER

Mussolini had not really expected to be appointed prime minister. He moved cautiously to shore up his support and to consolidate his power. His success was the result of the impotence of his rivals, his own effective use of his office, his power over the masses, and his sheer ruthlessness. On November 23, 1922, the king and Parliament granted Mussolini dictatorial authority for one year to bring order to local and regional government. Wherever possible, Mussolini appointed fascists to office.

Repression of Opposition Late in 1924, under Mussolini's guidance, Parliament changed the election law. Previously, parties had been represented in the Chamber of Deputies in proportion to the popular vote cast for them. According to the new election law, the party that gained the largest popular vote (if they won at least 25 percent) received two-thirds of the seats in the chamber. Coalition government, with all its compromises and hesitant policies, would no longer be necessary. In the election of 1924, the fascists won a great victory and complete control of the Chamber of Deputies. They used that majority to end legitimate parliamentary life. Laws passed in 1925 and 1926 permitted Mussolini, in effect, to rule by decree. In 1926, all other political parties were dissolved. By the close of that year, Mussolini had transformed Italy into a single-party dictatorial state.

Their growing dominance over the government had not, however, diverted the fascists from violence and terror. Fascists were put in charge of the police force, and the terrorist squads became a government

Benito Mussolini became famous for bombastic public speeches delivered in settings surrounded by his Fascist followers and military supporters.
AP Wide World Photos

militia. In late 1924, their thugs murdered Giacomo Matteotti (1885–1924), a leading noncommunist, socialist leader and member of Parliament. He had persistently criticized Mussolini and had exposed the criminality of the fascist movement. In protest against the murder, most opposition deputies withdrew from parliament. That tactic gave Mussolini an even freer hand. The deputies were refused readmission.

Thanks to effective Fascist Party propaganda, a cult of personality surrounded Mussolini. His skills in oratory and his general intelligence allowed him to hold his own with both large crowds and prominent individuals, foreign as well as Italian. Many respectable Italians tolerated and even admired Mussolini because they believed he had saved them from Bolshevism. Those who did have the courage to oppose him were usually driven into exile, and some, like Matteotti, were murdered.

Accord with the Vatican Mussolini made one important domestic departure that brought him significant political dividends. Through the Lateran Accord of February 1929, the Roman Catholic Church and the Italian state made peace with each other. Ever since the armies of Italian unification had seized papal lands in the 1860s, the church had been hostile to the Italian state. The popes had remained secluded in the Vatican after 1870 when the Italian army occupied Rome. The agreement of 1929 recognized the pope as the temporal ruler of the independent state of Vatican City. The Italian government agreed to pay an indemnity to the papacy for the territory it had confiscated. The state also recognized Catholicism as the religion of the nation, exempted church property from taxes, and allowed church law to govern marriage. The Lateran Accord brought further respectability to Mussolini's authoritarian regime.

MOTHERHOOD FOR THE NATION IN FASCIST ITALY

Fascist policy encouraged Italian women to have more children and to remain in the home to rear them for the good of the Italian state. To that end, the government instituted policies such as maternity leaves, insurance, subsidies to large families, and the dissemination of information about sound child-rearing practices. Other legislation outlawing contraception and abortion and discouraging the publication of information about sexuality and reproduction made it more difficult for women to limit the size of their families. Italian mothers were expected to see that their children attended fascist school programs. Government agencies provided modest benefits to mothers and their children, which tended to make them dependent on the government because Italian wages were low.

Despite the government's emphasis on the home and child rearing and the image of the father as earning a wage to support his family, women made up 25 percent of the Italian work force, a percentage of women workers second only to Sweden's. The fascist government nonetheless actively discouraged female participation in the work force or sought to keep women in lower skilled jobs. For example, although the fascists opened civil service jobs to women, they made it more difficult for women to compete with male workers. Laws favored the employment of skilled workers when, in Italy as elsewhere in Europe, most women worked in less skilled jobs. Laws that protected women from exploitation also limited their access to the labor market. In 1938, the government limited the number of women employees in both government and private offices to no more than ten percent. Although most of these exclusions were modified when Italy entered the Second World War in 1940, the policies had succeeded in degrading women's work. By 1940, women's participation in the Italian labor force was more part-time and low skilled than it had been before the fascists took power. For example, while the number of domestic servants declined elsewhere in Western Europe during the 1920s and 1930s, it increased in Italy, and most domestic servants were women.

JOYLESS VICTORS

Compared with events in Russia and Italy, the postwar political development of France and Great Britain seems tame. Neither experienced a revolution or a shift to authoritarian government. Yet this surface calm was largely illusory. Both France and Britain were troubled democracies. To neither did victory in war bring the good life in peace.

FRANCE: THE SEARCH FOR SECURITY

At the close of World War I, as after Waterloo, the revolution of 1848, and the defeat of 1871, the French voters elected a doggedly conservative Chamber of Deputies. The preponderance of military officers in blue uniforms among its members led to the nickname of the "Blue Horizon Chamber." The overwhelmingly conservative character of the chamber was registered in 1920 when it defeated Georges Clemenceau's bid for the presidency. The crucial factor had been, of all things, the alleged leniency of the Paris treaties and Clemenceau's failure to establish a separate Rhineland state under French influence. The deputies wanted to achieve future security against Germany and Russian communism. They intended to make as few concessions to domestic social reform as possible. The 1920s

were marked by frequent changes of ministries and drift in domestic policy. The political turnstile remained ever active. Between the end of the war in 1918 and January 1933, twenty-seven different cabinets took office in France.

New Alliances During the first five years after the conclusion of the Paris settlement, France accepted its role as the leading European power. The French plan was to enforce strictly the clauses of the treaty that were meant to keep Germany weak and also to build a system of eastern alliances to replace France's prewar alliance with Russia. In 1920 and 1921, three eastern states that had much to lose from a revision of the Versailles treaty—Czechoslovakia, Romania, and Yugoslavia—formed the Little Entente. France made military alliances with these states and with Poland. A border dispute with Czechoslovakia prevented the Poles from joining the Little Entente, but Poland's independence depended on preserving the Paris settlement.

This new system of eastern pacts was the best France could do, but it was far weaker than the old Franco-Russian alliance. Even combined, the new states were no match for the former power of tsarist Russia, and they were neither united nor reliable. Poland and Romania were more concerned about Russia than about Germany, and the main target of the Little Entente was Hungary. If a resurgent Germany threatened one of these states, it could not rely on the others for help.

The formation of this new alliance system heightened the sense of danger and isolation the two excluded powers, Germany and the Soviet Union, felt. In 1922, while the European states were holding an economic conference at Genoa, the Russians and the Germans met at nearby Rapallo and signed a treaty of their own. It established diplomatic and economic relations that proved useful to each of them. Although the treaty contained no secret political or military clauses, other governments suspected that such arrangements did exist. It is now known that the Germans did help train the Russian army and that their own army got valuable experience in the use of tanks and planes in the Soviet Union. Rapallo confirmed the French in their belief that Germany would not live up to the terms of the Versailles treaty and helped move them to strong action.

Quest for Reparations In early 1923, the Allies, and France in particular, declared Germany to be in technical default on payment of its reparations. Raymond Poincaré (1860–1934), France's powerfully nationalistic prime minister, decided to teach the Germans a lesson and force them to comply.

The French invasion of the German Ruhr (1923) began a crisis that brought strikes and rampant inflation in Germany. Here French troops have commandeered a German locomotive during one of the strikes.   UPI/CORBIS/Bettmann

On January 11, 1923, to ensure receipt of the hard-won reparations, the French government, in cooperation with Belgium, sent troops to occupy the Ruhr, Germany's mining and manufacturing district in the Rhineland. In response, the German government ordered passive resistance. The policy amounted to calling a general strike in the largest industrial region of Germany. Confronted with this tactic, Poincaré sent French civilians to run the German mines and railroads. France prevailed.

The Germans paid, but France's victory was costly. French heavy-handedness alienated the British, who took no part in the occupation. They became more suspicious of France and more sympathetic to Germany. The cost of the Ruhr occupation, moreover, vastly increased French as well as German inflation and hurt the French economy. The Ruhr invasion demonstrated how the uncertainties surrounding the Versailles treaty could harm even the nations it was intended to benefit.

In 1924, Poincaré's conservative ministry gave way to a coalition of leftist parties, the so-called *Cartel des Gauches*, led by Edouard Herriot (1872–1957). The new cabinet recognized the Soviet Union and adopted a more conciliatory policy toward Germany. This policy was the work of Aristide Briand (1862–1932), who was foreign minister for the remainder of the decade. He championed the League of Nations and tried to persuade France that its military power did not give it unlimited influence in the foreign affairs of Europe.

Under the leftist coalition, a mild inflation also occurred. It had begun under the conservatives, but picked up intensity in 1925. When the value of the franc fell sharply on the international money market in 1926, Poincaré returned to office as head of a national government of several parties. The value of the franc recovered somewhat, and inflation cooled. For the rest of the 1920s, the conservatives remained in power, and France enjoyed a general prosperity that lasted until 1931, longer than any other nation did.

GREAT BRITAIN: ECONOMIC CONFUSION

World War I profoundly changed British politics if not the political system. In 1918, Parliament expanded the electorate to include all men aged twenty-one and women aged thirty. (In 1928, the age for women voters was also lowered to twenty-one.) The prewar structure of parties and leadership shifted. A coalition cabinet of Liberal, Conservative, and Labour ministers had directed the war effort. The wartime ministerial participation of the Labour Party helped dispel its radical image. The war further divided the Liberal Party, however.

Until 1916, Liberal prime minister Herbert Asquith (1852–1928) had presided over the cabinet. As disagreements over war management developed, his fellow Liberal David Lloyd George (1863–1945) replaced him. The party split sharply between the followers of the two men. In 1918, against the wishes of both the Labour Party and the Asquith Liberals, Lloyd George decided to maintain the coalition through the tasks of the peace conference and the domestic reconstruction. In December 1918, the wartime coalition, now minus its Labour members, won a stunning victory at the polls, but the divisions among the Liberals meant that the new Parliament had many more Conservative than Liberal members. Lloyd George could thereafter remain prime minister only as long as his dominant Conservative partners wished to keep him.

During the election campaign, there had been much talk about creating "a land fit for heroes to live in." It did not happen. Except for the three years immediately after the war, the British economy was depressed throughout the 1920s. There was no genuine postwar recovery. Unemployment never dipped below ten percent and often hovered near eleven percent. There were never fewer than a million workers unemployed. The government expanded its insurance programs to cover unemployed workers, widows, and orphans. There was no similar meaningful expansion in the number of jobs available. From 1922 onward, accepting the "dole" with little expectation of future employment became a wretched and degrading way of life for thousands of poor British families.

The First Labour Government   In October 1922, the Conservatives replaced Lloyd George with Andrew Bonar Law (1858–1923), one of their own. A Liberal would never again be prime minister. Stanley Baldwin (1867–1947) soon replaced Law, who was dying from throat cancer. Baldwin decided to attempt to cure Britain's economic plight by abandoning free trade and imposing protective tariffs. The voters rejected that policy in 1923. In the election, the Conservative Party lost its majority in the House of Commons, but only votes from both Liberal and Labour party members could provide an alternative majority.

Labour had elected the second largest group of members to the Commons. Consequently, in December 1923, King George V (r. 1910–1936) asked Ramsay MacDonald (1866–1937) to form the first Labour ministry in British history. The Liberal Party did not serve in the cabinet, but provided the necessary votes to give Labour a working majority in the House of Commons.

The Labour Party was socialistic in its platform, but democratic and distinctly nonrevolutionary. The party had expanded beyond its early trade-union base. MacDonald himself had opposed World War I and for a time had also broken with the party. His own version of socialism owed little, if anything, to Marx. His program consisted of plans for extensive social reform rather than for the nationalization or public seizure of industry. A sensitive politician, if not a great leader, MacDonald understood the most important task facing his government was proving to the nation that the Labour Party was both respectable and responsible. His nine months in office achieved that goal, if little else of major importance. The establishment of Labour as a viable governing party signaled the permanent eclipse of the Liberal Party. It has continued to exist, but the bulk of its voters have drifted into either the Conservative or the Labour ranks.

The General Strike of 1926   The Labour government fell in the autumn of 1924 over charges of inadequate prosecution of a communist writer. Stanley Baldwin returned to office, where he remained until 1929. The stagnant economy remained uppermost in the public mind. Business and political leaders continued to believe all would be well if they could restore the prewar conditions of trade. A major element in these conditions had been the gold standard as the basis for international trade. In 1925, the Conservative government returned to the gold standard, abandoned during the war, in hopes of recreating the former monetary stability. The government, however, set the conversion rate for the pound too high against other currencies and thus, in effect, raised the price of British goods to foreign customers.

To make their products competitive on the world market, British management attempted to lower prices by cutting wages. The coal industry was the sector most directly affected by the wage cuts. It was inefficient and poorly managed and had been in trouble since the end of the war.

Labor relations in the coal industry long had been unruly. In 1926, after cuts in wages and a breakdown in negotiations, the coal miners went on strike. Soon thereafter, in May 1926, sympathetic workers in other industries engaged in a general strike lasting nine days. There was much tension but little violence. In the end, the miners and the other unions capitulated. With such high levels of unemployment, organized labor was in a weak position. After the general strike, the Baldwin government attempted to reconcile labor primarily through new housing and reforms in the poor laws. Despite the economic difficulties of these years, the standard of living of most British workers, including those receiving government insurance payments, actually improved. (See "Encountering the Past: The Coming of Radio: The BBC," page 894.)

Empire   World War I also modified Britain's imperial position. The aid the dominions, such as Canada and Australia, gave to the war effort

THE COMING OF RADIO: THE BBC

Radio was the first form of mass electronic communication. Radio, or wireless telegraphy, as it was called at the time, was first developed by the Italian inventor Guglielmo Marconi (1874–1937) in the 1890s. The first company devoted to radio communication was the Marconi Company, organized in Great Britain in 1897. Many other companies soon followed, including General Electric and RCA (the Radio Corporation of America) in the United States. The first American commercial station, KADA, opened in Pittsburgh in 1920, and radio flourished in the United States through advertising and popular programming from thousands of stations.

In Great Britain, the soon to be world-famous British Broadcasting Company (BBC) operated on very different principles. The BBC, founded in 1922, possessed a broadcasting monopoly granted by the British government. There was no advertising; instead, when people bought radios, they also had to purchase a radio license, and the funds generated paid the costs of broadcasting. About a million radios had been sold when the BBC first went on the air; by the end of the 1930s, almost everyone in Britain had access to a radio.

Because it was a monopoly, the management of the BBC could decide what image of Britain they wished to project over the radio waves. Unlike American radio stations, the BBC began with what some might consider an elitist mission: It set out to improve the level of British cultural life, not to broadcast the kind of popular music, dramas, or other programs that might too easily appeal to a mass audience. To preserve a sense of decorum, the early BBC broadcasters often dressed in white tie and tails even though their listeners could obviously not see them. In addition to news, beginning in 1923, the BBC also broadcast classical music and productions of the great plays from British literature and thus made them easily and inexpensively available to a mass audience. Yet even the BBC could not ignore popular taste, and after a few years it began to broadcast light music, sports, and even vaudeville acts.

The BBC also tapped into—some would say helped create—another aspect of popular culture: fascination with the British royal family and the intimate details of their lives. Radio enabled mil-

In 1932 King George V (r. 1910–1936) delivered the first royal Christmas address over the BBC to the British people.   Hulton-Deutsch Collection/CORBIS

lions of Britons for the first time to hear the voice of their monarch. In 1924, King George V (r. 1910–1936) became the first British sovereign ever to speak to the nation on radio; in 1932, he broadcast the first royal Christmas speech. Thereafter royal speeches on the BBC would become an enduring tradition and the monarchy a mass-market phenomenon.

The BBC in the 1920s and 1930s saw itself as transmitting official polite culture, though of an increasingly broad sort. In this it was not alone. Although the audience for radio was powerfully democratic, most European—and Asian—governments tried to monopolize or at least dominate the airways. Yet unlike the BBC, which strove to be above politics, the authoritarian governments operating in Europe from the 1920s onward would use their control of radio for their own political purposes.

- *In what ways was the BBC different from American commercial radio stations? How did the BBC affect the popularity of the British monarchy?*

demonstrated a new independence on their part. Empire was a two-way proposition. The idea of self-determination as applied to Europe filtered into imperial relationships. In India, the Congress Party, led by Mohandas Gandhi (1869–1948), was beginning to attract widespread support. The British started to talk more about eventual self-government for India. Moreover, during the 1920s, the government of India achieved the right to impose tariffs to protect its own industry rather than for the advantage of British manufacturers. British textile producers no longer had totally free access to the vast Indian market.

Ireland A new chapter was written in the unhappy relations between Britain and Ireland during and after the war. In 1914, the Irish Home Rule Bill had passed Parliament, but its implementation was postponed until after the war. As the war dragged on, Irish nationalists determined to wait no longer. On Easter Monday in April 1916, a nationalist uprising occurred in Dublin. It was the only rebellion of a national group to occur against any government engaged in the war. The British suppressed it in less than a week but then made a grave tactical blunder: They executed the Irish nationalist leaders who had been responsible for the uprising. Overnight those rebels became national martyrs. Leadership of the nationalist cause quickly shifted from the Irish Party in Parliament to the extremist **Sinn Fein**, or "Ourselves Alone," movement.

In the election of 1918, the Sinn Fein Party won all but four of the Irish parliamentary seats outside Ulster. They refused to go to the Parliament at Westminster. Instead, they constituted themselves into a *Dail Eireann*, or Irish Parliament. On January 21, 1919, they declared Irish independence. The military wing of Sinn Fein became the Irish Republican Army (IRA). The first president was Eamon De Valera (1882–1975), who had been born in the United States. What amounted to a guerrilla war broke out between the IRA and the British army, with the latter supported by auxiliaries known as the Black and Tans. There was bitterness and hatred on both sides.

In late 1921, the two governments began secret negotiations. In the treaty concluded in December 1921, the Irish Free State took its place beside the earlier dominions in the British Commonwealth: Canada, Australia, New Zealand, and South Africa. The six counties of Ulster, or Northern Ireland, were permitted to remain part of what was now called the United Kingdom of Great Britain and Northern Ireland, with provisions for home rule. No sooner had the treaty been signed than a

new civil war broke out between Irish moderates and diehards. The moderates supported the treaty; the diehards wanted to abolish the oath to the British monarch and establish a totally independent republic. The second civil war continued until 1923. De Valera, who supported the diehards, resigned the presidency and organized resistance to the treaty. In 1932, he was again elected president. The next year, the *Dail Eireann* abolished the oath of allegiance to the monarch.

During World War II, the Irish Free State remained neutral. In 1949, it declared itself the wholly independent Republic of Eire.

TRIALS OF THE SUCCESSOR STATES IN EASTERN EUROPE

It had been an article of faith among nineteenth-century liberals sympathetic to nationalism that only good could flow from the demise of Austria-Hungary, the restoration of Poland, and the establishment of nation-states throughout eastern Europe. These new states were to embody the principle of national self-determination and to provide a buffer against the westward spread of Bolshevism. They were, however, in trouble from the beginning.

Both France and Great Britain had long experience in liberal democratic government. Their primary challenges during the 1920s lay in responding to economic pressures and allowing new groups, such as the Labour Party, to share political power. In Germany, Poland, Austria, Czechoslovakia, and the other successor states, the challenge for the 1920s was to make new parliamentary governments function in a satisfactory and stable manner. Before the war, the elected parliaments of both Germany and Austria had not exercised genuine political power. The question after the war became whether those groups that had previously sat powerless in parliaments could assume both power and responsibility. Another question was how long conservative political groups and institutions, such as the armies, would tolerate or cooperate with the liberal experiments.

ECONOMIC AND ETHNIC PRESSURES

All the new states faced immense postwar economic difficulties. None of them possessed the kind of strong economy that nation-states such as France and Germany had developed in the nineteenth century. Indeed, political independence disrupted the previous economic relationships that each of them had developed as part of one of the prewar empires. None of the new states was financially independent; except for Czechoslovakia, all of them depended on foreign loans to finance economic development. Nationalistic antagonisms often prevented these states from trading with each other, and as a consequence, most became highly dependent on trade with Germany. The successor states of eastern Europe were poor and overwhelmingly rural nations in an industrialized world. The depression hit them especially hard, because they had to import finished goods for which they paid with agricultural exports whose value was falling sharply.

Finally, throughout eastern Europe, the collapse of the old German, Russian, and Austrian empires allowed various ethnic groups—large and small—to pursue nationalistic goals unchecked by any great power or central political authority. The major social and political groups in these countries were generally unwilling to make compromises lest they undermine their nationalist identity and independence. Each state included minority groups that wanted to be independent or to become part of a different nation in the region. Again, except for Czechoslovakia, all of these states succumbed to some form of domestic authoritarian government.

It is important to recognize these interwar economic difficulties and nationalistic pressures, because many of them reemerged in the region in the 1990s. Indeed, to a considerable extent, the breakup of Yugoslavia and Czechoslovakia, the present uncertainties in the former Soviet Union, and the efforts at political reorganization in the rest of the areas the Soviet Union once dominated constitute one more attempt by the peoples of eastern Europe to achieve political and economic stability in the wake of the upheaval in that region caused by the events surrounding World War I.

POLAND: DEMOCRACY TO MILITARY RULE

The nation whose postwar fortunes probably most disappointed liberal Europeans was Poland. For more than a hundred years, the country had been erased from the map. (See Chapter 17.) An independent Poland had been one of Woodrow Wilson's Fourteen Points. When the country was restored in 1919, nationalism proved an insufficient bond to overcome political disagreements stemming from class differences, diverse economic interests, and regionalism. Furthermore, large Ukrainian, Jewish, Lithuanian, and German minorities distrusted the Polish government and resented the domination of Polish culture in

Marshal Josef Pilsudski governed Poland from 1926 to 1935. Hulton Archive/Getty Images

their lives. The new Poland had been constructed from portions governed by Germany, Russia, and Austria for over a century. Each of those regions of partitioned Poland had different administrative systems and laws, different economies, and different degrees of experience with electoral institutions. A host of small political parties bedeviled the new Polish Parliament, and the executive was weak. In 1926, Marshal Josef Pilsudski (1867–1935) carried out a military coup. Thereafter, he ruled, in effect, personally until his death, when the government passed into the hands of a group of his military followers.

CZECHOSLOVAKIA: A VIABLE DEMOCRATIC EXPERIMENT

Only one central European successor state escaped the fate of self-imposed authoritarian government. Czechoslovakia possessed a strong industrial base, a substantial middle class, and a tradition of liberal values. During the war, Czechs and Slovaks had cooperated to aid the Allies. They had learned to work together and generally to trust each other. After the war, the new government had broken up large estates in favor of small peasant holdings. In the person of Thomas Masaryk (1850–1937), the nation possessed a gifted leader of immense integrity and fairness. The country had a real chance of becoming a viable modern nation-state.

There were, however, tensions between the Czechs and the Slovaks, who were poorer and more rural. Moreover, Czechoslovakia encountered discontent among its other non-Czech national groups, including Poles, Magyars, Ukrainians, and especially the Germans of the Sudetenland, which the Paris settlement had placed within Czech borders. The parliamentary regime might have been able to work through these problems, but extreme German nationalists in the Sudetenland looked to Hitler, who wanted to expand into eastern Europe, for help. In 1938, at Munich, the great powers first divided liberal Czechoslovakia to appease Hitler's aggressive instincts and then watched passively in early 1939 as he occupied much of the country, gave parts to Poland and Hungary, and manipulated a Slovak puppet state.

HUNGARY:
TURN TO AUTHORITARIANISM

Hungary was one of the defeated powers of World War I. In that defeat, it achieved its long-desired separation from Austria, but at a high political and economic price. In Hungary during 1919, Bela Kun (1885–1937), a communist, established a short-lived Hungarian Soviet Republic, which received socialist support. The Allies authorized an invasion by Romanian troops to remove the communist danger. The Hungarian landowners then established Admiral Miklós Horthy (1868–1957) as regent for the Habsburg monarch who could not return to his throne—a position Horthy held until 1944. After the collapse of the Kun government, thousands of Hungarians were either executed or imprisoned. It was, in part, in reaction to Kun's cooperation with socialists that Lenin ordered the Comintern to reject such cooperation in the future. Kun himself fled to Russia where Stalin later had him killed.

The Hungarians also deeply resented the territory Hungary had lost in the Paris settlement. The largely agrarian Hungarian economy suffered from a general stagnation. During the 1920s, the effective ruler of Hungary was Count Stephen Bethlen (1874–1947). He presided over a government that was parliamentary in form, but aristocratic in character. In 1932, he was succeeded by General Julius Gömbös (1886–1936), who pursued anti-Semitic policies and rigged elections. No matter

how the popular vote turned out, the Gömbös party controlled Parliament. After his death in 1936, anti-Semitism lingered in Hungarian politics.

AUSTRIA: POLITICAL TURMOIL
AND NAZI OCCUPATION

Austria's situation was little better than that of the other successor states. A quarter of the eight million Austrians lived in Vienna. Viable economic life was almost impossible, and the Paris settlement forbade union with Germany. Throughout the 1920s, the leftist Social Democrats and the conservative Christian Socialists contended for power. Both groups employed small armies to terrorize their opponents and to impress their followers.

In 1933, the Christian Socialist Engelbert Dollfuss (1892–1934) became chancellor. He tried to steer a course between the Austrian Social Democrats and the German Nazis, who had surfaced in Austria. In 1934, he outlawed all political parties except the Christian Socialists, the agrarians, and the paramilitary groups that composed his own Fatherland Front. He used troops against the Social Democrats, but was shot later that year during an unsuccessful Nazi coup. His successor, Kurt von Schuschnigg (1897–1977), presided over Austria until Hitler annexed it in 1938.

SOUTHEASTERN EUROPE:
ROYAL DICTATORSHIPS

In southeastern Europe, revision of the arrangements in the Paris settlement was less of an issue. Parliamentary government floundered there nevertheless. Yugoslavia had been founded by the Corfu Agreement of 1917 and was known as the Kingdom of the Serbs, Croats, and Slovenes until 1929. Throughout the interwar period, the Serbs dominated the government and were opposed by the Croats. The two groups clashed violently, but the Serbs had the advantage of having had an independent state with an army prior to World War I, whereas the Croats and Slovenes had been part of the Austro-Hungarian Empire. The Croats generally were Roman Catholic, better educated, and accustomed to reasonably incorrupt government administration. The Serbs were Orthodox, somewhat less well educated, and considered corrupt administrators by the Croats. Furthermore, although each group predominated in certain areas of the country, each had isolated enclaves in other parts of the nation. Bosnia-Herzegovina, in addition to Serbs and Croats, had a significant Muslim population. The Slovenes, Muslims, and other small national groups often played the Serbs and the Croats against each other. All of the political parties except the small Communist Party represented a particular ethnic group rather than the nation of Yugoslavia. The violent clash of nationalities eventually led to a royal dictatorship in 1929 under King Alexander I (r. 1921–1934), himself a Serb. He outlawed political parties and jailed popular politicians. Alexander was assassinated in 1934, but the authoritarian government continued under a regency for his son.

Other royal dictatorships were imposed elsewhere in the Balkans: in Romania by King Carol II (r. 1930–1940) and in Bulgaria by King Boris III (r. 1918–1943). They regarded their own illiberal regimes as preventing the seizure of power by more extreme antiparliamentary movements and as quieting the discontent of the varied nationalities within their borders. In Greece, the parliamentary monarchy floundered amid military coups and calls for a republic. In 1936, General John Metaxas (1871–1941) instituted a dictatorship under King George II (r. 1935–1947) that, for the time being, ended parliamentary life in Greece.

THE WEIMAR REPUBLIC IN GERMANY

The German **Weimar Republic** was born amid the defeat of the imperial army, the revolution of 1918 against the Hohenzollerns, and the hopes of German Liberals and Social Democrats. Its name derived from the city of Weimar, in which its constitution was written and promulgated in August 1919. While the constitution was being debated, the republic, headed by the Social Democrats, accepted the humiliating terms of the Versailles treaty, the part of the Paris settlement that applied to Germany. Although it had signed only under the threat of an Allied invasion, the republic was nevertheless permanently associated with the national disgrace and the economic burdens of the treaty.

Throughout the 1920s, the government of the republic was required to fulfill the economic and military provisions the Paris settlement imposed. It became all too easy for German nationalists and military figures, whose policies had brought on the tragedy and defeat in the war, to blame the young republic and the socialists for the military defeat and its grievous social and political results. In Germany, more than in other countries, all political groups shared the desire to revise the treaty, though they differed about the means. Some wished to oppose its provisions whenever good tactical opportunities arose; others simply assumed a position of total opposition to the treaty. Because of these revisionist desires, Germans had different degrees of loyalty to the political arrangements of the Weimar constitution, which many of them associated with the Paris settlement.

CONSTITUTIONAL FLAWS

The Weimar constitution was in many respects a highly enlightened document. It guaranteed civil liberties and provided for direct election, by universal suffrage, of the parliament, the *Reichstag*, and the president. It also contained, however, certain crucial structural flaws that eventually allowed its liberal institutions to be overthrown. It provided for proportional representation for all elections. This system made it relatively easy for small parties to gain seats in the *Reichstag*. Ministers were technically responsible to the *Reichstag*, but the president appointed and removed the chancellor. Perhaps most importantly, Article 48 allowed the president to rule by decree in an emergency. The constitution thus permitted a temporary presidential dictatorship.

LACK OF BROAD POPULAR SUPPORT

Beyond the burden of the Paris settlement and these potential constitutional pitfalls, the Weimar Republic did not command the sympathy or loyalty of many Germans. No social revolution had accompanied the new political structure. Many important political figures favored a constitutional monarchy. The schoolteachers, civil servants, and judges of the republic were generally the same people who had served the kaiser and the empire. Before the war, they had distrusted or even hated the Social Democratic Party, which figured so prominently in the establishment and the politics of the republic.

The officer corps was also deeply suspicious of the government and profoundly resentful of the military provisions of the peace settlement. Its leaders and other nationalistic Germans perpetuated the myth that the German army had been forced to sue for an armistice on foreign soil only because it had been stabbed in the back by civilians at home. Thus, many Germans in significant social and political positions wanted both to revise the peace treaty and to modify the system of government. The early years of the republic only reinforced these sentiments.

Major and minor humiliations, as well as considerable economic instability, hurt the new government. In March 1920, the right-wing *Kapp Putsch*, or "armed insurrection," erupted in Berlin. Led by a conservative civil servant and supported by army officers, the attempted coup failed, but the *putsch* collapsed only after the government had fled the city and German workers had carried out a general strike. In the same month, strikes took place in the Ruhr. The government sent in troops. Such extremism from both the left and the right would haunt the republic for all its days.

In May 1921, the Allies presented a reparations bill for 132 billion gold marks. The German republican government accepted this preposterous demand only after new Allied threats of occupation. Throughout the early 1920s, there were numerous assassinations or attempted assassinations of important republican leaders. Violence marked the first five years of the republic.

INVASION OF THE RUHR AND INFLATION

Inflation brought on the major crisis of the period. Borrowing to finance the war and the continued postwar deficit spending generated an immense rise in prices. Consequently, the value of the German currency fell. By early 1921, the German mark traded against the American dollar at a ratio of 64 to 1, compared with a ratio of 4.2 to 1 in 1914. German bankers contended that the mark could not be stabilized until the reparations issue had been solved. In the meantime, the printing presses kept pouring forth paper money, used to redeem government bonds as they fell due.

The French invasion of the Ruhr in January 1923 and the German response of economic passive resistance produced cataclysmic inflation. The Weimar government subsidized the Ruhr labor force, which had laid down its tools. Unemployment soon spread from the Ruhr to other parts of the country, creating a new drain on the treasury and also reducing tax revenues. By this point, the printing presses had difficulty providing enough paper currency to keep up with the daily rise in prices. In November 1923, an American dollar was worth more than 800 million German marks. Money was literally not worth the paper it was printed on. Stores were unwilling to exchange goods for the worthless currency, and farmers withheld produce from the market.

The social and economic consequences of the great inflation of 1923 were disastrous for many Germans. Middle-class savings, pensions, and insurance policies were wiped out, as were investments in government bonds. Simultaneously, debts

In 1923, Germany suffered from cataclysmic inflation. Paper money became worthless and children used packets of it as building blocks.   Bettmann/Hulton Deutsch/CORBIS/Bettmann

and mortgages could easily be paid off. Speculators in land, real estate, and industry made fortunes. Union contracts generally allowed workers to keep up with rising prices. Farmers who supplied food to the cities did well, as did food stores whose proprietors benefited from the barter that replaced cash transactions. The inflation, thus, was not a disaster to everyone. To the middle class and the lower middle class, however, the inflation was another trauma coming hard on the heels of the military defeat and the peace treaty. Only when the social and economic upheaval of these months is grasped can the later German desire for order and security at almost any cost be understood.

HITLER'S EARLY CAREER

Late in 1923, Adolf Hitler (1889–1945) made his first major appearance on the German political scene. He was born the son of a minor Austrian customs official. By 1907, he had gone to Vienna, where his hopes of becoming an artist were dashed when he failed to gain admittance to art school. He lived for a time off money his mother sent and, after her death, off his Austrian orphan's allowance. He also painted and sold postcards and worked as a day laborer. In Vienna, he became acquainted with Mayor Karl Lueger's (1844–1910) Christian Social Party and its anti-Semitic ideology.

Hitler also absorbed much of the rabid German nationalism, racism, and extreme anti-Semitism that flourished in Vienna. He came to hate Marxism, which he associated with Jews. During World War I, Hitler fought in the German army and was wounded; he was promoted to the rank of corporal and awarded the Iron Cross for bravery. The war gave him his first sense of purpose.

After the conflict, Hitler settled in Munich and lived there during a postwar year of violent tumult when Social Democrats briefly governed the city. There he became associated with a small nationalistic, anti-Semitic political party, which in 1920 adopted the name of National Socialist German Workers' Party, better known simply as the **Nazis**. The same year, the group began to parade under a red-and-white banner with a black swastika. It issued a platform, or program, known as the Twenty-Five Points, which called for the repudiation of the Versailles treaty, the unification of Austria and Germany, the exclusion of Jews from German citizenship, agrarian reform, the prohibition of land speculation, the confiscation of war profits, state administration of the giant business cartels, and the replacement of department stores with small retail shops. (See "Hitler Denounces the Versailles Treaty.") In the two years after the war, Hitler seems to have firmly adopted and frequently voiced anti-Semitism as a fundamental part of his political outlook.

Originally, the Nazis had called for a broad program of nationalization of industry in an attempt to compete directly with the Marxist political parties for the vote of the workers. When the tactic failed, the Nazis redefined the meaning of the word *socialist* in their name to suggest a nationalistic outlook. In 1922, Hitler said,

Whoever is prepared to make the national cause his own to such an extent that he knows no higher ideal than the welfare of his nation; whoever has understood our great national anthem, *Deutschland, Deutschland, Über Alles* ["Germany, Germany, Over All"], to mean that nothing in the wide world surpasses in his eyes this Germany, people and land, land and people—that man is a Socialist.[2]

This definition, of course, had nothing to do with traditional German socialism. The "socialism" that Hitler and the Nazis had in mind was not state ownership of the means of production, but the subordination of all economic enterprise to the welfare of the nation. It often implied protection for small economic enterprises. Increasingly, the Nazis discovered their party appealed to virtually any economic group that was at risk and under pressure. They often tailored their messages to the particular local problems these groups confronted in different parts of Germany. The Nazis also found considerable support among war veterans, who faced economic and social displacement in Weimar society.

Soon after the publication of the Twenty-five Points, the storm troopers, or **SA** (*Sturmabteilung*), were organized under the leadership of Captain Ernst Roehm (1887–1934). The SA was a paramilitary organization that initially provided its members with food and uniforms and eventually also paid them. In the mid-1920s, the SA adopted its infamous brown-shirted uniform. The storm troopers were the chief Nazi instrument for terror and intimidation before the party controlled the government. They were a law unto themselves. They attacked socialists and communists. The organization was a means of preserving military discipline and values outside the small professional army the Paris settlement allowed Germany to have. The existence of such a private party army was a sign of the potential for violence in the Weimar Republic. It also represented widespread contempt for the law and the institutions of the republic. In response to Nazi force, both the Social Democrat and the Communist parties organized paramilitary organizations of their own, but in neither size nor discipline could they rival the Nazis. All these paramilitary forces greatly weakened the Weimar Republic.

The social and economic turmoil following the French occupation of the Ruhr and the German inflation provided the fledgling Nazi Party with an opportunity for direct action against the Weimar Republic, which seemed incapable of giving Germany military or economic security. Because of his immense oratorical skills and organizational abilities, Hitler personally dominated the Nazi Party.

As Hitler established his dominance within the party, he clearly had the model of Mussolini in mind and spoke of the Italian dictator's accomplishments in glowing terms. Both men recruited from disillusioned veterans of the World War. Both adopted paramilitary modes of organization. Both disparaged liberal politics as incapable of achieving great national ends and righting the wrongs of the peace settlement. Both exalted the principle of obedience to the heroic leader. In late 1923, with the memory of Mussolini's march on Rome still fresh, Hitler attempted to seize power by force.

On November 9, 1923, Hitler and a band of followers, accompanied by General Ludendorff,

[2]Quoted in Alan Bullock, *Hitler: A Study in Tyranny*, rev. ed. (New York: Harper & Row, 1962), p. 76.

HITLER DENOUNCES
THE VERSAILLES TREATY

One of the chief complaints of the National Socialist movement was the unfairness of the Versailles treaty of 1919. Virtually all German public figures, including leaders of the Weimar Republic, hoped to see that settlement revised. Hitler and his followers made denunciation of the treaty their single most uncompromising declaration. In this speech of April 17, 1923, Hitler explained how the treaty had undermined the German nation.

■ *How might the French invasion of the Ruhr and the resulting inflation have made this speech particularly effective? To what extent was Hitler's condemnation of the control the Versailles treaty imposed on Germany correct? How does Hitler contrast his young Nazi movement with the young Weimar Republic? Why does the one appear a strong and the other a weak supporter of German national goals?*

With the armistice begins the humiliation of Germany. If the Republic on the day of its foundation had appealed to the country: "Germans, stand together! Up and resist the foe! The Fatherland, the Republic expects of you that you fight to your last breath," then millions who are now the enemies of the Republic would be fanatical Republicans. Today they are the foes of the Republic not because it is a Republic but because this Republic was founded at the moment when Germany was humiliated, because it so discredited the new flag that men's eyes must turn regretfully towards the old flag.

It was no Treaty of Peace which was signed, but a betrayal of Peace.

The Treaty was signed which demanded from Germany that she should perform what was for ever impossible of performance. But that was not the worst; after all that was only a question of material values. This was not the end: Commissions of Control were formed! For the first time in the history of the modern world there were planted on a State agents of foreign Powers to act as Hangmen, and German soldiers were set to serve the foreigner. And if one of these Commissions was "insulted," a company of the German army had to defile before the French flag. We no longer feel the humiliation of such

an act; but the outside world says, "What a people of curs!"

So long as this Treaty stands there can be no resurrection of the German people: no social reform of any kind is possible! The Treaty was made in order to bring 20 million Germans to their deaths and to ruin the German nation. But those who made the Treaty cannot set it aside. At its foundation our Movement formulated three demands:

1. Setting aside of the Peace Treaty.
2. Unification of all Germans.
3. Land and soil to feed our nation.

Our Movement could formulate these demands, since it was not our Movement which caused the War, it has not made the Republic, it did not sign the Peace Treaty.

There is thus one thing which is the first task of this Movement: it desires to make the German once more National, that his Fatherland shall stand for him above everything else. It desires to teach our people to understand afresh the truth of the old saying: He who will not be a hammer must be an anvil. An anvil are we today, and that anvil will be beaten until out of the anvil we fashion once more a hammer, a German sword!

From speech delivered in Munich, April 17, 1923 by Adolph Hitler from *The Speeches of Adolf Hitler, April 1922-August 1939*, trans. by Norman H. Baynes, 1969, pp. 56–57.

During a Nazi Party rally in Nuremberg in 1927, Adolf Hitler stops his motorcade to receive the applause of the surrounding crowd. In the late 1920s, the Nazi movement was only one of many bringing strife to the Weimar Republic. Heinrich Hoffman/Bildarchiv Preussischer Kulturbesitz

attempted a *putsch* from a beer hall in Munich. When the local authorities crushed the uprising, sixteen Nazis were killed. Hitler and Ludendorff were arrested and tried for treason. The general was acquitted. Hitler used the trial to make himself into a national figure. In his defense, he condemned the republic, the Versailles treaty, the Jews, and the weakened condition of his adopted country. He was convicted and sentenced to five years in prison, but was paroled after serving only a few months.

During his time in prison, Hitler dictated **Mein Kampf**, or *My Struggle*, from which he eventually made a great deal of money. In this book, not taken seriously enough at the time, he outlined key political views from which he never swerved, including a fierce racial anti-Semitism, opposition to Bolshevism, which he associated with Jews, and a conviction that Germany must expand eastward into Poland and Ukraine to achieve greater "living space." Such expansion assumed the resurgence of German military might. In effect, Hitler transferred the foreign policy goals and racial outlooks previously associated with German overseas imperialism to the politics of central and eastern Europe. The natural targets of implementing these ideas would be Jews, the successor states of eastern Europe, the Soviet Union, and any groups within

Germany that opposed Hitler's vision of national unity and purpose. In the mid-1920s, most observers discounted the likelihood of any German political party's carrying out such policies.

During his imprisonment, Hitler reached two other decisions. First, it appears that this was the moment when he came to see himself as the leader who could transform Germany from a position of weakness to strength. Second, he decided that he and the party must pursue power by legal means, but as Hitler emerged from his imprisonment, he was still a regional politician (albeit one who was transforming himself into a national figure).

THE STRESEMANN YEARS

Elsewhere, the officials of the republic were trying to repair the damage from the inflation. Gustav Stresemann (1878–1929) was primarily responsible for reconstructing the republic and giving it a sense of self-confidence. As chancellor from August to November 1923, Stresemann abandoned the policy of passive resistance in the Ruhr. The country simply could not afford it. Then, with the aid of the banker Hjalmar Schacht (1877–1970), he introduced a new German currency. The rate of exchange was one trillion of the old German marks for one new *Rentenmark*.

MAJOR POLITICAL EVENTS OF THE 1920s

1919 (August)	Constitution of the Weimar Republic promulgated
1920	*Kapp Putsch* in Berlin
1921 (March)	Naval mutiny leads Lenin to initiate his New Economic Policy
1921 (December)	Treaty between Great Britain and the Irish Free State
1922 (April)	Treaty of Rapallo between Germany and the Soviet Union
1922 (October)	Fascist march on Rome leads to Mussolini's assumption of power
1923 (January)	France invades the Ruhr
1923 (November)	Hitler's beer hall *Putsch*
1923 (December)	First Labour government in Britain
1924	Death of Lenin
1925	Locarno Agreements
1926	General strike in Britain
1928	Kellogg-Briand Pact
1929 (January)	Trotsky expelled from the Soviet Union
1929 (February)	Lateran Accord between the Vatican and the Italian state

Stresemann also moved against challenges from the left and the right. He supported the crushing of both Hitler's abortive *putsch* and smaller communist disturbances. In late November 1923, he resigned as chancellor and became foreign minister, a post he held until his death in 1929. He continued to exercise considerable influence over the affairs of the republic.

In 1924, the Weimar Republic and the Allies agreed to a new system of reparation payments. The Dawes Plan, submitted by the American banker Charles Dawes, lowered the annual payments and allowed them to vary according to the fortunes of the German economy. The last French troops left the Ruhr in 1925. (See Map 26–1.)

The same year, Friedrich Ebert (1871–1925), the Social Democratic president of the republic, died. Field Marshal Paul von Hindenburg (1847–1934), a military hero and a conservative monarchist, was elected as his successor. He governed in strict accordance with the constitution, but his election suggested that German politics had become more conservative. It looked as if conservative Germans had become reconciled to the republic. This conservatism was in line with the prosperity of the later 1920s. The new political and economic stability meant that foreign capital flowed into Germany, and employment rose smartly. In the steel and chemical industries, large combines spread. The prosperity helped broaden the acceptance of, and appreciation for, the republic.

In foreign affairs, Stresemann was conciliatory. He fulfilled the provisions of the Paris settlement, even as he attempted to revise it by diplomacy. He was willing to accept the settlement in the west, but was a determined, if sometimes secret, revisionist in the east. He aimed to recover German-speaking territories lost to Poland and in Czechoslovakia and possibly to unite with Austria, chiefly by diplomatic means. The first step, however, was to achieve respectability and economic recovery. That goal required a policy of accommodation and "fulfillment," for the moment at least.

LOCARNO

These developments gave rise to the Locarno Agreements of October 1925. The spirit of conciliation led foreign secretary Austen Chamberlain (1863–1937) for Britain and Aristide Briand for France to accept Stresemann's proposal for a fresh start. France and Germany both accepted the western frontier established at Paris as legitimate. Britain and Italy agreed to intervene against whichever side violated the frontier or if Germany sent troops into the demilitarized Rhineland. Sig-

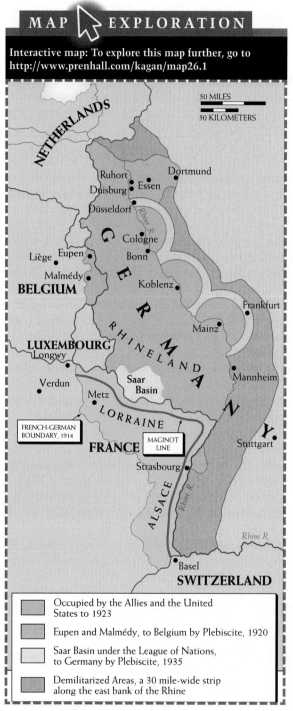

MAP EXPLORATION

Interactive map: To explore this map further, go to http://www.prenhall.com/kagan/map26.1

Map 26–1 GERMANY'S WESTERN FRONTIER The French-Belgian-German border area between the two world wars was sensitive. Despite efforts to restrain tensions, there were persistent difficulties related to the Ruhr, Rhineland, Saar, and Eupen-Malmédy regions that required strong defenses.

nificantly, no such agreement was reached about Germany's eastern frontier. The Germans signed treaties of arbitration with Poland and Czechoslovakia, however, and France strengthened its ties with the Little Entente. France supported German membership in the League of Nations and agreed to withdraw its occupation troops from the Rhineland in 1930, five years earlier than specified at Paris.

Locarno pleased everyone. Germany was satisfied to have achieved respectability and a guarantee against another Ruhr occupation, as well as the possibility of revision in the east. Britain was pleased to be allowed to play a more evenhanded role. Italy was glad to be recognized as a great power. The French were happy, too, because the Germans voluntarily accepted the permanence of their western frontier, also guaranteed by Britain and Italy, while France maintained its allies in the east.

The Locarno Agreements brought a new spirit of hope to Europe. Germany's entry into the League of Nations was greeted with enthusiasm. Chamberlain and Dawes received the Nobel Peace Prize in 1925, and Briand and Stresemann were awarded it in 1926. The spirit of Locarno was carried even further when the leading European states, Japan, and the United States signed the Kellogg-Briand Pact in 1928, renouncing "war as an instrument of national policy."

The joy and optimism were not justified. France had merely recognized its inability to coerce Germany without help. Britain had shown its unwillingness to uphold the Paris settlement in the east. Austen Chamberlain declared that no British government would ever "risk the bones of a British grenadier" for the Polish corridor. Germany remained unreconciled to the eastern settlement. It continued its clandestine military connections with the Soviet Union, which had begun with the Treaty of Rapallo, and planned to continue to press to revise the Paris settlement.

In both France and Germany, moreover, the conciliatory politicians represented only a part of the nation. In Germany, especially, most people continued to reject Versailles and regarded Locarno as only an extension of it. When the Dawes Plan expired in 1929, the Young Plan replaced it. Named after the American businessman Owen D. Young (1874–1962), who devised it on behalf of the Allies, this plan lowered German reparation payments, put a limit on how long they had to be made, and removed Germany entirely from outside supervision and control. The intensity of the outcry in Germany against the continuation of any reparations showed how far the Germans were from accepting their situation.

Despite these problems, major war was by no means inevitable. Europe, aided by American loans, was returning to prosperity. German leaders like Stresemann would unquestionably have continued to press for change, but they would certainly not have resorted to force, much less to a general war. Continued prosperity and diplomatic success might have won the loyalty of the German people to the Weimar Republic and moderate revisionism, but the **Great Depression** of the 1930s brought new forces into play.

IN PERSPECTIVE

At the close of the 1920s, Europe appeared finally to have emerged from the difficulties of the World War I era. The Soviet Union, deeply feared in the West as the source of further communist revolutions, was isolated by the other powers and had withdrawn into its own internal power struggles. Elsewhere, the initial resentments over the Versailles peace settlement seemed to have abated. The major powers were cooperating. Democracy was still functioning in Germany. The Labour Party was about to form its second ministry in Britain. France had settled into a less assertive international role. Mussolini's fascism seemed to have little relevance to the rest of the Continent. The successor states had not fulfilled the democratic hopes of the Paris conference, but their troubles were their own.

The European economy seemed finally to be on an even keel. The frightening inflation of the early years of the decade was over, and unemployment had eased. American capital was flowing into the Continent. The Young Plan had systemized reparation payments. Yet this economic and political stability proved illusory and temporary. What brought it to an end was the deepest economic depression in the modern history of the West. As governments and electorates responded to the economic collapse, the search for liberty yielded in more than one instance to a search for security. The political experiments of the 1920s gave way to the political tragedies of the 1930s.

REVIEW QUESTIONS

1. How did the Bolshevik revolution pose a challenge to the rest of Europe? Why did Lenin institute the New Economic Policy? Could the Russian Revolution have succeeded without Lenin? How did the Comintern affect Western socialist parties? How did Stalin overcome Trotsky and establish himself as head of the Soviet state? How did the Bolshevik revolution result in the split of the socialist parties in Western Europe?

2. What was fascism? How and why did the fascists obtain power in Italy? To whom did they

appeal? What were the differences between the fascist dictatorship of Mussolini and the communist dictatorship of Stalin? What was the status of women under these regimes?

3. Why were Britain and France "joyless victors" after World War I? What weakness did each have? How did World War I change British politics? How did Ireland win its independence?

4. Why did France find it difficult to achieve security after the Versailles treaty? Was the invasion of the Ruhr wise? Was the Locarno pact a success?

5. Why was Czechoslovakia the only generally viable democracy in eastern Europe? What forces worked against democracy in the region?

6. Was the failure of the Weimar Republic in Germany inevitable? Between 1919 and 1929, what were the republic's greatest strengths and weaknesses? Why did the Versailles Treaty loom so large in domestic German politics? What was the position of the Nazi Party in the late 1920s?

SUGGESTED READINGS

I. T. BEREND, *Decades of Crisis: Central and Eastern Europe before World War II* (2001). The best recent survey of the subject.

R. J. BOSWORTH, *Mussolini* (2002). A major new biography.

S. F. COHEN, *Bukharin and the Bolshevik Revolution: A Political Biography, 1888–1938* (1980). An examination of Stalin's chief opponent on the communist right.

I. DEUTSCHER, *The Prophet Armed* (1954), *The Prophet Unarmed* (1959), and *The Prophet Outcast* (1963). The classic biography of Trotsky.

G. FELDMAN, *The Great Disorder: Politics, Economics, and Society in the German Inflation, 1914–1924* (1993). The best work on the subject.

F. FURET, *The Passing of an Illusion: The Idea of Communism in the Twentieth Century* (1995). A brilliant account of how communism shaped politics and thought outside the Soviet Union.

B. HAMANN, *Hitler's Vienna: A Dictator's Apprenticeship* (1999). Probing study of the politics and society of Vienna as the young Hitler experienced them.

B. KENT, *The Spoils of War: The Politics, Economics, and Diplomacy of Reparations, 1918–1932* (1993). A comprehensive account of the reparations problem of the 1920s.

I. KERSHAW, *Hitler, 1889–1936: Hubris* (1998). The best treatment of Hitler's early life and rise to power.

R. McKIBBIN, *Classes and Cultures: England, 1918–1951* (2000). Viewing the era through the lens of class.

R. PIPES, *The Unknown Lenin: From the Secret Archive* (1996). A collection of previously unpublished documents that indicate the repressive character of Lenin's government.

J. F. POLLARD, *The Vatican and Italian Fascism 1929–32: A Study in Conflict* (1985). Provides the background to the Lateran pacts.

Z. STERNHELL, *The Birth of Fascist Ideology: From Cultural Rebellion to Political Revolution* (1994). A controversial examination of the roots of Mussolini's ideology.

DOCUMENTS CD-ROM

Society and Culture Between the Wars

27.1 Werner Heisenberg: Uncertainty
27.5 Neville Chamberlain Defends the Policy of Appeasement

Totalitarianism

28.1 Nadezhda K. Krupskaya: *What a Communist Ought to Be Like*
28.2 Benito Mussolini: from *The Political and Social Doctrine of Fascism*
28.3 Adolf Hitler: from *Mein Kampf*
28.4 Christopher Dawson: Religion and the Totalitarian State
28.5 The Russian Revolution
28.6 Socialist Marriage to Motherhood for the Fatherland

CHAPTER 27

EUROPE AND THE GREAT DEPRESSION OF THE 1930S

KEY TOPICS

- Financial collapse and depression in Europe
- The emergence of the National Government in Great Britain and the Popular Front in France in response to the political pressures caused by the Depression
- The Nazi seizure of power and the establishment of a police state and racial laws in Germany
- Forced industrialism and agricultural collectivization in the Soviet Union, and purges in the Soviet Communist Party and Soviet army under Stalin

I n Europe, unlike in the United States, the 1920s had not been "roaring." Economically, it had been a decade of insecurity, of a search for elusive stability, of a short-lived upswing, followed by a collapse in finance and production. The Great Depression that began in 1929 was the most severe downturn capitalist economies had ever experienced. High unemployment, low production, financial instability, and shrinking trade arrived and

Hitler's mastery of the techniques of mass politics and propaganda—including huge staged rallies like this one in 1938—was an important factor in his rise to power.   Art Resource/Bildarchiv Preussischer kulturbesitz.

would not depart. Business and political leaders despaired over the failure of the market mechanism to save them. Marxists and, indeed, many other observers thought the final downfall of capitalism was at hand.

European voters looked for new ways out of the doldrums, and politicians sought to escape the pressures that the depression had brought on them. One result of the fight for economic security was the establishment of the Nazi dictatorship in Germany. Another was the piecemeal construction of what became known as the mixed economy; that is, governments became directly involved in economic decisions alongside business and labor. In both cases, most of the political and economic guidelines of nineteenth-century liberalism were abandoned, and so were decency and civility in political life. ■

TOWARD THE GREAT DEPRESSION

Three factors combined to bring about the intense severity and the extended length of the Great Depression. First, there was a financial crisis that stemmed directly from the war and the peace settlement. Second, a crisis arose in the production and distribution of goods in the world market. These two problems became intertwined in 1929 and, so far as Europe was concerned, reached the breaking point in 1931. Finally, both difficulties became worse because neither the major Western European nations nor the United States offered strong economic leadership or acted responsibly. Without cooperation or leadership in the Atlantic economic community, the economic collapse in finance and production lingered and deepened.

THE FINANCIAL TAILSPIN

Most European nations emerged from World War I with inflated currencies. Immediately after the armistice, the unleashed demand for consumer and industrial goods drove up prices. The price and wage increases generally subsided after 1921. Yet the problem of maintaining the value of their national currencies still haunted political leaders—and intensified after the German financial disaster of 1923. The frightening German example of uncontrolled inflation helped explain the why most governments refused to run budget deficits when the depression struck. They feared inflation as a source of social instability and political turmoil the way that European governments since World War II have feared unemployment.

Reparations and War Debts   Reparation payments and international war-debt settlement further complicated the picture. Here France and the United States were the stumbling blocks. France had twice paid reparations as a defeated nation, once after 1815 and again after 1871. As a victor, it now intended both to receive reparations and to use them to finance its postwar recovery. The 1923 invasion of the Ruhr demonstrated French determination to exact reparations.

The United States was no less determined to be repaid the money it had loaned its allies. Moreover, the European Allies owed debts to each other. European nations intended to repay all these debts with German reparations. Most of the money that

the Allies collected from each other eventually went to the United States.

In 1922, Great Britain announced it would insist on payment for its own loans only to the extent that the United States required payments from Britain. The American government, however, would not relent. The reparations and the war debts made normal business, capital investment, and international trade difficult and expensive for the European nations. Governments exercised controls over credit, trade, and currency. Currency speculation drew funds away from capital investment in productive enterprise. The monetary problems reinforced the general tendency toward high tariff policies. If a nation imported too many goods from abroad, it might have difficulty meeting those costs and the expenses of debt or reparation payments. The financial and currency muddle thus discouraged trade and production and, in consequence, hurt employment.

American Investments   In 1924, the Dawes Plan reorganized the administration and transfer of reparations, which, in turn, smoothed the debt repayments to the United States. Thereafter, private American capital flowed into Europe—especially Germany. Much of the money, which provided the basis for Europe's brief prosperity after 1925, was in the form of short-term loans.

In 1928, this lending began to contract as American money was withdrawn from European investments into the booming New York stock market. In the Wall Street crash of October 1929—the result of virtually unregulated financial speculation—huge sums were lost. U.S. banks had made large loans to customers, who then invested the money in the stock market. When stock prices collapsed, the customers could not repay the banks. Consequently, within the United States, all kinds of credit that had been available shrank or disappeared, and many banks failed. Thereafter, little American capital was available to invest in Europe. Furthermore, American banks that were trying to cover domestic shortages did not renew loans already made to Europeans.

The End of Reparations   When the credit to Europe began to run out, a severe financial crisis struck the Continent. In May 1931, Kreditanstalt, a large bank in Vienna, collapsed. It was a primary lending institution for much of central and eastern Europe. Its collapse put severe pressure on the German banking system, which was saved only

MAJOR DATES OF THE ECONOMIC CRISIS	
1923	German inflation following French invasion of Ruhr
1924	Dawes Plan on reparations
1929 (June)	Young Plan on reparations
1929 (October)	Wall Street crash
1931 (May)	Collapse of Kreditanstalt in Vienna
1931 (June)	Hoover announces moratorium on reparations
1932	Lausanne Conference ends reparations

through government guarantees. In this crisis Germany was unable to make its next reparation payment as stipulated in the 1929 Young Plan. In June 1931, as the German difficulties mounted, American president Herbert Hoover (1874–1964) announced a one-year moratorium on all payments of international debts.

The Hoover moratorium was a prelude to the end of reparations. It was also a sharp blow to the French economy, for which the flow of reparations was important. The French agreed to the moratorium only because the German economy had all but collapsed. The Lausanne Conference in the summer of 1932, in effect, ended the era of reparations. The next year, the debts owed to the United States were settled either through small token payments or simply through default. Nevertheless, the financial politics of the 1920s had done its damage.

PROBLEMS IN AGRICULTURAL COMMODITIES

In addition to the dramatic financial turmoil and collapse, a less dramatic, but equally fundamental, downturn occurred in production and trade. The 1920s saw the market demand for European goods shrink relative to the Continent's capacity to produce goods. This meant idle factories and fewer jobs. Part of the problem originated within Europe, part outside. In both instances, the difficulty arose from agriculture. Better methods of farming, improved strains of wheat, expanded tillage, and more extensive transport facilities all over the globe vastly increased the world supply of grain. World wheat prices fell to record lows. This development was, of course, initially good for consumers. The collapse in grain prices, however, meant lower incomes for European farmers, especially those of central and eastern Europe.

Also, higher industrial wages raised the cost of the industrial goods farmers or peasants used. The farmers could no longer purchase those products. Moreover, farmers began to have difficulty paying off their mortgages and the debts they incurred each year to run their farms. Normally, they borrowed money to plant their fields, expecting to pay the debt when they sold the crops, but the fall in commodity prices made it difficult for the farmers to earn enough to repay those debts.

Farm problems became especially pressing in eastern Europe. Immediately after the war, the new governments there had undertaken land-reform programs. The democratic franchise in the successor states had led, in varying degrees, to the breakup of large estates and their replacement by small peasant-owned farms. This was especially true in Romania, Czechoslovakia, and parts of Yugoslavia.

The new small farms, however, proved to be inefficient, and the farmers who worked them were unable to earn sufficient incomes to buy consumer goods or new equipment for their farms. Protective tariffs often prevented the export of grain among European countries. The credit and cost squeeze on eastern European farmers and on their counterparts in Germany left many farmers disillusioned with liberal, democratic politics. Many German farmers, for example, supported the Nazis.

Outside Europe, similar problems affected other producers of agricultural commodities. The prices they received for their products plummeted. Government-held reserves of agricultural commodities accumulated to record levels. The glut involved the supplies of wheat, sugar, coffee, rubber, wool, cotton, and lard. The people who produced these goods in underdeveloped nations in Asia, Africa, and Latin America could no longer make enough money to buy finished goods from industrial Europe. As world credit collapsed, the economic position of these commodity producers worsened. Commodity production had simply outstripped world demand.

The collapse in agricultural prices and the financial turmoil resulted in stagnation and depression for European industry. European coal, iron, and textiles had depended on international markets. Unemployment spread from these industries to those producing finished consumer goods. The persistent unemployment in Great Britain and to a lesser extent in Germany during the 1920s had already meant "soft" domestic markets in those countries. Governments' attempts to lift the depression by reducing spending further weakened domestic demand. By the early 1930s, the Great Depression was growing on itself.

DEPRESSION AND GOVERNMENT POLICY

The Great Depression did not mean absolute economic decline, nor did it mean everyone was out of a job. People with work always well outnumbered those without work. New economic sectors, such as the production of automobiles, radios, and synthetics, and the service industries around them continued to develop during the depression, but the economic downturn made people anxious. People with jobs feared their own economic security and standard of living would suffer next. The depression also frustrated social and economic expectations. People with jobs improved their standard of living or were promoted much more slowly. They were working, but they seemed to be going nowhere. Their anxieties fueled social discontent.

The governments of the late 1920s and the early 1930s were not well fitted in either structure or ideology to confront these problems. Orthodox economic theory at the time called for cuts in government spending to prevent inflation. Eventually, the market mechanism was supposed to restore prosperity. One result of the economic crisis of the depression was the emergence of a body of economic thought first set forth in 1936 in John Maynard Keynes's (1883–1946) *General Theory of Employment, Interest, and Money*. Keynes advocated active government intervention in the economy. He believed the market would not always operate automatically and urged government spending to expand overall demand during an economic downturn. The statesmen of Europe and the United States were unaware of Keynes' ideas until the Great Depression was well underway.

JOHN MAYNARD KEYNES CALLS FOR GOVERNMENT INVESTMENT TO CREATE EMPLOYMENT

Since at least the late nineteenth century, European social critics had questioned whether capitalistic economies could function without major crises that resulted in unemployment and other social disruptions. Virtually all economists, however, believed that given enough time capitalistic economies would correct themselves. Consequently, when the Great Depression struck the worldwide economy, the governments of Western Europe and the United States initially undertook relatively modest actions to address it. They were doing what most economists at the time advocated. Socialists, of course, had long advocated government intervention. In 1936, however, John Maynard Keynes, a prominent British economist, published The General Theory of Employment, Interest and Money. *Keynes, who was not a socialist, believed that the Great Depression demonstrated that economic crises could be so severe that private investment would simply not take place and thus could not generate new economic activity that would revive employment and lift the economy out of depression. In the passage below, Keynes explains that although he believes in individual initiative, there are times it will not occur. Under those conditions he calls for the "socialisation of investment," which was his term for government spending to spark new economic activity that would expand employment. In the second paragraph, he argues that the role of such government investment or spending is to provide employment for those workers whom the private economy cannot employ. Keynes's book did not influence many policies during the Great Depression, but after World War II, many Western governments devised economic policies along the lines he advocated.*

■ *Why does Keynes believe the private economy will not always provide sufficient employment? Why does he call government spending the "socialisation of investment"? How much of his argument is analytical? How much political?*

(See "John Maynard Keynes Calls for Government Investment to Create Employment".)

Nonetheless, the severity of the depression, plus pressure from the new mass electorates, did lead governments across Europe to interfere with the economy as never before. Government participation in economic life was not new; we need only recall the mercantilistic policies of the seventeenth and eighteenth centuries and the government encouragement of railway building in the nineteenth century. From the early 1930s onward, however, government involvement increased rapidly. Private economic enterprise became subject to new trade, labor, and currency regulations. To restore employment and provide for defense the state had to set economic priorities. As in the past, state intervention generally increased as one moved from west to east across the Continent.

These new economic policies usually also involved further political experimentation.

CONFRONTING THE GREAT DEPRESSION IN THE DEMOCRACIES

The Great Depression ended the business-as-usual attitude that had marked the political life of Great Britain and France during the late 1920s. In Britain, the emergency led to a new coalition government and the abandonment of economic policies considered sacred for a century. The economic stagnation in France gave rise to a bold political and economic program sponsored by the parties of the left. The relative success of the British venture gave the nation new confidence in the democratic processes;

In some respects the foregoing theory is moderately conservative in its implications. For whilst it indicates the vital importance of establishing certain central controls in matters which are now left in the main to individual initiative, there are wide fields of activity which are unaffected. The State will have to exercise a guiding influence on the propensity to consume partly through its scheme of taxation, partly by fixing the rate of interest, and partly, perhaps, in other ways. Furthermore, it seems unlikely that the influence of banking policy on the rate of interest will be sufficient by itself to determine an optimum rate of investment. I conceive, therefore, that a somewhat comprehensive socialisation of investment will prove the only means of securing an approximation to full employment; though this need not exclude all manner of compromises and of devices by which public authority will co-operate with private initiative. But beyond this, no obvious case is made out for a system of State Socialism which would embrace most of the economic life of the community. It is not the ownership of the instruments of production which it is important for the State to assume. If the State is able to determine the aggregate amount of resources devoted to aug-

menting the instruments and the basic rate of reward to those who them, it will have accomplished all that is necessary. . . .

To put the matter concretely, I see no reason to suppose that the existing system seriously misemploys the factors of production which are in use. There are, of course, errors of foresight; but these would not be avoided by centralizing decisions. When 9,000,000 men are employed out of 10,00,000 willing and able to work, there is no evidence that the labour of these 9,000,000 men is misdirected The complaint against the present system is not that these 9,000,000 men ought to be employed on different tasks, but that tasks should be available for the remaining 1,000,000 men. It is in determining the volume, not the direction, of actual employment that the existing system has broken down.

John Maynard Keynes, *The General Theory of Employment, Interest and Money*. London: Macmillan & Co., Ltd., 1960 p. 379.

the new departures in France created social and political hostilities that undermined faith in republican institutions.

GREAT BRITAIN: THE NATIONAL GOVERNMENT

In 1929, a second minority Labour government, headed by Ramsay MacDonald, took office. As British unemployment rose to more than 2.5 million workers in 1931, the ministry became divided over what to do. In line with conventional economic theory, MacDonald wanted to slash the budget, reduce government salaries, and cut unemployment benefits. This was a bleak program for a Labour government. MacDonald's strong desire to make the Labour Party politically and socially respectable led him to reject more radical programs. Many of the cabinet ministers resisted MacDonald's proposals. They refused to penalize the poor and the unemployed. The prime minister requested the resignations of his entire cabinet and arranged for a meeting with King George V.

Everyone assumed the entire Labour ministry was about to leave office. However, to the surprise of his party and the nation, MacDonald did not resign. At the urging of the king and probably driven by his own ambition, MacDonald formed a coalition ministry, called the National Government, composed of Labour, Conservative, and Liberal

ministers. The bulk of the Labour Party believed their leader had sold them out and repudiated MacDonald's leadership. In the election of 1931, the National Government received a comfortable majority. After the election, however, MacDonald, who remained prime minister until 1935, was a tool of the Conservatives. They held a majority in their own right in the House of Commons, but the appearance of a coalition was useful for imposing unpleasant programs.

The National Government took three decisive steps to attack the depression. First, to balance the budget, it raised taxes, cut insurance benefits to the unemployed and the elderly, and lowered government salaries. Its leaders argued that since prices had also fallen, those cuts in benefits and pay did not appreciably cut real income. Second, in September 1931, Britain went off the gold standard. The value of the British pound on the international money market fell by about 30 percent. This move stimulated exports because it made British products cheaper for foreigners to buy. Third, in 1932, Parliament passed the Import Duties Bill, which placed a ten percent ad valorem tariff (a tax levied in proportion to the value of each imported good) on all imports except those from the empire. These steps were extraordinary. Gold and free trade, the hallmarks of almost a century of British commercial policy, were abandoned.

The policies of the National Government produced results. Great Britain avoided the banking crisis that hit other countries. By 1934, industrial production had expanded beyond the level for 1929. Britain was the first nation to restore that level of production. Of course, the mediocre British industrial performance of the 1920s made the task easier. The government also encouraged lower interest rates, which led to the largest private housing boom in British history. Industries related to housing and home furnishing prospered.

Britain had entered the depression with a stagnant economy and left the era with a stagnant economy. Those people who were employed generally improved their standard of living. Nonetheless, the hard core of unemployment remained. In 1937, the number of jobless had fallen to just below 1.5 million.

Yet the British political system was not fundamentally challenged. The unemployed protested, but social insurance, though hardly generous, did support them. To the employed citizens of the country, the Na-

In what was known as the "Jarrow Crusade" during the autumn of 1936 a group of approximately 200 protesters marched from the town of Jarrow in northeastern England to London to demonstrate their need for employment and the plight of their town where the previous year the shipyard had been closed.
Getty Images, Inc./Hulton Archive Photos

tional Government seemed to pursue a policy that avoided the extreme wings of both the Labour and the Conservative parties. When MacDonald retired as prime minister in 1935 (he remained in the cabinet as an elder statesman until his death in 1937), Stanley Baldwin again took office. He was succeeded in 1937 by Neville Chamberlain (1869–1940). Chamberlain is today best known for the disastrous Munich agreement with Hitler in 1938, but when he took office, he was considered one of the more progressive thinkers on social issues in the Conservative Party.

One movement in Britain did flirt with the extreme right-wing politics of the Continent. In 1932, Sir Oswald Mosley (1896–1980) founded the British Union of Fascists. He had held a minor position in the second Labour government, and its feeble attack on unemployment disgusted him. Mosley urged a program of direct action through a new corporate structure for the economy. His group wore black shirts in imitation of Mussolini's Italian Fascists and attempted to hold mass meetings. Even at the height of his popularity, however, Mosley gained only a few thousand adherents. Thereafter his anti-Semitism began to alienate supporters, and by the close of the 1930s, he was little more than a political oddity.

FRANCE: THE POPULAR FRONT

The unfolding of the Great Depression in France was the reverse of that in Britain. It came later and lasted longer. Only in 1931 did the economic slide begin to affect the French economy. Even then, unemployment did not become a major problem. Rarely were more than half a million French workers without jobs. One industry after another, however, lowered wages. The government raised tariffs to protect French goods and especially French agriculture. (Ever since that time, the government has carefully protected French farmers.) These measures helped maintain the home market, but did little to overcome industrial stagnation. Relations between labor and management were tense.

The first political fallout of the depression was the election of another Radical coalition government in 1932. Fearful of contributing to inflation as they had after 1924, the Radicals pursued a generally deflationary policy, lowering government spending and increasing interest rates. In the same year that the new ministry took office, reparation payments on which the French economy depended stopped. As the economic crisis tightened, parliamentary and political life became difficult.

Right-Wing Violence   Outside parliament, politics grew ugly. Various right-wing groups with authoritarian tendencies became active. These leagues included the Action Française, founded before World War I in the wake of the Dreyfus affair, and the veterans' group Croix de Feu, or "Cross of Fire." These and similar groups had a total of more than two million members. Some of them wanted a monarchy; others favored what would have amounted to military rule. They were hostile to parliamentary government, socialism, and communism. They wanted to set what they regarded as the greater good and glory of France above the petty machinations of political parties. They thus resembled the fascists and the Nazis.

The activities and propaganda of the right-wing leagues weakened loyalty to republican government and embittered French political life. They also led to an incident of extraordinary havoc that had grave political consequences.

This incident grew out of the Stavisky affair, the last of those curious scandals that punctuated the political fortunes of the Third Republic. Serge Stavisky (d. 1934) was a small-time gangster who appears to have had good connections within the government. In 1933, he became involved in a fraudulent bond scheme. When the police finally tracked him down, he committed suicide in suspicious circumstances in January 1934. The official handling of the matter suggested a political cover-up. It was alleged that people in high places wished to halt the investigation. To the right wing, the Stavisky incident symbolized all the seaminess, immorality, and corruption of republican politics.

Leon Blum (1872–1950) led the Popular Front to victory in the French elections of 1936. These demonstrators are carrying his portrait at a rally in Paris.   UPI/CORBIS/Bettmann

DEPRESSION YEARS
IN GREAT BRITAIN AND FRANCE

1929	Second Labour government comes to power in Britain with Ramsay MacDonald as prime minister
1931	Formation of National Government in Britain
1931	Britain goes off the gold standard
1932	Oswald Mosley founds British Union of Fascists
1933–1934	Stavisky affair in France
1934 (February 6)	Right-wing riots in Paris
1935	Stanley Baldwin becomes British prime minister
1936 (June 5)	Popular Front government in France under Leon Blum
1936 (June 8)	Labor accord in France
1937	Neville Chamberlain becomes British prime minister
1938	Popular Front replaced by Radical ministry in France

On February 6, 1934, a large demonstration of the right-wing leagues took place in Paris. The exact purpose and circumstances of the rally remain uncertain, but the crowd tried to storm the Chamber of Deputies, the lower house of the French parliament. Violence erupted between right and left political groups and between both of them and the police. Fourteen demonstrators were killed; scores of others were injured. It was the largest disturbance in Paris since the Commune of 1871.

After this clash, a government composed of all living former premiers replaced the Radical ministry of Edouard Daladier (1884–1970). Parliament permitted the ministry to deal with economic matters by decree. The major result of the right-wing demonstrations, however, was that the parties of the left, Radicals, Socialists, and Communists, began to realize that a right-wing coup might be possible in France.

Socialist-Communist Cooperation Between 1934 and 1936, the French left began to make peace within its own ranks. This was not easy. French Socialists, led by Léon Blum (1872–1950), had been the major target of the French communists since the split over joining the Comintern in 1920. Only Stalin's fear of Hitler as a danger to the Soviet Union made this new cooperation possible. Despite deep suspicions on all sides, what became known as the **Popular Front**, a coalition of all left-

wing parties, had been established by July 1935. Its purpose was to preserve the republic and press for social reform.

The election of 1936 gave the Popular Front a majority in the Chamber of Deputies. The Socialists were the largest single party for the first time in French history. They organized the cabinet as they had long promised they would do when they constituted the majority party of a coalition. Léon Blum became premier on June 5, 1936.

From the early 1920s, this Jewish intellectual and humanitarian had opposed the communist version of socialism. Cast as the successor to Jean Jaurès (1859–1914), who had been assassinated in 1914, Blum pursued socialism through a democratic, parliamentary government.

Blum's Government During May 1936, before the Popular Front came to power, strikes had begun to spread throughout French industry. Immediately after assuming office on June 6, the Blum government faced further spontaneous work stoppages involving over half a million workers who had occupied factories in sit-down strikes. These were the most extensive labor disturbances in the history of the Third Republic. They aroused new fears in the conservative business community, already frightened by the election of the Popular Front.

Blum acted swiftly to bring together representatives of labor and management. On June 8, he announced the conclusion of an accord that reorganized labor-management relations in France. Wages were immediately raised between 7 and 15 percent. Employers were required to recognize unions and to bargain collectively with them. Workers were given annual paid two-week vacations. The forty-hour week was established throughout French industry. Blum hoped to overcome labor hostility to French society, to establish a foundation for justice in labor-management relations, and to increase domestic consumer demand.

Blum followed his labor policy with other bold departures. He raised the salaries of civil servants and instituted a program of public works. Government loans were extended to small industry. Spending on armaments was increased, and some armament industries were nationalized. A National Wheat Board was set up to manage the production and sale of grain. Initially, Blum had promised to resist devaluation of the franc. By the autumn of 1936, however, international monetary pressure forced him to devalue. He did so again in the spring of 1937. The devaluations came too late to help French exports.

These moves enraged French bankers and businesspeople, who tended to be conservatives. In

March 1937, they brought enough influence to bear on the ministry to cause Blum to halt the program of reform. It was not taken up again. Blum's Popular Front colleagues considered the pause in reform an unnecessary compromise. In June 1937, Blum resigned. The Popular Front ministry itself held on until April 1938, when another Radical ministry under Daladier replaced it. Not until 1939 did French industrial production reach the level of 1929.

By the close of the 1930s, many people in France had begun to wonder whether the republic was worth preserving. The left remained divided. Businesspeople found the republic inefficient and too subject to socialist pressures. Many on the right hated the republic in principle. When the time came in 1940 to defend the republic, too many French citizens had lost faith in it.

GERMANY: THE NAZI SEIZURE OF POWER

The most remarkable political event that the uncertainty and turmoil of the Great Depression caused was the coming to power of the National Socialists (Nazis) in Germany. By the late 1920s, the Nazis were a major presence in the Weimar Republic, but were not yet real contenders for political dominance. The financial crisis, economic stress, and social anxiety the depression brought on rapidly improved their position. All the fragility of the Weimar constitution stood exposed, and the path opened for the most far-reaching event of the decade: the Nazi seizure of power.

DEPRESSION AND POLITICAL DEADLOCK

The outflow of foreign—especially American—capital from Germany beginning in 1928 undermined the brief economic prosperity of the Weimar Republic. The resulting economic crisis ended parliamentary government. In 1928, a coalition of center parties and the Social Democrats governed. All went well until the depression struck. Then the coalition partners disagreed on economic policy. The Social Democrats refused to reduce social and unemployment insurance. The more conservative parties, remembering the inflation of 1923, insisted on a balanced budget. The coalition dissolved in March 1930.

To resolve the parliamentary deadlock, President von Hindenburg appointed Heinrich Brüning (1885–1970) as chancellor. Lacking a majority in the Reichstag, Brüning governed through emer-

gency presidential decrees, as Article 48 of the constitution authorized him to do. The party divisions prevented the Reichstag from overriding the decrees. The Weimar Republic thus became an authoritarian regime.

German unemployment rose from 2,258,000 in March 1930 to more than 6,000,000 in March 1932. There had been persistent unemployment during the 1920s, but nothing of such magnitude or duration. The economic downturn and the parliamentary deadlock benefited the more extreme political parties. In the election of 1928, the Nazis had won only 12 seats in the Reichstag, and the Communists had won 54 seats. After the election of 1930, the Nazis held 107 seats and the Communists 77.

For the Nazis, politics meant the capture of power by terror and intimidation as well as by legal elections. Decency and civility in political life vanished. Thousands of unemployed joined the storm troopers (SA), which had 100,000 members in 1930 and almost 1 million in 1933. The SA freely and viciously attacked Communists and Social Democrats, who also fought each other. The Nazis held mass rallies that resembled religious revivals. They gained powerful supporters and sympathizers in business, military, and publishing circles. Some intellectuals were also sympathetic. The Nazis transformed this new enthusiasm born of economic despair and nationalistic frustration into impressive electoral results.

HITLER COMES TO POWER

For two years Brüning governed with the confidence of President von Hindenburg. The economy did not improve, however, and the political situation deteriorated. In 1932, the eighty-three-year-old president stood for reelection. Hitler ran against him and forced a runoff. The Nazi leader got 30.1 percent of the first vote and 36.8 percent in the runoff. Although Hindenburg remained in office, the results of the poll convinced him that Brüning no longer commanded sufficient confidence from conservative German voters.

On May 30, 1932, Hindenburg dismissed Brüning. The next day, Hindenburg appointed Franz von Papen (1878–1969) as chancellor. The new chancellor was one of a small group of extremely conservative advisers on whom the aged Hindenburg had become increasingly dependent. Others included the president's son and army officers. With the continued paralysis in the Reichstag, their influence over the president amounted to control of the government. Thus, only a handful of people made the crucial decisions of the next several months.

This group was determined to solve the political crisis outside of the politics of the Reichstag. Hitler himself had decided he would not participate in the government unless the president appointed him chancellor. He had no intention of forming a coalition with other parties, which was, in any case, an unlikely possibility.

Papen and the circle around Hindenberg wanted to find some way to use the Nazis without giving Hitler effective power. The government needed the mass popular support that only the Nazis seemed able to generate. The Hindenburg circle decided to convince Hitler that the Nazis could not come to power on their own. Papen removed the ban on Nazi meetings that Brüning had imposed. He also called a Reichstag election for July 1932. The Nazis won 230 seats and polled 37.2 percent of the vote. Hitler demanded to be appointed chancellor. Hindenburg refused. The government called another election in November, partly to wear down the Nazis' financial resources, which it did. The Nazis lost 34 seats, and their popular vote dipped to 33.1 percent. With Hiter's electoral support declining, the advisers around Hindenburg refused to appoint Hitler to office.

In November 1932, Papen resigned, and the next month General Kurt von Schleicher (1882–1934) became chancellor. Fear of civil war between the left and the right mounted as did the violence and disruptions that had marked German political life for months. Schleicher attempted to bypass Hitler and draw the Nazi Party into a coalition by trying to negotiate with another Nazi leader, but Hitler used the incident to make his own position in the party even stronger. Schleicher asked the president to permit him, in effect, to rule by emergency degree to buy time to achieve political stability. Schleicher, whose actual motives have never become fully clear, failed to win the trust or confidence of the Hindenberg circle, and the president refused his request. Schleicher then resigned on January 28. Hindenburg's advisors then persuaded the president to name Hitler chancellor under the illusion that he would be working for them. To control Hitler and to see he did little mischief, the Hindenburg circle appointed Papen vice chancellor and named other traditional conservatives to the cabinet. On January 30, 1933, Adolf Hitler achieved the goal he had long set for himself and became the chancellor of Germany. It is important to emphasize that this oucome had not been inevitable. As his most distinuished biographer has observed, "Hitler's rise from humble beginnings to 'seize' power by 'triumph of the will' was the stuff of Nazi legend. In fact, political miscalculation by those with regular access to the corridors of power

rather than any actions on the part of the Nazi leader played a larger role in placing him in the Chancellor's seat."[1] Hitler did not come to office on the tide of history, but through the blunders of conservative German politicians who hated the Weimar Republic and its rejection of traditional German political elites and who feared the domestic political turmoil the depression had spawned.

Hitler had, however, technically become chancellor by legal means. All the proper legal forms and procedures had been observed. As a result, the civil service, the courts, and the other agencies of the government could support him in good conscience. He had forged a rigidly disciplined party structure and had mastered the techniques of mass politics and propaganda. (See "Encountering the Past: Cinema of the Political Left and Right.) He understood how to touch the raw social and political nerves of the electorate. His support appears to have come from across the social spectrum and not, as historians once thought, just from the lower middle class. Pockets of resistance appeared among Roman Catholic voters in the country and small towns. Otherwise, support for Hitler was particularly strong among groups such as farmers, war veterans, and the young, whom the insecurity of the 1920s and the depression of the early 1930s had badly hurt. Hitler promised them security against communists and socialists, effective government in place of the petty politics of the other parties, and a strong, restored, purposeful Germany.

German big business once received much of the blame for the rise of Hitler. There is little evidence, however, that business contributions made any crucial difference to the Nazis' success or failure. Hitler's supporters were frequently suspicious of business and giant capitalism. They wanted a simpler world, one in which small property would be safe from both socialism and big business. These people supported Hitler and the Nazis rather than the Social Democrats because the latter were not sufficiently nationalistic. The Nazis won out over other conservative nationalistic parties because, unlike those conservatives, the Nazis did address social insecurities.

HITLER'S CONSOLIDATION OF POWER

Once in office, Hitler moved with almost lightning speed to consolidate his control. This process had three steps: the capture of full legal authority, the crushing of alternative political groups, and the purging of rivals within the Nazi Party itself.

[1] Ian Kershaw, *Hitler 1889–1936: Hubris* (New York: W. W. Norton & Company, 1999), p. 424.

CINEMA OF THE POLITICAL LEFT AND RIGHT

Before the invention of television, the cinema was the most powerful cultural vehicle for political regimes to project their power. Film directors of genius were drawn to the authoritarian governments of both the left and the right, and the films they made for these regimes, especially those of Soviet Russia and Nazi Germany, still impress moviegoers.

During the 1920s, the Soviet Union promoted the cinema as a propaganda tool. The greatest Soviet film director was Sergei Eisenstein (1898–1948). His most famous film, *The Battleship Potemkin*, which critics regard as one of the most important films of all time, depicts a mutiny on a warship during the Russian revolution of 1905. In *Potemkin*, Eisenstein portrayed the working class itself as the hero of both the film and, true to Marxist doctrine, of history itself.

As Stalin gained more and more power from the mid-1920s onward, he imposed rigid censorship on the arts. To work in the Soviet Union, Eisenstein had to make films that pleased Stalin, and this he did. However, such was Eisenstein's genius that he also made two movies that many film scholars consider masterpieces: *Alexander Nevsky*, which depicts the victory of a medieval Russian prince over invading Germans, and *Ivan the Terrible*, which some see, in its depiction of the sixteenth-century despotic tsar whom Stalin admired, as Eisenstein's surrender to Stalin and others as a portrayal of tyranny.

Leni Riefenstahl, (1902–2003) was by the early 1930s the most skilled documentary filmmaker in Germany and perhaps the world—an extraordinary accomplishment for a woman in a field dominated by men. Adolf Hitler asked her to make a documentary extolling the Third Reich after the Nazis took power in 1933. The results were *Triumph of the Will* (1934), about a Nazi Party rally, and

Leni Riefenstahl filming the 1936 Olympic Games in Berlin with Hitler on the reviewing stand. © Bettmann/CORBIS

Olympia (1938), about the Olympic Games held in Berlin in 1936. Both films display innovative, dramatically effective cinematic techniques and also the skilled political theatricality of the Nazi regime. These films dazzled audiences and are still shown in film classes as major works of twentieth-century cinematic art. Yet despite her artistry, Riefenstahl became marked—no matter how much she protested that she was a "pure" artist—as a producer of Nazi propaganda films. No American film studio would distribute her films to U.S. audiences.

After the defeat of Germany in 1945, Riefenstahl was imprisoned by the Allies under their de-Nazification program before being released in 1949. Thereafter, she attempted to rescue her career as a filmmaker, but the Nazi taint proved indelible. Instead, she became a noted photographer, especially of underwater photography. To the end or her life, Riefenstahl defends her films for the Third Reich as art, not propaganda.

- *Why were the Soviet and Nazi regimes so interested in the cinema? How did Leni Riefenstahl's films of Hitler and Nazi rallies affect her later career?*

917

The Reichstag fire in 1933 provided Hitler with an excuse to consolidate his power.　Bildarchiv Preussischer Kulturbesitz

Reichstag Fire　On February 27, 1933, a mentally ill Dutch communist set fire to the Reichstag building in Berlin. The Nazis quickly claimed the fire was part of an immediate communist threat to the government. The public believed the communists might attack the state now that the Nazis were in power. Under Article 48, Hitler issued an emergency decree suspending civil liberties and arrested communists or alleged communists. This decree remained in force for as long as Hitler ruled Germany.

The Enabling Act　In early March, another Reichstag election took place. The Nazis still received only 43.9 percent of the vote and won only 288 seats. The arrest and removal of all communist deputies, however, and the political fear the fire and the emergency decree aroused enabled Hitler to control the Reichstag. On March 23, 1933, the Reichstag passed an Enabling Act that permitted Hitler to rule by decree. Thereafter, his exercise of power had no legal limits. The Weimar constitution was never formally repealed or amended; the February emergency decree and the March Enabling Act simply made it a dead letter.

Perhaps better than anyone else, Hitler understood that he and his party had not inevitably come to power; so in a series of complex moves, Hitler outlawed or undermined any German institution that might have served as a rallying point for opposition. In early May 1933, the Nazi Party, rather than any government agency, seized the offices, banks, and newspapers of the free trade unions and arrested their leaders. In late June and early July, all other German political parties were outlawed. By July 14, 1933, the National Socialists were the only legal party in Germany.

During the same months, the Nazis took over the governments of the individual federal states in Germany. By the close of 1933, all major institutions of potential opposition had been eliminated.

Internal Nazi Party Purges   The final step in Hitler's consolidation of power involved the Nazi Party itself. By late 1933, the SA, or storm troopers, had approximately one million active members and a larger number of reserves. The commander of this party army was Ernst Roehm (1887– 1934), a possible rival to Hitler himself. The officer corps, on whom Hitler depended to rebuild the German army, were jealous of the SA leadership and feared the SA itself as a rival. So, to protect his own position and to shore up support with the regular army, on June 30, 1934, Hitler personally ordered the murder of key SA officers, including Roehm. Between June 30 and July 2, more than a hundred persons were killed, including former chancellor General Kurt von Schleicher and his wife. The German army, the only institution that might have prevented the murders, did nothing.

A month later, on August 2, 1934, President Hindenburg died. Thereafter, Hitler combined the offices of chancellor and president, making him head of state as well as head of the government. He was now the sole ruler of Germany and of the Nazi Party.

Soon after seizing power, the Nazi government began harassing German Jewish businesses. Non-Jewish German citizens were urged not to buy merchandise from shops owned by Jews.   Art Resource/Bildarchiv Preussischer Kulturbesitz

THE POLICE STATE
AND ANTI-SEMITISM

Terror and intimidation had been major instruments in the Nazi march to office. As Hitler consolidated his power, he oversaw the organization of a police state.

SS Organization   The chief vehicle of police surveillance was the **SS** (*Schutzstaffel*, or "protective force"), security units, commanded by Heinrich Himmler (1900–1945). This group had originated in the mid-1920s as a bodyguard for Hitler and had become a more elite paramilitary organization than the much larger SA. In 1933, the SS had approximately 52,000 members. It was the instrument that carried out the blood purges of the party in 1934. By 1936, Himmler had become head of all police matters in Germany and was among the Nazis closest to Hitler in power and influence.

Attack on Jewish Economic Life   The police character of the Nazi regime was all pervasive, but the people who most consistently experienced the terror of the police state were the German Jews.

A key plank of the Nazi program was an anti-Semitism based on biological racial theories stemming from late-nineteenth-century thought rather than from religious discrimination. Before World War II, the Nazi attack on the Jews went through three stages of increasing intensity. First, in 1933, shortly after assuming power, the Nazis excluded Jews from the civil service. They also tried to enforce boycotts of Jewish shops and businesses, but these campaigns won little public support.

Racial Legislation   Then in 1935, a series of measures known as the Nuremberg Laws robbed German Jews of their citizenship. The professions and the major occupations were closed to those defined as Jews. Marriage and sexual intercourse between Jews and non-Jews were prohibited. Legal exclusion and humiliation of the Jews became the order of the day. The definition of who was a Jew in this law was both confusing and complex because the Nazis could not produce regulations based solely on a

AN AMERICAN DIPLOMAT WITNESSES *KRISTALLNACHT* IN LEIPZIG

A key event in the Nazi attack on Jews in Germany occurred on November 9 and 10, 1938, during nights of destructive terror known as Kristallnacht. *David Buffum, the American consul in Leipzig, wrote an extensive report of what happened in that city. In addition to providing the information in the passage that follows, he observed that most German citizens seemed stunned by what had occurred and deeply disapproved of it, but as his observations of the events in the Leipzig Zoo indicate, Germans were intimidated by the Nazi tactics. Buffum also reported that many German Jews came to the American consulate to find aid for emigration or help in locating husbands and sons taken to concentration camps. Both the United States and the nations of Western Europe admitted only limited numbers of Jewish refugees from Germany and, later, from Nazi-occupied Europe. Compare the events recorded in this document with the predictions that Alexis de Tocqueville made to Count Arthur de Gobineau about what might happen when racial thinking affected mass politics. (See Chapter 24.)*

■ *Why did the Nazis claim that the destruction of life and property in Leipzig and other German cities arose from spontaneous actions? How did the Nazi perpetrators of* Kristallnacht *intimidate Jewish citizens? What aid that was available to other German citizens was denied to Jews during these destructive events? Why did other German citizens not oppose the Nazi actions against the Jews?*

At 3 A.M. on 10 November 1938 was unleashed a barrage of Nazi ferocity that has had no equal hitherto in Germany. . . .

Jewish shop windows by the hundreds were systematically and wantonly smashed throughout the entire city at a loss estimated at several

---

racial concept. The Nazi legal definitions of who was a Jew took into account the number of Jewish parents or grandparents, as well as whether a person practiced Judaisim. All persons with at least three Jewish grandparents were defined as Jews, but persons with two Jewish grandparents were considered Jewish only if they practiced Judaism, or if they were married to a Jew, or if they had been born to a marriage with one Jewish parent, or if they had been born out of wedlock with one Jewish parent.

Kristallnacht The persecution of the Jews increased in 1938. They were forbidden to engage in business. On November 9 and 10, 1938, under Nazi Party orders, thousands of Jewish stores and synagogues were burned or otherwise destroyed on what became known as ***Kristallnacht*** ("Crystal Night"), because so much smashed glass from shat-

tered windows and storefronts lay in the streets. (See, "An American Diplomat Witnesses Kristallnacht in Leipzig".) The Jewish community itself had to pay for the destruction and the cleanup, because the government confiscated the insurance money that was paid to cover the damages. In many other ways, large and petty, German Jews were harassed. This persecution allowed the Nazis to instill in the rest of the population the concept of a master race of pure German "Aryans" and also to display their own contempt for civil liberties.

The Final Solution After the war broke out, Hitler decided in 1941 and 1942 to destroy the Jews in Europe. More than six million Jews, mostly from eastern Europe, died as a result of that staggering decision, unprecedented in its scope and implementation. (See Chapter 29.)

millions of marks. . . . According to reliable testimony, the debacle was executed by SS men and Stormtroopers not in uniform, each group having been provided with hammers, axes, crowbars and incendiary bombs.

Three synagogues in Leipzig were fired simultaneously by incendiary bombs and all sacred objects and records desecrated or destroyed, in most cases hurled through the windows and burned in the streets. . . . All the synagogues were irreparably gutted by flames. . . . One of the largest clothing stores in the heart of the city was destroyed by flames from incendiary bombs, only the charred walls and gutted roof having been left standing. As was the case with the synagogues, no attempts on the part of the fire brigade were made to extinguish the fire. . . . It is extremely difficult to believe, but the owners of the clothing store were actually charged with setting the fire and on that basis were dragged from their beds at 6 A.M. and clapped into prison.

Tactics which closely approached the ghoulish took place at the Jewish cemetery where the temple was fired together with a building occupied by caretakers, tombstones uprooted and graves violated. . . .

Ferocious as was the violation of property, the most hideous phase of the so-called 'spontaneous' action has been the wholesale arrest and transportation to concentration camps of male German Jews between the ages of sixteen and sixty, as well as Jewish men without citizenship. . . . Having demolished dwellings and hurled most of the movable effects onto the streets, the insatiably sadistic perpetrators threw many of the trembling inmates into a small stream that flows through the Zoological Park, commanding horrified spectators to spit at them, defile them with mud and jeer at their plight. The latter incident has been repeatedly corroborated by German witnesses who were nauseated in telling the tale. The slightest manifestation of sympathy evoked a positive fury on the part of the perpetrators, and the crowd was powerless to do anything but turn horror-stricken eyes from the scene of abuse, or leave the vicinity. These tactics were carried out . . . without police intervention and they were applied to men, women, and children.

From *Nazism, 1919–1945: A Documentary Reader, Vol. 2, State, Economy and Society, 1933–39*, edited by J. Noakes and G. Pridham, new edition 2000, pp. 361–362. Reprinted by permission of University of Exeter Press.

RACIAL IDEOLOGY AND THE LIVES OF WOMEN

Hitler and other Nazis were less interested in increasing the national population, which was Mussolini's policy, than in producing racially pure Germans. In their role as mothers, German women had the special task of preserving racial purity and giving birth to more pure Germans who were healthy in mind and body. According to this view, women were to breed strong sons and daughters for the German nation. Nazi journalists often compared the role of women in childbirth to that of men in battle. Each served the state in particular social and gender roles. In both cases, the good of the nation was more important than that of the individual. (See "Hitler Rejects the Emancipation of Women," pages 922–923.)

Nazi racial ideology focused on women as the carriers and bearers of both the desired and undesired races. Nazi policy favored motherhood only for those whom its adherents regarded as racially fit for motherhood. As early as late 1933, the government raised the issue of what kind of persons were fit to bear children for the nation. This policy disapproved of fostering motherhood among those people Nazi racism condemned—particularly the Jews, but also Slavs and Gypsies. During the mass executions of Jews in the Holocaust, Jewish women were specifically targeted for death, in part to prevent them from bearing a new generation.

Nazi theorists also discriminated between the healthy and unhealthy, the desirable and undesirable, in the German population itself. The government sought to prevent "undesirables"

HITLER REJECTS THE EMANCIPATION OF WOMEN

—⚏—

According to Nazi ideology, a woman's place was in the home, producing and rearing children and supporting her husband. In this speech, Hitler urges this view of the role of women. He uses anti-Semitism to discredit those writers who urged the emancipation of women from their traditional roles and occupations. Hitler returns here to the "separate spheres" concept of the relationship of men and women. His traditional view of women was directed against contrary views that were associated with the Soviet experiment during the interwar years. Contrast the Nazi outlook on women and the family with the view expressed by the young Bolshevik Alexandra Kollontai in the document in Chapter 26.

■ *What social tasks does Hitler assign to women? Why does he associate the emancipation of women with Jews and intellectuals? How does he attempt to subordinate the lives of women to the supremacy of the state?*

The slogan "Emancipation of Women" was invented by Jewish intellectuals and its content was formed by the same spirit. In the really good times of German life the German woman had no need to emancipate herself. She possessed exactly what nature had necessarily given her to administer and preserve; just as the man in his good times had no need to fear that he would be ousted from his position in relation to the woman. . . .

If the man's world is said to be the State, his struggle, his readiness to devote his powers to the service of the community, then it may perhaps be said that the woman's is a smaller world. For her world is her husband, her family, her children, and her home. But what would become of the greater world if there were no one to tend and care for the smaller one? How could the greater world survive if there were no one to make the cares of the smaller world the content of their lives? No, the greater world is built on the foundation of this smaller world. This great world cannot survive if the smaller world is not stable. Providence has entrusted to the woman

from reproducing, a policy that led to both the sterilization and death of many women, often because of an alleged mental "degeneracy." Some pregnant women were forced to have abortions. The Nazis' population policy was, in effect, one of selective breeding, or antinatalism, that profoundly affected the lives of women.

To support motherhood among those whom they believed should have children, the Nazis provided loans to encourage early marriage, tax breaks for families with children, and child allowances. In this respect, Nazi legislation resembled that passed elsewhere in Europe during the decade. The subsidies and other family payments were sent to husbands rather than wives, to make married fatherhood seem preferable to bachelorhood. Furthermore, these policies were administered on the premise that only racially and physically desirable children received support.

Although Nazi ideology emphasized motherhood, in 1930 the party vowed to protect the jobs of working women, and the number of women working in Germany rose steadily under the Nazi regime. The Nazis recognized that in the midst of the depression many women needed to work, but the party urged them to pursue employment that was "natural" to their character as women. Such employment included agricultural labor, teaching, nursing, social service, and domestic service. The Nazis also intended women to be educators of the young. In that role, whether as mothers or as members of the serving professions, women became special protectors of German cultural values. Through cooking, dress, music, and stories, mothers were to instill a love for the nation in their children. As consumers for the home, women were to support German-owned shops, buy German-made goods, and boycott Jewish merchants.

the cares of that world which is her very own, and only on the basis of this smaller world can the man's world be formed and built up. The two worlds are not antagonistic. They complement each other, they belong together just as man and woman belong together.

We do not consider it correct for the woman to interfere in the world of the man, in his main sphere. We consider it natural if these two worlds remain distinct. To the one belongs the strength of feeling, the strength of the soul. To the other belongs the strength of vision, of toughness, of decision, and of the willingness to act. In the one case this strength demands the willingness of the woman to risk her life to preserve this important cell and to multiply it, and in the other case it demands from the man the readiness to safeguard life.

The sacrifices which the man makes in the struggle of his nation, the woman makes in the preservation of that nation in individual cases. What the man gives in courage on the battlefield, the woman gives in eternal self-sacrifice, in eternal pain and suffering. Every child that a woman brings into the world is a battle, a battle waged for the existence of her people. . . .

So our women's movement is for us not something which inscribes on its banner as its programme the fight against men, but something which has as its programme the common fight together with men. For the new National Socialist national community acquires a firm basis precisely because we have gained the trust of millions of women as fanatical fellow-combatants, women who have fought for the common life in the service of the common task of preserving life. . . .

Whereas previously the programmes of the liberal, intellectualist women's movements contained many points, the programme of our National Socialist Women's movement has in reality but one single point, and that point is the child, that tiny creature which must be born and grow strong and which alone gives meaning to the whole life-struggle.

From *Nazism, 1919–1945: A Documentary Reader, Vol. 2, State, Economy and Society, 1933–39*, edited by J. Noakes and G. Pridham, new edition 2000, pp. 361–362. Reprinted by permission of University of Exeter Press.

NAZI ECONOMIC POLICY

Besides consolidating power and pursuing anti-Semitic policies, Hitler still had to confront the Great Depression. German unemployment had helped propel him to power. The Nazis attacked this problem with a success that astonished and frightened Europe. By 1936, while the rest of the European economy remained stagnant, the specter of unemployment and other difficulties associated with the Great Depression no longer haunted Germany.

As far as the economic crisis was concerned, Hitler had become the most effective political leader in Europe. This success was perhaps the most important reason Germans supported his tyrannical regime. The Nazi success against the Great Depression gave the regime credibility. Behind the direction of both business and labor stood the Nazi terror and police. The Nazi economic experiment proved

that, by sacrificing all political and civil liberty, destroying a free trade-union movement, limiting the private exercise of capital, and ignoring consumer satisfaction, a government could achieve full employment to prepare for war and aggression.

Nazi economic policies supported private property and private capitalism, but subordinated all significant economic enterprise and decisions about prices and investment to the goals of the state. Hitler reversed the deflationary policy of the cabinets that had preceded him. He instituted a massive program of public works and spending. Many of these projects were related to rearmament. The government built canals, reclaimed land, and constructed an extensive highway system with clear military uses. It also sent unemployed workers back to farms if they had originally come from them. Other laborers were not permitted to change jobs without official permission.

In 1935, the renunciation of the military provisions of the Versailles treaty led to open rearmament and military expansion with little opposition, as explained in Chapter 28. These measures essentially restored full employment. In 1936, Hitler instructed Hermann Göring (1893–1946), who had headed the air force since 1933, to undertake a four-year plan to prepare the army and the economy for war. The government determined that Germany must be economically self-sufficient.

Armaments received top priority. This economic program satisfied both the yearning for social and economic security and the desire for national fulfillment.

With the crushing of the trade unions in 1933, strikes became illegal. There was no genuine collective bargaining. The government handled labor disputes through compulsory arbitration. It also required workers and employers to participate in the Labor Front, an organization intended to demon-

A CLOSER LOOK

The Nazi Party Rally
Young women were enthusiastic supporters among the crowd extending the Nazi salute in a 1938 rally.

The Nazi Party had used what later became the ever-present Swastika (or hooked cross) symbol since 1920. Hitler himself claimed to have chosen the symbol, which he and other Nazis associated with an allegedly racially pure Aryan past. In fact, many cultures had used the Swastika as a symbol. The Nazis adopted the Swastika as the German national flag in 1935.

Nazi rallies were intended to generate nationalistic group solidarity that would demonstrate that whatever other divisions might exist in the nation, loyalty to the Nazi Party and to the nation would be more important than any other group loyalty.

The image in the photo illustrates the gender divisions Nazi ideology fostered. Men were portrayed as defenders of the homeland. Women were to pursue traditional domestic roles and to bear children for the nation.

Bildarchiv Preussischer Kulturbesitz

strate that class conflict had ended. The Labor Front sponsored a "Strength Through Joy" program that provided vacations and other forms of recreation for the labor force.

ITALY: FASCIST ECONOMICS

The fascists had promised to stabilize Italian social and economic life. Discipline was a substitute for economic policy and creativity. During the 1920s, Mussolini undertook vast public works, such as draining the Pontine Marshes near Rome for settlement. The government subsidized the shipping industry and introduced protective tariffs. Mussolini desperately sought to make Italy self-sufficient. He embarked on the "battle of wheat" to prevent foreign grain from appearing in products on Italian tables. Wheat farming in Italy expanded enormously.

MAJOR DATES IN THE NAZI SEIZURE OF POWER

1928	National Socialists win 12 seats in the Reichstag
1930	National Socialists win 107 seats in the Reichstag
1930	Brüning appointed chancellor
1932 (April 10)	Hindenburg defeats Hitler for presidency
1932 (May 31)	Von Papen replaces Brüning
1932 (July 31)	National Socialists win 230 seats in the Reichstag
1932 (November 6)	Indecisive Reichstag election; National Socialists lose 34 seats
1932 (November 17)	Von Papen resigns
1932 (December 2)	Von Schleicher appointed chancellor
1933 (January 28)	Von Schleicher resigns
1933 (January 30)	Hitler appointed chancellor
1933 (February 27)	Reichstag fire
1933 (March 5)	National Socialists win 288 seats in the Reichstag
1933 (March 23)	Enabling Act passed
1933 (July 14)	National Socialists declared the only legal party
1934 (June 30)	Murder of SA leadership
1934 (August 2)	Death of Hindenburg
1935	Passage of Nuremberg Laws
1938 (November 9–10)	*Kristallnacht* (attacks on Jewish businesses and synagogues)

These policies, however, did not keep the Great Depression from affecting Italy. Production, exports, and wages fell. Even the increased wheat production backfired. So much poor marginal land that was expensive to cultivate came into production that the domestic price of wheat, and thus of much other food, actually rose.

SYNDICATES

Both before and during the depression, the fascists sought to steer an economic course between socialism and a liberal laissez-faire system. Their policy was known as **corporatism**. It was a planned economy linked to the private ownership of capital and to government arbitration of labor disputes. Major industries were first organized into syndicates representing labor and management. The two groups negotiated labor settlements within this framework and submitted differences to compulsory government arbitration. The fascists contended that class conflict would be avoided if both labor and management looked to the greater goal of productivity for the nation.

Whether this arrangement favored workers or managers is still in dispute. From the mid-1920s, however, Italian labor unions lost the right to strike and to pursue independent economic goals. In that respect, management clearly profited.

CORPORATIONS

After 1930, the industrial syndicates were reorganized into entities called *corporations*. These bodies grouped all industries relating to a major area of production, such as agriculture or metallurgy, from raw materials through finished products and distribution, into one entity. Twenty-two such corporations were established to encompass the whole economy. In 1938, Mussolini replaced the Italian Chamber of Deputies with a Chamber of Corporations.

This vast organizational framework did not increase production, but it did increase bureaucracy and corruption. The corporate state allowed the government to direct much of the nation's economic life without a formal change in ownership. Consumers and owners could no longer determine what was to be produced. The fascist government gained further direct economic power through the Institute for Industrial Reconstruction, which extended loans to businesses that were in financial difficulty. The loans, in effect, established partial state ownership of those businesses.

How corporatism might have affected the Italian economy in the long run is unknown. In 1935, Italy invaded Ethiopia, and economic life was put

An enormous propaganda effort accompanied the Soviet Five-Year Plans. This poster proclaims, "For the betterment of the Soviet people we are building an electricity plant."   Art Resource/Bildarchiv Preussischer Kulturbesitz

on a formal wartime footing. The League of Nations imposed economic sanctions, urging member nations to not to purchase Italian goods. The sanctions, which did not include a ban on selling oil to Italy, had little effect. Thereafter, taxes rose. During 1935, the government imposed a forced loan on the citizenry by requiring property owners to purchase government bonds. Wages continued to be depressed. As international tensions increased during the late 1930s, the Italian state assumed more direction over the economy. Instead of prosperity, fascism brought economic dislocation and a falling standard of living to Italy.

STALIN'S SOVIET UNION: CENTRAL ECONOMIC PLANNING, COLLECTIVIZATION, AND PARTY PURGES

While the capitalist economies of Western Europe floundered in the Great Depression, the Soviet Union undertook a tremendous industrial advance. As in past eras of Russian economic progress, the direction and impetus came from the top. Stalin far exceeded his tsarist predecessors in the intensity of state coercion and the terror he brought to the task. Russia achieved its stunning economic growth during the 1930s only at the cost

of literally millions—perhaps tens of millions—of human lives and the degradation of still other millions. Stalin's economic policy clearly proved that his earlier rivalry with Trotsky had been a personal, political power struggle rather than one over real ideological differences.

THE DECISION FOR RAPID INDUSTRIALIZATION

Through 1927, Lenin's New Economic Policy (NEP), as championed by Bukharin with Stalin's support, had charted Soviet economic development. The government permitted private ownership and enterprise in the countryside to ensure an adequate food supply for the workers in the cities and enough surplus grain to export in exchange for industrial equipment. Although by 1927 industrial production had reached the level it was in 1913, it had also begun to slow. During 1927, the Party Congress decided to push for rapid industrialization. As implemented through what has been termed "industrialization by political mobilization," this policy, which began in 1928, marked a sharp departure from the NEP and a rejection of the pockets of relatively free market operations within the larger Soviet economy.[2]

[2]Vladimir Andrle, *A Social History of Twentieth-Century Russia* (London: Arnold, 1994), p. 161.

The drive to rapid industrialization was a major pillar in Stalin's policy of "Socialism in One Country." His goal was to have the communist Soviet Union overtake the productive capacity of its enemies, the capitalist nations. This policy required the rapid construction of heavy industries, such as iron, steel, and machine tool making, building electricity-generating stations, and manufacturing tractors. Stalin's organizational vehicle for industrialization was a series of five-year plans, starting in 1928. The State Planning Commission, or *Gosplan*, oversaw the program, setting goals for production in every area of economic life and attempting to organize the economy to meet them. The task of coordinating all facets of production was immensely difficult and complicated. Deliveries of materials from mines or factories had to be assured before the next unit could carry out its part of the plan. Enormous economic disruption occurred as the *Gosplan* built power plants and steel mills and increased the output of mines. The plans consistently favored capital projects over the production of consumer goods. The number of centralized agencies and ministries involved in planning soared, and they often competed with each other.

The rapid expansion of the industrial base created the first genuinely large factory labor force in what had been Russia. Workers were recruited from the countryside and from the urban unemployed. New cities and new work districts in existing cities arose. More often than not, the workers themselves lived in deplorable conditions, crowded into shoddy buildings with inadequate sanitation, living space, and nourishment. Their lives were as bad as or worse than anything Marx and Engels had decried in the nineteenth century.

The government and the Communist Party undertook a vast program of propaganda to sell the five-year plans to the Russian people and to elicit their cooperation. The government boasted of the sheer size of the plants being constructed and the new towns being organized. Such efforts were necessary because most industrial workers were displaced peasants who had no previous factory experience and who often resisted industrial discipline. The party appealed to the idealism of the young in proclaiming its goals of rapidly modernizing the nation. Workers, such as a legendary coal miner named Stakhanov, who exceeded their assigned goals received rewards and publicity.

By the close of the 1930s, the results of the three five-year plans were impressive. The Russ-ian economy grew more rapidly than that of any other nation in the Western world during any similar period. Soviet industrial production rose approximately 400 percent between 1928 and 1940. Industries that had never before existed in Russia challenged their foreign counterparts. Hundreds of thousands of people populated new industrial cities. The social and human cost of this effort had, however, been appalling.

THE COLLECTIVIZATION OF AGRICULTURE

Agricultural productivity had always been a core problem for the emerging Soviet economy. Under the NEP the government purchased a certain amount of grain at prices it set itself. The rest of the grain was then supposed to be sold at market prices, which were higher than the government-set prices. Many peasant farmers of all degress of wealth tried to circumvent this system, often by keeping grain off the market in hopes that its price would rise. The scarcity of consumer goods available for purchase in the countryside also encouraged hoarding. With little to buy from what they earned by selling their grain, farmers had little incentive to sell it. Instead, many of them preferred to hoard grain, so that they could sell it in the future when they hoped more consumer goods would be available for them to purchase. The Soviet government, however, needed the grain immediately to feed its expanding urban workforce and to pay for imports from abroad. In 1928 and 1929, as a result of peasants hoarding their grains for better prices, the Soviet government confronted shortfalls of grain on the market and the prospect of food shortages in the cities and social unrest.

Stalin therefore decided to reverse the agricultural policies of the NEP. Toward the end of the 1920s Soviet communist economists and party officials devised an explanation for the difficulties they confronted in the agricultural sector. First, they asserted that the traditional peasant holdings were too small to produce enough grain for the country. Second, they claimed that a class-enemy was responsible for the hoarding and for what they regarded as speculation in the grain trade. This enemy was the group of relatively prosperous peasants, known as *kulaks*, who numbered somewhat less than five percent of the rural population and were often the most productive and efficient farmers. On the basis of these ideas, Stalin decided that Soviet agriculture must be collectivized to produce enough grain for domestic food and foreign export. Collectivization—the replacement

AP/Wide World Photos

Stalin used intimidation and propaganda to support his drive to collectivize Soviet agriculture. Communist Party agitators led groups of peasants, such as these shown on the left, to demand the seizure of the farms worked by the better-off and more successful farmers known as kulaks. The poster on the right shows an idealized Soviet collective farm on which tractors owned by the state have replaced peasant labor. In reality, collectivization provoked fierce resistance and caused famines in which millions of peasants died.

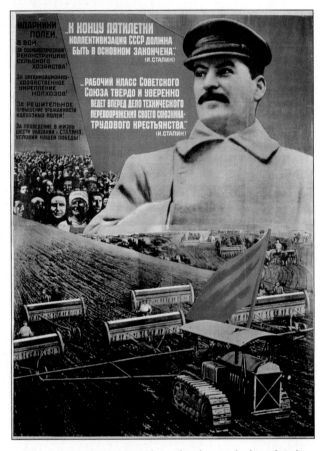

of private peasant farms with huge state-run and state-owned farms called collectives—would also put the Communist Party firmly in control of the farm sector of the economy and free up peasant labor to work in the factories of the expanding industrial sector. To carry out this policy, Stalin portrayed the small *kulak* minority in the countryside as the fundamental cause of the problem of agricultural shortages.

In 1929, unleashing unprecedented violence in the countryside, Stalin ordered a program of **collectivization** of agriculture that was only vaguely defined. As part of this plan, the government announced its determination to eliminate the *kulaks* as a class. At this point, however, the definition of a *kulak* came to embrace any peasants, whatever their wealth, who resisted collectivization and were thus regarded

Poster concerning the 1st 5 Year Plan with a photograph of Joseph Stalin (1879-1953), "At the end of the Plan, the basis of collectivisation must be completed," 1932 (colour litho) by Klutchis (fl. 1932). Deutsches Plakat Museum, Essen, Germany/Archives Charmet/The Bridgeman Art Library

STALIN CALLS FOR THE LIQUIDATION OF THE *KULAKS* AS A CLASS

The core of Stalin's agricultural policy undertaken in the late 1920s and early 1930s was the replacement of private farms with large collective farms run by the state. The greatest obstacle to this policy was the kulaks, *prosperous, productive peasants. In this speech of 1929, Stalin first explains why collective farms must replace small peasant farming to achieve an adequate food supply for the cities and the industrial workers. He then calls for the liquidation of the* kulaks *as a class. As might be expected, the* kulaks *resisted collectivization by destroying crops and farm animals. In turn, Communist Party agents killed millions of peasants to achieve collectivization.*

■ *What were the goals of the collectivization of farms in the Soviet Union? How did the* kulaks *stand in the way of collectivization? How does Stalin dehumanize the* kulaks *by discussing them entirely as a class and as part of the capitalistic system?*

Can we advance our socialized industry at an accelerated rate as long as we have an agricultural base, such as is provided by small-peasant farming, which is incapable of expanded reproduction, and which, in addition, is the predominant force in our national economy? No, we cannot. . . .

What, then, is the solution? The solution lies in enlarging the agricultural units, in making agriculture capable of accumulation, of expanded reproduction, and in thus transforming the agricultural bases of our national economy.

[T]he socialist way [to enlarge farming units], which is to introduce collective farms and state farms in agriculture, the way which leads to the amalgamation of the small-peasant farms into large collective farms, employing machinery and scientific methods of farming, and capable of developing further, for such agricultural enterprises can achieve expanded reproduction. . . .

The characteristic feature in the work of our Party during the past year is that we, as a Party, as the Soviet power,

(a) have developed an offensive along the whole front against the capitalist elements in the countryside;

(b) that this offensive, as you know, has brought about and is bringing about very palpable, positive results.

What does this mean? It means that we have passed from the policy of restricting the exploiting proclivities of the *kulaks* to the policy of eliminating the *kulaks* as a class. . . .

Until recently the Party adhered to the policy of restricting the exploiting proclivities of the *kulaks.* . . .

Could we have undertaken such an offensive against the *kulaks* five years or three years ago? Could we then have counted on success in such an offensive? No, we could not. That would have been the most dangerous adventurism. It would have been playing a very dangerous game at offensive. We would certainly have failed, and our failure would have strengthened the position of the *kulaks.* Why? Because we still lacked a wide network of state and collective farms in the rural districts which could be used as strongholds in a determined offensive against the *kulaks.* Because at that time we were not yet able to substitute for the capitalist production of the *kulaks* the socialist production of the collective farms and state farms. . . .

Now we are able to carry on a determined offensive against the *kulaks*, to break their resistance, to eliminate them as a class and substitute for their output the output of the collective farms and state farms. Now, the *kulaks* are being expropriated by the masses of poor and middle peasants themselves, by the masses who are putting solid collectivization into practice. Now, the expropriation of the *kulaks* in the regions of solid collectivization is no longer just an administrative measure. Now, the expropriation of the *kulaks* is an integral part of the formation and development of the collective farms. Consequently it is now ridiculous and foolish to discourse on the expropriation of the *kulaks.* You do not lament the loss of the hair of one who has been beheaded.

From Stalin, "Problems of Agrarian Policy in the USSR," Speech at a conference of Marxist students of the Agrarian question, December 27, 1929, in *Problems of Leninism*, pp. 391–393, 408–409, 411–412, as quoted in Robert V. Daniels, *A Documentary History of Communism*, rev. ed. (Hanover, NH and London: University Press of New England, 1984), pp. 224–227. Reprinted by permission.

as counterrevolutionary. The point of "dekulak-ization" was to remove from the countryside or to intimidate any peasants who might resist the policy of collectivization and direct central government control of agriculture.

Communist Party officials and army officers with troops at their command carried out the initial campaign of dekulakization and collectivization. Usually they would seek first to remove *kulaks* from a village while confiscating their land and would then attempt to coerce the remaining peasants into orgranizing a collective farm. Enormous rural turmoil and violence resulted. In March 1930, Stalin called a brief halt to the process, justifying the slowdown on the grounds of "dizziness from success." After the harvest of that year had been secured, however, the drive to collectivize the farms was renewed with vehemence.

From the onset of collectivization, peasants determined to keep their land, often with women in the lead, had sabotaged collectivization by slaughtering millions of horses and cattle between 1929 and 1933. Peasants who resisted peasants were killed outright. Others starved to death on their own farms when all the grain that they had produced was confiscated and removed by force. Over two million peasants were forcibly removed from their homes and deported in overcrowded cattle cars to distant areas of the Soviet Union or to prison camps where many of them died from disease, exposure, and malnutrition. Even if they survived that ordeal, they then had to patch together some kind of life as industrial workers or miners in Siberia or in another inhospitable province. Their children were treated as class-enemies and potential traitors.

During the drive toward collectivization, the Communist Party also targeted priests of the Russian Orthodox Church living in country villages. The Soviet Communist Party, atheistic in its ideology, had always opposed religion and the church, but only with collectivization were many rural priests attacked and churches closed or vandalized. Between 1926 and 1937, the number of priests recorded in the census of the Soviet Union dropped by more than one-half. Jewish rabbis, Catholic priests, Protestant ministers, and Muslim mullahs received the same harsh treatment.

By 1937, over 90 percent of Soviet grain production had been collectivized. The violent transformation of Soviet agriculture meant producers on collective farms could no longer decide what crops to produce or how much to sell them for. The Sovi-et government organized Motor-Tractor Stations which supplied the seed and equipment for several collective farms in a region and oversaw the collection and sale of grain. The heads of these stations were Communist Party political operatives, and they determined what payments the farmers eventually received for the grain they had produced. Alongside the state-run collective farms, by the middle of the 1930s, the government allowed farmers small household plots to grow food for their families and for local sale. In time these plots became an important part of the Soviet agriculture because peasants tended them so carefully and productively.

At the cost of millions of peasant lives, Stalin and the Communist Party, by the middle of the 1930s, had won the battle of the grain fields, but they had not solved the problem of producing enough food. That difficulty would plague the Soviet Union until its collapse in 1991 and remains a problem for its successor states.

FLIGHT TO THE SOVIET CITIES

An immediate consequence of Soviet collectivization was a flight of peasants, who lost their farms from the land to the cities. Between 1928 and 1932, approximately twelve million peasants left the countryside, a migration unprecedented in European history. Most of them were young males, leaving a disproportionate number of women and elderly people in the villages, where they lived in great poverty.

In the years after the drive toward collectivization, the populations of major cities in the Soviet Union grew rapidly. Moscow's population almost doubled. Between 1939 and 1980, the proportion of the Soviet population living on the land fell from two-thirds to one-third. Although all of Europe has become more urban in the twentieth century, in the Soviet Union urbanization arose directly from the violence the government inflicted on the countryside.

URBAN CONSUMER SHORTAGES

Much of the housing shortage that plagued the Soviet Union for the rest of its history originated in the 1930s. In the new industrial cities, workers lived in barracks. In the older cities, individuals and families had difficulty finding apartments. Those apartments they did find were tiny and several families often had to share kitchens, toilets, and baths. Such cramped quarters led people to

By the mid-1930s, Stalin's purges had eliminated many leaders and other members from the Soviet Communist Party. This photograph of a meeting of a party congress in 1936 shows a number of the surviving leaders with Stalin, who sits fourth from the right in the front row. To his left is Vyacheslav Molotov, longtime foreign minister. The first person on the left in the front row is Nikita Khruschev, who headed the Soviet Union in the late 1950s and early 1960s.   Itar-Tass/Sovfoto/Eastfoto

value even more what little privacy and few possessions they had, including pots and pans and bits of furniture.

For urban dwellers, in addition to the shortage of housing, the most fundamental fact of everyday Soviet life was a chronic shortage of the most basic consumer goods, including food and clothing—particularly shoes. From the end of the NEP through the collapse of the Soviet Union in 1991, city shops had few goods. Throughout the 1930s, Russians consumed less food each year than they had before the revolution, and the famines affected everyone's life. What goods did appear were often sold in stores reserved for party members. The small minority of party members and leaders lived much better than the general Soviet population. One of the most common experiences of Soviet citizens was standing in line for bread.

Except for certain showplaces in Moscow and Leningrad (formerly, and now again, St. Petersburg), Soviet cities generally lacked the kind of infrastructure that Western European cities had long enjoyed. The transport systems were too small for the rapidly expanding populations. Even cities as large and important as Stalingrad (today, Volgograd) lacked sewer systems in the mid-1930s. In the new industrial cities, even running water, paved streets, and electric lighting were rare. Urban crime and disease were widespread.

How did this Soviet society sustain itself? The black market flourished, and peasants raised food on tiny private plots. People bartered with each other and pilfered from the state. This whole informal mode of coping became known as the *blat*, but for much of the century, the Soviet people sustained themselves mainly through the conviction that they were enduring their present troubles to build a greater socialist future. During World War II, this emphasis changed to protecting the fatherland. After the war, the emphasis again shifted to a better future, but that future never came.

FOREIGN REACTIONS AND REPERCUSSIONS

Many foreign contemporaries looked at the Soviet economic experiment naïvely. While the capitalist world lay in the throes of the Great

Depression, the Soviet economy had grown at a pace never realized in the West. After a trip to Russia, the American writer Lincoln Steffens (1866–1936) reported, "I have seen the future and it works." Beatrice and Sidney Webb, the British Fabian socialists, spoke of "a new civilization" in the Soviet Union. These and similar observers ignored the shortages in consumer goods and the poor housing. More importantly, they had little idea of the social cost of the Soviet achievement. Millions of human beings had been killed, and millions more uprooted. Even with the recent opening of the Soviet archives, the total picture of suffering and human loss during those years will probably never be known; however, the deprivation and sacrifice of Soviet citizens far exceeded anything Marx and Enels had said about nineteenth-century industrialization in Western Europe.

The internal difficulties collectivization and industrialization caused led Stalin to make an important shift in foreign policy. In 1934, he began to fear the nation might be left isolated against future aggression by Nazi Germany. The Soviet Union was not yet strong enough to withstand such an attack. So that year he ordered the Comintern to permit communist parties in other countries to cooperate with noncommunist parties against Nazism and fascism. This reversed the Comintern policy Lenin established as part of the Twenty-One Conditions in 1919. The new Stalinist policy allowed the Popular Front Government in France to come to power.

THE PURGES

Stalin's decisions to industrialize rapidly, to move against the peasants, and to reverse the Comintern policy aroused internal opposition. Each was a departure from the policies of Lenin. In 1929, Stalin forced Bukharin, the fervent supporter of the NEP and his own former ally against Trotsky, off the Politburo. Little detailed information is known about further opposition to Stalin, but it seems to have lingered for a time among lower-level party followers of Bukharin and other opponents of rapid industrialization. Even at its most extensive, however, such opposition was modest.

Nonetheless, in 1933, with turmoil in the countryside and economic dislocation caused by industrialization, Stalin and others in the central Soviet bureauracy began to fear they were losing control of the country and the party apparatus and that ef-

---

MAJOR DATES IN SOVIET HISTORY DURING THE FIVE-YEAR PLANS AND PURGES

1927	Decision to move toward rapid industrialization
1928	First five-year plan begins
1929	Beginning of collectivization of agriculture
1929	Expulsion of Bukharin from Politburo affirms Stalin's central position
1930	Stalin's call for moderation in his policy of agricultural collectivization because of "dizziness from success"
1934	Assassination of Kirov
1936–1938	Major purge trials

---

fective rivals to their power and policies might emerge. These apprehensions, which were exaggerated, were largely a figment of Stalin's own paranoia and lust for power, but they resulted in the **Great Purges,** which remain one of the most mysterious and horrendous political events of the twentieth century. Few observers understood the purges at the time, and despite the recent opening of Soviet archives, they have still not been fully comprehended, either inside or outside the former Soviet Union.

The pretext for the onset of the purges was the assassination on December 1, 1934, of Sergei Kirov (1888–1934), the popular party chief of Leningrad and a member of the Politburo. In the wake of the shooting, thousands of people were arrested, and still more were expelled from the party and sent to labor camps. At the time, many thought that opponents of the regime had murdered Kirov, and Stalin routinely accused those whom he attacked of complicity in the crime. Today, many scholars believe that Stalin himself authorized Kirov's assassination because he was afraid of him. The available documentary evidence does not allow us to know for sure whether Stalin was involved, but he quickly used Kirov's death for his own purposes. Under Stalin, the Soviet Communist Party had already shown it could punish dissent within its ranks. The debates of the 1920s within the party and the expulsion of Trotsky had established a clear precedent for exercising firm discipline, and in the confusion surrounding the implementation of the five-year plans, persons accused of sabotage and disloyalty had been executed. The purges, however, went far beyond any of these precedents.

The purges that took place immediately after Kirov's death were just the beginning of a larger and longer process. Between 1936 and 1938, a series of spectacular show trials were held in Moscow. Former high Soviet leaders, including some who had belonged to the Politburo, such as Bukharin, publicly confessed to political crimes and were convicted and executed. It is still not certain why they made their palpably false confessions, although this seems to have been the kind of ritual confession of faults and short-comings that had long characterized internal Communist Party life. They had also been interrogated under the most difficult conditions, including torture, and feared for their families' lives. (In fact Stalin regularly arrested the wives, children, siblings, and in-laws of "traitors" and had them shot or sent to die in labor camps.) Other lower-level party members were tried in private and shot. Hundreds of thousands, perhaps millions, of ordinary Soviet citizens received no trial at all and were either executed or deported to slave labor camps. Within the party itself, thousands of members were expelled, and applicants for membership were removed from the rolls. After the civilian party members and leaders had been purged, the prosecutors turned against the government bureaucracy and the Soviet army and navy, convicting and executing thousands of officials and officers, including heroes of the civil war. The exact number of executions, imprisonments, interrogations, and expulsions is unknown, but ran well into the millions. While the purges went on, no one in the Soviet Union, except Stalin himself, was safe.

The rational explanations of the purges—to the extent that mass murder can ever be rationally explained—probably lie in two directions. First, over the several years the purges lasted, different portions of the party leadership moved against others. Initially, Stalin and the central Moscow leadership used the purges to settle old scores and to discipline and gain more control over lower levels of the party in the far-flung regions of the Soviet Union. In addition to increasing Stalin's authority, these central bureaucratic groups wanted to eliminate any opposition to their positions or policies. By 1937, however, Stalin seems to have become distrustful of the central party elite, his own supporters, and began to find or pretend to find enemies within its ranks. Moreover, by that date, local

communist groups were allowed to designate their own victims with little direction from Moscow. Thereafter, a self-destructive cascade of accusations, imprisonments, and executions occurred throughout the party and within its highest levels. The Communist Party leadership at all levels appeared to be consuming itself in an atmosphere of terror for its sake. This situation has been termed "centrally authorized chaos."[3]

Second, no matter how much tension and rivalry there were among the different levels and regions of the Communist Party, Stalin's primary motive in the purges was almost certainly fear for his own power and a ruthless determination to preserve and increase it. He and the deputies whom he allowed to survive the purges personally selected certain victims and determined the fate of their families. In effect, the purges created a new Communist Party that was absolutely subservient and loyal to Stalin. The "old Bolsheviks" of the October Revolution in 1917 were among his earliest targets. They and others active in the first years of the revolution knew how far Stalin had moved from Lenin's policies. New, younger recruits replaced the party members who were executed or expelled. The newcomers knew little about old Russia or the ideals of the original Bolsheviks. They had not been loyal to Lenin, Trotsky, Bukharin, or any other Soviet leader except Stalin himself.

IN PERSPECTIVE

By the mid-1930s, dictators of the right and the left had established themselves across much of Europe. Political tyranny was hardly new to Europe, but several factors combined to give these rulers unique characteristics. They drew their immediate support from well-organized political parties. Except for the Bolsheviks, these were mass parties. The roots of support for the dictators lay in nationalism, the social and economic frustration of the Great Depression, and political ideologies that promised to transform the social and political order. As long as the new rulers seemed successful, they did not lack support. Many citizens believed

[3]J. Arch Getty and Oleg V. Naumov, *The Road to Terror: Stalin and the Self-Destruction of the Bolsheviks, 1932–1939*, trans. by Benjamin Sher (New Haven, CT: Yale University Press, 1999), p. 583.

these leaders had ended the pettiness of everyday politics.

After coming to power, the dictators possessed a practical monopoly over mass communications. Through armies, police forces, and party discipline, they also monopolized terror and coercive power. They could propagandize large populations and compel people to obey them and their followers. Finally, as a result of the Second Industrial Revolution, they commanded a vast amount of technology and a capacity for immense destruction. Earlier rulers in Europe may have shared the ruthless ambitions of Hitler, Mussolini, and Stalin, but they had lacked the ready implements of physical force to impose their wills.

Mass political support, the monopoly of police and military power, and technological capacity meant the dictators of the 1930s held more extensive sway over their nations than any other group of rulers who had ever governed on the Continent. Soon the issue would become whether they would be able to maintain peace among themselves and with their democratic neighbors.

REVIEW QUESTIONS

1. Why did the Great Depression of the 1930s occur, and why was it more severe and longer lasting than previous depressions?

2. Why did Britain's National Government and France's Popular Front deal with the depression in different ways? Why did the Third Republic in France have so few supporters?

3. How did the Great Depression affect Germany? How did Hitler come to power?

4. How did Hitler's economic policies differ from those Britain, Italy, and France used to confront the depression? Why did some nations deal with the Great Depression more effectively than others?

5. How and why did Hitler, Mussolini, and Stalin use terror to achieve their goals? What were the particular characteristics of Nazi racial policy? How did this policy in its various guises affect Jewish life?

6. Why did Stalin decide that Russia had to industrialize rapidly? Why did this require the collectivization of agriculture? How did Stalin overcome the obstacles to collectivization? What were the causes of the purges in the Soviet Union?

SUGGESTED READINGS

W. S. ALLEN, *The Nazi Seizure of Power: The Experience of a Single German Town, 1930–1935*, rev. ed. (1984). A classic treatment of Nazism in a microcosmic setting.

A. APPLEBAUM, *Gulag: A History* (2003). A superbly readable account of Stalin's system of persecution and resulting prison camps.

M. BURLEIGH AND W. WIPPERMAN, *The Racial State: Germany 1933–1945* (1991). Emphasizes how racial theory influenced numerous areas of policy.

W. CHASE, *Enemies within the Gates?: The Comintern and Stalinist Repression, 1934–1939* (2001). Examines how Soviet policies destroyed the Comintern.

R. CONQUEST, *The Great Terror: Stalin's Purges of the Thirties* (1990). Still the most useful treatment of the subject.

V. DEGRAZA, *How Fascism Ruled Women: Italy, 1922–1945* (1993). A distinguished analysis.

B. A. ENGEL AND A. POSADSKAYA-VANDERBECK, *A Revolution of Their Own: Voices of Women in Soviet History* (1998). Long interviews and autobiographical recollections by women who lived through the Soviet era.

S. FITZPATRICK, *Everyday Stalinism, Ordinary Life in Extraordinary Times: Soviet Russia in the 1930s* (1999). A major study based on newly available materials.

S. FITZPATRICK, *Stalin's Peasants: Resistance and Survival in the Russian Village after Collectivization* (1994). An extensive social history.

R. GELLATELY, *Backing Hitler: Consent and Coercion in Nazi Germany* (2001). Controversial study emphasizing widespread support for Hitler.

J. A. GETTY AND O. V. NAUMOV, *The Road to Terror: Stalin and the Self-Destruction of the Bolsheviks, 1933–1939* (1999). A major collection of newly available documents revealing much new information about the purges.

R. F. HAMILTON, *Who Voted for Hitler?* (1982). An important examination of voting patterns.

J. JACKSON, *The Popular Front in France: Defending Democracy, 1934–1938* (1988). An extensive treatment.

I. KERSHAW, *Hitler*, 2 vols. (2000). The best biography now available.

C. KINDLEBERGER, *The World in Depression, 1929–1939* (1986). A classic, accessible analysis.

P. PULZER, *Jews and the German State: The Political History of a Minority, 1848–1933* (1992). A detailed study by a major historian of European minorities.

R. Service, *Stalin: A Biography* (2005). The strongest of a host of recent biographical studies.

R. Steigmann-Gall, *The Holy Reich: Nazi Conceptions of Christianity, 1919–1945* (2003). A probing discussion of Nazi manipulation of Christian ideas.

J. Stephenson, *Women in Nazi Germany* (2001). Analysis with documents.

E. WEBER, *The Hollow Years: France in the 1930s* (1995). Examines France between the wars.

DOCUMENTS CD-ROM

Society and Culture between the Wars

27.4 The Depression: Germany's Unemployed

Totalitarianism

28.7 Stalin's First Five Year Plan
28.8 Leader of the NAZI Women's Organization

PART 6: GLOBAL CONFLICT, COLD WAR, AND NEW DIRECTIONS
1939–2005

Politics and Government

1939	World War II begins
1941	Japan attacks Pearl Harbor, United States enters war
1942	Battle of Stalingrad
1945	Yalta Conference; Germany surrenders; atomic bombs dropped on Japan; Japan surrenders; United Nations founded
1947	Truman Doctrine
1948	Communist takeover in Czechoslovakia and Hungary; State of Israel proclaimed
1949	NATO founded; East and West Germany emerge as separate states
1950–1953	Korean War
1954	French defeat at Dien Bien Phu
1955	Warsaw Pact founded

Jewish children at Auschwitz, Poland

Society and Economy

1945–1951	Attlee ministry establishes the Welfare State in Great Britain
1947	Marshall Plan to rebuild Europe instituted
1949	Europe divided into Eastern and Western blocs
1957	European Economic Community founded
1960s	Rapid growth of student population in universities; migration of workers from eastern and southern to northern and western Europe; migration of non-European workers to northern and western Europe
1972	Club of Rome founded
1973–1974	Arab oil embargo
1975	Helsinki Accords

Gasoline shortage, 1973

Religion and Culture

1940	Koestler, *Darkness at Noon*
1943	Sartre, *Being and Nothingness*
1947	Camus, *The Plague*; Gramsci, *Letters from Prison*
1949	de Beauvoir, *The Second Sex*; Crossman, *The God That Failed*
1958	Pasternak forbidden to accept Nobel Prize for *Dr. Zhivago*; John XXIII becomes pope
1960s	The Beatles take world by storm
1962–1965	Second Vatican Council
1963	Solzhenitsyn, *One Day in the Life of Ivan Denisovich*
1968	Student rebellion in Paris
1974	Solzhenitsyn expelled from Soviet Union

The Beatles

1956	Khrushchev denounces Stalin; Suez crisis; Soviet invasion of Hungary
1961	Berlin Wall erected
1962	Cuban Missile Crisis
1963–1973	Major U.S. involvement in Vietnam
1968	Soviet invasion of Czechoslovakia
1979–1988	Soviet troops in Afghanistan
1985	Gorbachev comes to power in the Soviet Union
1989	Revolutions sweep across Eastern Europe
1990	German reunification; Yugoslavia breaks up
1991	Persian Gulf War; August coup in Moscow; Soviet Union dissolved
2001	United States attacked by terrorists
2003	United States invades Iraq
2005	Angela Merkl becomes first female chancellor in German history

Persian Gulf War

| 1980s and 1990s | Internal migration from Eastern to Western Europe; racial and ethnic tensions in Western Europe |
| 1990s | Changes in Eastern Europe and Soviet Union open way for economic growth and new trade relations across Europe |

Berlin Wall falls,
November, 1989

1978	John Paul II becomes pope
1980s	Growth of the environmental movement
1990s	Expanding influence of Roman Catholic Church in independent Eastern Europe
1990s	Feminists continue the critical tradition of Western culture
1990s	Era of the Internet begins
2005	Benedict XVI becomes pope

Internet use explodes in China

28

WORLD WAR II

KEY TOPICS

■ The origins of World War II
■ The course of the war
■ Racism and the Holocaust
■ The impact of the war on the people
of Europe
■ Relationships among the victorious allies
and the preparations for peace

The more idealistic survivors of World
War I, especially in the United States and
Great Britain, thought of it as "the war to
end all wars" and a war "to make the world safe
for democracy." Only thus could they justify the
slaughter, expense, and upheaval of that terrible
conflict. How appalled they would have been had

In August 1945 the United States exploded atomic bombs on the Japanese cities of Hiroshima and Nagasaki. A week later Japan surrendered. Without the bombs the United States would almost certainly have had to invade Japan, and tens of thousands of Americans would have been killed. Still, the decision to use the bomb remains controversial.   © CORBIS

they known that only twenty years after the peace treaties a second great war would break out, more global than the first. In this war, the democracies would be fighting for their lives against militaristic, nationalistic, authoritarian, and totalitarian states in Europe and Asia, and they would be allied with the communist Soviet Union in the struggle. The defeat of the militarists and dictators would not bring the peace they longed for, but the Cold War, in which the European states would become powers of the second class, subordinate to two new superpowers, partially or fully non-European: the Soviet Union and the United States. ■

AGAIN THE ROAD TO WAR (1933–1939)

World War I and the Versailles treaty had only a marginal relationship to the world depression of the 1930s. In Germany, however, where the reparations settlement had contributed to the vast inflation of 1923, economic and social discontent focused on the Versailles settlement as the cause of all ills. Throughout the late 1920s, Adolf Hitler and the Nazi Party denounced Versailles as the source of all of Germany's troubles. The economic woes of the early 1930s seemed to bear them out. Nationalism and attention to the social question, along with party discipline, had been the sources of Nazi success. They continued to influence Hitler's foreign policy after he became chancellor in January 1933. Moreover, the Nazi destruction of the Weimar constitution and of political opposition meant that Hitler himself totally dominated German foreign policy. Consequently, it is important to know what his goals were and how he planned to achieve them.

HITLER'S GOALS

From the first expression of his goals in a book written in jail, *Mein Kampf (My Struggle)*, to his last days in the underground bunker in Berlin where he killed himself, Hitler's racial theories and goals were at the center of his thought. He meant to go far beyond Germany's 1914 boundaries, which were the limit of the vision of his predecessors. He meant to bring the entire German people—the *Volk*—understood as a racial group, together into a single nation.

The new Germany would include all the Germanic parts of the old Habsburg Empire, including Austria. This virile and growing nation would need more space to live, or **Lebensraum**, that would be taken from the Slavs, who, according to Nazi theory, were a lesser race, fit only for servitude. The removal of the Jews, another inferior race according to Nazi theory, would purify the new Germany. The plans required the conquest of Poland and Ukraine as the primary areas for German settlement and for providing badly needed food. Neither *Mein Kampf* nor later statements of policy were blueprints for action. Rather, Hitler was a brilliant improviser who exploited opportunities as they arose. He never lost sight of his goal, however, which would almost certainly require a major war. (See "Hitler Describes His Goals in Foreign Policy.")

Germany Rearms   When Hitler came to power, Germany was far too weak to permit a direct approach to reach his aims. The first problem he set out to resolve was to shake off the fetters of Versailles and to make Germany a formidable military power. In October 1933, Germany withdrew from an international disarmament conference and also from the League of Nations. Hitler argued that because the other powers had not disarmed as they had promised, it was wrong to keep Germany helpless. These acts alarmed the French, but were merely symbolic. In January 1934, Germany signed a nonaggression pact with Poland that was of greater concern to France, for it undermined France's chief means of containing the Germans. At last, in March 1935, Hitler formally renounced the disarmament provisions of the Versailles treaty with the formation of a German air force, and soon he reinstated conscription, which aimed at an army of half a million men.

The League of Nations Fails   Growing evidence that the League of Nations could not keep the peace and that collective security was a myth made Hitler's path easier. In September 1931, Japan occupied Manchuria. China appealed to the League of Nations. The league dispatched a commission under a British diplomat, the earl of Lytton (1876–1951). The *Lytton Report* condemned the Japanese for resorting to force, but the powers were unwilling to impose sanctions. Japan withdrew from the League and kept control of Manchuria.

When Hitler announced his decision to rearm Germany, the League formally condemned that action, but it took no steps to prevent it. France and Britain felt unable to object forcefully because they had not carried out their own promises to disarm. Instead, they met with Mussolini in June 1935 to form the so-called Stresa Front, promising to use force to maintain the status quo in Europe. This show of unity was short lived, however. Britain, desperate to maintain superiority at sea, violated the spirit of the Stresa accords and sacrificed French security needs to make a separate naval agreement with Hitler. The pact allowed him to rebuild the German fleet to 35 percent of the British navy. Hitler had taken a major step toward his goal without provoking serious opposition. Italy's expansionist ambitions in Africa, however, soon brought it into conflict with the Western powers.

HITLER DESCRIBES HIS GOALS IN FOREIGN POLICY

From his early career, Hitler had certain long-term general views and goals. They were set forth in his Mein Kampf (My Struggle), *which appeared in 1925 and called for uniting the German* Volk *(people), more land for the Germans, and contempt for such "races" as Slavs and Jews. Here are some of Hitler's views about land.*

■ *On what basic principle is Hitler's policy founded? How does he justify his plans for expansion? Why is he hostile to France and Russia? Why does Hitler claim every man has a right to own farmland? Was that a practical goal for Germany in the 1930s? Could Hitler have achieved his goals without a major war?*

The National Socialist movement must strive to eliminate the disproportion between our population and our area—viewing this latter as a source of food as well as a basis for power politics—between our historical past and the hopelessness of our present impotence. . . .

The demand for restoration of the frontiers of 1914 is a political absurdity of such proportions and consequences as to make it seem a crime—quite aside from the fact that the Reich's frontiers in 1914 were anything but logical. For in reality they were neither complete in the sense of embracing the people of German nationality, nor sensible with regard to geomilitary expediency. . . .

As opposed to this, we National Socialists must hold unflinchingly to our aim in foreign policy, namely, to secure for the German people the land and soil to which they are entitled on this earth. . . .

The soil on which some day German generations of peasants can beget powerful sons will sanction the investment of the sons of today, and will some day acquit the responsible statesmen of blood-guilt and sacrifice of the people, even if they are persecuted by their contemporaries. . . .

Much as all of us today recognize the necessity of a reckoning with France, it would remain ineffectual in the long run if it represented the whole of our aim in foreign policy. It can and will achieve meaning only if it offers the rear cover for an enlargement of our people's living space in Europe. . . .

If we speak of soil in Europe today, we can primarily have in mind only Russia and her vassal border states. . . .

See to it that the strength of our nation is founded, not on colonies, but on the soil of our European homeland. Never regard the Reich as secure unless for centuries to come it can give every scion of our people his own parcel of soil. Never forget that the most sacred right on this earth is a man's right to have earth to till with his own hands, and the most sacred sacrifice the blood that a man sheds for this earth.

ITALY ATTACKS ETHIOPIA

In October 1935, Mussolini, using a border incident as an excuse, attacked Ethiopia. This attack made the impotence of the League of Nations and the timidity of the Allies clear. Mussolini's purposes were to avenge a humiliating defeat that the Italians had suffered in Ethiopia in 1896, to restore Roman imperial glory, and, perhaps, to distract Italian public opinion from domestic problems.

France and Britain were eager to appease Mussolini to offset the growing power of Germany. They were prepared to allow him the substance of conquest if he would maintain Ethiopia's formal independence. For Mussolini, however, the form was more important than the substance. His attack outraged opinion in the West, and the French and British governments were forced to at least appear to resist.

The League of Nations condemned Italian aggression and, for the first time, voted economic sanctions. It imposed an arms embargo that limited loans and credits to, and imports from, Italy.

Ethiopian Emperor Haile Selassie in 1936, as he delivered an address before the League of Nations. In the speech, he urged the body to save his country from invading Italian forces.

To avoid alienating Mussolini, however, Britain and France refused to embargo oil, the one economic sanction that could have prevented Italian victory. Even more important, Britain allowed Italian troops and munitions to reach Ethiopia through the Suez Canal. The results of this policy were disastrous. The League of Nations and collective security were discredited, and Mussolini was alienated. He now turned to Germany, and by November 1, 1936, he spoke publicly of a Rome-Berlin **Axis**.

REMILITARIZATION OF THE RHINELAND

The Ethiopian affair also convinced Hitler that the Western powers were too timid to oppose him forcefully. On March 7, 1936, he took his greatest risk yet, sending a small armed force into the demilitarized Rhineland. This was a breach not only of the Versailles treaty, but of the Locarno Agreements of 1925—agreements Germany had made voluntarily. It also removed a crucial element of French security. France and Britain had every right to resist, and the French especially had a claim to retain the only element of security left to them after the failure of the Allies to guarantee France's defense. Yet neither power did anything but register

a feeble protest with the League of Nations. British opinion would not permit support for France, and the French would not act alone. Internal division and a military doctrine that stressed defense and shunned the offensive paralyzed them. A growing pacifism further weakened both countries.

In retrospect, the Allies lost a great opportunity in the Rhineland to stop Hitler before he became a serious menace. The failure of his gamble, taken against his generals' advice, might have led to his overthrow; at the least, it would have made German expansion to the east dangerous if not impossible. Nor is there reason to doubt that the French army could easily have routed the tiny German force in the Rhineland. As the German general Alfred Jodl (1890–1946) said some years later, "The French covering army would have blown us to bits."[1]

A Germany that was rapidly rearming and had a defensible western frontier presented a completely new problem to the Western powers. Their response was the policy of **appeasement**, based on the assumption that Germany had real grievances and that Hitler's goals were limited and ultimately

[1]Quoted in W. L. Shirer, *The Collapse of the Third Republic* (New York: Simon & Schuster, 1969), p. 281.

acceptable. They set out to negotiate and make concessions before a crisis could lead to war.

Behind this approach was the universal dread of another war. Memories of the horrors of the last war were still vivid, and the prospect of aerial bombardment made the thought of a new war even more terrifying. A firmer policy, moreover, would have required rapid rearmament. British leaders especially were reluctant to pursue this path because of the expense and the widespread belief that the arms race had been a major cause of the last war. As Germany armed, the French huddled behind their newly constructed defensive wall, the Maginot Line, and the British hoped for the best.

THE SPANISH CIVIL WAR

The Spanish Civil War, which broke out in July 1936, made the new European alignment that found the Western democracies on one side and the fascist states on the other clearer. (See Map 28–1.) In 1931, the monarchy had collapsed, and Spain became a democratic republic. The new government followed a program of moderate reform that antagonized landowners, the Catholic Church, nationalists, and conservatives without satisfying the demands of peasants, workers, Catalán separatists, or radicals. Elections in February 1936 brought to power a Spanish Popular Front government ranging from republicans of the

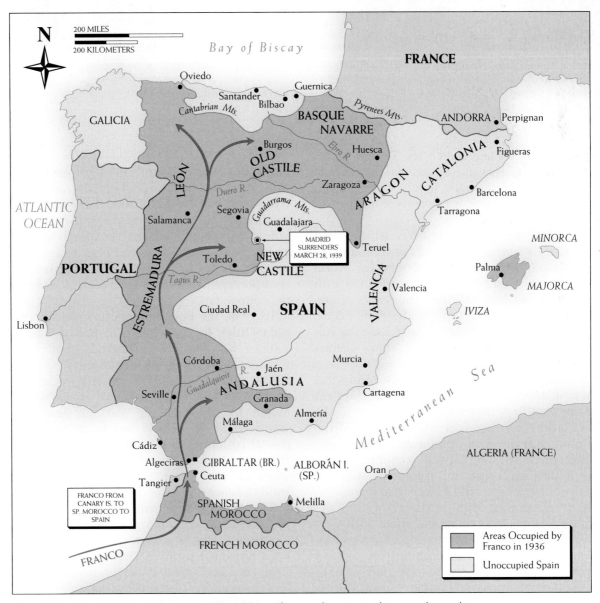

Map 28–1 **THE SPANISH CIVIL WAR, 1936–1939** The purple area on the map shows the large portion of Spain quickly overrun by Franco's insurgent armies during the first year of the war. In the next two years, progress came more slowly for the fascists as the war became a kind of international rehearsal for the coming World War II. Madrid's fall to Franco in the spring of 1939 had been preceded by that of Barcelona a few weeks earlier.

Picasso's surrealist painting depicts the horror of the terror bombing of the Basque town of Guernica by the German allies of General Francisco Franco's Nationalists during the Spanish Civil War.

Pablo Picasso, "Guernica", 1937. Oil on canvas. 11′5 1/2 × 25′5 3/4. Museo Nacional Centro de Arte Reina Sofia/© 2004 Estate of Pablo Picasso/Artists Rights Society (ARS), New York

left to communists and anarchists. The losers, especially the Falangists, the Spanish fascists, would not accept defeat at the polls. In July, General Francisco Franco (1892–1975) led an army from Spanish Morocco against the republic.

Thus began the Spanish Civil War, which lasted almost three years, cost hundreds of thousands of lives, and provided a training ground for World War II. Germany and Italy supported Franco with troops, airplanes, and supplies. The Soviet Union sent equipment and advisers to the republicans. Liberals and leftists from Europe and America volunteered to fight in the republican ranks against fascism.

The civil war, fought on blatantly ideological lines, profoundly affected world politics. It brought Germany and Italy closer together, leading to the Rome-Berlin Axis Pact in 1936. Japan joined the Axis powers in the Anti-Comintern Pact, ostensibly directed against international communism, but really a new and powerful diplomatic alliance. Western Europe, especially France, had a great interest in preventing Spain from falling into the hands of a fascist regime closely allied with Germany and Italy. Appeasement reigned, however. Although international law permitted the sale of weapons and munitions to the legitimate republican government, France and Britain forbade the export of war materials to either side, and the United States passed new neutrality legislation to the same end. When Barcelona fell to Franco early in 1939, the fascists had won effective control of Spain.

AUSTRIA AND CZECHOSLOVAKIA

Hitler made good use of his new friendship with Mussolini. He had always planned to annex his native Austria. In 1934, the Nazi Party in Austria assassinated the prime minister and tried to seize power. Mussolini had not yet allied with Hitler and was suspicious of German intentions. He quickly moved an army to the Austrian border, thus preventing German intervention and causing the coup to fail.

In 1938, the new diplomatic situation encouraged Hitler to try again. He perhaps hoped to achieve his goal by propaganda, bullying, and threats, but Austrian chancellor Kurt von Schuschnigg (1897–1977) refused to be intimidated. Schuschnigg announced a plebiscite for March 13, in which the Austrian people themselves could decide whether to unite with Germany. To forestall the plebiscite, Hitler sent his army into Austria on March 12. To his relief, Mussolini did not object, and Hitler rode to Vienna amid the cheers of his Austrian sympathizers.

The ***Anschluss***, or union of Germany and Austria, was another clear violation of Versailles. The treaty, however, was now a dead letter, and the West remained passive. The *Anschluss* had great strategic significance, however, because Germany now surrounded Czechoslovakia, one of the bulwarks of French security, on three sides.

In fact, the very existence of Czechoslovakia was an affront to Hitler. It was democratic and pro-Western; it had been created partly to check Germany and was allied both to France and to the Soviet Union. It also contained about 3.5 million Germans who lived in the Sudetenland, near the German border. These Germans had belonged to the dominant nationality group in the old Austro-Hungarian Empire and resented their new minority position. Supported by Hitler and led by Konrad Henlein (1898–1945), they made ever-increasing demands for privileges and autonomy within the Czech state. The Czechs made concessions, but Hitler really wanted to destroy Czechoslovakia. He told Henlein, "We must always demand so much that we can never be satisfied."[2]

As pressure mounted, the Czechs grew nervous. In May 1938, they received false rumors of an imminent attack by Germany and mobilized their army. The French, British, and Russians all warned they would support the Czechs. Hitler, who had not planned an attack at that time, was forced to publicly deny any designs on Czechoslovakia. The humiliation infuriated him, and he planned a military attack on the Czechs. The affair stiffened Czech resistance, but it frightened the French and British. The French, as had become the rule, deferred to British leadership. The British prime minister Neville Chamberlain (1869–1940) was determined not to allow Britain to go to war again. He pressed the Czechs to make concessions to Germany, but no concession was enough.

On September 12, 1938, Hitler made a provocative speech at the Nuremberg Nazi Party rally. His rhetoric led to rioting in the Sudetenland, and the Czechs declared martial law. German intervention seemed imminent. Chamberlain, aged sixty-nine, who had never flown before, made three flights to Germany between September 15 and September 29 in an attempt to appease Hitler at Czech expense and thus to avoid war. At Hitler's mountain retreat, Berchtesgaden, on September 15, Chamberlain accepted the separation of the Sudetenland from Czechoslovakia, and he and the French premier, Edouard Daladier (1884–1970), forced the Czechs to agree by threatening to abandon them if they did not. A week later, Chamberlain flew yet again to Germany, only to find that Hitler had raised his demands. He wanted cession of the Sudetenland in three days and immediate occupation by the German army.

Agreement at Munich. On September 29–30, 1938, Hitler met with the leaders of Britain and France at Munich to decide the fate of Czechoslovakia. The Allied leaders abandoned the small democratic nation in a vain attempt to appease Hitler and avoid war. Hitler sits in the center of the picture. To his right is British Prime Minister Neville Chamberlain.   Ullstein Bilderdienst

MUNICH

Chamberlain returned to England, and France and Britain prepared for war. At Chamberlain's request and at the last moment, Mussolini proposed a conference of Germany, Italy, France, and Britain. It met on September 29 at Munich. Hitler received almost everything he had demanded. (See Map 28–2, page 946.) The Sudetenland, the key to Czech security, became part of Germany, thus depriving the Czechs of any chance of self-defense. In return, Hitler agreed to spare the rest of Czechoslovakia. He promised, "I have no more territorial demands to make in Europe." Chamberlain returned to England with the Munich agreement and told a cheering crowd that he had brought "peace with honour. I believe it is peace for our time."

Even in the short run, the appeasement of Hitler at Munich was a failure. Czechoslovakia did not survive. Soon Poland and Hungary tore more territory from it, and the Slovaks demanded a state of their own. Finally, on March 15, 1939, Hitler broke his promise and occupied Prague, putting an end to the Czech state and to illusions that his only goal was to restore Germans to the Reich. Defenders of the appeasers have argued that their policy bought valuable time in which the West could prepare for war, but the appeasers themselves, who thought they were achieving peace, did not make that argument, nor does the evidence support it.

If the French and the British had been willing to attack Germany from the west while the Czechs fought in their own defense, their efforts might

[2]Quoted in Alan Bullock, *Hitler, a Study in Tyranny* (New York: Harper & Row, 1962), p. 443.

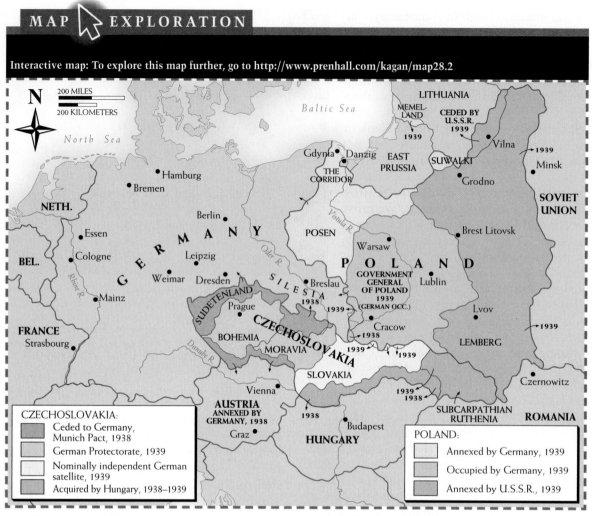

MAP EXPLORATION

Interactive map: To explore this map further, go to http://www.prenhall.com/kagan/map28.2

CZECHOSLOVAKIA:
- Ceded to Germany, Munich Pact, 1938
- German Protectorate, 1939
- Nominally independent German satellite, 1939
- Acquired by Hungary, 1938–1939

POLAND:
- Annexed by Germany, 1939
- Occupied by Germany, 1939
- Annexed by U.S.S.R., 1939

Map 28–2 **PARTITIONS OF CZECHOSLOVAKIA AND POLAND, 1938–1939** The immediate background of World War II is found in the complex international drama unfolding on Germany's eastern frontier in 1938 and 1939. Germany's expansion inevitably meant the victimization of Austria, Czechoslovakia, and Poland. With the failure of the Western powers' appeasement policy and the signing of a German-Soviet pact, the stage for the war was set.

have been successful. High officers in the German army were opposed to Hitler's risky policies and might have overthrown him. Even failing such developments, a war begun in October 1938 would have forced Hitler to fight without the friendly neutrality and material assistance of the Soviet Union—and without the resources of Eastern Europe that became available to him as a result of appeasement and Soviet cooperation. If, moreover, the West ever had a chance of concluding an alliance with the Soviet Union against Hitler, the exclusion of the Russians from Munich and the appeasement policy helped destroy it. Munich remains an example of shortsighted policy that helped bring on war in disadvantageous circumstances because of the very fear of war and the failure to prepare for it. (See "Churchill's Response to Munich.")

Hitler's occupation of Prague discredited appeasement in Britain. In the summer of 1939, a Gallup poll showed that three-quarters of the British public believed it was worth a war to stop Hitler. Though Chamberlain himself had not lost all faith in his policy, he felt he had to respond to public opinion, and he responded to excess.

Poland was the next target of German expansion. In the spring of 1939, the Germans put pressure on Poland to restore the formerly German city of Danzig and to allow a railroad and a highway through the Polish Corridor to connect East Prussia with the rest of Germany. When the Poles would not yield, the usual propaganda campaign began, and the pressure mounted. On March 31, Chamberlain announced a Franco-British guarantee of Polish independence. Hitler appears to have expected to fight a war with Poland, but not with

CHURCHILL'S RESPONSE TO MUNICH

—⟋⟍—

In the parliamentary debate that followed the Munich conference at the end of September 1938, Winston Churchill was one of the few critics of what had been accomplished. In the following selections from his speech, he expresses his concerns.

■ *What was decided at Munich? Why were the representatives of Czechoslovakia not at the meeting? Why did Chamberlain think the meeting was successful? Munich was the high point of the policy called appeasement. How would its advocates defend this policy? Churchill was a leading opponent of appeasement. What are his objections to it?*

I will begin by saying what everybody would like to ignore or forget but which must nevertheless be stated, namely, that we have sustained a total and unmitigated defeat, and that France has suffered even more than we have . . . .

We really must not waste time after all this long debate upon the difference between the positions reached at Berchtesgaden, at Godesberg and at Munich. They can be very simply epitomized if the House will permit me to vary the metaphor. One pound was demanded at the pistol's point. When it was given, £2 were demanded at the pistol's point. Finally, the dictator consented to take £1 17s. 6d. and the rest in promises of good will for the future. . . .

All is over. Silent, mournful, abandoned, broken, Czechoslovakia recedes into the darkness. She has suffered in every respect by her association with the Western democracies and with the League of Nations, of which she has always been an obedient servant. . . .

We have been reduced in these five years from a position of security so overwhelming and so unchallengeable that we never cared to think about it. We have been reduced from a position where the very word "war" was considered one which could be used only by persons qualifying for a lunatic asylum. We have been reduced from a position of safety and power—power to do good, power to be generous to a beaten foe, power to make terms with Germany, power to

give her proper redress for her grievances, power to stop her arming if we chose, power to take any step in strength or mercy or justice which we thought right—reduced in five years from a position safe and unchallenged to where we stand now. . . .

The responsibility must rest with those who have had the undisputed control of our political affairs. They neither prevented Germany from rearming, nor did they rearm ourselves in time. They quarreled with Italy without saving Ethiopia. They exploited and discredited the vast institution of the League of Nations and they neglected to make alliances and combinations which might have repaired previous errors, and thus they left us in the hour of trial without adequate national defense or effective international security. . . .

We are in the presence of a disaster of the first magnitude which has befallen Great Britain and France. Do not let us blind ourselves to that. It must now be accepted that all the countries of Central and Eastern Europe will make the best terms they can with the triumphant Nazi power. The system of alliances in Central Europe upon which France has relied for her safety has been swept away, and I can see no means by which it can be reconstituted. The road down the Danube Valley to the Black Sea, the road which leads as far as Turkey, has been opened.

"Churchill's Response to Munich" from *Blood, Sweat, and Tears* by Winston S. Churchill (New York: G.P. Putnam's Sons, 1941), pp. 55–56, 58, 60–61. Reproduced with permission of Curtis Brown Ltd., London on behalf of Winston S. Churchill. Copyright Winston S. Churchill. 1941.

the Western allies, for he did not take their guarantee seriously. He had come to hold their leaders in contempt. He knew both countries were unprepared for war and that large segments of their populations opposed fighting for Poland.

Moreover, France and Britain had no means to get effective help to the Poles. The French, still dominated by the defensive mentality of the Maginot Line, had no intention of attacking Germany. The only way to defend Poland was to bring Russia into the alliance against Hitler, but a Russian alliance posed many problems. Each side was profoundly suspicious of the other. The French and the British were hostile to communism, and since Stalin's purge of the Red Army, they were skeptical of the military value of a Russian alliance. Besides, the Russians could not help Poland without being given the right to enter Poland and Romania. Both nations, suspicious of Russian intentions—and with good reason—refused to grant these rights. As a result, Western negotiations for an alliance with Russia made little progress.

THE NAZI-SOVIET PACT

The Russians had at least equally good reason to hesitate. They resented being left out of the Munich agreement. The low priority that the West gave to negotiations with Russia, compared with the urgency with which Britain and France dealt with Hitler, annoyed them. The Russians feared, rightly, that the Western powers meant them to bear the burden of the war against Germany. As a result, they opened negotiations with Hitler, and on August 23, 1939, the world was shocked to learn of a Nazi-Soviet nonaggression pact.

The secret provisions of the pact, which were easily guessed and soon carried out, divided Poland between the two powers and allowed Russia to occupy the Baltic states and to take Bessarabia from Romania. The most bitter ideological enemies had become allies. Communist parties in the West changed their line overnight from ardently advocating resistance to Hitler to a policy of peace and quiet. Ideology gave way to political and military reality. The West offered the Russians immediate danger without much prospect of gain. Hitler offered Stalin short-term gain without immediate danger. There could be little doubt about Stalin's decision.

The Nazi-Soviet pact sealed the fate of Poland, and the Franco-British commitment guaranteed a general war. On September 1, 1939, the Germans invaded Poland. Two days later, Britain and France declared war on Germany. World War II had begun.

WORLD WAR II (1939–1945)

World War II was truly global. Fighting took place in Europe, North Africa, and Asia, on the Atlantic and the Pacific Oceans, and in the Northern and Southern Hemispheres. The demand for the fullest exploitation of material and human resources for increased production, the use of blockades, and the intensive bombing of civilian targets made the war of 1939 even more "total"—that is, comprehensive and intense—than that of 1914.

THE GERMAN CONQUEST OF EUROPE

The German attack on Poland produced swift success. The new style of "lightning warfare," or **blitzkrieg**, employed fast-moving, massed armored columns supported by airpower. The Poles had few planes and fewer tanks, and their defense soon collapsed. The speed of the German victory astonished the Russians, who hastened to collect their share of the booty before Hitler could deprive them of it.

On September 17, Russia invaded Poland from the east, dividing the country with the Germans. The Red Army then occupied the encircled Baltic countries. By July 1940, Estonia, Latvia, and Lithuania had become puppet republics within the Soviet Union. In June 1940, the Russians forced Romania to cede Bessarabia. In November 1939, the Russians invaded Finland, but the Finns resisted fiercely for six months. Although they were finally worn down and compelled to yield territory and bases to Russia, the Finns remained independent. Russian expansionism and the poor performance of the Red Army in Finland may well have encouraged Hitler to invade the Soviet Union in June 1941, just twenty-two months after the 1939 treaty.

Until the spring of 1940, the western front was quiet. The French remained behind the Maginot Line while Hitler and Stalin swallowed Poland and the Baltic states. Britain rearmed hastily, and the British navy blockaded Germany. Cynics in the West called it the phony war, or *Sitzkrieg*, but Hitler shattered the stillness in the spring of 1940. In April, without warning and with swift success, the Germans invaded Denmark and Norway. Hitler's northern front was secure, and he now had both air and naval bases closer to Britain. A month later, a combined land and air attack struck Belgium, the Netherlands, and Luxembourg. German airpower and armored divisions were irresistible. The Dutch surrendered in a few days; the Belgians, though aided by the French and the British, gave up less than two weeks later.

The British and French armies in Belgium were forced to flee to the English Channel to seek escape on the beaches of Dunkirk. The heroic efforts of hundreds of Britons manning small boats saved more than 200,000 British and 100,000 French soldiers. Casualties, however, were high, and valuable equipment was abandoned.

The Maginot Line ran from Switzerland to the Belgian frontier. Until 1936, the French had expected the Belgians to continue the fortifications along their German border. After Hitler remilitarized the Rhineland without opposition, the Belgians lost faith in their French alliance and proclaimed their neutrality, leaving the Maginot Line exposed on its left flank. Hitler's swift advance through Belgium, therefore, circumvented France's main line of defense.

The French army, poorly and hesitantly led by aged generals who did not understand how to use tanks and planes, collapsed. Mussolini, eager to claim the spoils of victory when he thought it was safe to do so, invaded southern France on June 10.

German troops parade down the Champs-Elysées after the fall of Paris in 1940.

THE COMING OF WORLD WAR II

1919 (June)	The Versailles treaty
1923 (January)	France occupies the Ruhr
1925 (October)	The Locarno Agreements
1931 (Spring)	Onset of the Great Depression in Europe
1931 (September)	Japan occupies Manchuria
1933 (January)	Hitler comes to power
1933 (October)	Germany withdraws from the League of Nations
1935 (March)	Hitler renounces disarmament, starts an air force, and begins conscription
1935 (October)	Mussolini attacks Ethiopia
1936 (March)	Germany reoccupies and remilitarizes the Rhineland
1936 (July)	Outbreak of the Spanish Civil War
1936 (October)	Formation of the Rome-Berlin Axis
1938 (March)	*Anschluss* with Austria
1938 (September)	The Munich conference and the partition of Czechoslovakia
1939 (March)	Hitler occupies Prague; France and Great Britain guarantee Polish independence
1939 (August)	The Nazi-Soviet pact
1939 (September 1)	Germany invades Poland
1939 (September 3)	Britain and France declare war on Germany

Less than a week later, the new French government, under the ancient hero of Verdun, Marshal Henri Philippe Pétain (1856–1951), asked for an armistice. In two months Hitler had accomplished what Germany had failed to achieve in four years of bitter fighting in the previous war.

THE BATTLE OF BRITAIN

The fall of France left Britain isolated, and Hitler expected the British to come to terms. He was prepared to allow Britain to retain its empire in return for a free hand for Germany on the Continent. The British had never been willing to accept such an arrangement and had fought the long and difficult war against Napoleon to prevent a single power from dominating the Continent. If there was any chance the British would consider such terms, it disappeared when Winston Churchill (1874–1965) replaced Chamberlain as prime minister in May 1940.

Churchill had been an early and forceful critic of Hitler, the Nazis, and the policy of appeasement. He was a descendant and biographer of the duke of Marlborough (1650–1722), who had fought Louis XIV in the eighteenth century. Churchill's sense of history, his feeling for British greatness, and his hatred of tyranny and love of freedom made him reject any compromise with Hitler. His skill as a

In August 1941, President Franklin Roosevelt and Prime Minister Winston Churchill met at sea and agreed on a broad program of liberal peace aims, called the Atlantic Charter, in the spirit of Woodrow Wilson's Fourteen Points.   The Granger Collection

speaker and a writer enabled him to inspire the British people with his own courage and determination and to undertake what seemed a hopeless fight. Hitler and his allies, including the Soviet Union, controlled all of Europe. Japan was having its way in Asia. The United States was neutral, dominated by isolationist sentiment, and determined to avoid involvement outside the Western Hemisphere.

One of Churchill's greatest achievements was establishing a close relationship with the American president Franklin D. Roosevelt (1882–1945). Roosevelt found ways to help the British despite strong political opposition. In 1940 and 1941, before the United States was at war, America sent military supplies, traded badly needed warships for leases on British naval bases, and even convoyed ships across the Atlantic to help the British survive.

As weeks passed and Britain remained defiant, Hitler was forced to contemplate an invasion, and that required control of the air. The first strikes by the German air force (**Luftwaffe**), directed against the airfields and fighter planes in southeast England, began in August 1940. If these attacks had continued, Germany might have gained control of the air and, with it, the chance of a successful invasion.

In early September, however, seeking revenge for some British bombing raids on German cities, the Luftwaffe switched its main attacks to London. For two months, it bombed London every night. Much of the city was destroyed, and about 15,000 people were killed. The theories of victory through airpower alone, however, proved false. Casualties

were much less than expected, and morale was not shattered. In fact, the bombings united the British people and made them more resolute.

The Royal Air Force (RAF) inflicted heavy losses on the Luftwaffe. Aided by the newly developed radar and excellent communications, the British Spitfire and Hurricane fighter planes destroyed more than twice as many enemy planes as the RAF lost. Hitler had lost the Battle of Britain in the air and was forced to abandon his plans for invasion.

THE GERMAN ATTACK ON RUSSIA

The defeat of Russia and the conquest of the Ukraine to provide *Lebensraum*, or "living space," for the German people had always been a major goal for Hitler. Even before the assault on Britain, he had informed his staff of his intention to attack Russia as soon as conditions were favorable. In December 1940, even while the bombing of England continued, he ordered his generals to prepare to invade Russia by May 15, 1941. (See Map 28–3.) He apparently thought a *blitzkrieg* victory in the east would also destroy the British hope of resistance.

Operation Barbarossa, the code name for the invasion of Russia, was aimed to destroy Russia before winter could set in. Success depended, in part, on an early start, but here Hitler's Italian alliance proved costly. Mussolini was jealous of Hitler's success and annoyed by how the German dictator had treated him. His invasion of France was a fiasco, even though the Germans were simultaneously crushing the main French forces. Hitler did not allow Mussolini to annex French territory in Europe or North Africa. Mussolini instead attacked the British in Egypt and drove them back some sixty miles. Encouraged by this success, he also invaded Greece from his base in Albania (which he had seized in 1939). As he told his son-in-law, Count Ciano: "Hitler always faces me with a fait accompli. This time I am going to pay him back in his own coin. He will find out in the newspapers that I have occupied Greece."[3]

In North Africa, however, the British counterattacked and invaded Libya. The Greeks themselves pushed into Albania. In March 1941, the British sent help to the Greeks, and Hitler was forced to divert his attention to the Balkans and Africa. General Erwin Rommel (1891–1944), later to earn the title of "Desert Fox," went to Africa and soon drove the British back into Egypt. In the Balkans, the German army swiftly occupied Yugoslavia and crushed Greek resistance. The price, however, was

[3]Quoted in Gordon Wright, *The Ordeal of Total War, 1939–1945* (New York: Harper & Row, 1968), pp. 35–36.

Map 28–3 **AXIS EUROPE, 1941** On the eve of the German invasion of the Soviet Union, the Germany-Italy Axis bestrode most of western Europe by annexation, occupation, or alliance—from Norway and Finland in the north to Greece in the south and from Poland to France. Britain, the Soviets, a number of insurgent groups, and, finally, America, had before them the long struggle of conquering this Axis "fortress Europe."

a delay of six weeks. The diversion Mussolini's vanity caused proved to be costly the following winter in the Russian campaign.

Operation Barbarossa was launched against Russia on June 22, 1941, and it almost succeeded. Despite their deep suspicion of Germany (and the excuse apologists for the Soviet Union later offered that the Nazi-Soviet pact was meant to give Russia time to prepare), the Russians were taken quite by surprise. Stalin appears to have panicked. He had not fortified his frontier, nor did he order his troops to withdraw when attacked. In the first two days,

the Germans destroyed 2,000 Russian planes on the ground. By November, the German army stood at the gates of Leningrad, on the outskirts of Moscow, and on the Don River. Of the 4.5 million troops with which the Russians had begun the fighting, they had lost 2.5 million; of their 15,000 tanks, only 700 were left. Moscow was in panic, and a German victory seemed imminent.

Yet the Germans could not deliver the final blow. In August, they delayed their advance while Hitler decided strategy. The German general staff wanted to take Moscow before winter. This plan probably would have brought victory. Unlike in Napoleon's time, Moscow was the hub of the Russian transportation system. Hitler, however, diverted a significant force to the south. By the time he was ready to return to the offensive near Moscow, it was too late. Winter devastated the German army, which was not equipped to face it.

Given precious time, Stalin restored order and built defenses for the city. Even more importantly, troops arrived from Siberia, where they had been placed to check a possible Japanese attack. In November and December, the Russians counterattacked. The *blitzkrieg* had turned into a war of attrition, and the Germans began to have nightmares of duplicating Napoleon's retreat.

HITLER'S PLANS FOR EUROPE

Hitler often spoke of the "new order" that he meant to impose after he had established his **Third Reich** (Empire) throughout Europe. The first two German empires were those of Charlemagne in the ninth century and Bismarck in the nineteenth. Hitler predicted that his own would last for a thousand years. If his organization of Germany before the war is a proper guide, he had no single plan of government, but relied on intuition and pragmatism. His organization of a conquered Europe had the same patchwork characteristics. Some conquered territory was annexed to Germany, some was not annexed, but administered directly by German officials, and other lands were nominally autonomous, but ruled by puppet governments.

Hitler's regime was probably unmatched in history for carefully planned terror and inhumanity. His plan of giving *Lebensraum* to the Germans was to be accomplished at the expense of people he deemed to be inferior. Hitler established colonies of Germans in parts of Poland, driving the local people from their land and employing them as cheap, virtually slave, labor. He had similar plans on an even greater scale for Russia. The Russians would be driven back to Central Asia and Siberia. Frontier colonies of German war veterans would keep them in check while Germans settled European Russia.

Hitler's long-range plans included germanization as well as colonization. In lands people racially akin to the Germans inhabited, like the Scandinavian countries, the Netherlands, and Switzerland, the German nation would absorb the natives. Such peoples would be reeducated and purged of dissenting elements, but there would be little or no colonization. Hitler even had plans to adopt selected people from the lesser races into the master race. For example, the Nazis planned to bring half a million Ukrainian girls to Germany as servants and find German husbands for them.

Hitler regarded the conquered lands as a source of plunder. From Eastern Europe, he removed everything useful, including entire industries. In Russia and Poland, the Germans simply confiscated the land itself. In the West, the conquered countries had to support the occupying army at a rate several times above the real cost. The Germans used the profits to buy up everything desirable, stripping the conquered peoples of most necessities. The Nazis were frank about their policies. One of Hitler's high officials said, "Whether nations live in prosperity or starve to death interests me only insofar as we need them as slaves for our culture."[4]

JAPAN AND THE UNITED STATES ENTER THE WAR

The American government was pro-British. The assistance that Roosevelt gave Britain would have justified a German declaration of war. Hitler, however, held back. The U.S. government might not have overcome isolationist sentiment and entered the war in the Atlantic if war had not been thrust on America in the Pacific.

Since the Japanese conquest of Manchuria in 1931, American policy toward Japan had been suspicious and unfriendly. The outbreak of the war in Europe emboldened the Japanese to accelerate their drive to dominate Asia. They allied themselves with Germany and Italy, made a treaty of neutrality with the Soviet Union, and forced defeated France to give them bases in Indochina. They also continued their war in China and planned to gain control of Malaya and the East Indies (Indonesia) at the expense of beleaguered Britain and the conquered Netherlands. The only barrier to Japanese expansion was the United States.

The Americans had temporized, unwilling to cut off vital supplies of oil and other materials for fear of provoking a Japanese attack on Southeast Asia and the East Indies. The Japanese occupation of Indochina in July 1941 changed that policy, which had already begun to stiffen. The United States froze Japanese assets and cut off oil supplies; the British and Dutch did the same. Japanese plans for expansion could not continue without the conquest of the Indonesian oil fields and Malayan rubber and tin.

In October, a war faction led by General Hideki Tojo (1885–1948) took power in Japan and decided to risk a war rather than yield. On Sunday morn-

[4]Quoted in Wright, p. 117.

The successful Japanese attack on the American base at Pearl Harbor in Hawaii on December 7, 1941, together with simultaneous attacks on other Pacific bases, brought the United States into war against the Axis powers. This picture shows the battleships USS *West Virginia* and USS *Tennessee* in flames as a small boat rescues a man from the water.   U.S. Army Photo

ing, December 7, 1941, while Japanese representatives were in Washington to discuss a settlement, Japan launched an air attack on Pearl Harbor, Hawaii, the chief American naval base in the Pacific. The technique was similar to the one Japan had used against the Russian fleet at Port Arthur in 1904, and it caught the Americans equally by surprise. The attack destroyed much of the American fleet and many airplanes. The American capacity to wage war in the Pacific was negated for the time being. The next day, the United States and Britain declared war on Japan. Three days later, Germany and Italy declared war on the United States.

THE TIDE TURNS

The potential power of the United States was enormous, but America was ill prepared for war. The army was tiny, inexperienced, and poorly supplied.

American industry was not ready for war. The Japanese swiftly captured Guam, Wake Island, and the Philippine Islands. By the spring of 1942, they had conquered Hong Kong, Malaya, Burma, and the Dutch East Indies. They controlled the southwest Pacific as far as New Guinea and were poised for an attack on Australia. It seemed that nothing could stop them.

In 1942, the Germans also advanced deeper into Russia, while in Africa Rommel drove the British back into Egypt until they stopped him at El Alamein, only seventy miles from Alexandria. Relations between the democracies and their Soviet ally were not close. German submarine warfare was threatening British supplies. The Allies were being thrown back on every front, and the future looked bleak.

The first good news for the Allied cause in the Pacific came in the spring of 1942. A naval battle

MAP 🖱 EXPLORATION

Interactive map: To explore this map further, go to http://www.prenhall.com/kagan/map28.4

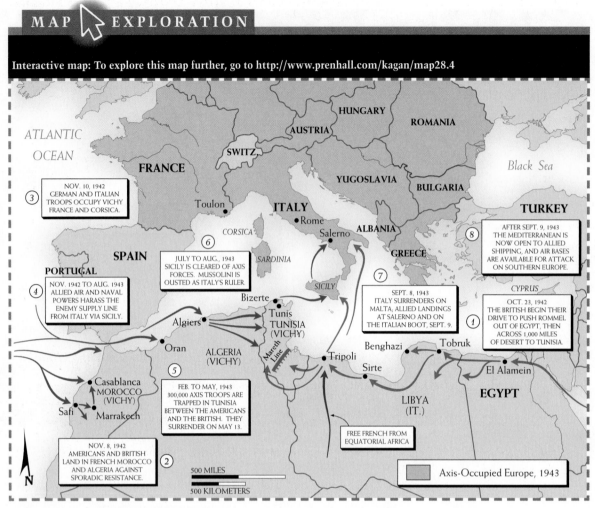

③ NOV. 10, 1942 GERMAN AND ITALIAN TROOPS OCCUPY VICHY FRANCE AND CORSICA.

④ NOV. 1942 TO AUG. 1943 ALLIED AIR AND NAVAL POWERS HARASS THE ENEMY SUPPLY LINE FROM ITALY VIA SICILY.

⑥ JULY TO AUG., 1943 SICILY IS CLEARED OF AXIS FORCES. MUSSOLINI IS OUSTED AS ITALY'S RULER.

⑤ FEB. TO MAY, 1943 300,000 AXIS TROOPS ARE TRAPPED IN TUNISIA BETWEEN THE AMERICANS AND THE BRITISH. THEY SURRENDER ON MAY 13.

② NOV. 8, 1942 AMERICANS AND BRITISH LAND IN FRENCH MOROCCO AND ALGERIA AGAINST SPORADIC RESISTANCE.

⑦ SEPT. 8, 1943 ITALY SURRENDERS ON MALTA; ALLIED LANDINGS AT SALERNO AND ON THE ITALIAN BOOT, SEPT. 9.

⑧ AFTER SEPT. 9, 1943 THE MEDITERRANEAN IS NOW OPEN TO ALLIED SHIPPING, AND AIR BASES ARE AVAILABLE FOR ATTACK ON SOUTHERN EUROPE.

① OCT. 23, 1942 THE BRITISH BEGIN THEIR DRIVE TO PUSH ROMMEL OUT OF EGYPT, THEN ACROSS 1,000 MILES OF DESERT TO TUNISIA.

FREE FRENCH FROM EQUATORIAL AFRICA

500 MILES
500 KILOMETERS

Axis-Occupied Europe, 1943

Map 28–4 **NORTH AFRICAN CAMPAIGNS, 1942–1945** Control of North Africa would give the Allies access to Europe from the south. The map illustrates this theater of the war from Morocco to Egypt and the Suez Canal.

in the Coral Sea sank many Japanese ships and gave security to Australia. A month later, the United States defeated the Japanese in a fierce air and naval battle off Midway Island. This victory blunted the chance of another assault on Hawaii and did enough damage to halt the Japanese advance. Soon American marines landed on Guadalcanal in the Solomon Islands and began to reverse the momentum of the war. The war in the Pacific was far from over, but the check to Japan allowed the Allies to concentrate their efforts on Europe.

More than twenty nations located all over the world were opposed to the Axis powers. The main combatants, however, were Great Britain, the Soviet Union, and the United States. The two Western democracies cooperated to an unprecedented degree, but suspicion between them and the Soviet Union continued. The Russians accepted all the aid they could get. Nevertheless, they did not trust their allies, complained of inadequate help, and de-

manded that the democracies open a "second front" on the mainland of Europe.

In 1942, American preparation and production were inadequate to invade Europe. German submarines made it dangerous to ship the vast numbers of troops such an invasion needed across the Atlantic. Not until 1944 were conditions right for the invasion, but in the meantime other developments forecast the doom of the Axis. (See "Encountering the Past: Rosie the Riveter and American Women in the War Effort.")

Allied Landings in Africa, Sicily, and Italy In November 1942, an Allied force landed in French North Africa. (See Map 28–4.) Even before that landing, after stopping Rommel at El Alamein, British field marshal Bernard Montgomery (1887–1976) had begun a drive to the west. Now, the Americans pushed eastward through Morocco and Algeria. The two armies caught the German

ROSIE THE RIVETER AND AMERICAN WOMEN IN THE WAR EFFORT

The induction of millions of men into the armed forces created a demand for new workers, especially in the defense industries. In response, millions of women entered the labor force, some of them taking jobs in defense plants to do work only men usually did. Economic pressures caused by the Great Depression of the 1930s had already brought many more women into the work force than had been common before. Most came from poor families and worked in white-collar jobs to support themselves or to help their families eke out a living. Even so, the heavy burden of housework and the widespread hostility to women working outside the home kept most women at home.

America's entry into the war changed things quickly. The need for vast amounts of equipment to wage the war called for and attracted new groups to seek work in the many enlarged and new factories. African Americans from the south came to northern and western cities to seek well-paying jobs, and women, too, came forward in greater numbers than ever before. Prejudices of various kinds had kept them from many opportunities, but the needs of war were too important. In October 1942, President Roosevelt made the new situation clear: "In some communities employers dislike to hire women. In others they are reluctant to hire Negroes. We can no longer afford to indulge such prejudice."

Many women changed jobs to work in the defense industries; others entered the work force for the first time, lured less by wages than by patriotism. Their brothers and boyfriends were risking their lives for their country and its ideals of freedom and democracy. They were eager to do their part to support them, to be, in the words of a current song, the woman "behind the man behind the gun." Another popular song, "Rosie the Riveter," told of a young woman working in an aircraft factory to provide protection for her boyfriend in the

Rosie the Riveter was one of the best known symbols of the U.S. war effort in World War II.   Printed by permission of the Norman Rockwell Family Agency. Copyright © 1943 the Norman Rockwell Family Entities

Marines. Rosie became one of the best known symbols of the war effort when she appeared on the cover of the *Saturday Evening Post* in a painting by Norman Rockwell. With her rivet gun on her lap she stamps on a copy of Hitler's *Mein Kampf*, the hated symbol of the evil enemy.

- *How did the war change women's place in American society? What attitudes did it need to overcome?*

army between them in Tunisia and crushed it. The Allies now controlled the Mediterranean and could attack southern Europe.

In July and August 1943, the Allies took Sicily. A coup toppled Mussolini, but the Germans occupied Italy. The Allies landed in Italy, and Marshal Pietro Badoglio (1871–1956), the leader of the new Italian government, declared war on Germany. Churchill had spoken of Italy as the "soft underbelly" of the Axis, but the Germans there resisted fiercely. Still, the need to defend Italy weakened the Germans on other fronts.

Battle of Stalingrad   The Russian campaign became especially demanding. In the summer of 1942, the Germans resumed the offensive on all fronts, but were unable to get far except in the south. (See Map 28–5.) Their goal was the oil fields near the Caspian Sea. Stalingrad, on the Volga, was a key point on the flank of the

In the battle of Stalingrad, Russian troops contested every street and building. Although the city was all but destroyed in the fighting and Russian casualties were enormous, the German army in the east never recovered from the defeat it suffered there.   Hulton Archives/Getty Images, Inc.

German army in the south. Hitler was determined to take the city, and Stalin was equally determined to hold it. The Battle of Stalingrad raged for months with unexampled ferocity. The Russians lost more men in this one battle than the Americans lost in combat during the entire war, but their heroic defense prevailed. Because Hitler again overruled his generals and would not allow a retreat, he lost an entire German army at Stalingrad.

Stalingrad marked the turning point of the Russian campaign. Thereafter, the Americans provided material help. Even more importantly, increased production from their own industry, allowed the Russians to gain and keep the offensive. As the Germans' resources dwindled, the Russians inexorably advanced westward.

Strategic Bombing   In 1943, the Allies also gained ground in production and logistics. The industrial might of the United States began to come into full force, and new technology and tactics reduced the submarine menace.

In the same year, the American and British air forces began a series of massive bombardments of Germany by night and day. The Americans were more committed to the theory of "precision bombing" of military and industrial targets vital to the enemy war effort, so they flew the day missions. The British considered precision bombing impossible and therefore useless. They preferred indiscriminate "area bombing," which they could do at night, to destroy the morale of the German people. Neither kind of bombing had much effect on the

war until 1944, when the Americans introduced long-range fighters that could protect the bombers and allow accurate missions by day.

By 1945, the Allies could bomb at will. Concentrated attacks on industrial targets, especially communication centers and oil refineries, did extensive damage and helped shorten the war. Terror bombing continued, too, with no useful result. The bombardment of Dresden in February 1945 was especially savage and destructive. It was much debated within the British government and has raised moral questions since. Whatever else it accomplished, the aerial war over Germany took a heavy toll of the German air force and diverted German resources from other military purposes.

THE DEFEAT OF NAZI GERMANY

On June 6, 1944 ("D-Day"), American, British, and Canadian troops landed in force on the coast of Normandy. The "second front" was opened. General Dwight D. Eisenhower (1890–1969), the commander of the Allied armies, faced a difficult problem. The European coast was heavily fortified. Amphibious assaults, moreover, are especially vulnerable to wind and weather. Success depended on meticulous planning, heavy bombing, and feints to mask the point of attack. The German defense was strong, but the Allies established a beachhead and then broke out of it. In mid-August, the Allies also landed in southern France. By the beginning of September, France had been liberated.

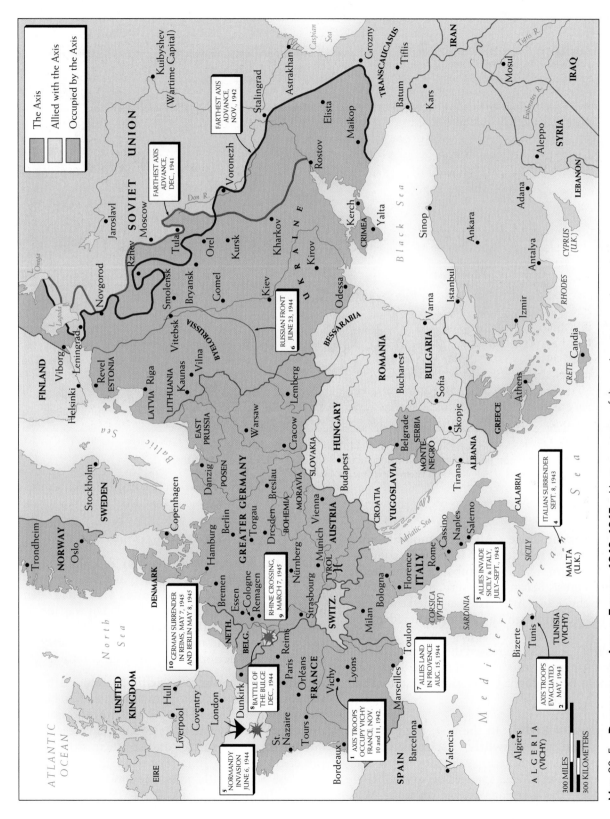

Map 28–5 DEFEAT OF THE AXIS IN EUROPE, 1942–1945 Here are some of the major steps in the progress toward Allied victory against Axis Europe. From the south through Italy, the west through France, and the east through Russia, the Allies gradually conquered the Continent to bring the war in Europe to a close.

The Axis
Allied with the Axis
Occupied by the Axis

FARTHEST AXIS ADVANCE, DEC, 1941

FARTHEST AXIS ADVANCE, NOV, 1942

RUSSIAN FRONT
JUNE 23, 1944
6

RHINE CROSSING,
MARCH 7, 1945
9

10 GERMAN SURRENDER
IN REIMS, MAY 7, 1945
AND BERLIN MAY 8, 1945

8 BATTLE OF
THE BULGE
DEC, 1944

5 NORMANDY
INVASION
JUNE 6, 1944

1 AXIS TROOPS
OCCUPY VICHY
FRANCE, NOV.
10 and 11, 1942.

7 ALLIES LAND
IN PROVENCE
AUG. 15, 1944

3 ALLIES INVADE
SICILY & ITALY,
JULY–SEPT., 1943

4 ITALIAN SURRENDER
SEPT. 8, 1943

2 AXIS TROOPS
EVACUATED,
MAY, 1943

300 MILES

300 KILOMETERS

957

Allied troops landed in Normandy on D-Day, June 6, 1944. This photograph, taken two days later, shows long lines of men and equipment moving inland from the beach to reinforce the troops leading the invasion.   Hulton Archive Photos/Getty Images, Inc.

The Battle of the Bulge   All went smoothly until December, when the Germans launched a counterattack in Belgium and Luxembourg through the Ardennes Forest. Because the Germans pushed forward into the Allied line, this was called the Battle of the Bulge. Although the Allies suffered heavy losses, the Bulge was the last gasp for the Germans in the West. The Allies crossed the Rhine in March 1945, and German resistance crumbled. This time there could be no doubt the Germans had lost the war on the battlefield.

The Capture of Berlin   In the east, the Russians swept forward no less swiftly, despite fierce German resistance. By March 1945, they were near Berlin. Because the Allies insisted on unconditional surrender, the Germans fought on until May. Hitler committed suicide in an underground bunker in Berlin on April 30, 1945. The Russians occupied Berlin by agreement with their Western allies. The Third Reich lasted only a dozen years instead of the thousand Hitler had predicted.

FALL OF THE JAPANESE EMPIRE

The war in Europe ended on May 8, 1945, and by then, victory over Japan was also in sight. The original Japanese attack on the United States had been a calculated risk against the odds. Japan was inherently weaker than the United States. The longer the war lasted, the more American superiority in industrial production and population counted.

Americans Recapture the Pacific Islands   In 1943, the American forces, still small in number, began a campaign of "island hopping." They did not try to recapture every Pacific island the Japanese held, but selected major bases and strategic sites along the enemy supply line. (See Map 28–6.) Starting from the Solomon Islands, they moved northeast toward Japan itself. By June 1944, they had reached the Mariana Islands, usable as bases to bomb the Japanese in the Philippines, China, and Japan itself.

In October of the same year, the Americans recaptured most of the Philippines and drove the

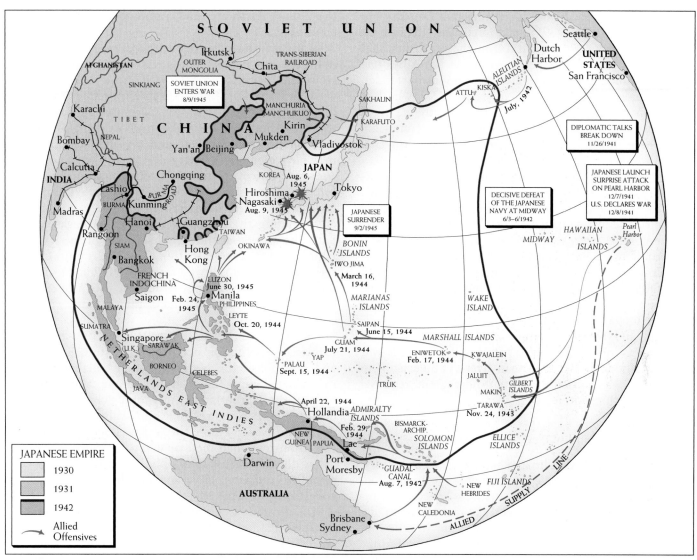

Map 28–6 **WORLD WAR II IN THE PACIFIC** As in Europe, the Pacific war involved Allied re-capture of areas that had been quickly taken earlier by the enemy. The enormous area represented by the map shows the initial expansion of Japanese holdings to cover half the Pacific and its islands, as well as huge sections of eastern Asia, and the long struggle to push the Japanese back to their homeland and defeat them by the summer of 1945.

Japanese fleet back into its home waters. In 1945, Iwo Jima and Okinawa fell, despite fierce Japanese resistance that included kamikaze attacks, suicide missions in which pilots deliberately flew their explosive-filled planes into American warships. From these new bases, closer to Japan, the Americans launched a terrible wave of bombings that destroyed Japanese industry and disabled the Japanese navy. Still the Japanese government, dominated by a military clique, refused to surrender.

Confronted with Japan's determination, the Americans made plans for a frontal assault on the Japanese homeland. They calculated it might cost a million American casualties and even greater losses for the Japanese. At this point, science and

technology presented the Americans with another choice.

The Atomic Bomb Since early in the war, a secret program had been in progress. Its staff, many of whom were exiles from Hitler's Europe, was working to use atomic energy for military purposes. On August 6, 1945, an American plane dropped an atomic bomb on the Japanese city of Hiroshima. The city was destroyed, and more than 70,000 of its 200,000 residents were killed. Two days later, the Soviet Union declared war on Japan and invaded Manchuria. The next day, a second atomic bomb hit Nagasaki. Even then, the Japanese cabinet was prepared to face an invasion rather than give up.

The unprecedented intervention of Emperor Hirohito (r. 1926–1989) finally forced the government to surrender on August 14 on the condition that Japan retain the emperor. Although the Allies had continued to insist on unconditional surrender, President Harry S. Truman (1884–1972), who had come to office on April 12, 1945, on the death of Franklin D. Roosevelt, accepted the condition. Peace was formally signed aboard the USS *Missouri* in Tokyo Bay on September 2, 1945.

Revulsion at the use of atomic bombs, as well as hindsight arising from the Cold War, have made the decision to use the bomb against Japanese cities controversial. Some have suggested the bombings were unnecessary to win the war and their main purpose was to frighten the Russians into a more cooperative attitude after the war. Others have emphasized the bureaucratic, almost automatic nature of the decision, once it had been decided to develop the bomb. To the decision makers and their contemporaries, however, matters were simpler. The bomb was a way to end the war swiftly and save American lives. The decision to use it was conscious, not automatic, and required no ulterior motive.

THE COST OF WAR

World War II was the most terrible war in history. Military deaths are estimated at some 15 million, and at least as many civilians were killed. If we include deaths linked indirectly to the war, from disease, hunger, and other causes, the number of victims might reach 40 million. Most of Europe and large parts of Asia were devastated. Yet the end of so terrible a war brought little opportunity to relax. The dawn of the atomic age made people conscious that another major war might extinguish humanity. Everything depended on concluding a stable peace, but even as the fighting ended, conflicts among the victors made the prospects of a lasting peace doubtful.

RACISM AND THE HOLOCAUST

The most horrible aspect of the Nazi rule in Europe arose not from military or economic necessity but from the inhumanity and brutality inherent in Hitler's racial doctrines. These were applied to several groups of people in Eastern Europe.

Hitler considered the Slavs *Untermenschen*, subhuman creatures like beasts who need not be treated as people. In parts of Poland, the upper and professional classes were entirely removed—jailed, deported, or killed. Schools and churches were closed. The Nazis limited marriage to keep down the Polish birthrate and imposed harsh living conditions.

In Russia, things were even worse. Hitler spoke of his Russian campaign as a war of extermination. Heinrich Himmler (1900–1945), head of Hitler's elite SS formations, planned to eliminate 30 million Slavs to make room for Germans; he formed extermination squads for this purpose. Six million Russian prisoners of war and deported civilians may have died under Nazi rule.

Hitler, however, had envisioned a special fate for the Jews. He meant to make all Europe *Judenrein*, or "free of Jews." For a time, he considered sending them to the island of Madagascar. Later, he arrived at the "final solution of the Jewish problem"—extermination. The Nazis built extermination camps in Germany and Poland and used the latest technology to achieve the most efficient means to kill millions of men, women, and children simply because they were Jews. (See "Mass Murder at Belsen, pages 962–963.) The most extensive destruction occurred in Eastern Europe and Russia, but the Nazis and their collaborators in occupied areas of western Europe, including France, the Netherlands, Italy, and Belgium, also deported Jews from these nations to almost certain death in the east. Before the war was over, perhaps 6 million Jews had died in what has come to be called the **Holocaust**. Only about a million European Jews remained alive, most of them in pitiable condition. (See Map 28–7.)

It is difficult to comprehend the massive Nazi effort to eradicate the Jews of Europe. This destruction took different forms in different regions of the Continent. To explore this central event of twentieth-century European history, we examine the fate of the Polish Jewish community, which before the Second World War was the largest in Europe, consisting of ten percent of Poland's population.

THE DESTRUCTION OF THE POLISH JEWISH COMMUNITY

A large Jewish community had dwelled within Poland for centuries, often in a climate of religious and cultural anti-Semitism. As a result of this anti-Semitism, Polish Jews had long lived in their own villages and later in their own urban neighborhoods. After the late-eighteenth-century partitions of Poland and the Congress of Vienna, most of Poland came under Russian rule. Through the policy of Official Nationalism (see Chapter 21), the nineteenth-century tsars identified loyalty to their government with membership in the Russian Orthodox Church. Other Christian groups, such as Lutherans and

Roman Catholics, were often treated with suspicion. Jews were treated worse and were subject to a wide variety of discriminatory legislation. Polish Jews did not experience any of the forms of Jewish emancipation that occurred in Western Europe. (See Chapter 24.)

Language, food, dress, and place of residence as well as religion distinguished Jews from the rest of the Polish population, almost all of whom were Roman Catholics. Hebrew was the Polish Jews' chief written language, and Yiddish their primary spoken language. Many Jews, particularly older ones, wore distinctive dress. They ate food different from that of most Poles. Many Polish Jews also moved to cities, and Jews were regarded as an urban people in a predominantly rural nation. Moreover, Jews were among the poorest people in Poland, often working as self-employed merchants, peddlers, and craftspeople, or in industries, such as textiles, clothing, and paper, that other Poles identified as Jewish-dominated. Few Polish Jews belonged to trade unions. These conditions made them vulnerable during the economic turmoil of the 1920s and especially of the 1930s.

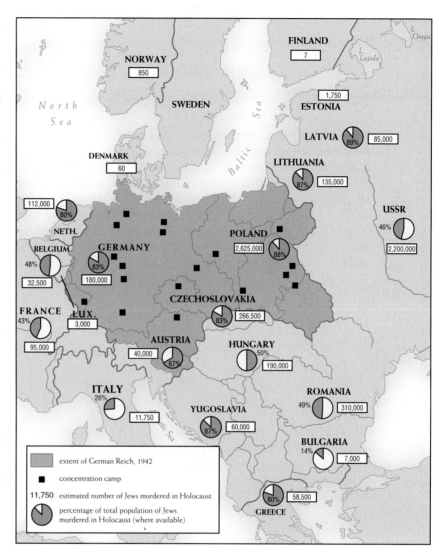

Map 28–7 **THE HOLOCAUST** The Nazi policy of ethnic cleansing—targeting Jews, Gypsies, political dissidents, and "social deviants"—began with imprisoning them in concentration camps, but by 1943 the *Endlösung*, or Final Solution, called for the systematic extermination of "undersirables."

POLISH ANTI-SEMITISM BETWEEN THE WARS

After the restoration of Poland following World War I, Polish leaders were divided about the role of Jews in Polish national life. Jozef Pilsudski (1867–1935), who dominated the interwar era, favored including Jews within the civic definition of the nation, and the constitution allowed Jews to participate in political life. After Pilsudski's death, political groups that equated citizenship with Polish ethnicity and embraced anti-Semitism came to the fore. Their ideology, no less than that of tsarist Russian Orthodoxy, defined Jews as outside the Polish nation.

No matter which political outlook dominated, discrimination against Jews existed throughout the culture and politics of interwar Poland. During

those years, the Polish government, supported by spokesmen for the Polish Roman Catholic Church, pursued policies that were anti-Semitic. The Polish government nationalized the matches, salt, tobacco, and alcohol industries and then enacted legislation that discriminated against hiring Jews for these government monopolies. Other laws made it difficult for Jews to observe the Sabbath while keeping their jobs. Regulations requiring businesses to be closed on Sunday meant Jewish shops had to close two days of the week. By the late 1930s, as ethnic nationalism became stronger, the government required businesses to display their owners' names prominently, which made it easy for people to avoid Jewish shops. Because Jews were excluded from the civil service, they moved into law and medicine, which provoked further resentment.

MASS MURDER AT BELSEN

Hitler's calculated plan to wipe out Europe's Jews, along with millions of other people he considered undesirable for racial and other reasons, was not widely known during the war. Care was taken to keep the mass murders secret. Even when news of them leaked out, many people were reluctant to believe what they heard, and participants in the crimes were naturally not eager to talk about them. Kurt Gerstein, a colonel in the SS, was part of the apparatus of extermination. However, unlike most people involved and at great risk to himself, he tried to tell the world what was taking place. The following is an account of what he saw at the death camp at Belsen in 1942.

■ *What were the reasons for Hitler's policy of exterminating millions of men, women and children? Why did many Germans take part in the process? Why did so conscientious a man as Colonel Gerstein not resist?*

A train arrived from Lemberg [Lvov]. There were forty-five cars containing 6,700 people, 1,450 of whom were already dead. Through the gratings on the windows, children could be seen peering out, terribly pale and frightened, their eyes filled with mortal dread . . . The train entered the station, and two hundred Ukrainians wrenched open the doors and drove the people out of the carriages with their leather whips. Instructions came through a large loudspeaker telling them to remove all their clothing, artificial limbs, glasses, etc. They were to hand over all objects of value at the counter . . . Shoes were to be carefully tied together, for otherwise no one would ever again have been able to find shoes belonging to each other in a pile that was a good eighty feet high. Then the women and girls were sent to the barber who, with two or three strokes of his scissors, cut off all their hair and dropped it into potato sacks. "That's for some special purpose or other on U-Boats, for packing or something like that," I was told by an SS-Unterscharfuhrer . . .

Then the column moved off. Headed by an extremely pretty young girl, they walked along the avenue, all naked, men, women, and children, with artificial limbs removed. I myself was stationed up on the ramp between the [gas] chambers with Captain Wirth.

Mothers with babies at their breasts came up, hesitated, and entered the chambers of death. At the corner stood a burly SS man with a priest-like voice. "Nothing at all is going to happen to you!" he told the poor wretches. "All you have to do when you get into the chambers is to

The path of assimilation into the larger culture that many European Jewish leaders had advocated during the nineteenth century hit a dead end in Poland because many Poles refused to regard even secular, assimilated Jews as fellow Poles. Nonetheless, many Jews attempted to embrace the social practices, dress, and language of the Polish majority without actually expecting to be considered Polish. They saw themselves as moving from a traditional style of life to a more modern and Polish one. Jewish newspapers and other magazines began to be published in Polish. Jews took advantage of their right to political participation, but they were divided into different factions and could not agree on how to defend Jewish life and culture in Poland. These divisions made the Jews of Poland more vulnerable when the Second World War broke out in 1939.

Whatever active anti-Semitism existed in Poland before the German invasion of 1939, it was the Nazis who tried to destroy the Polish Jewish community and Jewish communities elsewhere in Europe that fell under German control. In that respect, the Holocaust constitutes an event driven by German policy within the larger event of the Second World War.

breathe in deeply. That stretches the lungs. In-haling is necessary to prevent disease and epi-demics." When asked what would be done with them, he replied: "Well, of course, the men will have to work building houses and roads, but the women won't need to work. They can do house-work or help in the kitchen, but only if they want to." For some of these poor creatures, this was a small ray of hope that was enough to make them walk the few steps to the chambers with-out resistance. Most of them knew what was going on. The smell told them what their fate was to be. They went up the small flight of steps and saw everything. Mothers with their babies clasped to their breasts, small children, adults, men, women, all naked; they hesitated, but they entered the chambers of death, thrust forward by the others behind them or by the leather whips of the SS [Storm Troopers]. Most went in without a word . . . Many were saying prayers. I prayed with them. I pressed myself into a corner and cried aloud to my God and theirs. How gladly I should have gone into the chambers with them; how gladly I should have died with them. Then they would have found an SS officer in uniform in their gas chambers; they would have believed it was an accident and the story would have been buried and forgotten. But I could not do that yet. First, I had to make known what I had seen here. The chambers were filling up. Fill them up

well—that was Captain Wirth's order. The peo-ple were treading on each other's feet. There were 700–800 of them in an area of 270 square feet, in 1,590 cubic feet of space. The SS crushed them together as tightly as they possibly could. The doors closed. Meanwhile, the rest waited out in the open, all naked. "It's done exactly the same way in winter," I was told. "But they may catch their death!" I said. "That's what they're here for," an SS man said . . . The Diesel exhaust gases were intended to kill those unfortunates. But the engine was not working . . . The people in the gas chambers waited, in vain. I heard them weeping, sobbing . . . After 2 hours and 49 min-utes, measured by my stop watch, the Diesel started. Up to that moment, men and women had been shut up alive in those four chambers, four times 750 people in four times 1,590 cubic feet of space. Another twenty-five minutes dragged by. Many of those inside were already dead. They could be seen through the small win-dow when the electric light went on for a mo-ment and lit up the inside of the chamber. After twenty-eight minutes, few were left alive. At the end of thirty-two minutes, all were dead.

Pius XII and the Third Reich: A Documentation by Saul Friedlän-der. Copyright © 1966 by Alfred A. Knopf, Inc. Copyright © 1964 by Editions du Seuil. Originally published in French under the title Pie XII et le III Reich, Documents. Reprinted by permission of Georges Borchardt, Inc., for the author.

THE NAZI ASSAULT ON THE JEWS OF POLAND

The joint German-Soviet invasion of Poland brought millions of Jews under either German or Soviet authority. By conquering Poland, the Nazi government could carry out the destruction of Jew-ish communities to an extent far beyond anything possible in Germany itself. From the Nazi stand-point, the destruction of the Polish Jewish commu-nity held special importance. Polish Jewry was large and had produced many religious, cultural, and political leaders. It also constituted the single

most important source for Jewish emigration be-yond Eastern Europe. For the Nazis, Poland was the chief breeding ground for world Jewry.

By late autumn 1939, the Germans had begun to move against Polish Jews. The Nazi government first thought it might herd virtually all the Jews of occupied Europe into the Lublin region of Poland. By early 1940, the Nazis decided to move as many Jews as possible into ghettos, where they would be separated from the rest of the Polish population. The largest ghettos were Lodz and Warsaw, each of which had populations of several hundred thou-sand. The Nazis moved Jews from all over Poland

Roundup of Warsaw Jews. World War II resulted in the near-total destruction of the Jews of Europe, victims of the Holocaust spawned by Hitler's racial theories of the superiority and inferiority of particular ethnic groups. Hitler placed special emphasis on the need to exterminate the Jews, to whom he attributed particular wickedness. This picture shows a roundup of Jews in Warsaw, where there was a large Jewish population, ultimately on their way to concentration or death camps.   © Hulton-Deutsch Collection/CORBIS

and, eventually, other occupied regions by rail into these ghettos and then sealed them off with police guards and walls. Jewish councils, which were torn between responsibility to their communities and the need to respond to German orders, administered the ghettos. The Nazis confiscated and sold the personal property and businesses of the Jews who were herded into the ghettos. Jewish laborers were sent out to work as contract labor while their families remained in the ghettos. By 1941, the Polish Jews had lost their civic standing and property. They had been located in segregated communities within Poland where disease was rampant and the food supply meager. Approximately 20 percent of the population of both the Lodz and Warsaw ghettos died of disease and malnourishment.

The German invasion of the Soviet Union in June 1941 made the situation of Jews in Poland even worse. The advancing German forces killed tens of thousands of Jews in the Soviet Union during 1941 and hundreds of thousands more the next year. Bolsheviks and Jews became conflated in German thinking and propaganda. During the second half of 1941, the Nazi government decided to exterminate the Jews of Europe. From late 1941 through 1944, the Germans transported Jews from the ghettos by rail to death camps in Poland, including Kulmhof, Belzen, Sobibor, Treblinka,

Birkenau, and Auschwitz. One or more of the camps were in operation from 1941 to 1944, with Auschwitz being the last closed. In these camps, Jews were systematically killed in gas chambers.

By 1945, approximately 90 percent of the pre-1939 Jewish population of Poland had been destroyed. The tiny minority of Polish Jews who had survived faced bitter anti-Semitism under the postwar Soviet-dominated government. Many immigrated to Israel, leaving only a few thousand Jews within the borders of a nation where they had numbered in the millions and where they had created a rich religious, cultural, and political community. The largest Jewish community in Europe had virtually ceased to exist.

EXPLANATIONS OF THE HOLOCAUST

As interest in the Holocaust has grown since the 1960s, so has debate about its character and meaning. Was it a unique event of unprecedented and unparalleled evil, or was it one specific instance of a more general human wickedness that has found expression throughout history? Are its roots to be found in flaws in human nature as a whole, or are they unique to the experience of the West or, perhaps, to the German people? Some scholars point to the horrible mass murders committed in the twentieth century by communist regimes under Stalin in the Soviet Union and under Mao in China, each of which killed many more people than did Hitler, as evidence of the more general character of the phenomenon. Others argue that the Holocaust was unique because its goal was the annihilation of a whole people, from infants to the aged, just because of who they were. Some focus on the wickedness personified by Hitler, who was driven by his fixation on the myth of Jewish power and evil.

Perhaps we should think of the problem from the standpoint of two questions: Why were the Jews the main target of Hitler's policy of extermination? How was it possible to carry out such a vast mass murder? Surely, an essential part of an answer to the first question is the persistence of anti-Semitism in Christianity and Western culture, from the Church Fathers to Luther and to the teachings of churches in modern times. Some would combine this religious and historical anti-Semitism with the coming of the Enlightenment and the social sciences, which gave rise to pseudo-scientific racial theories that lent a new twist to the old hatred of the Jews. Pseudoscientific racism ap-

Auschwitz in Poland was the most notorious Nazi death camp. Railway lines led up to its gates, so that trains could unload boxcars of Jews into a future of almost certain death. Hulton Archive Photos/Getty Images, Inc.

pears to have been the most powerful influence on Hitler, but it could not have found widespread support without deeply rooted religious and social anti-Semitism.

For example, in at least one instance in Poland, Poles turned against their Jewish neighbors in outbursts of localized anti-Semitic violence. In July 1941, in the town of Jedwabne, in northeast Poland, non-Jewish Poles killed approximately 1,600 of their Jewish fellow townspeople. This horrendous incident suggests that although the Nazis carried out most of the atrocities against the Jews, a climate of either indifference or outright support existed in Poland as well as in other parts of Nazi-occupied Europe. Yet it must also be noted that between 1942 and 1945 the Council for Aid to Jews in Occupied Poland, known as ZEGOTA and sponsored by the Polish government in exile, protected and aided the escape of many thousands of Polish Jews.

As to how it was possible to murder six million people, part of the answer must lie in the parochial nationalism that arose during and after the French Revolution. For many people, nationalism divided the world into one's fellow nationals and all others. It encouraged, excused, and even justified terrible and violent acts performed on behalf of one's homeland. Another part of the answer may derive from the utopian visions also unleashed by some Enlightenment writers, who promised to achieve perfect societies through social engineering, regardless of the human cost. To this were added the scientific and technological advances that gave the modern state new power to command its people, to persuade them to obey by controlling the media of propaganda, and to enforce its will with efficient

MAJOR CAMPAIGNS AND EVENTS OF WORLD WAR II

September 1939	Germany and the Soviet Union invade Poland
November 1939	The Soviet Union invades Finland
April 1940	Germany invades Denmark and Norway
May 1940	Germany invades Belgium, the Netherlands, Luxembourg, and France
June 1940	Fall of France
August 1940	Battle of Britain begins
June 1941	Germany invades the Soviet Union
July 1941	Japan takes Indochina
December 1941	Japan attacks Pearl Harbor; United States enters war against Axis powers
June 1942	Battle of Midway Island
November 1942	Battle of Stalingrad begins
July-August 1943	Allies take Sicily, land in Italy
June 1944	Allies land in Normandy
May 1945	Germany surrenders
August 1945	Atomic bombs dropped on Hiroshima and Nagasaki
September 1945	Japan formally surrenders

brutality. All of these permitted the creation of a totalitarian state that, for the first time in history, could conduct mass murder on the scale of the Holocaust.

These questions and their possible answers are but suggestions meant to encourage further and deeper thought in what will surely be a continuing debate among scholars and the general public. World War II was unmatched in cruelty in modern times. When Stalin's armies conquered Poland and entered Germany, they raped, pillaged, and deported millions to the east. The British and American bombing of Germany killed thousands of civilians, and the atomic bombs dropped on Japan killed and maimed tens of thousands more. The bombings, however, were thought of as acts of war that would help defeat the enemy. Stalin's atrocities were not widely known in the West at the time or even today.

The victorious Western allies were shocked by what they saw when they came on the Nazi extermination camps and their pitiful survivors. Little wonder it was that they were convinced the effort to resist the Nazis and all the pain it had cost were well worth it.

THE DOMESTIC FRONTS

World War II represented an effort at total war by all the belligerents. Never in European or world history had so many men and women and such resources been devoted to military effort. One result was the carnage that occurred during the fighting. Another was an unprecedented organization of civilians on the home fronts. Each domestic effort and experience was different, but few escaped the impact of the conflict. Everywhere there were shortages, propaganda campaigns, and new political developments.

GERMANY: FROM APPARENT VICTORY TO DEFEAT

Hitler had expected to defeat all his enemies by rapid strokes, or *blitzkriegs*. Such campaigns would have required little change in Germany's society and economy. During the first two years of the war, in fact, Hitler demanded few sacrifices from the German people. Spending on domestic projects continued, and food was plentiful; the

Bombing of Cologne. The Allied campaign of aerial bombardment did terrible damage to German cities. This photograph shows the devastation it delivered to the city of Cologne on the Rhine. © Bettmann/CORBIS

967 CHAPTER 28 ■ WORLD WAR II 967

economy was not on a full wartime footing. Germany's failure to quickly overwhelm the Soviet Union changed everything. Food was no longer available from the east in needed quantities, Germany had to mobilize for total war, and the government demanded major sacrifices.

A great expansion of the army and of military production began in 1942. As minister for armaments and munitions, Albert Speer (1905–1981) directed the economy, and Germany met its military needs. The government sought the cooperation of major German businesses to increase wartime production. Between 1942 and late 1944, the output of military products tripled. As the war went on, more men were drafted from industry into the army, and military production suffered.

As the manufacture of armaments replaced the production of consumer goods, shortages of everyday products became serious. Prices and wages were controlled, but the standard of living of German workers fell. Food rationing began in April 1942, and shortages were severe until the Nazi government seized more food from occupied Europe. To preserve their own home front, the Nazis passed on the suffering to their defeated neighbors.

By 1943, labor shortages became severe. The Nazis required German teenagers and retired men to work in the factories, and many women joined them. To achieve total mobilization, the Germans closed retail businesses, raised the age of eligibility of women for compulsory service, shifted non-German domestic workers to wartime industry, moved artists and entertainers into military service, closed theaters, and reduced such basic public services as mail and railways. Finally, the Nazis compelled thousands of non-Germans do forced labor in Germany.

Hitler assigned women a special place in the war effort. The celebration of motherhood continued, with an emphasis on women who were the mothers of important military figures. Films portrayed ordinary women who became brave and patriotic during the war and remained faithful to their husbands who were at the front. Women were shown as mothers and wives who sent their sons and husbands off to war. The government pictured other wartime activities of women as the natural fulfillment of their maternal roles. As air-raid wardens, they protected their families; as factory workers in munitions plants, they aided their sons on the front lines. Women working on farms were providing for their soldier sons and husbands; as housewives, they were helping to win the war by conserving food. Finally, by their faithful chastity, German women were protecting racial purity. They were not to marry or to have sex with non-Germans. During the war domestic political propaganda went beyond what occurred in other countries. Hitler and other Germans genuinely believed that weak domestic support had led to Germany's defeat in World War I; they were determined not to let this happen again. Nazi propaganda blamed the outbreak of the war on the British and the Jews and its prolongation on Germany's opponents. It also stressed the power of Germany and the inferiority of its foes.

Propaganda minister Josef Goebbels (1897–1945) used both radio and films to boost the Nazi cause. Movies of the collapse of Poland, Belgium, Holland, and France showed German military might. Throughout the conquered territories, the Nazis used the same mass media to frighten inhabitants about the possible consequences of an Allied victory. Later in the war, Goebbels broadcast exaggerated claims of Nazi victories. As the German armies were checked on the battlefield, especially in Russia, propaganda became a substitute for victory. To stiffen German resolve, propaganda now aimed to frighten Germans about the consequences of defeat.

After May 1943, when the Allies began their major bombing offensive over Germany, the German people had much to fear. The bombing devastated one German city after another but did not undermine German morale. The bombing may even have increased German resistance by seeming to confirm the regime's propaganda about the ruthlessness of Germany's opponents.

World War II increased the power of the Nazi Party in Germany. Every area of the economy and society came under the direct influence or control of the party. The Nazis were determined that they, rather than the traditionally honored German officer corps, would profit from the new authority the war effort was giving to the central government. There was virtually no serious opposition to Hitler or his ministers. In July 1944, a group of army officers attempted to assassinate Hitler; the effort failed, and there was little popular support for this act.

The war brought great changes to Germany, but what transformed the country most was the experience of physical destruction, invasion, and occupation. Hitler and the Nazis had brought Germany to such a complete and disastrous defeat that only a new kind of state with new political structures could emerge.

FRANCE: DEFEAT, COLLABORATION, AND RESISTANCE

The terms of the 1940 armistice between France, under Pétain, and Germany, signed June 22, allowed the Germans to occupy more than half of France, including the Atlantic and English

A CLOSER LOOK

The Vichy Regime in France

After their surprisingly swift conquest of France in 1940, the Germans ruled one part of it directly from Paris, leaving the rest unoccupied until 1942, but firmly under the control of a collaborationist French government under Marshal Henri Philippe Pétain (1856–1951, see Map 28–3, page 951). This regime, based in the city of Vichy, pursued a reactionary policy, turning away from the democratic ways of the defeated Third Republic. The "Propaganda Centers of the National Revolution" published the poster below. "The National Revolution" was the name the Vichy regime gave to its program to remake France.

The house on the left, representing, the Third Republic, carries the name "France and Company," which implies that the Third Republic was run like a corrupt business firm. It tilts precariously on shaky supports: egoism, radicalism, capitalism, communism, Jewry, antimilitarism, parliament, and disorder. These, in turn, rest on what Vichy considered the Republic's basic flaws: laziness, demagogy, and internationalism instead of French patriotism.

The house on the right represents the Vichy government. Its name is "France," pure and simple. It sits, safe, strong, neat, and orderly, on solid columns: school, craftsmanship, the peasantry, and the military. These rest on equally firm bases: discipline, order, thrift, and courage. Underlying all are the three basic values—work, family, and fatherland—which Vichy made its national slogan to replace the liberty, equality, and fraternity that had been the motto of French republican regimes since the French Revolution.

Philippe Noyer, "Révolution nationale." Bibliothèque de Documentation International Contemporane.
© ARS-Artists Rights Society, New York

Channel coasts. To prevent the French from continuing the fight from North Africa, and even more to prevent them from turning their fleet over to Britain, Hitler left southern France unoccupied until November 1942. Marshal Pétain set up a dictatorial regime at the resort city of Vichy and collaborated with the Germans in hopes of preserving as much autonomy as possible.

Some of the collaborators believed the Germans were sure to win the war and wanted to be on the victorious side. A few sympathized with Nazi ideas and plans. Many conservatives regarded the French defeat as a judgment on what they saw as the corrupt, secularized, liberal Third Republic. Most of the French were not active collaborators but were demoralized by defeat and German power.

Many conservatives and extreme rightists saw in the Vichy government a way to reshape the French national character and to halt the decadence they associated with political and religious liberalism. The Roman Catholic clergy, which had lost power and influence under the Third Republic, gained status under Vichy. The church supported Pétain, and his government restored religious instruction in the state schools and increased financial support for Catholic schools. Vichy adopted the church's views on the importance of family and spiritual values. The government made divorce difficult and forbade it entirely during the first three years of marriage. The state encouraged and subsidized large families.

The Vichy regime also encouraged an intense, chauvinistic nationalism. It exploited prejudice against foreigners working in France and fostered resentment even against French men and women whom it regarded as not genuinely "French," especially French Jews. Anti-Semitism was not new in France, as the Dreyfus affair had demonstrated. Even before Germany undertook Hitler's "final solution" in 1942, the French had begun to remove Jews from positions of influence in government, education, and publishing. In 1941, the Germans began to intern Jews living in occupied France; soon they murdered individual Jews and imposed large fines collectively on the Jews of the occupied zone. In the spring of 1942, they began to deport Jews from France—ultimately more than 60,000—to the extermination camps of Eastern Europe. The Vichy government had no part in these decisions, but it made no protest, and its own anti-Semitic policies made the whole process easier to carry out.

Some French men and women, notably General Charles de Gaulle (1890–1969), fled to Britain after the defeat of France. There they organized the

French National Committee of Liberation, or "Free French." Until the end of 1942, the Vichy government controlled French North Africa and the navy, but the Free French began operating in Central Africa. From London, they broadcast hope and defiance to their compatriots in France. Serious internal resistance to the German occupiers and the Vichy government, however, began to develop only late in 1942. The Germans tried to force young people in occupied France to work in German factories; some of them joined the Resistance, but the number of all the resisters was small. Fear of German retaliation deterred many. Others disliked the violence that resistance to a powerful ruthless nation inevitably entailed. So long as it appeared the Germans would win the war, moreover, resistance seemed imprudent and futile. For these reasons, the organized Resistance never attracted less than five percent of the adult French population.

By early 1944, the tide of battle had shifted. The Allies seemed sure to win, and the Vichy government would clearly not survive; only then did a large-scale active movement of resistance assert itself. General de Gaulle spoke confidently for Free France from his base in London and urged the French people to resist their conquerors and the German lackeys in the Vichy government. Within France, Resistance groups joined forces to plan for a better day. From Algiers on August 9, 1944, the Committee of National Liberation declared the authority of Vichy illegitimate. French soldiers joined in the liberation of Paris and established a government for Free France. On October 21, 1945, France voted to end the Third Republic and adopted a new constitution as the basis of the Fourth Republic. The French people had experienced defeat, disgrace, deprivation, and suffering. Hostility and quarrels over who had done what during the occupation and under Vichy divided them for decades.

GREAT BRITAIN: ORGANIZATION FOR VICTORY

On May 22, 1940, the British Parliament gave the government emergency powers. Together with others already in effect, this measure allowed the government to institute compulsory military service, rationing, and economic controls.

To deal with the crisis, all British political parties joined in a national government under Winston Churchill. Churchill and the British war cabinet moved as quickly as possible to mobilize the nation. Perhaps the most pressing immediate need was to produce airplanes to fight the

Winston Churchill walks through the rubble-strewn streets of London after the city experienced a night of German bombing. Despite many casualties and widespread devastation, the German bombing of London did not break British morale or prevent the city from functioning. UPI/CORBIS/Bettmann

Germans in the Battle of Britain. Lord Beaverbrook (1879–1964), one of Britain's most important newspaper publishers, led this effort. The demand for more planes and other armaments inspired a campaign to reclaim scrap metal. Wrought-iron fences, kitchen pots and pans, and every conceivable metal object were collected for the war effort. This was only one successful example of the many ways the civilian population enthusiastically engaged in the struggle.

By the end of 1941, British production had already surpassed Germany's. To meet the heavy demands on the labor force, factory hours were extended, and many women joined the work force. Unemployment disappeared, and the working classes had more money to spend than they had enjoyed for many years. To avoid inflation caused by increased demand for an inadequate supply of con-

sumer goods, savings were encouraged, and taxes were raised to absorb the excess purchasing power.

The "blitz" air attacks in 1940–1941 were the most immediate and dramatic experience of the war for the British people. The German air raids killed thousands of people and left many others homeless. Once the bombing began, many families removed their children to the countryside. Ironically, the rescue effort improved the standard of living of many of the children, for the government paid for their food and medication. The government issued gas masks to thousands of city dwellers, who were frequently compelled to take shelter from the bombs in the London subways.

After the spring of 1941, Hitler needed most of his air force on the Russian front, but the bombing of Britain continued, killing more than 30,000 people by the end of the war. Terrible as it was, this toll was much smaller than the number of Germans Allied bombing killed. In England, as in Germany, however, the bombing may have made people more determined.

The British made many sacrifices. Transportation facilities were strained simply from carrying enough coal to heat homes and run factories. Food and clothing for civilians were scarce and strictly rationed. Every scrap of land was farmed, increasing the productive portion by almost four million acres. Gasoline was scarce, and private vehicles almost vanished.

The British established their own propaganda machine to influence the Continent. The British Broadcasting Company (BBC) sent programs to every country in Europe in the local language, to encourage resistance to the Nazis. At home, the government used the radio to unify the nation. Soldiers at the front heard the same programs their families did at home. The most famous program, second only to Churchill's speeches, was *It's That Man Again*, a humorous broadcast filled with imaginary figures that the entire nation came to treasure.

Strangely, for the broad mass of the population, the standard of living improved during the war. The general health of the nation also improved, for reasons that are still not clear. These improvements should not be exaggerated, but they did occur, and many connected them with the active involvement of the government in the economy and in the lives of the citizens. This wartime experience may have contributed to the Labour Party's victory in 1945; many feared a return to Conservative Party rule would also mean a return to the economic problems and unemployment of the 1930s.

THE SOVIET UNION: "THE GREAT PATRIOTIC WAR"

The war against Germany came as a great surprise to Stalin and the Soviet Union. The German attack violated the 1939 pact with Hitler and put the government of the Soviet Union on the defensive militarily and politically. It showed the failure of Stalin's foreign policy and the ineptness of his preparation for war. He claimed the pact had given the nation an extra year and a half to prepare for war, but this was clearly a lame and implausible excuse in light of the ease of Germany's early victories. Within days, German troops occupied much of the western Soviet Union. The communist government feared that Soviet citizens in the occupied zones—many of whom were not ethnic Russians—might welcome the Germans as liberators. The Stalinist regime had harshly oppressed these Soviet citizens.

No nation suffered more during World War II than the Soviet Union. Perhaps as many as 16 million people were killed, and vast numbers of Soviet troops were taken prisoner. Hundreds of cities and towns and well over half of the industrial and transportation facilities of the country were devastated. From 1942, thousands of Soviet prisoners worked in German factories as forced labor. The Germans also seized grain, mineral resources, and oil from the Soviet Union.

Stalin conducted the war as the virtual chief of the armed forces, and the State Committee for Defense provided strong central coordination. In the decade before the war, Stalin had already made the Soviet Union a highly centralized state; he had tried to manage the entire economy from Moscow through the five-year plans, the collectivization of agriculture, and the purges. The country was thus already on what amounted to a wartime footing long before the conflict erupted. When the war began, millions of citizens entered the army, but the army itself did not grow in influence at the expense of the state and the Communist Party—that is, of Stalin. He was suspicious of the generals, though he had presumably eliminated officers of doubtful loyalty in the purges of the late 1930s. As the war continued, however, the army gained more freedom of action, and eventually the generals were no longer subservient to party commissars. The power of Stalin and the nature of Soviet government and society, however, still sharply limited the army.

Soviet propaganda was different from that of other nations. Because the Soviet government distrusted the loyalty of its citizens, it confiscated radios to prevent the people from listening to German or British propaganda. In cities, the government broadcast to the people over loudspeakers in place of radios. During the war, Soviet propaganda emphasized Russian patriotism rather than traditional Marxist themes that stressed class conflict. The struggle against the Germans was called "The Great Patriotic War."

The regime republished great Russian novels of the past and printed more than half a million copies of Tolstoy's *War and Peace*, which was set during Napoleon's invasion of Russia, during the siege of Leningrad (Saint Petersburg). Authors wrote straightforward propaganda fostering hatred of the Germans. Serge Eisenstein (1898–1948), the great filmmaker (see Encountering the Past, Chapter 27), produced a vast epic entitled *Ivan the Terrible*, which glorified this brutal sixteenth-century tsar. Composers wrote music to evoke heroic emotions. The most important of these was Dimitri Shostakovich's (1906–1975) *Leningrad Symphony.*

The pressure of war led Stalin to make peace with the Russian Orthodox Church, and the Patriarch of Moscow urged resistance to the Germans. Stalin hoped this new policy would increase his support at home and in Eastern Europe, where the Orthodox Church predominated.

Within occupied portions of the western Soviet Union, an active resistance movement harassed the Germans. The swiftness of the German invasion had stranded thousands of Soviet troops behind German lines. Some escaped and carried on guerrilla warfare behind enemy lines. Stalin supported partisan forces in lands the enemy held for two reasons: He wanted to cause as much difficulty as possible for the Germans, and Soviet-sponsored resistance reminded the peasants that the Soviet government had not disappeared. Stalin feared the peasants' hatred of the communist government and collectivization might lead them to collaborate with the invaders. When the Soviet army moved westward, it incorporated the partisans into the regular army.

As its armies reclaimed the occupied areas and then moved across Eastern and Central Europe, the Soviet Union established itself as a world power second only to the United States. Stalin had entered the war a reluctant belligerent, but he emerged a major victor. In that respect, the war and the extraordinary patriotic effort and sacrifice it generated consolidated the power of Stalin and the party more effectively than the political and social policies of the previous decade.

PREPARATIONS FOR PEACE

The split between the Soviet Union and its wartime allies should cause no surprise. As the self-proclaimed center of world communism, the Soviet Union was openly dedicated to the overthrow of the capitalist nations. The Soviets muted this message, however, when the occasion demanded. On the other side, the Western allies were no less open about their hostility to communism and its chief purveyor, the Soviet Union. Although they had been friendly to the early stages of the 1917 Russian Revolution, they had intervened to try to overthrow the Bolshevik regime during the resulting civil war. The United States did not grant formal recognition to the USSR until 1933. The

Western powers' exclusion of the Soviets from the Munich conference and Stalin's pact with Hitler did nothing to improve relations between them during the war.

Nonetheless, the need to cooperate against a common enemy and strenuous propaganda efforts helped improve Western feeling toward the Soviet ally. Still, Stalin remained suspicious and critical of the Western war effort, and Churchill was determined to contain the Soviet advance into Europe. Roosevelt perhaps had been more hopeful that the Allies could continue to work together after the war, but even he was losing faith by 1945. Differences in historical development and ideology, as well as traditional conflicts over political power and influence, soon dashed hopes of a mutually satisfactory peace settlement and continued cooperation to uphold it.

THE ATLANTIC CHARTER

In August 1941, even before the Americans were at war, Roosevelt and Churchill met on a ship off Newfoundland and agreed to the Atlantic Charter. This broad set of principles in the spirit of Wilson's Fourteen Points provided a theoretical basis for the peace they sought. When Russia and the United States joined Britain in the war, the three powers entered a purely military alliance in January 1942, leaving all political questions aside. The first political conference was the meeting of foreign ministers in Moscow in October 1943. The ministers reaffirmed earlier agreements to fight on until the enemy surrendered unconditionally and to continue cooperating after the war in a united-nations organization.

TEHRAN: AGREEMENT ON A SECOND FRONT

The first meeting of the leaders of the "Big Three" (the USSR, Britain, and the United States) took place at Tehran, the capital of Iran, in 1943. Western promises to open a second front in France the next summer (1944) and Stalin's agreement to fight Japan when Germany was defeated created an atmosphere of goodwill in which to discuss a postwar settlement. Stalin wanted to retain what he had gained in his pact with Hitler and to dismember Germany. Roosevelt and Churchill were conciliatory but made no firm commitments.

The most important decision was the one that chose Europe's west coast as the main point of attack instead of the Mediterranean. That meant, in retrospect, that Soviet forces would occupy East-

NEGOTIATIONS AMONG THE ALLIES

August 1941	Churchill and Roosevelt meet off Newfoundland to sign Atlantic Charter
October 1943	American, British, and Soviet foreign ministers meet in Moscow
November 1943	Churchill, Roosevelt, and Stalin meet at Tehran
October 1944	Churchill meets with Stalin in Moscow
February 1945	Churchill, Roosevelt, and Stalin meet at Yalta
July 1945	Attlee, Stalin, and Truman meet at Potsdam

ern Europe and control its destiny. At Tehran in 1943, the Western allies did not foresee this clearly, for the Russians were still fighting deep within their own frontiers, and military considerations were paramount.

Churchill and Stalin   By 1944, the situation had changed. In August, Soviet armies were before Warsaw, which had revolted against the Germans in expectation of liberation, but the Russians halted and turned south into the Balkans, allowing the Germans to annihilate the Poles. The Russians gained control of Romania, Bulgaria, and Hungary, advances that centuries of expansionist tsars had only dreamed of achieving. Alarmed by these developments, Churchill went to Moscow and met with Stalin in October. They agreed to share power in the Balkans on the basis of Soviet predominance in Romania and Bulgaria, Western predominance in Greece, and equality of influence in Yugoslavia and Hungary. These agreements were not enforceable without American approval, and the Americans were hostile to such un-Wilsonian devices as "spheres of influence."

Germany   The three powers easily agreed on Germany—its disarmament, de-Nazification, and division into four zones of occupation by France and the Big Three. Churchill, however, began to balk at Stalin's demand for $20 billion in reparations as well as forced labor from all the zones, with Russia to get half of everything. These matters festered and caused dissension in the future.

Eastern Europe   The settlement of Eastern Europe was equally thorny. Everyone agreed the Soviet Union deserved to have friendly neighboring governments, but the West insisted they also be au-

tonomous and democratic. The Western leaders, particularly Churchill, were not eager to see Russia dominate Eastern Europe. They were also, especially Roosevelt, committed to democracy and self-determination.

Stalin, however, knew that independent, freely elected governments in Poland, Hungary, and Romania would not be friendly to Russia. He had already established a puppet government in Poland in competition with the Polish government-in-exile in London. Under pressure from the Western leaders, however, he agreed to include some Poles friendly to the West in it. He also signed a Declaration on Liberated Europe, promising self-determination and free democratic elections.

Stalin may have been eager to avoid conflict before the war with Germany was over. He was always afraid the Allies would make a separate peace with Germany and betray him, and he probably thought it worth endorsing some hollow principles as the price of continued harmony. In any case, he wasted little time violating these agreements.

YALTA

The next meeting of the Big Three was at Yalta in Crimea in February 1945. The Western armies had not yet crossed the Rhine, but the Soviet army was within a hundred miles of Berlin. (See Map 28–8, page 974.) The war with Japan continued, and no atomic explosion had yet taken place. Roosevelt, faced with a prospective invasion of Japan and heavy losses, was eager to bring the Russians into the Pacific war as soon as possible. As a true Wilsonian, he also suspected Churchill's determination to maintain the British Empire and Britain's colonial advantages. The Americans thought Churchill's plan to set up British spheres of influence in Europe would encourage the Russians to do the same and would lead to friction and war. To encourage Russian participation in the war against Japan, Roosevelt and Churchill made extensive concessions to Russia, ceding the Soviets Sakhalin and the Kurile Islands, and accommodating some of their desires in Korea and in Manchuria.

Again in the tradition of Wilson, Roosevelt emphasized a united-nations organization: "Through the United Nations, he hoped to achieve a self-enforcing peace settlement that would not require American troops, as well as an open world without spheres of influence in which American enterprise could work freely."[5] Soviet agreement on these points seemed worth concessions elsewhere.

[5]Robert O. Paxton, *Europe in the Twentieth Century* (New York: Harcourt Brace Jovanovich, 1975), p. 487.

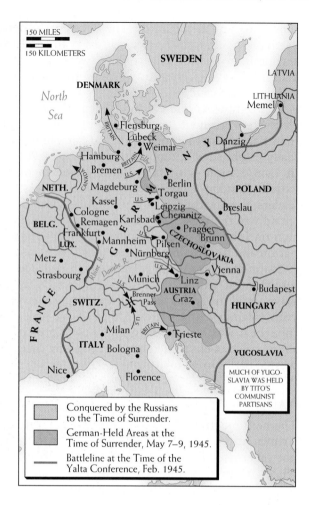

Map 28–8 YALTA TO THE SURRENDER "The Big Three"—Roosevelt, Churchill, and Stalin—met at Yalta in the Crimea in February 1945. At the meeting, concessions were made to Stalin concerning the settlement of eastern Europe because Roosevelt was eager to bring the Russians into the Pacific war as soon as possible. This map shows the positions held by the victors when Germany surrendered.

POTSDAM

The Big Three met for the last time in the Berlin suburb of Potsdam in July 1945. Much had changed since the previous conference. Germany had been defeated, and news of the successful explosion of an atomic weapon reached the American president during the meetings. The cast of characters was also different: President Truman replaced the deceased Roosevelt, and Clement Attlee (1883–1967), leader of the Labour Party that had just won a general election, replaced Churchill as Britain's spokesperson during the conference. Previous agreements were reaffirmed, but progress on undecided questions was slow.

Russia's western frontier was moved far into what had been Poland and included most of German East Prussia. In compensation, Poland was allowed "temporary administration" over the rest of East Prussia and Germany east of the Oder-Neisse River, a condition that became permanent. In effect, Poland was moved about a hundred miles west, at the expense of Germany, to accommodate the Soviet Union. The Allies agreed to divide Germany into occupation zones until the final peace treaty was signed. Germany remained divided until 1990.

A Council of Foreign Ministers was established to draft peace treaties for Germany's allies. Growing disagreements made the job difficult, and Italy, Romania, Hungary, Bulgaria, and Finland did not sign treaties until February 1947. The Russians were dissatisfied with the treaty that the United States made with Japan in 1951 and signed their own agreements with the Japanese in 1956. These disagreements were foreshadowed at Potsdam.

IN PERSPECTIVE

The second great war of the twentieth century (1939–1945) grew out of the unsatisfactory resolution of the first. In retrospect, the two wars appear to some people to be one continuous conflict, a kind of twentieth-century "Thirty Years' War," with two main periods of fighting separated by an uneasy truce. To others, that point of view over-

In February 1945 Churchill, Roosevelt and Stalin met at Yalta in the Crimea to plan for the organization of Europe after the end of the war. The Big Three are seated. Standing behind are Lord Leathers, Anthony Eden, Edward Stettinius, Alexander Cadogan, V. M. Molotov, and Averill Harriman.

simplifies by implying the second war was the inevitable result of the first and its inadequate peace treaties. The latter opinion seems more sound, for, whatever the flaws of the treaties of Paris, the world suffered an even more terrible war than the first because of failures of judgment and will by the victorious democratic powers.

Between the two wars, the United States, which had become the wealthiest and potentially the strongest nation in the world, disarmed almost entirely and withdrew into a shortsighted and foolish isolation. Therefore, it played no important part in restraining the angry and ambitious dictators who brought on the war. Britain and France refused to face the threat the Axis powers posed until the most deadly war in history was required to put it down. If the victorious democracies had remained strong, responsible, and realistic, they could have remedied whatever injustices or mistakes arose from the treaties without endangering the peace.

The second war itself was so plainly a world war that little need be said to indicate its global character. If the Japanese occupation of Manchuria in 1931 was not technically a part of that war, it was a significant precursor. Moreover, there were Italy's attack on the African nation of Ethiopia in 1935, the Italian, German, and Soviet interventions in the Spanish Civil War (1936–1939), and Japan's attack on China in 1937. These acts revealed that aggressive forces were on the march around the globe and the defenders of the world order lacked the will to stop them. The formation of the Axis incorporating Germany, Italy, and Japan guaranteed that when the war came, it would be fought around the world.

There was fighting and suffering in Asia, Africa, the Pacific islands, and Europe, and men and women from all the inhabited continents took part in it. The use of atomic weapons brought the frightful struggle to a close. Still, what are called conventional weapons did almost all the damage; their level of destructiveness threatened the survival of civilization, even without the use of atomic or nuclear devices.

The Second World War ended not with unsatisfactory peace treaties, but with no treaty at all in the European arena, where the war had begun. The world quickly split into two unfriendly camps: the western, led by the United States, and the eastern, led by the Soviet Union. This division, among other things, hastened the liberation of former colonial territories. The bargaining power of the new nations that emerged from them was temporarily increased as the two rival superpowers tried to gain their friendship or allegiance. It became customary to refer to these nations as "the Third World," or "developing countries," with the former Soviet Union and the United States and their respective allies being the first two. Time has shown that the differences among Third World nations are so great that the term is all but meaningless.

The surprising treatment the defeated powers of the Second World War received was also largely the result of the emergence of the Cold War. Instead of holding them back, the Western powers installed democratic governments in Italy, West Germany, and Japan, took them into the Western alliances designed to contain communism, and helped them recover economically. All three are now among the richest nations in the world.

REVIEW QUESTIONS

1. What were Hitler's foreign policy aims? Was he bent on conquest, or did he simply want to return Germany to its 1914 boundaries?

2. Why did Britain and France adopt a policy of appeasement in the 1930s? Did the West buy valuable time to rearm at Munich in 1938?

3. How was Hitler able to defeat France so easily in 1940? Why did the air war against Britain fail? Why did Hitler invade Russia? Could the invasion have succeeded?

4. Why did Japan attack the United States at Pearl Harbor? How important was American intervention in the war? Why did the United States drop atomic bombs on Japan? Was President Truman right to use the bombs?

5. How did experiences on the domestic front in Britain differ from those in Germany and France? What impact did "The Great Patriotic War" have on the people of the Soviet Union?

6. What was Hitler's "final solution" to the Jewish question? Why did he want to eliminate Slavs as well? To what extent can it be said the Holocaust was the defining event of the twentieth century?

SUGGESTED READINGS

O. BARTOV, *Mirrors of Destruction: War, Genocide, and Modern Identity* (2000). Remarkably penetrating essays.

A. BEEVOR, *The Spanish Civil War* (2001). Particularly strong on the political issues.

R. S. BOTWINICK, *A History of the Holocaust*, 2nd ed. (2002). A brief but useful account of the causes, character, and results of the Holocaust.

C. BROWNING, *The Origins of the Final Solution: The Evolution of the Nazi Jewish Policy* (2004). The story of how Hitler's policy developed from discrimination to annihilation.

W. S. CHURCHILL, *The Second World War*, 6 vols. (1948–1954). The memoirs of the great British leader.

A. CROZIER, *The Causes of the Second World War* (1997). An examination of what brought on the war.

J. C. FEST, *Hitler* (2002). Probably the best Hitler biography.

R. B. FRANK, *Downfall: The End of the Imperial Japanese Empire* (1998). A thorough, well-documented account of the last months of the Japanese Empire and why it surrendered.

J. L. GADDIS, *We Now Know: Rethinking Cold War History* (1998). A fine account of the early Cold War using new evidence emerging since the collapse of the Soviet Union.

J. L. GADDIS, P. H. GORDON, AND E. MAY (EDS.), *Cold War Statesmen Confront the Bomb: Nuclear Diplomacy since 1945* (1999). Essays on the effect of atomic and nuclear weapons on diplomacy since World War II.

M. GILBERT, *The Holocaust: A History of the Jews of Europe during the Second World War* (1985). The best and most comprehensive treatment.

M. HASTINGS, *The Second World War: A World in Flames* (2004). A fine account by a leading student of contemporary warfare.

A. IRIYE, *Pearl Harbor and the Coming of the Pacific War* (1999). Essays on how the Pacific war came about, including a selection of documents.

J. KEEGAN, *The Second World War* (1990). A lively and penetrating account by a master military historian.

W. F. KIMBALL, *Forged in War: Roosevelt, Churchill, and the Second World War* (1998). A study of the collaboration between the two great leaders of the West.

M. KNOX, *Common Destiny, Dictatorship, Foreign Policy, and War in Fascist Italy and Nazi Germany* (2000). A brilliant comparison between the two dictatorships.

M. KNOX, *Mussolini Unleashed* (1982). An outstanding study of fascist Italy in World War II.

S. MARKS, *The Illusion of Peace* (1976). A good discussion of European international relations in the 1920s and early 1930s.

W. MURRAY, *The Change in the European Balance of Power 1938–1939* (1984). A brilliant study of the relationship among strategy, foreign policy, economics, and domestic politics.

W. MURRAY AND A. R. MILLETT, *A War to Be Won: Fighting the Second World War* (2000). A splendid account of military operations.

P. NEVILLE, *Hitler and Appeasement: The British attempt to Prevent the Second World War* (2005). A defense of the British appeasers of Hitler.

R. OVERY, *Why the Allies Won* (1997). An analysis of the reasons for the Allied victory with emphasis on technology.

N. RICH, *Hitler's War Aims*, 2 vols. (1973–1974). The best study of the subject in English.

D. VITAL, *A People Apart: The Jews in Europe, 1789–1939* (1999). A major survey with excellent discussions of the interwar period.

R. WADE, *The Russian Revolution, 1917* (2000). A fine account that includes political and social history.

G. L. WEINBERG, *A World at Arms: A Global History of World War II* (1994). An excellent narrative.

DOCUMENTS CD-ROM

Society and Culture Between the Wars

27.3 A Room of One's Own

World War II

29.1 Adolf Hitler: *The Obersalzberg Speech*
29.2 Winston Churchill: *Their Finest Hour—House of Commons, 18 June 1940*
29.3 Franklin D. Roosevelt: *A Call for Sacrifice—28 April 1942*
29.4 NAZI SS Office
29.5 *The Buchenwald Report*
29.6 *Notes from the Warsaw Ghetto*

CHAPTER 29

THE COLD WAR ERA AND THE EMERGENCE OF A NEW EUROPE

KEY TOPICS

■ The origins of the Cold War and the division
of Europe into Eastern and Western blocs
following World War II

■ Major moments of Cold War tensions

■ Decolonization and the conflicts in Korea and
Vietnam

■ Polish protests against Soviet domination of
Eastern Europe

■ *Perestroika* and *glasnost* in the Soviet Union

■ The collapse of communism in Eastern
Europe and the Soviet Union

■ The civil war in Yugoslavia

■ The Rise of radical political Islamism

Since the end of World War II in 1945, two
often interrelated sets of fundamental, international political relationships have shaped
the experience of Europe, the United States, and
the wider global community. These were the **Cold
War** between the United States and the Soviet
Union and the long process of **decolonization**,
whereby the peoples of those regions of the world
formally or informally dominated by European

On September 11, 2001, a terrorist attack targeted the World Trade Center in New York City. In this photograph the first of the twin towers is in flames as the second plane heads directly toward the second tower. In a very brief time both towers collapsed with the loss of nearly 3,000 lives.   Masatomo Kuriya/CORBIS/Bettmann

nations and later by the United States have rejected that domination.

From the end of World War II in 1945 until the collapse of communist regimes in Eastern Europe between 1989 and 1991, the Soviet Union and the United States—two nuclear-armed superpowers—confronted each other in a simmering conflict known as the **Cold War**. While it lasted, this conflict dominated global politics and threatened the peace of Europe, which stood divided between the U.S.-dominated North Atlantic Treaty Organization (NATO) and the Soviet-dominated Warsaw Pact.

Decolonization very rapidly became enmeshed with the Cold War. As the nations of Europe retreated from empire, the rivalry between the two superpowers expanded into a contest for dominance in the postcolonial world. Superpower intervention aggravated local conflicts on every continent. In its efforts to limit communism, the United States became embroiled in bitter wars in Korea and Vietnam. The struggle between Israel and the Arab nations likewise became an arena of super-power conflict.

In the decade and a half since the collapse of the Soviet Union, the United States has remained the world's single superpower. It has become symbolically identified as embodying the political, economic, and cultural values of modern Western Civilization. In this role, it has replaced Europe as the object of anti-Western resistance. One of the numerous results of this new situation is the clash between the United States and radical political Islamism. The result has been the terrorist attacks on the United States on September 11, 2001, and the subsequent American intervention in Afghanistan and Iraq.

One way to think of the past sixty years is to see the history of Western Civilization as entering a new global era. Europe and later the United States had been active across the world scene since the end of the fifteenth century. Europe had created formal and informal regions of empire by the early twentieth century. However, commencing strongly in the 1930s and continuing to the present day, those once colonially dominated areas of the world have actively impacted upon the international relations and domestic politics of many European nations and of the United States rather than remaining regions largely subject to Western economic, political, and military influence. The give and take of political, economic, military, and cultural power has become far more reciprocal between the West and the rest of the global community. ■

THE EMERGENCE OF THE COLD WAR

The tense relationship between the United States and the Soviet Union began in the closing months of World War II. Some scholars attribute the hardening of the atmosphere between the two countries to Harry Truman's assumption of the presidency in April 1945, after the death of the more sympathetic Franklin Roosevelt, and to the American possession of an effective atomic bomb. Evidence suggests, however, that Truman was trying to carry Roosevelt's policies forward and that Soviet actions in Eastern Europe had begun to distress Roosevelt himself. Some have also argued that Truman did not use the atomic bomb to try to keep Russia out of the Pacific. On the contrary, he worked hard to ensure Russian intervention against Japan in 1945. In part, the coldness between the Allies arose from the mutual feeling that each had violated previous agreements. The Russians were plainly asserting permanent control of Poland and Romania under puppet communist governments. The United States was taking a harder line about German reparation payments to the Soviet Union.

In retrospect, however, and as more information emerges from the previously closed Soviet archives, it appears unlikely that friendlier styles on either side could have avoided a split that arose from basic differences of ideology and interest. The Soviet Union's attempt to extend its control westward into central Europe and the Balkans and southward into the Middle East continued the general thrust of the foreign policy of tsarist Russia. Britain had traditionally tried to restrain Russian expansion into these areas, and the United States inherited that task as Britain's power waned.

The Americans made no attempt to roll back Soviet power where it existed at the close of World War II. (See Map 29–1.) At the time, American military forces were the greatest in U.S. history, American industrial power was unmatched in the world, and atomic weapons were an American monopoly. In less than a year from the war's end, the Americans had reduced their forces in Europe from 3.5 million to 500,000. The speed of the withdrawal reflected domestic pressure to "get the boys home," but was also fully in accord with America's peacetime plans and goals, which included support for self-determination, autonomy, and democracy in the political sphere, and free trade, freedom of the seas, no barriers to investment, and an Open Door policy in the economic sphere. These goals reflected American principles and served American interests well. As the strongest, richest nation in the world—the one with the greatest industrial base and the strongest currency—the United States would benefit handsomely from an international order based on such goals.

Although postwar American hostility to colonial empires created tensions with France and Britain, the main conflict lay with the Soviet Union. The growth in France and Italy of large popular communist parties taking orders from Moscow led the Americans to believe that Stalin

to their security and their legitimate aims. They considered American objections to Soviet actions in Poland and other states as an effort to undermine regimes friendly to Russia and to encircle the Soviet Union with hostile neighbors. The Soviets could also use this point of view to justify their own attempts to overthrow regimes friendly to the United States in Western Europe and elsewhere.

Evidence of the new mood of postwar hostility between the former allies was soon apparent. In February 1946, both Stalin and his foreign minister, Vyacheslav Molotov (1890–1986), publicly spoke of the Western democracies as enemies. A month later, Churchill gave a speech in Fulton, Missouri, in which he declared that an "Iron Curtain" had descended on Europe, dividing a free and democratic West from an East under totalitarian rule. He warned against communist subversion and urged Western unity and strength against the new menace. In this atmosphere, difficulties grew.

CONTAINMENT IN AMERICAN FOREIGN POLICY

The resistance of Americans and Western Europeans to what they increasingly perceived as Soviet intransigence and communist plans for subversion and expansion took a clearer form in 1947. The American policy became known as one of **containment**, the purpose of which was to resist the extension of Soviet expansion and influence in the expectation that eventually the Soviet Union would collapse from internal pressures and the burdens of its foreign oppression. This strategy, which American policymakers devised in the late 1940s, would direct the broad outlines of American foreign policy for the next four decades, until the Soviet Union did collapse from exactly such pressures. Containment marked a major departure in American foreign policy and transformed the international situation during the second half of the twentieth century. The execution of the policy led the United States to enter overseas alliances, to make formal and informal commitments of support to regimes around the world it perceived as being anticommunist, to undertake enormous military expenditures, and to send large amounts of money abroad. In all these respects, the United States assumed unprecedented long-term foreign policy responsibilities. The United States thus became a permanent player in European international relations and in areas of the world where only European nations had been involved earlier in the century.

The Truman Doctrine Since 1944, civil war had been raging in Greece between the royalist government restored by Britain and insurgents supported

Map 29–1 **TERRITORIAL CHANGES IN EUROPE AFTER WORLD WAR II** The map shows the shifts in territory that followed the defeat of the Axis. No treaty of peace formally ended the war with Germany.

was engaged in a worldwide plot to subvert capitalism and democracy. From the Soviet perspective, extending the borders of the USSR and dominating the formerly independent successor states of Eastern Europe would provide needed security and compensate for the fearful losses the Soviet people had endured in the war. The Soviets could thus see American resistance to their expansion as a threat

by the communist countries, chiefly Yugoslavia. In 1947, Britain informed the United States it could no longer financially support its Greek allies. On March 12, President Truman asked Congress to provide funds to support Greece and Turkey, which was then under Soviet pressure to yield control of the Dardanelles, and Congress complied. In a speech to Congress that gave these actions much broader significance, the president set forth what came to be called the Truman Doctrine. He advo-

cated a policy of support for "free people who are resisting attempted subjugation by armed minorities or by outside pressures," by implication, anywhere in the world. (See "The Truman Doctrine Declared.")

The Marshall Plan   American aid to Greece and Turkey took the form of military equipment and advisers. For Western Europe, where postwar poverty and hunger fueled the menacing growth of

THE TRUMAN DOCTRINE DECLARED

In 1947, Britain informed the United States it could no longer support the Greeks in their fight against a communist insurrection. On March 12 of that year, President Truman asked Congress for legislation to support Greece and Turkey, which was also under Soviet pressure. The principle behind that request, which became known as the Truman Doctrine, appears in the selections that follow from Truman's speech to Congress.

■ *How does Truman relate the goals of the Second World War to the emerging Cold War with the Soviet Union? What qualities does Truman associate with free governments, and how were these qualities absent in the Soviet Union and its satellites in Eastern Europe? How does this speech establish guidelines that the United States might apply in parts of the world beyond Greece?*

One of the primary objectives of the foreign policy of the United States is the creation of conditions in which we and other nations will be able to work out a way of life free from coercion. This was a fundamental issue in the war with Germany and Japan. Our victory was won over countries which sought to impose their will, and their way of life, upon other nations.

To insure the peaceful development of nations, free from coercion, the United States has taken a leading part in establishing the United Nations. The United Nations is designed to make possible lasting freedom and independence for all its members. We shall not realize our objectives, however, unless we are willing to help free peoples to maintain their free institutions and their national integrity against aggressive movements that seek to impose upon them totalitarian regimes. . . .

At the present moment in world history, nearly every nation must choose between alternative ways of life. The choice is too often not a free one.

One way of life is based upon the will of the majority, and is distinguished by free institutions, representative government, free elections, guarantees of individual liberty, freedom of speech and religion, and freedom from political oppression.

The second way of life is based upon the will of a minority forcibly imposed upon the majority. It relies upon terror and oppression, a controlled press and radio, fixed elections, and the suppression of personal freedoms.

I believe that it must be the policy of the United States to support free peoples who are resisting attempted subjugation by armed minorities or by outside pressures.

I believe that we must assist free peoples to work out their own destinies in their own way.

I believe that our help should be primarily through economic and financial aid, which is essential to economic stability and orderly political processes.

From Senate Committee on Foreign Relations, *A Decade of American Foreign Policy: Basic Documents, 1941–1949* (1950), pp. 1235–1237.

communist parties, the Americans devised the European Recovery Program. Named the **Marshall Plan** after George C. Marshall (1880–1959), the secretary of state who introduced it, this program provided broad economic aid to European states on the sole condition that they work together for their mutual benefit. The Soviet Union and its satellites were invited to participate. Finland and Czechoslovakia were willing to do so, and Poland and Hungary showed interest. The Soviets, however, forbade them to take part.

The Marshall Plan restored prosperity to Western Europe and set the stage for Europe's unprecedented postwar economic growth. In addition to the vast program of American economic aid, the strong Christian Democratic movement that dominated the politics of Italy, France, and West Germany worked to keep communist influence at bay outside the Soviet sphere in Eastern Europe.

SOVIET DOMINATION OF EASTERN EUROPE

The Soviet determination to control Eastern Europe had both historical and ideological roots. Western European powers had invaded Russia

President Harry Truman greets Secretary of State George Marshall returning from Europe. Truman and Marshall were the architects of American foreign policy during the early years of the Cold War.   Hulton Archive Photos/Getty Images, Inc.

MAJOR DATES OF EARLY COLD WAR YEARS

1945	Yalta Conference
1945	Founding of the United Nations
1946	Churchill's Iron Curtain speech
1947	(March) Truman Doctrine regarding Greece and Turkey
1947	(June) Announcement of Marshall Plan
1948	Communist takeover in Czechoslovakia
1948	Communist takeover in Hungary
1948–1949	Berlin blockade
1949	NATO founded
1949	East and West Germany emerge as separate states
1950–1953	Korean conflict
1955	Warsaw Pact founded

---

twice in the nineteenth century (under Napoleon in 1812 and during the Crimean War of 1854–1856) and already twice more in the twentieth century. Tsarist Russia had governed most of Poland from the 1790s to 1915 and had intervened at the request of the Austrian Empire to put down the Hungarian revolution in 1849. Russia's interests in Turkey and the lands around the Black Sea were similarly long-standing. Given this history and the Soviet Union's extraordinary losses in World War II, it is not surprising that Soviet leaders sought to use their Eastern European satellites as a buffer against future invasions.

Stalin may have seen containment as a renewed Western attempt to isolate and encircle the USSR. In Eastern Europe, the Soviet Union found numerous supporters among those segments of the population who had opposed the various right-wing movements in those countries before the war and who had fought the Nazis during the war. In the autumn of 1947, Stalin called a meeting in Warsaw of all communist parties from around the globe. There they organized the Communist Information Bureau (Cominform), a revival of the old Comintern, dedicated to spreading revolutionary communism throughout the world. In Western Europe the establishment of the Cominform officially ended the era of the popular front during which communists had cooperated with noncommunist parties. Hard-liners who supported the Soviet line on every issue replaced communist leaders in the West who favored collaboration and reform.

THE CHURCH AND THE COMMUNIST PARTY CLASH OVER EDUCATION IN HUNGARY

—*m*—

Throughout Eastern Europe, the Roman Catholic church became one of the strongest opponents of the postwar Communist Party governments. It raised issues relating to church schools, free worship, participation in church-sponsored organizations, and the erection of new church buildings. One of the harshest clashes between the church and communism took place in Hungary. Following are two statements that illustrate the opposing positions of the church and the party. Cardinal Josef Mindszenty (1892–1975), the head of the Roman Catholic church in Hungary, was later imprisoned and became one of the best known political prisoners in Eastern Europe.

■ *How does Mindszenty relate the position of church-supported schools to the nature and rights of parenthood? How does he compare the actions of the Communist Party to those of Hitler? How does the Minister of Public Worship set party members against the church? How does he attempt to place loyalty to the party above private beliefs? What does the Communist Party fear from religious education and participation in religious activities by its members or their children?*

STATEMENT OF CARDINAL JOSEF MINDSZENTY, MAY 20, 1946

The right of the Church to schools is entirely in concord with the right of parents to educate their children. What is incumbent upon the parents in all questions of natural life is incumbent upon the Church with regard to the supernatural life. Parents are prior to the state, and their rights were always and still are, acknowledged by the Church. The prerogative of parents to educate their children cannot be disputed by the state, since it is the parents who give life to the child. They feed the child and clothe it. The child's life is, as it were, the continuation of theirs. Hence it is their right to demand that their children are educated according to their faith and their religious outlook.

It is their right to withhold their children from schools where their religious convictions are not only disregarded but even made the object of contempt and ridicule. It was this

In February 1948, in Prague, Stalin gave a brutal display of his new policy of bringing the governments of Eastern Europe under direct Soviet control. The communists expelled the democratic members of what had been a coalition government and murdered Jan Masaryk (1886–1948), the foreign minister and son of the founder of Czechoslovakia, Thomas Masaryk. President Edvard Beneš (1884–1948) was forced to resign, and Czechoslovakia was brought fully under Soviet rule. There and elsewhere in Eastern Europe, it was clear there would be no multiparty political system.

During the late 1940s, the Soviet Union required the other subject governments in Eastern Europe to impose Stalinist policies, including one-party political systems, close military cooperation with the Soviet Union, the collectivization of agriculture, Communist Party domination of educa-

tion, and attacks on the churches. (See "The Church and the Communist Party Clash over Education in Hungary.") Longtime Communist Party officials were purged and condemned in show trials like those that had taken place in Moscow during the late 1930s. The catalyst for this harsh tightening probably was the success of Marshal Josip (Broz) Tito (1892–1980), the leader of communist Yugoslavia, in freeing his country from Soviet domination. Stalin wanted to prevent other Eastern European states from following the Yugoslav example.

THE POSTWAR DIVISION OF GERMANY

Soviet actions, especially those in Czechoslovakia, increased the determination of the United States to go ahead with its own arrangements in Germany.

parental right which German parents felt was violated when the Hitler government deprived them of their denominational schools. The children came home from the new schools like little heathens, who smiled derisively or laughed at the prayers of their parents.

You Hungarian parents will likewise feel a violation of your fundamental rights if your children can no longer attend the Catholic schools solely because the dictatorial State closes down our schools by a brutal edict or renders their work impossible.

STATEMENT OF THE HUNGARIAN COMMUNIST MINISTER OF PUBLIC WORSHIP, JUNE 7, 1950

We must start a vast work of enlightenment, and in the first place explain to our party colleagues and also to all workers that any father who sends his child to religion classes places it in the hands of the enemy and entrusts his soul and thinking to the enemies of peace and imperialistic warmongers.

A part of our working people believes that participation of children in religious instruction is a private matter which has nothing to do with the political conviction of their parents. They are wrong. To send children to a reactionary pastor for religious instruction is a political movement against the People's Democracy, whether intentional or not. . . .

In carrying out the basic principles, religion within the party is no private matter, but we must make a difference between plain party members and party officials, and must not in any case make party membership dependent on the fact whether our party members are religious. In the first place, we must expect from our party officials, our leading men, that they do not send their children to religious instruction courses, do not take part in religious ceremonies and train their wives in the spirit of communistic conception.

Also, we must patiently endeavor to enlighten our members, and ensure through training and propaganda that they realize: "In going to Church, taking part in processions, sending our children to religious instruction, we unconsciously further the efforts of clerical reaction."

"The Church and the Communist Party Clash over Education in Hungary" from Colman J. Barry, ed., *Readings in Church History*, pp. 496–498. Copyright © 1965. Reprinted by permission of Ave Maria Press, Notre Dame, IN.

Disagreements over Germany   During the war, the Allies had never decided how to treat Germany after its defeat. At first they all agreed it should be dismembered, but they differed on how. By the time of Yalta, Churchill had come to fear Russian control of Eastern and central Europe and began to oppose dismemberment.

The Allies also differed on economic policy. The Russians swiftly dismantled German industry in the eastern zone, but the Americans acted differently in the western zone. They concluded that if they followed the Soviet policy, the United States would have to support Germany economically for the foreseeable future. It would also cause chaos and open the way for communism. They preferred, therefore, to try to make Germany self-sufficient, and this meant restoring, rather than destroying, its industrial capacity. To the Soviets, the restoration of a powerful industrial Germany, even in the western zone only, was frightening. The same difference of approach hampered agreement on reparations. The Soviets claimed the right to the industrial equipment in all the zones, and the Americans resisted their demands.

Berlin Blockade   When the Western powers agreed to go forward with a separate constitution for the western sectors of Germany in February 1948, the Soviets walked out of the joint Allied Control Commission. In the summer of that year, the Western powers issued a new currency in their zone. All four powers governed Berlin, though it was well within the Soviet zone. The Soviets feared the new currency, which was circulating in Berlin at better rates than their own currency. They chose to seal the city off by closing all railroads and

The Allied airlift in action during the Berlin Blockade. Every day for almost a year Western planes supplied the city until Stalin lifted the blockade in May 1949.

Art Resource/Bildarchiv Preussischer Kulturbesitz

highways that led from Berlin to West Germany. Their purpose was to drive the Western powers out of Berlin.

The Western allies responded to the Berlin blockade by airlifting supplies to the city for almost a year. In May 1949, the Russians were forced to reopen access to Berlin. The incident, however, was decisive. It increased tensions and suspicions between the opponents and hastened the separation of Germany into two states. West Germany formally became the German Federal Republic in September 1949, and the eastern region became the German Democratic Republic a month later. Ironically, Germany had been dismembered in a way no one had planned or expected. The two Germanys and the divided city of Berlin, isolated within East Germany, would remain central fixtures in the geopolitics of the Cold War until 1989. (See Map 29–2.)

NATO AND THE WARSAW PACT

Meanwhile, the nations of Western Europe had been drawing closer together. The Marshall Plan encouraged international cooperation. In March 1948, Belgium, the Netherlands, Luxembourg,

France, and Britain signed the Treaty of Brussels, providing for cooperation in economic and military matters. In April 1949, these nations joined with Italy, Denmark, Norway, Portugal, and Iceland to sign a treaty with Canada and the United States that formed the North Atlantic Treaty Organization (NATO), which committed its members to mutual assistance if any of them was attacked. The NATO treaty transformed the West into a bloc. A few years later, West Germany, Greece, and Turkey joined the alliance. For the first time in history, the United States was committed to defend allies outside the Western Hemisphere.

A series of bilateral treaties providing for close ties and mutual assistance in case of attack governed Soviet relations with the states of Eastern Europe. In 1949, these states formed the Council of Mutual Assistance (COMECON) to integrate their economies. Unlike the NATO states, the Soviets directly dominated the Eastern alliance system through local communist parties controlled from Moscow and the presence of the Red Army. The Warsaw Pact of May 1955, which included Albania, Bulgaria, Czechoslovakia, East Germany, Hungary, Poland, Romania, and the Soviet Union, gave formal recognition to this system. Europe was divided into two unfriendly blocs. The Cold War

Map 29–2 **OCCUPIED GERMANY AND AUSTRIA**   At the war's end, defeated Germany, including Austria, was occupied by the victorious Allies in the several zones shown here. Austria, by prompt agreement, was reestablished as an independent, neutral state, no longer occupied. The German zones hardened into an "East" Germany (the former Soviet zone) and a "West" Germany (the former British, French, and American zones). Berlin, within the Soviet zone, was similarly divided.

had taken firm shape in Europe. (See Map 29–3.) The strategic interests of the United States and the Soviet Union would not, however, permit the Cold War to be limited to the European continent. Major flash points would erupt around the world during the decades that followed, particularly in the Middle East and Asia. The establishment of a communist government in Cuba after 1959 would bring the conflict to the American hemisphere as well. In each case, the Cold War rivalry transformed what might otherwise have been regional conflicts into superpower strategic concerns.

THE CREATION OF THE STATE OF ISRAEL

One of the areas of ongoing regional conflict that became a major point of Cold War rivalry was the Middle East. Following World War I, Great Britain had exercised the chief political influence in the region under various mandates from the League of Nations. After World War II, both the Zionist movement, which sought to establish an independent Jewish state, and Arab nationalists, who sought to achieve self-determination, challenged British authority and influence.

British Balfour Declaration   The modern state of Israel was the achievement of the world Zionist movement, founded in 1897 by Theodor Herzl (see Chapter 24) and later led by Chaim Weizmann (1874–1952). In 1917, during World War I, Arthur Balfour (1846–1930), the British Foreign Secretary, declared that Britain favored establishing a national home for the Jewish people in Palestine, which was then under Ottoman rule. Between the wars, thousands of Jews, mainly from Europe, immigrated to what had become British-ruled Palestine. During this period, the *Yishuv*, or Jewish community in Palestine, developed its own political parties, press, labor unions, and educational system. Arabs already living in Palestine considered the Jewish settlers intruders, and violent conflicts ensued. The British tried, but failed, to mediate these clashes.

This situation might have prevailed longer, except for the outbreak of World War II and Hitler's

Map 29–3   **MAJOR COLD WAR EUROPEAN ALLIANCE SYSTEMS**   The North Atlantic Treaty Organization, which includes both Canada and the United States, stretches as far east as Turkey. By contrast, the Warsaw Pact nations were the contiguous Communist states of Eastern Europe, with the Soviet Union, of course, as the dominant member.

attempt to exterminate the Jews of Europe. The Nazi persecution united Jews throughout the world behind the Zionist ideal of a Jewish state in Palestine, and it touched the conscience of the United States and other Western powers. It seemed morally right to do something for the Jewish refugees from Nazi concentration camps.

The U.N. Resolution   In 1947, the British turned over to the United Nations the problem of the relationship of Arabs and Jews in Palestine. That same year, the United Nations passed a resolution dividing the territory into two states, one Jewish and one Arab. The Arabs in Palestine and the surrounding Arab states resisted this resolution. Not unnaturally, they resented the influx of new settlers. Many Palestinian Arabs were displaced and became refugees themselves.

Israel Declares Independence   In May 1948, the British officially withdrew from Palestine, and the Yishuv declared the independence of a new Jewish state called *Israel* on May 14. Two days later, the United States, through the personal intervention of President Truman, recognized the new nation, whose first prime minister was David Ben-Gurion (1886–1973). Almost immediately, Lebanon, Syria, Jordan, Egypt, and Iraq invaded Israel. The fighting continued throughout 1948 and 1949. By the end of its war of independence against the Arabs, Israel had expanded its borders beyond the limits the United Nations had originally set forth. Jerusalem was divided between Jordan and Israel. By 1949, Israel had secured its existence, but not the acceptance of its Arab neighbors. So long as Egypt, Jordan, Syria, Lebanon, Iraq, and Saudi Arabia, to name those nations closest, withheld diplomatic recognition from Israel, the peace was only an armed truce. (See Map 29–4.)

The Arab-Israeli conflict would inevitably draw in the superpowers. The dispute directly involved Europe because many of the citizens of Israel had emigrated from there, and Europe, like the United States, was highly dependent on oil from Arab countries. Furthermore, both the United States and the Soviet Union believed they had major strategic and economic interests in the region.

By 1949, the United States had established itself as a firm ally of Israel. Gradually, the Soviet Union began to furnish aid to the Arab nations. The bipolar tensions that had settled over Europe were thus transferred to the Middle East. Furthermore, the existence of the state of Israel would become one of the major points of contention between the United States and the governments of the various Arab states and later one of the chief complaints of radical political Islamists against the United States.

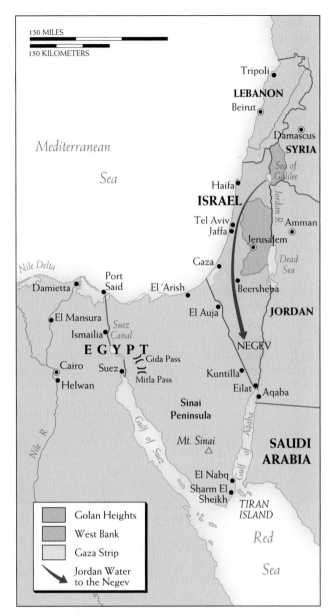

Map 29–4   **ISRAEL AND ITS NEIGHBORS IN 1949**   The territories gained by Israel in 1949 did not secure peace in the region. In fact, the disposition of those lands and the Arab refugees who live there has constituted the core of the region's unresolved problems to the present day.

THE KOREAN WAR

While early stages of the Cold War took place in Europe and the Arab-Israeli conflict developed in the Middle East, the United States confronted armed aggression in Asia. As part of a U.N. police action, it intervened militarily in Korea, following the same principle of containment that directed its actions in Europe.

Between 1910 and 1945, Japan, as an Asian colonial power, had occupied and exploited the formerly independent kingdom of Korea, but at the close of World War II, the United States and the Soviet

Union expelled the Japanese and divided Korea into two parts along the thirty-eighth parallel of latitude. Korea was supposed to be reunited. By 1948, however, two separate states had emerged: the Democratic People's Republic of Korea in the north, supported by the Soviet Union, and the Republic of Korea in the south, supported by the United States.

In late June 1950, after border clashes, North Korea invaded South Korea across the thirty-eighth parallel. The United States intervened, at first unilaterally and then under the authority of a U.N. resolution. Great Britain, Turkey, Australia, and other countries sent token forces. The Korean police action was technically a U.N.-sponsored venture to halt aggression. (It had been made possible when Stalin ordered the Soviet ambassador to boycott the United Nations when the key vote was taken.) For the United States, the point of the Korean conflict was to contain the spread and halt the aggression of communism.

Late in 1950, the Chinese, responding to the approach of U.N. forces near their border, sent troops to support North Korea. The American forces had to retreat. The U.S. policymakers believed, mistakenly, that the Chinese, who, since 1949, had been under the communist government of Mao Zedong (1893–1976), were simply Soviet puppets. Accordingly, the Americans viewed the movement of Chinese troops into Korea as another example of communist pressure against a noncommunist state, similar to what had previously happened in Europe. Today it is clear that Mao disliked Stalin and that tension existed between Moscow and the People's Republic of China, but that was little understood at the time.

On June 16, 1953, the Eisenhower administration concluded an armistice ending the Korean War and restoring the border near the thirty-eighth parallel. (See Map 29–5.) Thousands of American troops, however, are still stationed in Korea. The United States seemed to have successfully applied the lessons of the Cold War it had learned in Europe to Asia. The Korean War confirmed the American government's faith in containment. It also transformed the Cold War into a global rivalry that ranged well beyond Europe.

The formation of NATO and the Korean conflict capped the first round of the Cold War. In 1953, Stalin's death and the armistice in Korea fostered hopes that international tensions might ease. In early 1955, Soviet occupation forces left Austria after that nation accepted neutral status. Later that year, the leaders of France, Great Britain, the Soviet Union, and the United States held a summit conference in Geneva. Nuclear weapons and the future of a divided Germany were the chief items

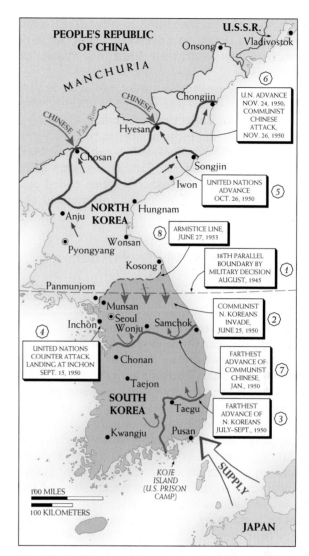

Map 29–5 **KOREA, 1950–1953** This map indicates the major developments in the bitter three-year struggle that followed the North Korean invasion of South Korea in 1950.

on the agenda. Despite public displays of friendliness, the meeting produced few substantial agreements, and the Cold War soon resumed.

THE KHRUSHCHEV ERA IN THE SOVIET UNION

No other nation had suffered greater losses or more deprivation during World War II than the Soviet Union. Many Russians had hoped the end of the war would signal a reduction in the scope of the police state and a redirection of the economy away from heavy industry to consumer products. They were disappointed. Stalin did little or nothing to modify the character of the regime he had created.

If anything, his determination to centralize his authority and a desire to undertake a new wave of internal purges continued until his death on March 6, 1953.

For a time, no single leader replaced Stalin. Rather, the *presidium* (the renamed Politburo) pursued a policy of collective leadership. Gradually, however, power and influence began to devolve on Nikita Khrushchev (1894–1971), who had been named party secretary in 1953. Three years later, he became premier. Khrushchev's rise ended collective leadership, but he never commanded the extraordinary powers of Stalin.

KHRUSHCHEV'S DOMESTIC POLICIES

The Khrushchev era, which lasted until the autumn of 1964, witnessed a retreat from Stalinism, though not from authoritarianism. Khrushchev sought to reform the Soviet system but to maintain the dominance of the Communist Party. Intellectuals were somewhat freer to express their opinions. Although Boris Pasternak (1890–1960), the author of *Dr. Zhivago* (1957), was not permitted to receive the Nobel prize for literature in 1958, another dissident author, Aleksandr Solzhenitsyn (b. 1918), could publish *One Day in the Life of Ivan Denisovich* (1963), a grim account of life in a Soviet labor camp under Stalin. Khrushchev also made modest efforts to meet the demand for more consumer goods and decentralize economic planning. In agriculture, he removed many of the more restrictive regulations on private cultivation and sought to expand the area available for growing wheat. At first, this program led to record grain production, but inappropriate farming techniques soon reduced yields. The Soviet Union had to import vast quantities of grain each year from the United States and other countries.

The Secret Speech of 1956 In February 1956, Khrushchev made an extraordinary departure from expected practice by directly attacking the policies

MAJOR DATES OF THE EARLY KHRUSHCHEV ERA

1953 Death of Stalin
1955 Austria established as a neutral state
1955 Geneva summit
1956 (February) Khrushchev's secret speech denouncing Stalin
      (Autumn) Polish crisis
      (October) Suez crisis
      (October) Hungarian uprising
1957 *Sputnik* launched

of the Stalin years. At the Twentieth Congress of the Communist Party, Khrushchev gave a secret speech (later published outside the Soviet Union) in which he denounced Stalin and his crimes against socialist justice during the purges of the 1930s. The speech stunned party circles, but it also opened the way for genuine, if limited, internal criticism of the Soviet government and for many of the changes in intellectual and economic life cited earlier. Gradually, Khrushchev removed the strongest supporters of Stalinist policies from the presidium. By 1958, all of Stalin's former supporters were gone, and none had been executed. (See "Khrushchev Denounces the Crimes of Stalin: The Secret Speech.")

Khrushchev's speech, however, had repercussions well beyond the borders of the Soviet Union. Communist leaders in Eastern Europe took it as a signal that they could govern with greater leeway than before and retreat from Stalinist policies. Indeed, Khrushchev's speech was simply the first of a number of extraordinary events in 1956.

THE THREE CRISES OF 1956

The Suez Intervention In July 1956, President Gamal Abdel Nasser (1918–1970) of Egypt nationalized the Suez Canal. Great Britain and France who had controlled the private company that had run the canal feared that this action would close the canal to their supplies of oil in the Persian Gulf. In October 1956, war broke out between Egypt and Israel. The British and French seized the opportunity to intervene militarily; however, the United States refused to support their action. The Soviet Union protested vehemently. The Anglo-French forces had to be withdrawn, and Egypt retained control of the canal.

The Suez intervention proved that without the support of the United States the nations of Western Europe could no longer impose their will on the rest of the world. It also appeared that the United States and the Soviet Union had restrained their allies from undertaking actions that might result in a wider conflict. The fact that neither of the superpowers wanted war constrained both Egypt and the Anglo-French forces.

Polish Efforts Toward Independent Action The autumn of 1956 also saw important developments in Eastern Europe that demonstrated similar limitations on independent action among the Soviet bloc nations. When the prime minister of Poland died, the Polish Communist Party leaders refused to replace him with Moscow's nominee, despite considerable pressure from the Soviets. In the end, Wladyslaw Gomulka (1905–1982) emerged as the

KHRUSHCHEV DENOUNCES THE CRIMES OF STALIN: THE SECRET SPEECH

In 1956, Khrushchev denounced Stalin in a secret speech to the Party Congress. The New York Times *published a text of that speech, smuggled from Russia.*

■ *What specific actions by Stalin did Khrushchev denounce? Why does Khrushchev pay so much attention to Stalin's creation of the concept of an "enemy of the people"? Why does Khrushchev distinguish between the actions of Stalin and those of Lenin?*

Stalin acted not through persuasion, explanation, and patient cooperation with people, but by imposing his concepts and demanding absolute submission to his opinion. Whoever opposed this concept or tried to prove his viewpoint and the correctness of his position was doomed to removal from the leading collective [group] and to subsequent moral and physical annihilation. . . .

Stalin originated the concept of "enemy of the people." This term automatically rendered it unnecessary that the ideological errors of a man or men engaged in a controversy be proved; this term made possible the usage of the most cruel repression violating all norms of revolutionary legality, against anyone who in any way disagreed with Stalin, against those who were only suspected of hostile intent, against those who had bad reputations.

This concept "enemy of the people" actually eliminated the possibility of any kind of ideological fight or the making of one's views known on this or that issue, even those of a practical character. In the main, and in actuality, the only proof of guilt used, against all norms of current legal science, was the "confession" of the ac-

cused himself; and, as a subsequent probing proved, "confessions" were acquired through physical pressures against the accused. . . .

Lenin used severe methods only in the most necessary cases, when the exploiting classes were still in existence and were vigorously opposing the revolution, when the struggle for survival was decidedly assuming the sharpest forms, even including civil war.

Stalin, on the other hand, used extreme methods and mass repressions at a time when the revolution was already victorious, when the Soviet State was strengthened, when the exploiting classes were already liquidated and Socialist relations were rooted solidly in all phases of national economy, when our party was politically consolidated and had strengthened itself both numerically and ideologically. It is clear that here Stalin showed in a whole series of cases his intolerance, his brutality and his abuse of power. Instead of proving his political correctness and mobilizing the masses, he often chose the path of repression and physical annihilation, not only against actual enemies, but also against individuals who had not committed any crimes against the party and the Soviet Government.

new Communist leader of Poland. He was the choice of the Poles, and he proved acceptable to the Soviets because he promised continued economic and military cooperation, and particularly because he continued Polish membership in the Warsaw Pact. Within those limits he halted the collectivization of Polish agriculture and improved relations with the Polish Roman Catholic Church.

The Hungarian Uprising Hungary provided the third trouble spot for the Soviet Union. In late Oc-

tober, demonstrations of sympathy for the Poles in Budapest led to street fighting. The Hungarian communists installed a new ministry headed by former premier Imre Nagy (1896–1958). Nagy was a Communist who sought a more independent position for Hungary. He went much further in his demands than Gomulka and directly appealed for political support from noncommunist groups in Hungary. Nagy called for the removal of Soviet troops and the ultimate neutralization of Hungary. He even called for Hungarian withdrawal from the

Warsaw Pact. These demands were wholly unacceptable to the Soviet Union. In early November, Soviet troops invaded Hungary; deposed Nagy, who was later executed; and imposed Janos Kadar (1912–1989) as premier.

The events of 1956 in the Middle East and Eastern Europe solidified the position of the United States and the Soviet Union as superpowers. In different ways and to differing degrees, the two superpowers had demonstrated this new political reality to their allies. The nations of Western Europe would be able to make independent policy among themselves within Europe, but were generally curtailed from independent action on the broader international scene. For approximately twenty-five years, the nations of Eastern Europe would be permitted virtually no autonomous actions in either the domestic or the international sphere.

LATER COLD WAR CONFRONTATIONS

After 1956, the Soviet Union began to talk about "peaceful coexistence" with the United States. With the 1957 launch of *Sputnik*, the first satellite to orbit the earth, the Soviet Union appeared to have achieved an enormous technological superiority over the West. In 1958, the two countries began negotiations toward limiting the testing of nuclear weapons. By 1959, tensions had relaxed sufficiently for Western leaders to visit Moscow and for Khrushchev to tour the United States. A summit meeting was scheduled for May 1960, and President Eisenhower was to go to Moscow.

Just before the Paris Summit Conference, the Soviet Union shot down an American U-2 aircraft that was flying reconnaissance over Soviet territory. Khrushchev demanded an apology from Eisenhower for this air surveillance. Eisenhower accepted full responsibility for the surveillance policy but refused to apologize publicly. Khrushchev then refused to take part in the summit conference, just as the participants arrived in the French capital. The conference, as well as Eisenhower's proposed trip to the Soviet Union, was thus aborted.

The Soviets did not scuttle the summit meeting on the eve of its opening simply because of the American spy flights. They had long been aware of these flights and had other reasons for protesting them when they did. By 1960, the communist world itself had split between the Soviets and the Chinese, who were portraying the Russians as lacking revolutionary zeal. Destroying the

summit was, in part, a way to demonstrate the Soviet Union's hard-line attitude toward the capitalist world.

THE BERLIN WALL

The aborted Paris conference opened the most difficult period of the Cold War. In 1961, the new U.S. president, John F. Kennedy (1917–1963), and Premier Khrushchev met in Vienna with inconclusive results.

Throughout 1961, thousands of refugees from East Germany crossed the border into West Berlin. This outflow of people embarrassed East Germany, hurt its economy, and demonstrated the Soviet Union's inability to control Eastern Europe. Consequently, in August 1961, the East Germans, with Soviet support, erected a concrete wall along the border between East and West Berlin, separating the two parts of the city. Despite speeches and symbolic support from the West, the wall halted the flow of refugees and brought the U.S. commitment to West Germany into doubt.

THE CUBAN MISSILE CRISIS

The most dangerous days of the Cold War occurred during the Cuban missile crisis of 1962. This event represented another facet of the globalization of the Cold War, on this occasion, into the Americas. Cuba lies less than 100 miles off the Florida coast, and the United States had dominated the island since the Spanish-American War in 1898. In 1957, Fidel Castro (b. 1926) launched an insurgency in

During the Cuban missile crisis of 1962, the American ambassador to the United Nations displayed photographs to persuade the world of the threat to the United States less than one hundred miles from its own shores. © CORBIS

Cuba, which toppled the dictatorship of Flugencio Batista (1901–1973) on New Year's Day of 1959. Thereafter Castro established a communist government, and Cuba became an ally of the Soviet Union. These events caused enormous concern within the United States.

In 1962, the Soviet Union secretly began to place nuclear missiles in Cuba. In response, the American government, under President Kennedy, blockaded Cuba, halted the shipment of new missiles, and demanded the removal of existing installations. After a tense week, during which nuclear war seemed a real possibility, the Soviets backed down, and the crisis ended. This adventurism in foreign policy undermined Khrushchev's credibility in the ruling circles of the Soviet Union and caused other non-European communist regimes to question the Soviet commitment to their security and survival. It also increased the influence of the People's Republic of China in communist circles and convinced Soviet military leaders of the need to strengthen their forces, so that they would be as strong as, or stronger than, those of the United States in any future confrontation.

If the Cuban missile crisis had led to war, the United States could have launched missiles over Europe or from European bases into the Soviet Union. The crisis thus threatened Europe directly, but it was the last major Cold War confrontation to do so. In 1963, the United States and the Soviet Union concluded a nuclear test ban treaty. This agreement marked the beginning of a lessening in the overt tensions between the two powers.

THE BREZHENEV ERA

By 1964, many in the Soviet Communist Party had concluded that Khrushchev had tried to do too much too soon and had done it poorly. On October 16, 1964, Khrushchev was forced to resign. He was replaced by Alexei Kosygin (1904–1980) as premier and Leonid Brezhnev (1906–1982) as party secretary. Brezhnev eventually emerged as the dominant figure.

1968: THE INVASION OF CZECHOSLOVAKIA

In 1968, during what became known as the Prague Spring, the government of Czechoslovakia, under Alexander Dubcek (1921–1992), began to experiment with a more liberal communism. Dubcek expanded freedom of discussion and other intellectual rights at a time when the Soviet Union was suppressing them. In the summer of 1968, the Soviet government and its allies in the Warsaw Pact sent troops into Czechoslovakia and replaced

---

MAJOR DATES OF LATER COLD WAR YEARS

1959	Khrushchev's visit to the United States
1960	Failed Paris Summit
1961	East Germany erects Berlin Wall
1962	Cuban missile crisis
1963	Test Ban Treaty between Soviet Union and the United States
1964	Khrushchev falls from power
1968	Soviet invasion of Czechoslovakia
1972	Strategic Arms Limitation Treaty

Dubcek with communist leaders more to its own liking.

At the time of the invasion, Soviet party chairman Brezhnev, in what came to be termed the *Brezhnev Doctrine*, declared the right of the Soviet Union to interfere in the domestic politics of other communist countries. Whereas the Truman Doctrine of 1947 had supported democratic governments and offered help to resist further communist penetration in Europe, the Brezhnev Doctrine of 1968 sought to sustain the communist governments of Eastern Europe and prevent any liberalization in the region. No further direct Soviet interventions occurred in Eastern Europe after 1968, yet the invasion of Czechoslovakia showed that any attempt at a greater liberalization could trigger Soviet military repression.

THE UNITED STATES AND DÉTENTE

Foreign policy under Brezhnev combined attempts to reach an accommodation with the United States with continued efforts to expand Soviet influence and maintain Soviet leadership of the communist movement.

Although the Soviet Union sided with North Vietnam in its war with the United States, which is discussed later in this chapter, Soviet support was restrained. Under President Richard Nixon (1969–1974), the United States began a policy of détente with the Soviet Union, and the two countries concluded agreements on trade and on reducing strategic arms. Despite these agreements, Soviet spending on defense, and particularly on its navy, grew, damaging the consumer sectors of the economy.

During Gerald Ford's presidency (1974–1977), both the United States and the Soviet Union along with other European nations signed the Helsinki Accords. The accords recognized the Soviet sphere of influence in Eastern Europe, but they also

In the summer of 1968, Soviet tanks rolled into Czechoslovakia, ending that country's experiment in liberalized communism. This picture shows defiant flag-waving Czechs on a truck rolling past a Soviet tank in the immediate aftermath of the invasion.   Hulton Archive Photos/Getty Images, Inc.

recognized the human rights of the signers' citizens, which every government, including the Soviet Union, agreed to protect. President Jimmy Carter (1977–1981), a strong advocate of human rights, sought to induce the Soviet Union to comply with this commitment, a policy that cooled relations between the two countries.

Throughout this period of détente, in addition to its military presence in Eastern Europe, the Soviet Union pursued an activist foreign policy around the world. During the 1970s, it financed Cuban military intervention in Angola, Mozambique, and Ethiopia. Soviet funds flowed to the Sandinista forces in Nicaragua and to Vietnam, which permitted the Soviets to use naval bases after North Vietnam conquered the south in 1975. The Soviet Union also provided funds and weapons to various Arab governments for use against Israel.

Each of these actions represented either Soviet support for what it viewed as its own strategic interests or an attempt to weaken the interests of the United States. Even more importantly, following its backing down in the Cuban missile crisis, the Soviet government was determined to build up its military forces. By the early 1980s, the Soviet Union possessed the largest armed force in the world and had achieved virtual nuclear parity with the United States.

THE INVASION OF AFGHANISTAN

It was at this moment of great military strength in 1979 that the Brezhnev government decided to invade Afghanistan, a strategic decision of enormous long-range consequences for the future of the Soviet Union as well as the United States. Although the Soviet Union already had a presence in Afghanistan, the Brezhnev government, for reasons that remain unclear, determined to send in troops to ensure its influence in central Asia and to install a puppet Afghan government.

The invasion brought a sharp response from the United States. The U.S. Senate refused to ratify a second Strategic Arms Limitation agreement that President Carter had signed earlier that year. The United States also embargoed grain shipments to the Soviet Union, boycotted the 1980 Olympic Games in Moscow, and sent aid to the Afghan rebels through various third parties, as did Pakistan, Saudi Arabia, and other Islamic nations. The U.S. Central Intelligence Agency became directly involved with the Afghan resistance forces, some of whom were radical Muslims. China, which felt threatened by the invasion, also helped the rebels.

Eventually, the Soviet forces bogged down in Afghanistan and could not defeat their guerrilla enemies. The Afghans killed approximately 2,000

Soviet troops a year and inflicted many other casualties. The morale and prestige of the Soviet army plummeted. At first, few Soviets knew about the problems in Afghanistan, but during the 1980s, the military failure became common knowledge in the Soviet Union. Although the Afghan war did not make daily headline news in the Western press, it sapped Soviet strength for ten years and demoralized the Soviet Union not unlike the way the Vietnam conflict did the United States.

COMMUNISM AND SOLIDARITY IN POLAND

Events in Poland commencing in 1980—a time when the Soviet government was becoming increasingly rigidified and involved in Afghanistan—challenged both the authority of the Polish Communist Party and the influence of the Soviet Union.

After the events of late 1956, when the Polish Communist Party had accommodated itself to Soviet domination, chronic economic mismanagement and persistent shortages of food and consumer goods plagued Poland for twenty-five years. In 1978, the election of Karol Wojtyla, cardinal archbishop of Kraków, as Pope John Paul II (d. 2005) proved important for Polish resistance to communist control and Soviet domination. An outspoken Polish opponent of communism now occupied a position of authority and enormous public visibility well beyond the reach of Soviet or communist control. The new pope visited his homeland in 1979 and received a tumultuous welcome.

In July 1980, the Polish government raised meat prices, leading to hundreds of protest strikes across the country. On August 14, workers occupied the Lenin shipyard at Gdansk on the Baltic coast. The strike soon spread to other shipyards, transport facilities, and factories connected with the shipbuilding industry. The strikers, led by Lech Walesa (b. 1944), refused to negotiate through any of the government-controlled unions. The Gdansk strike ended on August 31 after the government promised the workers the right to organize an independent union called Solidarity. In September, the head of the Polish Communist Party was replaced, the Polish courts recognized Solidarity as an independent union, and the state-controlled radio broadcast a Roman Catholic mass for the first time in thirty years.

The summer of 1981 saw events that were no less remarkable occur within the Polish Communist Party itself. For the first time in any European communist state, secret elections for the party congress were permitted with real choices among the candidates. A single party continued to govern Poland, but for the time being, the party congress permitted real debate within its ranks.

MAJOR DATES OF THE BREZHNEV ERA

1974 Solzhenitsyn expelled
1975 Helsinki Accords
1979 Soviet invasion of Afghanistan
1980 U.S. Olympic Games boycott
1981 Martial law declared in Poland in response to Solidarity
1982 Death of Brezhnev

This extraordinary Polish experiment, however, ended abruptly. In 1981, General Wojciech Jaruzelski (b. 1923) became head of the Polish Communist Party, and the army imposed martial law in December. The leaders of Solidarity were arrested. The Polish military acted to preserve its own position and perhaps to prevent a Soviet invasion similar to the one in Czechoslovakia in 1968. Martial law remained in effect until late in 1983, but the Polish Communist Party could not solve Poland's major economic problems.

RELATIONS WITH THE REAGAN ADMINISTRATION

Early in the administration of President Ronald Reagan (1981–1989), the United States relaxed its grain embargo on the Soviet Union and placed less emphasis on human rights. At the same time, however, Reagan intensified Cold War rhetoric, famously describing the Soviet Union as an "evil empire." More importantly, the Reagan administration increased U.S. military spending, slowed arms limitation negotiations, deployed a new missile system in Europe, and proposed the Strategic Defense Initiative (dubbed "Star Wars" by the press), involving a high-technology space-based defense against nuclear attack. The Star Wars proposal, although controversial in the United States, was a major issue in later arms control negotiations with the Soviet Union. Star Wars and the Reagan defense spending forced the Soviet Union to increase its own defense spending when it could ill afford to do so and contributed to the economic problems that helped bring about its collapse. Yet even during Reagan's first term (1981–1985), no major transformation of the Soviet Union seemed to be in the offing.

Meanwhile throughout these four decades of the Cold War between the United States and the Soviet Union, extraordinary events had been occurring in Africa and Asia.

DECOLONIZATION: THE EUROPEAN RETREAT FROM EMPIRE

The transformation of much of Africa and Asia from colonial domains into independent nations was the most remarkable global political event of the second half of the twentieth century. The numbers of people involved alone reveals the magnitude of the change. At the founding of the United Nations in 1945, approximately one-third of the population of the world was subject to the government of colonial powers. Since that time, more than eighty of those then non-self-governing territories have been admitted to U.N. membership as independent states. (See Map 29–6.)

Decolonization after 1945 was a direct result of both World War II itself and the rise of indigenous nationalist movements within Africa, Asia, and the Middle East. World War II drew the military forces of the colonial powers back to Europe. The Japanese overran European possessions in East Asia and demonstrated that the European presence there might not be permanent. After the dislocations of the war came the immediate postwar European economic collapse, which left the European colonial powers less able to afford to maintain their military and administrative positions abroad.

The war aims of the Allies had also undermined colonialism. It was difficult to fight against tyranny in Europe while maintaining colonial dominance abroad. The United States, and in particular Franklin Roosevelt, opposed the continuation of the colonial empires. This policy was, in part, a matter of principle, but it also recognized that both the political and economic interests of the United States were more likely to prosper in a decolonized world. The founding of the United Nations also assured the presence of an international body opposed to colonialism.

The Cold War complicated the process of decolonization. Both the United States and the Soviet Union opposed the old colonial empires, but both also worried about the potential alignment of the new nations and moved to create spheres of influence and, in some cases, alliances with the newly independent states. Certain nations, such as India, fiercely pursued policies of neutrality in hopes of receiving aid and support from both sides.

Major Areas of Colonial Withdrawal

Decolonization was a worldwide event lasting throughout the second half of the twentieth century and beyond. It involved such dramatic moments as the Dutch being forced from the East Indies in 1949 to be replaced by the independent nation of Indonesia, the Belgian withdrawal from the Congo in 1960, the liberation of Portuguese Mozambique and Angola in 1974 and 1975, and the end of all-white rule in Rhodesia (Zimbabwe) in 1979 and most remarkably in South Africa in 1994.

Each of these events was important, especially to the peoples involved, but the two largest colonial empires were the British and the French. Their retreat from empire produced the most far-reaching repercussions not only in former colonial nations, but in both Europe and the United States.

India

No anticolonial movement so gripped the imagination of the Western world as that carried out in India under the leadership of Mohandas Gandhi (1869–1948). The British had solidified their rule of India in the mid-eighteenth century (see Chapter 16), extending and consolidating it throughout the nineteenth. The British administration required the Indians themselves to pay for British rule. India supplied the raw materials for the British cotton mills. Other British policies pushed many Indians to migrate to British possessions in East Asia, Africa, and the Caribbean. For decades, the religious, ethnic, linguistic, and political divisions among Indians permitted the British to dominate the country through a divide-and-rule strategy.

As early as 1885, politically active Hindu Indians founded the Indian National Congress with the goals of modernizing Indian life and liberalizing British policy. Muslims organized the Muslim League in 1887, which for a time cooperated with the National Congress, but eventually sought an independent Muslim nation. After World War I, the Indian nationalist movement grew steadily in strength, in part because of British blunders, but more importantly because remarkable leaders pursued effective strategies.

Chief among these leaders was Gandhi, who had studied law in Britain and there began to encounter the ideas of liberal Western thinkers, including the American Henry David Thoreau (1817–1862) from whom he learned the concept of passive resistance. After being called to the bar in London in 1891, he returned briefly to India and then in 1893 went to South Africa where for over twenty years he worked on behalf of Indian immigrants. During those years he continued to read widely and became convinced of the power of passive resistance. Gandhi returned to India in 1915 and soon distinguished himself as a leader of Indian nationalism

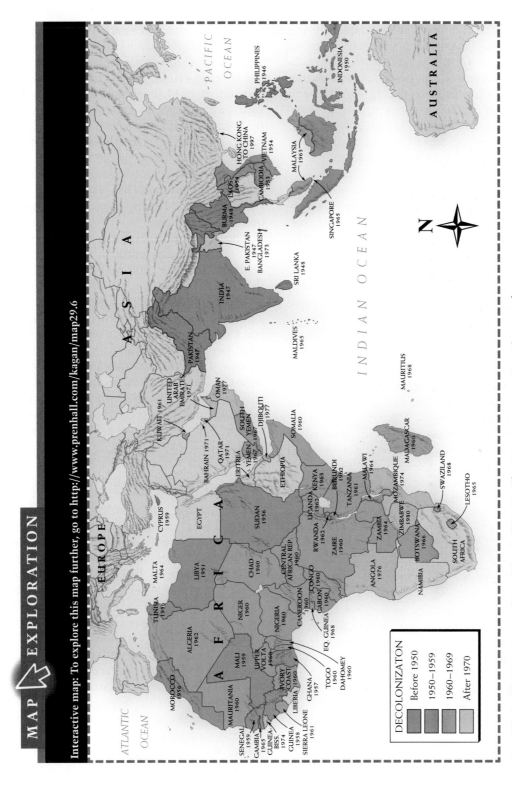

MAP EXPLORATION

Interactive map: To explore this map further, go to http://www.prenhall.com/kagan/map29.6

DECOLONIZATON

- Before 1950
- 1950–1959
- 1960–1969
- After 1970

Map 29–6 **DECOLONIZATION SINCE WORLD WAR II** The Western powers' rapid retreat from imperialism after World War II is graphically shown on this outline map covering half the globe—from West Africa to the southwest Pacific.

by his insistence on religious toleration. From the 1920s to the mid-1940s, he inspired a growing movement of passive resistance to British rule in India. In 1930, he lead a famous march to break the British salt monopoly by collecting salt from the sea. He was repeatedly arrested and jailed by the British authorities. To embarrass the British during these imprisonments and to gain worldwide publicity, he undertook long protest fasts during which he nearly died. In 1942, during World War II, Gandhi called on the British Government to leave India. In 1947, the British Labor government, weary of the incessant agitation and uncertain of its ability to maintain control in India, decided to do so.

Gandhi became and remains the most famous anticolonial leader of the twentieth century. His career demonstrates how such a leader could use ideas taken from the West against colonial regimes. His use of passive resistance became a model for Dr. Martin Luther King, Jr. (1929–1968) during the civil rights movement in the United States during the late 1950s and 1960s. (See "Gandhi Explains His Doctrine of Nonviolence.")

Gandhi and the Congress Party succeeded in forcing the British from India. However, they did not succeed in creating a single nation. Parallel to Gandhi's drive for an India characterized by diverse religions living in mutual toleration, the Muslim League led by Ali Jinnah (1876–1948) sought a distinctly Muslim state. What occurred in 1947 as the British left India was a partition of the country into the states of India and Pakistan. Sectarian warfare and hundreds of thousands of deaths marked the partition. A Hindu extremist assassinated Gandhi himself in 1948. It should also be noted that despite partition a vast Muslim population remained in India. Pakistan was initially a nation of two parts separated geographically by hundreds of miles of Indian territory. In 1971, East Pakistan broke away to become independent Bangladesh. As will be seen later in this chapter, the founding of Pakistan would be important for the emergence of political Islamism.

The partition of India and Pakistan illustrates an often-neglected factor in the process of decolonization. In many colonial regions, the retreat of the colonial powers opened the way for new or renewed conflicts among different ethnic and religious groups within the former colonial empires. For example, since partition, India and Pakistan have disputed the ownership of Kashmir in repeated armed clashes. Another example is the conflict over the former Portuguese colony of East Timor whose people have asserted a right to independence against the government of Indonesia, which occupied it for twenty years after Portugal withdrew in 1975.

FURTHER BRITISH RETREAT FROM EMPIRE

The British surrender of India marked the beginning of a long, steady retreat from empire. Generally speaking, the British accepted the loss of empire as inevitable. British decolonization sought first to maintain whatever links were economically and politically possible without conflict. Indeed, during the 1940s and 1950s, the British undertook various development programs in their remaining Asian, African, and Caribbean colonies. These investments paradoxically made the British government and public more aware of the actual costs of empire and may have led both to accept more easily the end of empire. Second, throughout decolonization the British hoped to oversee the creation of institutions in their former colonies that would assure representative self-government once they had departed.

In 1948, Burma and Sri Lanka (formerly Ceylon) became independent. As already observed, the formation of the state of Israel and Arab nationalist movements forced Britain to withdraw from Palestine. During the 1950s, the British tried, belatedly,

Ghandi led India from colonialism to independence. Part of his appeal was the simplicity of his life and dress.
CORBIS/Bettmann

GANDHI EXPLAINS HIS DOCTRINE OF NONVIOLENCE

The most famous device Indian nationalists used against British colonial rule in India was Gandhi's doctrine of nonviolence. He had come to believe in its power during his years in South Africa. Gandhi wrote this description of the meaning of nonviolence during World War II. Yet even while enunciating its meaning, he refused to associate himself with nonviolence in international relations. This reluctance may have stemmed from his recognition that the war against the Axis powers was a war against Nazi racism and Japanese imperialism, both of which were dangerous for colonial peoples of color.

■ *Why does Gandhi see nonviolence as evidence of strength? How does he refrain from extending nonviolence to external relations? How was Gandhi's doctrine transferable to other political movements, such as the American civil rights struggle?*

I do believe that, where there is only a choice between cowardice and violence, I would advise violence. . . .

But I believe that non-violence is infinitely superior to violence, forgiveness is more manly than punishment. . . .

Non-violence is the law of our species as violence is the law of the brute. The spirit lies dormant in the brute, and he knows no law but that of physical might. The dignity of man requires obedience to a higher law—to the strength of the spirit.

I have therefore ventured to place before India the ancient law of self-sacrifice. . . .

Non-violence in its dynamic condition means conscious suffering. It does not mean meek submission to the will of the evil-doer, but it means the pitting of one's whole soul against the will of the tyrant. Working under this law of our being, it is possible for a single individual to defy the whole might of an unjust empire to save his honour, his religion, his soul, and lay the foundation for that empire's fall or its regeneration. . . .

I have not the capacity for preaching universal non-violence to the country. I preach, there-fore, non-violence restricted strictly for the purpose of winning our freedom and therefore perhaps for preaching the regulation of international relations by non-violent means. But my incapacity must not be mistaken for that of the doctrine of non-violence. I see it with my intellect in all its effulgence. My heart grasps it. But I have not yet the attainments of preaching universal non-violence with effect. . . .

I do justify entire non-violence, and consider it possible in relation between man and man and nation and nation; but it is not "a resignation from all fighting against wickedness.' On the contrary, the non-violence of my conception is a more active more real fighting against wickedness than retaliation whose very nature is to increase wickedness. I contemplate a mental, and therefore a moral, opposition to immoralities. I seek entirely to blunt the edge of the tyrant's sword, not by putting up against it a sharper-edged weapon, but by disappointing his expectations that I should be offering physical resistance. . . .

Non-violence, therefore, presupposes ability to strike. It is a conscious deliberate restraint put upon one's desire for vengeance.

"Gandhi Explains His Doctrine of Non-Violence" from M. K. Gandhi, *Non-Violence in Peace and War*, Navajivan Publishing, 1942. Reprinted by permission of the Navajivan Trust.

to prepare their tropical colonies for self-government. Ghana (formerly the Gold Coast) and Nigeria—which became self-governing in 1957 and 1960, respectively—were the major examples of planned decolonization. In other areas, such as Cyprus, Kenya, and Aden (now part of Yemen), the British withdrew under the pressure of militant nationalist movements. In many areas, violence between the British and the forces demanding independence hastened this retreat.

The development of these former colonies in the second half of the twentieth century has followed two distinct paths. In general, political instability and poverty have characterized the history of the independent states in Africa. By contrast, Asia has been an area of overall political stability and remarkable economic growth, challenging the economies of both the United States and Western Europe.

THE TURMOIL OF FRENCH DECOLONIZATION

Although the British retreat from empire involved violence, at no point did the British "make a stand." Moreover, many groups in Britain, including the leadership of the Labour Party, had long been critical of colonialism. Such was not the case with France. Having been defeated by the Nazis and then liberated by the allied forces, France believed it must reassert its position as a great power. This determination led it into two disastrous attempts to maintain its colonial empire, in Algeria and Vietnam. As will be seen, the situation in Vietnam, because of the intervention of the United States, drew French decolonization directly into the tensions of the Cold War.

FRANCE AND ALGERIA

France had conquered the pirate's nest of Algiers in 1830 as Charles X (r. 1824–1830) futilely hoped the invasion would increase support for his monarchy. (See Chapter 20.) In late 1848, the French government made Algeria an integral part of France, establishing three administrative departments that were administered like those in France itself. Over the decades, as France consolidated and extended its position in Algeria, French soldiers and hundreds of thousands of Europeans from France and other Mediterranean countries settled there, primarily in the cities and on small farms. By the close of World War I, approximately 20 percent of the population was of European descent. Collectively these immigrants were termed the *pieds noirs* (meaning "black feet," a derogatory term). The voting structure was set up to give the French settlers as large a voice as the majority Arab Muslim population. The further one moved toward the south away from the coast and into the Sahara Desert, the greater the influence of the French military. Algerian Muslims were not

given posts in the administration. Shortly after World War I, the French extended the rights of full French citizenship to Algerian Muslims who had fought in the war, who were literate in French, or who owned land, but this rewarded only a few thousand of them.

During World War II, the forces of Free France dominated Algeria after 1942 while the Vichy regime still governed metropolitan France. The Free French government did little to change the colonial status quo. Moreover, in May 1945, during celebrations of the Allied victory in World War II, a violent clash broke out at Sétif between Muslims and French settlers. Matters rapidly got out of hand, and people on both sides were killed, but the French repressed the Muslims with a considerable loss of life. The Muslims of Algeria saw this incident the same way the Russian working classes viewed Bloody Sunday in 1905. (See Chapter 23.) It robbed the French administration of legitimacy and marked the beginning of conscious Algerian nationalism. Thereafter, many Algerian Muslims supported independence. To placate Muslim opinion, in 1947, the French established a structure for limited political representation of the Muslim population and undertook economic reforms. Not unsurprisingly, these steps proved ineffective.

Algerian nationalists soon founded the National Liberation Front (FLN). In late 1954, insurrections and soon open civil war broke out in Algeria as the FLN undertook highly effective guerrilla warfare. The government of the Fourth French Republic that had been founded in 1945 adamantly declared Algeria an integral part of France and refused to compromise with the insurgents. Thereafter a war

In 1959, Charles De Gaulle as President of the French Republic visited Algiers to great acclaim from its European inhabitants, known as *colons*. By 1962, however, he had sponsored a referendum that led to Algerian independence and the flight of most of those people. Loomis Dean/Getty Images, Inc.

lasting until 1962 ground on between the Algerian nationalists and the French. Both sides committed atrocities; hundreds of thousands of Algerians were killed. The war divided France itself with many French citizens, often of left-wing political opinion, objecting to the war, and the French military, still smarting from its defeats in World War II and in Indochina, determined to fight on. The presence of more than one million European settlers in Algeria, who saw any settlement with the nationalists as a betrayal, exacerbated the situation. The French government itself became paralyzed and lost control of the army. There was fear of civil war in France itself or of a military takeover. In Algeria, violence was spreading.

In the midst of this turmoil, General Charles de Gaulle (1890–1970), who had led the Free French forces during World War II and had briefly governed France immediately after the war, reentered French political life largely at the urging of the military. His condition for taking office was the end of the Fourth Republic and the promulgation of a new constitution, which enhanced the power of the president and created the Fifth Republic. The voters ratified this, and de Gaulle became president of France in December 1958. He then undertook a long strategic retreat from Algeria. The process was neither peaceful nor easy. In 1961, for example, it looked as if a group of officers known as the OAS (Organisation Armée Secrète) would attempt a coup in Paris. There were bombings, murders, and attempts on de Gaulle's life. In 1962, however, de Gaulle held a referendum in Algeria on independence, which passed overwhelmingly. Algeria became independent on July 3, 1962.

Once the FLN took over Algeria under the presidency of Mohammed Ben Bella (b. 1919), however, a second factor came into play in French domestic life. Hundreds of thousands of *pied noirs* settlers fled Algeria for France as did many Muslims who had supported the French and had good cause to fear reprisals. (Thousands of pro-French Muslims who did not flee were massacred.) The emigration of this latter group marked the beginning of a large, and largely unwelcome, Muslim population in France.

FRANCE AND VIETNAM

One of the reasons for the strong French stand against Algerian independence had been the loss of its south Asian empire in Indochina just before the Algerian insurrection broke out in 1954. Whereas the Algerian drive toward independence essentially involved only France and the populations of Algeria, the Indochina problem eventually drew the United States into war in Vietnam.

In its push for empire, France had occupied Indochina (which contained Laos, Cambodia, and Vietnam) between 1857 and 1893. By 1930, Ho Chi Minh (1892–1969) had turned a nationalist movement against French colonial rule into the Indochina Communist Party, which the French, for a time, succeeded in suppressing. World War II, however, provided new opportunities for Ho Chi Minh and other nationalists as they fought both the Japanese who occupied Indochina in 1941 and the pro-Vichy French colonial administration that collaborated with the Japanese until 1945. The war thus established Ho Chi Minh as a major anticolonial, nationalist leader. He was a communist to be sure, but he had achieved his position in Vietnam during the war without the support of Chinese or Soviet communists.

In September 1945, Ho Chi Minh declared the independence of Vietnam under the Viet Minh, a coalition of nationalists that the communists soon dominated. By 1947, a full-fledged civil war had erupted in Vietnam. (Cambodia and, to a lesser extent, Laos remained quiescent under pro-French or neutralist monarchies.)

Until 1949, the United States displayed minimal concern about the Indochina war. The establishment of the Communist People's Republic of China that year dramatically changed the U.S. outlook. The United States now saw the French colonial war against Ho Chi Minh as an integral part of the Cold War conflict. Even though the United States supported the French effort in Vietnam financially, it was not prepared, despite divisions among policymakers, to intervene militarily. In the spring of 1954, during an international conference in Geneva on the future of Vietnam, the French military stronghold of Dien Bien Phu fell to Viet Minh forces after a prolonged siege. France lost the will to continue the struggle, which had become increasingly unpopular with the French people.

By late June, a complicated and unsatisfactory peace accord divided Vietnam at the seventeenth parallel of latitude. North of the parallel, centered in Hanoi, the Viet Minh were in charge; below it, centered in Saigon, the French were in charge. This was to be a temporary border. By 1956, elections were to be held to reunify the country. In effect, the conference attempted to transform a military conflict into a political one.

VIETNAM DRAWN INTO THE COLD WAR

Unhappy with these arrangements, the United States, in September 1954, formed the Southeast Asia Treaty Organization (SEATO), a collective

MAJOR DATES
IN THE VIETNAM CONFLICT

1945 Ho Chi Minh proclaims Vietnamese independence from French rule

1947–1954 War between France and Vietnam

1950 U.S. financial aid to France

1954 Geneva conference on Southeast Asia opens

1954 French defeat at Dien Bien Phu

1954 Southeast Asia Treaty Organization (SEATO) founded

1955 Diem establishes Republic of Vietnam in the south

1960 Founding of National Liberation Front to overthrow the Diem government

1961 Six hundred American troops and advisers in Vietnam

1963 Diem overthrown and assassinated

1964 Gulf of Tonkin Resolution

1965 Major U.S. troop commitment

1969 Nixon announces policy of Vietnamization

1973 Cease-fire announced

1975 Saigon falls to North Vietnamese troops

security agreement that somewhat resembled the European NATO alliance, but without the integration of military forces or inclusion of all states in the region. Its membership consisted of the United States, Great Britain, France, Australia, New Zealand, Thailand, Pakistan, and the Philippines.

By 1955, American policymakers had begun to think about Indochina, and particularly Vietnam, largely in terms of the Korean example. The U.S. government assumed, incorrectly, that, like the government of North Korea, the government in North Vietnam was basically a communist puppet of the Soviets and the Chinese. That same year, French troops began to withdraw from South Vietnam. As they left, the various Vietnamese political groups began to fight for power among themselves.

The United States stepped into the turmoil in Vietnam with military and economic aid. Among the Vietnamese politicians, it chose to support was Ngo Dinh Diem (1901–1963), a strong noncommunist nationalist who had not collaborated with the French. Because the United States had been publicly and deeply committed to the French, however, Vietnamese nationalists would view any government it supported with suspicion. In October 1955, Diem established a Republic of Vietnam

in the territory for which the Geneva conference had made France responsible. Diem announced that the Geneva agreements would not bind his newly established government and that elections would not be held in 1956. The American government, which had not signed the Geneva documents, supported his position.

In 1960, the National Liberation Front was founded, with the goals of overthrowing Diem, unifying the country, reforming the economy, and ousting the Americans. It was anticolonial, nationalist, and communist. Its military arm was called the Viet Cong and was aided by the government of North Vietnam. Diem, a Roman Catholic, also faced mounting criticism from Buddhists and the army. His response to these pressures was further repression and dependence on an ever-smaller group of advisers.

DIRECT UNITED STATES INVOLVEMENT

The Eisenhower and Kennedy administrations continued to support Diem while demanding reforms in his government. The American military presence grew from about 600 advisors in early 1961 to more than 16,000 troops in late 1963. The political situation in Vietnam became increasingly unstable. On November 1, 1963, an army coup in which the United States was deeply involved overthrew and murdered Diem. The United States hoped a new government in South Vietnam would generate popular support. Thereafter, the United States sought to find a leader who could fulfill that hope. It finally settled on Nguyen Van Thieu (1923–2001), who governed South Vietnam from 1966 to 1975.

President Kennedy was assassinated on November 22, 1963. His successor, Lyndon Johnson (1963–1969), vastly expanded the commitment to South Vietnam. In August 1964, after an attack on an American ship in the Gulf of Tonkin, Johnson authorized the first bombing of North Vietnam. In February 1965, major bombing attacks began. They continued, with only brief pauses, until early in 1973. The land war grew until more than 500,000 Americans were stationed in South Vietnam.

In 1969, President Richard Nixon began a policy known as *Vietnamization*, which involved the gradual withdrawal of American troops from Vietnam while the South Vietnamese army took over the full military effort. Peace negotiations had begun in Paris in the spring of 1968, but a cease-fire was not finally arranged until January 1973. American troops left South Vietnam, and North Vietnam released its American prisoners of war. In early 1975, an evacuation of South Vietnamese troops from the northern part of their country turned into a rout when they were attacked by the North Vietnamese. On April 30, 1975, Saigon (renamed Ho Chi Minh City) fell to the Viet Cong and the North Vietnamese army. Vietnam was finally united. (See Map 29–7.)

The U.S. intervention in Vietnam, which grew out of a power vacuum left by French decolonization, affected the entire Western world. For a decade after the Cuban missile crisis, Vietnam largely diverted the attention of the United States from Europe. American prestige suffered, and the U.S. policy in Southeast Asia made many Europeans question the wisdom of the American government and its commitment to Western Europe. Many young Europeans and many people in the former colonial world as well as many Americans came to regard the United States not as a protector of liberty, but as an ambitious, aggressive, and cruel power trying to keep colonialism alive after the end of the colonial era. Within the United States, the Vietnam conflict produced enormous

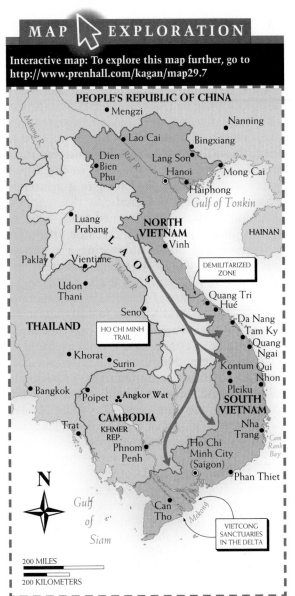

MAP EXPLORATION

Interactive map: To explore this map further, go to http://www.prenhall.com/kagan/map29.7

Map 29–7 **VIETNAM AND ITS SOUTHEAST ASIAN NEIGHBORS** The map identifies important locations associated with the war in Vietnam.

divisions and debates over American involvement in the rest of the world that persist to the present day.

THE COLLAPSE OF EUROPEAN COMMUNISM

The withdrawal of Soviet influence from Eastern Europe and the internal collapse of the Soviet Union are the most important European historical events of the second half of the twentieth century. They had virtually no parallel in modern European history. All of the other major governments that had disappeared in Europe earlier in the century had fallen either as the result of domestic revolution

U.S. armed forces patrol in Vietnam. At the war's peak, more than 500,000 American troops were stationed in South Vietnam. The United States struggled in Vietnam for more than a decade, seriously threatening its commitment to Western Europe. C. Simonpietri/CORBIS/Sygma

brought on by military defeat, as happened in tsarist Russia, Germany, and Austria after World War I and Italy during World War II, or military defeat followed by military occupation, as was the case with Germany after 1945 and the Third Republic in France in 1940. By contrast, the Soviet Union essentially imploded and then divided into separate successor states. There was no foreign invasion, no military defeat, and no internal revolution. Many of the factors leading to the Soviet collapse remain murky, but here is a relatively clear narrative of what occurred.

Under Brezhnev, who governed from 1964 to 1982, the Soviet government became markedly more repressive at home, suggesting a return to Stalinist policies. In 1974, the government expelled Aleksandr Solzhenitsyn. It also began to harass Jewish citizens, creating bureaucratic obstacles for those who wanted to emigrate to Israel. This internal repression gave rise to a dissident movement. Certain Soviet citizens dared to criticize the regime in public and accused the government of violating the human rights provision of the 1975 Helsinki Accords. The dissidents included prominent citizens, such as the Nobel Prize–winning physicist Andrei Sakharov (1921–1989). The Soviet government responded with further repression, placing some opponents in psychiatric hospitals and others under what amounted to house arrest. During the same period the structures of the Communist Party became both rigidified and corrupt, which increasingly demoralized younger Soviet bureaucrats and party members.

GORBACHEV ATTEMPTS TO REFORM THE SOVIET UNION

Although economic stagnation, party corruption, and the lingering Afghan war had long been undermining Soviet authority, what brought these forces to a head and began the dramatic collapse of the Soviet Empire was the accession to power of Mikhail S. Gorbachev (b. 1931) in 1985 after both of Brezhnev's two immediate successors, Yuri Andropov (1914–1984) and Konstantin Chernenko (1911–1985), died within thirteen months of each other. In what proved to be the last great attempt to reform the Soviet system, Gorbachev immediately began the most remarkable changes that the Soviet Union had witnessed since the 1920s. These reforms loosed forces that, within seven years, would force him to retire from office and would end both communist rule and the

Soviet Union as it had existed since the Bolshevik revolution of 1917. (See "Encountering the Past: Rock Music and Political Protest.")

Economic *Perestroika*   Gorbachev's primary goal was to revive the Russian economy to raise the country's standard of living. Initially, he and his supporters, most of whom he had appointed himself, challenged traditional party and bureaucratic management of the Soviet government and economy. Under the policy of ***perestroika***, or "restructuring," they reduced the size and importance of the centralized economic ministries.

During these same years, Gorbachev confronted significant labor discontent. A major strike by coal miners occurred in July 1989 in Siberia. Gorbachev had to settle their grievances quickly, because the economy desperately needed their output. He promised them better wages and wider political liberties.

By early 1990, in a clear abandonment of traditional Marxist ideology, Gorbachev began to advocate private ownership of property and liberalization of the economy toward free market mechanisms. Despite many organizational changes, the Soviet economy remained stagnate and even declined. The failure of Gorbachev's economic policies affected his political policies. To some extent, he pursued bold political reform because he failed to achieve economic progress.

Glasnost   Gorbachev allowed an extraordinary public discussion and criticism of Soviet history and Soviet Communist Party policy. This development

President Ronald Reagan and Premier Mikhail Gorbachev confer at a summit meeting in December 1989.   AP Wide World Photos

ROCK MUSIC AND POLITICAL PROTEST

Rock music, which epitomizes popular culture throughout the Western world, was a form of entertainment with a loud antiestablishment political message. Rock originated in the United States in the 1950s with African-American musicians and working-class and country music singers. By the early 1960s, rock also included folk singers who used their music to champion the civil rights movement and protest the war in Vietnam.

European rock groups both embraced and transformed American rock music. The most spectacularly successful European group was the Beatles. Though sporting long hair and attracting the politically active young, the Beatles's lyrics were more laid back than political.

During the 1970s, in both the United States and Europe, punk rock groups, with provocative names such as the Sex Pistols, became popular. Punk rock was deeply antiestablishment, but Western society, which was increasingly pluralistic, took punk rock in its stride.

In Eastern Europe and the Soviet Union, however, punk rock was literally revolutionary. There the ever more radical rock music of the 1970s and 1980s became a major vehicle for social and political criticism. In the face of communist cultural conformity, rock stars symbolized daring and personal heroism. Lyrics openly criticized communist governments, as in this example from "Get Out of Control," sung at a rock concert in Leningrad (now St. Petersburg) in 1986:

We were watched from the days of kindergarten.
Some nice men and kind women
Beat us up. They chose the most painful places
And treated us like animals on the farm.
So we grew up like a disciplined herd.
We sing what they want and live how they want
And we look at them downside up, as if we're
    trapped.
We just watch how they hit us
Get out of control!
Get out of control!
And sing what you want
And not just what is allowed
We have a right to yell![1]

This song became popular throughout Eastern Europe. It revealed how alienated the youth of the region had become from the official culture of the communist regimes. Rock music expressed and helped spread the disaffection that contributed to the collapse of communism throughout Eastern Europe at the end of the 1980s.

- *How did rock music evolve into an antiestablishment form of entertainment? Why was rock considered subversive in the Eastern bloc nations?*

The Russian rock group "Dynamic" performs in Moscow in 1987.
R. Podemi/TASS/Sovfoto/Eastfoto

[1]Quoted in Artemy Troitsky, *Back in the USSR: The True Story of Rock in Russia* (Boston: Faber & Faber, 1987), p. 127, as cited in Sabrina P. Ramet (ed.), *Social Currents in Eastern Europe: The Sources and Meaning of the Great Transformation* (Durham, NC: Duke University Press, 1991), p. 239.

The Polish trade union "Solidarity" in 1989 successfully forced the Polish Communist government to hold free elections. In June of that year Solidarity, whose members here are collecting funds for their campaign, won overwhelmingly. Bernard Bisson/CORBIS/Bettmann

was termed **glasnost**, or openness. The contributions to Soviet history of such figures from the 1920s and 1930s as Nikolai Bukharin, whom Stalin had executed in 1938, received official public recognition. Workers were permitted to criticize party officials and the economic plans of the party and the government. Censorship was relaxed and free expression encouraged. Dissidents were released from prison. In the summer of 1988, Gorbachev presided over a party congress that witnessed full debates.

Gorbachev soon applied *perestroika* to the political arena. In 1988, a new constitution permitted openly contested elections. After real political campaigning—a new experience for the Soviet Union—the Congress of People's Deputies was elected in 1989. One of the new members of the congress was Andrei Sakharov, the dissident physicist whom Brezhnev had persecuted. After lively debate, the Supreme Soviet, another elected body—although one the Communist Party dominated—formally elected Gorbachev president in 1989.

The policy of open discussion allowed national minorities within the Soviet Union to demand polit-

ical autonomy. Throughout its history, the Soviet Union had remained a vast empire of subject peoples. The tsars had conquered some of those groups, Stalin had incorporated others, such as the Baltic states, into the Soviet Union. *Glasnost* quickly brought to the foreground the discontent of all such peoples, no matter how or when they had been subjugated. Gorbachev proved inept in addressing these ethnic complaints. He badly underestimated the unrest that internal national discontent could generate.

1989: REVOLUTION IN EASTERN EUROPE

Solidarity Reemerges in Poland In the early 1980s, Poland's government relaxed martial law, and it eventually released all the Solidarity prisoners, although Jaruzelski remained president. In 1988, new strikes surprised even the leaders of Solidarity. This time, the communist government could not reimpose control. After consultations between the government and Solidarity, the union was legalized. Lech Walesa again took center stage, as a kind of mediator between the government and the more independent elements of the trade union movement he had founded.

Jaruzelski began some political reforms with the tacit consent of the Soviet Union. He promised free elections to a parliament with increased powers. When elections were held in 1989, the communists lost overwhelmingly to Solidarity candidates. Late in the summer, Jaruzelski, unable to find a communist who could forge a majority coalition in Parliament, turned to Solidarity and appointed the first noncommunist prime minister of Poland since 1945. Gorbachev expressly approved the appointment.

Toward Hungarian Independence Throughout 1989, as these events unfolded within Poland, one Soviet-dominated state after another in Eastern Europe moved toward independence. Early in the year, the Hungarian government opened its border with Austria, permitting free travel between the two countries. This breach in the Iron Curtain immediately led thousands of East Germans to move through Hungary and Austria to West Germany. In May, Janos Kadar, who had been installed after the Soviet intervention in 1956, was stripped of his position as president of the Hungarian Communist Party. Thousands of Hungarians gave an honorary burial to the body of Imre Nagy, whom Kadar had executed in 1958. The Hungarian Communist Party changed its name to the Socialist Party, permitted other parties to engage openly in politics, and promised free elections by October.

German Reunification In the autumn of 1989, popular demonstrations erupted in East German

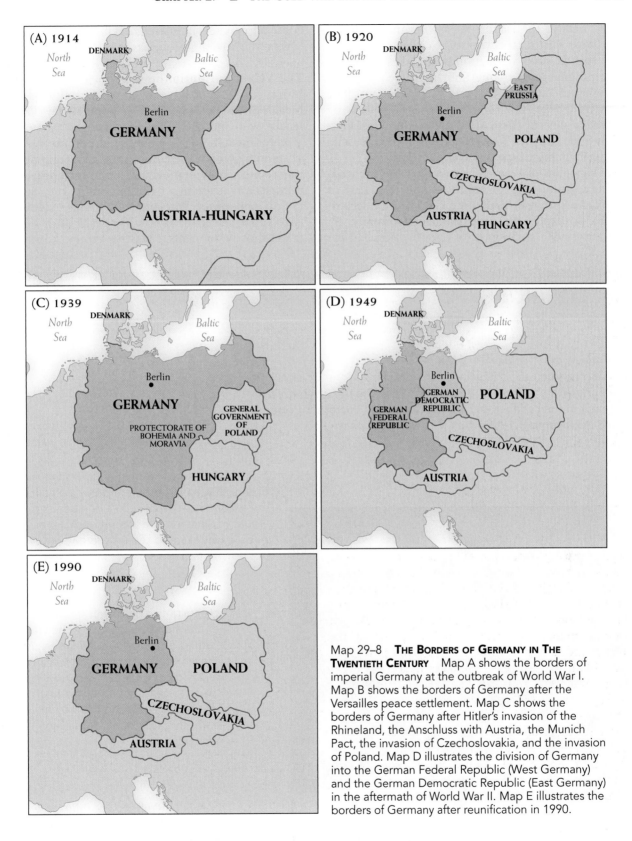

Map 29–8 **THE BORDERS OF GERMANY IN THE TWENTIETH CENTURY**   Map A shows the borders of imperial Germany at the outbreak of World War I. Map B shows the borders of Germany after the Versailles peace settlement. Map C shows the borders of Germany after Hitler's invasion of the Rhineland, the Anschluss with Austria, the Munich Pact, the invasion of Czechoslovakia, and the invasion of Poland. Map D illustrates the division of Germany into the German Federal Republic (West Germany) and the German Democratic Republic (East Germany) in the aftermath of World War II. Map E illustrates the borders of Germany after reunification in 1990.

cities. Adding to the pressure, Gorbachev told the leaders of the East German Communist Party that the Soviet Union would not use force to support them. With startling swiftness, the East German government resigned, making way for a younger generation of communist leaders who remained in office for only a few weeks. In November 1989, in one of the most emotional moments in European history since 1945, the government of East Germany ordered the opening of the Berlin Wall. That week, tens of thousands of East Berliners crossed into West Berlin to celebrate, to visit their families, and to shop with money the West German government gave them. Shortly thereafter, free travel began between East and West Germany. (See Map 29–8, page 1007.)

Within days of these dramatic events, West Germany and the other Western nations faced the issue of German reunification. Helmut Kohl (b. 1930), the chancellor of West Germany, became the leading force in moving toward full unification. Late in 1989, the European Economic Community accepted, in principle, the unification of Germany. By February 1990, some form of reunification had be-

come a forgone conclusion, accepted by the United States, the Soviet Union, Great Britain, and France.

The Velvet Revolution in Czechoslovakia Revolution in Czechoslovakia rapidly followed the breach of the Berlin Wall. The popular new Czech leader who led the forces against the party was Václav Havel (b. 1936), a playwright of international standing whom the communist government had imprisoned. In December 1989, the tottering communist government, together with the Soviet Union and other Warsaw Pact states, acknowledged that the invasion of 1968 had been a mistake. Shortly thereafter, Havel's group, known as

A CLOSER LOOK

Collapse of the Berlin Wall

No single structure so illustrated the divisions of the Cold War as the Berlin Wall, which was erected in 1961. The most symbolic moment in the collapse of communism across Eastern Europe came in November 1989 when that wall was breached.

English graffiti had been placed on the wall to ensure that an international television audience, which was largely English-speaking, would understand the aspirations of those people who wanted the wall to come down.

The sight of hundreds of Germans standing on top of the wall would have been unthinkable just days before. Armed East German and Soviet guards had for over a quarter-century prevented Germans from crossing the wall except at a few heavily guarded checkpoints.

The overwhelmingly youthful crowd indicates the repudiation by the new generation of Germans and Europeans of the Cold War divisions.

R. Bossu/Sygma/CORBIS

Civic Forum, forced Gustav Husak (b. 1913), who had been president of Czechoslovakia since 1968, to resign. On December 28, 1989, Alexander Dubcek became chairman of the Parliament, and the next day, Havel was elected president.

Violent Revolution in Romania   The only revolution of 1989 that involved significant violence occurred in Romania. There, in mid-December, the forces of President Nicolae Ceausescu (1918–1989), who had governed without opposition since 1965, fired on crowds that were protesting conditions in the country. By December 22, Bucharest was in full revolt. Ceausescu and his wife attempted to flee, but were captured, secretly tried, and shot on December 25.

The Soviet Stance on Revolutionary Developments   None of the revolutions of 1989 could have taken place unless the Soviet Union had refused to intervene militarily, in contrast to 1956 and 1968. As events unfolded, it became clear that Gorbachev would not rescue the old-line communist governments and party leaderships in Eastern Europe. In October 1989, he formally renounced the Brezhnev Doctrine. For the first time since the end of World War II, Eastern Europeans could shape their own political destiny without the fear of Soviet military intervention. Once they realized the Soviets would not act, thousands of ordinary citizens took to the streets to denounce Communist Party domination and assert their desire for democracy. The major question facing the Soviet Union became the peaceful withdrawal of its troops from Eastern Europe. The haphazard nature of that withdrawal and the general poverty to which those troops returned were other factors undermining the Soviet armed forces.

The peaceful character of most of these revolutions was not inevitable. It may, in part, have resulted from the shock with which much of the world responded to the violent repression of pro-democracy protesters in Beijing's Tiananmen Square by the People's Republic of China in May 1989. The Communist Party officials of Eastern Europe and the Soviet Union clearly decided in 1989 that they could not offend world opinion with a similar attack on democratic demonstrators.

THE COLLAPSE OF THE SOVIET UNION

Gorbachev clearly believed, as his behavior toward Eastern Europe in 1989 showed, that the Soviet Union could no longer afford to support communist governments in that region or intervene to uphold their authority while seeking to restructure its own economy. He also had concluded that the Communist Party in the Soviet Union must restructure itself and its relationship to the Soviet state and society.

Renunciation of Communist Political Monopoly   In early 1990, Gorbachev formally proposed to the Central Committee of the Soviet Communist Party that the party abandon its monopoly of power. After intense debate, the committee abandoned the Leninist position that only a single elite party could act as the vanguard of the revolution and forge a new Soviet society. (See "Gorbachev Proposes the Soviet Communist Party Abandon Its Monopoly of Power," page 1010.)

New Political Forces   Gorbachev confronted challenges from three major political forces by 1990. One consisted of those groups—considered conservative in the Soviet context—whose members wanted to preserve the influence of the Communist Party and the Soviet army. The country's economic stagnation and political and social turmoil deeply disturbed them. They appeared to control significant groups in the economy and society. During late 1990 and early 1991, Gorbachev, who himself seems to have been disturbed by the nation's turmoil, began to appoint members of these factions to key positions in the government. In other words, he seemed to be making a strategic retreat.

Gorbachev initiated these moves because he was now facing opposition from a second group—those who wanted much more extensive and rapid change. Their leading spokesman was Boris Yeltsin (b. 1931). He and his supporters wanted to move quickly to a market economy and a more democratic government. Like Gorbachev, Yeltsin had risen through the ranks of the Communist Party and had then become disillusioned with its policies. Throughout the late 1980s, he had been critical of Gorbachev. In 1990, he was elected president of the Russian Republic, the largest and most important of the Soviet Union's constituent republics. In the new political climate, that position gave him a firm political base from which to challenge Gorbachev's authority and increase his own.

The third force that came into play from 1989 onward was growing regional unrest in some of the republics of the Soviet Union. These republics had experienced considerable discontent in the past, but the military and the Communist Party had always managed to repress it. Initially, the greatest unrest came from the three Baltic republics of Estonia, Latvia, and Lithuania, which had been independent states until 1940 when the Soviet Union had occupied them in accord with secret provisions of the Soviet-German nonaggression pact of 1939.

GORBACHEV PROPOSES THE SOVIET COMMUNIST PARTY ABANDON ITS MONOPOLY OF POWER

On February 5, 1990, President Mikhail Gorbachev proposed to the Central Committee of the Soviet Communist Party that it abandon its position as the single legal party as provided in Article 6 of the Soviet constitution. His proposal followed similar actions by the communist parties of Eastern Europe. From the time of Lenin through Brezhnev, the Soviet Communist Party portrayed itself as the sole vanguard of the revolution. Gorbachev argued it should abandon that special role and compete for political power with other political parties. Within two years, the party was no longer in power, Gorbachev had resigned, and the Soviet Union no longer existed.

■ *Why did Gorbachev argue that the Soviet Communist Party must reform itself? To what extent did his speech call for the abandonment of traditional Communist Party goals? How did he think the Soviet Communist Party could function in a pluralistic political system?*

The main thing that now worries Communists and all citizens of the country is the fate of *perestroika*, the fate of the country, and the role of the Soviet Communist Party at the current, probably most crucial, stage of revolutionary transformation.

[It is important to understand] . . . that the party will only be able to fulfill the mission of political vanguard if it drastically restructures itself, masters the art of political work in the present conditions, and succeeds in cooperating with forces committed to *perestroika*.

The crux of the party's renewal is the need to get rid of everything that tied it to the authoritarian-bureaucratic system, a system that left its mark not only on methods of work and interrelationships within the party, but also on ideology, ways of thinking and notions of socialism.

The [newly proposed] platform says: our ideal is a humane, democratic socialism, expressing the interests of the working class and all working people; and relying on the great legacy of Marx, Engels and Lenin, the Soviet Communist Party is creatively developing socialist ideals to match present-day realities and with due account for the entire experience of the 20th century.

The platform states clearly what we should abandon. We should abandon the ideological dogmatism that became ingrained during past decades, outdated stereotypes in domestic policy, and outmoded views on the world revolutionary process and world development as a whole.

We should abandon everything that led to the isolation of socialist countries from the mainstream of world civilization. We should abandon the understanding of progress as a permanent confrontation with a socially different world. . . .

The party's renewal presupposes a fundamental change in its relations with state and economic bodies and the abandonment of the practice of commanding them and substituting for their functions.

The party in a renewing of society can exist and play its role as vanguard only as a democratically recognized force. This means that its status should not be imposed through constitutional endorsement.

The Soviet Communist Party, it goes without saying, intends to struggle for the status of the ruling party. But it will do so strictly within the framework of the democratic process by giving up any legal and political advantages, offering its program and defending it in discussions, cooperating with other social and political forces, always working amidst the masses, living by their interests and their needs.

From the *New York Times*, February 6, 1990, p. A16.

MAJOR EVENTS IN THE REVOLUTIONS OF 1989

January 11	Independent parties permitted in Hungary
April 5	Solidarity legalized in Poland and free elections accepted by government
May 2	Hungary dismantles barriers along its borders
May 8	Janos Kadar removed from office in Hungary
May 17	Polish government recognizes Roman Catholic Church
June 4	Solidarity victory in Polish parliamentary elections
July 25	Solidarity asked to join coalition government
August 24	Solidarity member appointed premier in Poland
October 18	Erich Honecker removed from office in East Germany
October 23	Hungary proclaims itself a republic
October 25	Gorbachev renounces Brezhnev Doctrine
November 9	Berlin Wall opened
November 17	Large antigovernment demonstration in Czechoslovakia crushed by police
November 19	Czechoslovak opposition groups organize into Civic Forum and demand resignation of communist leaders responsible for 1968 invasion
November 24	Czechoslovak communist leadership resigns
December 1	New Czechoslovak communist leaders denounce 1968 invasion; Soviet Union and Warsaw Pact express regret over 1968 invasion
December 3	Czechoslovak government announces ministry with noncommunist members
December 16–17	Massacre of civilians in Timisoara, Romania
December 22	Ceausescu government overthrown in Romania with many casualties
December 25	Announcement of Ceausescu's execution
December 28	Alexander Dubcek elected chairman of Czechoslovak Parliament
December 29	Václav Havel elected president of Czechoslovakia

That pact with Nazi Germany provided the only seemingly legal basis for the Soviet Union's continued control. In these republics, many local communist leaders began to see themselves as national leaders rather than as party stalwarts.

During 1989 and 1990, the parliaments of the Baltic republics tried to decrease Soviet control, and Lithuania actually declared independence. Gorbachev used military force to resist these moves. Discontent also arose in the Soviet Islamic republics in Central Asia and the Caucasus. Riots broke out in Azerbaijan and Tajikistan, where the army was used as a police force against Soviet citizens. Throughout 1990 and 1991, Gorbachev sought to negotiate new constitutional arrangements between the republics and the central government. His failure to effect such arrangements may have been the single most important reason for the rapid collapse of the Soviet Union.

The August 1991 Coup   The turning point in all of these events came in August 1991, when the conservative forces that Gorbachev had brought into the government attempted a coup. Troops occupied Moscow, and Gorbachev was placed under house arrest while on vacation in Crimea. The forces of political and economic reaction—led by people who, at the time, were associated with Gorbachev—had at last tried to seize control. The day of the coup, Boris Yeltsin climbed on a tank in front of the Russian Parliament building to denounce the coup and ask the world for help to maintain the Soviet Union's movement toward democracy.

Within two days, the coup collapsed. Gorbachev returned to Moscow, but in humiliation, having been victimized by the groups to whom he had turned for support. One of the largest public demonstrations in Russian history—perhaps even the largest—celebrated the failure of the coup in Moscow. From that point on, Yeltsin steadily became the dominant political figure in the nation. The Communist Party, compromised by its participation in the coup, collapsed as a political force. The constitutional arrangements between the central government and the individual republics were revised. In December 1991, the Soviet Union ceased to exist, Gorbachev left office, and the Commonwealth of Independent States came into being. (See Map 29–9, page 1012.)

The collapse of European communism in the Soviet Union and throughout eastern Europe has closed the era in which Marxism dominated European socialism that began in the 1870s with the German socialists' adoption of Marxist thought. The Bolshevik victory in the Russian Revolution

Map 29–9 **THE COMMONWEALTH OF INDEPENDENT STATES** In December 1991 the Soviet Union broke up into its fifteen constituent republics. Eleven of these were loosely joined in the Commonwealth of Independent States. Also shown is the autonomous region of Chechnya, which has waged two bloody wars with Russia in the last decade.

seemed to validate Marxism, and the policies of Lenin and Stalin sought to extend it around the world. Now the Soviet Union and the communist governments of Eastern Europe—heirs to the Bolshevik revolution—have vanished, and the economies they built have collapsed. As a result, Marxist socialism has been discredited, and socialism in general may find itself on the defensive in the future.

THE YELTSIN DECADE AND PUTIN

Boris Yeltsin emerged as the strongest leader within the new commonwealth. As president of Russia, he was head of the largest and most powerful of the new states. His popularity was high both in Russia and in the commonwealth in 1992, but within a year, he faced serious economic and political problems. The Russian Parliament, most of whom were former communists, opposed Yeltsin personally and his policies of economic and political reform. Relations between the president and Parliament reached an impasse, crippling the government. In September 1993, Yeltsin suspended Parliament, which responded by deposing him. Parliament leaders tried to incite popular uprisings against Yeltsin in Moscow. The military, however, backed Yeltsin, and he surrounded the Parliament building with troops and tanks. On October 4, 1993, after pro-Parliament rioters rampaged through Moscow, Yeltsin ordered the tanks to attack the Parliament building, crushing the opposition.

These actions consolidated Yeltsin's authority. The major Western powers, deeply concerned by the turmoil in Russia, supported him. In December 1993, Russians voted for a new Parliament and approved a new constitution. By 1994, the central government found itself at war in the Islamic

A Chechen fighter points his rifle at the head of a Russian prisioner of war outside the Chechen capital Grozny in August 1996.
Mindaugas Kulbis/AP Wide World Photos

province of Chechnya in the Caucasus, a conflict that has continued to the present with the Russian government unable to assert its firm control.

During the mid-1990s, to dismantle the Soviet state and economy, former state-owned industries were privatized. This complicated process involved much corruption and opportunism by individuals determined to profit from the emerging economic organization. One result was the creation of a small group of enormously wealthy individuals, whom the press dubbed "the oligarchs." While these people amassed vast wealth, the general Russian economy remained stagnant. In 1998, Russia defaulted on its international debt payments. Political assassinations occurred. The economic downturn contributed to further political unrest. In the face of these problems and in declining health, Yeltsin resigned the presidency in a dramatic gesture just as the new century opened. His successor was Vladimir Putin (b. 1952).

Putin renewed the war against the rebels in Chechnya, which has resulted in heavy casualties and enormous destruction there, but has also strengthened Putin's political support in Russia itself. After the terrorist attacks on the United States in September 2001, Putin supported the American assault on Afghanistan, largely because the Russian government was afraid that Islamic extremism would spread beyond Chechnya to other regions in Russia and to the largely Muslim nations that bordered Russia in Central Asia and the Caucasus.

The Chechen war spawned one of the major acts of recent terrorism in Russia. In September 2003, a group of Chechens captured an elementary school in Beslan, a community in the Russian republic of North Ossetia (in the north Caucasus) on the opening day of the term. Approximately 1,200 students, teachers, and parents were held hostage for several days. When government troops stormed the school, approximately 330 of the hostages were killed.

In the wake of this event and as part of his determination that the central government will dominate Russia's economy and political life, Putin has sought to diminish local autonomy and centralize power in his own hands. The central government has also moved against leading oligarchs. Putin appears to fear their independent influence. He has also used the attacks on them to generate support from the broad Russian public who regard the oligarchs as thieves and find themselves in economic hardship.

The internal situation in Russia remains uncertain. Despite Putin's concentration of power, Russia remains more democratic than it ever was under the Soviet system. Yet the economy continues to stagnate. Corruption and violent crime are rife and growing. Foreign investment remains inadequate. Observers both inside and outside Russia see it as a nation in decline with many of its most basic economic, social, and educational systems in decay. Since the 1980s, life expectancy in Russia has fallen from 74.4 years to 72.3 years for women and from 63.8 years to 59.9 years for men, and demographers expect the country's population to fall sharply during the twenty-first century. For the next decade or longer, Russia may resemble

Mexico during the 1920s and 1930s, when that country endured almost two decades of political instability in the wake of its revolution and had to finance itself by selling off its natural resources, mainly oil, to foreign buyers.

THE COLLAPSE OF YUGOSLAVIA AND CIVIL WAR

Yugoslavia was created after World War I. Its borders included seven major national groups—Serbs, Croats, Slovenes, Montenegrins, Macedonians, Bosnians, and Albanians—among whom there have been ethnic disputes for centuries. The Croats and Slovenes are Roman Catholic and use the Latin alphabet. The Serbs, Montenegrins, and Macedonians are Eastern Orthodox and use the Cyrillic alphabet. The Bosnians and Albanians are mostly Muslims. Most members of each group reside in a region with which they are associated historically—Serbia, Croatia, Slovenia, Montenegro, Macedonia, Bosnia-Herzegovina, and Kosovo—and these regions constituted individual republics or autonomous areas within Yugoslavia. Many Serbs, however, lived outside Serbia proper.

Tito (1892–1980), had acted independently of Stalin in the late 1940s and pursued his own foreign policy. To mute ethnic differences, he encouraged a cult of personality around himself and instituted complex political power sharing among these different groups. After his death, economic difficulties undermined the authority of the central government, and Yugoslavia gradually dissolved into civil war.

THE BREAKUP OF YUGOSLAVIA

June 1991	Slovenia declares independence; Croatia declares independence
September 1991	Macedonia declares independence
April 1992	War erupts in Bosnia and Herzegovina after Muslims and Croats vote for independence
April 1992	Serbia and Montenegro proclaim a new Federal Republic of Yugoslavia
November 1995	Peace agreement reached in Dayton, Ohio
March 1998	War breaks out in Kosovo, a province of Serbia
March 1999	NATO bombing of Serbia begins

In the late 1980s, the old ethnic differences came to the foreground again in Yugoslav politics. Nationalist leaders—most notably Slobodan Milosevic (b. 1941) in Serbia and Franjo Tudjman (b. 1922) in Croatia—gained authority. The Serbs contended that Serbia did not exercise sufficient influence in Yugoslavia and that Serbs living in Yugoslavia but outside Serbia encountered systematic discrimination, especially from Croats and Albanians. Ethnic tension and violence resulted. During the summer of 1990, in the wake of the changes in the former Soviet bloc nations, Slovenia and Croatia declared independence from the central Yugoslav government, and several European nations, including, most importantly, Germany, immediately granted them recognition. The full European community soon did likewise.

Destruction of Sarajevo. An elderly parishioner walks through the ruins of St. Mary's Roman Catholic Church in Sarajevo. The church was destroyed by Serb shelling in May 1992.   Reuters/CORBIS/ Bettmann

From this point on, violence escalated. Serbia—concerned about Serbs living in Croatia and about the loss of lands and resources there—was determined to maintain a unitary Yugoslav state that it would dominate. Croatia was equally determined to secure independence. Croatian Serbs demanded safeguards against discrimination and violence, providing the Serbian army with a pretext to move against Croatia. By June 1991, full-fledged war had erupted between the two republics. Serbia accused Croatia of reviving fascism; Croatia accused Serbia of maintaining a Stalinist regime. At its core, however, the conflict was ethnic; as such, it highlights the potential for violent ethnic conflict within the former Soviet Union.

The conflict took a new turn in 1992 when Croatian and Serbian forces determined to divide Bosnia-Herzegovina. The Muslims in Bosnia—who had lived alongside Serbs and Croats for generations—soon became crushed between the opposing forces. The Serbs in particular, pursuing a policy called "ethnic cleansing," a euphemism redolent of some of the worst horrors of World War II, killed or forcibly removed many Bosnian Muslims.

More than any other single event, the unremitting bombardment of Sarajevo, the capital of Bosnia-Herzegovina, brought the violence of the Yugoslav civil war to the attention of the world. The United Nations attempted unsuccessfully to mediate the conflict and imposed sanctions that had little affect. Early in 1994, however, a shell exploded in the marketplace in Sarajevo, killing dozens of people. Thereafter, NATO forced the Serbs to withdraw their artillery from around Sarajevo.

The events of the civil war came to a head in 1995 when NATO forces carried out strategic air strikes. Later that year, under the leadership of the United States, the leaders of the warring forces negotiated a peace agreement in Dayton, Ohio. The agreement was of great complexity but recognized an independent Bosnia. NATO troops, including those from the United States, have enforced the terms of the agreement.

Toward the end of the 1990s, Serbian aggression against ethnic Albanians in the province of Kosovo again drew NATO into Yugoslav affairs. For months, through television and other media, the world watched the Serbian military deport Albanians from Kosovo where Albanians constituted a majority of the population. The tactics closely resembled those the Serbs previously used in Bosnia. There were many casualties, atrocities, and deaths. Early in 1999, NATO again carried out an air campaign and sent troops into Kosovo to safeguard the ethnic Albanians. This air campaign was the largest military action in Europe since the close of World War II. In 2000, a revolution overthrew Slobodan Milosevic. The new Yugoslav government turned the former leader over to the International War Crimes Tribunal at the Hague where his trial has dragged on without a verdict.

THE RISE OF RADICAL POLITICAL ISLAMISM

On September 11, 2001, Islamic terrorists attacked the United States, crashing hijacked civilian domestic aircraft into the twin towers of the World Trade Center in New York City, the Pentagon in Washington, D. C., and a Pennsylvania field with a vast loss of life and property. These events and those flowing from them not only transformed American foreign policy toward the Middle East but have also changed European relations with the United States.

In retrospect, we can see that those attacks were the result of forces that had been affecting not only the United States but the Western world for at least a half century. The end of the Cold War has been succeeded by a new political world in which both the United States and the nations of Europe, including the Russian Federation, are endangered by terrorist attacks from nongovernmental or non-state-based organizations. These groups are guided by ideologies in the Islamic world that have filled a political and ideological vacuum left by the end of the Cold War.

Radical Islamism is the term scholars use to describe an interpretation of Islam that came to have a significant impact in the Muslim world during the decades of decolonization. It is only one—and by no means the most popular—interpretation of Islam. The ideas informing radical Islamism extend back to the 1930s and resistance to British rule in Egypt, but for many years, those had little impact on the politics of the Middle East.

ARAB NATIONALISM

Radical Islamism arose primarily in reaction to the secular Arab nationalism that developed in countries like Egypt and Syria in the 1920s and 1930s. Although Arab and other Middle Eastern nationalists, like nineteenth-century modernizers in the Ottoman Empire, believed that the path to independence and strength lay in adopting the technology and imitating the political institutions of the West. These advocates of radical Islam wanted to reject Western ideas and create a society based on a rigorous interpretation of Islam and its teachings. (See Chapter 22.)

In the wake of World War II, many of the foremost leaders of Arab nationalism against Western direct and indirect dominance, such as Gamal Abdul Nasser of Egypt, were sympathetic to socialism or to the Soviet Union. Because socialism and communism were Western ideologies, left-leaning Arab nationalism was no less Western in its orientation than were nationalists friendly to the United States. Moreover, Soviet communism was overtly atheistic and hence doubly offensive to devout Arab Muslims.

Nationalism forged by nondemocratic Middle Eastern governments, usually traditional monarchies or authoritarian regimes dominated by the military, brought different results to the various Arab nations. Oil made Saudi Arabia wealthy and powerful and the small Gulf states, such as Kuwait, rich but not powerful. Other states, such as Jordan, Syria, and Egypt, which lacked oil, remained burdened by large impoverished populations.

Arab governments defining themselves according to the values of nationalism worked out arrangements with local Muslim authorities. For example, the Saudi royal family turned over its educational system to adherents of a rigorist, puritanical form of Islam called *Wahhabism* while modernizing the country's infrastructure. The Egyptian government attempted to play different Islamic groups off against one another. These governments retained the support of prosperous, devout middle-class Muslims while doing little about the plight of the poor. In general, Muslim religious leaders were hostile to the Soviet Union and its influence in the Islamic world.

THE IRANIAN REVOLUTION

The Iranian Revolution of 1979 transformed the Middle East. The Ayatollah Ruhollah Khomeini (1902–1989) managed to unite both the middle and lower classes of a major Middle Eastern nation to overthrow a repressive but a modernizing government that had long cooperated with the United States. For the first time, a religiously dominated government defining itself and its mission in distinctly Islamic, as well as nationalistic, terms took control of a major state. Iran's revolutionary government was a theocracy, that is, there was no separation of religion and government or, in European terms, of church and state. The Iranian constitution gave the clergy, acting on behalf of God, the final say in all matters.

By challenging the Westernization of Iranian society, the Iranian Revolution shocked the world. It also challenged the largely secular presuppositions of Arab nationalists in states such as Egypt, Saudi Arabia, and Algeria that had failed to satisfy the needs of their own underclasses. In the mid-twentieth century, Arabs and other Middle Eastern peoples had turned to nationalism in reaction against European colonial powers. Those who grew up under nationalist leadership and still found themselves politically and economically disadvantaged, however, reacted against nationalism. The Iranian Revolution, which many thought would spread throughout the Islamic world, attracted them.

The Iranian Revolution both embodied and emboldened the forces of what is commonly called Islamic *fundamentalism*, but is more correctly termed Islamic or Muslim *reformism*. This is the belief that a reformed or pure Islam must be established in the contemporary world. Most adherents of this point of view would emphasize personal piety and religious practice. However, a minority wish to see their states strictly governed the way Iran purports to be by Islamic law or the Shari'a. In fact, the Iranian clergy made numerous compromises to the practical demands of everyday government and the oil industry, but their public message to the world was that Iran is a strict Islamic state hostile to the West in general and the United States—"the Great Satan"—in particular. The Iranian Revolution also opposed the state of Israel on both religious and nationalistic grounds.

The conservative Arab governments feared the Iranian Revolution would challenge their legitimacy. They consequently began to pay much more attention to their own religious authorities and cracked down on radical reformist or fundamentalist Muslims. In Egypt, such actions followed the assassination in 1981 of President Anwar Sadat (b. 1918) by a member of the Muslim Brotherhood.

AFGHANISTAN AND RADICAL ISLAMISM

The Russian invasion of Afghanistan of 1979, discussed earlier in this chapter, introduced a major new component into this already complicated picture, illustrating the convergence of Cold War and Islamist politics. The Soviet Union sought to impose a communist, and hence both Western and atheist, government in Afghanistan. Muslim religious authorities declared *jihad*, literally meaning "a struggle" but commonly interpreted as a religious war, against the Soviet Union. The Afghan resistance to the Soviets thus became simultaneously nationalistic, universalistic, and religious.

Thousands of Muslims, mostly fundamentalist in outlook, arrived in Afghanistan from across the Islamic world to oust the Soviets and their Afghan puppets. Conservative Arab states and the United States supported this effort, which succeeded when all Soviet forces withdrew in 1989. The conservative Arab states saw the Afghan war as an opportunity both to resist Soviet influence and to divert the energies of their own religious extrem-

Taliban fighters brandish machine-guns and rocket launchers near the Tora Bora mountains in Afghanistan, the site of a major battle with U.S. forces in late 2001.   Knut Mueller/Das Fotoarchiv/Peter Arnold, Inc.

ists. The United States saw the Afghan war as another round in the Cold War. The militant Muslim fundamentalists saw it as a religious struggle against an impious Western power.

The Taliban and Al Qaeda The Soviet withdrawal created a power vacuum in Afghanistan that lasted almost a decade. By 1998, however, rigorist Muslims known as the *Taliban* had seized control of the country. They imposed their own version of Islamic law, which involved strict regimentation of women and public executions, floggings, and mutilations for criminal, religious, and moral offenses. The Taliban also allowed groups of Muslim terrorists known as *Al Qaeda*, which means "Base," to establish training camps in their country. The terrorists who attacked the United States on September 11, 2001, came from these camps.

The ideology of these groups had emerged over several decades from different regions of the Islamic world but had been inculcated in Pakistan. The Pakistani government had long assigned considerable control over education to Islamic schools, or *madrasas*, that taught reformed Islam, rejection of liberal and nationalist secular values, intolerance toward non-Muslims, repudiation of Western culture, hostility to Israel, and hatred of the United States.

Jihad Against the United States Once the jihad against the Soviet Union had succeeded, radical Muslims, largely educated in these Pakistani schools, turned their attention to the United States,

the other great Western power. The event that brought about this redirection was the Persian Gulf War of 1991. The occasion for that conflict was the invasion of Kuwait by Iraq, under Saddam Hussein (b. 1937). The conservative Arab governments, most importantly Saudi Arabia, not only supported the United States, but permitted it to construct military bases on their territory. Islamic extremists who had fought in Afghanistan, one of whom was Osama Bin Laden (b. 1957), saw the establishment of U.S. bases in Saudi Arabia, which was the home of the prophet Muhammed and contained Islam's two holiest cities, Mecca and Medina, as a new invasion by Western Crusaders. The bases added a new grievance to the already long list of radical Muslim complaints against the United States.

The United States became a target because of its secular public morality, its international wealth and power, its military strength, its ongoing support for Israel, and its adherence to the U.N. sanctions imposed on Iraq after the Gulf War. Certain Muslim religious authorities declared a jihad against the United States, thus transforming opposition to American policies and culture into a religious war. Through the 1990s, terrorists attacks were directed against targets in or associated with the United States. These included bombings of the World Trade Center in New York City in 1993, of a U.S. army barracks in Saudi Arabia in 1996, of U.S. embassies in East Africa in 1998, and of the USS *Cole* in the Yemeni port of Aden in 2000. These attacks resulted in a considerable loss of life.

A TRANSFORMED WEST

The attacks on the United States on September 11, 2001, transformed and redirected American foreign policy into what the administration of President George W. Bush (b. 1946) termed "a war on terrorism." In late 2001, the United States attacked the Taliban government of Afghanistan, rapidly overthrowing it. The defeat of the Taliban destroyed Al Qaeda's Afghan bases but not its leadership, which appears to have survived, although it was dispersed and remains in hiding.

Following the Afghan campaign, the Bush administration set forth a policy of preemptive strikes and intervention against potential enemies of the United States. The administration argued that the danger of weapons of mass destruction developed by governments such as that of Iraq falling into the hands of international terrorist organizations posed so severe a danger to the security of the United States that the nation could not wait to respond to an attack, but must take preemptive action. This argument, which aroused controversy both at home and abroad, marked a major departure from previous United States foreign policy. It is a direct result of the attacks on the United States that occurred on September 11.

Baghdad, April 2003. American forces pull down a statue of Iraqi leader Saddam Hussein in Al Ferdous Square, Baghdad. Onlookers cheer and wave. One man points the sole of his shoe at Hussein in a sign of disrespect.
Markus Matzel/Das Fotoarchiv/Peter Arnold, Inc.

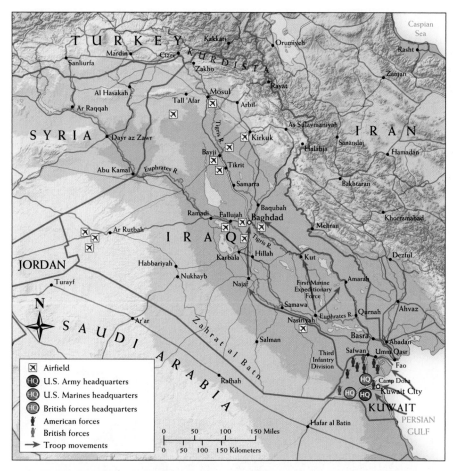

Map 29–10 **INVASION OF IRAQ**   On March 20, 2003, American and British troops poured into Iraq from bases in Kuwait, crossing the Iraqi border to the east near Safwan. The American Third Infantry Division used armored bulldozers to create wide gaps in the Iraqi defensive line.

In 2002, the Bush administration turned its attention to Saddam Hussein's government in Iraq. Since the defeat of Iraq in 1991 by an international coalition led by the United States, Saddam Hussein, contrary to widespread expectations, had remained in power and had continued to oppress his own people. Throughout the 1990s, the Iraqi government had also resisted the work of United Nations inspectors charged with discovering and destroying weapons of mass destruction found in Iraq or facilities capable of manufacturing such weapons. The Iraqis eventually expelled the United Nations inspectors in 1998, and the United Nations was unable to reinsert them for almost five years.

The United States government adopted a policy of regime change in Iraq during the last years of the Clinton administration (1993—2001) though it did little to carry out that policy. In the wake of the September 11, 2001, attacks, however, the Bush administration determined to overthrow Saddam Hussein and remove any threat from supposed

Iraqi weapons of mass destruction. In late 2002 and early 2003, the United States and British governments sought to obtain passage of United Nations Security Council resolutions that would require Iraq to disarm on its own or to be disarmed by military force. These efforts failed. France and Russia threatened to veto the measure, and a majority of the Security Council voted against it. Nonetheless, the United States and Great Britain, backed by token forces from some fifty other nations, invaded Iraq in late March 2003. After three weeks of fighting, the Iraqi army and with it the government of Saddam Hussein collapsed. The announced goals of the invasion, in addition to toppling the Iraqi regime, were to destroy Iraq's capacity to manufacture or deploy weapons of mass destruction and to bring consensual government to the Iraqi people.

The invasion of Iraq was undertaken in the face of considerable opposition from France, Germany, and Russia. It also provoked large antiwar demonstrations in the United States and throughout the

On July 7, 2005, a series of bombs rocked the London transport system with the loss of over 50 lives. This photo shows the remains of a London bus on which a suicide bomber took more than a dozen lives near Russell Square, London.
Sion Touhig/CORBIS/Bettmann

world. Both the war and the diplomatic difficulties preceding it disrupted the long-standing Atlantic alliance. Moreover, French and German opposition to the war created strains within Europe and particularly within NATO and the European Union, as other European governments either strongly supported or opposed the United States and Britain. As a result, the war in Iraq would appear to mark a new and divisive era in relations between the United States and Europe, and between the United States and the rest of the world.

Once the invasion of Iraq had been carried out and the occupation commenced, Al Qaeda terrorists struck in Europe itself. On March 11, 2004, at least 190 people were killed in train bombings in Madrid, Spain. The terrorist attack occurred just before the Spanish election. The Spanish government, which had supported the American invasion of Iraq, unexpectedly lost the election. The new government then soon withdrew Spanish troops from Iraq. The Madrid bombings were the largest act of terrorism against civilians in Europe since World War II. The attack demonstrated that terrorist attacks can directly influence European political processes.

The Iraq War and the bloody insurgency that has followed it remain controversial. The coalition forces found no weapons of mass destruction in Iraq. Government commissions in the United States and Britain have criticized the intelligence information used to justify the invasion. More than 2000 American troops and thousands of Iraqis have been killed. Many more have been injured. (See Map 29–10, page 1019.)

In 2004, however, President Bush was reelected. In March 2005, thousands of Iraqis braved threats to vote in the first meaningful election held in Iraq since the 1950s, later in October 2005 would vote to ratify a new constitution. Meanwhile in May 2005, the British government of Prime Minister Tony Blair was also reelected, though with a much reduced parliamentary majority. However, on July 7, 2005, terrorist bombings struck the London bus and subway system with a considerable loss of life. Once more, as in Spain, terrorism struck a major European city. The British government, unlike the Spanish, continued to retain its armed forces in Iraq.

As this book goes to press the United States and many of its historic post–World War II allies remain deeply divided. NATO has survived and in 2004 expanded its membership to include Poland, the Czech Republic, and Hungary. Yet the exact purpose of NATO in a world without the Soviet threat remains ill-defined.

Many Europeans see themselves, their values, and their emerging political community as different from Americans and their values and political community. Despite these immediate problems, the long-term relationship between Europe and the United Sates will no doubt survive. It is more than likely that events beyond Europe and the Atlantic community, particularly the wider conflict between the West and radical political Islam, will largely determine the shape of relations between the United States and Europe, just as the division between a democratic West and a communist eastern block once did in the past.

IN PERSPECTIVE

In 1900, the major European nations dominated the world. Their wealth in terms of manufacturing, investment banking, and consumer demand profoundly influenced the lives of millions of people on every continent. Their military power, particularly their navies, and their colonial administrators controlled most of Africa and much of Asia. Many Europeans were emigrating, especially to the Americas. Wherever Europeans traveled or governed, they could expect that people on other continents would look to Europe as a model for industrial development, accumulation of wealth, and high culture in the arts and sciences. It was the apex of the European era that began at the close of the fifteenth century. In 1900, almost no one could have predicted the enormous human tragedies that would occur in Europe during the next half century or the retreat from world dominance that would mark the European experience during the rest of the twentieth century.

World War II resulted in the political collapse of Europe. In the wake of the war, the United States and the Soviet Union emerged as two superpowers, both of them equipped with nuclear weapons. From that time until the collapse of the

Soviet Union in 1991, the U.S.-Soviet rivalry dominated world affairs. Local flashpoints became regions for rivalry and conflict between the two nuclear powers.

While the Cold War profoundly influenced international relations, the process of decolonization spread around the globe. One nation after another in Africa and Asia became free of direct European colonial rule. Scores of new nations emerged. Both the Soviet Union and the United States frequently filled the political, economic, and military vacuum the departure of the European colonial rulers left. This situation led each nation into major military interventions—the United States in Vietnam and the Soviet Union in Afghanistan—that had significant domestic consequences in each nation.

By the middle of the 1980s, the economy and political structures of the Soviet Union could no longer bear the burden of the Cold War. The effort to reform Soviet structures Mikhail Gorbachev commenced concluded with the surrender of political monopoly by the Soviet Communist Party. Simultaneously the Soviet Union retreated from eastern Europe, and the states that Soviet-controlled Communist parties formerly dominated achieved independence. By 1991, the Soviet Union had collapsed internally. The loosely structured Confederation of Independent States replaced it. Many former Soviet republics became completely independent states, some of which were hostile to Russia.

Since the collapse of the Soviet Union, the United States has remained the single superpower. Just after the turn of the new century, the United States suffered a major and unprecedented terrorist attack on its soil. Thereafter, the United States responded with unprecedented intervention in the Middle East. The political structures of that region were themselves the result of the decisions the Western powers took after World War I at the Versailles peace conference in 1919. In that regard, the conflict between the United States and many groups in the Middle East, most prominently radical political Islamists, represents one more chapter in the long, unfolding twentieth-century story of the global interaction between regions of the world European power once dominated and the West. The ongoing ramifications of decolonization have continued in the wake of the end of the Cold War.

REVIEW QUESTIONS

1. How did the United States and the Soviet Union come to dominate Europe after 1945? How would you define the policy of *containment*?

In what areas of the world did the United States specifically try to contain Soviet power from 1945 to 1982? Why were 1956 and 1962 crucial years in the Cold War?

2. How did Khrushchev's policies and reforms change the Soviet state after the repression of Stalin? Why did many people consider Khrushchev reckless?

3. Why did the nations of Europe give up their empires? How did World War II affect the movement toward decolonization? How did Gandhi lead India toward independence? How did French decolonization policies differ from Britain's? How did the United States become involved in Vietnam?

4. What internal political pressures did the Soviet Union experience in the 1970s and early 1980s? What steps did the Soviet government take to repress those protests? What role did Gorbachev's attempted reforms play in the collapse of the Soviet Union? What were the major events in Eastern Europe—particularly Poland—that contributed to the collapse of communism? What are the major domestic challenges to the new Confederation of Independent States?

5. Was the former Yugoslavia a national state? Why did it break apart and slide into civil war? How did the West respond to this crisis?

6. How did the American response to the attacks of September 11, 2001, divide the NATO alliance? Why do some European nations feel able to dissent from the U.S. position in the Middle East when they rarely did so during the Cold War?

7. What were the major causes for the rise of radical political Islamism? In what ways is the present U.S. intervention in the Middle East a result of decolonization and in what ways are other factors at work?

SUGGESTED READINGS

A. AHMED, *Discovering Islam. Making Sense of Muslim History and Society*, rev. ed (2003). An excellent and readable overview of Islamic–Western relations.

R. BERNSTEIN, *Out of the Blue: The Story of September 11, 2001 from Jihad to Ground Zero* (2002). An excellent account by a gifted journalist.

R. BETTS, *France and Decolonization* (1991). Explores the complexities of the French case.

A. BROWN, *The Gorbachev Factor* (1996). Reflections by a thoughtful observer.

R. CONQUEST, *Reflections on a Ravaged Century* (2001). Thoughtful discussion of the Soviet Union and future developments in Europe.

C. ELKINS, *Imperial Reckoning: The Untold Story of Britain's Gulag in Kenya* (2005). A study of the violence involved in Britain's eventual departure from Kenya.

M. ELLMAN AND V. KONTOROVICH, *The Disintegration of the Soviet Economic System* (1992). An overview of the economic strains in the Soviet Union during the 1980s.

G. FULLER, *The Future of Political Islam* (2003). A good overview of Islamist ideology by a former CIA staff member.

J. L. GADDIS, *The United States and the Origins of the Cold War, 1941–1947* (1992). A major discussion.

M. GLENNY, *The Balkans, 1804–1999: Nationalism, War and the Great Powers* (1999). A lively narrative by a well-informed journalist.

W. HITCHCOCK, *Struggle for Europe: The Turbulent History of a Divided Continent, 1945–2002* (2003). The best overall narrative now available.

A. HORNE, *A Savage War of Peace: Algeria 1954–1962* (1987). A now dated but classic narrative.

T. JUDAH, *The Serbs: History, Myth and the Destruction of Yugoslavia* (1997). A clear overview of a complex event.

J. KEAY, *Sowing the Wind: The Seeds of Conflict in the Middle East* (2003). A balanced account.

N. R. KEDDIE, *Modern Iran: Roots and Results of Revolution* (2003). Chapters 6–12 focus on Iran from 1941 through the 1978 revolution.

J. KEEP, *Last of the Empires: A History of the Soviet Union, 1945–1991* (1995). An outstanding one-volume survey.

G. KEPEL, *Jihad: The Trail of Political Islam* (2002). An extensive treatment by a leading French scholar.

R. MANN, *A Grand Delusion: America's Descent into Vietnam* (2001). The best recent narrative.

D. E. MURPHY, S. A. KONDRASHEV, AND G. BAILEY, *Battleground Berlin: CIA vs. KGB in the Cold War* (1997). One of the best of a growing literature on Cold War espionage.

W. E. ODOM, *The Collapse of the Soviet Military* (1999). A study more wide ranging than the title suggests.

B. PAREKH, *Gandhi: A Very Short Introduction* (2001). A useful introduction to Gandhi's ideas.

T. R. REID, *The United States of Europe: The New Superpower and the End of American Supremacy* (2004). A journalist's exploration of the impact of the European Union on American policy.

J. SPRINGHALL, *Decolonization since 1945: The Collapse of European Empires* (2001). Systematic treatment of each major former colony.

B. STANLEY, *Missions, Nationalism, and the End of Empire* (2003). Discusses the often ignored role of Christian missions and decolonization.

M. VIORST, *In the Shadow of the Prophet: The Struggle for the Soul of Islam* (2001). Explores the divisions in contemporary Islam.

DOCUMENTS CD-ROM

The Cold War and its Aftermath

30.1 Nikita S. Khrushchev: *Address to the Twentieth Party Congress*
30.2 George Kennan, from *Memoirs: 1925–1950*
30.3 Bosnia: The Two Faces of War
30.4 The Non-Aligned Movement
30.6 The Wall in My Backyard

THE WEST AT THE DAWN OF THE TWENTY-FIRST CENTURY

- **THE TWENTIETH-CENTURY MOVEMENT OF PEOPLE**
  Displacement Through War
  • External and Internal Migration
  • The New Muslim Population
  • European Population Trends

- **TOWARD A WELFARE STATE SOCIETY**
  Christian Democratic Parties •
  The Creation of Welfare States •
  Resistance to the Expansion of the
  Welfare State

- **NEW PATTERNS IN WORK AND EXPECTATIONS OF WOMEN**
  Feminism • More Married Women
  in the Work Force • New Work
  Patterns • Women in the New
  Eastern Europe

- **TRANSFORMATIONS IN KNOWLEDGE AND CULTURE**
  Communism and Western Europe
  • Existentialism • Expansion of
  the University Population and
  Student Rebellion • The
  Americanization of Europe •
  A Consumer Society •
  Environmentalism •

- **ART SINCE WORLD WAR II**
  Cultural Divisions and the Cold
  War • Memory of the Holocaust

- **THE CHRISTIAN HERITAGE**
  Neo-Orthodoxy • Liberal Theology
  • Roman Catholic Reform

- **LATE-TWENTIETH-CENTURY TECHNOLOGY: THE ARRIVAL OF THE COMPUTER**
  The Demand for Calculating
  Machines • Early Computer
  Technology • The Development of
  Desktop Computers

- **THE CHALLENGES OF EUROPEAN UNIFICATION**
  Postwar Cooperation • The
  European Economic Community
  • The European Union • Discord
  over the Union

- **IN PERSPECTIVE**

KEY TOPICS

- Migration in twentieth-century Europe
- Europe's Muslim minority
- Changing status and role of women in Europe
- New cultural forces and the continuing influence of Christianity
- The impact of computer technology
- The movement toward the European Union

---

he Cold War defined the life of the West during most of the second half of the twentieth century. This affected not only political developments and military alliances but the lives of millions of Europeans and Americans. For almost half a century, the easy travel throughout the world that many people take for granted today and that enriches the lives of thousands of

The most important accomplishment of the European Community was the launching on January 1, 1999, of the Euro, a single monetary unit that replaced the national currencies of most of its member nations. In Frankfurt, Germany people crowded around a symbol of the new currency. AP Wide World Photos

American students every year was impossible. Vast areas were closed off. The Iron Curtain separated families. Most of Eastern Europe was cut off from the material and technological advances that marked the second half of the century.

Yet despite these problems, European society, especially in the West, changed remarkably after World War II, as did, of course, the United States. Western Europe enjoyed unprecedented prosperity, peace, and technological advances. During the same years Europe also took unprecedented steps toward economic cooperation and political union. ■

THE TWENTIETH-CENTURY MOVEMENT OF PEOPLE

In the twentieth century, the movement of peoples transformed European society and the character of many European communities. The Soviet communists' forced removal of Russian peasants and the Nazi's deportations and execution of European Jews were only the most dramatic examples of this development. The Second World War and the subsequent economic transformation of the Continent brought further extensive migrations. The most pervasive trend in this movement of peoples was the continuing shift from the countryside to the cities. Today, except for Albania, at least one-third of the population of every European nation lives in large cities. In Western Europe, city dwellers are approximately 75 percent of the population.

Other vast forced movements of peoples by governments, however, were little discussed during the Cold War. During the century, millions of Germans, Hungarians, Poles, Ukrainians, Bulgarians, Serbs, Finns, Chechens, Armenians, Greeks, Turks, Balts, and Bosnian Muslims were displaced.

This forced displacement transformed parts of Europe. Stalin literally moved whole nationalities from one area of the Soviet Union to another and killed millions of people in the process. The Nazis first displaced the Jews and then sought to exterminate them. Throughout Eastern Europe, cities that once had large Jewish populations and a vibrant Jewish religious and cultural life lost any Jewish presence. The displacement of Germans after World War II transformed cities that had been German into places almost wholly populated by Czechs, Poles, or Russians. For example, the present Polish city of Gdansk was once the German city of Danzig, and today's Russian city of Kaliningrad had been the German Königsberg before 1945.

DISPLACEMENT THROUGH WAR

World War II created a vast refugee problem. An estimated 46 million people were displaced in central and Eastern Europe and the Soviet Union alone between 1938 and 1948. Many cities in Germany and in central and Eastern Europe had been bombed or overrun by invading armies. The Nazis had moved hundreds of thousands of foreign workers into Germany as slave laborers. Millions more were prisoners of war. Some of these people returned to their homeland willingly; others, particularly Soviet prisoners fearful of being executed by Stalin, had to be forced to go back. Hundreds of thousands of Baltic, Polish, and Yugoslav prisoners found asylum in Western Europe.

Changes in borders after the war also uprooted many people. For example, Poland, Czechoslovakia, and Hungary forcibly expelled millions of ethnic Germans from their territories to Germany. This transfer of over 12 million Germans in effect "solved" the problem of German minorities living outside of Germany's national boundaries that had been one of Hitler's excuses for aggression against neighboring countries. In another case of forced migration, hundreds of thousands of Poles were transferred to within Poland's new borders from territory the Soviet Union annexed. Other minorities, such as Ukrainians in Poland and Italians on the Yugoslav coast, were driven into their ethnic homelands. As one historian has commented, "War, violence, and massive social dislocation turned Versailles's dream of national homogeneity into realities."[1]

EXTERNAL AND INTERNAL MIGRATION

Between 1945 and 1960, approximately half a million Europeans left Europe each year. This was the largest outward migration since the 1920s, when around 700,000 persons had left annually. In the second half of the nineteenth century, most immigrants were from rural areas. After World War II, they often included educated city dwellers. Immediately after the war, some governments encouraged migration because they were afraid that, as in the 1930s, their economies would not be able to provide adequate employment for all their citizens.

Decolonization in the postwar period led many European colonials to return to Europe from overseas. The most dramatic example of this phenomenon was the more than one million French colonials who moved to France after the end of the Algerian war in 1962 (see Chapter 29). Britons returned from parts of the British Empire, Dutch returned from Indonesia in the late 1940s, Belgians from the Congo in the 1960s, and Portuguese from Mozambique and Angola in the 1970s.

Decolonization also led non-European inhabitants of the former colonies to migrate to Europe. Great Britain, for example, received thousands of

[1] Mark Mazower, *Dark Continent: Europe's Twentieth Century* (New York: Knopf, 1999), p. 218.

immigrants from its former colonies in the Caribbean, Africa, and the Indian subcontinent. France received many immigrants from its empire in Africa, Indochina, and the Arab world. This influx has proved to be a long-term source of social tension and conflict. In Britain, racial tensions were high during the 1980s. France faced similar difficulties, which contributed to the emergence of the National Front, an extreme right-wing group led by Jean-Marie Le Pen (b. 1928) that sought to exploit the resentment many working-class voters felt toward North African immigrants. In 2002, Le Pen won enough votes to become one of the two candidates in the run-off election for the French presidency, although he lost overwhelmingly to Jacques Chirac (b. 1932) in the final ballot. Similar pressures have arisen in Germany, Austria, Italy, the Netherlands, and even Denmark. Such tension did not result only from immigration from Africa and Asia; internal European migration—from the Balkans, Turkey, and the former Soviet Union, often of people in search of jobs—also changed the social and economic face of the Continent and led to a backlash. However, the growing Muslim presence in Europe has produced some of the most serious ethnic and political tensions.

THE NEW MUSLIM POPULATION

As recounted earlier in this textbook, well into the twentieth century the European relationship with most of the Muslim world was at arm's length or colonialist. Muslims from the Ottoman Empire, the greatest Muslim state, rarely traveled in Europe, and few Europeans traveled in the empire. Europeans encountered Muslims mainly as subjects, in colonies, such as Algeria, Egypt, the Indian subcontinent, sub-Saharan Africa, and the East Indies. In all these regions from at least the mid-nineteenth century onward, Christian missionaries often clashed with Muslim religious teachers.

At the same time, most Europeans, except for a few communities in the Balkans and the former Soviet Empire, regarded themselves and their national cultures as either Christian or secular. Indeed, until recently most Europeans paid little attention to Islam.

That indifference began to change in the 1960s and had dissolved by the end of the twentieth century as a sizable Muslim population settled in Europe. This highly diverse immigrant community had become an issue in Europe even before the events of September 11, 2001.

The immigration of Muslims into Europe, and particularly Western Europe, arose from two chief sources: European economic growth and decolonization. As the economies of Western Europe began to recover in the quarter century after World War II, a labor shortage developed. To fill this demand, Western Europe imported laborers, many of whom came from Muslim nations. For example, Turkish "guest workers" were invited to move to West Germany—on a temporary basis, it was presumed—in the 1960s, and Britain welcomed Pakistanis. The aftermath of decolonization and the quest for a better life led Muslims from East Africa and the Indian subcontinent to settle in Great Britain. The Algerian war brought many Muslims to France. Today there are approximately 1.3 million Muslims in Great Britain, 3.2 million in Germany, and 4.2 million in France. Smaller but still significant numbers have settled in Italy, Spain, Sweden, Denmark, and the Netherlands, nations that previously had had generally homogeneous populations.

These Muslim immigrant communities share certain social and religious characteristics. Originally, many Muslims came to Europe expecting they would eventually return to their homes, an expectation their host countries shared. Neither the immigrants nor the host nations gave much thought to assimilation. Moreover, except for Great Britain, where all immigrants from the Commonwealth may vote immediately upon settling there, European

Muslim women wearing headscarves, France. The presence of foreign-born Muslims whose labor is necessary for the prosperity of the European economy is a major issue in contemporary Europe. Many of these Muslims, such as these women, live in self-contained communities. Figaro Magazine/Torregano/Getty Images, Inc.—Liaison

governments made it difficult for Muslim, or any other, immigrants to take part in civic life. Unlike the United States, few European countries had any experience dealing with large-scale immigration. The Muslim communities have, therefore, generally remained unassimilated and self-contained. This apartness has provided internal community support for Muslim immigrants, but has also prevented them from fully engaging with the societies in which they live. Many of their children have not learned European languages well, and Muslim women tend to remain confined to their homes.

Yet the world around these communities has changed. Many of the largely unskilled jobs that the immigrants originally filled have disappeared. Most of the Muslim immigrants to Europe, unlike many who have settled in the United States and Canada, were neither highly skilled nor professionally educated. As a result, they and their adult children who may have grown up in Europe find it difficult to get jobs in the modern service economy. Furthermore, as European economic growth has slowed, European Muslims have become the target of politicians, such as Le Pen in France, who seek to blame the immigrants for a host of problems from crime to unemployment.

The radicalization of parts of the Islamic world has also touched the Muslim communities in Europe. Although Turkish Muslims living in Germany come from a nation that has been secularized since the 1920s and thus tend to be less religiously observant than Pakistani Muslims dwelling in Great Britain, Muslims from both countries have been involved in radical Islamic groups, and some belonged to organizations involved in the September 11, 2001, attacks on the United States. By contrast, the French government has exerted more control over its Muslim population. However, that policy appeared to have failed badly when in the autumn of 2005 immigrant youth, largely Muslim, carried out riots in various parts of France. These were the most serious civil disturbances in France since 1968.

Nonetheless, European Muslims are not a homogeneous group. They come from different countries, have different class backgrounds, and espouse different Islamic traditions. Many European Muslims and Muslim clerics disagree strongly with each other. At the same time, these Muslim communities, so often now marked by deep poverty and unemployment, have become a major concern for European social workers who disagree among themselves about how their governments should respond to them.

EUROPEAN POPULATION TRENDS

During the past quarter century, the population of Europe, measured in terms of the European birthrate, has stabilized in a manner that has dis-

turbed many observers. Europeans are having so few children that they are no longer replacing themselves. Whereas in the 1950s European women on average bore 2.1 children, that rate fell to 1.9 in the 1980s and to 1.4 at present, which is below the replacement level. In Mediterranean countries, such as Greece, Spain, and Italy, the rate is even lower. This situation stands in stark contrast to the growth in population in the United States during the past decade when the birthrate reached approximately 2.1. If the current rates more or less hold, by the middle of this century, the United States will have more people than Europe for the first time in history.

There is no consensus on why the European birthrate has declined. One reason often cited is that women are postponing having children until later in their childbearing years. Nonetheless, in response to public opinion, governments have been trying to limit immigration into Europe at a time when it may need new workers.

This falling birthrate means that Europe will face the prospect of an aging population. The energy and drive that youth can provide may shift to the other side of the Atlantic. An aging population is unlikely to give rise to economic innovation. The internal European market, now larger than the internal American market, will shrink. In contrast to the late nineteenth century (see Chapter 23), Europe itself will have fewer Europeans, and Europe's share of the world's population will also decline. Part of Europe's influence on the world in the nineteenth and early twentieth centuries was simply a consequence of the size of its population.

TOWARD A WELFARE STATE SOCIETY

During the decades spanning the Cold War, the U.S. involvement in Vietnam, and the Soviet domination of Eastern Europe, the nations of Western Europe achieved unprecedented economic prosperity and maintained or inaugurated independent, liberal democratic governments. Most of them also confronted problems associated with decolonization and with maintaining economic growth.

The end of the Second World War saw vast constitutional changes in much of Western Europe, except for Portugal and Spain, which remained dictatorships until the mid-1970s. Before or during the war, Germany, Austria, Italy, and France had experienced authoritarian governments. The construction of stable, liberal, democratic political frameworks became a major goal of their postwar political leaders, as well as of the United States.

All concerned recognized that the earlier political structures in those nations had failed to resist the rise of right-wing, antidemocratic movements. The Great Depression had shown that democracy requires a social and economic base, as well as a political structure. Most Europeans came to believe that government ought to ensure economic prosperity and social security. Success at doing so, they hoped, would stave off the kind of turmoil that had brought on tyranny and war and could lead to communism.

CHRISTIAN DEMOCRATIC PARTIES

Except for the British Labour Party, the vehicles of the new postwar politics were not, as might have been expected, the democratic socialist parties. Outside Scandinavia, those parties generally did not prosper after the onset of the Cold War. Both communists and conservatives opposed them. Rather, various Christian democratic parties, usually leading coalition governments, introduced the new policies.

These parties were a major new feature of postwar politics. They were largely Roman Catholic in leadership and membership. Catholic parties had existed in Europe since the late nineteenth century. Until the 1930s, however, they had been conservative and had protected the social, political, and educational interests of the church. They had traditionally opposed communism but proposed few positive programs of their own. The postwar Christian democratic parties of Germany, France, Austria, and Italy, however, were progressive and welcomed non-Catholic members. Democracy, social reform, economic growth, and anticommunism were their hallmarks.

The events of the war years largely determined the political leadership of the postwar decade. On the Continent, those groups and parties, including communist parties, that had been active in the resistance against Nazism and fascism held an initial advantage. After 1947, however, in a policy the United States naturally favored, communists were systematically excluded from Western European governments.

The most immediate postwar domestic problems included not only those the physical damage of the conflict created but often also those that had existed in 1939. The war, however, opened new opportunities to solve those prewar difficulties.

THE CREATION OF WELFARE STATES

The Great Depression, the rise of authoritarian states in the wake of economic dislocation and mass unemployment, and World War II, which involved more people in a war effort than ever before, changed how many Europeans thought about social welfare. Governments began to spend more on social welfare than they did on the military. This reallocation of funds was a reaction to the state violence of the first half of the century and was possible because the NATO defense umbrella, which the United States primarily staffed and funded, protected Western Europe.

The modern European welfare state was broadly similar across the Continent. Before World War II, except in Scandinavia, the two basic models for social legislation were the German and the British. Bismarck had introduced social insurance in Germany during the 1880s to undermine the German Social Democratic Party. In effect, the imperial German government provided workers with social insurance and thus some sense of social security while denying them significant political participation. In early-twentieth-century Britain, where all classes had access to the political system, social insurance was targeted toward the poor. In both the German and British systems, workers were insured only against the risks from disease, injury on the job, and old age. Unemployment was assumed to be only a short-term problem and often one that workers brought on themselves. People higher up in the social structure could look out for themselves and did not need government help.

After World War II, the concept emerged that social insurance against predictable risks was a social right and should be available to all citizens. In Britain, William B. Beveridge (1879–1963) famously set forth this concept in 1942. Paradoxically, making coverage universal, as Beveridge recommended, appealed to conservatives as well as socialists. If medical care, old-age pensions, and other benefits were available to all, they would not become a device to redistribute income from one part of the population to another.

The first major European nation to begin to create a welfare state was Britain, in 1945–1951 under the Labour Party ministry of Clement Attlee (1883–1967). The most important element of this early legislation was the creation of the National Health Service. France and Germany did not adopt similar health care legislation until the 1970s, because their governments initially refused to make coverage universal.

The spread of welfare legislation (including unemployment insurance) within Western Europe was related to both the Cold War and domestic political and economic policy. The communist states of Eastern Europe were promising their people social security as well as full employment. The capitalist states came to believe they had to provide similar security for their people, but, in fact, the social security of the communist states was often more rhetoric than reality.

RESISTANCE TO THE EXPANSION OF THE WELFARE STATE

Western European attitudes toward the welfare state have reflected three periods that have marked economic life since the end of the war. The first period was one of reconstruction from 1945 through the early 1950s. It was followed by the second period—almost twenty-five years of generally steady and expanding economic growth. The third period brought first an era of inflation in the late 1970s and then one of relatively low growth and high unemployment from the 1990s to the present. During each of the first two periods, a general conviction existed, based on Keynesian economics, that the foundation of economic policy was government involvement in a mixed economy. From the late 1970s, more people came to believe the market should be allowed to regulate itself and that government should be less involved in, though not completely withdraw from, the economy.

The most influential political figure in reasserting the importance of markets and resisting the power of labor unions was Margaret Thatcher (b. 1925) of the British Conservative Party who served as Prime Minister from 1979 to 1990. She cut taxes and sought to curb inflation. She and her party were determined to roll back many of the socialist policies that Britain had enacted since the war. Her administration privatized many industries that Labour Party governments had nationalized. She also curbed the power of the trade unions in a series of bitter and often violent confrontations. Her goal was to make the British economy more efficient and competitive. Although her administration roused enormous controversy, she was able to push these policies through parliament. Furthermore, over time the British Labour Party itself largely came to accept what was at the time known as the Thatcher Revolution. (See "Margaret Thatcher Asserts the Need for Individual Responsibility.")

While Thatcher redirected the British economy, the government-furnished welfare services now found across continental Europe began to encounter resistance. The funding on which they are based assumed a growing population and low unemployment. As the proportion of the population consuming the services of the welfare state—the sick, the injured, the unemployed, and the elderly—increases relative to the number of able-bodied workers who pay for them, the costs of those services have risen.

The leveling off of population growth in Europe discussed in the previous section has thus imper-

Margaret Thatcher, a shopkeeper's daughter who became the first female prime minister of Great Britain, served in that office from May 1979 through November 1990. Known as the "Iron Lady" of British politics, she led the Conservative Party to three electoral victories and carried out extensive restructuring of the British government and economy.   AP Wide Wold Photos

iled the benefits of the welfare state, which Europeans have come to take for granted. Furthermore, during the past two decades, significant levels of unemployment in major Western European nations have increased welfare payments. The low fertility rates across the Continent mean the next working generation will have fewer people to support the retired elderly population. Middle-class taxpayers have also become reluctant to support existing systems.

The general growth of confidence in the ability of market forces rather than government intervention to sustain social cohesion has also spread in the past twenty-five years and has raised questions about the existing welfare structures. Governments across the Continent, including those normally associated with left-of-center politics, such as the British Labour Party and the German Social Democratic Party, have limited further growth of the welfare state and have reduced benefits. In that respect, Europeans in the next few decades may look at the second half of the twentieth century as the Golden Age of welfare states and may find their own societies dealing with social welfare differently.

MARGARET THATCHER ASSERTS THE NEED FOR INDIVIDUAL RESPONSIBILITY

No single European political figure so challenged and criticized the assumptions of the welfare state and of state intervention in general than Margaret Thatcher, British Prime Minister from 1979 to 1990. Known as the "Iron Lady," Mrs. Thatcher repeatedly demanded that people take individual responsibility rather than rely on state-sponsored support. Yet her administration did not dismantle the key structures of the British welfare state.

■ *How and why does Mrs. Thatcher contend that there is no such thing as society? Does she criticize all government aid to citizens? How does she emphasize the reciprocal character of social relationships? How does she argue in favor of personal and private charity to aid persons in need?*

I think we have gone through a period when too many children and people have been given to understand "I have a problem, it is the Government's job to cope with it!" or "I have a problem, I will go and get a grant to cope with it!" "I am homeless, the Government must house me!" and so they are casting their problems on society and who is society? There is no such thing! There are individual men and women . . . there are families and no government can do anything except through people and people look to themselves first. It is our duty to look after ourselves and then also to help look after our neighbour and life is a reciprocal business and people have got the entitlements too much in mind without the obligations, because there is no such thing as an entitlement unless someone has first met an obligation and it is, I think, one of the tragedies in which many of the benefits we give, which were meant to reassure people that if they were sick or ill there was a safety net and there was help, that many of the benefits which were meant to help people who were unfortunate—"It is all right. We joined together and we have these insurance schemes to look after it." That was the objective . . . But it went too far. If children have a problem, it is society that is at fault. There is no such thing as society. There is living tapestry of men and women and people and the beauty of that tapestry and the quality of our lives will depend upon how much each of us is prepared to take responsibility for ourselves and each of us prepared to turn round and help by our own efforts those who are unfortunate.

This extract derives from a transcript of the original interview rather than the published text. Reprinted with permission from margaretthatcher.org, the official website of the Margaret Thatcher Foundation.

NEW PATTERNS IN WORK AND EXPECTATIONS OF WOMEN

Since World War II, the work patterns and social expectations of European women have changed enormously. In all social ranks, women have begun to assume larger economic and political roles. More women have entered the "learned professions," and more are filling major managerial positions than ever before in European history. Yet certain more or less traditional patterns continue to describe the position of women in both family and economic life. Despite enormous gains during the second half of the twentieth century, and despite the collapse of those authoritarian governments whose social policies inhibited women from advancing into the mainstream of society, gender inequality remained a major characteristic of the social life of Europe at the opening of the twenty-first century.

FEMINISM

Since World War II, European feminism, although less highly organized than in America, has set forth a new agenda. The most influential postwar work on women's issues was Simone de Beauvoir's

(1908–1986) *The Second Sex*, published in 1949. In that work, de Beauvoir explored the difference being a woman had made in her life. (See "Simone de Beauvoir Urges Economic Freedom for Women.") She was part of the French intellectual establishment and thus wrote from a privileged position. Nonetheless, she and other European feminists argued that, at all levels, European women experienced distinct social and economic disadvantages. Divorce and family laws, for example, favored men. European feminists also called attention to the social problems that women faced, including spousal abuse.

Simone de Beauvoir, here with her companion, the philosopher Jean-Paul Sartre, was the major feminist writer in postwar Europe.   Keystone_Paris/ Getty Images Inc./Hulton Archive Photos

In contrast to earlier feminism, recent feminism has been less a political movement pressing for specific rights than a social movement offering a broader critique of European culture. Several new feminist journals appeared during the 1970s, many of which are still published: *Courage, Emma—Magazine by Women for Women*, and *Spare Rib*. A statement in *Spare Rib*, an English magazine, captures the spirit of these publications:

Spare Rib aims to reflect women's lives in all their diverse situations so that they can recognize themselves in its pages. This is done by making the magazine a vehicle for their writing and their images. Most of all, *Spare Rib* aims to bring women together and support them in taking control of their lives.[2]

This emphasis on women controlling their own lives may be the most important element of recent European feminism. Whereas in the past feminists sought and, in significant measure, gained legal and civil equality with men, they are now pursuing personal independence and issues that are particular to women. In this sense, feminism is an important manifestation of the critical tradition in Western culture.

MORE MARRIED WOMEN IN THE WORK FORCE

One of the patterns that seemed firmly established in 1900 has reversed itself. The number of married women in the work force has risen sharply. Both middle-class and working-class married women have sought jobs outside the home. Because of the low birthrate in the 1930s, few young single women were employed in the years just after World War II. Married women entered the job market to replace them. Some factories changed their work shifts to accommodate the needs of married women. Consumer conveniences and improvements in health care also made it easier for married women to enter the work force by reducing the demands childcare made on their time. At the same time, all surveys indicate that the need to provide care for their children is the most important difficulty women face in the workplace. This situation is a main reason why so many women remain in part-time employment.

In the twentieth century, children were no longer expected to contribute substantially to family income. They now spend more than a decade in compulsory education. When families need more income than one worker can provide, both parents work, bringing many married women with children into the work force. Such financial necessity led many married women back to work. Evidence also suggests that married women began to work to escape the boredom of housework and to enjoy the companionship of other adult workers.

NEW WORK PATTERNS

The work pattern of European women has been far more consistent in the twentieth century than it had been in the nineteenth. Single women enter the work force after their schooling and continue to work after marriage. They may stop working to care for their young children, but they return to work when the children begin school. Several factors created this new pattern, but women's increasing life expectancy is one of the most important.

When women died relatively young, child rearing filled a large proportion of their lives. As a longer life span has shortened that proportion, women throughout the West are seeking ways to lead satisfying lives after their children have grown. Decisions about when to have children and how many have also shaped the late-twentieth-century work pattern for women. Many women have begun to limit the number of children they bear or to forgo childbearing and child rearing altogether.

[2]Quoted in Bonnie S. Anderson and Judith P. Zinsser, *A History of Their Own: Women in Europe from Prehistory to the Present*, Vol. 2 (New York: Harper Perennial, 1988), p. 412.

SIMONE DE BEAUVOIR URGES ECONOMIC FREEDOM FOR WOMEN

Simone de Beauvoir was the most important feminist voice of mid-twentieth-century Europe. In The Second Sex, *published in France in 1949, she explored the experience of women coming of age in a world of ideas, institutions, and social expectations shaped historically by men. Much of the book discusses the psychological strategies that modern European women had developed to deal with their status as "the second sex." Toward the end of her book, de Beauvoir argues that economic freedom and advancement for women are fundamental to their personal fulfillment.*

- *Why does de Beauvoir argue that economic freedom for women must accompany their achievement of civic rights? Why does the example of the small number of professional women illustrate issues for European women in general? How does she indicate that even professional women must overcome a culture in which the experience of women is fundamentally different from that of men? Do de Beauvoir's comments seem relevant for women at the opening of the twenty-first century? What similarities do you see to the views of Priscilla Wakefield (Chapter 15) and Mary Wollstonecraft (Chapter 17)?*

According to French law, obedience is no longer included among the duties of a wife, and each woman citizen has the right to vote; but these civil liberties remain theoretical as long as they are unaccompanied by economic freedom. . . . It is through gainful employment that woman has traversed most of the distance that separated her from the male; and nothing else can guarantee her liberty in practice. Once she ceases to be a parasite, the system based on her dependence crumbles; between her and the universe there is no longer any need for a masculine mediator. . . .

When she is productive, active, she regains her transcendence; in her projects she concretely affirms her status as subject; in connection with the aims she pursues, with the money and the rights she takes possession of, she makes trial of and senses her responsibility. . . .

There are . . . a fairly large number of privileged women who find in their professions a means of economic and social autonomy. These come to mind when one considers woman's possibilities and her future . . . [E]ven though they constitute as yet only a minority; they continue to be the subject of debate between feminists and antifeminists. The latter assert that the emancipated women of today succeed in doing nothing of importance in the world and that furthermore they have difficulty in achieving their own inner equilibrium. The former exaggerate the results obtained by professional women and are blind to their inner confusion. There is no good reason . . . to say they are on the wrong road; and still it is certain that they are not tranquilly installed in their new realm: as yet they are only halfway there. The woman who is economically emancipated from man is not for all that in a moral, social, and psychological situation identical with that of man. The way she carried on her profession and her devotion to it depends on the context supplied by the total pattern of her life. For when she begins her adult life she does not have behind her the same past as does a boy; she is not viewed by society in the same way; the universe presents itself to her in a different perspective. The fact of being a woman today poses peculiar problems for an independent human individual.

The age at which women have decided to bear children has risen, to the early twenties in Eastern Europe and to the late twenties in Western Europe. In urban areas, women have fewer children and have them later in life than rural women do. These various personal decisions leave many years free to develop careers and stay in the work force.

WOMEN IN THE NEW EASTERN EUROPE

Many paradoxes surround the situation of Eastern European women now that communists no longer govern the region. Under communism, women generally enjoyed social equality, as well as a broad spectrum of government-financed benefits. Most women (normally well over 50 percent) worked in these societies, both because they could and because they were expected to. No significant women's movements existed, however, because communist governments regarded them with suspicion, as they did all independent associations.

The new governments of the region are free, but have shown little concern with women's issues. Indeed, the economic difficulties the new governments face may endanger their funding of health and welfare programs that benefit women and children. For example, a free market economy may limit the extensive maternity benefits to which Eastern European women were previously entitled. Moreover, the high proportion of women in the work force could leave them more vulnerable than men to the region's economic troubles. Women may be laid off before men and hired later than men for lower pay.

TRANSFORMATIONS IN KNOWLEDGE AND CULTURE

Knowledge and culture in Europe were rapidly transformed in the twentieth century. Institutions of higher education enrolled a larger and more diverse student body, making knowledge more widely available than ever before. Also, movements such as existentialism challenged traditional intellectual attitudes. Environmental concerns also raised new issues. Throughout this ferment, representatives of the Christian faith tried to keep their religion relevant.

COMMUNISM AND WESTERN EUROPE

Until the final decade of the twentieth century, Western Europe had large, organized communist parties, as well as groups of intellectuals sympathetic to communism. After the Bolshevik victory in the Russian Revolution and the subsequent civil war, the Western European socialist movement divided into independent democratic socialist parties and Soviet-dominated communist parties that followed the dictates of the Third International. In the 1920s and 1930s, those two groups fought each other with only rare moments of cooperation, such as that achieved during the French Popular Front in 1936.

The Intellectuals During the 1930s, as liberal democracies floundered in the face of the Great Depression and as right-wing regimes spread across the Continent, many people saw communism as a vehicle for protecting humane and even liberal values. European university students were often affiliated with the Communist Party. They and older intellectuals visited the Soviet Union and praised what they saw as Stalin's achievements. Some of these intellectuals may not have known of Stalin's terror. Others simply closed their eyes to it, believing humane ends might come from inhumane methods. Still others defended Stalinist terror. During the late 1920s and the 1930s, communism became a substitute religion for some Europeans. One group of former communists, writing after World War II, described their attraction toward, and later disillusionment with, communism in a book entitled *The God That Failed* (1949).

Four events proved crucial to the intellectuals' disillusionment: the great Soviet public purge trials of the late 1930s, the Spanish Civil War (1936–1939), the Nazi-Soviet pact of 1939, and the Soviet invasion of Hungary in 1956. Arthur Koestler's (1905–1983) novel *Darkness at Noon* (1940) recorded a former communist's view of the purges. George Orwell (1903–1950), who had never been a communist, but who had sympathized with the party, expressed his disappointment with Stalin's policy in Spain in *Homage to Catalonia* (1938). The Nazi-Soviet pact destroyed Stalin's image as an opponent of fascism. Other intellectuals, such as the French philosopher Jean-Paul Sartre (1905–1980), continued to believe in the Soviet Union during and after the war, but the Hungarian Revolution cooled their ardor. The Soviet-led invasion of Czechoslovakia in 1968 simply confirmed a general disillusionment with Soviet policies by even left-wing Western European intellectuals.

Yet disillusionment with the Soviet Union or with Stalin did not always mean disillusionment with Marxism or with radical socialist criticisms of European society. Some writers and social critics looked to the establishment of alternative communist governments based on non-Soviet models. During the decade after World War II, Yugoslavia provided such an example. Beginning in the late 1950s, radical students and a few intellectuals found inspiration in the Chinese Revolution. Other groups hoped a European Marxist system would de-

George Orwell (1903–1950), shown here with his son, was an English writer of socialist sympathies who wrote major works opposing Stalin and communist authoritarianism.
Felix H. Man/Bildarchiv Preussischer Kulturbesitz

velop. Among the more important contributors to this non-Soviet tradition was the Italian communist Antonio Gramsci (1891–1937), especially in his work *Letters from Prison* (published posthumously in 1947). The thinking of such non-Soviet communists became important to Western European communist parties, such as the Italian Communist Party, that hoped to gain office democratically.

Another way to accommodate Marxism within mid-twentieth-century European thought was to redefine the basic message of Marx himself. During the 1930s, many of Marx's previously unprinted essays were published. These books and articles, written before the *Communist Manifesto* of 1848, are abstract and philosophical. They make the "young Marx" appear to belong more nearly to the humanist than to the revolutionary tradition of European thought. Since World War II, works such as *Philosophic Manuscripts* of 1844 and *German Ideology* have been widely read. Today, many people are more familiar with them than with the

Manifesto or *Capital*. They allowed some people to consider themselves sympathetic to Marxism without also seeing themselves as revolutionaries or supporters of the Soviet Union. With the collapse of the communist governments of Eastern Europe and the Soviet Union, what influence Marxism will continue to have on European intellectual life in the future is unclear.

EXISTENTIALISM

The intellectual movement that perhaps best captured the predicament and mood of mid-twentieth-century European culture was **existentialism**. Like the modern Western mind in general, existentialism, which has been termed the "philosophy of Europe in the twentieth century," was badly divided; most of the philosophers associated with it disagreed with each other on major issues. The movement represented, in part, a continuation of the revolt against reason that began in the nineteenth century.

Roots in Nietzsche and Kierkegaard Friedrich Nietzsche (1844–1900), discussed in Chapter 24, was a major forerunner of existentialism. Another was the Danish writer Søren Kierkegaard (1813–1855), who received little attention until after World War I. Kierkegaard was a rebel against both Hegelian philosophy and Danish Lutheranism. In works such as *Fear and Trembling* (1843), *Either/Or* (1843), and *Concluding Unscientific Postscript* (1846), he maintained that the truth of Christianity could be grasped only in the lives of those who faced extreme situations, not in creeds, doctrines, and church structures.

Kierkegaard also criticized Hegelian philosophy and, by implication, all academic rational philosophy. Philosophy's failure, he felt, was the attempt to contain life and human experience within abstract categories. Kierkegaard spurned this faith in the power of mere reason. "The conclusions of passion," he declared, "are the only reliable ones."[3]

The intellectual and ethical crisis of World War I brought Kierkegaard's thought to the foreground and also created new interest in Nietzsche's critique of reason. The war led many people to doubt whether human beings were actually in control of their own destiny. Its destructiveness challenged faith in human rationality and improvement. Indeed, the war's most terrible weapons—poison gas, machine guns, submarines, high explosives—were the products of rational technology. The pride in rational human achievement that had characterized nineteenth-century European civilization lay in ruins. The sunny faith in rational

[3]Quoted in Walter Kaufman, ed., *Existentialism from Dostoyevsky to Sartre* (Cleveland: World Publishing Company, 1962), p. 18.

human development and advancement had not withstood the horror of war.

Questioning of Rationalism   Existentialist thought thrived in this climate and received further support from the trauma of World War II. The major existential writers included the Germans Martin Heidegger (1889–1976) and Karl Jaspers (1883–1969) and the French Jean-Paul Sartre (1905–1980) and Albert Camus (1913–1960). Their books are often difficult or obscure. Although they frequently disagreed with each other, they all, in one way or another, questioned the primacy of reason and scientific understanding as ways to come to grips with the human situation. Heidegger, a philosopher deeply compromised by his association with the Nazis, argued, "Thinking only begins at the point where we have come to know that Reason, glorified for centuries, is the most obstinate adversary of thinking."[4]

The Romantic writers of the early nineteenth century had also questioned the primacy of reason, but their criticisms were much less radical than those of the existentialists. The Romantics emphasized the imagination and intuition, but the existentialists dwelled primarily on the extremes of human experience. Death, fear, and anxiety provided their themes. The titles of their works illustrate their sense of foreboding and alienation: *Being and Time* (1927), by Heidegger; *Nausea* (1938) and *Being and Nothingness* (1943), by Sartre; *The Stranger* (1942) and *The Plague* (1947), by Camus. The touchstone of philosophic truth became the experience of the individual under extreme conditions.

According to the existentialists, human beings are compelled to formulate their own ethical values and cannot depend on traditional religion, rational philosophy, intuition, or social customs for ethical guidance. The opportunity and need to define values endow humans with a dreadful freedom. (See "Sartre Discusses His Existentialism.")

The existentialists were largely protesting against a world in which reason, technology, and politics produced war and genocide. Their thought reflected the uncertainty of social institutions and ethical values in the era of the two world wars. Since the 1950s, however, their works and ideas have found their way into university curriculums around the

world, making them objects of study, if not the source of intellectual ferment they had been. They continue to be discussed in philosophy and literature classes, but their popularity has receded.

European intellectuals were attracted to communism and existentialism before and just after World War II, but in the 1960s, the turmoil over Vietnam and the youth rebellion brought other intellectual and social issues to the fore. Even before the collapse of communism, these had begun to redirect European intellectual interests.

EXPANSION OF THE UNIVERSITY POPULATION AND STUDENT REBELLION

As rapid changes in communications technology vastly expanded access to information, more Europeans received some form of university education. In 1900, only a few thousand people were enrolled in universities in any major European country. By 2000, that figure had risen to hundreds of thousands, although university education is still less common in Europe than in the United States. Higher education is now available to people from a variety of social and economic backgrounds, and, for the first time, to women.

One of the most striking and unexpected results of this rising post–World War II population of students and intellectuals was the student rebellion of the 1960s. This development is still not well understood. Student uprisings began in the early 1960s in the United States and grew with opposition to the war in Vietnam. The student rebellion then spread into Europe and other parts of the world. It was al-

In 1968 a student rebellion in Paris threatened to bring down the government of Charles De Gaulle. This was only one example of the explosion of student activity that rocked the West in the late 1960s. © Bettmann/CORBIS

SARTRE DISCUSSES HIS EXISTENTIALISM

Jean-Paul Sartre, dramatist, novelist, and philosopher, was the most important French existentialist. In the first paragraph of this 1946 statement, Sartre asserted that all human beings must experience a sense of anguish or the most extreme anxiety when undertaking a major commitment. That anguish arises because, consciously or unconsciously, they are deciding whether all human beings should make the same decision. In the second paragraph, Sartre argued that the existence or nonexistence of God would make no difference in human affairs. Humankind must discover the character of its own situation by itself.

■ *How might the experiences of fascism in Europe and the fall of France to the Nazis have led Sartre to emphasize the need of human beings to choose? Why does Sartre believe existentialism must be related to atheism? Why did Sartre regard existentialism as optimistic?*

The existentialist frankly states that man is in anguish. His meaning is as follows—When a man commits himself to anything, fully realizing that he is not only choosing what he will be, but is thereby at the same time a legislator deciding for the whole of mankind—in such a moment a man cannot escape from the sense of complete and profound responsibility. There are many, indeed, who show no such anxiety. But we affirm that they are merely disguising their anguish or are in flight from it. Certainly, many people think that in what they are doing they commit no one but themselves to anything: and if you ask them, "What would happen if everyone did so?," they shrug their shoulders and reply, "Everyone does not do so." But in truth, one ought always to ask oneself what would happen if everyone did as one is doing; nor can one escape from that disturbing thought except by a kind of self-deception. The man who lies in self-excuse, by saying, "Everyone will not do it" must be ill at ease in his conscience, for the act of lying implies the universal value which it denies. By its very disguise his anguish reveals itself.

Existentialism is nothing else but an attempt to draw the full conclusions from a consistently atheistic position. Its intention is not in the least that of plunging men into despair. And if by despair one means—as the Christians do—any attitude of unbelief, the despair of the existentialist is something different. Existentialism is not atheist in the sense that it would exhaust itself in demonstration of the nonexistence of God. It declares, rather, that even if God existed that would make no difference from its point of view. Not that we believe God does exist, but we think that the real problem is not that of His existence; what man needs is to find himself again and to understand that nothing can save him from himself, not even a valid proof of the existence of God. In this sense existentialism is optimistic. It is a doctrine of action, and it is only by self-deception, by confusing their own despair with ours that Christians can describe us as without hope.

From Jean-Paul Sartre, *Existentialism and Humanism*, trans. by Philip Mairet (London: Methuen), in Walter Kaufman, ed., *Existentialism from Dostoyevsky to Sartre* (New York: Meridian Books, 1956), pp. 292, 310–311.

most always associated with a radical political critique of the United States, although Eastern European students resented the Soviet Union even more. The movement was generally antimilitarist. Students also questioned middle-class values and traditional sexual mores and family life.

The student movement peaked in 1968, when American students demonstrated forcibly against U.S. involvement in Vietnam. In the same year, students at the Sorbonne in Paris almost brought down the government of Charles de Gaulle, and in Czechoslovakia, students were in the forefront of the liberal socialist experiment. These protests failed to have an immediate effect on the policies of the governments at which they were directed. The United States stayed in Vietnam until 1973, de Gaulle remained president of France for another year, and the Soviets suppressed the Czech experiment.

By the early 1970s, the era of student rebellion seemed to have passed. Students remained active in European movements against nuclear weapons and particularly against the placement of American nuclear weapons in Germany and elsewhere in Europe. From the mid-1970s, however, although often remaining political radicals, they generally abandoned the disruptive protests that had marked the 1960s.

THE AMERICANIZATION OF EUROPE

During the past half century, through the Marshall Plan, the leadership of NATO, the stationing of huge military bases, student exchanges, popular culture, and tourism, the United States has exerted enormous influence on Europe, especially Western Europe. The word *Americanization*, an often pejorative term in European publications, refers, in part, to this economic and military influence, but also to concerns about cultural loss. Many Europeans feel that American popular entertainment, companies, and business methods threaten to extinguish Europe's unique qualities. Many American firms now have European branches. Large American corporations, such as McDonald's, Starbucks, Apple computers, and the Gap, have outlets in European cities from Dublin to Moscow. American liquor companies and distilleries now sell their goods in Europe. Casual American clothing, such as blue jeans and baseball caps, is ubiquitous in Europe. Shopping centers and supermarkets, first pioneered in America, are displacing neighborhood markets in European cities. American television programs, movies, computer games, and rock and rap music are readily available. Furthermore, as Europe moves toward greater economic cooperation, English has become the common language of business, technology, and even some academic fields—and it is American English, not British. (See Encountering, the Past: Toys from Europe Conquer the United States.)

A CONSUMER SOCIETY

Although European economies came under pressure during the 1990s and experienced high levels of unemployment, the consumer sector has expanded to an extraordinary degree during most of the last half century.

The consumer orientation of the Western European economy emerged as one of the most important characteristics differentiating it from Eastern Europe. Those differences produced political results. In the Soviet Union and the nations it dominated in Eastern Europe, economic planning overwhelmingly favored capital investment and military production. These nations produced inadequate food for their people and few consumer goods. Long lines for staples, such as food and clothing, were common. Au-

McDonald's restaurants like this one in Moscow are a symbol of American popular culture in Europe. © John Dakers; Eye Ubiquitous/CORBIS

tomobiles were a luxury. Housing was inadequate. Consumer goods were shoddy.

By contrast, by the early 1950s, Western Europeans enjoyed an excellent food supply that has continued to improve. Also, in a sign of the strength of Western Europe's economy, if not the healthfulness of its diet, fast-food outlets have multiplied.

Western Europe has enjoyed a similar expansion of consumer goods and services. Automobile ownership has soared. Refrigerators, washing machines, electric ranges, televisions, microwaves, videocassette recorders, cameras, computers, CD players, DVD players, and other electronic consumer items are taken for granted. Like their American counterparts, Western Europeans now have a whole gamut of products, such as disposable diapers and prepared baby foods, to help them raise children. They take foreign vacations year round, prompting the expansion of ski resorts in the Alps and beach resorts on the Mediterranean.

This vast expansion of consumerism, which, as we noted in Chapter 15, began in the eighteenth century, became a defining characteristic of Western Europe in the late twentieth century. It stood in marked contrast to the consumer shortages in Eastern Europe. Yet through even the limited number of

TOYS FROM EUROPE CONQUER THE UNITED STATES

Today many Europeans criticize what they term *Americanization*—the intrusion of popular American products and restaurant chains onto the European scene. Yet over the past half century one European toy—LEGO building blocks manufactured in Denmark—has shaped the experience of childhood for many children in the United States and the rest of the world, entering their lives and imaginations no less powerfully than the cartoon figures associated with the American Disney Corporation.

In 1932, in the midst of the depression, Ole Kirk Christiansen opened a small business in Billund, Denmark, that manufactured household goods and wooden toys. The toys sold so well that two years later the firm renamed itself LEGO from the Danish *LEg GOdt* meaning "Play well." The company remained small, producing only wooden toys, until 1947 when it began to make molded plastic toys. It only sold its products in Denmark.

In 1955, LEGO introduced LEGO Bricks—plastic building blocks of the familiar stud-and-tube type—that it sold in sets under the name LEGO System of Play. That system, which the firm patented in 1958, allowed children to combine LEGO Bricks in an almost endless number of ways, limited only by their own imaginations and that of their parents. The company also extended its market across and began to sell in the United States in 1961.

Thereafter, the success of LEGO as a toy and as a company fed on itself. The company added many new features to the original concept of interlocking building blocks. For example, wheels enabled children to use LEGO kits to build their own trucks, trains, and similar mobile toys.

In 1968, the LEGO Company, no doubt following the example of the Disney Corporation in the United States, opened an amusement park in Billund in which the rides were designed to look like huge LEGO toys. By the end of the century, LEGO had opened similar parks in England, the United States, and Germany.

However, the company remained focused on making toys for children. It designed new toys,

Children across the world play with LEGO toys.   Tom Prettyman/PhotoEdit

such as plastic figures with human heads to ride in LEGO vehicles, and whole LEGO villages, castles, and pirate ships. By the 1990s, LEGO had become the largest toy manufacturer in Europe and a part of modern culture. Museums displayed LEGO products and art built from LEGO blocks. Contests were held to construct the largest or most unusual LEGO structures. In 1999, *Fortune* magazine included the LEGO brick among the "Products of the Century," and in 2002, LEGO persuaded European and American management consultants that working with LEGO blocks would help business executives think more clearly about corporate planning. Perhaps most astonishing is that during a half century of tumultuous change, children around the world have continued to play with these little pieces of plastic.

- *How has LEGO been an example of the European penetration of popular culture around the world? Why has the influence of LEGO on children's toys been less controversial than the appearance of American fast-food chains in Europe?*

Source: Factual information derived from the official Lego Company Web site: *www.lego.com/eng/info/history*.

radios, televisions, movies, and videos available to them, people in the East grew increasingly aware of the discrepancy between their lifestyle and that of the West. They associated Western consumerism with democratic governments, free societies, and economic policies that favored the free market and limited government planning. Thus, the expansion of consumerism in the West, which many intellectuals and moralists deplored, helped generate the discontent that brought down communism in Eastern Europe and the Soviet Union.

ENVIRONMENTALISM

After World War II, shortages of consumer goods created a demand that fueled postwar economic reconstruction and growth into the 1950s and 1960s. In those expansive times, public debate about the ethics of economic expansion and efficiency and their effects on the environment was muted. Concerns about pollution began to grow in the 1970s, and by the 1980s, environmentalists had developed real political clout. Among the most important environmental groups were the German Greens. The Greens formed a political party in 1979 that immediately became an electoral force. During these same years, concern for environmental issues, such as global warming and the pollution of water and the atmosphere, commanded the attention of governments outside Europe and of the United Nations.

Several developments lay behind this new concern for the environment. The Arab oil embargo of 1973–1974 pressed home two messages to the industrialized West: Natural resources are limited, and foreign, potentially hostile, countries control critical resources. By the 1970s, too, the environmental consequences of three decades of economic expansion were becoming increasingly apparent. Fish were dying in the Thames River in England. Industrial pollution was destroying life in the Rhine River between Germany and France. Acid rain was killing trees from Sweden to Germany. Finally, long-standing worries about nuclear weapons merged with concerns about their environmental effects, strengthening antinuclear groups and generating opposition to the placement of nuclear weapons in Europe.

The German **Green movement** originated among radical student groups in the late 1960s. Like them, it was anticapitalist, blaming business or pollution. The Greens and other European environmental groups were also strongly antinuclear. Unlike the students of the 1960s, the Greens avoided violence and mass demonstrations, seeking instead to become a significant political presence through the electoral process.

The 1986 disaster at the Chernobyl nuclear reactor in the Soviet Union heightened concern about environmental issues and raised questions that no European government could ignore. The Soviet government had to confront casualties at the site and relocate tens of thousands of people. Radioactive fallout spread across Europe. Environmentalists had always contended that their issues transcended national borders. The Chernobyl fire proved them right.

After Chernobyl, European governments, East and West, began to respond to environmental concerns. Some observers believe the environment may become a major political issue across the Continent. In Western Europe, environmental groups command many votes. Economic and political integration opens the possibility of transnational cooperation on environmental matters. As the European Economic Community solidifies, it and its member nations will likely impose more environmental regulations on business and industry. The nations of Eastern Europe have been forced to face the cleanup of vast areas of industrial development polluted during the communist era and to try to combine environmental protection with economic growth.

ART SINCE WORLD WAR II

It is impossible to cover even briefly the expansive and varied world of Western art since the end of World War II. However, we can note how both the Cold War and the memory of the horrors of the Second World War influenced Western art.

Tatjiana Yablonskaya, *Bread*, 1949. Ria Novosti/Sovfoto/Eastfoto

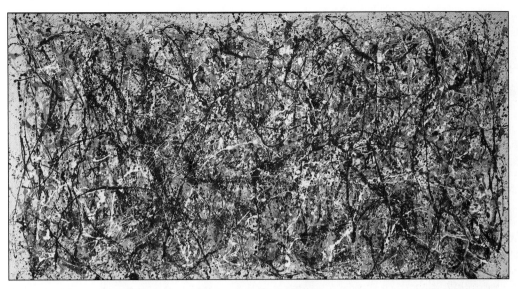

Jackson Pollock, *One (Number 31, 1950)*.   Oil and enamel on unprimed canvas, 8 ft. 10 in. × 17 ft. 5⅝ in.
(269.5 × 530.8 cm). The Museum of Modern Art/Licensed by Scala-Art Resource, NY. Sidney and Harriet Janis
Collection Fund (by exchange). Photograph © 2000 The Museum of Modern Art, New York. 00007.68. © 2004
The Pollock-Krasner Foundation/Artists Rights Society (ARS), New York

CULTURAL DIVISIONS AND THE COLD WAR

Although they may seem like products from different centuries, the Soviet painter Tatjiana Yablonskaya's (b. 1917) sun-strewn *Bread* (1949) and the American Jackson Pollock's (1912–1956) dizzyingly abstract *One* (Number 31, 1950) were painted only one year apart. The stark differences between these two works mirror the cultural divisions of the early Cold War.

Bread, measuring over six feet high and twelve feet wide, is a monumental example of socialist realism. Established, on Stalin's orders, as the official doctrine of Soviet art and literature in 1934, socialist realism sought to create optimistic and easily intelligible scenes of a bold socialist future, in which prosperity and solidarity would reign. Manual laborers and prominent historical and political figures were painted in a traditional and often rigid figurative manner. Under Soviet control after World War II, socialist realism became the dominant artistic model throughout Eastern Europe, only waning when Nikita Khrushchev liberalized Soviet cultural policy in the late 1950s.

The looping skeins of paint in *One* (Number 31, 1950) may seem completely different from the kind of "realistic" propaganda visible in *Bread*, but Pollock's painting is in fact a central document of postwar American cultural life. Flinging paint from sticks and brushes onto his floor-bound canvas, Pollock freed his lines from representing any figure or outline. The result, in *One* (Number 31, 1950), which is over 8 feet high and 17 feet wide, is a writhing tangle of pure visual energy. In the politically charged atmosphere of the early Cold War, critics saw Pollock's exuberant "drip" paintings as the embodiment of American cultural freedom and celebrated the Wyoming-born Pollock as a kind of artist cowboy.

Lurking behind such interpretations was the awareness that the Soviets had imposed socialist realism on Eastern Europe and the Nazis had persecuted avant-garde artists. As skeptical as many viewers might have been about the merits of abstract art (*Time* magazine, for instance, dismissed Pollock as "Jack the dripper" in 1947), many people in the West saw it as the antithesis of socialist, realist totalitarianism.

Indeed, New York City—not Paris—emerged as the international center of modern art after World War II, a position it retains today. As the home of growing collections of twentieth-century art and dozens of European artists who had fled from the Nazis, New York became a fertile training ground for young artists such as Pollock. Just as American political and economic structures became models for the postwar redevelopment of Western Europe, so did American cultural developments. By the time Pollock's first posthumous retrospective toured Europe in 1958, much European painting resembled an elegant imitation of his frenetic lines.

Yablonskaya and Pollock together illustrate the two central poles of twentieth-century art: realism and abstraction. Although artistic style is no longer as closely associated with political programs as it once was, these two poles still frame the work of countless artists today.

Rachel Whiteread's *Nameless Library* in Vienna commemorates the thousands of Austrian Jews killed in the Nazi Holocaust.   Corbis/Bettmans ©Reuters NewMedia Inc./CORBIS

MEMORY OF THE HOLOCAUST

The British sculptor Rachel Whiteread (b. 1963) is one of the leading artists of today's Europe. Her work illustrates how European art is breaking out of the modernist contours that were set at the beginning of the twentieth century. On one hand, Whiteread's art returns to what seem like familiar forms; on the other, it forces us to view these forms in ways that are as new to us as cubism was to the public in its day.

Whiteread's work is associated with minimalism in contemporary art. This movement, which originated in architecture and interior design, seeks to remove from the object being portrayed as many features as possible while retaining the object's form and the viewer's interest. Minimalist art aims to be as understated as possible. In Whiteread's hands, the minimal becomes the austere, and her work often exudes melancholy and loss.

Whiteread began her career by focusing on objects from everyday life. She would make a plaster cast of an object's interior space. Initially her subjects were small—a hot water bottle, a piece of furniture, or the space under a chair. In 1993, however, she made a cast of the interior space of an entire house that was about to be torn down in London. She left the work untitled, but it became known as *House*. It presents interior space as solid but temporary, subject to the passage of time. Like many of Whiteread's subjects, the object that has been molded—in this case the demolished house—no longer exists, and even the sculpture itself will eventually disappear. *House* stood on the site for only two and a half months before being razed, like the actual house itself, as part of an urban redevelopment plan.

Whiteread's most important public work, and one designed to endure, is *Nameless Library*, the Judenplatz Holocaust Memorial in Vienna, which commemorates the deaths of 65,000 Austrian Jews under the Nazis. This memorial, which resembles a vast haunting tomb, is cast in concrete and embodies the outline of books whose spines are turned inward, thus remaining forever unread and as unopenable as the library's huge concrete doors are. Whiteread has said the molded, unopened books, which have been compared to the ghost of a library, symbolize the loss both of Jewish contributions to culture and of Jewish lives in the Holocaust.

THE CHRISTIAN HERITAGE

In most ways, Christianity in Europe has continued to be as hard-pressed during the twentieth century as it had been in the late nineteenth. Material prosperity, political ideologies, environmentalism, gender politics, and simple indifference have replaced religious faith for many people. Still, despite the loss of much of their popular support and legal privileges and the low rates of church attendance, the European Christian churches continue to exercise social and political influence. In Germany, the churches were one of the few major institutions that the Nazis did not wholly subdue. Lutheran clergy, such as Martin Niemöller (1892–1984) and Dietrich Bonhoeffer (1906–1945), were leaders of the opposition to Hitler. After the war, in Poland and elsewhere in Eastern Europe, the Roman Catholic Church opposed communism.

In Western Europe, religious affiliation provided much of the initial basis for the Christian Democratic parties. The churches have also raised critical questions about colonialism, nuclear weapons, human rights, war, and other issues. Consequently, even in this most secular of ages, Christian churches have influenced state and society.

NEO-ORTHODOXY

Liberal theologians of the nineteenth century often softened the concept of sin and portrayed human nature as close to the divine. The horror of World War I destroyed that optimistic faith. Many Europeans felt that evil had stalked the Continent.

The most important Christian response to World War I appeared in the theology of Karl Barth (1886–1968). In 1919, this Swiss pastor published *A Commentary on the Epistle to the Romans*, which reemphasized the transcendence of God and the dependence of humankind on the divine. Barth portrayed God as wholly other than, and different from, humankind. In a sense, Barth was returning to the Reformation theology of Luther, but the work of Kierkegaard had profoundly influenced his reading of the reformer. Like the Danish writer, Barth regarded the lived experience of men and women as the best testimony to the truth of Luther's theology. Those extreme moments of life Kierkegaard described provided the basis for a knowledge of humanity's need for God.

This view challenged much nineteenth-century writing about human nature. Barth's theology, which came to be known as neo-Orthodoxy, proved influential throughout the West in the wake of new disasters and suffering.

LIBERAL THEOLOGY

Neo-Orthodoxy did not, however, sweep away liberal theology, which had a strong advocate in Paul Tillich (1886–1965). This German-American theologian tended to regard religion as a human, rather than a divine, phenomenon. Whereas Barth saw God as dwelling outside humankind, Tillich believed that evidence of the divine had to be sought in human nature and human culture.

Other liberal theologians, such as Rudolf Bultmann (1884–1976), continued to work on the problems of naturalism and supernaturalism that had troubled earlier writers. Bultmann's major writing took place before World War II, but was popularized after the war by the Anglican bishop John Robinson in *Honest to God* (1963). Another liberal Christian writer from Britain, C. S. Lewis (1878–1963), attracted millions of readers during and after World War II. This layman and scholar of medieval literature often expressed his thoughts on theology in the form of letters and short stories. His most famous work is *The Screwtape Letters* (1942). In recent years, however, European religious thought has produced few major Protestant voices.

ROMAN CATHOLIC REFORM

Among Christian denominations, the most significant postwar changes have been in the Roman Catholic Church. Pope John XXIII (r. 1958–1963) initiated these changes, the most extensive in Catholicism for more than a century and, some would say, since the Council of Trent in the sixteenth century. In 1959, Pope John summoned the Twenty-First Ecumenical Council (the Emperor Constantine had called the first council in the fourth century), which came to be called Vatican II. The council finished its work in 1965 under John's successor, Pope Paul VI (r. 1963–1978). Among many changes in Catholic liturgy, the council introduced, Mass was now celebrated in the vernacular languages rather than in Latin. The council also encouraged freer relations with other Christian denominations, fostered a new spirit toward Judaism, and gave more power to bishops. In recognition of the growing importance to the church of the world outside Europe and North America, Pope Paul appointed several cardinals from the former colonial nations, transforming the church into a truly world body.

In contrast to these liberal changes, however, Pope Paul and his successors have firmly upheld the celibacy of priests, maintained the church's prohibition on contraception and abortion, and opposed moves to open the priesthood to women. The church's unyielding stand on clerical celibacy has caused many men to leave the priesthood and many men and women to leave religious orders. The laity has widely ignored the prohibition on contraception.

John Paul II, the former Karol Wojtyla, archbishop of Kraków in Poland, was elected in 1978 after the death of John Paul I, whose reign lasted only 34 days. The youngest pope since Pius IX (r. 1846–1878), John Paul II (1920–2005) pursued a three-pronged policy during his long pontificate. First, he maintained traditionalist doctrine, stressing the authority of the papacy and attempting to limit doctrinal and liturgical experimentation.

Second, taking a firm stand against communism, he supported the spirit of freedom in Eastern Europe that brought down the communist regimes. As a cardinal in Poland, he had clashed with the communist government. After his election, he visited Poland, lending support to Solidarity. His Polish origins helped make him an important factor in the popular resistance to Eastern Europe's communist governments that developed during the 1980s. He thus opened a new chapter in the relationship between church and state in modern Europe.

Third, John Paul II encouraged the growth of the church in the non-Western world, stressing the need for social justice, but limiting the political activity of priests. (See "Pope John Paul II Discusses International Social Justice," page 1046.) The pope's concern for the expansion of Roman

A CLOSER LOOK

The Copenhagen Opera House

The New Opera House opened in Copenhagen, Denmark in 2005. The structure has come to symbolize free enterprise in the European Union because its full cost was covered by private, rather than government, funding.

Henning Larson, a Dane, was the architect. His design, however, has been criticized for being subtly commercial because some observers see the opera house as resembling the grill of an automobile.

AP Wide World Photos

The construction of the Copenhagen Opera House reclaimed areas of decaying dockland in the city. In this respect, it symbolizes similar projects that have been undertaken in other major European ports where docks have been relocated in the late twentieth century.

Throughout his pontificate John Paul II continued a close relationship with his native Poland to which he made several visits. The earliest of these was important in demonstrating the authority of the church against Polish communist authorities. Shown here in his Polish visit of June 1999, the pope would celebrate mass before several hundred thousand Poles after the collapse of communism which had occurred a decade earlier. AP Wide World Photos

Catholicism beyond Europe and North America recognized and encouraged what appears to be a transformation in Christianity as a world religion. Whereas in Europe Christian observance whether Roman Catholic, Protestant, or Orthodox had declined sharply during the twentieth century, Christianity has grown rapidly and fervently in Africa and Latin America. Observers estimate that within a few years, over half of the world's Christians will live in those two continents. Recognizing these changes, John Paul II created more cardinals from non-Western nations.

John Paul II died in 2005. His successor was his closest collaborator, the German Cardinal Joseph Ratzinger (b. 1927), who took the name Benedict XVI. He is expected to continue the conservative theological and cultural policies of his predecessor.

LATE-TWENTIETH-CENTURY TECHNOLOGY: THE ARRIVAL OF THE COMPUTER

During the twentieth century, technology crossed international borders the way popular culture did. As with other areas of European life and society, American technology had an unprecedented impact on the Continent, whether in the guise of the first airplanes or Henry Ford's method of producing affordable automobiles. It seems certain, however, that no single American technological achievement of the twentieth century will so influence Western life on both sides of the Atlantic, as well as throughout the rest of the world, as the computer.

THE DEMAND FOR CALCULATING MACHINES

Beginning in the seventeenth century, thinkers associated with the scientific revolution—most famously, the French mathematician and philosopher Blaise Pascal (1623–1662)—attempted to construct machines that would carry out mathematical calculations that human beings would find essentially impossible because of the tedium and the amount of time they involved. Starting in the late nineteenth century, the governments of the consolidating nation-states of Europe and of the United States confronted new administrative tasks that involved collecting and organizing vast amounts of data about national censuses, tax collection, economic statistics, and the administration of pensions and welfare legislation. During the same years, private businesses sought calculating machinery to handle and organize growing amounts of economic and business data. Such machines became technologically possible through the development of complex circuitry for electricity, the most versatile mode of energy in human history. Moreover, inventions that were dependent on electricity, including the telephone, the telegraph,

POPE JOHN PAUL II DISCUSSES INTERNATIONAL SOCIAL JUSTICE

Pope John Paul II issued his encyclical, The Social Concerns of the Church, *in 1988. In the passages given here, he attempted to set concerns for justice among developed and developing nations into the larger context of Christian moral theology.*

■ *How does the pope relate the fate of the poorest nations to the international system of trade and finance? What evidence is there that the pope did not favor radical social action by Roman Catholic clergy? How does this encyclical illustrate the pope's concerns for non-European parts of the world?*

The Church's social doctrine is not a "third way" between liberal capitalism and Marxist collectivism, nor even a possible alternative to other solutions less radically opposed to one another: rather, it constitutes a category of its own. Nor is it an ideology, but rather the accurate formulation of the results of a careful reflection on the complex realities of human existence, in society and in the international order, in the light of faith and of the Church's tradition. Its main aim is to interpret these realities, determining their conformity with or divergence from the lines of the Gospel teaching on man and his vocation, a vocation which is at once earthly and transcendent; its aim is thus to guide Christian behavior. It, therefore, belongs to the field, not of ideology, but of theology and particularly moral theology. . . .

The international trade system today frequently discriminates against the products of the young industries of the developing countries and discourages the producers of raw materials. There exists, too, a kind of international division of labor, whereby the low-cost products of certain countries which lack effective labor laws or which are too weak to apply them are sold in other parts of the world at considerable profit for the companies engaged in this form of production, which knows not frontiers. . . .

[H]umanity today is in a new and more difficult phase of its genuine development. It needs a greater degree of international ordering, at the service of the societies, economies and cultures of the whole world. . . .

It is desirable, for example, that nations of the same geographical area should establish forms of cooperation which will make them less dependent on more powerful producers; they should open their frontiers to the products of the area; they should examine how their products might complement one another; they should combine in order to set up those services which each one separately is incapable of providing; they should extend cooperation to the monetary and financial sector. . . .

The Church well knows that no temporal achievement is to be identified with the Kingdom of God, but that all such achievements simply reflect and in a sense anticipate the glory of the Kingdom, the Kingdom which we await at the end of history, when the Lord will come again. But that expectation can never be an excuse for lack of concern for people in their concrete personal situations and in their social, national, and international life, since the former is conditioned by the latter, especially today.

underwater cables, and the wireless, created a new communications industry that in and of itself also required the organization of large databases of customer information to deliver their services. By the late 1920s, companies like National Cash Register, Remington Rand, and International Business Machines Corporation (IBM) had begun to manufacture such business machinery.

EARLY COMPUTER TECHNOLOGY

As has happened so often in history, warfare was the chief catalyst of change. After World War I and during World War II, the major powers developed new weapons that required exact mathematical ballistic calculations to effectively strike targets with bombs delivered by aircraft or long-range guns.

The first machine genuinely recognizable as a modern digital computer was the Electronic Numerical Integrator and Computer (**ENIAC**), built and designed at Moore Laboratories of the University of Pennsylvania and put into use by the U.S. Army in 1946 for ballistics calculation. The ENIAC was an enormous piece of equipment with 40 panels, 1,500 electric relays, and 18,000 vacuum tubes. It also used thousands of punch cards, and a separate tabulator had to print the data from them. Further computer engineering occurred at the Institute for Advanced Research in Princeton, New Jersey, in laboratories at the Massachusetts Institute of Technology, and in other laboratories the U.S. government and private businesses, especially IBM, ran. The other primary sites for computer development were laboratories in Britain.

THE DEVELOPMENT OF DESKTOP COMPUTERS

During the 1950s, however, the transistor revolutionized electronics, permitting a miniaturization of circuitry that made vacuum tubes obsolete and allowed computers to become smaller. Yet computers still had to be programmed with difficult computer languages by persons expertly trained to use them.

By the late 1960s, however, two innovations transformed computing technology. First, control of the computer was transferred to a bitmap covering the screen of a computer monitor. The mouse, invented in 1964, eased the movement of the cursor around the computer screen. Second, engineers at the Intel Corporation—then a California start-up company—invented the microchip, which became the heart of all future computers.

The bitmap on the screen, operated through the mouse, in effect embedded complicated computer language in the machine, hidden from the user, who simply manipulated images on the screen with the mouse. Almost anyone could thus learn to operate computers. At the same time, the tiny microchip, itself a miniature computer or microprocessor, permitted computer technology to abandon the mainframe and move to still smaller computers. At the Xerox Corporation, engineers devised a small computer using a mouse, but the machine never achieved commercial success. By 1982, IBM had produced a small personal computer, but temporarily lost the race for commercialization to a then small company called Apple Computer Corporation. The design features originally developed at Xerox informed the ideas of the Apple engineers, who, in early 1984, produced a small, highly accessible, commercially successful computer, known as the Macintosh, that would fit on a desktop in the home or office. IBM soon adopted the Apple concept with different engineering and marketing approaches and manufactured a product called the Personal Computer, or PC. By the mid-1980s, for a relatively modest cost (and one that has continued to drop), individuals had available for their own personal use in their offices or homes computers with far more power than the old mainframes. The Apple Macintosh and the IBM PC transformed computers into objects of everyday life and, in doing so, began to transform everyday life itself. Nonetheless, the chief contemporary users of computers remain governments followed by the telephone industry, banking and finance, automobile operation, and airline reservation systems.

Despite the potential democratizing character of computer technology, the computer revolution has also introduced new concepts of "haves" and "have-nots" to societies around the world. Computers, whatever their possible shortcomings, enable their users to do things that nonusers cannot do. Whether in poor school districts in the United States or in poor countries of the former Soviet bloc, students

The earliest computers were very large. Here in a 1946 photograph J. Presper Eckert and J. W. Mauchly stand by the Electronic Numerical Integrator and Computer (ENIAC) which was dedicated at the University of Pennsylvania Moore School of Electrical Engineering.   CORBIS/Bettmann

who graduate without computer skills will have difficulty making their way in the world's rapidly computerizing economy. Some commentators also fear that boys are more likely than girls to receive technological training in computers. Nations whose governments and businesses become networked into the world of computers will prosper more fully than those whose access to computer technology is deficient. In that regard, the possession of computers and the ability to use them will probably determine future economic competition, just as they have determined recent military competition.

THE CHALLENGES OF EUROPEAN UNIFICATION

The unprecedented steps toward economic cooperation and unity Western European nations took during the second half of the twentieth century were the single most important European success story of that era. The process originated from American encouragement in response to the Soviet domination of Eastern Europe and from the Western European states' own sense that they lacked effective political and economic power. Furthermore, leaders in France and Germany who recoiled from the disastrous peace that followed World War I were determined that something different would arise from the political collapse of Europe after World War II. They understood that cooperation, rather than revenge, must inform the future of Europe.

POSTWAR COOPERATION

The mid-twentieth-century Western European movement toward unity could have occurred in at least three ways: politically, militarily, or economically. Economic cooperation, unlike military and political cooperation, involved little or no immediate loss of sovereignty by the participating nations. Furthermore, it brought material benefits to all the states involved, increasing popular support for their governments. Moreover, the administration of the Marshall Plan and the organization of NATO gave the countries involved new experience in working with each other and demonstrated the productivity and efficiency that mutual cooperation could achieve.

The first effort toward economic cooperation was the formation of the European Coal and Steel Community in 1951 by France, West Germany, Italy, and the Benelux countries (Belgium, the Netherlands, and Luxembourg). The community both benefited from and contributed to the immense growth of material production in Western Europe during this period. Its success reduced the suspicions of government and business groups about coordination and economic integration.

THE EUROPEAN ECONOMIC COMMUNITY

It took more than the prosperity of the European Coal and Steel Community to draw European leaders toward further unity, however. The unsuccessful Suez intervention of 1956 and the resulting diplomatic isolation of France and Britain persuaded many Europeans that only by acting together could they significantly influence the United States and the Soviet Union or control their own national and regional destinies. So, in 1957, through the Treaty of Rome, the six members of the Coal and Steel Community agreed to form a new organization: the **European Economic Community (EEC)**. The members of the Common Market, as the EEC was soon known, envisioned more than a free-trade union. They sought to achieve the eventual elimination of tariffs, a free flow of capital and labor, and similar wage and social benefits in all their countries.

The Common Market achieved stunning success during its early years. By 1968, well ahead of schedule, the six members had abolished all tariffs among themselves. Trade and labor migration among the members grew steadily. Moreover, non-member states began to copy the EEC and, later, to seek to join it. In 1959, Britain, Denmark, Norway, Sweden, Switzerland, Austria, and Portugal formed the European Free Trade Area. By 1961, however, Britain had decided to join the Common Market. Twice, in 1963 and 1967, President Charles de Gaulle of France vetoed British membership. He argued that Britain was too closely tied to the United States to support the EEC wholeheartedly. Finally, in 1973, Great Britain, Ireland, and Denmark became members. Throughout the late 1970s, however, and into the 1980s, momentum for expanding EEC membership slowed. Norway and Sweden, with relatively strong economies, declined to join. Although in 1982, Spain, Portugal, and Greece applied for membership and were eventually admitted, sharp disagreements and a sense of stagnation within the EEC continued.

THE EUROPEAN UNION

In 1988, the leaders of the EEC reached an important decision. By 1992, the EEC was to be a virtual free-trade zone with no trade barriers or other restrictive trade policies among its members. In 1991, the Treaty of Maastricht made a series of specific proposals that led to a unified EEC currency (the Euro) and a strong central bank. The treaty was submitted to referendums in several European states. Denmark initially rejected it, and it passed only narrowly in France and Great Britain, making clear that it needed wider popular support. When the treaty finally took effect in November 1993, the EEC was renamed the **European Union**. Throughout the 1990s, the Union's influence grew. Its most notable achievement was the launching in early 1999 of the **Euro**, which by 2002 had become the common currency in twelve of the member nations.

In May 2004, the European Union added ten new nations raising the total number of members to twenty-five. (See Map 30–1.) Membership in the European Union indicated that a nation had achieved economic stability, and genuinely democratic institutions. Nonetheless, several of the new members states from the former Soviet bloc are relatively poor and will require much economic support from the Union.

DISCORD OVER THE UNION

The 2004 expansion of the European Union may mark for some time the high point of European integration. During that year the leaders of the member nations adopted a new constitutional treaty for the Union. This treaty, generally known as the European Constitution, was a long, detailed, and highly complicated document involving a bill of rights and complex economic and political agreements among all the member states. It would have transferred considerable decision-making authority from the governments of the individual states to the central institutions of the European Union, many of which are located in Brussels, Luxembourg, and Strasbourg. To become effective, all the member states had to ratify the constitution either by their parliaments or through national referendums.

To the surprise of many in the European elite, in the spring of 2005, referendums held in France and the Netherlands heavily defeated the new constitutional treaty. Britain, where support for further European integration was lukewarm at best, immediately postponed holding its own referendum. Public opinion in other nations also soured on the constitutional treaty. Furthermore, immediately after these events, discord erupted over the Union's internal budget. These events marked an unprecedented crisis for the European Union and for the project of European integration.

Several factors appear to have brought the European Union to this pass. First, for at least the past

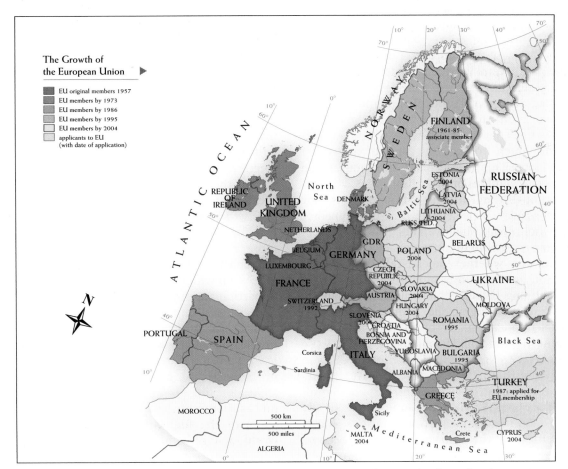

Map 30–1   **THE GROWTH OF THE EUROPEAN UNION**   This map traces the growth of membership in the European Union from its founding in 1957 through the introduction of its newest members in 2004. Note that Turkey though having applied for membership has not yet been admitted.

fifteen years, a gap has been growing between the European political elites who have led the drive toward unity and the European voting public. The former have either ignored the latter or have moved the project along with only narrow majorities. Second, the general Western European economy has stagnated for the last decade with relatively high rates of unemployment, especially among the young. Voting against the constitution was a way to voice discontent with this situation. Third, many of the smaller member states of the European Union have felt that France and Germany have either ignored them or taken them for granted. Fourth, some nations have come to believe that they were placed at an economic disadvantage when the Euro replaced their former national currencies because the rates of exchange were unfairly calculated. Fifth, many people in the various states, large and small, have become increasingly reluctant to cede national sovereignty and the authority to make economic decisions to the bureaucracy in Brussels. Britain, for example, would like to see less economic regulation. France, on the other hand, is loath to see the European Union gain the power to revise the French labor code with its extensive protections and benefits for workers.

Finally, another large issue has informed the internal skeptics of the current European Union. Over the past several years, the leaders of the major member states have grown more favorable to the eventual admission of Turkey as a member state. If Turkey were admitted, Europe would have to integrate into the Union a state whose population is larger and much poorer than that of any other member state. This would place enormous social and economic burdens on the other states. Furthermore, although the Turkish government has long been seen as adamantly secular, the Turkish people are overwhelmingly Muslim. This "Islamic factor" has become increasingly controversial among those Europeans who, whether they are religiously observant or not, believe European culture to be Christian, and among those secular Europeans who are deeply concerned about the political, economic, and social implications of the Continent's already significant Muslim population.

It seems inconceivable that the effort to unify in Europe will either halt or be reversed. At the present time, however, it also seems certain that all future developments will move much more slowly and will require complicated negotiations. Moreover, the future of the European Union has become enmeshed in often bitter and divisive debates within the member states over social policies, the future of their economies, and what role the state should play in economic affairs.

A woman stands between a "yes" and a "no" campaign poster in reference to France's referendum on the EU constitution in a street of Rennes, western France, Friday May 27, 2005, two days before the vote.   AP Wide World Photos

IN PERSPECTIVE

The twentieth century was the most destructive in human history. The wars of the first half of the century killed millions of Europeans and disrupted the fabric of European society. The Bolsheviks, Fascists, and National Socialists sought to remake whole societies according to utopian visions that resulted in repression and death on a mass scale, and drove millions of Europeans from their ancestral homes.

With the defeat of National Socialism and Fascism, society in Western Europe developed along more peaceful lines with a powerful economic and cultural influence coming from the United States. Migration and the economic growth of the second half of the century reshaped the society of many Western nations. Welfare systems provided an extensive social safety net. The role and opportunities for women in society expanded. More and more Europeans across the Continent attended universities. The end of Soviet domination began a process in which Eastern Europe increasingly came to participate in the affluence of the West with its myriad consumer goods.

By the close of the century, Europe, like much of the rest of the world, had entered a new technological revolution through the computer and advances in medical care. Economic growth slowed in the 1990s, but most of Europe outside the former communist-dominated regions continued to enjoy some of the highest standards of living in the world, under liberal democratic governments.

The efforts to unify Europe have transformed the Continent and the everyday lives of its citizens. The future of the European Union, however, now stands at a crossroads.

REVIEW QUESTIONS

1. How did migration affect twentieth-century European social life? What internal and external forces led to migration?
2. In what specific ways was Europe Americanized in the second half of the twentieth century? How do you explain the trend toward a consumer society?
3. How have women's social and economic roles changed in the second half of the twentieth century? What changes and problems have women faced since the fall of communism in Eastern Europe?
4. How did the pursuit and diffusion of knowledge change in the twentieth century? What have been the effects of the communications revolutions? Has Western intellectual life become more unified or less so? Why?
5. What did Nietzsche and Kierkegaard contribute to existentialism? How was existentialism a response to the crises of the twentieth century?
6. What were the technological steps in the emergence of the computer? What changes will computers bring in the next decade?
7. What were the major steps in the emergence of the European Union? Why is the Union now facing a crisis?

SUGGESTED READINGS

G. AMBROSIUS AND W. H. HUBBARD, *A Social and Economic History of Twentieth-Century Europe* (1989). An excellent one-volume treatment of the subject.

B. S. ANDERSON AND J. P. ZINSSER, *A History of Their Own: Women in Europe from Prehistory to the Present*, vol. 2 (1988). A broad-ranging survey.

G. BOCK AND P. THANE (eds.), *Maternity and Gender Politics: Women and the Rise of the European Welfare States, 1880s–1950s* (1991). Explores the emergence of welfare legislation.

E. BRAMWELL, *Ecology in the 20th Century: A History* (1989). Traces the environmental movement to its late-nineteenth-century origins.

P. E. CERUZZI, *A History of Modern Computing* (2003). A comprehensive survey.

S. COLLINSON, *Beyond Borders: West European Migration Policy and the 21st Century* (1993). Explores a major contemporary European social issue.

R. CROSSMAN (ED.), *The God That Failed* (1949). Classic essays by former communist intellectuals.

D. DINAN, *Europe Recast: A History of the European Union* (2004). A major overview.

C. FINK, P. GASERT, AND D. JUNKER, *1968: The World Transformed* (1998). The best collection of essays on a momentous year.

B. GRAHAM, *Modern Europe: Place, Culture, Identity* (1998). Thoughtful essays on the future of Europe by a group of geographers.

H. S. HUGHES, *Sophisticated Rebels: The Political Culture of European Dissent, 1968–1987* (1988). Thoughtful essays on recent cultural critics.

P. JENKINS, *Mrs. Thatcher's Revolution: The Ending of the Socialist Era* (1988). The best work on the subject.

P. JENKINS, *The Next Christendom: The Coming of Global Christianity* (2002). A provocative analysis.

T. JUDT, *Past Imperfect: French Intellectuals, 1944–1956* (1992). An important study of French intellectuals and communism.

T. JUDT, *Pastwar: A History of Europe since 1945* (2005). The most recent authoritative overview.

R. MALTBY (ED.), *Passing Parade: A History of Popular Culture in the Twentieth Century* (1989). Essays on a topic just beginning to receive scholarly attention.

R. MARRUS, *The Unwanted: European Refugees in the 20th Century* (1985). An important work on a disturbing subject.

D. MEYER, *Sex and Power: The Rise of Women in America, Russia, Sweden, and Italy* (1987). A lively, useful survey.

N. NAIMARK, *Fires of Hatred: Ethnic Cleansing in Twentieth-Century Europe* (2002). A remarkably sensitive treatment of a tragic subject.

M. POSTER, *Existential Marxism in Postwar France* (1975). An excellent and clear work.

H. ROWLEY, *Tête-á-Tête: Simon de Beauvoir and Jean-Paul Sartre* (2005). A highly critical joint biography.

S. STRASSER, C. McGOVERN, AND M. JUDT, *Getting and Spending: European and American Consumer Societies in the Twentieth Century* (1998). An extensive collection of comparative essays.

F. THEBAUD (ED.), *A History of Women in the West, Vol. 5: Toward a Cultural Identity in the Twentieth Century* (1994). A collection of wide-ranging essays of the highest quality.

DOCUMENTS CD-ROM

Society and Culture between the Wars

27.2 Jean-Paul Sartre: Existentialism

The Cold War and its Aftermath

30.5 Stokeley Carmichael: What We Want

ENERGY
AND THE MODERN WORLD

No single technological factor so determines the social relationships and standard of living of human beings as energy. The more energy a society can command for each of its members, the stronger and more influential it will be. Throughout recorded human history, those societies that have found ways to improve their access to sources of energy, and have then efficiently applied the energy, have dominated both their immediate environments and much of the world beyond. Indeed, the possession of, or the lack of, efficient, inexpensive sources of energy in large measure determines which nations will be wealthy and which will be poor.

ANIMALS, WIND, AND WATER

For civilization to advance technologically, energy had to be applied to tasks. The earliest source of such energy was animal power, which was used all over the world except among the peoples on the American continent prior to the arrival of the Europeans. Oxen, water buffalo, and horses were the major draft animals. Of these, horses were the most efficient.

Throughout the world until the eighteenth century, however, wind and water furnished most of the energy for machinery. Sailing ships had been used since ancient times for travel, fishing, and the transport of goods. The wind also worked mills that pumped water and ground grain. Waterwheels proved to be highly flexible machines and by the eighteenth century constituted the major sources of mechanical power in Europe and much of the rest of the world. But wind and water were uncertain sources of energy. The wind could cease; drought could dry up streams. Water-powered machinery had to be located near the stream furnishing the water. Consequently, most of the mills employing such machinery were located in the countryside.

Although animals, wind, and water provided energy for relatively complicated machines capable of manufacturing and transporting high-quality goods, the economic and political transformations that have driven the history of the world for the past two and a half centuries could only have occurred through a qualitative as well as quantitative leap in the manner in which human beings commanded energy. The twin sources of this world-transforming energy have been fossil fuels and electricity.

Until the second half of the eighteenth century, fossil fuels—coal, petroleum, and, to a lesser extent, natural gas—contributed only a small portion of human energy requirements. Their use as meaningful sources of energy required a series of inventions that allowed the energy of heat to be changed into mechanical energy.

STEAM POWER AND THE AGE OF COAL

Although peoples living near coal deposits had used it as a household fuel for a very long time, only the invention of the steam engine, patented by James Watt in 1769, established a major industrial demand for coal. The steam engine first permitted the pumping of water from coal mines to increase production. But as the industrial uses for the steam engine grew, the invention itself drove the demand for greater quantities of coal as fuel.

Coal-fueled steam power changed the face of human society during the nineteenth century and continues to provide the energy for the most powerful turbogenerators at the dawn of the twenty-first century. Steam-powered machines could be made larger and more flexible than those powered by wind or water, and so long as coal was available, they could run steadily day and night. Steam engines, in contrast to waterwheels, were transportable. Factories could be moved away from streams in the countryside to urban areas where a ready work force existed. And goods produced in factories powered by steam engines could be carried around the world by steam-powered locomotives and ships. Those expanding markets in turn called forth more steam-powered factories and even greater use of coal. Furthermore, steam-powered factories could also produce military weapons that could be placed on steam-powered naval vessels constructed of iron and steel in vast coal-fueled blast furnaces. When Theodore Roosevelt sent the U.S. fleet around the

Until the eighteenth century, sailing ships were powered by wind alone. In this fourteenth-century manuscript illustration, sailors navigate with the help of an astrolabe. Bibliotheque Nationale, Paris, France/Bridgeman Art Library International

world, it was a testimony to the power of coal and steam as well as to the power of the American navy.

The age of steam was the age of coal. The nations possessing large coal deposits dominated much nineteenth-century economic life as the nations that possess oil reserves dominate much contemporary economic life. For many decades, Great Britain dominated the world's production and delivery of coal, which was transported over the entire world. Its domination was challenged only in the late nineteenth century as the United States and later Russia and China began to produce vast quantities of the fuel. Coal remained the chief fuel for the United States until after World War I and for Western Europe until after World War II. It remains the chief fuel for China.

Coal generated a rising standard of living in Europe and the expansion of European and later American power, but coal also generated a number of social problems. The most shocking conditions of exploited labor occurred in coal mines, where parliamentary reports of the 1840s described and illustrated half-clad women and children drawing coal carts from the depths of the mines to the surface. Throughout the nineteenth and twentieth centuries, thousands of miners died in mining disasters. Work in the mines injured the health of miners, as did the pollution sent into the atmosphere by coal fires from both factories and homes. By the early twentieth century, observers had begun to note the damage to the environment caused by strip mining of coal and the later abandonment of the regions.

THE INTERNAL COMBUSTION ENGINE: THE AGE OF OIL

As with coal, the impact of petroleum, the second major fossil fuel, also depended on the invention of machinery to use it. Originally, the use for oil was limited to kerosene, the fuel used for lighting around much of the world by 1900. It was upon the world demand for lamp oil that John D. Rockefeller founded the Standard Oil Company. The invention of the internal combustion engine in 1882 by Rudolf Daimler and the diesel engine in 1892 by Rudolf Diesel transformed the demand for oil. Toward the close of the nineteenth century, extensive oil production had begun in the United States, with Russia, Romania, Sumatra, Mexico, Iran, and Venezuela starting to tap their own oil resources before World War I.

Just as the steam engine had spurred the expansion of the coal industry, the internal combustion engine drove the oil industry. Fuel oil would begin to replace coal, not so much because it was cheaper but rather because it was more efficient, easier to store and transport, and cleaner to burn. Initially, fuel oil tended to be used in those countries where it could be produced relatively near the point of use. Until the end of World War II, the United States was the primary world producer and user of oil. As fuel for the internal

Until 1924, Henry Ford had disdained national advertising
for his cars. But as General Motors gained a competitive
edge by making yearly changes in style and technology,
Ford was forced to pay more attention to advertising. This
ad was directed at "Mrs. Consumer," combining appeals
to both female independence and motherly duties.   Ford
Motor Company

combustion engine, oil became the driving force of
automobiles, locomotives, airplanes, ships, factory
machinery, and electric generators. It revolutionized
agricultural machinery and world food production,
but as a fuel for transportation, it fostered a social
transformation over much of the world.

Starting in the United States and then spreading
elsewhere, owning an automobile introduced a new
mobility factor into social relationships. People
could move easily across long distances to join a
new community or to start a new job. Inexpensive
gasoline for cars and public transport buses permitted the development of suburbs ever farther removed from traditional urban centers. In turn,
retailing moved away from city centers to shopping
malls. At the same time, wherever the mechanization of farming through improved farm machinery
took place, there usually followed a movement of
people from farming communities to urban areas.

ELECTRICITY INCREASES
THE DEMAND FOR OIL

The manufacture of automobiles and other forms
of transport using the internal combustion or
diesel engine was central to all modern industrial
life. As those industries expanded, so did the construction of extensive road systems. These in turn
created new demands for fuel oil.

But the greatest demand for fuel oil arose from
the application of electricity to the needs of everyday life. Electricity proved to be the most flexible
and versatile source of energy for the twentieth
century, and its generation provided the single
greatest source of demand for both coal and oil.
Electricity generation would also employ new
modes of water power in the forms of hydroelectric
generators.

The scientific basis for the production of electric energy was Michael Faraday's study of electro-
magnetic induction. In 1831, he demonstrated that
mechanical energy under the proper conditions
could be converted into electric energy. Even more
important, the reverse was also true. Electricity
could be generated in one location and applied far
away wherever electrical lines could be extended.
The applications of electrical power have appeared
to be restricted only by the limitations of the in-
ventive imagination.

During the second half of the nineteenth century, a whole host of inventors, such as Thomas
Alva Edison, worked through the production and
application of electrical power to service large regions. Electricity found applications across the
spectrum of human society, actions, and enterprises. Access to electricity in the course of the twentieth century became the key factor for an
improved standard of living. A fundamental moment in the decision by Japan to modernize during
the late nineteenth century was the construction
of the Tokyo Electric Light Company in 1888. The
extension of electrical lines into the American
countryside was one of the major accomplishments of Franklin Roosevelt's New Deal. Electrical power transformed the workplace, but even
more strikingly it transformed homes. Without access to electrical power, domestic households
could not make use of any of the growing array of
labor-saving appliances such as electric washing
machines, electric irons, electric stoves, and electric vacuum cleaners. Electric lights brightened
whole cities. Electricity replaced both coal and oil
as the source of power for many locomotives; it
powered public tram systems and opened the way

for the telegraph, the telephone, the wireless, the motion picture camera, and television. It planted the seeds for the computer revolution in communication and information. Electricity allowed manufacturing plants and office complexes to be built wherever electric lines could be carried. Indeed, the spread of access to electrical power has been the single best indication of economic advancement for any nation or region.

Yet within this era of ever-expanding electrification, coal and oil—the fundamental fossil fuels—would still provide the underpinnings of the world's energy. In fact, more oil and coal are used to generate electricity than for any other single purpose. Throughout the twentieth century, the demand for these fuels led to the refinement of their production techniques to permit the extraction of coal from ever-deeper seams and the strip mining of it from regions where previously it would have been economically unproductive to do so. The effort to discover, extract, and transport oil would have major consequences for the world's physical and geopolitical environment far into the twentieth century.

OIL AND GLOBAL POLITICS IN THE TWENTIETH CENTURY

As the century began, the United States was by far the largest producer and exporter of petroleum. Yet by the 1920s, the American government began to worry about running out of oil. So, too, did the British, who depended on imported oil for all of their military and industrial needs. During the 1920s and 1930s, both governments encouraged oil companies to forge agreements for the drilling and export of oil from the Middle East. These arrangements fit into the pattern of formal and informal colonialism that still characterized the interwar period.

After World War II, Western Europe, the Soviet Union, and the nations of the Warsaw Pact began to turn from coal to oil as the basis for economic growth. (Japan followed this course during the 1960s.) By 1947, the United States had begun to import more oil than it produced. These two developments—a new dependence on oil by the industrialized nations and the expanded search for oil by the West—formed the basis for the new role that the nations of the Middle East would play in the world economy as the chief oil exporters. Simultaneously, as the world's industrialized economies were growing dependent on Middle East oil production, nationalistic leaders in that region were denouncing former colonial domina-

In 1989, when a supertanker spilled 35,000 tons of crude oil into Alaska's Prince William Sound, rescue workers struggled to save the lives of seabirds and animals. Nevertheless, thousands died.   Ron Levy/Liaison Agency, Inc.

tion and rejecting relationships with the West and with Israel, a country that received strong political support from the United States and Western Europe. The stage was thus set for oil to play a new role in the geopolitical conflicts of the Cold War era.

Playing a major role in those conflicts was the Organization of Petroleum Exporting Nations (OPEC), founded in 1960. Regardless of their differences, OPEC members were united in two things: First, they deeply resented former colonial control of their oil supplies, and second, they were determined that their own governments, not foreign oil companies, would control those vital resources. (Mexico had brought its own petroleum industry under state control before World War II.) In 1973, during the Yom Kippur War, OPEC acted, sharply raising oil prices to nations whose governments supported Israel. The action caused severe economic consequences in the West and spurred new efforts to develop local oil reserves in politically safe locations such as in the North Sea. OPEC would attempt similar actions on other occasions, most successfully in 1979. In that year, a revolution in Iran overthrew the government, which had long been supported by the United States. OPEC cut off oil shipments to the West, causing severe dislocations. Concerns about securing oil supplies in the West were again sparked by the Persian Gulf War and other political tensions in the region.

In addition to the political problems associated with Middle East oil production, the industrial world's reliance on oil has had severe environmental consequences. Generally, when the United States dominated oil production, the oil refineries were located near the source of oil production. As the exploitation of oil reserves moved to the Middle East and then later in the century to Alaska and to the North Sea, oil refineries became separated from the drilling locations. Crude oil was shipped to refineries on enormous tankers. More than once, these supertankers have hit shoals or gone aground, causing large oil spills, calamitous to both animals and humans.

THE PROMISE AND DANGER OF NUCLEAR ENERGY

Following World War II, nuclear power became a new source for the generation of electrical energy. The power of the atom, first released in the 1940s for military purposes, held the promise of virtually infinite quantities of energy. The world would no longer be dependent on finite supplies of fossil fuel located in politically tense regions of the world. The generation of such energy, however, required the most complex sets of machinery ever devised to produce electrical energy. France and Great Britain began to build nuclear reactors in the 1950s with the United States, the Soviet Union, and various other European nations following in the 1960s. Nations outside the West, such as India and Pakistan, looked to the construction of nuclear power stations as a means of moving more rapidly toward the achievements of industrialization and a rising standard of living through extensive electrification. Nations with limited supplies of fossil fuel, such as Japan, hoped nuclear energy would solve their energy supply problem. The oil shock of the mid-1970s brought new enthusiasm to the adoption of nuclear energy, but the economic downturn of the late 1970s and early 1980s slowed the construction of nuclear-generating stations. The construction of breeder reactors, which would produce their own

fuel in the process of generating electrical energy, seemed to promise a world liberated from dependence on a finite supply of fossil fuels. Furthermore, unlike coal and oil, which have many uses besides that of fuel, uranium had no other economic use. The workers in the field of atomic energy were scientists and engineers rather than the kind of industrial labor force that produced coal and oil.

Yet the technology of nuclear energy production proved to be exceedingly dangerous. The atomic reactors produced spent radioactive waste that would remain hazardous for hundreds of years. After many years of warnings of such danger, the Chernobyl nuclear generating plant in the former Soviet Union caused enormous, lasting damage in the spring of 1986. In 1979, the possibility of a similar disaster had occurred at the Three Mile Island plant in Pennsylvania. Both the promise and danger of nuclear power continue to inform the political life of all nations using such power. It is wholly unclear, for example, what will be done with the radioactive spent fuel. Furthermore, the construction of nuclear generating plants has allowed nations that lack atomic weapons to train scientists and other experts who might be able to use that knowledge to develop atomic weapons. Whereas in the United States and Europe the military uses of atomic power came first and were followed by peaceful energy uses, the reverse has been the case in nations such as India and Pakistan. Despite its initial promise, nuclear power has contributed far less to energy production than we originally imagined.

The problem of energy remains with us in the new century. Environmental pollution and all the issues surrounding the nuclear generation of energy will demand increasing attention and expenditure of public funds. Similarly, the political pressures and tensions surrounding the oil supplies of the Middle East will not disappear, as advanced nations seek to secure and protect energy reserves while the nations that possess those reserves seek to secure a rising standard of living for themselves.

■ *Trace the transformation of energy used in the West from wind and water to petroleum. How did coal transform both the industry and the military power of the West? How did inventions, such as the internal combustion engine, change the demands on sources of energy? Why did the rise of electrical power increase the need for petroleum? What opportunities and dangers has nuclear energy posed?*

GLOSSARY

absolutism Term applied to strong centralized continental monarchies that attempted to make royal power dominant over aristocracies and other regional authorities.

Acropolis (ACK-row-po-lis) The religious and civic center of Athens. It is the site of the Parthenon.

Act of Supremacy The declaration by Parliament in 1534 that Henry VIII, not the pope, was the head of the church in England.

agape (AG-a-pay) Meaning "love feast." A common meal that was part of the central ritual of early Christian worship.

agora (AG-o-rah) The Greek marketplace and civic center. It was the heart of the social life of the *polis*.

Agricultural Revolution The innovations in farm production that began in the eighteenth century and led to a scientific and mechanized agriculture.

Albigensians (Al-bi-GEN-see-uns) Thirteenth-century advocates of a dualist religion. They took their name from the city of Albi in southern France. Also called *Cathars.*

Anabaptists Protestants who insisted that only adult baptism conformed to Scripture.

anarchism The theory that government and social institutions are oppressive and unnecessary and society should be based on voluntary cooperation among individuals.

Anschluss (AHN-shluz) Meaning "union." The annexation of Austria by Germany in March 1938.

anti-Semitism Prejudice, hostility, or legal discrimination against Jews.

apostolic primacy The doctrine that the popes are the direct successors to the Apostle Peter and as such heads of the church.

Apostolic Succession The Christian doctrine that the powers given by Jesus to his original disciples have been handed down from bishop to bishop through ordination.

appeasement The Anglo-French policy of making concessions to Germany in the 1930s to avoid a crisis that would lead to war. It assumed that Germany had real grievances and Hitler's aims were limited and ultimately acceptable.

Areopagus The governing council of Athens, originally open only to the nobility. It was named after the hill on which it met.

arete (AH-ray-tay) Manliness, courage, and the excellence appropriate to a hero. It was considered the highest virtue of Homeric society.

Arianism (AIR-ee-an-ism) The belief formulated by Arius of Alexandria (ca. 280–336 C.E.) that Jesus was a created being, neither fully man nor fully God, but something in between. It did away with the doctrine of the Trinity.

aristocratic resurgence Term applied to the eighteenth-century aristocratic efforts to resist the expanding power of European monarchies.

Arminians (are-MIN-ee-ans) A group within the Church of England who rejected Puritanism and the Calvinist doctrine of predestination in favor of free will and an elaborate liturgy.

Asia Minor Modern Turkey. Also called *Anatolia.*

asiento (ah-SEE-ehn-tow) The contract to furnish slaves to the Spanish colonies.

assignats (as-seen-YAHNTS) Government bonds based on the value of confiscated church lands issued during the early French Revolution.

Atomists School of ancient Greek philosophy founded in the fifth century B.C.E. by Leucippus of Miletus and Democritus of Abdera. It held that the world consists of innumerable, tiny, solid, indivisible, and unchangeable particles called *atoms.*

Attica (AT-tick-a) The region of Greece where Athens is located.

Augsburg (AWGS-berg) **Confession** The definitive statement of Lutheran belief made in 1530.

Augustus (AW-gust-us) The title given to Octavian in 27 B.C.E. and borne thereafter by all Roman emperors. It was a semireligious title that implied veneration, majesty, and holiness.

Ausgleich (AWS-glike) Meaning "compromise." The agreement between the Habsburg Emperor and the Hungarians to give Hungary considerable administrative autonomy in 1867. It created the Dual Monarchy, or Austria-Hungary.

autocracy (AW-to-kra-see) Government in which the ruler has absolute power.

Axis The alliance between Nazi Germany and fascist Italy. Also called the *Pact of Steel.*

banalities Exactions that the lord of a manor could make on his tenants.

baroque (bah-ROWK) A style of art marked by heavy and dramatic ornamentation and curved rather than straight lines that flourished between 1550 and 1750. It was especially associated with the Catholic Counter-Reformation.

Beguines (bi-GEENS) Lay sisterhoods not bound by the rules of a religious order.

benefice   Church offices granted by the ruler of a state or the pope to an individual. It also meant *fief* in the Middle Ages.

bishop   Originally a person elected by early Christian congregations to lead them in worship and supervise their funds. In time, bishops became the religious and even political authorities for Christian communities within large geographical areas.

Black Death   The bubonic plague that killed millions of Europeans in the fourteenth century.

blitzkrieg (BLITZ-kreeg)   Meaning "lightning war." The German tactic early in World War II of employing fast-moving, massed armored columns supported by airpower to overwhelm the enemy.

Bolsheviks   Meaning the "majority." Term Lenin applied to his faction of the Russian Social Democratic Party. It became the Communist Party of the Soviet Union after the Russian Revolution.

bourgeois   A French word used as an adjective describing something associated with the middle class or as a noun to describe a middle class person.

boyars   The Russian nobility.

Bronze Age   The name given to the earliest civilized era, c. 4000 to 1000 B.C.E. The term reflects the importance of the metal bronze, a mixture of tin and copper, for the peoples of this age for use as weapons and tools.

Bund   A secular Jewish socialist organization of Polish Jews.

Bundesrat (BUHN-dees-raht)   The upper house of the German federal parliament whose members are appointed by the various state governments.

Caesaropapism (SEE-zer-o-PAY-pi-zim)   The direct involvement of the ruler in religious doctrine and practice as if he were the head of the church as well as the state.

cahiers de doléances (KAH-hee-ay de dough-LAY-ahnce)   Meaning "lists of grievances." Petitions for reforms submitted to the French crown when the Estates General met in 1789.

caliphate (KAH-li-fate)   The true line of succession to Muhammad.

capital goods   Machines and tools used to produce other goods.

Carbonari (car-buh-NAH-ree)   Meaning "charcoal burners." The most famous of the secret republican societies seeking to unify Italy in the 1820s.

categorical imperative   According to Emmanuel Kant (1724–1804), the internal sense of moral duty or awareness possessed by all human beings.

catholic   Meaning "universal." The body of belief held by most Christians enshrined within the church.

Catholic Emancipation   The grant of full political rights to Roman Catholics in Britain in 1829.

censor   Official of the Roman republic charged with conducting the census and compiling the lists of citizens and members of the Senate. They could expel senators for financial or moral reasons. Two censors were elected every five years.

Chartism   The first large-scale European working-class political movement. It sought political reforms that would favor the interests of skilled British workers in the 1830s and 1840s.

chiaroscuro (kyar-eh-SKEW-row)   The use of shading to enhance naturalness in painting and drawing.

civic humanism   Education designed to promote humanist leadership of political and cultural life.

civilization   A form of human culture marked by urbanism, metallurgy, and writing.

classical economics   The theory that economies grow through the free enterprise of individuals competing in a largely self-regulating marketplace with government intervention held to a minimum.

clientage (KLI-ent-age)   The custom in ancient Rome whereby men became supporters of more powerful men in return for legal and physical protection and economic benefits.

Cold War   The ideological and geographical struggle between the United States and its allies and the USSR and its allies that began after World War II and lasted until the dissolution of the USSR in 1989.

collectivization   The bedrock of Stalinist agriculture, which forced Russian peasants to give up their private farms and work as members of collectives, large agricultural units controlled by the state.

coloni (CO-loan-ee)   Farmers or sharecroppers on the estates of wealthy Romans.

Commonwealthmen   British political writers whose radical republican ideas influenced the American revolutionaries.

Concert of Europe   Term applied to the European great powers acting together (in "concert") to resolve international disputes between 1815 and the 1850s.

conciliar theory   The argument that General Councils were superior in authority to the pope and represented the whole body of the faithful.

condottieri (con-da-TEE-AIR-ee)   Military brokers who furnished mercenary forces to the Italian states during the Renaissance.

congregationalist   A congregationalist puts a group or assembly above any one individual and prefers an ecclesiastical polity that allows each congregation to be autonomous, or self-governing.

Congress System   A series of international meetings among the European great powers to promote mutual cooperation between 1818 and 1822.

conquistadores (kahn-KWIS-teh-door-hez)   Meaning "conquerors." The Spanish conquerors of the New World.

conservatism   Support for the established order in church and state. In the nineteenth century, it implied support for legitimate monarchies, landed aristocracies, and established churches. Conservatives favored only gradual, or "organic," change.

Consulate French government dominated by Napoleon from 1799 to 1804.

consuls (CON-suls) The two chief magistrates of the Roman state.

Consumer Revolution The vast increase in both the desire and the possibility of consuming goods and services that began in the early eighteenth century and created the demand for sustaining the Industrial Revolution.

containment The U.S. policy during the Cold War of resisting Soviet expansion and influence in the expectation that the USSR would eventually collapse.

Convention French radical legislative body from 1792 to 1794.

Corn Laws British tariffs on imported grain that protected the price of grain grown within the British Isles.

corporatism The planned economy of fascist Italy that combined private ownership of capital with government direction of Italy's economic life and arbitration of labor disputes. All major areas of production were organized into state-controlled bodies called *corporations*, which were represented in the Chamber of Corporations that replaced the Chamber of Deputies. The state, not consumers and owners, determined what the economy produced.

corvée (cor-VAY) A French labor tax requiring peasants to work on roads, bridges, and canals.

Council of Nicaea (NIGH-see-a) The council of Christian bishops at Nicaea in 325 C.E. that formulated the Nicene Creed, a statement of Christian belief that rejected Arianism in favor of the doctrine that Christ is both fully human and fully divine.

Counter-Reformation The sixteenth-century reform movement in the Roman Catholic Church in reaction to the Protestant Reformation.

coup d'état (COO DAY-ta) The sudden violent overthrow of a government by its own army.

creed A brief statement of faith to which true Christians should adhere.

Creoles (KRAY-ol-ez) Persons of Spanish descent born in the Spanish colonies.

Crusades Religious wars directed by the church against infidels and heretics.

culture The ways of living built up by a group and passed on from one generation to another.

cuneiform (Q-nee-i-form) A writing system invented by the Sumerians that used a wedge-shaped stylus, or pointed tool, to write on wet clay tablets that were then baked or dried (*cuneus* means "wedge" in Latin). The writing was also cut into stone.

Curia (CURE-ee-a) The papal government.

Cynic (SIN-ick) **School** A fourth-century philosophical movement that ridiculed all religious observances and turned away from involvement in the affairs of the *polis*. Its most famous exemplar was Diogenes of Sinope (ca. 400–325 B.C.E.).

deacon Meaning "those who serve." In early Christian congregations, deacons assisted the presbyters, or elders.

decolonization The process of European retreat of colonial empires following World War II.

deism A belief in a rational God who had created the universe, but then allowed it to function without his interference according to the mechanisms of nature and a belief in rewards and punishments after death for human action.

Delian (DEE-li-an) **League** An alliance of Greek states under the leadership of Athens that was formed in 478–477 B.C.E. to resist the Persians. In time the league was transformed into the Athenian Empire.

deme (DEEM) A small town in Attica or a ward in Athens that became the basic unit of Athenian civic life under the democratic reforms of Clisthenes in 508 B.C.E.

demesne (di-MAIN) The part of a manor that was cultivated directly for the lord of the manor.

divine right of kings The theory that monarchs are appointed by and answerable only to God.

Domesday (DOOMS-day) *Book* A detailed survey of the wealth of England undertaken by William the Conqueror between 1080 and 1086.

domestic system of textile production Method of producing textiles in which agents furnished raw materials to households whose members spun them into thread and then wove cloth, which the agents then sold as finished products.

Donatism The heresy that taught the efficacy of the sacraments depended on the moral character of the clergy who administered them.

Duce (DO-chay) Meaning "leader." Mussolini's title as head of the Fascist Party.

Duma (DOO-ma) The Russian parliament, after the revolution of 1905.

electors Nine German princes who had the right to elect the Holy Roman Emperor.

émigrés (em-ee-GRAYS) French aristocrats who fled France during the Revolution.

empiricism (em-PEER-ih-cism) The use of experiment and observation derived from sensory evidence to construct scientific theory or philosophy of knowledge.

enclosure The consolidation or fencing in of common lands by British landlords to increase production and achieve greater commercial profits. It also involved the reclamation of waste land and the consolidation of strips into block fields.

encomienda (en-co-mee-EN-da) The grant by the Spanish crown to a colonist of the labor of a specific number of Indians for a set period of time.

ENIAC The Electronic Numerical Integrator and Computer. The first genuine modern digital computer, developed in the 1940s.

Enlightenment The eighteenth-century movement led by the *philosophes* that held that change and reform were both desirable through the application of reason and science.

Epicureans (EP-i-cure-ee-ans)   School of philosophy founded by Epicurus of Athens (342–271 B.C.E.). It sought to liberate people from fear of death and the supernatural by teaching that the gods took no interest in human affairs and that true happiness consisted in pleasure, which was defined as the absence of pain. This could be achieved by attaining *ataraxia*, freedom from trouble, pain, and responsibility by withdrawing from business and public life.

equestrians (EE-quest-ree-ans)   Literally "cavalrymen" or "knights." In the earliest years of the Roman Republic those who could afford to serve as mounted warriors. The equestrians evolved into a social rank of well-to-do businessmen and middle-ranking officials. Many of them supported the Gracchi.

Estates General   The medieval French parliament. It consisted of three separate groups, or "estates": clergy, nobility, and commoners. It last met in 1789 at the outbreak of the French Revolution.

Etruscans (EE-trus-cans)   A people of central Italy who exerted the most powerful external influence on the early Romans. Etruscan kings ruled Rome until 509 B.C.E.

Eucharist (YOU-ka-rist)   Meaning "thanksgiving." The celebration of the Lord's Supper. Considered the central ritual of worship by most Christians. Also called *Holy Communion*.

Euro   The common currency created by the EEC in the late 1990s.

European Economic Community (EEC)   The economic association formed by France, Germany, Italy, Belgium, the Netherlands, and Luxembourg in 1957. Also known as the *Common Market*.

European Union   The new name given to the EEC in 1993. It included most of the states of Western Europe.

excommunication   Denial by the church of the right to receive the sacraments.

existentialism   The post–World War II Western philosophy that holds human beings are totally responsible for their acts and that this responsibility causes them dread and anguish.

Fabians   British socialists in the late 19th and early 20th century who sought to achieve socialism through gradual, peaceful, and democratic means.

family economy   The basic structure of production and consumption in preindustrial Europe.

fascism   Political movements that tend to be antidemocratic, anti-Marxist, antiparliamentary, and often anti-Semitic. Fascists were invariably nationalists and exhalted the nation over the individual. They supported the interests of the middle class and rejected the ideas of the French Revolution and nineteenth-century liberalism. The first fascist

regime was founded by Benito Mussolini (1883–1945) in Italy in the 1920s.

fealty   An oath of loyalty by a vassal to a lord, promising to perform specified services.

feudal (FEW-dull) **society**   The social, political, military, and economic system that prevailed in the Middle Ages and beyond in some parts of Europe.

fief   Land granted to a vassal in exchange for services, usually military.

foederati (FAY-der-ah-tee)   Barbarian tribes enlisted as special allies of the Roman Empire.

folk culture   The distinctive songs, sayings, legends, and crafts of a people.

Fourteen Points   President Woodrow Wilson's (1856–1924) idealistic war aims.

Fronde (FROHND)   A series of rebellions against royal authority in France between 1649 and 1652.

Führer (FYOOR-er)   Meaning "leader." The title taken by Hitler when he became dictator of Germany.

gabelle (gah-BELL)   The royal tax on salt in France.

Gaul (GAWL)   Modern France.

German Confederation   Association of German states established at the Congress of Vienna that replaced the Holy Roman Empire from 1815 to 1866.

ghetto   Separate communities in which Jews were required by law to live.

glasnost (GLAZ-nohst)   Meaning "openness." The policy initiated by Mikhail Gorbachev (MEEK-hail GORE-buh-choff) in the 1980s of permitting open criticism of the policies of the Soviet Communist Party.

Glorious Revolution   The largely peaceful replacement of James II by William and Mary as English monarchs in 1688. It marked the beginning of constitutional monarchy in Britain.

gold standard   A monetary system in which the value of a unit of a nation's currency is related to a fixed amount of gold.

Golden Bull   The agreement in 1356 to establish a seven-member electoral college of German princes to choose the Holy Roman Emperor.

Great Depression   A prolonged worldwide economic downturn that began in 1929 with the collapse of the New York Stock Exchange.

Great Purges   The imprisonment and execution of millions of Soviet citizens by Stalin between 1934 and 1939.

Great Reform Bill (1832)   A limited reform of the British House of Commons and an expansion of the electorate to include a wider variety of the propertied classes. It laid the groundwork for further orderly reforms within the British constitutional system.

Great Schism   The appearance of two and at times three rival popes between 1378 and 1415.

Green movement   A political environmentalist movement that began in West Germany in the 1970s and spread to a number of other Western nations.

grossdeutsch (gross-DOYCH) Meaning "great German." The argument that the German-speaking portions of the Habsburg Empire should be included in a united Germany.

guild An association of merchants or craftsmen that offered protection to its members and set rules for their work and products.

hacienda (ha-SEE-hen-da) A large landed estate in Spanish America.

Hegira (HEJ-ear-a) The flight of Muhammad and his followers from Mecca to Medina in 622 C.E. It marks the beginning of the Islamic calendar.

heliocentric (HE-li-o-cen-trick) **theory** The theory, now universally accepted, that the earth and the other planets revolve around the sun. First proposed by Aristarchos of Samos (310–230 B.C.E.). Its opposite, the geocentric theory, which was dominant until the sixteenth century C.E., held that the sun and the planets revolved around the earth.

Helots (HELL-ots) Hereditary Spartan serfs.

heretic (HAIR-i-tick) A person whose beliefs were contrary to those of the Catholic Church.

hieroglyphics (HI-er-o-gli-phicks) The complicated writing script of ancient Egypt. It combined picture writing with pictographs and sound signs. Hieroglyph means "sacred carvings" in Greek.

Holocaust The Nazi extermination of millions of European Jews between 1940 and 1945. Also called the "final solution to the Jewish problem."

Holy Roman Empire The revival of the old Roman Empire, based mainly in Germany and northern Italy, that endured from 870 to 1806.

home rule The advocacy of a large measure of administrative autonomy for Ireland within the British Empire between the 1880s and 1914.

Homo sapiens (HO-mo say-pee-ans) The scientific name for human beings, from the Latin words meaning "Wise man." *Homo sapiens* emerged some 200,000 years ago.

honestiores (HON-est-ee-or-ez) The Roman term formalized from the beginning of the third century C.E. to denote the privileged classes: senators, equestrians, the municipal aristocracy, and soldiers.

hoplite **phalanx** (FAY-lanks) The basic unit of Greek warfare in which infantrymen fought in close order, shield to shield, usually eight ranks deep. The phalanx perfectly suited the farmer-soldier-citizen who was the backbone of the *polis*.

hubris (WHO-bris) Arrogance brought on by excessive wealth or good fortune. The Greeks believed it led to moral blindness and divine vengeance.

Huguenots (HYOU-gu-nots) French Calvinists.

humanism The study of the Latin and Greek classics and of the Church Fathers both for their own sake and to promote a rebirth of ancient norms and values.

humanitas (HEW-man-i-tas) The Roman name for a liberal arts education.

humiliores (HEW-mi-lee-orez) The Roman term formalized at the beginning of the third century C.E. for the lower classes.

Hussites (HUS-Its) Followers of John Huss (d. 1415) who questioned Catholic teachings about the Eucharist.

Iconoclasm (i-KON-o-kla-zoom) A heresy in Eastern Christianity that sought to ban the veneration of sacred images, or icons.

id, ego, superego The three entities in Sigmund Freud's model of the internal organization of the human mind. The id consists of the amoral, irrational instincts for self-gratification. The superego embodies the external morality imposed on the personality by society. The ego mediates between the two and allows the personality to cope with the internal and external demands of its existence.

Iliad (ILL-ee-ad) **and the** ***Odyssey*** (O-dis-see), **The** Epic poems by Homer about the "Dark Age" heroes of Greece who fought at Troy. The poems were written down in the eighth century B.C.E. after centuries of being sung by bards.

imperator (IM-per-a-tor) Under the Roman Republic, it was the title given to a victorious general. Under Augustus and his successors, it became the title of the ruler of Rome meaning "emperor."

imperialism The extension of a nation's authority over other nations or areas through conquest or political or economic hegemony.

imperium (IM-pear-ee-um) In ancient Rome, the right to issue commands and to enforce them by fines, arrests, and even corporal and capital punishment.

indulgence Remission of the temporal penalty of punishment in purgatory that remained after sins had been forgiven.

Industrial Revolution Mechanization of the European economy that began in Britain in the second half of the eighteenth century.

Inquisition A tribunal created by the Catholic Church in the mid-twelfth century to detect and punish heresy.

insulae (IN-sul-lay) Meaning "islands." The multi-storied apartment buildings of Rome in which most of the inhabitants of the city lived.

intendents (in-TEN-duhnts) Royal officials under the French monarchy who supervised the provincial governments in the name of the king.

Intolerable Acts Measures passed by the British Parliament in 1774 to punish the colony of Massachusetts and strengthen Britain's authority in the colonies. The laws provoked colonial opposition, which led immediately to the American Revolution.

investiture controversy The medieval conflict between the church and lay rulers over who would control bishops and abbots, symbolized by the ceremony of "investing" them with the symbols of their authority.

Ionia (I-o-knee-a)   The part of western Asia Minor heavily colonized by the Greeks.

Islam (IZ-lahm)   Meaning "submission." The religion founded by the prophet Muhammad.

Italia irredenta (ee-TAHL-ee-a ir-REH-dent-a)   Meaning "unredeemed Italy." Italian-speaking areas that had been left under Austrian rule at the time of the unification of Italy.

Jacobins (JACK-uh-bins)   The radical republican party during the French Revolution that displaced the Girondins.

Jacquerie (jah-KREE)   Revolt of the French peasantry.

Jansenism   A seventeenth-century movement within the Catholic Church that taught that human beings were so corrupted by original sin that they could do nothing good nor secure their own salvation without divine grace. (It was opposed to the Jesuits.)

Judah (JEW-da)   The southern Israelite kingdom established after the death of Solomon in the tenth century B.C.E.

Julian Calendar   The reform of the calendar by Julius Caesar in 46 B.C.E. It remained in use throughout Europe until the sixteenth century and in Russia until the Russian Revolution in 1917.

July Monarchy   The French regime set up after the overthrow of the Bourbons in July 1830.

Junkers (YOONG-kerz)   The noble landlords of Prussia.

jus gentium (YUZ GEN-tee-um)   Meaning "law of peoples." The body of Roman law that dealt with foreigners.

jus naturale (YUZ NAH-tu-rah-lay)   Meaning "natural law." The Stoic concept of a world ruled by divine reason.

Ka'ba (KAH-bah)   A black meteorite in the city of Mecca that became Islam's holiest shrine.

Keynesian economics   The theory of John Maynard Keynes (CANES) (1883–1946) that governments could spend their economies out of a depression by running deficits to encourage employment and stimulate the production and consumption of goods.

kleindeutsch (kline-DOYCH)   Meaning "small German." The argument that the German-speaking portions of the Habsburg Empire should be excluded from a united Germany.

Kristallnacht (KRIS-tahl-NAHKT)   Meaning "crystal night" because of the broken glass that littered German streets after the looting and destruction of Jewish homes, businesses, and synagogues across Germany on the orders of the Nazi Party in November 1938.

kulaks (koo-LAKS)   Prosperous Russian peasant farmers.

Kulturkampf (cool-TOOR-cahmff)   Meaning the "battle for culture." The conflict between the Roman Catholic Church and the government of the German Empire in the 1870s.

laissez-faire (lay-ZAY-faire)   French phrase meaning "allow to do." In economics the doctrine of minimal government interference in the working of the economy.

Late Antiquity   The multi-cultural period between the end of the ancient world and the birth of the Middle Ages, 250–800 C.E.

latifundia (LAT-ee-fun-dee-a)   Large plantations for growing cash crops owned by wealthy Romans.

Latium (LAT-ee-um)   The region of Italy in which Rome is located. Its inhabitants were called *Latins*.

League of Nations   The association of sovereign states set up after World War I to pursue common policies and avert international aggression.

Lebensraum (LAY-benz-rauhm)   Meaning "living space." The Nazi plan to colonize and exploit the Slavic areas of Eastern Europe for the benefit of Germany.

levée en masse (le-VAY en MASS)   The French revolutionary conscription (1792) of all males into the army and the harnessing of the economy for war production.

liberal arts   The medieval university program that consisted of the *trivium* (TRI-vee-um): grammar, rhetoric, and logic, and the *quadrivium* (qua-DRI-vee-um): arithmetic, geometry, astronomy, and music.

liberalism   In the nineteenth century, support for representative government dominated by the propertied classes and minimal government interference in the economy.

Logos (LOW-goz)   Divine reason, or fire, which according to the Stoics was the guiding principle in nature. Every human had a spark of this divinity, which returned to the eternal divine spirit after death.

Lollards (LALL-erds)   Followers of John Wycliffe (d. 1384) who questioned the supremacy and privileges of the pope and the church hierarchy.

Lower Egypt   The Nile delta.

Luftwaffe (LUFT-vaff-uh)   The German air force in World War II.

Magna Carta (MAG-nuh CAR-tuh)   The "Great Charter" limiting royal power that the English nobility forced King John to sign in 1215.

Magna Graecia (MAG-nah GRAY-see-a)   Meaning "Great Greece" in Latin, it was the name given by the Romans to southern Italy and Sicily because there were so many Greek colonies in the region.

Magyars (MAH-jars)   The majority ethnic group in Hungary.

Mandates   The assigning of the former German colonies and Turkish territories in the Middle East to Britain, France, Japan, Belgium, Australia, and South Africa as de facto colonies under the vague supervision of the League of Nations with the hope that the territories would someday advance to independence.

mannerism   A style of art in the mid to late sixteenth century that permitted artists to express their own "manner" or feelings in contrast to the symmetry and simplicity of the art of the High Renaissance.

manor   Village farms owned by a lord.

Marshall Plan   The U.S. program named after Secretary of State George C. Marshall of providing economic aid to Europe after World War II.

Marxism   The theory of Karl Marx (1818–1883) and Friedrich Engels (FREE-drick ENG-ulz) (1820–1895) that history is the result of class conflict, which will end in the inevitable triumph of the industrial proletariat over the bourgeoisie and the abolition of private property and social class.

Mein Kampf (MINE KAHMFF)   Meaning *My Struggle*. Hitler's statement of his political program, published in 1924.

Mensheviks   Meaning the "minority." Term Lenin applied to the majority moderate faction of the Russian Social Democratic Party opposed to him and the Bolsheviks.

mercantilism   Term used to describe close government control of the economy that sought to maximize exports and accumulate as much precious metals as possible to enable the state to defend its economic and political interests.

Mesopotamia (MEZ-o-po-tay-me-a)   Modern Iraq. The land between the Tigris and Euphrates Rivers where the first civilization appeared around 3000 B.C.E.

Messiah (MESS-eye-a)   The redeemer whose coming Jews believed would establish the kingdom of God on earth. Christians considered Jesus to be the Messiah (*Christ* means Messiah in Greek).

Methodism   An English religious movement begun by John Wesley (1703–1791) that stressed inward, heartfelt religion and the possibility of attaining Christian perfection in this life.

millets   Administrative units of the Ottoman Empire that were not geographic but consisted of ethnic or religious minorities to whom particular laws and regulations applied.

Minoans (MIN-o-ans)   The Bronze Age civilization that arose in Crete in the third and second millennia B.C.E.

missi dominici (MISS-ee dough-MIN-ee-chee)   Meaning "the envoys of the ruler." Royal overseers of the king's law in the Carolingian Empire.

mobilization   The placing of a country's military forces on a war footing.

modernism   The movement in the arts and literature in the late nineteenth and early twentieth centuries to create new aesthetic forms and to elevate the aesthetic experience of a work of art above the attempt to portray reality as accurately as possible.

moldboard plow   A heavy plow introduced in the Middle Ages that cut deep into the soil.

monasticism   A movement in the Christian church that arose first in the East in the third and fourth centuries C.E. in which first individual hermits and later organized communities of men and women (monks and nuns) separated themselves from the world to lead lives in imitation of Christ. In the West the Rule of St. Benedict (c. 480–547) became the dominant form of monasticism.

Monophysitism (ma-NO-fiz-it-ism)   A Christian heresy that taught that Jesus had only one nature.

monotheism   The worship of one universal God.

Mycenaean (MY-cen-a-an)   The Bronze Age civilization of mainland Greece that was centered at Mycenae.

"mystery" religions   The cults of Isis, Mithra, and Osiris, which promised salvation to those initiated into the secret or "mystery" of their rites. These cults competed with Christianity in the Roman Empire.

nationalism   The belief that one is part of a nation, defined as a community with its own language, traditions, customs, and history that distinguish it from other nations and make it the primary focus of a person's loyalty and sense of identity.

natural selection   The theory originating with Darwin that organisms evolve through a struggle for existence in which those that have a marginal advantage live long enough to propagate their kind.

naturalism   The attempt to portray nature and human life without sentimentality.

Nazis   The German Nationalist Socialist Party.

Neolithic (NEE-o-lith-ick) **Revolution**   The shift beginning 10,000 years ago from hunter-gatherer societies to settled communities of farmers and artisans. Also called the Age of Agriculture, it witnessed the invention of farming, the domestication of plants and animals, and the development of technologies such as pottery and weaving. The earliest Neolithic societies appeared in the Near East about 8000 B.C.E. "Neolithic" comes from the Greek words for "new stone."

Neoplatonism (KNEE-o-play-ton-ism)   A religious philosophy that tried to combine mysticism with classical and rationalist speculation. Its chief formulator was Plotinus (205–270 C.E.).

New Economic Policy (NEP)   A limited revival of capitalism, especially in light industry and agriculture, introduced by Lenin in 1921 to repair the damage inflicted on the Russian economy by the Civil War and war communism.

New Imperialism   The extension in the late nineteenth and early twentieth centuries of Western political and economic dominance to Asia, the Middle East, and Africa.

nomes   Regions or provinces of ancient Egypt governed by officials called *nomarchs*.

oikos (OI-cos)   The Greek household, always headed by a male.

Old Believers   Those members of the Russian Orthodox Church who refused to accept the reforms of the seventeenth century regarding church texts and ritual.

Old Regime   Term applied to the pattern of social, political, and economic relationships and institutions that existed in Europe before the French Revolution.

optimates (OP-tee-ma-tes)   Meaning "the best men." Roman politicians who supported the traditional role of the Senate.

orthodox   Meaning "holding the right opinions." Applied to the doctrines of the Catholic Church.

Ottoman Empire   The imperial Turkish state centered in Constantinople that ruled large parts of the Balkans, North Africa, and the Middle East until 1918.

Paleolithic (PAY-lee-o-lith-ick) **Age, The**   The earliest period when stone tools were used, from about 1,000,000 to 10,000 B.C.E. From the Greek meaning "old stone."

Panhellenic (PAN-hell-en-ick) ("all-Greek")   The sense of cultural identity that all Greeks felt in common with each other.

Pan-slavism   The movement to create a nation or federation that would embrace all the Slavic peoples of Eastern Europe.

papal infallibility   The doctrine that the pope is infallible when pronouncing officially in his capacity as head of the church on matters of faith and morals, enumerated by the First Vatican Council in 1870.

Papal States   Territory in central Italy ruled by the pope until 1870.

parlements (par-luh-MAHNS)   French regional courts dominated by hereditary nobility. The most important was the *Parlement* of Paris, which claimed the right to register royal decrees before they could become law.

parliamentary monarchy   The form of limited or constitutional monarchy set up in Britain after the Glorious Revolution of 1689 in which the monarch was subject to the law and ruled by the consent of parliament.

patricians (PA-tri-she-ans)   The hereditary upper class of early Republican Rome.

Peloponnesian (PELL-o-po-knees-ee-an) **Wars**   The protracted struggle between Athens and Sparta to dominate Greece between 465 and Athens final defeat in 404 B.C.E.

Peloponnesus (PELL-o-po-knee-sus)   The southern peninsula of Greece where Sparta was located.

peninsulares (pen-in-SUE-la-rez)   Persons born in Spain who settled in the Spanish colonies.

perestroika (pare-ess-TROY-ka)   Meaning "restructuring." The attempt in the 1980s to reform the Soviet government and economy.

petite bourgeoisie (peh-TEET BOOSH-schwa-zee)   The lower middle class.

pharaoh (FAY-row)   The god-kings of ancient Egypt. The term originally meant "great house" or palace.

Pharisees (FAIR-i-sees)   The group that was most strict in its adherence to Jewish law.

philosophes (fee-lou-SOPHS)   The eighteenth-century writers and critics who forged the new attitudes favorable to change. They sought to apply reason and common sense to the institutions and societies of their day.

Phoenicians (FA-nee-shi-ans)   The ancient inhabitants of modern Lebanon. A trading people, they established colonies throughout the Mediterranean.

physiocrats   Eighteenth-century French thinkers who attacked the mercantilist regulation of the economy, advocated a limited economic role for government, and believed that all economic production depended on sound agriculture.

Plantation Economy, The   The economic system stretching between Chesapeake Bay and Brazil that produced crops, especially sugar, cotton, and tobacco, using slave labor on large estates.

Platonism   Philosophy of Plato that posits preexistent Ideal Forms of which all earthly things are imperfect models.

plebeians (PLEB-bee-ans)   The hereditary lower class of early Republican Rome.

plenitude of power   The teaching that the popes have power over all other bishops of the church.

pogroms (PO-grohms)   Organized riots against Jews in the Russian Empire.

polis (PO-lis) (plural, *poleis*)   The basic Greek political unit. Usually, but incompletely, translated as "city-state," the Greeks thought of the *polis* as a community of citizens theoretically descended from a common ancestor.

politique   Ruler or person in a position of power who puts the success and well-being of his or her state above all else.

polygyny (po-LIJ-eh-nee)   The practice of having two or more wives or concubines at the same time.

polytheism (PAH-lee-thee-ism)   The worship of many gods

pontifex maximus (PON-ti-feks MAK-suh-muss)   Meaning "supreme priest." The chief priest of ancient Rome. The title was later assumed by the popes.

Popular Front   A government of all left-wing parties that took power in France in 1936 to enact social and economic reforms.

populares (PO-pew-lar-es)   Roman politicians who sought to pursue a political career based on the support of the people rather than just the aristocracy.

positivism   The philosophy of Auguste Comte that science is the final, or positive, stage of human intellectual development because it involves exact descriptions of phenomena, without recourse to unobservable operative principles, such as gods or spirits.

post-impressionism A term used to describe European painting that followed impressionism; the term actually applies to several styles of art all of which to some extent derived from impression or stood in reaction to impressionism.

Pragmatic Sanction The legal basis negotiated by the Emperor Charles VI (r. 1711–1740) for the Habsburg succession through his daughter Maria Theresa (r. 1740–1780).

predestination The doctrine that God had foreordained all souls to salvation (the "elect") or damnation. It was especially associated with Calvinism.

presbyter (PRESS-bi-ter) Meaning "elder." A person who directed the affairs of early Christian congregations.

Presbyterians Scottish Calvinists and English Protestants who advocated a national church composed of semiautonomous congregations governed by "presbyteries."

proconsulship (PRO-con-sul-ship) In Republican Rome, the extension of a consul's imperium beyond the end of his term of office to allow him to continue to command an army in the field.

Protestant Ethic The theory propounded by Max Weber in 1904 that the religious confidence and self-disciplined activism that were supposedly associated with Protestantism produced an ethic that stimulated the spirit of emergent capitalism.

Ptolemaic (tow-LEM-a-ick) **System** The pre-Copernican explanation of the universe, with the earth at the center of the universe, originated in the ancient world.

Punic (PEW-nick) **Wars** Three wars between Rome and Carthage for dominance of the western Mediterranean that were fought from 264 B.C.E. to 146 B.C.E.

Puritans English Protestants who sought to "purify" the Church of England of any vestiges of Catholicism.

Qur'an (kuh-RAN) Meaning "a reciting." The Islamic bible, which Muslims believe God revealed to the prophet Muhammad.

racism The pseudoscientific theory that biological features of race determine human character and worth.

raison d'état (RAY-suhn day-TAH) Meaning "reason of state." Concept that the interests of the state justify a course of action.

realism The style of art and literature that seeks to depict the physical world and human life with scientific objectivity and detached observation.

Reformation The sixteenth-century religious movement that sought to reform the Roman Catholic Church and led to the establishment of Protestantism.

regular clergy Monks and nuns who belong to religious orders.

Reichstag (RIKES-stahg) The German parliament, which existed in various forms, until 1945.

Reign of Terror The period between the summer of 1793 and the end of July 1794 when the French revolutionary state used extensive executions and violence to defend the Revolution and suppress its alleged internal enemies.

relativity The scientific theory associated with Einstein that time and space exist not separately but as a combined continuum whose measurement depends as much on the observer as on the entities that are being measured.

Renaissance The revival of ancient learning and the supplanting of traditional religious beliefs by new secular and scientific values that began in Italy in the fourteenth and fifteenth centuries.

reparations The requirement incorporated into the Versailles Treaty that Germany should pay for the cost of World War I.

revisionism The advocacy among nineteenth-century German socialists of achieving a humane socialist society through the evolution of democratic institutions, not revolution.

robot (ROW-boht) The amount of labor landowners demanded from peasants in the Habsburg Monarchy before 1848.

Romanitas (row-MAN-ee-tas) Meaning "Roman-ness." The spread of the Roman way of life and the sense of identifying with Rome across the Roman Empire.

romanticism A reaction in early-nineteenth-century literature, philosophy, and religion against what many considered the excessive rationality and scientific narrowness of the Enlightenment.

SA The Nazi parliamentary forces, or storm troopers.

sans-culottes (SAHN coo-LOTS) Meaning "without kneebreeches." The lower-middle classes and artisans of Paris during the French Revolution.

Schlieffen (SHLEE-fun) **Plan** Germany's plan for achieving a quick victory in the West at the outbreak of World War I by invading France through Belgium and Luxembourg.

Scholasticism Method of study based on logic and dialectic that dominated the medieval schools. It assumed that truth already existed; students had only to organize, elucidate, and defend knowledge learned from authoritative texts, especially those of Aristotle and the Church Fathers.

scientific induction Scientific method in which generalizations are derived from data gained from empirical observations.

scientific revolution The sweeping change in the scientific view of the universe that occurred in the sixteenth and seventeenth centuries. The new scientific concepts and the method of their construction became the standard for assessing the validity of knowledge in the West.

scutage Monetary payments by a vassal to a lord in place of the required military service.

Second Industrial Revolution The emergence of new industries and the spread of industrialization from Britain to other countries, especially Germany and the United States, in the second half of the nineteenth century.

secular clergy Parish clergy who did not belong to a religious order.

seigneur (sane-YOUR) A noble French landlord.

Sejm (SHEM) The legislative assembly of the Polish nobility.

serfs Peasants tied to the land they tilled.

Shi-a (SHE-ah) The minority of Muslims who trace their beliefs from the caliph Ali who was assassinated in 661 C.E.

Sinn Fein (SHIN FAHN) Meaning "ourselves alone." An Irish political movement founded in 1905 that advocated complete political separation from Britain.

social Darwinism The application of Darwin's concept of "the survival of the fittest" to explain evolution in nature to human social relationships.

Sophists (SO-fists) Professional teachers who emerged in Greece in the mid–fifth century B.C.E. who were paid to teach techniques of rhetoric, dialectic, and argumentation.

soviets Workers and soldiers councils formed in Russia during the Revolution.

spinning jenny A machine invented in England by James Hargreaves around 1765 to mass-produce thread.

SS The chief security units of the Nazi state.

Stoics (STOW-icks) A philosophical school founded by Zeno of Citium (335–263 B.C.E.) that taught that humans could only be happy with natural law. Human misery was caused by passion, which was a disease of the soul. The wise sought *apatheia*, freedom from passion.

studia humanitatis (STEW-dee-a hew-MAHN-ee tah-tis) During the Renaissance, a liberal arts program of study that embraced grammar, rhetoric, poetry, history, philosophy, and politics.

Sturm und Drang (SHTURM und DRAHNG) Meaning "storm and stress." A movement in German romantic literature and philosophy that emphasized feeling and emotion.

suffragettes British women who lobbied and agitated for the right to vote in the early twentieth century.

summa (SUE-ma) An authoritative summary in the Middle Ages of all that was allegedly known about a subject.

Sunna (SOON-ah) Meaning "tradition." The dominant Islamic group.

Sunnis Those who follow the "tradition" (sunna) of the Prophet Muhammed. They are the dominant movement within Islam to which the vast majority of Muslims adhere.

symposium (SIM-po-see-um) The carefully organized drinking party that was the center of Greek aristocratic social life. It featured games, songs, poetry, and even philosophical disputation.

syncretism (SIN-cret-ism) The intermingling of different religions to form an amalgam that contained elements from each.

syndicalism French labor movement that sought to improve workers' conditions through direct action, especially general strikes.

Table of Ranks An official hierarchy established by Peter the Great in imperial Russia that equated a person's social position and privileges with his rank in the state bureaucracy or army.

tabula rasa (tah-BOO-lah RAH-sah) Meaning a "blank page." The philosophical belief associated with John Locke that human beings enter the world with totally unformed characters that are completely shaped by experience.

taille (TIE) The direct tax on the French peasantry.

Ten lost tribes The Israelites who were scattered and lost to history when the northern kingdom of Israel fell to the Assyrians in 722 B.C.E.

tertiaries (TER-she-air-ees) Laypeople affiliated with the monastic life who took vows of poverty, chastity, and obedience but remained in the world.

tetrarchy (TET-rar-key) Diocletian's (r. 306–337 C.E.) system for ruling the Roman Empire by four men with power divided territorially.

Thermidorian Reaction The reaction against the radicalism of the French Revolution that began in July 1794. Associated with the end of terror and establishment of the Directory.

thesis, antithesis, and synthesis G. W. F. Hegel's (HAY-gle) (1770–1831) concept of how ideas develop. The *thesis* is a dominant set of ideas. It is challenged by a set of conflicting ideas, the *antithesis*. From the clash of these ideas, a new pattern of thought, the *synthesis*, emerges and eventually becomes the new thesis.

Third Estate The branch of the French Estates General representing all of the kingdom outside the nobility and the clergy.

Third Reich (RIKE) Hitler's regime in Germany, which lasted from 1933 to 1945.

Thirty-Nine Articles (1563) The official statement of the beliefs of the Church of England. They established a moderate form of Protestantism.

three-field system A medieval innovation that increased the amount of land under cultivation by leaving only one-third fallow in a given year.

transportation The British policy from the late eighteenth to the mid–nineteenth centuries of shipping persons convicted of the most serious offenses to Australia as an alternative to capital punishment.

transubstantiation   The doctrine that the entire substances of the bread and wine are changed in the Eucharist into the body and blood of Christ.

tribunes (TRIB-unes)   Roman officials who had to be plebeians and were elected by the plebeian assembly to protect plebeians from the arbitrary power of the magistrates.

ulema (oo-LEE-mah)   Meaning "persons with correct knowledge." The Islamic scholarly elite who served a social function similar to the Christian clergy.

Upper Egypt   The part of Egypt that runs from the delta to the Sudanese border.

utilitarianism   The theory associated with Jeremy Bentham (1748–1832) that the principle of utility, defined as the greatest good for the greatest number of people, should be applied to government, the economy, and the judicial system.

utopian socialism   Early-nineteenth-century theories that sought to replace the existing capitalist structure and values with visionary solutions or ideal communities.

vassal   A person granted an estate or cash payments in return for accepting the obligation to render services to a lord.

vernacular   The everyday language spoken by the people as opposed to Latin.

vingtième (VEN-tee-em)   Meaning "one-twentieth." A tax on income in France before the Revolution.

Vulgate   The Latin translation of the Bible by Jerome (348–420 C.E.) that became the standard bible used by the Catholic Church.

Waldensians (wahl-DEN-see-ens)   Medieval heretics who advocated biblical simplicity in reaction to the worldliness of the church.

war communism   The economic policy adopted by the Bolsheviks during the Russian Civil War to seize the banks, heavy industry, railroads, and grain.

war guilt clause   Clause 231 of the Versailles Treaty, which assigned responsibility for World War I solely to Germany.

water frame   A water-powered device invented by Richard Arkwright to produce a more durable cotton fabric. It led to the shift in the production of cotton textiles from households to factories.

Weimar (Why-mar) **Republic**   The German democratic regime that existed between the end of World War I and Hitler's coming to power in 1933.

White Russians   Those Russians who opposed the Bolsheviks (the "Reds") in the Russian Civil War of 1918–1921.

zemstvos (ZEMPST-vohs)   Local governments set up in the Russian Empire in 1864.

Zionism   The movement to create a Jewish state in Palestine (the Biblical Zion).

Zollverein (TZOL-fuh-rine)   A free-trade union established among the major German states in 1834.

INDEX

—m—

Italic page numbers refer to illustrations.

M

SINGLE PC LICENSE AGREEMENT AND LIMITED WARRANTY

READ THIS LICENSE CAREFULLY BEFORE OPENING THIS PACKAGE. BY OPENING THIS PACKAGE, YOU ARE AGREEING TO THE TERMS AND CONDITIONS OF THIS LICENSE. IF YOU DO NOT AGREE, DO NOT OPEN THE PACKAGE. PROMPTLY RETURN THE UNOPENED PACKAGE AND ALL ACCOMPANYING ITEMS TO THE PLACE YOU OBTAINED THEM [[FOR A FULL REFUND OF ANY SUMS YOU HAVE PAID FOR THE SOFTWARE]]. *THESE TERMS APPLY TO ALL LICENSED SOFTWARE ON THE DISK EXCEPT THAT THE TERMS FOR USE OF ANY SHAREWARE OR FREEWARE ON THE DISKETTES ARE AS SET FORTH IN THE ELECTRONIC LICENSE LOCATED ON THE DISK:*

1. GRANT OF LICENSE and OWNERSHIP: The enclosed computer programs and data ("Software") are licensed, not sold, to you by Prentice-Hall, Inc. ("We" or the "Company") and in consideration of your purchase or adoption of the accompanying Company textbooks and/or other materials, and your agreement to these terms. We reserve any rights not granted to you. You own only the disk(s) but we and/or our licensors own the Software itself. This license allows you to use and display your copy of the Software on a single computer (i.e., with a single CPU) at a single location for academic use only, so long as you comply with the terms of this Agreement. You may make one copy for back up, or transfer your copy to another CPU, provided that the Software is usable on only one computer.

2. RESTRICTIONS: You may not transfer or distribute the Software or documentation to anyone else. Except for backup, you may not copy the documentation or the Software. You may not network the Software or otherwise use it on more than one computer or computer terminal at the same time. You may not reverse engineer, disassemble, decompile, modify, adapt, translate, or create derivative works based on the Software or the Documentation. You may be held legally responsible for any copying or copyright infringement which is caused by your failure to abide by the terms of these restrictions.

3. TERMINATION: This license is effective until terminated. This license will terminate automatically without notice from the Company if you fail to comply with any provisions or limitations of this license. Upon termination, you shall destroy the Documentation and all copies of the Software. All provisions of this Agreement as to limitation and disclaimer of warranties, limitation of liability, remedies or damages, and our ownership rights shall survive termination.

4. LIMITED WARRANTY AND DISCLAIMER OF WARRANTY: Company warrants that for a period of 60 days from the date you purchase or adopt the accompanying textbook, the Software, when properly installed and used in accordance with the Documentation, will operate in substantial conformity with the description of the Software set forth in the Documentation, and that for a period of 30 days the disk(s) on which the Software is delivered shall be free from defects in materials and workmanship under normal use. The Company does not warrant that the Software will meet your requirements or that the operation of the Software will be uninterrupted or error-free. Your only remedy and the Company's only obligation under these limited warranties is, at the Company's option, return of the disk for a refund of any amounts paid for it by you or replacement of the disk. THIS LIMITED WARRANTY IS THE ONLY WARRANTY PROVIDED BY THE COMPANY AND ITS LICENSORS, AND THE COMPANY AND ITS LICENSORS DISCLAIM ALL OTHER WARRANTIES, EXPRESS OR IMPLIED, INCLUDING WITHOUT LIMITATION, THE IMPLIED WARRANTIES OF MERCHANTABILITY AND FITNESS FOR A PARTICULAR PURPOSE. THE COMPANY DOES NOT WARRANT, GUARANTEE OR MAKE ANY REPRESENTATION REGARDING THE ACCURACY, RELIABILITY, CURRENTNESS, USE, OR RESULTS OF USE, OF THE SOFTWARE.

5. LIMITATION OF REMEDIES AND DAMAGES: IN NO EVENT, SHALL THE COMPANY OR ITS EMPLOYEES, AGENTS, LICENSORS, OR CONTRACTORS BE LIABLE FOR ANY INCIDENTAL, INDIRECT, SPECIAL, OR CONSEQUENTIAL DAMAGES ARISING OUT OF OR IN CONNECTION WITH THIS LICENSE OR THE SOFTWARE, INCLUDING FOR LOSS OF USE, LOSS OF DATA, LOSS OF INCOME OR PROFIT, OR OTHER LOSSES, SUSTAINED AS A RESULT OF INJURY TO ANY PERSON, OR LOSS OF OR DAMAGE TO PROPERTY, OR CLAIMS OF THIRD PARTIES, EVEN IF THE COMPANY OR AN AUTHORIZED REPRESENTATIVE OF THE COMPANY HAS BEEN ADVISED OF THE POSSIBILITY OF SUCH DAMAGES. IN NO EVENT SHALL THE LIABILITY OF THE COMPANY FOR DAMAGES WITH RESPECT TO THE SOFTWARE EXCEED THE AMOUNTS ACTUALLY PAID BY YOU, IF ANY, FOR THE SOFTWARE OR THE ACCOMPANYING TEXTBOOK. BECAUSE SOME JURISDICTIONS DO NOT ALLOW THE LIMITATION OF LIABILITY IN CERTAIN CIRCUMSTANCES, THE ABOVE LIMITATIONS MAY NOT ALWAYS APPLY TO YOU.

6. GENERAL: THIS AGREEMENT SHALL BE CONSTRUED IN ACCORDANCE WITH THE LAWS OF THE UNITED STATES OF AMERICA AND THE STATE OF NEW YORK, APPLICABLE TO CONTRACTS MADE IN NEW YORK, AND SHALL BENEFIT THE COMPANY, ITS AFFILIATES AND ASSIGNEES. HIS AGREEMENT IS THE COMPLETE AND EXCLUSIVE STATEMENT OF THE AGREEMENT BETWEEN YOU AND THE COMPANY AND SUPERSEDES ALL PROPOSALS OR PRIOR AGREEMENTS, ORAL, OR WRITTEN, AND ANY OTHER COMMUNICATIONS BETWEEN YOU AND THE COMPANY OR ANY REPRESENTATIVE OF THE COMPANY RELATING TO THE SUBJECT MATTER OF THIS AGREEMENT. If you are a U.S. Government user, this Software is licensed with "restricted rights" as set forth in subparagraphs (a)-(d) of the Commercial Computer-Restricted Rights clause at FAR 52.227-19 or in subparagraphs (c)(1)(ii) of the Rights in Technical Data and Computer Software clause at DFARS 252.227-7013, and similar clauses, as applicable.

Should you have any questions concerning this agreement or if you wish to contact the Company for any reason, please contact in writing: Legal Department, Prentice Hall, One Lake Street, Upper Saddle River, NJ 07458. If you need assistance with technical difficulties, call: 1-800-677-6337.